THE PUBLIC SCHO

LATIN GRAMM

FOR THE USE OF
SCHOOLS, COLLEGES, AND PRIVATE STUDENTS.

BY
BENJAMIN HALL KENNEDY, D.D.

REGIUS PROFESSOR OF GREEK IN THE UNIVERSITY OF CAMBRIDGE, AND CANON OF ELV.

Nihil ex grammatica nocuerit nisi quod supervacuum ert: neque enim
obstant hae disciplinae per illas euntibus, sed circa illas haerentibus.
QUINTIL. *Inst. Orat.* lib. i. cap. iv

Revised & Updated
Simon Wallenberg Press
2007

© 2007 Simon Wallenberg ISBN 1-84356-033-X
        The Public School Latin Grammar
        Benjamin Hall Kennedy

This is an updated version of The Public School Latin Grammar with Chapters from the and Revised Latin Grammar has been rearranged, revised and improved by the Simon Wallenburg Press.

The Shorter Revised Latin Primer - Eight Edition Published London 1908 - This Edition Revised Improved & Enlarged by Simon Wallenberg Press 2007

A Wallenberg Grammar Book

Published by the Simon Wallenberg Press
wallenberg.press@gmail.com

Copyright revision: Simon Wallenberg
© Book Block & Cover design Wallenberg Press, Printed in the United States of America & The United Kingdom.

Printed on acid-free paper.

Benjamin Hall Kennedy
(November 6, 1804 – April 6, 1889)

Was an English scholar. He was born at Summer Hill, near Birmingham, the eldest son of Rann Kennedy (1772–1851), of a branch of the Ayrshire family which had settled in Staffordshire.

Rann was a scholar and man of letters, several of whose sons rose to distinction. Benjamin was educated at Shrewsbury School, and St John's College, Cambridge. After a brilliant university career he was elected fellow and classical lecturer of St John's College in 1828. Two years later he became an assistant master at Harrow, whence he went to Shrewsbury as headmaster in 1836. He retained this post until 1866, the thirty years being marked by a long series of successes for his pupils, chiefly in classics.

When he retired from Shrewsbury a large collection was made, and was used partly on new school buildings and partly on the founding of a Latin professorship at Cambridge. The first holders were both Kennedy's old pupils, HAJ Munro and JEB Mayor. In 1867, Kennedy was elected Regius Professor of Greek at Cambridge and canon of Ely Cathedral.

From 1870 to 1880 he was a member of the committee for the revision of the New Testament. He supported the admission of women to university, and took a prominent part in the establishment of Newnham and Girton colleges.

In politics, he had liberal sympathies. Among a number of classical schoolbooks published by him are two, a Public School Latin Primer and Public School Latin Grammar, which were for long in use in nearly all English schools. He died near Torquay.

His other chief works are: Sophocles, Oedipus Tyrannus (2nd ed., 1885), Aristophanes, Birds (1874); Aeschylus, Agamemnon (2nd ed1882), with introduction, metrical translation and notes; a commentary on Virgil (3rd ed., 1881); and a translation of Plato, Theaetetus (1881).

He contributed largely to the collection known as Sabrinae Corolla, and published a collection of verse in Greek, Latin and English under the title of Between Whiles (2nd ed., 1882), with many autobiographical details.

Kennedy's Books remain popular right up to the present day for students of the Latin Language.

All of Benjamin hall Kennedy's language Books in their Revised and updated editions are published by the Simon Wallenberg Press.

PREFACE

TO

THE FIFTH EDITION.

————◆◇◆————

§ 1. BY AN AGREEMENT between the Proprietors and Mr. John Peile, Fellow and Tutor of Christ's College, Cambridge, it is arranged that the 'Public School Latin Grammar,' with the books akin to it, shall hereafter be revised by Mr. Peile as joint and, in due time, sole Editor. Mr. Peile's merits as a classical and Sanskrit scholar, and as an able teacher, are widely known. Those who have the advantage of nearer acquaintance with him will be assured that the maintenance and improvement of these books, as means of public instruction, could not be placed in safer keeping.

————————

§ 2. The First Edition of this Grammar, published in January 1871, was introduced by the following Preface :—

'The " Public School Latin Grammar" is simply a development of the Primer, in conformity with the design of those, who, after accepting the latter book, entrusted to the same Editor the preparation of the former. The difference between the elementary compendium and the higher work is such as might be justly expected. Whilst the general principles and many of the paradigms are in both the same, in the Grammar the subject-matter is arranged more systematically, the body of examples very much increased, the illustration wider, and a large amount of information is added, which in the Primer does not appear at all.

'Yet a Grammar of this size does not profess to be an exhaustive treatise on its subject. Competent and careful students, who combine its use with the reading of authors and the practice of composition, so as to master its contents, ought indeed to become Latin scholars of considerable width and power; but they will still find much to learn in the field of Latin, which must be gathered from special monographies by eminent scholars, some of whom are occasionally cited in the following pages.

'At the present time, when the science of Comparative Philology has made such advance, that good living scholars know far more of the history and organism of the Latin language than was known to Quintilian and the old grammarians, the publication of a Higher Latin Grammar, without reference to the facts and principles of that science, would be a retrogressive and senseless act. It must, however, be remembered that the chief end and aim of a Classical Latin Grammar is, to impress upon the minds of students the forms and constructions found in classical authors. Its office, therefore, is to use Comparative Philology as a guide and auxiliary in teaching Latin, not to teach Comparative Philology itself through the medium of Latin. This principle has been kept in view by the Editor throughout his work. The just mean is always hard to observe ; but he may venture to say that he has not strayed from it wilfully. In the Appendix, indeed, and in a few other places, he has thought it not inexpedient to cite some of the most important affinities between Latin and other Aryan languages and dialects ; but only with a view to point the path of future study, not to furnish the student with a sufficient knowledge of the several subjects there noticed.'

3. The following passages are taken from the Preface to the Second Edition, published in 1874 :—

'Competent and candid critics are aware that a book of this size, in spite of its title, is not meant for school use in the same sense as the Primer and other lesson-books of a similar kind. As a school-book (for there is no limit to its use by any students who are capable of good private reading) masters *can* use it in two ways : (1) by enforcing general or occasional reference to its principles and rules in reading Latin authors ;

(2) by requiring definite portions to be prepared for periodical examinations conducted on paper as well as orally.

'The present opportunity has been used to enlarge and improve several departments of the Grammar, especially those of Soundlore and Derivation. To discuss the physiology of articulate sound has never entered into my plan. Were I competent to undertake this, which is not the case, I should hardly deem it suited to a book applying specially to Latin, but rather appropriate to a more general work treating of the Prolegomena to Grammar.

'On the other hand, I have striven to bring out somewhat more prominently than before the leading facts of Comparative Philology, so far as they concern three kindred languages— Latin, Greek, and Sanskrit. The Sanskrit words in this Edition are generally cited in their modern form. The term Primitive Root is, however, used; in what sense, and by what right, appears in a Supplementary Note at the close of the Appendix.

'As I am now, by the kindness of those whom I was bound to consult, authorised to attach my name to this Preface, I think it right to notice the chief objections made to the books on Latin Grammar with which I have been occupied.

'When the Primer was published, seven years ago, it was right that it should be criticised, and certain that it would be impugned ; nor could we expect that all criticism would be equally candid and intelligent, or that every assailant would choose his weapons from the armories of truth and reason only.

'The chief objection urged against the Primer was this : that it was too abstract and difficult for the use of children beginning Latin. There would have been some weight in this argument, if the purpose of the book had been rightly described. But it was really designed as a class-book, not for Elementary Schools and First Forms, but for all Forms in Public Schools below the grade of those boys who could pass with advantage to the use of a fuller Grammar. Other companion books were in preparation for the instruction of children at home or under private care ; and these have since been published.

'It was, secondly, stated as a charge against the Primer, and subsequently against this Grammar (in which the teaching of the Primer is contained), that they " bristle with new, hard, and uninviting terms." This charge, urged as it has been with much persistence, and little concern for truth, must now be met by some remarks on the terminology of Grammar, together with a statement of my own feelings and practice in regard to it.

§ 4. 'Every science must have its own terminology. Grammar is a science; and in Latin Grammar, as one of its departments, there exist, I believe, more than three hundred technical terms. Most of these are either actually Greek words, as Syntax, Prosody, &c., or translated from Greek into Latin, as the names of the Cases and Parts of Speech. Others are purely Latin, as Gerund, Supine, Active, Passive Voice. Of these various terms, whatever the original unfitness of some, the larger number have struck their roots in literature so deeply and widely that any attempt to extirpate them would be quixotic. Many, indeed, are in themselves unmeaning or inadequate (as Gerund, Supine, Deponent, Accusative, Genitive, Ablative); but the learner by gradual experience is enabled to use them practically, which is after all the end we wish to reach, though the road to it might at several points have been improved. A few terms, which are not only vicious, but really confusing, and at the same time unessential, I have exchanged for better substitutes. Among those so rejected are Neuter Verb, Neutropassiva, Neutralia Passiva, Substantive Verb. Again, we find a considerable number of cumbersome Greek terms (Heteroclita, Heterogenea, Aptota, Diptota, Triptota, Tetraptota, with many of the names given to what are called Figures of Speech), which are of little use to learners. These may either be omitted, or, at least, dismissed to some unconspicuous corner.

'This statement affords ample proof that no disposition existed to place in the student's hands a Grammar " bristling with hard and uninviting terms," though it is not unnatural to ask what those "inviting" terms are which, like the " crustula " of the "blandi doctores " in Horace's time, have magic power enough to attract young learners, " elementa velint ut discere prima."

'But there is one important truth which many would-be critics either ignore or forget. Grammar is not only a science, but a science capable of constant improvement; and improvement in science usually brings with it some change in terminology, or some addition to it. Now, in every division of Grammar,—Soundlore, Wordlore, Syntax, and Prosody,—vast strides have been made in this century through the fruitful labours of scholars, chiefly German, some English ; whom I would gladly recount here, were I not afraid of omitting some name or names from so large a list. Accordingly it will be found by those who study the works to which I allude, that the terminology in each division has been more or less modified, more or less enriched.

§ 5. ' As respects my own contributions to Latin Grammar, in the treatment of Soundlore and Wordlore I claim little originality. If I have compiled judiciously and correctly from the works of great comparative philologers, so as to explain and illustrate usefully the received facts of Latin word-formation, I shall be amply satisfied with such credit. Again, in the Prosody of this Grammar I have no share beyond the Table of Metres and one of the Notes on Metre, containing little more than tabular enumeration. The rest I owe to the kindness of my friend Mr. Munro, whose recognised eminence as a scholar needs no praise from me to enhance it.

' But the Analysis of Sentences (Simple and Compound) which constitutes the Syntax of this book, has been, to a great extent, the fruit of personal study, personal thought, personal labour. Sketched out in the Syntax of my " Elementary Latin Grammar," it is filled in, though far from reaching the fullness of perfection, in the present Grammar.

' I speak from long personal experience when I say that any capable mind, which has fully mastered the principles of those pages (348–500, especially 348–359 and 434–500), will be able, in reading any part of Horace, Cicero, Livy, or Tacitus, to move through their longest periods with a firm intellectual step, realising, and, if need be, stating the *raison d'être* of every constructed word, especially (for this is the most crucial test) the *raison d'être* of mood and tense in every Subjunctive Verb. The same mind, so prepared, and applying itself to write Latin, will be free from the risk of using any wrong construction. Not that the mastery of a grammatical Syntax alone will give the student stylistic power and skill in composition. These belong to the *vis divinior*, to inspiration drawn by a gifted nature from the study of the best Latin authors themselves. To such study, combined with practice, no scholar will hesitate to assign by far the largest share in the formation of a good style whether of prose or of poetry. But, in the course of reading, the student cannot afford to neglect any valuable help ; and of all appliances none is so valuable, none so indispensable, as a sound, well-arranged, and lucid Grammar.

§ 6. ' The study of any language with its grammar contains more or less, according to the character of the language chosen, the study of every language and its grammar, the study of language in general and its grammar. The Greek and Latin languages (illustrated by their sister, the Sanskrit) are best adapted for this purpose, because their forms and constructions, themselves grand, are fixed in two grand literatures. One who studies these languages and their grammars cannot help studying to a great extent, coordinately with them, his or her own native language and its grammar. And the best mode and course of study will be that which is so conducted as to make such co-ordination as effectual and as widely instructive as possible. The principal reason why translation into Greek and Latin Verse as well as Prose deserves to be retained in the practice of classical instruction I hold to be this,—that it is a valuable exercise in the acquirement not only of those two dead languages, but of the learner's native living language at the same time.

§ 7. ' A book like the " Public School Latin Grammar " does not pretend to exhaust the subjects of which it treats—subjects on which many large volumes may be, and have been, written—but it carries the student very far on his road, and points and smooths the path of future acquirement.

§ 8. ' I return to speak of my Latin Syntax, by which alone, so far as I know, my works on Grammar have obtained the favour and confidence of eminent scholars engaged in public instruction.

' The treatment of Latin Syntax has in the present century passed through a revolution scarcely less considerable than the treatment of Etymology.

' The means by which this revolution has been wrought are: (1) the application to the whole doctrine of Syntax of the correlative logical terms Subject-Predicate and Subject-Object, with the principles they imply ; (2) the distinction between the Simple and Compound Sentence, and between the several kinds of each, with the consecution of tenses in them ; (3) the distinction between Oratio Recta and Oratio Obliqua, with the various affections which clauses subordinate to Oratio Obliqua receive.

'We owe to the perspicacity and learned labours of various writers, chiefly German, the reforms made in Latin Syntax. I cannot assign to each his due share. The Grotefends, Krüger, Zumpt, O. Schulz, Ramshorn, Kühner, Madvig, Key, have each their special merits. Of these I place Raphael Kühner in the first rank ; and I am much indebted to Grieben's "Lateinische Satzverbindungen." In our own country the scholastic study of this part of Grammar was usefully promoted by the Exercise-books of T. Kerchever Arnold.

'These reforms brought into the teaching of Latin Syntax, besides the terms already named, a certain number more, perhaps from forty to fifty, including the names given to the several varieties of the Simple and Compound Sentence, with their subdivisions ; including also the terms Protasis and Apodosis in sentences which, like the Conditional, take these parts.

§ 9. 'As regards the new terms which my own improvements have suggested, three alone have frequent and important practical use ; the value of which I insist on as very great. These are, (1) Prolative (Infinitive) ; (2) Copulative Verbs, introduced first in my "Elementary Grammar"; (3) Suboblique (clause or verb), a convenient abridgment of the necessary phrase "Subordinate to Oratio Obliqua."

'Further, it appeared that the doctrine of copulative predication in Grammar required, for its clear statement, the use of some terminology from which the term predicate itself should be excluded ; and this was at length found in the term used by Mr. C. P. Mason, (predicative) Complement.

'I say then, generally, that a new term proposed in Grammar is not to be condemned because it is new; but, if at all, for one of three reasons: that it is superfluous ; or that it is inadequate ; or because a better term is suggested. As respects myself, I repeat that I have not the least disposition to use hard terms ; and I say that those which I have introduced are unjustly so described. But I cannot adopt the poor pedantry which refuses to facilitate and abridge discourse by the use of suitable terms ; to write, for instance (after due explanation) "Collective Subject" rather than "Nominative Singular of a Substantive which implies a multitude of persons or things": and "Composite Subject" rather than "two or more singular Nominatives agreeing with one plural Verb."

§ 10. 'My "Elementary Latin Grammar," first published in 1843, obtained, after twenty years, approval so wide, that its circulation approached 8,000 copies annually: and, during those years, not a single complaint affecting its terminology was heard either from the public press or from the eminent teachers who used it in their schools. Such attacks broke out when it was adopted as the groundwork of a new school grammar; and their justice may be tested both by this fact, and by comparing the imaginary difficulty imputed to a few new terms in the Primer, with the many and great obstacles existing in its chief predecessor, Lilly's Grammar.'

§ 11. In the Preface to the Third and Fourth Editions certain portions of Syntax were discussed. Those discussions, being of signal importance to the right appreciation of Latin Compound Construction, will here be repeated generally: but with partial suppression of some topics and enlargement of others.

I. The Doctrine of Predication.

§ 12. This Doctrine is treated (§§ 100–106) in agreement with the principles now received in all Continental Latin Grammars, and in most Grammars of the English language, but with some slight variations in the mode of treatment. Logic and Grammar are akin to one another; but their spheres are different. Logic is the Grammar of reasoning: it develops 'the laws of thought.' Grammar is the Logic of language: it displays the rules and idioms of discourse. The Correlation and the Terms Subject-Predicate are necessary to both sciences. But the scope of these terms is not the same in both.

If we take a Simple Sentence, such as 'beneficium male collocatum nocet (noxium est) hominum societati,' we see that the Logical Subject of this proposition is 'beneficium male collocatum,' but the Grammatical Subject of the sentence is 'beneficium,' of which 'male collocatum' is an adjunct. Again, the Logical Predicate is 'noxium,' the Grammatical Predicate 'nocet' or 'noxium est,' of which 'hominum societati' is an adjunct. Hence appears the propriety and necessity (if confusion is a thing proper and necessary to be avoided) of distinguishing the terms Subject and Predicate in Grammar by the epithet 'Grammatical.' As for the terms Subject-

Predicate themselves, they have now so firm a footing in the science of Grammar that they cannot be excluded from it, if their exclusion were desirable. See 'Predicate' in Index I.

The Subject is 'id quod Praedicato subjectum est' : the Predicate is 'id quod de Subjecto praedicatum est.' The combination of the two (as Kühner says: 'Ausführliche Grammatik der Lat. Spr.,' Part iii. § 1) is rightly calle the Predicative Relation, because the Predicate (or Verbal   ion) is the kernel of speech, to which the Substantival notion stands in subjection, and is therefore called Subject ; often indeed expressed by the endings of the Verb (am·o, ama-s, &c.).

When I was preparing my 'Elementary Latin Grammar' forty years ago, being in some dread of interference with Logic, I took for my type of simple predication, 'homo est mortalis.' But, when the Primer was compiled in 1866, the four Oxford scholars engaged in that work unanimously held that (in Grammar) Subject and Finite Verb are the true norm (homo moritur), and that Incomplete Predication (of the form homo est mortalis) should be taken afterwards as the large exception. This settled the question then, in accordance (as before noticed) with the practice of all continental writers : and a verdict thus authoritatively and generally pronounced is surely entitled to acceptance.

II. Complement (of Predication).

§ 13. This suitable and useful term was first suggested by Mr. C. P. Mason in his 'English Grammar,' to designate that which *completes* the sense of a Simple Sentence when the verb is one 'of *incomplete* Predication' (called 'Copulative' in this Grammar, p. 351).

In sentences such as 'homo moritur (est mortalis),' we have seen above that the Grammatical Predicate is (not 'mortalis,' but) 'moritur' or 'est mortalis.' Donaldson's expedient, of using the terms 'primary, secondary, tertiary' predicate, I cannot approve. It confounds confusion, invades the domain of Logic gratuitously, and carries into the rules of Grammar the use of a word (predicate), which, however necessary to the preamble of Syntax, as the correlative of Subject, may be replaced afterwards by the term Finite Verb (or Verb of the Sentence) with great advantage. All confusion is happily avoided by the term 'Complement,' which is wide enough to include every word or phrase capable of completing the construction of a Copulative Verb, whether finite or infinitive. See the Examples on p. 352.

III. Relations in the Simple Sentence.

§ 14. Mr. Mason, in his 'English Grammar,' following Becker's 'Organism der Sprache,' treats of the Relations of Words in the Simple Sentence. The 'Public School Latin Grammar' does the same. One of our critics regards these Relations as 'spurious children of Logic and Grammar.' But he has failed to interpret the procedure rightly. It is as purely grammatical as any procedure can be, which admits (what no grammarian can now exclude) the correlations Subject-Predicate and Subject-Object.

Two of Mr. Mason's 'Relations,' the Predicative (I.) and the Objective (III.), are the same, in title and extent, as those of this Grammar. His 'Attributive' Relation contains the Qualitative (II.), but is more extensive : his 'Adverbial' Relation contains the Circumstantive (V.), but is more extensive.

Mr. Mason was dealing with English, a language of rare inflexions, using Prepositions in their stead. I deal with Latin, a largely inflected language. But even in English the Genitive should not be merged in the Attributive Relation, and the Dative Case in the Adverbial (Circumstantive): much less in Latin. For, true as it is that numerous instances of the Genitive are attributive in character, and that many Datives might be replaced by Preposition with case (*i.e.* adverbially) ; still there remain very many examples of each case which cannot be so represented, and this fact, combined with that signal distinction between forms of construction, which merits distinct treatment in Grammar, leads to the conclusion that the Dative and Genitive Cases ought to rank as separate Relations. The Dative is therefore classed here under the 'Receptive' (IV.), and the Genitive under the 'Proprietive' Relation (VI.).

Relation VII., that of 'the Prolative Infinitive,' appeared for the first time in the 'Public School Latin Primer.' It comprises all the instances in which the Infinitive *extends* (profert) the construction of words capable of being followed in dependence by a Copulative Infinitive with Nominative Com-

plement. See § 180. In the 'Elementary Latin Grammar'
the Infinitive with some of these Verbs (soleo, possum, &c.)
was called Objective ; with others (videor, dicor, &c.) Predicative (*i.e.* complemental). But these shifts never satisfied: for
if, in 'soleo errare,' the Infinitive is Object of 'soleo,' it is an
unique Object : and if, in 'videor errare,' the Infinitive is predicatively complemental (which in some sense it is), its character
as a 'Complement' is widely distinct from that of an Adjective
or Substantive (which qualify the Subject), and from every other
instance in p. 352. And how, on the same principle, can we
analyse without the most unpleasant confusion such sentences
as these ?—

Marcus putatur velle fieri philosophus. Sapientis est velle
fieri doctiorem.

At length a conviction was reached, that this usage of
Grammar (common to all Aryan languages at least) deserves
separate classification as a specialty of the Infinitive Verb-noun.

Madvig's mode of treating this construction is not essentially
different in principle. Under one head (§ 180) this Grammar
gives what he sets forth in three places (§ 389, § 393, § 400). He
treats in one and the same chapter of the Infinitive in Oratio
Recta and Oratio Obliqua. Deeming it right and important to
keep Simple and Compound Construction apart, we consider in
Chapter III. the Infinitive of Oratio Recta, in Chapter IV.
that of Oratio Obliqua. But when Madvig speaks of the
Infinitive as joined to these (extensible) Verbs 'um den
Begriff zu ergänzen und die Handlung zu ergeben' (*to complete
the idea and supply the action*), this is exactly what is meant by
the Prolative Relation of the Infinitive : and it is very much
the same as the use of the Infinitive, in German and English,
with those Verbs which some grammarians have very inadequately called 'auxiliary' (ich will, soll, kann, muss, &c.
kommen : I will—shall—can—must, &c. come). The construction belongs also to French, a Romance (latinistic)
language. For though French inflects (with Latin) *I will
come, I would come,* by 'je viendrai, je viendrais,' it falls in
with Latin, German, English, in saying je peux—je veux—je
désire—j'ose, &c. venir. It is unquestionably true that after
many of these Verbs the Infinitive may be called an Object by
anybody who wishes to do so, as in 'vincere scis, tu sais
vaincre,' 'cupis abire, tu désires partir,' &c. The use of the

Verb-noun as an Object is recognised in § 179. But the reasons in favour of accepting a distinct Relation wherever the test of 'esse,' &c. with Nominative will apply are decidedly preponderant. If an example be adduced like this in Horace, *C.* i. 2 :—

hic magnos potius triumphos
hic a m e s dici pater atque princeps,

and if it be asked whether, as *triumphos* is Object of a m e s, *dici* does not also stand in the same construction, the reply is— that Latin writers, especially poets, often construct one Verb with dependence of two kinds : so Verg. *Aen.* iii. 234 :—

sociis tunc arma capessant
e d i c o et dira bellum cum gente gerendum.

'Ames,' in the lines of Horace, first takes an Accus. Object *triumphos*, and then a Prolative Infin. *dici*, with its complements. The example belongs to that kind of construction which grammarians have called Zeugma. See § 61.

Our last Relation, the Annexive (VIII.), is in kind different from the other seven. It is really no more than a compendious *method*, by which a word B is noted as assignable to the same Relation with a preceding word A. It is a convenient substitute for those cumbersome and yet incomplete rules which in the old School Grammars were meant to account for the cases, moods, &c. of words linked to others by various conjunctions. See Supplementary Note II. p. 579.

§ 15. There are two great facts in Grammar which the student of language should always bear in mind :—

(1) Few Definitions are free from examples which occasionally stray beyond the precincts there laid down, to enter those of another Definition. For instance : a Substantive may sometimes become an Adjective (rex, regina, raptor, victor, victrix, &c.) : an Adjective or Participle often becomes a Substantive (sapiens, utile, utilia, adulescens, sponsus, dictum, &c.) : a Verb contains a Noun among its forms : a Noun sometimes takes the functions of a Verb : an Adverb becomes a Preposition, a Preposition an Adverb : Declensions encroach upon one another ; and so on.

(2) A Norm or Rule may be liable to numerous exceptions:

and yet, even if the excepted instances could be shewn to equal or even exceed in number the instances which obey the rule, the Norm ought to remain paramount, and not to be extended in order to recognise such instances as normal. See § 101.

Thus, referring to (1), all Annexed Words belong to some one or more of the other Relations also. Every Complement, belonging, as such, to I. will fall under some other Relation also. Of those which occur in the examples, p. 354, the first six fall under II., the seventh and eighth under VI., the tenth under IV., the ninth and eleventh under V. Most examples of Relation VI. and some of IV. V. are akin to II., being attributive in sense, but excluded from II. because they appear as caseforms, and not in attributive concord.

§ 16. The foregoing observations shew that, in the mode of treating these Relations, there is no spurious intrusion of Logic into Grammar. The Dative is not merged in the category of Circumstance, nor the Genitive in that of Attribution (Qualitative). Each case has its own sphere : the Nominative (as Subject-case) and the First Concord are in I., the Accusative as Case of nearer Object is in III., the Dative as remoter Object-case in IV., the Ablative (with the Accusative depending on Prepositions) in V., the Genitive in VI. The Concords 2, 3, 4, come under II.; the peculiar use of the Infinitive under VII., the linking by Conjunctions under VIII. Afterwards, the Vocative and all Interjectional usages lying out of the Sentence are separately treated, and then the theory of the Relative. Grammar is followed, Grammar kept in view, throughout.

Experience proves that such a synopsis of the Simple Sentence *does* materially help many students to read with more profitable appreciation the rules that follow, and, reviewed again at the close, will map the subject in their minds more lucidly and more enduringly.

IV. Ellipse of the Finite Forms of 'Sum.'

§ 17. This topic is considered in the note on p. 428 : see also § 99, Munro *on Lucr.* ii. 1, with the authorities there cited. The ellipse occasionally creates misinterpretation, participles finitely used being sometimes mistaken for mere participles (Hor. *C.* i. 37. 25; ii. 9. 15), and again mere participles having been regarded as finite : thus in Verg. *B.* ii. 40 :—

a

praeterea duo nec tuta mihi valle reperti
capreoli, sparsis etiam nunc pellibus albo,
bina die siccant ovis ubera; quos tibi servo.

Wagner and Ribbeck have a semicolon after 'albo,' thus apparently making 'reperti' finite: but the tenour of the passage indicates that 'capreoli siccant' is the principal predication, and 'reperti' a mere participle.

The ellipse of 'esse' in oblique construction, when the participles perfect, future, or gerundive occur as accusatives in dependence, is familiar to every reader of Latin authors in prose and poetry. But the Prolative construction, by which the Nominatives of these Participles are used as Infinitives without 'esse,' is not by any means so generally and so well understood by young scholars. They are therefore advised to study with care the note on § 180 in this Grammar, and to collect other examples of this construction (the Participles in the Nominative as Infinitives without 'esse'), which are not duly recognised in Madvig's Grammar. It may perhaps be more clearly exhibited by setting side by side the Accusative (Oblique) and the Nominative (Prolative) constructions in a few examples.

    a. T. Manlium locutum ferunt,
       T. Manlius locutus fertur, Liv.
    b. Ferunt Promethea coactum . . .
       Fertur Prometheus coactus . . . Hor.
    c. Delectum habendum putant,
       Delectus habendus putatur.
    d. Omnes secuturos verisimile est,
       Omnes secuturi videntur.
    e. Graeciam collisam narrant,
       Graecia collisa narratur, Hor.
    f. Memorant quendam solitum . . .
       Memoratur quidam solitus, . . . Hor.
    g. Credimus Athon ve
       Creditur Athos velificatus, Iuv.
    h. Ferunt genetricem adfatam Iovem,
       Fertur genetrix adfata Iovem, Verg. ix. 82.

In every one of these examples 'esse' is to be mentally supplied—its construction being Oblique (§ 194) in each former—Prolative (§ 180) in each latter line.

V. § 18. Some nice points of Syntax have been either over-looked or inadequately treated. Such are the Substantival constructions with ut and quod, in place of an Infinitive Clause. See §§ 195–6. Still more unfortunate has been the treatment of constructions ranked in this Grammar under the title Petitio Obliqua, § 197. A disposition is shewn by some writers to make these mere varieties of the Adverbial (Final) Clause with ut, ne, although their prominence and importance in Narratio Obliqua (§ 230) prove their just rank as one of the three varieties of dependent Substantival Clauses, which constitute Oratio Obliqua. The Statement (Accusative and Infinitive) and the Question assert themselves, as it were, and cannot be ignored : but the Dependent Petition has to wage a sort of rivalry with other constructions of ut, ne, in order to obtain its just place in Grammar, as representing an Oblique 'permission, command, or request.' The examples which Madvig cites in §§ 403–4, shewing the juxtaposition in Narratio Obliqua of indirect statements, commands, and questions, might have shewn him the true order in which the three ought to be treated.

' Si pacem populus Romanus cum Helvetiis faceret, in eam partem *ituros* atque ibi *futuros Helvetios*, ubi eos Caesar constituisset atque esse voluisset : sin bello persequi perseveraret, *reminisceretur* et veteris incommodi populi Romani et pristinae virtutis Helvetiorum . . . quare *ne committeret* ut is locus, ubi constitissent, ex calamitate populi Romani . . . nomen caperet.' —Caes. *B. G.* i. 13.

' Cum vellet, *congrederetur; intellecturum* quid invicti Germani . . . . virtute possent.'—Caes. *B. G.* i. 38.

' Duces pronuntiare iusserunt : " *ne* quis ab loco *discederet ;* illorum *esse praedam* atque illis *reservari* quaecumque Romani reliquissent : proinde omnia in victoria posita *existimarent.*" '— Caes. *B. G.* v. 34.

' Cicero respondit : " non *esse consuetudinem* populi Romani accipere ab hoste armato condicionem : si ab armis discedere velint, se adiutore *utantur* legatosque ad Caesarem *mittant; sperare,* pro eius iustitia quae petierint impetraturos." '—Caes. *B. G.* v. 42.

' Nuntia Romanis : " *caelestes* ita *velle* ut mea Roma caput orbis terrarum sit : proinde rem militarem *colant; sciantque* et ita posteris *tradant*, nullas opes humanas armis Romanis resistere posse." '—Liv. i. 16.

'Exprobrant multitudini : "*saginare plebem* populares suos, ut iugulentur. *hoccine patiendum fuisse*, si ad nutum dictatoris non responderit vir consularis? *fingerent* mentitum ante, atque ideo non habuisse quod tum responderet : cui servo umquam mendácii poenam *vincula fuisse?*" '—Liv. vi. 17.

'Blaesus multa dicendi arte, "non per seditionem et turbas *desideria* militum ad Caesarem *ferenda*," ait ; " neque *veteres* ab imperatoribus priscis neque *ipsos* ab divo Augusto tam nova *petivisse*; et parum in tempore incipientes principis *curas onerari* : si tamen tenderent in pace temptare quae ne civilium quidem bellorum victores expostulaverint, *cur* contra morem obsequii, contra fas disciplinae vim *meditentur? decernerent* legatos seque coram mandata *darent*." '—Tac. *Ann.* i. 19.

'Eo in metu arguere Germanicum omnes, *quod non* ad superiorem exercitum *pergeret*, ubi obsequia et contra rebellis auxilium: " Satis superque missione et pecunia et mollibus consultis *peccatum* ; vel si vilis ipsi salus, *cur* filium parvulum, *cur* gravidam coniugem inter furentes et omnis humani iuris violatores *haberet?* illos saltem avo et reipublicae *redderet*." '—Tac. *Ann.* i. 40. See do. do. ii. 15.

'post paulo scribit sibi *milia quinque*
esse domi chlamydum ; partem vel *tolleret* omnes.'
Hor. *Epist.* i. 6. 43.

Compare Verg. *Aen.* iv. 683 :

date volnera lymphis *Abluam*, &c.

Aen. vi. 884 :

manibus *date* lilia plenis Purpureos *spargam* flores, &c.

The true construction, 'date abluam,' *grant me to wash away*, 'date spargam,' *grant me to scatter*, &c., has in each place been recognised fully by no commentator except Ladewig. If commentators who have fallen into error respecting them had been familiar with the principles of 'Petitio Obliqua,' they would have seen that the Subjunctives depend as Objects on 'date,' like 'colamus' in the following lines of an Inscription to Silvanus found at Aime in France :

tu me meosque reduces Roman sistito·
*da*que Itala rura te *colamus* praeside.—Coll. Orell. 1613.

Had 'sinite' been written instead of 'date' (and there is no real difference) the mistake would not have been made.

VI. § 19. Chapter VI. of Part I., Division ii. (§§ 61–99), on the Uses of Words, though subjoined to Wordlore, may be read by those who have already studied Latin Syntax to some extent in a shorter Grammar with suitable practice. It unavoidably contains many topics (as, Ellipsis and Zeugma, Prepositions, Correlation, Mood), which belong in principle to the construction of Sentences, and which many grammarians, as Madvig, intermingle with the rules of Syntax, thereby, we think, sadly breaking the continuity, and obscuring the doctrine of these latter, as intended to develop the construction of Sentences, Simple and Compound.

To those who study this Grammar we strongly recommend the adoption of the following order, in studying the laws of Words constructed in Sentences; *i.e.* Syntax.

(1) Wordlore, Division ii., Chapter VI., Sections i.–viii. (§§ 61–89).

(2) Wordlore, Division ii., Chapter II., Section x. (Numerals, §§ 32–34).

(3) Syntax, Chapters I., II., III., IV., Section i. (§§ 100–189).

(4) Uses of the Verb (Wordlore, §§ 90–99).

(5) Syntax continued (§§ 190–250).

The whole Chapter on the Uses of Words may be reperused with advantage at the close of such a course.

VII. § 20. The systematic order in which the Doctrine of Sentences is drawn out is the chief characteristic feature of this Grammar.

Chapter I. of Part II. (§ 100) sets forth :

(1) The distinction of Sentences as Simple or Compound.

(2) The three forms of the Simple Sentence :

Statement (enuntiatio): Will-speech (petitio): Question (interrogatio).

(3) The forms which these three severally take when, being subordinated in compound construction, they become Substantival Clauses :—

Oblique Statement : Oblique Will-speech : Oblique Question.

Chapter II. (§§ 101–106) contains :

The Analysis of the Simple Sentence, and the eight Relations comprised in it: adding to these the Interjectional use of the Vocative and other Cases similarly interposed.

Chapter III. (§§ 107–188) contains:
Rules and Examples of construction in the Simple Sentence (Agreement: Cases: Infinitive with Gerunds and Supines).

Chapter IV. (§§ 189–240) treats of:
The Compound Sentence, in five Sections.
Section I. takes up the topic begun in Chapter I., and shews:
(1) Subordinate Clauses, of three kinds;
Substantival (§ 100): Adverbial: Adjectival:
(2) Adverbial Clauses, of seven kinds:
(3) Adjectival Clauses, being in some kinds substitutes for Adverbial (see § 204).

Section II. states the laws of Mood in subordination to Oratio Obliqua, actual and virtual, with examples.

Section III. contains:
Rules and Examples of the construction of the three varieties of Substantival Clauses:
(1) Oblique or Indirect Statement (enuntiatio obliqua).
(2) Oblique or Indirect Will-speech (petitio obliqua).
(3) Oblique or Indirect Question (interrogatio obliqua).

Section IV. contains:
Rules and Examples of Adverbial and Adjectival Clauses treated in connexion with one another.

Section V. forms a Supplement, treating of:
(1) Consecution of Tenses:
(2) Narratio Obliqua:
(3) Reflexive Pronouns in Clauses:
(4) Participial Construction.

VIII. § 21. The scheme of Latin construction thus shewn forms an edifice of its doctrine, from which no stone can be taken away or displaced without damage to the whole fabric.[1]

---

[1] Let me here state my meaning more distinctly.

1. I consider it *desirable* that the Uses of Words and the Rules of Construction should be kept generally distinct: but I deem it *essential* that the Uses of the Verb and the Doctrine of Moods should be learnt *before* the Laws of Compound Construction. This opinion is illustrated in Appendix II. to the 'Public School Latin Primer' (years 1878 &c.).

Nor can a single fact or principle laid down in it be denied by any one who is able to recognise facts in language, and to deduce principles from them correctly.

(1) The Simple Sentence has three Varieties :

1. Vales : 2. Vale : 3. Valesne?

Can this be denied?

(2) Each Variety can be subjoined (with some formal change) to a principal Predication ; such junction being a 'Compound Sentence,' the subordinate or dependent member in which we term 'the Clause.'

1. Audio (constat) *te valere.*

2. Opto (optandum est) *ut valeas.*

3. Quaero (quaeritur) (dic) *valeasne.*

Can this be denied?

(3) Each of these Clauses is related as Object or Subject to the Verb on which it depends.

1. I hear (it is evident)—What? *That you are well.*

2. I wish (my wish must be)—What? *That you be well.*

3. I ask (it is asked) (say)—What? *Whether you are well.*

Can this be denied? (See it even in Madvig, § 208b, 398a.)

2. It is essential that Syntax should take for its starting-point the three forms of a simple sentence and their transformation into clauses when they become subordinate.

3. It is essential that the study of Simple and that of Compound Sentences should be treated in distinct parts of the Grammar, and that the rules for the Simple Infinitive, with Gerunds and Supines, should be included under the Simple Sentence, leaving the Infinitive Clause (though it may be cursorily mentioned) to take its proper place at the head of Compound Construction.

4. It is essential that the Doctrine of Compound Construction should take for its starting-point the threefold distinction of Substantival, Adverbial, and Adjectival Clauses, shewing the intimate relation of the two latter classes.

5. It is essential that the Substantival Ut-clause and the Substantival Quod-clause should be shewn in their true place as succursal to the Infinitive Clause, with due notice of the relation which they severally imply to Consecutive and Causal Construction.

6. It is highly important that (while the term Conjunctive is given to the Mood generally) the term Subjunctive should be confined to its subordinate use.

7. The distinction of Compound and Complex Sentences, which some English grammarians use, is superfluous in Latin. That of Coordinate and Subordinate Clauses (§ 100) answers the purpose adequately.

(4) Therefore each of these Clauses has the property of a Substantive, and is justly termed 'Substantival.'

Can this be denied?

(5) Of other Subordinate Clauses, those which answer the adverbial questions—*how, for what purpose, why, when, on what condition*, &c.—are justly termed Adverbial Clauses (Consecutive, Final, &c.). See § 189 B.

There can be no just reason to deny this.

[All Relative Clauses—formed by qui or a particle explicable by a case of qui, as quo, unde, cur, &c., may be called Adjectival, having the attributive nature of Adjectives. But in this Grammar (§ 189 C, § 204, &c.) the term is applied only to those Relative Clauses which determine Mood to be Subjunctive: such as: Quis est tam impius *qui* parentem feriat? = ut feriat?—Missi sunt *qui* specularentur = ut specularentur :— Miseret me tui *qui* tantum desipias = quum . . . desipias : and the like. The larger power of the term Adjectival, as belonging to any Relative Clause, should not be forgotten, though its use is needed here alone to complete the analogy.]

This classification of Clauses, as Substantival, Adverbial, and Adjectival, is recognised by the soundest German grammarians, Krüger, Kühner, Feldbausch, Grieben, and many others. Its omission is among the chief faults of Madvig's Syntax.

(6) Returning to Substantival Clauses (2), we observe that each of the Clauses is *indirect*, i.e. dependent on a Verb, which is itself *direct*, i.e. independent. This *indirect speech* is called by general consent of grammarians 'Oratio Obliqua,' and that on which it depends is called 'Oratio Recta' (direct speech). Thus it appears, that all three forms of the Substantival Clause constitute Oratio Obliqua. This is allowed, though haltingly and inadequately, by Madvig, § 403, Obs. 1. The chief reason why oblique statement (te valere) has been 'specially called' Oratio Obliqua is this : that ordinary discourse in prose consists mainly of statements. Another reason is, that the indirect expression of the Imperative (bidding-speech or will-speech) is not so manifestly distinguishable from other forms as the Infinitive Clause (te valere), about which there can be no mistake. See what is said above of Petitio Obliqua. The student is strongly advised to keep this larger sense of the term Oratio Obliqua always in mind, and to fortify it by careful

study of Oblique Narration, as used by Livy, Sallust, and Tacitus. He may also consult with advantage the Syntaxis Vergiliana in our edition of Virgil, pp. 664, &c.

(7) The limits of Oratio Obliqua being thus established as coincident with Substantival Clauses, we pass to the Mood of Verbs in subsequent Clauses depending on them, which we therefore call 'Suboblique,' that is, 'Subordinate to Oratio Obliqua.' The rules on this subject are given in §§ 190–193, because the constructions resulting from them occur in many of the examples cited in the sections following.

The Conjunctive is, by its nature, the Thought-mood or mood of conception. Hence, when a finite verb in secondary dependence forms part of the same conception as the Oratio Obliqua in primary dependence, it is put in the Subjunctive (dependent Conjunctive). See Example in § 190 I. So also :

Apud Hypanim fluvium Aristoteles ait b e s t i o l a s quasdam n a s c i, quae unum diem *vivant*, Cic. *T. D.* i. 39. Perspicuum est, non e s s e u t i l i a, quae *sint* turpia, Cic. *Off.* iii.

With the other examples on p. 437 of this Grammar, and those in 'Public School Latin Primer,' p. 167. This doctrine is laid down in all Latin grammars.

IX. § 22. So also Rule 193, which states that a subjunctive is used in dependence on another Verb in the Conjunctive Mood, is in the nature of a corollary to Rule 190, and is not disputed. Rule 191 relates to implied or virtual Oratio Obliqua. The doctrine on this subject I have somewhere seen described as a mystery, too abstruse for anybody to understand or study. Now the differential calculus, or logarithms, or even decimal fractions, remain a mystery to those who have not taken the trouble to learn them. But Grammars are written for those who are willing to learn, and who wish to know well what they profess to know at all. It seems, therefore, that a few words here may not be wasted in the endeavour to clear up a subject which, after all, has nothing in it mysterious. For this purpose, it is best to begin with the simplest obvious examples. Compare, then, the two following places in Cicero's Treatise 'De Officiis' :

(1) Cyrenaici . . . virtutem c e n s u e r u n t esse l a u-d a n d a m, *quod* efficiens *esset* voluptatis, iii. 33.

(2) L a u d a t Africanum Panaetius, *quod fuerit* abstinens, ii. 22.

We say that ' virtutem esse laudandam' (actually) *is* Oratio Obliqua, on which 'quod esset' depends, and is therefore Subjunctive, being 'suboblique.' We say that 'laudat' (virtually) *contains* Oratio Obliqua, and that 'quod fuerit,' depending on it, is 'virtually suboblique.'

Such is our proposition. Let us consider it.

First, as to 'quod esset' in sentence (1).

'Virtutem esse laudandam' is Oratio Obliqua in its principal form of Accus. with Infin. (Infinitive Clause), and a Finite Verb really depending on such a form will be Subjunctive because the reason given for virtue being praiseworthy as well as the fact itself is referred to the mind of the Cyrenaics, and for this purpose the Thought-mood (Conjunctive) is employed. Such is the rationale of a Subjunctive 'actually subordinate to Oratio Obliqua,' or (for brevity's sake) 'suboblique.'

Secondly, as to 'quod fuerit,' in Sentence (2).

Do we utter 'a mystery' when we say, that a person who is said to praise another, is said *to think* and *to express* something; that 'laudat' necessarily contains the meaning 'putat esse laudandum' with the meaning 'ait esse laudandum'? Enough that it contains the latter. Laudat then contains 'virtual (i.e. implied) Oratio Obliqua': and the Finite Verb depending on it (quod fuerit), being really subordinate to a virtual Oratio Obliqua, or (for brevity's sake) 'virtually suboblique,' is referred to the mind of Panaetius by becoming Subjunctive. He gives the reason why he praises.

Such is one of the simplest instances of 'virtual Oratio Obliqua.'

X. § 23. Here it will be right to deal with a plausible objection, which may lead some not unintelligent minds to question the merit of the terminology used. Why, they may perhaps say, is a term which itself needs explanation, and which suggests a merely formal cause, interposed between the learner's understanding and the true logical reason of the Thought-mood, viz. that it refers the proposition to the *mind* of the Subject?

The answer to this objection has already been suggested in another part of this Preface. Every science is taught and learnt through the medium of terms. It is the teacher's business to see that his pupils do learn—do know—the meaning and force of such terms. It is a learner's business to acquire their meaning and force, either from his teacher (if he has one) or from his books (if he studies privately). If he uses terms, of which he has not learnt the true meaning, he walks in the dark, and the results can only be ignorance and error. A good teacher will be always on his guard against this danger. If he asks a question, and is answered by a correct term, which he is sure the learner understands, he may say 'quite right,' and pass on. If he doubts this, he should cross-examine. For instance,

As to passage (1):
Q. Why is 'esset' Subjunctive?
A. It is suboblique.
Q. How so?
A. It is subordinate to the Oratio Obliqua 'virtutem esse laudandam.'
Q. And this Oratio Obliqua itself?
A. It is subordinate to the principal sentence 'Cyrenaici censuerunt.'
Q. To what then is the Clause 'quod efficiens esset voluptatis' referred?
A. To the mind of the Subject 'Cyrenaici.'

As to passage (2):
Q. Why is 'fuerit' Subjunctive?
A. It is virtually suboblique.
Q. How so?
A. It is subordinate to an Oratio Obliqua implied in 'laudat.'
Q. How would you express this Oratio Obliqua?
A. Ait esse laudandum (or some equivalent).
Q. To what then is the Clause 'quod fuerit abstinens' referred?
A. To the mind of the Subject Panaetius.

If the question were in class, and the catechumen failed to answer, the teacher would probably explain publicly, and re-examine privately, till he was sure the matter was understood.

If our imaginary disputant, returning to the charge, says: May not this cross-examination be cut short? is not all contained in the last question and answer? No, we reply: for we are not teaching Logic only, but also Latin: Latin construction,

Latin procedure, with its *rationale.* The attempt to teach the *rationale* without the forms which lead to it would be a double failure : grammar would manifestly be sacrificed, and Logic (we believe) would gain nothing by the sacrifice.

XI. § 24. Some persons imagine they have solved all 'the mystery' of such constructions as (2) by saying that 'The Subjunctive is used in Causal and Relative Sentences to denote an alleged reason or act.' These words we quote from one such writer.[1]

'Causal and Relative Sentences' certainly do (for obvious reasons) supply the most numerous instances of 'virtually

---

[1] It may be instructive to cite this writer's 'ipsissima verba,' as an instance of error growing out of the attempt to defend error. He says :

'The Subjunctive is also used in Causal and Relative Sentences to denote an alleged reason or act, as "Laudat Panaetius Africanum, quod fuerit abstinens," "Panaetius praises Africanus, *because he says that he was* self-restraining." Fuit for fuerit would mean "because he actually was self-restraining," without implying that Panaetius said so. So "iniuria quae tibi facta est," "the injury which has been done you" ; but "iniuria quae tibi facta sit," "the injury which you say has been done you." Cic. *in Caec.* 58.'

(1) The translation here marked in italic type I would rather leave to the judgment of scholars than characterise it myself. The correct version is '*alleging that he was*' or (better still) '*on the ground that he was.*'

(2) 'Fuit' for 'fuerit' would not have been joined by Cicero to such a context as 'laudat quod,' that is to say, where the principal verb is one which by its own nature (as laudo, queror, accuso, &c.) contains Oratio Obliqua, and is used in any person but the first. If the verb has no such nature, as in the well-known passage 'Themistocles noctu ambulabat, quod somnum capere non posset,' *T. D.* iv. 19, Cicero could have written 'poterat,' if he had wished to refer the clause to his own statement.

(3) Any good scholar, on reading this writer's next citation (from Cic. *in Caec.* 58) would perceive at once that it is fallacious ; that the context, when supplied, must account for the use of 'quae sit facta.' And such is the case. Cicero writes : 'Hic tu, si laesum te a Verre esse dices, patiar et concedam : *si iniuriam tibi factam quereris*, defendam et negabo. Deinde *de iniuria, quae tibi facta sit*, neminem nostrum graviorem vindicem esse oportet quam te ipsum, cui facta dicitur.' Then, a few sentences later : 'Quid si *ne iniuriae quidem, quae tibi ab illo facta sit*, causa remanet ?'

It would be quite enough to say that for 'si iniuriam tibi factam quereris' Cicero might have used the not less frequent 'quereris quod iniuria tibi facta sit,' and that 'de iniuria quae tibi facta sit' is a mere abridgement of suboblique' construction : and I suppose this writer has been misled by Madvig, who, in his very faulty treatment of Mood, mentions such examples only. But the principle is general, and applies also to Temporal, Conditional, and Concessive Clauses : as witness the following examples :

Darius ejus pontis, *dum* ipse *abesset*, custodes reliquit, Nep. *Milt.* 3. At memoria minuitur. Credo, *nisi* eam *exerceas*, aut *si sis* natura tardior, Cic. *C. M.* 7. Utilitas efflorescit ex amicitia, *etiamsi* tu eam minus *secutus sis*, Cic. *Lael.* 27.

This last example is gnomic in its nature. See xv.

Moreover, it is not true that the Subjunctive, by its own *independent* right, 'denotes an alleged reason or act.' If this were so, then the compound sentence 'Laudat Africanum Panaetius, *nam fuerit* abstinens' would be good Latin, and might express 'Panaetius praises Africanus, for he was self-denying': quod absurdum est, as geometricians say.

The truth (overlooked by the writer in question) is that this power belongs to the Mood *in subordination* only, when it is truly Subjunctive ; and it belongs to it only *in its relation to* the previous predication, which is never to be left out of question. If such predication is itself subordinate, that is, conveys the thought of another subject going before it, as in (1), then the Subjunctive also shares that thought. If the Subjunctive, as in (2), depends on a principal Indicative (and is not Consecutive, or otherwise controlled), its presence denotes that in that principal predication the idea of Oratio Obliqua is *implied*. In other words, it is not the dependent mood alone which is then to be considered, but *the principal predication together with its dependence.* In the sentence cited in the note, 'posset' conveys to 'ambulabat' the accessary notion of a reason given for the act by Themistocles : 'poterat' would confine 'ambulabat' to the statement of Cicero.

XII. § 25. I proceed to support my explanation of this doctrine by citing a large number of examples, which will be more instructive if divided into three classes :

'de iniuria, de qua quereris quod tibi facta sit.' But also 'de iniuria, quae tibi facta sit' is really subordinate to the Oratio Obliqua 'neminem . . . vindicem esse': and, when 'facta sit' is afterwards used, Cicero merely cites his own phrase, the import of which is known from the previous context. See Example 57, below.

First : Examples in which the text does not exhibit formal 'oratio obliqua'; but a slight addition or a slight change of form at once exhibits it without any difference of sense.

Secondly : Examples where 'oratio obliqua' is implied in the meaning of the principal construction as one of expressed feeling : *praise, blame, complaint, accusation, reproach, boasting, giving thanks, promising, indignation, anger, menace, regret,* &c.

Thirdly : Examples in which no such connexion exists between the principal Sentence and the Clause as to exhibit a *manifest* 'Oratio Obliqua'; but we say, on the ground of analogy, that an accessory meaning is conveyed to the principal construction from the fact of its relation to the Clause.

CLASS I.

1. Ne iustitiam quidem recte quis dixerit per se optabilem, sed *quia* iucunditatis vel plurimum *afferat.*—Cic. *d. Fin.* i. 16. (Dixerit only wants the dropped *esse* to make this an example of actual oratio obliqua.)

2. Te felicem dicis amasque
 Quod nusquam tibi *sit* potandum.—Hor. *S.* ii. 7, 31.
  (*Esse te felicem.*)

3. Recte est igitur surgetque? negabit,
 Quod latus aut renes morbo *temptentur* acuto.—Hor. *S.* ii. 3, 162. (Negabit *recte esse.*)

4. Hanc reperiebat causam, *quod* apud Germanos ea consuetudo *esset* ut &c.—Cæs. *B. G.* i. 50. (*Causam esse.*)

5. Cum contemplor animo, reperio quattuor causas, cur senectus misera videatur : unam, *quod avocet* a rebus gerendis ; alteram, *quod* corpus *faciat* infirmius ; tertiam, *quod privet* omnibus fere voluptatibus ; quartam, *quod* haud procul *absit* a morte.—Cic. *C. M.* 5. (*Esse* being supplied with 'causas,' 'unam' &c., oratio obliqua exists throughout.)

6. Ille laborem
 Excusare Philippo et mercennaria vincla
 Quod non mane domum *venisset,* denique *quod* non
 Providisset eum.—Hor. *Ep.* i. 7, 66. (Excusare=*dicit in causa esse.*)

7. Bene maiores nostri accubitionem epularem amicorum, *quia* vitae coniunctionem *haberet*, convivium nominarunt.—Cic. *C. M.* 13. (Nominarunt=*esse dixerunt.*)

8. Caesar sua senatusque in Ariovistum beneficia commemoravit, *quod* rex *appellatus esset* a senatu, *quod* amicus, &c.—Caes. *B. G.* i. 43. (Commemoravit= *multa esse dixit.*)

9.   Huic me, *quaecumque fuisset,*
   Addixi.—Verg. *Aen.* iii. 652. (Addixi me=*dixi me adhaesurum.*)

10. Videor mihi gratum fecisse Siculis, *quod* eorum iniurias meo labore, inimicitiis, periculo *sim persecutus.*—Cic. *Verr.* ii. 6. (Videor mihi=*puto me.*)

11. Commodissimum visum est C Valerium Procillum . . . *quod* in eo peccandi Germanis causa non *esset,* ad eum mittere.—Cæs. *B. G.* i. 47. (Visum est=*putavit esse.*)

12. Mirabile videtur *quod* non *rideat* haruspex cum haruspicem viderit ; hoc mirabilius *quod* vos inter vos risum tenere *possitis.*—Cic. *N. D.* i. 26. (Mirabile videtur=*mirandum esse putant.*)

13. Thucydides libros suos tum scripsisse dicitur, *cum* a republica remotus atque in exilium *pulsus esset.*—Cic. *d. Or.* ii. 15. (Th. scripsisse dicitur=*Thucydidem scripsisse dicunt.*)

14. *Quidquid peperisset* decreverunt tollere.—Ter. *And.* ii. 1, 6. (Tollere=*ut tollerent.*)

15. Helvetii constituerunt ea *quae* ad proficiscendum *pertinerent* comparare.—Caes. *B. G.* i. 3. (Comparare= *ut compararent.*)

Class II.

16. Nemo extulit eum verbis, *qui* ita *dixisset,* ut qui adessent intellegerent quid diceret.—Cic. *d. Or.* i. 14. (Extulit verbis=*laudandum esse dixit.*)

17. Athenienses Lacedaemoniorum victorias suae culpae tribuebant, *quod* Alcibiadem e civitate *expulissent.* —Nep. *Alc.* 6.

18. Caesar temeritatem cupiditatemque militum reprehendit, *quod* sibi ipsi *iudicavissent* quo procedendum aut quid agendum videretur.—Caes. *B. G.* vii. 52.

19. Nec vero quisquam potest iure reprehendere, *quod* mare non *transierim.*—Cic. *Att.* viii. 12, 3.

20. Haedui questum veniebant, *quod* Harudes, qui nuper in Galliam transportati essent, fines eorum *popularentur.* —Caes. *B. G.* i. 37.

21. Saepe illi deplorare solebant, tum *quod* voluptatibus *carerent* . . . tum *quod spernerentur* ab eis, a quibus essent coli soliti.—Cic.

22. Hospitem inclamavit, *quod* sese absente mihi fidem habere *noluisset.*—Plaut. *Asin.* 583.

23. Graviter Haeduos accusat *quod* . . . non *sublevetur* . . . *quod sit destitutus,* queritur.—Caes. *B. G.* i. 16.

24. Theophrastus moriens accusasse naturam dicitur, *quod* hominibus tam exiguam vitam *dedisset.*—Cic. *T. D.* iii. 28.

25. Vercingetorix proditionis insimulatus est *quod* castra propius Romanos *movisset, quod* cum omni equitatu *discessisset, quod* sine imperio tantas copias *reliquisset, quod* eius discessu Romani tanta opportunitate et celeritate *venissent.*—Caes. *B. G.* vii. 20.

26. Caesar centuriones incusavit, *quod* aut quam in partem aut quo consilio ducerentur, sibi quaerendum aut cogitandum *putarent.*—Caes. *B. G.* i. 40.

27. Themistocles graviter castigavit Lacedaemonios, *quod* non virtute sed imbecillitate sociorum potentiam *quaererent.*—Iust. ii. 15.

28. Cato obiecit ut probrum M. Nobiliori, *quod* is in provinciam poetas *duxisset.*—Cic. *T. D.* i. 2.

29. Litterae ipsae videntur quasi exprobrare *quod* in eà vita *maneam,* in qua nihil insit, nisi propagatio miserrimi temporis.—Cic. *Fam.* vi. 15.

30. Non tam exitu bellorum, *quod vincatis,* quam principiis, *quod* non sine causa *suscipiatis,* gloriamini.—Liv. xlv. 22.

31. Caesari decima legio per tribunos militum gratias egit, *quod* de se optimum iudicium *fecisset.*—Caes. *B. G.* i. 41.

32. Themistocles domino navis quis sit aperit, multa pollicens *si se conservasset.*—Nep. *Them.* 8.

33. Xerxes ei praemium proposuit, *qui invenisset* novam voluptatem.—Cic. *T. D.* v. 7.

34.   Beroen digressa reliqui
Aegram, indignantem, tali *quod* sola *careret*
Munere, nec meritos Anchisae *inferret* honores.—Verg.
Aen. v. 650.

35. Augebat iras, *quod* soli Iudaei non cessissent.—Tac. *H.*
v. 10.

36. Atqui voltus erat multa et praeclara minantis,
Si vacuum tepido *cepisset* villula tecto.—Hor. *S.* ii. 3, 9.

37.   Aeneas . . . minatur
Exitium, *si* quisquam *adeat.*—Verg. *Aen.* xii. 760.   See
viii. 649.

38. An paenitet vos, *quod* salvum atque incolumem exercitum *traduxerim?*—Caes. *B. G.* ii. 32.

Class III.

39. Nec fluminibus aggesta terra semper laudabilis, *quando
senescant* sata quaedam aqua.—Plin. *N. H.* xvii. 4.
(Laudabilis=*ea quae laudari debeat.*)

40. Eo id laudabilius erat, *quod* animum eius tanta acerbitas patria nihil a pietate *avertisset.*—Liv. vii. 5. (Eo
laudabilius erat=*eo magis laudandum esse plebs putavit.*)

41. Lycurgus populo creandi *quos vellet* magistratus potestatem
permisit.—Iust. iii. 3. (Permisit=*dari iussit.*)

42. Conon a colloquio Artaxerxis prohibitus est, *quod* eum
more Persarum adorare *nollet.*—Iust. vi. 2. (Conon
prohibitus est=*edictum est ut Conon prohiberetur.*)

43. Unus ex eis domum abiit, *quod* fallaci reditu in castra
iureiurando se *exsolvisset.*—Liv. xxii. 61. (Abiit=*abire
licitum esse putavit.*)

44. Augebat Tyriis animos Didonis exemplum, *quae* Carthagine condita tertiam partem orbis *quaesisset.*—Iust.
xi. 10. (Augebat . . . exemplum=*animari se dicebant
Didonis exemplo.*)

45. Si quis erat dignus describi *quod* malus aut fur . . . *foret*
. . . notabant.—Hor. *S.* i. 4, 3. (Describi=*qui descri-
beretur.*)

46   Mercatique solum, facti de nomine Byrsam,
Taurino *quantum possent* circumdare tergo.—Verg. *Aen.*
i. 367. (i.e. mercati sunt, *pacti tantum fore quantum,*

&c. 'Poterant' might have been written, if the
mere fact, not the thought of the purchasers were
to be expressed.)

47. Pascentes illae tantum prodire volando
Quantum acie *possent* oculi servare sequentum.—Verg.
Aen. vi. 199. (Prodire=*prodire se volebant.* Again
'poterant' might have been used of the mere fact.)

48. Perdiccas rex Macedoniae moriens filio monstravit locum
quo condi *vellet.*—Just. vii. 2. (Monstravit implies the
addition *eum esse dicens.*)

49. Sapiens non dubitat, *si* ita melius *sit,* migrare de vita.
—Cic. *Fin.* i. 19. (Non dubitat migrare=*migrandum
sibi esse decernit.*)

50. Tribunos omnes patricios creavit populus contentus eo,
quod ratio plebeiorum *habita esset.*—Liv. iv. 6. (Contentus eo=*satis esse putans.*)

51. Consulem cura anceps agitare : nolle deserere socios,
nolle minuere exercitum, *quod* aut moram sibi ad
dimicandum aut in dimicando periculum afferre *posset.*
—Liv. xxxiv. 12. (Oratio obliqua· is evidently latent
here: most simply we may say ' deserere '='se deserere,'
' minuere '='se minuere.')

52. Ille nescio qui, qui in scholis nominari solet, mille et
octoginta stadia *quod abesset* videbat.—Cic. *Ac. Pr.* ii.
25. (i.e. *videre dicebatur a nominantibus.*)

53. *Quoniam* Miltiades ipse pro se dicere non *posset,* verba
pro eo fecit frater eius Tisagoras.—Nep. *Milt.* 7.
(Fecit=*facienda a se putavit* ; but the example is a daring
one.)

54. Re nuntiata ad suos, *quae imperarentur* facere dixerunt.
—Caes. *B. G.* ii. 32. (This sentence is remarkably con-
densed. At full it is : 'the envoys of the Aduatuci, *after
reporting the matter to their constituents,* came back and
said they would do what was ordered them.' ' Facere ' is,
in fact, oratio obliqua, ' suos ' being understood as subject.)

55. Brutus terram osculo contigit, scilicet *quod* ea communis mater omnium mortalium *esset.*—Liv. i. 56. (Con-
tigit=*contingendam esse putavit.*)

56.   Alter

Sublegit *quodcumque iaceret* inutile, quodque
Posset cenantes offendere.—Hor. *S.* ii. 8, 11. (Sublegit
contains the notion, that the slave ' *sublegendum esse
vidit.*')

57. Ex his, *qui* arma ferre *possent* ad milia xcii.—Caes. *B. G.*
i. 29. (In the previous sentence we read : 'in tabulis
nominatim ratio confecta erat, qui numerus domo
exisset eorum, *qui* arma ferre *possent.*' This reference
to a construction preceding in the text, illustrates
our general subject here—a Latin author's habit of
adapting mood to a construction existing in his mind,
but only implied in his text. See note at page xxix.

58. Numa Camenis eum lucum sacravit, *quod* earum ibi
concilia cum coniuge sua Egeria *essent.*— Liv. i. 21.
(Sacravit=*sacrum esse voluit.*)

59.   Non equidem extimui Danaum *quod* ductor et Arcas,
Quodque a stirpe *fores* geminis coniunctus Atridis.—Verg.
Aen. viii. 130. (Non extimui=*non extimescendum
esse putavi.*)

60. Poetus omnes libros, *quos* frater suus *reliquisset*, mihi
donavit.—Cic. *Att.* ii. 1. (Donavit=*donare se dixit.* His
words would be: dono tibi libros, quos frater meus reliquit.)

XIII. § 26. Looking at Example 60, we observe that the reference to the mind of the subject Poetus is indicated not only
by the subjunctive 'reliquisset,' but also by the subjective or reflexive pronoun 'suus.' Cicero might have written, 'quos
frater eius reliquerat,' if he had been satisfied with making the
statement his own, as in the sentence 'Themistocles ambulabat,' &c., he might have written 'poterat' for 'posset,' if he
had not wished to refer the act to the mind of Themistocles.
See also Examples 47, 48, 56. As to suus see § 231 B. and
Ex. 31, 32, 43, 51, 54. We venture to cite in illustration of it
a modern version of the two famous epigrams respecting
George I., who, on coming to the English throne, sent cavalry
to Oxford, and gave a library to Cambridge.

Diversis Diversa, 1.

Dum populi spectat mores, et mente gemellas
Mox academias invigilante notat,

Cur equitum mittit tibi rex, Oxonia, turmam?
   Quod tu, docta licet, *sis* male fida *sibi.*
Idem, Granta, libros mittit tibi, praemia iusta,
   Quod tu fida *sibi sis*, male docta tamen.

Diversis Diversa, 2.

Cur equitum mittit tibi rex, Oxonia, turmam?
   Quod vis regicolis pro ratione *valet.*
Cur mittat tibi, Granta, libros hinc collige, *quod* vis
   Unica poplicolis in ratione *sita est.*[1]

In the first epigram the reasons are subjectively stated, being referred to the mind of the king. In the second they are stated as the writer's own observations.

XIV. § 27. Looking at Example 59, we observe that the virtually suboblique clause is rarely found after a principal Verb in the First Person. Thus Cic. *Rosc. Am.* 47, *quod* viris fortibus, quorum opera eximia in rebus gerendis exstitit, honos *habitus est*, laudo. On this account it seldom occurs after Verbs of joy, because they usually appear in that Person: gaudeo (gratulor) quod salvum te recepisti. But, if the writer speaks of a feeling entertained by himself in a past time, the Subjunctive may follow, as 'quod fores' in 59. It must also be remembered that the Exceptions (noticed § 193, and further exemplified on p. 437) of Indicative Clauses apparently, but not really, depending on Oratio Obliqua, are very numerous, especially in Caesar. Thus too the Clause with 'quod' depending on Verbs of feeling may be Indicative, if the *fact* in the Clause is more strongly emphasised than the *expression* of feeling which it arouses: as in Liv. iv. 3, *quod spiratis, quod*

---

[1] The English originals are:

JACOBITE EPIGRAM.

The king, observing with judicious eyes
The state of both his universities,
To Oxford sent a troop of horse : for why?
That learned body wanted loyalty.
To Cambridge books he sent, as well discerning
How much that loyal body wanted learning.

HANOVERIAN REPLY.

The king to Oxford sent a troop of horse ;
For Tories own no argument but force.
On the other hand to Cambridge books he sent,
For Whigs allow no force but argument.

vocem *mittitis, quod* formas hominum *habetis,* indignantur. So Cic. *Verr.* i. 47. Utrum reprehendis, *quod* libertus patronum *iuvabat* eum, qui tum in miseriis erat, an *quod* alterius patroni mortui voluntatem *conservabat,* a quo summum beneficium acceperat?

To the examples in XII. may be added those which appear on pp. 437 II., 459 (foot), where 'suboblique' should be 'virtually suboblique'; also the examples in the 'Public School Latin Primer,' p. 168.

The construction of Subjunctives in dependence on formal Oratio Obliqua and on other Subjunctives is not controverted, and need not therefore be here specially exemplified. It appears indeed in almost every page of great Latin prose writers, and is noted by italics in the examples of Compound Construction (§ 194, &c.) in this Grammar.

XV. § 28. Madvig, whose great merit is the nice observation of particular idioms, notices (§ 370), that the Second Person of the Conjunctive is used (like 'man' in German, 'on' in French) to express an undefined subject (*some one, any one*). Thus often in principal construction : Quem neque gloria nec pericula excitant, nequiquam *hortere,* Sall. *Cat.* 58. Canes venaticos *diceres,* Cic. *Verr.* iv. 13. It appears also in Clauses dependent on some general statement, which we call Gnomic. *Cum* animum ab istis imaginibus ad veritatem *traduxeris,* nihil relinquitur, Cic. *T. D.* v. 5. Bonus segnior fit, *ubi neglegas,* Sall. *Iug.* 31. Cum aetas extrema advenit, tum illud quod praeteriit effluxit ; tantum remanet, *quod* virtute et recte factis *consecutus sis,* Cic. *d. Or.* iii. 52. Mens, quoque et animus, nisi tamquam lumini oleum *instilles,* extinguuntur senectute, Cic. *C. M.* 11. Virtutem necessario gloria, *etiamsi* tu id non *agas,* consequitur, Cic. *T. D.* i. 38. Gerundive and other Impersonal Verbs have a gnomic character, and are sometimes used with Subjunctive clauses dependent on them. Suae cuique utilitati, *quod* sine alterius iniuria *fiat,* serviendum est. Cic. Tibi ipsi dicendum erit aliquid *quod non sentias* aut faciendum *quod* non *probes,* Cic. *Fam.* iv. 9. Est enim sapientis, *quidquid* homini accidere *possit,* id praemeditari ferendum modice esse, si evenerit. Maioris omnino est consilii providere, nequid tale accidat ; animi non minoris fortiter ferre, *si evenerit,* Cic. *Phil.* xi. 3. Dicere fortasse *quae sentias,* non licet ; tacere plane licet, Cic. *Fam.* iv. 9.

XVI. § 29. In quitting the topic of Virtual Oratio Obliqua, on which I have dwelt longer than I expected, I have to say that this is one of the few terms for which I am responsible. I should have been equally content to call it 'contained' or 'implied,' or 'informal' Oratio Obliqua : all which mean one and the same thing.

The point at issue is this :

Are they right, who like Madvig (§ 357, § 368–9, § 404) put forward first the usage

(α) Principal Sentence (Indic.) + Clause (Subjunct.)
and follow this up with

(β) Princ. Sent. (Indic.) + O. Obliqua + Clause (Subjunct.)
thus making (β) a corollary or special case of (α)?

Or are they right, who give the converse order, and make (α) a corollary or special case of (β)?

Having had this question in view for half a century or more, I have never for a moment doubted that the just grammatical order is that which appears in this book (§§ 190–191), from (β) to (α), not from (α) to (β); that this is the order in which teachers and students ought to pursue the doctrine of Oblique Construction in Latin; taking the Infinitive Clause (Accus. and Infin.) as its first—most representative—most normal form (§ 100, § 190, § 194).

XVII. § 30. Yet, although Madvig has failed to treat the doctrine in this order, I shall now cite incidental passages from his book, which indicate an inadequately developed consciousness of that order being the true one.

(1) When treating of the Accusative (§ 322) Madvig says : 'In the indefinite infinitive expression, when the connexion between the subject and predicate is not of itself asserted, the subject and the predicative noun stand in the accusative, e.g. hominem currere, *that a man runs*; esse dominum, *to be lord*.' This just view, properly followed up, ought to have led him to place the Accus. and Infin. in the front of Compound Construction. But he lost sight of its true importance in his Second Part.

(2) In his Chapter on the Conjunctive, where most of his paragraphs are useful, as isolated remarks, but uninstructive, in so far as they are out of place and unsystematic—he says (§ 348, Obs. 3): 'The same holds'—to our mind the connexion

he suggests has no real existence—'of other conditional propositions, which do not contain a condition applying to the leading proposition, but complete an idea contained in it, which has the force of an infinitive or otherwise dependent proposition, *so that the conditional clause belongs to the "oratio obliqua,"* e.g. Metellus Centuripinis, nisi statuas Veneris restituissent, graviter minatur (Cic. *Verr.* ii. 67—minatur se iis malum daturum nisi—Minatur is stated absolutely without any condition). Iugurtha iram senatus timebat, ni paruisset legatis (Sall. *Iug.* 25—ne senatus irasceretur). Nulla maior occurrebat res quam si optimarum artium vias traderem meis civibus (Cic. *de Div.* ii. 1, e.g. Nullam rem putabam maiorem esse.)'

Need I say that in this passage—occurring before he has introduced those rules and examples on the Subjunctive clause before referred to—Madvig does, in point of fact, though but partially, teach the very doctrine which is drawn out in this Grammar, and which in this part of the Preface I have been maintaining and exemplifying,—the doctrine of Virtual Oratio Obliqua, exhibited in his three cited examples? He has, unhappily, failed to recognise its wide scope and great importance, and so to give it due prominence afterwards.

The late Professor Key, a learned and ingenious scholar, in his Latin Grammar (1201–1204) states first the doctrine of Oratio Obliqua (too narrowly, because he has not based it on the triple form of simple sentences and dependent Substantival clauses) and then adds (1205): 'Without a formal use of the " Oratio Obliqua," a verb in a dependent clause may be in the Subjunctive Mood, when it expresses the thoughts or words or alleged reasons of another.' He then cites the example, Cic. *T. D.* v. 36 (given by us, p. 459) Aristides, &c. and the two following : Fabio dicta dies est, *quod* legatus in Gallos *pugnasset,* Liv. vi. 1. Aedem Iovi vovit, *si* eo die hostes *fudisset,* Liv. xxxi. 21 : (in which obviously : Fabio dicta dies est=*Fabius accusatus est,* and vovit contains *se dedicaturum*).

Thus, by saying 'without a *formal* use of the Obliqua Oratio,' Key recognises an *informal* (or virtual) use of it, as I do ; and postpones this rightly to the formal use. I could cite German grammarians, were it worth while, whose treatment implies the same principles : for instance, Middendorf and Grüter, Frei, Billroth, Ellendt, &c. But *the term* (Virtual O. O.) was, I repeat, introduced by me thirty-six years ago.

It rests upon its own fitness: I can but deprecate, if it exist anywhere, the spirit complained of by Horace, when he says:

Indignor quicquam reprehendi, non quia crasse
Compositum illepideve putetur, sed quia nuper.

Ep. ii. i, 76.

XVIII. § 31. The question, whether the (independent) Thought-mood should be called Subjunctive or Conjunctive, stands as follows:

The Greek grammarians of Alexandria used the term ἔγκλισις ὑποτακτική, modus subjunctivus. Why? Because in Greek there are two forms of the Thought-mood, one of which they called εὐκτική, Optative, the other ὑποτακτική, Subjunctive. Neither of these terms corresponds exactly to the uses of the respective forms. The term Optative expresses only one use of the first:—that of *praying* or *wishing*, ἔλθοι, *may it come*: but it has also a dependent use, ὅτι ἔλθοι, *that it was come*; and by the convenient accession of the modal particle ἄν it gains an independent or enunciative power ἔλθοι ἄν, like the Latin 'veniret,' *it would come*. The second form ἔλθῃ was called ὑποτακτική because it never did acquire enunciative power; the modal ἄν was not extended to it, but only the conjunction ἄν, *if*, the conjunctional relative ὅς ἄν &c., *whosoever*, &c., in dependent construction. It has, however, an independent power as succursal to the imperative, in hortative sense 1st pers. plur., ἔλθωμεν, *let us come*; and as interrogative, in dubitative sense, —τί φῶ, *what can I say*? In spite of these two exceptional uses, it is manifest that the term ὑποτακτική, subjunctive, is, for the Greek mood, fully defensible, because its principal and (so to say) normal use is *dependence*. German grammarians, however, call it Conjunctive; wisely we think, for the maintenance of analogy

But for calling the Latin Thought-mood, generally, Subjunctive, there seems to be, from a right point of view, no reasonable defence. Key, indeed, has taken a point of view, which, if it were right, would supply one. His words are (Gr. §§ 427–8):

'The Subjunctive Mood, as its name implies, is used in secondary sentences subjoined to the main verb. In some sentences it is not uncommon to omit the main verb, and then the Subjunctive Mood seems to signify *power, permission, duty, wish, purpose, result, allegation, hypothesis*; whereas in fact these notions belong to the verb which is not expressed. Thus the phrase "quid faciam?" is translated by *what should I do* or *what am I to do?* but the full phrase is "quid vis faciam?" *what do you wish me to do?* (!)'

This theory Key, perhaps, borrowed from Hermann, who applies it (De emendanda ratione Grammaticae Graecae) to explain the two exceptional uses before noticed of the Greek Subjunctive: supposing ἴωμεν=ἄγε ἴωμεν, and τί φῶ=σήμηνον or οὐκ οἶδα τί φῶ. This farfetched caprice of an ellipsis is bad enough as used by Hermann: but when applied to all the independent usages of the Latin Thought-mood it has not, I think, been accepted by any grammarian but Key himself. I therefore consider the adoption of the term Subjunctive, as a name for that mood generally, to be an unwise and unjustifiable violation of propriety in the choice of terms. Such no doubt is the opinion of that multitude of grammatical writers who take the term Conjunctive in its stead, though, unhappily, they neglect to assign a distinct name to that dependent use, which is really Subjunctive. To this neglect is due, in great measure, their vague and unsatisfactory method of treating Compound Construction in Latin; a method propagated, through Madvig, to some English scholars.

See Uses of the Verb, §§ 90–99 of this Grammar, Appendix ii. to the 'Public School Latin Primer,' and the Preface to my Second Edition of Virgil.

XIX. § 32. The small number of terms for which this Grammar is specially responsible will be seen in its Index. Care has been taken to make them etymologically appropriate, and useful for their several purposes. On such points I have always invited expression of opinion by correspondence. It has been justly urged, that the term Factitive (adopted from German writers for that class of verbs which join a complement to their object, § 106, § 131)—is bad in etymology. I have therefore now written Factive: but I feel inclined to prefer the term 'Appositive Verbs': i.e. such as *append* to their object a complement resembling an apposition: populus Numam *regem creavit: puto te felicem* (*philosophum*). The point merits further consideration.

XX. § 33. Among the numerous books which in the course of my grammatical labours have been consulted with profit, I desire specially to mention the various writings of Mr. Thring, of Uppingham. His 'Elements of Grammar taught in English' is an admirable companion book to the 'Public School Primer' for early instruction in Latin.[1]

B. H. KENNEDY.

CAMBRIDGE : *Oct.* 5, 1879.

CONTENTS.

[Numerals following § represent the marginal numeration. Numerals without § represent the pages. The matter printed in Italics belongs to the Footnotes.]

§ 1-5, p. 1. . . . . . . .INTRODUCTION.

1. Divisions of Grammar; the Latin Language; Families of Language; the Semitic Family; the Aryan Family and its branches. 2. The Italic Branch; its Dialects; Latin; Languages derived from Latin; English; its formation; Influence of Greek on Latin. 3. Sketch of Latin Literature; Table of Classical Authors. 4. *Abbreviations in this Grammar.*

§ 6-99, p. 5. . . . *PART I.—ETYMOLOGY.*

§ 6, p. 5. Divisions of Etymology; Primitive Sounds and Roots.

§ 7-12, p. 5. . DIVISION I.—PHONOLOGY OR SOUNDLORE.

5. i. Alphabet; Capital and Small Letters; Vowels; Consonants. 6. Divisions of the Consonants; ii. Quantity, short, long, doubtful; iii. Syllabation. 7. iv. Accentuation; *Middle Tone.* 8. v. Punctuation; vi. Relations of the Letters; Scheme of Vowels; Scheme of Consonants. 9. vii. Memoranda from the History of the Alphabet; the Letters c, g, k, q, h, f, v, z, y, x; the Aspirate sounds ch, th, ph, rh; the three Letters of the Emperor Claudius. viii. the Semiconsonants i–j and v–u. 10. i-consonans and i-vocalis; v-consonans and v-vocalis. ix. Sound and quality of the Vowels; three primitive Vowels a, i, u. 11. a the standard Vowel; introduction of e, o; comparative strength of Vowels; lengthening of Vowels; Final short and long Vowels. x. Phonetic Decay in old Italian Language; Classical Latin a reaction. 12. xi. Vowel-change; strengthening or weakening. xii. Formation and Decay of Diphthongs; Guna and Vṛiddhi; full list of Diphthongs; ui, yi. A i (a e) and its changes. 13. O i (o e) and its changes; e i and its changes; a u, e u, o u. 14-17. xiii. Vowel-strengthening in Root-syllables, Suffixes and Endings. 18. xiv. Vowel-strengthening in Disyllabic Perfects; xv. Compensation. 19. xvi. Nasalization; xvii. Vowel-weakening; Euphony; Selection; e as final. 20. xviii. The Vowel ă and its weakenings, A) in Root- and Stem-syllables; B) in Suffixes; C) in Cases and Personal Endings. 21. xix. Weakening into ŏ as influenced by Selection. 21-24.

xx. Weakening into ŭ as influenced by Selection. 22. *Dialectic use of o and u in final syllables. Formidulosus, &c.* 23. *Gerundive forms oŋdus, &c.* 24–28. xxi. Change into ĕ as influenced by Selection. 29–31. xxii. Selection of ĭ. 30. Vincular ĭ. *Note.* 32. Recapitulation. 32–35. xxiii. Vowel-change by Assimilation and Dissimilation of Vowels to each other. 35–39. xxiv. Vowel-weakening in the second Member of Compounds ; 35. Loose and Fast Compounds ; Some Compounds unweakened. 36. In others, a weakened into u ; a into e ; 37. a into i ; 38. e into i ; 39. e into u ; ae into ī ; o e into ĭ ; o e into ū ; a u into o ; a u into u ; a u into o e. 40. xxv. Reduplication. 41–44. xxvi. Changes of concurrent Consonants. 41. Complete Assimilation of Consonants ; Regressive. 42. Progressive. Partial Assimilation of Consonants. *Formation of Comparatives and Superlatives.* 43. Dissimilation of Consonants. 44. xxvii. Loss of Initial letters. 45. xxviii. Loss of Final Letters. 47–50. xxix. Loss of Inner Consonants by Concurrence with other Consonants. 50–52. xxx. Loss of Inner Vowels before Consonants. 52–55. xxxi. Hiatus, Elision, Contraction and Coalition of Vowels. 54. xxxii. Loss of Inner Vowels with Consonants. 55–56. xxxiii. The Shortening of Vowels in Latin. 56–58. xxxiv. Exclusion of Consonants followed by Contraction of Vowels. *Peculiar Contractions in Verbs.* 59–68. xxxv. Relations of the Consonants in Latin and kindred Languages. 58–60. The Guttural Surds c (k) q. 59. *Labialism and Dentalism.* 60. *Sound of ce, ci.* 61. The Guttural Sonant g. 61–62. The Aspirates h, f. 63. The Labial Mutes p, b ; the Dentals t, d. 64–66. The Nasals n, m ; the Liquids l, r, and the Sibilant s. 66. The Soft Labial Spirant v. 67. *Sound of V-consonans ;* I-consonans. 68. The Double Consonant x. *Words which have lost an initial letter.*

§ 13–99, p. 69. . DIVISION II.—MORPHOLOGY or WORDLORE.

§ 13, p. 69. . . . . . . SUBDIVISIONS.

§ 14–16, p. 69. *CHAPTER I.*—WORDS AND THEIR FLEXION.

69. i. Stem-flexion : Word ; Stem ; Root ; Suffix. 70. Prefix ; Character ; Flexion ; Definition of Stem ; of Root. 70–73. ii. Classification of Words. 70. I. Nouns ; Noun Substantive. 71. Noun Adjective ; Attribution ; Pronoun ; Apposition ; Names, Abstract and Concrete. Common Names. Collective Nouns. Adjectives for Substantives. Numerals. 72. Declension ; Accidents of Nouns ; II. Verb Finite and Infinite ; Conjugation, Accidents of Verb ; III. Particles ; Adverb ; Preposition. 73. Conjunction ; Interjection ; Parts of Speech ; Absence of Articles.

§ 17–34, p. 73. . . . *CHAPTER II.*—NOUNS.

§ 17–21, p. 73. . . . . . . SECTION I.

73. i. Number in Nouns. 73–79. ii. Gender of Nouns. 74. Distinct Generic Names ; Mobilia. 75. Verbals of double Gender ; Patronymics. 75–77. Words Common of two Genders. 75. Appellatives. 76. Names of Animals. 77. Epicoena. 77–79. Gender shown by meaning. 80. iii. The Cases ; Declension ; Case in ancient and modern language. *Order of the Cases.* 81. iv. The Five Declensions. 82–84. v. Formation of the Cases. 85. vi. Endings of the Five Declensions.

§ 22, p. 86. . SECTION II.—i. FIRST DECLENSION; A-NOUNS.

86. Nouns contained in First Decl. ii. Table. iii. Cases in First Decl. 87–89. iv. Greek Nouns in First Decl.

§ 23, p. 89. SECTION III.—i. SECOND DECLENSION; O-NOUNS.

89. Nouns contained in Second Decl. ii. Table. 90. iii. Cases. 91. iv. Clipt Nouns in er. 92. v. Greek Nouns in Second Decl. vi. Gender. 93. vii. Table of Adjectives in Decl. II. and I.

§ 24, p. 94. . SECTION IV.—i. THIRD DECLENSION, CONSONANT AND I-NOUNS.

94. The two Divisions; their occasional confusion; its cause; ii. Nominative Endings in the Consonant Declension. 95. Vowel of True Stem. 95–103. iii. Syllabus of Cons. Stems, with Genders. 95–96. *A.* Mute Guttural Stems. 96–99. *B.* Mute Dental Stems. 99. *C.* Mute Labial Stems. 99–101. *D.* Nasal Stems. 101–103. *E.* Liquid and Sibilant Stems. 103. *F.* u- and v-stems. *G.* Greek e- o- and y-stems. 104. iv. I-stems: Imparisyllaba and Parisyllaba. v. Grouping of I-nouns with Gender. 104–106. *A)* Parisyllable I-nouns in Is (ĕr). 104–106. *Nature of i. B)* Parisyllable I-nouns Fem. in ēs (Is). 106–107. *C)* Neuter I-nouns in ĕ, ăl, ăr. 107–108. *D)* Clipt I-nouns Imparisyllable. 108–109. vi. Notes on the Cases. 109. *Gen. Pl. varying with form of Noun. Summary of Gender in Third Decl.* 110–112. vii. Table of Third Decl. 112–115. viii. Greek Nouns in Third Decl. 114–115. Greek Table. 115–119. ix. Adjectives in Third Decl. 115. Consonant Adjectives; Table. 116–119. Adjectives not purely Consonantal. Four Groups. 118–119. Table of these Adjectives.

§ 25, p. 119. . SECTION V.—i. FOURTH DECLENSION; U-NOUNS.

119. ii. Table. 120. iii. Confusion of U- and O-nouns. 121. iii. Cases in Fourth Decl. 121. iv. Gender in Fourth Decl.

§ 26, p. 121. SECTION VI.—i. FIFTH DECLENSION. E-NOUNS, FEM.

ii. Table. 122. iii. Cases in Fifth Decl. iv. Gender of dies.

§ 27–28, p. 123. . . SECTION VII.—IRREGULAR NOUNS.

123. i. Irregularity; Abundance; Defect. 123–125. ii. Abundance in Substantives; of Declension; of Case-forms. 125–130. iii. Defect in Substantives. 125. *A.* Defect of Number. I) Substantives Singular only. 126–128. II) Plural only. 128–129. III) Substantives which change their meaning in Plural. 129–130. *B.* Defect of Case. Substantives Defective in Case. 131. iv. Irregularity in Adjectives; Abundance; Defect.

§ 29–30, p. 131. . . SECTION VIII.—COMPARISON.

131–132. i. Comparison of Adjectives; 132. Degrees of Comparison; ii. Examples; iii. Notes on Comparison. 133. iv. Irregular Comparison. 133–135. v. Defective Comparison. 135. vi. Comparison of Adverbs. 136. vii. Irregular Comparison in Adverbs.

§ 31, p. 136. . . . . SECTION IX.—PRONOUNS.

136. i. Pronouns Substantive or Adjective; their Persons. 136–137. ii. Classification of Pronouns: *A.* Substantival: 1. Personal; 2. Reflexive; *B.* 3. Possessive; *C.* 4. Demonstrative; 5. Definitive; 6. Relative; *a.* Interrogative; *b.* Indefinite; *c.* Compound Pronouns; 7. Pronominalia; 138–142. iii. Tables of Declension. 142–143. Observations on certain Pronouns. 143–145. *Ancient Caseforms of Pronouns.* 144–146. iv. Correlation of Pronouns.

§ 32–34, p. 147. . . . SECTION X.—NUMERALS.

147. i. Numeralia; ii. Symbols of Number: *Note on these*; iii. The Four Chief Numeral Series—Cardinal, Ordinal, Distributive Numerals, Quotientive Adverbs. 148–149. iv. Minor Numeral Series. 150–151. v. Declension of Numerals. 150–153. *Numeral Table; Numeral Roots.* 153–155. vi. Use of the Numerals. 156–157. Compound Numeration. 157–158. viii. Expression of Fractions; the As and its parts; Calculation of Inheritance.

§ 35–53, p. 158. . . . *CHAPTER III.*—THE VERB.

§ 35–40, p. 158. . . . SECTION I.—i. THE VERB FINITE AND INFINITE.

ii. The Voices. 159. iii. Deponent Verbs. iv. Verbs Transitive and Intransitive; Impersonal and Reflexive uses of the Verb. 160. v. Verbs Quasi-Passive and Semi-Deponent; Passive Participles from Active Verbs. 160–161. The Moods—Indicative, Conjunctive, Imperative. 161–164. vii. The Tenses. 161–163. Tense-forms Inflected or Combinate. 163. Table of Tense-forms. *Conjunctive Tenses.* 164. Combinate or Periphrastic Forms; Tenses Primary and Historic. viii. Number and Person. 164–166. ix. The Verb Infinite; Infinitive; Gerunds; Gerundive; Supines; Participles.

§ 41–50, p. 166. . . . SECTION II.—THE CONJUGATION OF VERBS.

166. i. The three Stems in Verbs; Parts derived from them severally. 167. ii. The Verb of Being 'sum' (esse); *Forms of sum, esse.* 168. Its Table. 169–182. iii. The Four Conjugations of Regular Verbs; Weak and Strong Conjugations; the Stems in each. 169. *Quantity of the Vowel Characters.* 170–171. Mode of Conjugating Verbs Active, Passive, and Deponent. 171. Verbs in io of Conj. 3. 172–182. Tables of the Four Conjugations—Active, Passive, and Deponent. 180. Of Io-Verbs in Conj. 3. 180–182. iv. Combinate or Periphrastic Conjugation. 181–183. *Correspondence of the Latin Verb.* 183–189. v. Conjugation of Irregular Verbs. 184. Possum. 184–185. Fero. 186. Fio. 187. Volo, nolo, malo. 188. Eo, queo, nequeo. 189. Edo. 189–191. Conjugation of Defective Verbs. 189. Praeteritiva, coepi, odi, memini. *Capio,* &c. 190. Novi, aio. 191. Inquam, ovare, quaeso. 192–194. Impersonal Verbs. 192. Impersonal Verbs Active. 193. Impersonal Verbs Passive. 194. Impersonals Gerundive.

§ 51, p. 194. SECTION IV.—THE FORMS OF THE THREE STEMS IN VERBS.

194–196. i. The Present Stem and its Affections. 196. Inceptive or Inchoative Verbs in sco. 196–199. ii. The Perfect Stem and its varieties of formation. 199–202. iii. The Supine Stem and its varieties of formation.

§ 52, p. 202. . . . SECTION V.—COMPOSITION OF VERBS.

202–203. i. Prepositions compounded with Verbs, separable and inseparable; their Euphonic Mutations; Examples. 202. *Sus, subs.* 203. *The form obs.* 204. Scheme of Vowel-changes in the three Stems of Compound Verbs. 205. ii. Verbs compounded with Adverbs; with Nominal or Verbal Elements.

§ 53, p. 205. SECTION VI.—SYLLABUS OF STEM-FORMATION IN VERBS.

205. *A*) The First Conjugation; Imitative Verbs; Frequentative Verbs; Deminutive Verbs; *B*) Second Conjugation; *C*) Fourth Conjugation. 206. Desiderative Verbs; *D*) Third Conjugation. 206–208. Stem-table of A-verbs; *Compounds; Deponent A-verbs.* 209–214. Stem-table of E-verbs, *Compounds.* 214–216. Stem-table of I-verbs, *Compounds.* 216–227. Stem-table of Consonant and U-verbs, *Compounds.* 216–217. Cons. Verbs with reduplicated Perfect-stem. 217–218. With strengthened Perf. stem. 219–221. With agglutinated Perf. Stem in ui, vi. 221–224. With agglutinated s in Perf. stem. 221–223. Guttural Stems. 223. Dental Stems. 224. Labial, Nasal, and Liquid Stems. 224–225. U-verbs. 225–227. Deponent Verbs in Third Conjugation. 226–227. *Inchoative Verbs.* 227. *Homonymous Verb-forms.*

§ 54–58, p. 228. . *CHAPTER IV.*—PARTICLES.

228. Four Classes of Particles; their intimate connexion.

§ 55, p. 228. . . . . . SECTION I.—ADVERBS.

228–232. Interrogative Adverbs referring to Place, Time, Number, Manner, Degree, Cause, Quality, &c. *Table of Adverbs corresponding to these severally.*

§ 56, p. 232. . . . SECTION II.—PREPOSITIONS.

232. Relations expressed by Prepositions. 1) Prepositions which take Accusative Case. 233. 2) Prepositions which take Ablative Case. 3) Prepositions which take either case.

§ 57, p. 233. . . . SECTION III.—CONJUNCTIONS.

233. Conjunctions, Coordinative or Subordinative; Conjunctions with both uses. *A.* List of Coordinative Conjunctions. 234. *B.* List of Subordinative Conjunctions.

§ 58, p. 234. . . . . SECTION IV.—INTERJECTIONS.

234. Interjections expressing various Emotions. 235. Interjectional Nouns; Verbs; Adverbs; Phrases. Cases found with Interjections.

§ 59, p. 235–253. . CHAPTER V.—DERIVATION AND COMPOSITION OF WORDS.

p. 235 . . . SECTION I.—DERIVATION OF NOUNS.

236. i. Staminal Suffix. ii. Root or Rudiment. iii. Suffixes. 237. iv. Rudimental Words. 237–248. v. Syllabus of Suffixes; *Examples.* 247. Formation of Deminutives; *Examples.* vi. Patronymics. 249. vii. Names of Countries. 249–251. viii. Nominative Endings of derived Words according to their meanings; *Examples.* 252. Adjectives derived from Particles; *Examples.* 252–253. Adjectives derived from Proper Names: Personal; Gentile; *Roman Names.*

p. 254. . SECTION II.—DERIVATION OF VERBS.

254. Verbs derived from Verbs; Verbs derived from Nouns.

p. 255–259. SECTION III.—DERIVATION OF PARTICLES.

255. i. Primitive Particles. ii. Particles derived from Nouns; from Pronouns; from other Particles. *Particles compounded with other Particles.* 256–257. iii. Denominative Adverbs in the form of Cases. 257–258. Denominative Adverbs with Adverbial Endings. 258. v. Derivation of Pronominal Particles. 259. vi. Other Particles. *Note on some of them.*

§ 60, p. 259–266. SECTION IV.—COMPOSITION OF WORDS.

260. i. Parts of a Compound, Fundamental and Determinative; *Parathetic and Synthetic Composition.* ii. Varieties of Composition, Constructive, Attributive, Adverbial, and Possessive. 260–263. *Synthetically compounded Substantives, Adjectives and Verbs.* 263. Decomposita. 263–266. *Verbs compounded with Prepositions; their various senses, &c.*

§ 61–99, p. 267. . CHAPTER VI.—USES OF WORDS.

§ 61, p. 267. SECTION I.—i. FIGURATE CONSTRUCTION.

267–269. ii. Ellipsis; Zeugma; Pleonasm; *Examples*; Attraction; Synesis. 269–270. iii. Other Variations. 270. iv. Metaphor; Metonymy.

§ 62, p. 270. . SECTION II.—USES OF THE SUBSTANTIVE.

270. i. Singular Appellatives used collectively for Plurals. 271. ii. Plural words used with Singular collective sense in prose and poetry. iii. Plural used to express a 'genus,' when individuals are implied. iv. Plural of Proper Names expressing typical characters. v. Abstract Substantives used in Plural. 272. vi. Abstract Substantives for Concrete. 272–273. vii. Idioms of Substantives. 274–275. viii. Ellipse of Substantives.

63, p. 275. . . SECTION III.—USES OF THE ADJECTIVE.

275–278. i. Adjectives used as Substantives. 278. ii. Adjectives used adverbially in Predicative Construction. iii. Partitive Attributes.

iv. Multiplication of Attributes. 279. v. Possessive Attributes. vi. Idioms of the Superlative. 280. vii. Intensive Phrases. 281. viii. Adjectives used in Passive and Active Sense.

§ 64–69, p. 281. . SECTION IV.—USES OF PRONOUNS.

281. i. Personal and Possessive Pronouns. 282–285. ii. Demonstrative Pronouns h i c, i l l e, i s t e, i s, i d e m. 285–287. iii. The Reflexive Pronouns s e, s u u s. 287–289. iv. The Definitive Pronoun i p s e. 289–291. v. The Indefinite Pronouns q u i s, q u i, a l i q u i s, a l i q u i, q u i s p i a m, q u i s q u a m, q u i d a m, q u i v i s; the Pronoun q u i s q u e. 291. vi. The Universal Relatives q u i s q u i s, q u i c u m q u e, &c. 292. vii. Pronominalia ; a l t e r, u t e r, &c.; a l i u s, &c.

§ 70–72, p. 293. . SECTION V.—USES OF PREPOSITIONS.

293–299. Examples of Prepositions taking an Accusative Case. 299–304. Examples of Prepositions taking an Ablative Case. 304–306. Examples of Prepositions taking Accusative and Ablative. 306. Prepositions used as Adverbs. 307. Notes on Prepositions.

§ 73–76, p. 307. SECTION VI.—CORRELATIVE CONSTRUCTION.

307–310. i. Pronominal Correlation. ii. 310–312. Correlations of Manner with ut, &c. 312–313. iii. Correlations of Likeness and Unlikeness with a t q u e, ac., &c. 314–315. iv. Correlations of Degree with quam. 314. Q u a m with Positive and Superlative Adjectives, &c. Q u a m after Adverbs. 315. Idioms of Comparative.

§ 77–82, p. 316. . . SECTION VII.—COORDINATION.

316–320. i. Coordination by Conjunctions. 316. Annexive Conjunctions. 317. Distributive Association ; Ordinative Particles. 318. Disjunctive Particles ; Adversative. 320. Causal ; Illative. 320–322. ii. Coordination by the Relative and its Particles. 321–322. Idioms of q u o d.

§ 83–85, p. 323. . SECTION VIII.—NEGATIVE WORDS.

323–324. i. N e and its Compounds. 324. ii. Doubled Negatives. 325–326. iii. N e . . . q u i d e m, n e d u m, n o n m o d o, &c.

§ 86–89, p. 326. . SECTION IX.—QUESTIONS AND ANSWERS.

I. Questions Single or Disjunctive. 326–327. i. Single Interrogation without Particle ; ii. with Particle ; uses of a n, n e s c i o a n, &c. 328–329. iii. Disjunctive Interrogation with u t r u m, &c. 329. II. Answers. i. Affirmative Answers. 330. ii. Negative Answers.

§ 90–99, p. 330. . SECTION X.—USES OF THE VERB.

331. i. The Indicative Mood and its Tenses ; Use of Mood ; Relations of Tenses. 332–333. Uses of the Present. 333. Uses of the Perfect. 334. Uses of the Imperfect and Pluperfect. Tenses in Roman Letter-writing. 335. Uses of the Simple Future and Future Perfect ; of the Future Periphrastic Conjugation. 336. Idioms of the

Contents.

Indicative Past Tenses in Predications of duty, necessity, &c. 337. ii. The Imperative Mood and its Tenses. 338. iii. The Conjunctive Mood and its Tenses. 338–341. iv. Uses of the Pure Conjunctive ; Potential. 339. Dubitative, Concessive, Optative, Hortative uses. 340. Permissive and exhorting use of 2nd Pers. Conjunctive ; Prohibitive use. 341. v. Examples of Pure Conjunctive. 342–343. vi. The Subjunctive ; Subordinate Subjunctive Clauses. 343–344. vii. Particles and Pronouns which introduce Clauses. 344–346. viii. Consecution of Tenses with Examples. 346–347. ix. Ellipses of the Verb.

§ 100–250, p. 348. . . *PART II.—SYNTAX.*

§ 100, p. 348. *CHAPTER I.*— The Doctrine of Sentences.

348. Sentences Affirmative or Negative ; Simple or Compound. In a Compound Sentence, Principal Sentence and Clauses ; Coordinate and Subordinate Clauses. Three Forms of a Simple Sentence— Enuntiation, Petition, Interrogation. 349. Oratio Recta and Obliqua. Substantival Clauses ; their Three Kinds—Enuntiatio Obliqua, Petitio Obliqua, Interrogatio Obliqua.

§ 101–106, p. 349. *CHAPTER II.*—The Simple Sentence.

349. i. Members of a Simple Sentence, Grammatical Subject and Grammatical Predicate. 350. What the Subject may be. What the Predicate. Examples of Predication with Subject and Verb. Omission of Pronoun Subject. ii. Incomplete Predication ; Verbs which do not predicate completely. S u m, e s s e (complete only when implying absolute existence), usually requires a Complement. 351. Examples. Incomplete Verbs called Copulative. List of Copulative and Factive Verbs. 350–351. *Incomplete Predication and its Terms.* 352. What the Complement may be. Examples of Copulative Predication. *Phrase, Enthesis, Clause.* 353. iii. Relations in the Simple Sentence. *Note on these.* I. Predicative Relation ; Subject and Predicate. II. Qualitative Relation—Attribute, Apposite. *Adjuncts of Substantives.* 354. Four Varieties of Qualitative Relation—Epithetic, Enthetic, Adverbial, Complemental. III. Objective Relation ; Object, Accusative governed by Transitive Verbs ; Verbs with two Objects, Person and Thing ; Verbs with two Accusatives, one Oblique Complement of the other. IV. Receptive Relation ; Dative of Recipient. 355. Predicative Dative or Dative of Purpose. *Trajective Words.* V. Circumstantive Relation ; Adverbs ; Ablative Case, &c. 356. VI. Proprietive Relation ; Genitive Case. VII. Prolative Relation ; Predication extended by Infinitive. VIII. Annexive Relation ; Conjunctions. 357. iv. Ecthesis by Interjections and Vocative Case. v. Notice of the Relative Pronoun. 358. vi. Conversion of Active Sentences into Passive form.

§ 107–188, p. 359. *CHAPTER III.*—Constructions of the Simple Sentence.

§ 107. I. Agreement. II. Case-Construction. III. Verb-Construction.

§ 108–114, p. 359. . . . . Section I.—Agreement.

359. Agreement what. i. The Four Concords : I. Verb with Subject ; Examples. II. Adjective with Substantive ; III. Substantive with

Substantive. 360. Examples of II. III. 361. IV. Relative with Antecedent; Examples. ii. Ellipsis of Subject. 361–362. iii. Attraction of Verb. 362. iv. Synesis in first and second Concords; of Gender; of Number; Collective Nouns. 363. v. Composite Subject. 364–367. vi. Idioms of Attribution and Apposition. 364. Adjective agreeing with Verb-Noun. 365. Adjectival Pronoun substantively used as Subject. Adverbial Attribution and Apposition. Neuter Adjectives Substantival. 366. Number and Gender of Apposites. Peculiar forms of Apposition. 367. Attribute with more than one Noun. Noun with more than one Attribute or Apposite. 367. vii. Synesis and Ellipsis in Relative Construction. 368. Attraction in Relative Construction. viii. Construction of Qualis; Quantus; Quot. 369. Abnormal Constructions. 369–370. *Examples of the Rules of Agreement.*

§ 115–176, p. 370. . . SECTION II.—CASE-CONSTRUCTION.

§ 115–117, p. 370. . . *A.*—THE NOMINATIVE CASE.

370. i. The Nominative as Subject; ii. As Complement. 371. iii. With Interjections.

§ 118–119, p. 371. . . . *B.*—THE VOCATIVE CASE.

371. i. Vocative without or with Interjection; ii. The Nominative for the Vocative.

§ 120–132, p. 372. . . . *C.*—THE ACCUSATIVE CASE.

372. i. The Accusative the Case of the Contained or Attained Nearer Object: Agent and Object: Objective Propositions. ii. Accusative of the Nearer or Attained Object of Transitive Verbs. Examples. 373–374. iii. Contained Object (Cognate Accusative): its various instances. 374. Part Affected (Respect). iv. Medial Object in Poetry. 375. v. Accusatives of Time, Space, Measure. vi. Accus. of Place Whither. 376. vii. Transitive Verbs used Intransitively. 376–378. Intransitive Verbs used Transitively. 376. Verbs expressing State. 377. Compounds of Intransitive Verbs become Transitive; Test of Active Transitive Verb its power of becoming Passive. viii. Personal and Impersonal Passives. 378. Preposition of Compound Verb repeated with Accusative. Compounds with two Accusatives. 278. ix. Idiomatic uses. Verbals with Accusative. Unconstructed Accusative. 379. x. Exclamatory Accusative with or without Interjection. 379–380. xi. Accusatives of two Objects with Verbs of *asking, teaching,* &c. 380–381. xii. Oblique double Accusative. 381–383. *Examples of Accusative.*

§ 132–142, p. 382. . . . *D.*—THE DATIVE CASE.

382–383. i. Three chief uses of Dative—I. As Remoter Object. II. As Recipient or Acquisitive. III. As expressing Purpose. 384–386. ii. Dative of Remoter Object. Words which govern it. 386–388. Verbs which vary Construction with Meaning. 388–389. Adjectives with Dative Object. 389–390. iii. Recipient or Acquisitive Dative (Commodi et Incommodi). 390–391. iv. Predicative Dative. 391–394. *Examples of Dative.*

§ 143–161, p. 392. . . . *E.*—THE ABLATIVE CASE.

392. i. Uses of Ablative—I. Instrumental; II. Locative; III. Ablative Proper. 393. ii. Instrumental Ablative. 393–394. Ablative of Cause. 395. Of Instrument: of Personal Agent. 395. Of Price. 396–398. Of Matter. 398–402. iii. Locative Ablative. 398. Ablative of Respect: of Measure. 399. Of Manner: of Condition: of Quality. 400–401. Of Time. 401–402. Of Place Where. 402. Of Direction. 403–405. iv. Ablative Proper. 403. Ablative of Place Whence: of Separation. 403–404. Of Origin. 404–405. Of the Thing Compared. 405–406. v. Ablative Absolute. 406–411. *Examples of Ablative.*

§ 162–176, p. 407 . . . *F.*—THE GENITIVE CASE.

407–408. i. Main Function of Genitive. ii. Its twofold Use: Subjective and Objective. 408. Both these dependent on one Noun. 409. iii. *A*) Subjective Genitive; Possessive; Descriptive; Partitive. Phrases for Genitive. 410. Attributive Nature of Subjective Genitive. 411–413. Genetivus Auctoris et Possessoris. 413–415. Genetivus Descriptionis. 414. Genitive of the Fact charged. 415. Genetivus Qualitatis. 416–417. Genitive of Value and Price. 416. Constructions with interest, refert. 417–418. Genetivus Rei Distributae, or Partitive. 418–420. Genetivus Rei Demensae or of Quantity. 420. Genitive of Plenty and Want. 421–423. iv. *B*) Objective Genitive dependent, 421. on Substantives; 421–422. on Adjectives; 422–423. on Verbs. 423. Genitive of Cause. 423–427. *Examples of Genitive.*

§ 177–188, p. 424. . . SECTION III.—VERB-CONSTRUCTION.

424–425. i. The Infinitive. 426. ii. The Infinitive Present and Past as Subject. 427. iii. As Object. 427–428. iv. Prolative Infinitive: extends Construction of Verbs. *Construction of Copulative Infinitives.* 428. Use of coepit &c. with Impersonal Infinitives. Prolative Infinitive extending Adjectives. 428–429. Cases of the Infinitive, Gerunds, and Supines. 428. v. Gerundial Construction: the Gerunds. 429. Their Case-construction; Gerundial Attraction; their Dependence. vi. Impers. Gerundive Construction. vii. Personal Gerundive Construction. 430–431. viii. Notes on Gerundial Construction. 431. The two Supines—Accusative Supine; Ablative Supine. 432. Note on the Annexive Relation. 431–434. *Examples of Infinitive, Gerunds, and Supines.*

§ 189–240, p. 434. . *CHAPTER IV.*—COMPOUND CONSTRUCTION.

§ 189, p. 434. . . SECTION I.—SUBORDINATION OF CLAUSES.

434. Clauses of three Kinds—Substantival, Adverbial, Adjectival or Relative.

§ 190–193, p. 435. . . SCTION II.—SUBOBLIQUE CONSTRUCTION.

435. i. Oratio Obliqua. ii. In a Clause dependent on it (*i.e.* Suboblique), the Verb is Subjunctive. iii. Virtual Oratio Obliqua. In a Clause dependent on it (*i.e.* virtually Suboblique), the Verb is Subjunctive. 486. iv. A Verb dependent on Conjunctive is generally Subjunctive. v. Exceptions to the Law of Mood in dependence. 437. *Examples of Suboblique Construction.*

§ 194–203, p. 437. • SECTION III.—SUBSTANTIVAL CLAUSES.

437. I) Enuntiatio Obliqua: has three Forms—Infinitive Clause; Ut-clause; Quod-clause. 437–440. i. Infinitive Clause. 440–441. ii. Ut-clause. 441–442. Quod-clause. 442. II. Petitio Obliqua: Verbs which introduce it. 443. Quominus; Quin; Construction with Predications of Fear and Caution. 444–447. III. Interrogatio Obliqua. 448–449. Dependent Constructions with various Verbs. 444–451. *Examples of Substantival Clauses.*

§ 204–227, p. 452. • • • SECTION IV.—ADVERBIAL AND ADJECTIVAL CLAUSES.

452. Why taken in connexion. i. Relative Clauses, why called Adjectival; Particles equivalent to Pronouns; Mood in Relative Clauses. ii. Consecutive Clauses: why so called; with ut, ut non, &c., after Demonstratives or without them. 452–453. Adverbial Consecutive Clauses. 453. Use of Perfect Subjunctive in Historic Consecution; Idioms of Adverbial Consecution: Tantum abesse ut... 454–457. Adjectival Consecutive Clauses; when they occur; after what Predications, &c. 456. Use of quin for qui non. 457. Limitative use of qui; Occasional Definiteness of Relative with Indicative. 454–456. *Examples of Consecutive Clauses.* 457. iii. Final Clauses: what they express; Adverbial Final Clauses with ut, ne, &c. 458. Demonstratives used with them; Adjectival Final Clauses. 457–458. *Examples of Final Clauses.* 458–461. iv. Causal Clauses; Adverbial Causal Clauses: of admitted Cause, quoniam, &c. with Indicative usually. 459. Of alleged Cause, quod, quia, with Indicative, if not Suboblique; Of conceived Cause, cum, with Subjunctive. 459–460. v. Idioms of Causal construction; non quod, &c.; non quin. 461. Adjectival Causal Clauses. 459–461. *Examples of Causal Clauses.* 461–467. vi. Temporal Clauses; four Groups of Temporal Conjunctions. 462–463. When Subjunctive is required in Temporal Clauses. 463. Iterative Subjunctive. 461–464. *Examples of Temporal Clauses.* 465–467. Uses of the Conjunction cum, when. 465–466. *Examples of cum with Indicative and with Subjunctive.* 467–479, vi. Conditional Sentences. 467. Conditional Conjunctions; Normal Forms of the Conditional Sentence. 468–469. Class Alpha, Sumptio Dati; Examples. Class Beta, Sumptio Dandi. Class Gamma, Sumptio Ficti. 469–470. Various Forms of Gamma. 467–468. *Examples of the three Classes, Distinctions.* 470–472. Conjunctive Protasis with Indicative Apodosis: *Four Idioms with Examples.* 472. Indicative Protasis with Conjunctive Apodosis. 473. Abnormal Relation of Tenses; Protasis without si. 473–474. Si in various senses. 474. Si combined with Pronouns and Particles. 474–475. Idiomatic uses of Si. 475. Sive, seu. 475–477. Negative condition; Nisi, ni, si non. 477–478. *Examples.* 477–478. Conditional Sentences in Oratio Obliqua; *Examples.* 479. Modo, dum, dummodo, Conditional; *Examples.* 479. vii. Concessive Sentences; Concessive Conjunctions of several Classes. 480–482. Mood in Concessive Clauses. 480–482. Idioms of Concessive Conjunctions. 481–482. *Examples of Concessive Sentences.* 482–483. viii. Comparative Sentences; Conjunctions that introduce these. 483. Comparative Idioms. 482–483. *Examples of Comparative Sentences.*

§ 229–240, p. 483. . . . SECTION V.—SUPPLEMENT TO COMPOUND CON-
STRUCTION.

I. 483–486. Consecution of Tenses. 483. Consecution of Present
Past. 484. Of Historic Present; of Future with Future; three
varieties. 485. Of Future after Primary and Historic Tenses; of
Subordinated Conditional Sentences. 486. Of *might have, ought,
must have*; Consecution when Infinitive, &c., intervene.

II. 487–489. Narratio Obliqua, how used by Historians; *Examples.*
487–488. Idioms. 488–489. *Examples of the Conversion of Oratio
Recta into Oratio Obliqua.*

III. 489–495. i. The Reflexive Pronouns s e, s u u s, in Clauses. 489.
I p s e supplies them; s e, s u u s are Subjective; i s, i l l e, &c. Objective.
Pronominal reference to be interpreted by 'the Reason of the Thing.'
490. Se, s u u s connected with the use of Subjunctive: with the mind of
the Subject. ii. Their use in various Clauses. 490–492. In Substantival Clauses: Ordinary Instances. 491. Reference when a Clause
has a new Subject capable of being referred to Subjectively; Vari-
ation of Reference in Clauses of Prayer, Exhortation, &c. 492.
Se, s u u s, when referred to a Case governed by a Passive Verb. 492–
494. Pronominal Reference in Adverbial and Adjectival Clauses: in
Final; Consecutive; Causal; Conditional; Relative Clauses. 494. iii.
When Oratio Obliqua intervenes. iv. When in Clauses more than one
Subject is referred to. 494–495. I p s e assisting the use of Reflexive
Pronouns in two ways. 495. Its Appositive use; I n t e r i p s o s; I n t e r s e.

IV. 495–501. Participial Construction. 495–496. Nature of Participle; want of Participles; how supplied. 496. Uses of Participles;
Participle as an abbreviated Clause; Attributive or Absolute. 497.
Construction of Abl. Absolute; Participial Construction abbreviates,
1) Relative Clauses; 2) Adverbial Clauses; Consecutive; *Translation of English* 'without' *and Verb.* 498. Final, by Fut. Participle;
Causal; Temporal; Conditional. 499. Concessive; with n i s i, e t s i,
&c.; Comparative with q u a s i, t a m q u a m, &c. 499–501. Notes on
Participial Construction.

§ 241–250, p. 501. . . *CHAPTER V.*—ARRANGEMENT OF WORDS AND
STRUCTURE AND CONNEXION OF SENTENCES.

501–502. Order of Words; Parts of Sentence. 503–504. Notes on
the Order of Words. 504–505. Connexion of Sentences. 505–510.
The PERIOD in Latin, Simple or Complex. 506–510. Its Style and
Rhythm. 508. Subject and Object in Periods. 510. Narrative Style;
Qualities of Style. 510–511. Distinctions of Prose Style. *Styles of
Various Authors.*

§ 251–269, p. 511. . . *PART III.—LATIN PROSODY.*

511. Prosody; Quantity and Rhythm. 512–513. Quantity of
Syllables; Position. 512. *Syllables long by nature or position.*
513–516. Quantity of Inner Syllables. 516–520. Quantity of Final
Syllables. 520–521. Quantity of Words in Composition. 521–522.
Elision. 523–524. Exceptions to the Law of Elision; Hiatus. 524–525.
Metre; Verse; Foot; Arsis and Thesis; Principal Feet. 525–527.
Verses: Dactylic Hexameter. *List of Feet.* 527–531. Caesura;
Synaphea. 527–528. *Technical Terms.* 531–532. The Elegiac
Distich; *its Rhythm.* 533–546. Lyric Metres. 533. *Catullus,
Horace.* 533–534. Iambics of Horace and Catullus; Scazon; Epodes
of Horace. 534–535. Minor Horatian Metres; Three Lyric Types;

Asclepiad Metres: 536–537. Glyconics of Catullus ; Sapphic Stanza in Horace and Catullus. 537–538. The Hendecasyllable of Catullus. The Alcaic Stanza in Horace. 538. The Galliambus of Catullus. 539–541. Table of Metres : I. Single Verses ; Dactylic Rhythms ; Trochaic Rhythms ; Iambic Rhythms. 539–540. Ionic Rhythms. 541–543. Mixed Rhythms ; Logaoedic. 543. Asynartete. Anapaestic Rhythm : Saturnian Verse. II. Strophic Metres ; Dicola Disticha. 544. Dicola Tetrasticha. 545. Tricola Tetrasticha. 546. Metres of the Comic Poets.

p. 547. . . . . . . APPENDIX.

547–551. *A.* Latin Orthography. 551–553. *B.* Latin Pronunciation. 554–555. *C.* Affinities in the Aryan Family. 555. Grimm's Law. 556–563. *D.* Ancient Dialects of Italy. 556–559. (A) The Umbrian Dialect. 559–561. (B) The Oscan Dialect. 561–563. (C) Specimens of Ancient Latin. 563–564. *E.* Poetic Forms and Idioms. 565. *F.* Supplement to Figurate Construction (§ 61). 566–572. *G.* Money ; Weight ; Measure. 572–575. Computation of Time ; Roman Calendar. 575–576. Siglarium Romanum (Abbreviations). 577–582. Supplementary Notes : I. On Sanskrit Roots. II. On Relations in the Simple Sentence.

p. 583 . . . . . . INDICES.

I. INDEX OF SUBJECTS 583
II. LATIN INDEX 591

THE

PUBLIC SCHOOL LATIN GRAMMAR.

———◆———

INTRODUCTION.

GRAMMAR has two chief divisions:

1
Divisions of Grammar.

(1) ETYMOLOGY (ἐτυμολογία, true wordformation), the doctrine of Letters and Words.

(2) SYNTAX (σύνταξις, construction), the doctrine of Sentences and Discourse.

PROSODY (προσῳδία), which treats of Quantity, Rhythm, and Metre, is not a necessary part of Grammar, but is usually appended to it.

The Latin Language, so called from the Latini, or people of Latium, in Italy, who used it, was the prevalent scion of the Italic branch of the great Indo-European or Aryan family.

2
The Latin Language.

1. Various languages were formed by various races of mankind in their several habitations. When migrating bodies sought new seats, they carried with them their native language, which, amidst the changes wrought by time, always retained traces, more or less strong, of kinship to other branches of the primitive stock. Such kindred languages constitute a Family. Among the families of human speech, two have been most operative in the work of civilisation—the Semitic and the Indo-European or Aryan.

The Semitic family (to which we owe the origin of alphabetic writing) occupied south-western Asia; comprising the Aramaic (Syriac and Chaldee), Hebrew, Phoenician, and Arabic branches.

The Aryan race was seated in central Asia; whence, by a long series of migrations, it sent forth language to most parts of Europe, and to various regions of the Asiatic continent. The European branches of this family are: (1) the Keltic; (2) the Teutonic or German; (3) the Sclavonic; (4) the Lithuanian; (5) the Italic (Latin); (6) the Hellenic (Greek). The Asiatic branches are: (1) the Indic or Sanskrit, in India; (2) the Iranian (of which the Zand is the chief scion) or speech of Persia, Bactria and adjoining districts.

B

2. The Italic branch, like the Hellenic, was from early times divided into various dialects. The principal of these were the Umbrian in the north-east of Italy, the Sabellian and the Oscan in the central districts, and the Latin in Latium. Umbrian, Sabellian, Oscan, and others were destined to fade away, leaving a few scattered monuments of their former existence. Latin survived to be the parent of learning and language in Western Europe. Rome, founded on the Tiber by Latins, according to tradition, B.C. 754, became, on the fall of Alba, the head of the Latin race and name (nomen Latinum) ; and the clannish pride of the Romans led them to call their language, and afterwards their literature, Latin rather than Roman.

3. By Roman conquest and dominion the Latin speech was extended, with dialectic varieties, to all Italy and to other neighbouring countries. From this source are derived the following modern languages : Italian, French (in both its divisions, *Oc* and *Oil*), Spanish, Portuguese, Wallachian, and the Romansch of the Swiss Grisons. They bear the common title of Romanic or Romance languages. All are more or less alloyed with the Teutonic dialects which barbarian conquest carried into Western and Southern Europe in the fifth and following centuries.

3
English. English is the single instance of a Teutonic language largely alloyed, without being disorganised, by the speech of Romanic conquerors. When the Romans quitted Britain in the fifth century, the island, after a brief interval, was overrun by Teutonic hordes (Saxons, Angles, and Jutes), who formed no fusion with the Keltic natives, but either extirpated them gradually, or drove them (as Wälsche, Welsh, or foreigners) into mountainous and barren districts. The rest of the country south of the Tweed came to be called England (Angle-land), and its speech (Anglo-Saxon) was the parent of the later English. The conversion of the Saxons to the Christian faith brought into England some knowledge of Latin, and incorporated many Latin words with the English tongue. By the Norman conquest, A.D. 1066, a dominant race came in, who, though comparatively few in number, filled most places of rank, power, and influence. Hence their speech—Norman-French, a Romanic dialect—became that of courtly society and of law; Latin, its mother-tongue, became the vehicle of religious service and learned intercourse ; whilst English continued to be spoken by the great bulk of the population. In the fusion of these varieties, by which modern English was gradually formed, the usage of the yeomanry and peasantry prevailed over that of the nobles, the law, and the church. English is structurally a Teutonic language, and the number of Teutonic words holds to those of Latin origin a proportion of about two to one. This shews that, without a knowledge *of* Latin, it is impossible to gain a thorough knowledge of English. It must also be remembered that the Teutonic element in English has itself a distant kinship to Latin.

4
Influence of Greek. The influence of Greek civilisation upon Latin was immense. Besides their original affinity the Greek race came into influential contact with the Latin at two distinct eras. The first of these *was*

when the Greek colonies in Sicily and Italy became active in commerce and literature. This activity may be dated as beginning about 550 B.C. The Aeolic city of Cumae in Campania appears to have been the chief medium of communication between Rome and the Greek colonies, and to the influence then exercised may perhaps be ascribed those facts of language which led grammarians to derive Latin from the Aeolic Greek Dialect. Hence too the Romans probably drew the peculiarities which characterise the Latin Alphabet, as the letter Q and the V consonant, which the Aeolic Greeks had kept in the Dorian alphabet at Cumae.

Again, when literary activity began at Rome in the third century B.C., Grecian literature supplied most of the forms and much of the matter. Rome had no models to furnish. Inscriptions, laws, crude annals, with fragments of ritual songs and coarse farces, are all it has to shew within its first five centuries. The credit of authorship is ascribed first to Livius Andronicus, who wrote dramas for the stage B.C. 240. He was succeeded by a crowd of authors, among whom may be mentioned Naevius, Ennius, the father of epic poetry at Rome, and Lucilius, whose subject and reputed invention, satire, is the most original product in Latin literature. But of these writers mere fragments remain. The comedies of Plautus (Plaut.)[1] and Terentius (Ter.), founded on those of the later Attic stage, with the remnant *De Re Rustica* of the elder Cato, are the only literary works extant in Latin before 85 B.C., the date of Cicero's earliest writings. From this time to A.D. 14 extends what is usually called the Golden Age of Latin. Its most eminent authors are :—

(marginal note: 5 Sketch of Latin Literature.)

Prose.		Poetry.	
Cicero	C. (or Cic.)	Lucretius...........	Lucr.
Caesar...............	Caes.	Catullus	Cat.
Cornelius Nepos...	N. (or Nep.)	Vergilius	V. (or Verg.)
Sallustius...........	Sall.	Horatius	H. (or Hor.)
Livius	L. (or Liv.)	Tibullus	Tib.
Varro	Varr.	Propertius	Prop.
Vitruvius...........	Vitr.	Ovidius	Ov.

The so-called Silver Age, to A.D. 117, contains among others :

Prose.		Poetry.	
Seneca...............	Sen.	Manilius	Man.
Quintilianus	Qu.	Phaedrus...........	Phaed.
Plinius the elder...	Pl. N. H.	Seneca...............	Sen. Tr.
Plinius the younger	Plin.	Lucanus	Lucan.
Valerius Maximus	V. Max.	Persius	Pers.
Velleius Paterculus	Vell.	Silius Italicus......	S. It.
Tacitus	Tac.	Valerius Flaccus	V. Fl.
Suetonius	Suet.	Statius...............	St.
Florus ?	Fl.	Iuvenalis...........	Iuv.
Q. Curtius ?	Curt.	Martialis...........	Mart.

---

[1] The letters following the names shew the abbreviations used for them in this Grammar.

The next period, extending to the fall of the Western Empire, A.D. 476, has been termed the Brazen Age. The writers who come nearest to the classic style during this period, are :—

Prose.		Poetry.	
A. Gellius	Gell.	Ausonius............	Aus.
Iustinus	Iust.	Claudianus	Claud.
Appuleius	App.		
Eutropius	Eutr.		
Macrobius	Macr.		

In the Iron Age, which succeeded, Boëthius may be named as the most successful imitator of classic purity.[1]

---

[1] Other abbreviations used in this Grammar:

Pr. Primitive (Sound or Root).

Sk. Sanskrit.
Gr. Greek.

E. L. Early Latin (before 186 B.C.).
R. L. Republican Latin (from 186 to 30 B.C.)
I. L. Latin of Imperial Age (from 30 B.C. to 170 A.D.).
C. L. Classical Latin.
L. L. Later Latin.

U. Umbrian.
O. Oscan.
S. Sabellian.
F. Faliscan.
V. Volscian.
M. Lucr. Munro on Lucretius.
C. Corssen (Aussprache).
Curt. G. Curtius (Gr. Etymologie).

Three dots (...) following a word imply that other derived or kindred words are to be included.

In Sanskrit words:

c′ represents the palatal sound *ch* (as in 'church'): *ric′* is sounded 'rich.' G. Curtius represents it by *k′*.

s′ represents the slightly aspirated sibilant, which often corresponds to Greek κ and Latin c, q. Sk. *das′an,* Gr. δέκα, L. decem. Sk. *dis′,* Gr. δεικ-, L. doc-eo, &c. G. Curtius represents it by *ç*.

ri is a Sanskrit vowel, which may be written *ar.* See p. 578.
j is the Sanskrit letter=English j (Curtius *g′*).
y=English y-consonant (Curtius *j*).
Ex.—yuj, *to yoke* (Curt. *jug′*).

PART I.

LATIN ETYMOLOGY.

ETYMOLOGY comprises:—

    I. PHONOLOGY or SOUNDLORE, the doctrine of Sounds.

    II. MORPHOLOGY or WORDLORE, the doctrine of Words.[1]

By a Primitive Sound or Root is meant one which careful induction assigns to that ancient, though no longer extant, Aryan language from which the Sanskrit is derived. Such induction is obtained by comparison of the Sanskrit with all other kindred languages, especially with Zand, Greek, Latin, Gothic, and Lithuanian. See Supplementary Notes following Appendix.

DIVISION I.

PHONOLOGY OR SOUNDLORE.

i. Soundlore treats of the sounds and relations of Letters and Syllables.

1. The Latin Alphabet now in use contains the same Letters as the English, omitting W.
The Letters have two forms:

    1) The Capital, Uncial, or ancient form.

    2) The Small, or later form, which came into common use in the eighth or ninth century: after which the Capitals were chiefly used for inscriptions, and as initial letters of sentences and proper names.

    1) A B C D E F G H·I (J) K L M N O P Q R S T

    2) a b c d e f g h i (j) k l m n o p q r s t

    (U) V X Y Z.

    (v) u x y z.

2. Six of the Letters are VOCALES, Vowels (self-sounding), a, e, i, o, u, y: the rest are CONSONANTES, Consonants, which are sounded only with a vowel.

---

[1] The terms Phonology and Morphology are taken from Schleicher's *Vergleichende Grammatik der Indogermanischen Sprachen.*

3. Consonants are divided into Mutes, Nasals, Liquids, Spirants, and Double Consonants.[1]

The Nasals are n, m; Liquids, r, l; Spirants, f, h, j, s, v; Double Consonants, x, z : the rest are Mutes.

Note 1. **y** and **z** are only used in words borrowed from the Greek.

Note 2. **i+j** and **u+v** are two pairs; each pair constituting one ancient letter in double form. See § **12**. viii.

Sylla-
bles:
Diph-
thongs.

4. A *SYLLABLE* (συλλαβή) consists of one or more letters pronounced in a single breath; i-lex.

5. A *DIPHTHONG* (δίφθογγος) is the combined sound of two vowels meeting in the same syllable; au-lae.

There are in Latin three usual diphthongs, ae (or æ), oe (or œ), au; and three seldom used, ei, eu, ui.

8
Quan-
tity.

ii. *QUANTITY* is the time of uttering a Syllable.

1. Every Syllable is considered Short (‿) or Long (‾) in Quantity, according as its vowel is short or long; that is, according as it is uttered with a single or double time (mora) :

Short by nature . .	ă ŏ in . .	ămŏr.
Long by nature . .	ē ū in . .	ēsū.
A Vowel may be { Short by position before another vowel . .	ĭ in . . .	pĭos.
Long by position before two consonants or a double consonant .	ē ō in . .	pērnōx.
Diphthongs are long	au, ae in .	caūdaē.

2. A Vowel is called Short or Long by Nature, when the reason of its quantity is other than position.

3. A Syllable is called Doubtful (‿̄) when its Vowel may be short or long : Sidŏnius.

4. A Vowel, naturally short, may be made long in poetry, if it stands before **cr, gr, tr, dr, pr, br, fr, cl, pl**, or **fl** : tenĕbrae, quădrŭplex. Such a Vowel is called Doubtful by position. In prose the syllable is pronounced short, tenĕbrae.

9
Syllaba-
tion.

iii. *SYLLABATION* is subject to the following rules:

1. Every syllable must contain a vowel.
2. A word may begin with any vowel but **y**.
3. A word may end with any vowel, and with any of the consonants, **l, m, n, r, s, t, x**. A few words end in **b, c, d**.

---

[1] Checks are another term for Mutes; Trills for Liquids; Fricatives (as generated by the friction of the breath) for Spirants (See Max Müller's *Lectures on Language*). Mutes have also been called Momentaneous or Explosive Consonants, as distinguished from Nasals, Liquids, and Spirants, which are Continuous.

4. Priscian's rule is that inner syllables end with a vowel, if a single consonant follows : cla-ma-tur ; or if two or more consonants follow, which can begin a word : lu-di-crus, e-sca, ma-gnus, scri-ptus, scri-psi, a-stra. Custom extends this rule to such instances as so-mnus, A-bdera, rhy-thmus, etc. But, if the consonants cannot begin a word, they are divided between the syllables : gal-lus, punc-tum, of-fen-do, am-plis-simus, ex-per-tus.

5. In compound words a syllable ends with the end of one part : ab-igo, res-publica.

6. The last syllable is called Ultima, the last but one Penultima or Penult, the last but two Antepenultima or Antepenult. An inner syllable is called open if it ends with a vowel, close if it ends with a consonant. A word of one syllable is called Monosyllable; a word of two syllables, Disyllable, etc.

vi. *ACCENTUATION* has the following laws:[1]

1. The tone of a syllable is called ACCENT. There are two strong accents, the Acute (´) or sharp quick stress, and the Circumflex (ˆ) or deep lengthened stress. Syllables without either are sometimes called Baryton (Grave in tone), sometimes Atonic.

2. Monosyllables, with vowel short by nature, have the Acute Accent : ós, vír, dúx; those with Vowel long by nature have the Circumflex : ôs, môs, lêx.

3. Words of several syllables are not accented on the Ultima, but on one of the two preceding syllables. Only, when a word loses a final vowel, if the Penult had an accent, that accent remains on the same syllable : illínc for illímce, audîn for audîsne.

4. Disyllables have the Acute on the Penult, when either both syllables are short by nature, as bónă, or the first is long by position, or the last long by nature or position, as ínter, móres, ámant.

5. Disyllables have the Circumflex on the Penult, when the Penult is long by nature, and the last short by nature and not lengthened by position : mâtĕr, mûsă.

6. Words of more than two syllables have the Acute on the Antepenult, when the Penult is short, as hómĭnes, amplíssĭmos. But the accent remains on the Penult in unweakened compounds of făcio, as benefácis, and in contracted genitives : ingéni.

7. Words of more than two syllables have their Accent on the Penult when long; namely, the Acute when the Penult is long by position only, clamántur; or when the last syllable also is long, amárant; the Circumflex, when the Penult is long by nature, and the last short by nature, and not lengthened by position : clamâre.

8. ENCLITICS, que, nĕ, ve, etc. bring forward the accent of the word to which they are subjoined : hómines, hominésque; próna, pronáque. Prepositions are PROCLITIC, that is, without an accent of their own before their cases . circa moénia; but, moénia círca.

Note. The Accents are not marked on words, but understood.[2]

---

[1] Latin Accentuation Is a subject too large, intricate and unsettled to be fully discussed in a book like the present. Students who wish to pursue it more minutely are referred to the works of Ritschl and Corssen, and to the Latin Grammars of Krüger and Kühner. Only a few general rules are given here.

[2] Corssen allows a second accent, which he calls a Middle Tone (i.e. semiacute), to

11
Punctu-
ation.

v. PUNCTA, the Signs of Punctuation, or Stops.

These are the same in Latin as in English : Comma (,) ; Semi-colon (;) ; Colon (:) ; Full Stop (.) ; Note of Interrogation (?) ; Note of Admiration (!). The mark (··) is placed over e or i when it does not coalesce with a preceding vowel : aër, Teïus. But none of these were used anciently except the Full Stop (punctum).

12
Schemes
of the
Letters.

vi. The Relations of the Letters may be thus shewn :

I. VOWELS.

Standard vowel

a

Sharp medial   **e**   **o**   Flat medial
Sharp semiconsonant   **i**   ⊢   **u**   Flat semiconsonant
Medial (see vii. 11).

II. CONSONANTS.

Note.—Tenues and Mediae are by some called severally Surds and Sonants. Guttural mutes are also called k-sounds, Dental mutes t-sounds, Labial mutes p-sounds.	MUTES (Momentaneous)		NASALS	LIQUIDS	SPIRANTS			DOUBLE
	Tenues or Sharp	Mediae or Flat	(Continuous)		Sibilant	Aspirate	Semivowel	
GUTTURAL, or Throat-sounds . . .	c (k, q)	g	n·	··	··	h	··	x
DENTAL, or Teeth-sounds . . .	t	d	n	r, l	s	··	j	z
							f v	
LABIAL, or Lip-sounds	p	b	m					

N is guttural when it precedes **g, c,** or **q.** The Spirants **f, v,** if sounded as in English, are labiodental.[1]

---

certain words of more than three syllables, when there is an interval between the accented syllables. Such words are—

1) Plurisyllable Compounds, in which the Middle Tone will fall generally on the first syllable, as in vérsipellis, mísericordia, úndeviginti, éffrenatus, súblevare, etc. ; sometimes on the second, as in supérbiloquentia, repándirostrum.

2) Plurisyllables, in which, by Derivation or Flexion, the accent of the primitive word has been shifted to a suffix. Such a Middle Tone will generally be on the first syllable ; as in lóngitudo, pópulabundus, sérvitutem. This theory implies, in rare instances, the possibility of two Middle Tones, as in cónfidéntiloquius. See Corssen, ii. 824.

[1] Sanskrit has two more classes of Consonants : (a) Palatal, a modification of the Gutturals ; (b) Cerebral or Lingual, a modification of the Dentals. Thus, in Sanskrit J is Palatal.

vii. Memoranda from the History of the Alphabet. History of Alphabet.

1. The Romans modified the form of the third Greek letter from Γ to C, and gave it the sound K, instead of G. The sound and letter G were afterwards introduced about 250 B.C. C. was kept as the abbreviation of Gaius; Cn. of Gnaeus.

2. The use of C as sharp made K superfluous, and the Romans almost ceased to use it; but it was kept in a few abbreviations: K. for Kaeso; Kal. for Calendae and Calumnia: also Kar. for Kartago.

3. The other Phoenician guttural surd Koph or Koppa (which the Dorian Alphabet of Cumae possessed) was kept by the Romans as Q, and ultimately confined to words in which parasitic **u** or **v** follows the guttural.

4. The Rough Breathing was raised to the rank of a letter, obtaining the form and position of the Greek Eta, H.

5. The letter **f** was purely Italian, its ancient sound being not exactly that (which it now has) of Phi (ph), nor that (which its form suggests) of the Greek Digamma (w). In the Etruscan Alphabet it has the form 8; but the Romans gave it that of the Digamma, (ϝ) F.

6. Vau (V nearly = English w) was adopted by the Romans as a semi-vowel, and took the position held by Upsilon next to T.

7. There is some evidence that the ancient Romans used **z** (zeta), but afterwards supplied it by **s** or **ss** : so that **y, z** were added at the end of the Alphabet in Cicero's age to represent the Greek v, ζ, and are only used in latinized Greek words: lyra = λύρα, zona = ζώνη.

8. The history of **x** is obscure. It appears in a few early inscriptions : but, though in power equal to Greek ξ (**cs**), it took the place and form of Chi : when and why, are doubtful points. See Corssen (*Ausspr.* I. 6).

9. The long vowels Eta and Omega were omitted as unnecessary.

10. The Aspirate sounds χ, θ, φ, as foreign to Italian utterance, were left out; but the study of Greek in Cicero's age led to the use of **ch, th, ph,** which represent those letters in latinized Greek words: parochus, thesaurus, philosophus; also of **rh** : rhetor.

11. The Emperor Claudius invented and introduced three letters : (1) ⅃ to represent **u-**consonant; (2) Ɔ (antisigma) to represent ψ (**ps**); (3) Ⱶ to represent a vowel having a middle tone between **i** and **u**, as in lĭbet—lŭbet, gradĭbus—gradŭbus, maxĭmus— maxŭmus. They did not remain in use; but the first and last appear in inscriptions.

viii. The Semiconsonants i (j) and u (v).

1. The consonantal character of **i** (**j**) is shewn by the two facts, i (j). that, when it begins Latin words before a vowel it makes position in verse after words ending with a consonant, and that it makes no hiatus after words ending with a vowel or with **m.** Thus in

Sub Ioue iam ius est

sub, iam are long by position, and -ĕ, -**am** are not elided before **i.**

1) **ɪ** is a vowel (ɪ-vocalis) when it ends a syllable; ni-ti; or when it stands in a syllable before a consonant, in-it, sic-cis; or when it is a syllable; ab-i-to.

ɪ is a consonant (ɪ-consonans) when it begins a syllable before a vowel; ie-iu-no; its sound being that of English y-consonant (= German j), a faint protraction of the vowel-sound **ɪ**.

2) In Greek words, however, Ĭŏle, ĭambus, and in a few Latin words, ĭ-ens, ĭeram, ɪ-vocalis remains open before a vowel.

3) The sign J was introduced in a late age, to represent ɪ-con-sonans, and most editors do not use it. Its English and French sibilant sounds (*John*, *Jean*) are not classical, but crept in before the Middle Ages.

4) **ɪ**-consonans is omitted before **ɪ** by the compounds of ĭacio, āb-icio cōn-icio prō-icio rē-icio, etc.; though the long quan-tity of the first syllable is kept; **ɪ** being =**j ɪ**. See Munro on Lucr. i. 34, ii. 951. In Lucr. Verg. êĭce, rêĭce. But rĕ-ĭcere, Plaut.

5) Poets sometimes harden ɪ-vocalis into ɪ-consonans: āb-ĭĕ-te, ār-ĭĕ-te, pār-ĭĕ-te, for ab-ĭ-ete, etc. Sound ab-yĕte, ar-yĕte, etc., trisyll. So Horace has consīl-ium (=consīl-yum), Virgil has flūv-iorum (=flūv-yorum), trisyll. M. Lucr. ii. 991.

V (U).   2. The sign V was employed by the Romans as vowel and con-sonant. In a latter age **u** became the vowel sign, **v** the consonant sign. If uva (= oowa) be sounded, it appears that **u**-consonans (=w) is only a faint protraction of the labial vowel **u** ; whence the modern name Double-u.

1) V-consonans is vocalized in cautum for cavitum, fautum for favitum, lautum for lavitum, and in auceps for aviceps, nauta for navita, naufragus for navifragus.

2) Poets sometimes vocalize **u**-consonans before a vowel: sil-u-ae: sometimes they harden **u**-vocalis into **u**-consonans: gen-ua for ge-nu-a, ten-ui-a for te-nu-ia. M. *Lucr.* iv. 1157.

3) Parasitic **u** follows **q, ng,** and **s** : sequor; lingua; suavis. This usage is derived from ancient groups **kv, gv, sv** : but as the sign **u** so used neither forms a syllable nor creates position, it must be regarded, not as a proper letter, but as a kind of link between the guttural (or sibilant) and labial sounds.[1]

ix. *Sound* and *Quality* of the Vowels.

Sound and quality of Vowels.   1. Vowels have not one short and one long sound only; but various shades of these, in close or open syllables.

(Thus the sound of **u** varies in the following words: *credŭlŭs, bŭsy, fŭll, ūse, Jūne,* and in the French words, *commŭn, commūne.*)

2. The old sounds of the Latin vowels probably differed little from those of the vowels in modern Italian. Proceeding from the thinnest and sharpest sound **ɪ**, to the thickest and flattest **u**, the following words may represent their general distinction : the first four being pronounced as in French, the fifth as in Italian, Zŭloo.

Quĭnīne, dĕmēsne, păpā, prŏmōte, Zŭlū.

3. The three primitive vowels are **a, ɪ, u.** Sanskrit has **e** and **o** only as diphthongs arising from **aɪ, au.**

[1] In many modern editions of Latin authors, V alone is used as the Capital form of con-sonant and vowel, and **u** alone as the Cursive form of both. In this grammar *v* is retained as a cursive.

1) The standard vowel is ă, issuing from the throat through the opened mouth : ĭ is the thin sharp palatal, sounded between the tongue and the lower palate ; ŭ is the thick flat labial, sounded by a low interior whistle through the protruded lips. Each has its long and short sound, with shades of these.

2) The want of intervening sounds to represent the strengthening of ĭ and ŭ, and the primary weakenings of ă, called into use two subsidiary vowels ; ĕ medial between ă and ĭ, and ŏ medial between ă and ŭ. Both these are narrower gutturals than **a** ; **e** sounding along the upper palate and tending to the sharpness of **i** ; and **o** sounding from the lower throat with a fullness which its form marks, but tending to the labialism and flatness of **u**.[1]

3) The strongest short vowel is ă, into which none other passes.

4) The weakest is ĭ : for which reason it often stands as a vincular vowel before suffixes : reg-ĭ-to, flag-ĭ-to, leg-ĭ-bus : but sometimes **e** or **u** takes its place; soci-ĕ-tas, teg-ŭ-mentum.

5) That ŏ is stronger than ĕ may be seen by comparing pondus with pendere, tŏga with tĕgere, vŏlo with vĕlim, velle.

6) Though ŭ has various shades of strengh, as in pŭto, sŭmŭs, augŭr, augŭrium, declining almost to the weakness of ĭ, as in optŭmus (optĭmus, vii. 11), yet on the average it is not seen to be weaker than ĕ. Such examples as pignŭs, pignĕris, pignŏris etc., might seem to shew ŭ stronger than ĕ, ŏ : but it must be remembered that this ŭ corresponds not to Greek *v*, but to Greek *o* : that ŭs is really a weak syllable, and ŭ, like ĭ, gives a facility to the rejection of **s** in old Latin poetry, which ĕ does not afford.

7) When a vowel from being short becomes long, it is doubled in time and strength ; ĭĭ = ī, ĕĕ = ē, etc.

8) As final short vowels, ă and ĕ predominate; ĭ, ŏ are rarely final ; ŭ never, except by the rejection of **s** in old Latin poetry.

As final long vowels, ī and ō predominate : ē and ā are less frequent ; and ū least frequent of all.

x. Phonetic Decay in old Italian language.
(See Corssen, I. 347.)

1. Phonetic Decay tends to lighten diphthongs, to shorten and weaken vowels, to silence or throw out light vowels, to cast off or assimilate consonants.

2. This tendency is especially shewn in Umbrian and its cognate dialects ; also in the old Latin, of which our knowledge is derived chiefly from inscriptions, partly from the testimonies of grammarians, and from the most ancient manuscripts.

3. Classical Latin (see § 5) may be regarded as in some measure a reaction, by which, during a long literary period, the process of Phonetic Decay in Latin was arrested. After the age of Suetonius, about A.D. 120, decay recommenced and continued for nearly 1000 years, till the modern Romanic languages gradually emerged from the darkness of those centuries.

---

[1] Vowels are here spoken of as sounded with consonants : ăd, dă. All vowels issue from one primary vowel, a faint sigh in the depths of the throat. Its first scarce distinguishable strengthenings may be compared thus : max-*i*-mos, max-*ŭ*-mos, max-*ĕ*-mos, max-*ŏ*-mos, max-*ă*-mos.

Vowel-change.

xi. VOWELCHANGE.

1. Vowels are liable to change in the Flexion, Derivation, and Composition of words.

2. Syllables may be either s t r e n g t h e n e d or w e a k e n e d by Vowelchange.

3. The general tendency of Italian dialects was to weaken vowel sounds. But sometimes a syllable is strengthened by assuming a stronger for a weaker vowel. Thus the tonic syllable in t o g a is stronger than in t e g o.

Diph-thongs.

xii. Formation and Decay of Diphthongs.

1. Diphthongs and long Vowels in Sanskrit arise from the intro-duction of a vowel to strengthen a short sound. Thus ă by strengthening ĭ produces ê ; ă by strengthening ŭ produces ô ; and this process is called Guna (distinction). If â strengthens (âi, âu), the process is called Vṛiddhi (augmentation).

2. In Latin (as in Greek) ĕ and ŏ are themselves capable of strengthening ĭ and ŭ. Thus the full list of diphthongs proper is

ai	**ei**	**oi**
au	**eu**	**ou**

3. **ui** is an improper diphthong, only found in the words c u i, h u i c, h u i, p h u i.

4. **yi** in Greek words for *υι* is very rare : as I l i t h y i a (Εἰλειθυῖα).

5. The six diphthongs proper existed in ancient Latin, as shewn by inscriptions : but before the classic age all except au had de-cayed into other long sounds, namely :—

> **ai** into **ae**, rarely passing into ē (**ei**) ī
> **oi** — **oe**, often — — ū (**ei**) ī
> **ei** — ē or ī
> **eu** — ū
> **ou** — ū

Note. Corssen observes (I. 674), that the history of **ai, oi, ei,** has peculiar interest, because, as these diphthongs often sprang from the addition of a suffix which begins with a vowel to a stem which ends with a vowel, they illustrate the laws of flexion as well as the progress of phonetic decay.[1]

6. The diphthong **ai** prevailed in old Latin: a i d i l i s, R o m a i, f i l i a i, &c.; and is found even in the imperial age. But about B.C. 200 **ae** came into use, and gradually became the classical form. For this, as a rustic variety, in the age of Lucilius, is found ē : ē d u s, prē tor, Cē cilius, &c.; which became more prevalent in later Latin, and in modern language has superseded **ae** : *secular, premium.*

1) Examples occur of **eis** for Dat. and Abl. Plur. Ending **ais**, which in classical Latin became īs : t a b u l e i s p u b l i c e i s = t a b u l i s p u b l i c i s.

---

[1] This history is gained from the careful comparison of Latin Inscriptions extending for about 400 years from B.C. 260 to A.D. 150. In the present chapter and in § 20 such results alone are generally mentioned as suffice to explain the varieties of form which appear in classical authors.

a) Old poets, as Lucretius, often use the Gen. in ā-ĭ, dividing it into two syllables, materiā-ī. Virgil rarely: aulā-ī, Aen. iii. 354.

b) The vowels are divided in Gā-ĭ-ŭs, Gā-ī, and in the Greek words Agla-ĭ-ă, Lā-ĭ-ŭs. In others, as Achaia, Aiax, Graius, Maia, and in aio, maior, ı is ı-cons. (Achā-ya, ā-yo, mā-yor, ...).

7. The diphthong oı (oe) is of much rarer use than aı (ae). Oı is found as late as the first century B.C. in stem-syllables. But it passed into oe early, as aı into ae, by strengthening ı. Also, by weakening o, it passed into (uı, ue =) ū. Thus we find moi-nera, moenera, mūnera; loidos, loedus, lūdus; ποινή, poena, punire; coirare, coerare, curare (also courare); oitier, oetier, ūti. M. Lucr. ii. 829.

1) In the Imperial age oe began to be corrupted into (ee) ē: pomērium, fēderatus. This, as in ae, grew more and more usual, and prevails in modern language: *penal, federal,* &c.

2) In Case-endings, oı from old times was liable to pass into eı and ı: puer-oi, puer-ei, puer-i; puer-ois, puer-eis, puer-is.

a) In prŏīn, prŏīnde, the vowels coalesce: in Trō-ĭ-ŭs they remain separate (Hiatus). In Troia ı is ı-cons. (Trō-ya).

8. Eı is either a diphthong, as in a few old words, deiva, deicere, leiber; in the old Italian Dative ending eı, virtutei; in Dat. Abl. Pl. endings eıs for oıs; and in Nom. Pl. ending eı for oı of Decl. 2: or it is a middle sound between ē and ī, as when the form eıs represents a compromise between the Acc. Plur. endings īs, ēs, of I-nouns: ur̥bīs, urbēs, urbeis.

1) Eı is found as diphthong or middle sound in inscriptions of all ages; ē sometimes taking its place, but ī prevailing over both.

a) In the words dein, deinde, deinceps, e-ı may coalesce in poetry, or, as some think, e is elided.

b) In names in -eıus, ı is ı-cons.; Pompeius = Pompē-yus.

c) Greek ει appears in Latin generally as ī: Tydīdes for Τυδείδης; but often as ē before a vowel; Alexandrēa or Alexandrīa, Darēus or Darius, Thalēa or Thalīa.

d) In some Greek words e is open before ı (Hiatus): Tēïus, Plēïas, Nerĕïdes.

9. Au was retained in all ages of Latin. But it often passed (by the process ou, oo) into ō: cōdex, plōstrum, Clōdius, Plōtius, &c., and (in Italian) *oro, toro, tesoro,* &c.; sometimes (by the process ou, uu) into ū: clūdo. M. Lucr. ii. 829.

10. Eu in Latin words is very rare. Heu, eheu, *alas,* are imitative words. In neu, seu, ceu, u is a vocalised v (neve, seve, ceve). On neuter, neutiquam, see Prosody.

a) In Greek words eu remains: Euripides, Eurus.

Note.—Greek au and eu before a vowel are written with vowel or consonant: Agaue or Agave; Euander or Evander.

11. Ou occurs on old Inscrr.: *doucere, iousit, Louceria;* but had decayed into ū before the classical age.

(On the pronunciation of Diphthongs, see Appendix *B*.)

xiii. *VOWELSTRENGTHENING* in Root-syllables, Suffixes, and Endings.

A) Root-syllables (see Supplemental Notes after Appendix).

a) Primitive or Italian ŭ, strengthened by ă (ŏ, ĕ) in the manner of Guna, or by ā, (ō, ē) in the manner of Vṛiddhi, subsides from a diphthongal sound into ū or ō; the series of possible change being **ŭ, au, ou, eu, ū (ō).**

jŭg, *to yoke*	(ŭ) iŭ(n)g-ĕre ... iŭg-u-m, iŭg-are .... **(eu)** ζευγ- (ū) iūg-i-s, iūg-er-a, iū-mentu-m.
krŭ, *hear*	(ŭ) clŭ-ĕre. **(au)** lau-s, laud-are .... **(ū, ō)**, lū- s-cin-ia, glō-r-ia ....
krŭ, *be raw*	(ŭ) rŭ-di-s. **(au)** rau-du-s, rau-du-s-culu-m. **(ū)** crū-du-s ... crū-d-eli-s ... crū-s-tu-m, crū-s-ta.
lŭ, *wash*	(ŭ) lŭ-ĕre ... lŭ-tu-m .... **(au)** lăv-ere with **v-** cons. ... lautus. **(ou)** λού-ειν, di-lŭv-iu-m ... with **v-**cons. for **v-**voc. **(ū, ō)**, lō-tu-s ... pol-lū-tu-s ... lū-s-tru-m, lū-s-tr-are ....
plŭ, *flow*	(ŭ) plŭ-it. **(ou)** plŭv-ia ... for E. L. *plov-ia* ... **(ū, ō)**, plū-vi ... plō-r-are ....
(pŭ-s, *nur- ture, thrive*)	(ŭ) pŭ-er ... pŭ-ella ... pŭ-s-illu-s ... disci-pŭ-lu-s, pŭ-m-ilu-s, pŭ-tu-s. **(au)** παῖς for πă-υς. **(ū)** pū-su-s, pū-s-io, pū-pu-s, pū-pa, pū-p- ula, pū-p-illu-s, pū-m-ilio, pū-ber, pū-bes.
pŭ, *cleanse*	(ŭ) pŭ-tu-s, pŭ-t-are ... am-pŭ-t-are. **(au)** pa-eni- t-et for *pav-ine-t-et*. **(ou)** po-ena for pov- ina. **(ū)** pū-ru-s ... pū-n-ire ....
pŭ, *stink*	(ŭ) pŭ-ter pŭ-tris .... **(au)** pa-e-d-or for *pav-i-d-or*. **(ū)** pū-s pū-r- ... pū-t-ēre ....
rŭ, *bray*	(ŭ) rŭ-d-ĕre ... rŭ-d-en-s. **(au)** rāv-u-s ... rau- cu-s .... **(ū)** rū-m-or.
rŭdh, *be red*	(ŭ) rŭb-er, rŭb-ēre ... rŭ-tilu-s ... ἐρυθ-ρός. **(eu)** ἐρεύθ-ω. **(ū, ō)** rūb-ig-o or rōb-ig-o, rūf- u-s ....
rŭk, *give light*	(ŭ) lŭc-er-na, λυκ-. **(ou)** E. L. *Louc-ina.* **(eu)** λευκός. **(ū)** lūx lūc- ... lūc-ēre ... Lūc-ina, di-lūc-ulu-m ....
skŭ, *hide*	(ŭ) scŭ-tu-la ... cŭ-ti-s. **(au)** căv-ēre, cau-tu-s ... cau-s-sa or cau-sa. **(ou)** E. L. *cou-r-are* or *coi-r-are* for *cov-ĭ-r-are*. **(eu)** κεύ-θω. **(ū)** cū-ra, cū-r-are ... E. L. *cō-r-are*, cū- s-to-s, scū-tu-m, ob-scū-ru-s. See C. I. 356.
sŭ, *sew*	(ŭ) sŭ-ere. (diphthongal in Sk. Goth. and Lith.). (ū) sū-t-or, sū-bula.

tŭ, *swell* . | (ŭ) tŭ-m-ēre, tŭ-m-idu-s, tŭ-mu-lu-s. (au in Sk.), tae-d-et for *tav-i-d-et.* So ta-e-ter. O. *tau-ta.* (ou) O. *tou-to.* (ū, ō) tō-tu-s, tū-ber. U. *tu-ta, to-ta.* These old Italian words mean '*a community,*' a *people.*'

dŭc-, *lead* . | (ŭ) dux dŭc- ... edŭc-are .... (ou) E. L. *douc-ĕre.* (ū) dūc-ĕre ... .

flŭ-, *flow* . | (ŭ) flŭ-ĕre ... con-flŭ-g-es. (ou) flūv-ĭdu-s, flŭv-iu-s (from flou-v-). (ū) flū-men, flū-t-are.

nŭ-, *nod* . | (ŭ) nŭ-ĕre. (eu) νεύω. (ū) nū-tu-s, nū-t-are ... nū-men.

Add the prim. root dyu, *shine* (=div), whence (ŏ for ŭ) iŏ-cu-s. (ou), O. *Diouv-ei,* whence the weakened words, E. L. *Diŏv-is,* U. *Juv-e,* Iŏv-is, iŭv-at, ... (ū) Iū-p-piter, Iū-n-o, iū-c-undu-s....

b) Primitive or Italian ĭ, strengthened by ă (ŏ, ĕ), or by ā (ō, ē), subsides from a diphthongal sound into ī or ā; the series being ĭ, **ai, oi, ei,** ī (ē).

dĭk, *shew*. | (ĭ) dĭc-are ... dĭc-io, con-dĭc-io, dĭc-is, caussi-dĭc-u-s ... iu-dex, iu-dĭc- ... di-dĭc-i, dĭg-i-tu-s, dig-nu-s ... pro-dĭg-iu-m; ... δὶκ-η .... (ei) δεικ- E. L. *deic-ĕre.* (ī) dīc-ĕre, dīx-i ...

dĭv, *shine* . | (ĭ) re-dĭv-ivu-s, dĭ-u, inter-dĭ-u-s, nu-dĭ-u-s, dĭ-es, dĭ-ur-nu-s, ho-dĭ-er-nu-s, dĭ-es-piter, nun-dĭ-na-e. (ē=ai) Sk. *dēv-a-s, a god.* (ei) θεῖος, E. L. *deivos, deiv-a.* (ī) dīv-us, dī-us (weakened form dĕ-us), Dī-a-na, I-anus for *Di-anus.* In bĭ-du-um, trĭ-du-um, &c., du is a weakened form of div.

ĭ, *go* . . | (ĭ) ĭ-t-er, ad-ĭ-tu-s, &c., in-ĭ-t-iu-m. ... (ē=ai) Sk. *ē-mi.* (oi) οἶ-μ-ο-ς. (ei) εἶ-μ-ι, E. L. *ei-re.* (ī) ī-re, ī-bo, ī-vi. ...

ĭ, *that* . | (ĭ) ĭ-s, ĭ-b-i, ĭ-dem.... (ei) E. L. *ei-eis.* (ī) ī-dem.

kĭ, *lie down* | (ĭ) quĭ-es, quĭ-e-sc-ĕre, quĭ-e-tus .... (ei) κεῖμαι, E. L. *cei-vi-s.* (ī) cī-vi-s.

slĭ, *smear* . | (ĭ) lĭ-n-ĕre (-ire), lĭ-tu-s, lĭ-tu-ra. (ei) E. L. *lei-t-er-a.* (ī) lī-mu-s ... lī-m-ax, lī-n-ea, lī-t-er-a or li-tt-er-a. (G. *schleim,* Engl. *slime.*)

spĭc (= spăk), *spy* | (ĭ) -spĭc-ere -spĕc-ere ... (ei) E. L. *peic-u-s.* (ī) pīc-u-s, su-spīc-io? (G. *specht.* Engl. *wood-pecker; pie.*)

trĭ, *three* . | (ĭ) trĭ-bu-s, trĭ-dens ... tĕr, trĕ-centi. (ei) τρεῖς. (ī) trī-s, trī-ni, trī-du-um.

fĭd, *to trust* | (ĭ) fĭd-es, fĭd-eli-s, per-fĭd-u-s .... (oi) E. L. *foid-u-s,* foedus, foed-er-a-tu-s, πέποιθα. (ei) πείθω, E. L. *feidus.* (ī) fīd-ĕre, fīd-us ....

lĭb, *to choose* | (ĭ) lĭb-et. (oi) E. L. *loeb-er.* (ei) E. L. *leib-er.* (ī) līb-er ....

c) Primitive or Italian **ă**, sometimes represented by **ĕ, ĭ, ŏ,** or **ŭ**, is strengthened into **ā**, which sometimes sinks to **ē** or **ō**.

(1) ă (ĕ, ĭ, ŏ, ŭ).   (2) ā.   (3) ē.   (4) ō.

ăk, *sharpen*	(1) ἀκ- ăc-u-s, ăc-u-ĕre. (2) āc-er. (4) ἀκωκή, ὠκ-ύς, ōc-i-or… .
ăg, *drive* .	(1) ἀγ-ăg-ĕre… ăg-i-li-s…. (2) amb-āg-es, āc-tu-s. (3) ēg-i, στρατηγός … . (4) paedăgōg-u-s.
bhă *throw* bhă-s ∫*light*	(1) fĕ-n-es-tra, fă-t-eri, fă-t-uu-s, infĭ-ti-a-s, fax făc-, făc-ĕre … făc-ie-s, fă-ber, φă-ος, φă-ναι. (1) fā-s, fā-s-ti, fā-ri, fā-bula, fā-ma, fā-c-und-us … fā-tu-m, fā-nu-m. (3) fē-t-i-ali-s, *fē-s-ia-e* = fē-r-ia-e, fē-s-tu-s, φημί, φήμη.
bhrăg, *break*	(1) fra(n)g-ĕre … frăg-ili-s, frăg-or, nau-frăg-us, … . (2) refrāg-ari, suf-frāg-iu-m …frāc-tu-s. (3) frēg-i, Ϝρηγ- … . (4) ἔρρωγα.
kăr, *want* .	(1) căr-ēre. (2) cār-us.
găn, *beget* .	(1) gĕn-us … gĕn-ui, γἔν- γŏν- gĕn-ĕr, pro-gĕn-ie-s, gĕn-iu-s, in-gĕn-iu-m, indi-gĕn-a, gĕn-i-tor, γυνή. (2) gnā-tu-s, nā-tu-s … nā-t-io, nātura, gnā-vu-s, i-gnā-vu-s … . (3) γνήσιος.
gnă, *know*	(1) nŏ-t-a, nŏ-t-are, cŏ-gnĭ-t-us … . (2) gnā-ru-s, i-gnā-ru-s, nā-r-r-are. (4) nō-tu-s, i-gnō-tu-s, ignō-r-are … nō-r-ma … nō-bili-s … nō-men, a-gnō-men, i-gnō-min-ia … ἔγνωκα.
ḱăl, *hide* .	(1) clĕ-p-ĕre (clĭ-p-eu-s), cel-la, oc-cŭl-ĕre, cu-cul-lu-s, -cĭl-iu-m, c-la-m, κλοπή. (2) cāl-ig-o. (3) cēl-are. (4) κλώψ.
lăb, *slip* .	(1) lăb-are, lăb-e-facere. (2) lāb-i … lāb-es.
mă, *measure*	(1) mă-nu-s, μετρεῖν, mĕ-tru-m, mĕ-d-imnu-s, mĕ-t-ĕre, mŏ-dïu-s, mŏ-d-u-s, mŏ-d-er-ari, mŏd-es-tu-s … . (2) mā-ne, im-mā-ni-s, mā-tu-ru-s, Mā-tu-ta. (3) mē-ta, mē-t-īri … mē-n-sa, mē-n-sura, mē-n-si-s, se-mē-s-tri-s … . (4) mō-s mōr-, mōr-osu-s.
păk, *fasten*	(1) păc-i-sc-i, pa(n)g-ĕre, pe-pĭg-i, πăγ-. (2) pāx pāc-, pāc-are, re-pāg-ulu-m, pāg-u-s, pāg-ina, com-pāg-es, pro-pāg-o. (3) -pēgi, πηγ-.
răg, *direct* .	(1) rĕg-ere, rĕg-io, -rĭgĕre, rŏg-u-s. (2) Sk. *rājan.* (3) rēx rēg- … rēg-ula … . (From rĕgere perhaps rĭg-ēre, rĭg-i-du-s … .)
să, *sow* .	(1) să-tu-s, să-t-io (sĕ-rĕre) … . (2) Să-t-ur-nu-s. (3) sē-vi, sē-men … .
snă, *float,* *bathe*	(1) nă-t-are. (2) nā-re … nā-r-i-s, nā-s-u-s, năs-turt-iu-m (nasum torquens). (3) νῆσος, νήχω.

stă, *stand* .	(1) stă-tor, stă-ti-m (but E. L. *stā-ti-m*), stă-ti-o, stă-tu-s, stă-tu-ĕre, stă-tu-a, stă-bulum-m, stă-bili-s : stĕ-t-i, super-stĭ-t- .... (2) stā-turu-s, stā-tura, stā-men, and in Conjug. stā-re, stā-bam .... (3) στῆναι ....
star, *strew*.	(1) stĕr-(n)ĕre (στορ-), (2) strā-vi, strā-tu-s, strā-men ... stlā-ta, stlā-t-ariu-s, (4) στρω-ννύ-ναι, στρῶ-μα.

d) The following are strengthened from (1) ă (ĕ or ĭ) to (3) ē (ī).

Pr. hăr, *seize*	(1) (h)ĕr-us, (h)ĕr-a, (h)er-c-i-sc-ĕre, hĭr-und-o, hĭr-ud-o, E. L. *hir* (χερ-) (3) (h)ēr-es, (h)er-ēd-
kăr, *create*	(1) Cĕr-es, crĕ-are, cre-sc-ĕre ..., (3) crē-vi, in-crē-mentu-m ... .
săd, *sit* .	(1) sĕd-ēre ... as-sĭd-uu-s, (3) sēd-es, sēd-i, sēd-ulu-s, sīd-ĕre... .
săr, *join* .	(1) sĕr-ĕre ... sĕr-ie-s, sĕr-a, ser-tu-m, (3) sēr-ia, sēr-u-s, sēr-iu-s.
skăr, *sever*	(1) cĕr-(n)ĕre ... cer-tu-s, ... scrĕ-are, (3) crē-vi, dis-crē-tu-s ..., ex-crē-mentu-m, crī-bru-m, crī-men, dis-crī-men ... . κρίνω.
stăg, *cover*	(1) στέγω, τέγ-ος, tĕg-ere, tĕg-es, (3) tēg-ula, tēx-i.
văr ⎱ *cover* văl ⎰ *choose*	(1) val-lu-m, vĕr-ēri, vĕl-le, văl-ĕre, văl-idu-s, (3) vēl-u-m, vēl-are ... : vēr-us, vēr-ax ... .

From another root văl, implying motion, come

(1) vŏl-are, (3)vēl-ox, vēl-es, vēl-it-ari.

e) The following are strengthened from (1) Pr. ă (ŏ) to (4) ō.

Pr. săr, *be whole*	(1) săl-us săl-u-t-, săl-u-ber, sal-vu-s..., (4) sōl-ari, sōl-a-c-iu-m.
svăn, *sound*	(1) sŏn-u-s, sŏn-are ... (4) per-sōn-a.
svăp, *sleep*	(1) sŏp-or ... som-nu-s, (4) sōp-ire.
svăr, *sun*	(1) sĕr-enu-s, σέλ-ας, σελ-ήνη, Σείρ-ιος, (4) sōl (Sk. *sūr-a-s*).
văk, *call* .	(1) vŏc-are, (4) vōx vōc-, vōc-ali-s (con-vīc-iu-m ?).

f) C. cites also many examples of ĭ (ĕ) rising to ī and of ŭ rising to ū in Latin without diphthongal accretion. Such are

(α) lĭqu-ēre ... lĭqu-or, (β) līqu-i, līqu-or.

(α) sĕc-are ... (β) sīc-a, sīc-ar-iu-s.

(α) stĭl-u-s, stĭm-ulu-s ... (β) instīg-are.

(α) ὑγ-ρό-ς, (β) ū-v-ĕre, ū-m-or ... .[1]

---

[1] The examples in pp. 14–17 are selected from a large number in Corssen's great work, I. 348–550. The instances cited are the most important of those in which the short as well as the long vowel occurs in words of classical use. Forms from old Italian dialects and from other languages are here given only so far as they illustrate diphthongal strengthening. Other roots of great interest will be found in Corssen's pages : as

Păr, pŭr, *fill*: whence plēre, plūs, plēnus, popŭlus, plebs.

Măr, *glitter*: whence măre, marmor, Mars, Mamers.

Măr, *fade*: whence marcēre, mors, mŏri.

Bhŭ, *be born*: whence fŭ-, fŏre, fē-, fētus, fēmină, fēcundus, fēnus.

B) Vowelstrengthening in Suffixes, Case-endings, and Personal-endings, will appear in the Sections which treat of Declension, Conjugation, and Derivation :

hon-ōs honōr-is, Cer-ēs, pulv-īs, nub-ēs, lig-ōn-is, matri-mōn-ium, matr-ōn-a ; — mens-ār-um, de-ōr-um ; — am-ās, am-ā-mus, am-ā-ris, fu-ē-runt, fu-ī.

Disyllabic Perfects.

xiv. Vowelstrengthening in Perfects.

1) Most Verbs with vowel character **a, i, o**, and some with **e**, formed the Perf. in **vi**, and lengthened the character :

nā-vi, nē-vi, nō-vi, lī-vi.

2) Of **u**-verbs, C. says that their Present-stem anciently received the strengthenings **ou, ū**, before it was weakened into **ŭ** ; and that the Perf. passed through the forms -**ūvi, ūi** before it was weakened into **ŭi**. Thus plouo, plūo became plŭo : and plūvi, plūi became plŭi. The only exceptions are batŭo, -grŭo, metŭo, rŭo, which seem never to have lengthened **u** before a vowel : and fuo, which in the Perf. became fouī (poet. fōvi), fūi, and ultimately fŭi.

3) As to the formations

căveo	cāvi	fŏveo	fōvi
făveo	fāvi	mŏveo	mōvi
păveo	pāvi	vŏveo	vōvi

C. thinks that (to avoid the concurrence -**vui**) **ŭ** was thrown out, and the root-vowel then strengthened : căvui, căv-i, cāvi.

4) As to the following three—

sĕdeo sēdi ; vĭdeo vīdi (E.L. veidi) ; vĕnio vēni

he assumes the existence of old forms sĕd-ĕre, vĭd-ĕre, vĕn-ĕre, which in the Perfect were strengthened as the following Consonant Verbs :

făc-	fēci	fră(*n*)g-	frēgi	căp-	cēpi
iăc-	iēci	lĕg-	lēgi (lēxi)	rŭ(*m*)p-	rūpi
lĭ(*n*)qu-	līqui	ĕd-	ēdi	scăb-	scābi
vĭ(*n*)c-	vīci	fŏd-	fōdi	ĕm-	ēmi
ăg-	ēgi	fŭ(*n*)d-	fūdi		

He brings reasons against the common assumption that in such Perfects the long vowel compensates for a lost reduplication. And, in fact, the practice of vowelstrengthening in Italian Soundlore is so well established, that no such assumption is necessary to explain the quantity. Yet fefici (O. *fefāci*) is known as an older form than fēci, while pēgi from pango and tūdi from tundo appear as secondary forms for pepĭgi and tutŭdi. We may also compare Greek forms, as ἄγηγον or ἤγαγον with ēgi, ἐδωδή with ēdi, οἶδα with vīdi or veidei, and be led to doubt whether, in some instances at least, a loss of reduplication may not have caused the root-vowel to be strengthened in Latin.

Compensation.

xv. *COMPENSATION.*

Compensation is usually said to happen when a naturally short vowel is lengthened in order to maintain the quantity of a syllable after the loss of a consonant : vĭd-sum, vīsum. But such compensation is not always made : segĕt-s, segĕs.

xvi. Strengthening of the Present Stem in Verbs by Insertion of a Nasal.

Some Verb-stems have the short vowel of their Present-stem strengthened by *NASALISATION*; that is, by adding **n** to the Stem-vowel before a Guttural or Dental, **m** before a Labial character :

frăg-	frango	pĭg-	pingo	scĭd-	scindo
iŭg-	iungo	pŭg-	pungo	tŭd-	tundo
lĭg-	ling-	strĭg-	stringo	pĭs-	pinso
lĭqu-	linquo	tăg-	tango	cŭb-	cumbo
mĭg-	mingo	vĭc-	vinco	lăb-	lambo
nĭgu-	ninguo	fĭd-	findo	rŭp-	rumpo
păg-	pango	fŭd-	fundo		

As the Nasal for the most part disappears in Derivation, it was evidently not so strongly sounded as in modern utterance.

Guttural **n** is called by grammarians **n** adulterinum.

(On the strengthening of the Present-Stem by Suffixes, see § 52.)

xvii. Vowelweakening.

1. Pr. roots are formed with each of the Pr. vowels, ă, ĭ, ŭ : but those with ă are by far the most numerous.

2. The standard vowel ă is weakened into ĭ and ŭ in all Aryan languages : but in those which have ĕ and ŏ the weakening of ă into ĭ passes through ĕ, and the weakening of ă into ŭ passes through ŏ :

Pr. sămă   E.L. sĕmŏ-l   C.L. sĭmŭ-l

3. Italian dialects shew such weakening largely; in Root-syllables, in Suffixes, and in Endings of Case and Person.

4. The general object of all such changes is Euphony (εὐφωνία), the more easy and convenient utterance of the sounds of speech.

5. In pursuit of this object certain principles are applied; among them Assimilation and Dissimilation, hereafter noticed; also Selection, which occurs when a certain vowel is chosen as the most suitable before a particular consonant. Thus, **v** has a preference for **o**; **l** and the labials chiefly for **u**; **r** for **e**; **n** and **t** for **i**. Grouped consonants often prefer **e** :

Iŭvis	becomes	Iŏvis	*Mĕnerva*	becomes	Mĭnerva
volt	—	vult	*alĕtem*	—	alĭtem
epŏpa	—	ŭpŭpa	*volle*	—	velle
pepĭri	—	pepĕri	*faciundus*	—	faciendus

Note. **E** is the easiest and smoothest Latin vowel, being neither so sharp and thin as ĭ, nor so flat and thick as ŏ and ŭ. Hence it prevails as a final vowel, and in several instances is so used when final consonants are cast off : venērĕ for venērunt ; utarĕ for utarĭs ; dictatorĕ for dictatorē-d or dictatorī-d. Also for ĭ final in Neuter Nouns : mare for mari-.

But when Masculine or Feminine Nouns drop final **n**, the stronger vowel **o** becomes final in Nom. Sing. : homŏ̄ (homŏn-, homĭn-), virgō (virgŏn-, virgĭn-).

xviii. The Vowel ă and its Weakenings.

A) In Root and Stem syllables.

1) Corssen (II. 6) cites about 270 Latin words which have kept Pr. ă in the syllable of the root or stem :

ăcus, ăqua, trăho, daps, lăbor, păteo, mădeo, măneo, ango, pando, ămo, sal, văleo, palleo, mălus, căreo, carmen, hasta, ăveo, grăvis.

2) He cites about 215 words which have weakened Pr. ă to ĕ in the syllable of the root or stem :

dĕcem, nĕco, ĕquos, sĕquor, tĕgo, tĕpeo, fĕbris, pĕto, ĕdo, sĕnex, frĕmo, mĕl, quĕror, tĕro, vespa, sĕverus.

And others which have passed from ă through ĕ to ĭ :

dĭgitus, ignis, quinque, pinguis.

3) He cites about 190 words which have weakened Pr. ă into o in the syllable of the root or stem :

vŏco, mox, lŏquor, rŏgo, ŏpus, ŏb, nŏta, fŏdio, tŏno, vŏmo, mŏla, ŏrior, vŏro, post, nŏvem.

And others which have passed from a through o to u :

nummus, unguis, fungus, multus, culmen, vulnus.

a) Pr. ă is weakened to ĕ and ŏ in some roots :

nex, nĕco, nŏceo ; tĕgo, tŏga.
bĕne, bŏnus ; mens, mŏneo ; pendo, pondus.
fĕro, fors, fortis ; verto, vorto ; vŏlo, velle, volt (vult).
prĕces..., prŏcus, posco ; cello, collis, columen.

b) Pr. ă, kept in Latin, also becomes ĕ in

fătisco, fessus ; grădior, gressus.

c) Pr. ă, kept in Latin, also becomes ŏ in

ăpiscor, ŏpus ; scăbo, scobs ; pars, portio ; făveo, fŏveo.

d) Pr. long ā becomes ō in some words and many suffixes :

dōnum, vōx, mōs :
-tōr, -ōs, -ōr, -mōn, -ōn, and Imperative **-to.**

B) In Suffixes.

It may be stated as a general rule that Latin suffixes with the vowels ĕ, ĭ, ŏ, ŭ, are weakened from Pr. suffixes with **a.**

Exceptions are very few :

tĭ- in such words as mentĭ- partĭ- potĭ-.
nĭ- in such words as ignĭ- panĭ-.
vĭ- in words like ovĭ- avĭ-.
tŭ- (sŭ-) in Supines and Nouns, as statŭ-, dictŭ-, casŭ-.

All which are in Pr. form.

C) In Cases and Personal Endings.

Cases (except the Locative Singular) and Personal Endings, with vowels **e, i, o, u,** are for the most part weakened from Pr. forms with **a.** See §§ 20, 39, and Schleicher, *Vergleich. Gramm. der Indogerm. Spr.,* § 205.

xix. Weakening into ŏ as influenced by Selection.

1. **v** following has determined Pr. **ǎ** to become **ŏ** in
    nŏvem, nŏvus, Iŏvis, ŏvis.

2. **v** preceding has probably done this in vŏco : while in vŏlo,
    volvo, volnus (vulnus) and vŏmo, the consonants which
    follow may also have had influence.

    E. L. has *vŏco* for vǎco, *vŏto* for vĕto, vorto, voltur.   M.
    Lucr. i. 20.

3. Pr. **sva** is changed to **so** in
    sŏror (for *svasar*, 'sister'), sŏpor, sŏcer, sŏnus, sol,
    sŏdalis;
    and has passed to **sŭ** in sŭ-sur-rus.   See p. 17. C. II. 64.

4. **L** shews a preference for **o** before it in many words :
    dŏlus, sŏlum, sŏlium, tollo, &c.

    but especially in E. L. suffixes :
    poc-ŏl-om, tab-ŏl-a, Pseud-ŏl-us, po-pŏl-us.

    which afterwards changed **ŏ** into **ŭ**.

5. Inner **r** often prefers **ŏ** to **ŭ** : fŏre, fŏrem from fŭ-o; so
    ancŏra from Gr. ἄγκυρα (but generally Greek υ was kept
    before **r** : pur-pŭr-a) :
    especially in the Suffix of Neut. Substantives with Nom.
    S. **ŭs** or **ŭr** : corp-ŭs corp-ŏr-, eb-ŭr eb-ŏr-.
    Some keep **ŭr-** : fulg-ŭr-, gutt-ŭr-, murm-ŭr-, sulf-
    ŭr- ; and the Masc. words aug-ŭr-, turt-ŭr-, vult-ŭr-.
    (But most Neuters in **ŭs** are inflected by **ŏr-**.   See p. 25.)

6. The Comparative Suffix was anciently **ōs ōr-**, then **ōr ōr-**,
    for all genders : finally, and in C. L., it became
    M.F. meli-ŏr meli-ōr-, N. meli-ŭs meli-ōr-.   Note
    p. 42.

xx. Weakening into ŭ as influenced by Selection.

1. C. says : 'In Latin root-syllables, suffixes, and flexional ,end-
    ings, **ŭ** has arisen generally from **ŏ**.'

    a) before **s** and **m** final :
    deŭs (θεύς), genŭs (γένος), bellum (bellom), filium (filiom).

    b) before inner **l**, or a labial :
    popŭlus, upŭpa, colŭmen, Hecŭba.

    c) before grouped consonants, the first of which is a Liquid,
    Nasal or Sibilant :
    pulsus, palumbes, fungus, rursum, luscus.

2. About 230 B.C. the **ŏ** of case-endings generally passed into **ŭ** :
    but **ŏ** was kept in some instances :

    a) hoc, tot, quod, quot, always.   So com- con-.

β) after **u, v,** as late as the Augustan age :

equos, equom, servos, servom, aevom.   So quom.

The Emperor Claudius seems to have promoted the use of the combinations **uu, vu,** which in Republican times were generally avoided.   See C. II. 97–101.

3. Rustic dialects kept **o** frequently : hence it returned into use in L. L., and reappears in modern Italian : *popŏlo, secŏlo.*[1]

4. Selection of **u** appears

A) before Labials and **l** :

1) in place of **o** :

hūmanus	utrŭbi	consŭl
ŭmerus	bŭbīle	adŭlescens
nummus	bŭbulcus	epistŭla
volŭmus	būbus	exsŭl
quaesŭmus	rūbigo	titŭlus
sŭmus	ūpilio	singŭli

Bŏvile is another form for bŭbile.

2) in place of Gr. *α, ε* :

hŭmus (χαμαί)   scopŭlus (σκόπελος)
pessŭlus (πάσσαλος)   Sicŭlus (Σίκελος)

3) in place of **ă, ĕ** :

ă : occŭpo, aucŭpor, contŭbernium ; **ĕ** : quincŭplex.

4) as middle sound, approaching to **y** :

clŭpeus or clĭpeus : lacrŭma or lacrĭma.   See xxi.

Note 1. When **y** or **ĕ** came before the suffix **ŏlŏ- ŏl-, ŏ** was not changed into **ŭ** :

(1) fili-ŏlu-s, basi-ŏlu-m, Cori-ŏl-i, vi-ŏl-entus.
(2) alve-ŏlu-s, lacte-ŏlu-s, laure-ŏla, Pute-ŏl-i.[2]

Note 2. When **v** came before **ŏl, ŏ** was kept as late as the Augustan age, after which it often became **ŭ** :

parv-ŏlu-s, parv-ŭlu-s : serv-ŏlu-s, serv-ŭlu-s.

But friv-ŏlu-s was never changed.

---

[1] As to the dialectic use of **o** and **u** in final syllables, C. says :
1) Lat. and F. received **o** as the pure Gr. **o**.
    O. and S. as **o** inclining to **u**.
    U. as a middle tone, or **u** inclining to **o**.
2) Lat. changed **o** to **u** about 300 . . . 200 B.C.
    F. still earlier.
    O. about 300 B.C., but before **m** not till 130 B.C.
    S. before 200 B.C.
    V. never.
    New U. returned from **u** to **o** between 300 and 130 B.C.
[2] MSS. shew formid-ul-osus and formid-ol-osus, sanguin-ul-entus and sanguin-ol-entus, vin-ul-entus and vin-ol-entus ; the forms with ul- having the advantage. Somn-ul-entus is decidedly better than somn-ol-entus.

B) Before grouped consonants, of which the first is a Liquid, Nasal, or Sibilant :

1. In place of **o**.

   1) pullus, cucullus, and the Deminutives ampulla, homullus, Catullus, Marullus, &c.

      But before **ll**, **e** is more frequent than **u**.   See xxi. D. 6.

      fulcio ..., hiulcus, pulcher ..., sulcus ..., Vulcanus ;

      fulgeo ..., mulgeo..., vulgus ... .

      culpa ..., bulbus.

      adultus ..., cultus ..., multa ..., pul(t)s, ultra ... vultur, vultus, vult :—vulsi.

      culmen, fulmen, ulmus ; ulna.

      Fulvius, pulvis, vulva, ulva.

Here too **ol** after **v** held its ground long :

      Volcanus, volgus, voltur, voltus, volt, volsus.

   2) amurca, furca, urceus, murmur, furnus, eburnus, purpura, Surrentum, ursus, rursus.

   3) umbo, nummus, aerumna, alumnus, autumnus, columna, Clitumnus, Vertumnus.

   4) uncia, uncus, hunc, Aurunci ; fungus, unguis ... .

The Demin. suffix **-unculo-** : ranunculus, virguncula.

   5) Promunturium ; nuntio (noventio), Corss. I. 51 ; nundinae.

The Personal Ending **-unt** was anciently **onti- ont**, as *ecfociont* for effugiunt on the Columna Rostrata, *consentiont, dederont,* &c., on old inscriptions. The classical form of 3d Pers. Pl. Perfect **-runt** for **-ront** first appears in the Senatusconsult. de Bacc. B.C. 186, consoluerunt; the weakened form in **-re** somewhat earlier, fecere. When **u** or **v** came before **-ont**, **o** was kept to a later time. Thus in the MSS. of Plautus appear ruont, perpluont, vivont; and in Lucretius loquontur, dissoluont, vivont.

The inner suffix **-unt-** (*οντ-*) appears in a few words : sc euntem ..., chironomunta (Juv.); Acherunta (Plaut. Lucr.).

The suffix **-un-do-** (for **-on-do-**) appears in

      har-undo, hir-undo, sec-undus, ori-undus, rot-undus, fa-c-undus, fē-c-undus, verē-c-undus, furi-b-undus, treml-b-undus, vagā-b-undus ;

      and in Gerundive Participles.[1]

---

[1] Of the Gerundive forms -ondu-s, -undu-s, -end-us, C. (I. 180) shews that

(1) No existing E. L. Inscrr. contain -ond-us ; but, as it was the tendency of L. L. to resume the o of E. L., and in L. L. appear such forms as secondus, verecondus, while Italian also has *secondo, rotondo,* it may justly be assumed that -on-do- was the first weakening of Pr. -an-d-ya.

(2) The forms -undus -endus appear side by side in E. L. and R. L. to the Christian era. So in Plaut. Ter. Lucr. : in the Senatuscons. de Bacc., the Lex Iulia.

(3) The form -endus prevails in prose : but Sallust likes -undus. Cicero, Caesar, Livy, use it often, chiefly in io-verbs of the 3rd as well as 4th Conj. : moriundum, partiundus, &c. It prevails especially in legal and statistic phrases : rerum repetundarum, iure dicundo, belli gerundi, agris dividundis.

Rarer forms are frundes for frondes, frunte for fronte, dupundius for dupondius.

Later language resumed **o** :

It. *fronde, fronte, pondo, mondo.*

6) The Demin. forms arbuscula, corpusculum, rumusculus.

aplustre, indu-stria (endo) :
also arbustum, onustus, robustus, venustus ;

which C. would derive from weakened forms arbus, onus, robus, venus.

2. The words in which **u** appears to represent **e** are few : as mulsum (μέλι) ; sepultus from sepĕl-ire ; urgeo (ἔργω) .... .

Note. Long **ū** for Pr. **ā** or its substitute **ō** appears in various suffixes : -tūro-, -tūra, -sūro-, -sūra, -ūno-, -ūna, -ūco-, -ūca, -ūceo-, -ūcio- :

i-tūrus, prae-tūra, pas-sūrus, men-sūra, Nept-ūnus, fort-ūna, cad-ūcus, fest-ūca, pann-ūceus, Vin-ūcius.
compared with
prae-tōr (anc.), patr-ōnus, fer-āx, fer-ōx, mer-ācus, clo-āca, gallin-āceus.

xxi. Change into ĕ as influenced by Selection.

It has been shewn that

A) ĕ has affinity with **r**.

B) ĕ is a convenient vowel for the close of words and for final syllables.

Also it must be noted that

C) ĕ has affinity with the combinations **st, ss, ll.**

D) ĕ is a convenient letter for the syllable of Reduplication.

These causes determine a great number of instances in which **e** appears for other vowels in suffixes and endings.

A) ĕ chosen with **r**.

1) In Decl. 1 and 2, before the suffix **ro- ra-**, ĕ takes the place of Pr. **ā** or of **o**, sometimes of **ŭ** : Examples are—

Words which retain vowel and suffix throughout :

numĕru-s, umĕru-s, utĕru-s ; camĕra, littĕra, tessĕra ;

and the Fem. Adjectives,

lacĕra, libĕra, misĕra, tenĕra, altĕra.

Words which drop the vowel of the suffix in Nom. and Voc. Sing. Masc. :

genĕr, puĕr, socĕr (ἑκυρός), vespĕr.
lacĕr, libĕr, misĕr, tenĕr, altĕr.

Words which drop the vowel of the suffix in Nom. and Voc. Sing. Masc., and drop ĕ in all their other forms :

agĕr, apĕr, fabĕr, magistĕr ;
Afĕr, rubĕr, nigĕr, ŭtĕr.

In some of these (as magistĕr and utĕr) ĕ represents Pr. ă, while in others it is perhaps a transposed representant of the dropt ŏ.

In some words with suffix ro- ra- Greek α was kept before r :
canthărus, cithăra.

2) Similarly, in Decl. 3, e comes before r in many forms :
Words in ĕr ĕr-, which keep e throughout :

carcĕr, cadavĕr, pipĕr, papavĕr, tubĕr :
celĕr, degenĕr, paupĕr, ubĕr.

Words in tĕr, cĕr, bĕr ; which keep e (= Pr. ă) only in Nom. and Voc. Sing. Masc., dropping it in the other cases :

fratĕr, matĕr, patĕr, ventĕr, imbĕr ;
acĕr, alacĕr, salubĕr, putĕr, silvestĕr.

Numerous words of Decl. 3, which take Nom. S. ŭs (= ŏs), have in the Oblique Cases the suffix ĕr- :

fun-ĕr-is, gen-ĕr-is, op-ĕr-is, Ven-ĕr-is, vet-ĕr-is.

but some keep ŏ-r- :
corp-ŏr-is, frig-ŏr-is, pect-ŏr-is.

a few use ĕr- and ŏr- :
pign-ŭs, pign-ĕr-is and pign-ŏr-is : fenŭs, fen-ĕr-is and fen-ŏr-is ;
tempĕri for tempŏri : whence tempĕro, tempĕries.

Vomĕr or vomĭs, Gen. vom-ĕr-is, points to an original form in es, which sometimes weakens the consonant and becomes ĕr, sometimes weakens the vowel and becomes ĭs : see xxii. 2. and compare the forms

Cerēs Cerĕr-, cinĭs cinĕr-, pulvĭs pulvĕr-.

3) Verbs having ĕr in their root do not weaken e into ĭ in compounds :

affĕro, congĕro, desĕro, puerpĕra.

for the same reason
pepĕri not (pepĭri) ; reppĕri not (reppĭri).

similarly the compounds of iūro become de-iĕro, pe-iĕro, weakening ū into ĕ.

When the Perfect receives suffixes which begin with r, ĭ is changed into ĕ or ē :

(E. L. *dedi-sont dedĕ-ront*) dedĕrunt or dedēre.
(E. L. *dedi-so*), dedĕ-ro.

B) **E** has a tendency to take the place of other vowels in final syllables before weak consonants, **n, m, s, t.**

1) In Decl. 3, the Nom. S. -ĕn (for Pr. -an) becomes -ĭn- in the Oblique Cases :

pectĕn, agmĕn, crimĕn, oscĕn, tubicĕn.
Gen. pectĭn-is, agmĭn-is, crimĭn-is, oscĭn-is, tubicĭn-is.

2) *a.* Septem (Sk. *saptan,* Gr. ἑπτα); novem (Sk. *navan,* Gr. ἔννεα), decem (Sk. *das'an,* Gr. δέκα).

β. In Decl. 3 -**em** is the Accus. S. Ending of Cons. Nouns :
reg-em, virgin-em, passer-em.

it prevails in I-nouns against -**im**:
civ-em, font-em, serpent-em.

but -**im** is retained by some :
bur-im, sit-im, tuss-im, vim.

while others use both forms. See § **24,** 5.
febr-im febr-em, messim messem.

Tim is kept by the numerous Adverbs having that form :
as ad fatim, partim. But saltem or saltim.

M as a final letter faded in L.L. as it had faded in U., and passed out of use in modern Italian, leaving **e** final generally : *sette, nove,* &c.; but *undeci, dodeci,* ... from undecim, duodecim, ...

3) On such forms as nub-es, sed-es, see § **20, 24.**
Some I-nouns have two forms of Nom. S., -ĭs and ēs :
fel-ĭs fel-ēs, vall-ĭs vall-ēs, verr-ĭs verrēs;

but **s,** like **m,** disappeared in L.L. and Italian, leaving **e** final : *nube, valle,* &c.

4) In old Italian dialects, except O., also in E. L., final **t** in Verbal forms was weak and sometimes disappeared. Before it the Perfect character ī was sometimes changed into ē : at a later time to the middle sound **ei** : finally in classical times settling into ĭ. Thus are found the various forms :
(*dedē, dedīt, dedēt, dedeit*), dedĭt.

In L. L. and in Italian, this **t,** like **m** and **s,** disappeared again, leaving final **e** ; *disse, fece.*

C) **E** has a tendency to become itself a final letter in the place of other·vowels.

1) In the Voc. S. of O-nouns it supersedes ŏ :
dominĕ, lupĕ, Romulĕ.

2) In the Neut. S. Nom. Accus. of I-nouns it supersedes ĭ :
marĕ, retĕ ; tristĕ, necessĕ.

3) When final consonants are cast off :
quinque (Sk. *panc'a,* Gr. πέντε).

illĕ, istĕ, ipsĕ (illus, istus, ipsus).
Abl. S. of Decl. 3 : quaestorĕ (quaestorid or quaestored).

-rĕ for **runt** in Perf. dedēre (dedĕrunt).
-rĕ for **-rĭs** in 2nd Pers. S. Pass. : loquare for loquaris.

-vĕ for **vĭs** in nevĕ, sivĕ.
magĕ for magĭs; potĕ for potĭs.
In L. L. instances occur even of a Gen. S. in **e** for **ĭs.**

By this gradual rejection of final consonants the classical system of case-inflexion was broken down and the uniform declension introduced which prevails in modern Italian.

D) **E** has a tendency to take the place of other vowels before grouped and double consonants.

1) **E** appears before **x** (= **cs, gs**) in the final syllable of Nouns of Decl. 3 which are inflected with the suffixes **ĭc- ĭg-** (= **ĭco- ĭgo-**, as explained by Corssen) :

codex, cortex, imbrex, remex ; simplex, supplex.
Gen. codĭcis, cortĭcis, remĭgis ; simplĭcis, supplĭcis.

2) **E** appears before **ps, bs** in the final syllable of Nouns of Decl. 3, which are inflected with the suffixes **ĭp- (up-) ĭb-** : such are

municeps, auceps, caelebs, particeps.
Gen. municĭpis, aucŭpis, caelĭbis, particĭpis.

Compounds of căpŭt, with Nom. -ceps for -cĭpit-s, have Gen. -cĭpĭtis ;

praeceps, Gen. praecĭpĭtis.

3) When a Noun with that suffix **ti-** (which appears in hos-ti-s, tes-ti-s) would have the accent on an antepenult syllable (álă-ti-, équŏ-ti-), the vowel of the penult is weakened usually into **ĭ** (alĭtĭ-, equĭtĭ-), sometimes into **ĕ** (abiĕtĭ- segĕtĭ-). The **ĭ** of the suffix being dropt, the forms then become (alĭt- equĭt- segĕt- abiĕt-): and when the Nom. S. is formed by the addition of **-s,** they become (alit-s equit-s seget-s abiet-s): but, **e** being preferred to **ĭ** in a final suffix, (alit-s equit-s) become (alet-s equet-s). After which, by the rule of euphony, the dental falls out before **s,** and the Nominatives then become

alĕs, equĕs ; Gen. alĭt-is, equĭt-is;
segĕs, Gen. segĕt-is; tegĕs, Gen. tegĕt-is.
but abiēs, ariēs, pariēs, Gen. abiĕtis, ariĕtis, pariĕtis, on account of **ĭ** preceding.

Note. In this class, the vowels **e, ĭ** generally represent Pr. or Latin **ă** (see above), but in a few **ĭ** is the root-vowel :

comes, comĭt- (root ĭ, *to go*).

In pedĕs pedĭt-, probably also in segĕs, tegĕs, the vowel is adopted by analogy, forming a suffix ĭ-t- or ĕ-t-. See Footnote, p. 30.

4) The same principle applies to a few words derived from sĕd- sĭd-, *to sit* (Pr. săd) :
(obsed-s) obsĕs obsĭd-; (praesed-s) praesĕs, praesĭd-;
(desed-s) desĕs desĭd-; (resed-s) resĕs resĭd-.

5) E before **nt** appears in the suffix **mento-** :
ar-mentu-m, la-mentu-m, monu-mentu-m.

and for Greek α in
talentum, Agrigentum, Tarentum.

6) E is frequent before **ll** :
cello, pello, vello, velle,

and the Demin. forms : puella :
but in these ı is also used : sigillum.

In other groups with ı the vowel **u** prevails, see xix. : but e is not excluded : celsus, excelsus.

7) Equester, pedester, for (equet-ter, pedet-ter).

8) (făt-) fessus ; (grăd-) gressus.

9) The Neuter suffix (**os**) **us** weakens its vowel into e before another suffix beginning with **t** :
fun-us fun-es-tus ; scel-us, scel-es-tus.
temp-us temp-es-tas ; intemp-es-tus.

The existence of an old Neuter Noun modus is shown by
mod-es-tus ; mod-ĕr-ari :

so the Masc. Noun honōs forms
hon-ēs-tus, hon-ēs-tas :

but o becomes **u** in
ang-us-tus, aug-us-tus, on-us-tus, rob-us-tus, ven-us-tus.
maius, mai-es-tas, is like temp-us, temp-es-tas.

C. forms pot(i)os, pot-es-tas : others
poten(t)s (potent-tas) pot-es-tas :

he cites Prae-n-este as Superl. from a supposed (prae-no-), meaning '*the town on the highest prominence.*'

10) The comparative forms mag-is-ter, min-is-ter, sin-is-ter, in L. L. appear with **es** for **ıs** ; whence Italian *maestro.* In some other words also, as antestes, L. L. writes **est-** for **ıst-**.

Modern Italian is not uniform in the choice between e and ı. We find
fermo, selva, segno, trenti ; but
principe, sinistra, vittoria, carissimo.

E) On the use of ĕ for ă, ŏ, ŭ in the reduplicated syllable of Perfects see xxv.

xxii. The Selection of i.

A) The thinnest and sharpest vowel i has a strong affinity with dental consonants ; chiefly with n and s, but also with t and d.

B) Hence it is largely used as a vincular vowel, linking stem with suffix and suffix with suffix.

C) The existence of a middle sound between ĭ and ŭ caused the orthography of many words to fluctuate.

A) 1. Affinity of i with n.

I represents Greek α before n in

balĭneum, bucĭna, fascĭno, machĭna, patĭna, trutĭna.

It represents Greek ι before n in

adamantĭnus, coccĭnus, coccĭneus, crystallĭnus.

It stands before the suffix no- in numerous Latin words : [1]

fiscĭna, fuscĭna, pagĭna, sarcĭna, pampĭnus, sucĭnum, fagĭnus, fagĭneus, gemĭnus, myrrhĭnus.

In mĭno- (Pr. mana) and tĭno- (Pr. tana):

termĭnus, femĭna ; fruimĭno, amamĭnor.
crastĭnus, diutĭnus, pristĭnus.

In the suffix ĭn- (Pr. an L. ēn, ĕn) before vowels :

pect-ĭn-is, sangu-ĭn-is, osc-ĭn-is.

In the suffix ĭn- (Pr. an L. ōn, ŏn) before vowels :

hom-ĭn-is, marg-ĭn-is, ord-ĭn-is, virg-ĭn-is, Apoll-ĭn-is.

In the suffix mĭn- (Pr. man L. mĕn) before vowels :

flu·mĭn-is, no-mĭn-is, nu-mĭn-is.

A striking instance of the affinity of ĭ with n appears in the fact that it was inserted in the Greek word μνᾶ, which so became mĭna. Similar insertions occur in Daph-ĭ-ne, luc-ĭ-nus or lych-ĭ-nus (M. Lucr. p. 211), gum-ĭ-nasium probably in Catullus.

So the affinity of ŭ with m is shewn in the occasional forms drac-ŭ-ma for δράχμη, Alc-ŭ-mēna, Tec-ŭ-messa, &c., and with l in Aesc-ŭ-lapius, Herc-ŭ-les.

Mĭnerva, anciently Mĕnerva.

Though e prevails before grouped consonants, yet there are many instances of it being sharpened into i before n with another consonant :

intus, inter, indu- ... quinque ... tingo ... vindico ...

so when n follows another consonant :

ignis, pignus, signum, tignum.

2. Affinity of i with s is shewn

In the forms cinĭs (cinĕr), cucumĭs (cucumĕr), pulvĭs (pul-vĕr), vomĭs (vomĕr), pubĭs (pubĕr) : also acipensĭs (acipensĕr). See C. II. 278.

---

[1] In fact the suffix no- takes, in true Latin words, no *short* vowel but ĭ before it. Such words as balănus, cottăna, platănus, raphănus, Rhodănus are not native of Italy.

In the Gen. ending -**is** (Pr. **as**).

In the occasional use of **i-sc-** for **e-sc-** in Inceptive Verbs:

lucisco for lucesco.

3. Affinity of **i** with **t** is shewn

In the adoption of **i** before many Verb and Noun suffixes beginning with **t**:

ag-ĭ-to, ag-ĭ-te, ag-ĭ-tis, gen-ĭ-tus, gem-ĭ-tus, domĭ-tum, merĭ-tum, vetĭ-turus, dolĭ-turus, fru-ĭ-turus, gen-ĭ-tor (but genetrix), habĭ-tare, strepĭ-tare:— laetĭ-tia, planĭ-ties, verĭ-tas, altĭ-tudo, penĭ-tus, largĭ-ter, sempĭ-ternus.

4. Affinity of ĭ with **d** is shewn

In the adoption of ĭ before the suffix **do-** :

candĭ-dus, torp-ĭ-dus, flu-ĭ-dus, viv-ĭ-dus.
herbĭ-dus, gravĭ-dus, morbĭ-dus, gelĭ-dus.

Note. When an E-verb forms a Substantive with suffix **d-on- d-ĭn-**, the vowel before that suffix is ē :

albē-do, dulcē-do, gravē-do :

but libī-do, by assimilation.

B) Use of **i** as a linking Vowel.[1]

1. The large use of ĭ before suffixes beginning with **n, t, d**, and its own aptitude for this purpose, led to its adoption before many other suffixes as a link-vowel in the place of others: as before **co-, c-un-do-, culo-, cro-** ; **b-un-do-, bulo-, bili-, men, men-to-, monia.**

(Verbalia) alĭ-ca, velĭ-co, medĭ-cus, rubĭ-cundus, cubĭ-culum, ridĭ-culus, veh-ĭ-culum, pudĭ-bundus, fur-ĭ-bundus, patĭ-bulum, cred-ĭ-bilis, terrĭ-bilis, flexĭ-bilis, spec-ĭ-men, al-ĭ-mentum, querĭ-monia.

(Denominativa) aulĭ-cus, bellĭ-cus, annĭ-culus, ludĭ-cer, currĭ-culus, anĭ-cula, aegrĭ-monia, caerĭ-monia.

But Verbal **ā** is kept :

irā-cundus, caenā-culum, vagā-bundus, amā-bilis, gravā-men, sacrā-mentum.

Sometimes **ē** : verē-cundus, flē-bilis.

---

[1] Corssen is right in principle, when he considers this ī to be a weakening of the final vowel of Stems with vowel-character; as in aulĭ-cus from aula: bellĭ-cus from bello- ; ridĭ-culus from ride- ; anĭ-cula from anŭ-. But he seems to go back too far when (II. 314 and elsewhere) he speaks, for instance, of the ī in regĭmen as weakened 'from the original final ă of the 3rd Conjugation.' He might surely have applied here and in other Derivatives of Consonant Nouns as well as Verbs the principle which he admits, for example, in ped-ĕs, ped-ĭt- from the root ped- (Pr. pad, Gr. ποδ-), and in the use of the suffix ĭ-co- (II. 211. 205) ; namely, that the usage of vowel-stems, which adopt I so generally as a light link-vowel, has thus created *a uniform suffix* (einheitliches Suffix) applied, by *linguistic analogy* (Sprachbewusstsein), to Consonant stems also. This is, in fact, all that is meant when the use of vowels (ĭ, ŭ, ĕ) is cited in this Grammar as 'vincular :' and in this sense the term will be still kept as convenient.

The same convenience recommends the term 'Clipt Stem' to express a vowel-stem without its vowel character. But 'mord' is in fact the root of mord-ēre. Hence, to say that momord-i, morsum, come from a theoretic verb mord-ēre, as C. does, and *to* say that they are formed from the Root of the extant Verb, are but two ways of saying one and the same thing ; and the latter is the shorter way.

2. A similar adoption of ĭ is frequent in Compound Words at the close of the prior element.

(1) terrĭ-gena, silvĭ-cola, aurĭ-fex, signĭ-fer, fatĭ-dicus; cornĭ-ger, arcĭ-tenens, luctĭ-ficus; munĭ-ceps, sortĭ-legus; parrĭ-cida, luc-ĭ-fer, rur-ĭ-cola; (2) horrĭ-sonus, terrĭ-ficus; miserĭ-cors; (3) undĭ-que, indĭ-dem, sicĭ-ne ... hicĭ-ne ....

Ante, bene, male vary:

antĭ-cipo, anti-stes; but antĕ-cedo, antĕ-venio ...
beni-gnus, benĭ-volus; but also benĕ-volus ...
mali-gnus, malĭ-ficus; but also malĕ-ficus ....

E-verbs compounded with dicere, facere keep ē or weaken it to ĕ:

valēdicere, arēfactus, tepĕfactus.

3. The Suffixes **lo-, ro-, cro-, bro-, bulo-, tro-, tĭlo-,** &c., often change their vowel into ĭ before the Nom. ending **s**; thus causing Adjectives in **us, a, um** to pass into the I-declension.

gracil-ŭs, gracil-ĭs; hilar-ŭ-s, hilar-ĭ-s.
steril-ŭ-s, steril-ĭ-s; indecōr-ŭ-s, indecōr-ĭ-s.
seques-tĕr -tră -trum; seques-ter -trĭs -trĕ.

On this preference of ĭ the Adjectival forms in **li-s, ri-s, cri-s, bri-s, bili-s, tri-s** are founded.

By the passing also of ŏ- ŭ-s into ĭ- ĭ-s arises a double form of numerous Adjectives:

imberb-ŭ-s, imberb-ĭ-s; unanim-ŭ-s, unanim-ĭ-s
decliv-ŭ-s, decliv-ĭ-s; effren-ŭ-s, effren-ĭ-s.

In bicornĭ-s, **u** of the stem passes into ĭ.   See § 28.

4. Before the Ending **-bus** of Dat. Abl. Pl. we have

i for **o**, in quĭ-bus, hī-bus (Plaut.), and other old forms.
ĭ in I-nouns, as navĭ-bus (navĕ-bos on the Duellian Column).
ĭ vincular in Cons. Nouns, as reg-ĭ-bus, virgin-ĭ-bus.
ĭ for ŭ generally in U-nouns, as cantĭ-bus, cornĭ-bus; except those in **-cu-s**, and artus, partus, tribus; which keep ŭ.

C) The last-cited examples point to that middle sound between ĭ and ŭ, which the Emperor Claudius wished to mark by a distinct sign. See p. 9. This exists almost exclusively before labials, affecting chiefly such words as the following :—

(1) ĭmo- or ŭmo- :

lacrĭma	lacrŭma	victĭma	victŭma
aestĭmo	aestŭmo	existĭmo	existŭmo
legitĭmus	legitŭmus	maritĭmus	maritŭmus
maxĭmus	maxŭmus	decĭmus	decŭmus
monĭmentum	monŭmentum	testĭmonium	testŭmonium.

(2) ĭp- or ŭp-, ĭb- or ŭb- :

mancĭpium	mancŭpium	recĭpero	recŭpero
lĭbet	lŭbet	ritĭbus	ritŭbus.

(3) ĭf- or ŭf-

aurĭfex	aurŭfex	pontĭfex	pontŭfex
manĭfestus	manŭfestus	sacrĭfico	sacrŭfico

Also capitalis or caputalis and a few more words.

Inscriptions shew that the forms with ŭ prevailed in E. L. and R. L., those with ɪ in and after the Augustan age, for which the Monument of Ancyra, as edited by Mommsen, is the best authority.

Recapitulation. The principles thus laid down respecting the adaptation of certain vowels to certain consonants in Latin are supported by the usage of other Italian dialects so far as known. See Corssen, II. 60–225.

These principles affect short vowels much more than long; suffix vowels more than root vowels; grave much more than accented vowels.

The general results are :

A, the strongest vowel, into which none other is changed, is not itself appropriate to any particular consonant, though its natural kinship is to gutturals first, and least to labials.

O is appropriate (1) to **v**, (2) to **l**, **r**.

U is appropriate to **l** and the Labials.

E is appropriate to **r**.

I is appropriate to the Dentals **n**, **t**, **d**, **s**.

Again :

E and **u** are appropriate to grouped consonants.

E is convenient for final syllables and the end of words.

E is a convenient letter for the syllable of Reduplication in Verbs.

I is adapted, by its lightness, to link stems with suffixes, and suffixes with each other. **U**, **e**, sometimes take its place.

All these appropriations arise from euphonic assimilation, intended to make utterance less troublesome.

Again :

The extensive weakening of Pr. **a** through **o** to **u** and through **e** to **i**, is characteristic of Italian language. In L. L. a reaction occurred, by which **o** and **e** recovered much of their lost ground, and in modern Italian **o** very often appears where **u** stood anciently : often **e** where Latin had **i** :

> *molto, mosca, polvere, sepolcro, fondere, rompere, sono* (sum), &c., *bevere* (bibere), *disse* (dixit), *senza* (sine), *verde* (viridis).

Assimi-
lation
and Dis-
simila-
tion.

xxiii. Vowelchange by Assimilation and Dissimilation of Vowels to each other.

By Assimilation a letter is changed so as to become the same as another, or so as to become more suitable to it.

When a letter is changed so as to become unlike another, this change is called Dissimilation.

Every such change has euphony for its object.

Assimilation may affect adjoining or disjoined letters.

It may be Regressive, when the following letter operates to change the preceding : or Progressive, when the former letter operates to change one which follows.

I. Assimilation of Vowels.

A) Assimilation of adjoining Vowels.

(An adjoining vowel is never assimilated so as to be the same as its neighbour; but only so as to be suitable to it.)

a. Regressive.

1) In the conjugation of the Verb-roots ĭ, *go*, quĭ, *can*, and their compounds, ĭ before **a, o, u** is changed into **e**:

eam ... eo, eunt; queam ... queo, queunt.

ĭ before **e** in their Participles is used rarely: as Nom. S. i e n s, q u i e n s, but in the Oblique Cases usually **ie** becomes **eŭ**:

euntis ... queuntis ...

So i e n d u m ... usually passes into e u n d u m ... .

As **ie** is an admissible combination, it is probable that the order of change was **ĭ-ont- ĭ-ond-**, then **e-unt-**, **e-und-**, which remained in this old verb after **ent- end-** had come in generally.

A m b i o, one of the compounds of e o, is conjugated like a u d i o.

2) The Pronoun-root ĭ (ĭs), and its strengthened compound i d e m, in the same manner change ĭ to ĕ before **a, o, u**: hence we get

eà, eam, eum, eo, eos;

eadem, eandem, eundem, eodem, eosdem, easdem.

3) D e u s, d e a (for d i v-u s, a, from Pr. dĭv), is an assimilation of the same nature. In Nom. P. d i (dei) are used; in D. Abl. d i s (deis); but not d i i, d i i s.

But D i a n a is classical: D e a n a L. L.

4) T e a t e, T e a n u m, for *Tiati- Tiano-* O.
    n a u s e a (ναυσία); c o c h l e a (κοχλίας).

but ĭ remains in p i u s ... v i a (veha).

b. Progressive.

1) By the influence of ĕ or of ĭ preceding it, **o** is prevented from passing into **u** in the suffix **ŏlo-**; see p. 22.

2) Substantives in **-ĭa**, Decl. I., pass into **-ĭes**, Decl. 5:

avarit-ia avarit-ies; mater-ia mater-ies.[1]

3) In Numeral Adverbs, from Pr. **ĭ-yans**, comes **-ĭens (-ĭēs)**:

quot-iens (quot-ies); dec-iens (dec-ies).

4) In Verbs the Mood-suffix **ĭa** becomes **ĭe**:

(es-ia-m) = siem = sim;

(ama-s·ia-m = ama-ie-m = ama-im) amem.

---

[1] The Fifth Declension is a mere offshoot of the First. The ending **ā**, Decl. I., was originally long, as a q u i l ā in old Latin poetry. Hence came ĭē by assimilation from ĭā, and, with addition of Nom. S. Ending **s**, ĭēs: luxuriā, luxuriē-s.

B) Assimilation of disjoined Vowels.

(Regressive and complete always in Classical Latin.)

1) **u** is often assimilated to a subsequent **ɪ** :

Aemĭlius	(aemŭlus)	Esquĭliae	(aescŭlus)
consĭlium	(consŭlo)	exĭlium	(exŭlo)
-cĭlium	(-cŭlere)	facĭlis	(facŭl)
simĭlis	(simŭl)	Quĭris	(Cŭres)
manĭbiae	(manŭbiae)		

2) **o** is assimilated to a subsequent **ɪ** in

inquĭlinus   (incŏlo) | upilio   (οἰόπολος)

3) **ᴇ** is assimilated to a subsequent **ɪ** in

Duilius (Duel-l-ius, Bellius), Brundĭsium (Brundēsium),
mĭhi (mĕhi), tĭbi (tĕbi), sĭbi (sĕbi) ;
nĭhil (nĕhil), nĭmius (nĕ-mi-u-s), *unmeasured.* See C. II. 366
famĭlia (O. *famel*, whence famŭl, famŭlus).[1]

u is assimilated to **o** in
      sŏboles, when written for sŭboles.

o is assimilated to **ŏ** in
      bĕnĕ (bŏno-)

ᴇ is assimilated to **ŭ** in
      tŭgurium (tĕgere).

And long **ē** to **ō** in
      sōcors (sēcors).

II. Dissimilation of Vowels.

Dissimilation of Vowels.

1) It has been shewn that in E. L. and R. L. **u**, **v** were avoided before **u**, whence such forms as vivont, avos, servom, &c., antiquom, suom, &c., continued in use to the Augustan age. **Uv** was not so much avoided.   We find indeed *floviom, conflovont* in E. L., but also in R. L., Cluvius, Iuventius.

2) The concurrence **ɪɪ** was avoided in E. L. and R. L. by writing i-ei ; as *fili-ei* 'sons ;' *peti-ei,* &c., *ieis* and *eeis* ; also *adi-ese* in Senatuscons. de Bacc., but in I. L. this repugnance faded ; and we find iis consiliis, &c. on the Monument of Ancyra.

In C. L. **ɪɪ** is avoided by writing ** e** for **ɪ** in

anxi-ĕtas, ebri-ĕtas, pi-ĕtas, sati-ĕtas, soci-ĕtas, vari-ĕtas, abi-ĕtis
    ..., ari-ĕtis ..., pari-ĕtis ... vari-ĕgare, li-ēn, Ani-ēn, ali-ēnus,
    lani-ēna,

and in many Proper Names :
      Cati-ēnus, Labi-ēnus.

---

[1] Few words have been more debated, as to their derivation and consequent orthography, than suspĭcio (suspĭtio) and convĭcium (convĭtium). Each form has good documentary evidence in its favour, and perhaps the strongest argument for t is that, while ci often appears in I. L. and L. L. for ti, converse examples are hardly to be found. Yet Corssen is strongly in favour of suspĭcio, as an assimilation of a strengthened form suspēcio, and of convĭcium, as an assimilated form from convōcium.   Fleckeisen on the other side assumes suspĭtio from suspicitio, and convitium from convocitium. Sub iudice lis est.   There are strong arguments against each view ; but for the present Corssen's seems the less objectionable.

It is avoided in the compounds of i a c i o by casting out one ĭ, and allowing to the other the power of jĭ. See pp. 10, 38.

Peior is perhaps by dissimilation for pid-ior (compare *piḍ*, 'injure')

In the Pronouns ĭs, īdem, the forms ĭi, ĭis were avoided by writing ĕi, ĕis : but ĭi, ĭis were tolerated in Imperial times.

3) **o-o** was tolerated in I. L.

But cŏ-ŏpia becomes cōpia ; and
coptato is in the Lex Iulia for co-optato. ́ M. Lucr. v. 342.

xxiv. Vowelweakening in the Second Member of Compound Words.

Composition of words forms either loose or fast Compounds.

If the two members are so joined that, although the first is proclitically connected with the second, nevertheless they can be separated, the compound is loose. Thus Márs-pater is a loose compound ; but becoming Máspiter, it is fast ; because the parts are inseparable. In old language compounds are often found in a state of separation : M. Lucr. i. 452.

ob vos sacro	(Festus)	obsecro vos
sub vos placo	„	supplico vos
facit are	(Lucr.)	arefacit
per mihi gratum est	„	pergratum est mihi
per mihi placet	„	mihi perplacet

Such compounds as satisfacere, circumdare, &c., may be considered loose ; while proficere, tradere, &c. are fast.

The fast Compounds hitherto cited, Maspĭter, profĭcere, tradere, weaken the root-vowel of the second member. But this weakening, though of frequent occurrence, is not universal in fast Compounds. Thus attraho, though a fast Compound, is not weakened.

We have now to see what compound words do weaken the second member of the composition.

   1. *a*) Numerous words keep their root-vowel **a** unweakened in the second member of their compounds ; such are most Verbs of Conj. 1. :

      agitare, amare, gravare, vagari;

   many of Conj. 2. :

      ardēre, iacēre, manēre, pallēre, patēre, pavēre, valēre;

   many Nouns :

      ànimus, avus, faber, palma, par.

Some words, as will be seen, weaken a part of their compounds, but not all : from mandare, commendo, but demando.

Likewise some compounds are not weakened in earlier Latin which are weakened later : M. Lucr. ii. 951, 1135.

   aspargere, dispargere (Lucr.) ;
   afterwards aspergere, dispergere.

b) **A** is weakened (through **o**) into **u** in the second member of some compounds :

a. before **l** :

calcare	. .	con-culco : in- pro-culco.
salsus	. .	insulsus.
saltare	. .	ex-sulto : de- in-sulto.
saltum	. .	de-sultum : as- dis- ex- in- prae- pro- sub-sultum.

Note. Salire anciently was weakened by **u**, dissuluit (Lucr.) ; but later it took **i** by assimilation : de-silio.

β. Before Labials :

căp-	. . .	occŭpare : nuncŭpare : aucŭp- : mancŭp-.
tăberna	.	contŭbernium.
lăvĕre	. .	dilŭvies, al- col- il-lŭv-ies, -ium.

γ. After **qu**, by assimilation :

quătere	. .	concŭtio, de- dis- in- per- suc-cŭtio -cussi ...
quāre	. .	cūr (for quor).

δ. Before **ss** :

as, assis	.	decussis : nonussis : centussis.

Note. **O** (from Pr. **a**) is weakened into **u** in
consŭl, exsŭl, praesŭl, insŭla, consŭlo.

Long **ā** is weakened into **ū** in the suffix **-ugo** (**-āgo**) :
aerūgo, albūgo, ferrūgo, lanūgo.

c) **A** is weakened into **ĕ** in the second member of many compounds :

tam	. .	autem, item.
-dam	. .	idem, itidem ... quidem, tandem ....
ăpisci	. .	indĕpisci.
cănere	. .	oscĕn, cornĭcĕn, fidĭcĕn ... accentus ...
băcillus	. .	imbecillus ...
grădi	. .	aggrĕdior ... con- de- di- e- in- prae- pro- trans- re-grĕdior : aggressus ....
lăcere	. .	illĕcebrae, illectus, paelex.
păcisci	. .	depĕcisci (or depăc-) : but compacisci.
păti	. .	perpĕtior, perpessus.
fătigare	. .	defĕtigo (or defăt-).
fătisci	. .	defĕtisci, defessus.
dăre	. . .	addĕre, de- e- pro- red- tra-dĕre ....
(Sk. *dhâ*)	.	abdĕre, con- abscon- in- sub- cre- ven-dĕre.
părare	. .	(impĕro ...; paupĕr ..., propĕro, aequipĕro, vitu-pĕro ...?) but appăro, com- prae- rĕ- sē-păro.
părio	. .	compĕrio, repĕrio : (apĕrio, opĕrio ?) puerpĕra, vipĕra ...
ăger	. .	peregre (i), peregrinus ; but peragrare.
arma	. .	inermis.
arcēre	. .	coerceo, exerceo ....
ars	. . .	iners, sollers, quinquertium.
ăgere	. .	remex.
annus	. .	biennis, biennium, tri- dec-ennis -ennium ...
aptus	. .	ineptus ; adeptus.

as, assis . tressis, bessis, bicessis … .
barba . . imberbis.
canděre . accendo, incendo … succendo … .
cantus . . accentus, concentus.
căpere . . particeps, princeps … auceps, manceps … .
captus . . acceptus, con- de- ex- in- prae- re- sus-ceptus… .
caput .· . anceps, biceps, triceps, centiceps, praeceps … .
carpere . . discerpere, con- de- ex-cerpere.
castus . . incestus.
damnare . condemnare ; indemnatus, indemnis.
făcere . . artifex, opifex, carnifex.
factus . . affectus … con- de- ef- in- prae- re- suf-fectus :
but labefactus … with many more.
fallere . . refello.
fassus . . confessus, dif- pro-fessus.
farcire . . confercio, confertus, infercio, refercio, refertus.
jăcere . . obex (for ob-iex).
iactus . . adiectus, con- de- dis- in- ob- re- sub-iectus
lactare . . delecto, oblecto.
·mandare . commendo, but demando.
pandere . dispendo, dispessus (but expando).
parcere . . comperco, compesco, dispesco (but com-parsit).
pars . . . expers, impertio, dispertio, bi- tri-pertitus (-par-
titus).
·partus . . compertus, repertus (apertus, opertus).
passus . . perpessus.
·patrare . . impetro, perpetro.
raptus . . abreptus, cor- di- sur-reptus.
sacrare . . consecro, ob- ex- re-secro (consacro, Mon. Anc.).
scandere . ascendo, conscendo, de- ex-scendo.
·spargere . aspergo, con- di- in- re-spergo.   See p. 35.
stare . . antistes, superstes (-stĭt-).
tractare . contrecto, de- ob-trecto ; but retracto (con-
tracto, Lucr.).

Note. o (Pr. a) is weakened into e in
potis . . hospes, sospes (pĭt-) … but compos, impos.

Long ā is weakened into ē in
hālare .. . anhēlo (redhālo, Lucr. vi. 523).

d) A is weakened (through e) to ĭ in the second member of
many compounds :

ăgere . . adĭgo, ab- ex- red- sub-ĭgo (but circumăgo, perăgo,
satăgo), nav-ĭg-o.   Part. P. -actus.
ăpisci . . adĭpiscor, indĭpiscor.
ămicus . . inĭmicus … .
cădere . . accĭdo, con- de- ex- in- oc- re-cĭdo … decĭduus,
occĭduus, … stilicĭdium.
·cănere . . accĭno, concĭno, prae- pro- re- suc-cĭno, vaticĭnium,
luscĭnia … .
·căput . . occĭput, sincĭput, ancĭpit- praecĭpit- … .
·căpere . . accĭpio, con- de- ex- in- per- prae- re- sus-cĭpio,
… praecĭpuus, princĭpium … .
dătus . . addĭtus … de- prae- pro- red- tra-dĭtus.

Pr. dhâ . . abdĭtus, con- ē- sub- cre- ven-dĭtus.

făcere . . affĭcio, con- de- ef- in- of- prae- pro- re- suf-fĭcio;
cpp. with -ficus -ficium, beneficus ... beneficium
..., but benefacio, calefacio, and all similar cpp.

făcilis . . diffĭcilis.

făcies . . superfĭcies.

făcetus . . infĭcetus.

fătēri . . confĭteor, dif- pro-fĭteor, infĭtiae, infĭtior.

hăbēre . . adhĭbeo, co- ex- in- per- pro- red-hĭbeo; but
post-hăbeo.

iăcere . . adĭcio, ab- con- e- pro- re- in- ob- sub-ĭcio. On
forms in MSS. with e, and on dissice, see M.
Lucr. ii. 951.

lăcere . . allĭcio, e- il- pel-lĭcio.

lătēre . . delĭtesco.

mănus . . commĭnus, emĭnus.

nam . . . enim, etenim.

păter . . Iuppĭter, Diespĭter, Maspĭter.

plăcēre . . displĭceo : but perplăceo.

răpere . . abrĭpio, arrĭpio, cor- de- di- e- prae- pro- sur-rĭpio.

rătus . . irrĭtus.

sălire . . adsĭlio, de- ex- in- pro- re- sub-sĭlio.

săpere . . desĭpio, insĭpiens ; resĭpisco.

stāre . . instĭtor, iustĭtium, solstĭtium.

stătuere . constĭtuo, de- in- prae- pro- re- sub-stĭtuo.

(stan-) . . destĭno, obstĭno, praestĭno, obstĭnatus.

frangere . effringo, in- con- per- re-fringo. Part. P. -fractus.

pangere . compingo, impingo. Part. P. -pactus.

tangere . . attingo, con- per-tingo. Part. P. -tactus.

fascĭnare . praefiscĭnē (i).

as, assis . semis, semisses.

Note. **o** (Pr. **a**) is weakened to ĭ in

pŏtis . . . hospĭta, sospĭta, hospĭtium ....

Long **ā** is weakened into ī in the suffix -īgo (-āgo) :
fulīgo, robīgo, ulīgo, &c.

2. *a*) **E** is kept in the second member of many compounds :

ĕdo, fremo, gemo, meto, peto, seco, sequor, tremo, tego,
veho, venio, gen-, ped- ;

and those with **er**,

fero, gero, sero, tero.

b) **E** is weakened into ĭ in the second member of several compounds :

ĕgēre . . indĭgeo, indĭgus.

ĕmere . . adĭmo, exĭmo, per- red-ĭmo, (but coĕmo).

lĕgere . . collĭgo, de- di- e- se-lĭgo. But intellĕgo, neglĕgo,
sublĕgo. Also perlĕgo, prae- re-lĕgo from lĕgere,
to read.

mĕdius . . dimĭdius.

prĕmere . comprĭmo, de- im- op- re- sup-prĭmo.

rĕgere . . arrĭgo, cor- de- e-rĭgo.

sĕdēre . . assĭdeo, con- de- dis- in- ob- prae- re- sub-sĭdeo ;
assĭduus, praesĭdium, subsĭdium.

tĕnēre . . abstĭneo, attĭneo, con- de- dis- ob- re- per-tĭneo ;
                contĭnuus, pertĭnax, protĭnus, protĭnam.
dĕdi . . . addĭdi, &c.
stĕti . . . adstĭti, &c.

In close syllables compounds resume **e** :
        ademptus, collectus, compressus, directus, **consessus,**
           retentus.

Long **ē** is weakened into **ī** in
    lēnire . . delīnio (also delēnio).
    tēla . . . subtīlis.

c) **E** is changed to **ŭ** in
    temnere . contŭmelia (contŭmax ?)

3. **o** is kept in the second member of compounds generally:
convoco, abrōdo.   But
    lŏcus . . ilĭco.
    gnōtus . . agnĭtus, cognĭtus.

4. **u** is kept in the second member of compounds: ac- incŭbo,
elūceo ; except that **ū** is weakened into **ĕ** in
    iūrare . . de-iĕro, pe-iĕro.

5. The diphthong **ae** is often kept, as exaestŭo, obaeratus ;
but melts into **ī** in
    aequus . . inīquus.
    aestumare . existimo.
    caedere . . abscīdo, accīdo, con- de- in- oc- prae- suc- re-cīdo,
           homicīdium, parricīda … .
    laedere . . allīdo, col- il-līdo.
    quaerere . acquīro, anquīro, con- dis- in- per- re-quīro, inquī-
           sitio … .

6. The diphthong **oe** (**oi**) sinks to **ĭ** in
    coenum[1] . inquĭnare, coinquĭnare.

In E. L. it sank to **ū** in lūdere, ūti, mūnus, mūnio, pūnio,
etc., and their compounds.   See xii.

7. The diphthong **au** is generally kept: inauro, adaugeo: but
it sinks to **ō** in
    faux . . . suffōcare ;
    plaudere . explōdo, supplōdo (but applaudo) ;
to **ū** in
    causa . . accūso, incūso, recūso ;
    fraus . . (frustra, frustrare) defrūdare : see M. Lucr. vi. 187.
    claudere . conclūdo, dis- ex- in- oc- prae- re-clūdo ;
and to **oe** in
    audire . . oboedire.

Note. The other Italian dialects exhibit the same general laws
of Vowelchange as the Latin.

---

[1] Obscenus (obscoenus) is usually derived from coenum. This, however, is by
no means certain.

XXV. *REDUPLICATION.*

Reduplication in language is a practice as old as language itself.
The infant from instinct or imitation forms words by repeating
the syllables: pa-pa, ma-ma, ta-ta; often unconsciously weakening
the first: pŭ-pā, mĕ-mā, tĭ-tā: and the mother or nurse amuses
or lulls the infant by similar repetitions: ding-dong, by-bye, &c.
Various emotions express themselves in the same manner: aha!
oho! &c. See Pott (*Die Doppelung*).
Thus arose the habit of modifying words

A) By doubling a root merely:

B) By prefixing to it its first consonant and vowel.

> After which it came to pass, that the reduplicative syllable
> might be either strengthened or weakened, and the root
> itself weakened (rarely strengthened) after reduplication, in
> consequence of accentual change.

A) Reduplication by doubling the Root merely :

a) bar-bar-us (bulbul Pers.), cu-cu-lus, la-la-re, Mar-mar, cin-
cin-nus, tin-tin-nare, ul-ul-are, cur-cul-io, gur-gul-io, furfur, mur-mur, tur-tur.   So quisquis, utut, ubiubi, &c.

b) The Root is weakened in

> car-cer, mar-mor.

B) Reduplication by prefixing the first two letters of the Root.
(This is specially important in Greek and Latin on account of
its use in forming the Perfect Tense of Verbs.)

a) Without vowelchange :

> cŭ-cul-lu-s, (*pŏ-pŏl-u-s*), sŭ-sur-ru-s, and the following Per-
> fects ; cŭ-curr-i, dĭ-dĭc-i, mŏ-mord-i, pĕ-pend-i, pŏ-posc-i,
> pŭ-pŭg-i (pu-*n*-go), scĭ-cĭd-i (sci-*n*-do), spŏ-pond-i (spon-
> deo), tĕ-tend-i, tŏ-tond-i, tŭ-tŭd-i.

b) Redupl. weakened, Root unchanged ; in occasional forms

> cĕ-curr-i, mĕ-mord-i, pĕ-posc-i, pĕ-pŭg-i, spĕ-pond-i.

c) Redupl. unchanged ; Root strengthened.

> pă-pā-ver, tŭ-tūd-i (rare).

d) Redupl. strengthened ; Root weakened.

> Mā-mers, Mā-mer-cus, Mā-mŭr-iu-s, pā-pĭl-io, pō-pŭl-us
> (*poplar*), pū-bl-icu-s.

e) Redupl. unchanged ; Root weakened,

> pŏ-pŭl-us (*people*).

f) Redupl. and Root weakened.

> cĭ-cind-ela (candela), cĭ-con-ia ; tĭ-tŭ-lu-s ; bĭ-bĕ-re (po Pr.
> *pā, drink*), gi-gn-ere (Pr. *găn*, gĕn, *engender*), si-stĕ-re
> (sta-), sĕ-rĕ-re (for sĕ-sĕ-re, Root *sa*).

The reduplicative syllable is weakened in many Perfects by
changing its vowel to ĕ (see xxi.) :

dĕ-d-i (dă-), stĕ-t-i (sta-) : fĕ-fell-i (fallo), pĕ-pĕr-i (pă-rio),
pĕ-perc-i (parco) : tĕ-tŭl-i (tol-l-o, Pr. *tal*) : cĕ-cĭd-i
(cado), cĕ-cĭn-i (cano), pĕ-pĭg-i (pa-*n*-go), tĕ-tĭg-i (ta-*n*-
go) : cĕ-cīd-i (caedo).

Obs. A consonant is lost in si-stĕ-re (for sti-ste-re), sci-cid-i,
usually scĭd-i (for sci-scĭd-i), spŏ-pond-i or spĕ-pond-i (for spo-
spond-i or spe-spond-i), pŏ-pŭl-are (for spo-spŭl-are from spŏlium).
A vowel is lost in dĕ-d-i (for de-de-i) : gi-gn-o (for gi-gĕn-o).
A vowel and consonant are lost in stĕ-t-i (for ste-ste-i).

xxvi. Changes of Concurrent Consonants.

Assimi-
lation of
Conson-
ants.

(The sign × is used to express 'becomes.')

I. Complete Assimilation of Consonants.

A) Regressive Assimilation :

(dq) × **cq** (adquiro) acquiro	**(bm)** × **mm** (submoveo) summoveo
„ „ „ (quidque) quicque	„ „ „ (sub-mus) summus
(dl) × **ll** (adludo) alludo	**(gm)** „ „ (flagma) flamma
„ „ „ (sĕd-*u*-la) sella	**(nm)** „ „ (inmotus) immotus
(nl) „ „ (conloco) colloco	**(br)** × **rr** (subripio) surripio
„ „ „ (coron-*u*-la) corolla	**(nr)** „ „ (inrideo) irrideo
„ „ „ (un-*u*-lus) ullus	
(rl) „ „ (perlicio) pellicio	**(ds)** × **ss** (fod-sa) fossa
„ „ „ (ager-*u*-lus) agellus	„ „ „ (adsurgo) assurgo
(tn) × **nn** (pet-na) penna	„ „ „ (cedsi) cessi
(dn) „ „ (adnuo) annuo	**(ts)** „ „ (concutsi) concussi
„ „ „ (merced-narius) mercennarius.	

The following Assimilations also occur in the Composition of
Particles with Verbs :

(bc) × **cc** (obcurro) occurro	**(bp)** × **pp** (obpono) oppono
(dc) „ „ (adcedo) accedo	**(dp)** „ „ (adpeto) appeto
(bg) × **gg** (obgero) oggero	**(bf)** × **ff** (obfero) offero
(dg) „ „ (adgravo) aggravo	**(cf)** „ „ (ecfugio) effugio
(dt) × **tt** (adtendo) attendo	**(df)** „ „ (adficio) afficio
	(sf) „ „ (disfiteor) diffiteor

a) **(nd)** × **nn** occurs in Plautus :

dispennite for dispendite ; distennite for distendite.

So in Oscan ; *opsannam* = operandam.

β) **mn**, though stable in C. L., often yields to assimilation in
modern language :

L. columna, It. *colonna*, Fr. *colonne.*

γ) That final **m** of a proclitic word assimilated itself in utterance to a following **n**, is testified by Cic. Or. 45 and Quint.
viii. 3. 45. Thus etiam nunc was sounded etian-nunc.[1]

---

[1] The sharpening of an inner syllable by doubling a consonant (rel ligio, relliquiae,
millia, querella, bracchium, Iuppiter, littera) must not be confounded with
Assimilation. See Appendix A. : also C. I. 227. II. 466.

B) Progressive Assimilation :

(ferse) ferre ; (farsis) farris ; (τύρσις) turris.

So C. forms (miser-timus × miser-simus) miserrimus.

(**ls**) × **ll** ; (vol-se) velle ; (mel-tis × mel-sis) mellis, &c. (facil-timus × facil-simus) facillimus (C.).

(**st**) × **ss** : (duris-timus) durissimus : where duris is contracted from durius (C.).[1]

(This assimilation occurs in some Supines, according to C.'s view: fissum, fossum, passum, &c. See xxxi.)

Adapta-
tion.

II. Partial Assimilation of Consonants (Adaptation).

1. The Sonant **g** becomes **c**, and the Sonant **b** becomes **p**, before **s or t** :

(reg-si) × rexi (= rec-si)   (scrib-si) × scripsi
(reg-tum) × rectum   (scrib-tum) × scriptum

a) But a b, s u b, o b, may remain in composition :

absens, subter, obtineo (but also apsens, optineo)

And **bs** final may be kept in Nouns :

caelebs, plebs, trabs, urbs (but also pleps, urps, &c.).

Obs. **x** = **cs** = any Guttural with **s** : any Guttural except **c** being supposed to become **c** before **s**, and so to form **x** :

(dīc-si) × dīxi   (sūg-si × sūc-si) × sūxi
(făc-s) × fax   (lēg-s × lēc-s) × lēx
(coqu-si × coc-si) × coxi   (ungu-si × unc-si) × unxi

The following Verbs deserve special attention :

trah-ĕre Perf. (trah-si trac-si) traxi (from a lost Pr. *tragh ?*)
veh-ĕre — (veh-si vec-si) vexi : Sk. *vah* (a lost Pr. *vagh ?*).

---

[1] The formation of Latin Comparatives and Superlatives may be briefly stated here.
I. Comparatives.
  1) (Sk. *yãns, yas*) Lat. (-ios) × -ior -ius is added to the Clipt Stem :
      (dur-iōs) d u r-i ŏr, d u r-i ŭs ; (ingent-iōs) i n g e n t-i ŏr, i n g e n t-i ŭs.
      (mag-iōs, mag-ior, &c.), m a-i o r, m a-i u s :—m a g ĭs for mag-ius.
      (root min- ; min-ior, &c.), m i n-o r, m i n u s.
      (root ple-=Sk. *prĕ* : ple-ior, ple-ius, plo-ius, plous), p l ū s, p l ū r-.
  2) (Sk. *tara*) Lat. tero- is added to Roots and Stems :
      a l-t e r, u-t e r, d e x-t e r, s i n i s-t e r, i n-t e r :—p a r i-t e r, a l i-t e r, &c.
  3) Both Suffixes are used in
      m a g-i s-t e r, m i n-i s-t e r :—d e x-t e r-i o r, i n-t e r-i o r, &c.
II. Superlatives.
  1) (Sk. *ta*) to-, in q u a r-t u-s, q u i n-t u-s, q u o-t u-s, &c.
  2) (Sk. *ma*) mo-, in s u m-m u-s, i-m u-s, p r i-m u s, m i n i-m u-s, p l u r i-m u-s ; (ex-t e r-m u-s) × e x t r e-m u-s ; (p o s-t e r-m u-s) × p o s t r e-m u-s ; (super-m u-s) × s u p r e-m u-s.
  3) (Sk. *tama*) tĭmo- in c i-t i m u-s, u l-t i m u-s, o p-t i m u-s, i n-t i m u-s, ex-ṭ i m u-s, p o s-t u m u-s, d e x-t i m u-s, s i n i s-t i m u-s.
      passes into simo- in (p e-d-t i m o-) p e s s i-m u-s, (m a g-t i m o-) m a x i m-u s, p r o x i m u-s.
      passes into (simo-) lĭmo- in f a c i l l i m u-s, &c.
      — — (simo-) rimo- in m i s e r r i m u-s, &c.
  In most Adjectives tĭmo- is added to the contracted comparative is (ĭ-ōs) and as-similated :
      (d u r-i s-t i m o-) × d u r i s s i m u-s. So tristissimus, felicissimus, &c.

viv-ĕre Perf. (vigv-si vic-si) vixi : Sk. *jīv* (Pr. *gvigv-*).
flu-ere — (flugv-si, fluc-si) fluxi (from a lost form *flug-vĕre*).
stru-ere — (stru-ic-si) struxi (probably from a form *stru-ic-ĕre*).

Add the nasalized ninguĕre with its Noun nix, *s-now* (Pr. *snigh*, Sk. *snih*, ' to stick'). Nix (ningv-s) drops **v** in Nom. Sing. and **ng** in the other cases, forming Gen. niv-is, &c.

2. Liquids and Nasals [1] take Sonants before them in preference to Surds :

(po-pl-icus) × pu-bl-icus   (ili-cn-us)   × ili-gn-us
(qua-tr-a)   × qua-dr-a   (cy-cn-us)   × cy-gn-us
(ne-cl-ego) × ne-gl-ego   (se-cm-entum) × se-gm-entum

Through some feeling of euphony (nec-otium) becomes neg-otium.

3. **N** becomes **m** before the Labials **p, b, m**; but remains before **f, v** :

impleo, imbuo, immitto ; but infero, inveho.

4. A Labial Mute becomes **m** before **n** :

(sop-nus) × somnus ; (Sab-nium) × Samnium.

5. **M** often becomes **n** within words before a Guttural or Dental ; and, if kept, is sounded as **n** :

clan-culum   prin-ceps   eun-dem
clan-destinus   quen-dam   ean-dem.

So quon-iam for quom-iam.

But in some instances **m** must be kept : quemque, quemquam, unumquemque, namque, numquis.
In others **m** is better than **n** : quamquam, tamquam, cumque, umquam, numquam.

6. When Dental Mutes meet, the former often becomes **s** :

(edit, ed-t) × ēst   (claud-trum) × claustrum
(rod-trum) × rostrum   (plod-trum) × plostrum.

In Supines and Superlatives sometimes both become **s** :

(fod-tum) fossum ; (pat-tum) passum ; (duris-timus) durissimus.

III. Dissimilation of Consonants.

Dissimilation of Consonants.

The recurring sound of the same Consonant in succeeding syllables is sometimes avoided by changing it in one place.

a) caeluleus, caelulus are changed into caeruleus, caerulus.

b) Palilia is sometimes written Parilia : Remuria × Lemuria.

---

[1] The assimilation of Sonant to Nasal explains the sound of **gn** in French -**gne** final, as cygne. Its sound in French and Italian before interior vowels = **n-y** : thus, agneau, agnello (=an-yo, an-yello).

c) The suffixes **ali- eli- ili- uli-** are chosen for Adjectives derived from Nouns, if the root contains **r** : and the suffix **-ari** is chosen if the root contains **l** :

austr-ali-s	al-ari-s
cardin-ali-s	capill-ari-s
liber-ali-s	coll-ari-s
reg-ali-s	sol-ari-s
crud-eli-s	stell-ari-s
puer-ili-s	tutel-ari-s
cur-uli-s	vulg-ari-s

Obs. But in the suffix **-ario**, **r** is not changed :

　　　　ordin-ariu-s, temer-ariu-s.

Trans-position. *Note* 1. Consonants are sometimes transposed within a word for the sake of euphony :

| pristis   for (pistris) | colurnus for (corulnus) |
| extremus „ (extermus) | |

Euphonic Insertion. *Note* 2. When **m** is followed by **s** or **t**, **p** is euphonically inserted to strengthen the syllable :

　　　　hiem-p-s, em-p-tor, sum-p-si, sum-p-tum.[1]

The change *temptare* for tentare, though supported by inscriptions and good MSS., is censured by Corssen as an etymological blunder : the formation of the Verb being Pr. *tan*, L. ten, whence ten-d-ĕre, ten-tu-s, ten-t-are.

s seems to be euphonically inserted in mon-s-trum, mon-s-tro, &c. (from mon-eo).

(On the euphonic insertion of a Vowel in m-ĭ-na, drac-ŭ-ma, &c., see xxii.　On the insertion of **e** in ag-e-r, nig-e-r, &c., see xxi.)

⁂　The Loss of Letters will next be considered.

Loss of Initial Letters. **xxvii.** Loss of Initial Letters ('Ἀφαίρεσις).

	lost by	*shewn in*
c	lamentum...	c-lamare
	laus ; luscinia ...	c-luere
	vapor ...	κ-απνός.
g	nasci, natus ...	g-nasci g-natus : Sk. *jan* Gr. γεν-
	noscere, notus ...	g-noscere, i-gnotus : Sk. *jnâ* Gr. γνο-[2]
	narrare	(g-narigare) from g-narus
	lac	Gr. γα-λακ-τ-

---

[1] The euphonic insertion of b between m and l or r, and that of d between n and r, occur in Greek (as μέμ-β-λωκα, γαμ-β-ρός, ἀν-δ-ρός), but not in classical Latin, except in hi-b-ernus for (hiem-rinus, Gr. χειμερινός).　But they came in later, and exist in numerous modern words: as number, humble, remember, cinder, tender, &c.

[2] Cicero, though a Greek scholar, was unacquainted with the forms gnasci, gnoscere, and knew so little of etymology, that he treats the g in ignotus, ignavus, ignarus as a mere euphonic substitute.　See Or. 47.　He would naturally do the same in agnatus, cognatus, prognatus, agnomen, cognomen, &c.

	lost by	*shewn in*
g	vivere	Sk. *j-îv* (Pr. *gvîv*). See p. 43.
p	lanx ; lătus	Gr. π-λακ-, π-λατύς.
d	viginti	for dvi-ginti. In d-vis, d-vellum, d-vonus, **d-v** becomes **b** ; bis, bellum, bonus. See Cic. *Or.* 45. But duellum in Latin poetry : Eng. *dŭel.* M. Lucr. ii. 662.
	Iuppiter : Ianus	See p. 15.
v	rosa (radix, rigo)	Gr. ϝ-ρόδον, Aeol. βρόδον.
	lupus	Sk. *v-arka-s*, Gr. λύκος.
st	lis, locus	for st-lis (G. *streit*, Eng. *strife*) ; st-lo-cus (Sk. *stha-la*).
s	torus	Gr. σ-τορ-, Sk. *s-tar*, ' *to strew.*'
	fallere	Gr. σ-φάλλειν, Sk. *s-phal.*
	tegere	Sk. *s-thag*, Gr. στέγειν.
	taurus	Sk. *s-thûras*, ' strong ' : Eng. *steer.*
	cutis, cavus, caelum, casa, cavere, causa, cauda, &c.	Sk. *s-ku, to hide.*

for other instances, see Corssen I.: also pp. 14–17.

α) Tŭli, fĭdi, scĭdi, cast off the syllable of reduplication.

β) Sum, sumus, sim...cast off the initial vowel **e**.

γ) When the Verb-form est follows a word ending with a vowel or **m** or with **s** after a vowel, it often loses **e**, and attaches itself enclitically to the preceding word. This occurs chiefly in the Comic poets, but also in later writers both of prose and poetry, and on Inscriptions : itast, ibist, quomst, quidemst, temulentast, nactust for nactus est, culest for qualis est (Plaut.).

The Second Person, es, is subject to the same change, but not after **m** : homos for homo es, meritus for meritus es.

xxviii. Loss of Final Letters ('Αποκοπή).

Loss of Final Letters.

A) Final **e** is dropt :

a) By enclitic nĕ :

mēn for menĕ, tūn for tunĕ, dixtin for dixtinĕ : quīn (qui-nĕ), sīn (sī-nĕ).

Sometimes the word before nĕ loses **s** :

aĭn for aisne, vidĕn for videsne, satĭn for satisne :

b) In ceu, neu, seu (ce-ve, nē-ve, se-ve or sive).

c) In the Imperatives

dīc, dūc, făc, fĕr (dicĕ, &c.)

So, in poetry, congĕr for congĕrĕ ; ingĕr for ingĕrĕ.

d) Neuter Substantives in ālĕ (ālĭ-), ārĕ (ār-ĭ) drop ĕ (ĭ) and shorten **a** :

torăl for torāle ; calcăr for calcāre.

But they resume **ā** in the increasing Cases : torālis, calcāris.

e) Many other I-nouns clip **ĭ** in Nom. Sing., some without taking **s**: (par-i-) × par; others before they take the **s**: (stirpi-) × stirp-s, (arci-) × arx.

f) Facŭl for facĭle.

g) Ac for atque; nec for neque : mage for magis.

h) The Pronoun hic, with the Adverbs hīc, illic, istic, hinc, illinc, &c., have dropt **ĕ**. Thus illinc is for illimcĕ.

Note.—Ab (ἀπό), sub (ὑπό) have lost a final vowel.

B) Final Consonants are sometimes lost :

a) Substantives with final **ōn** drop **n** in the Nom. Sing., resuming it in the Oblique Cases :

ratio, virgo; Gen. ration-is, virgĭn-is.

b) A final Consonant has béen dropt in Acc. and Nom. S. by the following Neuter Substantives :

cor (cord-) Gen. cordis (Gr. καρδία)
far (fars-) — farr-is (for fars-is)
fel (felt-) — fellis (Gr. χόλος)
lac (lact-) — lactis (Gr. γά-λακτ-)
mel (melt-) — mellis (for meltis, Gr. μέλι μέλιτος)
os (ost-) — ossis (for ostis, Gr. ὄστεον)

c) The Latin Ablative S. cast off final **d** :

(praeda-d) × praedā : (Gnaivo-d) × Gnaeo
(dictatore-d) × dictatore : (mari-d) × mari
(senatu-d) × senatu

Also Adverbs in **ē** and some Prepositions :

(*facilumē-d*) × facillimē; (*exstra-d*) × extrā.

d) On **-rĕ** for **-runt** and for **-rĭs** in Verbs, see xxi.
venē-rĕ for venĕ-runt ; uta-rĕ for uta-ris.

e) Particles often drop final letters in composition :

amb- am- for ambi ; co- for com- ; di- for dis- ; pro- for prod- ; re- for red- ; sē- for sēd- ; tra- for trans.

So hau for haud or haut : hau-scio for haud scio (Plaut.).

Pos- (pos-t) drops **s** in pomoerium, pomeridianus.
The Prepositions ā for ăb, ē for ex, are long by Compensation.

C) Consonant and Vowel, or Vowel and Consonant, are dropt.
dein, exin, proin for deinde, exinde, proinde, Cic. Or. 45.
nihil for nihilum : non for (noenum ne-unum) ; sat for satis.

O-nouns with Nom. **er** have dropt **os (us)** :

magister for magister-os.
famul (O. *famel*) for famulus, Lucr. iii. 1048.

Note. The three consonants oftenest final are **m, s, t.** All these fell off frequently in E. L. (Roscio for Roscius and for Roscium), again in L. L., and ultimately in modern Italian. See p. 26.

Final **m**, with its vowel, was so weak that poets took no note of it metrically before a word beginning with a Vowel. Thus in Virgil's verse

monstr*um* *h*orrend*um* infor*me* ingens cui lumen ademptum

the letters printed in italics do not count in the metre, and the verse runs thus :

monstr orrend inform ingens cui lumen ademptum.

Final **s**, on the other hand, after a short vowel, was neglected by poets as late as Lucretius before words beginning with a consonant, as testified by Cicero in the following passage : 'Ita enim loquebantur : Qui est omnibu' princeps, non, omnibus princeps : et, Vita illa dignu' locoque, non, dignus, Or. 48. He also testifies that this weakness of **s** had existed in common parlance even when the vowel before it was long : ' Sine vocalibus saepe brevitatis causa contrahebant, ut ita dicerent, multi' modis ; vas' argenteis ; palmi' et crinibus ; tecti' fractis,' Or. 45.

Final **t** also was often dropt in ancient Verb-forms : dedē for dedit. See p. 26, and C. I. 188.

xxix. Loss of Inner Consonants by concurrence with other Consonants.[1]

When this loss occurs for euphonic reasons, if a syllable previously long by position alone is left short by the removal of one consonant, compensation is often made by lengthening the vowel : (pic-nus) × pīnus : but not always ; (lac-nius) × lănius.
The sign of length (–) will here shew the compensated syllables.

A) Exclusion of Guttural Mutes.

1. A Guttural Mute is excluded in Verbal formations when it occurs between a Liquid and one of the letters **s, t, m.**

(farc-si) × farsi	(fulc-si) (fulg-si) } × fulsi
(differc-tum) × differtum	(fulc-tum) × fultum
(sparg-si) × sparsi	(indulg-si) × indulsi
(torqu-tum) × tortum	(indulg-tum) × indultum
(torqu-mentum) × tormentum	(fulg-men) × fulmen

2. Occasional instances of Gutturals excluded :

c between **n** and a Dental Mute :

quintus (quinc-tus)   quindecim (quinc-decim)

But quinctus may be kept, as tinctus, sanctus.

c before **m** : lāma (lăc-) ; tēmo (τεκ-) ; lūmen (lŭc-).

c — **n** : arānea (ἀράχ-νη) ; lāna (lăc-) ; plānus (πλăκ-) ; rāna (răc-) ; vānus (văc-) ; dēni (dĕc-) ; lūna (lŭc-) ; quīni (quinc-), in which **n** before **c** is also cast out.

---

[1] Many combinations are troublesome to utter: guttural with labial mute, or labial mute with guttural ; surd with its sonant, or sonant with its surd, and so on. When the addition of a suffix in derivation produces such combinations, they are usually avoided by excluding the first consonant: scalprum for scalp-brum, ful-crum for fulc-crum, &c.

c before **s** : ursus (Sk. *arkshas,* Gr. ἄρκτος).

g — **j** : āio (ăg-io); māior (măg-ior); Māius (Măg-ius); pulēium (puleg-ium).

g — **l** : mōles (μογ-) but mŏlestus; pīla, *pillar, pier* (pĭg-? comp. pepĭgi).

g — **m** : contāminare (tag-); exāmen (ăg-); flāmen (flăg-); rīma (rĭg-, riⁿgi); iūmentum (iŭg-, iuⁿgere); sūmen (sūg-).

g — **v** : māvis, māvult (măg-e-); lĕvis (leg-vis); brĕvis (breg-vis).

x — **d** : sēdecim (sex-decim).

x — **n** : sēni (sex-ni).

x — **v** : sēviri or sexviri.

x — **l** :}
x — **m** :} tēla (tex-), subtēmen (tex-).[1]

The same principle applies in āla (ax-); māla (max-); pālus, pāla, (pax-); tālus (tax-). See Cic. Or. 45.

B) Exclusion of Dental Mutes.

1. Dental Mutes often fall out before **s.**

  1) In the Flexion of Nouns.

  Dental Mute Stems, including Pres. Participles in **n(t)s,** are by far the most numerous class in the 3rd Declension : and as all but a few take the Nom. S. ending **s,** they drop the dental **t** or **d** before the sibilant :

  (virtūt-s) × virtū-s; (comĭt-s) × comĕ-s
  (custōd-s) × custō-s; (văd-s) × vās
  (part-i part-s) × pars ; (dent-i- dent-s) × dens.

  The rule of quantity here is, that long stems remain long, short remain short, in the Nom. S. : excepting

  (pĕd-s) pēs with its compounds, (văd-s) vās,

  abiēs, ariēs, pariēs for (abiĕt-s, &c.)

  with a few Greek words which drop **n** as well as **t** :

  elephās (elephant-s); Simoīs (Simoent-s)

  See § **24.** Syllabus.

---

[1] Since x=cs or gs, the changes from x to s in Sestius (Sextius), sescenti (sexcenti), mistus (mixtus), are really instances of the loss of a guttural mute before s ; of c in the first two examples, of g in the third (μιγ-). Again

discere (dic-sc-ere), miscēre (mig-sc-ēre)

are similar omissions before sc.

This seems to justify the assumption that when x falls out before l, the c departs first, then the s :

tex-la, tĕs-la, tēla

and so in the other instances.

That s would fall out before l is shewn in qualus (quas-), pīla, *mortar* (pins-), and in Fr. Bâle (Basle). Corssen however (I. 64) confines himself to saying of these instances that x falls out before l, m, and that c does not fall out before l. The alternative above stated he does not notice.

2) In the Flexion of Verbs.

a) A certain number of Verbs throw out **d**, a few **t**, before the Perfect·Suffix **s-i** :

ardēre (ard-si) arsi   ludĕre (lud-si) lusi
ridēre (rid-si) risi   radĕre (rad-si) rasi
sentīre (sent-si) sensi   flectĕre (flect·si) flexi

Assimilation occurs in
cedĕre (ced-si) cessi and its compounds.
decutĕre (decut-si) decussi, with other compounds of quatio.

Compensation occurs in none but
divĭdĕre (divid-si) divīsi- ; mittĕre (mitt-si) mīsi.

b) In the Supine formation also the Dental is often lost. Whenever **t** or **d** is brought before the suffix **tum**, that suffix is changed to **sum**. But whether stem or suffix parts with its dental first, is a disputed point. Corssen's order is
t-tum (or **d-tum**), **-s-tum**, **-sum**.

However this be, **t-tum** (or **d-tum**) usually becomes **-sum**, losing the Dental :
(vert-tum) versum ; (cud-tum) cusum ;
(sent-tum) sensum ; (rad-tum) rasum.

But **-ssum** by Assimilation in a few Verbs :

sĕd-ēre sessum   cēd-ĕre cessum   fŏd-ĕre fossum
făt-ēri fassum   fi(*n*)d-ĕre fissum   păt-i passum
mĕt-ĕre messum   sci(*n*)d-ĕre scissum   grăd-i gressum

Also mitt-ĕre, missum, which drops **t** between two Dentals.

Compensation occurs in a few Verbs with their Compounds.

vĭd-ēre vīsum   ĕd-ĕre ēsum   ŏd-ĕre ōsum
căd-ĕre cāsum   fu(*n*)d-ĕre fūsum   (also gavīsum from
divĭd-ĕre divīsum   tu(*n*)d-ĕre tūsum   gaudēre = ga-vĭd-ēre)

Obs. 1. Observe also that **-tum** of the Supine becomes **-sum** after these combinations, **ll, rr, rc, rg** :
fall-ĕre falsum ; curr-ĕre cursum ;
parc-ĕre parsum ; sparg-ĕre sparsum.

Obs. 2. The euphonic rule for Dentals before the suffix **-tum** in Supines applies equally to Dentals before Noun-suffixes beginning with **t** in Derivation :
(tond-tor) tonsor ; (vert-tura) versura ; (offend-tio) offensio ;
(cad-tus) casus.

2. Occasional Exclusion of Dental Mutes.

d before **c** : (hŏd-ce) × hōc ; (quŏd-circa) × quōcirca.
— — **gn** : a-gnoscere, a-gnatus, &c.
— — **m** : cae-mentum (caed-) ; ra-mentum (rad-).
— — **n** : fī-nis (fĭd-).
— — **v** : sua-vis (suad-).

C) Exclusion of **n**.

n before **c** : When the Suffix -**cĭn** is added to Nasal stems : latro-cinium, sermo-cinari.

— — **gn** : i-gnoscĕre, i-gnavus, &c. co-gnoscere, &c.

— — **s** : -**ēs** for -**ens** in Numeral Adverbs ; quotiēs, deciēs, miliēs, &c., for quotiens, &c. after the Augustan age : before which time -**ens** was used. (semen-stris) × semestris ; mostellaria from monstrum ; (formonsus, formossus) × formosus ; (sanguin-suga) × sanguisuga ;[1] (quam si, quan-si) × quăsi.

Note. **N** before **s** was very weak in E. L. and R. L. Inscrr. give the forms *co-sol, ce-sor, castre-sis,* &c. ; even **as, es** for the endings **ans, ens** : *infas, doles.* So Ital. *mese* (mensis) ; Fr. *peser* (pensare).

nt before **n** : This omission is seen in Numerals when -**ceni** is written for -**centni** : vicēni.

— — **s** : -**cesimus** -**gesimus** for -**cent-simus**, -**gent-simus** : vice-simus, trige-simus, &c.

nd - **l** : scala (scand-la).

Note. The exclusion of **p** seems doubtful. Corssen cites ā-mentum, ă-mes, as derived from ăp-. (Ribbeck has ammentum.)

D) Exclusion of **r** :

r before **b** : fune-bris (funer-) ; mulie-bris (mulier). In fe-bris (ferv-) **rv** fall out.

— — **j** : (per-iūro) × pe-iĕro.

— — **s** : prō-sa for prorsa ; pe-stis for per(d)-stis.

— — **t** : sempĭ-ternus (semper-).

E) Exclusion of **s** :

s before **d** : iū-dex (ius-dicere) ; (is-dem) × īdem.

— — **l** : corpu-lentus (corpus) ; virŭ-lentus (virus) ; quā-lus (quas-).

— — **m** : ō-men (os-) ; rē-mus (res-, ἐρετ-) ; dū-mus (dus-) ; Că-mena (cas-) ; multĭ-modis.

— — **n** : cē-na (cĕs-) ; ahē-neus (ahĕs-) ; pōne (pos-ne) : audin, vin, potin, satin, &c. for audisne, &c.

Loss of
Inner
Vowels.

xxx. Loss of Inner Vowels before Consonants (Συγκοπή).

a : pal-ma (παλάμη, pal-u-ma) ; cup-ressus (κυπάρισσος, cup-e-rissus) ; nomenc-lator (c-a-lare, c-u-lare).

o : p-te for pŏte : meopte :

suffix **trīno**- for (-**torīno** -**tĕrīno**) : doct-rina, pist-rinum.

u : 1) (man-u-ceps) × man-ceps ; (quat-u-or) × quat-er ; (man-u-suesco) × mansuesco.

---

[1] Probably an I-noun sangui-s (shewn in exsanguis) was a byform of sanguis (sanguen) sanguin-. So anguis, *snake*, probably had a byform anguis anguin- shewn in the Demin. anguilla.

2) The suffix -**culo**-, **culeo**- may exclude **u** :

orac-lum poet. for oraculum ; vinc-lum for vinculum ;
nuc-leus for nuculeus : so fig-lïnus for fic-ŭ-lïnus.

The suffix **pulo**- loses **u** in some words :

discip-lina, temp-lum, extemp-lo ;

so amp-lus, dup-lus, &c.

3) All Deminutive words ending in -**llus** -**lla** -**llum** have excluded **u** before the second **l** : and then formed the assimilation **ll** :

whether Primary Deminutives :

agellus (ager-u-lus), olla (aul-u-la)'; villum (vin-u-lum) ;
ullus (un-u-lus) ; stella (ster-u-la) ; hilla (hir-u-la) ;

or Secondary :

porcellus (porcul-u-lus) ; cistella (cistul-u-la) ;
quantillus (quantul-u-lus) ; tantillus (tantul-u-lus).

4) The Verbal suffixes -**bam**, -**bas**, -**bo**, -**bis**, &c., have lost
u : being for fu-am, fu-as, fu-o, fu-is, &c.

e : 1) The Suffixes **bĕro**- **bĕri**- **cĕro**- **cĕri**- **tĕro**- **tĕri** often exclude **e** in flexion and derivation :

creb-ro, celeb-ris, mac-rum, ac-riter, dext-ra, put-re.

Hence Nouns with suffixes **bro**- **cro**- **tro**- form Deminutives regularly in **e-llo**- :

flab-rum, flabellum ; dolab-ra, Dolabella ; luc-rum
lŭcellum ; plaust-rum, plostellum ; cast-rum castellum : (for flaber-u-lum, Dolaber-u-la, &c.).

2) **e** is often excluded when **d**, **f**, **g**, **p**, come before **er** :

Evand-rus, vaf-re, nig-resco, Ap-rilis, inf-ra.

Hence the regular formation of such Deminutives as

flagellum from flag-rum (flager-u-lum)
capella — cap-ra (caper-u-la).

3) In salictum for salic-ētum, carectum for caric-
ētum, **e** has been shortened and excluded.

4) The Suffix **gĕno**- excludes **e** in many words :

benig-nus, mali-g-nus, privig-nus : so g-nascor.

5) E-verbs compounded with facere sometimes exclude **e** :

cal-facere, ol-facere.

Note. Ferris, 2nd Pers. Pres. Pass. of fero, ferre Infin. (for
fer-se), velle (for vol-se) from volo, and ēs-se (for ed-se), from
ĕdo, if formed as classical Verbs in general, would be (fer-ĕ-ris,
fer-ĕ-re, vol-ĕ-re, ed-ĕ-re). It cannot be said, however, that they
have lost **e,** but that, like esse, posse (from sum), they never
took it.

1: 1) The words nau-ta, nau-fragus, &c., au-ceps, auspex, &c., also cau-tum, fau-tum, &c. have excluded ĭ.
But navĭ-ta, navĭ-fragus are used in poetry : and cav-
ĭ-tum, fav-ĭ-tum, &c., are found in old Latin.

2) Fero forms fers, fertur, &c. not (fer-ĭ-s, fer-ĭ-tur, &c.).

3) Edo forms ēs for ed-ĭ-s, ēst for ed-ĭ-t, estur for
ed-ĭ-tur.

4) Volo forms volt, vult (vol-ĭt), voltis, vultis (vol-ĭ-tis).
The formation of vis is supposed to be
(volis, vol-s, vil-s) vīs.

5) The vowel ĭ is lost by

purgare (pur-ĭg-are), iurgari (iur-ĭg-ari) ;
audēre (av-ĭd-ēre) ; gaudēre (gav-ĭd-ēre) :

also in the suffix **mno- mna** for (**mĕno-**) **mĭno- mĭna** :
alum-nus, Vertum-nus, colum-na, &c.

6) Corssen derives

iuxta   from (iug-ista, *in nearest junction*).
exta   — (ex-istă, *the most outward entrails*).
praesto — (prae-isto, *in most forwardness*).

7) (ced-i-te) × cette ; (opi-ficina) × officina
(bidiv-um, tridiv-um, &c.) × biduum, triduum, &c. :
(posi-v-i) × posui :
(semi-caput, sim-ciput) × sinciput :
(mater-itera, *second mother*) × matertera :
(nasi-torqu-t-iu-m) × nasturtium : see M. Lucr. ii. 401.
(nep-ĭ-tis weakened from nep-otis) × neptis.

8) Puer-tia is poetic for puerĭtia : misertus for mis-
erĭtus : -postus in compounds for -posĭtus.
Rarer poetic omissions of ĭ are

lam-na, cal-dus, sol-dus, strig-libus, &c. for lamĭna, &c.

Balneum is more usual than balĭneum ; audacter
than audacĭter : valĭdē and valdē are used, but
with some difference of meaning.

xxxi. Elision, Contraction and Coalition of Vowels.

Hiatus.

Hiatus (the open concurrence of Vowels) is avoided within
words in three ways.

Elision.

1) First : Hiatus is avoided by Elision (Συναλοιφή), the cutting
off of the former vowel :

(ne-ullus) × nullus   (ante-ea) × antea
(ne-unquam) × nunquam   (quinque-unc-s) × quincunx
(ne-usquam) × nusquam   (semi-uncia) × semuncia

In semianimis the ĭ of semi becomes a consonant.

a) Elision includes the cutting off of **m** with its vowel within a word as well as at the end of a word in metre.

(venum-eo) × vēneo; (animum adverto) × animadverto; (septem-unc-s) × septunx.   So sept-ennis, dec-ennis, dec-ussis, &c.

b) The Preposition **com** (cum) in composition elides **m** only before a vowel, leaving the vowel open :

co-ĕmo   co-eo   co-haereo

But com-ĕdo.

Circum does this before **i** : as circu-it, circu-itus ;
but keeps **m** before other vowels :

circumago   circumerro

2) Secondly : Hiatus is avoided by Contraction (Συναίρεσις, **Contrac-**
Κρᾶσις) : by which two concurring vowels unite into one long **tion.**
vowel, rarely into a diphthong.

a) If the concurring vowels are the same, the same vowel lengthened results from their contraction :

(cŏ-ŏpis) × cōpis	(tibĭ-i-cen) × tibīcen
(prŏ-ŏles) × prōles	de-eram × dēram
(dii) × dī	de-ero × dēro
filii × filī (Gen. S.)	de-esse × dēsse

b) If the vowels differ, the former usually absorbs the latter.

cŏ-alescere × cōlescere	(semi-as) × semīs
(prŏ-ĕmo) × prōmo, (de-ĭgo) × dēgo	fili-e × filī
victŭ-i × victū	si-em × sīm
(indŭ-itiae) × indūtiae	(ama-im, ame-im) × amēm

In some instances, the latter absorbs the former :

(ama-o) × amo	diei × dĭī as well as dĭē
(fu-io) × fĭo	(glacie-alis) × glacialis.

c) Remarkable contraction of **ā** with parasitic **u** appears in cūr for (quor) quare ; and culest (Plaut.) for qualis est.[1]

(On Contraction after exclusion of Spirants, see xxxiv.)

3) Thirdly : Hiatus is avoided in poetry by Coalition ; which **Coali-**
grammarians called Συνίζησις, 'settling together,' or Συνεκφώνησις, **tion.**
'uttering together ;' when, without written contraction, vowels were scanned and uttered as forming one syllable : dĕ͡in, prŏ͡in, aurĕ͡a, omnĭ͡a, Pelĕ͡o, pitŭ͡ita, antĕ͡hac.   See Prosody.

Note. Dĕ͡ero, dĕ͡eram, dĕ͡esse, are sometimes ranked here.

---

[1] Still more remarkable are the instances (cited by C.) where **ĭ**, before a vowel, re-presents an old **ī** contracted from **ŭĭ** (like fĭo ; compare fĭeri).   These are : (1) clĭens (clŭiens) ; (2) industrius (endostrŭ-ĭus) ; and (3) the word noticed by Festus, incĭens, 'propinqua partui' (incu-iens ; compare κύειν, ἔγκυος) ; whence Fr. *enceinte*.   This shews the usually received derivation of the latter word, incincta, incinta (given in Ducange's *Glossarium in voce*) to be quite erroneous.

xxxii. Loss of Inner Vowels with Consonants.

1. (homi-ni-cīda) × homicīda ; (lapi-di-cidīna) × lapi-cidīna
(sti-pi-pendium) × stipendium ; (pau-ci-per) × pauper
(tru-ci-cīdare) × trucīdare ; (tri-num-nundĭnum) × trinundĭnum
(no-men-cupo) × nuncupo ; (prae-vo-co) × praeco
(ae-vi-tas) × aetas ; (manu-hi-biae) × manibiae.
(vene-ni-ficium) × veneficium ; patro-no-cinium × patrocinium.

2. (consue-ti-tudo) × consuetudo ; (mansue-ti-tudo) × mansuetudo ;
(hebe-ti-tudo) × hebetudo ; (calamit-at-osus) × calamitosus.

3. (bicipit-s, bicip-e-s) × biceps ; (praecipit-s praecipe-s) × praeceps, &c. ; (locu-lo-ples) × locuples.

4. (unus-decem) × undecim ; (quinque-decem) × quindecim.

5. The second syllable of semi, *half,* and the first syllable of
decem, *ten,* are often lost in the formation of numeral words :
se-squi- for semisque, selibra for semilibra : viginti for dvi-de-centi,
triginta for tria-de-centa, &c. : bi-c-essis for bi-dec-essis, &c.

6. (per-ri-gere) × pergere ; (sus-ri-gere) × surgere ;
sur-pui poet. for sur-ri-pui.

7. possum = potis (pote) sum ; potes = potis (pote) es, &c.

mālo, &c. for (mage-volo, &c.).

vendere for venumdare[1] : narrare (narare) for (g-nar-ig-are).

(re-ce-cĭdi) × reccĭdi or rēcĭdi ; (re-pe-pĕri) × reppĕri ;
(re-pe-pŭli) × reppŭli ; (re-te-tŭli) × rettŭli.

Compounds of reduplicated Verbs drop the syllable of reduplication :
dif-fĭdi, in-cĭdi, ob-tĭgi, pro-tendi.

Except those of disco, posco, and some of curro :
dedidici, expoposci, praecucurri.

8. The syllable **si** is cast out by Syncope from Perfect-stem
forms of Verbs, chiefly in Comic poetry, but also in that of the best
age :[1]

a) Perf. Act. 2nd Pers. Sing. and Plur.
dixti for (dic-si-sti) ; duxti for (duc-si-sti)
misti for (mi-si-sti) ; scripsti for (scrip-si-sti)
accestis for (acces-si-stis).

b) Pluperfect Conj. :
exstinxem for (exting-si-sem)
vixet for (vic-si-set)
erepsemus for (erep-si-semus).

---

[1] A large number of examples of this omission, chiefly from the old Scenic poets, but
many Augustan, are given by Corssen, ii. 553. . . .

c) Infin. Perf. :

> surrexe for (surreg-si-se) ; traxe for (trac-si-se)
> divisse for (divi-si-se) ; iusse for (ius-si-se).

d) Besides the Verbs which classically form a Perfect-stem with the character **s**, some other Verbs did this in old Latin : cap-ere, fac-ere, rap-ere, tan-gere, aud-ēre. As the old formation of the Perf. Conj. and Fut. Perf. with character **s** was **si-sim, si-so**, such Verbs, by dropping **si**, formed these tenses in **sim, so** :

> faxim for (fac-si-sim) ; faxo for (fac-si-so)
> clepsit for (clep-si-sit) ; ausint for (au-si-sint).

e) A-verbs in old Latin formed these two Tenses sometimes by casting out a syllable and then doubling **s** :

> negassim for (nega-vi-sim) : rogassit for (roga-vi-sit)
> servasso for (serva-vi-so) : locassint for (loca-vi-sint).

A few such forms are found from E-verbs and I-verbs :

> prohibessit = prohibuerit ; ambissint = ambiverint.

Note. This Future in **asso**, mistaken, it would seem, for a Present, gave birth to Infinitives in **assere**, used by Plautus :

> impetrassere, oppugnassere, reconciliassere.

Sometimes even to Passive forms :

> turbassitur, Cic. ; compare faxitur, Liv.

xxxiii. The Shortening of Vowels in Latin.

1. Between the First Punic War (B.C. 260) and the Augustan age (B.C. 30) the Quantity of Vowels underwent a generally shortening process, especially in final syllables. This is shewn by comparing

The extant specimens of old Saturnian Verse.

The fragmentary remains of the old Dactylic and Iambic poets (Ennius, &c.).

The Comedies of Plautus and Terence.

The poetic remains of Lucilius and Cicero.

The poetry of Lucretius and Catullus.

The Augustan poetry (Virgil, Horace, Ovid, &c.).

2. The Comedies of Plautus (B.C. 180) are a most important stage in this enquiry : because, though they contain a large number of long syllables afterwards shortened, they also exhibit numerous examples of the shortening process always going on : and among these some which are repudiated by the taste of Augustan poets.

Such Plautine shortenings mark the direction in which the current of popular parlance was setting, whilst in Augustan literature these corruptive tendencies are suppressed for a while by the study of Greek models and a fine sense of what was really good in Roman antiquity.

3. Examples of Final Syllables with Quantity varying in Early Latin, in Plautus, and in the Augustan age.

	E. L.	Plaut.		Aug.
1. **a** Nom. Fem.	ā	ā	ă	ă
2. **a** Neut. Pl.	ā	ā	ă	ă
3. **e** Abl. Decl. 3.	ē	ē	ĕ	ĕ
4. **e** Infin.	ē	(ē)	ĕ	ĕ
5. **at** ⎫	ā	ā	ă̆.	ă
et ⎬ 3rd Pers. S.	ē	ē	ĕ	ĕ
it ⎭	ī	ī	ĭ	ĭ
6. **is** Nom.	ī	ī	ĭ	ĭ
7. **ris** 2nd Pers. S. Conj. . . .	ī	ī		ĭ̄
8. **bus** Dat. Abl. Pl.	ū	ū	ŭ	ŭ
9. **mus** 1st Pers. Pl.	ū	ū	ŭ	ŭ
10. **ar** in Nouns	ā	ā		ă
11. **ar** in Verbs	ā	ā	ă	ă
12. **or** in Nouns	ō	ō		ŏ
13. **or** in Verbs	ō	ō	ŏ	ŏ
14. **al** in Nouns	ā	ā		ă

Yet Augustan poetry, especially the Hexameter, supplies many instances in which the antiquarian long quantity of a word was adopted to suit metrical convenience: graviā (Verg.) arāt (Hor.) vidēt (Verg.) velīt (Hor.) tondebāt (Verg.) ignīs (Hor.) pectoribūs (Verg.) negabamūs (Ov.) trahōr (Tibull.), &c.

4. The words which Plautus shortens by the license of common parlance are mostly Iambic words, which he thus slurs into pyrrhichs, we might almost say into monosyllables. Such are

> locĭ, merĭ, dolĭ, bonŏ, domŏ, virŏ, domĭ, forĕs, pedĕs, herĭ, probĕ, amă, rogă, pută, cavĕ, manĕ, tacĕ, valĕ, abĭ, adĭ, bibĭ, dedĭ, stetĭ, darĭ, loquĭ.

Augustan poetry preserves the traces of this popular usage (which generally it rejected) in such words as benĕ, modŏ, nisĭ, quasĭ, mihĭ, tibĭ, sibĭ, ibĭ, ubĭ, pută, cavĕ, valĕ, &c. : and to its influence we may perhaps refer such abnormal quantities as palŭs, polypŭs in those writings of Horace which he himself calls 'sermoni propiora.'[1]

Exclusion of Consonants with Contraction.

xxxiv. Exclusion of Consonants followed by Contraction of Vowels.

s : dēxtans for (de-s-extans) = $\frac{5}{6}$ of the as : nī for nĭ-s-ĭ.

i-consonans : bīgae for bĭ-i-ugae ; quadrīgae for quadrĭ-i-ŭgae : cuncti for co-i-uncti : aes for (Pr. *ayas*).

h : cōrs for cŏ-h-ors ; vēmens for vĕ-h-ĕmens ; prendo for pre-h-endo ; praeda for (prae-h-eda) ; nēmo for (nĕ-h-ĕmo for nĕ-hŏmo) ; nīlum for nĕ-hīlum ; nīl for nĭ-h-il ; mi for mĭ-h-ĭ ; īmus for (ĭ-h-ĭmus for in-ĭ-ĭmus) ; dēbeo for de-h-ĭbeo ; praebeo for prae-h-ĭbeo.

---

[1] On this subject, besides Corssen, the student should especially consult Ritschl's Plautus and Opuscula ; C. W. Müller's Plautinische Prosodie ; and Munro's Lucretius : also the Prosody in this Grammar by the last-named scholar.

q : dodrans (for dequadrans), ¾ of the as, is formed by the following process, according to Corssen (dequa × dequo × doquo × docu- × doc- × do-).[1]

v : There are two modes of suppressing **v** with contraction : and in some words each mode would lead to the same result.

1. The short vowel after **v** may be excluded, **v** vocalised (becoming **u**), and then contracted with the preceding vowel.

2. **v** may be excluded and contraction ensue.

1. First Mode.

This is shewn where the diphthong **au** results :

> auceps (ăv-ĭ-ceps); auspex (av-i-spex)
> nauta for nav-ĭ-ta; naufragus for nav-ĭ-fragus
> cautum for căv-ĭ-tum; fautum for făv-ĭ-tum
> audeo (ăv-ĭ-deo); gaudeo (gav-ĭ-deo)

and may be inferred (as shewn by lōtum, lūtum for lautum) in most instances where **ō, ū** result (for **ov = ou** or for **uv = uu**) :

> fōtum (fŏv-ĭ-tum); fōmentum (fŏv-ĭ-mentum)
> mōtum (mŏv-ĭ-tum) ; mōmentum (mŏv-ĭ-mentum)
> iūtum (iŭv-ĭ-tum); iūmentum (iŭv-ĭ-mentum)
> ūpilio, ōpilio (ŏv-ĭ-pilio); prūdens for prov-ĭ-dens
> curia (co-vĭria); decuria (decu-vĭria)
> Iupiter (Iov-ĭ-piter); bobus or bubus (bov-ĭ-bus)
> brūma (brev-ĭ-ma, breuma)
> nunc (nov-um-ce) ; nuper (nov-ĭ-per)
> iūnior (iuv-ĕ-nior) ; ūdus (uv-ĭ-dus).

In nundĭnae (nov-endinae, noundinae), nuntio (nov-entio, noun-tio), and contio (co-ventio, countio), the vocalization of **v** seems to take place before the exclusion of the vowel.

2. Second Mode.

> *a*) (dīs, Ter. once) for dī-v-es ; dītior for dī-v-itior ;
> dītissimus for dī-v-ĭtissimus : oblītus (obli-v-itus) :
> hornus (ho-v-ernus) :
> praes (prae-v-ĭ-des, prae-i-des, praeds) :
> Cloelius (Clo-v-i-lius, Cloilius) :
> mālo, mālle, &c. for ma-v-olo, ma-v-elle, &c.
> nōlo, nōlle, &c., (ne-v-olo, ne-v-olle, &c.) :
> sis for si vis; sultis, for si vultis, elides iv.

> *b*) Many Adverbs are formed by the contraction of a Pronoun
> or Particle with the Participle vorsus, vorsum :

> horsum (ho-vorsum); prors-us -um (provors-us
> -um); hence prosa for prorsa (pro-vorsa); alior-
> sum (alio-vorsum); rurs-us -um (revors-us -um);
> sursum (sus-vorsum); intrors-us -um for (intro-vors-
> us -um): rusum, susum, introsum. M. Lucr. iii. 45.

---

[1] Bes, or bessis, bes-ses (dvi-esses), two thirds of the as, is another curious abbreviation ; representing bis trientes, twice one third.

c) This form of Contraction prevails especially in the Perfect-stem Tenses of Pure Verbs.

a. When the Perfect-stem ends in **āv, ēv, ōv**, the **v** may be excluded before **is** or **er** (but not before **ĕrĕ**), contraction ensuing :

> amāsti for amav-isti; implēssem for implev-issem; nōsse for nov-isse.
> amāram for amav-eram; implēro for implev-ero; nōrunt for nov-erunt.

And in Lucr. **āt** for **avit** : inritāt, i. 70.

These contractions are not used in the forms of lāvi, cāvi, fāvi, pāvi, fōvi, vōvi : but in those of mōvi and iūvi they sometimes occur in poetry :

> adiūris for adiūveris; mōstis for movistis; admōrunt for admoverunt; summōsses for submovisses.

β. When the Perfect-stem ends in **īv**, the **v** is often excluded, and contraction usually follows before **is** :

> audĭ-eram for audiveram; audĭ-ero for audiv-ero, audissem for audivissem.

So, in **eo** and its compounds :

> ĭeram, ĭero; issem, isse, &c.

Sīris is used for sīveris from sĭnĕre, sīvi.

The contraction of -**iĭt** into -**īt** occurs; obīt for obiit.

Anciently the Perfect ending **īt** was itself long, being often exhibited as **eit** in E. L.[1] See M. Lucr. iii. 1042.

---

[1] Peculiar contractions are seen in the formation of the Tenses of Verbs.

A) Forms of (esum) s u m, compounded with other Verbs :

Indic. Mood. Fut. 1. (eso) e r o : Imperf. (esa-m) e r a m.
Conj. Mood. (Mood-vowel ia=ie). Pres. (es-ia-m, es-ie-m) s i e m, sim. Imperf. (esa-ia-m, esa-ie-m, es-ai-m, es-e-m) e s s e m. Infin. es-se.

Forms of fuo (shewn in fŏre=fūre, fuisse, &c.), compounded with other Verbs.
Indic. Mood. Imperf. (fuam). Perf. f u - i, whence fu-ero, fu-eram, &c.

B) Tenses of a m o (ama-o):

Ind. M. Fut. 1. (ama-fuo) a m a b o. Imp. (ama-fuam) a m a b a m. Perf. (ama-fui) a m a v i. Fut. 2. (amav-eso) a m a v e r o. Plup. (amav-esam) a m a v e r a m.
Conj. M. Pres. (ama-ia-m, am-ai-m) a m e m. Imp. (ama-esem) a m a r e m. Perf. (amav-esim) a m a v e r i m. Plup. (amav-esem) a m a v i s s e m.
Infin. (ama-se) a m a r e : (amav-ese) a m a v i s s e.

C) Passive Present-stem forms are derived generally from the Active by adding se (*self*), and making euphonic change :
Pres. Ind. (amo-se) a m o r ; (amas-se) a m a r - i s ; (amat-se) a m a t - u r, &c.

D) Inf. Pass. (amase-se) a m a r i - e r, a m a r i ; (regese-se) r e g i - e r, r e g i.

The Conj. Pres. endings am, as, at, &c. of the Third Conjugation (regam, regas, &c.) represent the Primitive Conjunctive in *ā*; and Fut. forms in es, et, &c. (reges, reget, &c.) are contracted from *a-ia-s*, &c., as in (esa-ia-s) e s ē s. See C. II. 729.

xxxv. Relations of the Consonants in Latin and kindred Languages. Relations of Consonants.

I. The Guttural Surds **c, q.** Gutturals C, Q.

1) **c** corresponds to Sk. *s′, k, c′*; to Gr. κ or π :

L.	Sk.	Gr.
centum	*s′ata*	ἕ-κατον
decem	*das′an*	δέκα
canis	*s′van*	κυών (κυν-)
iecur	*yakart*	ἧπαρ
voco	*vac′*	Ϝέπω.

2) **Qu** sometimes corresponds to Sk. *s′v*, Gr. π (κ) τ :

L.	Sk.	Gr.
equos	*as′vas*	ἵππος
		ἴκκος (for ἴκϜος.

More frequently **qu** corresponds to Sk. *c′, k*, Gr. π, τ (κ) :

L.	Sk.	Gr.
quattuor	*c′atvâras*	τέτταρες (for τέτϜαρες)
		πίσυρες (O. *petora*)
linquo	*ric′*	λιπ-
sequor	*sac′*	ἐπ- for σ-επ
que	*ka*	καί τε
quis	*kas*	τίς (U. *pis*).

Some think that *kv* should always be assumed as the primitive of **qu**; but Corssen maintains that **c** (**k**) could develop **u** after it in Italian language as a transition-step to the labial **p**: and he thinks that even in Indic *kv* is developed from *k*.

3) The Labialism by which π and **p** represent Pr. *k*, prevailed in Umbrian and Oscan. U. *peturpursus*＝quadrupedibus; O. *pitpit*＝quidquid. Hence (from O. *petora*, four) come the names Petreius, Petronius: and (from O. *pom-t-is*＝quinque) Pontius (＝Quinctius), Pompeius, Pompeii, Pomponius, Pompilius.[1]

4) In two instances **c, qv** seem to correspond to Sk. *p*, Gr. π :

L.	Sk.	Gr.
coquo	*pac′*	πέπ-τω
quinque	*panc′a*	πέντε, πέμπε.

Here some think the primitive roots were *kak* or *kvak; kanka* or *kvankva*. Fick, however, supposes coquo to be for (poquo), quinque for (pinque), by assimilation.

5) In proof that **qu** could be developed from **c**, Corssen cites

huiusque for huiusce; inquilinus from incolo; inquinare from coenum; quom＝cum; querquetum for quercetum; Quirites from Cures; sterquilinium from stercus.

---

[1] Perhaps other instances of Labialism (p for k) in Latin are dialectic (Sabine): as lupus (Sk. *var-kas*, Gr. λύκος); popina for coquina; palumbes＝columba: Epŏna (for Equŏna): spolium (Gr. σκῦλον): and one or two more doubtful, as pavo (Gr. ταῶς).

Of Dentalism in Latin (t for k) the traces are few and dubious: as talpa (for s-talpa, s-calpa): stercus (Gr. σκώρ); studeo, studium (Gr. σπεύδω, σπουδή).

6) **Q** is found in E. L. for **qu**, chiefly before **u**, as *pequnia, qum, qur, quius* : rarely before other letters : as *neqidem, qe.*

7) To avoid **quu**, before the Aug. age **cu** was often used :

ecus, cocus, anticus, execuntur, secundus.

So locūtus, secūtus.

Ne-cŭbi, si-cŭbi, ali-cŭbi, &c., take the place of n e - q u ŭ b i, &c.

8) **Qu** becomes in Greek κου, κυ, κ, sometimes κο :

Τορκουατος, Κουιρινος, Ταρκυνιος, Τραγκυλλος, Κοιντος.

9) **Qu** was uttered as in English : **c** as **k**.[1] Their sounds appear in '*come quicker.*'

The assibilation or soft sound of **ci, ce** did not prevail in Latin before the 7th century of our era.

---

[1] I. The following facts shew that the assibilated sound of ce, ci, was not used in C. L.

1. Greek represented c by k before ε, η, ι : as

κεντυρία, Πίκεντες, κῆνσος, φήκιτ, Κίκερων.

2. Latin represented Greek κ by c before e, i, y : as

Cecrops, cerasus, Cilix, Cimon, cithara, Cybele.

3. Gothic represents c by k before these vowels : as

kerker, keller, kirsche.

4. Quintilian cites c h e n t u r i o n e s as a way of spelling c e n t u r i o n e s.

An Inscription A.D. 326 gives

s c h e n i c o s for scenicos, and also s c e n i c o r u m.

Another, A.D. 408, has p a c h e for pace.

5. Qu could not represent an assibilated c ; therefore such forms on Inscrr. in L. L. as (on the one hand)

h u i u s q u e for huiusce ; r e q u i e s q u e t for requiescit

and (on the other)

s i c i s for siquis ; c i n t u s for quintus

shew that up to their date ce, ci kept the hard guttural sound.

6. In the imitative verbs c r o c i o, g l o c i o, c must have had the hard sound.

7. Finally, no grammarian has told us that c was uttered in one way before e, i, in another before the remaining vowels. This silence goes to prove that no such difference existed in C. L.

In the Umbrian and Volscian dialects there had existed a soft ç, as U. *façia,* V. *fasia,* for f a c i a t.

And in the late Imperial times such tendency dawns in a few words on Inscrr. :

p r o v i n s i a for provincia ; L u z i a e for Luciae ; F e l i s s i o s a for Feliciosa.

But it was not until the 7th century A.D. that popular utterance so far relaxed its energy as to adapt generally the guttural consonant to the palatal vowel, and propagate that sibilant sound of ce, ci which, for instance, transmutes the classical Kikero into

It.	G.	Fr. Eng.
Chichero	Shishero	Sisero.

II. The assibilation of inner ti before a vowel began earlier. It had existed in dialects : as U. *purdinçust* for *purdintiust*: O. *Bansae* for Bantiae. The grammarian *Pompeius* in the 5th century testifies that Titius, for instance, was sounded Titsius, Consentius says that etiam was pronounced eziam. In the next century we meet with ἀκτζιο for actio, Constanzo for Constantio : soon after with iustizia, milizia, preparing the way for modern Italian, which writes *Firenze* (Florentia), *Piacenza* (Placentia), *palazzo* (palatium).

II. The Guttural Sonant **G**.

G.

1) **G** usually corresponds to Sk. **j** or **g**, Gr. γ :

L.	Sk.	Gr.
gen-	*jan*	γεν- γον-
ag-o	*aj*	ἀγ-
teg-o	*sthag*	στέγ-ω

Sometimes to Sk. *s'*, Gr. κ :

viginti	*vins'ati*	Ϝεικοσι.

Sometimes to Sk. *kh, h*, Gr. χ, γ :

unguis	*nakhas*	ὄνυχ-
li(n)go	*lih*	λείχω
ego	*aham*	ἐγώ

2) Parasitic **u** follows **g** in anguis, sanguis, unguis, lingua, linquo, stinguo, tinguo, unguo, urgueo. In pinguis (πα-χύς) **u** is a suffix.

In all these, except urgueo, the guttural **n** adulterinum strengthens **g**, giving it a nasal twang: as in the Verbs cited p. 19.

3) **G** was guttural in C. L.; as in Eng. *go, gave, give, get, beget, begin*. Its palatal assibilations before **e, i**, whether hard, as in Eng. *gentle, giant, rage*, It. *gentil, Ginevra, gioia, ragione*, or soft, as in Fr. *gentil, géant, gîte, rage*, began towards the 5th century with the use, as in Italian, of **gi** (= Eng. **j**) before another vowel : *Giove, Giulia, giallo*.

III. The Aspirates : **h, f**.

Aspi-rates.

It belongs not only to Indic language but also to Greek to aspirate the medial mutes **g, d, b**, as well as the tenues **k, t, p**. Thus arise the medial aspirates **gh, dh, bh** ; to which the partially corresponding sounds in Greek are χ, θ, φ, severally. Latin has neither class of aspirates : the letters which it uses for the purpose of correspondence are principally **h, f**, and the medial **b**.

1. **H**, when sounded at all, was sounded as the Greek Rough Breathing, but corresponds to it only in words borrowed from the Greek : Hebe, Homerus, hora, &c.

H.

a) In some words **h** corresponds to Sk. *h*, Gr. χ : as

L.	Sk.	Gr.
hiemps	*himam*	χεῖμα
heri	*hyas*	χθές
veho (via)	*vah*	ὀχέω
ans-er (for h-ans-er)	*hạnsa*	χήν, *goose* (= χανσ-) [1]

---

[1] The Teutonic names of this bird, *goose, gander, gos* (Anglo-Sax.), *gans* (Germ.), compared with the Greek χήν, seem to shew that *ghans* is the Prim. form. There can be no doubt that Greek χ indicates a Prim. *gh* in all these words : and this is also shewn in the Latin Perf. of veho : vexi for vegh-si.

b) **H** represents dialectic **f** in some words, as haedus, hario-lus, hircus, hordeum, horreum, hostis, also in mihi. So in Spanish, *hijo*=filius ; *hablar*=fabulari.

c) **H** has no position in Latin metre ; and a tendency to get rid of this aspirate, as a troublesome sound, is manifest in the history of Latin. Hence the fluctuation in the orthography of many words in MSS. and Inscrr. : harena, arena ; harundo, arundo ; haruspex, aruspex ; have, ave ; haedus (aedus) ; hariolus (*ariolus*) ; Hadria (*Adria*) ; heres (eres) ; hĕrus, hĕra, and ĕrus, ĕra ; hedera (edera) ; holus (olus) ; Hammon (Ammon) ; Hister (Ister). But the forms *humerus, humor,* &c. for umerus (ὦμος), umor (from uvēre), are not good.

c) The loss of **h** was propagated in L. L. Hence in modern Italian it is not sounded, and has generally disappeared as an initial letter.

F.   2. The Italian Labiodental Aspirate **f** is described by Quintilian as a very strong rough sound: ‘ Illa quae est sexta nostrarum paene non humana voce vel omnino non voce potius inter discrimina dentium efflanda est,’ xii. 10. This description does not seem to imply that the ancient pronunciation of **f** was materially different from our own : but it does imply what is probable on other grounds, that φ was different from our **f**, not, like this, labio-dental, but a pure labial aspirated.

F is seldom the inner letter of a root. As an initial it corresponds to Sk. *bh*, Gr. φ, chiefly: Sk. *dh*, Gr. θ, sometimes ; Sk. *gh*, Gr. χ, rarely.

	L.	Sk.	Gr.
1)	fero	*bhar*	φέρω
	fui (fe-, &c.)	*bhû*	φύω
	flag- (fulg-)	*bhrâj*	φλέγω
	frigo	*bhrajj*	φρύγω
	fugio	*bhuj*	φεύγω
	frater	*bhrâtar*	φρατήρ

See *bha*, p. 16. To Pr. *bh*, C. also refers the **f** in many words : fovere, favilla ; favere ...; famulus ... (O. *faama,* ‘house’) ; fervere ... furere ...; fidere ... ; fiber ; forare ; furvus ; fundus ...; frequens : compare also fagus (φηγός) ; folium (φύλλον) ; frango (Ϝραγ-) ; frigus (Ϝρῖγος).

	L.	Sk.	Gr.
2)	foris	*dvâr*	θύρα
	fumus	*dhûmas*	θύος
	rufus	(*rudh*)	ἐρυθρός
	firmus	*dhar*	(θαλ- θελ-)[1]

From this last root C. deduces a large number of words : fere, ferme, frenum, forum, furca, fulcio, &c.

---

[1] Lat. -fendo, Gr. θείνω are referred to Sk. *han.* Probably on this account Prof. Monier Williams, in his Lexicon, refers *han* to a Prim. *dhan*, though so many of its forms indicate an original *ghan.*

The Preposition **af** which appears in Latin Inscrr. is by Corssen distinguished from a b, and derived from Sk. *adhi*.

	L.	Sk.	Gr.
3)	fel (comp. bilis)	(*hari*, 'greenish yellow')	χολή
	fu(*n*)do	(*ghu?*)	χέϝω

To Pr. **gh** C. refers fulvus (helvus), hostis (fostis), hariolus ('inspector of the hira or *entrail*'), haedus (faedus), hordeum (fordeum), fames, far, frio, furfur.

IV. The Labial Mutes **p, b.**   Labials
P, B.

These were sounded anciently as in modern language.

P corresponds generally to Pr. *p*, Gr. π.   But see I.

B corresponds often to Pr. *b*, Gr. β ; but, as already shewn (I. and III.), it has several other special relations.

Thus it is developed not only from **dv** (as in bis, bellum, bonus, see p. 45), but also from **gv** :

L.	Sk.	Gr.
bos, bov-	*gaus*	βοῦς
faba	(*bhas*, 'eat')	φαγ-
(for fag-va)		

As an inner Consonant **b** represents Sk. *bh* regularly, *dh* rarely.

L.	Sk.	Gr.
nubes	*nabhas*	νέφος
uber	*údhar*	οὔθαρ

So **b** = φ (*bh*) in ambo (ἄμφω), ambi- (ἀμφί), glaber (γλαφυρός), nubo (νύμφη), scribo (γράφω), sorbeo (ῥοφέω), umbilicus (ὄμφαλος) : in the suffixes **-bus** (-φι), **-bam, -bo, -bro, -bra, -bulo, -bili, -bi** (tibi, sibi, ubi, &c.), **-bis** (nobis, vobis).

Again **b** = θ (*dh*) in ruber (ἐρυθ-), plebs (πλῆθος), and in abies, arbor, urbs, verbena, verbum, barba, &c.

V. The Dental Mutes **t, d**, retain their ancient sounds, corresponding to Sk. *t, d* (or *dh*), Gr. τ, δ (or θ).   Dentals
T D.

a) The sonant mute stands regularly for the aspirate in medius (Sk. *madhyas*, Gr. μέσσος for μεδ-yos), vidua (Sk. *vidhavâ*), -děre (Sk. *dhâ*, Gr. θε-).   In-latēre (λαθεῖν), pati (παθεῖν), **t** seems to represent Pr. *dh* ; but this is very exceptional.

b) Final **d** in C. L. is only used in a few particles (apud, ad, haud, sed), and pronouns (id, illud, aliud, quod, quid, quidquid, &c.).   Some of these are occasionally found in MSS. and Inscrr. with **t** for **d**, as aput, haut, set, aliut.   This shews that final **d** had a hard sound.   On final **t**, see p. 26.

c) The assibilation of inner **di**, as of **ti**, before a vowel, began in the Imperial age, and is represented in Italian by **zz**, as *mezzo* for medio.

VI. The Nasals **n, m,** correspond in sound to Pr. *n* and *m,* Gr. *ν* and *μ*.

a) **N** has in Latin a twofold use :

1) As a Dental ; initial, final, and before a vowel :
2) As a Guttural (adulterinum) ; before **g, c, qu**. It is weak and slightly uttered before **s** and **ts**, especially when these are final. See p. 50.

b) In Latin the Labial Nasal **m** often takes the place which belongs to *ν* in Greek as a final suffixed Consonant :

(μοῦσαν) × musam ; (ἀπῆν) × aberam.

(μουσά-ων) × musarum ; (δόμων) × domorum.

In the First Pers. Plur. of Act. Verbs **s** corresponds to *ν* :

(εἴδομεν) × vidimus.

In the Third Pers. Plur. **nt** :

(ἀπῆσαν) × aberant.

VII. The Liquids and the Sibilant.

1) Though **r** (littera canina, the growling letter) is one of the roughest sounds, and **l** one of the softest, they are intimately related to each other. **L** is a lisped **r** : compare barbarus with balbus, and κόραξ with κόλαξ (Aristoph.)

Accordingly the interchange of these letters is frequent in Indic, Greek and Latin. Some roots have **l** in all three: *lagh, ligh, lu* ; many have **r** in all: *bhar, mar, sarp, star, hard,* &c.

2) The derivation in L. and Gr. of **l** from Pr. **r** is exemplified in

L.	Sk.	Gr.
linquo	*ric'*	λιπ-
luceo	*ruc'*	λυκ-
cluo	*s'ru*	κλύω
volo	*var*	βουλ-
ulna	*aratni*	ὠλένη
sal	*sara*	ἅλς
levis	*raghus*	ἐλαχύς

See the derivatives of *svar*, p. 17.

Lat. **r** from Sk. *l* is shewn in rumpo from *lup* (old form *rup*).

3) Comparing Latin and Greek, we find, on the one hand,

lacer (ῥάκος), lilium (λείριον): so luscinia (Fr. rossignol) :

on the other,

grando (χάλαζα), hirundo (χελιδών), arx (ἀλκ-), vermis (ἔλμις), strigilis (στλεγγίς) :

with a great number of words in which the letters correspond, especially those with **l** : as

leo (λέων), lēvis (λεῖος), oleum (ἔλαιον), silva (ὕλη), &c.

but also some with **r** : as

aranea (ἀράχνη), rivus (ῥόος), taurus (ταῦρος), &c.

4) In Latin words the order Mute-Vowel-Liquid often appears where the corresponding Greek forms have Mute-Liquid-Vowel :

bardus (βραδύς), caro (κρέας), cerno (κρίνω), dulcis (γλυκύς), pulmo (πλευμών), sorbeo (ῥοφέω), torqueo (τρέπω). So tri and ter, trinus and ternus, porro for (protro), &c.

5) Frequent interchange is found between the Liquids and the Dental **d** :

d and **l** :

lacrima (δάκρυ, *tear*), lingua (E.L. *dingua*, 'tongue'), levir (Sk. *devar*, Gr. δαήρ), olere (ὄδωδα, odor), Ulixes ('Ὀδυσσεύς), adeps (ἀλείφω). Meditor (μελετάω) is not so certain.

d and **r** :

meridies for (medi-dies); and ar- for ad in old compounds: arbiter (ad-bitere), arcesso for (ad-ci-esso).

6) As to the sound of **l**, we learn from Priscian the opinion of the elder Pliny : '**L** triplicem, ut Plinio videtur, sonum habet : exilem, quando geminatur secundo loco posita, ut ille, Metellus ; plenum quando finit nomina vel syllabas, et quando aliquam habet ante se eadem syllaba consonantem, ut sol, silva, flavus, clarus ; medium in aliis, ut lectum, lectus,' I. 7. 38.

7) The lightness of inner **l** caused it to be often sharpened by doubling :

loquella, querella, &c.

8) On its affinity to **u**, see xx. In French this goes so far that **u** often takes the place of **l**, forming diphthongs *au, eau, eu, ou* :

(ad illu) × *au* ; (ad illos) × *aux* ; (alter) × *autre*.
(cheval-s) × *chevaux* ; (chevel-s) × *cheveux*.
(bel) × *beau* ; (castellum) × *chateau* ; (fol, mol, sol) × *fou, mou, sou*.

a) No relation is more important in Latin Wordlore than that which arose between the letters **r** and **s**, changing the sibilant between vowels into the canine liquid. Varro mentions it : 'In multis verbis in quibus antiqui dicebant **s** postea dictum **r**, ut in carmine Saliarium sunt haec : ... foedesum, plusima, meliosem, asenam,' vii. 26. In the Carmen Arvale the Lares are called Lases. Cicero says (Fam. ix. 21) that L. Papirius Crassus was the first to call himself Papirius (B.C. 336) : before which all his clan were called Papisii. So the Auselli became Aurelii, the Fusii Furii, the Numisii Numerii, the Pinasii Pinarii, the Spusii Spurii, the Volesi Valerii, the Vetusii Veturii. Thus we have Halesus, Falisci, and Falerii ; Etrusci, Tusci, and Etruria. **R and S.**

Hence in roots these changes appear :

(asa) × ara ; (asena, fasena) × harena ; (fesiae) × feriae ; (nases) × nares, comp. nasus ; (geso) × gero ; (hausio) × haurio ; (seso) × sero ; (uso) × uro ; (hesi) × heri, comp. χθές, hesternus.

So spes and spero ; quaero and quaeso ; vis, vires ; glis, gliris ; flos, floris, &c. ; nefarius from nefas, &c.

Hence almost all the Noun-flexions in **r**-, as **ĕr- ŏr- ōr- ŭr-** from Nominatives in **es, is, ŭs, ōs (or), ūs**, belong to stems which are really not **r**-stems, but **s**-stems : the old forms, many of which are found in old Inscrr., being, for instance (*aesis, foedesis, pignosis* or *pignesis, arbosem, floses, plusima, maioses*), &c.

The Case-endings -**arum** -**orum** were (-*asum*, -*osum*).

The Verb-forms -**eram** -**ero** were (-*esam* -*eso*), -**ris** -**re** -**ri** were (-*sis* -*se* -*si*). In the Passive endings -**or** -**ur**, &c., **r** represents the pronoun **se**.

Dir-imo is for dis-emo, dir-ibeo for dis-hibeo.

b) The **r** for **s** between vowels very often corresponds to the loss of Greek σ between vowels :

(ausosa) × aurora (αὐ-ώς, Sk. *ûshas*); (ausis) × auris (οὖ-ας); (visus) × virus (Ϝι-ός, Sk. *vishas*); (nusus) × nurus (νυός, Sk. *snushâ*); (sosor) × soror (ŏ-αρ, Sk. *s'vasar*, ' sister'); (genesis) × generis (γένε-ος); (musis) × mu-ris (μυ-ός); (deasum) × dearum (θεά-ων); (esam) × eram (ἐ-ῆν), &c.

c) **R** is for **s** before a consonant in M i n e r v a (Sk. *manas*, 'mind') ; v e r n a (Sk. *vas*, ' dwell') ; v e t e r n u s from vetus, d i u r n u s, h o d i-e r n u s from d i e s :

And as final in the ending **ŏr** for **os** : color, honor, labor, &c., for colos, honos, labos, &c.

S.

aa) The Greeks, who avoided sibilation as much as possible, substituted generally the rough breathing for primitive **s** at the beginning of words. Not so the Italians. Hence Latin initial **s** before a vowel corresponds often to Sk. *s*, Gr. aspirate :

salix (ἑλίκη), sex (ἕξ), sedes (ἕδος), semi- (ἡμί-), serpo (ἕρπω), simul (ἅμα, ὁμοῦ), sollus (ὅλος), silva (ὕλη), se (ἕ), suus (ἑϜός), suavis (ἡδύς), sub (ὑπό), super (ὑπέρ), sudor (ἱδρώς), sus (ὗς), &c.

Sometimes initial **s** corresponds to Greek ' spiritus lenis : '

si (εἰ), sero (εἴρω), serum (ὑρός).

bb) **Sc**, **sp**, **st** initial generally correspond in Greek and Latin, unless **s** is dropt, as in t e g o (στέγω). See p. 45.

cc) **s** initial was probably sounded more sharply than as an inner letter : hence c a u s s a as well as c a u s a appears in MSS. and Inscrr., and other occasional doublings of **s** are found.

dd) **s** falls out in C e r e a l i s for (Ceresalis) ; in v ē r (ἔ-αρ for Ϝέσαρ) ; in v i-m, v-i ; in the cases of s p e-s for (spe-r-es = spe-s-es), in those of d i e s, d i e i for (die-s-i), &c., and in other forms.

The Spirant v.

VIII. The soft Labial Spirant **v**.

a) **v**-consonans has the same relation to **f** that **b** has to **p** : it corresponds to Pr. **v**, Gr. digamma, like which it was sounded : and this sound was probably that of Eng. **w**.[1] Corssen thinks its

---

[1] That Latin v-consonans had the sound of English w always, is probable for the following reasons :

ɪ) By a slight change in the position of the speech organs the vowel **i** passes into **y**-cons. By a precisely parallel change the vowel **u** becomes, not Eng. **v**, but Eng. **w**.

initial sound was that of Eng. **v**, its inner sound that of Eng. **w.**

L.	Sk.	Gr.
vomo	*vam*	Ϝεμέω
volvo	*val*	Ϝελύω
voco	*vac'*	Ϝέπω
video	*vid* ('know')	Ϝιδ-
vestis	*vasis*	Ϝεσθής
novus	*navas*	νέϜος
ovis	*avis*	όϜις

So vis (Ϝίς), viola (Ϝίον), vinum (Ϝοῖνος), bos bov- (βοϜς βοῦς), navis (ναϜς, ναῦς), ver (Ϝῆρ), vespera (Ϝεσπέρα, ἑσπέρα), Vesta (Ϝεστία, ἑστία), radix (Ϝρίζα, ῥίζα, βρίζα), &c.

b) As the Greeks lost the use of Ϝ, they represented initial **v** sometimes by ου, sometimes by β,

Varro (Οὐάρρων or Βάρρων).

On the vocalization of **v** see p. 10 ; on its omission, see pp. 57, 58.

IX. **ɪ**-consonans (J).

The Spirant J.

On the sound and uses of ɪ-consonans (j), see viii. 1, and xii. 6. It corresponds to Sk. *y*, sometimes to Gr. ζ, as iugum (Sk. *yuj*, Gr. ζυγόν).

a) A form of **ɪ** taller than the adjoining letters (I), appears in late Republican and Augustan Inscrr. to express

1) long **ī**-voc. :[1]
DĪVO, EI, STIPENDĪS.

2) ɪ-cons.; both between vowels and initially :
MAIOR, CVIVS, EIVS ; IVS, IVLIA.

A more corrupt form II is also found :
CVIIVS, COIIVGI.

b) That which is merely a general fact, has been wrongly set down as a rule of sound : namely, that a vowel before ɪ-cons. is long. Corssen has shewn that in all words which can be traced (for iēiunus is obscure) where a vowel is long before ɪ-cons., it is so by its own nature :

ā-io, Gā-ius, Mā-ius, pē-ior, pē-iero, &c.

---

2) Greek ου (as in Οὐελέα for Velia in Dion. Hal.) expresses Gr. digamma and Lat. v ; and this sound cannot be interpreted as Eng. v, but as w. The occasional substitution of β, by Plutarch chiefly, proves nothing to the contrary : but only means that, ου being a clumsy representation of Ϝ and v, β was taken as the nearest labial instead.

3) A. Gellius cites a grammarian, who says that Deus Vaticanus presided over infancy, and that the two first letters of his name (Va) are that sound which the infant first utters. The sound then is Eng. wā not vā, which the infant, having no teeth, cannot utter.

Corssen's opinion is that Latin initial v may have had that middle sound between w and v, which German w has in some localities ; the upper teeth being brought near to the lower lip, but not pressed upon it. This view we cannot accept.

[1] It was shewn (p. 33) that ei was long used to express ī with a leaning to ē. Lucilius tried to mark long vowels by writing them twice, as Maarcus for Mārcus. This appears on some Inscrr. but did not last long. It was followed in Cicero's time by the Apex or mark over a long vowel, like (ʹ) or (ʹ), which frequently appears on a, e, o, u ; not on i.

In bĭ-iugus, quadrĭ-iugus, trĭ-iuges, &c., ĭ, being naturally short, remains so.

c) Progressive assimilation has changed ĭ-cons. to ĭ in cello, fallo, pello for (cel-yo, fal-yo, pel-yo), as ἄλλος in Greek for (ἀλ-γος), σφάλλω for (σφάλ-yω).

d) On Iuppiter, Iuno, Ianus, &c. for D-iupiter, &c., see p. 15. This passage from **dj** to **j** shews distinctly how the assibilation arose by which ĭ-cons., afterwards taking the sign **j**, became a compound palatal sibilant in English and (with **gĭ** for Eng. **j**) in Italian; while in French it becomes purely palatal. So, from Latin diurnus we get

Eng.	It.	Fr.
journey	*giorno*	*journée*

X.

X. The Double Consonant **x**.

X (= **cs**) corresponds to Gr. ξ. See vii. 8.
Republican as well as L. L. Inscrr. shew **xs** :

> *deixserit, duxserit, vixsit.*

In L. L. **x** passed into **ss** or **s**, and appears as **ss** in Italian ; so *disse* for dixit.[1]

---

[1] A more ample list is here added of Latin words which have lost initial letters.

1. C. : vapor, vapidus, vappa (*κϝαϖ*) ; vermis ; verrere ; lamentum, laus, luscinia ; ludere (*κϝῐϙ*); libum ; raudus (c-rudus, ' raw ') ; nidor (*κνίσσα*).

G. : lac (*γαλακτ-*); nasci . . . ; narrare . . . ; noscere . . .; Naevius ; niti ; vivere.

P. : lanx ; lātus ; lāter ; laetus ; livere ; linter.

D. : ruere ; runa ; racemus ; bellum . . . bis . . . bonus ; viginti . . . ; iuvare . . . ; Iuppiter, Iuno, Ianus . . . ; iuvenis ; iam ; iacĕre.

S. : cavus, caula, cavea, caulis, causa, cauda, casa, castrum, cassis, cutis ; cernere . . . ; cortex ; culter ; carpere ; cilium ; caedere ; clavis, claudere ; cena ; gradi ; -gruere ; parcere ; pannus ; picus ; pituita ; penuria ; pellere ; puls ; palpare ; palpebra ; parra ; pulex ; palea ; pandere ; populare ; fallere ; fides ; fungus ; torus ; temetum ; tegere ; tundere ; tonare ; taurus ; tueri ; tergere ; torpere ; turdus ; turba, turbo, turma ; truncus ; talpa ; turgere ; trux, trucidare ; macula ; mordere ; memor . . . ; mirus . . . ; mittere ; ninguere ; nex ; nare, nares, nasus ; nurus, nutrix ; limus, linere, linea, littera, limax, lubricus ; rivus, Roma, Reate.

St. : lis, lātus, locus.

V. : laqueus ; lacer, lacerare ; lupus.

2. Observe, on xxix., that derivatives sometimes lose radical consonants belonging to the words from which they are derived : currus, curulis ; mamma, mamilla ; offa ofella ; quattuor, quater ; villa, vīlicus ; in-loco, īlico ; stilla, stīlicidium ; mille, mīlia (but millia on the Ancyra monument). See M. Lucr. i. 313, and, on religio, i. 63.

DIVISION II.

MORPHOLOGY.

MORPHOLOGY or WORDLORE treats of Words.

It is subdivided as follows :—

CHAP.   I. Words : their Parts, Kinds, and Flexion in general.
—   II. Nouns : their Parts, Kinds, and Declension.
—   III. Verbs : their Parts, Kinds, and Conjugation.
—   IV. Particles : their Kinds.
—   V. Derivation and Composition of Words.
—   VI. Supplement on the Uses of Words.

CHAPTER I.

WORDS AND THEIR FLEXION.

i. Stem-flexion.

1. WORDS are called in Grammar the *PARTS OF SPEECH.*

Words are either Simple, as flagrare, flamma, or Compound, as con-flagrare, flamm-i-fer.
Every Word has Meaning and Form.   Form helps to determine Meaning.

2. Every Word has *STEM* and *ROOT.*

Word, Stem and Root may be (but seldom are) the same : as tu, *thou* ; aqua, *water.*
Word and Stem may be (but usually are not) the same, while Root differs : flamma, *flame* : Root, flag-, *blaze.*
Root and Stem are often the same : ăg-ere, *to act.*   Such words are called Radical or Primitive : all others are Derivatives.
A Compound Word has only one Stem, but as many Roots as it has composing parts.   Thus the Stem of conflagrare is con-flagra-, the two Roots, cum and flag-.

3. Every true element in a word following the Root, is called a *SUFFIX* : thus in flamma (for flag-ma) -ma is a Suffix ; in flag-rare -r, -a, -re are Suffixes.
Suffixes may need a connecting Link or Vincular, which is not elemental : reg-ĭ-bus, quer-ĭ-monia.   The final Suffix, which converts a Stem into a Word, is called an Ending, as -re in flag-r-a-re.   But the Suffix -ma in flam-ma is not called an Ending, because flamma is itself a Word.   When it forms flamma-s, s is an Ending, and, specially, a Case-ending.

4. A syllable placed before a Word to modify its meaning, *not* being a root-word, is called a *PREFIX*. Thus in te-tend-i, cin-cinnus, -**te** and **cin**- are Prefixes. But Particles in composition, as de- se- re-, are not called Prefixes, being themselves roots.

5. The last letter of a Root, as **g** in flag-, is the Root-character. The last letter of a Stem, as **a** in flagra- and flamma, is the Stem-character : and this (being of chief importance in Grammar) is called the *CHARACTER* of the Word.

6. *FLEXION*, or Stem-flexion, is the method of inflecting a Stem, that is, of making such changes in its form as may indicate changes in its meaning and use. This is usually done by suffixing a Flexional Ending to the Stem : flagra-**re**, flamma-**rum**. Such suffixed Endings sometimes need a Vincular, as **ĭ** in reg-**ĭ**-bus ; sometimes they cause a mutilation of the Stem, as flamm-**ĭs** for flamma-**ĭs** (which is for flamma-**bus**). Sometimes change in a letter of the Stem itself is an inflexion : as flammā from flammă. Sometimes both Letter-change and Ending are used ; ăg-, ēg-**ĭ**. Sometimes Prefix, Letter-change, and Ending : căn-, cĕ-cĭn-**ĭ**.

7. How then is a Stem defined ?

A Stem is that part of a Word which is virtually contained in every change of form, though the character is often liable to be hidden through the operation of the laws which determine Letter-change. So the character of flamma is hidden in the form flamm-is ; the character of virgĭn- is hidden in the form virgo : the character of dirig- in the form direxi.

8. And how is a Root defined ?

A Root is the primitive element in any word ; that part which the word has in common with all other kindred words. Thus, in agito, the Stem is agita-, but the Root is **ag**-, which it has in common with ag-o, ag-men and many other kindred words. The Root-character and Root-vowel are more liable to be hidden through Letter-change than even the Stem-character. Thus the Root **ag**- is contained in the words actio, examen, redigo, but obscured in each word by some mutation.

15
Classes
of
Words.

ii. Classification of Words.

Words are of three kinds :

   I. Nouns.   II. The Verb.   III. Particles.

Nouns.   I. A *NOUN* (Nomen) is the name of something perceived or conceived.

Nouns are of three kinds : Substantives ; Adjectives ; Pronouns.

1. A Noun *SUBSTANTIVE* (Nomen Substantivum) is a name simply denoting something perceived or conceived : psittacus, *the parrot* ; nix, *snow* ; virtus, *valour, virtue* ; Caesar, *Caesar.*

2. A Noun *ADJECTIVE* (Nomen Adjectivum) is a name indicating a quality perceived or conceived as inherent in something denoted by a Substantive. Accompanying the Substantive, it is said to be an Attribute, or in Attribution to it: psittacus loquax, *the talkative parrot*; nix alta, *the deep snow*; vera virtus, *true valour*; Caesar inclutus, *the renowned Caesar*. In such examples it is also called an Epithet.

3. A *PRONOUN* (Pronomen) is a relational Substantive or Adjective which abbreviates discourse by avoiding the repetition of Names. Thus a speaker avoids his own name by using the Pronoun ego, *I*. He addresses another as tu, *thou* or *you*. A person once mentioned he afterwards names as is or ille, *he*. He speaks of his own horse as meus equus, *my horse*; of his companion's dog as canis tuus, *your dog*.

　1) One Substantive may qualify another, and is then said to be an Apposite, or in Apposition, to it: psittacus avis loquax, *the parrot, a talkative bird*, where avis, *bird*, is an Apposite, or in Apposition, to psittacus, *the parrot*.

　2) Names given to the qualities of things are called Abstract (Abstracta): candor, *whiteness*, virtus, *valour*. In contradistinction to these, Names of things to which such qualities belong are called Concrete (Concreta): nix, *snow*; vir, *a man*.

　3) Concrete Names Individual or Proper (Nomina Propria), are such as can only be applied to single persons, places, or objects · Caesar, Roma, Bucephălus, Cerbĕrus.

　4) Names are called Appellative (Appellativa) when they belong in common to a number of individuals which thus constitute a class: vir, *a man*, urbs, *a city*, ager, *a field*, canis, *a dog*, arbor, *a tree*.

　5) Names expressing in the Singular Number a plurality of things, are called Collective Nouns or Nouns of Multitude: turba, *crowd*, populus, *people*, gens, *clan*, exercitus, *army*.

　6) A quality, without a substantive name, may sometimes suffice to describe an object. That is, Adjectives may stand as Substantives. In Natural History, the Adjective words Mineral, Vegetable, Annual, Mammal, express sufficiently the things meant. So in Latin: sapiens, *a wise man* (vir); calida, *warm water* (aqua); natalis, *a birthday* (dies); utile, *the useful*, convey their meaning without Substantives.

　7) *NUMERALS* (Numeralia) are a class of Adjectives expressing Number: unus, *one*; duo, *two*, &c., centum, *a hundred*, mille, *a thousand*, &c. These, like other Adjectives, can appear as Substantives: milia multa, *many thousands*. The ancients marked them as Pronouns.

8) A Substantive, or any word put for a Substantive, is called a Noun-term.

9) Nouns have a Flexion called *DECLENSION*; and four Accidents (Accidentia) : Number, Gender, Person, and Case. A Noun inflected through all its Cases is said to be Declined.

The Verb.

II. The *VERB* (Verbum) is the Word which makes Predication, that is, which declares or states something about a Subject, and so forms a Sentence : ago, *I do*; dicimus, *we say*: consul triumpavit, *the consul triumphed.*

1. The Verb has two parts :

1) The Verb Finite (Verbum Finitum), which is personal;

2) The Verb Infinite (Verbum Infinitum), consisting of Verbal Nouns : principally the Infinitive (Infinitivum), which is a kind of Substantive; and Participles (Participia), which are a kind of Adjectives.

2. The Verb has a Flexion called *CONJUGATION*. It has five Accidents : Voice, Mood, Tense, Number, and Person. A Verb inflected through certain forms is said to be Conjugated.

Particles.

III. *PARTICLES* (Particulae) are the uninflected help-words of discourse ; and are of four kinds: Adverb, Preposition, Conjunction, Interjection.

1. An *ADVERB* (Adverbium) is a particle which helps to determine the force of a Verb or Adjective, sometimes of a Substantive, sometimes of another Adverb : Quam turpiter interfectus est Socrates, tam bonus civis et vere philosophus; *how shamefully was Socrates put to death, so good a citizen and truly a philosopher.*

1) Adverbs which ask and answer the questions, 'when, where, whence, whither,' &c., are Pronominal Adverbs :

quando? ubi? quo? nunc hic illuc

2) Adverbs which ask and answer the question 'how often,' are Numeral Adverbs :

quotiens? semel bis ter quater quinquiens

2. A *PREPOSITION* (Praepositio) is a particle which, used with a Noun-case, helps to define its relation to some other Noun: Ego sto ad fores, tu in conclavi, *I stand at the door, you in the apartment.*

1) Many Prepositions can be used as Adverbs : such are,

ante, *before* ; circum, *around* ; intra, *within.*

2) The Cases used with Prepositions are the Accusative and the Ablative.

3. A *CONJUNCTION* (Coniunctio) is a particle which helps to shew the connection of words, clauses, and sentences: Oves et aves, *sheep and birds* ; edimus ut vivamus, *we eat that we may live.*

4. An *INTERJECTION* (Interiectio) is an exclamatory particle used to express feeling or call attention:

O, *O!*   heu, eheu, *alas!*   en, ecce, *lo!*

The Parts of Speech, recounted, appear to be

16
Parts of Speech.

1. Substantive	5. Adverb
2. Adjective	6. Preposition
3. Pronoun	7. Conjunction
4. Verb	8. Interjection
which are inflected.	which are uninflected.

Note.—Latin has no Articles : and, when a Latin Substantive is to be rendered in English, the context and collocation alone shew what English Article, if any, must be supplied. Thus : lux may mean ' a light,' or ' the light,' or ' light ' in general, according to the place in which it stands.

CHAPTER II.

NOUNS.

SECTION I.

i. *NUMBER* in Nouns.

17
Number.

The Substantive is declined by Number and Case ; the Adjective by Number, Gender, and Case, agreeing in these with the Substantive which it qualifies.

The Numbers (Numeri) are two: 1. Singular (Singularis): mensă, *table*; 2. Plural (Pluralis): mensae, *tables.*

Sanskrit, Greek, and Sclavonic have a Dual Number; of which in Latin the only traces are the words duo, *two*, ambo, *both.*

ii. *GENDER* of Nouns.

18
Gender.

The Genders (Genera) are two: 1. Masculine (Masculinum) ; 2. Feminine (Femininum). A Substantive which is neither Masc. nor Fem. is said to be Neuter (Neutrum), i.e. Neither of the two.

A Substantive which may be Masc. or Fem. is called Common (Commune) of both Genders.

(The lively imagination of the East ascribed sex to inanimate objects, the sun, moon, stars, trees, &c. Hence the distinctions of Gender in Sanskrit, Greek, and Latin : which are found not only in the Romanic languages, but also in German and other Teutonic dialects, English alone excepted.)

A. The Gender of words which imply sex is expressed in Latin in four ways.

Distinct Generic names.

I. First : Distinct words are used, as in English, for many of the most familiar relations :

homo	*man*	mulier	*woman*
mas	*male*	femina	*female*
maritus vir }	*husband*	uxor femina }	*wife*
pater	*father*	mater	*mother*
frater	*brother*	soror	*sister*
vitricus	*stepfather*	noverca	*stepmother*
gener	*son-in-law*	nurus	*daughter-in-law*
patruus	*uncle* {on father's side}	amita	*aunt*
avunculus	*uncle* {on mother's side}	matertera	*aunt*
senex	*old man*	anus	*old woman*
verna	*house slave*	ancilla	*maid-servant*
taurus	*bull*	vacca	*cow*
aries vervex	*ram* *wether* }	ovis	*ewe*
catus	*he-cat*	fel-es(is)	*she-cat*
verres maialis }	*boar*	scrofa	*sow*
haedus	*kid*	capella	

Homo (*human being*), though never used with a feminine epithet, may comprehend woman as well as man.

Mulier is the Roman law-term for *woman*, especially for *a married woman*, distinct from virgo.

Femina, *female* (ἡ φύουσα, genetrix), is applied to all animals.

Maritus and uxor are the law-terms for *husband* and *wife*.

Vir is constantly used for maritus, as Mann in German.

Senex (with its comparative senior) is the only word corresponding to Fem. anus. It occurs rarely as a Fem. Adjective.

Substantiva Mobilia.

II. Secondly : Many words, called Substantiva Mobilia, have a Masculine and a Feminine form, as in English, *lion, lioness,* &c. Such are

1)	avus, 2.	*grandsire*	avia, 1.	*grandmother*
	nepos, 3.	*grandson*	neptis, 3.	*granddaughter*
	puer, 2.	*boy*	puella, 1.	*girl*
	socer, 2.	*father-in-law*	socrus, 4.	*mother-in-law*

So, poeta *poet*, poetria; cliens *client*, clienta; rex *king*, regina; caupo *vintner*, copa; fidicen, *lute-singer*, fidicina;

tibīcen *flute-player*, tibīcĭna; leo *lion*, lea, leaena; gallus *cock*, gallīna; Cres *Cretan*, Cressa; Threx *Thracian*, Threissa; Libys *Libyan*, Libyssa; Cilix *Cilician*, Cilissa; Phoenix, *Phoenician*, Phoenissa; Laco *Laconian*, Lacaena; Tros *Trojan*, Troas : and others.

2) Many Masculines of the Second Declension in **-us -er** have Feminines of the First Declension in **-a -ra** :

a. de-**us a**	domin-**us a**	cerv-**us a**	urs-**us a**
div-**us a**	er-**us a**	equ-**us a**	vitul-**us a**
fili-**us a**	serv-**us a**	iuvenc-**us a**	γ. arbit-**er ra**
nat-**us a**	libert-**us a**	lup-**us a**	magist-**er ra**
marit-**us a**	patron-**us a**	mul-**us a**	minist-**er ra**
spons-**us a**	β. agn-**us a**	porc-**us a**	cap-**er ra**
privign-**us a**	asin-**us a**	simi-**us a**	colub-**er ra**

3) Verbals of the Third Declension in **-tor -sor** often have Feminines in **-trix**, as vic-tor, vic-trix. So

adiu-tor -trix	moni-tor -trix	expul-sor expul-trix
crea-tor -trix	fau-tor -trix	ton-sor ton-strix, &c.

4) Patronymica, or Names formed from those of parents or ancestors, have the following Endings :

Ending of Parent Name	Patronymic Ending Masc.	Fem.
-us, 2. and some of Decl. 3. . .	-ĭdes	-ĭs
-eus (ευς)	-īdes	-ĕĭs
-ius, 2. and some of Decl. 3. . .	-iădes	-iăs
-as, 1. and some of Decl. 3. . .	-ădes	—

Examples :

Tantal-ĭdes *son*	Tantal-ĭs *daughter*	Thest-iădes *son*	Thest-iăs *daughter*
of Tantalus.		*of* Thestius.	

Thes-īdes *son*	Thes-ēis *daughter*	Anchis-iădes, *son of* Anchis-es.
of Theseus.		Aene-ădes, *son of* Aeneas.

Other Female Patronymic Endings are **-īne, ōne** :

Neptunīne, *daughter of* Neptunus, Acrisiōne, *daughter of* Acrisius.

III. Thirdly : Substantiva Communia, Words Common of both Genders, are of two classes. *Substantiva Communia.*

1. Appellatives used of both sexes. Such in English are the words *parent, child, infant, cousin, companion, guide, guardian, hostage, witness*, &c.

These include names of animals, found Masc. or Fem., without change of form : gender being shown either by the epithets applied to them, or by their apposition to other words : bos, sus, &c.

2. Words having no relation of sex, but varying their gender according to sense or usage : dies, *day*, callis, *path*.

1. Appellativa Communia.

1) Appellatives of Common Gender should not be grouped indiscriminately : community of gender being in some the rule, in others an exception. When the sexes are included in the Plurals, the gender is Masculine by the rule which gives priority to that sex: 'sacerdotes casti,' *chaste priests*, in Virgil, including both sexes.

Coniunx, *wife*, is usual ; coniunx, *husband*, poetic.

The following words are freely used of either sex :

auctor	*author*	municeps	*burgess*
civis	*citizen*	nemo	*nobody*
comes	*companion*	parens	*parent*
custos	*guardian*	sacerdos	*priest (priestess)*
dux	*guide, leader*	satelles	*body-guard*
exul	*banished one*	vates	*seer*

The following are usually Masculine, but occasionally Feminine :

adulescens	*young person*	hostis	*enemy*
antistes	*president*	infans	*infant*
hospes	*host (hostess)*	iuvenis	*young person*

Yet the Feminine forms antistita, hospita, are also found.

The following, usually Masculine, rarely take Feminine epithets:

affinis	*akin*	iudex	*judge*
artifex	*artist*	interpres	*interpreter*
augur	*augur*	miles	*soldier*
contubernalis	*tent-mate*	patruelis	*cousin*
heres	*heir*	testis	*witness*
incola	*inhabitant*	vindex	*avenger*
index	*informer*		

The following, usually Masculine, are found in apposition to females, but not with Feminine epithets :

accola	*dweller-near*	obses	*hostage*
advena	*new-comer*	opifex	*worker*
aurīga	*charioteer*	praeses	*president*
auspex	*omen-taker*	transfuga	*deserter*
homo	*human being*		

Add to these successor, rector, sponsor.

2) Nomina Animantium.

    a) animans, Masc., *a rational being* ; Fem. or Neuter, *an animal.*

        quadrupes (properly Adjective) is usually Fem., but in several places Masc., rarely Neuter.

        ales, *bird* (properly Adjective), is generally Fem., yet often Masc.

b) The following are of both genders, preferring that subjoined :

anguis	*snake* (m.)	grus	*crane* (f.)
anser	*goose* (m.)	perdix	*partridge*
bos	*ox* or *cow* (m.)	serpens	*serpent* (f.)
camēlus	*camel*	sus	*swine* (f.)
canis	*dog*	tigris	*tiger* or *tigress* (f.)
damma	*deer*		

c) accipiter, *hawk*, Masc., is once Fem. in Lucretius.
    bubo, *owl*, Masc., is once Fem. in Virgil.
    elephantus, Masc., is once Fem. in Plautus.
    lynx, Fem., is once Masc. in Horace.
    talpa, *mole*, Fem., is once Masc. in Virgil.

2. For Common Nouns of the second kind see the Declensions.

IV. Fourthly : Names of Animals only found in one gender, which necessarily comprises both sexes, are called Epicoena (ἐπίκοινα, *common to both*). [Epicoena.]

Among Masculine Epicoena are :

crabro	*hornet*	pavo	*peacock*
cycnus, olor	*swan*	piscis	*fish*
glis	*dormouse*	stelio	*lizard*
mugil, mullus	*mullet*	vermis	*worm*
mus	*mouse*	vespertilio	*bat*
papilio	*butterfly*	vultur	*vulture*

with all not before specified in -us, -ex, -er: corvus, *rook*, milvus, *kite*, turdus, *thrush*, culex, *gnat*, passer, *sparrow*.
    The reading 'fecundae leporis,' Hor. *S.* ii. 4. 44 cannot be relied on. Lepus, *hare*, is therefore a Masculine Epicene.

Among Feminine :

avis	*bird*	apis	*bee*
anas	*duck*	vulpes (is)	*fox*

with all not before specified in -a, -ix, -do: aquila, *eagle*, rana, *frog*, cornix, *raven*, coturnix, *quail*, hirundo, *swallow*, &c.
    If the sex must be expressed, this is done by using the words femina, mas (mascula): 'femina piscis,' Ovid.: 'vulpis mascula,' Plin. So in English, *he-goat, she-goat, cock-sparrow, hen-sparrow*, &c.

B. The Gender of Latin substantives which do not imply sex is often shewn by the meaning or the form of the word. [Gender shewn by Meaning.]
    1. The general correspondence of Gender with Meaning is as follows :—

(1) Masculine	(2) Feminine	(3) Neuter
Males	Females	Indeclinable words.
Months (mensis m.)	Plants (planta f.)	
Winds (ventus m.)	Countries (terra f.)	
Mountains (mons m.)	Islands (insula f.)	
Rivers (fluvius m.)	Cities (urbs f.)	
People (populus m.)		

Examples

Masc. : Iulius, Aprilis, Notus, Haemus, Liris, Achivi.

Fem. : Andromache, laurus, Germania, Cyprus, Athenae.

Neut. : fas, instar, alpha, vivere.

Exceptions to the Rules of Gender as shewn by Meaning :

A) Mountains :

Fem. :

Decl. 1. Aetna ; Hybla ; Ida ; Oeta ; Calpe ; Cyllene ; Pholoe ; Pyrene ; Rhodope.
Decl. 3. Alpis (usually Plur.) ; Carambis.

Neut. :

Decl. 2. Pelion ; and Plurals implying mountain ranges (iuga) : Gargara ; Ismara ; Maenala ; Taygeta ; and others.
Decl. 3. Soracte.

B) Rivers :

Fem. :

Decl. 1. Allia ; Albula ; Druentia ; Duria (*the Dora*) ; Matrona ; Lethe.
Decl. 3. Styx.

AA) Plants :

Masc. :

Decl. 2. acanthus ; amaracus ; asparagus ; boletus ; calamus ; carduus ; hyacinthus ; intubus ; iuncus ; muscus ; narcissus ; oleaster.

Neut. :

Decl. 2. Nouns in **um** : apium ; ligustrum ; lilium ; thymum.
Decl. 3. acer ; cicer ; papaver ; piper ; robur ; siler ; siser ; suber ; tus.

Common :

Decl. 2. balanus ; cytisus ; lotus ; rubus ; spinus.
Decl. 3. larix ; rumex.

BB) Countries :

Masc. :

Decl. 2. Pontus.

Neut. :

Decl. 2. Nouns in **um** :

Illyricum ; Latium ; Noricum ; Samnium.

CC) Cities :

Masc. :

Decl. 2. All Plurals in **1** :

Corioli ; Delphi ; Gabii ; Puteoli ; Veii ; Argi (for **Argŏs**). Also, Canopus ; Orchomenus ; Stymphālus.

Decl. 3. Nouns in **as ant-** : Acragas; Taras ; **ēs, ēt** : Tunes ; several in **ō ōn-** : Frusino ; Hippo ; Narbo (Martius); Sulmo; Vesontio; some in **ōn-** : Brauron; **ūs unt-** : Hydrus; Pessinus.

But of this last class most are Fem. : Amathus; Opus; Myus; Rhamnus, &c.   Selinus is common.

Martial has 'Narbo pulcherrima,' of another Narbo.

Croto (also Croton, and Crotona f.), Marathon are common.

Neut. :

Decl. 2. Nouns in **um, ŏn, ă** (Pl.) :

Tarentum ; Tusculum ; Ilion ; Arbēla ; Leuctra ; Susa.

Decl. 3. Most in **ĕ, ur, os** :

Caere ; Bibracte ; Reate ; Tergeste ; Tibur ; Argos.

Also Praeneste, which Virgil and Juvenal have Fem. in Abl. by Synesis.   Anxur is Masc. in Mart. with reference to the hill, 'candidus Anxur;' Neut. in Hor. with reference to the town; 'impositum saxis late candentibus Anxur.'

Amphipolis, Trapezus are Neut. in Pliny with reference to 'oppidum.'

Some have double form and gender : Sagunt-us f. -um, n.

Note 1. Names of precious stones are, some Fem. in reference to gemma, others Masc. in reference to lapis.

Fem. :

amethystus; sapphirus :—iaspis; onyx; sardonyx (usually).

Masc. :

beryllus :—adamas.

Common :

chrysolithus; smaragdus, *emerald.*

Note 2. Synesis (agreement with meaning, not with form) sometimes gives to a Noun an attribute of a different Gender :

'Eunuchus acta est' (i.e. fabula Eunuchus), Ter.   'Centauro magna' (i.e. nave Centauro), Verg.   'Alta cremata est Ilion,' Ov. *Met.* xiv. 466.

So, Female names in **um** of Decl. 2 are Fem.: 'Mea Glycerium,' Ter.   'Mea Silenium,' Plaut.

Note 3. Some Fem. and Neut. words imply men without changing their gender :

operae, *workmen*; excubiae, *night sentinels* ; vigiliae, *watchmen*; auxilia, *auxiliaries* : so mancipium n. means *a slave*, considered as a piece of goods.

Similarly, prostibulum, scortum are Neuter words contemptuously applied to profligate women.

2. Correspondence of Gender with Form appears in the Declensions.

19
Case.

iii. CASE in Nouns.

1. The Cases (Casus) in each Number are six: Nominativus, Vocativus, Accusativus, Genetivus, Dativus, Ablativus. (On the Locative Case see below, and § 20.)

		Answers the question	Example:
1)	NOMINATIVE .	Who or What?. Quis dedit? . . } Vir, / *Who gave?* . . } *A man.*	
2)	VOCATIVE (Case of one addressed) . . . . . . { O vir, / { *O man.*	
3)	ACCUSATIVE .	Whom or what? Quem video? . } Virum, / *Whom do I see?* } *A man.*	
4)	GENITIVE .	Whose or whereof? Cuius donum? } Viri, / *Whose gift?* . } *A man's.*	
5)	DATIVE . . .	To or for whom or what? Cui datum? . } Viro, / *To whom given?* } *To a man.*	
6)	ABLATIVE . .	By, with, &c., whom or what? A quo datum? } A viro, / *By whom given?* } *By a man.*	

2. Case (Gr. πτῶσις) is the form given to a Noun or Pronoun to shew the relation in which it stands to some other word. Grammarians·represented that form which a Noun takes when it is the Subject of a sentence, by an upright line, and likened the other forms to lines *falling* away from the perpendicular. These they called *Cases* (cado): and their series, *the declension*, or *sloping down*, of the word. Afterwards, the Nominative was called Casus Rectus, *the Upright Case,* and the others (except the Vocative) Casus Obliqui, *Oblique Cases*; whereas the Stem is more properly the upright line, and the several Cases, including the Nominative and Vocative, are deflections from it. So, from the Stem nuc- (*walnut-tree*) the Cases are: Nom. V. nuc-s (=nux), Acc. nuc-em, G. nuc-is, D. nuc-i, Ab. nuc-e.

3. The Relations which Cases fail to express are supplied by Prepositions; and in the languages of modern Europe the use of Prepositions prevails, and Declension is comparatively rare. Thus the Romanic languages have only one Case-form in each Number for Nouns; English, two; but the Possessive in English is of very limited use. Sanskrit has the six Latin Cases and two more, the Instrumental and the Locative. Greek has only five; but it preserves traces of the Instrumental and the Locative. Latin retains many fragments of the Locative Case.[1]

---

[1] The order in which the cases were ranked by ancient Grammarians, imitated, as it has been, by modern writers, is vicious and misleading. The Vocative has been separated from the Nominative, with which it is almost identical, and has thus assumed an importance which ought not to be given to it. The Accusative, so often concurring with both, has been separated from both. The Dative and Ablative, so often identical in form, have been thrown apart. The only motive for this misarrangement was the desire to place the Genitive next to the Nominative, because its variations indicate those of Declension. But this is better done by giving the Stem and Character, which appear in the Genitive Plural of Nouns: thus homo, homin-, shewn in homiN-um.

iv. The Five Declensions.

There are Five Declensions of Latin Nouns, which shew the Character of their Stems by the letter before -**rum** or -**um** in the Genitive Plural.

I.	A-stems have Character	. **A** .	. mens**A**-rum.
II.	O-stems —	**0** .	. domin**0**-rum.
III.	Consonant-stems } —	a Consonant	virgi**N**-um.
	I-stems —.	**I** .	. ov**I**-um.
IV.	U-stems —	**U** .	. grad**U**-um.
V.	E-stems —	**E** .	. di**E**-rum.

a) The Declensions fall into two groups : namely

(I) The A- E- and O-declensions (1. 5. 2.)
(II) The Consonant and Semiconsonant (I, U) declensions (3. 4.)

(I) The primary vowel **a** is appropriate to Fem. words (Decl. 1) ; weakened to **e**, it forms another more limited Fem. Decl. (5) ; weakened to **o** (which in a later age partly became **u**), it forms a Masc. Decl. (2) in **o-s** (**u-s**), including also Neuters in **o-m** (**u-m**).

(II) In Consonant Nouns the stem and suffix are often linked by the vowel **i** : duc-ĭ-bus. Sometimes this happens in the Nom. Sing. : can-i-s, iuven-i-s, which thus appear like I-nouns. On the other hand, I-nouns often drop that light vowel in the Nom. Sing. and so wear the appearance of Consonant Nouns : stirp-s, par-s. These causes made it so hard for grammarians to draw the line of distinction accurately between these two classes that they included them in one Decl. (3).

U-nouns (4), which contract some cases, escape this confusion, but are liable to another ; for the affinity of **u** and **o** has caused some of their case-forms to be often mixed up with those of the O-Decl. (2).

Obs. Pronouns are peculiar and irregularly declined Nouns, which are with most convenience treated separately.

b) 1. In Neuter Nouns, the Nominative, Vocative, and Accusative are the same in each Number severally ; and in the Plural they end in ă. The A- and E-declensions have no Neuters : the U-declension has very few.

2. The Vocative in words not Greek is the same as the Nominative, except in the Singular of Nouns in -**us** of Decl. 2, which have Vocative-ending **e** : domin-ĕ, fili (for fili-ĕ).

3. The Dative and Ablative Plural are always alike.

---

[1] The Consonant before -**um** is the Character in Consonant-nouns. This may be any Mute (except **k, q**), Nasal, or Liquid ; or the Sibilant represented by r.

v. Formation of the Cases.

The Cases are generally formed by suffixing an Ending to the Stem; a vincular ĭ is sometimes required in Consonant-nouns; while in many instances Letter-change occurs in the formation. See Bücheler (*Lat. Declension*).

NOMINATIVE SINGULAR : Primitive ending **s**.

Decl. 1. A-nouns, except Greek Masc. names, do not take **s**: mensă: but Gr. Borea-s, alipte-s.

Decl. 2. O-nouns, not Neuter, take **s**: dominŭ-s for domi-nŏ-s.
But some stems in **-ĕro-** drop **o**, rejecting **s**:
    puer for puerŏ-s, tener for tenerŏ-s.

And nouns, in which **-ro** follows a mute or **f**, drop **o**, reject **s**, and insert **e** before **r**:
    magist-e-r for magistr-ŏ-s, nig-e-r for nigr-ŏ-s.

Decl. 3. Mute Consonant-nouns take **s**:
    iudex for iudic-s; pes for ped-s; princep-s.

Liquid and Nasal nouns do not take **s**: consul, passer, virgo (virgin-). Hiem-p-s alone takes **s**, inserting **p**.
In numerous words with Nom. in s, inflected in ĕr-, ŏr-, ōr-, ūr, **s** belongs to the stem and is not a Case-ending; its place in flexion being taken by **r**: flos floris for (flosis), aes aeris for (aesis).
I-nouns take **s** if the vowel is not dropt:
    avi-s, nube-s[1] for (nubi-s), gravi-s:

also when the vowel is dropt (which happens in many stems) if the Consonant before the Character is a Mute:
    audax for (audaci-s), serpen-s for (serpenti-s).

If the stem ends in **ri-** after a Mute, **ĭ** is dropped, and **e** inserted before **r**: imb-e-r for (imbri-s), ac-e-r for acri-s: but the forms in **ris** are also used by Adjectives.

Decl. 4. U-nouns take **s**: gradu-s.

Decl. 5. E-nouns take **s**: die-s.

ACCUSATIVE SINGULAR : Primitive Ending **m**, Greek *ν* or *α*.

All Declensions take the Ending **m** for Masc. and Fem. Nouns, **o** passing into **u**, and **ĭ** generally into **e**: Cons.-stems insert **e**:

1. mensa-m	3. virgin-e-m	4. gradu-m
2. dominu-m for domi-	tussi-m	5. die-m
no-m	nube-m	
	orbe-m	

---

[1] Corssen, referring to the Noun pub-es -is, with its byform puber -ĕris, also to such Nouns as Cer-es -ĕris, pulv-is -eris, &c., contends that I-nouns in -**ēs**, like nubes, sedes, were originally S-stems.

Obs. In all Neuter Nouns, the Nominative and Accusative have the same form. See iv. b. This, in O-nouns, is **o-m = um** : bellum for bell-om.

In Cons-, I-, and U-nouns it is the Noun-stem :

3. siser, marmor, sinapi ; 4. cornu ;

often with vowel-change : genus for (genes), frigus for (frigos) melius for (melios), marĕ for (marī-) : or dropping **ı** : animal for (animalĭ-), calcar for (calcarĭ-).

GENITIVE SINGULAR : Primitive Ending generally **as**.

As the Greek, so the old Latin language weakened **as** into **ŏs** ; which was further weakened into **ıs** This ending is taken by Consonant-, I-, and U-nouns :

3. virgin-is, tuss-is for tussi·   4. gradūs for gradu-is.

That A-nouns anciently had it, argued from familia-s in paterfamilias, &c., and similar forms found in E. L. That it was used in E-nouns is shewn by the form Diespiter, and rabies (Gen.) in Lucr. iv. 1079. But the endings (**a-ı**) **ae**, (**o-ı**) **ı**, and **e-ı** were afterwards taken by A-, O-, and E-nouns severally.

A-ı remained long in use, and abounds in Lucretius, as vitā-ı, and is used in a few words by Virgil. (**O-ı**) is not found in use ; it passed into **ı** at an early time, and is also found as (**eı**) in R. L. till near the Augustan age. Lucilius proposed to reject Gen. S. (**eı**) and write Nom. Pl. (**eı**) ; but his distinction was not observed.

In E-nouns **e-ı** remains. Hence

1. mens-ae. 2. domin-i. 5. die-i.

DATIVE SINGULAR : Primitive ending **aı**.

This Ending is only taken by A-, O-, and E-nouns :

1. mensae (anc. mensai) for (mensa-ai) ; 2. domino (anciently dominoi) for (domino-oi) ; 5. diei for (die-ei).

In the rest the Locative **ı** has superseded the Dative Ending :

3. virgin-i   tuss-i for (tussi-i)   4. gradu-i

LOCATIVE : Primitive Ending **ı**.

The Locative Singular remains in Latin in such forms as
militiae, belli, domi, humi, vesperi, ruri, Tiburi, luci ;
the Adverbial forms ubi, ibi, &c.
and in the names of towns, &c., of the A- and O-declensions :

Romae for Roma-i, Tarent-i, Milet-i, &c.

The Loc. Plur. is confounded with Dat. and Abl. in **ıs** or **bus**. The Sing. Loc. in Cons.-nouns often passes into the Abl. **ĕ** ; Carthaginĕ for Carthaginī, Lacedaemone for Lacedaemoni.

Vesperĕ also is used for vesperī.

ABLATIVE SINGULAR : Primitive ending **t**.

In Oscan and old Latin this ending became **d** :

1. sententia-d   2. poplico-d   3. conventioni-d mari-d   4. senatu-d

This **a** (often noticeable in Plautus) was dropped after B.C. 186, and the Ablative became the Stem of the word, lengthened in the Vowel-Declensions (though ĭ is often weakened into ĕ: urb-ĕ), and in the Consonant-Declension ending in ĕ: contion-ĕ.

NOMINATIVE PLURAL : Primitive ending **as.**

This became -**es** in the Consonant-, U-, and E-declensions :

3. virgin-ēs   4. gradūs for (gradu-es)
   orb-ēs for (orbi-es)   5. di-es for (die-es)

Instances of **es** in the O-Decl. occur in E. L.
But in the A- and O-declensions, by dropping **s** and contracting vowels, as in the Gen. Sing., the endings **ae, ĭ,** were obtained :

1. mensae for (mensa-es).   2. domini for (domino-es).

The form (**eĭ**) for **ĭ** occurs in Latin as late as the age of Caesar.

ACCUSATIVE PLURAL : Primitive ending **s,** added to the Accusative Singular in Masc. and Fem. Nouns.
The change of **m** into **n** before **s** makes the Latin forms **ans, ons, (e)ns, ins, uns, ens.** Hence, by excluding the weak nasal, with compensation, are obtained **ās, ōs, ēs, īs, ūs, ēs** :

1. mens-as   3. virgin-es   4. gradūs
2. domin-os   orb-īs   5. dies

This shews why the Accus. Plural of I-nouns is correctly written -**īs,** though the analogy of the Nom. has led to the use of **ēs** (**eĭs**).
The Primitive ending of Accus. Nom. and Voc. Plural in Neuter Nouns was **â,** which was weakened into **ă** in Greek and Latin :

2. bell-ă.   3. nomin-ă, reti-ă.   4. cornu-ă.

GENITIVE PLURAL : Primitive endings **âm, sâm.**

The former of these became -**um** in Consonant-, I-, and U-nouns :

3. virgin-um   orbi-um   4. gradu-um

The latter, as -**sum,** was adopted in A- O- and E-nouns :

1. mensā-rum for (mensa-sum)   5. diē-rum for (die-sum)
2. dominō-rum for (domino-sum)

DATIVE AND ABLATIVE PLURAL : Primitive ending **bhyâs.**

This, corrupted into **bus** (for **b-ĭos**), became the ending of these Cases in Consonant- I- U- and E-nouns :

3. virgin-ĭ-bus   orbĭ-bus   4. arcŭ-bus   5. diē-bus

and occasionally in the A-nouns :

6. deā-bus, filiā-bus, &c.

But in most A-nouns, it became (**aĭs**)**īs** : 1. mensīs.
In O-nouns, (**oes, oĭs**)**īs,** usually (**eĭs**) before Augustus, after whose time **īs** prevailed ; 2. dominīs ; bellīs.
We find **iĭ** contracted : pecunis (Cic.), provincis (Inscr.).

21.   14. ENDINGS OF THE FIVE DECLENSIONS OF SUBSTANTIVES.

	I. A-NOUNS	II. O-NOUNS		III. CONS.-NOUNS		III. I-NOUNS		IV. U-NOUNS		V. E-NOUNS
	F. (M.)	M. (F.)	N.	M. F.	N.	M. F.	N.	M. (F.)	N.	F.
SINGULAR.										
Nom.	ă	ŭs ĕr	um	s, r...	s, r...	s...	e, ĭ...	ŭs	ū	ēs
Voc.	=N.	ĕ	=N.	=N.	=N.	=N.	=N.	=N.	=N.	=N.
Acc.	am	um	=N.	em	=N.	em (im)	=N.	um	=N.	em
Gen.	ae	ī	ī	ĭs	ĭs	ĭs	ĭs	ūs	ūs	ĕī (ē)
Dat.	ae	ō	ō	ī	ī	ī	ī	ŭī (ū)	ŭī (ū)	ĕī (ē)
Abl.	ā	ō	ō	ĕ	ĕ	ĭ, ĕ	ĭ, ĕ	ū	ū	ē
(*Loc.*)	ae	ī	ī	ī ĕ	ī ĕ	ī	ī	ŭī (ū)	ŭī (ū)	ĕī (ē)
PLURAL.										
Nom.	ae	ī	ă	ēs	ă	ēs	ă	ūs	ŭă	ēs
Voc.	=N.	=N.	=N.	=N.	=N.	=N.	=N.	=N.	=N.	=N.
Acc.	ās	ōs	=N.	ēs	=N.	īs ēs	=N.	ūs	=N.	ēs
Gen.	Arum	Orum		-um		Ium		Uum		Erum
Dat.	īs	īs		ĭbŭs		ĭbŭs		ŭbŭs, ĭbŭs		ēbŭs
Abl.	=Dat.	=D.		=D.		=D.		=D.		=D.

In Declension II., of the Masculine Substantives with N. V. S. in -ĕr (for er-us), some keep ĕr before the Endings, as puer (for puer-us). Most drop e in all but N. V. S.: magister, magistr-.

SECTION II.

i. First Declension: **A**-Nouns.

The First Declension contains Latin and latinized words with the Nominative Singular in ă. These are Feminine: Musă, *muse*, mensă, *table*; excepting Male Names and Appellatives: Messallă, Belgă, *Belgian*, scribă, *secretary*, poetă, *poet*; also Hadriă, *Adriatic-gulf*; which are Masculine.

It also contains Greek Appellatives and Names, Proper and Patronymic, in ēs, ās, Masculine: aliptēs, *a trainer*, Aenēās, Atrīdēs; in ē, à, ă, Feminine: crambē, Agāvē, Nemĕā, Iphigenĭă.

[In Tables of Declension and Conjugation byforms of equal authority are placed beside others: **an am**; byforms comparatively rare are added between brackets: **ēn (am)**.]

ii. Table.

	1. *table*, f.	2. *secretary*, m.	3. *goddess*, f.	4. *son of Atreus*, m.
		SINGULAR.		
Nom.	mens-**ă**	scrib-**ă**	de-**ă**	Atrīd-**es** (**ă**)
Voc.	mens-**a**	scrib-**a**	de-**a**	Atrid-**ē ā** (**ă**)
Acc.	mens-**am**	scrib-**am**	de-**am**	Atrid-**ēn**
Gen.	mens-**ae**	scrib-**ae**	de-**ae**	Atrid-**ae**
Dat.	mens-**ae**	scrib-**ae**	de-**ae**	Atrid-**ae**
Abl.	mens-**ā**	scrib-**ā**	de-**ā**	Atrid-**ē ā**
		PLURAL.		
Nom.	mens-**ae**	scrib-**ae**	de-**ae**	Atrid-**ae**
Voc.	mens-**ae**	scrib-**ae**	de-**ae**	Atrid-**ae**
Acc.	mens-**as**	scrib-**as**	de-**as**	Atrid-**as**
Gen.	mens-**Arum**	scrib-**Arum**	de-**Arum**	Atrid-**um**
Dat.	mens-**is**	scrib-**is**	de-**ābus**	Atrid-**is**
Abl.	mens-**is**	scrib-**is**	de-**ābus**	Atrid-**is**

Fem. Adjectives in ă, as bonă, teneră, nigră, are declined as mensă.

iii. Cases in the First Declension.

a) The old Gen. S. in **as** remains in the phrases paterfamilias, materfamilias, filiusfamilias, found in good writers from Terence to Suetonius: and in the Plur. patres (matres, filii) familias. Familiae is also used with pater, &c., by Livy always: and familiarum is written with patres, &c.[1]

b) The old Gen. S. in **ai** appears in Inscrr. It is used as a disyllable āī by Ennius, Plaut. Lucr. Verg. (aulāī, aurāī, aquāī, pictāī).

---

[1] Alcumēna-s (Gen.) is cited from Plautus. The Gen. form in **a-es**, found chiefly in late Inscrr. of I. L. or later R. L., may be an imitation of Gr. ης.

c) The Gen. Plur. is formed in **-um** rather than **-arum** (which can however be used), by the following :

1) Patronymic Names in **-des**,

Aenea-des, Aenea-dum.

2) Many Names of Tribes, People, &c.,

Lapith-ae, Lapith-um.

3) Compounds of col- gen- (in poetry),

caelicol-a, caelicol-um ; terrigen-a, terrigen-um.

4) Amphor-um from amphor-a, drachm-um from drachm-a, when used with Numerals :

terna milia amphorum, 3,000 *amphors*; mille drachmum, 1,000 *drachms*.

d) The form in **ăbus** of Dat. Abl. Pl. might serve to distinguish the Fem. from the Masc. not only in dea, but in many other Substantiva Mobilia. For this purpose it is ascribed by grammarians to numerous words :

filia, nata, liberta, conserva, domina, era, mima, nympha, asina, equa, mula, anima :

and in some of these, especially filia, nata, liberta, it often occurs in Inscrr. and legal forms. But, generally, there is little authority for the use of this Case-ending by classical authors, in any words but deabus, duabus, ambabus.

e) The Locative Case in **ae** (for **a-i**) is formed in the Sing. by militia, and Names of Towns :

militiae, *at the wars*, Romae, *at Rome*.

in **īs** by Plural Names of towns :

Athenis, *at Athens*.

iv. Greek Nouns in First Declension.

	Nom.	Voc.	Acc.	Gen.	Dat.	Abl.
M.	alipt-es	ē ă	ēn (am)	ae	ae	ē (ā)
	Pers-es ă	ē ă	ēn am	ae	ae	ē ā
	Aeet-es ă	ē ă	ēn (am)	ae	ae	ē (ā)
	Aene-as	ā	ān am	ae	ae	ā
	Marsy-as (ă)	ā ă	am ān	ae	ae	ā
F.	music-ă (ē)	ă (ē)	am (ēn)	ae (ēs)	ae	ā (ē)
	cramb-ē	ē	ēn	es	ae	ē
	Helen-ē (ă)	ē ă	ēn am	ēs ae	ae	ē ā
	Agav-ē	ē	ēn	ēs	ae	ē
	Neme-ā	ā	ān (am)	ae	ae	ā
	Iphigenī-ă	ă	ăn am	ae	ae	ā
	Electr-ă	ă	ăn am	ae	ae	ā

The Plural of Appellatives follows that of mensa.

a) Many Greek Nouns of this Decl. were latinized early, and seem to have soon exchanged the Greek endings ης, ας, η, ᾱ, first for ā, then, as shortening came into vogue, for ă, following the practice of the Aeolic dialect :

Masc. pirată (πειρατής)   Fem. aură (αὖρα)
poetă (ποιητής)   epistulă (ἐπιστολή)

Such words are :

Masc., like s c r i b a :

> athleta, bibliopola, citharista, nauta, &c.

Fem., like m e n s a :

> ancora, apotheca, aula, bibliotheca, comoedia, tragoedia, scaena, &c.

b) Words introduced later have much variety, fluctuating between the Greek and Latin form; and poetic usage in these often differs from that of prose.[1] Thus we find :

A) Masc. Greek Nouns :

1) Patronymics, like A t r i d -**ēs ă** :

> Aeneades, Pelides, Tydides, &c. (ă being rare).

2) Appellatives, like a l i p t ē s :

> anagnostes, geometres, Olympionīces, sophistes.

3) Gentile Names, like P e r s -**ēs ă** :

> Scyth-**es a**, Sauromat-**es**, Sarmat-a ;

with many in **ītes ītă, ōtes ōtă** :

> Abderīt-**es a**, Epirot-**es a**.

These sometimes pass to Decl. 3. with Accus. S. **em, ēn**.

4) Like A e e t -**ēs ă** :

> Anchis-**es a**, Lycamb-**es a**, Orest-**es a**, Thyest-**es, a**.

5) Like A e n e ā s :

> Anaxagoras, Diagoras, Lysias, Boreas, &c.

6) Like M a r s y -**ās ă** :

> Cinyr-**as a**, Dam-**as a**, Damoet-**as a**, Iarb-**as a**, Leonid-**as a**, Mid-**as a**.

B) Fem. Greek Nouns :

1) Like m u s i c -**ă ē** :

> dialectic-**a e**, grammatic-**a e**, physic-**a e**, rhetoric-**a e**.

2) Like c r a m b ē :

> aloe, epitome, hyperbole, &c.

3) Like H e l e n -**ē ă** :

> Alcumen-**ă**, Erigon-**ă**, Hecat-**ă**, Led-**ă**, Nymph-**ă**, Semel-**ă**; which also take **ē** : Circ-**ē**, Cybel-**ē**, Dirc-**ē**, Europ-**ē**, Eurydic-**ē**, Penelop-**ē**; which also take **ă**.

---

[1] Cicero, as a rule, prefers Latin forms to Greek, and sometimes introduces the latter with acknowledgment of their origin ('quae h y p e r b o l e dicitur'), or with an apology, as *Epp. ad Att.* vii. 3: 'Reprehendendus sum quod homo Romanus P i r a e e a scripsi, non P i r a e e u m ; sic enim omnes nostri locuti sunt'

Also local names, Aetn-ă, Cret-ă, Id-ă, Ithac-ă, Liby-ă, may take ē for ă in poetry.

 4) Like Agavē :

  Calliope, Danae, Euterpe, Hebe, Lethe, Melpomene, Oenone, Persephone, Procne, &c.

 5) Like Nemeā :
   Malea, Midea.

 6) Like Iphigeniă :
   Medea; and the local Names Aegina, Lerna, Ossa.

 7) Like Electrā :
   Cassandra.

Note. Many Nouns in **es**, which in Greek belong to the First Decl., having the form of Patronymics without really being such, pass over to the Third Decl. in Latin, forming Gen. -**is** :

 Alcibiades, Euclides, Euripides, Miltiades, Simonides.

Yet these and many other names, Greek and barbarian, which take Gen. **is**, fluctuate between the First and Third Declension in the ending of the Accus. S. (**ēn, em**). Such are :

 Achilles, Aristoteles, Archimedes, Artaxerxes, Cleanthes, Datames, Diogenes, Diomedes, Euphrates, Mithridates, Phrahates, Polynices, Polycrates, Socrates, Tiridates, Xerxes, &c.

SECTION III.

i. Second Declension: O-Nouns.

The Second Declension contains

 1) Latin and latinised Nouns in **ŭs** (for **ŏs**) chiefly Masculine: dominŭs, *lord*;

 2) Clipt Masculine Nouns in **ĕr** (for **ĕr-ŏs, r-ŏs**; see p. 82): puer, *boy*, magister, *master*; to which add vĭr (for vĭr-os), *man*;

 3) Neuter Nouns in **um**: bellum, *war*.

 4) Greek Nouns in **ŏs**, Masc. and Fem.; in **ōs, Masc.**; in **ŏn**, Neuter; used chiefly by the poets.

ii. Table:

SINGULAR.

	lord, m.	*boy,* m.	*master,* m.	*war,* n.
Nom.	domin-**us**	puer	magister	bell-**um**
Voc.	domin-**e**	puer	magister	bell-**um**
Acc.	domin-**um**	puer-**um**	magistr-**um**	bell-**um**
Gen.	domin-**i**	puer-**i**	magistr-**i**	bell-**i**
Dat.	domin-**o**	puer-**o**	magistr-**o**	bell-**o**
Abl.	domin-**o**	puer-**o**	magistr-**o**	bell-**o**

23
Second
Declen-
sion.

PLURAL.

Nom.	domin-**i**	puer-**i**	magistr-**i**	bell-**a**
Voc.	domin-**i**	puer-**i**	magistr-**i**	bell-**a**
Acc.	domin-**os**	puer-**os**	magistr-**os**	bell-**a**
Gen.	domin-**orum**	puer-**orum**	magistr-**orum**	bell-**orum**
Dat.	domin-**is**	puer-**is**	magistr-**is**	bell-**is**
Abl.	domin-**is**	puer-**is**	magistr-**is**	bell-**is**

SINGULAR.

	son, m.	*bushel,* m.	*God,* m.	*command,* n.
Nom.	fili-**us**	medimn-**us**	de-**us**	imperi-**um**
Voc.	fil-**i**	medimn-**e**	de-**us**	imperi-**um**
Acc.	fili-**um**	medimn-**um**	de-**um**	imperi-**um**
Gen.	fil-**i** (**ii**)	medimn-**i**	de-**i**	imper-**i** (**ii**)
Dat.	fili-**o**	medimn-**o**	de-**o**	imperi-**o**
Abl.	fili-**o**	medimn-**o**	de-**o**	imperi-**o**

PLURAL.

Nom.	fili-**i**	medimn-**i**	di (de-**i**) [1]	imperi-**a**
Voc.	fili-**i**	medimn-**i**	di (de-**i**)	imperi-**a**
Acc.	fili-**os**	medimn-**os**	de-**os**	imperi-**a**
Gen.	fili-**orum**	medimn-**um**	de-**orum**, de-**um**	imperi-**orum**
Dat.	fili-**is**	medimn-**is**	dis (de-**is**)	imperi-**is**
Abl.	fili-**is**	medimn-**is**	dis (de-**is**) [1]	imperi-**is**

Vir, *a man*; Acc. S. vĭrum, &c.; Gen. Pl. virorum or virum.
And its Compounds, semivir, decemvir, triumvir, &c.

SINGULAR (no Plural).

Irregular Decl.

	sea, n.	*venom,* n.	*common-people,* n. (m.)
N.V.Ac.	pelag-**us**	vīr-**us**	vulg-**us**
Gen.	pelag-**i**	vīr-**i** (rare)	vulg-**i**
D. Abl.	pelag-**o**	vīr-**o**	vulg-**o**

Pelag-**ē**, *seas*, occurs in Lucr.; vulgus has an Accus. vulg-**um**, m.
Pelagus (πέλαγος, Pl. πελάγ-εα, η) is a Greek Neuter Noun.

iii. Cases in the Second Declension.

1) The endings **os, om** were used even to the Augustan age, after
v̇, u, qu, as shewn by Inscrr. and MSS. Thus were written av-ŏs,
av-om, div-om, mortu-ŏs, mortu-om, aequ-om, &c.

2) The Vocative in ĕ is a weakening of ŏ (Pr. ă), and resembles
English forms in **ie, y** (Willie, Johnny, &c.).
Male names in **ius** contract this case into **i**: Claudi, Mercuri,
Demetri, Vergili. Pompēī (from Pompeius) is further contracted by Horace into Pompēī. So Vultēī, from Vulteius. Filius,
son, is the only Appellative which forms this contraction. Others
are regular: fluvie, *O river*; and Adjectives: Cynthie, *O Cyn-
thian* (Apollo). But meus (for mius), Voc. mi for mie.

---

[1] Dii, diis are sometimes written, but pronounced as dī, dīs.

3) The Gen. Sing. of Substantives with Nom. **ius, ium,** was contracted into **i** (by prose-writers as well as poets) till the Augustan age, and is so written by Virgil and Horace. Propertius and Ovid are the first who wrote **ii,** which then became the usual form ; but the poets Manilius, Persius, and Martial prefer **i.**

4) Humus, *ground,* bellum, *war,* vesper, *evening,* and Singular Names of towns, form the Locative Case in **i** :

humi, *on the ground*	Ephesi, *at Ephesus*
belli, *at the wars*	Mileti, *at Miletus*
vesperi (vesperĕ), *at evening*	Tarenti, *at Tarentum*

Plural names of towns form the Locative in **īs** : Gabiis, *at Gabii ;* Veiis, *at Veii.*

5) The Genitive Plural Ending **um** is preferred to **orum** :

a) by words signifying coins, sums, weights, and measures :

Gen. Pl.	from Nom. Sing.
nummum . . .	nummus, *a coin*
denarium . . .	denarius, *ten-as-piece*
sestertium . . .	sestertius, *sesterce*
talentum . . .	talentum, *a talent* (a sum and weight)
stadium . . .	stadium, *furlong*
modium . . .	modius, *peck*
medimnum . . .	medimnus (also um, n.), *bushel*

b) by many names of people: Argivum, Danaum, Pelasgum, &c. from Argivus, &c.

c) as a licence, chiefly in poetry, by a great number of words, such as deus and its compounds, divus, vir and its compounds, faber, *engineer,* socius, *ally,* liberi, *children,* &c.: also by numeral and compound Adjectives: 'denum talentum'; 'magnanimum Rutulum'; 'omnigenumque deum monstra.'—Verg.

iv. Clipt Nouns in **ĕr.**

1) The Clipt-nouns from Stems in **ĕro-,** like puer, are

gener, *son-in-law*	vesper, *evening*
socer, *father-in-law*	Liber, *Bacchus*
adulter, *paramour* (lascivious, Adj.)	

and Adjectives,

asper, *rough* (rarely aspr-)	miser, *wretched*
lacer, *torn*	prosper, *prosperous*
līber, *free* (whence liberi, *children* of freemen)	tener, *tender*

with the many compounds of fero, gero ; frugifer, *fruitful,* corniger, *horned.* Add satŭr, satŭra, satŭrum, *full, satiated.* Ibēr (Hibēr), Celtiber, *Spaniard,* form their cases in **ēr-o-** :

Ibērum, Celtibērum, &c.

2) Clipt-nouns from Stems in **ro-** after a mute or **f**, like magister :

ager, *field*	cancer, *crab*	faber, *architect*
aper, *wild boar*	caper, *he-goat*	līber, *book*
arbiter, *umpire*	coluber, *snake*	minister, *attendant*
auster, *south-wind*	culter, *knife*	

With Proper Names, as I s t e r or H i s t e r, *the Danube*, Alexander, E u a n d e r, T e u c e r, &c. ; and these Adjectives :

aeger, *sick*	macer, *lean*	sacer, *sacred*
Afer, *African*	niger, *black*	scaber, *rough*
ater, *jet-black*	piger, *slow*	sinister, *on left hand*
Calaber, *Calabrian*	impiger, *active*	taeter, *foul*
creber, *frequent*	integer, *entire*	vafer, *cunning*
glaber, *smooth*	pulcher, *beautiful*	noster, *our*
ludicer, *sportive*	ruber, *red*	vester, *your*

α) M u l c i b e r, *Vulcan*, and dexter, *on the right hand*, are declined with and without **e** in the other forms :

　　M u l c i b ĕr-i or Mulcibri (also Mulcibĕris, Mulcibris 3.) ;
　　dexter, dextĕra or dextra, dextĕrum or dextrum.

β) Some Substantives use the form in **us** as well as that in **er**:
E u a n d e r or E u a n d r u s (whence Voc. E u a n d r ĕ) in Virgil;
M a e a n d e r or M a e a n d r u s : *puerus* (anc.).

v. Greek Nouns in the Second Declension.

SINGULAR.

Nom.	Del-**ŏs**, f.	Ath-**ōs**, m.	Androge-ōs (**ŭs**), m.	Peli-**ŏn**, n.
Voc.	Del-**ĕ**	Ath-**ōs**	Androge-ōs	Peli-**ŏn**
Acc.	Del-**ŏn um**	Ath-ōn (**ō**)	Androge-ō **ōn** (**ōnǎ**)	Peli-**ŏn**
Gen.	Del-**ı**	Ath-**ō**	Androge-ō (**ı**)	Peli-**ı**
D.Abl.	Del-**o**	Ath-ō (**ōne**)	Androge-ō	Peli-**o**

α) The Greek Nom. and Accus. forms of Personal and Local
Names, with a few Appellatives, in **ŏs**, **ŏn**, Masc. Fem., and **ŏn**,
Neut., are frequently used in Latin poetry, but rare in prose :

　　Meleagrŏs ; scorpiŏs ; Cnidŏs ; Troilŏn ; Samŏn ; Iliŏn, &c.

Virgil has A t h ŏn (as from Athŏs) : Chaŏs n. 3., Abl. Chaō :
and P a n t h ū, Voc. of P a n t h ū s.
　On Nouns in **eus** see § **24.**

β) The Greek Genitive Plural in ōn (ων) is found in Latin.
Sallust has 'colonia Theraeōn,' 'Philaenōn arae,' for The-
raeorum, Philaenorum.　So Georgicōn for Georgicorum,
from Georgică, *the Georgics*.

vi. Gender in the Second Declension.

Besides the Nouns of which the meaning determines the Gender,
as stated in § **18.** ii., only four genuine Latin words in this Decl.
are Fem.　They are:

alvus, *paunch*
colus, *distaff* (See Decl. 4.)
humus, *ground*
vannus, *winnowing-fan*

The following Greek words are Fem. :

arctus, *the bear-constellation*
atomus, *atom*, C. *Fin.* i. 6.
carbasus, *linen curtain* or *sail*
dialectus, *dialect*
pharus, *lighthouse*, Stat. *S.* v. 101.

and many others are cited by grammarians, but without good classical authority for their use.

Barbitos, *lute*, is common.

vii. Table of Adjectives in Decl. II. and I.

Adjectives of three Endings, in -**us** -**a** -**um**, -**er** -**ĕra** -**ĕrum**, and -**er** -**ra** -**rum**, follow the Second and First Declensions.

Table of Adjectives in the Second and First Declensions.

	MASC.	FEM.	NEUT.	
	like	like mensa	like bellum	
like	dominus . bonus	bona	bonum	*good*
	puer . . . tener	tenera	tenerum	*tender*
	magister . niger	nigra	nigrum	*black*

SINGULAR.

		M.	F.	N.
1)	N.	bon-**us**	bon-**a**	bon-**um**
	V.	bon-**e**	bon-**a**	bon-**um**
	Acc.	bon-**um**	bon-**am**	bon-**um**
	G.	bon-**i**	bon-**ae**	bon-**i**
	D.	bon-**o**	bon-**ae**	bon-**o**
	Abl.	bon-**o**	bon-**ā**	bon-**o**

PLURAL.

		M.	F.	N.
	N.	bon-**i**	bon-**ae**	bon-**a**
	V.	bon-**i**	bon-**ae**	bon-**a**
	Acc.	bon-**os**	bon-**as**	bon-**a**
	G.	bon-**orum**	bon-**arum**	bon-**orum**
	D.	bon-**is**	bon-**is**	bon-**is**
	Abl.	bon-**is**	bon-**is**	bon-**is**

SINGULAR.

		M.	F.	N.
2)	N.	tener	tener-**a**	tener-**um**
	V.	tener	tener-**a**	tener-**um**
	Acc.	tener-**um**	tener-**am**	tener-**um**
	G.	tener-**i**	tener-**ae**	tener-**i**
	D.	tener-**o**	tener-**ae**	tener-**o**
	Abl.	tener-**o**	tener-**ā**	tener-**o**

PLURAL.

	M.	F.	N.
N.	tener-i	tener-ae	tener-a
V.	tener-i	tener-ae	tener-a
Acc.	tener-os	tener-as	tener-a
G.	tener-orum	tener-arum	tener-orum
D.	tener-is	tener-is	tener-is
Abl.	tener-is	tener-is	tener-is

SINGULAR.

		M.	F.	N.
3)	N.	niger	nigr-a	nigr-um
	V.	niger	nigr-a	nigr-um
	Acc.	nigr-um	nigr-am	nigr-um
	G.	nigr-i	nigr-ae	nigr-i
	D.	nigr-o	nigr-ae	nigr-o
	Abl.	nigr-o	nigr-ā	nigr-o

PLURAL.

	M.	F.	N.
N.	nigr-i	nigr-ae	nigr-a
V.	nigr-i	nigr-ae	nigr-a
Acc.	nigr-os	nigr-as	nigr-a
G.	nigr-orum	nigr-arum	nigr-orum
D.	nigr-is	nigr-is	nigr-is
Abl.	nigr-is	nigr-is	nigr-is

SECTION IV.

i. Third Declension: **CONSONANT**- and I-Nouns.

The Third Declension has two chief Divisions:

> I. Nouns with Character a Consonant, either
> Mute, Nasal, Liquid, or Sibilant.
> II. Nouns with Character I-vocalis.

A few Consonant-nouns, as c a n i s, i u v e n i s, v a t e s, seem as if they were I-nouns; many I-nouns, as p a r e n s, c o h o r s, seem as if they were Consonant-nouns; and many appear to fluctuate between the two divisions, as c i v i t a s, s e r v i t u s. The cause of this uncertainty lies in the unstable nature of i-vocalis; which, being sometimes staminal, sometimes vincular, easily changed into ĕ, easily lost, does not always furnish a sure criterion of the class to which the Noun belongs, by its presence or absence.

I. CONSONANT STEMS.

ii. Nominative Endings in the Cons. Declension.

1) In this Declension the Nominative-endings are numerous; the chief being **s, n, l, r** (Sibilant, Nasal, and Liquids), of which **s,** including **x (cs),** is the prevalent ending.

2) Nominatives which end in **o** have dropt **n**.

Those in **c, t, a, e,** are Neuter words without final suffix.

3) The vowel of the true Stem is often shewn both in the Noun-stem and the Nominative: dux dŭc-, fax făc-, &c. Sometimes the Noun-stems, and not the Nominative, shews the root-vowel: iudex iudĭc- (true form dĭc-), comĕs comĭt- (true form it-). Sometimes the Nominative, and not the Noun-stem, shews it: auspex auspic- (true form spĕc-) ; obses obsĭd- (true form sĕd-). Sometimes neither of the two: remex remĭg- (true form is ăg-, of which the ă is weakened into ĭ in the open syllable, to ĕ in the close). So auceps aucŭp-, princeps princĭp- (true form in each căp-), nomĕn nomĭn- (Primitive *nâman*).

iii. Syllabus.

Syllabus of Cons. Stems.

In the following Syllabus the chief stems are given, with Nom. endings, and distinctions of Gender (M. F. N. C.). Greek stems which include no true Latin words, are kept separate : but where the same stem comprises words in both languages, Greek are added to Latin words, and marked with an asterisk. This stands before the Gender when all of that Gender are Greek words.

A. Mute Guttural Stems.

To form the Nom. S., the stem adds **s,** with which the guttural melts into **x, ĭ** being generally changed into **ĕ.**

1) Latin Guttural Stems, with a few Greek marked *.

Stem.	Nom. S.	
ăc-	-ax	F. fax, *torch* : *M. Corax.
āc-	-āx	F. pax, *peace* : fornax, *furnace*; M. Aiax; C. līmax, *snail.*
		*M. Thrax, *Thracian* ; Phaeax, *Phaeacian*, thōrax, *breastplate.*
ĕc-	-ex	F. nex, *death* ; (prĕc-), *prayer*, has no Nom. G. Sing. Adj. faenisex, *haycutter.*
		(Variant C. ; sĕnex, *old person*, inflected sĕn- for senĕc-. Demin. senec-io.)
ēc-	-ēx (-ēc)	M. vervex, *wether.* N. halec, *fish-pickle* (also F. halex).
ĭc-	-ex	M. ăpex, *peak* ; caudex or cōdex, *trunk, writing-book*, &c.; cīmex, *bug*; cŭlex, *gnat*; extispex, *entrail-viewer*; frŭtex, *shrub*; lătex, *liquid*; mū-rex, *purple-shell, purple*; podex; pollex, *thumb*; pontifex, *pontiff*; pūlex, *flea*; pūmex, *pumice*; rā-mex, *bloodvessel*; saurex or sōrex, *shrew-mouse*; vertex or vortex, *summit, eddy.*
		F. cārex, *sedge* ; īlex, *scarlet oak* : paelex, *concubine* ; vītex (a shrub).
		C. cortex, *bark* ; forfex, *shears* ; illex, *decoyer* ; imbrex, *tile* ; rŭmex, *sorrel* ; sĭlex, *basalt* ; with words applicable to either sex ; artifex, auspex, carnifex, index, iūdex, opifex, vindex. See p. 76.

Stem.	Nom. S.	
Ĭc-	-ix	M. călix, *cup* ; fornix, *arch* ; *Cĭlix, *Cilician.* F. appendix ; coxendix, *hip* ; ĭlix, *fern* ; fŭlix, *gull* ; natrix, *water-snake* ; pix, *pitch* ; sălix, *wil- low* ; struix, *heap* ; (vĭc-is), *change* (no Nom. S.); *hystrix, *porcupine.* C. lărix, *larch* ; vārix, *swoln vein.*
Īc-	-īx	F. cervix, *neck* ; cicatrix, *scar* ; cornix, *raven* ; coturnix, *quail* ; lōdix, *blanket* ; meretrix ; nu- trix, *nurse* ; rādix, *root* ; vībix, *weal* ; and many more. *M. Phoenix, *Phoenician* (also a name) ; phoenix (a fabulous bird).
ŏc-	-ōx	F. vox, *voice.*
ŭc-	-ux	F. crux, *cross* ; nux, *walnut-tree.* M. tradux, *layer* (of vine) : C. dux, *leader, guide.*
ūc-	-ūx	F. lux, *light.* M. Pollux.
ĕg-	-ex	M. grex, *herd* ; Lelex (one of the Lelĕges).
ēg-	-ēx	M. rex, *king* ; F. lex, *law.* Adj. exlex (Acc. exlegem), *outlawed.*
ĭg-	-ix	F. strix, *screech-owl* ; M. Ambiorix, Dumnorix, Biturix, &c. (Keltic names).
ĭg-	-ex	M. rēmex, *rower.*
ŏg-	-ox	M. Allobrox, *Allobrogian* (Keltic tribe).
ŭg-	-unx	C. coniunx or coiux, *wife ; husband.* p. 76.
ūg-	-ūx	F. (frūg-), *fruit, produce* : no Nom. S.

2) Greek Guttural Stems.

Stem.	Nom. S.	
ŏc-	-ox	M. Cappadox, *Cappadocian.*
y̆c-	-yx	M. călyx, *bud, husk* ; Eryx.
ȳc-	-ȳx	M. bombyx, *silkworm* ; Cēyx.
y̆ch-	-yx	F. ŏnyx ; sardonyx ; (both precious stones).
nc-	-nx	F. lynx (M. in Hor.).
y̆g-	-yx	M. Iāpyx (a wind) ; Phryx, *Phrygian.* F. Styx (river in hell).
ng-	-nx	F. phălanx ; sȳrinx ; Sphinx.

B. Mute Dental Stems.

The Stem adds **s** in Nom. S., before which the Dental is excluded : aetas for (aetat-s), nox for (noct-s).

Sometimes **n** is excluded with **t**: elephas for (elephant-s).

Short ĭ may become ĕ: milĕs for (milit-s).

1) Latin, with Greek words.*

Stem.	Nom. S.	
ăt-	-as	F. anas, *duck* (Cic. *N.D.* ii. 48, anătum ova : var. r. anĭtum).
āt-	-ās	F. aetas, *time, age* ; aestas, *summer* ; calamitas, *calamity* ; civitas, *citizenship, body of citizens,* *city* ; cupiditas, *desire* ; pietas, *piety* ; tempestas,

Stem.	Nom. S.	
		season, weather, storm; voluptas, *pleasure*; with many other Derivatives. See p. 108.
		M. Maecenas.
ĕt-	-ēs	M. ariēs, *ram*; pariēs, *house-wall.* F. abiēs, *firtree.*
ĕt-	-ĕs	M. (indigĕs), *native* (no Nom. S.).
		F. segĕs, *corn-crop*; tegĕs, *mat.*
		C. interprĕs, *interpreter.*
ĭt-	-ĕs	M. amĕs, *pole*; caespĕs, *turf*; coclĕs, *one-eyed person*; caelĕs, *celestial*; equĕs, *horseman, on horseback*; pedĕs, *foot-soldier, on foot*; fomĕs, *fuel*; gurgĕs, *whirlpool*; limĕs, *boundary*; palmĕs, *vine-tendril*; poplĕs, *knee*; stipĕs, *trunk*; termĕs, *bough* (cut off); tramĕs, *cross-path*; velĕs, *skirmisher.*
		F. mergĕs, *sheaf.*
		C. antistĕs; comĕs; hospĕs; milĕs; satellĕs. See p. 76.
		Adj. alĕs, *winged* (Abl. S. ī, ĕ), used as Subst. *bird,* (Gen. Pl. in poetry alituum for alitum); divĕs, *rich*; praepĕs, *fast-flying*; sospĕs, *safe*; superstĕs, *surviving.* Also Caerĕs, *of Caere.*
īt-	-īs	M. Dīs, *Pluto.*
ēt-	-ēs	F. quiēs, *rest*; inquiēs, *restlessness* (only Nom. S.); requiēs, *repose* (also declined as an E-noun, Acc. requiem, Abl. requiē). Adj. inquiēs, *restless.*
		*M. lebēs, *chaldron*; magnēs, *magnet*; Crēs, *Cretan*; also Names of men which have a second form in ēs, ĭs : Chremēs, Darēs, Thalēs.
		Adj. locuples, *wealthy.*
ĭt-	-ŭt	N. capŭt, *head*; with its compounds occipŭt, sincipŭt. See p. 109. 5.
		Adj. Compounds of capŭt in -ceps for -cipĕs (-cipit-s), cipit-: biceps, triceps, praeceps, &c.
ōt-	-ōs	M. nepōs, *grandson*; *Erōs; *Aegocerōs; *rhinocerōs.
		F. dos, *dowry.* C. sacerdōs, *priest* or *priestess.*
ŏt-	-ŏs	Adj. compŏs, *possessing*; impŏs, *without power.*
ūt-	-ūs	F. iuventūs, *youth*; senectūs, *old age*; salūs, *weal, safety*; servitūs, *slavery*; virtūs, *virtue, valour.* Servitūs admits Gen. Pl. servitutium.
ŭt-	-us	Adj. intercus, *under the skin.*
ct-	-c -x	N. lac, *milk.* See p. 107. M. Astyanax.
nt- rt-	-ns -rs	M. Arruns; Acheruns, Plaut.; Ufens; Mars, Mavors.
ăd-	-ās	M. vās, *personal surety.*
ĕd-	-ēs	M. pēs, *foot.* F. Its compound (compĕs), *fetter,* is Fem. (with reference to catena). C. quadrupēs (also N.). Adj. bipēs, tripēs, alipēs.
ēd-	-ēs	F. mercēs, *hire, pay.* C. herēs, *heir.* Adj. exherēs, *disinherited.*
aed-	-aes	M. praes, *bondsman* (in money).
ĭd-	-ĕs	C. obsĕs, *hostage*; praesĕs, *president.* Adj. desĕs, *lazy*; resĕs, *reposing.*

H

Stem.	Nom. S.	
Ĭd-	-Ĭs	M. lapĭs, *stone*. F. cassĭs, *helmet*; cuspĭs, *point*; promulsĭs, *antepast*. Adj. tricuspĭs. (On Greek words in **ĭs, ĭd-**, see below.)
ōd-	-ōs	C. custōs, *guardian*.
ŭd-	-ŭs	F. pecus, *head of cattle, beast*.
ūd-	-ūs	F. incūs, *anvil*; palūs, *marsh, pool* (Livy has Gen. Pl. palūdium).
aud- rd-	-aus	F. fraus, *deceit*; laus, *praise*.
rd-	-r	N. cor, *heart*. Adj. compounds concors, discors, excors, misericors, socors, vecors, are I-nouns. *Note.* C. vat-es, *seer*, has the form of an I-noun; but its root is vat-, Gen. Pl. vat-um.

2) Greek Dental Stems.

ăt-	-ă	N. aenigmă, *riddle*; emblemă, *mosaic*; epigrammă, *epigram*; poemă, *poem*; toreumă, *embossed-work*, &c. Such words are irregularly declined in the Plural: having G. Pl. -t-orum or -t-um, D. Abl. -t-is (sometimes -t-ĭbus), as G. Pl. emblemat-orum, D. Pl. emblemat-is. Martial has the Greek Gen Pl. epigrammatōn.
Ĭt-	-Ĭs	F. Charĭs, *a Grace*.
ēth-	-ēs	M. Parnēs, (a mountain).
ant-	-ās	M. adamas, *adamant*; elephas, *elephant*. The Names Atlās, Calchās, Pallās (son of Mezentius in the Aeneid), &c. have Voc. ā; Atlā, Calchā, Pallā. Corybās, Corybantĕs (Pl.), (the priests of Cybele).—Acc. S. -antem or -antă. Acc. Pl. -antēs or -antăs.
ent-	-īs	M. Simoīs, (river of Troy in the Iliad).
ont-	-ōn -ō }	M. chamaeleon; Anacreon, Charon, Creon, Phaethon, Xenophon. Attempts were made (Plaut. Ter. Cic.) to latinize this form by writing **o** for **on**; Xenopho, Creo, Antipho, Ctesipho, Demipho. Terence inflects the three last in **ōnĭ-**.
unt-	-ūs	Names of towns: F. Opūs, Trapezūs, &c. M. Pessinūs. C. Selinūs. Sometimes latinized into 2. n. **-untum, -ontum**: Hydruntum (Hydrūs), Liv., Sipontum (Sipūs), Cic.
nth-	-ns	F. Tīryns.
ăd-	-ăs	F. lampăs, *torch* (Pl. Nom. lampadĕs, Ov.); Pallăs, Dryăs, Maenăs, Naiăs, &c. Acc. S. ă (**em**), Dat. ĭ in poetry. D. Abl. Pl. -ăsĭ, -ăsĭn in poetry, as Troasin, Ov. M. Arcăs, *Arcadian*. Pl. Nom. Arcadĕs, Verg. Acc. Arcadăs, Cic.
Ĭd-	-Ĭs	This form comprises numerous words. Some are Appellatives; F. aegis, amystis, aspis, pyramis, tyrannis, &c. The rest are Names: 1) Local: (*a*) towns: F. Aulis, Chalcis, &c.; (*b*) countries: F. Doris, Locris, Persis, &c. (really Adjectives); (*c*) rivers: M. Phasis, Thybris, &c. 2) Personal: (*a*) F. Patronymic: Brisēĭs, Chry-

Stem.	Nom. S.	
		sēĭs, Colchĭs, Minoĭs, Nerĕĭs, Titanĭs. (*b*) F. Amaryllĭs, Bacchĭs, Chrysĭs, Lycorĭs, Phyllĭs, Semiramĭs, Thaĭs, Thetĭs. Classes (*a*), (*b*) take Acc. S. -**ĭdem** or -*ida* generally: but some also take -*ĭn*, **ĭm**: Alcestĭn, Isĭn, Irim. (*c*) M. Adonis, Alexis, Anubis, Busiris, Daphnis, Osiris, Phalaris, Paris, Thyrsis, Zeuxis. Acc. S. **ĭm** *ĭn*; or **ĭdem** *ĭdă*.
		The Voc. S. of all these stems is in *ĭ*: Colchĭ, Phyllĭ, Alexĭ, Osirĭ.
		Many fluctuate between the Cons. and I-declension: tigris, tigri- or tigrid-; Thybris Thybri- or Thybrid-.
ŏd-	-ūs	M. tripūs (τρίπους), *tripod*; Melampūs; Oedipūs. The last name is variously declined: (1) as an O-noun, Voc. Acc. Oedipĕ, Oedipum. (2) as an A-noun, Oedipod-ēs, Acc. -*ēn*, Abl. -*ē*. (3) as here; Oedip-ūs, Acc. Gen. -ŏdem or ŏdă, -ŏdis.
ўd-	-ўs	F. chlamўs, *mantle*; pēlamўs, *tunny-fish*. M. Iapўs, Pl. Iapўdes (an Illyrian race).

C. Mute Labial Stems.

The Stem takes **s** in Nom. S.

1) Latin Labial Stems (Greek marked *).

Stem.	Nom. S.	
ăp-	-aps	F. (daps), *banquet* (no Nom. S.). M. *Laelaps (name of a dog in Ovid).
ĭp-	-eps	C. adeps (also adips), *fat*; and the compounds from capio; forceps, *tongs*; municeps; particeps; princeps. See p. 76.
ĭp-	-ips	F. (stips), *a small coin, dole.*
ŭp-	-eps	M. auceps, *fowler*; manceps (both from capio).
ŏp-	-ops	F. (ops), *help* (no Nom. S.). *M. Pelops; *Aethiops, *Ethiopian.* Adj. inops, *resourceless*, Abl. S. inopi.

2) Greek Stems.

Stem.	Nom. S.	
ōp-	-ōps	M. hydrops, *dropsy*; Cyclops: (Acc. S. **em**, *a*, Pl. *ăs*).
ўp-	-yps	M. gryps, *griffin.*
ăb-	-abs-aps	M. Arabs (Araps).
ўb-	-ybs	M. Chalybs.

D. Nasal Stems.

There is only one **m**-stem, hiem-p-s; which takes **s** in Nom. S., inserting euphonic **p**, according to the best authorities. **ɴ** takes **s** in one Latin word only, sangui-s for sanguin-s: it remains the Nom. Ending in all Neuter, and many Masc. words: in all Fem. and some Masc. words **n** is dropt, and the Nom. Ending becomes **o**; but in Neuter and some Masc. Nouns ĭn- becomes ĕn.

1) Latin Nasal Stems.

Stem.	Nom. S.	
ĕm-	-m-p-s	F. hiemps, *winter*.
ĭn-	-ĕn	M. flamĕn, *priest* (of some deity); pectĕn, *comb*, and the compounds of cănere, fidĭcen, *lutist*; tibīcen, *flute-player*; līticen, *clarion-player*; tubĭcen, *trumpeter*; oscen, *ominous* (bird).
		N. gluten, *glue*, and numerous Verbal Substantives: agmen, carmen, culmen, nōmen, nūmen, regĭmen, semen, stamen, tegmen, volūmen, &c.
ĭn-	-is	M. sanguĭs, *blood*; (pollis) *mill-dust, powder*. Other forms are sanguĕn, pollĕn: and probably I-stems, sangui- polli-, existed anciently.
ĭn-	-o	M. homo, *human being* (homon- hemon- are old forms): turbo, *whirlwind, top*; Apollo.
		C. nemo, *nobody*.
		F. Many in **-do, -go**: grando, *hail*; harundo, *reed*; hirundo, *swallow*, hirudo, *leech*, testudo, *tortoise*; indago, *net*; origo, *origin*; robigo, *mildew*; virgo, *virgin*; Carthago, &c.: and numerous abstracts: cupīdo, libīdo, fortitudo, magnitudo, vicissitudo, &c.
		Caro, *flesh*; carn- (for carĭn- or caron-), becoming an I-noun, Gen. Pl. carnium.
		M. cardo, *hinge*; ordo, *order*; Cupido, the deity *Cupid*; C. margo, *margin*.
ŏn-	-ō	M. Concretes in **ō ōn-**: agaso, *groom*; baro, *simpleton*; bibo, *toper*; bufo, *toad*; carbo, *coal*; crabro, *hornet*; epulo, *banquetter*; latro, *robber*; leo, *lion*; ligo, *spade*; mucro, *point* (of dagger); upilio or opilio, *shepherd*; pāpilio, *butterfly*; praedo, *pirate*; pugio, *poniard*; sermo, *discourse*; stelio, *lizard*; tiro, *recruit*; vespertilio, *bat*; also unio, *pearl*; ternio, *tré*, senio, *sice*, &c., in dice-play: Names; Capito, Cicero, Naso, Pollio, &c., but F. Iuno.
		F. Abstracts in **io ion**: (*a*) from Adjectives: communio, perduellio, *treason*, rebellio; (*b*) from Pres. Stem. of Verbs: lĕgio, rĕgio, &c.; (*c*) from Supine Stem, a very large class: actio, dictio, lectio, positio, &c. Some take concrete meaning: natio, *a nation*; oratio, *a speech*, &c.
		Note. C. Can-is, *dog*, iuven-is, *young person*, are really Nasal Stems (Pr. *kvan, yuvan*): but take i in Nom. S. Their Gen. Pl. is in **-um**.

2) Greek Nasal Stems.

Stem.	Nom. S.	
ān-	-ān	M. Acarnān, *Acarnanian*; Pān; Paeān (name of Apollo: hymn to Apollo); Titān.
ēn-	-ēn	M. rēn-es, Pl. *kidneys, reins, loins* (Gen. Pl. **um**, or **ium**); splēn, *spleen, milt* (for which liēn is a Latin form): attagēn (a bird). The river Aniō is inflected Aniēn- from a byform Aniēn.
		F. Sirēn.

Stem.	Nom. S.	
ĕn-	-ēn	M. Hymēn ; Philopoemēn.
īn-	-īn -īs	M. delphīn, *dolphin* (also delphin-us, 2.)
		F. Eleusīs, Salamīs.
ōn-	-ōn	M. Solōn, Telamōn, Tritōn, &c. Cithaerōn, Helicōn. Names of men were generally latinised by taking Nom. S. **o** : Hiero, Milo, Plato, Zeno, &c. But Alcōn, Cimōn, &c. keep **n**.
		F. Babylōn ; Calȳdōn ; Marathōn, &c.
ŏn-	-ōn	M. Ariōn ; Amphiōn ; Iasōn ; Ixiōn ; Memnōn, &c.
		F. Amazōn ; Gorgōn ; sindōn, *fine linen*.
		Rarely latinised with Nom. S. in **o** : M. Macedo, *Macedonian*.
		Note. Greek Nasal Nouns have Acc. S. *ă* or **em** (Pan always Pană) ; Pl. *ăs* generally.

E. Liquid and Sibilant Stems.

L and **r** proper do not take **s** in Nom. S. : as consul, aequor. Sibilant Stems are numerous, many of them retaining their **s** in Nom. S. and changing it to **r** in the inflected cases : Venus, Venĕris ; flos, flōris, &c. Others change **s** to **r** in the Nom. S. also : lar, lăris ; meliŏr, meliōris. Vowel-change often occurs in Nom. S. : ĕbŭr for ĕbŏr.

1) Latin Stems (Greek *).

Stem.	Nom. S.	
ăl-	-al	M. sal, *salt* (rarely N.) ; Hannibăl, Hiempsăl, &c.
ĭl-	-ĭl	M. pugĭl, *boxer* ; vigĭl, *watchman* ; mugĭl (also mugili-s), *mullet.*
		Adj. vigĭl, *wakeful*, Abl. S. ī.
ōl-	-ōl	M. sōl, *the sun.*
ŭl-	-ŭl	M. consul ; praesul, *president* ; C. exul, *banished one.*
ell-	-ĕl	N. fel, *gall* ; mel, *honey*, &c.
ăr-	-ăr	M. Caesar ; lar, *household-god* (anc. Pl. Lases).
		N. par, *pair* ; baccar (a plant) ; iubar, *sun-beam* ; instar, *likeness* (only Nom. Acc. S.) : *nectar, *nectar*. (Adj. pār, with compounds, is an I-stem.)
arr-	-ār	N. far, *flour.*
ĕr-	-ĕr	M. acipens-er or acipensis, *sturgeon* ; agger, *mound* ; anser, *goose* ; asser, *pole* ; carcer, *prison* (Pl. *starting place*) ; later, *brick* ; passer, *sparrow* ; with the Plurals Celeres, *the knightly body-guards* ; proceres, *nobles* ; see p. 127.
		F. mulier, *woman.* C. tuber (a fruit tree).
		N. ăcer, *maple* ; cadāver, *carcase* ; cĭcer, *chickpea* ; papāver, *poppy* ; pĭper, *pepper* ; sĭler, *withy* ; sĭser, *skirret* ; sūber, *cork* ; tūber, *a hump, a truffle* ; ūber, *a teat* ; also ĭter or (itĭner), *journey*, Gen. itineris ; Pl. iugera, *acres* ; (verber), *stripe*, Abl. S. verbĕre, with full Pl.

Stem.	Nom. S.	
		The M. form vesper-ĕ, i, seems to be of this Decl., but its other cases (vesper, &c.) are of the 2nd. Plautus uses vesperi (and luci, temperi, mani) with Prep.: 'de vesperi suo,' &c. And Corssen does not consider them to be Locative but true Abl. Cases. Virgil has vespere Abl.: 'vespere ab atro,' Aen. v. 19.
		Adj. degener, *degenerate* ; pauper, *poor.*
ĕr-	-ēr	N. ver, *spring.*
ŏr-	-ŏr	N. aequor, *level surface, sea* ; marmor, *marble, sea* ; ador, *spelt* (whence F. adōrea, i.e. donatio, a dole of spelt given to victorious soldiers : hence '*victory*,' '*glory*'), has only Nom. Acc. S.
		M. Archaic words, as Marcipor (Marci puer), *slave of Marcus* : Lucipor, *slave of Lucius*, &c.
ōr-	-ŏr (anc. -ōr)	M. olŏr, *swan* : with a large number of Verbal Substantives, some formed from root or Pres. stem : amor, *love* ; ardor, *heat* ; calor, *warmth* ; dolor, *grief, pain*, &c. ; others, very numerous, from Supine stem : cultor, *tiller, worshipper* ; domitor, *tamer* ; victor, *conqueror*, &c.
		F. soror, *sister* ; uxor, *wife.*
		Adj. Acc. S. primōrem, Pl. primōres, *chief persons.*
ŏr-	-ŭr	ĕbŭr, *ivory* ; fĕmŭr, *thigh* ; iĕcŭr, *liver* (also iecinŏr- iocinŏr- iociněr-) ; rōbŭr, *hard wood, oak* (old form probably robus, whence robustus).
ŭr-	-ŭr	M. furfŭr, *bran* ; (lemŭr) *goblin* (chiefly Plur.) ; vultŭr, *vulture* ; turtŭr, *turtle-dove* ; *Ligŭr or Ligŭs, *Ligurian* ; C. augŭr.
		N. guttŭr, *throat* ; fulgŭr, *lightning* ; murmŭr ; sulfŭr, *sulphur.*—Adj. cicŭr, *tame.*
ūr-	-ūr	M. fūr, *thief.*
ās-	-ās	N. vas, *vessel* (Pl. vasa, vasorum, vasis) ; fas, *(divine) right* ; nefas, *wrong, impiety* : (both words have only Nom. Acc. S. ; but V. uses fandi, nefandi, as their Gen.).
ær-	-æs	N. æs, *copper, brass, bronze.*
ĕr-	-ēs	F. Cēres (goddess of corn).
		Adj. pubēs (pubĕris), *of ripe age* : impubēs (impubĕris), *under age.* See p. 115.
ĕr-	-ĭs	M. cucumĭs, *cucumber* (also cucumĭ-) ; vomĭs (vomĕr), *ploughshare* : acipensĭs.
		C. cinĭs, *ash, cinder* ; pulvĭs, *dust.*
ĕr-	-ŭs	F. Venus.
		N. foedus, *treaty* ; funus, *funeral* ; genus, *race, kind* ; glomus, *ball* (of thread, &c.) ; holus (olus), *green stuff* ; lătus, *side* ; munus, *gift, office* (Nom. Acc. Pl. munera or munia) : onus, *burden* ; pondus, *weight* ; raudus (rūdus), *bit* (of brass, &c.) ; scelus, *crime, wickedness* ; sidus, *constellation* ; vellus, *fleece* ; (viscus, rarely Sing.), *bowel* ; ulcus, *sore* ; vulnus, *wound.* Sěcus, *sex* (only Nom. Acc. S.). This **us** is for anc. **os.**

Stem.	Nom. S.	
ŏr-	-ŭs	M. lepus, *hare.*
		N. corpus, *body* ; dĕcus, *grace,* dedecus, *disgrace* ; facinus, *deed, crime* ; fēnus, *usury, interest* (also ĕr-) ; frīgus, *cold* ; lītus, *shore* ; nĕmus, *forest, grove* ; pectus, *breast* ; pignus, *pledge* (also ĕr-) ; stercus, *dung* ; tempus, *time* ; *temple* (of head) ; tergus (also tergum 2.), *back.* This **us** was anc. **os**.
ŏr-	-ōs -ŏr	F. arbōs or arbŏr, *tree.*
ōr-	-ōs -ŏr (anc. ōr)	M. colōs, usually colŏr, *colour, complexion* ; honōs or honŏr, *honour, office* ; lăbōs or lăbŏr, *toil* ; lepōs or lepŏr, *wit, good humour.* So odŏr, *scent* ; pavŏr, *alarm* ; rumŏr, *report* (rarely odōs, &c.). See p. 102.
ōr-	-ōs	M. flōs, *flower* ; mōs, *custom* ; rōs, *dew.*
		N. ōs, *mouth, face.* On comparatives meliŏr, meliŭs (anc. meliōs), see pp. 21, 42.
ūr-	-ūs	F. tellūs, *land, earth.*
		N. crūs, *leg* ; iūs, *right* ; iūs, *gravy, broth* ; pūs, *foul matter* ; rūs, *country* ; tūs, *frankincense.*
tr-	-tĕr	M. pater, *father* ; frater, *brother* ; accipiter, *hawk.*
		F. mater, *mother.*

2) Greek R-Stems.

ĕr-	-ēr	M. aēr, *atmosphere* (Acc. S. aĕră or aĕrem) : aethēr, *sky* (Acc. S. aethĕră).
ēr-	-ēr	M. cratēr, *mixing-bowl.* (Acc. S. ă, Pl. ăs.)
ŏr-	-ŏr	M. rhetŏr, Castŏr, Hectŏr, Nestŏr, &c. (Acc. S. ă or **em**, Pl. ăs). This ŏr is latinized from Gr. ωρ.

F. **u**- and **v**-Stems.

ŭ-	-ūs	C. grūs, *crane* ; sūs, *swine* (Dat. Abl. Pl. sūbus or suibus).
ŏv-		M. Iuppiter Iŏv-, *Iupiter.*
		C. bōs bŏv-, *ox* or *cow* (Gen. Pl. boum ; Dat. Abl. bōbus or būbus).

G. Greek **E**- **O**- and **Y**-Stems.

ĕ-	-ŏs	N. epos, *epic poem* ; melos, *lyric* (Gen. S. -eos, Nom. Acc. Pl. melē, contracted from melĕa). So cetē, *whales* ; pelagē, *seas* ; Tempē, (a vale in Thessaly). Chaŏs belongs here : but Virgil has Abl. Chao, 2.
ō-	-ōs	M. herōs herō-, *hero* (Acc. S. herŏă, Nom. Pl. herōĕs, Acc. herōăs).
ŏ-	-ō	F. echō (Gen. echūs for echŏ-ōs ; the other cases in ō ; so Io, Ino. Dido, Sappho, also form ōn-).
y̆-	-y̆s	M. Coty̆s Coty̆- ; Phorcy̆s Phorcy̆- ; Tiphy̆s Tiphy̆- ; F. Eriny̆s Eriny̆-, Acc. S. -ă. Pl. -ăs.

(A few Adjective and other I-stems are included in the foregoing tables, on account of their connexion with other words.)

iv. I-stems.

Nouns of the Third Declension are either (1) Imparisyllaba (unequal in the number of their syllables), having more syllables in the Gen. Sing. than in the Nom. : or (2) Parisyllaba, having the same number of syllables in those Cases.

Of Imparisyllabic Substantives, the greater number are Cons:nant Nouns : but many are Clipt I-nouns : especially those which have a Labial, Nasal, or Liquid before s in the Nom. Sing. as urbs, bidens, cohors, pars. Of Parisyllabic Substantives, all are I-nouns but a very few, already cited : canis, iuvenis, senex, vates : pater, mater, frater, accipiter, &c.

Adjectives of both kinds in this Decl. are I-nouns except a few.[1]

v. Grouping of I-nouns.

I-nouns come under four chief Heads :

A) Parisyllabic I-nouns, with Nom. Sing. ĭ-s (a few ĕr for -rĭ-) : Fem. Masc. or Common.

B) Parisyllabic I-nouns in ē-s (ĭ-s) perhaps from original sibilant-stems : chiefly Fem.

C) Neuter I-nouns of Adjectival nature, Parisyll. in ĕ, Imparisyll. in äl, är.

D) Clipt I-nouns Imparisyllabic : Fem. Masc. or Common.

A) I-nouns under the first Head are grouped according as they form the Accus. Sing. in im or em, and the Abl. Sing. in ī or ĕ.

1. Acc. S. im : Abl. ī.

1) F. *cannabĭs, *hemp* (Abl. ĕ in Persius); tussĭs, *cough*; sitĭs, *thirst* (S. only); burĭs, *ploughtail* (only Acc. S.); ravĭs, *hoarseness* (only Acc. S.); * tigrĭs, *tiger* (also as a Consonant Noun, tigrĭd-).

Names of Towns : Hispalĭs, *Seville*; Neapolĭs, *Naples*; Amphipolĭs; Memphĭs.

Vīs, *force* (an S-stem), Acc. S. vim, Abl. vi, casting out s (Gen. Dat. wanting); Pl. vīres, &c., changing s into r.

*Greek I-nouns: poesĭs, *poetry*; mathesĭs, *science*; Charybdĭs: Voc. S. ĭ, Acc. ĭn or im ; poesĭ, poes-ĭn (im).

The Greek Gen. in *eŏs* is rare: poeseŏs : and Gen. Pl. *eōn* : metamorphoseōn.

---

[1] Many Latin I-nouns correspond to Pr. I-nouns: anguis, ignis, ovis, ars, dos, gens, mens, and others. In some ĭ represents Pr. a : axis, foris, imbris, nubes panis, pellis, penis, unguis. In others ĭ is a Latin suffix to a Pr. root : can-i-s iuven-i-s, Iov-i-s, vat-i-s; mitis, turpis, brevis, gravis, lĕvis, pinguis, suavis, tenuis. In mensis (Gr. μήν), sĭ is suffixal. In a few, as arx, daps, there is a Pr. root with Nom. suffix s. In some of these forms ĭ, not belonging to the original Nom., has been developed in the other Cases ; but in most of the Imparisyllabic I-nouns it has been dropt in Nom. Very many Latin I-nouns, especially the great bulk of Adjectives, have been formed in accordance with prevalent analogies.

Observe the adverbial phrases ad amussim, examussim, *by rule, accurately*; ad fatim, affătim, *abundantly*; from disused nouns amussis, fatis. Hence it is probable that adverbs in **tim, sim**, partim, sensim, &c., are similarly cases of lost I-nouns.

2) M.: cucumis, *cucumber* (also inflected as a Cons.-noun cucumer-, like Ceres, pulvis, cinis).

Names of Rivers: Albis, *the Elbe*; Tiberis, *Tiber*; Liris, Phasis, &c.

2. Acc. S. im or **em. Abl. ī** or **ě.**

This group is wholly Feminine :

F. puppis, *poop*; febris, *fever*; turris, *tower* : **im** (**em**); **ě, ī.**

securis, *hatchet*; **im** (**em**); ī	restis, *rope*; **im** (**em**); ě
messis, *harvest*; **em** (**im**); ě	clavis, *key*; **em** (**im**); ī ě
sementis, *seed-time*; **em** (**im**);	navis, *ship*; **im, em**; ī, ě
ī, ě	pelvis, *pan*; **im, em**; ě ī

3. Acc. S. em; **Abl. ě** or **ī.**

M. axis, *axle*; ě (ī)   ignis, *fire*; ī, ě
fustis, *cudgel*; ě, ī   unguis, *claw*; ě (ī)

F. bilis, *bile*; classis, *fleet*; avis, *bird*; ě (ī)
strigilis, *scraper*; ī (ě)

Supellectilis (res), *furniture*, properly an Adj., is clipt in Nom. S. into supellex. In Abl. S. it has ī or ě.

C. amnis, *river*; ě (ī)   civis, *citizen*; ī (ě)
finis, *end*; ě (ī)   anguis, *snake*; ě (ī)

Finis, originally Fem., is so used only in the Sing., and rarely.

a) M. imber imbrĭ- m. *shower*, Abl. ī, ě.

The Month-names September, October, November, December; Abl. ī : are used adjectively.

b) Many Adjectives have Substantival use :

M. aedilis, *edile*, ě (ī); aequalis, *contemporary*, ī; annalis, ī (chiefly Plur. *annals*); aqualis, *water-can*, ī; natalis, *birthday*, ī (ě); rivalis, *rival*, ě (ī); familiaris, *intimate friend*, ī (ě); molaris, *grinder*, ī (chiefly Plur.).

F. bipennis, *double axe*, ě ī; novalis, *fallowed field*, ě ī; triremis, *trireme*, ī ě; volucris, *bird*, ě.

C. affinis, *kinsperson*, ě ī; iuvenis, *young person*, ě; contubernalis, *tentmate*, ě ī; patruelis, *cousin on father's side*, ě, ī; sodalis, *companion*, ī ě; canalis, *canal, channel*, ī.

c) Any such Adjectives, if they become Proper Names, have Abl. Sing. in ě: Iuvenale, Latiare, Maluginense, Martiale.

d) In this group must be ranked the Masc. and Fem. forms of Adjectives in ĭs, ĭs, ĕ, and in ĕr, ĭs, ĕ : as tristĭs, ĭs, ĕ ; acĕr, acrĭs, acrĕ. But the Neuter forms tristĕ, acrĕ, belong to Head *C*). All have Abl. S. ī, very rarely ĕ.

4. Acc. **em** : Abl. ĕ.

M. orbis, *circle, world* ; fascis, *bundle* ; piscis, *fish* ; caulis, *stalk* ; collis, *hill* ; follis, *bellows* ; vermis, *worm* ; clunis, *hind-leg* ; crinis, *hair* ; panis, *loaf* ; torris, *brand* ; ensis, *sword* ; mensis, *month* ; postis, *door-post* ; vectis, *lever* ; uter, *leathern bottle* ; venter, *belly* ; with the Plural words casses, *nets* ; antes, *front vine-rows* ; manes.

F. scobis (or scobs), *saw-dust* ; rudis, *foil* ; sudis (no Nom. S.), *stake* ; trudis, *pike* ; ninguis, *snow* (Lucr.) ; con-vallis, *hollow vale* ; pellis, *hide* ; Alpis, *Alp* ; apis, *bee* ; auris, *ear* ; irauris, *earring* ; naris, *nostril* ; cutis, *cuticle* ; neptis, *granddaughter* ; pestis, *plague* ; ratis, *raft* ; vestis, *garment* ; vitis, *vine* ; ovis, *ewe* : with the Plur. words fores, *door* ; grates, *thanks* ; nates ; fides, *lutestrings* (has Abl. S. fidĕ).

C. corbis, *basket* ; callis, *path* ; funis, *rope, cable* ; torquis (es), *collar* ; hostis, *enemy* ; pedis, *crawler* ; scrobis (or scrobs), *ditch* ; testis, *witness* ; linter or lunter, *boat* ; also sentis, *thorn* ; vepris, *bramble*.[1]

B) Nom. S. **es**, Acc. **em**, Abl. ĕ.

All Latin words of this form are F. except M. verres, *boar-pig*.

F. aedes, *temple* (Pl. *house*) ; caedes, *lopping, bloodshed* ; cautes, *rock* ; clades, *defeat* ; compages, *structure* ; fames, *hunger* (Abl. ē) ; feles, *cat* ; indoles, *native disposition* ; labes, *fall, mischief* ; lues, *pest* ; meles, *badger* ; moles, *pile* ; nubes, *cloud* ; palumbes, *pigeon* ; plebes, *the com-mons* (also plebs : see *Decl.* 5) ; proles, *offspring* (Gen. Pl. **um**) ; pubes, *young population* ; rupes, *crag* ; saepes, *hedge* ; sedes, *seat* ; soboles or suboles, *offspring* ; sordes, *dirt* (Pl. *meanness*) ; strages, *slaughter* ; strues, *heap* ; tabes, *taint, consumption* (no Pl.) ; valles, *vale* ; vulpes, *fox* ; and the Plural words lactes, *small entrails* ; ambages, *evasive language or conduct* (has Abl. S. ĕ, Gen. Pl. **um**).

Several of these have a byform in **is** : aedis, caedis, felis, melis, vallis, vulpis, and some more.

The older words are supposed to be S-stems converted into I-stems by exclusion of staminal **s** (as puber-is pubes).

C) Neuter Nouns : Nom. S. ĕ (for ĭ-) ; ăl (for ālĭ-) ; ăr (for ārĭ-). Abl. ī. Neut. Pl. ĭă.

---

[1] Ísolated variations of Case occur in some. See M. Lucr. i. 978. IIII. Varro says that o vi as well as o ve was used in his time. Neptī is found in Tac.

1.) N. măre, *sea* ; rēte, *net* ; aplustre, *flag* ; conclave, *apartment* ; insigne, *ensign* ; praesepe, *stall, crib* ; ancīle, *small shield* ; bubīle, *ox-stall* ; caprīle, *goat-house* ; cubīle, *bedchamber, couch* ; equīle, *stable* ; hastīle, *spear* ; mantīle, *napkin* ; monīle, *necklace* ; ovīle, *sheepfold* ; focāle, *neckwrapper* ; novāle, *fallow* ; penetrāle, *inner shrine* ; cochleāre, *spoon* ; altaria (Pl.), *high altar* ; talaria (Pl.), *ankle-rings*. Also caepe, *onion* (takes Plur. from byform caepa, f. 1).

Lac, *milk*, is for lac-te, līke rete.

Retis c. is a rare form for rete ; praesēpis, f. for praesēpe. Some local names ending in tĕ take Abl. ĕ usually : Bibracte, Reate, Soracte.

Abl. marĕ for marī is in Lucr. Ov. Abl. retĕ is frequent.

2) N. animăl ; cervicăl, *bolster* ; minutăl, *minced meat* ; torăl, *sofa-cover* ; tribunăl ; vectigăl, *toll, revenue*. See Baccanăl, bidentăl, capităl, Lupercăl, Minervăl, puteăl in Dictionary.

3) N. calcăr, *spur* ; exemplăr, *pattern* ; lacūnăr, laqueăr, *ceiling* ; lupānăr ; pulvīnăr, *cushioned seat* ; torculăr, *wine-press*.

Observe par, pări-, *pair*.

Note. Almost all words in *C*) except mare, rete, are evidently Neuter Adjectives, derived from Substantives. Those in 2) 3) have dropt ĕ : toral for torale, exemplar for exemplare. This makes it probable that mare, rete are likewise adjectival.

D) Clipt I-nouns : Gen. Pl. **i-un.**.

The vagueness of the distinction between Clipt I-nouns and Cons.-nouns has been noticed already, see p. 94. One test of an I-noun, **ı** before **um** in Gen. Plur., may fail, if an I-noun loses **ı** (as in apum, volucrum), if a Cons.-noun takes **ı** (as in civitatium, paludium), or if no Gen. Plur. is found, as in many words, chiefly monosyllabic in Nom. Another test, **īs** (= **ēs, eis**) in Acc. Pl. m. f. or **ıa** n., may not occur in MSS. or Inscrr. The safest course, therefore, is to rank Imparisyllaba with Cons.-nouns (as pax, lux, sol, &c.), where no test of an I-noun is ascertained : unless some strong analogy points to an exception.

Guttural before **ı** :
F. faex faecĭ-, *lees* ; (faux) faucĭ-, *jaw* ; calx calcĭ-, *heel* ; falx falcĭ-, *pruning-hook, scythe* ; lanx lancĭ-, *dish* ; arx arcĭ-, *citadel* ; merx mercĭ-, *merchandise*. Add nix nivĭ-, *snow*.

M. Deunx deuncĭ-, quincunx quincuncĭ-, &c., (parts of **as**).

Labial before **ı** :
F. stirps stirpĭ- (also stirpes and stirpis), rarely M., *trunk* ; trabs (or trab-es) trabĭ-, f. *beam* ; urbs (or urps) urbĭ-, f. *city*.

Nasal before **ı** :
F. caro carnĭ- (for carĭni-), *flesh*. See Cons.-Nouns.

R (for **s**) or **s** before **i** :

M. glis gliri-, *dormouse* ; mus muri-, *mouse* ; and, by probable
analogy, mas mări-, *male* ; as assi-.

F. vis viri-, *force* : see p. 104.

N. os ossi-, *bone* (but Nom. Pl. ossa for oss-ia).

Dental before **i** :

These are the most numerous : many being Adjectival.

a) M. Gentile words in **ās āti-, īs īti-** (clipt from āti-s, ītis) :
Aquinas, *man of Aquinum* ; Arpinas, *man of Arpinum* ;
Quiris, (man of Cures) *Roman* ; Samnis, *Samnite*, &c. ;
(optimas, primas, summas, used in Plur.) ; Penat-es (Plur.),
household gods.

Adj. nostras, *of our country* ; vestras, *of your country* ;
cŭias, *of what country.*

b) F. lis liti-, *strife.*

c) Nouns in **ans anti-, ens enti-**, mostly participial.

M. amans, *lover* ; dextans, dodrans, quadrans, sextans, triens
(parts of as) ; cliens, *client* ; dens, *tooth*, and compounds,
(but F. bidens, *sheep*) ; oriens (sol), *east* ; occidens (sol),
west ; rudens, *cable* ; torrens, *torrent.*

F. gens, *clan, nation* ; lens, *lentil* ; mens, *mind, intellect.*

C. animans ; infans ; parens ; serpens.　See p. 76.

All words in *a*) *c*) not being monosyllabic in Nom. S., can drop **i**
in Gen. Pl. ; as optimatum for optimatium, infantum for in-
fantium, parentum for parentium.

d) Nouns in **ons onti-** :

M. fons, *fountain* ; mons, *mountain* ; pons, *bridge.*

F. frons, *forehead* ; (spons), *free choice* (only Abl. sponte).

e) Nouns in **ls lti-, rs rti-, cs (x) cti-** : Fem.

F. puls, *pulse* ; ars, *art* ; pars, *part* ; cohors, cors, *cohort,
court* ; fors (S.), *chance* ; mors, *death* ; sors, *lot* ; nox,
night.

f) Nouns in **ns ndi-** : Fem.

F. frons, *leaf* ; glans, *acorn* ; iuglans, *walnut.*

Notes
on the
Cases.

vi. Notes on the Cases.

1. Instances occur of a Gen. Pl. in **ium** from Cons. Nouns in
ās āt-, ūs ūt-, ūs ūd- : more rarely from those in **x, ps** : civitatium (always in Livy, sometimes in Cicero), aetatium, simultat-
ium, &c., servitutium, virtut-ium, palud-ium, fornac-ium,
forcip-ium.　Alituum for alit-um in Virgil is a bold license
for the sake of metre.[1]

---

[1] Old poets often dropt, metrically, the s of Gen. S. : as
　　　Quid dubitas quin omni' sit haec rationi' potestas?—Lucr. ii. 53.
On the dropping of final m in Acc. S. anciently, see pp. 28, 46.

No Gen. Plur. is found of the following words : bes (bessis), cor, cos, fel, fors, glos, lac, lux, mel, nex, os (ōr-), pax, pix, praes, pus, ros, rus, sal, sol, tus, vas (vadis), ver, (vix). Canis, iuvenis, strues, vates, have Gen. Pl. **um**: also panis, in the opinion of some grammarians : apis, volucris have Gen. Pl. **um**, sometimes **ium**. Sedum occurs from sedes ; mensum (rarely mensuum) from mensis ;[1] but also **ium**.

Some Plural words in **ālia, īlia, āria**, especially names of festivals, follow Decl. 2. in their Gen. Plur. : as Compitali-orum ; vectigali-orum, Suet. ; ancili-orum, Hor. ; lacunari-orum, Vitr.

Vās vās- forms its Plural as Decl. 2. vasa, vasorum, vasis.

2. The Accus. Plur. in **īs** (= **es, eis**) is proper to I-nouns, as civīs, parentīs, and is found side by side with **ēs, eis** till the Aug. age, after which **ēs** prevailed. So trīs or tres.

A Nom. Pl. in **īs** or **eis** occurs sometimes in the MSS. of Plautus and Lucretius ; aedīs, aurīs, familiarīs, &c. ; and in old Inscrr.

A Gen. S. in **us** and es is archaic only, as (*patrus, Apolones*).

3. The Dat. Sing. had an old form in **ē**, retained in some classical phrases : ' triumviri auro argento aere flando feriundo.' See Cic *Fam.* vii. 13. ' Iure Romae dicundo,' L. xlii. 28. Virgil has orĕ for ori, *G.* i. 430. Another old form is **ei**. So urbei, uxorei, &c. On the tomb of Scipio Barbatus is ' forma virtutei parisuma.'

4. On the Locative case in **ī**, see § **20**. Instances are luci, ruri, temperi, Carthagini, Tiburi (also Tiburĕ, Abl.), Pl. Gadibus.

5. Forms of clipt I-nouns with Abl. S. **ī** are found ; sorti frequently (Nom. sortis, Plaut.) ; parti, Plaut. Ter. : some even of Cons.-nouns, capiti (Catull. Tib.), occipiti (Pers.) ; and others.[2]

---

[1] It is notable that of Nouns which have Gen. S. of the form $\smile \smile$ (dŭcĭs) the great majority take **um** in Gen. Pl. : fācum, dŭcum, crŭcum, nŭcum, prĕcum, grĕgum, pĕdum, ăpum, ŏpum, cănum, sĕnum, pătrum, Lărum, bŏum, gruum, suum, struum. But of those which have Gen. S. of the form $\angle \smile$, the great majority take **ium** in the Gen. Pl. : falcium, litium, artium, &c. : exceptions are vōcum, lēgum, rēgum, and a few others. So Gen. S. $\angle \smile \smile$ or $\smile \smile \smile$ gives Gen. Pl. in **um** : supplĭcum, princĭpum, vigĭlum. (Compēs) compedium is an exception. But a trisyllabic or plurisyllabic Gen. S. with long penult. gives in most Adjectives Gen. Pl. in **ium** : ferac-ium, felic-ium, &c. ; and in Substantives often leads to the fluctuation noticed above, (1 *a*). Comparatives are an exception, because io-r-ium would be a bad combination. The same is true of io-n-ium. Hence mel-io-rum, act-io-num, &c.

[2] Gender is shewn in the lists. The general results are (not including those settled by meaning):

F. Mute Latin Cons. stems, and clipt I-stems with mute before **ī**.
    N-stems in do ; go ; io (abstr.) ; with caro. Also merges ; hiemps ; tellūs ; arbŏr. Parisyll. I-nouns in īs, ēs ; pp. 105, 106. See Exceptions below and in lists.

M. Most in ex, ĭc- ; ĕs ĭt- ; ns ; all in unx ; Concreta in ō : Nouns in l ; ĕr ĕr- ; īs ĕr- ; īs īri- ; ter tri- ; ŏr ōr- ; ōs ōr- ; ūr : Greek Appellatives, except those in ăs, ĭs, ўs (F.) : ă, ŏs, ĕ (N.). Also calix, fornix, grex, paries, pēs, lapĭs, sanguĭs, turbo, cardo, ordo, pecten, furfŭr, turtŭr, vultŭr, lepŭs, mūs, ās : with the parisyll. I-nouns marked M. in pp. 105, 106.

N. Nouns in ĕn ĭn- ; ĕ ; ăr ; ăl āli- ; ŏr ŏr- ; ŭr ōr- ; ŭr ŭr- ; ŭs ĕr- ; ŭs ŏr- ; ŭs ūr-. Alsǫ halec, caput, lac, cŏr, mel, fel, vēr, itĕr, cadavĕr, ubĕr, verbĕr, papavĕr, acĕr, cicĕr, pipĕr, &c. (see p. 101), aes, far, ōs (ōris), ŏs (ossis), vās (vāsis).

C. These will be found in the lists : and many on p. 76.

vii. Table:

I. CONSONANT-NOUNS.

1. MASCULINE AND FEMININE.

1) MUTE GUTTURAL STEMS.

SINGULAR.

	judge, c.	*root*, f.	*voice*, f.	*king*, m.	
N.V.	iudex	radix	vox	rex	— [1]
Acc.	iudĭc-	radīc-	vōc-	rēg-	**em**
Gen.	iudic-	radic-	voc-	reg-	**ĭs**
Dat.	iudic-	radic-	voc-	reg-	**ī**
Abl.	iudic-	radic-	voc-	reg-	**ĕ**

PLURAL.

N.V.A.	iudic-	radic-	voc-	reg-	**ēs**
Gen.	iudiC-	radiC-	voC-	reG-	**um**
D.Abl.	iudic-	radic-	voc-	reg-	**ĭbus**

2) MUTE DENTAL STEMS.

SINGULAR.

	summer, f.	*companion*, c.	*virtue*, f.	*foot*, m.	
N.V.	aestas	comĕs	virtūs	pēs	—
Acc.	aestāt-	comĭt-	virtūt-	pĕd-	**em**
Gen.	aestat-	comit-	virtut-	ped-	**ĭs**
Dat.	aestat-	comit-	virtut-	ped-	**ī**
Abl.	aestat-	comit-	virtut-	ped-	**ĕ**

PLURAL.

N.V.A.	aestat-	comit-	virtut-	ped-	**ēs**
Gen.	aestaT-	comiT-	virtuT-	peD-	**um**
D.Abl.	aestat-	comit-	virtut-	ped-	**ĭbus**

3) LABIAL-MUTE, NASAL, AND ʊ-STEMS.

SINGULAR.

	chief, c.	*beam*, f.	*lion*, m.	*virgin*, f.	*crane*, c.	
N.V.	princeps	trabs	leo	virgo	grus	—
Acc.	princĭp-	trăb-	leōn-	virgĭn-	grŭ-	**em**
Gen.	princip-	trab-	leon-	virgin-	gru-	**ĭs**
Dat.	princip-	trab-	leon-	virgin-	gru-	**ī**
Abl.	princip-	trab-	leon-	virgin-	gru-	**ĕ**

PLURAL.

N.V.A.	princip-	trab-	leon-	virgin-	gru-	**ēs**
Gen.	princiP-	traB-	leoN-	virgiN-	grU-	**um**
D.Abl.	princip-	trab-	leon-	virgin-	gru-	**ĭbus**

[1] For Nom. S. Endings, see § 20 and p. 94.

4) LIQUID AND SIBILANT STEMS.

SINGULAR.

	love, m.	*dew,* m.	*woman,* f.	*cinder,* c.	*father,* m.	
N.V.	amŏr	rōs	muliĕr	cinĭs	pater	—
Acc.	amōr-	rōr-	muliĕr-	cinĕr-	patr-	**em**
Gen.	amor-	ror-	mulier-	ciner-	patr-	**ĭs**
Dat.	amor-	ror-	mulier-	ciner-	patr-	**ī**
Abl.	amor-	ror-	mulier-	ciner-	patr-	**ĕ**

PLÙRAL.

N.V.A.	amor-	ror-	mulier-	ciner-	patr-	**ēs**
Gen.	amoR-	roR-	mulieR-	cineR-	patR-	**um**
D.Abl.	amor-	ror-	mulier-	ciner-	patr-	**ĭbus**

2. NEUTER.

SINGULAR.

	head	*name*	*right*	*work*	*body*	
N.V.A.	capŭt	nomĕn	iūs	opŭs	corpŭs	—
Gen.	capĭt-	nomĭn-	iūr-	opĕr-	corpŏr-	**ĭs**
Dat.	capit-	nomin-	iur-	oper-	corpor-	**ī**
Abl.	capit-	nomin-	iur-	oper-	corpor-	**ĕ**

PLURAL.

N.V.A.	capit-	nomin-	iur-	oper-	corpor-	**ă**
Gen.	capiT-	nomiN-	iuR-	opeR-	corpoR-	**um**
D.Abl.	capit-	nomin-	iur-	oper-	corpor-	**ĭbŭs**

II. ɪ-NOUNS.

1. MASCULINE AND FEMININE.

SINGULAR.

	cough, f.	*ship,* f.	*harvest,* f.	*fire,* m.	*shower,* m.
N. V.	tuss-ĭs	nav-ĭs	mess-ĭs	ign-ĭs	imb-ĕr
Acc.	tuss-**im**	nav-**im em**	mess-**em (im)**	ign-em	imbr-em
Gen.	tuss-ĭs	nav-ĭs	mess-ĭs	ign-ĭs	imbr-ĭs
Dat.	tuss-ɪ	nav-ɪ	mess-ɪ	ign-ɪ	imbr-ɪ
Abl.	tuss-ɪ	nav-ɪ e	mess-e	ign-ɪ e	imbr-ɪ (e)

PLURAL.

N. V.	tuss-ēs	nav-ēs	mess-ēs	ign-ēs	imbr-ēs
Acc.	tuss-ēs ɪs	nav-ēs ɪs	mess-ēs ɪs	ign-ēs ɪs	imbr-ēs ɪs
Gen.	tuss-**ɪum**	nav-**ɪum**	mess-**ɪum**	ign-**ɪum**	imbr-**ɪum**
D.Abl.	tuss-ɪbus	nav-ɪbus	mess-ɪbus	ign-ɪbus	imbr-ɪbұs

SINGULAR.

	ewe. f.	cloud, f.	tooth, m.	city, f.	mouse, m.	
N. V.	ovis	nubes	dens	urbs	mus	—
Acc.	ov-	nub-	dent-	urb-	mur-	em
Gen.	ov-	nub-	dent-	urb-	mur-	ĭs
Dat.	ov-	nub-	dent-	urb-	·mur-	ī
Abl.	ov-	nub-	dent-	urb-	mur-	ĕ

PLURAL.

N. V.	ov-	nub-	dent-	urb-	mur-	ēs
Acc.	ov-	nub-	dent-	urb-	mur-	ēs īs
Gen.	ov-	nub-	dent-	urb-	mur-	ĭum
D. Abl.	ov-	nub-	dent-	urb-	mur-	ĭbŭs

The ending of the Accusative Plural of I-nouns fluctuates in MSS. between **īs** and **ēs**, the form **īs** prevailing.

2. NEUTER.

SINGULAR.

	net	sofa-cover	spur	bone
N. V. A.	ret-ĕ	torăl	calcăr	ŏs
Gen.	ret-ĭs	torāl-ĭs	calcār-ĭs	oss-ĭs
Dat.	ret-ī	toral-ī	calcar-ī	oss-ī
Abl.	ret-ī (ĕ)	toral-ī	calcar-ī	oss-e

PLURAL.

N. V. A.	ret-ĭa	toral-ĭa	calcar-ĭa	oss-a
Gen.	ret-ĭum	toral-ĭum	calcar-ĭum	oss-ĭum
D. Abl.	ret-ĭbus	toral-ĭbus	calcar-ĭbus	oss-ĭbus

Greek Nouns.

viii. Greek Nouns in Decl. 3.

Nominative Sing.

The tendency to latinise Greek names is shewn by dropping the *ν* in such words as Plato, Macedo, Antipho, and in Apollo Apollĭn- (Gr. Ἀπολλων-), draco dracon- (Gr. δρακοντ-): but Nepos retains **n** in Cimon, Conon, Dion, Timoleon, &c. : and it is usually kept in local names: Babylon, Lacedaemon. Gr. ωρ becomes ŏr: Hectŏr, rhetŏr; Gr. εις becomes **īs**: Simoïs Simoent- ; Sardīs (Plur.). Other endings are kept.

Vocative Sing.

The Nominatives **ĭs, ўs, ās, eus, ēs** give

Vocatives   **ĭ, ў, ā, eū, ē (ēs)**

Parĭ, Daphnĭ, Thybrĭ, Phyllĭ ; Cotў, Tiphў ; Atlā, Pallā ; Peleu, Theseu ; Chremē (ēs), Periclē (ēs), Hercules.

Accusative Singular (Greek α, ν).

Prose writers, rarely poets, latinise this Case by using the Latin ending **m**: lampadem, tyrannidem, Phrygem, Paridem, Osirim. But the Greek *ă* is used in some words by both: aethera (always), aera (rarely **-em**). Cicero writes Pana, hebdomada: and in poetry names of persons and places in *ă* abound: Agamemnŏnă, Hectŏră, Palladă, Phyllidă, Babylōnă, Salamīnă, &c.; likewise appellatives: heroă, Cyclopă, lampadă, tyrannidă, aegidă, &c.

Names in **is** fluctuate between the formations **im** *ĭn* and **ĭdem** *ĭdă*. Patronymics: Briseis, Nais, Nereis, Aeneis, &c., and many Female names, Amaryllis, Phyllis, &c. have *ĭdă*: but exceptions occur; Alcestin, Mart.; Isin, Ov.; Irim, Verg., &c. On Nouns in **is im** (*ĭn*) see p. 104.

Names in **ēs ētĭ-** (or **ēs, ĭ-**) also fluctuate. From Dares Darēn, Daretă (Verg.), Daretem: Chremes, Chremem (*en*) and Chremētem (*a*); Thales, Thalēn and Thaletem (*a*).

Similarly Gen. Sing. **ētis** and **ĭs**.

Many names in **ēs** have Acc. S. **em** (*ēn*): Socratem (*ēn*); Xerxem (*ēn*): others **em** only: Aristotelem, Cic.

Names in **clēs** have **em** or *ĕa*, rarely *ēn*: Pericles, Periclem or Periclĕa: rarely Periclēn.

Of Names in **eus** see the Decl. below.

See also the Syllabus of Cons. Nouns.

Genitive Singular.

Poets often use Gr. *-ŏs* for **ĭs**: Palladŏs, Thetidŏs, Peleŏs. A Gen. in **i** is taken by many Names in **eus, ēs**.

See Table of Declension.

Dative Singular.

The short *ĭ* is sometimes found in poetry: Daphnidĭ, Palladĭ.

Nominative Plural.

Poets sometimes use the Greek *ĕs*: Arcadĕs, Phrygĕs, Naiadĕs, Erinyĕs (Verg.).

The Neuter Plural words Tempē, cetē, melē, pelagē (*ē* for *ea*) are occasionally found.

Accusative Plural.

Prose writers sometimes have *ăs*: Arcadas, Cyclopas, Cic.; Senonas, &c., Caes.; Macedonas, Liv. Poets often: as heroăs, lampadăs, lyncăs, Naiadăs, Nereidăs, Erinyăs.

Genitive Plural.

Catullus has Chalybōn for Chalybum; Curtius Malieōn for Maliensium; Martial epigrammatōn for epigrammatum: but Cic. has poematorum, transferring the word to Decl. 2.

Dat. Abl. Plural.

The Greek ending *sĭ* (*sĭn*) is very rarely used by poets: Troăsin, Dryăsin, Charĭsin, Lemniăsin, Ov.

Nouns in *mă* are declined in the Plural after Decl. 2: Cic. uses poematīs, aenigmatīs, emblematīs, &c.

I

ix. Greek Table.　(Greek Endings italic.)

I) Consonant Stems.　See Syllabus.

Sing. Nom. V.— ; Acc. **em** (*ă*) ; Gen. **ĭs** (*ŏs*) ; D. **ī** (*ĭ*) ; Abl. **ĕ**.
Plur. Nom. V. *ĕs* ; Acc. *ăs* (**es**) ; Gen. **um** ; D. Abl. **ĭbus** (*sĭ* rare).

Examples :

M. Phryx Phrȳg-, lebēs lebēt-, gigas gigant-, aēr aĕr-, herōs
herō-.　So Atlas Atlant-, but with Voc. S. *ā*.　See p. 98.

F. chlamȳs chlamȳd-, lampăs lampăd-.
C. lynx lync-.
On Neuters in *mă măt-*, as poema, see p. 98.
On Neuter E-stems and Fem. O- and Y-stems, see p. 103.

II) I-stems.　See p. 104.

Sing. Nom. **ĭs** ; Voc. *ĭ* ; Acc. **ĭm** *ĭn* ; Gen. **ĭs** (*eŏs*) ; D. Abl. **ī**.
Plur. Nom. V. **ēs** ; Acc. **īs ēs** ; Gen. **ĭum** (*eōn*) ; D. Abl. **ĭbus**.

Examples :

F. basis, poesis, Charybdis, Nemesis, Lachesis, Syrtis.
M. Anubis, Albis, Athesis.
Acinaces, m. *scimitar*, is declined as nubes : but Names in
ēs are subject to flexional variations.

III) Heteroclite or Fluctuating Declension.

1) Third Decl. mixed with First and Second.

a) Nom. S. **ēs** ; Voc. *ē* ; Acc. **em** (*ēn*) ; Gen. **ĭs**, **ī** ; D. **ī** ; Abl. **ĕ**.
Examples :

M. Aristoteles ; Archimedes ; Demosthenes ; Euripides ; Thucydides ; Xerxes.

Hercules has Voc. **ēs** and Abl. **ĕ** (Hor.).

b) Nom. S. **clēs** ; Voc. **clēs** *clē* ; Acc. **clem** (*clēn*), *cleă* ; Gen.
clĭs, clī ; Dat. **clī** ; Abl. **clē**.
Examples :

M. Callicles, Damocles, Pericles, Sophocles, Themistocles.

c) Nom. S. *eūs* ; Voc. *eū* ; Acc. **eum**, *ĕa* ; Gen. **ĕi**, **ēi**, **ī** (*eŏs*) ; D.
ĕo, **ēŏ**, *ēi* ; Abl. **ĕo**, **ēŏ**.
Examples :

M. Nereus ; Orpheus ; Peleus ; Perseus ; Theseus ; Tydeus.
Acc., *ēa*, *ĕă* occur in poetry : Idomenēa, Orphéa (Verg.).
The Greek Gen. *eŏs* is confined to poets after the Aug. age.
With this Decl. of Perseus compare Perses, p. 87.　Livy
uses the former for the last Macedonian king : Cicero the
latter.

d) The two Masculine names Achilles, Ulixes, have a
peculiar flexion :

Nom. S. **ēs** ; Voc. *ē* ; Acc. **em**, *ēn*, *ĕa* ; Gen. **ĭs**, *ĕŏs*, **ĕi**, **ī** ; D. *ēi*,
ī ; Abl. **ē** **ĕ**, **ī**.

2) Consonant Declension mixed with I-declension :

a) Nom. S. ēs ; Voc. *ē* ; Acc. **em** (*en*), **ētem**, *ēta* ; Gen. **ĭs, ētis** ; D. **ī, ētī** ; Abl. **ē, ētĕ.**

Examples : M. Chremes, Dares, Laches, Thales.

b) Nom. S. **ĭs** ; Voc. *ĭ* ; Acc. **im,** *ĭn* ; **ĭdem,** *ĭdă* ; Gen. **ĭdĭs** (*ĭdŏs*) ; D. **ĭdī** ; Abl. **ĭdĕ.**

Plur. Nom. V. **ēs, ĭdes** ; Acc. **ēs, īs,** *ĭdăs* ; Gen. **ium, ĭdum** ; D. Abl. **ĭbus, ĭdĭbus** (*sĭ* rare).

Examples : tigris ; Paris, &c. See p. 98.

Fem. names, especially Patronymics, follow chiefly the Cons.-forms : but with much variance. See Neue (*Formenlehre,* I. 300, &c.).

x. Adjectives in the Third Declension.

Adjectives in Decl. 3.

1. The Declension of Adjectives is distinguished from that of Substantives only by having Case-endings which represent different Genders. Therefore Consonant Adjectives which have no distinct generic Case-forms are merely declined like corresponding Substantives. They are a very small class, of which the principal are

Cons. Adjectives.

(caeles) caelĭt-	*heavenly*	particeps particĭp-	*sharing*
dives divĭt-	*rich*	princeps princĭp-	*chief*
sospĕs sospĭt-	*safe*	caelebs caelĭb- m.	*unmarried*
superstĕs superstĭt-	*surviving*	paupĕr paupĕr-	*poor*
desĕs desĭd-	*slothful*	pubĭs } pubĕr-	*of age*
resĕs resĭd-	*reposing*	pubēs }	
compos compŏt-	*possessing*	impubĭs } impubĕr-	*not of age*
impos impŏt-	*unpossessing*	impubēs }	

An I-noun im pubis (ĭs, ĕ) is more frequently used.

Sospes is once Neuter in Iuv.: 'Nec umquam depositum tibi sospes erit,' xiii. 177.

Dis (Ter.) contracted from dives, becomes an I-noun, Abl. diti ; Neut. Pl. ditia ; Gen. Pl. ditium.

Table :

SINGULAR.

N. V.	divĕs	paupĕr	—
Acc.	divĭt-	paupĕr-	**em**
Gen.	divit-	pauper-	**is**
Dat.	divit-	pauper-	**ī**
Abl.	divit-	pauper-	**ĕ**

PLURAL.

N. A. V.	divit-	pauper-	**ēs**
Gen.	divit-	pauper-	**um**
D. Abl.	divit-	pauper-	**ĭbus**

I-noun Adjectives. 2. Adjectives and Participles, not purely Consonantal, may be classed in four groups, shewn in the following Table :—

		SINGULAR.					

		Nom. Voc.		Acc.		Gen.	Dat.	Abl.
		M. F.	N.	M. F.	N.			
I.	1.	ĭs	ĕ	em	ĕ	ĭs	ī	ī
	2.	ĕr r-ĭs	r-ĕ	r-em	r-ĕ	r-ĭs	r-ī	r-ī
II.		s(x ns ...)		em	s(x ns ...)	ĭs	ī	ī (ĕ)
III.		ŏr	ŭs	em	ŭs	ĭs	ī	ĕ
IV.		r, l, s ...		em	—	ĭs	ī	ī

		PLURAL.					

	Nom. Voc.		Acc.			Gen.	·Dat. Abl.
	M. F.	N.	M. F.		N.		
I.	ēs	ia	ēs īs		ia	ium	ĭbus
II.	ēs	ia	ēs īs		ia	ium	ĭbus
III.	ēs	ă	ēs īs		ă	um	ĭbus
IV.	ēs	—	ēs īs		—	um	ĭbus

The Ending of Accusative Plural fluctuates between **īs** (for **eis**) and **es**, as in Substantival **ı**-stems. Even Comparatives have both forms, though with Abl. S. **ĕ** : Neut. Pl. **ă.**

I) The first group contains

  1) A large number of Adjectives declined as I-nouns with Nom. **ĭs** *m. f.,* **ĕ** *n.* : dulcis, *sweet* ; pinguis, *fat* ; mitis, *mild* ; tristis, *sad* ; grandis, *great* ; viridis, *green* ; turpis, *base* ; segnis, *lazy* ; sublimis, *lofty* ; agilis, *active* ; nobilis, *noble* ; aequalis, *equal* ; fidelis, *faithful* ; servilis, *slavish* ; vulgaris, *common* ; lĕvis, *light* ; lēvis, *smooth,* &c.

Instances of Ablative in **ĕ** are very rare in this class : 'nobilĕ viro,' Cic. ; ' caelestĕ, bimestrĕ, perennĕ,' Ov.

  2) A small number in **ĕr, -rĭs, -rĕ** : as acĕr, acrĭs, acrĕ, *keen.*

Celer, celĕris, celĕrĕ, *swift,* is the only Adjective of this kind which retains **e** before **r** through all the Cases. Its Gen. Pl. ends in **ium** when it is merely adjectival, but in **um** when it signifies the ancient body-guard at Rome, called C e l e r e s.

The Adjectives which, besides a c e r (acris), cast out **e** before **r** in the Cases, are

cele-ber	-bris	-bre *famous*	eques-ter	-tris	-tre *on horse*
salu-ber	-bris	-bre *healthy*	pedes-ter	-tris	-tre *on foot*
ala-cer	-cris	-cre *brisk*	palus-ter	-tris	-tre *marshy*
volu-cer	-cris	-cre *swift, winged*	pu-ter	-tris	-tre *putrid*
campes-ter	-tris	-tre *of the plain*	terres-ter	-tris	-tre *of land,*
silves-ter	-tris	-tre *woody*			*of earth.*

The forms in **-bris, -cris, -tris,** may be Masc. ; but **-ber, -cer, -ter** are usual in prose. These latter forms were also of Common Gender anciently.

September, October, November, December, are like celeber, but have no Neuter Cases.

The Masc. and Fem. forms of this group are like i g n i s, i m b e r (Abl. ī) ; the Neuter like r e t e.

II) This group comprises many Adjectives :

1) Adjectives in **ax ācĭ-; ox ōcĭ-; ix īcĭ-** :

audax, *bold*, ferax, *fruitful*, &c. ; ferox, *haughty*, velox, *swift*, &c.; felix, *happy*, pernix, *fleet* : including words in **ix**, Fem. in Sing. but taking also Neuter endings in Plur.: victrix, Pl. victrices, victricia. So ultrix, corruptrix.

Adjectives under 1) rarely take Abl. S. **ĕ.**

Like these are declined :

a) Compounds of c a p u t : anceps, *double* ; biceps, *two-headed*; praeceps, *headlong*, &c. (for -cipĕs) -cipitĭ-.

b) Compounds of c o r : concors, *agreeing* ; discors, *disagreeing*; misericors, *merciful* ; socors or secors, *stupid*; vēcors, *insane* : -cordĭ-.

c) par parĭ-, *equal* ; hebes hebetĭ-, *dull* (no Gen. Pl.); teres teretĭ- (no Gen. Pl.), *smooth-rounded* ; praepes praepetĭ-, *fast-flying*; trux trucĭ-, *cruel*.

But the compounds of par, dispar, *unlike*, impar, *unequal*, take Abl. S. **ĕ** or **ī**, Gen. Pl. **um.**

2) Adjectives and Participles used adjectively in **ns ntĭ- rs rtĭ-** :

ingens, *huge* ; prudens, *sage* ; praesens, *present*; absens, *absent*; recens, *fresh*; sapiens, *wise*; praestans, *excellent* ; insons, *innocent*; iners, *inactive* ; expers, *void*, &c. In these the Abl. in **ĕ**, though less frequent than **ī**, is often found.

a) So those in **ās ātĭ-** : nostras, vestras, cuias, &c. See p. 108.

b) Numerals in **plex plici-**: simplex, duplex, multiplex,, &c.

c) Derivatives of dens: tridens tridentĭ-, *three-pronged*; these have no Neut. Pl.

d) Locuples locupletĭ-, *wealthy*; Abl. S. ĕ (ī); Gen. Pl. **um** or **ium.**

Note. Present Participles, when they keep their Verbal force, take ĕ in Abl. S.: for instance, when used absolutely: regnante Romulo, imperante Augusto: if used as mere Adjectives they usually take Abl. S. ī.

But rare instances occur of Participles with Abl. ī used verbally, and of Participles with Abl. ĕ used adjectively.

Obs. The Gen. Pl. in **ntĭ-um, rtĭ-um, atĭ-um, etĭ-um** is liable to an occasional loss of ĭ: recentum, sapientum, locupletum, amantum, nostratum, &c.

III) This group contains Comparative Adjectives in ŏr ōr- *m. f.* ŭs ōr- *n.*: melior, praestantior, sapientior, &c.
Abl. S. ĕ as a rule, rarely ī.
Vetŭs vetĕr-, *ancient*, has the same endings: Abl. ĕ (rarely ī); Neut. Pl. ă, Gen. Pl. **um.**

IV) Group IV. has no Neut. Plur.   Abl. S. ī, Gen. Pl. **um.**

a) Compounds of pēs: alipēs, Abl. S. alipedĭ.   As a Neuter Subst. quadrupes has Pl. quadrupedia.

b) Compounds of color: concolor concolōr-, *of the same colour*; discolor discolōr-, *of different colour.*   Neut. Pl. ĭă (rare).

c) alĕs alĭt-, *winged* (Ovid has alitĕ).

degener degenĕr-, *degenerate*	uber ubĕr-, *fruitful*
inops inŏp-, *destitute*	vigil vigĭl-, *wakeful*
memor memŏr-, *mindful*	
immemŏr, *unmindful*	

d) redux redŭc-, *returned*
supplex supplĭc-, *suppliant* } Abl. S. ī, ĕ.

Obs. The Neuter Comparative plus plur- has Abl. S. plurĕ, Neut. N. V. A. plura, Gen. Pl. plurium.
Its compound complures has complura or compluria.

Table of Adjectives. Table of Adjectives not purely consonantal:

SINGULAR.

	M. F.	N.	M. F.	N.	M. F.	N.
N.V.	trist-ĭs	trist-ĕ	felix		ingens	
Acc.	trist-em	trist-ĕ	felic-em	felix	ingent-em	ingens
Gen.	trist-ĭs		felic-ĭs		ingent-ĭs	
Dat.	trist-ī		felic-ī		ingent-ī	
Abl.	trist-ī		felic-ī		ingent-ī (ĕ)	

PLURAL.

N.V.	trist-**ēs**	trist-**ĭă**	felic-**ēs**	felic-**ĭă**	ingent-**ēs**	ingent-**ĭă**
Acc.	trist-**ēs īs**	trist-**ĭă**	felic-**ēs īs**	felic-**ĭă**	ingent-**ēs īs**	ingent-**ĭă**
Gen.		trist-**ium**		felic-**ium**		ingent-**ium**
D.Abl.		trist-**ĭbus**		felic-**ĭbus**		ingent-**ĭbus**

SINGULAR.

	M.	F.	N.		M.	F.	N.
N.V.	celer	celer-**ĭs**	celer-**e**		acer	acr-**ĭs**	acr-**e**

Other cases of Sing., and the Plural, as tristis.

	SINGULAR.		PLURAL.	
	M. F.	N.	M. F.	N.
N.V.	meli-**ŏr**	meli-**ŭs**	melior-**ēs**	melior-**ă**
Acc.	melior-**em**	meli-**ŭs**	melior-**es (īs)**	melior-**ă**
Gen.	melior-**ĭs**		melior-**um**	
Dat.	melior-**ī**		melior-**ĭbus**	
Abl.	melior-**ĕ (ī)**		melior-**ĭbus**	

	SINGULAR.		PLURAL.
	M. F.	N.	M. F.
N.V.	inops		inop-**ēs**
Acc.	inŏp-**em**	inops	inop-**es īs**
Gen.	inop-**ĭs**		inop-**um**
D. Abl.	inop-**ī**		inop-**ĭbus**

SECTION V.

i. The Fourth Declension: U-Nouns.

U-Nouns add **s** to the Stem in the Nominative Sing. of Masc. (Fem.) words, gradŭ-s ; but not in that of Neuter words, which are three only : cornu, *horn* ; genu, *knee* ; veru, *spit*. The endings of the other Cases, uncontracted, appear in the declension of grus, p. 110 ; but the forms, contracted as in the following Table, are used by all U-nouns except grus, sus.

ii. Table.

SINGULAR.

	step, m.	*tribe*, f.	*knee*, n.
N.V.	grad-**ŭs**	trib-**ŭs**	gen-**ū**
Acc.	grad-**um**	trib-**um**	gen-**u**
Gen.	grad-**ūs**	trib-**ūs**	gen-**ūs**
Dat.	grad-**uī ū**	trib-**uī ū**	gen-**ū**
Abl.	grad-**ū**	trib-**ū**	gen-**ū**

PLURAL.

N.V.A.	grad-**ūs**	trib-**ūs**	gen-**ua**
Gen.	grad-**ŭum**	trib-**ŭum**	gen-**ŭum**
D.Abl.	grad-**ĭbus**	trib-**ŭbus**	gen-**ĭbus**

iii. Confusion of O- and U-nouns.

a) On account of the near relation of the flat vowels *o*, *u*, the U-declension is invaded by many forms of the O-declension, 2.

Thus senati, tumulti, occur in Sallust ; and in poets from the earliest time down to Lucretius many such forms are found : adventi, aesti, fructi, geli, gemiti, ornati, piscati, quaesti (frequent), sumpti, victi, &c.

b) Ficus, f. *fig-tree*, an O-noun of Decl. 2., fluctuates in

Gen. S. ī or ūs, Abl. S. o or u.
Nom. Pl. ī or ūs, Acc. Pl. os or ūs.

Laurus, f. *bay-tree*, cupressus, *cypress-tree*, are similarly declined : also pinus, *pine*, but with Abl. S. in u only : and cornus, *cornel*, but with Gen. S. in ı only.

Myrtus, f. *myrtle*, an O-noun, has Nom. Pl. ī or ūs ; Acc. Pl. ōs or ūs.

Quercus, f. *oak*, is a U-noun, but Gen. Pl. quercorum, Cic.

Colus, 2. f. *distaff*, Gen. S. ī or ūs, D. o, Abl. o or u. Nom. Pl. ūs, Acc. ūs or os.

So domus, f. *house*, fluctuates between Decl. 4 and Decl. 2.

SINGULAR.		PLURAL.
N. V.	domŭs	domūs
Acc.	domum	domos (ūs)
Gen.	domūs	domuum, domorum
Dat.	dom-ui, o	domĭbus
Abl.	dom-o u	domĭbus

Domi (or domui), *at home*, is the Locative.   It can be used with an Attribute : domi meae, *at my house* ; domi Caesaris, *at Caesar's house*.   Also domui alienae, *at another's house*.

Pecu, 4. n. is a disused Nom. (=pecus, pecoris), cases of which are found : Dat. S. pecui. Abl. pecu. Pl. Nom. Acc. pecua (Dat. Abl. pecubus ?).

Gelus, 4. m. *frost*, is a disused Nom., Gen. S. geli. Abl. gelu. Gelum, 2. n. is also extant.

Tonitrus, 4. m. Abl. S. tonitru. Nom. Acc. Pl. tonitrus (also tonitrua from a byform tonitruum 2. n.). Dat. Abl. tonitribus. (Ossua, ossuum, from a disused ossu, 4. n. = os *bone*, are only found in old Inscrr.)   Sub diu for sub divo, Lucr. v. 211.

iv. Cases in the Fourth Declension.

1) The *Gen*. Sing. of Neuter Nouns is now shewn to be like that of others, in ūs, though old grammarians held it to be in ū.

2) The Dat. **ui** is generally contracted into **u** : usu for usui : 'parce metu ;' 'victu invigilant,' Verg.   It is much used with esse, habere, &c., 'usui esse,' *to be useful* ; 'derisui habere,' &c.

3) In the Dat. Abl. Pl. **ŭbus** is generally weakened into **ĭbus**. The only Nouns which exclude **ĭbus**, are acus, arcus, and tribus : **ŭbus** is however usual in artus (Pl.), *limbs*; lacus; partus, *birth*; portus, *harbour*; specus, *cave*; veru : and found in genu, tonitrus, Quinquatrus.   Other nouns have **ĭbus** alone.

v. Gender in the Fourth Declension.

The Feminine Nouns of the U-declension (besides those determined by meaning as females or plants) are : acus, *needle, point*; domus, *house*; manus, *hand*; porticus, *porch*; tribus, *tribe*; Idus (Pl.), *the Ides* (of the month); Quinquatrus (Pl.), a byform of Quinquatria, *the feast of Minerva*.

Specus, m. is rarely f. (Pl. specua is found in E. L.).

Obs. Most Nouns of this Decl. are Derivatives ; either from Substantives: consul-atus, magistr-atus, sen-atus, &c., signifying *office* : or from the Supine Stem of Verbs, with abstract meaning : actus, auditus, eventus, visus, &c.   To these latter often correspond forms rather less abstract in **-io** 3. f., actio, auditio, visio, &c. ; and others concrete in **um** 2. n. : (actum), eventum, visum, &c.

SECTION VI.

i. The Fifth Declension : **E**-Nouns.

E-nouns add **s** to the Stem in the Nominative : in the other cases closely corresponding with dea in the First Declension.

26
Fifth
Declen-
sion.

	SINGULAR.			PLURAL.	
Decl. 1. dea	dea-m	dea-i	deae	dea-rum	dea-bus
Decl. 5. die-s	die-m	die-i	die-s	die-rum	die-bus

ii. Table.

SINGULAR.

	day, c.	*thing,* f.	*faith,* f.
N. V.	di-ēs	r-ēs	fid-ēs
Acc.	di-em	r-em	fid-em
Gen.	di-ēi	r-ei	fid-ei
Dat.	di-ēi	r-ei	fid-ei
Abl.	di-ē	r-ē	fid-ē

PLURAL.

N. Ac. V.	di-ēs	r-ēs	none
Gen.	di-ērum	r-ērum	
Dat. Abl.	di-ēbus	r-ēbus	

iii. Cases in the Fifth Declension.

1) **Dies** and **res** are the only nouns fully declined. Acies, *edge*, *army*, facies, *face*, effigies, *image*, glacies, *ice* (Verg.), series, species, *form*, spes, *hope*, have the first three Plural Cases.[1] All others are Singular only : being in sense either abstract or collective. Many are byforms of A-nouns :

materia, 1., materies, 5., *mother-stuff*, *matter*
mollitia, 1., mollities, 5., *softness*, *effeminacy*.

So amaritia, es ; avaritia, es ; barbaria, es ; duritia, es ; luxuria, es ; segnitia, es, &c.

Other words are caesaries, *(clipt)* *hair* ; caries, *rot* (in wood) ; congeries, *mass* ; esuries, *hunger* ; macies, *wasting disease* ; pauperies, *poverty* ; pernicies (or permities), *bane*, *ruin* ; progenies, *offspring* ; rabies, *fury*, *madness* ; sanies, *corrupt matter*, *gore* ; scabies, *the scab*, *mange*, or *rot* ; superficies, *surface* ; temperies, *climate*, *temper*, *moderation* ; intemperies, *immoderation* (Pl. intemperiae of the 1st. Decl.).

2) A few Nouns of Decl. 3. confuse some cases with Decl. 5. Thus famēs, *hunger*, has Abl. famē ; tabes, Abl. tabē, in Lucr. Requies, *rest*, has Acc. requiem and requietem, Gen. requietis, Dat. requieti, Abl. requie. Plebes or plebs has Gen. plebis, plebei, plebi, Dat. plebi or plebei.

3) An example of the old Gen. Sing. in ēs survives in Lucr. iv. 1083 : ' Quodcumque est r a b i e s unde illaec germina surgunt.'

4) The e of Gen. Dat. ei is long after i : diēi, progeniēi ; ɔut short, classically, after a Consonant : fid-ĕi, rĕi (spĕi ?). But in old Latin it was long in these also : ' plenu' fidēi,' Enn., Lucr. ; rēi (or reii). Plautus and Terence make ei in rēi, spēi coalesce by synizesis.

5) Ei was also contracted into ē, anciently into ī, diei, dĭē, dĭī ; plebei, plebi. ' Constantis iuvenem fide ;' ' commissa fide,' Hor. ' Munera laetitiamque dii,' Verg. A. Gellius cites from old Latin authors such instances as acii, fami, luxurii, pernicii, progenii, &c.

6) the phrases ' die crastini,' ' die proximi,' ' die septimi,' are examples of the Locative Case in this Decl. So cotidie, postridie.[2]

iv. Gender in the Fifth Declension.

All E-nouns are Fem. except dies, which, when it means *a day*, is usually, and in the Plur. always, Masc. So its compound meridies, *noon*, is Masc. classically. But, if it means *time*, dies is Fem. : ' Longa dies illi quid profuit ?' Iuv. x.

---

[1] Some other forms appear anciently or in post-classical writings, as *speres* for sp es : facierum ; specierum, speciebus.
[2] No Adjectives belong to the 4th and 5th Declensions.

SECTION VII.

i. Irregular Nouns.

1) Irregularity (ἀνωμαλία) is said to exist in a word if it departs in any respect from the normal constitution of its class.

2) A Substantive is normally constituted when it has two Numbers, with six Cases in each, all of the same gender, following one pattern of Declension. A Substantive is said to be irregular, so far as it departs from this constitution.

3) Irregularity may consist in Abundance (more forms than usual) or Defect (fewer forms than usual).

A word may be Abundant in one respect and Defective in another. Thus, vulgus, 2, is Abundant in having two Genders and two forms of Accusative : Defective in having no Plural.

ii. Abundance in Substantives.

Abundance is shewn in

1) Substantives which, with the same Clipt-stem and meaning, are formed after more than one Declension. See § **25.** 6.

a) With difference of Gender :

Decl. 1. f. and 2. n.

alimoni-a um, *nurture*; cingul-a um (us, m.), *belt*; essed-a um, *chaise*; margarit-a um, *pearl*; mend-a um, *fault*; mulctr-a um, *milking-pail.*

Note ostrea, *oyster,* f.; Pl. ostrea, *oysters,* n.

Decl. 1. f. and 2. m.

vesper-a, vesper, *evening* ; acin-a, us, *berry.*

Decl. 1. f. and 3. m.

cratēra, cratēr, *mixing-bowl.*

Decl. 1. f., 2. n., and 3. n.

gausap-a, **um,** ĕ, *frieze cloth or coat.*

Decl. 1. f. and 3. n.

caepa, caepe, *onion* (Pl. from caepa).

Decl. 2. n. and 5. f.

diluvi-um, es, *deluge.*

Decl. 2. n. and 3. f.

consorti-um, o, *companionship* ; contagi-um, o, *contagion.*

Decl. 2. n., 3. n., and 3. f.

praesepium, praesepe, praesepis, *crib, stall* (Pl. 3. n.).

Decl. 2. n., 3. n., and 3. m.

tapetum, tapete, tapes, *carpet.*

Decl. 2. n. and 3. n.

    tergum, tergus (or-), *back* (rarely 2 m.)

Decl. 2. n. and 4. m.

    angiport-um, us, *lane*; conat-um, us, *endeavour*; event-um, us, *issue*; *event* (p. 121, *Obs.*); incest-um, us, *incest*; suggest-um, us, *pulpit*. Fretum, *frith*, has an ancient form fretus, 4.

Obs. The old root pen-, *interior* (whence penes, penitus, penetrare, penetrale, penates), has a Substantive exhibited in several forms, all classical : penu-s, 4. f., penu-s, 2. m., penu-m, 2. n., and penus penor-, 3. n., *provision, store of food* : as, 'magna penus,' Lucil. ; 'penus annuus,' Plaut. ; 'penum erile,' Afran. ; 'frumenta penus-que,' Hor.

b) With the same Gender :

Decl. 1. and 3. f.

    cassida, cassis, *helmet* ; fulica, fulix, *coot*; iuvent-a, ūs, *youth* ; senect-a, ūs, *old age*.

Decl. 2. and 3. m.

    delphinus, delphin ; elephantus, elephas ; Mulciber (beri, bri, and beris, bris) ; Oedipus (i and odis) ; scorpius, scorpio.

Decl. 3. and 5. f.

    colluvio, colluvies, *conflux* ; paupertas, pauperies, *poverty*.

Decl. 2. and 3. n.

    iugerum (iuger), *acre* ; nihilum, nihil, *nothing*. Necessus, necessum, necesse, *necessity*. See Corssen, ii. 238.

Decl. 1. and 5. (see § **26**).

On Greek names of two Declensions, see § **24**. ix.

Obs. Names of trees have Nom. **us**, f., their fruits **um**, n. usually.

cerasus	*cherry-tree*	cerasum	*cherry*
prunus	*plum-tree*	prunum	*plum*

So malus, *apple-tree*, malum, *apple* ; pirus, *pear-tree*, pirum, *pear* : but amygdala, *almond-tree*, amygdalum, *almond*.

2) Substantives, chiefly of Decl. 2, which vary their Gender, and with it their Case-forms, in the Plural.

  a) locus, *place*, m. . . . loci, m. . . . . . loca, n.

      (loci often means *topics, places in books*, but not exclusively)

    iocus, *jest*, m. . . . ioci, m. . . . . ioca, n.

    sibilus, *hiss*, m. . . . sibili, m. . . . . sibila, n.

    carbasus, *canvas*, f. . . (carbasi) . . . . carbasa, n.

    Tartarus, *hell*, m. . . . . Tartara, n.

Like T a r t a r u s are formed many names of mountains, referred in **Sing.** to m o n s, m., in Pl. to i u g a, n. :

    Ismar-us, Pl. -a ; Maenal-us, Pl. -a ; Tayget-us, Pl. -a.

b) rastrum, *harrow*, n. . . . rastri, m. . . . rastra, n.
    frenum, *bit*, n. . . . freni, m. . . . frena, n.
    caelum, *heaven*, n. . . caeli, m. (Lucr.)
    porrum, *leek*, n. . . . porri, m.

c) In Decl. 3 :
    siser, *skirret*, n. . . . siseres, m.

Many examples of words in one Decl. which borrow cases from another are given in §§ **21** . . . **26** : plebes, fames, requies, domus, fraus, &c. See especially § **25**.

Note. The compounds respublica, *commonwealth*, iusiurandum, *oath*, decline both elements : rempublicam, reipublicae, republicā, &c. ; iurisiurandi, iureiurando.

iii. Defect in Substantives.

Defect is of Number or Case.

A. DEFECTIVA NUMERO are :

I) Nouns which have no Plural Number (Singular only).

1. Words which seem, by their nature, to need no Plural, are Nomina Propria, Abstracta, Collectiva, and Materialia.

Yet Proper Names may take a Plural, when several of one name are mentioned, duodecim Caesares, *the twelve Caesars* ; Cn. et L. Scipiones, *the Scipios Gnaeus and Lucius* ; also if, as types of a class, they become Appellatives : 'Non omnes possumus esse Cicerones,' *we cannot all be Ciceros*. 'Sint Maecenates, non derunt, Flacce, Marones,' Mart.

Abstracta take a Plural, when various instances of their occurrence are implied : odia, *hatreds*, amicitiae, *friendships*, invidiae, *envies*, impietates, &c.

So Collectiva may take a Plural, if several instances are implied : populi, *peoples*, senatūs, *senates*, mundi, *worlds*, &c.

Materialia may take a Plural, when more than one kind is implied : vina, *wines*. Also when objects made of the material are meant : cerae, *waxen tablets* or *waxen busts* ; æra, *bronzes* ; marmora, *works in marble*. Other metals, as aurum, *gold*, argentum, *silver*, are not used in the Plural, because objects of show were not usually made in them. Argentum, Sing., is used for the collective *silver plate* of an owner.

As we say *fish, meat, lamb, cheese*, &c., so the Romans expressed objects of ordinary consumption in the Singular : 'Villa mea abundat porco, haedo, agno, gallinā, caseo, melle,' C. Faba, Sing., is used for *beans*, rosa for *roses*, glans for *acorns*, &c.[1] Similarly, miles for milites, eques for equites : gemma, *jewelled cups*, tegula, *tiles*.

On the other hand, poets use in the Plural many words which might appear to confine their meaning to the Singular : mella, tura, farra, hordea, nives, grandines, rores, soles, rura, corda, colla, pectora, ora, silentia, crepuscula, ligna, &c. So they pluralize local

---

[1] The word *pea* in English is a modern corruption of the true form '*peas*,' L. pis-um, Fr. pois. In Shakespere we find 'a peas or a bean.' The plural is *pease* or *peasen*.

names : Esquiliae, *the Esquiline hill*; Capitolia, *the Capitol*, Palatia, *the Palatine*, &c.

2. Generally, in Latin, the Plural has a large and liberal use. Yet the following words may be mentioned as Singular only, no good authority or analogy sanctioning a Plural form :

acetum	*vinegar*	lac	*milk*	pus	*matter*
ador	*spelt*	letum	*death*	salus	*safety*
aether	*sky*	limus	*mud*	sanguis	*blood*
argentum	*silver*	meridies	*noon*	supellex	*furniture*
aurum	*gold*	merum ⎱	*wine*	venia	*pardon*
fames	*hunger*	nectar ⎰		ver	*spring*
ferrum	*iron*	oleum	*oil*	vesper	*evening*
garum	*pickle*	plumbum	*lead*	virus	*venom*
humus	*ground*	pontus	*sea*	vulgus	*populace*

It is unsafe to say of Abstracts, like pietas, infantia, pueritia, experientia, sapientia, that they are Singular only ; because, if any such words are not found Plural in classical authors, so many Plurals are found resembling them that the possibility of their Plural use cannot be confidently denied.

Abstracts of the Fifth Declension are not, however, used in the Plural, but their corresponding forms of the First Declension.

Plural only.

II) Nouns never, or rarely found Singular (Plural only). These are numerous in Latin.

1) Names of People or Tribes, individuals of which are seldom mentioned : Aborigines ; and the three original tribes of Rome, Ramnes, Tities, Luceres. But most of such names may occur as Singular : Arpinas, Samnis, Gallus, Saxo ; thus Hor. 'infidelis Allobrox ;' 'Marsus et Appulus ;' 'Dacus et Aethiops.'

2) Mountain, Island, &c. groups : Alpes (Alpis rare) : Acroceraunia (iuga) : Aegates, Baleares, Cyclades (insulae). So the street Carinae (the Keels) at Rome ; Tempe, (vale in Thessaly).

3) Many names of Cities and Towns are Plural, as consisting of parts : 1. Athenae, Baiae, Cumae, Mycenae, Syracusae, Thebae ;[1] 2. Argi, Delphi, Gabii, Philippi, Pompeii, Veii : Ecbatana, Leuctra, Susa ; 3. Cures, Gades, Sardis ; or from the name of the people, as Leontini :[2] or from a Plural Appellative, as Aquae Sextiae, Fundi, Ostia, Centumcellae.

4) Names of recurring Calendar days : Calendae or Kalendae ; Nonae ; Idus, 4. And of Holidays, Festivals, Games, &c. : as Latinae, Sementivae (feriae), Quinquatrus ; nundinae (feriae), *market day*; Circenses (ludi) ; Feralia, Floralia, Liberalia, Megalesia, Dionysia, Nemea, Olympia, Pythia, Saturnalia (festa). To this class belong nuptiae (epulae), *wedding*; repotia (festa), *feast after a wedding*; sponsalia (sacra or

---

[1] Cicero writes Cyrenae, Mytilenae for the Greek forms in ē.
[2] Most of the considerable towns in and around France take their names from the old Gallic tribes of which they were the capitals : Paris (Lutetia Parisiorum) ; Amiens (Ambiani) ; Limoges (Lemovices) ; Bourges (Bituriges) ; Orleans (Aureliani) ; Tours (Turones) ; Rouen (Rotomagi) ; Soissons (Suessiones) ; Langres (Lingones) ; Sens (Senones) ; Nantes (Nannetes) ; Tréves (Augusta Treverorum), &c.

festa), *betrothal* ; iusta (sacra), *funeral rites* ; parentalia (festa), *funeral banquet* ; inferiae (epulae), *offering to the dead.*

5) Neuter Greek names for treatises or poems : ethica, *ethics* ; metaphysica, *metaphysics* ; Georgica, *the Georgics*, &c. (scripta).

6) Masculine Collective Names of persons seldom or never so named individually : Decl. 2. gemini, *twins* ; liberi, *the children* of a free Roman ; one being unus (una) e liberis or liberorum : inferi, *dwellers below* ; superi, *gods above* ; posteri, *posterity* ; Decl. 3. maiores, *ancestors* ; minores, *descendants* ; caelites, *heavenly deities* ; lemures, *goblins* ; penates, *household-gods* ; optimates, primores, proceres, *chiefs, nobles* (the last six rarely S. : 'Agnosco procerem,' Iuv.) ; manes,[1] *ghost* or *ghosts.*

7) Parts of the human body, subsisting plurally, and seldom or never separately mentioned : cani (capilli), *grey hairs* ; cervices 3. *neck* (also cervix) ; lactes 3. *small guts* ; exta 2. (outermost) *entrails* ; intestina 2. viscera 3. *entrails* (viscus used) ; ilia 3. *groin, bowels* ; praecordia 2. *midriff, heart* ; pantīces 3. *paunch.* The words genae, *cheeks* ; tempora 3. *temples* ; fauces 3. *jaws* ; renes 3. *kidneys,* imply that the Sing. may be used, if necessary. Hence gena (Suet.), tempus (Verg.) : Abl. fauce often in poetry (Hor. Ov. &c.) : ren is not found in classical Latin ; but can be used technically.

Artus 4. *the limbs* ; Sing. once in Lucan.

8) Many other words, which may be generally distinguished thus :

a) Plural Nouns implying individuals, which are not cited in the Singular except in rare instances marked (s.) :

Decl. 1. antae, *pilasters* ; clitellae, *packsaddle* ; dirae, *curses, furies* (s.) ; gerrae, (wattled twigs) *nonsense* ; habenae, *reins* (s. in Hor.) ; plăgae, *nets* ; scalae, *stairs* ; thermae, *warm baths* ; valvae, *folding doors*.

Decl. 2. fori, *hatches* (of a ship) ; acta, *transactions* ; arma, *arms* ; bellaria, *dessert* ; crepundia, (rattling) *toys* ; cibaria, *food* ; munia, *duties* ; pascua, *pastures* ; sata, *cornfields* ; scruta, *second-hand wares* ; tesqua, *wilds.*

Decl. 3. antes, m. *front vine rows* ; casses, m. *nets* (s.) ; compedes, f. *fetters* (s.) ; fides, f. *lute-strings* (s.) ; obices, c. *bars* (s.) ; sentes, c. *thorns* (s.) ; vepres, c. *brambles* (s.) ; magalia, mapalia, n. *huts, village.*

b) Plural Nouns implying parts not similar and separable.

Decl. 1. balneae, *bath-house* (balnea, *baths*) ; bigae, *chariot and pair* ; cunae, *cradle* ; divitiae, *riches* ; epulae, *banquet* ; exsequiae, *burial* ; exuviae, *spoils* (*stript from the dead*) ; induviae, *clothes* ; lapicidinae, *stonequarry* ; manubiae

---

[1] The word M a n e s belongs to Italian, probably to Etruscan, religion. Departed spirits were deified under the title of di m a n e s or m a n e s ; and the word is sometimes used, as a true Plural, of all such spirits ; sometimes as a Singular-Plural, of the spirit or ghost of an individual. Thus, 'Quae vis deorum est manium,' Hor. ; 'Sunt aliquid manes,' Prop. ⁚ 'Callimachi manes,' Prop. ; 'Verginiae manes,' Liv.

or manibiae, *prize money* (in war): phalerae, *trappings*;
parietinae, *ruins*; quadrigae, *chariot and four* (s.); quisquiliae, *rubbish*; reliquiae, *remnant*; salinae, *saltwork*;
scopae, *besom, broom.*

Decl. 2. cancelli, *railing* (in court); clathri, *grating*; codicilli,
ledger; adversaria, *notebook*; compita, *cross-road* or *roads*
(s.): cunabula, *cradle*; donaria, *treasury*; multicia, *fine
raiment*; serta, *wreath, garland.*

Decl. 3. ambages, (circuits) *evasive language* or *conduct*; fraces,
f. *oil-lees*; fores, f. *door* (s.); pugillares, m. *writing-tablet*;
sordes, f. *dirt, meanness* (s.); altaria, *high altar*; brevia,
shoals; moenia, *town-walls.*

c) Plural Nouns implying repetition or continuation.

Decl. 1. angustiae, *straits* (s.); argutiae, *subtleties, acuteness*;
blanditiae, *flattery* (s.); decimae, *tithes*; deliciae (s.), *delight, darling*; excubiae, *nightwatch*; facetiae, *pleasantry*
(s.); feriae, *holidays*; ineptiae, *follies* (s.); inimicitiae,
enmity (s.); insidiae, *ambush, treachery*; minae, *threats*;
nugae, *trifles*; praestigiae, *jugglery*; primitiae, *first-
fruits*; tricae, *tricks*; tenebrae, *darkness*; vindiciae, *claim.*

Decl. 2. fasti, *annals*; flabra, *blasts* (also flamina); lamenta,
lamentations; oblivia, *forgetfulness.*

Decl. 3. grates, f. *thanks*; verbera, *stripes* (s.); tormina,
gripes.

III) Nouns which vary their meaning in the Plural.

SINGULAR.		PLURAL.	
aedes	*temple*	aedes	*house*
aqua	*water*	aquae	*mineral springs*
auxilium	*help*	auxilia	*auxiliary forces*
bonum	*good* (abstr.)	bona	*goods, property*
carcer	*prison*	carceres	*starting-place* (s)
castrum castellum }	*fort*	castra	*camp*
cera	*wax*	cerae	*waxen tablets* or *busts*
comitium	*Assembly-place*	comitia	*the Assembly at Rome*
copia	*plenty*	copiae	*forces, resources*
facultas	*faculty*	facultates	*means*
finis	*an end*	fines	*boundaries*
fortuna	*fortune*	fortunae	*gifts of fortune*
gratia	*favour*	gratiae	*thanks* (s)
hortus	*garden*	horti	*pleasure-grounds*
impedimentum	*hindrance*	impedimenta	*baggage*
littera	*a letter*	litterae	*epistle, literature*
loculus	*box*	loculi	*money-case*
ludus	*play*	ludi	*public games*
lustrum	*five years*	lustra	*lairs, dens*
natalis	*birth-day*	natales	*origin*
opera	*exertion*	operae	*workpeople* (s)
opis (Gen.)	*help*	opes	*power, wealth* [*faction*
pars	*a portion*	partes	*part in a play; side* or

SINGULAR.		PLURAL.	
rostrum	*beak*	rostra	*the Roman pulpit*
sal	*salt*	sales	*wit* (s)
tabula	*board*	tabulae	*writing tablets*
torus	*couch*	tori	*muscles*
balneum, 2.	*bath*	balneae, 1.	*bath-house*
epulum. 2.	*sacred feast*	epulae, 1.	*banquet*

B. DEFECTIVA CASIBUS.   Defectiva Casibus.

In many Nouns the exigencies of language have called into use a portion only of the ordinary Case-forms.[1]

A) The following Nouns have the full Plural; but in the Singular they have only

a) Four Cases :

N.V. vis, Acc. vim, Abl. vi ; *force*, 3. f.   Pl. vir-**es ium**, &c.

	Nom.	Acc.	Gen.	Dat.	Abl.				
(dap-)		**em**	**is**	**i**	ŏ	*banquet*, 3. f.	} Pl. **es**		**um**, &c.
(frug-)		**em**	**is**	**i**	ĕ	*fruit*, 3. f.			

b) Three Cases :

	Acc.	Gen.	Dat.	Abl.				
(op-)	**em**	**is**	—	ŏ	*help*, 3. f.	} Pl. **es**	**um**, &c.	
(prec-)	**em**	—	**i**	ĕ	*prayer*, 3. f.			
(sord-)	**em**	**is**	—	ŏ	*dirt*, 3. f.	Pl. **es**,	**ium**, &c.	
(vic-)	**em**	**is**	—	e	*change*, 3. f.	Pl. **es**	—, &c.	
——	visc-**us**	**ĕris**	—	ĕre	*entrail*, 3. n.	Pl. **a**	**um**, &c.	

c) Two Cases :

	Acc.	Gen.	Dat.	Abl.			
(verber-)	—	**is**	—	ŏ	*stripe*, 3. n.	Pl. **a**	**um**, &c.

d) One Case : being Ablatives of Decl. 3 :

ambage, f. | casse, m. | fauce, f. | obice, c. | compede, f. | iugere, n.

B) Many Nouns with full Singular have only N. V. Acc. Plural. Such are farra, mella, murmura, rura, tura, &c., 3. n. ; metus, situs, &c., 4. m. ; acies, effigies, facies, species, spes, 5. f.

Astus, *cunning*, 4. m., has Nom. Abl. Sing. and Nom. Acc. Plur.

C) The following Nouns, without Plural, have in the Singular

a) Four Cases:

Nom. V.	Acc.	Gen.	Dat.	Abl.		
(dicio on-) .	**em**	**is**	**i**	ŏ	*power*, 3. f.	
lu-**es** .	. **em**	—	—	ŏ	*wasting disease*, 3. f.	
mān-ĕ .	. ĕ	—	—	ŏ (ī)	*morning*, 3. n.	

---

[1] Words having one Case only in either number were called by the old grammarians MONOPTOTA ; those with two, DIPTOTA ; those with three, TRIPTOTA ; those with four, TETRAPTOTA : (from πτῶσις, *case*, and the several numerals).

b) Three Cases :[1]

Nom. V.	Acc.	Gen.	Dat.	Abl.		
fors . . .	—	—	—	fort-e	*chance,*	3. f.
fas . . .	fas	—	—	—	*right (by divine law),*	3. n.
nefas . .	nefas	—	—	—	*wrong (by divine law),*	3. n.

c) Two Cases :

Nom.		Gen.	Dat.	Abl.		
instar . .	instar	—	—	—	*likeness,*	3. n.
nihil, nīl .	nihil, nīl	—	—	—	*nothing,*	3. n.
opus . .	opus	—	—	—	*need,*	3. n.
—	—	impetis	—	impete	*force,*	3. m.
—	venum	—	veno	—	*sale,*	2. n.

d) Nouns using only one Case are numerous :

Nom. glos, 3. f. *sister-in-law* ; inquies, 5. f. *restlessness.*

Acc. secus, 3. n. *sex,* with epithet virile or muliebre.
   pessum, *to the bad* (for ped-sum), 4. m. in connexion with
    Verbs (pessum dare, pessum ire, &c.).

Gen. dĭcis (causā), 3. *for form's sake* : non nauci, 2. *not
   worth a nutshell, worthless.*

Dat. despicatui, frustratui, ludificatui habere, *to despise, baffle, ridicule* ; indutui gerere, *to wear* ; ob-
   tentui esse, *to be a show,* &c., 4.

Abl. sponte (meā, suā, &c.), 3. f. *by choice, spontaneously.*
   accitu, admonitu, iussu, iniussu, coactu, concessu, ductu,
    hortatu, mandatu, permissu, rogatu, &c. 4.
   noctu, *by night* ; diu, lucu, *by daylight,* 4.
   in promptu esse, in procinctu stare, *to be in readi-
    ness,* 4.
   natu maior, *elder* ; natu minor, *younger,* 4.
   pondo, 2. *by weight,* understands librarum, and is used
    with any Numeral : corona ducentum pondo, *a crown
    of* 200 *pounds' weight.*

D) The following Nouns, without Singular, have in Plural

a) Two Cases :

N. Acc. suppetiae, -as, *succour* ; grates, *thanks* (gratibus, Tac.).
Gen. repetundarum, Abl. repetundis, 1. f. *extortion* (under-
    stand rerum, rebus).
Acc. foras, *out of doors,* Abl. foris, *abroad,* 1. f.

b) One Case :

Acc. ad incitas redigere, *to drive to extremities,* 1. f.
—   infitias ire, *to deny,* 1. f.
Abl. (gratiis) gratis, *freely* ; ingratiis, *against will,* 1. f.

E) Indeclinable, with one form for any Case, are

Names of letters ; alpha, beta, &c.
Various words from other languages : Adam.
Infinitives : amare, vivere.

---

[1] Necesse 3. n. (Nom. Acc.), *necessity,* Gen. necessis (Lucr.) ; Plautus has necessum,
necessus. See p. 124, and M. *Lucr.* ii. 710, vi. 815.

iv. Irregularity in Adjectives.

28
Adjec-
tiva
Abun-
dantia.

I) Some Adjectives have two forms, one like bonus, the other like tristis or ingens :

acclivis (us)	*steep*	imbecillus is	*weak*
biiugis (us)	*two-yoked*	imberbis (us)	*beardless*
effrenus (is)	*unbridled*	inermus is	*unarmed*
unanimus is	*of one mind*	opulentus (opulens)	*wealthy*
hilaris (us)	*cheerful*	violentus (violens)	*violent*

So exanim-**us, is** ; semianim-**us, is** ; sublim-**is, us** ; and others.
The Adverb luculenter implies an old form luculens.

II) *a.* Some are Defective in Number :

Defec-
tiva.

pauci, *few*, is rarely Sing. (Hor. *ad Pis.* 203).
plerique, *most*, is found Sing. with Collective words :
　‘pleraque nobilitas’ (for plerique nobiles), Sall.

b. Some are Defective in Case and Number :

a) Two Cases :
Nom. S. pernox, Abl. pernocte, *all night.*

b) One Case ;
Nom. S. damnas, *condemned*, for damnat(u)s, with esto : but
　used also idiomatically as Nom. Pl. with sunto ;
exspes, *hopeless* ; potis, pote, *able, possible.*

c. Of some the Nominatives are not found, but other Cases only:
(sons), *guilty* ; sontes, *the guilty* : but insons, *innocent*, has full
Cases.
　Macte, Voc. S., macti, Voc. Pl., are used with esto, este, *be
blessed, be lucky*, &c. : ‘Macte (macti) virtute esto (este),’ *good luck
to you for your valour*, Liv.　See M. Lucr. v. 1339.

d. The dat. S. frugi (*for good*) is used as an indeclinable Adjective of all Cases : frugi servus, *a good ·honest slave.*　Opposed to
this is the indeclinable Adjective nequam, *good for nothing* ; probably for ne quam frugem (habet), *no good.*　See pp. 129, 133.
These idioms are drawn from the colloquial language of Italian
farmers in early times.

SECTION VIII.

i. Comparison of Adjectives.

29
Compa-
rison of
Adjec-
tives.

The same quality may be perceived in several objects.　If three be taken, the quality may be perceived
in the second more than in the first, and in the third
most of all.　These relations are expressed by the
flexion called *COMPARISON* in Adjectives and Adverbs.

The Degrees of Comparison are therefore three:

I. The POSITIVE Degree shews quality absolutely perceived: vir procerus, *a tall man*; or equally in two: vir tam procerus quam Lucius, *a man as tall as Lucius.*

II. The COMPARATIVE Degree shews quality perceived more in one of two than in the other: vir procerior quam Lucius, *a man taller than Lucius.*

III. The SUPERLATIVE Degree shews quality perceived most in one of several: vir omnium procerissimus, *the tallest man of all.*

The formation of the Comparative and Superlative is explained in p. 42, *Note*.

ii. Examples :

Comparison of Adjectives.

Pos.		Compar.		Superl.	
dur-us	*hard*	dur-**ior**	*harder*	dur-**issimus**	*hardest*
trist-is	*sad*	trist-**ior**	*sadder*	trist-**issimus**	*saddest*
fel-ix	*happy*	felic-**ior**	*happier*	felic-**issimus**	*happiest*
lib-er	*free*	lib-er-**ior**	*more free*	lib-er-**rimus**	*most free*
nig-er	*black*	nig-r-**ior**	*blacker*	nig-er-**rimus**	*blackest*
salub-er	*healthy*	salub-r-**ior**	*healthier*	salub-er-**rimus**	*healthiest*
simil-is	*like*	simil-**ior**	*more like*	simil-**limus**	*most like*

Like similis are formed facilis; gracilis; humilis; difficilis; dissimilis. But utilis and others have Sup. -**issimus**.

Maturus, *early*, has Sup. maturrimus or maturissimus.

iii. Notes on Comparison.

a) The Comparative may imply a degree *too high* (excess): durior (i.e. durior aequo), *too harsh.*

b) The Superlative may express not only the highest, but a *very high* degree (Elative sense): ' vir doctissimus,' *a very learned man* (i.e. in the highest grade of learning).

c) The Superlative form before the Augustan age was generally -**ŭmus**, after which -**ĭmus** prevailed: maxŭmus, maxĭmus ; optŭmus, optĭmus. See p. 31, *C.*

d) Participles Present and Past often have Comparative Flexion like other Adjectives :

amans	amantior	amantissimus
paratus	paratior	paratissimus

iv. Irregular Comparison.

1) Forms from various Roots.

bonus	*good*	melior	*better*	optimus	*best*
malus	*bad*	peior	*worse*	pessimus	*worst*
parvus	*small*	minor	*less*	minimus	*least*
multus	*much*	(plus, n.)	*more*	plurimus	*most*

The Comparative of multus has no M. F. form in the Sing., but full Plural: plur-es a, plur-ium, plur-ibus.

Lucr. has parvissima, i. 615.   See M.

2) Variant Stem-forms.

mag-nus, *great* ; maior, *greater* ; maximus, *greatest.*

frugi, *honest* ; frugalior, frugalissimus.

nequam, *worthless* ; nequior, nequissimus.

dives ⎫	*rich*	divitior	divitissimus
(dis) ⎭		ditior	ditissimus

Adjectives compounded with **-dicus -ficus -volus** (from dico, facio, volo) form their comparison in **-entior -entissimus**, as if from Participles in **-ens**.

maledicus	*slanderous*	maledicentior	maledicentissimus
magnificus	*splendid*	magnificentior	magnificentissimus
benevolus	*benevolent*	benevolentior	benevolentissimus

Similarly :

egenus,	*needy,*	egentior,	egentissimus
providus,	*foreseeing,*	providentior,	providentissimus.

v. Defective Comparison.

1) Comparison without Positive Form :

a) The Comparison of Position springs from Prepositions, and is not fully represented by Positive Adjectives :

Preposition.		Positive Adj.	Comparative.	Superlative.
e, ex	*out of*	(exter)	exterior	extremus
intra	*within*	(inter)	interior	intimus
supra	*above*	(super)	superior	supremus, summus
infra	*below*	(infer)	inferior	infimus, imus
(prae)	*before*	—	prior	primus
post	*after*	(poster)	posterior	postremus (postumus)
cis	*on near side*	(citer)	citerior	citimus
ultra	*beyond*	(ulter)	ulterior	ultimus
prope	*near*	—	propior	proximus
de	*down from*	(deter)	deterior	deterrimus *worst*

aa) Of the Positive forms, (inter, citer, ulter, deter) are not used.

Super(us), infer(us) are used in Neut. Sing. with mare (mare superum, mare inferum); and in Plur.

Exter(us) is rare in Sing., but not infrequent in Plur.

Poster(us) is used (but not in Nom. Sing. Masc.): pos-
tera aetas; postero die: and Plur. posteri. See
p. 127.

Prior, primus are from a lost form pri-s. Some derive
them from προ: (pro-ior) = prĭor; (pro-imus) = prīmus.

bb) Of the Comparatives, deterior means *worse* (than something good, i.e. *fallen off*); peior *worse* (than something
bad).

cc) Of the Superlatives, summus has the sense '*highest*;'
or supremus, poet. On the other hand, supremus is used
for '*last*,' and summus, poet.: 'venit summa dies,' Verg.

Postremus, *hindmost (last)*: postumus, *coming after, last born,
born after the father's death.*

Four Superlatives can express the notion '*last*:' ultimus (*yon-
dermost, farthest*), extremus (*outermost*); which are most
usual: also postremus and supremus.

To these Comparisons may be added:

dexter, *on the right*, dexterior, dexterrimus or dextimus.
sinister, *on the left*, sinisterior, (sinistimus).

b) —　　　ocior *swifter*, ocissimus *swiftest*.
　　—　　　potior *preferable*, potissimus.

In the Greek ὠκύς (ocis), *swift*, and the Defective Adj. potis,
pote, are shewn the original Positives of these forms.

2) Comparison without Comparative Form.

The Adjectives bellus, consultus, diversus, falsus, inclitus, invictus, invitus, meritus, novus, par, persuasus,
sacer, are found with Superl., but without Comparative.

Vetus, Sup. veterrimus (veterior, Plaut.; but vetustior is
usual).

3) Comparison without Superlative Form.

a)　　senex　　*old*　　senior　　　　　　—
　　　iuvenis　　*young*　iunior (for iuvenior)　　—

Senior has a kind of Pos. force: '*one who has become old.*'

Elder is expressed by natu maior, or maior: *eldest* by
natu maximus, or maximus. So *younger* is natu
minor, or minor; *youngest*, natu minimus, or minimus.

b) Adjectives in **bĭlĭs** have Comparative without Superl.:
except a few: amabilis, mobilis, nobilis: amabilissimus,
&c.

c) Also the following:

adolescens, aequalis, agrestis, alacer, arcanus, astutus, ater,
caecus, capitalis, civilis, crispus, declivis, diuturnus, deses,
exilis, longinquus, opimus, popularis, proclivis, pronus,
propinquus, regalis, rusticus, salutaris, satur, segnis, serus,
supinus, surdus, taciturnus, teres, vicinus, &c.

Note. (satior) satius, *better, fitter*, is a Comparative from the Adverbial word satis, *enough.*

4) Absence of Comparative Flexion.

A great number of Adjectives have no Comparative Flexion : some being incapable of it by their meaning (Incomparabilia) : merus, vernus ; some unsuited to it by their form : memor, tremulus ; while for others no reason can be assigned but usage.[1]

Among Adjectives excluded from Comparison by their form are most of those in **eus, ius, uus** : idoneus, anxius, arduus ; (but not those in **quus** : antiquus, antiquior, antiquissimus).

Rare instances occur of Comparative Flexion by such Adjectives : assiduissimus, Cic. ; strenuissimus, Tac.   And Iuvenal has ' Egregius cenat meliusque miserrimus horum,' xi. 12.

Any Adjectives, not Incomparabilia, can be modified Comparatively by the addition of the Adverb magis : 'Quid magis est durum saxo, quid mollius unda,' Ov. ; and Superlatively by the Adverbs maxime, summe, also admodum, perquam, valde, and others.

vi. Comparison of Adverbs.

1) ADVERBS in ē, ō, ĕ, tĕr, derived from Adjectives, often follow their Comparison, with Comparative Ending ŭs, Superlative ē (ō, um) :

Adj.	Adv.			
dignus	dignē	*worthily*	dignius·	dignissimē
vafer	vafrē	*cunningly*	vafrius	vaferrimē
tutus	tuto	*safely*	tutius	tutissimē (ō)
facilis	facilĕ	*easily*	facilius	facillimē
fortis	fortiter	*bravely*	fortius	fortissimē
constans	constanter	*firmly*	constantius	constantissimē
audax	audacter	*boldly*	audacius	audacissimē
But				
meritus	merito	*deservedly*	—	meritissimō (ē)
uber	(ubertim)	*abundantly*	uberius	uberrimē

[1] Adjectiva Incomparabilia are too numerous to be set down at full, and are indeed best learnt by reading and practice.   Among them may be mentioned : (1) those which express colour, matter, time, place, nationality, descent : albus (but viridis has Compar. flexion), aureus, aestivus, campester, Romanus, paternus, &c. (2) Deminutives, parvulus, vetulus, &c. (3) Compounds of e, per, sub, ve : egelidus, perfacilis, subobscurus, vesanus, &c. (many compounds of prae are comparable, as praeclarior). (4) Compounds of animus, arma, color, genus, gradus, inguen, lex, modus, sonus, somnus (but the compounds of ars, cor, mens are comparable : inertior, misericordior, dementior). (5) Compounds of fero, gero : signifer, belliger, &c. (6) Most adjectives in -ĭcus, -ĭmus, -ĭnus, -īnus, -ōrus, -īvus, -bundus, -āris, -ālis, -ĭlis ; exceptions are, divinus, familiaris, hospitalis, liberalis, civilis, and a few more. (7) Also the following with many more : almus, canus, caducus, calvus, claudus, compos, impos, cicur, dispar, impar, ferus, fessus, gnarus, gnavus, ieiunus, lacer, lassus, mancus, mediocris, merus, mirus, mutilus, mutus, nefastus, rudis, sospes, trepidus, trux, vagus, vivus, volucer, volgaris, &c.
Comic poets invent jocular forms of Comparison : exclusissimus, ipsissimus, oculissimus, patruissimus, ridiculissimus.

2) Irregular Comparison is in most forms represented adverbially :

Adj.	Adv.		Compar.		Superl.	
bonus	benĕ	*well*	melius	*better*	optimē	*best*
malus	malĕ	*ill*	peius	*worse*	pessimē	*worst*
magnus	magnoperĕ	*greatly*	magĭs	*more*	maximē	*most*
parvus	{paulum	*a little*	}minus	*less*	{minimē	*very little*
	{parum	*too little*			{minimum	*least*
multus	multum	*much*	plus	*more*	plurimum	*very much*
—	—	—	ocius	*quicker*	ocissimē	*very quickly*
–	—	—	prius	*sooner*	{primum	*first*
					{primo	*at first*
—	—	—	potius	*rather*	potissimum	*preferably*
—	—	—	deterius	*worse*	deterrimē	*very badly*
—	intus	*within*	interius	—	intimē	
—	post	*after*	posterius	—	postremo	
—	prope	*nearly*	propius	–	proximē	

Also :

—	saepe	*often*	saepius	—	saepissimē	
—	diu	*long*	diutius	—	diutissimē	
—	penitus	*deeply*	penitius	—	penitissimē	
—	satis	*enough*	sătius	—	—	
—	secus	*otherwise*	sētius	—	—	
—	temperi	*betimes*	temperius	—	—	
—	nuper	*lately*	—	—	nuperrimē	

Magis means '*more in degree* ;' plus, '*more in quantity.*' 'Lucio magis carus sum :' ' Lucius me plus diligit.'

SECTION IX.

i. Pronouns (Pronomina).

1. A Pronoun, being a substitute for a Noun, may be
 (1) Substantive : (2) Adjective : (3) Capable of being both.

2. A Pronoun may be
 (*a*) 1st Person : (*b*) 2nd Person : (*c*) 3rd Person : (*d*) Of all Persons.

ii. Classification of Pronouns.

A. The Pronouns purely Substantival are:

1. The PERSONAL Pronouns ego, *I*, nos, *we*, of the First Person ; and tu, *thou*, vos, *ye*, of the Second.

2. The REFLEXIVE Pronoun, se, *himself, herself,* or *themselves*, which has no Nominative, and is always referred to a Subject of the Third Person, Singular or Plural.

B. The Pronouns Proper purely Adjectival are:

The POSSESSIVE Pronouns, which correspond to the Personal and Relative Pronouns:

meus, *my, mine*	corresponding to . . .	ego
noster, *our*	—	nos
tuus, *thy, thine*	—	tu
vester, *your*	—	vos
suus, *his, her,* or *their own*	—	se
cuius, *whose*	—	qui

with the Gentilia, nostras, *of our country,* vestras, *of your country* ; cuias, *of what country?*

Suus, like se, is referred to a Subject of the Third Person.

C. The remaining Pronouns are Adjectival, but often used as Relational Substantives. These are:

1. The DEMONSTRATIVE Pronouns (of the Third Person):

ĭs, ĕa, ĭd, *that* (or *he, she, it*)
hic, haec, hōc, *this* (near me)
istĕ, ista, istud, *that* (near you)
illĕ, illa, illŭd, *that, yon* (aloof from us).

2. The DEFINITIVE Pronouns (of all Persons):

ipsĕ, ipsa, ipsum, *self*
īdem, ĕadem, ĭdem, *same.*

3. The RELATIVE Pronoun (of all Persons):

quī, quae, quŏd, *who* or *which.*

Akin to this are:

a. The INTERROGATIVE Pronouns:

quĭs, quĭd? qui, quae, quod? *who* or *what?*
ŭter? *whether of two?*

b. The INDEFINITE Pronouns:

quis, quă (quae), quid ; qui, quae, quod, *any.*
ŭter, *either of two.*

c. The various COMPOUNDS of quis, qui, uter.

4. PRONOMINALIA, or Adjectives of a Pronominal nature: as alius, alter, &c., talis, tantus, &c., qualis, quantus, &c., aliquantus, &c. See v.

Tables
of De-
clension.

iii. Tables of Declension of Pronouns.

A. PERSONAL (OF EITHER GENDER).

FIRST PERSON.

SINGULAR.	PLURAL.
Nom. ego, *I*	nos, *we*
Acc. me, *me*	nos, *us*
Gen. mei, *of me*	nostri, *or* nostrum, *of us*
Dat. mihi, *to* or *for me*	nobis, *to* or *for us*
Abl. me, *from* or *with me*	nobis, *from* or *with us*

SECOND PERSON.

N. V. tu, *thou*	vos, *ye*
Acc. te, *thee*	vos, *you*
Gen. tui, *of thee*	vestri, *or* vestrum, *of you*
Dat. tibi, *to* or *for thee*	vobis, *to* or *for you*
Abl. te, *from* or *with thee*	vobis, *from* or *with you*

REFLEXIVE.

SINGULAR AND PLURAL.

Nom. (none).
Acc.   se, *or* sese, *himself, herself, itself,* or *themselves.*
Gen.   sui, *of himself,* &c.
Dat.   sibi, *to himself,* &c.
Abl.   se, *or* sese, &c., *from himself,* &c.

B. POSSESSIVE.

1) declined in Gender, Number, and Case, like b o n u s :

meus, mea, meum, *my, mine* ;	suus, sua, suum, *his,* &c., *their, own* ;
tuus, tua. tuum, *thy, thine* ;	cuius, cuia, cuium, *whose.*

meus has Vocative Masc. mī.[1]

2) declined in Gender, Number, and Case, like n i g e r :

noster, nostra, nostrum, *our* ; | vester, vestra, vestrum, *your.*

The Demonstratives have no Possessives corresponding to them ; but their Genitives supply the want : eius vacca, *his (her) cow.*

3) Gentilia (of 3rd Decl.) :

nostr-as -ati- ; vestr-as -ati- ; cui-as -ati- ?

The affix **met** (*self*) may be appended to all the cases of ego, tu (except the Plural Genitives and the form tu itself), also to se, sibi : egomet, nosmet, temet, vobismet, semet, sibimet : often with a case of ipse added : nobismetipsis, semetipsum. Tu takes affix **te**, -tute ; also tutemet. The affix **met** is appended to the cases of suus, after which a case of ipse often follows : 'Intra suamet ipsum moenia compulere,' *they drove him within his own walls,* L. vi. 36. Also meamet : Sall., Plaut.

The affix **pte** is appended to the Ablatives Sing. of the Possessives : 'Meopte ingenio,' Plaut. 'Suapte manu,' *with his own hand,* Cic. See M. *Lucr.* vi. 755.

[1] The only Pronouns capable of having a Vocative are tu, vos ; and meus, noster.

C. 1. DEMONSTRATIVE.

a. UNEMPHATIC.

Is, *that,* or *he, she, it.*

	SINGULAR.				PLURAL.		
	M.	F.	N.		M.	F.	N.
N.	is	ea	id		ei (ii)	eae	ea
Ac.	eum	eam	id		eos	eas	ea
G.		eius			eorum	earum	eorum
D.		ei			eis (iis)		
Ab.	eo	eā	eo		eis (iis)		

b. EMPHATIC.

Hic, *this (near me),* or *he, she, it.*

	SINGULAR.				PLURAL.		
N.	hic	haec	hoc		hi	hae	haec
Ac.	hunc	hanc	hoc		hos	has	haec
G.		huius			horum	harum	horum
D.		huic			his		
Ab.	hoc	hac	hoc		his		

Iste, *that (near you),* or *he, she, it.*

	SINGULAR.				PLURAL.		
N.	iste	ista	istud		isti	istae	ista
Ac.	istum	istam	istud		istos	istas	ista
G.		istīus			istorum	istarum	istorum
D.		isti			istis		
Ab.	isto	istā	isto		istis		

Ille, *that (yonder),* or *he, she, it.*

	SINGULAR.				PLURAL.		
N.	ille	illa	illud		illi	illae	illa
Ac.	illum	illam	illud		illos	illas	illa
G.		illīus			illorum	illarum	illorum
D.		illi			illis		
Ab.	illo	illā	illo		illis		

2. DEFINITIVE.

1) Idem, *same.*

	SINGULAR.				PLURAL.		
Nom.	īdem	eadem	ĭdem		īīdem	eaedem	eădem
Acc.	eundem	eandem	ĭdem		eosdem	easdem	eădem
Gen.		eiusdem			eorundem	earundem	eorundem
Dat.		eidem			isdem *or* eisdem		
Abl.	eodem	eādem	eodem		isdem *or* eisdem		

2) Ipse, *self.*

	SINGULAR.			PLURAL.	
Nom.	ipse	ipsa	ipsum	ipsi	ipsae	ipsa
Acc.	ipsum	ipsam	ipsum	ipsos	ipsas	ipsa
Gen.		ipsīus		ipsorum	ipsarum	ipsorum
Dat.		ipsi			ipsis	
Abl.	ipso	ipsā	ipso		ipsis	

Plautus has the forms eumpsĕ, eampse, eāpse, &c. Also reapse, *in reality*, for re ipsā.

a) The affix **-c** (for **cĕ**) is added to iste and ille, making a pronominal declension as follows :—

SINGULAR.

N.	istic	istaec	istoc *or* istuc	illic	illaec	illoc *or* illuc
Acc.	istunc	istanc	istoc *or* istuc	illunc	illanc	illoc *or* illuc
Abl.	istoc	istac	istoc	illoc	illac	illoc

PLURAL.

N. Acc.	—	—	istaec	—	—	illaec

Cĕ sometimes appears at full : istiusce, illosce, &c.
So from hic, hunce, huiusce, hosce, &c. : and hicine? hocine? &c.

b) The Interjection ecce, *lo!* coalesces in comic poetry with cases of is, ille, iste : ecca, eccum, eccam, &c. ; eccilla, eccillum, &c. ; eccistam, &c. En, *lo!* also coalesces with ille into the Accusative forms, ellum, ellam, ellos, ellas.

3. RELATIVE.

Qui, *who* or *which.*

	SINGULAR.			PLURAL.		
Nom.	qui	quae	quod	qui	quae	quae
Acc.	quem	quam	quod	quos	quas	quae
Gen.		cuius		quorum	quarum	quorum
Dat.		cui			quĭbus *or* quīs	
Abl.	quo	quā	quo		quĭbus *or* quīs	

a) INTERROGATIVE.

Quis? qui? *who* or *which?*

SINGULAR.

Nom.	quis		quid }
	qui	quae	quod }
Acc.	quem	quam	quid }
	quem	quam	quod }
Gen.		cuius	
Dat.		cui	
Abl.	quo	quā	quo

b) INDEFINITE.

Quis, qui, *anyone.*

SINGULAR.

Nom.	quis	(qua)	quid }
	qui	quae (qua)	quod }
Acc.	quem	quam	quid }
	quem	quam	quod }
Gen.		cuius	
Dat.		cui	
Abl.	quo	quā	quo

In the Plural like the Relative.
Indefinite Pl. Nom. Qui, quae, qua *or* quae.
The forms Quis, quid, are Substantival ; Qui, quod, Adjectival.

a) Add to these Uter? *whether of the two?*

	SINGULAR.			PLURAL.		
Nom.	uter	utra	utrum	utri	utrae	utra
Acc.	utrum	utram	utrum	utros	utras	utra
Gen.		utrĭus		utrorum	utrarum	utrorum
Dat.		utri			utris	
Ab.	utro	utrā	utro		utris	

Uter is also Indefinite : *either of two.*

Neuter, neutra, neutrum, *neither of the two,* is declined as uter.

c) COMPOUND PRONOUNS.

1. *a*) quisnam, quidnam : quinam, quaenam, quodnam, *who, what?*
   b) uternam, utranam, utrumnam, *whether of the two?*

2. ecquis, ecqua, ecquid : ecqui, ecquae, ecquod, *anyone?*
So numquis, siquis, nē quis, &c.

3. *a*) aliquis, aliqua, aliquid : aliqui, aliqua, aliquod, *some one.*
   b) alteruter, *one or other*; Gen. alterutrius or alterius utrius, &c.

4. quispiam, quaepiam, quippiam (quodpiam), *anyone* (positively).

5. quisquam, quicquam, *anyone at all* (with n o n, h a u d, vix, &c.).

6. quidam, quaedam, quiddam (quoddam), *a certain one.*

7. *a*) quicumque, quaecumque, quodcumque, *whosoever, what-soever.*[1]
   b) utercumque, utracumque, utrumcumque, *whichever of two.*

8. quisquis, *whosoever,* quidquid, *whatsoever* ; Acc. (quemquem), quidquid ; (G. cuicuimodi) ; Abl. (quoquo, quaquā, quoquo), &c. ; Pl. D. Abl. (quibusquibus). Some of these forms are rare.

9. *a*) quivis, quaevis, quidvis (quodvis), *any you will.*
   b) utervis, utravis, utrumvis, *whether of the two you will.*

10. *a*) quilibet, quaelibet, quidlibet (quodlibet), *any you please.*
    b) uterlibet, utralibet, utrumlibet, *whether of the two you please.*

11. *a*) quisque, quaeque, quicque (quodque), *each.*
    b) unusquisque, unaquaeque, unumquicque (-quodque), *each one* : Acc. unumquemque, unamquamque, &c. Gen. uniuscuiusque, &c.
    c) uterque, utraque, utrumque, *both, each of two.*

Obs. These Compounds are declined as the Simple forms, the undeclined affix or prefix accompanying each Case : Gen. cuiusnam, alicuius, cuiuscumque, utriusvis, &c. &c.

---

[1] Poets often disjoin the affix cumque from the Relative : Quae te cumque domat Venus, Hor.

4. PRONOMINALIA.

Alius, *another*.

	SINGULAR.			PLURAL.		
Nom.	ălĭus	alia	aliŭd	alii	aliae	alia
Acc.	alium	aliam	aliud	alios	alias	alia
Gen.		alīus		aliorum	aliarum	aliorum
Dat.		alii			aliis	
Ab.	alio	alĭā	alio		aliis	

Alter, *one of two* (*the one, the other*).

Nom.	alter	altera	alterum	alteri	alterae	altera
Acc.	alterum	alteram	alterum	alteros	alteras	altera
Gen.		alterĭus		alterorum	alterarum	alterorum
Dat.		alteri			alteris	
Ab.	altero	alterā	altero		alteris	

Solus, *alone*.

Nom.	sōlus	sola	solum	soli	solae	sola
Voc.	sole	sola	solum	soli	solae	sola
Acc.	solum	solam	solum	solos	solas	sola
Gen.		solīus		solorum	solarum	solorum
Dat.		soli·			solis	
Ab.	solo	solā	solo		solis	

Tōtus, *whole*, is declined like sōlus : also, unus, *one*, ullus, *any at all*, nullus, *none*. See Numeralia.

Nĭhĭl, *nothing* (N. Acc.) is undeclined.

Nēmo, *nobody*, Acc. nemĭnem ; G. nullīus ; D. nemini ; Abl. nullo. Plural, nulli, &c.

The Plural word plērīque, *most* ; from an E. L. Adj. plērus.

Nom.	plerique	pleraeque	plerăque
Acc.	plerosque	plerasque	plerăque
D. Abl.		plerisque	

The Gen. in use is plurim-orum, arum, orum.
The phrase plerique omnes=paene omnes, *almost all*.

Also the following words, with their compounds :

quālis, *of what kind?* tālis, *such* (like tristis).
quantus, *how great?* tantus *so great* (like bonus).
quŏt, *how many?* tŏt, *so many* (undeclined).

iv. Observations on certain Pronouns.

I. The Interrogative forms quis? qui? (Indefinite quis, qui) differ in this respect : quis is substantival, asking usually the nature, name, &c. ; qui adjectival, asking quality. Quis is also Fem. in the comic poets, and grammarians refer the Fem. quae to the form qui. Quid always has a substantival, quod an adjectival use : quod vinum? but quid vini? *what wine?*

2. Quis, qui, Indefinite, is rarely found except as Enclitic after a particle, as ecquis, siquis, numquis, &c.; or with a second case of its own : ' siquis quem fraudavit.' It enters into composition with the prefix **ali-** *one or other* (aliquis), the indefinite affixes **-piam -quam** (quispiam, quisquam), and the distributive **-que** (quisque) ; qui takes the definitive **-dam** (qui-dam).

3. The Interrogative quis, qui becomes Universal (*-soever*) by self-duplication (quisquis), and by taking the affix **-cumque** or **-cunque** (quicumque, quicunque). It is also modified by the appended Verb-forms, vis, *you will*, libet, *it pleases* (quivis, quilibet). It becomes Emphatic by adding the precative affix **-nam** (quisnam? quinam?). Some of these affixes are likewise taken by the Interrogative Pronominals qualis, quantus, quot, and the Interrogative Adverbs ubi, quo, quando, quotiens, &c. See v.

4. U ter (for cuter = κότερος), *whether of two*, with its compounds, forms a dual series parallel to quis, &c. But the Relative qui is used in correlation to it. It takes many of the same affixes as qui.[1]

---

[1] The following note treats chiefly of the cognate and ancient Case-forms of the Latin Pronouns.

　I. The Personal Pronouns and the Reflexive.

　　1. Nominative Singular.

　　The Prim. roots of the two Personal Pronouns and the Reflexive are severally *ma, tu* (or *tva*), *sva*.

　　How the root *ma* connects itself with the Nom. Sing. Sk. *aham*, Gr. ἐγώ, L. ego, is a doubtful question.

　　Pr. *tu* (Sk. *tvam*) becomes Gr. τὐ (σὐ), L. tū.

　　2. Accusative Singular.

　　Sk. *mâm* or *mâ*, Gr. μέ (ἐμέ), L. mē.

　　Sk. *tvâm* or *tvâ*, Gr. (τέ for τϝε) σέ, L. tē.

　　Gr. ἔ (for σϝε), L. sē, point to a Pr. *svâm*. But Sanskrit has only an undeclined form *svayam*, which may be joined to cases of Personal Pronouns.

　　3. Dative Singular.

　　Sk. *ma-hyam* (for Pr. *ma-bhyam*) becomes L. mihĭ (U. *mehê*, E. L. *mihe, mihei*).

　　　Sk. *tu-bhyam* becomes L. tibĭ (U. *tefê*, E. L. *tibe, tibei*).

　　Hence sibĭ (E. L. *sibe, sibei*) points to a Pr. but not extant (*sva-bhyam*).

　　4. Ablative Singular.

　　Sk. and Pr. *ma-t, tva-t* and by analogy (Pr. *sva-t*) become in E. L. *me-d, te-d, se-d* ; afterwards mē, tē, sē.

　　These forms in **-d** were also used for the Accus. Sing. in E. L.

　　5. Nominative and Accusative Plural.

　　Unaccented Accus. forms in Sk. *nas* (for *mas*?) and *vas* (for *tvas*), appear to be the originals of the Latin cases nōs, vōs. See Schleicher, § 266. In the Carmen Arvale *enos* appears for Acc. nos.

　　6. Dative and Ablative Plural.

　　Schleicher explains the suffix **bis** (-*bei-s*) in nōbīs, vōbīs, as the Plural of **bi (bei)**, attached to the stems nos- vos- (see above), which become nō- vō-. Festus cites a form (*nis*).

　　7. Genitive Singular and Plural.

　　The Sk. Gen. S. is (1) *mama*, (2) *tava*. But Pr. forms *mas, tvas*, (*svas*) are traceable in very ancient L. forms *mis, tis*.

　　The forms classically used for these cases are nothing more than the Neuter Genitives of the Possessive Pronouns : mei, tui, sui ; nostri, vestri ; nostrum (for nostrorum), vestrum (for vestrorum). Thus ' vive memor mei (nostri)' is lit. *live mindful of what is mine (ours)* ; i.e. *of me (us)*.

v. Correlation of Pronominal Words.

A) Certain Pronouns, Pronominal Adjectives and Adverbs, are correlated to one another in several classes : namely

---

II. The Possessive Pronouns.

These are derived from the Personal Roots.

Tuus, suus correspond severally to Gr. τεός (for τϝεός or τεϝός), ἑός (for σϝεός or σεϝός). E. L. forms are *tovos*, *sovos*. The scenic poets use the cases as monosyllables.

Noster, vester are formed with the Comparative Suffix **ter** (like dexter, sinister), as are Gr. ἡμέ-τερ-ος, ὑμέ-τερ-ος.

III. The Demonstrative, Relative, &c. Pronouns.

The Flexion of these Pronouns has many features in common.

1. (1) Nominative Singular Masc.

a. The stem ī-, as an I-noun, takes the ending **s**, forming the Nom. **ĭs**. It corresponds to Sk. *sa*, Gr. ὁ. In E. L. we find (*ēīs*). It has an O-stem (*io-*) for most cases.

Its comp. īdem has E. L. forms (*ĭsdem, isdem, ēīdem*).

Is-tĕ, another compound (stem isto-), has in Plautus the form *is-tus*.

I-psĕ, also a compound (for is-pse), is found as *i-ps-us*.

Illĕ is for *oll-us* (stem ollo- or illo-), from an Italian root.

The stem ho- or hi- takes in most cases the affix -ce (c), becoming in Nom. S. Masc. h i c (for *hi-ce* or *his-ce*). An E. L. form is (*hec*).

b. Qui qui-s Interrog. and Indef. (stem qui- or quo-) corresponds to Sk. Interrog. *ka, ka-s* ; Gr. τίς, O. *pis*.

Qui, as the Relative, is peculiar to Latin. E. L. forms are (*que, quei*). Quei continued in use to the time of Caesar. *Queique* is an old form of quisque. *Quirquir* is cited by Varro for quisquis.

c. Alius has an old I-form *alis, alid*.

Uter (for cuter) corresponds to Pr. *katara*, Gr. κότερος : quot, tot, to Sk. *kati, tati.*

(2) Nom. S. Fem.

E a is by assimilation for i a from stem (*io-*) : the same change from **i** to **e** is made in most cases of is, idem.

An old form (*sapsa*) for ea ipsa is cited from Pacuvius.

Ista, ipsa, illa are regularly formed from the O-stems, but quae (O. *pai*, E. L. *quai*), haec (E. L. *hai-ce*) are irregular flexions in which the forms *hă quă* are strengthened by the vowel **i**. The analogy of these is followed by istaec, illaec (for ista-ce, illa-ce). Quă is kept usually in the Indef. Pronoun and its compounds : siqua, numqua, ecqua, aliqua.

(3) Nom. Accus. S. Neuter.

The following Pronouns weaken the Prim. Neuter suffix **t** into **d** : id ; ĭdem (for id-dem); qui-d ; quo-d ; and illud, istud, aliud (anc. *alid*) : in these three **o** is also weakened into **u**. Hoc is for (ho-d-ce). The rest take um ; ipsum, utrum, alterum, &c.

2. Accusative Singular.

E. L. forms of **ĭs** (*em, im* from the I-stem; *sum, sam* from the Pr. *sa*) are cited from the old poets for eum, eam, severally.

Also eumpse, eampse occur for eum ipsum, eam ipsam.

Hunc is for (*hom-ce, honc*) ; hanc for (*ham-ce*). Quem belongs to the I-stem qui : quam and quod to the O-stem quo-.

3. Genitive Singular.

The flexion of this case in all these Pronouns is a variation of Sk. *asya*. They strengthen the stem with **i** and then take **us** for the Case-ending. Thus are obtained

(*ii-us*) by dissimilation eius (in E. L. *ei-ius, eIus*).

(*illoi-us, illei-us*) illīus or illĭus. So ipsīus, istīus, unīus, nullīus, totīus ; utrīus ; alīus ; alterīus ; solīus : (alterĭus, solĭus occur rarely).

(*hoi-us*) huius ; (*quoi-us*) cuius.

In the scenic poets quoius is used as one syllable, suppressing **u** : hence the forms q u o i-m o d i for (quoismodi), and c u i c u i m o d i for (cuiscuismodi).

(1) Interrogative; (2) Demonstrative; (3) Definitive; (4) Inde-finite; (5) Relative.

Examples :

(1) quis? qui? *who, what?* (2) is, *he, that,* &c. (3) ipse, *self*; idem, *the same*; alius, *another*; (4) quis, qui, *any*; quis-piam, *anyone*; aliquis, *some or other*; quisquam, *any at all* (used only with non, haud, si, num, &c.); quidam, *a certain one*; (5) qui, *who.*

(1) uter? *whether of two?* (2) is; (3) alter, *one of two, the other*; (4) alteruter, *one or the other*; (5) qui.

(1) qualis? *of what kind?* (2) talis, *such*; (3) — ; (4) — ; (5) qualis, *as.*

(1) quantus? *how great?* (2) tantus, *so great*; (3) tantusdem; (4) aliquantus, *of some size*; (5) quantus, *as (great).*

---

4. Dative Singular.

The Locative ending **i** appears to have been generally used instead of the Dative ending **ei** in all these Pronouns; but the ending **ei** occurs in old forms.

The forms in use are : 1) e-i (also anc. *eiei eei*); illi (for illo-i), &c., huic (for hoi-ce): 2) c u i (for *quo-i,* or *quo-ei,* which is found in E. L.)

The O-noun forms of the Gen. and Dat. Sing. of some Pronominals occur rarely : as nulli consili, Ter. ; aliae pecudis, Cic. ; loquitur alterae, Ter. ; toto orbi, Prop. : also Gen. illi, illae, isti, ipsi, &c. in Plaut. and Lucr.

5. Ablative Singular.

This case follows the O-stem. But qui is used adverbially (*how*); also when the Pre-position c u m follows it : quicum for quocum : quique for quōque in Lucr.

6. Nominative Plural.

a) From is, E. L. forms before Plautus are (*eeis, ieis, eis*): afterwards in R. L. iei, ei: in the scenic poets ēi (i). In I. L. ii (pronounced i) was allowed.

From idem the forms *eisdem, isdem, eidem* are found as Nominatives Plural before Caesar. Once in Plautus ĕidem. Iidem was admitted in I. L.

From hic the forms (*heis, heisce, hisce*) appear in E. L. ; hei in R. L. to the Aug. age : then hi ; which, like the irregular Fem. form hae (for *hai*), rejects c (ce) to avoid con-fusion. But the forms (*haec, illaec, istaec*) are found in E. L. as Fem. Nominative Plural.

The Neut. Pl. haec is strengthened with **i**, being, as well as the Fem. S., for (*ha-i-ce*).

b) An old Pl. q u e s from quis is found in Senatus-consultum de Bacchana'ibus, &c., Pacuvius, and Cato : but quei in R. L. is Pl. of quis and qui ; also qui, which became general : and Fem. quae (for *quai*). The Neut. quae, like haec, is a strengthened form : quā remains often in the Indef., and always in aliquā.

Grammarians tell us that in plebeian speech the initial vowel was often cast off in such forms as istae, istuc, &c., which were sounded stae, stuc, &c.

7. Accusative Plural.

These forms are regular from O- and A-stems Except the Neuter forms haec, quae. See 6.

8. Genitive Plural.

This Case is formed in all as from O-nouns. Horumce, harumce appear in the scenic poets as horunc, harunc ; once in Plaut. quoium seems to be Gen. Pl. from qui ; and also in two ancient laws.

Dative Ablative Plural.

a) From 'is' the forms are various. Thus, from I-stem, ībus, Plaut. ; ĭbus, Lucr. : and Fem. eābus, Cat. From O-stem, (E. L. *eieis, eeis*) ; i e i s in R. L. to Aug. ; ēis or īs in the scenic poets and Lucr. ; once in Plaut ēis. Under Aug. we find Is for iis (ieis) pro-nounced as one syllable.

So, from idem, ēisdem or īsdem, once in Juv. ĕisdem : iisdem (disyll.) is found.

From hic, hībus is cited once from Plaut. : usually hīis (E. L. *heisce*).

From ille (E. L. *oloes*, m. *olaes*, f.) illis (*olleis, illeis*). Old forms in *ibus* are cited.

b) From qui, quis, the only forms are quībus (from I-stem) and quīs (from O-stem) in all Genders.

(1) quot? *how many?* (2) tot, *so many*; (3) totidem, *just so many*; (4) aliquot, *some*; (5) quot, *as (many)*.

Derived from this are :

quotus, *one of how many?* (Demonstr. tŏtus, Lucr. v. 652.)
quotusquisque = *how few?* Demonstr. pauci, *few*.
quotiens, *how often?* Demonstr. totiens, *so often*; Indef. aliquotiens, *several times* : Rel. quotiens, *as (often)*.

(1) ubi, *where?* (2) ibi, *there*; hic, *here*, &c.; (3) ibidem, *in the very place*; alias, *elsewhere*; (4) ubi, *in any place*; alicubi, *in some place*; (5) ubi, *where*.

(1) unde, *whence?* (2) inde, *thence*; hinc, *hence*, &c.; (3) indidem, *from the same side*; aliunde; (4) unde, *from any quarter*; alicunde, *from some quarter*; (5) unde, *whence*.

(1) quo, *whither?* (2) eo, *thither*; huc, *hither*, &c.; (3) eodem, *to the same place*; alio, *to another place*; (4) quo, *anywhither*; aliquo, *somewhither*; (5) quo, *whither*.
So quā, *in what direction?* eā, *in that d.*; hac, *in this d.*, &c.

(1) quam, *how?* (2) tam, ita, *so*; (3) itidem, *in the same way*; aliter, *otherwise*; (4) aliquam; (5) quam, *as*.
With other series, as quando, *when?* tum, *then*, &c.

B) The Universal Pronouns (6) also are severally correlated to the above, and to other forms which imply (7) Choice ; (8) Distribution ; (9) Exclusion ; (10) Inclusion.

Examples :

(6) quisquis, quicumque, *whosoever, whatsoever*; (7) quivis, quilibet, *any you will*; (8) quisque, *each*; (9) nemo, *nobody*; nullus; (10) omnes, *all*.

(6) utercumque, *whichever of two*; (7) utervis, uterlibet, *which of two you will*; (8) uterque, *each of two*; (9) neuter, *neither*; (10) ambo, *both*.

(6) qualisqualis, qualiscumque, *of whatever kind*.

(6) quantusquantus, quantuscumque, *how great soever*; (7) quantusvis, quantuslibet, *as great as you will*.

(6) quotquot, quotcumque, *as many as, however many*; (7) quotlibet (rare) ; (8) unusquisque, singuli, *each one*; (9) nulli, *none*; (10) universi, *the entire number*.

(6) ubiubi, ubicumque, *wheresoever*; (7) ubivis, ubilibet, *where you will*; (8) ubique, *everywhere*; (9) nusquam, *nowhere*.

(6) undeunde, undecumque, *whencesoever*; (7) undevis, undelibet, *whence you will*; (8) undique, *from every side* (utrimque, *from both sides*).

(6) quoquo, quocumque, *withersoever*; (7) quovis, quolibet, *whither you will*. (So quaqua, quacumque ; quavis, qualibet : usquequaque, &c.)

(6) quamquam, quamcumque, *howsoever*; (7) quamvis, quamlibet, *how you will*; (8) — ; (9) neutiquam, *in no way*; (10) omnino, *in every way*.

(6) quandocumque, *whensoever*; (7) quandolibet; (8) quandoque; (9) numquam, *never*; (10) semper *always*.

SECTION X.

i. Numeralia.

NUMERALS (Numeralia) are Nouns and Adverbs used in the expression of Number.

ii. Latin symbols of Number:[1]

I	V	X	L	C	IƆ or D	CIƆ or M
1	5	10	50	100	500	1000

By these symbols the Romans exhibited any required Number.
A smaller symbol before a larger is subtracted : IV = 5 − 1.
A smaller after a larger is added : VI = 5 + 1.
Equal symbols are added together : II = 1 + 1 ; XX = 10 + 10.
But a smaller symbol before M multiplies M : IIM = 2000.
Usually such a number was expressed by words, not by symbols :
duo milia or bis mille.

The symbol IƆ is multiplied by ten as often as Ɔ is subjoined.
Thus,

$$IƆƆ = 10 \times 500 = 5,000$$
$$IƆƆƆ = 10 \times 5,000 = 50,000.$$

As often as the symbol C is prefixed to I, equalling the number of suffixed Ɔ, the total is doubled. Thus,

$$CIƆ = \text{twice} \quad 500 = 1,000$$
$$CCIƆƆ = \text{twice} \quad 5,000 = 10,000$$
$$CCCIƆƆƆ = \text{twice} \quad 50,000 = 100,000 \quad \&c.$$

iii. The four chief Numeral Series:

I. CARDINAL Numerals (Cardinalia), which are Adjectives answering the question Quot, *how many?*

II. ORDINAL Numerals (Ordinalia), which are Adjectives answering the question Quotus, *which in order of number?*

---

[1] The Numeral symbols were not originally letters, except, perhaps, M, the initial of mille. The sign of unity was a perpendicular line, afterwards I. The sign of 10 was cruciform, and became X, of which the half (5) passed into V. These three signs are found in Etruscan inscriptions. Then, to represent 50, 100, and 1000, the Romans took three Greek letters, which they did not use in their alphabet, Chi, Theta, and Phi. An old figure of Chi, in the shape of a right angle, became L, 50. Θ was corrupted into C, the initial of centum, 100. Φ, which stood for 1000, was broken into the form CIƆ ; and half of this, IƆ, was taken for 500, sometimes closing up into the form D. (See Mommsen, *Unteritalische Dialekten*, pp. 19, 33, and Ritschl, *Rhein. Museum*, 1869, p. 12, &c.) Ritschl also considers M to be modified from the symbol CIƆ. It is generally admitted that the words decem (Sk. *daśan*, Gr. δέκα) and digitus (δάκτυλος) are cognate : and Curtius adds to these dextera (Sk. *dakshina*, Gr. δεξία), referring to the verb δέχομαι, *to receive* ; but Pott, more speciously, to the verb of *shewing* or *teaching*, doceo (Sk. *diś*, Gr. δεικ-). This points to the fact that numeration began with counting the fingers, and indicates the origin of the decimal system. It is therefore not unlikely that the unit sign I represented the outstretched forefinger, and X the hands or forefingers crossed.

III. DISTRIBUTIVE Numerals (Distributiva), which are Adjectives answering the question Quoteni, *how many each* or *each time?*

IV. Numeral ADVERBS (Quotientiva), answering the question Quotiens, *how often?*

iv. Numeral Series of minor extent:

1. MULTIPLICATIVA, compounded with a root of number and the suffix plic-. They answer the question quotuplex, *how many fold?* and only nine are classically known : though many more might be formed by analogy :

simplex	*simple*	triplex	quincuplex	decemplex
duplex	*double*	quadruplex	septemplex	centuplex

Also sescuplex or sesquiplex.

2. PROPORTIONALIA, formed from a root of number and the suffix **pul-o=plo-** (*more*), answer the question quotuplus, *how many more?* The words in this series classically used are :

simplus	triplus	quincuplus	octuplus
duplus	quadruplus	septuplus	

Also sescuplus, *as much and half as much more*, from sesqui (for sinsemisque, 1½).

Sesquialter has the same meaning as sescuplus.

3. From the Ordinals come

Adjectives in **anus**, which often imply *a soldier* of the legion designated by the Numeral: primanus . . . decumanus . . . vicesimanus, unaetvicesimanus, &c.[1] *a soldier of the 1st, 10th, 20th, 21st, &c. legion.*

But note also : tertiana, quartana febris, *a tertian, quartan ague or fever* : decumanus ager, *tithepaying land* ; decumanus, *a tithe farmer* ; decumanus fluctus, *the tenth* (i.e. largest) *wave* : hence decumana porta in a Roman camp, *the largest gate* (at the back, remote from the enemy).

Adjectives in **arius**, implying class or rank : primarius, secundarius, &c.

Obs. Miliarius lapis, *a milestone* ; because the Roman 'mile' measured 'mille passus,' 1000 paces = 5000 feet.

4. From the Distributives come

Adjectives in **arius**, which mean '*containing* or *consisting of so many each* :' binarius, ternarius, &c. Numerus binarius, the number 2. Versus senarius, septenarius, octonarius, *a verse of 6, 7, 8 feet* : nummus quinarius, denarius, *a coin of 5, 10 asses.* In Plautus, lex quina vicenaria is used to express the law which made debts irrecoverable if contracted by youths under 25 years of age.

Singularis, from singuli, means *unparalleled, remarkable.*

5. Substantives and Adjectives compounded with the Numeral roots exist in great number :

---

[1] It is remarkable that una of unaetvicensima (legio) and analogous Fem. forms remain in these Adjectives.

bīmus, *two years old*; trīmus, *three* . . . quadrīmus, *four* . . . ;
from hĭm- *winter*, with bi- tri- &c.

bimenstris, trimenstris, semenstris, '*of* 2, 3, 6 *months* (also
written bimestris, &c.), from mensis and bi- tri- &c.

biennis, triennis, quadriennis, quinquennis . . . decennis, '*of*
2, 3, 4, 5 . . . 10 *years*,' from annus with bi- tri- &c. ;
but quinquennalis, '*happening once in* 5 *years*.'

biennium, triennium, quinquennium . . . decennium . . . 2. n.
'*a term of* 2, 3, 4, 5 . . . 10 *years*.'

biduum, triduum, quatriduum . . . '*a term of* 2, 3, 4 . . .
days (for bidium, &c.), from dies with bi- tri- &c.

binoctium, trinoctium, &c. are rare.

bivium, trivium, quadrivium, '*a place where* 2, 3, 4 *roads*
(viae) *meet*.'

Compounds of as, assis are tressis (*of* 3 *asses*), quinquessis,
octussis, nonussis, decussis, centussis, &c.

The official terms duumvir, triumvir, &c., *one of a commission
of two, three*, &c., are used in both numbers : but may
also be written in Plur., duoviri, tresviri, &c.

To these may be added a very large list of Adjectives similarly compounded :

biceps, triceps . . .	biformis, triformis . . .	bilinguis, trilinguis . . .
bicolor, tricolor . . .	bifidus, trifidus . . .	bipes, tripes . . .
bicorpor, tricorpor . . .	biiugis, triiugis . . .	biremis, triremis . . .
bidens, tridens . . .	bilibris, trilibris . . .	bisulcus, trisulcus . . .

The word '*balance*' is derived from bilanx (double-dish).

6. The Verbs fari, partiri with the Quotientiva form two series
of Adverbs implying partition :

bifariam, trifariam, quadrifariam, &c. } in 2, 3, 4, &c. parts.
bipartito, tripartito, quadripartito, &c. }

Obs. The words unio (whence Engl. *onion*), binio, ternio, qua-
ternio, senio, are post-classical. But senio is used for the *sice-
throw* (called also Venus) in dice-play.

7. The Ordinals form two series of Numeral Adverbs implying
sequence :

primum . . .   tertium   quartum . . .
primo . . .   tertio   quarto . . .

Primum may mean '*in the first place*,' or '*for the first time*.'
When it means 'in the first place,' it is usually followed by
deinde, in *the second place* ; then by other adverbs, tum, deinceps,
leading up to postremo, *lastly*, or denique, *in fine*.

When it means '*for the first time*,' its sequence is : iterum, *for the
second time*, tertium, quartum . . . postremum.

Some of these words are used with titles of office to express the
second, third, &c. time of a man's holding it : 'L. Corn. Scipio
consul iterum . . . tertium consul,' &c.

Primo usually means '*at the beginning*,' *at the first*, and may be
followed by dein, *next*, post, postea, &c. But primo is sometimes
used like primum, *in the first place*, followed by dein, tertio, quarto,
&c.

v. Declension·of the Numerals.[1]

	M.	F.	N.	
1) Sing. Nom.	un-**us**	**a**	**um** *one.*	Plural
Voc.	un-**e**	**a**	**um**	as
Acc.	un-**um**	**am**	**um**	bonus.
Gen.		un-**ĭus**		
Dat.		un-**i**		
Abl.	un-**o**	**ā**		

Like unus : ullus (for unulus), *any* ; nullus (for ne unulus), *none.*
The Ordinalia and Distributiva are declined as bonus.

NUMERAL

ARABIC	ROMAN SYMBOLS	CARDINALIA
1	I	unus, a, um
2	II	duo, ae, o
3	III	tres, tria
4	IV	quattuor
5	V	quinque
6	VI	sex
7	VII	septem
8	VIII	octo
9	VIIII *or* IX	novem
10	X	decem
11	XI	undecim
12	XII	duodecim
13	XIII	tredecim ; decem et tres ; tres et decem
14	XIV	quattuordecim ; decem et quattuor
15	XV	quindecim
16	XVI	sedecim ; sexdecim ; decem et sex
17	XVII	decem et septem ; s. et d. ; septemdecim
18	XVIII	duodeviginti (decem et octo)
19	XVIIII *or* XIX	undeviginti (decem et novem)
20	XX	viginti
21	XXI	unus et viginti ; viginti unus
22	XXII	duo et viginti ; viginti duo
28	XXVIII	duodetriginta (octo et viginti)
29	XXIX	undetriginta (novem et viginti)
30	XXX	triginta
40	XL	quadraginta
50	L	quinquaginta
60	LX	sexaginta
70	LXX	septuaginta
80	LXXX	octoginta
90	XC	nonaginta
98	IIC	nonaginta octo ; octo et nonaginta
99	IC	nonaginta novem ; undecentum
100	C	centum
101	CI	centum et unus ; centum unus
136	CXXXVI	centum et triginta sex ; c. tr. s.
200	CC	ducenti, ae, a
300	CCC	trecenti . . .
400	CCCC	quadringenti . . .
500	IƆ *or* D	quingenti . . .
600	IƆC *or* DC	sescenti . . .
700	IƆCC *or* DCC	septingenti . . .
800	IƆCCC *or* DCCC	octingenti . . .
900	IƆCCCC *or* DCCCC	nongenti . . .
1,000	CIƆ *or* M	mille
2,000	CIƆCIƆ *or* MM	duo milia (bis mille)
5,000	IƆƆ	quinque milia
10,000	CCIƆƆ	decem milia
50,000	IƆƆƆ	quinquaginta milia
100,000	CCCIƆƆƆ	centum milia ; centena milia
1,000,000	CCCCIƆƆƆƆ	deciens centum milia ; deciens

[1] See note on page 152.

2) Plur. Nom.

	M.	F.	N.
Nom.	duo	duae	duo *two.*
Acc.	duos (duo)	duas	duo
Gen.	duorum	duarum	duorum
D. Abl.	duobus	duabus	duobus

3) Plur. N. tres, tria ; Acc. tris (tres), tria ; G. trium ; D. Abl. tribus.

4) Plur. Nom. Acc. milia; G. milium ; D. Abl. milibus.

Duo for duos is classical. Duum is a form of Gen. much used with weights, measures, numbers; as duum nummum ; duum amphorum ; duum milium.

TABLE.

ORDINALIA -us, -a, -um	DISTRIBUTIVA. -i, -ae, -a	QUOTIENTIVA (-iens or -ies)
primus	singuli	semel.
secundus (*or* alter)	bini	bis.
tertius	terni *or* trini	ter.
quartus	quaterni	quater.
quintus	quini	quinquiens *or* quinquies.
sextus	seni	sexiens.
septimus	septeni	septiens.
octavus	octoni	octiens.
nonus	noveni	noviens.
decimus	deni	deciens.
undecimus	undeni	undeciens.
duodecimus	duodeni	duodeciens.
tertius decimus (decimus et tertius)	terni deni	terdeciens *or* tredeciens.
quartus decimus (decimus et quartus)	quaterni deni	quattuordeciens *or* quater d.
quintus decimus	quini deni	quindeciens *or* quinquiens d.
sextus decimus	seni deni	sedeciens *or* sexiens deciens.
septimus decimus	septeni deni	septiensdeciens.
duodevicensimus (octavus decimus)	duodeviceni	duodeviciens *or* octiens d.
undevicensimus (nonus decimus)	undeviceni	undeviciens *or* noviens d.
vicensimus (vigensimus) *or* vicesimus	viceni	viciens.
unus et vicensimus (primus et vic. ; vic. pr.)	viceni singuli	semel et viciens *or* v. s.
alter et vicensimus (v. a. ; duo et vic.)	viceni bini	bis et viciens *or* v. b.
duodetricensimus (octavus et vicensimus)	duodetriceni	octiens et viciens.
undetricensimus (nonus et vicensimus)	undetriceni	noviens et viciens.
tricensimus (trigensimus) *or* tricesimus	triceni	triciens.
quadragensimus	quadrageni	quadragiens.
quinquagensimus	quinquageni	quinquagiens.
sexagensimus	sexageni	sexagiens.
septuagensimus	septuageni	septuagiens.
octogensimus	octogeni	octogiens.
nonagensimus	nonageni	nonagiens.
nonagensimus octavus	nonageni octoni	nonagiens octiens.
undecentensimus	undecenteni	undecentiens?
centensimus *or* centesimus	centeni	centiens.
centensimus primus	centeni singuli	centiens semel.
centensimus trincensimus sextus	centeni triceni seni	centiens triciens sexiens.
duocentensimus	duceni	ducentiens.
trecentensimus	treceni	trecentiens.
quadringentensimus	quadringeni	quadringentiens.
quingentensimus	quingeni	quingentiens.
sexcentensimus ; sesc.	seceni	sescentiens.
septingentensimus	septingeni	septingentiens.
octingentensimus	octingeni	octingentiens.
nongentensimus	nongeni	nongentiens.
millensimus *or* millesimus	singula milia	miliens.
bis millensimus	bina milia	bis miliens.
quinquiens millensimus	quina milia	quinquiens miliens.
deciens millensimus	dena milia	deciens miliens.
quinquagiens millensimus	quinquagena milia	quinquagiens miliens.
centiens millensimus	centena milia	centiens miliens.
quingentiens millensimus	quingena milia	quingentiens *miliens.*
miliens millensimus	decies centena milia	deciens centiens miliens.

Ambo, *both,* is declined as duo : but without contraction.
Mille, *thousand,* is undeclined.

---

[1] The whole Numeral system contains only 14 roots : those of the ten first Cardinal Numbers (unus . . . decem); mille; semel; and those of primus, secundus. All other Numerals come from these.

Formation of Numerals.

A) Cardinalia.

Unity is expressed in Latin by two forms : (1) u-nu-s; (2) sim-, which appears in singuli, simplex, semel.

1) Unus (E.L. *oinus*) seems to be the Demonstr. Pronoun i gunized (becoming ai, oi=û) and taking the suffix **no**-, so as to imply '*consisting of that,*' '*that and no other=one.*' The Sk. word for *one* is *ekas*, the same pronoun compounded with the interrogative Pron. *ka*, ' who or what,' meaning '*that whatsoever.*' In Zand the form is *aiva* or *aëva*, corresponding to Gr. οἶος, οἱ̂ος, ' *alone.*'

2) Sim- represents Sk. *sa-ma*, which is the Superl. of the Demonstr. Pron. *sa*, thus expressing ' *that especially.*' Singulus (for sim-culus), a deminutive expressing ' *that particular.*' ' *that small unit,*' is used as Plural ; very rarely Singular. It would seem as if singulus and unus had changed places in usage : for although singulus is well suited to the Cardinal series, it belongs to the Distributive, which, having in every other instance the suffix **no**- (bini, terni, &c.), might claim unus as its proper head. This however only occurs when Pluralia-tantum are numbered : as una (bina, trina, &c.) castra; unae (binae, trinae, &c.) litterae, aedes, &c.

From sim- comes sem-e-l; also sim-u-l, sim-ili-s: *sama* is contained also in Gr. εἷς (ἕν-ς), μία, ἵν, in which the Masc. sam-s, becoming san-s and so ἑνς, passes into εἷς, and the Fem. sam-ya becomes sm-ya, m-ya, and so μία.

For the names of the Cardinalia from 2 to 10 see Table.

The Cardinalia from 11 to 17 are additive Compounds of the first nine with decem, 10 : un-decim, duo-decim, &c.

The principal forms for 18, 19 are Subtractive : duodeviginti (2 off 20); undeviginti (1 off 20) ; and these forms reappear in 28, 29 ; 38, 39, &c. to 99, undecentum : 98 only being excepted.

The Cardinalia, which are multiples of 10, are multiplicative Compounds of the Numerals 2 . . . 10 with decentî or degenta (10):—20 (d-videcenti 2×10=) viginti ; 30 (triadecenta 3×10=)=triginta ; 40 (quatora'decenta 4×10=) qu'adraginta, &c. ; but in 70, septuaginta, a byform septuo is used for septem ; and in 90, nonaginta, nona- seems to be contracted from novena. It must be observed that all these forms in ā are probably Neuters Plur. which classically retain the ancient long ā. Centum alone is Neut. Sing. and stands for (decen- decentum 10×10), dropping the first three syllables, as in English the word *wig* has dropt the two first syllables of *periwig*. The Sk. form is *s'ata* (=*kata*), Gr. ἑκατόν, perhaps for (δεκα- δέκατον).

The Multiples of centum from 200 to 900 are Compounds of the first nine Numerals with the form -centi, among which quadr-*in*-genti is strangely formed on the analogy of quingenti, &c. ; octingenti goes back to the Pr. form (*aktau*) ; and nongenti is for (novingenti).

The form expressing 1000 is different in the several branches of the Aryan family : Ind. *sahasra*: Gr. χίλιοι ; L. mille ; Goth. *thusund*, &c.

The root of mille is questionable. Some refer it to Sk. *mil*, Gr. ὁ-μιλ-, *to associate, assemble.*

B) Ordinalia :

Primus (Sk. *prathamas*, Gr. πρῶτος) is Superl. of prae, pro (Sk. *pra*, Gr. πρό. Compare πρίν).

Secundus is Present Participle of sequor (Sk. *sak*, Gr. ἑπ-).

The next four assume the Superl. suffix (*ta*) to-, euphonized in tert-i-u-s (for ter-tu-s, τρίτος), by inserting i. Octa-v-us (ὄγδοφος) seems to be the Adj. of Sk. *ashtau*: and the retention of av (rather than ov) is a remarkable instance of dissimilation. Nonus is a contraction of novenus, a Distributive form in this instance appearing among the Ordinals, as **unus** (see above) among the Cardinal numerals.

vi. Use of the Numerals.

A) Cardinalia.

a) Since the Singular itself implies unity, unus without other Numerals always has emphasis : 'Amicitiae vis est in eo ut unus quasi animus fiat ex pluribus,' *the essence of friendship is that one soul as it were is formed of several*, C. Lael. 25. But, 'Matronae annum, ut parentem, Brutum luxerunt,' *the matrons mourned Brutus for one year, as a father*, L. ii. 7.

b) Unus may take a Superlative force, or emphasise Superlatives : 'Demosthenes unus eminet inter omnes oratores,' *Demosthenes stands unrivalled among orators*, C. Or. 29. 'P. Nigidius, unus omnium doctissimus,' *Publius Nigidius, the most learned of men*, C. Fam. iv. 13. It is likewise used emphatically with some Pronouns and Pronominals : 'Hoc non quivis unus ex populo poterat agnoscere,' *it was not any individual from among the people that could recognise this*, C. Br. 93. 'Nemo unus erat vir quo magis innisa res Romana staret,' *there was no one man on whom the Roman commonwealth more leaned for its support*, L. ix. 16. On the Plural use of unus see p. 155. The Voc. Sing. une is used by Catullus, xxxvii. 17.

c) Mille is used (1) as an undeclined Substantive; rarely with Sing. Verb : 'Amplius mille hominum cecidit,' *more than one*

In the Ordinals of 20, 30 .... to 90 the Superl. ending -sĭmu-s -sŭmu-s is taken, forming -ent-simus (or ent-sumus), -en-simus (or -en-sumus), before the Aug. age, afterwards -ēsimus: as vicensimus (or vicensumus), vicesimus, &c.

This form is adopted, by mere analogy, in cent-ensimus and its Compounds, ducentensimus, &c., and in mill-ensimus.

C) Numeral Adverbs.
Semel: see *A*): bis for (d-vis); ter by transp. for tri: quater (for quat-v-or). All others are formed with the final suffix **-iens** : quinquiens, &c. In the multiples of 10, **-iens** takes the place of **-inta** : viciens, triciens, quadragiens, &c. In 100 and its multiples it follows **nt** : centiens, ducentiens . . . From mille, miliens.

After the Aug. age **n** usually fell out, and the forms became quinquies. . . . milies. So toties, quoties: in R. L. totiens, quotiens.

D) Distributiva.
Singuli : see *A*) : bi-ni (for d-vi-ni), ter-ni or trī-ni : quater-ni : qui-ni (for quinc-ni), se-ni ; septe-ni, octo-ni, nove-ni, de-ni (for dece-ni), &c.

Afterwards the suffix **-eni** is taken by all Distributiva below 1,000.

The form milleni is not used, but instead of it milia is multiplied by the previous Distributives : singula milia, bina milia, &c. See Numeral Table.

Ningulus, an E.L. word (for ne-singulus),=nullus.

The following table shews the resemblance of the Numerals in seven Indo-European languages : Latin, Sanskrit, Greek, Lithuanian, Welsh (Cymraeg), Gothic, and German.

Lat.	Sk.	Gr.	Lith.	W.	Goth.	Germ.
unus	ekas	εἶς	véna	un	aina	eins
duo	dvi	δύο	dva	dau	twai	zwei
tri-	tri	τρι-	tri	tri	thrija	drei
quattuor	c'atvâras	τέτϝαρες	keturi	pedwar	fidvôr	vier
quinque	panc'an	πέντε (πέμπε)	penki	pump	fimf	fünf
sex	shash	ἕξ	szeszi	chwech	saihs	sechs
septem	saptan	ἑπτα	septyni	saith	sibun	sieben
octo	ashtau	ὀκτω	asztuni	wyth	ahtau	acht
novem	navan	ἐννεϝα	devyni	naw	niun	neun
decem	das'an	δέκα	deszinti	deg	taihun	zehn
centum	s'ata	ἑκατόν	szimta	cant	hund	hundert

thousand men fell, Nep. *Dat.* 8 : frequently with Plural verb :
'Mille passuum erant inter urbem castraque,' *there was an
interval of a mile between the city and the camp*, L. xxi. 61. So
mille nummum. (2) As undeclined Adjective constantly : 'Mille
rates,' *a thousand ships*, Ov. *Met.* xii. 7.

The Plural milia (or millia) is only a Substantive, followed
usually by a Genitive : 'Quattuor milia hominum et quingenti
Capitolium occupavere, *four thousand five hundred men seized the
Capitol*, L. iii. 15. If smaller Numerals intervene between milia
and the Substantive, the latter may agree with the smaller : 'Tria
milia et septingenti pedites ierunt,' *there marched* 3,700
infantry, L. xxxv. 40.

'Mille as Abl. is peculiarly used in the following place :

'Cum octo milibus peditum, mille equitum,' L. xxi. 61.

d) The Numerals sescenti and mille are idiomatically used
by Latin authors to express indefinitely large numbers : ' Ses-
centas uno tempore epistolas accepi,' *I received* 600 *letters at once*,
C. *Att.* vii. 2. 'Aiax milies oppetere mortem quam illa perpeti
maluisset,' *Ajax would rather have died* 1,000 *times than have en-
dured that treatment*, C. *Off.* i. 31. 'Mille pro uno Kaesones
exstitisse plebs querebatur,' *the plebeians were grumbling that for
one Kaeso there were now* 1,000, L. iii. 14.

Poets use centum for this purpose. 'Non, mihi si linguae
centum sint oraque centum,' *not if I had a hundred tongues and
a hundred mouths*, Verg. *G.* ii. 44. 'Caecuba servata centum cla-
vibus,' *the Caecuban wine guarded by a hundred keys*, Hor. *C.* ii.
14. 26.

Tres stands for *a few* in Plautus. 'Te tribus verbis volo. Vel
trecentis,' *I want three words with you. Three hundred if you will*,
Trin. iv. 2.

B) Ordinalia.

a) Alter may be used for *second* : 'Alter ab undecimo tum me
iam ceperat annus,' *my twelfth year* (lit. *next from the eleventh*) *had
then commenced*, Verg. *B.* viii. 39. 'Unus et alter,' *one or two*.

Secundus expresses no more than the numerical order : alter
implies that the second is in kind the same as the first. So, 'Denique haec (Pelopidas) fuit altera persona Thebis, sed tamen
secunda ita, ut proxima esset Epaminondae,' *in short, Pelopidas
was the second personage in Thebes, but holding the second rank so
as to be very near Epaminondas*, Nep. *Pel.* 4. See Hor. *C.* i. 12. 18.

b) Ordinals are used in computing time : 'Anno post urbem
conditam septingentensimo quinquagensimo quarto natus
est Christus,' *Christ was born* 754 *years after the foundation of
Rome*. 'Ab illo tempore annum iam tertium et quinquagen-
simum regnat,' *from that time he has now been reigning* 53 *years*,
C. *p L. Man.* 3. Hora quota est ? *what o'clock is it ?* Hora prima,
secunda, tertia, &c., 7, 8, 9. *&c. o'clock*. Horā nonā, *at 3 o'clock*.

c) The Ordinals are used with quisque : 'tertio quoque anno,
every third year, &c. But 'alternis diebus,' *every other day*.

C) Distributiva.

a) These apply the Number they express to *each* of several
persons or things or times : 'Data ex praedā militibus aeris

octogeni bini sagaque et tunicae,' *the soldiers received from the spoil eighty-two asses each, with cloak and tunic,* L. x. 30 (i.e. militibus singulis). 'Germani singulis uxoribus contenti sunt,' *the Germans are satisfied with one wife each,* Tac. *G.* 18 (i.e. Germani singuli). 'Ursae pariunt plurimum quinos,' *bears bring forth at most five cubs at a birth,* Pl. *N. H.* (i.e. ursae singulae).

b) When the Distributive singuli is expressed in Latin with one Noun, the Cardinal can be used with the other : 'Singulis censoribus denarii trecenti ad statuam praetoris imperati sunt,' *each censor had 300 denars imposed on him for the statue of the praetor,* C. *Verr.* ii. 55. But the Distributive is much more usual in this position : 'Verberibus mulcant sexageni singulos,' *they punish with stripes, 60 soldiers each centurion,* Tac. *Ann.* i. 32. 'Antonius quingenos denarios singulis militibus dat,' *Antonius gave each soldier 500 denars,* C. *Fam.* x. 31.

Singuli incedunt, *they advance one by one.* Singulis diebus eadem fiunt, *the same happens every day.*

Quotannis may be used for singulis annis, *every year*; cotidie for singulis diebus ; and viritim, *man by man,* for any Masc. case of singuli.

Plautus has 'singulum vestigium,' *Cist.* iv. 2.

c) The Distributives are often multiplied by the Adverbs : 'Bis bina quot sunt?' *how many are twice two?* Cic. 'Decrevere pontifices ut virgines ter novenae per urbem euntes carmen canerent,' *the pontiffs decreed that three choirs of maidens, nine in each, should sing in procession through the city,* L. xxvii. 37.

d) Uni (not singuli), trini (not terni), and the Distributives bini, quaterni, quini, &c., are used with Substantives of Singular sense and Plural form : 'Una castra iam facta ex binis videbantur,' *one camp seemed now to have been formed out of two,* Caes. *B. C.* i. 24 : 'trinis castris,' Caes. *B. G.* vii. 66. So, 'unae nuptiae,' unae litterae, &c. ; but, 'tres liberi,' *three children.* On this principle the following expressions are legitimate : 'uni Ubii,' *the Ubii alone,* Caes. : 'unos sex dies,' *six days only,* Plaut. 'Lacedaemonii iam septingentos annos unis moribus vivunt,' *the Lacedaemonians have now been living 700 years with one set of habits,* C. *p. Flacc.* 26.

e) Bini is used to express *a pair* : 'Pamphilus binos habebat scyphos sigillatos,' *Pamphilus had a pair of embossed cups,* C. *Verr.* iv. 14. 'Bina manu crispans hastilia,' *brandishing a couple of spears,* Verg. *Aen.* i. 317.

f) Poets sometimes use the Distributives in a multiplicative sense : 'Septeno gurgite,' *with sevenfold torrent,* Lucan. viii. 444. Frequently for the Cardinals : 'centenas manus,' *a hundred hands,* Verg.

But when Virgil writes Per duodena regit mundum sol aureus astra, *the golden sun through 12 signs guides the world,* the Distributive is correct, because each year is implied, *G.* i. 231.

g) The Gen. Pl. of Cardinals and Distributives is usually contracted into **um** : 'quingentum iugerum ;' 'senum septenumve annorum.'

vii. Compound Numeration.

a) In the Table of Numerals the most approved forms are set down ; those less usual but not inadmissible are bracketed.

b) In Compound Numbers above 20, either the smaller number with et precedes the larger, or the larger without et precedes the smaller : 'Romulus septem et triginta regnavit annos,' *Romulus reigned 37 years,* C. *Rep.* ii. 10. 'Macedo Alexander tertio et tricensimo anno mortem obiit,' *Alexander of Macedonia died in his thirty-third year,* C. *Ph.* v. 17. 'Septuaginta et tres amissi,' *73 were lost,* L. xxxv. 1. 'Plinius scripsit sub Nerone naturae historiarum libros triginta septem,' *Plinius in the reign of Nero wrote 37 books of natural history,* Plin. *Ep.* iii. 5. 'Dentes triceni bini viris attribuuntur,' *thirty-two teeth are assigned to a man,* Pl. *N. H.* vii. 16. But 'et' occurs after the larger Numeral : 'viginti et duos annos,' C. *Cat. M.* 9. Also the smaller occurs before the larger without et : 'Quattuor quadraginta illi debentur minae,' *44 minas are due to him,* Plaut. *Most.* iii. 1. 'Septimo quinquagensimo die rem confeci,' *I finished the affair in 57 days,* C. *Fam.* xv. 4. Unus, when it occurs with viginti, &c., generally stand^s first, and the Noun last : unus et viginti homines ; unum et triginta millia. But exceptions occur : 'Viginti unus tribuni,' L. xxii. 49. 'Viginti unam muscas,' *21 flies,* Pl. *N. H.* xxx. 10. 'Diebus viginti uno,' Pl. *N. H.* xxix. 6.

c) In Compound Numbers above 100, the larger with or without et generally precedes the smaller : 'Leontinus Gorgias centum et septem complevit annos,' *Gorgias of Leontini completed 107 years,* C. *Cat. M.* 5. 'Annum magnum esse voluerunt omnibus planetis in eundem recurrentibus locum, quod fit post duodecim milia nongentos quinquaginta quattuor annos,' *they would have a great year to be when all the planets come back into the same place, which happens after 12,954 years,* Cic. 'Sescentensimum et quadragensimum annum urbs Roma agebat, cum primum Cimbrorum audita sunt arma,' *Rome was in its 640th year when the arms of the Cimbri were first heard,* Tac. *G.* 37. 'Olympiade centensimā quartādecimā Lysippus fuit,' *Lysippus lived in the 114th Olympiad,* Pl. *N. H.* xxxiv. 8. 'Aristidis arbitrio quadringena et sexagena talenta quotannis Delum sunt collata,' *under the control of Aristides 460 talents were annually contributed to the treasury at Delos,* Nep. *Ar.* 3.

d) The multiples of 1,000 are expressed by the Cardinals (or Distributives) multiplying milia : duo, tria, &c., ; decem, viginti, &c. ; centum, ducenta, &c. milia ; (or bina, terna, &c.), milia.

Poets and some prose writers of the silver age use bis, ter, &c. with mille : 'bis mille equos,' Hor. ; 'quinquiens mille quadringenta stadia,' Pl. *N. H.* And so with smaller Numerals : 'Hic (Caesar) deciens senos tercentum et quinque diebus addidit,' *Caesar added 60 days to 305,* Ov. *F.* iii. 163.

e) The multiples of 100,000 are expressed by the Numeral Adverbs joined to centum milia or centena milia, as stated in the following passage : 'Non erat apud antiquos numerus ultra centum, milia; itaque et hodie multiplicantur haec, ut deciens centena milia aut saepius dicantur,' *the ancients had no number beyond* 100,000 ; *wherefore to the present day these figures are multiplied, so as to use the form* ' *ten times a hundred thousand,' and the like in progression*, Pl. *N. H.* xxxiii. 10.

Thus we find : 'viciens centum milia passuum,' 2,000,000 = *miles*, Caes. : 'bis et triciens centum milia passuum,' 3,200,000 *miles*, Suet. 'quinquiens miliens centum milia,' 500,000,000, Pl.; 'octagiens quinquiens centena sexaginta octo milia,' 8,568,000 Pl. In cipher the thousands were written with a line above them, and the hundred thousands with side lines also. Thus 999,999 in writing is: noviens centena nonaginta novem milia nongenti nonaginta novem; in cipher: $\mid$ IX $\mid$ XCIX IɔCCCCXCIX.

aa. Unus is often used in Compound Numbers for the Ordinal primus : 'Plato uno et octogensimo anno scribens mortuus est,' *Plato died while writing in his* 81*st year*, C. *Cat. M.* So unetvicensimus, unaetvicensima or unetvicensima. Duoetvicensimus is rare.

viii. Numeral Expression of Fractions.

Frac-tions.

The Romans expressed fractions in the following ways :[1]

1) If the numerator is 1, it is not expressed : as dimidia pars = $\frac{1}{2}$, tertia pars = $\frac{1}{3}$, &c.

2) If the numerator is greater than 1, and less than the denominator by more than 1, it is expressed as in English, suppressing 'partes :' duae quintae = $\frac{2}{5}$; tres septimae = $\frac{3}{7}$, &c.

3) If the numerator is less than the denominator by 1 only, the latter may be suppressed, 'partes' being expressed : duae partes = $\frac{2}{3}$; tres partes = $\frac{3}{4}$; quinque partes = $\frac{5}{6}$, &c.

4) A fraction may be expressed by the multiplication of two fractions : dimidia tertia = $\frac{1}{2} \times \frac{1}{3} = \frac{1}{6}$; quarta septima = $\frac{1}{4} \times \frac{1}{7} = \frac{1}{28}$, &c.

5) A fraction may be expressed by the addition of two fractions : as pars dimidia et tertia = $\frac{1}{2} + \frac{1}{3} = \frac{5}{6}$; pars quarta et septima = $\frac{1}{4} + \frac{1}{7}$ = $\frac{11}{28}$.

6) The Roman unit of weight, length, or measure was called a s.

The 'as' (unit) of weight, called libra, *pound*
 — — — of length — pes, *foot*
 — — — of area — iugerum, *acre*

was in each case divided into 12 parts, called unciae.[2]

Hence fractions of 12 were named, according to the number of unciae they contained, as follows :—

---

[1] Dimidio maior means ' *half as much larger,'* altero tanto maior, *as large again*, i.e. *twice as large*. The following passage from Pl. *N. H.* vi. (cited by F. Schultz) may be a useful exercise in fractional computation, while it shews the great ignorance of geography which existed in Pliny's time :—

'Apparet Europam paulo minus dimidia Asiae parte maiorem esse quam Asiam ; eandem altero tanto et sexta parte Africae ampliorem quam Africam. Quod si misceantur omnes summae, liquido patebit Europam totius terrae tertiam esse partem et octavam paulo amplius, Asiam vero quartam et quartamdecimam, Africam autem quintam et insuper sexagensimam.'

[2] Hence *inch* as well as *ounce* is derived from uncia.

uncia	$= 1$ unc.	$\frac{1}{12}$ of the unit
sextans	$= 2$ —	$\frac{2}{12} = \frac{1}{6}$,, ,,
quadrans	$= 3$ —	$\frac{3}{12} = \frac{1}{4}$,, ,,
triens	$= 4$ —	$\frac{4}{12} = \frac{1}{3}$,, ,,
quincunx	$= 5$ —	$\frac{5}{12}$,, ,,
semissis	$= 6$ —	$\frac{6}{12} = \frac{1}{2}$,, ,,

septunx	$= 7$ unc.	$\frac{7}{12}$ of the unit.
bes	$= 8$ —	$\frac{8}{12} = \frac{2}{3}$,, ,,
dodrans	$= 9$ —	$\frac{9}{12} = \frac{3}{4}$,, ,,
dextans	$= 10$ —	$\frac{10}{12} = \frac{5}{6}$,, ,,
deunx	$= 11$ —	$\frac{11}{12}$,, ,,

By this notation inheritance was calculated : 'heres ex asse,' *universal heir* : 'heres ex semisse,' *heir to half the estate*; 'heres ex dimidia et quadrante,' *heir to three-fourths*, &c.

The Uncia was also subdivided, viz. :—

scripulum	$= \frac{1}{24}$ unc.	$= \frac{1}{288}$ of unit	sicilicus $= \frac{1}{4}$ unc. $= \frac{1}{48}$ of unit.
sextula	$= \frac{1}{6}$ —	$= \frac{1}{72}$,,	semuncia $= \frac{1}{2}$ — $= \frac{1}{24}$,,

Sescuncia or Sescunx (uncia semisque) $= 1\frac{1}{2}$ uncia $= \frac{1}{8}$ of unit.
Sesquialtera ratio $= 1\frac{1}{2} : 1 = 3 : 2$.

CHAPTER LII.

THE VERB.

SECTION I.

35
Verb
Finite
and In-
finite.

i. The Verb Finite and Infinite. See page 72.

I. The Verb Finite is so called, because its forms are *limited* by Mood and Person, as well as Tense.

II. The forms of the Verb Infinite are not limited by Mood and Person.

Note. Any Finite form is called a PERSONAL VERB, because it agrees with a Nominative in the 1st, 2nd, or 3rd Person.

36
Voices.

ii. The Voices of the Verb.

There are in Verbs two classes of form, which grammarians have called *VOICES* (Voces, Genera) :

1) The Active Voice (Vox Activa), from agere, *to do.*

2) The Passive Voice (Vox Passiva), from pati, *to suffer.*

1) The Active Voice indicates that a Subject *is* or *does* something :

sum, *I am*   amo, *I love*
valeo, *I am well*   moneo, *I advise*

2) The Passive Voice indicates generally that a Subject *suffers* something (*has* something *done* to it):

amor, *I am loved*   moneor, *I am advised*

iii. Deponent Verbs.

Many Verbs, though Passive in most of their forms, have an Active meaning:

venor, *I hunt*   vereor, *I fear*

These are called by grammarians, DEPONENT VERBS (Deponentia).[1]

iv. Transitive and Intransitive Verbs.

1) In order that it may be fully conjugated (like amo and moneo), in both Voices, a Verb must be Transitive.
Intransitive Verbs are fully conjugated in one Voice only.

2) A Verb is called TRANSITIVE when its action *passes on* (transit) to an Object in the Accusative (Objective) Case: moneo Lucium, *I advise Lucius*; Lucius me audit, *Lucius hears me.* A Deponent Verb may be Transitive, though conjugated in the Passive Voice only: venamur lepores, *we hunt hares*; lepores nos verentur, *hares fear us.*

3) An INTRANSITIVE Verb, Active or Deponent, requires no Object: surgo, *I rise*; proficiscor, *I go.*
Those which express state or condition are called Static Verbs: aegroto, *I am sick*; sto, *I stand*; irascor, *I am angry.*
An Accusative Object, called Cognate or Contained, may be joined to an Intransitive Verb, if it expresses the function contained in the Verb itself: ludere ludum insolentem, *to play a haughty game*; aegrotare mirum morbum, *to be sick of a strange disease.* See Syntax (Accusative).
The construction called IMPERSONAL allows Intransitive Verbs to be used in the Third Persons Singular and in the Infinitive of the Passive Voice: surgitur (a nobis or ab illis being understood), *we (they) rise* (literally, *there is rising by us* or *by them*). See § 50.

4) The Subject of a Transitive Verb may become its Object: (ego) verto me, *I turn myself*; (tu) vertis te, *you turn yourself*; (is) vertit se, *he turns himself.* This Pronoun Object is sometimes omitted, as in English, and the Verb is thus used intransitively: iam verterat fortuna, *fortune had now turned*, Liv.
On the other hand, the Passive, like the Greek Middle Voice, has often a reflexive use: vertor, *I turn myself*; lavor, *I wash myself.* Probably this was the primary sense of the Passive.
Some Deponents originate thus: glorior, *I boast* (*myself*); vescor, *I feed* (*myself*). Others grow out of Passive Verbs: gravor, *I grudge, am loth* (lit. *am grieved*).

---

[1] The term 'Deponent' is bad, though inveterate in Latin grammar. Medial (Media) would be a better name for these Verbs.

v. Quasi-Passive and Semi-Deponent Verbs.

1) A few Verbs, of Active form, are used in Passive sense, and are called QUASI-PASSIVE Verbs :

exsulo, 1. *I am banished.*
vapulo, 1. *I am beaten*
fio, *I become* or *am made,*   Passive of facio, *I make.*
pereo, *I am lost* or *destroyed*   —   perdo, *I lose or destroy.*
veneo, *I am on sale*   —   vendo, *I sell.*
liceo, 2. *I am put to auction* (but liceor, *I bid at an auction*).

The Participles perditus and perdendus, venditus and vendendus, are in use. Verbero, *I beat*, has a Passive verberor, but vapulo often took its place in popular speech.

2) Some Verbs, otherwise Active, take a Passive form with Active meaning in their Perfect Participle and the Tenses derived from it :

audeo, 2. *I dare*   ausus sum, *I dared*
gaudeo, 2. *I rejoice*   gavisus sum, *I rejoiced*
soleo, 2. *I am wont*   solitus sum, *I was wont*
fido, 3. *I trust*   fisus sum, *I trusted*
fio, *I become*   factus sum, *I became*

These are called SEMI-DEPONENT Verbs.

3) Some Verbs have an Active Perfect, with a Passive Perfect Participle, active in sense :

ceno, cenavi, *I supped*   cenatus, *having supped*
iuro, iuravi, *I swore*   iuratus, *having sworn*
prandeo, prandi, *I dined*   pransus, *having dined*
nubo, nupsi, *I was wedded*   nupta, *wedded*

Other Passive Participles from Active Verbs are :

adultus, *grown up,*   from adolesco, adolevi
cretus, *sprung*   —   cresco, crevi
suetus, *accustomed*   —   suesco, suevi (with compounds)
obsoletus, *out of date*   —   obsolesco, obsolevi
placitus, *pleasing*   —   placeo, placui.
potus, *having drunk,* from an old stem po-
perosus, *hating,* from perodi ; exosus, *hating* or *hated utterly*
pertaesus, *tired,* from pertaedet.

Also coalitus (coalesco), deflagratus, exoletus, initus, inveteratus, propensus. See M. *Lucr.* ii. 383 ; iii. 772.

37 Moods.

vi. The Moods of the Verb.

MOODS (Modi) express the *manner* of action in a Finite Verb.

There are three Moods of the Verb Finite :

1) The *INDICATIVE* Mood declares a fact or condition as real or absolute :

gaudeo quod (si) abest, *I am glad that (if) he is absent.*

2) The *CONJUNCTIVE* Mood states a fact or condition as conceived or contingent :

gaudeam si absit, *I shall be glad if he be absent*;
velim absit, *I would wish he were absent*:
vellem abesset, *I could wish he had been absent.*

This Mood, in principal construction, we call the PURE Conjunctive, gaudeam, velim, vellem. When it depends on another Verb, it is called SUBJUNCTIVE, absit, abesset.
The English version of the Conjunctive generally requires the use of an auxiliary Verb, *may, might, would, should, shall*, &c.
The Subjunctive is often rendered by the English Indicative : nescio quid velis, *I know not what you wish*; tam stulti sunt ut nihil intellegant, *they are so foolish that they understand nothing*; also by the English Subjunctive : dubito num intellegat, *I doubt if he understand*; but often it must be expressed by an auxiliary verb *may, might*: ĕdimus ut vivamus, *we eat that we may live.*
The right rendering of this Mood is not learnt from tables, but by exemplification, reading, and practice.

3) The *IMPERATIVE* Mood is for command and entreaty : huc curre, *run hither*; memento venias, *you must remember to come.* See p. 163.

vii. The Tenses of the Verb.

TENSES (Tempora) are forms which indicate the *time* of action or state in Verbs.

1. Tense-forms are either INFLECTED or COMBINATE.

An Inflected Tense-form is a distinct word obtained by modifying the Stem of the Verb : ama-bo, ama-v-eram.
A Combinate Tense-form is obtained by connecting a Participle of the Verb with a Tense-form of an auxiliary Verb. The only auxiliary Verb ordinarily used for this purpose in classical Latin is the Verb of Being, sum, esse, *to be*, which, combined with the Participles in us, supplies various Tenses, especially the Perfect Tenses in the Passive Voice : amatus sum, fui, &c.

2. The English language has very few inflected Tenses ; as

Pres.	love, lovest, loves ;
Past	loved, lovedst :

but its Verb is enlarged by combining with Infinitive and Participial forms nine auxiliary Verbs and several Prepositions : namely,

α.	be (am, was, &c.)	have (had)	must
	do (did)	let	shall (should)
	can (could)	may (might)	will (would)

β. to ; about to ; by ; in.

M

Hence English is richer in its power of expressing Time than Latin ; and most Latin forms admit various English equivalents. As grammatical tables cannot supply all the English equivalents for each Verb-form, a thorough knowledge of the Latin Verb is gained only by the practical work of reading and intertranslating.

3. Time is Present, Past, or Future.

Action or state may be *simply* present, past, or future.

For each simple time Latin has an inflected Indicative Tense-form in the Active Voice ; and, in the Passive, inflected forms for the Present and Future, and a combinate form for the Simple Past. Thus, in the Indicative Mood,

SIMPLE PRESENT.	SIMPLE PAST.	SIMPLE FUTURE.
	ACTIVE.	
ămo, *I love*	amāvi, *loved*	amābo, *shall love*
	PASSIVE.	
ămor, *I am loved*	amātus sum, *was loved*	amābor, *shall be loved*

4. But it is often necessary to describe action and state with more complex relations of time; and this the English language, by its numerous auxiliary verbs, can do more fully than Latin. Such relations are (in the Indicative Mood) :

	ACTIVE.	PASSIVE.
I. Present in		
Present	am loving*	am being-loved*
Past	*was loving*	*was being-loved*
Future	shall-be loving*	shall-be (being) loved*
II. Past in		
Present	have loved*	have-been loved*
Past	*had loved*	had-been loved†
Future	*shall-have loved*	shall-have-been loved†
III. Future in		
Present	am about-to-love†	am about-to-be-loved‡
Past	was about-to-love†	was about-to-be-loved‡
Future	shall-be about-to-love†	shall-be about-to-be-loved‡

Latin has inflected Tense-forms for three only of these relations in the Active ; and for one only in the Passive :

Indic. Act.	amābam, *I was loving*
— —	amāveram, *I had loved*
— —	amāvero, *I shall have loved*
— Pass.	amābar, *I was being loved*

To express the English marked *, the Simple Tense-forms are used : amo, amor; amabo, amabor; amavi, amatus sum (fui).

To express that marked †, Combinate forms are needed : amatus eram (fueram) ; amatus ero (fuero) ; amaturus sum, fui, ero (fuero).

For the English marked ‡, and other temporal relations still more complex, the help of particles is required in Latin:

> *the woman is about to be killed*
> in eo est mulier ut trucidetur :
> *the woman was about to be killed*
> in eo erat mulier ut trucidaretur.

If this be thrown into oblique statement (*I think, I thought that,* &c.), the Passive Infin. iri with Supine may be used; or futurum (fore) ut with Subjunctive:

> puto (putavi) mulierem trucidatum iri
> puto futurum ut mulier trucidetur
> putavi fore ut mulier trucidaretur.

5. Action is either Incomplete (Infecta) or Complete (Perfecta).

The names of the Finite Tenses are:

1) Of Incomplete Action :

> Present ; Future Simple ; Imperfect.

2) Of Complete Action :

> Perfect ; Future Perfect ; Pluperfect.

The subjoined Table shews their form in the three Moods of each Voice. (See Scheme.)

	ACTIVE			PASSIVE		
	Indic.	Conjunc. [1]	Imper.	Indic.	Conjunc.	Imper.
1) Present	amo	amem	amā	amor	amer	amāre
Fut. S.	amabo		amāto	amabor		amātor
Imperfect	amabam	amarem		amabar	amarer	
2) Perfect	amavi	amaverim		amatus sum	amatus sim	
Fut. P.	amavero			amatus ero		
Pluperf.	amaveram	amavissem		amatus eram	amatus essem	

The Imperative *to*-forms are generally regarded as strengthening varieties, implying *must*. Some (as Madvig, Ferd. Schultz, &c.) treat them in this sense as = Future forms. We do the same, but merely for the sake of convenience.

---

[1] Gossrau (*Latein. Sprachl.* § 146) rightly says that the Conjunctive Tenses are not *temporal* in the same sense as those of the Indicative ; the Pluperfect being the only one which never loses its proper expression of time. But his mode of escape from this difficulty is so far from commendable, that to discuss it would be lost time. The distinction used in this grammar, of Pure Conjunctive in a principal sentence, and Subjunctive in a dependent clause, seems to be the simplest and easiest as far as it goes. But the difficulty still remains of having to call the Conjunctive (or Subjunctive) forms by the names of the Indicative Tenses, from which some of them diverge in use so widely. The only way of

Obs. The defects of this Tense-system are in part supplied by the Combinate or Periphrastic Conjugation of sum with the Participles in -rus, -dus (see § **47**) :

amaturus sum ero eram fui, &c. sim essem fuerim, &c.
amandus sum ero eram fui, &c. sim essem fuerim, &c.

6. Tenses are Primary or Historic.

The Primary Tenses are the Present and the Futures : the Historic are the Imperfect, Pluperfect, and Simple Past (*I loved*). When Present-Past (*I have loved*), the Perfect is Primary.

It is a great advantage of Greek, as compared with Latin, that it has inflected forms for both these relations :

Simple Past (Aorist) . . ἐφίλησα, *I loved*
Present Past (Perfect) . πεφίληκα, *I have loved*

39
Number and Person.

viii. Number and Person in the Verb.

The Tenses of the Finite Verb have two *NUMBERS*, Singular and Plural; with three *PERSONS* in each Number, distinguished by Pronominal endings.

The First Person expresses one or more speaking ;
The Second   ,,   ,,   ,,   spoken to ;
The Third   ,,   ,,   ,,   spoken of :

SINGULAR.	PLURAL.
ego am-o, *I love*	nos amā-mus, *we love*
tu amā-s, *thou*[1] *lovest*	vos amā-tis, *ye*[1] *love*
is amă-t, *he loves*	ii ama-nt, *they love*

The **o** in amo represents a Primitive form *ă-mi*. Hence the characters of the three Persons are severally **m, s, t.** Pronoun Nominatives, being understood in the Personal endings, are commonly omitted : am-o, *I love*; ama-s, *you love*; ama-t, *he loves*, &c.

In the Imperative Mood there is no First Person ; and in its Present Tense the Second Person only is used.

40
The Verb Infinite.

ix. The Verb Infinite contains :

1. Infinitive, Gerunds, and Supines ; which are Substantival ;

2. Participles, which are Adjectival.

---

avoiding it seems to be, to use for the Conjunctive forms, when cited in Syntax, a numeral notation easy to be remembered :

amem ; moneam ; regam ; audiam : C_1 or S_1
amaverim ; monuerim ; rexerim ; audierim : C_2 or S_2
amarem ; monerem ; regerem ; audirem : C_3 or S_3
amavissem ; monuissem ; rexissem ; audissem : C_4 or S_4.

[1] English usage has adopted *you* for the Second Person of both Numbers instead of *thou* and *ye*, which are now used only in prayer or by poets.

1. *A*) The *INFINITIVE* (Infinitivum) describes action or state in a general manner, without personal relation.   <small>Infinitive.</small>

It has Tense-forms :

   1) For Incomplete Action (Present and Imperfect) :

     Act. amā-re, *to love, be loving, have been loving*
     Pass. amā-ri, *to be loved.*

   2) For Complete Action (Perfect and Pluperfect) :

     Act. amav-isse, *to have loved*
     Pass. amat-us, a, um, esse, *to have been loved.*

   3) For Future in Present Action :

     Act. amat-urus, a, um, esse, *to be about to love*
     Pass. amat-um iri, *to be about to be loved* (where amatum, being Supine, is invariable).

   4) For Future in Past Action :

     Act. amat-urus, a, um, fuisse, *to have been about to love.*

B) The *GERUNDS* (Gerundia) are cases of a Verbal Substantive with suffix -**ndo**-, Decl. 2. n.   <small>Gerunds.</small>
The *GERUNDIVE* (Gerundivum) is a Participle or Verbal Adjective with the same suffix :

GERUNDS.	GERUNDIVE.
Acc. ama-**ndum,** *loving*	Nom. S. ama-**ndus, a, um** (*meet*)
Gen. ama-**ndi,** *of loving*	*to be loved*
Dat. ama-**ndo,** *for loving*	declined as bonus.
Abl. ama-**ndo,** *by* or *in loving*	

The Gerundive is used to express meetness or necessity, either impersonally, as eundum est, *one must go* ; or personally : vita tuenda est, *life should be protected.* If a Case of the Person is added, that Case is usually the Dative : eundum est mihi, *I must go* ; vita nobis tuenda est, *life should be protected by us.*

C) *SUPINES* (Supina) are Accusative and Ablative of a Verb-noun of Decl. 4, with suffix -**tu** (su) or -**to** (so) :   <small>Supines.</small>

     amā-**t-um,** *to love*   amā-**t-ū,** *in loving*

2. *PARTICIPLES* (Participia) are so called because they take part of the properties of Verbs, and part of the properties of Adjectives. Besides the Gerundive, three other Participles are found in Verbs :   <small>Participles.</small>

Active Pres. and Imperf. ama-**ns,** *loving* . . . . as ingens
  —   Future . . . . ama-**t-ūrŭs,** *about to love* } as bonus
Passive Perfect . . . . ama-**t-ŭs,** *having been loved* }

a) The three Participles wanting may be thus supplied :

Act. Part. Perf. *having loved,* cum amavisset (or by Abl. Absolute)

Pass. — Pres. *being loved,* qui amatur, or dum amatur

— — Fut. *about to be loved,* qui amabitur.

b) Some Verbs form Participials in **-bundus** or **-cundus**, expressing 'fulness,' as vagabundus, *wandering,* iracundus, *wrathful* ;

in **-bĭlis**, expressing 'possibility,' parabĭlis, *procurable* ;

in **-ĭlis**, expressing 'capacity,' docĭlis, *teachable* ;

in **-ax**, expressing 'inclination,' loquax, *talkative* ;

in **-ĭdus**, expressing 'active force,' rapĭdus, *hurrying,* cupĭdus, *desirous.*

c) Deponent Verbs, though of Passive form, have the Active Participles in **-ns, urus**, and also use their Perfect Participle in an Active sense :

Pres. vena-ns, *hunting*

Fut. venā-t-ūrŭs, *about to hunt*

Perf. venā-t-ŭs, *having hunted*

But many Deponents use their Perfect Participle passively as well as actively, as pollicitus, *promised* or *having promised,* from polliceor, *I promise.* Others of this kind are abominatus, auspicatus, adeptus, comitatus, commentus, conatus, confessus, dignatus, dimensus, effatus, emensus, expertus, exsecratus, fabricatus, frustratus, imitatus, impertītus, machinatus, meditatus, mentītus, merĭtus, moderatus, modulatus, nactus, oblītus, opinatus, orsus, exorsus, pactus, partītus, populatus, professus, ratus, sortītus, testatus, testificatus, ultus, velificatus, veneratus, &c.

SECTION II.

41
The
three
Stems in
Verbs.

i. The Conjugation of Verbs.

1) In order to conjugate a Verb of Active form, three elements must be known :

1. The *PRESENT STEM* . . . ama-
2. The *PERFECT STEM* . . . amāv-
3. The *SUPINE STEM* . . . amāt-

2) To conjugate a Verb of Passive form (which has no Perfect Stem) the Present Stem and Supine Stem must be known :

1. Pres. Stem . . . vena-
2. Sup. Stem . . . venāt-

The last letter in each Stem (a, v, t) is its Character.

a) From the Present Stem are derived :

Present, Future Simple, Imperfect, Imperative, Infinitive Present, in each Voice;

Gerunds, Gerundive, and Participle Present in the Active Voice.

β) From the Perfect Stem are derived :

Perfect, Future Perfect, Pluperfect, Infinitive Perfect, in the Active Voice.

γ) From the Supine Stem are derived :

Supines, Future Participle in the Active Voice ; Perfect Participle Passive ; and therefore all the Combinate Tenses in the Passive Voice.

ii. The Verb of Being, sum,[1] esse.

Before other Verbs, it is convenient to shew the conjugation of the irregular *VERB OF BEING*, sum, esse, fui, *to be*, which enters into their Combinate Tenses as an auxiliary Verb.

This Verb is formed from two roots:

es- (Sk. *as*) *to be* ;
fu- (Sk. *bhû*) *to be* or *become.*

The forms of the Present Stem (except forem, fore) belong to the first of these ; the Perfect, Future Participle, and Future Infinitive, with forem, fore, to the second ; the other Tenses are compounded of both.

---

[1] The Root of Being, Sk. *as* Gr. ἐσ- L. es-, is found in all branches of the Aryan family, variously modified.

1) The root 'es-' forms

Present Indic.

L.	s-*u*-m	ĕs (for es-s)	est	sŭmus	es-tis	sunt
Sk.	*as-mi*	*as-i*	*as-ti*	*s-mas*	*s-tha*	*s-anti*
Gr.	εἰμί (ἐσμί)	εἶ (ἐσ-σί)	ἐστί	ἐσμέν (ἐσμές)	ἐστέ	εἰσί (ἐντί)

Fut. Indic. L. ĕro (for *es-io*), Gr- ἔσο-μαι.
Imperf. L. ĕram (for *es-am*), Sk. (simple Aor. in am), Gr. ἔην (for ἐσ-ην).
Pres. Conjunc. L. (siem) sim (for *es-iem*), Sk. *s-yâm*, Gr. ε-ίην (for ἐσ-ιην).
The forms siem, sies, siet are occasionally found.
Imperf. Conjunc. L. essem. See p. 58.

Imperative.

	Pres.			Future	
	S.	Pl.	S.		Pl.
L.	ĕs	este	esto	estote	sunto
Sk.	*e-dhi* (for *as-dhi*)	*s-ta*	*astu*		*s-antu*
Gr.	ἰσ-θι	ἐστε	ἔστω		ἔστων

The Infinitive es-se is, as that of every Active Verb, the Dative (or Loc.) Case of a Verb-noun.

2) The Root fu-, Sk. *bhû*, Gr. φυ- forms
Imperf. Conjunc. forem (for *fu-sem*) : Infin. fore (for *fu-se*).
Fut. Partic. fut-urus.

It also forms the Perfect Stem fu- (for fuv-), and its derived Tenses, by agglutinating the tenses of sum. See p. 58.
The English forms 'am,' 'art,' 'is,' 'are,' belong to the root *as* : 'be' to the root *bhû.*

Tense	Mood		1. I	2. thou	3. he, she, it	1. we	2. ye	3. they	
Present	INDIC.	{	sum / *am*	ĕs / *art*	est / *is*	sŭmŭs / *are*	estĭs / *are*	sunt / *are*	
	CONJ.	{	sim	sīs	sĭt	sīmŭs	sitĭs	sint . *be or may be.*	
S. Fut.	INDIC.	{	ĕro / *shall*	erĭs / *wilt*	erĭt / *will*	erĭmŭs / *shall*	erĭtĭs / *will*	erunt	*will . . . . be.*
Imperfect	INDIC.	{	ĕram / *was*	erās / *wast*	erăt / *was*	erāmŭs / *were*	erātĭs / *were*	erant / *were*	
	CONJ.	{	essem / *(was) or may*	essēs / forēs	essĕt / forĕt	essēmŭs / forēmŭs	essētĭs / forētĭs	essent / forent	} *were or might be*
Perfect	INDIC.	{	fuī / *was or have been*	fuisti / *wast &c.*	fuĭt / *was &c.*	fuĭmŭs / *were*	fuistĭs / *were*	fuērunt or ērĕ / *were (have been).*	
	CONJ.	{	fuĕrim / *(was) or may*	fuerĭs / *mayst*	fuerĭt / *may*	fuerĭmŭs / *may*	fuerĭtĭs / *may*	fuerint	*may . . have been.*
Fut. Perf.	INDIC.	{	fuĕrō / *shall*	fuerĭs / *wilt*	fuerĭt / *will*	fuerĭmŭs / *shall*	fuerĭtĭs / *will*	fuerint	*will . . have been.*
Pluperfect	INDIC.	{	fuĕram / *had*	fuerās / *hadst*	fuerăt / *had*	fuerāmŭs / *had*	fuerātĭs / *had*	fuerant	*had . . . . been.*
	CONJ.	{	fuissem / *(had been) should*	fuissēs / *wouldst*	fuissĕt / *would*	fuissēmŭs / *should*	fuissētĭs / *would*	fuissent	*would . . have been.*

IMPERATIVE MOOD.

Pres. S. ĕs, *be thou.*
— Pl. estĕ, *be ye.*
Fut. S. estō, *thou must be.*
     estō, *he (she, it) must be.*
— Pl. estōtĕ, *ye must be.*
     suntō, *they must be.*

INFINITIVE.

Pres. Imperf. essĕ, *be, or was being.*
Perf. Plup. fuissĕ, *was, have (or had) been.*
Fut. fōrĕ, or fŭtūrŭs, ā, um, essĕ, *will be.*

Like sum are its compounds absum, adsum, dēsum, insum, intersum, obsum, praesum, prōsum, subsum, sŭpersum. Prōsum takes **d** before **e** : prōdest, prōd-essĕ. Absum forms Participle absens ; praesum, praesens.

PARTICIPLES.

Pres. (ens, not used).
Fut. fŭtūrŭs, ā, um, *about to be.*
(Sum has no Gerund or Supines.)

iii. Latin Verbs are customarily divided into four
Classes, called *CONJUGATIONS*, according to their Pre-
sent Character, that is, the last letter of their Present-
Stem.

a) One of these Conjugations, having for its Present-Character
either a Consonant or the Semiconsonant **u**, is called the Strong
Conjugation, because it keeps that Character in all Present-Stem
forms, without suffering contraction :

reg-ĕ-re   indu-ĕ-re.

Consonant Verbs, which, with a few exceptions, are the oldest in
Latin, ought, strictly, to be the First Conjugation ; but from ancient
times they have been named and ranked as the 3rd, which title
they cannot now lose without great inconvenience, on account of
the large number of Dictionaries and other books of reference in
which they, like the Declensions, are cited numerically.

b) The other three Conjugations are called Pure, because their
Character is a Vowel (**a, e, i**). They are also called Weak, or Contracted, because in some Present-Stem Forms the Vowel Character
unites by Contraction with a following Vowel : amă-o, amo;
amă-im, amem, &c. So

ama-ĕ-re, amāre ; mone-ĕ-re, monēre ; audi-ĕ-re, audīre.[1]

c)   A-verbs are called the 1st Conjugation.
          E-verbs   —   —   2nd   —
          I-verbs   —   —   4th   —

Consonant and U-verbs being the 3rd Conjugation. See *a*).

d) The Character of the Verb is therefore the letter which stands
before **re** of the Infinitive in the Weak Conjugations, or before ĕ-**re**
in the Strong Conjugation :

Conj. 1. amA-re, *love*   Conj. 3. { reG-ĕre, *rule*
  — 2. monE-re, *advise*   { indU-ĕre, *put on*
  — 4. audI-re, *hear*

e) In Conjugation 3 are included some Verbs which exhibit **i** in
many Present-Stem forms : caP-*i*-o, paT-*i*-or; this **i** not being,
however, the Character of the Verb.

---

[1] Although the assumption of a Vincular absorbed by contraction would account for
most of the forms in which the Characters **a, e, i** are long before a Consonant, it cannot
safely be affirmed that this is the true principle of formation. It is perhaps more correct
to say that these Characters are generally strengthened in this position. The practical
rules are :

1) The Characters **e, i** are short before a Vowel : monĕam, audĭes. But **ă** with a
following Vowel forms Contraction : ama-o, am-o, ama-im, amem.

2) The Characters, **a, e, i** are long when final : amā, monē, audī ; or before a
Consonant : amās, amāmus ; monēs, monēmus ; audīs, audīmus (anciently amāmūs, &c.). Exceptions are : (1) before **t** final, though originally long
(amāt, monēt, audīt), these Characters become short in Latin usage : amăt,
monĕt, audĭt ; (2) the Verb dă-, *give*, keeps **a** short before a Consonant :
dăre, dăbo, dăbam, dăto, but dā.

3) The Mood-vowels, **a, e, i**, follow generally the same law as the Characters :
audiās, audiāmus ; amēs, amarēmus ; velīs, velīmus ; but audiăt
amarĕt, velĭt (anciently audiāt, amarēt, velīt).

f) The three Stems in each Conjugation are as follows :—

ACTIVE VERBS.			DEPONENT VERBS.	
Present.	Perfect.	Supine.	Pres.	Sup.
1. amA-	amaV-	ămaT-	venA-	venaT-
2. monE-	monU-	monĭT-	verE-	verĭT-
3. reG-	rex- (for reGs)	recT-	uT-	us-
4. audI-	audiv-	audīT-	partI-	partīT-

The Present Stem of a Pure Verb, without its Character, is called a **Clipt Stem** : am-, mon-, aud-, ven-, ver-, part-.

Method of Conjugating.

g) A Latin Verb is sufficiently described by naming—

(1) the Present Indic. 1st Person ;
(2) the Infinitive Pres. ;
(3) the Perfect Indic. 1st Person ;
(4) the Supine in **um** :

amo, amāre, amāvi, amātum ;

but it is useful, in conjugating, to mention some other forms.

CONJUGATION OF THE ACTIVE VOICE.

	1st Conj.	2nd Conj.	3rd Conj.	4th Conj.
1 Pers. Ind. Pr.	am-o	mon-eo	reg-o	aud-io
2 Pers. Ind. Pr.	am-ās	mon-ēs	reg-ĭs	aud-īs
Infinitive	am-āre	mon-ēre	reg-ĕre	aud-īre
Perfect	am-āvi	mon-ui	rex-i	aud-īvi
Gerund in **dum**	am-andum	mon-endum	reg-endum	aud-iendum
— **di**	am-andi	mon-endi	reg-endi	aud-iendi
— **do**	am-ando	mon-endo	reg-endo	aud-iendo
Supine in **um**	am-ātum	mon-ĭtum	rect-um	aud-ītum
— **u**	am-ātu	mon-ĭtu	rect-u	aud-ītu
Partic. Present	am-ans	mon-ens	reg-ens	aud-iens
— Future	am-āturus	mon-ĭturus	rect-urus	aud-īturus

CONJUGATION OF THE PASSIVE VOICE.

	1st Conj.	2nd Conj.	3rd Conj.	4th Conj.
1 Pers. Ind. Pr.	am-or	mon-eor	reg-or	aud-ior
2 Pers. Ind. Pr.	am-āris	mon-ēris	reg-ĕris	aud-īris
Infinitive	am-āri	mon-ēri	reg-i	aud-īri
Perfect	am-ātus sum	mon-ĭtus sum	rect-us sum	aud-ītus sum
Partic. Perfect	am-ātus	mon-ĭtus	rect-us	aud-ītus
Gerundive	am-andus	mon-endus	reg-endus	aud-iendus[1]

Deponent Verbs have Passive Conjugation, but Active meaning, Gerunds, Supines, and Participles Active. As Intransitive Verbs have no personal Passive, so Intransitive Deponents, as vagor, 1. *wander*, have no Gerundive Adjective.

---

[1] The Gerundive is ranked under the Passive Voice because none but Transitive Verbs can use it adjectively. But we agree with Pott, that it may be ascribed to both voices. If a horse is 'ferox ante domandum,' *wild before being broken in,* his rider is 'cautus ante domandum,' *cautious before breaking him in.* To the bees is ascribed 'amor habendi :' of their wax may be said what Virgil says of rich soil, 'ad digitos lentescit habendo,' *it yields to the fingers in being handled.*

CONJUGATION OF DEPONENTS.

	hunt	*fear*	*use*	*divide*
1 Pers. Pres. Ind.	vĕn-or	vĕr-eor	ūt-or	part-ior
2 Pers. Pres. Ind.	ven-āris	ver-ēris	ut-ĕris	part-īris
Infinitive Pres. .	ven-āri	ver-ēri	ut-i	part-īri
Perfect	ven-ātus sum	ver-ĭtus sum	ūs-us sum	part-ĭtus sum
Gerund in **dum** .	ven-andum	ver-endum	ut-endum	part-iendum
— **di** .	ven-andi	ver-endi	ut-endi	part-iendi
— **do** .	ven-ando	ver-endo	ut-endo	part-iendo
Gerundive . . .	ven-andus	ver-endus	ut-endus	part-iendus
Supine in **um**. .	ven-ātum	ver-ĭtum	ūs-um	part-ītum
— **u** . .	ven-ātu	ver-ĭtu	ūs-u	part-ītu
Partic. Pres. . .	ven-ans	ver-ens	ut-ens	part-iens
— Perf. . .	ven-ātus	ver-ĭtus	ūs-us	part-ītus
— Fut. . .	ven-āturus	ver-ĭturus	ūs-urus	part-īturus

Verbs in *i-o* of the Third Conjugation, in their Present-Stem forms, retain this *i* generally; but not before **i**, final **e**, and short **ĕr.**   These are the following Verbs, with their compounds :

Fŭg*io*, făc*io*, and iăc*io*,
Compounds of spĕc*io* and lăc*io*,
Păr*io*, fŏd*io*, and quăt*io*,
Cŭp*io*, căp*io*, răp*io*, săp*io* ;
(Deponents) grăd*ior*, păt*ior*, mŏr*ior*,
And, in some tenses, pŏt*ior*, ŏr*ior*.

Their form of Conjugation is :

	Active.	Passive.	Deponent.
1 Pers. Pres. Ind. . .	cap-*i*-o	cap-*i*-or	pat-*i*-or
2 Pers. Pres. Ind. . .	cap-ĭs	cap-ĕris	pat-ĕris
Infinitive Pres. . . .	cap-ĕre	cap-i	pat-i
Perfect	cēp-i	capt-us sum	pass-us sum
Gerund in **dum** . . .	cap-*i*-endum		pat-*i*-endum
— **di**	cap-*i*-endi		pat-*i*-endi
— **do**	cap-*i*-endo		pat-*i*-endo
Gerundive		cap-*i*-endus	pat-*i*-endus
Supine in **um** . . .	capt-um		pass-um
— **u**	capt-u		pass-u
Partic. Pres.	cap-*i*-ens		pat-*i*-ens
— Perf.		capt-us	pass-us
— Fut.	capt-urus		pass-urus

Note 1.—In the Scheme, Latin forms are given at full, with the corresponding English of one Verb.   English must be supplied, on the same principle, to the other Verbs.

Note 2.—The Masculine Participles amatus, amati, &c., are set down alone to avoid confusion ; but the Gender of a Participle follows that of the Noun with which it agrees :

is auditus est,   ea audita est,   id auditum est,
he was heard,   *she was heard,*   *it was heard.*

And so in all Persons and Cases of both Numbers,

ACTIVE VOICE.

	INDICATIVE MOOD					
	SINGULAR.			PLURAL.		
	1.	2.	3.	1.	2.	3.
Present.	*I*	*thou*	*he, &c.*	*we*	*ye*	*they*
	love	*lovest*	*loves*	*love*	*love*	*love*
	ăm -(a)o	-ās	-ăt	-āmŭs	-ātĭs	-ant
	mŏn -eo	-ēs	-ĕt	-ēmŭs	-ētĭs	-ent
	rĕg -o	-ĭs	-ĭt	-ĭmŭs	-ĭtĭs	-unt
	aud -io	-īs	-ĭt	-īmŭs	-ītĭs	-iunt
Fut. Simple.	*shall*	*wilt*	*will*	*shall*	*will*	*will—love, &c.*
	amā -bō	} -bĭs	-bĭt	-bĭmŭs	-bĭtĭs	-bunt
	monē -bō					
	reg -am	} -ēs	-ĕt	-ēmŭs	-ētĭs	-ent
	audi -am					
Imperfect.	*was*	*wast*	*was*	*were*	*were*	*were—loving, &c.*
	amā -bam					
	monē -bam	-bās	-băt	-bāmŭs	-bātĭs	-bant
	regē -bam					
	audiē -bam					
Perfect.	*loved*	*lovedst*	*loves*	*loved*	*loved*	*loved, &c.*
	or have	*hast*	*has*	*have*	*have*	*have—loved, &c.*
	amāv -ī					
	monu -ī	-istī	-ĭt	-ĭmŭs	-istĭs	-ērunt
	rex -ī					*or* -ērĕ
	audīv -ī					
Fut. Perfect.	*shall*	*wilt*	*will*	*shall*	*will*	*will—have loved, &c.*
	amāv -ĕrō					
	monu -ĕrō	-ĕrĭs	-ĕrĭt	-ĕrĭmŭs	-ĕrĭtĭs	-ĕrint
	rex -ĕrō					
	audīv -ĕrō					
Pluperfect.	*had*	*hadst*	*had*	*had*	*had*	*had—loved*
	amāv -ĕram					
	monu -ĕram	-ĕras	-ĕrăt	-ĕrāmŭs	-ĕrātĭs	-ĕrant
	rex -ĕram					
	audīv -ĕram					

I. Examples of Indicative and Imperative Moods.

A) (Pres. and Fut. Active) : lĕgo, *I read :* quid ăgis? *what are you doing?* lego, *I am reading :* lege sis, *read, if you please :* lego, *I do read :* iamdiu lego, *I have been reading long :* quid facies? *what will you do?* legam, *I shall read :* leges Iliădem, *you will read the Iliad, I hope :* legam, *I will read it :* cum lēgero semel, *when I shall have read it once :* relĕge sodes, *read it again, pray :* relegito, *you must read it again :* de manibus non deposueris antequam relēgeris, *you will not put it out of your hands till you have read it again.*

B) (Past Tenses Active) : quid agebas heri? *what were you doing yesterday?* legebam, *I was reading :* quid agebas ruri? *what did you do in the country?* legebam, *I used to read :* legebam dum lux erat, *I read while it was light :* legere te iusseram, *I told you to read :* legebam, *I did read :* legeres Iliădem, *you were to read the Iliad :* lēgi heri, *I read it yesterday :* legistine Iliadem? *have you read the Iliad?* lēgi, *I have read it :* lĕgere debuisti, *you ought to have read it :* lēgi, *I did read it :* lēgeram pridie, *I had read it the day before.*

FOUR CONJUGATIONS.

PASSIVE VOICE.

INDICATIVE MOOD.

SINGULAR.			PLURAL.		
1.	2.	3.	1.	2.	3.
I	*thou*	*he, &c.*	*we*	*ye*	*they*
am	*art*	*is*	*are*	*are*	*are—loved, &c.*
am -ŏr	-ārĭs	-ātŭr	-āmŭr	-āmĭnī	-antŭr
mon -eŏr	-ērĭs	-ētŭr	-ēmŭr	-ēmĭnī	-entŭr
reg -ŏr	-ĕrĭs	-ĭtŭr	-ĭmŭr	-ĭmĭnī	-untŭr
aud -iŏr	-īrĭs	-ītŭr	-īmŭr	-īmĭnī	-iuntŭr

shall	*wilt*	*will*	*shall*	*will*	*will—be loved, &c.*
amā -bŏr					
monē -bŏr	-bĕr-ĭs (ĕ)	-bĭtŭr	-bĭmŭr	-bĭmĭnī	-buntŭr
reg -ăr					
audi -ăr	-ēr-ĭs (ĕ)	-ētŭr	-ēmŭr	-ēmĭnī	-entŭr

was	*wast*	*was*	*were*	*were*	*were—being loved*
amā -băr					
monē -băr					
regē -băr	-băr-ĭs (ĕ)	-bātŭr	-bāmŭr	-bāmĭnī	-bantŭr
audiē -băr					

was	*wast*	*was*	*were*	*were*	*were—loved*
have	*hast*	*has*	*have*	*have*	*have—been loved*
amātŭs, monĭtŭs, rectŭs, audītŭs			amātī, monĭtī, rectī, audītī		

sum	ĕs	est	sŭmŭs	estĭs	sunt
(fui)	(fuisti	(fuĭt)	(fuĭmŭs)	(fuistĭs)	(fuērunt, ĕ)

shall	*will*	*will*	*shall*	*will*	*will—have been*
amātŭs, monĭtŭs, rectŭs, audītŭs			amātī, monĭtī, rectī, audītī *[loved*		

ĕrō	ĕrĭs	ĕrĭt	ĕrĭmŭs	ĕrĭtĭs	ĕrunt
(fuĕro)	(fuĕrĭs)	(fuĕrĭt)	(fuĕrĭmŭs)	(fuĕrĭtĭs)	(fuĕrint)

had	*hadst*	*had*	*had*	*had*	*had—been loved*
amātŭs, monĭtŭs, rectŭs, audītŭs			amātī, monĭtī, rectī, audītī		

ĕram	ĕrās	ĕrăt	ĕrāmŭs	ĕrātĭs	ĕrant
(fuĕram)	(fuĕras)	(fuĕrăt)	(fuĕrāmŭs)	(fuĕrātĭs)	(fuĕrant)

Note 1.—In the Second Pers. Pres. Ind. Passive it is not so usual to write rĕ for rĭs, on account of the confusion with Infin. Act. and Imperat. Pass. Cicero has very few instances, chiefly Deponent forms, though in the other tenses he decidedly prefers the forms in -rĕ.

2.—Poets sometimes write the Simple Futures of I-verbs, Act. -ĭbo, -ĭbis, &c., Pass. -ĭbor, -ĭberis (e), &c. ; and the Imperfects, Act. -ĭbam, -ĭbas, &c., Pass. -ĭbar, -ĭbaris (e), &c. ; as audĭbo, audĭbor; audĭbam, audĭbar. These were the ancient forms. M. *Lucr.* v. 934.

3.—The Perf. Partic. used with sum expresses that something was and is complete : with fui, that something was complete at some past time : ' leges quae latae sunt . . . quae promulgatae fuerunt,' C. *p. Sest.* 25. See Madvig, *Opusc.* ii. p. 218.

4.—On the exclusion of **v**, followed by contraction, from Perfect Stems in āv-, ēv-, ŏv-, ūv-, īv-, see p. 58. The forms in -ii, -ieram, -iero, -issem, -isse, are used in prose as well as poetry. I it, from eo, is found ; but most disyllabic forms keep **v** : as quīvi, sīvi.

SCHEME OF THE

ACTIVE VOICE.

IMPERATIVE MOOD.							
	Present.			**Future.**			
	S. 2.	Pl. 2.		S. 2.	S. 3.	Pl. 2.	Pl. 3.
love	*thou*	*ye*		*thou*	*he, &c.*	*ye*	*they, &c.*
am	-ā	-āte	am	-ātō	-ātō	-ātōte	-antō
mon	-ē	-ēte	mon	-ētō	-ētō	-etōte	-entō
reg	-ĕ	-ĭte	reg	-ĭtō	-ĭtō	-ĭtōte	-untō
aud	-ī	-īte	aud	-ītō	-ītō	-ītōte	-iuntō

must love, &c.

		CONJUNCTIVE MOOD.					
		SINGULAR.			**PLURAL.**		
		1.	2.	3.	1.	2.	3.
Present.	am	-em	-ēs	-ĕt	-ēmŭs	-ētĭs	-ent
	mone	-am	-ās	-ăt	-āmŭs	-ātĭs	-ant
	reg	-am	-ās	-ăt	-āmŭs	-ātĭs	-ant
	audi	-am	-ās	-ăt	-āmŭs	-ātĭs	-ant
Imperfect.	amā	-rem					
	monē	-rem	-rēs	-rĕt	-rēmŭs	-rētĭs	-rent
	regĕ	-rem					
	audī	-rem					
Perfect.	amāv	-ĕrim					
	monu	-ĕrim	-ĕrĭs	-ĕrĭt	-ĕrĭmŭs	-ĕrĭtĭs	-ĕrint
	rex	-ĕrim					
	audīv	-ĕrim					
Pluperfect.	amāv-	-issem	-issēs	-issĕt	-issēmŭs	-issētĭs	-issent
	monu-						
	rex-						
	audīv-						

II. Pure Conjunctive.

A) (Potential and Conditional use): mirum fortasse videatur, *perhaps it may seem wonderful* : ita amicos pares, *thus you may gain friends* : quaerat quispiam, *some one may ask* : dixerit aliquis, *somebody may (might) say* : pace tua dixerim, *I would say with your leave* : pro certo affirmaverim, *I can aver for a fact* : crederes victos, *you would have supposed them vanquished* : velim esse tecum, *I would like to be with you* : nolim te abire, *I should not like you to go away* : nollem id factum, *I could wish it had not been done* : mallem aliud factum, *I would rather something else had been done.*

B) (Dubitative use): quid faciam? *what must (can, shall) I do?* quid facerem? *what should (could) I have done?* faveas tu hosti? *must (should) you favour an enemy?*

C) (Concessive use) : naturam expellas, *you may drive out nature* : fuerit sapiens, *suppose he were wise* : ne fuerit sapiens, *suppose he were not wise* : fuisset anceps fortuna, *fortune might have been doubtful.*

D) (Optative use) : vivas, *may you live* : valeant cives mei, *may my countrymen flourish* : di bene vertant, *heaven prosper it* : moriar (ne vivam) si mentior *may I die if I speak falsely* : ita vivam ut te amo, *so may I live as I love you=upon my life I love you.*

E) (Hortative use) : imitemur bonos, *let us imitate the good* : desinant furere, *let them (or they should) cease to rave* : rem tuam curares, *you should have been minding your own business* : mortem pugnans oppetisset, *he should have died fighting.*

FOUR CONJUGATIONS.

PASSIVE VOICE.

IMPERATIVE MOOD.

Present.			Future.		
S. 2.		Pl. 2.	S. 2.	S. 3.	Pl. 3.
be thou		*ye—loved*, &c.	*thou*	*he*	*they*
amā	-re	-mĭnī	amā -tŏr	-tŏr	-ntŏr
monē	-re	-mĭnī	monē -tŏr	-tŏr	-ntŏr
reg	-ĕre	-ĭmĭnī	rĕg -ĭtŏr	-ĭtŏr	-untŏr
audī	-re	-mĭnī	audī -tŏr	-tŏr	-untŏr

must be loved, &c.

CONJUNCTIVE MOOD.

	SINGULAR.			PLURAL.		
	1.	2.	3.	1.	2.	3.
am	-ĕr	-ēr-ĭs(ĕ)	-ētŭr	-ēmŭr	-ēmĭnī	-entŭr
mone	-ăr	-ār-ĭs(ĕ)	-ātŭr	-āmŭr	-āmĭnī	-antŭr
reg	-ăr	-ār-ĭs(ĕ)	-ātŭr	-āmŭr	-āmĭnī	-antŭr
audi	-ăr	-ār-ĭs(ĕ)	-ātŭr	-āmŭr	-āmĭnī	-antŭr

amā	-rĕr					
monē	-rĕr	-rēr-ĭs(ĕ)	-rētŭr	-rēmŭr	-rēmĭnī	-rentŭr
reg-ĕ	-rĕr					
audī	-rĕr					

amātŭs, monĭtŭs, rectŭs, audītŭs			amātī, monĭtī, rectī, audītī		
sim	sīs	sĭt	sīmŭs	sītĭs	sint
(fuĕrĭm)	(fuĕris)	(fuĕrĭt)	(fuĕrĭmŭs)	(fuĕrĭtĭs)	(fuĕrint)

amātŭs, monĭtŭs, rectŭs, audītŭs			amātī, monĭtī, rectī, audītī		
essem	essēs	essĕt	essēmŭs	essētĭs	essent
(fuissem)	(fuissēs)	(fuissĕt)	(fuissēmŭs)	(fuissētĭs)	(fuissent)

III Subjunctive.

Fit ut aegrotem, *it happens that I am sick :* evēnit ut aegrotarem, *it fell out that I was sick:* necesse est eas (necesse erit eas), *you must go :* opus est ut eas (oportet eas), *it behoves you to go :* opus erat ut ires (oportuit ires), *it behoved you to go :* metuo ne eas, *I fear you will go :* metuebam ne ires, *I feared you would go,* *I fear you are not going :* metuebam ut ires, *I feared you were not going :* cura ut eas (fac eas), *mind you go :* sine eamus, *suffer us to go :* oro ut eas, *I beg that you go :* oravi ut ires, *I begged you would go :* utinam eas! *O that you may go!* utinam ires! *O that you had been going!* utinam ne isses! *O that you had not gone!* scio cur veniat, *I know why he comes:* scio cur venerit, *I know why he came :* sciebam cur veniret, *I knew why he came :* sciebam cur venisset, *I knew why he had come :* non tam amens est ut eat, *he is not so mad as to go :* non tam amens fuit ut iret, *he was not so mad as to go :* edo ut vivam, *I eat that I may live :* vivebant ut ederent, *they lived that they might eat:* laudant me quod eam, *they praise me because I go :* laudant me quod ierim, *they praise me because I went :* laudabant me quod irem, *they praised me because I went :* laudabant me quod issem, *they praised me because I had gone :* quae cum ita sint, ibo, *since this is the case, I will go :* quae cum ita essent, ivi, *since this was the case, I went :* aegrotabam cum irem, *I was ill when I went :* convalui cum issem, *I got well when I had gone :* exspecta dum redeam, *wait till I return :* nusquam ibo antequam redeat, *I will go nowhere before he returns :*

SCHEME OF THE

ACTIVE VOICE.

VERB

INFINITIVE.					
Pr. Impf. *to love*, &c.		Perf. Plup. *to have loved*, &c.		Future. *to be about to love*, &c.	
amā	-rĕ	amāv	-issĕ	amāt	-ūrŭs
monē	-rĕ	monu	-issĕ	monĭt	-ūrŭs
regĕ	-rĕ	rex	-issĕ	rect	-ūrŭs } essĕ
audī	-rĕ	audīv	-issĕ	audīt	-ūrŭs

Gerunds. *loving*, *of, by*, &c.		Supines. *to love, in loving*, &c.		Partic. Pres. *loving*, &c.		Partic. Fut. *about to love*, &c.	
amand	-um -ī -ō	amāt	-um -ū	ama	-ns	amatūr	-ŭs -ă -um
monend	-um -ī -ō	monĭt	-um -ū	mone	-ns	monitūr	-ŭs -ă -um
regend	-um -ī -ō	rect	-um -ū	reg-*e*	-ns	rectūr	-ŭs -ă -um
audiend	-um -ī -ō	audīt	-um -ū	audi-*e*	-ns	auditūr	-ŭs -ă -ūm

ut peccaverit, carus est tamen, *though he has sinned, yet he is dear*: quamvis peccasset, carus fuit, *though he had sinned, he was dear*: clamas tanquam surdus sim, *you bawl, as though I were deaf*: clamabas quasi surdus essem, *you were bawling, as if I had been deaf*: emo libros quos legam, *I buy books to read*: emi libros quos legerem, *I bought books to read*: non is sum qui te deseram, *I am not one to forsake you*: non is fuit qui me desereret, *he was not one to forsake me*: quis est quin fleat aliquando? *who is there that weeps not sometimes?* nemo fuit quin fleret, *there was no one but wept*: nihil dubito quin gaudeant, *I have no doubt they rejoice*: non dubitabam quin gauderent, *I had no doubt they rejoiced*: nihil obstat quominus eam, *nothing hinders me from going*: per me stetit quominus ires, *I was the cause of your not going*: vetitus est ne iret, *he was forbidden to go*: dubito an verum sit, *I doubt it may be true*: nescio an verum sit, *I rather think it is true*: felicem esse puto qui rei nullius indigeat, *I consider him to be happy who wants nothing*: ais te cum redeam adfuturum, *you say you will be present when I return*: ait se cum redierim adfuturum, *he says he will be present when I have returned*: aiebant se cum rediissem adfore, *they said they would be present when I had returned*: nego quicquam esse utile, quod non sit honestum, *I say that nothing is expedient which is not morally right*: aedes quas emisset exornari iussit, *he ordered the house which he had bought to be decorated*: exprobratur mihi quod Iliadem nondum legerim, *I am reproached with not having yet read the Iliad*: exprobratum est mihi quod Iliadem nondum legissem, *I was reproached with having not yet read the Iliad*: Themistocles noctu ambulabat, quod somnum capere non posset, *Themistocles used to walk by night, because (he said) he could not sleep*.

IV. Pure Conjunctive and Subjunctive in Combination.

Velim rescribas, *I should wish you to write back*: vellem adesses, *I could wish you were here*: nollem accidisset, *I could wish it had not happened*: mallem quidvis faceres, *I would rather you did anything*: mallem aliter fecisset, *I would rather he had done otherwise*: quidvis potius paterer, quam mentirer, *I would suffer anything rather than tell a falsehood*: praestes quod receperis, *you should perform what you have undertaken*: praestaret quod recepisset, *he should perform what he had undertaken*: eant quo velint, *they may go where they will*: irent quo vellent, *they might go where they would*: quis miretur quod homines liberi servire nolint? *who can say he wonders that free men do not wish to be slaves?* eam si iubeas, eam si iusseris, ierim si iusseris, *I shall go if you bid me*: irem si iuberes, *I would go if you bade me*: issem si iussisses, *I would have gone, had you told me*: non iturus essem, nisi tu iussisses, *I should not have been about to go, unless you had bidden me*.

(Examples of this kind, noted and imitated, teach the right rendering of the Conjunctive Mood, in its various uses, better than English given in Tables.)

FOUR CONJUGATIONS.
PASSIVE VOICE.
INFINITE.

Pr. Impf.		Perf. Plup.			Future.		
to be loved, &c.		*to have been loved, &c.*			*to be about to be loved, &c.*		
amā	-rī	amāt	-ŭs		amāt	-um	
monē	-rī	monĭt	-ŭs	essĕ	monĭt	-um	īrī
reg	-ī	rect	-ŭs		rect	-um	
audir	-ī	audīt	-ŭs		audīt	-um	

Gerundive.				Partic. Perf. Plup.			
(meet) *to be loved, &c.*				*loved* or *having been loved, &c.*			
amand	-ŭs	-ă	-um	amāt	-ŭs	-ă	-um
monend	-ŭs	-ă	-um	monĭt	-ŭs	-ă	-um
regend	-ŭs	-ă	-um	rect	-ŭs	-ă	-um
audiend	-ŭs	-ă	-um	audīt	-ŭs	-ă	-um

V. The Verb Infinite.

ACTIVE.	PASSIVE.
legere utile est	legi libros utile est
to read is useful	*it is useful that books be read*
librum legere coepi	liber legi coepit
I have begun to read the book	*the book has begun to be read*
memini me legere	memini librum legi
I remember that I read	*I remember the book being read*
aio me legisse	aio librum lectum esse
I say that I have read	*I say that the book has been read*
memineram me legisse	memineram librum lectum esse
I remembered that I had read	*I remembered the book had been read*
videor mihi lecturus esse	dicitur liber lectus esse
I think I am going to read	*the book is said to have been read*
aio me lecturum esse	aio libros lectum iri
I say that I will read	aio futurum ut libri legantur
	I say the books are going to be read
aiebam me lecturum esse	aiebam fore ut libri legerentur
I said that I would read	*I said that the books would be read*
aiebam me lecturum fuisse	aio futurum fuisse ut legerentur
I said that I would have read	*I say they would have been read*
putor lecturus fuisse	
it is supposed I should have read	
legendum est nobis	legendus est liber
we must read	*the book must be read*
consuetudo legendi	cupido librorum legendorum
the habit of reading	*the desire of reading books*
cupidus sum legendi	cupidus sum libri legendi
I am desirous of reading	*I am desirous of reading the book*
aptus est legendo (ad legendum)	aptus est libris legendis
he is fit for reading	aptus est ad libros legendos
inter legendum	*he is fitted for reading books*
in the course of reading	
oblector legendo	oblector libris legendis
I amuse myself with reading	*I amuse myself with reading books*
in legendo versor	in libris legendis versor
I am engaged in reading	*I am engaged in reading books*
eo lectum Iliadem	librum unicuique legendum
I am going to read the Iliad	*a book to be read by everybody*
lecturus sum Iliadem	librum utilem lectu
I am about to read the Iliad	*a book useful to read*
Iliadem legens oblector	Iliade lecta gaudeo
I am charmed with reading the Iliad	*I rejoice in having read the Iliad*

N

SCHEME OF THE
DEPONENT

	INDICATIVE MOOD.						
	SINGULAR.			PLURAL.			
	1.	2.	3.	1.	2.	3.	
	I	*you*	*he*, &c.	*we*	*ye*	*they*	
Present.	vēn -ŏr	-ār-ĭs(ĕ)	-ātŭr	-āmŭr	-āmĭnī	-antŭr	*hunt,* &c.
	vĕr -eŏr	-ēr-ĭs(ĕ)	-ētur	-ēmur	-ēmini	-entur	
	ūt -ŏr	-ĕr-ĭs(ĕ)	-ĭtur	-ĭmur	-ĭmini	-untur	
	part -iŏr	-īr-ĭs(e)	-ītur	-īmur	-īmini	-iuntur	
Fut. Simple.	venā -bŏr vere -bor } -bĕr-is(e)		-bĭtur	-bĭmur	-bĭmini	-buntur	*shall (will) hunt,* &c.
	ut -ăr parti -ar } -ēr-is(e)		-ētur	-ēmur	-ēmini	-entur	
Imperfect.	venā -băr vere -bar utē -bar partiē-bar } -bār-is(e)		-bātur	-bāmur	-bāmini	-bantur	*was hunt-ing,* &c.
Perfect.	vēnātŭs, vĕrĭtŭs, ūsŭs, partītŭs			vēnātī, vĕrĭtī, ūsī, partītī			*hunted or have h.*
	sum　　ĕs　　est (fui, &c.)			sŭmus　　estis　　sunt			
Fut. Perf.	venatus, veritus, usus, partitus			venati, veriti, usi, partiti			*shall (will) have hunted.*
	ĕro　　erĭs　　erĭt (fuero, &c.)			erĭmus　erĭtis　erunt			
Pluperfect.	venatus, veritus, usus, partitus			venati, veriti, usi, partiti,			*had hunted.*
	eram　　erās　　erăt (fueram, &c.)			erāmus　erātis　erant			

IMPERATIVE MOOD.

	Present.			Future.			
	S. 2.	Pl. 2.		S. 2.	S. 3.	Pl. 3.	
hunt,&c.	*thou*	*ye*		*thou*	*he*	*they*	*must hunt,* &c.
	venā -re	-mĭnī		venā -tŏr	-tŏr	-ntŏr	
	vere -re	-mini		vere -tor	-tor	-ntor	
	utĕ -re	-ĭ-mini		utĕ -tor	-tor	-untor	
	partī -re	-mini		partī -tor	-tor	-untor	

Note.—Some Deponents have an Active form also, as comitari or comitare.

FOUR CONJUGATIONS.

VERBS.

CONJUNCTIVE MOOD.

	Singular 1.	2.	3.	Plural 1.	2.	3.
$C_1 S_1$	ven -ĕr	-ēr-ĭs(ĕ)	-ētur	-ēmur	-ēmini	entur
	vere -ăr	-ār-is(e)	-ātur	-āmur	-āmini	antur
	ut -ar	-ār-is(e)	-ātur	-āmur	-āmini	antur
	parti -ar	-ār-is(e)	-ātur	-āmur	-āmini	antur
$C_2 S_2$	vena -rĕr, verē -rer, utĕ -rer, partī-rer	-rēr-is(e)	-rētur	-rēmur	-rēmini	-rentur
$C_3 S_3$	venatus, veritus, usus, partitus: sim (fuerim, &c.)	sīs	sĭt	venati, veriti, usi, partiti: sīmus	sītis	sint
$C_4 S_4$	venatus, veritus, usus, partitus: essem (fuissem, &c.)	essēs	essĕt	venati, veriti, usi, partiti: essēmus	essētis	essent

VERB INFINITE.

INFINITIVE.

Pres. Impf.		Perf. Plup.		Future.	
venā -rī	*to hunt, &c.*	venāt-ŭs esse	*to have hunted, &c.*	venāt-ūrŭs esse	*to be about to hunt, &c.*
verē -ri		verĭt -us esse		verĭt -urus esse	
ut -i		us -us esse		ūs -urus esse	
partī -ri		partīt-us esse		partīt-urus esse	

PARTICIPLES.

Pr. Impf.		Gerundive.		Perf. Plup.		Future.	
vena -ns	*hunting, &c.*	venand -ŭs	*meet to be hunted, &c.*	venāt -ŭs	*having hunted, &c.*	venāt-ūrŭs	*about to hunt, &c.*
vere -ns		verend -us		verĭt -us		verĭt -urus	
ūt-*e* -ns		ūtend -us		ūs -us		ūs -urus	
parti-*e* -ns		partiend-us		partīt -us		partīt-urus	

Gerunds.		Supines.	
venand -um -ī -ō	*hunting, &c. of, for, by hunting, &c.*	venāt-um -ū	*in order to hunt; in hunting.*
verend -um -i -o		verĭt-um -u	
utend -um -i -o		ūs-um -u	
partiend -um -i -o		partīt-um -u	

VERB in Ĭ-O OF CONJUG. III.

(Present-Stem Forms.)

ACTIVE.

Indic. Pres.	căp*i*-o, cap-ĭs, -ĭt, -ĭmus, -ĭtis, cap*i*-unt.
— Fut.	cap*i*-am, -ēs, -ět, -ēmus, -ētis, -ent.
— Imperf.	cap*i*-ēbam, -ēbas, -ēbat, -ēbamus, -ēbatis, -ēbant.
Conj. Pres.	cap*i*-am, -ās, -ăt, -āmus, -ātis, -ant.
— Imperf.	cap-ěrem, -ěres, -ěret, -ěrēmus, -ěrētis, -ěrent.
Imper. Pres.	cap-ě, -ĭtě.
— Fut.	cap-ĭto, -ĭtōtě, -*i*-untō.
Infin. Pres.	cap-ěrě.
Gerund.	cap*i*-endum, -endī, -endō.
Part. Pres.	cap*i*-ens.

DEPONENT.

Indic. Pres.	păt*i*-or, pat-ěris, -ĭtur, -ĭmur, -ĭmĭnī, -*i*-untur.
— Fut.	pat*i*-ăr, -ēr-is(ě), -ētur, -ēmur, -ēmini, -entur.
— Imperf.	pat*i*-ēbar, -ēbār-ĭs(e), -ēbātŭr, -ēbāmŭr, -ēbāmini, -ēbantur.
Conj. Pres.	pat*i*-ăr, -ār-is(e), -ātur, -āmur, -āmini, -antur.
— Imperf.	pat-ěrer, -ěrēr-ĭs(e), -ěrētŭr, -ěrēmŭr, -ěrēmini, -ěrentŭr.
Imper. Pres.	pat-ěre, -ĭmini.
— Fut.	pat-ĭtor, -*i*-untor.
Infin. Pres.	pat-ī.
Gerund.	pat*i*-endum, -endi, -endo.
Gerundive.	pat*i*-endus.
Part. Pres.	pat*i*-ens.

The Passive of cap*i*-o is similar, omitting Gerund and Part.

a) Pŏtior follows the Fourth Conjugation, but in some forms wavers between the Third and Fourth: potĭtur or potītur, potĭmur or potīmur, potěrer or potīrer.

b) In ŏrior the forms orīri and orīrer (rarely orěrer) are classical; but others (orěris, orĭtur, &c.) follow the Third Conjugation.

c) Grădior, mŏrior were originally I-verbs; and exhibit various i-forms in older Latin (as -grediri -gredirer, moriri). In classical Latin they became Consonant-Verbs wholly. Morior, orior, have Future Participles morĭturus, orĭturus.

iv. Combinate or Periphrastic Conjugation.

The Participles in **-urus, -dus,** may be combined with all the Tenses of the Verb sum. These forms are called, 1) 'Coniugatio Periphrastica Futuri'; 2) 'Coniugatio Periphrastica Gerundivi:'[1] as

---

[1] So also the Passive Combinate Tenses (amatus sum, eram, &c.) might be called 'Coniugatio Periphrastica Praeteriti.'

SINGULAR.

1) C. P. F. 2) C. P. G.

amaturus, a, um, amandus, a, um,
&c. &c. &c. &c.

Pres.	sum	es	est	sim	sis	sit
S. Fut.	ero	eris	erit			
Imp.	eram	eras	erat	essem	esses	esset
Perf.	fu-i	-isti	-it	fu-erim	-eris	-erit
Fut. P.	fu-ero	-eris	-erit			
Plupf.	fu-eram	-eras	-erat	fu-issem	-isses	-isset

Indic. M. Conj. M.

PLURAL.

amaturi, ae, a, amandi, ae, a,
&c. &c. &c. &c.

Pres.	sumus	estis	sunt	simus	sitis	sint
S. Fut.	erimus	eritis	erunt			
Imp.	eramus	eratis	erant	essemus	essetis	essent
Perf.	fu-imus	-istis	-erunt	fu-erimus	-eritis	-erint
Fut. P.	fu-erimus	-eritis	-erint			
Plupf.	fu-eramus	-eratis	-erant	fu-issemus	-issetis	-issent

Indic. M. Conj. M.

INFINITE FORMS.

amaturus, a, um, &c. amandus, a, um, &c.
amaturi, ae, a, &c. amandi, ae, a, &c.

Pres. Imp. esse
Perf. Plup. fuisse.

---

[1] *A*) Correspondence of the Latin Verb.

The Latin Verb corresponds in many points with the Sanskrit and the Greek : but there are also some in which it shews Italian peculiarities.

The points of agreement are chiefly—

1) The Active Personal Endings.
2) The use of Mood Vowels generally.
3) The use of Reduplication, though more limited in Latin.
4) The form of the Present Participle Active.
5) The correspondence of many Roots.

But Latin Conjugation departs from Sanskrit and Greek in the following respects :—

1) It has only two Voices and two Numbers.
2) It has lost the Augment, the distinction of Perfect and Aorist Tense, and that of Optative and Conjunctive Mood.
3) Its Passive Personal Endings are formed by agglutinating 'se.'
4) Most of its Tenses are formed by Verbal agglutination.
5) Most of its Infinitive and Participial forms are peculiar to it.

B) Personal Endings.

a) The Personal Endings of the two principal Active Moods generally correspond thus :

	SINGULAR.			PLURAL.		
	1.	2.	3.	1.	2.	3.
L.	m, o ;	s	t	mus	tis	nt
Sk.	*mi, m* ;	*si, s*	*ti, t*	*mas, ma*	*than, ta*	*nti*
Gr.	μι, ν, ω ;	ς	σι, τι	μεν, (μις)	τε	ντι

In translating, it is only required to construe each part of the Verb sum with each Participle : as amaturus sum, *I am about to love*; amandus sum, *I am* meet *to be loved* (or, *I am to be loved*). So futurus sum, *I am about to be* ; futurus sim, eram, essem, &c.

Examples :

Nos scripturi sumus (erimus) ea quae agenda sunt (erunt).
Vos dicturi eratis (fuistis) ea quae agenda erant (fuere).
Dux deliberaturus est (erit) quid agendum sit.
Dux deliberaturus erat (fuit) quid agendum esset.
Illud puto statuendum esse, quid nos acturi simus.
Illud putavi statuendum esse, quid vos acturi essetis.

These do not include the peculiar endings of the Latin Perfect Indicative, which are noticed later.

b) The Endings of the Imperative Active also coincide :

	1		2		
L.	a, &c.	te	to	tote	nto
Sk.	*a*	*ta*	*tu*		*ntu*
Gr.	ε	τε	τω		ντων

The Ending **to** was in E.L. *tod*; in Oscan *tud*; in Umbrian *tu*.
The Passive Personal Endings formed by agglutinating s e are noticed p. 58.

c) The Imperative Passive Endings are so formed :

amator for amato-se   amantor for amanto-se

Similar agglutination of Passive forms appears in the Umbrian and Oscan dialects ; also in the Sclavonic and Lithuanian languages.
The Second Persons Plural in -**mini** are to be regarded as Participles (like Gr. -μενοι) with which the Verb of Being est is, este, is to be understood:—**mino** is an old ending of the Imper. Fut. Pass. 2nd Person, as arbitramino, Plaut. *Epid.* v. 2., where -**minor** is called by Ritschl a traditional fiction.

C) Formation of the Tenses.

a) Present Tense Active.
The Present Stem is prefixed to the Personal Endings ; but
the A-verb contracts **ao** into **o** in (amao) amo :
the I-verb takes vincular *u* in 3. Plur., audi-*u*-nt.
the Consonant Verb takes a vincular in all persons but 1. Sing. ; *i* in 2. 3. Sing. and 1. 2. Plur. ; *u* in 3. Plur. : reg-*ĭ*-s, reg-*ĭ*-t, reg-*ĭ*-mus, reg-*ĭ*-tis, reg-*u*-nt.
On the quantities, see p. 169, *Note.*

b) Future Simple Active.
Here is found variety of formation.
The A- and E-verbs form this tense by agglutinating -**bo**, which represents the Pres. verb fuio. The personal inflexion is like that of the Cons.-Verb in Present Tense : ama-bo, mone-bo, -bis, -bit, &c.
The Cons. and I-verbs take between Stem and Ending in the 1st Pers. S. the Conjunctive mood-vowel **a** (Sk. *ā*): as veham (Sk. *vahām*), audiam : in the other Persons they take the Optative mood-vowel **e** (Sk. *e*): vehēs, vehĕt (anc. vehĕt), vehēmus, vehētis, vehent. So audiēs, &c.
But I-verbs in E. L. took the forms -**bo**, -**bis**, &c. : as audībo, audībor, &c. : and these are sometimes found in poetry. Even such forms as *regebo*, &c., appear on old Inscrr. ; and Quintilian says that *dicem, faciem* were written by the elder Cato for dicam, faciam.

c) Imperfect Indic. Active.
This Tense in all Conjugations takes the form -**bam** -**bas**, &c., representing fuam, fuas, &c., the old Imperf. of fuo. In A- and E-verbs this is at once agglutinated to the Present-stem ama-bam, mone-bam ; but in the Cons. and I-verbs **ê** connects them : reg-ē-bam, audi-ē-bam: a formation which seems due to mere analogy. Here too the form -**ibam** for -**iebam** occurs in old Latin and in poetry.

v. Conjugation of Irregular Verbs.

Certain Verbs are called Irregular (Anomala) :
1) Some because they take tenses from more than one stem :
sum, possum, fero, fio ;
2) Others because some of their forms are subject to peculiar
changes : volo, nolo, malo, ; eo, queo, nequeo ; ĕdo.

---

d) Present (and Fut.) Conjunctive.

The E- I- and Cons.-Verbs take the old Sk. Conjunctive vowel *á*, adding **am, as,**
&c. to the Present Stem : moneam, moneas, &c. ; audiam, audias, &c. ;
regam, regas, &c.

But as ama-am, &c., would be inadmissible, -**am** in A-Verbs seems to have been
weakened into -**im** ; whence ama-im, amem, &c.

The **a** of the Stem is also found in old Latin to be weakened into **u** in duim (Cic.),
for dem (da-im). Thus, in Plautus, perduim, creduim (also creduam). The
ending **im**, which appears in sim, velim, is also found in old and poetic forms of
other verbs : edim, Hor. ; comedim, Cic. ; carint ; effodint ; temperint (Plaut.).

e) Imperfect Conjunctive.

Esem (=erem) is agglutinated to the Present-stem : forming (ama-esem)amārem ;
(mone-esem) monērem ; (reg-ĕsem) regĕrem ; (audi-esem) audīrem.

f) Perfect Indicative.

Perfect-stem with **i, isti,** &c. On these end-forms much has been written, and their
origin is still disputed. Curtius (with Schleicher), Corssen, Lübbert, and Herzog
have taken different views, which may be compared in the work of the last-
named scholar (*Untersuchungen über die Bildungsgeschichte der Griech. und
Latein. Sprache*). In so doubtful a matter it may be allowable to surmise that
this tense, like the rest of its Class, is formed by agglutination, the Present forms
of the Verb ĕs- (sum) being added to the Perfect-stem of each Verb, and synco-
pation ensuing in most Persons. This theory would give :

amav-es-m-i	passing into	amav-i
amav-es-s-i	— —	amav-is-t-i
amav-es-t	— —	(amav-īs-t) amav-īt, amav-ĭt
amav-es-mus	— —	amav-ĭ-mus
amav-es-tis	— —	amav-istis
amav-es-unt	— —	amav-ĕrunt, -ērunt, -ēre

Forms in *ā* for ī, *āt* for īt, belong to E.L. and R.L. Poets use -ĕrunt : stetĕrunt,
Verg. ; vertĕ-runt, Hor., &c.

g) The other Perfect-stem Tenses are formed by agglutinating es-im, es-o (ero)
and es(s)em severally to the Perfect-stem :

Perf. Conj. amav-erim ; Fut. Perf. amav-ero ; Plup. Conj. amav-issem
(sharpened from -ĕsem).

D) The Verb Infinite.

The Infinitive Pres. Act. ama-re (for ama-se), Perf. amav-is-se (for amav-i-se),
are Verb-nouns formed by adding the Dative or Locative element -se to the Present and Perfect Stems severally.

The Present Active Participle in **ns (nt-s)** corresponds to the Greek Participle in
ντ-, Sk. *t* (*nt* when nasalized ; Nom. S. *n*).

The Supines and Passive Participle in **tu- to- (tus)** correspond to the Sk. Participial in *ta.*

The Future Participle in -**turus** corresponds to the Sk. agentive ending *tar* (tor) :
amaturus (amator).

The Gerundive in -**ndo (ndus)** seems to have a double suffix : (1) Pres. Partic. in
nt, (2) **do**-. The vincular *e* which connects these with the Present-Stem of Cons.
and I-verbs was anciently *u* ; which remained in legal documents to the Aug.
age : regendus, regundus ; feriendus, feriundus : but oriundus always.

On the old Passive Infinitive form **ier** (which passed into **i**), see p. 58. Gossrau
says that Lange has collected 336 instances of its use in inscriptions, laws, old
writers, and poets : of the latter, 187 are in Plautus, 46 in Lucretius, and 6 in
Virgil. Pure Verbs are those which shew it oftenest.

On the archaic and poetic forms which omit **si**, see p. 54.

Possum. I. Possum, *I can*, is assimilated from pot-sum = potis (or pote) sum, *I am able*: Perf. potui for pote-fui. See p. 168.

SCHEME.

	Indic.	Conjunc.		Indic.	Conjunc.
Present.	S. possum potĕs potest P. possŭmus potestis possunt	possim possis possit possīmus possītis possint	**Perf.**	potui potuisti potuit potuimus potuistis [-e potuĕr-unt	potuerim potueris potuerit potuerĭmus potuerĭtis potuerint
Fut. S.	S. potero poteris poterit P. poterĭmus poterĭtis potĕrunt	as Pres.	**Fut. P.**	potuero potueris potuerit potuerĭmus potuerĭtis potuerint	as Perf.
Imp.	S. poteram poteras poterat poteramus poteratis poterant	possem posses posset possemus possetis possent	**Plup.**	potueram potueras potuerat potueramus potueratis potuerant	potuissem potuisses potuisset potuissemus potuissetis potuissent

Infin. Pr. Impf. posse (for pot-es-se); Perf. Plup. potuisse.

Potens is an Adjective rather than a Participle, '*powerful, able.*'

Some archaic forms are found in the elder poets: as poterint, potessem, potesse, possiem, possies, &c. The Impersonal Passive potestur is in Lucr. and Plaut. This, and the Passive forms of queo, nequeo, coepi, desino, are only used before an Infinitive Passive. See Munro on Lucr. i. 1045. Potis sum, es, est, &c. are found in poetry.[1]

Fero. II. Fero (Sk. *bhar*, Gr. φερ-), *bring, bear.*

The peculiarities of this Verb are:

1) In the Present-stem forms it casts out vincular ĭ before **s** and **t**: as fers, fert, fertur, &c.: also ĕ between **r** and **r**: as ferrem, ferrer, ferre. The Imperative fer rejects final ĕ.

2) It takes its Perfect-stem tŭl- from the root tŏl-, and the Supine-stem lāt- (for t-lat-) from another form of the same root (*tal-* or *tla-*). For Cpp. see p. 217.

---

[1] *Potis,* pote (originally Adjectives) are also used adverbially. Their origin is Sk. *pati,* 'lord,' whence Gr. πόσις, πότνια (*lord* and *lady*).

SCHEME.

PRESENT-STEM TENSES ACTIVE.					
	Indic.	Conjunc.	Imper.	Infin.	Part.
Present.	S. *fĕro*	feram		*ferre*	ferens
	fers	feras	*fer*		
	fert	ferat			
	P. ferĭmus	ferāmus			
	fertis	feratis	*ferte*		
	fĕrunt	ferant			
Fut. S.	S. feram			laturus	laturus, a,
	feres	as Present	*ferto*	esse	um
	&c.		&c.		
Imperf.	S. ferebam	*ferrem*			
	ferebas	*ferres*			
	&c.	&c.			
PRESENT-STEM TENSES PASSIVE.					
Present.	S. feror	ferar		*ferri*	lātus, a, um
	ferris	ferār-is (e)	*ferre*		
	fertur	feratur			
	P. ferĭmur	ferāmur			
	ferimini	feramini	ferimini		[um
	feruntur	ferantur			ferendus, a,
Fut. S.	S. ferar			latum iri	
	ferēr-is (e)	as Present	*fertor*		
	&c.		&c.		
Imperf	S. ferebar	*ferrer*			
	ferebar-is	*ferrer-is* (e)			
	(e) &c.	&c.			

PERFECT-STEM TENSES (ACTIVE).

tŭl-i, tul-ero, tul-eram, tul-issem, &c. ; tulisse : regularly, as rex-i, &c.

SUPINE-STEM TENSES (PASSIVE).

lātus . . sum (fui, &c.), ero, eram, sim, essem, &c. : regularly, as rect-us sum (fui), &c.

III. Fio (Sk. *bhû*, Gr. φυ-), *am made, become.*   Fio.

The Quasi-passive fio is used as the Passive of facio in the Present-Stem Tenses.

The Supine-Stem Tenses are formed by factus regularly.

SCHEME.

		Indic.	Conjunc.	Imper.	Infin.	Part.
Present.		S. fīo fīs fīt P. (fīmus) (fītis) fīunt	fīam fīas fīat fīamus fīatis fīant	fī (fīte)	*fīeri*	factus, a, um [um faciendus, a,
Fut. S.		S. fīam fīes &c.	as Present	(fīto) &c.	fŭturus esse fŏre	fŭturus, a, um
Imperf.		S. fīebam fīebas &c.	*fīerem* *fīeres* &c.			
Perf.		S. factus sum &c.	factus sim &c.		factus esse	factus, a, um

The bracketed forms are hardly found.

Fio (fu-i-o) is only a strengthened form of fu-. Hence fore and futurus may be assigned to this Verb as well as to sum, by which they are borrowed. This appears from the constant usage of Latin authors : 'Neque ego ea, quae facta sunt, fore quum dicebam, divinabam futura,' C. *Fam.* vi. 1. 5 ; 'Quid fiat, factum, futur-umve sit.' C. *d. Or.* ii. 26. 113.

The ĭ is long except before ĕr, and in fĭt. Comic poets often lengthen ĭ in fierem, fieri.

Fio, being the Passive of facio, appears as such in many Compounds : liquefio, calefio, satisfio ; with Prepositions only in a few instances, as in some forms of confieri. defieri, interfieri, effieri, superfieri. Also infit, *begins (to speak)*, Verg.

IV. V. VI. Vŏlo, nōlo, mālo.

Volo, *I wish, I will* (Sk. *var*, Gr. βολ- βουλ-), has the following peculiarities :

1) Its stem-vowel fluctuates between o, u, e.

2) It rejects *i* in three Persons of Pres. Indic. (2. 3 S. 2 Pl.), and *e* in Impf. Conj. and Infin. Pres.

3) It rejects a consonant in Pres. Indic. 2nd Pers. vis. (Corssen says that this cons. is not l but the prim. r. See *Krit. Nachträge*, 287.)

4) It assimilates s to preceding l in vellem, &c. for vel-sem, &c. and in vel-le for vel-se.

5) The Pres. Conj. takes the ending im, is, &c. instead of am.

Nolo is compounded of ne (non) with volo : Malo of magis or mage and volo.

Māvelim, māvelle, &c., also nēvis, nēvelle, appear in E. L.
Volt, voltis were used before Augustus.
Noli is formed from nolis, 2nd Pers. Conj.

SCHEME.

		Indicative.			Conjunctive.		
Present.	S. vŏlo	nōlo	mālo	*vĕlim*	*nōlim*	*mālim*	
	vīs	nonvis	mavis	velis	nolis	malis	
	vult	nonvult	mavult	velit	nolit	malit	
	P. *volumus*	*nolumus*	*malumus*	velīmus	nolīmus	malīmus	
	vultis	*nonvultis*	*mavultis*	velītis	nolītis	malītis	
	volunt	nolunt	malunt	velint	nolint	malint	
Fut. S.	S. volam						
	voles	noles	males		as Present		
	&c.	&c.	&c.				
Imp.	S. volebam	nolebam	malebam	*vellem*	*nollem*	*mallem*	
	volebas	nolebas	malebas	*velles*	*nolles*	*malles*	
	&c.	&c.	&c.	&c.	&c.	&c.	
Perf.	S. vŏlui	nōlui	mālui	voluerim	noluerim	maluerim	
	voluisti	noluisti	maluisti	volueris	nolueris	malueris	
	&c.	&c.	&c.	&c.	&c.	&c.	
Fut. P.	S. voluero	noluero	maluero				
	volueris	nolueris	malueris		as Perfect		
	&c.	&c.	&c.				
Plup.	S. volueram	nolueram	malueram	voluissem	noluissem	maluissem	
	volueras	nolueras	malueras	voluisses	noluisses	maluisses	
	&c.	&c.	&c.	&c.	&c.	&c.	

IMPERATIVE.

(volo and malo, none)

	S. 2	3.	P. 2.	3.
Pres.	*nolī*	—	*nolīte*	—
Fut.	*nolīto*	*nolīto*	*nolītote*	nolunto

INFINITIVE.

Pres Impf.	*velle*	*nolle*	*malle*
Perf. Plup.	voluisse	noluisse	maluisse

PARTICIPLES.

Pres.   volens   nolens (rare)

Gerunds are hardly found.

a) Pervŏlo, *wish much,* has pervĕlim, pervellem, pervelle.

b) Vin is used for visne, *will you?* sis for si vis; sultis for si
vultis, *if you please:* capsis for cape si vis.

Eo.

VII. E o (for Ĭo), *go.*

The root is Ĭ- (Sk. Gr.), *to go*, which becomes **e** before **a, o, u.**

SCHEME.

		Indic.	Conjunc.	Imper.	Verb Infinite.	
Present.		S. *eo* īs ĭt P. īmus ītis *eunt*	*eam* *eas* *eat* *eamus* *eatis* *eant*	I ite	INFINITIVE. (Pr. Impf.) ire (Perf. Plup.) ivisse or isse	PARTICIPLES. (Pres. Impf.) iens *euntem* &c.
Fut. S.		S. ĭbo ĭbis ĭbit P. ĭbimus ĭbitis ĭbunt	as Present	ĭto ĭto ĭtote *eunto*	(Future) ĭturus esse	(Future) ĭturus
Imperf.		S. ĭbam ĭbas &c.	īrem īres &c.		GERUND.	SUPINES.
Perf.		S. īvi *or* ĭi īvisti, isti &c.	ĭerim ĭeris &c.		*eundum* *eundi* *eundo*	1. ĭt-um 2. ĭtu

The remaining Tenses are formed as in a u d - i v i. The **v** is usually dropt by ivi and its Compounds: ii, iisti or isti, ieram, issem, &c.; redii, rediero, redistis, redisse, &c.

The Impersonal Passive ĭtur, ĭtum est, īri, &c., is often used: Iri with Supine supplies a Future Passive to Verbs. Also the Active e o forms a periphrasis with Supine.

> iniurias istas ultum eunt
> *they are going to avenge those wrongs*
> aiunt iniurias istas ultum iri
> *they say that those wrongs are going to be avenged*

(literally : *there is a-tending to avenge those wrongs*).

Ambio, *go round, canvass,* follows the Conjugation of audio.

Queo,
nequeo.

VIII. IX. Queo ; nequeo.

Queo, *can* (Stem qui-), n e q u e o, *cannot*, are like e o, so far as their forms extend ; but have no Imperative and no Gerunds.

queo quīs quivi quīre . . . . quĭtum quiens (queuntis)
nequeo nequis nequivi nequire . nequĭtum nequiens (nequeuntis)

The Indicative and Conjunctive forms are like those of eo.

Queor, nequeor, are found in old writers with an Infin. Pass. : subpleri queatur, Lucr. i. 1045; 'quĭta est,' Ter. *Hec.* iv. i. 59; 'nequĭtur,' Plaut. *Rud.* iv.

X. Ědo (Sk. *ad*, Gr. ἐδ-), *eat.*

This Verb is anomalous only by the occasional mutation of forms, which omit the Vincular, and either assimilate or omit **d**.

2nd Pers. S. Pres. Act.	*ēs*	for ed-ĭ-s (ed-s).		
3rd „ „ „	*est*	for ed-ĭ-t (ed-t).		
2nd Pers. Pl. „ „	*estis*	for ed-ĭ-tis (ed-tis).		
Imperf. Conj. „	*essem*	for ed-ĕ-rem (ed-sem), &c.		
Imperat Pres. „	*este*	for ed-ĭ-te (ed-te)		
„ Fut. „	*esto, estote*	for edĭto, edĭtote		
Inf. Pres. . „	*esse*	for ed-ĕ-re (ed-se)		
3rd Pers. S. Pres. Pass.	*estur*	for ed-ĭ-tur (ed-tur)		

The other forms of this Verb are regular; except that e d i m, e d i s, &c., are sometimes found for e d a s, e d a t, &c.

vi. Conjugation of Defective Verbs.

DEFECTIVE VERBS are without some of the usual parts of a Verb. In this strict sense a great number of Verbs are Defective; but those commonly so called by grammarians are the following:

I. Praeteritiva: Verbs which, having no Present-Stem forms in use, express these by Perfect forms.

1) coepi,[1] (*have begun* =) *begin*, from c o - a p - *i* - o (Obsolete)
2) ōdi, (*have hated* =) *hate*, from ŏd - *i* - o (Obsolete)
3) mĕmĭni, (*have minded* =) *remember*, from men- (Obs.)

SCHEME.

	Indic.	Conjunc.	Imper.	Infin.
Perfect.	coepi coepisti &c. ōdi ōdisti &c. memĭni meministi &c.	coeperim coeperis &c. ōderim ōderis &c. meminerim memineris &c.		coepisse ōdisse meminisse
Fut. Perf.	coepero ōdero meminero		memento	coepturus esse ōsurus esse
Pluperf.	coeperam ōderam memineram	coepissem ōdissem meminissem		

---

[1] The obsolete Verb apio, *get, acquire*, of which c o e p i o, c o e p i, is a compound, appears in the forms a p i s c o r, a p t u s, a d i p i s c o r, a d e p t u s, and probably also in a p i s,

a) A Participle c o e p t u s forms Perfect c o e p t u s s u m : as 'comitia haberi coepta sunt,' Cic. C o e p t u r u s is used by Pliny, Quintilian, &c.

The Pres. Stem c o e p i o itself is used in older Latin (Plaut. Ter.). Cŏ-ēpit is in Lucretius (iv. 619), where see Munro.

b) The obsolete Verb ŏd*i*o, odĕre, probably meant *to repel.* O s u s s u m is a rarer form of ōdi. O s u r u s is used. E x o s u s, p e r o s u s, *hating greatly*, have Passive sense in L.L.

c) M e m i n i has a Compound c o m m e m i n i. It is the Perf. of an obs. verb m e n o (măno) = Sk. *man*, 'think,' which appears in c o m m i n i s c o r c o m m e n t u s ; m e n s ; m e n t i o ; m e n t i o r, and numerous Greek and other forms.

Novi.

4) N ō v i (*have come to know*), Perfect of n o s c o, *know*, is used as a Praeteritive (*I know*), like Gr. οἶδα. Hence n o v e r a m, n o r a m, *knew* ; n o v e r o, *shall know* ; n o v i s s e, n o s s e, *to know*, &c.

Aio.

II. A i - o, *I say, affirm* (Sk. *ah*, for Pr. *agh*).

		Indic.	Conjunc.	Imper.
Present.		ai-o ă-is ă-it — — ai-unt	— ai-as ai-at — — ai-ant	a-i (rare)
Imperf.		ai-ebam ai-ebas &c.		

The Participle a i - e n s is very rare ('negantia sunt contraria aientibus,' Cic.).

A i b a m, found in some MSS. of Plautus, is of doubtful validity. A i n' t u? *do you say so ?* was a familiar expression.

Inquam.

III. I n q u a m, *say I* (inquit, *saith he*, &c.), for i n q u i o.

---

o p i s, o p u s, o p e r a, &c., o p t o. Its Sk. root is *áp* (Pr. *ap*). The kinship of a p i o, c o e p i o, and c a p i o (cepi), cannot but be recognised, when we observe the similarity of meaning as well as form : for not only is the sense of *acquiring* in c a p i o, a c c i p i o, p e r - c i p i o, &c., but also that of *beginning* in i n c i p i o (incepi) and o c c i p i o (occepi, sometimes written occoepi). Hence it seems probable that c a p i o is only the adoption in Italian speech, as a simple form, of the compound c o - a p - (*get together*, and so *take*), bearing the same relation to a p - that c o m p r e h e n d o does to p r e h e n d o. The old word remained, in the sense of *beginning*, at first in all forms (as shewn in Plautus, &c.), afterwards in the Perfect only ; which sense the new Verb recognised in its own compounds i n c i p i o, i n c e p i, o c c i p i o, o c c e p i ; as well as in its derivative o c c u p o : 'interdum rapere occupat,' *now and then she is the first to snatch them*, Hor. The passage of compound Verbs to Simple is shewn in p r o m o, s u m o, s u r g o, and other instances.

SCHEME.

	Indic.	Conjunc.	Imper.
Present	inquam inquis inquit inquĭmus — inquiunt	— — inquiat? — — —	
Fut. S.	— inquies inquiet		inquito
Imp.	inquiebat		
Perf.	— inquisti inquiit?		

Inquam and sum are the only two Verbs which retain **m** (Sk. *mi*, Gr. μι) in the Pres. Indic.

Inquam is not placed in construction, but interposed between parts of construction, as *quoth* in English.

Its etymology is doubtful (R. Sk. *khyâmi*, ' I say').

IV. Fari, *to speak*, has these forms :   **Fari.**

 Indic. Pres..   . fatur, *speaks*
 Fut.   .   .   .   . fabor, fabitur
 Perf., &c.   .   . fatus, sum, eram, &c.
 Imperat. .   .   . fare
 Infin. .   .   .   . fari
 Gerund   .   .   . fandi, fando.   Gerundive, fandus
 Supine   .   .   . fatu
 Part. Pres. .   . fantem, fantis, &c.   Part. Perf. fatus

Its Compounds affari, effari, (inter prae pro)-fari, can use the same forms and a few more: 'affamur,' Ov. ; 'affamini,' Curt. ; 'affabar,' Verg. ; 'effabere,' Lucan ; ' effabimur,' Cic. ; 'praefantes,' Catull. ; praefarer, praefamino, &c.

V. Ovare, *to rejoice, triumph*, has some Third Persons Sing. **Ovare.**
(ovat, ovet, ovaret), and the Partic. Pres. ovans. Persius has ovatus.

VI. Quaeso, *I beg*; 1st P. Pl. quaesumus.   **Quaeso.**

VII. Verb-forms used in the Imperative and Infinitive :   **Imperative Forms.**

		hail!	*hail!*	*farewell!*	*come!*	*be off!*
Imperative .	S.	salvē	hăvē (or avē)	vălē	ăgĕ	ăpage
„	Pl.	salvete	havete	valete	agite	
„	S.	salveto	haveto	valeto		
Fut. S. .	.	salvebis		valebis		
Infin. .	.	salvere	havere	valere		

Add S. cĕdŏ, Pl. cĕdite, cette, *pray tell me, give me,* &c.

VIII. Impersonal (or Unipersonal) Verbs.

IMPERSONAL VERBS are conjugated in the Third Persons Singular of the Finite Verb, and in the Infinitive.

A. Active Impersonals have no Passive Voice.

1) The principal of these are of the Second Conjugation :

oportet, taedet, miseret,	*it behoves, disgusts, moves pity*
piget, pudet, paenitet,	*it irks, shames, repents*
decet *atque* dedecet,	*it beseems, misbeseems*
libet, licet, *et* liquet,	*it pleases, is lawful, is clear*
attinet *et* pertinet,	*it relates, belongs.*

Table of Impersonal Verbs (Second Conj.) :

		Indic.	Conj.	Infin.
	1. oport			
	2. taed			
	3. miser			
me, te, eum, 4. pig		-et	-eat	-ēre . . Pres.
nos, vos, eos 5. pud		-ebit	. . . . . .	. S. Fut.
	6. paenit	-ebat	-ēret .	. . . Imperf.
	7. dec	-uit	-uerit	-uisse . Perf.
	8. dedec	-uerit	. . . . .	. Fut. Perf.
mihi, &c. . . 9. lib		-uerat	-uisset	. . . . Pluperf.
	10. lic			
ad me, &c. . 11. attin				
	12. pertin			

The following Perfects are also used : 2. pertaesum est; 3. miseritum est; 4. pigitum est; 5. puditum est; 9. libitum est; 10. licitum est.

Miserescit is used; sometimes miseretur.

Gerundives pigendus, pudendus, paenitendus : Participles miseritus, pertaesus, attinens, pertinens, are used. Paenitens, decens, libens, licitus, are used as Adjectives.

The Persons are expressed by the Case : as

Sing.	oportet me ire[1]	*it behoves me*		*I*	
	oportet te ire	— — *you*		*you*	
	oportet eum ire	— — *him*	*to go =*	*he*	*ought to go*
Pl.	oportet nos ire	— — *us*		*we*	
	oportet vos ire	— — *you*		*ye*	
	oportet eos ire	— — *them*		*they*	

Sing.	licet mihi ire	*it is allowed me*		*I*	
	licet tibi ire	— — *you*		*you*	
	licet ei ire	— — *him*	*to go =*	*he*	*may go*
Pl.	licet nobis ire	— — *us*		*we*	
	licet vobis ire	— *you*		*ye*	
	licet iis ire	— — *them*		*they*	

And so in the other Tenses.

---

[1] C. derives oportet (op-portet) from Gr. πορ-, '*it is the part* ;' pudet, paenitet, from Sk. *pu* ; taedet, from Sk. *tu* (see pp. 14, 15) ; decet from Sk. *diś*. Libet or lubet : Sk. *lubh*, 'desire.' Licet : Sk. *riç*, Gr. λιπ- L. linquere, *leave*. The same relation exists between '*to leave*' and the noun *leave* in English. '*I give you leave*'='*I leave it to you* ;' '*I have leave*'='*it is left to me*.' Piget is unexplained.

2) Some Personal Verbs are used impersonally with special meaning :

accidit	*it happens*			delectat	*it charms*	
conducit	*it profits*			iuvat	*it delights*	me, te,
contingit	*it befalls*	mihi		fallit	*it eludes*	eum, &c.
evenit	*it turns out*	tibi		fugit	*it escapes*	
convenit	*it suits*	ei		interest	*it concerns*	meā, tuā,
expedit	*it is expedient*	nobis		rēfert	*it imports*	eius, &c.
placet	*it pleases*	vobis		est	*it is a fact*	
restat	*it remains*	iis, &c.		fit	*it comes to pass*	
succurrit	*it occurs*			constat	*it is acknowledged*	
vacat	*there is leisure*			praestat	*it is best*	

So usu venit, in mentem venit, &c.

3) Some Impersonals express changes of season and weather: such are

fulgurat	*it lightens*	ningit	*it snows*	lucescit	*it dawns*
tonat	*it thunders*	pluit	*it rains*	illucescit	*it gets light*
grandinat	*it hails*	rorat	*there falls dew*	vesperascit	*it gets late*

Impersonals of Class 3) may be explained by regarding the cognate Noun as Subject: nix ningit, *snow snows*=nix est, *snow occurs.* This may be sometimes said in Class 1): pudet me facti = pudor facti me pudet=pudor facti me habet. All of Class 2) and most of Class 1) have for their Subject either an Infinitive Verb-noun or a dependent Clause.

B. 1) Intransitive Verbs may be used impersonally in the Passive Voice: luditur, from ludo, *I play.*

	Ind.	Conj.	Infin.
Present . .	luditur	ludatur	ludi
Simple Fut..	ludetur		lusum iri
Imperf. . .	ludebatur	luderetur	
Perfect . .	lusum est	lusum sit	lusum esse
Fut. Perf. .	lusum erit		
Pluperf. . .	lusum erat	lusum esset	lusum fuisse

The Persons may be expressed by an Ablative Case with the Preposition a or ab following the Verb :

Present Indicative.

Sing.	luditur a me	*there is playing by me*	= *I play*
	luditur a te	— —	*thee* = *thou playest*
	luditur ab eo	— —	*him* = *he plays*
Pl.	luditur a nobis	— —	*us* = *we play*
	luditur a vobis	— —	*you* = *ye play*
	luditur ab iis	— —	*them* = *they play*

And so in the other Tenses.

The Case is generally understood, and the Verb is rendered usually as expressing the First or Third Person Plural ; *we play,* or *they play* : sometimes, *one plays* ; as the French, *on joue.*

2) The Neuter Gerundive is similarly used to express duty or necessity, with a Dative or Ablative of the Person :

Present Indicative.

Sing.	ludendum est mihi	*there must be playing by me*			= *I*	
	ludendum est tibi	—	—	—	*thee*	= *thou*
	ludendum est ei	—	—	—	*him*	= *he*
Pl.	ludendum est nobis	—	—	—	*us*	= *we*
	ludendum est vobis	—	—	—	*you*	= *ye*
	ludendum est iis	—	—	—	*them*	= *they*

must play

And so in the other Tenses.

In this construction the case often occurs; but here too it may be absent, and *we, they*, or *one* supplied, as in the former instance. So French, *on doit jouer.*

SECTION III.

The Forms of the three Stems in Verbs.

i. The Present-Stem.

1. The only Verb-roots which have Indicative Present-Stem forms unchanged immediately before Personal endings are :

The root ĕs (sum, *es-mi*) in the forms es-t, es-tis, es-te, es-to (es-se).

The root vŏl in the forms vol-t, vol-tis.

The root fĕr in the forms fer-s, fer-t, fer-tis, fer, fer-te, fer-to, (fer-re).

The root dă, *give*, in the forms dă-t, dă-mus, dă-tis, da-nt, dă-te, dă-to, (dă-re). But in Sk. and Gr. this root is reduplicated.

2. The only Verb-roots which, with Vowel character, have Present-stem forms merely strengthening that character before Personal endings are :

The root stă, *stand, station*, in the forms stā-s, stā-t (classically stă-t), stā-mus, stā-tis, stā-nt, stā, stā-te, stā-to, (stā-re). In Sk. and Gr. it is reduplicated.

The roots fle, *weep*, ne, *spin*, ple, *fill*, in the same forms, flē-s, nē-s, -plēs-, &c.

The root ĭ, *go,* in the forms ī-s, ī-t (classically ĭt), ī-mus, ī-tis, ī, ī-te, ī-to (ī-re). In ĕo, ĕam, &c., ĭ is strengthened, but the endings also contain a strengthening suffix.

The root quĭ, *can* (with its compound nequĭ), the forms of which resemble those of ĭ.

(*Note.* fī-, being contracted and so properly long, is not an example here.)

3. In all other A- E- and I-Verbs (Conj. 1. 2. 4.) the Vowel character is itself a first suffix, attached to what we call the Clipt-Stem [1] (am-, mon-, aud-), and preceding all flexional suffixes. This

---

[1] On the Term Clipt-Stem and the reason of its use, see Note, p. 30.

is true of U-Verbs also; but these, unlike the rest, are not strengthened in the Present-stem: indŭ-ĭs, indŭ-ĕ, indŭ-ĕre: but audī-s, audī, audī-re.

4. With respect to Consonant Verbs (Conj. 3),

Some scholars think that every root-vowel was primitively short. Such was certainly the case with some roots which in Latin Verbs have the long vowel: dīcere (E. L. *deicere*), dūcere (E. L. *doucere*), fīdere (E. L. *feidere*), compared with veridĭcus, dux dŭcis, fĭdes.

These, however, like Latin Verbs in general, follow the Scheme of Conjugation before given; in which the formative suffix of Indic. Pres. 1st P. Sing. **ô** contains a conjugative element (Sk. *â-mi*).

Certain other affections of the Present Stem in Verbs of the 3rd (Cons.) Conjugation, distinguishing it from the True Stem, come into notice here.

A) Strengthening by the insertion of a nasal before the Character (Nasalisation).   See § 12. xvi.

To the examples there given many may be added, which, though keeping the nasal in the Perfect-Stem, lose it in derived or kindred forms: fi-*n*-g- (fictum); fre-*n*-d- (fressum), -he-*n*-d- (χαδ-, -hĕdera); iu-*n*-g- (iŭgum); lă-*m*-b- (lăbium); li-*n*-g- (lĭgurrio); ma-*n*-d- (māla); mi-*n*-g- (mictum); mu-*n*-g- (mūcus); ni-*n*-g- (nix); pa-*n*-d- (passus); pi-*n*-s- (pistor); sa-*n*-cire (săcer); sca-*n*-d- (scala); sti-*n*-g- (στίξ); a-*n*-g- (ἀγών).

B) Suffix *n* (Sk. *na*) joined to a Vowel or Liquid Stem:

Strengthened Stem	True Stem	Shewn in Perf.
lĭ-*n*-	li- or le-	lī-vi or lē-vi
sĭ-*n*-	si-	sī-vi
posĭ-*n*- } pōn- }	posi-	(posī-vi) pos-ui } posĭ-tum (Sup.) }
cer-*n*-	cer- (cre-)	crē-vi
sper-*n*-	sper- (spre)	sprē-vi
ster-*n*-	star- (stra)	strā-vi
tem-*n*-	tem-	tem-si

In E. L. are found such forms as dă-*n*-unt for dant, solĭ-*n*-unt for solent, nequĭ-*n*-unt for nequeunt, obĭ-*n*-unt for obeunt.

C) The Suffix **sc**, added to the True Stem, makes the Verb Inceptive or Inchoative (1) when the True Stem ends in a Vowel. Thus: from pa-, pa-*sc*-ĕre; from fati-, fati-*sc*-ĕre; from ira-, ira-*sc*-i; from na-, na-*sc*-i; from cre-, cre-*sc*-ĕre; from quie-, quie-*sc*-ĕre; from no-, no-*sc*-ĕre; from hi-, hi-*sc*-ĕre.

(2) When the True Stem ends with a Cons.-, vincular *i* is required: from ap-, ap-*i*-*sc*-i; from men-, men-*i*-*sc*-i; from obliv-, obliv-*i*-*sc*-i; from pac-, pac-*i*-*sc*-i; from profic- profic-*i*-*sc*-i; from ulc-, ulc-*i*-*sc*-i; from nac- (also nasalised), na-*n*-c-*i*-*sc*-i; from experrig- (also syncopated), experg-*i*-*sc*-i.

C is excluded by di-*sc*-ĕre for dic-*sc*-ere; d by ve-*sc*-i for ved-*sc*-i.

Obs. The foregoing examples are mostly from stems which are not in use as actual words : but Inceptive or Inchoative Verbs derived from existing Verbs or Nouns are a very large class, all of the 3rd Conjugation, and express *the beginning* of action.

Those derived from Verbs add *sc-* or *-i-sc-* to the Present-stem :

laba-*sc*-ĕre	from	labā-re, 1.
palle-*sc*-ĕre	—	pallē-re, 2.
trem-*i*-*sc*-ĕre	—	trem-ĕre, 3.
obdormī-*sc*-ĕre	—	obdormī-re, 4.

Those derived from Nouns add *e-sc-* (rarely *a-sc-*) to the Clipt Stem :

dur-*esc*-ĕre	from	durus
mit-*esc*-ĕre	—	mitis
macr-*esc*-ĕre	—	măcer
plum-*esc*-ĕre	—	pluma
vesper-*asc*-ĕre	—	vespera

For a fuller list see Syllabus.

D) A few Present-stems are reduplicated. On Reduplication see § 12. xiv. Thus

bĭ-bĕ-re	for	pi-pĕ-re (Stem *pa*, po)
gi-gn-ĕre	—	gi-gen-ĕre (Stem gen, Sk. *jan*)
si-stĕ-re	—	sti-stĕ-re (Stem *sta*)
se-rĕ-re	—	si-sĕ-re (Stem *sa*)

E) The Liquid **l** is doubled in the Present-stem of
cel*l*ĕre, fal*l*ĕre, pel*l*ĕre, tol*l*ĕre.

F) **T** is added to the True Stem in
flec*t*ĕre, nec*t*ĕre, pec*t*ĕre, plec*t*ĕre.

G) A few Present Stems are written with *g* or *gu* indifferently :
ningĕre or nin*gu*ĕre, tingĕre or tin*gu*ĕre, ungĕre or un*gu*ĕre. So in Conj. 2. urgēre or ur*gu*ēre.

H) The appearance of *ĭ*[1] in certain Verbs of Conj. 3. (cap*i*o, pat*i*or, &c.), as an extension of the Present-Stem, has been noticed.

(Peculiarities of special Consonant Verbs will be found in the Syllabus.)

Forma-
tion of
Perfect
Stem.

ii. The Perfect-Stem.

The Perfect Stem of Latin Verbs is formed in various ways.

A) By reduplicating the Present-Stem without or with vowel-change of Stem : the reduplicative syllable being in some instances dropt.

B) By lengthening the vowel of the Present-Stem, without or with vowel-change.

---

[1] This **i** represents a Conjugative suffix *ya* in Sanskrit, of which the â falls away in Latin : so that **c a p - i - o, p a t - i - o r**, &c., may be represented as= **c a p - y o, p a t - y o r**, &c. See Schleicher, p. 577. v.

C) By adopting the Present-stem as Perfect-stem.
D) By suffixing to the Present-stem **v** or **u**, representing **fu-**.
E) By suffixing to the Present-stem **s**, representing **es-**.

A) Perfect-stem formed by Reduplication.

a) The Reduplicative syllable consists of the first two letters of the Stem : in which case there is no vowel-change of the Stem.

In E-verbs the Clipt-stem is thus sometimes reduplicated : mŏ-mord-i from mord-e-; pĕ-ɪ end-i from pend-e-; spŏ-pond-i (for spo-spond-i) from spond-e-; tŏtond-i from tond-e-.

In Consonant Verbs the True Stem : cŭ-curr-i from curr- ; dĭ-dic-i from di-sc- (for dic-sc-) ; pĕ-pend-i from pend-; pŏ-posc-i from posc- ; pŭ-pŭg-i from pu-*n*-g-; tĕ-tend-i from tend-; tŭ-tŭd-i from tu-*n*-d-. Fĭd-i is for (*fĭ-fĭd-i*) from fi-*n*-d-; scĭd-i for (*sci-scĭd-i*) from sci-*n*-d-.

b) The Reduplicative syllable is the first consonant with **ĕ** ; in which case some weakening of the stem-vowel also takes place, unless this vowel be **e** in a close syllable, as above in pĕpendi, tĕtendi.

The only instances in A-verbs are dĕ-d-i from dă- ; stĕ-t-i from sta- : which seem to cast out the stem-vowel. But they probably are for dedei, stestei, and so have weakened **a** into **e**.

In Consonant Verbs the instances are :

pĕ-perc-i from parc-; pĕ-pĭg-i from pa-*n*-g-; tĕ-tĭg-i from ta-*n*-g-; cĕ-cĭd-i from căd-; cĕ-cīd-i from caed- ; cĕ-cĭn-i from căn-; mĕ-mĭn-i from mĕn-; pĕ-pĕr-i from par-*ĭ*-; fĕ-fell-i from fall- ; pĕ-pul-i from pel-*l*-. Tŭli from tol-*l*- is for te-tul-i, which is found in old Latin. *Cĭ-cŭl-i* is from cel-*l*- ; but both are obsolete : the Cp. percell- forms percŭli. Other forms of E. L. are *fefici* from fac-, *tetĭni* from ten-.

B) Perfect-stem formed by lengthening the vowel of the Present-stem.   See § 12. xiv. p. 18.

a) The Vowel of the Clipt Stem is lengthened without other change in these Pure Verbs :

iūv-i from iŭva- ; lāv-i from lăva-; sēd-i from sĕde-; vīd-i from vĭde-; cāv-i from căve- ; fāv-i from fave- ; pāv-i from păve-; fōv-i from fŏve- · mōv-i from mŏve-; vōv-i from vŏve-.

b) The Vowel of the True Stem is lengthened without other change in these Consonant Verbs :

vīc-i from vi-*n*-c- ; līqu-i from li-*n*-qu- ; fūg-i from fŭg-*i*-; lēg-i from lĕg-; ēd-i from ĕd-; fōd-i from fŏd-*i*-; fūd-i from fu-*n*-d-; rūp-i from ru-*m*-p-; scāb-i from scăb-; ēm-i from ĕm-.

c) The Present-stem vowel is changed and lengthened in the following Consonant Verbs :

fēc-*i* ; iēc-*i* from iăc-*i*- ; ĕg-*i* from ăg- ; frēg-*i* from fra-*n*-g- ; cēp-*i* from căp-*i*- ; and in -pēg-i from some compounds of pa-*n*-g-.

C) Perfect-stem formed by adopting the Present-Stem.

a) The Clipt Present-stem becomes Perfect-stem in these E-verbs :

prande- prand-i ; strīde- strīd-i ; ferve- ferv-i (also ferbui). and in the I-verbs :

compĕri- compĕr-i ; repĕri- reppĕr-i ;

unless r e p p e r i is syncopated from r e p e p e r i.

b) The Present-stem becomes Perfect-stem in these Consonant forms :

bĭb-i ; cūd-i ; īc-i ; -fend-i ; lamb-i ; mand-i ; prehend-i; pand-i ; psall-i ; scand-i ; solv-i ; verr-i ; vell-i ; vert-i ; vīs-i ; volv-i ; -cand-i (-cend-i in Comp.).

Likewise in U-verbs classically : rŭ-i, metŭ-i.

But on these see § 12. xiv. p. 18.

D) *a*. Perfect-stem formed by suffixing **v** (=fu-) to a strengthened Vowel character.

This is done by most A- and I-verbs :

amā-v-i　　　audī-v-i

and by some E-verbs :

delē-v-i　　　flē-v-i

Also by the Verbs which have suffixed a Consonant to a True Vowel stem.　See p. 195.

crē-v-i ; sī-v-i ; lē-v-i or lī-v-i ; nō-v-i ; sprē-v-i ; strā-v-i ; pā-v-i ; quiē-v-i ; sē-v-i.

Likewise a few Verbs in Conj. 3. assume the Perf. and Supine forms of Conj. 4. :

cup-*i*- cup-īv-i ; pet- pet-īv-i ; ter- ter-īv-i or trīvi ; quaer- for quaes- quaes-īv-i ; arcess- arcess-īv-i ; and so capess-facess- lacess-.

b. Perfect-stem formed by suffixing **u** (=fu-) to the Present Stem.

a) To a Clipt Stem :

In a few A-verbs :

crepa- crep-u-i ; cuba- cub-u-i : and so from doma-, sona-, veta-, seca-, mica-, tona-, frica- ; neca-, plica-.

But some of these also take a-v-i.　See Syllabus.

In most E-verbs :

mone-　　　　mon-u-i

In the I-verbs aperi- aper-u-i ; operi- oper-u-i ; sali- sal-u-i.

Note. Inceptive Verbs, derived from Verbs, follow the *forma-*tion of their Primitive Verb : but those in **esc- isc-** derived from Nouns, if they have a Perfect, form it in u-i : o b d u r e s c- o b d u r-u - i.

b) To a True Consonant Stem :

in most Verbs with character **l, m** :

> al- al-u-i ; gem- gem-u-i ; &c.

also in

> elic-*i* elic-u-i; rap-*i* rap-u-i; strep- strep-u-i; frend- frend-u-i;
> stert- stert-u-i; cum*b*- cub-u-i; pon- pos-u-i; pins- pins-u-i;
> ser-, *join*, ser-u-i ; compesc- compesc-u-i ; gign- (= gen-)
> gen-u-i ; tex- tex-u-i.

E) Perfect-stem formed by suffixing **s** (= **es**) to the Present-stem.

This may be called the Aorist formation, resembling as it does the Greek Aorist form in σα.

As this formation brings **s** into concurrence with other consonants, the laws of euphony must be applied as set forth in § 12. xxvi. and § 12. xxix : where it is shewn that

> a guttural with **s** produces **x**: dixi, rexi; **b** before **s** becomes **p**: scripsi ; dentals are cast out, Compensation or Assimilation often ensuing: risi, sensi ; and gutturals are cast out after **r, l**: mersi, fulsi. Also **p** is inserted between **m** and **s**: sum*p*si.

a) **s** is suffixed to the Clipt-stem of many E-verbs and some I-verbs :

> auge- auxi ; luce- luxi, arde- arsi ; &c.
> farci- farsi ; vinci- vinxi ; sanci- sanxi, &c.

> In iube- iussi the assimilation is peculiar ; mane- mansi is an unusual formation : in haere- haesi and hauri- hausi **r** (= **s**) has fallen out before **s**.

b) **s** is suffixed to most Consonant Stems with a Mute character, and to some with **m, r, (s)** : duc- duxi ; teg- texi ; sparg- sparsi ; ced- cessi ; nub- nupsi ; com- compsi ; ur- ussi, &c. See Syllabus.

iii. The Supine-Stem.

Formation of Supine Stem.

This has the suffix **t**, which is added to the True or Clipt Stem, without or with *i* before the ending -**um**. A Vowel Character (**a, e, i**) is, with some exceptions, lengthened.

I. **T** is suffixed to the Stem without mutation of Consonants, but with lengthening of a Vowel Character

1) In those Pure Verbs which add **v** to the True Stem in the Perfect :

> amā-t-um   flē-t-um   audī-t-um

including some which strengthen the Pres. Stem with a suffix : p. 95 :

> crē-t-um   quiē-t-um   nā-t-um
> sprē-t-um   irā-t-um   nō-t-um
> strā-t-um

But in the following Supines the Stem vowel is not lengthened :

> lĭ-t-um (lĭno)   sĭ-t-um (sĭno)
> ĭ-t-um (eo)   să-t-um (sĕro)

Pa-s-t-um (pasco, pavi, from root pa) keeps **s** irregularly.

2) In Verbs of Conj. 3., which adopt in the Perfect the Character **ı** of Conj. 4.: cupī-tum ; petī-tum ; quaesī-tum ; trī-tum ; arcessī-t-um ; capessī-t-um ; facessī-t-um ; lacessī-tum.

3) In U-verbs : indū-t-um (indu-ĕre).

Except rŭ-t-um or ru-ĭ-t-um (ru-ĕre) : lu-ĭ-t-um (lu-ĕre) ; fru-ĭ-tum (fru-i).

4) In Consonant Verbs with the Characters **c** (after a Vowel) **x p, n, m** (with euphonic **p**), **r, l** (after **a, u**) : dic-tum, duc-tum, nac-tum, tex-tum, ap-tum, comp-tum, par-tum, al-tum, consul-tum, &c.

Also stru-c-t-um (from stru-ere for stru-ic-ĕre).

For Exceptions see III.

On the Vowel-change which occurs in the close syllable of many Supines : affec-tum (afficere), cul-tum (colere). See § 12. xxiv.

5) In stā-t-um (stā-re), sometimes stă-t-um.

But dă-t-um (dă-re) keeps **ă** short.

II. **т** is added to the Stem with mutation of Consonants.

1) The Guttural Characters **g, gv, qv, h,** in Conj. 3. become **c** when **t** follows (see § 12. xxvi. II.) : a-c-t-um (ag-ĕre) ; fra-c-t-um (fra*n*g-ĕre) ; un-c-t-um (ungu-ĕre) ; co-c-t-um (coqu-ĕre) ; -li-c-t-um (li*n*qu-ĕre) ; tra-c-t-um (trah-ĕre) ; ve-c-t-um (veh-ĕre). Also vi-c-t-um (viv-ĕre) ; experre-c-t-um (experg-isci) ; pis-t-um (pins-ĕre). See Syllabus.

2) **qv** is vocalized into **-cu** in

lo-cū-t-um (loqu-i)   se-cū-t-um (sequ-i)

3) The Labial character **b** becomes **p** :

nu-p-t-um (nub-ĕre)   scri-p-t-um (scrib-ĕre)

4) **v** is vocalized into **u** in

sol-ū-t-um (solv-ĕre)   vol-ū-t-um (volv-ĕre)

5) **R** (primitively **s**) becomes **s** again :

ge-s-t-um (ger-ĕre)   u-s-t-um (ur-ĕre)
que-s-t-um (quer-i)

6) Exclusion of the preceding Character occurs in

ul-t-um (ulc-isci)   oblī-t-um (obliv-isci)

III. **т** is joined to the Stem by *ĭ*, in the following Verbs of Conj. 3. with Nasal Character : frem-*ĭ*-t-um, gem-*ĭ*-t-um, gen-*ĭ*-t-um, vom-*ĭ*-t-um.

Also in elic-*ĭ*-t-um, fug-*ĭ*-t-um, bib-*ĭ*-t-um, cub-*ĭ*-t-um, strep-*ĭ*-t-um, mol-*ĭ*-t-um, coal-*ĭ*-t-um (coalesc-ĕre), pos-*ĭ*-t-um, lu-*ĭ*-t-um, ru-*ĭ*-t-um, fru-*ĭ*-t-um.

IV. **т** is added to the Clipt Stem without mutation of Consonants in the following :

A-verbs : seca- sec-t-um ; frica- fric-t-um ; eneca- enec-t-um.

E-verbs : doce- doc-t-um ; tene- ten-t-um ; misere- miser-*ĭ*-t-um (or miser-t-um).

I-verbs : amici- amic-t-um ; sanci- sanc-t-um (or sanc-ī-tum); vinci- vinc-t-um ; saepi- saep-t-um ; aperi- aper-t-um ; comperi-

comper- com-t-um ; experi- exper-t-um ; opperi- opper-t-um ; ori-
or-t-um ; reperi- reper-t-um ; sali- sal-t-um ; sepeli- sepul-t-um
(with vowel-change) ; vĕni- ven-t-um.

The Participle mor-t-u-us from mori-or is an irregular formation,
in the nature of an Adjective, from mor-s, mor-ti-, *death*.

V. **T** is joined to the Clipt Stem with mutation of Consonants :

1) A- and E-verbs in **v-a-**, **v-e-**, vocalise **v**, and form contractions
u-u × **ū** ; **a-u** × **au** or **ō** ; **o-u** × **ō** :
    A-verbs : iuva- iū-t-um ; lava- lau-t-um, lō-t-um.
    E-verbs : cave- cau-t-um ; fave- fau-t-um ; fove- fō-t-um ; move-
mō-t-um ; vove- vō-t-um.

2) The Consonant is changed by Assimilation in the following :
    E-verbs : auge- auc-t-um ; torre- tos-t-um ; sorbe- sorp-t-um.
    I-verb : hauri- haus-t-um (hau-sum).

3) The Consonant is excluded in the following :
    E-verbs : indulge- indul-t-um ; misce- mis-t-um (mix-tum) ; tor-
que- tor-t-um.
    I-verbs : farci- far-t-um ; fulci- ful-t-um ; sarci- sar-t-um.

VI. **T** is joined to the Clipt Stem by *i* :

1) In the A-verbs crepa- crep-*ĭ*-t-um ; cuba- cub-*ĭ*-t-um ;
plica- plic-*ĭ*-t-um (or -atum); doma- dom-*ĭ*-t-um; sona- son-*ĭ*-t-um;
tona- ton-*ĭ*-t-um ; veta- vet-*ĭ*-t-um.

2) In most E-verbs : mone- mon-*ĭ*-t-um.

VII. **T** joined to the True Stem becomes **s** :

1) In Dental Verbs of Conj. 3. :
    a) The Dental is excluded : **cs** becomes **x**, and a short Vowel is
        lengthened by Compensation :
flect- flexum ; nect- nexum ; amplect- amplexum ; ūt- ūsum ; vert-
versum ; pend- pensum ; fu-*n*-d- fūsum ; căd- cāsum ; caed-
caesum ; divĭd- divīsum.

So clau-sum, cū-sum, -fen-sum, fi-sum, prehen-sum, scan-sum,
&c. But tend- ten-sum or ten-tum ; tu-*n*-d- tun-sum or
tū-sum ; nīt- nī-sum or nixum.

    b) The Dental becomes assimilated to **s** :
ced- cessum ; fi-*n*-d- fissum ; sci-*n*-d- scissum ; met- messum ;
fre-*n*-d fressum ; fod-*i*- fossum ; pat-*i*- passum ; quat-*i*- quassum.

Add to these mitt- missum ; pand- passum (or pansum),
and, with vowel-change, fat-*i*-sc- fessum ; grad-*i*- gressum.

2) In Guttural Verbs, the Guttural falling out between **r** and **s** :
parc- parsum ; sparg- sparsum ; merg- mersum ; térg- tersum.

3) In Verbs with Character **rr** or **ll**, dropping one Liquid :
    curr- cursum ; verr- versum ; fall- falsum ; cell- celsum.
And, with Vowel-change,
        pell- pulsum ; percell- perculsum ; vell- vulsum.

4) The following are special instances :
        fig- fixum ; flu- (flugv-)fluxum ; lab- lapsum ; prem- pressum.

VIII. **т** joined to the Clipt Stem becomes **s** :

1) After Dentals :

a) The Dental being excluded, &c.

E-verbs : arde- arsum; morde- morsum; pende- pensum; prande- pransum; ride- risum; suade- suasum; sponde- sponsum; tonde- tonsum; vĭde- vīsum; aude- ausum.

But gaude- (for gav-ĭd-e-), gavīsum.

In I-verbs : senti- sensum; assenti- assensum; ordi- orsum.

b) The Dental being assimilated to **s** :

sede- sessum; fate- fassum.

2) After Gutturals following **r** or **l** :

mulce- mulge- mulsum; terge- tersum.

3) In special instances :

iube- iussum; cense- censum; haere- haesum; mane- mansum; meti- mensum (mentior may have been the original Present).

Note. The importance of the Supine-Stem lies in the Participles derived from it, not in the Supines themselves, which are comparatively little used by Latin authors.

SECTION IV.

Composition of Verbs.

I. The Prepositions compounded with Verbs are :

A) Separable :—

ab	ante	e	inter	prae	subter
abs	circum	ex	ob	praeter	super
a	cum	e	per	pro	trans
ad	de	in	post	sub	

B) Inseparable :—

ambi- (amb-), *around, about*;　　　sēd- sē, *apart.*
dis-, di-, *in different parts or ways*;　　sus,[1] *up* (susque deque).
rĕd-, rĕ-, *back, again*;

To which some add por (= Gr. προτί), an or in (= ἀνά).

Prepositions in Composition are subject to various mutations.

A) 1) A, ab, abs, are written

a before **m, v** : amitto, avoco.

abs before **c, t** : abscedo, abscondo, absterreo.

as before **p** : asporto.

au before **f** : aufero, aufugio.　But afui, afore.

ab before other letters : abeo, abdo, abĭgo, abiungo, ablūdo, abnuo, abrādo, absisto, abundo.

2) Ad remains before **b, d, h, i, m, v,** and vowels :

adbibo, addo, adhibeo, adiungo, admitto, advoco, adeo, adoro.

Becomes **a-** before **gn, sc, sp** :

agnosco, ascendo, aspicio (but ad may remain).

---

[1] On sus, see Corssen ii. 580. He derives it from sup-us (= supinus), related to Greek ὕψι, a locative form, out of which grew sup-s-i, sup-s, sus.

Is assimilated before other letters :
> accendo, affero, alludo, annuo, appono, acquiro, arrideo, assisto, attendo.   But adfero, adnuo, &c., are also used.

3) **Cum, in-,** are written com-, im-, before **p, b, m** :
> comparo, combibo, committo ; impello, immergo.

Assimilated before **l, r** : colludo, corrōdo, illīdo, irruo.

Cum becomes **co-** before vowels, **h,** and **gn** :
> Coeo, cohaereo, cognosco. So ignosco. Note comĕdo.

Con-, in-, before other consonants, in- before vowels and **h** :
> concurro, condo, confero, coniungo, connecto, conquiro, construo, contingo, convoco, incumbo, induco, ineo, inhio, infringo, ingero, iniungo, innuo, inquiro, insisto, intono, invado. Con-, in-, may remain before **p, l** : conpono, inludo.

4) **Ec, ex, e,** are assimilated before **f** : effero, efficio.

Ex before vowels, **h, c, q, p, s, t** :
> exeo, exhibeo, excedo, exquiro, expello, extruo, extraho.

E before others : educo, eludo, emitto, erumpo, evoco.

5) **Ob,**[1] **sub,** are assimilated before **c, g, p, f** : occurro, oggannio, oppono, offero, succedo, suppono, suggero, sufficio.

They remain before other letters :
> obdo, obeo, obicio, oblĭno, obruo, obsisto, obtineo, obvenio, subduco, subiungo, subrideo, subsido, subtraho.

Note omitto, operio, ostendo, surripio, summoveo, summitto.

6) **Per** is changed only in the Verbs pellicio, pelluceo, peiero.

7) **Trans** becomes **tra** before **d, n,** and i-consonans :
> trado, trano, traicio.

Tran- before **s** : transcribo.

Remains before others : transfero, transeo, transmitto.

8)

Ante	de	post	prae	super
circum	inter	praeter	pro	subter

remain in composition with Verbs : except
> intel-lego   prod-eo   prod-igo   prod-esse, &c.

Pro, usually long, is shortened in a few compounds :
> prŏfari, prŏfiteri, prŏficisor.

B) 1) **Amb-** (ἀμφί) becomes am- before **p** : amputo, amplector.

2) **Dis-** is assimilated before **f** : differo.

Remains before gutturals, labials, **t,** i-consonans, and **s** with vowel : discerpo, dispello, distraho, disicio, dissero.   But diiudico.

Di- before **s** with consonant, and before other consonants :
> diruo, distringo, divello.

Observe dĭr-ibeo for dis-hibeo, dĭr-imo for dĭs-imo.

---

[1] The form **obs** wants authority. Such words as obtineo, obtuli, &c. compared with abstineo, abstuli, shew that it has no euphonic use. Obsolesco, often cited as a compound of olesco, is really (with exolesco, insolesco) a compound of soleo (solesco) ; ob-stinare is a strengthened form of ob-stare ; oscen is from os, for ob would make it occen ; ostendo is, we believe, for ob-os-tendo, *stretch before the face=shew* : obtendo is itself a distinct compound. And, if in the two places of Plautus, where (instead of the usual obtrudo) obstrudo is given, the reading is correct, here too ob-os-trudo may be the real compound : as in each place it is used of putting food into the mouth. We cannot, therefore, accept Corssen's view, i. 121.

3) Rĕd- stands in redamo, redarguo, reddo, redeo, redhibeo, redĭmo, redigo, redoleo, redundo.
Rĕ- in other compounds, as remitto.

4) Sēd- appears only in seditio and its derivatives: sē- in Verbs, secubo, seduco, seiungo, sepono, sevoco.

5) Sus- is used before ci, p, t :
suscipio, suscĭto, suspendo, sustineo, sustuli.
su- before sp : suspicio, suspiro.

6) Por- is noted in porricio, porrigo, portendo, polliceor, pollingo, polluceo, polluo, possideo.

7) An- (according to Key) in anhelo, anquiro, intumesco, &c.

Note. The following scheme shews the Vowel-changes in the three Stems of Compound Verbs with vowels, **a, e.**　See § 12. xxiv.

Simple Verb	Comp. Present	Comp. Perfect	Comp. Supine.	Simple Verbs in question.
1. *a*	*i*	*ē*	*a*	ago, frango, pango.
2. *a*	*i*	*ĭ*	*a*	tango, cado.
3. *a*	*ĭ*	*ĭ*	*e*	rapio, cano.
4. *a*	*ĭ*	*ē*	*e*	facio, iacio, lacio, capio.
5. *a*	*ĭ*	*ĭ*	*u*	salio.
6. *a*	*ĭ*		*e*	fateor.
7. *e*	*ĭ*	*ĭ*	*e*	teneo.
8. *e*	*ĭ*	*ē*	*e*	sedeo, specio, lego, rego, emo, premo.
9. *e*	*ĭ*	*ĭ*		egeo.

Examples :

1) ăgo	subĭgo	subēgi	subactum	*subdue.*
frango	effrĭngo	effrēgi	effractum	*break open.*
pango	compĭngo	compēgi	compactum	*fasten together*
2) tango	attĭngo	attĭgi	attactum	*reach.*
cădo	occĭdo	occĭdi	occāsum	*die.*
3) răpio	surrĭpio	surrĭpui	surreptum	*steal.*
căno	concĭno	concĭnui	concentum	*sing in unison·*
4) făcio	refĭcio	refēci	refectum	*repair.*
iăcio	deĭcio	deiēci	deiectum	*throw down.*
lăcio	illĭcio	illexi	illectum	*entice.*
căpio	accĭpio	accēpi	acceptum	*receive*
5) sălio	prosĭlio	prosĭlui	prosultum	*spring forth.*
6) făteor	confĭteor	—	confessus	*confess.*
7) tĕneo	sustĭneo	sustĭnui	sustentum	*sustain.*
8) sĕdeo	obsĭdeo	obsēdi	obsessum	*besiege.*
spĕcio	perspĭcio	perspexi	perspectum	*look through.*
lĕgo	dilĭgo	dilexi	dilectum	*love.*
rĕgo	dirĭgo	direxi	directum	*direct.*
ĕmo	exĭmo	exēmi	exemptum	*take out.*
prĕmo	reprĭmo	repressi	repressum	*repress*
9) ĕgeo	indĭgeo	indĭgui	—	*need.*

Exceptions appear in the Notes to the Syllabus.

II. A few Verbs are compounded with Adverbs, with Nominal, or with Verbal elements: benefacio, malefacio, satisfacio, satisfio, satisdo; venumdo, vendo, veneo, pessumdo, valedico, calefacio, calefio, with a large number of other compounds of facio, fio.

SECTION V.

53
Syllabus
of Stem-
Forma-
tion.

Syllabus of Stem-Formation in Verbs.

A) The FIRST or A-CONJUGATION contains many Verbs, Active and Deponent. Most of the Active are Transitive; most of the Deponents Intransitive.

[Many A-verbs are derived from Nouns; many from Verbs. Among the former are Imitative Verbs in -**isso**: attic-isso, graec-isso, com-issor. Among the latter

Imita-
tive
Verbs.

1) Frequentative Verbs, which express repeated or intense action, formed either in -**to**, -**so**, from Supine-stems: canto, *sing much* (cano, cantum), curso, *run often* (curro, cursum); so adiuto; apto; capto; dicto; iacto; gesto; lacto; nuto; occulto; rapto; tento; tracto; vecto; voluto; cesso; merso; penso; prenso; presso; pulso; quasso; verso; grassor;—or by adding **i-to**, **i-tor** to the Clipt Stem: rog-*i*-to, *ask often* (rog-o), min-*i*-tor, *threaten much* (min-or): (so agito, cogito, mussito, strepito, visito): sometimes to the Supine Stem: haes-*i*-to, lus-*i*-to. Frequentatives may be formed from Frequentatives: cant-*i*-to; curs-*i*-to; dict-*i*-to.

Fre-
quenta-
tive
Verbs.

2) Deminutive Verbs in -**illo**, from Present-stems: conscrib-illo, *scribble*; sorb-illo, *sup up*.]

Demi-
nutive
Verbs.

	Perf.	Sup.
A-verbs form	-**āvi**	**ātum**

Variant Verbs are cited in the Syllabus; Deponents in the Notes.

B) The SECOND or E-CONJUGATION contains fewer Verbs than the First, and very few Deponents. Its Verbs are principally Intransitive. Several have by-forms in -**ĕre**, 3. used by poets: ferv-ĕre, frig-ĕre, fulg-ĕre, strid-ĕre, turg-ĕre. A large number pass into the Inceptive or Inchoative form in -sco, 3.

Many Verbs of this Conjugation are without Supine; some without Perfect also. Inchoatives in Perfect and Supine follow the formation of the Verb from which they spring.

E-verbs should regularly form -**ēvi**, **ētum**; but they usually have -**ŭi**, -**ĭtum**. Most of them are cited in the Syllabus.

C) The FOURTH or I-CONJUGATION has not a large number of Active Verbs, and few Deponents. Most are Transitive.

[Desiderative Verbs are of this Conjugation, formed from Supine Stems with Suffix -ŭr-io :

> es-ŭr-io, *desire to eat, am hungry.*
> script-ŭr-io, *desire to write.*]

	Perf.		Sup.
I-verbs form	**-īvī**		**-ītum**

Only Variant and Deponent I-Verbs are cited in the Syllabus.

D) The THIRD CONJUGATION contains Consonant Verbs and U-verbs : Consonant Verbs in each class are placed in the order of their character : Guttural (**c, g, qu, h,** &c.) ; Dental (**t, d**) ; Labial (**p, b**) ; Nasal (**m, n**) ; Liquid (**l, r, s**).

Nearly all Simple Verbs of this Conjugation are cited.
(Most Compounds of all Verbs cited are mentioned at the foot.
The formation of Perfect and Supine is the same in the Compounds as in the Simple Verb, unless otherwise stated.
S. means Stem : L. S. lengthened Stem, as in mōv-i : Cp. Compound : Cpp. Compounds.)

A) First Conjugation : A-verbs :[1]

(am-are am-āvi am-ātum)

Redupl. | **-atum** :

1. dăre	dĕdi	dătum	*give, put*
2. stāre	stĕti	statum	*stand*

L.S. | **-tum** :

3. iŭv-are	iūvi	iūtum	*help, please*
4. lăv-are	lāvi	lŏtum	*wash*

---

[1] A-Verbs.

1. Dăre is the only Verb which keeps short **ă** (except in dā).
The Cpp. circumdăre, *set round*, pessumdăre, *ruin*, venumdăre, *set for sale*, satisdăre, *give security*, keep ă, and form dĕdi, dătum. All its other Cpp. pass over to the Cons. Decl. -do -dĭs -dĕre, &c., with meanings of several, which (as in circumdăre) do not represent '*giving*,' but '*placing*' or '*setting*.' Hence it seems clear that this Verb, whether as dăre or -dĕre, contains within its forms *two* Verbs, which in Sanskrit and Greek are distinct : namely, Sk. dā (*dadāmi*), Gr. (δο) δίδωμι, *give*, and Sk. dhā (*dadhāmi*), Gr. (θε) τίθημι, *set, put*. Some of the Cpp. must be ascribed to the latter Verb : circumdo, abdo, condo, indo, obdo, &c. : while others, dedo, reddo, trado, &c. may be more easily assigned to the former. See M. Lucr. iv. 41.

2. Cpp. (ad con ex in ob per prae re)-sto -stĭti. See sisto 3. (Ante circum-)sto -stĕti. Disto, super-sto, have no Perf. or Sup. The Sup. statum has **ă** short in 'stăta tempora,' also stător, stătus, stătura, stătim. But in Cpp. long quantity prevails : constāturus, exstāturus. Praestitum, L. xliii. 18 : praestiturus has some authority. R. Pr. *sta*, Sk. *sthā*, Gr. στα.

3. Iuvaturus, Sall. Cp. adiuvo. R. Sk. *div*, 'shine.'

4. Lavavi, Ter. lavatum : lautum : whence Adj. lautus, *sumptuous*. Older form lavĕre, Verg. Hor. : still older luĕre (distinct from lu- *loose*). See this and its Cpp. R. Gr. λυ-. See Curt. *Gr. Et.* p. 371.

5. Simple necare, -avi -atum : necui, Phaedr. : from nex, *violent death* ; Gr. νεκύς, *corpse*. R. Sk. *nas*, 'perish.'

-ui | -tum :

5. enĕc-are	enecui	enectum	*kill*
6. frĭc-are	fricui	frictum	*rub*
7. sĕc-are	secui	sectum	*cut*

-ui | -ĭtum :

8. crĕp-are	crepui	crepĭtum	*creak, prattle*
9. cŭb-are	cubui	cubĭtum	*lie down*
10. dŏm-are	domui	domĭtum	*tame*
11. sŏn-are	sonui	sonĭtum	*sound*
12. tŏn-are	tonui	tonĭtum	*thunder*
13. vĕt-are	vetui	vetĭtum	*forbid*

6. Cp. perfrico. A Supine fricatum is used by frico and Cpp. effrico, refrico.   R. Sk. ghar. Gr. χρι-. See Curt. *Gr. Etym.* p. 203.

7. Secaturus is found.   Cpp. (dis ex re sub)-seco.

8. Cpp. discrepo, *differ* ; increpo, *chide* ; (con per) crepo.   Rarely -avi -atum.

9. Cpp. accubo, occubo ; (ex in re se)-cubo. Rarely -avi -atum. Cumbĕre 3. is a nasalised byform. R. Sk. *s'î*, ' *lie down*,' Gr. κει-.

10. Cpp. (e per) domo. R. Sk. *dam*, Gr. δαμ-, *tame*.

11. Sonaturus, Hor. Cpp. (in per re) -sono. R. Sk. *svan*, ' to sound.'

12. Cp. intono -ui -atum. Adj. attonitus, R. Sk. *tan*, Gr. τεν-, *to stretch*. Tonĕre, sonĕre 3. are old and poetic forms.

13. Vetavit, Pers. ; but some read notavit.

14. Simple Verb has plicavi; plicui is rare : plicitum and plicatum.   Cpp. applico, complĭco, explico, implico, take both forms of Perf. and Sup. The Verbs duplico, multiplico, supplico are not Cpp. and have -avi -atum.   Gr. πλέκω. See plecto 3.

15. Cpp. dimico, *combat*, dimicavi ('dimicui,' Ov.), dimicatum ; emico, emicui.

a) The Inchoative Verbs formed from A-verbs are :

From gelare : congel-ascĕre -avi -atum, *freeze*.
— labare : lab-ascĕre (no Perf. or Sup.), *begin to waver*.
— hiare : hiscĕre . . (no Perf. or Sup.), *gape, whisper* ; M. Lucr. iv. 66.
— . . . . dehiscĕre   „   „   „   „

b) Deponent A-verbs (all conjugated regularly in **-ari, -atus**).

Those marked * have also an Active form in **-o, -are**, in general peculiar to old Latin ; but an original Active may be ascribed to all.

abomin-ari, *abhor*
*adminicul-ari, *prop, support*
advers-ari, *oppose*
*adul-ari, *flatter*
aemul-ari, *rival*
alucin-ari, *dote*
*alterc-ari, *wrangle*
amplex-ari, *embrace*
ampull-ari, *talk big*
ancill-ari, *act as handmaid*
apric-ari, *sun oneself*
aqu-ari, *fetch water*
*arbitr-ari, *think, deem*
architect-ari, *build*
argument-ari, *prove*
*argut-ari, *quibble*
*aspern-ari, *despise*
assent-ari, *comply, flatter*
adstipul-ari, *support*
auction-ari, *hold an auction*
*aucup-ari, *catch*
avers-ari, *dislike*

*augur-ari, } *soothsay*
*auspic-ari, }
auxili-ari, *aid*
*bacch-ari, *revel* (as a Bacchanal) (de)
*bell-ari, *make war*
*bubulcit-ari, *tend kine*
*cachinn-ari, *laugh loud*
calumni-ari, *cavil, chicane*
cavill-ari, *banter*
caupon-ari, *sell by retail*
caus-ari, *allege*
comiss-ari, *revel*
*comit-ari, *accompany*
*comment-ari, *remark*
*communic-ari, *impart*
contion-ari, *harangue*
conflict-ari, *contend*
con-ari, *endeavour*
consili-ari, *counsel*
consol-ari, *comfort*
*conspic-ari, *behold*
*contempl-ari, *view*

convici-ari, *revile*
*conviv-ari, *feast*
cornic-ari, *chatter*
*crimin-ari, *accuse*
*cunct-ari, *delay*
*depecul-ari, *pillage*
despic-ari, *despise*
devers-ari, *lodge*
digladi-ari, *combat*
*dign-ari, *deem worthy*
dedign-ari, *disdain*
*domin-ari, *rule*
elucubr-ari, *work out, compose*
epul-ari, *feast*
*exsecr-ari, *curse*
*fabric-ari, *fashion*
*fabul-ari, *talk* (con-)
famul-ari, *serve*
f-ari, *speak* (af- ef- prae- pro-)
*fener-ari, *lend on interest*
feri-ari, *keep holiday*
*fluctu-ari, *fluctuate*

-avi (ui) | -ĭtum or -ātum :

14. plĭc-are　　plicavi (-ui)　　plicĭtum (-atum) *fold*

-ui or -avi | -ātum.

15. mĭc-are　　micui (-avi)　　-micātum　　　*glitter*

---

frument-ari, *lay in corn*
*frustr-ari, *baffle*
*frutic-ari, *sprout*
fur-ari, *steal*
gesticul-ari, *make gestures*
glori-ari, *boast*
graec-ari, *live sumptuously* (*like Greeks*)
grass-ari, *advance, attack*
grat-ari, } *congratulate*
gratul-ari, } (con)
gratific-ari, *do a kindness*
grav-ari, *grudge*
hariol-ari, *divine*
helu-ari, *eat gluttonously*
hort-ari, *exhort* (ad- ex-)
hospit-ari, *lodge*
*iacul-ari, *dart* (e-)
imagin-ari, *imagine*
imit-ari, *imitate*
indign-ari, *disdain*
infiti-ari, *deny*
insidi-ari, *plot*
interpret-ari, *explain*
*ioc-ari, *jest*
*laet-ari, *rejoice*
*lacrim-ari, *weep*
lament-ari, *lament*
latrocin-ari, *rob*
lenocin-ari, *pander*
licit-ari, *bid* (in auction)
lign-ari, *collect timber*
lucr-ari, *make gain*
*luct-ari, *struggle* (col- ob- re-)
*ludific-ari, *make mock*
*luxuri-ari, *wanton*
machin-ari, *contrive*
materi-ari, *fell timber*
*medic-ari, *heal*
*mendic-ari, *beg*
medit-ari, *con, plan* (prae)
merc-ari, *buy*
*meridi-ari, *take-siesta*
*met-ari, *measure*
*min-ari, } *threaten*
*minit-ari } (com-)
mir-ari, *wonder* (ad- de-)
*miser-ari, *pity* (com-)

*moder-ari, *rule, restrain*
modul-ari, *tune*
*moriger-ari, *comply*
*mor-ari, *delay* (com- de- im- re-)
*muner-ari, *reward* (re-)
*mutu-ari, *borrow*
negoti-ari, *do business*
*nict-ari, *wink*
nidul-ari, *make nest*
*nundin-ari, *market*
nug-ari, *trifle*
*nutric-ari, *nurture*
obvers-ari, *be present* (to sight or mind)
odor-ari, *scent out*
*omin-ari, *forebode*
oper-ari, *work*
*opin-ari, *think*
*opitul-ari, *help*
*opson-ari, *buy meat*
*oscit-ari, *yawn*
*oscul-ari, *kiss*
oti-ari, *be at leisure*
pabul-ari, *forage*
*pacific-ari, *make peace*
*pal-ari, *wander*
*palp-ari, *stroke, flatter*
pandicul-ari, *stretch oneself*
parasit-ari, *play the buffoon*
patrocin-ari, *patronise*
percont-ari, } *inquire*
percunct-ari, }
peregrin-ari, *dwell as a stranger*
periclit-ari, *venture, be in peril*
philosoph-ari, *philosophize*
*pigner-ari, *take-pledge*
pigr-ari, *be lazy*
pisc-ari, *fish* (ex-)
pollicit-ari, *promise*
*popul-ari, *lay waste* (de)
praed-ari, *plunder*
*praestol-ari, *wait for*
praevaric-ari, *walk crooked, play the rogue*
prec-ari, *pray* (com- de- im-)

*proeli-ari, *fight a battle* (de-)
ratiocin-ari, *reason*
record-ari, *remember*
refrag-ari, *vote against, oppose*
*rim-ari, *rake out, search*
rix-ari, *wrangle*
rustic-ari, *live in the country*
*savi-ari, *kiss*
scit-ari, } *inquire*
*sciscit-ari, }
scrut-ari, *search out* (per-)
scurr-ari, *play the buffoon*
*sect-ari, *follow* (as- con- in-)
sermocin-ari, *discourse*
sol-ari, *comfort*
spati-ari, *walk* (ex-)
specul-ari, *look out*
*stabul-ari, *be in a stall*
*stipul-ari, *bargain* (ad- re-)
stomach-ari, *be angry*
suffrag-ari, *vote with*
suspic-ari, *suspect*
tergivers-ari, *shuffle*
test-ari, { *call to witness,*
testific- { *bear witness* (at- ari, { con- de- ob- pro- testari)
tric-ari, *make difficulties*
trist-ari, *be sad*
trutin-ari, *poise in the scales*
*tumultu-ari, *make an uproar*
*tut-ari, *defend*
urin-ari, *dive*
vad-ari, *hold to bail*
*vag-ari, *wander* (di- e- per-)
vaticin-ari, *prophesy*
*velific-ari, *sail*
velit-ari, *skirmish*
*vener-ari, *venerate* (de)
ven-ari, *hunt*
verecund-ari, *be shy*
vers-ari, *be engaged, dwell* (con- de- di-)
*vocifer-ari, *cry out*

Most of these Verbs are derived from Nouns, a few from Verbs. Adulare (i) may be the same word as adorare, but applied to meaner subjects (dog, flatterer, &c.); on aemulor, imitor, see Corss. *Kr. B.* 253: cunctor, R. Sk. *s'ank*, ' hesitate:' contemplari is primarily an augural word, *to observe the heavens* (templa caeli): populare probably for spo-spulare, from spolium, Gr. σκῦλον.

B) Second Conjugation: E-verbs:[1]

E-verbs.

(Verbs which have also an Inchoative form of Conj. 3. are printed in italics.)

Redupl. | -**sum** :

1. mord-ēre	mŏmordi	morsum	*bite*
2. pend-ēre	pĕpendi	pensum	*hang*
3. spond-ēre	spŏpondi	sponsum	*contract*
4. tond-ēre	tŏtondi	tonsum	*shear*

L. S. | **tum** :

5. căv-ēre	cāvi	cautum	*beware*
6. făv-ēre	fāvi	fautum	*favour*
7. fŏv-ēre	fōvi	fotum	*cherish*
8. mŏv-ēre	mōvi	motum	*move*
9. vŏv-ēre	vōvi	votum	*vow*
10. *păv-ēre*	pāvi	—	*quake*

L. S. | **sum** :

11. sĕd-ēre	sēdi	sessum	*sit*
12. vĭd-ēre	vīdi	visum	*see*

1 | **sum** :

13. prand-ēre	prandi	pransum	*dine*

1 | no Sup.

14. conīv-ēre	conivi	—	*blink*
15. strīd-ēre	stridi	—	*creak*
16. *fervēre*	ferbui	—	*boil*

---

[1] E-verbs.

1. Mĕmordi is used. Cpp. (ad prae re-)mordeo -mordi -morsum. See Corss. *Krit. B.* 430. R. Sk. *mard.*

2. Pendēre is the Intrans. Verb corresponding to the Trans. pendĕre 3. *hang*: whence pondus, *weight*, and Frequent. pensare, *ponder.* Cpp. appendeo, impendeo, (de pro-)pendeo -pendi -pensum.

3. Spopondi, euphonic for spo-spondi; Spĕpondi is found. Cpp. despondeo, *betroth*, respondeo, *answer*, -spondi -sponsum. See Corss. *Krit. N.* 112. The Verb means 'to give a legal contract,' 'sponsionem facere.'

4. Also tĕtondi. Cpp. attondeo, detondeo -tondi -tonsum. The Verbs 1-4 shew that Compounds drop the reduplicative syllable. R. τέμνω, Curt. *Gr. Et.* p. 221.

5. Cp. praecaveo. R. Sk. *sku,* 'hide.'

6. 7. See Corss. *Krit. B.* 56, 57.

8. Cpp. (a ad com de di e pro rĕ sĕ sum-)moveo. See Curt. *Gr. Et.* 324.

9. Cp. devoveo.

10. Inchoative expavesco, expāvi, *become terrified.*

11. Cpp. (circum super-)sedeo. But assĭdeo, possĭdeo, and (con de dis in ob prae re sub-)sĭdeo -sēdi -sessum. R. Sk. *sad,* Gr. ἑδ-.

12. Cpp. (in per prae pro-)video. R. Sk. *vid,* Gr. Fιδ-.

13. Prandeo is 'to eat the prandium' (pri-, dies-?) or earlier meal (answering to the present English 'luncheon,' French 'déjeuner à la fourchette'), distinguished from cena, which answers to the present English 'dinner,' formerly 'supper.'

14. Also conixi. The form nīv- is corrupted from gnigv-, g twice falling out; R. Sk. *jânu,* γόνυ, genu, *knee.* See C. *Krit. B.* 56.

15. Byform stridĕre.

16. Byform fervĕre, whence another Perf. fervi. Ferbui is euphonic for fervui, R. Sk. *ghar,* Gr. θερ-. See C. *Krit. B.* 165. 203. Inch. defervesco, deferbui: effervesco, efferbui.

-ēvi | -ētum :

17.	del-ēre	delēvi	delētum	*blot out*
18.	fl-ēre	flēvi	flētum	*weep*
19.	n-ēre	nēvi	nētum	*spin*
20.	-plēre	plēvi	plētum	*fill*
21.	vi-ēre	(viēvi)	viētum	*bind with twigs*
22.	ci-ēre	—	—	*stir up*
23.	-ŏlēre	-olēvi	(olĭtum)	*grow,* &c.
24.	*su-ēre*	suevi	suetum	*be wont*

-ui | -ĭtum :

25.	arc-ēre	arcui	(-artum)	*ward off*
26.	coerc-ēre	coercui	coercĭtum	*restrain*
27.	exerc-ēre	exercui	exercĭtum	*exercise*
28.	căr-ēre	carui	carĭtum	*be without, be in want of*
29.	deb-ēre	debui	debĭtum	*owe*
30.	*dŏl-ēre*	dolui	dolĭtum	*grieve*
31.	hăb-ēre	habui	habĭtum	*have*
32.	iăc-ēre	iacui	iacĭtum	*lie*
33.	lĭc-ēre	licui	licĭtum	*be bid for*
34.	mĕr-ēre	merui	merĭtum	*serve, earn*
35.	mŏn-ēre	monui	monĭtum	*advise*
36.	nŏc-ēre	nocui	nocĭtum	*hurt*
37.	pār-ēre	parui	parĭtum	*appear, obey*
38.	plăc-ēre	placui	placĭtum	*please*
39.	praeb-ēre	praebui	praebĭtum	*afford*
40.	terr-ēre	terrui	terrĭtum	*affright*

17. Some make this Verb de-olēre, comparing abolēre. More probably it is a Cp. of le-, *smear*, True Stem of lĭno.
18. Cpp. affleo, defleo. Compare Gr. φλε- φλυ-, L. flu-. See Curt. 302.
19. Gr. *ve*-. Eng. *needle*, G. nadel.
20. Cpp. compleo, impleo, oppleo, suppleo, (ex re)-pleo, R. Sk. *prî*, Gr. πλε-.
21. Hence vitis, vimen.
22. R. Sk. *s'i*, 'sharpen.' The Perf. and Sup. are formed from cire 4.
23. The root of growth, ol-(=Sk. *ar*, L. al- ar- or-), is distinct from the root of smell, ol (=od). Olesco has the Cpp. adolesco, *grow up*, adolevi, adultum : inolesco -evi, *grow in*: whence ind-oles ; and subolesco, whence suboles. The Transitive Verbs adoleo, *inflame sacrificially*, aboleo, *abolish*, with their Inchoatives (adolesco, abolesco), have a distinct sense, and may possibly be derived from the word o l e u m, implying an old practice of using *oil* to make the sacrifices burn speedily: Verg. iv. 244: Pingue super oleum infundens ardentibus extis.
24. Suēre is found in Lucr., but suesco is the Verb in classical use. Cpp. assuesco, (con de in)-suesco, suevi, suetum. Also mansuesco -suevi -suetum, *grow mild, tame*. See Curt. 251 ; M. *Lucr.* i. 60, iv. 1282.
25. 26. 27. R. Gr. ἀλκ-, ἀρκ-.
30. Inchoatives : (con in)-dolesco -dolui.
31. Cpp. debeo (dehibeo) ; praebeo ; (prae-hibeo) ; (ad co ex in per pro red)-hĭbeo -hibui -hibitum. But posthabeo.
32. Cpp. (ad circum sub)-iaceo. The intransitive Verb corresponding to iacio, *cast*. See this in Conj. 3.
33. See Curt. 456 ; and p. 192 of this Gr.
34. See Curt. 332.
35. Cpp. (ad con prae)-moneo. R. Sk. *man*.
37. Cpp. appareo, compareo, *appear*.
38. Cpp. displiceo -plicui -plicitum ; (com per)-placeo. Sk. *prî*.
40. Cpp. absterreo ; (con de ex per)-terreo. R. Sk. *tras*, Gr. τρε-.

41. *tăc-ēre*	tacui	tacĭtum	*be silent*
42. *văl-ēre*	valui	valĭtum	*be strong, be well*

-ui | -tum :

43. *dŏc-ēre*	docui	doctum	*teach*
44. misc-ēre	miscui	{ mistum / mixtum	} *mingle*
45. tĕn-ēre	tenui	tentum	*hold*
46. *torr-ēre*	torrui	tostum	*scorch, roast*

-ui | -sum :

47. cens-ēre	censui	censum	*value, vote*

-ui | no Sup.

48. *ĕg-ēre*	egui	—	*want*
49. mĭn-ēre	-minui	—	*jut*
50. ŏl-ēre	olui	—	*smell*
51. sorb-ēre	sorbui	—	*suck up*
52. stŭd-ēre	studui	—	*study*
53. *ăc-ēre*	acui	—	*be sour*
54. *ār-ēre*	arui	—	*be dry*
55. *căl-ēre*	calui	—	*be hot*
56. *call-ēre*	callui	—	*be hard-skinned*
57. *cand-ēre*	candui	—	*glow white*
58. *clār-ēre*	clarui	—	*be bright, illustrious*
59. *flōr-ēre*	florui	—	*bloom*
60. *frond-ēre*	frondui	—	*be in leaf*
61. *horr-ēre*	horrui	—	*shudder, be rough*
62. *langu-ēre*	langui	—	*be faint*
63. *lăt-ēre*	latui	—	*lie hid*

---

41. Cpp. (con ob re)-ticeo, ticui: no Sup.: usually -ticesco, -ticui.
42. Cp. praevaleo: others form Inch. (con e in re)-valesco -valui -valitum.
43. Cpp. (ad de e)-doceo. R. Sk. *dis'*, Gr. δεικ-.
44. For mic-sc-eo, Cpp. commisceo, immisceo, (ad inter per re)-misceo, R. Sk. *mis'r*, Gr. μιγ.
45. Cpp. attineo (con de dis ob per re sus)-tineo -tinui -tentum, R. Sk. *tan*, Gr. τεν-.
46. R. Pr. *tarsh*, 'be dry,' Gr. τερσ-. Inch. torresco, Lucr. iii. 890.
47. Cpp. accenseo, recenseo, succenseo. Censitus occurs on Inscrr.: hence recensitus.
48. Cp. indig-eo -ui, Gr. ἀχήν.
49. Cpp. emin-eo -ui :·immineo, no Perf. ; promineo.
50. Cpp. (red sub)-oleo. Subst. odor. R. Gr. ὄζω, ὄδωδα.
51. Cpp. (ab ex ob re)-sorbeo. Gr. ῥοφε-.
52. Gr. σπεύδω.
53. Inch. acesco -acui. Cp. coacesco. R. Gr. ἀκ-, *sharpen*.
54. Inch. aresco. Cp. exar-esco -ui.
55. Inch. cal-esco -ui. Cpp. (con per)-cal-esco -ui, *grow hot*.
56. Inch. Cpp. occall-esco, percall-esco -ui.
57. Inch. Cpp. (ex in)-cand-esco -ui. Cando 3. (used in Cpp. only in the Trans. form. See Corss. *K. B. 111.*)
58. Inch. claresco, Cp. inclar-esco -ui, *become bright, illustrious*.
59. Inch. floresco, Cp efflor-esco -ui, *bloom*.
60. Inch. frond-esco, Cp. refrond-esco -ui, *come into leaf again*.
61. Cpp. (ab ex in)-horreo, Inch. horresco. Cpp. cohorresco, (ex in per)-horr-esco -ui, *shudder*. R. Pr. *harsh*, 'to bristle,' Gr. φρίσσω.
62. Inch. languesco, Cpp. (e ob re)-langu-esco -ui, *grow faint*. R. Gr. λαγ-.
63. Inch. lat-esco, Cp. delit-esco -ui. Frequent. latito 1. See C. *Kr. B.* 79.

64.	*lĭqu-ēre*	lĭcui	—	*melt*
65.	*măd-ēre*	madui	—	*be wet*
66.	*marc-ēre*	marcui	—	*fade*
67.	*nit-ēre*	nitui	—	*shine*
68.	*pall-ēre*	pallŭi	—	*be pale*
69.	*păt-ēre*	patui	—	*be open*
70.	*pūt-ēre*	pūtui	—	*smell rank*
71.	*putr-ēre*	putrui	—	*be rotten*
72.	*rĭg-ēre*	rigui	—	*be stiff*
73.	*rŭb-ēre*	rubui	—	*be red*
74.	*sĭl-ēre*	silui	—	*be silent*
75.	*sord-ēre*	sordui	—	*be dirty*
76.	*splend-ēre*	splendui	—	*glitter*
77.	*squāl-ēre*	squalui	—	*be filthy*
78.	*stŭp-ēre*	stupui	—	*be amazed*
79.	*tāb-ēre*	tabui	—	*pine*
80.	*tĕp-ēre*	tepui	—	*be lukewarm*
81.	*tĭm-ēre*	timui	—	*fear*
82.	*torp-ēre*	torpui	—	*be torpid*
83.	*tŭm-ēre*	tumui	—	*swell*
84.	*vĭg-ēre*	vigui	—	*be vigorous*
85.	*vĭr-ēre*	virui	—	*be green*

No Perf. | No Sup. :

86.	ăv-ēre	*long*	93.	pigr-ēre	*be sluggish*
87.	claud-ēre	*limp*	94.	poll-ēre	*be powerful*
88.	clu-ēre	*be called*	95.	vĕg-ēre	*excite*
89.	dens-ēre	*thicken*	96.	aegr-ēre	*be sick*
90.	foet-ēre	*be fetid*	97.	alb-ēre	*be white*
91.	frend-ēre	*gnash teeth*	98.	calv-ēre	*be bald*
92.	maer-ēre	*mourn*	99.	căn-ēre	*be grey*

---

64. Inch. liquesco ; Cp. deliqu-esco, delicui, *begin to melt.*
65. Inch. mad-esco -ui, *become moist.* Gr. μαδ-.
66. Inch. marcesco, *fade,* R. Pr. *mar,* Gr. μορ-.
67. Cp. eniteo. Inch. nitesco, enitesco -ui, *shine forth.*
68. Inch. pallesco, Cpp. (ex im)-pall-esco -ui, *grow pale.* R. Gr. πελ·
69. Inch. pat-esco -ui. R. Gr. πετα-.
70. Inch. pūtesco -ui, *become foul* ⎫
71. Inch. putr-esco -ui, *become rotten* ⎬ R. Sk. *pûy.* Gr. πύ-θω.
72. Inch. rig-esco -ui. Cpp. (di ob)-rig-esco -ui, *grow stiff.*
73. Inch. rub-esco, Cp. erub-esco -ui, *blush.* R. Pr. *rudh,* Gr. ἐρυθ-.
74. Inch. sil-esco -ui, *become silent.*
75. Inch. sord-esco -ui, *become mean, worthless.*
76. Cp. resplendeo. Inch. splend-esco, exsplend-esco -ui, *shine out.*
78. Inch. stup-esco, obstup-esco -ui, *stand amazed.* See Curt. 218.
79. Inch. tabesco ; Cpp. (ex in)-tab-esco -ui, *begin to pine.* See Curt. 238.
80. Inch. tep-esco -ui. R. Sk. *tap.*
81. Cpp. (prae sub)-timeo. Inch. Cpp. (ex per)-tim-esco -ui.
82. Inch. torp-esco, Cp. obtorp-esco -ui, *grow torpid.* See Corss. *K. B.* 438.
83. Inch. tum-esco, Cp. intum-esco -ui, *begin to swell.* R. Sk. *tu.*
84. Inch. vig-esco -ui. R. Sk. *uksh,* 'grow strong,' Gr. ὑγ-. But see Curt. 186.
85. Inch. vir-esco, Cp. revir-esco -ui, *become green again.*
86. See Curt. 309.
88. R. Sk. *s'ru,* Gr. κλυ-.
96. Inch. aegresco, *become sick.*
97. Inch. albesco, exalbesco, *become white.*

100. *flacc-ēre*	be flabby		
101. *flāv-ēre*	be yellow		
102. *hĕb-ēre*	be dull		
103. *lact-ēre*	be milky		
104. *līv-ēre*	be livid		
105. *mūc-ēre*	be mouldy		
106. *renīd-ēre*	smile		
107. *scăt-ēre*	bubble up		
108. *sĕn-ēre*	be old		
109. *ūm-ēre*	be moist		
110. *ūv-ēre*	be dank		

-si | -tum :

111. polluc-ēre	polluxi	polluctum	*make a feast*
112. *aug-ēre*	auxi	auctum	*increase*
113. indulg-ēre	indulsi	indultum	*indulge*
114. mulg-ēre	mulsi	mulctum	*milk*
115. torqu-ēre	torsi	tortum	*twist*
116. *lūg-ēre*	luxi	—	*mourn*

-si | sum :

117. mulc-ēre	mulsi	mulsum	*soothe*
118. terg-ēre	tersi	-tersum	*wipe*
119. *ard-ēre*	arsi	arsum	*take fire*
120. rīd-ēre	risi	risum	*laugh*
121. suād-ēre	suasi	suasum	*persuade*
122. iŭb-ēre	iussi	iussum	*command*
123. măn-ēre	mansi	mansum	*remain*
124. *haer-ēre*	haesi	haesum	*stick*

si | no Sup. :

125. alg-ēre	alsi	—	*be cold*
126. *fulg-ēre*	fulsi	—	*glitter*
127. *turg-ēre*	tursi	—	*swell*
128. urg-ēre	ursi	—	*urge*
129. *frīg-ēre*	-frixi	—	*be cold*
130. *lūc-ēre*	luxi	—	*shine*

100. See Corss. *Kr. B.* 28.   Byform scatĕre, 3. Lucr. v. 40.
108. Inchoative, sen-esco, consen-esco -ui, *grow old.*
(The other Verbs from 96 to 111 form Inchoatives, which denote beginning of state : but are without Perf. and Sup. except incanesco, which has Perf. incanui.)
112. Cpp. (ad ex)-augeo.   Inch. augesco.   R. Sk. *uksh.*
113. See Corss. *K. Beitr.* 382.   This derivation from ἀλέγω is very doubtful.
114. Cp. immulgeo.   R. Sk. *marj,* Gr. ἀ-μελγ-.
115. Cpp. (con de dis ex in re)-torqueo.   R. τρεπ-.
116. See Curt. 182.   The Subst. luctus points to a Sup. of that form.
117. Cpp. (de per)-mulceo.   See Curt. 327.
118. Cpp. (abs de)-tergeo.   See Corss. *K. B.* 437.
119. Inch. ard-esco, exard-esco -arsi.   Corss. derives from aridus, *K. B.* 111.
120. Cpp. arrideo, irrideo, (de sub)-rideo.   R. Sk. *krīḍ,* 'play.'
121. Cpp. (dis per)-suadeo.   R. Sk. *svad,* 'sweeten,' Gr. ἁδ-.
122. From ius- hibere.
123. Cpp. (per re)-maneo.   R. Gr. μεν-.
124. Cpp. cohaereo, (ad in)-haereo.   Inch. haere-sco, haesi and Cpp.
126. Cpp. affulgeo, effulgeo, refulgeo.   Inch. fulg-esco, fulsi.   Byform fulgĕre, 3. R. Sk. *bhrāj,* Gr. φλεγ-.
128. Cp. adurgeo.   R. Pr. *varj,* 'to press,' Gr. ϝειργ-.
129. Inch. frigesco, Cp. refrigesco -frixi.   R. Gr. ῥιγ-.
130. Cpp. colluceo (e re sub)-luceo.   Inch. lucesco, Cp. illucesco -luxi, *dawn.* R. Sk. *ruč,* Gr. λυκ-.

Semideponent :

131. aud-ēre	ausus sum	—	*dare*
132. gaud-ēre	gavīsus sum	—	*rejoice*
133. *sŏl-ēre*	solĭtus sum	—	*be wont*

Deponent :

134. lĭc-ēri	licĭtus	—	*bid for*
135. mĕr-ēri	merĭtus	—	*deserve*
136. mĭser-ēri	miserĭtus	—	*pity*
137. tu-ēri	tuĭtus	—	*view, protect*
138. vĕr-ēri	verĭtus	—	*fear, respect*
139. r-ēri	rătus	—	*think*
140. făt-ēri	fassus	—	*confess*
141. mĕd-ēri	—	—	*heal*

C) Fourth Conjugation : I-verbs :[1]

(aud-īre, aud-īvi (ii), aud-ītum.)

Variant:

-īvi (ii) | -tum :

1. sĕpĕl-īre	sepelivi	sepultum	*bury*
2. īre (eo)	ivi	ĭtum	*go*
3. quīre	quivi	quĭtum	*be able*

-ui | -tum :

4. săl-īre	salui	(saltum)	*leap, dance*
5. ăpĕr-īre	aperui	apertum	*open*
6. ŏpĕr-īre	operui	opertum	*cover*

-i | tum :

7. compĕr-īre	compĕri	compertum	*find*
8. repĕr-īre	reppĕri	repertum	*discover*

(C. S.-) -tum :

9. vĕn-īre	vēni	ventum	*come*

---

131. Corss. derives from ăvid-us.
132. Corss. derives from a form gavidus. R. Gr. γαϝ-.
133. Probably connected with the forms Sk. sarva-s, E. L. sollus, Gr. ὅλος, &c. Cp. assoleo. An Inch. form solesco must be assumed whence in-solesco, ex-solesco, ob-solesco -ēvi (insolens, exoletus, obsoletus).
134. Cp. polliceor, *promise.* See 33.
135. Cpp. commereor, (de pro)-mereor.
137. Cpp. (con in)-tueor. See Corss. *K. B.* 437.
138. Cpp. (re sub)-vereor. R. Pr. *var*, 'cover.'
140. Cpp. diffiteor, diffessus ; (con pro)-fiteor -fessus. R. Gr. φα-.
141. Medicatus is used as Partic. of medeor.

[1] I-Verbs.
2. Cpp. (ab ad ante circum co ex in inter ob per prae praeter prod red sub trans)-eo. Also vēn-eo, vēn-īre (venum ire), *to be sold*, quasi-passive of vendere (venum-dare), *to sell* : has no Sup. : Pass. Partic. venditus, vendendus. Ambio, as audio.
3. Cp. nequeo. See p. 188.
4. Salii is used. Cpp. (ad de ex in pro re sub)-silio -silui or -silii, -sultum. R. Pr. *sar*, Gr. ἅλλ-.
5–8. These Verbs with experior, opperior, peritus, periculum, belong to a lost verb perire, *try.* R. Pr. *par*, 'accomplish.' Comperior is used by Sallust.
9. Cpp. (ad circum con de e in inter ob per prae pro re super sub)-venio. R. Sk. gam. See Corss. *Kr. B.* 58.

-si | -tum :

10. ămĭc-īre	amixi	amictum	*clothe*
11. farc-īre	farsi	fartum	*stuff*
12. fulc-īre	fulsi	fultum	*prop*
13. sanc-īre	sanxi	sanctum	*consecrate*
14. sarc-īre	sarsi	sartum	*mend*
15. vinc-īre	vinxi	vinctum	*bind*
16. saep-īre	saepsi	saeptum	*hedge in*
17. haur-īre	hausi	haustum	*drain*
18. rauc-īre	rausi	—	*be hoarse*

-si | -sum :

19. sent-īre	sensi	sensum	*feel*

No Perf. | No Supine :

20. caecut-īre	*be blind*	27. glŏc-īre	*cluck*
21. crŏc-īre	*croak*	28. grunn-īre	*grunt*
22. dement-īre	*be distracted*	29. hinn-īre	*neigh*
23. fĕr-īre	*strike*	30. inept-īre	*be silly*
24. fĕrōc-īre	*be wild*	31. prūr-īre	*itch*
25. gest-īre	*be eager*	32. singult-īre	*sob*
26. gann-īre	*yelp.*		

Deponent :

-ītus :

33. bland-īri	blandītus	*fawn, flatter*
34.*larg-iri	largītus	*bestow*
35.*ment-iri	mentītus	*speak falsely*
36.*mōl-iri	molītus	*plan*
37.*part-iri	partītus	*divide*
38. pŏt-iri	potītus	*get possession of*
39.*pūn-iri	punītus	*punish*
40.*sort-iri	sortītus	*allot, take by lot*

-tus (from C. S.) :

41.*expĕr-iri	expertus	*experience*
42. oppĕr-iri	oppertus	*wait for*
43. ŏr-iri	ortus	*arise*

---

10. Also amicui.
11. Cpp. differcio (con in re)-fercio -fersi -fertum.
12. Cpp. effulcio, suffulcio.   Derived from furca, *prop*, C.
13. Sa-*n*-c-io is nasalised, as sa-c-er shews. R. Gr. σά-ος.
14. Cp. resarcio.
15. Cp. devincio.
16. Gr. σηκός. Saepes, praesaepe, saepire, shew the same labialism as lupus. &c., p. 59.
17. Also hausum. Cp. exhaurio.
19. Cpp. (con per)-sentio.
21. It is evident that the **c** in the verbs crocire, *croak*, glocire, *cluck*, must have had the hard k-sound.
33-40. These are derived from Nouns.   Cpp. subblandior : (di e)-largior : ementior : (e re)-molior : (im dis)-pertior.
43. Orior, Gr. ὀρ- has Cpp. (ad co ex ob)-orior -ortus.

-sus (from C. S.) :

44.*assent-īri	assensus	*agree*
45. mēt-iri	mensus	*measure*
46. ord-iri	orsus	*begin*

Cons. and U-verbs.

D) Third Conjugation : Consonant [1] and U-verbs :

I. Consonant Verbs.

1) Verbs with Reduplicated Perfect-Stem. (Compounds drop Reduplication; except those of disco, posco, sisto, -dere, and sometimes of curro.)

Redupl.	-tum :		
1. disc-ĕre	didĭci	—	*learn*
2. posc-ĕre	poposci	—	*demand*
3. pa-*n*-g-ĕre	pepĭgi	pactum	*fasten*
4. pu-*n*-g-ĕre	pupŭgi	punctum	*prick*
5. ta-*n*-g-ĕre	tetĭgi	tactum	*touch*
6. sist-ĕre	-stĭti	(-stĭtum)	*stop*
7. -d-ĕre	-dĭdi	-dĭtum	*put, give*
8. tend-ĕre	tetendi	tentum	*stretch*
9. căn-ĕre	cecĭni	cantum	*sing*

44-46. Assentior from sentire : metior, Sk. *mâ*, Suff. **-ti** : Cpp. (de di e)-metior -mensus. This Participle is difficult. Perhaps the Pres. also was nasalised, but dropt **n** to avoid confusion with mentior. Cp. of ordior, exordior -orsus. R. or- with suff. **d-i**. Virgil uses nutriri as Depon.: 'nutritor olivam,' *G.* ii. 425.

Inchoative from Verbs of Conj. 4.

dormi-	edormi-sco	edormivi	edormitum	*sleep out*
—	obdormi-sco	obdormivi	obdormitum	*fall asleep*
sci-	sci-sco	scivi	scitum	*ratify*
—	consci-sco	conscivi	conscitum	*resolve*
—	desci-sco	descivi	descitum	*revolt*
—	resci-sco	rescivi	rescitum	*learn*

[1] Consonant Verbs.

1. Cpp. (ad con de e per prae)-disco For dic-sc-o. See p. 195.
2. Cpp. (de ex re)-posco. For porc-sc-o. R. Sk. *prac'h*, 'ask, pray.' Hence, prec-ari, procus.
3. Cpp. compingo, impingo -pēgi -pactum; oppango, oppēgi. (De re)-pango. R. Sk. *pas'*, Gr. παγ-, whence also pac-i-sc-or, pax, pignus, &c.
4. Cpp. (com dis ex inter)-pungo. On the probable common origin of pungere, pingere, pix, &c., and Gr. πεύκη, πικρός, ποικίλος, from a Pr. R. *pik, puk, to prick, dot,* &c., see Curt. *Gr. Et.* I. 133, 4. Compare Engl. *peak, pike, pick, peck, poke, pock.* (Can Sk. *pis'* be cited here?)
5. Cpp. attingo, attĭgi, attactum; (con ob)-tingo -tĭgi -tactum. The root-form tăg-o is used by Plautus: also attĭgo (Gr. ταγ-: compare tingere). See Curt. 217.
6. Sisto, redupl. of sto, is trans. or intrans., but its Cpp. are intrans. (ab ad con de ex in ob per re sub)-sisto -stĭti. Sup. (-stĭtum, -stātum) is very rare.
7. Cpp. of -do -dĕre (for dăre) are (ab ad con de e in ob per pro red sub tra)-do -didi -ditum. Also credo (Sk. *s'rad-dadhâmi,* 'put trust, believe'), -dĭdi, -dĭtum, *trust,* and vendo -dĭdi -dĭtum, *sell.* See dăre. The Partic. praedĭtus, *endued,* is a relic of praedĕre, not otherwise occurring.
8. Cpp. attendo (con dis in ob prae sub)-tendo -tendi -tentum : (de ex os pro re) -tendo -tendi -tentum, sometimes -tensum. R. Sk. *tan,* Gr. ταν- τεν-, with suffix **d**.
9. Cpp. occĭno, succĭno -cinui -centum ; so (con prae)-cino. Intercĭno, recĭno, no Perf. or Sup. Occecini is found.

10. păr-ĕre	pepĕri	partum	*bring forth*
11. toll-ĕre	sustŭli	sublātum	*take up*

Redupl. | **-sum** :

12. parc-ĕre	peperci	parsum	*spare*
13. căd-ĕre	cecĭdi	cāsum	*fall*
14. caed-ĕre	cecīdi	caesum	*cut, beat, kill*
15. pend-ĕre	pependi	pensum	*weigh*
16. tu-*n*-d-ĕre	(tutŭdi)	tūsum	*thump, pound*
17. curr-ĕre	cucurri	cursum	*run*
18. fall-ĕre	fefelli	falsum	*deceive*
19. pell-ĕre	pepŭli	pulsum	*drive*
20. (-cell-ĕre)	(cecŭli)	(-culsum)	*push*

2) Verbs with Present-stem strengthened in Perfect.

(S–) | **-tum** :

21. făc-ĕre (*i*-o)	fēci	factum	*make, do*
22. iăc-ĕre (*i*-o)	iēci	iactum	*throw*
23. li-*n*-qu-ĕre	līqui	-lictum	*leave*

---

10. Fut. Part. pariturus.

11. The old Perfect tetŭli is used by Plaut. and Lucr. Tuli, with dropt reduplication, is used as the Perfect of fero. See Irregular Verbs, p. 184. Latum, used as Sup. of fero, is for t-latum from Sk. *tul*, Gr. τλα-, L. tol-, *lift, endure*. The Cpp. of fero are : (ante circum de per prae pro re trans)-fero -tuli -latum ; affero attuli allatum ; aufero abstuli ablatum ; confero contuli collatum ; differo distuli dilatum ; effero extuli elatum ; infero intuli illatum ; offero obtuli oblatum ; suffero sustuli sublatum (which two forms are borrowed by tollo).

12. Cp. comparco -parsi -parsum : or with ℮ ; comperco, &c. Curtius compares Gr. σ-παρνός.

13. Cpp. accĭdo, occĭdo, succĭdo -cĭdi. So (con ex in inter pro re)-cĭdo : occasum is the only Sup. Recĭdi for rececidi.

14. Cpp. accīdo, occīdo, succīdo -cīdi -cīsum. So (con de ex in prae re)-cīdo.

15. Cpp. appendo, impendo -pendi -pensum. So (dis ex per re sus)-pendo.

16. Cpp. (con ob re)-tundo -tŭdi -tūsum or tunsum. R. Sk. *tud*, 'to strike, push, bruise.'

17. Cpp. (ante circum in inter pro re super)-curro -curri. So succurro. Accurro, occurro and (con de dis per trans)-curro have -curri or cŭcurri : ad (ex prae) -curro prefer -cucurri. All have -cursum. Probable R. Pr. *karsh*, 'draw.' Cecurri is found.

18. Cp. refello, refelli ; no Sup. R. Sk. *sphal*, Gr. σ-φάλλω (sphal-yo), *make to fall.*

19. Cpp. (com de dis ex per pro re)-pello -puli -pulsum. So appello, impello. Aspello, no Perf. or Sup. Reppuli for repepuli.

20. (Cello cecŭli) are not used. Cp. percello, perculi, perculsum, *to thrill.* R. Sk. *kal*, 'to push.'

21. Cpp. (con de in inter per prae pro re)-fĭcio -fēci -fectum ; so afficio, officio, sufficio : but (satis bene male)-făcio -fēci -factum. Facio is compounded with many verbal elements : (are assue cale collabe commone labe lique made mansue pate putre stupe obstupe tabe tepe treme tume)-facio -feci -factum, together with many more ; the passive forms of which are similar compounds of fio.

22. Cpp. (ab ad con de dis e in ob pro re sub tra)-icio -ieci -iectum. See Munro on Lucr. ii. 951 ; Curt. 403.

23. The Supine is only found in the Cpp. (re dere)-linquo -liqui -lictum. R. Sk. *ric*, Gr. λιπ-.

24. vi-*n*-cĕre	vīci	victum	*conquer*
25. ăg-ĕre	ēgi	actum	*do*
26. fra-*n*-g-ĕre	frēgi	fractum	*break*
27. lĕg-ĕre	lēgi (lexi)	lectum	*read, choose*
28. căp-ĕre (*i*-o)	cēpi	captum	*take*
29. ru-*m*-p-ĕre	rūpi	ruptum	*break*
30. ĕm-ĕre	ēmi	emptum	*buy, take*
31. scăb-ĕre	scābi	—	*scratch*

(S–) | -**sum** :

32. ĕd-ĕre	ēdi	ēsum	*eat*
33. fŏd-ĕre (*ĭ*-o)	fōdi	fossum	*dig*
34. fu-*n*-d-ĕre	fūdi	fūsum	*pour*

Exceptions :

(S–) | Ĭ-**tum** :

35. fŭg-ĕrĕ (*ĭ*-o)	fūgī	fŭgĭtŭm	*fly*

(S) | -Ĭ-**tum** :

36. bĭb-ĕre	bĭbi	bibĭtum	*drink*

(S) | -**tum** :

37. īcĕre	(īci)	ictum	*strike*

Lost Redupl. | -**sum** :

38. fi-*n*-d-ĕre	fĭdi	fissum	*cleave*
39. sci-*n*-d-ĕre	scĭdi	scissum	*cut*

(S.) | -**sum** :

40. vert-ĕre	verti	versum	*turn*
41. -cend-ĕre	-cendi	-censum	*set alight*

---

24. Cpp. (con de e per re)-vinco.

25. Cpp. (circum per)-ago -egi -actum ; (ab ad ex red sub trans transad)-igo -egi -actum ; cŏigo=cōgo, cŏegi, cŏactum ; dēigo=dēgo degi, prodigo prodegi, no Sup. ; ambigo, no Perf. or Sup. ; satago sategi, no Sup. R. Sk. *aj,* Gr. αγ-.

26. Cpp. confringo, effringo ; (de in per prae re)-fringo -fregi -fractum. Gr. ϝραγ-.

27. Lego, *read,* Cpp. (per prae re)-lego -legi -lectum. Lego, *choose* : sub-lĕgo -lēgi -lectum, (col de e se)-lĭgo -lēgi -lectum ; intellego, neg-lego, -lexi -lectum ; and di-lĭgo -lexi -lectum. Gr. λεγ-.

28. Cpp. (con de ex in inter per prae re sus)-cipio -cepi -ceptum. So accipio. But antecapio. See p. *190.* Note.

29. Cpp. corrumpo, irrumpo ; (di e inter per pro)-rumpo. R. Sk. *lup,* ' to tear.'

30. Cpp. (ad dir ex red)-ĭmo -ēmi -emptum ; coĕmo, (inter per)-ĕmo. The rest (como, demo, promo, sumo) form -psi -ptum. Emo seems, in some of its uses, to be the Causal of eo. Compare intereo with interemo ; pereo with peremo.

32. Cpp. (ad com ex per)-ĕdo -ēdi -ēsum. See Irregular Verbs, p. 189.

33. Cpp. (con de in per)-fodio. Also effodio.

34. Cpp. (con de in per pro re)-fundo. Also affundo, effundo, offundo, suffundo ; Gr. χυ-, with nasalised suff. **d** : pointing to a lost root *ghu.*

35. Cpp. aufugio, diffugio, effugio : (con per pro re trans)-fugio. R. Sk. *bhuj,* Gr. φυγ-.

36. Cpp. combibo, ebibo, imbibo. R. Sk. *pâ,* Gr. πο-, Present-stem redupl. ; the **p** being softened to **b**.

38. Cp. dif-findo.

39. Cpp. (ab di ex re)-scindo. R. Sk. *c'hid.*

40. Cpp. (a ad con de di e in ob per prae re sub)-verto. R. Pr. *vart.*

41. Cpp. accendo, incendo, succendo -cendi -censum.

42. cūd-ĕre	cūdi	cūsum	*hammer*
43. -fend-ĕre	-fendi	-fensum	*strike*
44. mand-ĕre	mandi	mansum	*chew*
45. pand-ĕre	pandi	pansum	*spread*
46. prehend-ĕre	prehendi	prehensum	*take, grasp*
47. scand-ĕre	scandi	scansum	*climb*
48. sīd-ĕre	sīdi	—	*settle*
49. lamb-ĕre	lambi	—	*lick*
50. verr-ĕre	verri	versum	*sweep*
51. vell-ĕre	{velli / vulsi}	vulsum	*rend, pluck*
52. psall-ĕre	psalli	—	*play (chords)*
53. vīs-ĕre	vīsi	vīsum	*visit*
54. fīdere	fisus sum	—	*trust*

3) Verbs with agglutinated Perfect-stem in **-ui** or **-vi**.

a. **-ui | -tum** :

55. compesc-ĕre	compescui	—	*restrain*
56. răp-ĕre (*i*-o)	rapui	raptum	*seize*
57. *ăl-ĕre*	alui	altum	*nourish*
58. cŏl-ĕre	colui	cultum	*till*
59. consŭl-ĕre	consului	consultum	*consult*
60. occŭl-ĕre	occului	occultum	*hide*
61. sĕr-ĕre	serui	sertum	*set in row*
62. pins-ĕre	pinsui	pistum	*pound*

42. Cpp. (ex in pro)-cudo -cudi -cusum. Hence incus incūd-, *anvil.*
43. Cpp. (de of)-fendo. Hence infensus, infestus, manifestus (for -fendtus). Sk. han (Pr. *dhan?*), Gr. θεν-.
45. Cpp. (dis ex prae)-pando -pandi -pansum or passum.
46. Also prend-ĕre, prendi, prensum. Cpp. apprehendo (com de re)-prehendo or -prendo, &c. Gr. χαδ- χανδάνω.
47. Cpp. (ad con de in tran)-scendo -scendi -scensum. R. Sk. *skand.*
48. See sed-ĕre, of which sidĕre is a variant form. Cpp. (ad con in re sub)-sido -sidi.
49. Latin root lab-.
50. Cp. everro. See Corss. *Kr. B.* 403.
51. Cpp. (con di per re)-velli -vulsum : (a e)-velli or -vulsi -vulsum. See Corss. *Kr. B.* 325.
53. From Sup. of video. Cpp. (in re)-viso.
54. Cpp. (con dif)-fido, of which the Perfects (con dif)-fīdi are in use as well as (con-dif)-fisus sum.
55. For comperc-sc-ere.
56. Cpp. (ab de di e)-ripio -ripui -reptum. So arripio, corripio, surripio. Pott and Corssen take *rap* to be the original form of Sk. *lup.* 'to tear,' also shewn in ru-m-pere.
57. *Al, ol,* is the root of growth=Pr. *ar* : shewn in al-ere al-tus, olescere, and nume-rous words. Inch. co-al-esco -ui -itum, *unite, curdle.* See Curt. 359.
58. Cpp. (ex in re)-colo. See accolo. R. Pr. *kar*, 'make.'
59. Corssen (*Nachtr.* 280) agrees with Mommsen in adopting Pr. *sar*, 'move,' L. sal-, as the root of con-sul-ere, exsul, praesul, &c. He gives consulere a sense=con-venire, and makes consul (for consul-us) its derivative.
60. Occŭlo, cēlare, cella, clam, and Gr. καλύπτω (κρύπτω) καλία, are evidently cog-nate and point to a common Pr. *kal*, 'hide,' which appears in Sk. as *kŭl.* Curtius compares also clepere and color.
61. Cpp. (con de dis ex in)-sero. So assero. Gr. εἴρω. See Curt. 355.
62. Sometimes pisere, pisi. R. Sk. *pish*, 'crush.'

63. tex-ĕre	texui	textum	*weave*
64. deps-ĕre	depsui	—	*knead, tan*

-ui | ĭ-tum :

65. elĭc-ĕre (*i*-o)	elicui	elicĭtum	*tice forth*
66. stert-ĕre	stertui	—	*snore*
67. strĕp-ĕre	strepui	strepĭtum	*rattle*
68. cumb-ĕre	cŭbui	cubĭtum	*lie down*
69. frĕm-ĕre	fremui	fremĭtum	*roar*
70. *gĕm-ĕre*	gemui	gemĭtum	*groan*
71. *trĕm-ĕre*	tremui	—	*tremble*
72. vŏm-ĕre	vomui	vomĭtum	*vomit*
73. gign-ĕre	gĕnui	genĭtum	*beget*
74. pōn-ĕre	posui	posĭtum	*place*
75. mŏl-ĕre	molui	molĭtum	*grind*
76. velle (volo)	vŏlui	—	*wish*
77. nolle (nolo)	nōlui	—	*wish not*
78. malle (mālo)	mālui	—	*wish rather*

-ui | -sum :

79. mĕt-ĕre	messui	messum	*mow, reap*
80. frend-ĕre	frendui	fressum	*gnash, bruise*
81. (-cell-ĕre)	(-cellui)	(-celsum)	*push*

b. **-vi | -tum :**

These include the Verbs, before noticed, in which the Present Stem is so modified as to become consonantal : while the True Stem, which is pure, is shown in the Perfect and Supine forms.

a.
82. lĭn-ĕre	lēvi	lĭtum	*smear*
83. sĭn-ĕre	sīvi	sĭtum	*allow*
84. cern-ĕre	crēvi	crētum	*sift*

---

63. Cpp. (con in ob per prae re sub)-texo. R. Sk. *taksh* (for Pr. *tak*), 'fashion.' Gr. τευχ-.
64. Gr. δέφω.
65. See lacere.
67. Cpp. (ob per)-strepo.
68. Cpp. (con de dis in pro re)-cumbo. See cubare.
69. Cp. infremo. R. Sk. *bhram*, Gr. βρέμ-ω.
70. Cpp. (con in)-gemo. Inchoative : gemisco. Cpp. (con in)-gemisco, gemui.
71. Inchoative tremisco. Cpp. (con in)-tremisco, tremui. R. Sk. *tras*, Gr. τρε-. Suff. **m.**
72. Cpp. (e re)-vomo. R. Sk. *vam*, Gr. ϝεμ-ε-.
73. Cp. progigno. Redupl. of gen-. Sk. *jan*, Gr. γεν-. Gĕno is found in old Latin.
74. Cpp. (ante com de dis ex inter post prae pro re se trans)-pono. See p. 195.
75. Cp. permŏlo. Gr. μυλ-, L. mŏla, *a mill*. Hence *malt*?
76–78. See Irregular Verbs, p. 186.
79. Cp. demĕto. (Sk. *mâ*, 'measure'?)
80. The Sup. shews the nasalisation of Pres. St. See frendēre.
81. Cpp. (ante ex prae)-cello cellui. Hence the Adjectives celsus, excelsus, praecelsus. R. Sk. *kal*, 'push,' shewn also in procul, procella, culter, celer, κέλλω, βούκολος, and others. See 20.
82. Cpp. (per ob sub)-lino -levi -lĭtum. Also collĭno, illĭno. Another form is linire. R. Sk. *lĭ*.
83. Cp. desino, (desīvi) desii, also desītus sum.
84. Cpp. (de dis ex se)-cerno. R. Gr. κρι-. Hence L. cribrum, *sieve*.

	85. spern-ĕre	sprēvi	sprētum	*spurn*
	86. stern-ĕre	strāvi	strātum	*strew*
	87. sĕr-ĕre	sēvi	sătum	*sow*
	88. cresc-ĕre	crēvi	crētum	*grow*
	89. quiesc-ĕre	quiēvi	quiētum	*rest*
	90. suesc-ĕre	suēvi·	suētum	*be wont*
	91. (g)nosc-ĕre	(g)nōvi	(g)nōtum	*know*
	92. pasc-ĕre	pāvi	pastum	*feed*
β.	93. cŭp-ĕre (*i*-o)	cupīvi	cupītum	*desire*
	94. pĕt-ĕre	petīvi	petītum	*demand*
	95. quaer-ĕre	quaesīvi	quaesītum	*seek*
	96. rud-ĕre	rudīvi	rudītum	*bray*
	97. săp-ĕre (*i*-o)	sapīvi	—	*savour*
	98. tĕr-ĕre	trīvi	tritum	*rub, bruise*
γ.	99. arcess-ĕre	arcessīvi	arcessītum	*fetch*
	100. incess-ĕre	incessīvi	incessītum	*attack*
	101. căpess-ĕre	capessīvi	capessītum	*take in hand*
	102. făcess-ĕre	facessīvi	facessītum	*cause*
	103. lăcess-ĕre	lacessīvi	lacessītum	*provoke*

4) Verbs forming Perfect-Stem with agglutinated -**s** (for **es-**).

a. Guttural Stems :

-**si** | -**tum** :

104.	dīc-ĕre	dixi	dictum	*say*
105.	dūc-ĕre	duxi	ductum	*lead*
106.	-lăc-ĕre (*i*-o)	-lexi	-lectum	*entice*

85. Spernere, properly '*to kick.*' Curt. 289.
86. Cpp. (in pro)-sterno. R. Pr. *star*, Gr. στορ-.
87. Cpp. (con in)-sero -sēvi -sĭtum.
88. Cpp. (con de ex in)-cresco. Also accresco, succresco. Cresco is Inchoative of creo, Sk. *kṛi*, 'make.'
89. Cpp. acquiesco, (con re)-quiesco. Sk. *s'ĭ*, Gr. κει-.
90. Cpp. assuesco, (con de in)-suesco. Sk. *svadhâ*, 'self-will.' R. *sva*, 'self.'
91. Nosco has dropt **g** which reappears in agnosco, agnovi, agnĭtum ; cognosco, cognovi, cognĭtum, ignosco, ignovi: Adj. ignotus. Dignosco, internosco have no Sup. This Verb, with potum, potus, are the only remnants of a Latin O-verb. Sk. *jnâ*, Gr. γνο-.
92. Cp. depasco.
93. Cupiret, Lucr.
94. Cpp. (com ex re)-peto. So appeto, oppeto. Curtius refers to Sk. *pat*, Gr. πετ-, *fly*.
95. For quaesĕre or quaesire., Cpp. (con dis ex in per re)-quiro -quīsivi -quīsītum. So perquiro, conquiro.
96. Sk. *ru*, *rud* ; Gr. ὠρύω. Persius has rŭdere : but rŭdens, *cable*.
97. Or sapui. Cp. desipio -ui. Inchoative resipisco -sipui, *grow wise again*. This word, compared with sucus, shews labialism, as lupus, popina, &c.
98. Cpp. (de con pro)-tero -trivi -tritum. Also attero. Perf. terivi and terui are found. Connected with Gr. τείρω, τέρην. L. tener.
99-103. These Verbs are formed with a suffix ess- which expresses eager action. Arcess- is for acci-ess-, and is sometimes written accers- : incess- for inci-ess- : both from root ci, *rouse* : capess- from cap- : facess- from fac- : lacess- from lac- Perfect and Supine shew that the Present-Stem was originally -io. Perfects incessi, facessi, lacessi, are cited.
104. Cpp. (ad benĕ contra e in inter malĕ prae vale)-dico. R. Sk. *dis'*, Gr. δεικ-.
105. Cpp. (ab ad circum con de di e in intro ob per pro re se sub tra)-duco.
106. Cpp. *al-licio, il-licio, pel-licio, pro-licio* -lexi -lectum ; but elicio, elicui, elicitum.

107. -spĕc-ĕre (*i*-o)	-spexi	-spectum	*espy*
108. cŏqu-ĕre	coxi	coctum	*cook*
109. cing-ĕre	cinxi	cinctum	*surround*
110. fi*n*g-ĕre	fi*n*xi	fictum	*fashion*
111. -flīg-ĕre	-flixi	-flictum	*smite*
112. frīg-ĕre	frixi	frictum	*roast, fry*
113. iung-ĕre	iunxi	iunctum	*join*
114. ling-ĕre	-linxi	·linctum	*lick*
115. mung-ĕre	-munxi	-munctum	*wipe*
116. pi*n*g-ĕre	pi*n*xi	pictum	*paint*
117. plang-ĕre	planxi	planctum	*beat*
118. rĕg-ĕre	rexi	rectum	*rule*
119. stri*n*g-ĕre	stri*n*xi	strictum	*bind*
120. sūg-ĕre	suxi	suctum	*suck*
121. tĕg-ĕre	texi	tectum	*cover*
122. -stingu-ĕre	-stinxi	-stinctum	—
123. tingu-ĕre	tinxi	tinctum	*stain*
124. ungu-ĕre	unxi	unctum	*anoint*
125. ningu-ĕre	ninxi	—	*snow*
126. ang-ĕre	(anxi)	—	*squeeze*
127. clang-ĕre	—	—	*rattle*
128. trăh-ĕre	traxi	tractum	*draw*
129. vĕh-ĕre	vexi	vectum	*carry*
130. vīv-ĕre	vixi	victum	*live*
131. stru-ĕre	struxi	structum	*pile*

107. Cpp. (circum con de di in per pro re)-spĭcio -spexi -spectum. So aspicio, suspicio. R. Sk. *spas'*, Gr. σκεπ-.

108. Cpp. (con de in per)-coquo. R. Sk. *pac'*, Gr. πεπ-. See p. 59.

109. Cpp. (dis prae re)-cíngo. So accingo, succingo.

110. Cpp. affingo, effingo, re-fingo, Gr. θιγ-.

111. Cpp. (con in)-fligo, affligo. Profligare, *rout*, is of Conj. 1.

112. R. Sk. *bhrajj*, Gr. φρυγ-.

113. Cpp. (ad con dis in se sub)-iungo. R. Sk. *yuj*, Gr. ζυγ-.

114. Cp. pol-lingo, *anoint* (*a corpse*), pollinxi, pollinctum. Sk. *rih* or *lih*, Gr. λειχ-.

115. Cp. emungo, *wipe the nose, clean out.* R. Sk. *muc'*.

116. Cpp. appingo, depingo. See pungere. R. Sk. *pinj*.

117. Gr. πληγ-. L. plāga.

118. Cpp. arrĭgo, corrĭgo, dirĭgo ; (e por)-rigo -rexi -rectum. Also pergo, perrexi, per-rectum ; surgo, *rise*, surrexi, surrectum, with its compounds : (as con ex in re)-surgo -surrexi -surrectum. R. Gr. ὀρεγ-.

119. Cpp. astringo, (con de di ob per prae re sub)-stringo. From praestringĕre comes praestigiae, *juggleries* (for praestrigiae). Gr. στραγγ-.

120. Cp. exsugo.

121. Cpp. (con de ob pro re)-tego. Latin has dropt s. R. Sk. *sthag*, Gr. στεγ-.

122. Stinguo has the sense of *pricking* and also of *quenching.* Cpp.: (1) (di in)-stinguo ; (2) (ex re)-stinguo. Gr. στίζω.

123. Gr. τέγγω.

124. Cpp. (in per)-unguo. Tinguo, unguo may be written ti n g o, u n g o.

125. A primitive *s-nih-* must be assumed, from which, by casting off **s** and nasalizing, comes the form ningu-, and again nix, nivis, &c. Gr. νίφω. Hence Germ. schnee, Eng. *snow.* R. Sk. *snu.*

126. R. Sk. *anj*, Gr. ἀγχ-.

128. Cpp. attraho ; (con de dis ex per pro re sub)-traho.

129. Cpp. (a ad circum con de e in praeter re sub)-veho. R. Sk. *vah*, Gr. ϝοχε-.

130. Prim. *gvîv*, Sk. *jîv*, whence vigv-, the True Stem of vivo, which drops the *second* **v** in Perf. and Sup. Corssen, *B.* 72. Inchoative : reviv-isc-o, revixi, re-victum.

131. See Corssen, *B.* 72. Cpp. (ad con de ex in ob sub)-struo -struxi -structum.

-si | -sum :

a.	132. fīg-ĕre	fixi	fixum	*fix*
	133. flu-ĕre	fluxi	fluxum	*flow*
ß.	134. merg-ĕre	mersi	mersum	*drown*
	135. sparg-ĕre	sparsi	sparsum	*sprinkle*
	136. terg-ĕre	tersi	tersum	*wipe*

b. Dental Stems :

-si | -sum :

137. flect-ĕre	flexi	flexum	*bend*
138. nect-ĕre	{nexi / nexui}	nexum	*twine*
139. pect-ĕre	pexi	pexum	*comb*
140. plect-ĕre	—	-plexum	{*plait* / *smite*}
141. mitt-ĕre	mīsi	missum	*send*
142. quăt-ĕre (*i-*o)	—	quassum	*shake*
143. cēd-ĕre	cessi	cessum	*yield*
144. claud-ĕre	clausi	clausum	*shut*
145. divĭd-ĕre	divīsi	divisum	*divide*
146. laed-ĕre	laesi	laesum	*hurt*
147. lūd-ĕre	lūsi	lusum	*play*
148. plaud-ĕre	plausi	plausum	*clap hands*
149. rād-ĕre	rāsi	rasum	*shave*
150. rōd-ĕre	rōsi	rosum	*gnaw*
151. trūd-ĕre	trūsi	trusum	*thrust*
152. vād-ĕre	-vāsi	-vasum	*go*

---

132. Cpp. affigo, suffigo ; con- de- in- prae- re- trans-figo.
133. Enlarged forms flug- and flugv- account for the Perfect fluxi and for flu-v-ius. Cpp. (circum con de dif ef in per prae praeter pro re)-fluo -fluxi -fluxum. Also affluo, diffluo, effluo. The noun fluctus points to an older Sup. in -tum.
134. Cpp. immergo ; (de e sub)-mergo.
135. Cpp. conspergo, dispergo ; (ad in re)-spergo -spersi -spersum. In old L. these keep **a.**
136. For stergĕre. So C. and Meyer. Compare s-trigilis, *flesh-scraper.* See ter-gĕre.
137. This and the next three are Guttural Verbs, strengthened by a suffix **t**; but, as **t** falls out before **s**, and also influences the Supine, they may be treated as Dental Verbs. Cpp. (circum de in re)-flecto.
138. Cpp. (ad con in sub)-necto -nexui -nexum. See meto.
139. Cp. depecto depexi depexum.
140. Gr. πλεκ-.
141. Cpp. dimitto, immitto, ŏmitto ; (a ad com de e inter per prae praeter pro re sub trans)-mitto -misi -missum.
142. Cpp. (con dis ex in per)-cutio -cussi -cussum. So repercutio.
143. Cpp. (abs ante con de dis ex in inter prae pro re se)-cedo. So accedo, succedo.
144. Cpp. (con dis ex in inter prae re se)-cludo -clusi -clusum. So occludo, Gr. κλείω.
146. Cpp. allīdo, collīdo, elīdo, il-līdo -lisi -lisum.
147. Cpp. alludo, colludo, illudo, (de e) -ludo -lusi -lusum.
148. Cpp. applaudo -plausi - plausum, (ex sup)-plodo -plosi -plosum.
149. Cpp. (ab e)-rado. So corrado. R. Sk. *rad.*
150. Cpp. (de prae)-rodo. So arrodo, corrodo. Sk. *rad.*
151. Cpp. (abs de ex in ob pro)-trudo.
152. *Cpp. (e in per)-vado.*

c. Labial Stems :

-si | -tum :

153. carp-ĕre	carpsi	carptum	*pluck*
154. clĕp-ĕre	clepsi	cleptum	*steal*
155. { rēp-ĕre	repsi	reptum	*creep*
{ serp-ĕre	serpsi	—	*crawl*
156. { scalp-ĕre	scalpsi	scalptum	*scratch*
{ sculp-ĕre	sculpsi	sculptum	*grave*
157. glūb-ĕre	glupsi	gluptum	*peel*
158. nūb-ĕre	nupsi	nuptum	*wed*
159. scrīb-ĕre	scripsi	scriptum	*write*

d. Nasal Stems :

-si | -tum :

160. cōm-ĕre	compsi	comptum	*dress hair*
161. dēm-ĕre	dempsi	demptum	*take away*
162. prōm-ĕre	prompsi	promptum	*take forth*
163. sūm-ĕre	sumpsi	sumptum	*take up*
164. temn-ĕre	tempsi	temptum	*despise*

-si | -sum :

165. prĕm-ĕre	pressi	pressum	*press*

e. Liquid (Sibilant) Stems :

-si | -tum :

166. gĕr-ĕre	gessi	gestum	*carry on*
167. ūr-ĕre	ussi	ustum	*burn*

II. U-verbs :

-ui | -ūtum :

168. ăcu-ĕre	acui	acūtum	*sharpen*
169. argu-ĕre	argui	argūtum	*prove*

---

153. Cpp. (con de dis ex)-cerpo -cerpsi -cerptum.
154. Gr. κλέπτω.
155. Cpp. (ad ob per sub)-repo. Correpo, irrepo. Serpsi is not found in Classical Latin. R. Pr. *sarp*.
156. Cpp. (ex in)-sculpo.
157. Gr. γλύφω.
158. Nubo is classically applied to the woman only, except in a jocular sense: as Martial viii. 12 : ' uxori nubere nolo meae.' It has Perf. nupta sum as well as nupsi. That the verb is originally transitive, meaning to *veil* or *cover*, is shewn by various passages and by the Compound obnubo. Hence the bride who covers herself with the flammeum is said nubere (se).
159. Cpp. (ad circum con de ex in per prae pro re sub tran)-scribo.
160–163 are Cpp. of ĕmo, *take*, but differing from it in the Perfect. Cpp. of promo : (de ex)-promo -prompsi -promptum. Cpp. of sumo : (ab as con de in re)-sumo -sumpsi -sumptum.
164. Cp. contemno contempsi contemptum.
165. Cpp. imprĭmo, supprĭmo ; (com de ex op re)-primo -pressi -pressum.
166. Cpp. (con di e in)-gero. So aggero, suggero.
167. Cpp. (ad ex in per)-uro. Corssen (*Kr. Nachträge,* 117) derives amburo, com-buro -bussi -bustum, together with the Noun bustum, from Sk. *prush. plush,* ' to burn.'
168. Cp. exacuo, exacui. On the original long quantity of **u** in U-verbs, see p. 18.
169. Cp. redarguo. Sk. *arjuna-s, clear,* Gr. ἀργός.

170. exu-ĕre	exui	exūtum	*put off*
171. indu-ĕre	indui	indūtum	*put on*
172. imbu-ĕre	imbui	imbūtum	*tinge*
173. lu-ĕre	lui	lūtum	*wash, atone*
174. minu-ĕre	minui	minūtum	*lessen*
175. nu-ĕre	nui	nūtum	*nod*
176. spu-ĕre	spui	spūtum	*spit*
177. statu-ĕre	statui	statūtum	*set up*
178. sternu-ĕre	sternui	sternūtum	*sneeze*
179. su-ĕre	sui	sūtum	*sew*
180. tribu-ĕre	tribui	tribūtum	*assign, pay*
181. solv-ĕre	solvi	solūtum	*loose, pay*
182. volv-ĕre	volvi	volūtum	*roll*

-ui | -ŭtum :

183. ru-ĕre	rui	rŭtum (ruĭtum)	
184. batu-ĕre	batui	—	*beat*
185. -gru-ĕre	-grui	—	
186. metu-ĕre	metui	—	*fear*
187. plu-ĕre	plui	—	*rain*

Deponent Verbs in Conj. 3 :

a. 188. fung-i	functus		*perform*
189. nīt-i	nisus (nixus)		*strive*
190. plect-i	-plexus		*twine*
191. păt-i (*i*-or)	passus		*suffer*
192. ūti	usus		*use*
193. grăd-i (*i*-or)	gressus		*step*

170–1. Latin -uo in these Verbs corresponds to Gr. δύω. Curt. 621. But see Corss.
Beitr. 496. Hence ind-uviae, ex-uviae.
172. Corssen considers bu in imbuo a weakened form of *pā po-*, 'to drink.'
173. Cpp. (ab di e per pol pro sub)-luo -lui -lūtum. Fut. Part. luiturus. Luo is the
weak form which appears strengthened in Gr. λούω and L. lav-ĕre, lavare
(see A-verbs). Curt. 370. See solvere.
174. Cpp. (com de di im)-minuo. R. Sk. *mi*, Gr. μι-ν-.
175. Cpp. (ab an in re)-nuo. Gr. νεύω.
176. Cpp. (con de ex re)-spuo -spui. Gr. πτύω, hence p-i-tuĭta for s-pituĭta.
177. From status. Cpp. (con de in pro re sub)-stituo -stitui -stitūtum.
179. Cpp. (as con dis re)-suo. R. Sk. *siv*.
180. From tribus, *tribe* : Root tri, *three*. Applied first to the state-payments of the
three original Tribes at Rome. Cpp. (con dis re)-tribuo. So attribuo.
181. Cpp. (ab dis ex per re)-solvo. For se-luere, from a verb lu-, loose=Sk. *lû*, Gr.
λυ-, but not otherwise shewn in L.
182. Cpp. (ad circum con de e in ob per pro re)-volvo. Gr. Ϝελύω.
183. Cpp. (di e ob pro sub)-ruo -rui -rūtum. So corruo, irruo. Fut. Part. rui-
turus.
185. Cpp. (con in)-gruo.
186. Metūtum appears in Lucr. v. 1139.
187. Cp. depluo.
(The word delibutus, *steeped*, belongs to a disused Verb delibuo.)
188. Cpp. (de per)-fungor.
189. Cpp. (ad con e in ob re sub)-nitor -nixus. For g-nitor. R. Sk. *jânu*, Gr. γόνυ,
knee.
190. See plectĕre. Cpp. amplector, complector, *embrace*.
191. Cp. perpetior, perpessus.
192. In old Latin the form oitier appears. Cp. abutor abusus.
193. Cpp. aggredior (con de di e in prae pro re trans)-gredior -gressus.

194. lāb-i	lapsus	*glide, fall*
195. mŏr-i (*i*-or)	mortuus	*die*
196. quĕr-i	questus	*complain*
197. fru-i	fruitus	*enjoy*
198. lŏqu-i	locutus	*speak*
199. sĕqu-i	secutus	*follow*
β. 200. apisc-i	aptus	*obtain*
201. -menisc-i	-mentus	*have in mind*
202. expergisc-i	experrectus	*wake up*
203. fatisc-i	fessus	*be weary*
204. (g)nasc-i	(g)natus	*be born*
205. irasc-i	iratus	*be angry*
206. nancisc-i	nactus	*find*
207. oblivisc-i	oblītus	*forget*
208. pacisc-i	pactus	*bargain*
209. proficisc-i	profectus	*set out*

194. Cpp. (de di e praeter pro sub re)-lābor -lapsus. So allabor, collabor, illabor.
195. Cpp. (de e)-morior -mortuus. Fut. Part. moriturus. So immorior. R. Sk. *mar*. Mortuus is an Adj. used participially.
196. Cp. conqueror conquestus.
197. For frugv-i, hence fructus ; but Fut. Part. fruiturus. Cp. perfruor perfruitus.
198. Cpp. (e ob pro)-loquor -locutus. So alloquor, colloquor.
199. Cpp. (con ex in ob per pro sub)-sequor -secutus. R. Sk. *sac'*, Gr. ἑπ-.
200. Cpp. (ad ind)-ipiscor -eptus. R. Sk. *åp*.
201. Cpp. comminiscor commentus ; reminiscor, no Part. R. Sk. *man*.
202. The Cp. expergisci experrectus is evidently weakened from exporgisci exporrectus : from exporrigi, *to stretch oneself out* (on awakening). See rego.
203. Cp. defetiscor defessus.
204. Cp. (con e in)-nascor -natus, Fut. Part. nasciturus. Observe cognatus, prognatus. See gignere, 73.
206. Nanctus is also used : and nanciam is cited as an old form.
207. From liv-ēre, *to be of a dark colour*; hence oblivisci, *to become darkened, to forget*. So Corssen, *Nachtr.*, 34.
208. See pango. Cpp. (com de)-paciscor or -peciscor. R. Sk. *pas'*.
209. From prō fāc- (*make forward*).

(Inchoative Verbs derived from other Verbs have been mentioned in the Notes to the Syllabus.)

A) Inchoatives derived from Nouns are very numerous : examples are—

1) Having a Perfect, but no Supine.

From vesper			
From vesper	vesperasco	vesperavi	} *grow towards evening*
— —	advesperasco	advesperavi	
— —	invesperasco	invesperavi	
— creber	crebresco	crebui	} *become frequent*
— —	increbresco	increbui	
— —	percrebresco	percrebui	
— crudus	recrudesco	recrudui	*become sore again*
— durus	duresco	durui	} *grow hard*
— —	induresco	indurui	
— —	obduresco	obdurui	
— macer	macresco	mācrui	*grow lean*
— maturus	maturesco	maturui	*become ripe*
— mutus	obmutesco	obmutui	*become mute*
— niger	nigresco	nigrui	*become black*
— notus	innotesco	innotui	*become known*
— surdus	obsurdesco	obsurdui	*become deaf*
— vanus	vănesco	vānui	} *vanish away*
— —	evănesco	evānui	
— vilis	vilesco	vilui	} *become cheap*
— —	evilesco	evilui	

210.	ulcisc-i	ultus	*avenge*
211.	vesc-i	—	*feed*
γ. 212.	līqu-i	—	*melt*
213.	ring-i	—	*grin*

2) Without Perfect or Supine :

puer	puerasco (re)	curvus	incurvesco
ignis	ignesco	iuvenis	iuvenesco (re)
integer	integrasco	mitis	mitesco
arbor	arboresco	mollis	mollesco
dives	ditesco	pinguis	pinguesco
dulcis	dulcesco	pluma	plumesco
grandis	grandesco	sterilis	sterilesco
gravis	gravesco (in)	tener	tener-esco -asco (in)
niger	nigresco	lentus	lentesco

3) Some are of uncertain origin :

glisco, *increase*   fatisco (Gr. χα-), *fall open*, &c.

Conquinisco, conquexi, *stoop*, is an old and remarkable Inchoative Verb.

Obs. Other Verbs of Conj. 3. without Perfect and Supine are :

ambigo, *doubt* ; clango ; furo, *rage* ; plecto, *strike.*

B) Homonymous words are such as are written alike, though differing in sense and generally in origin.

1) Verbs having the same First Person Present Ind. in different Conjugations.

Conj. 1.		Conj. 3.		Conj. 1.		Conj. 3.	
appello	*call*	appello	*land*	fundo	*found*	fundo	*pour*
compello	*address*	compello	*compel*	mando	*entrust*	mando	*chew*
colligo	*bind*	colligo	*collect*	obsĕro	*bolt*	obsĕro	*sow over*
consterno	*alarm*	consterno	*strew*	vŏlo	*fly*	vŏlo	*wish*
effero	*make wild*	effero	*bear out*				

With difference of Quantity :

Conj. 1.		Conj. 3.		Conj. 1.		Conj. 3.	
cōlo	*strain*	cŏlo	*till*	edŭco	*train*	edūco	*lead out*
dīco	*dedicate*	dĭco	*say*	lēgo	*bequeath*	lĕgo	*read*, &c.
indīco	*point out*	indĭco	*proclaim*		with Compounds.		
praedīco	*declare*	praedĭco	*foretell*				

2) The same form of Perfect :

					Perfect.
acesco, 3.	*grow sour*	acuo, 3.	*sharpen*		acui
cerno, 3.	*sift*	cresco, 3.	*grow*		crēvi
frigeo, 2.	*am cold*	frigo, 3.	*roast*		frixi
fulgeo, 2.	*glitter*	fulcio, 4.	*prop*		fulsi
luceo, 2.	*shine*	lugeo, 2.	*mourn*		luxi
mulceo, 2.	*soothe*	mulgeo, 2.	*milk*		mulsi
paveo, 2.	*dread*	pasco, 3.	*feed*		pāvi

3) The same form of Supine :

					Supine.
cerno, 3.	*sift*	cresco, 3.	*grow*		cretum
pando, 3.	*spread*	patior, 3.	*suffer*		passum
pango, 3.	*fasten*	paciscor, 3.	*bargain*		pactum
teneo, 2.	*hold*	tendo, 3.	*stretch*		tentum
verro, 3.	*sweep*	verto, 3.	*turn*		versum
video, 2.	*see*	viso, 3.	*visit*		visum
vivo, 3.	*live*	vinco, 3.	*conquer*		victum

CHAPTER IV.

PARTICLES.

**54
Particles.**

There is a close intimacy between the four classes of Particles. Prepositions are Adverbs used with Noun-cases, and many can be used without case, as mere Adverbs. On the other hand, some Adverbs (as procul, simul) can take cases. Many Pronominal Particles are Adverbs when interrogative, but Conjunctions when relative. Interjections are Adverbs hanging loose on the sentence: and some resemble Prepositions by taking a Noun-case.

SECTION I.

**55
Adverbs. .**

Adverbs.[1]

i. The relations expressed by *ADVERBS* are Place; Time; Number; Order; Manner; Degree; Cause; Quality. Some Adverbs (which may be called Logical) are used for questioning, denying, affirming, or otherwise modifying the form of discourse.

ii. Interrogative Adverbs refer to

I. Place :

1. ubi? *where?*	4. quā? *by which way?*
2. quo? *whither?*	quatenus? *how far?*
3. quorsum? *whitherward?*	

([1] The following List contains most of the Pronominal and Primitive Adverbs, with samples of the large classes derived from Nouns and Verbs.
The Dual Adverbs derived from u t e r have an asterisk.)

I. Adverbs of Place :

1. Adverbs corresponding to the questions Ubi? ubinam? *Where?* *Utrubi? *In which place* (of two)?
ibi, illic, istic, *there*; hic, *here*; hic illic, *here and there*: inibi, *therein*; ibidem, *in the same place*; alibi, *elsewhere*; alicubi, *somewhere*; -ubi, uspiam, *anywhere*; usquam, *anywhere at all*; ubiubi, ubicumque, *wheresoever*; ubivis, ubilibet, *where you will*; *utrulibet, *in either place*; *utrubique, *in both places*; †neutrubi, *in neither place*; ubique, usquequaque, *everywhere*; nusquam, *nowhere*; prope, *near*; procul, *aloof, afar*; ante, prae, *in front*; post, pone, *behind*; circa, circum, *around*; cis, citra, *on this side*; ultra, *beyond*; contra, *over against*; iuxta, iuxtim, *adjoining*; intra, *within*; extra, *without*; super, *above*; subter, *beneath*; supra, *above*; infra, *below*; supernĕ, *above*; infernĕ, *below*; passim, *here and there, everywhere*; foris, *abroad*; peregre, *in foreign parts*; praesto, *at hand*; ruri, *in the country*; domi, *at home*; humi, *on the ground*; belli, militiae, *at the wars*; comminus, *close at hand*; eminus, *at a distance*.

2. Adverbs corresponding to the question Unde? *Whence?*
inde, illim, illinc, istim, istinc, *thence*; hinc, *hence*; hinc inde, hinc illinc, *from this side and that*; indidem, *from same place*; aliunde, *from another place*; alicunde, *from some place*; -unde, *from any place*; undeunde, undecumque, *from whatever place*; undevis, undelibet, *whence you will*; undique, *from all sides*; *utrimque, *from both sides*; domo, *from home*; rure, *from the country*; intus, intrinsecus, *from within, within*; extrinsecus, *without*; altrinsecus, *from one or other side*:

II. Time :

    1. quando ? *when ?*   3. quousque ? *to what limit ?*

    2. quamdiu ? *how long ?*   quoad ? *until when ?*

       Also quam dudum ? quam pridem ? *how long ago ?*

---

desuper, *from above* ; subtus, *from beneath* ; caelitus, *from heaven* ; divinitus, *from the deity* ; penitus, *from far within* ; funditus, *from the base* ; radicitus, stirpitus, *from the roots.* (These last four words may mean *utterly.*)

3. Adverbs corresponding to the questions Quo? quonam? *Whither?* *Utro? *To which place* (of two)?

eo, illuc, illo, istuc, isto, *thither* ; huc, *hither* ; huc illuc, *hither and thither* ; eodem, *to the same place* ; alio, *to another place* ; aliquo, *somewhither* ; -quo, quopiam, *anywhither* ; quoquam, *anywhither at all* ; nequoquam, *nowhither* ; quoquo, quocumque, *whithersoever* ; quovis, quolibet, *whither you will* ; *utrovis, *to which place you will* (of two) ; *utroque, *to both places* ; *neutro, *to neither place* ; citro, *to this side* ; ultro, *to yon side, farther* ; ultro citroque, *to and fro* ; intro, *to within* ; porro, *forward* ; retro, *backward* ; domum, *home* ; rus, *into the country* ; foras, *out of doors.*

Ultro (root ul-s) properly means *to yon side* : idiomatically it gains these senses : *going farther, yet farther, without instigation, of free motion.*

The questions quoad ? quousque ? *how far ?* are answered by usque, *all the way* ; eo usque, *that far* ; huc, adhuc, huc usque, *thus far.*

4. Adverbs corresponding to the question Quors-um(us) ? *Whitherward ?*

illorsum, istorsum, *thitherward* ; horsum, *hitherward* ; aliorsum, *to another quarter* ; aliquors-um(-us), *to some quarter* ; quoquo versus, *to whatever quarter* ; *utroque versum, *to both quarters* ; intrors-um(-us), *inwards* ; sursum, *upwards* ; deors-um, *downwards* ; sursum deorsum, susque deque, *up and down* ; prors-um (-us), *straightforwards* ; rursum prorsum, *backwards and forwards* ; retrors-um (-us), rursum(-us), rursum vorsum, *backwards* ; seors-um(-us), *apart* ; exadvers-us (-um), *over against* ; dextrorsum, *to the right* ; sinistrors-um, *to the left* ; pessum, *to ruin* ; incassum, *to no purpose.*

5. Adverbs corresponding to the question Qua? quanam? *By which way? in which direction?*

ea, illa, illac, *that way* ; hac, *this way* ; eadem, *the same way* ; alia, *another way* ; aliqua, *some way* ; -qua, *any way* ; quaquam, *any way at all* ; quadam, *a certain way* ; quaque, *every way* ; quaqua, quacumque, *whatever way* ; quavis, qualibet, *any way you will* ; *utravis, *utralibet, *either way* ; haudquaquam, nequaquam, *by no means* ; recta, *straight on* ; dextra, *by the right road* ; sinistra, *by the left road.*

The question Quatenus? *How far?* is answered by

eatenus, *that far, so far* ; hactenus, *thus far* ; aliquatenus, *to some extent* ; quadamtenus, *to a certain extent* ; usquequaque, *to the fullest extent.*

Obs. The distinctions between the Particles ibi, illic, istic, hic ; inde, illinc, istinc, hinc ; eo, illuc, istuc, huc, &c., correspond to the distinctions between their Pronouns is, ille, iste, hic. In the series of time, nunc corresponds to hic, tunc to is.

The Indefinites -ubi -unde -quo -qua -quando belong to the Indefinite Pronoun quis, qui, being chiefly used with Particles, as si-c-ubi, si-c-unde, siquo, &c., ne-c-ubi, ne-c-unde, nequando, &c., where ubi, unde, resume the c of the Relative.

Uspiam, quopiam, &c., are used, like quispiam, in affirmative clauses ; usquam, quoquam, &c., like quisquam, in negative or dubitative clauses.

II. Adverbs of Time :

1. Adverbs answering the question Quando? ecquando? *When?*

tum, tunc, ibi, ibi tum, *then* ; etiamtum, *even then* ; nunc, *now* ; etiamnunc or etiamnum, *even now* ; inde, deinde, exinde, dein, exin, *thereafter, next* ; hinc, abhinc, dehinc, *henceforth, from this time* ; alias, *at another time* ; -quando, *at any time* ; aliquando, *at some time* ; umquam, *ever* ; numquam, *never* ; nonnumquam, *sometimes* ; numquam non, *always* ; quandocumque, quandoque, *at whatever time* ; quondam, olim, *some time or other* (*formerly* or *hereafter*).—Iam, *now, already* ; iam tum, *even then* ; iamnunc, nunciam, iamiam, et iam, *even now* ; diu, *long* ;

III. Number :

quotiens? *how many times ? how often ?*

IV. Manner : (*how ?*)

quomodo? quemadmodum? (quî? ut?)

---

dudum (for diudum), *a while ago* ; pridem, *at a former time* ; iamdiu, iamdudum, iampridem, *long ago* ; haud dudum, haud pridem, *not long ago* ; interdum, *now and then* ; nondum, hauddum, *not yet* ; vixdum, *hardly yet* ; tandem, *at length* ; demum, *at last* ; mox, *by and by, soon* ; propediem, *presently* ; protenus, protinam, *forthwith* ; interim, interea, *meanwhile* ; ante, antea, prius, *before* ; antehac, antidhac, *heretofore* ; post, postea, (postidea), *after, afterwards* ; posthac, *hereafter* ; postilla, *after that time* ; postmodo, *soon after.*—Modo, *now, lately, soon* ; nuper, *newly, lately* ; recens, *freshly, lately* ; denuo, *afresh, again* ; commodum, *just now* ; antiquitus, *of old* ; primitus, *from the first* ; simul, *at the same time* ; semper, usque, usquequaque, *always* ; perpetuo, *continually* ; sero, *late* ; cito, *speedily* ; actutum, *briskly* ; confestim, *in a trice* ; continuo, *without stop* ; extemplo, *on the moment* ; ilico (in loco), *on the spot* ; ilicet, *straightway* ; statim, *instantly* ; repente, derepente, subito, *suddenly* ; quam primum, *as soon as possible* ; obiter, *by the way.*—Hodie, *to-day* ; heri, here, *yesterday* ; cras, *to-morrow* ; pridie, *the day before* ; postridie, *the day after* ; perendie, *the next day but one* ; nudius tertius, *the third day back*, &c. ; mane (mani), *in the morning* ; diluculo, *at dawn* ; meridie, *at noon* ; vesperi, vespere, *at even* ; interdiu, luci, lucu, *in the daytime* ; nocti, noctu, *in the nighttime.* The Abl. brevi, also perbrevi, means either *in a short time* or *in a few words* (brevi dictione).

a) The questions quam dudum? quam pridem? *how long ago?* are answered by diu ; dudum ; pridem ; iamdiu ; iamdudum ; iampridem ; haud dudum ; haud pridem ; haud ita pridem.

2. Adverbs answering the question, Quamdiu? *How long ?*

diu, *long* ; perdiu, *very long* ; tamdiu, *so long ;* aliquamdiu, *some length of time* ; tantisper, *so long* ; aliquantisper, *for some time* ; parumper, paulisper, *for a little time* ; adhuc, *so far, hitherto* ; semper, *always* ; in perpetuum, *for ever* ; amplius, *longer* ; non amplius, haud amplius, non iam, *no longer.*

The questions quousque, quoad, *to what limit of time?* are answered by usque, usquequaque, *continually* ; adhuc, *hitherto* ; eo usque, *so long*, &c.

III. Adverbs of Number :

Answering the question, Quotiens? *How often ?*

totiens, *so often* ; aliquotiens, pluriens, *several times* ; identidem, *repeatedly* ; interdum, subinde, *now and then* ; iterum, *a second time* ; saepe, saepius, *often* ; persaepe, saepissime, *very often* ; plerumque, *generally* ; crebro, *frequently* ; raro, *seldom* ; cotidie, indies, *daily* ; quotannis, *annually* ; semel, *once* ; bis, *twice* ; ter, *thrice*, &c. &c. See NUMERALIA.

a) Ordinal Adverbs answering the question Quo ordine ?

primum, *first* ; primo, *in the first place* ; deinde, *in the next place* ; tum, *then, afterwards* ; denique, *finally* ; postremo, *in the last place* ; deinceps, *next in order* ; secundo, *in the second place* ; tertio, *in the third place*, &c. ; porro, *farther* ; insuper, *moreover* ; necnon, *also* ; praeterea, *besides* ; quin, *furthermore.*

IV. Adverbs of Manner :

Answering the question Quomodo? quomodonam? quemadmodum? quî? ut? *How ?*

adeo, ita, sic, *so* ; aeque, adaeque, *equally, as much* ; item, itidem, pariter, perinde, proinde, similiter, iuxta, *in like manner* ; contra, *contrariwise* ; aliter, secus, *otherwise.*

V. Degree :

    1. quam ? *how ?*   2. quantum ? *how much ?*

VI. Cause : (*why ? wherefore ?*)

        quare ? cur ? quamobrem ?

VII. Quality :

        qualiter ? *in what kind of way ?*

V. Adverbs of Degree :

1. Adverbs answering to the question Quam ? *How ?*

tam, *so* ; omnino, prorsus, *altogether* ; admodum, oppido, penitus, planē, perquam, sanē, sanēquam, valdē, valdequam, *very, quite* ; vementer, *exceedingly* ; longē, *far* ; magis, *more* ; maximē, *most, very* ; minus, *less* ; minimē, *least, not at all* ; potius, *rather* ; potissimum, *chiefly* ; in primis, apprime, praecipuē, praesertim, *especially* ; etiam, vel, *even* ; ferē, *almost, generally* ; fermē, paenĕ, *almost* ; propĕ, propemodo, propemodum, *nearly, almost* ; aegrē, vix, *scarcely, hardly* ; dumtaxat, *merely* ; modŏ, *only* ; saltem, *at least* ; solum, solummodŏ, tantum, tantummodŏ, *only* ; utique, *in fact, at all events.*

2. Adverbs answering to the question Quantum ? *How much ?*

tantum, *so much* ; aliquantum, *considerably* ; multum, *much* ; permultum, plurimum, *very much* ; plus, *more* ; satis, sat, *enough* ; abundē, affatim, *plentifully* ; nimis, nimium, *too much* ; paulum, *little* ; paululum, *very little* ; parum, *little, too little* ; minus, *less* ; minimum, *least, very little* ; quantulum, quantillum, *how little* ; tantulum, tantillum, *so little.*

a) The question Quanto ? *By how much ?* is answered by tanto, eo, *by so much* ; aliquanto, *by a good deal* ; multo, nimio, *by a great deal* ; paulo, *by a little* ; nihilo, &c.

b) The question Quanto opere, *How greatly ?* by tanto opere, *so greatly* ; magno opere, *greatly* ; maximo opere, *very greatly.*

VI. Adverbs of Cause :

Answering the question Quare ? cur ? quamobrem ? *Why ? wherefore ?*

eo, ideo, idcirco, propterea, *on that account* ; ergo, igitur, itaque, *therefore* ; proin, proinde, *accordingly.*

VII. Adverbs of Quality (chiefly formed from Adjectives : but also many from Substantives, Verbs, and Particles).

Answering the question Qualiter ? *In what kind of way ?*   Examples are :

benĕ, *well* ; malĕ, *ill* ; ritĕ, *duly* ; iucundē, *pleasantly* ; gravatē, *grudgingly* ; rectē, *rightly* ; pulchrē, *finely* ; latē, *widely* ; longē latēque, *far and wide* ; publicē, *publicly* ; miserē, *wretchedly* ; splendidē, *nobly,* &c. &c. &c. ; audacter, *boldly* ; feliciter, *happily* ; fortiter, *bravely* ; amanter, *lovingly* ; decenter, *becomingly* ; sapienter, *wisely,* &c. &c. &c. ; privatim, *privately* ; raptim, *hurriedly* ; sensim, *gradually* ; furtim, *stealthily* ; paulatim, pedetentim, *little by little* ; nominatim, *by name* ; singulatim, sigillatim, *individually* ; viritim, *man by man* ; tributim, *tribe by tribe* ; vicissim, *by turns* ; seorsim, *apart,* &c. &c. &c. ; falso, *falsely* ; consulto, *deliberately* ; tuto, *safely* ; falso, *falsely* ; fortuito, *casually* ; gratuito, *without fee* ; improviso, inopinato, necopinato, *unexpectedly* ; liquido, *clearly* ; merito, *deservedly,* &c. ; olam, clanculum, *secretly* ; palam, *openly* ; unā, simul, *together* ; bifariam, bipartito, *in two parts* ; trifariam, tripartito, &c. ; temere, *at hazard* ; fortĕ, *by chance* ; spontĕ, *by choice* ; ritĕ, *duly* ; temperi, *seasonably* ; frustra, *in vain* ; perperam, *badly* ; gratiis, gratis, *freely* ; ingratiis, *unwelcomely* ; coram, *face to face* ; alioqui(-n), ceteroqui(-n), *in other respects* ; nequiquam, *to no purpose* ; incassum, *fruitlessly* ; praefiscine, *without offence.* This adverb is derived from prae, fascino, *barring the evil eye, under favour.* 'Praefiscine dixerim,' Plaut. *Asin.* ii. 4. 84.

For Comparison of Adverbs see § **30.**

VIII. The Logical Interrogative Adverbs, which expect affirmative or negative answers, are :

-ně (enclitic)? an? anně? num? numně? utrum? utrumně? nonně? annon?

SECTION II.

56 Prepositions.

Prepositions.

A *PREPOSITION* is an exponent of relation between one Noun and another.

i. The primary relations are those of Place, Time, Number. From these spring many others, which are figurative or logical.

The relation of Place includes that of Person or Thing, when Person or Thing represents Place : apud regem, *at the king's court*; ante me, *in front of me*; ad bellum, *to the war*.

The relation of Time includes that of Person or Thing, when Person or Thing represents Time : post Romulum, *after the time of Romulus*; ante tubas ferrumque, *before the invention of trumpets and steel*.

Some Prepositions are used with Verbs of Motion, some with Verbs of Rest ; many with both.

Several Prepositions are so used with a Case, as to form Adverbial Phrases, which are to all intents true Adverbs : admodum, invicem, obviam, ab integro, de novo, ex tempore, &c.

Table of Prepositions.

ii. Twenty-nine Prepositions take the Accusative Case, twelve the Ablative, and four the Accusative or the Ablative.

1) The following Prepositions take the Accusative Case :—

ad	*to, at, &c.*	ob	*over against, on account of*
advers-us(um)	*against, toward*		
ante	*before*	penes	*in the power of*
apud	*near, at, with*	per	*through*
circum	*around*	pone	*behind*
circa	*around, about*	post	*after, behind*
circiter	*about*	praeter	*beside*
cis, citra	*on this side of*	prope, *near*, propius, proxime	
contra	*against*	propter	*on account of, nigh*
erga	*towards*	secundum	*next, according to*
extra	*outside of*	supra	*above*
infra	*below*	trans	*across*
inter	*between, among*	ultra	*beyond*
intra	*within*	versus, versum	*towards*
iuxta	*next to*		

Logical Adverbs, used to modify Discourse, are

(1) nempe, scilicet, videlicet, *namely, of a sooth*; nimirum, *to be sure*; (2) quidem, equidem, *indeed*; certe, *certainly, at least*; tamen, attamen, *yet, nevertheless*; nihilominus, *nevertheless*; (3) fors, forsan, forsitan, fortasse, fortassis, *perhaps*; (4) immo, *nay but, nay rather*; (5) certo, *assuredly*; ita, etiam, *yes, even so*; ně (often spelt nae), *yea, verily*; planě, *evidently*; profecto, *doubtless*; saně, *quite so*; utique, *in sooth*; vero, *truly, yes indeed*; quippe, *to be sure*; (6) non, *not, no*; haud (haut), *not, no* (the reverse); minimě, *by no means*; ně, *not, lest*; nedum, *not to say, much less*; ne . . . quidem, *not even*.

Versus follows its Case; as, Urbem versus, *towards the city.* Other Prepositions occasionally follow their Case.

2) The following take the **Ablative Case** :—

a, ab, abs	*by* or *from*	ex, e	*out of, from*
absque	*without*	palam	*in sight of*
clam	*unknown to*	prae	*before, owing to*
coram	*in the presence of*	pro	*before, for*
cum	*with*	sine	*without*
de	*from, concerning*	tenus	*as far as*

Ab stands before vowels and **h**; a and often ab before consonants; abs sometimes before q, rarely before c, t ; but abs te is usual.

Ex stands before vowels and **h** ; ex and e before consonants.

Clam is used with Accusative by the Comic poets.

Cum is attached to the Personal and Reflexive Pronouns, sometimes to the Relative : as mecum, nobiscum, tecum, vobiscum, secum, quocum, or quicum, quibuscum.

3) The following take the **Accusative or the Ablative** :—

in	*into, against* (Acc.), *in* (Abl.)	super	*over, upon*
sub	*up to, under* (Acc.), *under* (Abl.)	subter	*under*

In and sub with Accusative imply motion; with Ablative, rest.

SECTION III.

Conjunctions.

CONJUNCTIONS are of two Classes :

A. Coordinative, or those which link words and sentences without affection of Mood.

B. Subordinative, or those which link sentences, with affection of Mood.

The following are used in Coordination as well as Subordination : quippe, si, seu, sive, nisi, etsi, etiamsi, tametsi, quamquam, quamvis, quasi, tanquam, sicut, velut, ceu.

A. Coordinative Conjunctions are :—

Annexive : et, -que,[1] *and, both, also,* &c.; atque, ac, *and*; neque, nec, *nor, neither* : and the adverbial words item, *also,* etiam, quoque,[2] *also, even* ; necnon, *moreover.*

Disjunctive : aut, vel, -ve,[1] *or, either* ; sive, seu, *either, or.*

Adversative : sed, at (ast), verum, *but*; autem,[2] *but, now* ; ceterum, *but* ; atqui, *but yet*; vero,[2] *truly, but*; tamen, *yet, nevertheless* ; attamen, verumtamen, *however, but yet.*

Causal : nam, namque, enim,[2] etenim, *for*; enimvero, *for in truth.*

---

[1] -que -ve are enclitics, always attached to the word which they affect, or to some other in the same clause.

[2] Quoque, autem, vero, enim (and the adverb quidem) never stand first in a clause, but usually after one or more words : autem, vero, enim, after the first word usually ; quoque, quidem, after the word which they affect.

Illative : ergo, itaque, igitur, *therefore.*

Conclusive: quare, quamobrem, quapropter, quocirca, *wherefore.*

Comparative : ut, uti ; velut, veluti ; sicut, sicuti ; ceu ; quemadmodum ; quomodo, all rendered *as* ; atque, ac, *as* ;
quam, *than, as* ; quasi, tamquam, *as, as it were* ; utpote, *as
being.*

B. Subordinative Conjunctions are :—

Consecutive : ut, *so that* ; (ut non) ; quin, *but that, that not.*

Final : ut, *in order that* ; ut ne, ne (for ut ne), *in order that
not* ; utinam, *O that* ; utinam ne, &c. ; quo, *in order that* ;
quominus, *in order that not.*

Causal : quod, quia, *because* ; quoniam, quando, quandoquidem,
since ; siquidem, *inasmuch as* ; quom or cum, *since.*

Temporal : quom or cum, *when* ; ubi, quando, *when* ; ut,
when, from the time that ; dum, donec, *while, whilst* ;
dum, donec, *until* ; quoad, *whilst* ; quoad, *until* ; antequam, priusquam, *before that* ; postquam, *after that* ; simul
ac, simul (omitting ac), *as soon as* ; quotiens, *as often as* ;
and others.

Conditional : si, *if* ; sin (for si-nĕ), *but if* ; sive, seu, *or if, whether* ; nisi, *unless* ; ni, *unless* ; si modo, si tantum, *if only,*
or modo, tantum (omitting si) ; dum, dummodo, *provided
that,* or modo (omitting dum).

Concessive : etsi, etiamsi ; tametsi, tamen etsi, *although, even
if* ; quamquam, utut, *however* ; quamvis, *although,* lit.
how you will ; cum, ut, licet, *although.*

Comparative : quasi, *as if* (for quam si) ; ut si, ac si, velut si,
as if ; or velut (dropping si) ; tamquam, *as though* (for
tamquam si) ; ceu, *as if* (dropping si).

Obs. In Subordinative Conjunctions must be included

All Interrogative Pronouns and Particles used obliquely :

The Relative Pronoun with its Particles ubi, unde, quo, qua, &c.,
inasmuch as both these classes link sentences with affection of
Mood.

SECTION IV.

Interjections.

INTERJECTIONS strictly so called (interiecta, inserted
in the sentence without affecting its form) express :

Invocation : O, heus, oho or ohe, eia or heia ; pro (proh),
eho, ehodum, *hark, halloa,* &c.

Designation : en, ecce, *lo ! behold !*

Surprise : O, hem, em, ehem, babae, and the comic words au;
hui ; va (vah) ; eia ; bombax ; atat or attat ; attate ; attat tatae.

Disgust : (comic) phui, aha, *faugh* ; phy, *pooh !*

Satiety : ohe, oiei, *enough !*

Laughter : (comic) aha (haha), hahahae.

Joy : O, io, eia, euge, evoe, eupoe, papae, *huzza ! joy !* &c.,
and the comic words euax, eugepae (εὐγεπαῖ).

Praise: eu, euge, eia, *bravo! well done!* &c.

Pain and Sorrow: heu, eheu, hei or ei, vae, ah or a, *alas! woe!* ilicet, *all's up!*

Deprecation: pro (proh), *forbid it!*

Call to Silence : st, *hush!*

Several Nouns, Verbs, and Adverbs are used in exclamation or invocation, like Interjections. Such are :

1) Nouns: pax, *hush!* malum, *plague!* nefas, infandum, *monstrous!* indignum, horrendum, miserum, miserabile, turpe.

The Vocative macte, Plur. macti, is used with an Ablative or Genitive : as macte esto virtute, *go on and prosper.* It is perhaps the Participle of a lost Verb macĕre. M. Lucr. v. 1339.

2) Verbs : quaeso, *prithee!* precor, oro, obsecro, *pray;* amabo, *do, please;* sis (si vis), sultis (si vultis), *please :* sodes (si audies?), *if you'll be so good :* agesis, agedum, agitedum, *come now ;* cedo (Pl. cette), *give me ;* apage, *away, avaunt.*

3) Adverbs: profecto, *really;* nae (or nē), *truly,* used with the Nominative of a Pronoun: nae ego velim...nae illi errant,&c.

(*a*) The following expressions are elliptical :

mehercule[1]	= me, Hercule, iuves, *so help me, Hercules.*
mecastor, ecastor	= me, Castor, iuves, *so help me, Castor.*
edepol, pol	= me, dee Pollux, iuves, *so help me, Pollux.*
medius fidius	= me, deus Fidius, iuves, *so help me, God of faith* (Ζεὺς Πίστιος).
pro Iuppiter	= prohibeas,[2] Iuppiter, *Jove forbid.*
pro di immortales	= prohibeatis, di immortales : *heaven forefend!*

(*b*) O, a, heu, eheu, hem, eia, en, ecce, pro are found with Accusative ; hem, hei, vae, with Dative ; O, a, heu, heus, eho, and others are often accompanied by a Vocative. The Vocative itself is in the nature of an Interjection, lying out of the construction of the sentence.

CHAPTER V.

DERIVATION AND COMPOSITION OF WORDS.

SECTION I.

Derivation of Nouns.

i. The Suffixes used in the Flexion of Stems are shewn in the preceding Chapters. We have next to shew those by which a Stem is derived from a Root, or one Stem from another.

59 Suffixes of Derivation.

---

[1] Mehercle, hercle, are abridged forms.

[2] The etymology of pro (proh) here given is not disproved by the phrase 'pro deum atque hominum fidem,' which may represent another ellipsis, 'prohibeatur deum atque hominum fidem violari.'

That Suffix in a derived Stem, which contains the Stem-character, is the staminal Suffix. Thus in the word **crudelitas**, Stem cru-d-eli-tat-, **tāt** is the staminal Suffix.

It commonly happens that a word comes immediately from another, which is itself derived from a third, and so on, till a root or rudimental form is reached. Every word (including the root) is the Theme of such as are immediately derived from it. Thus,

Theme of **crudelitas** : Adj. **crūdelis**; Stem crūdeli-.
Theme of **crudelis** : Adj. **crūdus**; Stem crūdo- for crŭ-ĭdo-.
Theme of **crudus** : Root cru-, Sk. *kravi*, Gr. κρεϝ-, *raw flesh.*

Beginning from the Root, the order is :

crŭ-, crŭ-ĭdŏ- (= crū-du-**s**), crŭ-ĭd-ēlĭ- (= crū-d-ēlĭ-**s**), crŭ-ĭd-ēlĭ-tāt- (= crū-d-ēlĭ-ta-**s**).

Here the suffixes are **ĭdŏ (ĭd-)**, **ēlĭ, tāt**; to each of which the ending **s** is joined to form the Nominative Case.

The words of such a series may form branch-lines of derivation by other suffixes.

Thus from **cru-** come crŭ-or, *gore*, cru-entu-s, *gory* ; from this the Verb cru-ent-a-re : from crudus come cru-d-i-ta-s and cru-d-esc-ere : from crudelis the Adv. cru-d-eli-ter : crudelitas merely forms its own Cases.

ii. Root or Rudiment.

The determination of Roots, though greatly assisted by Comparative Philology, is a work of vast labour and difficulty, demanding the nicest conjectural criticism, and often baffling all conjecture. Very many roots are indeed determined beyond question ; ĕs, ĭ, *to go*, ĭ, *that*, dă, stă, ăg, ăp, &c. : others are open to doubt ; căp (see p. 190): while in făc, which heads, perhaps, the largest group of Latin words, **c** is now held to be a suffix, added to the root fă = Sk. *bhâ*, Gr. φα-, *to give light*, under which stand new groups, including fax, facies, fateor, fari, fas, &c., with their derivatives. Hence it is often safer, in deriving words, to call their ultimate form a rudiment rather than a root.

iii. Suffix.

The derivation and distribution of Latin Suffixes, with their meaning, when they have one, are a special topic too wide to be fully treated here. The Syllabus which follows, with the subjoined examples, will supply considerable information. It adopts Düntzer's method (*Lat. Wortbildung und Composition*), though not his order ; corrected throughout by reference to the views of Schleicher (*Compend.* §§ 215–231) and Corssen (*Ausspr.* I. 566, &c.). Bopp, Leo Meyer, and Fick's Lexicon have also been consulted.

Suffixes are simple or compound : but the parts of a compound suffix often cohere so regularly in a class of words, that, having been once shewn as compound, it may be cited without inconvenience as if it were simple. Such are **tudon. mento. cundo, bundo,** &c.

iv. Rudimental Words.

Rudimental words are such as append their Case-endings to the real or seeming Root, unstrengthened or strengthened.   Such are

a) gru-s, su-s; re-s; bov- (bos), Iov-; crux, dux, nex, nux, pix, prĕc-, dĭc-, grex, pes, vas (văd-), adips, caelebs, dap-, ŏp-, stĭp-, with many compound words, auspex, haruspex, obex, index, iudex, artifex, tradux, coiux, manceps, princeps, praeses, praepes, crassipes, &c.   *b*) lux, pax, vox, lex, rex, &c. *c*) sal, sol, lar, par, ver, ius, crus, tus, rus, spes, mos, ros, flos, os (or-) : also farr- (far), fell- (fel), melt- (mel), ost- (os, *bone*), cord- (cor).

v. Syllabus of Suffixes (with examples at the foot).

In the List of Suffixes and their Examples the abbreviations used are :

S. Substantive.   *V.* Verbalia (words derived from Verbs).
A. Adjective.   *D.* Denominativa (words derived from Nouns).

Unc. (uncertain) implies that root or roots are unknown.

&c.
&c. &c.   } placed after Examples cited, indicate that many
&c. &c. &c.   } others exist of the same class, and that in
                   } some instances the number is very large.

Every Suffix ending in **ŏ** must be taken as including the forms ŭs, ă, um; that is, A-nouns as well as O-nouns.

I. Vowels and **v.**[1]

Of Vowel Suffixes (besides the characters **ă, ŏ, ĭ, ŭ, e**), the most important is **ĭŏ**, including, as it does, a large class of Abstract Substantives in ĭă, ĭum, and of Possessive Adjectives in ĭŭs.

S.   *a*) **ă**   *β*) **ŏ**   *γ*) **ē, ĭē**   *δ*) **ŭ**   *ε*) **ĭ**   *ζ*) **ĕŏ**
        η) **ĭŏ**   *θ*) **ŭŏ, vŏ, īvŏ, vĭ.**

---

[1] I. Vowels and **v.**

Substantives.

a) Masc. *V.* scrib-a, adven-a, incol-a, terrigen-a, &c.

β) *V.* merg-us, *cormorant*; tŏr-us, *couch*; fūg-a, *flight*; talp-a, *mole*; pronūb-a, *bridesmaid*; iŭg-um, *yoke*, &c. &c. *D.* nimb-us, *cloud*; nerv-us; taur-us; lŭp-us; ŏr-a, *coast*; săl-um, *brine*, &c.

γ) *V.* fĭd-es, effĭg-ies, spĕc-ies, &c.   *D.* pauper-ies . . .

δ) *V.* ăc-us, *D.* nŭr-us.

ε) *V.* arx, falx, nix, ăp-is, rūp-es, &c.   *D.* nox, nūb-es, măr-e, &c.

ζ) Mostly *D.* calc-eus, *shoe*; trăb-ea, *striped robe*; flamm-eum, *bridal veil*, &c.   *V.* ŏl-ea, *olive*.

η) A few Masc. *V.* lud-ius, *player* . . . *D.* sim-ius, *ape.* A large number of Fem. *D.* av-ia, *grandmother*; and abstracts of *Quality* : audac-ia, *boldness*; ignav-ia, *sloth*; victor-ia, *victory*; absent-ia, *absence*, &c. &c, A large number are Neut. most *V.* denoting '*the Effect* :' benefic-ium, *benefit*; conub-ium, *marriage*; gaud-ium, *joy*, &c. &c. &c. : some *D.* minister-ium, *service*; sen-ium, *old age*; sav-ium, *kiss*, &c. &c.   Words like arbitr-ium, augur-ium, &c., should be ranked as *V.*

θ) **ŭŏ** : *D.* patr-uus, *uncle* on father's side; ian-ua, *house-door*; **vŏ** : *V. D.* cer-vus; ri-vus; lar-va, *mask, spectre*; ar-vum, *plough-land*; **īvŏ** : ol-iva, *an olive*; sal-iva, *spittle*; **vĭ** : *V.* ci-vis.

A.   *a*) ŏ   *β*) ĭ   *γ*) ĕŏ   *δ*) ĭŏ   *ε*) ŭŏ, vŏ, īvŏ, tĭvŏ, vĭ.

II. c.

c is a stable suffix, denoting Individuality in Substantives : Permanent Condition or Relation in Adjectives. Often, however, the individuality or condition denoted is of a disparaging kind : as in s e n e x, s e n e c-i o, c i m e x, c u l e x, p u l e x ; c a e c u s, f l a c c u s, l u s c u s, m a n c u s, t r u n c u s, &c. So in **c-ulo c** is deminutive, but in **c-undo** it denotes permanent activity.

S.   *a*) cĭ ĭc   *β*) cŏ cĭŏ ĭcŏ tĭcŏ   *γ*) āc ōc   *δ*) īc īcŏ
     ε) ūcŏ.

A.   *a*) cŏ ĭcŏ tĭcŏ lĭcŏ   *β*) ācĭ ōcĭ   *γ*) ācŏ ācĕŏ

Adjectives :

a) **ŏ**: *V.* fid-us, *faithful* ; viv-us, *alive* . . . with Cpp. naufrăg-us, *shipwrecked* ; profug-us, *fugitive* . . . *D.* re-us, *accused* ; nov-us, *new* ; me-us, tu-us, su-us . . .

β) **ĭ**: ĭ-s ; quī-s ; qui ; iug-is . . . Cpp. bimar-is . . .

γ) **ĕŏ**: *D.* implying ' *Formed of* :' aur-eus, *golden* ; argent-eus, *of silver* ; ' *Exhibit-ing* :' lūt-eus, *muddy* ; lūt-eus, *of deep yellow* ; ' *Belonging to* :' virgin-eus, *maiden, maidenlike*, &c.

    Note.—ĕŏ represents Gr. ειος, Pythagor-ēus, El-ēus, *of Elis.*

δ) **ĭŏ**: *D.* imply generally ' *Having the quality* ' of, or ' *Belonging to* :' mart-ius, patr-ius, reg-ius, pluv-ius, &c. &c. ; some Cpp. egreg-ius, exim-ius. Aer-ius, aether-ius are Greek, having the sense of L. ĕŭs. Alius, Gr. ἄλλος=al-yus ; medius, Gr. μέσσος=med-yus ; **ĭ** being ĭ-consonans. Add plebe-ius=plebe-yus.

ε) **ŭŏ**: *V.* with some in **vŏ, īvŏ**, chiefly *V.*, may imply ' *Active quality* :' contig-uus, *adjoining* ; contin-uus, &c. ; gna-vus, *knowing* ; proter-vus, *frolicsome* ; sae-vus, *raging*, &c. ; noc-uus or noc-ivus,, *hurtful*, &c. : or may have Passive use : divid-uus, *parted* ; ingen-uus, *freeborn* ; mut-uus, *exchanged* (between two per-sons or parties), *mutual* ; relic-uus, *left* ; rig-uus, irrig-uus, *watered* ; vid-uus, *widowed* ; ca-vus, *hollow* ; sal-vus *safe* ; adopt-ivus, *chosen, adoptive* ; especially those in **t-īvŏ**, having the Supine or participial suffix **t** : captivus, *captured* ; fes-tivus, *festive* ; fugi-tivus, na-tivus, praeroga-tivus, vo-tivus, &c. &c. Aes-tivus, *of summer*, supposes a verb aedĕre (Gr. αιθ-), *to heat* ; tempes-tivus, *season-able*, is abnormal ; mor-tuus (=mor-tivus), *dead* ; ann-uus is a rare Denom. ; mens-tr-uus seems to be for mens-trius from mensis, *month.* **vĭ**: brevis, Gr. βραχύς ; gravis, Sk. *gurus*, Gr. βαρύς ; lĕ-vis, Sk. *laghus*, Gr. ἐλαχύς, *light* ; lē-vis, Gr. λειϝός, *smooth* ; sua-vis, Sk. *svâdus*, Gr. ἡδύς.

II. c.

Substantives.

a) **cĭ**: lanx, merx (faeci- fauci- . . .): **ĭc** (ix). *V.* appendix : **ĭc** (ex), *V.* vert-ex, vort-ex, *D.* ram-ex. See pp. 95–6 (most unc.).

β) **cŏ**: *V.* fŏ-cus, *hearth* ; fū-cus, *drone* ; es-ca, *food*, *D.* ĭuven-cus -ca ; **cĭŏ-**, *V.* sola-cium ; *D.* un-cia (from unus) ; **ĭcŏ**: *D.* vil-ĭcus, *steward* ; vil-ica, *steward's wife* ; man-ĭca, *handcuff* ; ped-ĭca, *fetter, springe*, &c. ; **tĭcŏ**, *V.* can-tĭcum : *D.* viaticum, *provision for journey.*

γ) *D.* forn-ax, *furnace* ; lim-ax, *snail* ; cel-ox, *yacht.*

δ) **īc**, p. 96 (most unc. rad-ix, &c.): but *V.* in **trīc- trix**, Fem. as mere-trix, vic-trix, &c. (see **R**) ; **īcŏ**: *V. D.* mend-īcus, -īcă, *beggar* ; lect-īca, *litter*, and others.

ε) lact-ūca, *lettuce* (some unc.).

Adjectives.

a) **cŏ**: *V. D.* par-cus, pau-cus, pris-cus, rau-cus, sic-cus, &c. (some unc.): **ĭcŏ**: most *D.* imply ' *Pertaining to* :' bell-ĭcus, publ-ĭcus, &c. : some *V.* med-ĭcus, *of healing* (as Subst. *physician*). Many Gentilia ; Scythĭcus, &c. **tĭco** : *D.* rus-tĭcus, aqua-tĭcus, &c. *V.* vena-tĭcus ; **lĭco** : *D.* fame-lĭcus.

β) **ācĭ**: *V.* imply ' *Inclined to*,' ' *Capable of* :' aud-ax, *daring* ; ĕd-ax, *devouring* ; fĕr-ax, *fruitful*, &c. &c. ; **ōcĭ** : *V.* ' *Inclined to* :' fĕr-ox, *haughty* ; vĕl-ox, *swift.*

γ) **ācŏ**: mer-ācus, *pure* (op-ācus, *shady*, unc.) ; Subst. clo-āca, *sewer* (clu=lu). **ācĕŏ**: *D.* ' *Consisting of* :' farr- aceus, *of flour*, and some others.

δ) ῐcŏ ῐcῐŏ tῐcῐŏ   ε) ῑcῐ   ζ) ūcŏ ū̆cĕŏ   η) ῐăcŏ.

III. G.

In many words which have **g** before the final vowel or case-ending, this cons. is known to be a root-character: as in l e x, r e x, s t r i x, f r u g -, c o n i u x, a n g u - i s, c o m p ā g - e s, c o n t ā g - e s, m e r g - u s, r ŏ g - u s, f ŭ g - a, p l ă g - a, p l ā g - a, t ŏ g - a, i ŭ g - u m, and others. (Pinguis, as compared with Sk. *pí*, Gr. πι-, seems to shew a suffix **g**, but not if compared with Gr. παχύς. See Curt. *Gr. Et.* 276.) This suggests the probability that in uncertain words, as v a g - u s, a l g - a, and others, **g** is radical rather than suffixal. On the other hand, it is probable that the root *ăg* is suffixal (ῐg, āg, īg, ūg) in various words. Its presence in r e m e x (remum agere), a u r ī g a (aureas agere), p r o d ῐ g u s, and a m b ā g e s, is obvious: in con-fluges, c o a g u l u m, s t r a g e s, s t r a g u l u s, it may be conjectured: also in n u g a e, for nŏv-ῐg-ae, *novelties = trifles* as opposed to s e r i a (from serus), *long-considered matter*: 'hae nugae seria ducunt in mala.' V a l g u s, v o l g u s are deduced by some from Sk. roots. (May not the latter be referred to the former word?) Finally, the root *ag* may be supposed in **agon, egon, ugon**: see **N.** Compare the Greek ὁδηγός, χορηγός, &c.

On fastig-ium, vestig-ium, see C. *Ausspr.* II. 427, *Kr. B.* 197, 361.

IV. T.

This is the most efficient suffixal letter in Aryan language. If we include its representation by **s** and **d,** it enters into the formation of all Participles and Participial Adjectives, and into that of all Verbal Substantives with Participial theme: by the suffixes **tŏ (sŏ, dŏ), tŭ (sŭ), tῐ (sῐ), tῐōn (sῐōn), ntῐ,** &c. Besides which it forms important groups of Denominative Substantives; concrete by the suffixes **ῐt ĕt,** abstract by the suffixes **tāt tūt,** and others.

(For the suffixes into which **n** enters, see **N**: for d ŏ, d ῐ see **D.** The suffixes **sŏ, sŭ, sῐ** are included here.)

S.   α) tă̆ ῐtă̆   β) tŏ (sŏ) ῐtŏ   γ) tŭ (sŭ) ῐtŭ ă̄tŭ ῑtū ultū

δ) ῐcŏ: *V.* am-ῑcus, *friendly* (Subst. *friend*); pud-ῑcus, *modest*; apr-ῑcus, *sunny*; from Particles; ant-iquus, *ancient*; post-ῑcus, *hinder*; ῐcῐŏ: *D.* imply 'Consisting of:' later-ῑcius: '*of brick,*' &c. '*Pertaining to*;' natal-ῑcius, *belonging to a birthday,* &c. but nov-ῑcius, *newly arrived* (*novice*), Juv.: tῐcῐŏ (sῐcῐŏ): *V.* (Sup. St.) Participial: advec-ticius, *imported*; conduc-ticius, *hired*; trala-ticius, *transferred,* &c. The quantity of ti, si is probably variable.

ε) (fel-ix, pern-ix, both unc.)

ζ) ūcŏ: *V.* only cad-ūcus, *falling*; ūcĕŏ: *D.* only pann-uceus, *rugged.*

η) Greek *D.* card-iăcus, *dyspeptic*: Aegypt-iăcus. &c.

IV. T.

Substantives.

α) *D.* nau-ta, nav-ῑta.

β) *V.* numerous: lec-tus, *bed*; sec-ta, *sect*; fa-tum, *fate*; cau-sa, *cause*; pen-sum, *task*; mer-itum, *desert*; ius-sum, *command,* &c. &c. *D.*: liber-tus, *freedman*; iuven-ta, *youth*; salic-tum, *willow-bed*; carec-tum, *sedge-bed*; virgul-tum, *thicket,* &c. The last three have tum for ĕtum. See δ) below.

γ) tŭ (sŭ), ῐtŭ: *V.* (Sup. St.) fle-tus, *weeping*; mo-tus, *motion*; ic-tus, *stroke*; crucia-tus, *torture*; mugī-tus, *bellowing*; hab-ĭtus, *habit*; strep-itus, *noise*; nex-us, *connexion*; vi-sus, *sight,* &c. &c. (Pr. st.) hal-ĭtus, spir-itus, *breath*; tum-ultus, *uproar.* But *D.* in ă̄tŭ denote *Office, Position, Corporate Body,* &c.: consul-atus, *consulship*; sen-atus, *senate*; re-atus, *state of accusation*; equit-atus, *cavalry,* &c.

   δ) ētŏ ε) tĭ (sĭ) ζ) ŏt ĭĕt ĭt η) tāt ĭtāt ŏtāt estāt
   θ) tūt ĭtūt ι) tĭŏ (sĭŏ) ĭtĭŏ ĭtĭē κ) ātŏ ūtŏ ītŏ λ) ōt
   μ) tĕŏ.

A α) tŏ (sŏ) ĭtŏ β) ātŏ γ) ētŏ δ) ītŏ ε) ōtŏ
     ūtŏ ζ) ātĭ ītĭ η) tĭ ŏtĭ ĭt.

V. D.

This cons. is a principal element in several important compound Suffixes, Verbal and Denominative, which appear under **N.** Besides those, its leading use is in the Participial Adjective suffix ĭdŏ.

S. α) dŏ ĭdŏ β) dĭ γ) ēd ōd δ) ŭd.
A. α) dŏ ĭdŏ β) dĭ.

VI. P.

It is doubtful whether any true suffix can be shewn with **p,** except **pŭlŏ,** in which the root *pur, pul,* ple-, *to fill,* is probably contained: mani-pul-us, po-pul-us, cra-pula, du-plus, &c. : du-pl-ex, &c. in which pl-ex (not from plico) is a compound suffix pul-ic(s).

δ) ace-tum, *vinegar*; with many neuter *D.* denoting '*Place of growth*;' myrt-etum, *myrtle-grove*; oliv-etum, *olive-yard,* &c.

ε) *V.* gens, mens, sors, &c.; vec-tis, ves-tis, vi-tis, mes-sis. *D.* men-sis, nep-tis.

ζ) *V.* seg-ĕs, ar-iĕs (see C. *Nachtr.* 268–270): and *D.* in ĕs ĭt-, al-ĕs, equ-ĕs, ped-ĕs, &c. p. 97.

η) Numerous Abstract *D.* liber-tas, auctor-itas, car-itas, pi-etas, soci-etas (ⵀ by dissimilation after **l**), &c. &c. &c. On hon-estas, &c., see **R**: pot-estas, eg-estas may be for -ent-tas.

θ) Abstract *D.* iuven-tus, senec-tus, vir-tus, serv-itus.

ι) *D.* nun-tius, nun-tia, trist-itia, serv-itium, calv-ities, amar-ities, iust-itia, &c. &c.

κ) pal-atum, *palate*; Mat-uta, *goddess of Morn*; pitu-ita, *phlegm.*

λ) dos, *dowry*; nepos, *grandson.*

μ) lin-teum, *towel.*

Adjectives.

α) *D.* numerous: ius-tus, *just*; mul-tus, *much*; sex-tus, *sixth,* &c. &c. *V.* tac-itus, *silent*; sal-sus, *salted*; with all Perf. Participles of Conj. 3., most of 2. and others; tac-tus, doc-tus, admon-ĭtus, atton-ĭtus, ius-sus, pressus, &c. &c. &c.

β) *D.* numerous: barb-atus, *bearded*; ferr-atus, *iron-clad,* &c. &c. *V.* most Participles of Conj. 1. am-atus, arm-atus, &c. &c. &c.

γ) *V.* fac-etus: and many Participles, defl-etus, decr-etus, &c.

δ) *D.* crin-ītus, *rich-haired*; mell-ītus, *honied,* &c. *V.* most Participles of Conj. 4. and others, aud-itus, per-itus, tr-itus, &c. &c. &c.

ε) *D.* aegr-otus, *sick*; nas-utus, *sharp-nosed,* &c. *V.* Participles of Verbs in **uo,** ac-utus, arg-utus, &c.

ζ) *D.* nostras, Arpinas, &c. Quiris, Samnis, &c. p. 108.

η) for-tis, hebes, dives, p. 116, &c.

V. D.

Substantives.

α) *V.* mŏ-dus; cau-da; cica-da; tae-da; crep-ĭda.

β) *V.* laus, cla-des.

γ) *V.* her-es, merc-es, (cust-os?)

δ) *D.* pec-us ud-.

Adjectives.

α) *D.* absur-dus, cru-dus; fum-idus, *smoky*; gel-idus, *chilly, frosty*; herb-idus, *grassy*; morb-idus, *diseased*; sol-idus; suc-idus, *juicy,* and others: *V.* many from Verbs (chiefly, but not solely, of Conj. 2.): ac-idus, alg-idus, ar-idus, av-idus, call-idus, ferv-idus, pall-idus, tab-idus, tim-idus, torr-idus, val-idus, um-idus, &c. &c.; cup-idus, flu-idus, grav-idus, rab-idus, rap-idus, vīv-idus.

β) *D.* gran-dis; viri-dis.

VII. **B.**

S.　　*α*) **bŏ.**　　*β*) **bĭ.**
A.　　**bŏ.**

on **bundŏ** see **N**; on **bĭlĭ bĕrĭ**, &c., see **L, R.**

VIII. **M.**

This Nasal has an important place in Latin Wordlore. It ter-
minates, as in Sk., the Accus. Sing. of all Masc. and Fem. Nouns,
and the first three cases of Neut. O-nouns. The Suffix **mŏ** enters
into the Superl. form of the Adj. **Mĭn (mĕn), mentŏ** have concrete use, implying Instrument : **mōnĭŏ** implies Permanent State :

S. *α*) **mŏ ĭmŏ tĭmŏ**　　*β*) **mĭn (mĕn) ĭmĭn (ĭmĕn) ŭmĭn**
　　(**ŭmĕn**)　　*γ*) **mentŏ ĭmentŏ ŭmentŏ āmentŏ**　　*ε*)
　　mōn ŭmōn　　*ε*) **mōnĭŏ ĭmōnĭŏ**　　*ζ*) **umnŏ.**

A. *α*) **mŏ**　　*β*) **ĭmŏ (ŭmŏ) tĭmŏ (tŭmŏ) sĭmŏ (sŭmŏ) rĭmŏ**
　　(**rŭmŏ**) **lĭmŏ (lŭmŏ) ĭssĭmŏ (ĭssŭmŏ) ēsĭmŏ (ēsŭmŏ).**

VII. **B.**

Substantives.
　　α) mor-bus, tu-ba, tur-ba, ver-bum.
　　β) plebs, pu-bes.

Adjectives :
　　pro-bus (προ-φυής), super-bus (ὑπερ-φυής?).

VIII. **M.**

Substantives.
　　α) *V.* ar-mus, *shoulder-joint*; fu-mus, *smoke*; ra-mus, *bough*; an-ĭmus, *mind*;
　　an-ĭma, *breath*; fa-ma, *fame*; flam-ma, *flame*; spu-ma, *foam*; vic-tima, *victim*;
　　ar-ma, *arms*, &c.　*D.* bru-ma, *mid-winter* (brevi-ma).
　　β) *V.* Neut. (numerous): imply '*Means, Instrument* or *Concrete Effect*:' (1) when
　　the theme has active force: flū-men, *stream*; lū-men, *light*; lenī-men, levā-men,
　　assuagement; nū-men, *nod, deity*; nutrī-men, *nutriment*; reg-ĭmen, *govern-
　　ment*; solā-men, *comfort*; teg-men, *covering* : (2) when the theme has a pas-
　　sive sense: ag-men, *a marching body* (quod agitur); nō-men, *name* (quod nos-
　　citur); strā-men, *straw* (quod sternitur); sē-men, *seed* (quod seritur); exā-men,
　　swarm of bees (quod exigitur, *which is driven out*) or *tongue of balance* (quod
　　exigitur, *which is adjusted*). So crīmen, *a charge* ; doc-ūmen, *lesson*, &c. &c. &c.
　　Some suppose Verbs not in use: albū-men, gra-men, *grass* (ger-ere or gen-ere?
　　Compare ger-men, *sprout*). (Many unc. abdō-men, bitū-men, lī-men and others.
　　Flāmen, *priest*, Masc. from flag- φλεγ-, *lighter of sacrificial fire*.)
　　γ) This Suffix is an enlargement of the last, and has the same general meanings and
　　varieties : *V.* (1) Act. argū-mentum, *proof*; ar-mentum, *plough-cattle*; complē-
　　mentum, *what fills up*; fō-mentum, *poultice* (quod fŏvet), fer-mentum (quod
　　fervet); nutrī-mentum, ornā-mentum, al-ĭmentum, teg-ūmentum.　(2) Pass. cae-
　　mentum, *hewn stone* (quod caeditur); frag-mentum; rā-mentum, *shaving* (quod
　　raditur), testā-mentum, *will*, &c. &c. &c.　From non-extant Verbs: calceā-men-
　　tum, *shoe*; rudī-mentum, *first training, rudiment* (compare erudire); palud-
　　āmentum, *military cloak*.
　　δ) ser-mo, *discourse* : (Lucu-mo, *prince, priest*, in Etruria).
　　ε) *D.* acr-imonia, *sharpness*; aegr-imonia, *melancholy*; parc-imonia (rather than
　　pars-imonia), *thrift*; matr-imonium, *marriage*, &c.　*V.* quer-imonia, *complaint* :
　　al-imonium, *nourishment*, &c.
　　ζ) *V.* al-umnus, *nursling*; col-umna, *column*.

Adjectives.
　　α) *V.* al-mus, *genial*; fir-mus, *firm*.　*D.* On Superl. suffix **mŏ** see p. 42.　So the
　　　　Ordinal Numerals septimus, decimus, &c. p. 152.
　　β) *D.* plur-ĭmus, ci-tĭmus, pes-sĭmus, acer-rĭmus, humil-lĭmus, dur-issĭmus, quin-
　　　　quag-ensĭmus, cent-ensĭmus (ŭmus), &c. &c.　See pp. 42, 153.

γ) ĭtĭmŏ (ĭtŭmŏ)   δ) īmŏ   ε) mĭ.

IX. N.

The Nasodental **n** is not less important than the Dentals **t, d** in forming Latin Suffixes. Three uses may be distinguished : (1) when **n** is followed by a vowel in a staminal suffix (**nă, nŏ, ĭnŏ, ānŏ, īnŏ,** &c.) or by two vowels (**nĕŏ, ĭnĕŏ,** &c.) : (2) when it is itself, in Substantives, the Stem-character (**ĕn, ĭn, ēn, ŏn, ōn**) ; here it does not, like **t, d,** fall out before a Nom.-Ending **s**, but rejects **s**, remaining itself in the form **ĕn** or **ēn** (pectĕn, tegmĕn, liēn), but rejected by the stems **ŏn ōn**, which become **ō** in Nom. Sing. (homo, natio, Plato) : (3) when it stands chiefly in Adjectives before **t, d** or **s** (**entŏ, entĭ, endŏ, ensĭ,** &c.), rarely before **g** (quadringenti): being sometimes the final letter of a preceding suffix (**men-tŏ**), sometimes, perhaps, the strengthening Nasal (**ntĭ, nsĭ**).

S. (1) α) **nă**   β) **nŏ ĭnŏ**   γ) **ānŏ ōnŏ ūnŏ ēnŏ ĭlēnŏ**
        δ) **īnŏ**   ε) **nĭ**

   (2) ζ) **ĕn (ĭn) mĕn (mĭn)**   η) **ŏn (ĭn)**   θ) **gŏn āgŏn**
        īgŏn ūgŏn (gĭn)   ι) **dŏn ēdŏn īdŏn ūdŏn (dĭn)**
        tūdŏn ĭtūdŏn (dĭn)   κ) **ōn ĭōn cĭōn tĭōn sĭōn**

   (3) λ) **entĭ antĭ**   μ) **undŏn (dĭn).**
        See **mentŏ** under **M.**

γ) *D.* leg-itĭmus, mar-itĭmus (-ŭmus).

δ) *D.* matr-īmus, *having mother alive* ; patr-īmus : (op-īmus, *having wealth, rich*).

ε) cō-mis, sublīmis (*seen from underneath* 'limis oculis ?' i.e. *lofty.* Compare obliquus).

IX. N.

Substantives.

α) *V.* ver-na, *houseslave.*

β) *V.* som-nus, dom-inus, pen-na, pag-ina, reg-num. . . . *D.* pi-nus, *pine-tree.*

γ) **ānŏ**: *D.* Silv-anus, *god of forests* ; membr-ana, *parchment* ; (gra-num, *a grain*) ; **ōnŏ**: *V.* col-onus, *farm-tenant. D.* patr-onus, *patron* ; matr-ona, *matron* ; **ūnŏ**: *D.* trib-unus, *tribune* ; fort-una, *fortune* ; **ēnŏ**: *V.* hab-ena, *rein* ; *D.* lani-ena, *butcher's shop* ; (ven-enum, *poison*) ; le-aena, *lioness*, &c. ; **ĭlēnŏ**: *V.* cant-ilena, *ditty.*

δ) **īnŏ**: *V.* inquil-inus, *lodger* ; ru-ina, *fall, ruin* ; rap-ina, *plunder* ; cŭ-lina, *kitchen* ; *D.* gall-ina, *hen* ; medic-ina, *medical art* ; discipl-ina, *teaching, school*, &c.

ε) *V.* fi-nis, *end* ; cri-nis, *parted hair.*

ζ) *V.* pect-en, *comb.* For the suffix mĕn (mĭn), &c. see **M.**

η) *D.* hom-o, *man* ; turb-o, *whirlwind, top.*

θ) **gŏn**: *D.* vir-go, *virgin* ; **āgŏn**: *V.* vor-ago, *gulph* ; *D.* farr-ago, *mess of flour* ; (im-ago, *image ?*) ; **īgŏn**: *V.* or-igo, *origin* ; vert-igo, *twirl* ; **ūgŏn**: *D.* aer-ugo, *copper-rust* ; lan-ugo, *down*, &c. (Genitives gĭnis.)

ι) **dŏn**: or-do, *order ?* **ēdŏn**: *V.* dulc-edo, *sweetness* : torp-edo, *numbness* ; **īdŏn**: *V.* cup-ido, *desire* ; **ūdŏn**: *D.* test-udo, *tortoise, penthouse* ; **ĭtūdŏn**: *D.* alt-itudo, fort-itudo, lat-itudo, long-itudo, viciss-itudo ; vale-tudo (for valentudo ?), &c. &c. (Genitives dĭnis.)

κ) **ōn**: m. *D.* commilit-o, *fellow-soldier* ; epul-o, *banqueter*, &c. &c. : *V.* bib-o, *toper* ; erro, *vagabond* ; **ĭōn**, many masc. *D.* lud-io, *player* ; sēn-io, *sice*, &c. *V.* pŭg-io, *poniard.* Fem. *V.* (Pres. St.): condĭc-io, leg-io, opĭn-io, suspic-io, &c. Some *D.* commun-io, *communion* ; consortio, rebellio, &c. ; **cĭōn**: homuncio ; **tĭōn, sĭōn**: Fem. *V.* (Sup. St.), a very numerous class of words : aestimatio, admonī-tio, sortī-tio, ac-tio, na-tio, ora-tio, posses-sio, ul-tio, vi-sio, &c. &c. &c.

λ) *V.* adulesc-ens, serp-ens, torr-ens, anim-ans, inf-ans, &c. *D.* tri-ens, quad-rans, &c.

μ) hir-undo, *swallow* ; har-undo, *reed.*

A. (1) *a*) **nŏ ĭnŏ nĕŏ gĭnŏ gnŏ tĭnŏ**   *β*) **ānŏ ānĕŏ**
          tānĕŏ   *γ*) **ēnŏ ĭēnŏ oenŏ ūnŏ**   *δ*) **īnŏ, tīnŏ**   *ε*) **nĭ**

(3) *ζ*) **entŏ ŭlentŏ ŏlentŏ ĭlentŏ (gĭntŏ centŏ gentŏ)**
      η) **antĭ entĭ ĭlentĭ ŭlentĭ**   *θ*) **ensĭ ĭensĭ ensĭlĭ**
      ι) **undŏ endŏ andŏ**   *κ*) **cundŏ**   *λ*) **bundŏ.**

X. s.

The Sibilant in a large class of words, chiefly *V*., represents the
Dental **t** (**sŏ, sĭ, sĭōn, sŏr, sōrĭŏ, surŏ**). When **s** is a Stem-character,
in many words, especially in the older, it remains in Nom. Sing. **flos,
ros, opus, nemus, Venus, pulvis,** &c., but oftener becomes **r** in the
suffix **ōs ōr** : **pudor, auctor,** &c. : while in some words both forms
were used : **honōs** or **honŏr, labōs** or **labŏr, lepōs** or **lepŏr** : so
amos, colos occur.   In the Oblique Cases **s** becomes **r** : **flōris,
rōris, opĕris, Venĕris, honōris,** &c.   But if in derivation such
words come before a Mute, then **s** is resumed : **flos-culus, opus-
culum, venus-tus, hones-tus : hes-ternus** (from **heri** for **hes-i,**
Gr. χθές) : not before a vowel : **flor-eus, pulver-ulentus;** see **R**.
On the falling out of **n** before **s** in various words (**quotiens, semenstris, formonsus, vicensumus,** &c.), see p. 50.

S. *a*) **să**   *β*) **sŏ sĭ sĭŏ ēsĭŏ ĭsōn**

Adjectives.

   a) *D*. **mag-nus, sa-nus, va-nus, ver-nus, no-nus, u-nus, octo-nus, ter-nus; acer-nus,**
      of maple; **colur-nus** (for **corulinus**), *of hazel*; **adamant-īnus; ahe-neus,** *of brass*;
      ebur-neus, *of ivory*; (**ido-neus,** *fit*); **olea-ginus,** *of olive*; **beni-gnus,** *kind, boun-
      tiful*; **cras-tīnus,** *of the morrow*; **pris-tīnus,** *of olden time.*

   β) *D*. **arc-anus,** *secret*; **font-anus,** *of a fountain*; **quart-anus**; **cotidi-anus,** *daily*;
      suburb-anus, *near the city*; **subterr-aneus,** *underground*; *V*. **supervac-aneus**;
      collec-taneus, *gathered together*; **consen-taneus,** *adapted,* &c.

   γ) *V*. **eg-enus,** *needy*: *D*. **ali-enus,** *foreign*; **terr-enus,** *earthly*; (**ser-enus**); **op-
      port-unus,** *at hand*; (**amoenus,** *agreeable*).

   δ) *D*. **can-īnus,** *of a dog*; **div-inus,** *of a deity, divine*; **mar-inus,** *of the sea*, &c. &c.;
      libert-inus, *of freedman-class*; **matut-inus,** *of morn*; **vesper-tinus,** *of evening,* &c.

   ε) **seg-nis,** *lazy.*

   ζ) *D*. **cru-entus,** *bloody*; **vi-olentus,** *violent*; **lut-ulentus,** *muddy*; **mac-ilentus,** *wasted*;
      (**corp-ulentus** for **corpor-ulentus**).   For the forms **vi-ginti, tri-ginta,** &c. **du-centi,
      quin-genti,** &c., see Numeralia.

   η) *V*. Adjectives and Participles in **ens, ans,** denoting '*Present activity* :' **abs-ens,
      eleg-ans, impud-ens, prud-ens, am-ans, praest-ans, cand-ens, dilig-ens, negleg-ens,
      audi-ens,** &c. &c., (**petul-ans**).   *D*. **pest-ilens.**

   θ) *D*. **for-ensis,** *of the forum*; **Athen-iensis,** *of Athens*; **ut-ensilis,** *for use*; observe
      di nov-ensiles, the meaning of which term is questionable.

   ι) *V*. Gerundive Participles in **undus** (anc.), **endus, andus**; **reg-undus, audi-endus,
      am-andus,** &c. &c. &c.   They denote '*Present activity.*' See Syntax.

   κ) *V*. **cundŏ** is a suffix compounded of the suffixes **cŏ** and **ndŏ,** and denotes
      '*Permanent action*' or '*Present activity* :' **fa-cundus,** *eloquent*; **iu-cundus,**
      pleasant; **vere-cundus,** *bashful,* &c. &c. &c.

   λ) *V*. **bundŏ** is compounded of **bŏ** and **ndŏ,** and denotes '*Production of Present
      activity* :' **popula-bundus,** *engaged in laying waste*; **vaga-bundus,** *given to wan-
      der*; **mori-bundus,** *on the point of dying,* &c.   It is found with an Object : '**vita-
      bundus castra hostium,**' *striving to avoid the enemy's camp*, Liv.

X. s.

Substantives.

   a) *V*. **lixa,** *sutler* (**lic-ēre** ?).

   β) *V*. **na-sus,** *nose*; **noxa,** *harm,* &c. (see **T**); **mes-sis,** *harvest*; **ama-sius,** *sweet-
      heart*; **Megal-esia,** *feast of Cybele*; **equi-iso,** *groom.*

γ) **iscŏ istŏ estrŏ astrŏ**　　　　　δ) **ĕs** (*ĭs, ŭs*) = **ĕr**

ε) **ŏs** (*ŭs*) = **ŏr**　　ζ) **ōs** (*ŏr*) = **ōr**　　η) **uscŏ ustŏ**

A. α) **sŏ sĭŏ**　　β) **ōsŏ ĭōsŏ cōsŏ cŭlōsŏ** &c.　　　γ) **strĭ**

　　　estrĭ astrŏ ĭstrŏ　　δ) **estĭ estĭcŏ**　　ε) **uscŏ**　　ζ) **estŏ**

　　ustŏ　　ŋ) **ĭōs** (*ĭŏr*) = **ĭōr**.

XI. R.

This Liquid occurs in many Suffixes, sometimes without a second consonant in the same Suffix (**rŏ, ārĭ, ārĭŏ,** &c.), often in sequence of one of the mutes, **c, t, b** (**crŏ, trŏ, brŏ,** &c.). On its relations to **l** and to **s** see pp. 64. 65, and **s** above.

S. α) **rŏ**　　β) **ĕrŏ ŭrŏ**　　γ) **cĕrŏ (crŏ)**　　δ) **bĕrŏ (brŏ)**

　　ε) **tĕrŏ (trŏ)**　　ζ) **rŭ**　　η) **rĭ**　　θ) **ĕr ercŏ ertŏ**

γ) lent-iscus, *lentisk* ; ar-ista, *ear of corn* ; fen-estra, *window* ; *D.* in -aster, -astrum are of a deminutive nature : ole-aster, *wild olive* ; api-astrum, *wild parsley, mint* ; parasit-aster, *a would-be parasite.*

δ ε ζ) Nouns increasing in ĕr- from Nominatives in ĭs, ŭs, in ŏr- from ŭs, and in ŏr- from ōs, will be found at pp. 25, 102.

η) moll-usca : (loc-usta).

Adjectives.

α) *V.* las-sus, anxius, &c. &c.　See **T.**

β) **ōsŏ** (for **onsŏ** or **ontĭŏ,** as οὐσία for ὀντία), numerous ; *D.* anim-osus, form-osus, &c. &c. &c. ; capt-iosus, cur-iosus, &c. ; belli-cosus, siti-culosus, monstr-uosus, &c.

γ) *V.* illu-stris ; *D.* palu-stris, silv-estris : sin-ister.

δ) *D.* agr-estis, cael-estis, dom-esticus.

ε) *D.* cor-uscus, *glittering.*

ζ) *D.* funestus from funus, ĕr- ; scelestus from scelus, ĕr- ; honestus from honos, ŏr- (so tempestas from tempus, ŏr-) ; but onustus from onus, ĕr- ; venustus from Venus, ĕr- ; vetustus from vetus, ĕr- ; modestus points to a lost Neut. modus. Augustus from augur, and robustus from robur, shew that, even in Subst. with Nom. ŭr, the original ending was ŭs.

η) This is the Suffix of Comparatives : mel-ĭōr (anc. meliŏr, meliōs).　See p. 21.

XI. R.

Substantives.

α) *V.* cu-ra, *care* ; ser-ra, *saw* ; lab-rum, *lip* ; (aurora, *morning,* p. 66).

β) *V.* num-erus, *number* ; arbit-er, *umpire* ; gen-er, *son-in-law* ; op-era, *aid* ; iug-erum, *acre.　D.* um-erus, *shoulder* ; sat-ura, *satire.*

γ) *V.* Neuter words implying ʻ *That which effects action* :ʼ simula-crum, *likeness* ; sepul-crum, *a grave* ; lu-crum, *gain* ; ful-crum (for fulc-crum), *prop,* &c. &c. **Cŭlŏ (clŏ)** is another form : cena-culum, *dining-room.* See **L.** The suffix comes from the root Sk. *kar,* L. cre-o, *to make.*

δ) *V.* ʻ *That which effects action* :ʼ fa-ber, *engineer* ; dola-bra, *hatchet* ; late-bra, *hiding-place* ; cri-brum, *sieve* ; scalprum (for scalp-brum, *chisel*). *D.* candela-brum, *candlestick.* Root Sk. *bhar,* Gr. φερ-. **Bŭlŏ** is another form : turi-bulum, *censer.*

ε) The Suffix **tĕr (trŏ)** has two uses in Latin, both from one root, Sk. *tar,* Gr. τορ- (shewn in τέρμα, terminus, trames, trans, in-tra-re, pene-tra-re, &c.), *go beyond, penetrate, attain.* (1) It corresponds to the comparative suffix Sk. *tara,* Gr. τερο-, used to express a relation between two : shewn in the Gr. Compar. -τερος, L. ter : magis-ter, minis-ter, mater-tera, &c. &c. and in Adverbs. (2) Like **crŏ** and **brŏ,** it denotes in *V.* ʻ *That which effects the action* :ʼ cul-ter, *knife* ; mulc-tra, *milkpail* ; ara-trum, *plough* ; claus-trum, *barrier* ; ros-trum, *beak* (rod-) ; ras-trum, *harrow* (rād-) : in mon-s-trum, *prodigy,* **s** is euphonically inserted.

ζ) *V.* cur-rus, *chariot.*

η) *V.* au-ris, *ear* ; na-ris, *nostril.*

θ) *D.* ans-er (for h-anser ; Sk. *hansa,* Gr. χήν), *gander* ; pass-er, *sparrow* ; muli-er, *woman* ; nov-erca, *stepmother* ; *V.* it-er, *journey* ; cad-av-er, *corpse.*

bĕrĭ brĭ   κ) tĕrĭ (trĭ)   λ) tĕr tr   μ) ĭnĕr ĭnŏr   ν) băr
ξ) ŏr ŭr   o) ārĭ   π) ārĭŏ   ρ) ŏr = ōr   σ) tŏr = tōr (sōr)
trīc-   τ) tōrĭŏ (sōrĭŏ)   υ) ūrŏ ūrĭ ūrĭŏ   φ) tūrŏ (sūrŏ).

A. α) rŏ   β) ĕrŏ ŭrŏ   γ) cĕrŏ (crŏ)   δ) bĕrŏ (brŏ)
tĕrŏ (trŏ)   ε) estĕrĭ (estrĭ)   ζ) ārŏ ōrŏ ērŏ   η) cĕrĭ (crĭ)
θ) bĕrĭ (brĭ)   ι) tĕrĭ (trĭ)   κ) ārĭ   λ) ārĭŏ   μ) tōrĭŏ
(sōrĭŏ)   ν) tūrŏ (sūrŏ).

ι) *V.* fe-bris, *fever.*

κ) (lin-ter or lunter, *boat ?*)

λ) See above ε). This suffix corresponds to the Sk. *tara*, denoting chiefly relation-
ships : pa-ter, ma-ter, fra-ter. Observe (Sk. *svasar*, Gr. ὄαρ, L. soror for sosor).

μ) (itiner), *journey* ; (iociner), *liver:* (facinŭr-) facinus, *deed, exploit, crime.*

ν) iu-bar, *sunbeam.*

ξ) *D.* aequ-ŏr, *level surface, sea* ; (unc. iecur, ebur, robur, Gen. -ŏris). *V.* fulg-ur,
ligtning ; Gen. -ŭris. (Unc. augur, turtur, vultur.)

o) *D.* mol-aris (lapis), *grindstone:* many Neut. from Adjectives : alve-are, *hive* ;
calc-ar, *spur,* &c. &c.

π) Properly Adj. libr-arius, *copyer of books* ; den-arius, *a ten-as piece* ; Aulul-aria (name
of a Comedy of Plautus) ; tabul-arium, *record-office* ; pom-arium, *orchard,* &c.&c.

ρ) *V.* or from prim. rudiment : am-ŏr, *love* ; cru-ŏr, *blood* ; clam-ŏr, *outcry* ; trem-ŏr,
trembling ; um-ŏr, *moisture* ; (ux-ŏr, *wife ?*), Gen. ōrīs, &c. &c. &c. Many had
character **s** originally : umōs, lepōs, &c. See **S.**

σ) *V.* a numerous class, denoting '*an Agent :*' ara-tŏr, ora-tŏr, pisca-tŏr, moni-tŏr,
ac-tŏr, vic-tŏr, spon-sŏr, mes-sŏr, Gen. ōris, &c. &c. &c. The Fem. form is
trīc trix : moni-trix, vic-trix, tons-trix, &c. &c.
D. gladia-tŏr, via-tŏr, fund-ĭ-tŏr, ianĭ-tŏr, and some others.

π) From Verbal Adjectives Neut. : denote chiefly locality : audi-torium, *lecture-room* ;
dever-sorium, *hostel,* &c. See below μ).

υ) *V.* fĭg-ura, *shape* ; sec-uris, *axe* ; *D.* pen-uria, *penury* ; promunt-urium, *promon-
tory.*

φ) *V.* (Sup. St.) na-tura, *nature* ; sepul-tura, *burial* ; men-sura, *measure* ; cae-sura,
cutting, &c. : official terms : dicta-tura, *dictatorship* ; quaes-tura, *quaestorship* ;
cen-sura, *censorship.* Others imply '*the work of an Agent* (tor, sor) :' pic-tura,
painting ; ton-sura, *shaving,* &c.

Adjectives.

α) *V.* cla-rus, gna-rus.

β) *V.* glab-er, *smooth* ; intĕg-er, lăc-er, săc-er, scăb-er, *rough* : *D.* sătur.

γ) *V.* ludi-cer.

δ) *V.* cre-ber, *frequent.*

ε) *D.* The Derivatives have the Compar. suffix *tara* : al-ter, u-ter, dex-ter, sinis-ter,
nos-ter, ves-ter, ex-ter, in-ter, &c. (So in Adverbs ali-ter, pari-ter, &c.) See
above ε).

ζ) *V.* av-arus, *covetous* ; can-orus, od-orus, son-orus (unc. aust-erus ; sev-erus ;
sin-cerus, pro-cerus ?).

η) *V.* volu-cer, medio-cris (acer, alacer ?).

θ) *V.* cele-ber ; lugu-bris ; salu-ber ; *D.* fene-bris, fune-bris, mulie-bris (drops r). This
suffix is from Sk. R. *bhar,* Gr. φερ-.

ι) *D.* 1. eques-ter, pedes-ter, palus-ter, seques-ter (secus), semes-tris (for semenstris) : 2. camp-estris, silv-estris, terr-ester (tris).

κ) *D.* in **ārĭ** are a large class and imply '*Belonging to* ;' they are used for forms in
ālĭ if **l** is before in the word : consul-aris ; famili-aris ; milit-aris ; sol-aris ;
vulg-aris, &c. &c. &c. They form Substantives in **ăr ārĭ.** See above o).

λ) The suffix **ārĭŏ** is an enlargement of **ārĭ.** The Adjectives derived from
Nouns and Particles imply *character, quality, class,* &c. : agr-arius, *of land* ;
greg-arius, *of a herd* ; numm-arius, *of coin* ; necess-arius ; prec-arius ; volunt-
arius, &c. &c. Hence Substt. See above π).

μ) These are chiefly formed from Verbal Nouns of the Agent in tor (sor) and imply
'*Belonging to* :' ama-torius, ora-torius, cen-sorius, &c. &c. &c.

ν) This is the Fut. Participle Act. of Verbs, denoting '*Intended activity* :' amā-turus,
dă-turus, placĭ-turus, ĭ-turus, fŭ-turus, lŭ-surus, mis-surus, &c. &c. &c.

XII. **L.**

This soft Liquid is chiefly used in Deminutive Suffixes of *D.* (ŭlŏ, ŏlŏ, ellŏ, &c.) : and it often denotes *weakness, lightness, &c.* in Suffixes of Verbalia (ŭlŏ, ĭlĭ, tĭlĭ). But after a long Vowel it has the same firmness as **r**, to which it is often equivalent. Thus the Suffixes ālĭ ārĭ are virtually the same : but the former is always preferred unless **l** occurs in the Stem (hiem-alis but lun-aris) : but ārĭŏ is never changed into ālĭŏ (agr-arius). The Suffix **bŭlŏ** is a softened form of **bĕrŏ** (**brŏ**) ; **bĭlĭ** of **bĕrĭ** (**brĭ**), both from root *bhar,* φερ- ; **cŭlŏ** (as distinguished from the double Demin. **c-ŭlŏ**) is a softened form of **cĕrŏ** (**crŏ**) from root *kar.*

(1) Not formally Deminutive.

S. *a)* ă   *β)* lŏ ŭlŏ ŭlĕŏ   *γ)* cŭlŏ (clŏ)   *δ)* bŭlŏ

    ε) ēlŏ   *ζ)* ĭlŏ illŏ   *η)* lĭ ĭlĭ   *θ)* ālĭ īlĭ ēlĭ.

A.   *a)* ŭlŏ ŭlĕŏ   *β)* ĭlŏ

XII. **L.**

(1)

Substantives.

a) V. assec-la, masc. *follower.*

β) D. vio-la, *violet* (Gr. ἴον) ; pi-lum, *pestle* ; neb-ula, *cloud.* V. cŭc-ulus, *cuckoo* : ang-ulus, *corner* ; fig-ulus, *potter* ; oc-ulus, *eye* ; cop-ula, *link* ; spec-ula, *watch tower* ; exem-p-lum (for exim-ulum), tem-p-lum (for tem-ulum), &c. &c. In these and others some deminutive influence may be surmised, and in many unc. (cat-ulus, cum-ulus, fam-ulus, scop-ulus, Gr. σκόπελος, stim-ulus, vit-ulus, fist-ula, ins-ula, mer-ula, &c.). See 3). On rēg-ula, *rule* ; tēg-ula, *tile,* see pp. 16, 17. Pŏ-pŭl-us, e-pul-ae, probably contain the root *par* (*prĭ*) *pul ple.* See **P.**

γ) V. (Pres. St.) numerous : implying ‘*Instrument, means of action,*’ are Neut. : gu-berna-culum, *helm* ; ora-culum (-clum), *oracle* ; specta-culum, *sight* ; vehi-culum, *vehicle* ; peri-culum, *trial, peril,* &c. &c. &c. In vinculum (vinclum), *chain* ; torcŭlum, *press,* **c** (**qu**) has fallen out after **c** : and it is not improbable that the same occurs in ia-culum, *javelin* ; spe-culum, *mirror.* Unc. are (graculus, *jackdaw* ; surculus, *shoot* ; baculum, *walking-stick,* Gr. βα-? saeculum, *an age, generation,* &c.). See **cĕrŏ** (**crŏ**) in **R.**

δ) V. (same meaning) : fā-bula, *story* ; sū-bula, *awl* ; lati-bulum, *hiding-place* ; pā-bulum, *fodder* : voca-bulum, *word, name,* &c. D. turi-bulum, *censer.*

ε) V. (Pres. St.) cand-ela, *candle* ; (redupl.) cicind-ela, *glowworm* ; suad-ela, *persuasion* : (with **ll**) loqu-ella, *saying* ; quer-ella, *complaint* ; (Sup. St.) corrupt-ela, *corruption* ; tut-ela, *guardianship* or (concrete) *guardian, ward.* D. client-ela, *clientage.*

ζ) (unc. aqu-ila) ; D. cap-illus, *hair* ; anc-illa, *maidservant* ; arg-illa, *clay* ; scint-illa, *spark* ; V. pist-illum, *pestle* ; vex-illum, *banner,* &c. (probably deminutive of lost forms, or formed by analogy).

η) V. cau-lis, *stalk* ; col-lis, *hill* ; strig-īlis, *flesh-brush.*

θ) D. Adjectival words formed into Subst. ālĭ, Masc. : nat-alis, *birthday* ; riv-alis, *rival* (unc. can-alis, *canal* ; feti-alis, *sacred envoy* ; sod-alis, *comrade*), &c. Neut. foc-ale, *neckwrapper* ; penetr-ale, *inner shrine* ; anim-al, &c. p. 107, with Plur. names of Feasts : Consu-alia, Luperc-alia, Termin-alia, &c. &c. p. 126. īlĭ, Masc. aed-ilis, *edile* ; Apr-ilis, *April,* &c. Neut. cub-ile, hast-ile, ov-ile, sed-ile, &c. p. 107. Plur. Par-ilia, *feast of Pales* ; Suovetaur-ilia, *Feast with sacrifice of swine, sheep,* and *steer.* ēlĭ: patru-ēlis, *cousin* on father’s side.

Adjectives.

a) D. būb-ulus, *of an ox* ; caer-ulus, caer-uleus, *sky-blue* ; edent-ulus, *toothless.* V. (Pres. St.) denoting ‘*Tendency* :’ bib-ulus, cred-ulus, garr-ulus, pat-ulus, quer-ulus, strid-ulus, sed-ulus, trem-ulus, &c., all with demin. character : (unc. aem-ulus).

β) D. nub-ilus, *cloudy* ; rut-ilus, *reddish.*

γ) ĭlĭ   δ) bĭlĭ ĭbĭlĭ   ε) tĭlĭ (sĭlĭ)

ζ) ātĭlĭ   η) ālĭ īlĭ ūlĭ ēlĭ.

(2) Deminutive.

S. and A.

I. *a*) ŭlŏ (anc. ŏlŏ, which remains after ĕ, ĭ).

b) ellŏ, illŏ, ullŏ, primarily deminutive, are not purely suffixal, but contain the Stem-character l, n or r assimilated to l of the Suffix : in some words they are perhaps used by analogy.

c) ellŏ, illŏ, secondary Deminutives for ŭl-ŭlŏ.

d) ellŭlŏ, illŭlŏ, secondary Deminutives, when derived from *b*), tertiary, when derived from *c*).

γ) *V.* (Pres. St.) denoting *Tendency* or *capacity*: ag-ilis, *nimble*; hab-ilis, *apt*; deb-ilis, *weak*; fac-ilis, *easy*; diffic-ilis, *difficult*; nub-ilis, *marriageable*; ut-ilis, *useful*, &c. *D.* hum-ilis, *lowly*; sim-ilis, *like*; ster-ilis, *barren*: (unc. grac-ilis, *slender*).

δ) *V.* (Pres. St.) denoting chiefly '*Passive capability* :' mira-bilis, *wonderful*; muta-bilis, *changeable*; fle-bilis, *mournful*; prob-a-bilis, *approvable*; credi-bilis, *credible*; no-bilis, *noble*, &c. &c. &c. Terri-bilis, *terrible*, has Active force. (Sup. St.) flex-ibilis, *flexible*; plaus-ibilis, *commendable*; sens-ibilis, *perceivable*. Add poss-ibilis, *possible* (of the Silver age).

ε) *V.* (Sup. St.) Some denote only '*Passive quality*,' differing little from the Perf. Part. : al-tilis, *fattened*; coc-tilis, *baked*; fic-tilis, *fashioned*; fis-silis, *cleft*; mis-silis, *sent*; nex-ilis, *twined*; tor-tilis, *twisted*; versa-tilis, *made to revolve*, &c. : others denote '*Passive capacity* :' flex-ilis, *flexible*; diffu-silis, *expansive*; tac-tilis, *that may be touched*: others '*Active quality* :' pen-silis *hanging*; ses-silis, *squab*; vol-atilis, *flying*, &c. Abnormal: fer-tilis, *fruitful*, indicating an old word fert-us (fut-tilis, *futile* ?).

ζ) *D.* aqu-atilis, fluvi-atilis, *river-dwelling*, &c.

η) ālĭ: *D.* (numerous) denote '*Belonging to*,' &c. : aequ-alis, dot-alis, fat-alis, furi-alis, liber-alis, marti-alis, mort-alis, reg-alis, triumph-alis, &c. : vit-alis, voc-alis, &c. &c. &c. īlĭ: *D.* civ-ilis, er-ilis, host-ilis, puer-ilis, scurr-ilis, sen-ilis, serv-ilis, vir-ilis, &c. Subtī-lis for sub-telis, *of the woof, fine, subtle.* ūlĭ: *D.* cur-ulis, *like a chariot* (applied to the 'sella' of certain magistrates, which had that shape); trib-ulis, *of the tribe.* The Adj. ed-ulis, *eatable*, is abnormal. ēlĭ: *D.* crud-elis, *cruel*; fīd-elis, infid-elis. See above θ).

(2) Deminutive Nouns.

I. *a*) O and A-nouns form Deminutives by joining ulus (a, um) to the Clipt Stem unless ĕ, ĭ, l, n, or r precede the ending:

> riv-us, riv-ulus; frigid-us, frigid-ulus; cist-a, cist-ula; scut-um, scut-ulum.

After ĕ, ĭ, ŏlŭs (a, um) is used :

> alve-us, alve-ŏlus: aure-us, aure-ŏlus; line-a, line-ŏla; horre-um, horre-ŏlum; fili-us, fili-ŏlus; glori-a, glori-ŏla; savi-um, savi-ŏlum.

Guttural and Dental Nouns add ŭlŭs (ă, um) to the True Stem :

> rex, rēg-ulus; cornix, cornīc-ula; adolescens, adolescent-ulus, adolescent-ula; caput, capĭt-ulum : lapid-u-lus becomes lapillus.

b) ŭlŭs (ă), ĭnŭs (ă), īnus (ă), ēnŭs (ă), become ellŭs (ă):

> pŏpulus, popellus; fābula, fabella; ăsĭnus, asellus; gĕmĭnus, gemellus; pătĭna, patella; cătīnus, catellus; cătēna, catella.

ĕr (ră or ĕră, rum) become ellŭs (ă, um):

> līber, libellus; mĭser, misellus; capra, căpella; ŏpera, opella; labrum, lăbellum.

G-nus, g-num, and ulum usually form illus, illum :

> pug-nus, pŭg-illus; signum, sĭgillum; pōculum, pōcillum; (but scamnum, scabellum).

e) Substantival Deminutives **ŏllŏ, ālŏ** (for **axŭlŏ**), **ŭlŏŏ**, and Adjectival **aulŏ (aullŏ), aulŭlŏ (aullŭlŏ)**, are rare.

II. *a)* The double Deminutive **o-ŭlŏ.**

β) **ŏĭŏn** is a rare Suffix : as homun-cio.

γ) **uncŭlŏ** in a few words is joined by analogy to Stems not Nasal : av-unculus, fur-unculus, ran-unculus.

Note 1. Care must be taken not to class among Deminutives words which are not such : as Verbals in culum : iăculum, pōculum, &c. It is probable that umbra-culum and taberna-culum should be ranked with these rather than with Deminutives.

2. Sometimes the meaning of a Deminutive differs altogether from that of its theme : avunculus, *uncle* (on mother's side), from avus, *grandfather*; osculum, *kiss*, from os, *mouth.*

3. Deminutives sometimes express *endearment,* sometimes *scorn* : usually *smallness* only. They keep the Gender of their Primitives.

4. Latin Deminutives have importance in the Romance languages, which form many words from them : as L. luscini-ola, It. usignuolo, Fr. rossignol, *nightingale*; L. api-cula, Fr. abeille, *bee* ; L. agn-ellus, Fr. agneau, *lamb*; L. gem-ellus, Fr. jumeau, *twin.*

vi. Patronymica, Names derived from Parents or Ancestors, are noticed at p. *75.*

---

c) Porcellus from porculus, cistella from cistula, cōdic-illus from codic-ulus (codex), pauxillus from pauculus, are secondary Deminutives.

d) Porcellulus from porcellus, cistellula from cistella, pauxillulus from pauxillus, are tertiary Deminutives.

e) Coron-ula, corolla ; palus for (paxulus) paxillus ; equ-us, equ-uleus or equ-ulus ; pauc-ulus, paullus ; whence paullulus.

II. *a)* Other Consonant Nouns add culus (a, um) to the Stem :

frater, frater-culus ; pauper, pauper-culus ; animal, animal-culum ; flos, flos-culus ; mus, mus-culus ; opus, opus-culum ; cor-culum for cord-culum.

And from Comparative Adjectives :

grandius-culus, *rather older* ; melius-culus, *a little better* ; plus-culum, *somewhat more.*

on becomes **un** :

homo, homun-culus ; virgo, virgun-cula ; ratio, ratiun-cula.

os becomes **us** in arbos, rumor :

arbus-cula, rumus-culus.

Bos (bovis) forms būcula, *heifer,* for bovi-cula.

I-nouns take cŭlŭs (ă, um), and usually shorten **i** :

piscis, piscĭ-culus ; levis, levĭ-culus ; pars, part-ĭcula ; rete, retĭ-culum ; venter, ventrĭ-culus. In a few Deminutives **i** is long, as canīcula, cutīcula, febrīcula.

From anguis, *snake,* comes anguilla, *eel.*

U-nouns join ĭ-cŭlus (ă, um) to the Clipt Stem :

versus, vers-ĭculus ; anus, an-ĭcula ; cornu, corn-ĭculum. Lacus-culus, domun-cula, are abnormal exceptions.

E-nouns add cŭlă to the Stem :

diē-cula, rē-cula.

Nubē-cula, plebē-cula, vulpē-cula, from Nouns of Decl. 3, are formed as though from E-nouns.

vii. Names of Countries are usually formed from the name of the people with ending **ia.**

Ital-i, Ital-ia; Graec-i, Graecia; Gall-i, Gallia; Arab-es, Arab-ia; Arcad-es, Arcad-ia, &c.

Some with the ending **ĭs** :

Pers-ae, Pers-is; Colch-i, Colch-is; Aeol-es, Aeol-is, &c.

Exceptions : Africa, Iudaea, Illyricum, and some others.

viii. Nominative Endings of Derived Words, according to their several meanings.[1]

I. Substantives :

(I.) Abstract :

1) *Action; Faculty.*

V. tio, sio ; tus, sus 4 ; io (fem.) ; tura, sura.

2) *State; Habit; Effect:*

V. ŏr ōr- ; ŭs ŏr-, ŭs ĕr- ; ies, ium; īna; mōnia; mōnium; ēla (ella) ; tēla ; ĭdo, ēdo ; īgo.

3) *Quality; Qualified Condition; Function:*

D. ia, ies, ium ; ĭtia, ĭties, ĭtium ; ntia; tas ; tūs ; tūdo; ēla ; īna ; io (fem.) ; mōnia ; mōnium ; ēdo ; āgo, ūgo ; ātus 4 ; tūra, sūra.

(II.) Concrete :

1) *Personal Agent; Individual:*

V. tor, sor (masc.), trix (fem.) ; ātus 2 ; o ōn- (masc.) ;
D. tor (masc.), trix (fem.) ; ātus 2 ; arius 2 ; ĕs, ĭt- ; o, io (masc.).

2) *Efficient Thing (Means, Instrument).*

V. ĕn ; mĕn ; mentum; (ulum) culum, crum ; bulum, brum, bra ; trum.

D. bulum, brum (in a few instances).

---

[1] Examples :

I. (I) 1) actio, visio ; actus, visus ; oblivio ; sepultura, versura.
2) furor; decus ; pondus ; congeries, colloquium ; ruina ; querimonia ; alimonium ; suadela ; corruptela ; libido, torpedo ; vertigo.
3) concordia, pauperies, consortium ; saevitia, mollities, calvitium ; ignorantia, intellegentia ; celeritas, aedilitas, libertas ; senectus ; latitudo, mansuetudo ; clientela ; disciplina ; communio; castimonia ; matrimonium ; pinguedo ; farrago, lanugo ; consulatus, comitatus ; pictura, censura.

(II) 1) *V.* doctor, cursor, adiutrix ; legatus; comedo :—*D.* viator, funditor, ianitrix ; candidatus; sicarius ; eques, miles ; naso, centurio.
2) *V.* unguen ; lenimen ; lenimentum ; speculum ; operculum, lavacrum ; vocabulum, delubrum, latebra ; aratrum, feretrum :—*D.* acetabulum (umbraculum, tabernaculum may perhaps be taken as Verbalia).

3) *Thing effected:*

> *V.* tum, sum.

4) *Locality :*

> *D.* etum ; ctum ; ltum ; stum ; arium ; torium ; trina, tri-
> num ; īna.

5) *Object :*

> *V.* ex, ĭc- ;   *D.* āle, ăl ; āre, ăr, īle.

Deminutives appear above, p. 247, and are not repeated here.

Obs. Under other Endings, us 2 ; ius 2 ; a ; um ; is 3 ; ēs **3,**
&c., are comprised Derivatives various in meaning and origin, but
almost all concrete.

II. Adjectives :

(I.) Verbalia :

1) With Active sense .

> ns (Pres. Part.) ; urus (Fut. Part.) ; cundus ; bundus ; ax ;
> idus ; īcus, ūcus ; uus, īvus ; ŭlus ; tĭlis (a few) ; ber, bris ;
> cer, cris ; āneus.

2) With Passive sense :

> tus, sus (Perf. Part.) : ĭlĭs ; bĭlis ; tĭlis, sĭlis ; uus ; tīvus ;
> tīcius ; tāneus.

3) With sense Active or Passive .

> ndus (Gerundive).

(II.) Denominativa : with the meanings

1) ' *Belonging to :*'

> ius ; ĭcus ; tĭcus ; ānus ; iānus ; āneus ; ēnus, ēneus ; ensis,
> iensis ; ālis, āris, ārius ; īlis, ēlis, ūlis ; atilis ; īnus ; ĭvus ;
> ster, stris, stis ; timus ; nus.

2) '*Made*' or ' *consisting of :*'

> eus ; ĭnus ; nus, neus ; icius ; āceus ; ūceus.

---

3) meritum, visum. (Visio, *the seeing* ; visus 4, *the faculty of sight,* or *the fact of
sight :* visum, *the thing seen.*)

4) quercetum ; salictum ; virgultum ; arbustum ; viridarium ; praetorium ; tonstrina,
pistrinum ; officina.

5) vortex ; torale, puteal ; laqueare, calcar ; bubīle ; but *V.* sĕdile.

II. (I) 1) constans, fulgens ; dicturus, mansurus ; iracundus, verecundus ; errabundus ;
tenax ; timidus ; pudicus ; caducus ; nocuus, nocivus ; garrulus ; volatilis ;
saluber, lugubris ; volucer ; consentaneus, succedaneus.

2) notus, fessus ; docilis ; amabilis (terribilis, Act.) ; sutilis, fossilis ; mutuus ; vo-
tivus ; conducticius ; collectaneus.

3) notandus, delendus, gerundus.

(II) 1) regius, oratorius ; bellicus ; fanaticus, rusticus ; montanus, decumanus ; Caesa-
rianus ; spontaneus ; terrenus ; aēneus ; castrensis, Carthaginiensis ; hiemalis,
solaris, gregarius, senarius ; erilis, crudelis, tribulis ; aquatilis ; marinus,
libertinus ; aestivus ; pedester ; caelestis ; maritimus, legitimus ; pater-nus. (Observe colurnus by transposition for corul-nus, from corulus, *hazel.*)

2) ferreus ; faginus, fagineus ; querqus ; latericius ; hordeaceus ; pannuceus.

3) '*Full of;*' '*abounding in :*'

ōsus; olentus, ulentus, olens; idus.

4) '*Endued with*' (analogous to Perf. Part.).

ātus, ītus, ūtus.

5) '*Having the nature of :*'

stus; gnus.

6) Adjectives of Time have the endings tĭnus, tīnus; ernus, urnus.

ix. Adjectives are also derived from Particles; some from Adverbs, some from Prepositions.[1]

3) frondosus; fraudulentus, violentus, violens; herbidus. The ending o s u s often implies faultiness: glori-osus, *full of* (vain)*-glory, boastful*; fam-osus, (*full of fame*, but) *ill-famed*; mor-osus, (*full of moralities*, but) *peevish, morose.* Ul-entus, ul-ens probably combine the root of growth, **ol, ul**, with **ent-** the participial suffix. Cru-entus, *bloody*, omits **ol.**

4) auratus, togatus, auritus (from auris), astutus.

5) honestus, funestus, scelestus, robustus, venustus; abiegnus, benignus, malignus.

6) annotĭnus; hornotĭnus; serotĭnus; matutīnus, vespertīnus; aet-ernus, hib-ernus, di-urnus, noct-urnus.

Adverbs with their Derivative Adjectives :

diu; diutĭnus	hodie; hodiernus	perendie; perendĭnus
diuturnus	nimis; nimius	repente; repentĭnus
cras; crastĭnus	nuper; nuperus	simul; similis
heri; hesternus	peregre; peregrinus	temere; temerarius

Also semp-i-ternus from semper.

Prepositions with corresponding Adverbs and Adjectives are derived from various rudiments :

an-	an-te (for old Abl. anted or antid).
	(anter-us) anter-ior :—antīquus.
pos-	pos-t (for pos-te=old Abl. postid). See M. *Lucr.* iv. 1186.
	poster-us, poster-ior, postre-mus :—post-īcus.
cĭ-	ci-s; ci-tra; ci-tro :
	(citer) citer-ior, citi-mus.
ul-	ultra; ultro :
	(ulter-us) ulter-ior, ulti-mus :—ultroneus.
com	contra; contro-:
	(conter-us) :—contr-arius.
ec-	ex, e; extra; (extris) extrin-secus:
	exter-us, exter-ior, extre-mus :—externus; extraneus; extrarius.
in	in-tus; inter; intra; intro, (intris) intrin-secus :
	(inter-us) inter-ior, inti-mus :—intestinus :— internus, inferus, infer-ior, infimus, imus :—infernus.
pri-	prae; praeter:
	prior, primus; priscus; pristĭnus.
pro	pro-pe; propter:
	propior, proximus :—propinquus :—probus : pronus.
sup-	sub sus-; super, supra; subter:
	super-us, super-ior, supre-mus :—supinus. See Footnote, p. 202.
de	(di-s):
	(deter-us), deter-ior, deterrimus.
rĕ-	retro.
	Key derives reci-procus from re, pro, with suffix **cŏ** appended to each.
sē-	sīne.
clam :	
	clandestinus (lost form clan-dus).
tar- :	appears in tran-s, -ter, -tra.

x. Adjectives derived from Proper Names.

A) From Personal Names :[1]

1) Suffix **ius** :

This is the ending of Roman Nomina Gentilia (clan names) : Cornelius, Fabius, Iunius, Iulius, Tullius. As such, it is used substantively. But it is used adjectively to describe a law brought in, a road or public edifice made, by a member of any gens, as lex Roscia, via Appia, aqua Iulia, theatrum Pompeium, &c. A law brought in by two colleagues bore the twofold name, as lex Papia Poppaea de maritandis ordinibus.

2) Suffixes **anus, ianus, īnus,** imply '*belonging to*' the person : Caesar-*i*-anus, Cinn-anus, Sull-anus, August-anus (or August-ianus), &c. ; Plaut-inus, Verr-inus, &c., and 'oratio Metell-ina,' C. *Att.* i. 13.

3) Suffix -**ĕus** is poetical : Caesar-eus, Hercul-eus, Romul-eus, &c. Horace has Romula gens. Augustus is used adjectively, as domus Augusta ; historia Augusta ; so columna Traiana, portus Traianus.

4) Suffixes **ēus īus,** for Gr. -ειος, and **ĭcus** for Gr. -ικος, are used in personal Adjectives from the Greek : Pythagorēus, Aristotelīus, Socrat-īcus, &c.

B) Gentilia : from Names of People, Cities, Towns, &c.

These are properly Adjectives ; but often used Substantively.

1) Suffix **anus,** chiefly from Places in **a** or **ae** : Alba-nus, Roma-nus, Theba-nus ; but also from some Places in um or i : as Tuscul-anus, Puteol-anus.

2) Suffix **īnus,** from Places in **ia, ium** : Amer-inus (Ameria), Aric-inus (Aricia), Clus-inus (Clusium). Observe also Praenest-inus (Praeneste), Reat-inus (Reate), Tarent-inus (Tarentum).

---

[1] *Roman Names.*—A Roman of distinction had at least three names : the Praenomen, individual name ; the Nomen, name shewing the Gens or clan ; the Cognomen, surname, shewing the Familia or family. Thus, L. Iunius Brutus expressed Lucius of the Gens Iunia and Familia Brutorum. To these were often added Agnomina, titles either of honour (Africanus, Asiaticus, Coriolanus, Creticus, Isauricus, Macedonicus, Numidicus, Magnus, Maximus, &c.), or expressing that a person had been adopted from another Gens : Aemilianus, (*adopted from the Gens Aemilia*), Domitianus, Licinianus, Mucianus, Octavianus, Salvianus, Seianus, Terentianus, Titianus, and many more. The full name of Augustus (originally an Octavius) when adopted by his uncle's will and adorned by the Senate with a title, was Gaius Iulius Caesar Octavianus Augustus.

The Roman Gentes were either patrician (Cornelia, Iulia, &c.) or plebeian (Licinia, Memmia, Coruncania, &c.) : or there might be a patrician and plebeian gens of the same race, as of the Claudii. Theoretically they are referred to ancestors, whose Nomina give them their titles ; being themselves due to various circumstances. Some Gentes are derived from *Numerals* : Quinctia, Quinctilia (Pompeia, Pompilia, Pomponia, Pontia), Sestia, Septimia, Octavia, Nonia, Decia : so Postumia. Some from *Colours* : Albia, Caesia, Flavia, Fulvia, Helvia, Livia, Rubria, Rutilia. Some from *Animals* : Aquillia, Asinia, Apronia, Caninia, Canuleia, Ovidia, Porcia, Verria. Many from *Personal peculiarities* : Caecilia, Calidia, Catia, Claudia, Cordia, Curtia, Digitia, Genucia, Hirtia, Iuventia, Licinia, Naevia, Opimia, Pedia, Plancia, Plautia, Silia, Spuria, Stertinia, Turpilia, Varia, Valgia, Vegetia, Vitellia, &c. Others are derived from *Office, business, station, birthplace.*

3) Suffix **as** from Places in **na nae num no** : Fiden-as (Fidenae), Arpin-as (Arpinum), Aquin-as (Aquin-um), Capēn-as (Capena), Frusin-as (Frusino). Also Anti-as (Antium), Arde-as (Ardea). These are declined in **āt-**, like nostras, vestras, optimates, Penates.

4) Suffix **ensis** from Places in **o**, and from some in **a ae um** : Narbon-ensis, Cann-ensis, Mediolan-ensis. Some take **i-ensis** : Athen-i-ensis, Carthagin-i-ensis.

The same Suffix may represent Gr. εύς, as Chalcid-ensis (Χαλκιδεύς). But **eus** is also kept : Demetrius Phalereus, Zeno Citieus or Citiensis. We find Zeuxis Heracleotes for Heracleensis.

5) Peculiar Latin Adjectives of Place are :
Caer-es (it-) from Caere : Camers, from Camerinum : Veiens, from Veii ; Tiburs from Tibur : but, when things are qualified, the usual forms are Caeret-anus, Camert-inus, Veient-anus, Tiburt-inus.

6) The Suffixes **ius** (ιος), **aeus** (αιος), **enus** (ηνός) belong to Adjectives derived from the Names of Greek Places : Corinthius, Rhodius, Lacedaemonius, Larissaeus, Smyrnaeus, Cyzicenus.

7) The Greek Suffixes **ātes ītes ōtes** are rare in Latin : Spartiates, Tegeates (but the Adjective forms are Spartanus, Tegeaeus) ; Abderites (but also Abderitanus) ; Epirotes, Heracleotes.

8) Feminine Gentile Names are in **a ĭs ăs** : Cressa, *Cretan*, Ausonis, *Ausonian*, Troas, *Trojan woman*.

C) Names of People are either derived from Names of Countries and of Cities : Latinus (Latium), Romanus (Roma), Siceliotes (Sicilia), or they are Primitive : Afer, Gallus, Syrus, Thrax, Cres (*Cretan*). Such Names form Adjectives in **ĭcus ius aeus ensis**, &c. : Africus, Gallicus, Syrius, Thracius, Cretaeus, Cretensis, Creticus, &c.

With Personal Names the primitive is often used adjectively, as poeta Hispanus, miles Gallus, &c. Poets use it with Appellatives : Marsus aper, venena Colcha, flumen Rhenum, flumen Medum, Hor.; and so Fem. Adjectives : Ausonis ora, Cressa pharetra, Verg.

---

or *residence*, &c. : Antistia, Aurelia, Cluentia, Coelia, Coponia, Cornificia, Curia, Duilia or Duillia, Falcidia, Flaminia, Fonteia, Furnia, Gabinia, Hortensia, Maria, Nautia, Scribonia, Servia, Silvia, &c. The Gens Iulia is traced back to Iulus ; Titia to Titus ; Tullia to Tullus, &c.

The Cognomina are similarly distinguishable : in the oldest times the birthplace or residence often gave a Cognomen ; which sometimes descended to the Family, Camerinus, Sabinus, but usually not, as Auruncus, Caeliomontanus, Fidenas, Privernas, Siculus, Soranus, Tuscus, &c.

Colours give rise to Cognomina : Albus, Flavus, Niger, Pullus, Rufus, Rutilus. *Animals* : Asina, Bestia, Buteo, Canina, Catulus, Catullus, Corvus, Cossus, Galba, Gallus, Lupus, Merula, Mus, Noctua, Porcina, Pulex, Taurus, Verres, Vitulus. *Vegetables* : Caepio, Cicero, Piso ; Lactucinus. *Parts of the Body* : Arvina, Axilla, Barbula, Crus, Denter, Nerva, Sura, Sulla (for Surula), Scapula : and with Suffix **on** (**o**) indicating size or prominence of the feature : Capito (*big-head*), Fronto (*big-brow*), Labeo, (*thick lips*), Mento (*chinny*), Naso(*big nose* : but Nasica, *sharp nose*), Pedo (*splay foot*), &c. *Implements* : Caligula, Carbo, Caudex, Dolabella, Fusus, Malleolus, Marculus, Marcellus, Pera, Pulvillus, Scipio, Stolo, Spinther, &c. *Office, station, business, ability*, &c. : Albinus, Bubulcus, Camillus, Cursor, Cornicen, Cunctator, Figulus, Hortator, Metellus,

SECTION II.

Derivation of Verbs.

A) Verba Verbalia.

Inchoativa (Inceptiva) in **sco** 3.　§ 53, p. 209, &c.
Imitativa in **isso** I.
Frequentativa in **so, ito** I.　　　⎫
Deminutiva in **illo** I.　　　　　　⎬ § 53, p. 205.
　　　　　　　　　　　　　　　　　⎭
Desiderativa in **urio** 4.　§ 53, p. 206.

B) Verba Denominativa.

Most Verbs in Conj. 1 and 4 are from Substantives or Adjectives :
the greater number being Transitive.

laud-are I.	*praise*	dit-are I.	*enrich*
milit-are I.	*serve in war*	liber-are I.	*set free*
nomin-are I	*name*	sollicit-are I.	*make anxious*
fin-ire 4.	*end*	insan-ire 4.	*be mad*
vest-ire 4.	*clothe*	moll-ire 4.	*soften*
pisc-ari I.	*fish*	laet-ari I.	*rejoice*
mol-iri 4.	*contrive*	larg-iri 4.	*bestow*

Suffixes **ul ol cin it ĭg-** (=**ăg-**) **ĭc-** occur in Conj. 1 :

grat-ul-ari	*congratulate*	nav-ig-are	*sail*
vi-ol-are	*do violence*	mit-ig-are	*soften*
sermo-cin-ari	*discourse*	claud-ic-are	*limp*
debil-it-are	*weaken*	commun-ic-are	*impart*

So iur-g-are for iur-ig-are, pur-g-are for pur-ig-are.

Most in Conj. 2 are from Substantives ; a few from Adjectives :
the greater number being Intransitive :

　　　　call-ēre, luc-ēre, flor-ēre, flav-ēre.

A few U-verbs 3 are Denominativa :

　　　　acu-ĕre, metu-ĕre, minu-ĕre, tribu-ĕre.

Obs. Some Roots have a Trans. and an Intrans. Verb corresponding to each other: fugare, *to put to flight* ; fugĕre, *to fly.* So cae-
dĕre, cadĕre ; iacĕre, iacēre ; liquare, liquēre ; pendĕre, pendēre ;
plăcare, plăcēre ; sēdare, sĕdēre and sīdĕre.

Natta, Paterculus, Rex, Regulus, Salinator, Vespillo. *Personal peculiarities, characteristics
or accidents* : Ahenobarbus, Ambustus, Balbus, Barbatus, Brutus, Caecus, Caesar, Cato,
Celer, Celsus, Cerco, Cinna, Cincinnatus, Claudus, Cornutus, Crispus, Crassus, Curvus,
Dentatus, Felix, Festus, Flaccus, Flamma, Frugi, Geminus, Glabrio, Gurges, Laha-
tus, Lentulus, Lepidus, Longus, Nepos, Nobiliòr, Paetus, Pansa, Pilatus, Paullus,
Pollio, Potitus, Plancus, Plautus, Poplicola, Postumus, Priscus, Proculus, Pulcher, Scaeva,
Scaevola, Strabo, Torquatus, Tremulus, Trigeminus, Tubero, Varro, Varus, Verrucosus,
Vetus, Vulso.

Many Cognomina in **anus inus** were originally Adjectives derived from an earlier
Cognomen : Augurinus, Censorinus, Mamercinus, Paetanus, Rufinus, Silanus, &c.

An Agnomen of honour sometimes became a Cognomen of the family. Thus in the
Valerian clan (which had also the Agnomina Poplicola and Maximus) we find a family be-
coming Corvini from Valerius Corvus, and another branch Messallae from the capture of
Messana. Of many Cognomina as well as Nomina the origin cannot be traced.

SECTION III.

Derivation of Particles.

i. Primitive Particles in Latin are few. Of these most belong also to kindred language. Such are

> ab; ante; ambi- ; di- dis- ; ex ; in, indu- in- ; pro ; pri- prae ; per per- (παρά and περί) ; ob (ἐπί?) sub ; cum co- (σύν?, κοινός) ; et, at ; aut (?) ; que ; ne ; an ; si ; semi- ; sem- or sim- ; heri.

A few cannot be traced with certainty beyond Italian language. Such are

> ad ; de ; re- ; sē- ; sine ; cis ; uls ; haud ; cras ; sat.

ii. Most Latin Particles are either derived or compounded.

1) Derived Particles are either

>   *a*) Denominative (from Substantives, Adjectives, or Participles) ; or
>
>   *b*) Pronominal (from Pronouns).
>
>   *c*) A few only are from other Particles.

Derived Adverbs in general are either Cases of their themes, or formed from them with peculiar Endings, in the manner of Cases.

The Cases which chiefly form Particles are the Accusative, the Ablative, the Locative.

2) Particles may be compounded of the same or various Parts of Speech.[1]

---

[1] From the List in pp. 228, &c. the student will be able to select examples of compounded Particles.

I. Relative:

1) with its own Particles and Elements: quamquam, quoquo, ubiubi, utut, &c. : quacumque, undecumque, utcumque, quotiescumque, &c. : quŏque, ubique, undique, utique, usque, usquequaque, umquam, uspiam, usquam : quippe : quousque : (with uter) utrubi, utrimque, utroque, &c.

2) with Prefix *ne* : neque ; nec ; nequaquam, nequiquam, neutiquam ; numquam, nuspiam, nusquam, neutrubi, nēcubi.

3) with Prefix *ali-* ; aliquo, aliquam, aliquantum, alicubi, aliquoties ; with other Demonstrative Prefixes: tamquam, sicuti, sicut, namque, nempe, atque ; with Prepositions: antequam, perquam, postquam, praequam, praeterquam, praeut, prout ; with Conjunctions : at-qui, nun-cubi, si-cubi, si-cunde, &c. : with Adjectives : alioqui, ceteroqui, priusquam.

4) with Demonstrative Suffixes : quonam, quanam, ubinam, utinam, &c. ; with suffixed Prepositions : quoad, quapropter, quocirca, quatenus, aliquatenus, &c. ; with Conjunctions : quasi, quin, &c. ; with Verbs : quamvis, quovis, quolibet, ubivis, &c. ; with Nouns : quomodo ; quare, cur ; quemadmodum, quamobrem, quominus, utpote, &c.

II. Demonstratives :

Compounded with each other: hi-c, illi-c, &c. : hin-c, illin-c, &c. ; hu-c, illu-c, &c., alibi, aliu-ta, i-ta (for ita-d), i-tem, si-c, e-nim, etenim ; ast (at-set C. ?), au-tem, tamen (tam in?) ideo : With Prepositions: adeo, adhuc, dein, exin, proin, abhinc, dehinc, inibi, interibi, postibi ; interim ; anteā, antideā, antehac, antidhac, posteā, postideā, posthac, postillā, intereā, praetereā, praeterhac, hacpropter (compare quapropter); hactenus, eatenus ; horsum (hovorsum), illorsum, &c. From dein is formed dein-ceps (capio).

Igitur is of obscure derivation.

iii. Denominative Adverbs in the form of Cases.

A) In the form of Accusative :

a) From Substantives :

1) Uncompounded : (perhaps) partim, *partly* ; foras (pl.), *out of doors* ; and (rarely) vicem, *in the stead* ; diu, *a long time* (for dium).

2) Compounded with Particles, admodum, affatim, comminus, eminus, invicem, incassum, obiter, obviam, propediem, propemodum, postmodum.
Clam, coram, palam, perperam, saltem or saltim are of questionable origin.

b) From Adjectives :

1) in **am** : bifariam, &c. p. 149 : multifariam, plurifariam, *in many parts* ; promiscam, protinam (Plaut.): in **as** : alias.

2) in **um** : ceterum, circum, clanculum, commodum, demum, nimium, solum, verum : —multum, paullum, parum, tantum, quantum, &c., primum, secundum, iterum, &c., plerumque ; with many Superl. minimum, plurimum, potissimum, postremum, summum, ultimum, &c. (Non, *not*, anc. noen-um for ne-unum).

3) in **ĕ** (from real or supposed Adj. in **ĭs**) : abundĕ, facilĕ, apprimĕ, impunĕ, propĕ, paenĕ, saepĕ, &c. On procliv-i, -e, see Madv. *C. Fin.* 14 ; M. *Lucr.* ii. 455.

4) in **ŭs, ĭs** (Comparative) : plus, minus, melius, potius, saepius, magis (nimis?), &c. &c. &c.　Also secus, tenus, protenus.

5) Recens for recenter is a special instance.

Obs. 1. Add to these the Compounds with vorsum (versum), as aliorsum, prorsum, rursum, &c.　Some of these often use the Nom. form : prorsus, rursus, &c.

Obs. 2. Poets freely use Neuter Adjectives Sing. (sometimes Plur.) adverbially : ' perfidum ridens Venus,' Hor. ; ' crassum ridet Vulfenius,' Pers. ; ' dulce loquentem Lalagen,' Hor. ; ' suave locus resonat,' Hor. ; ' sedet aeternumque sedebit,' Verg. ; ' sera comantem narcissum,' Verg.　See p. 374.

B) In the form of Ablative :

a) From Substantives :

1) in **o** : modŏ (o being shortened) ; ergō, numerō ; and the Compounds, extemplō, profectō, postmodŏ, saepenumerō ; magnopere or magno opere, &c., ilicō (in loco), oppidō (ἐπὶ πέδῳ ?).

[The peculiar words anteā (for ante ea), antehac (for ante haec), &c., have been variously explained.　Some scholars, as Bücheler, take the Pronouns to be Ablatives, dating from a time when the Prepositions ante, post, inter, praeter, &c., may have been constructed with that case : and they cite arvorsum eād in the *Senat. Cons. de Bacch.*, also apud sēd, inter sēd, which are found.　But Corssen, who discusses the matter, *Ausspr.* ii. 455, &c., takes the Pronouns to be Accus. Pl. with the ancient long quantity, and eād, sēd, mēd, eā, hāc, to be Accus. also, the **d** growing out of a temporary confusion of Accus. and Abl. forms at an era when the Abl. was losing its old final **d.**　This view seems right.]

2) in ŏ : fortĕ, iurĕ, ritĕ, spontĕ.

3) in ĭs (pl.) : gratis or gratiis ; ingratis or ingratiis ; foris. M. *Lucr.* iii. 935.

b) From Adjectives and Participles :

1) in ā (orig. Abl. ād, underst. parte or viā) : dextrā, laevā, sinistrā : the Pronouns eā, hac, aliā, &c.

To this formation belong all the Prepositions in ā, which are really Ablatives Fem. (circā, citrā, ultrā, contrā, &c.).

2) in ō orig. ōd (but citŏ) : certo, composito, continuo, consulto, falso, merito, raro, subito, tuto, vero, &c. &c., bipartito, &c., inopinato, necopinato ; primo, secundo, &c. : immo : Superl. meritissimo, postremo, supremo, ultimo, praesto : omnino, from a lost omninus : Cp. denuo (de novo).

To this formation belong the Prepositional Adverbs citro, ultro, intro, porro, retro, contro- from Adjectives in -ter (from *tara,* comparative suffix).

3) in ī : brevi, perbrevi (dicto or tempore).

4) in īs : alternis (vicibus) ; paucis (verbis) ; imprimis or in primis ; cum primis.

C) In the form of Locative (Place or Time) ; heri ; domi ; humi ; ruri ; temperi ; vesperi or vespere ; mane (mani) ; diu, *by day* ; noctu or nocti ; ho-die ; pri-die ; postri-die ; peren-die (πέραν), *the day after to-morrow* ; cotidie. Pl. quot-annis.

(The forms diu, *long,* perdiu and perdius, *all day,* interdius, interdiu, *in the daytime,* are by C. considered to be Accusative.)

iv. Denominative Adverbs with Adverbial Endings.

These Endings are principally

ē (ĕ) ; tĕr (ŏr), īter ; tĭm, sĭm ; tus ; iens or ies.

1) Adverbs in ē are derived from Adjectives and Participles of the **o**-declension :

alt-ē, caut-ē, miser-ē, pulchr-ē, &c. &c. &c.

Benĕ, malĕ were shortened early, like modŏ.

Obs. ē appears to be an anc. Abl. for e-d. See p. 46.

2) Adverbs with the Compar. ending **ter,** īter are derived chiefly from Adjj. of the Cons. and I-declensions :

audac-ter (audac-iter), difficul-ter, felic-īter, fortī-ter, mollī-ter, parī-ter, &c. &c. **Tĭ** falls out : decen-ter for decenti-ter, &c. Ali-ter is from the old form alis.

Some O-Adjj. form Advv. in **ter** as well as in ē :

dur-ē and dur-īter : human-ē and human-īter ; luculent-ē and luculen-ter, &c.

3) Adverbs in **tĭm, sĭm** are derived

a) from Perf. Participles :

coniunc-tim, minu-tim, praeser-tim, ráp-tim ; pede-tentim, *step by step* (pedem tendere) ; sta-tim, *immediately* ; cursim, pas-sim, sen-sim, seor-sim, &c. &c.

b) from Substantives or Adjectives :

fur-tim, uber-tim ; vicis-sim ; singul-tim, &c.

Obs. Some form **ē** as well as **im** :

gravat-ē or -im ; separat-ē or im, &c.

4) Adverbs in **tus** are from (1) Substantives : cael-ĭ-tus; fund-ĭ-tus ; radic-ĭ-tus ; pen-ĭ-tus : (2) Adjectives : divin-ĭ-tus : (3) Prepositions : in-tus ; sub-tus. Mord-ĭcus, *with the teeth*, is peculiar.

5) On the Numeral Adverbs in **1ens** (**1ēs**) see § **33**.

v. Derivation of Pronominal Particles.

Pronominal Stems give birth to various Case-form Particles (Conjunctions and Adverbs), and again to various inseparable Elements, which enter into the composition of other Particles.

1) The Interrogative and Relative Stem **quŏ, quĭ** (Prim. *ka*) : whence the Case-form Particles

quom or cum, quam, quod ; quō, quī, quā ; and the Elements *u- um- us-* (whence u-bi, un-de, us-que, umquam, &c.) [1] *-que* (*-pe?*) *-cumque.*

The Demonstrative Stems

2) **ĭ, ĭŏ** : whence the Particles eā, eo, and (with Suff.) i-bi : and the Element *im* which with *-de* forms the Particle in de.

3) **tŏ, tă** : whence the Particles tam, tum, and (with Suff. *ĭ* for *ce*) tun-c : also the Elements *-tem -tă -tĭ, -tŏ.*

By composition of **ĭ** with **tŏ** is formed the Pronoun iste (for istus), whence the Particles isti-c, istu-c, istim, istin-c, &c. Also ĭ-ta, ĭta-que, ĭ-tem, ĭ-ti-dem, &c.

4) **nŏ, nă** : whence the Particles nam, num, and (with Suff. **c**) nun-c ; ne : and the Elements *-nam, -num, -ne.*

5) **hŏ, hĭ** (anc. **sŏ, sĭ**) : whence (with **c**) the Particles hi-c, hu-c, ha-c, si-c : and the Elements *ho-, him-* : whence the Particle hin-c.

6) **ol, ul, il,** forms the Pronoun ille (for ol-us), and gives birth to its Particles, illi-c, illu-c, ill-im, illin-c, illa-c, and ōlim.

7) **ăl, ălĭ** : compounded with **ĭ, ĭŏ** gives rise to the Pronominals alius (al-is) al-ter, and forms or enters into numerous Particles, aliō, aliā, al-ibi, ali-ter, &c.

8) **cĭ** forms the Prep. ci-s and the Element *cĕ* (*c*), which becomes a Suffix to so many Pronouns and Particles.

Note. Other Particles formed by Pronom. Stems in Composition with each other, with their own Elements, and with various Prefixes and Suffixes, are shewn in the Footnote, p. 255.

---

[1] Corssen formerly (*Kr. B.* 1.) adopted the common view, that u-bi, un-de, u-ti (ut), u-ter and Cpp. are from the Rel. **quo-**, dropping the guttural. But in *Kr. N.* 26, he subscribes to the opinion of H. Weber, that their root is a Demonstr. Pron. **u**, which assumes also Interrog. and Rel. power : and that -c-u-bi, -c-un-de, -c-u-ter are distinct Rel. formations. The question must be regarded as still ' sub iudice.'

Obs. 1. The Dual Pronoun u-ter (Gr. πότερος or κότερος) forms Particles of its own and in composition with many above named.

Obs. 2. Corssen forms e-t, a-t, au-t, au-tem, by composition of the Prim. Pronom. Stem ă with the Stem tŏ. This may also be the strengthening element e in e-nim, e-quidem, ec-ce (for e-ce).

Obs. 3. The Particles dum, iam, with the Elements -dam, -dem, -do, -dĕ, -dum, also -iam, have been usually assigned to a Pronominal Stem; but Corssen (*Kr. Beitr.* p. 197, &c.) derives all these forms (with diu, dius) from the Sanskrit Root *div, to shine,* whence dyus = dies. Compare propediem.[1]

The Elements -pe and -iam form the compound Element -piam.

vi. Some other Particles.

With the suffix per are formed aliquant-is-per, paul-is-per, tant-is-per,[2] parum-per, nuper (novi-per) and sem-per, *once for all, always,* from root *sama,* as sem-el, singuli, simplex, &c.

As a prefix, per is intensive : per-multum, per-iucunde, &c. &c.

C. derives de-mu-m, de-ni-que from Adjectives formed by de : immo from an Adjective in-mus.

Mox (μόγ-ις?), vix, saepe, procul, haud or hau, are obscure. On the last see C. *Ausspr.* i. 205.

The Conj. licet is a Verb : its compounds ilicet (ire licet), scilicet (scire licet), videlicet (videre licet), are sentences.

Dumtaxat (dum taxat), '*while one estimates*' = *merely,* is a clause.

Vel, vĕ is from velle, *to choose.* Nimirum, *no doubt* = mirum est ni.

Fors is a Subst. used adverbially, (it is) *a chance, perchance* : and in forsit, forsitan, *perhaps* (for fors sit, for sit an). Fortassis = forte an si vis, for which is used fortasse, *perhaps.*

Prepositions are compounded together in de-super, in-super.

SECTION IV.

The Composition of Words.

i. Composition takes place when two words are so joined as to form one word.

---

[1] The Particles formed by this class of enclitics are:

a) quon-dam ; β) quĭ-dem, ibĭ-dem, utrobĭ-dem, indĭ-dem, itĭ-dem, indentĭ-dem, prĭ-dem and Cpp. tan-dem, tanti-dem, tantun-dem : γ) un-de and Cpp., in-de, ali-un-de, quam-de ; δ) quan-do and Cpp. aliquan-do, &c. : ε) du-dum (for diu-dum), ne-dum, non-dum, nec-dum, haud-dum, nihil-dum, vix-dum, primum-dum, etiam-dum, inter-dum : also with the Imperatives age-dum, mane-dum, *stay a bit,* fac-dum, *do just,* ades-dum, &c.). ζ) iamiam, et-iam, nunc-iam, quon-iam, us-p-iam, nus-p-iam. C. forms qui-a from qui-iam. On iamiam, see M. *Lucr.* iii. 894.

Donec is for do-ni-que, do-ni- being an Adjectival form from the root diu-s. M. *Lucr.* v. 997. Donicum in Plautus = donec cum.

Other compounds of diu-s are tamdiu, quamdiu, aliquamdiu, perdiu, interdiu and interdius, nudius.

[2] The suffix ' is (= ius)' is used in Comparison of Degree (mag-is), Time (paul-is-) or Place (sin-is-ter). It is found also as us (minus, secus, &c.).

(Only Nouns and Verbs are here considered: the Composition of Particles being shewn in Section III.)

The latter word in Composition is Fundamental, the former Determinative.

Sometimes the words are so joined that one actually agrees with the other :[1]

res-publica ; ius-iurandum ; tres-viri :

or that the second actually governs the first :

senatus-consultum ; veri-similis.

Such compounds can be severed :

resque publica ; senatusve consulta.

But generally one part or both lose the form of words :

magnanimus ; Troiugena ; artifex.

ii. Composition of Words may be (1) *constructive*, when one of the parts in a Noun or a Verb has the nature of a Case governed by the other part : (2) *attributive*, when the first part in a Substantive attributively qualifies the second : (3) *adverbial*, when the first part adverbially modifies the second : (4) *possessive*, when Adjectives are so compounded as to imply 'having' the fundamental part in some qualified manner, or 'not having' it.[2]

A) Substantives are compounded

1) *constructively* ; when the parts are

S. × V. : agri-cola (qui agrum colit) :

---

[1] *Parathetic* Compounds, in which either the parts actually agree, or the first is governed by the second, are very few : as (1) iusiurandum, *oath* ; (2) agricultura ; aurifodinae, *gold-mine* ; iurisconsultus, *civil lawyer*, ludimagister, *schoolmaster* ; pater- mater-filius-familias ; plebi-scitum ; (3) verisimilis , (4) lucrifacere, pessumdare, venumdare, vilipendere.

In Pronouns we find such forms as alteruter, quotusquisque, quisquis, &c. ; and in Numerals *additive* Compounds : as duo-decim, tertius-decimus, &c. ; *subtractive* ; as un-de-viginti, duo-de-triginta, &c. ; *multiplicative* : as ducenti, treceni, &c.

[2] Examples of *Synthetic* Composition.

A) Substantives :

S. × V. The Verb-roots which form constructive Compounds with determinative Substantives are principally these : ăg- caed- căpi- căn- col- făci- (fĭc-) dīc- lĕg- spĕci- : as remex, remigium, navigium ; homi-cida, parri-cida (-cidium) ; auceps, aucupium, manceps (-cipium), municeps (-cipium), particeps (-cipium) ; bucina, fĭdi-cen (-cĭna), tĭbĭ-cen (-cĭna), tubi-cen, galli-cinium, *cock-crowing* ; caelicola, ruricola ; aedificium, arti-fex (-ficium), carnifex, opifex, pontifex ; sacrificium ; veneficium ; causs-idicus, *pleader* ; iudex, iudicium ; florilegium, sortilegus, sorti-legium, spicilegium ; auspex, auspicium, exti-spex (-spicium), haruspex. Other examples are : funambulus, *rope-dancer* ; nomenclator, *namecaller* (călare) ; nau-frăgium, *shipwreck* ; caprimulgus, *goat-milker* ; puer-pera (-perium) from parĕre, also vi-pera (for vivi-para) : stipendium (for stipi-pendium), libripens ; faenisex ; iustitium, *stoppage of law-courts* (ius sistere), solstitium ; lectisternium ; nas-turtium ; aedituus (aedem tuens), &c.

S. × *S.* : viti-sator (vitium sator).

2) *attributively* ; when the parts are

A. × *S.* or *N.* (Numeral) × *S.* : pleni-lunium : tri-ennium.

3) *adverbially* ; when the parts are

N. × *V.* or *P.* × *V.* : prin-ceps ; in-ĕdia.

Note. *P.* × *S.* may be (1) *constructive*: inter-montium ; or (2) *adverbial* : com-mercium ; nihil (ne-hilum, ni-hilum, Lucr. iv. 516).

B) Adjectives are compounded

1) *constructively* ; when the parts are

S. × *V.* : armi-ger ; melli-fluus.

P. × *S.*, when *S.* is in the nature of a governed Case : exspēs.

2) *adverbially*, when the parts are

A. × *V.* : *N.* × *V.* : *P.* × *V.* : omni-potens ; bi-fĭdus ; bene-volus.

N. × *A.* : *P.* × *A.* : semi-vivus, septem-geminus ; immemor.

S × *V.* Substantives of this form are few : caprificus, *wild fig* ; iuglans (Iovis glans) ; manupretium ; rupicapra, *chamois*.

A × *S.* Substt. few : latifundium ; privilegium ; viviradix ; medi-astīnus.

N. × *S.* numerous : see § 33 with bi- tri- &c.: as ilibra, biduum, biennium, &c. ; decempeda, *ten-foot pole* ; teruncius, *three-ounce coin* ; also with semi- sesqui- : sembella (for semi-libella), selibra (for semilibra), semideus, semihomo, semihora, semivir ; semuncia, sescuncia, sesquihora, sesquimensis, &c.

N. × *V.* : *P.* × *V.* : rare : for such words as accola, incola, advena, convena, ambages, coiux, conviva, dedecus, incus, indigena, ingenium, indoles, proles, suboles, obiex or obex, obses, perfuga, transfuga, praefica, praeses, &c. may be treated as derivatives of the Compound Verbs accolo, incolo, advenio, &c., or, at least, as coordinate with these.

P. × *S.* (1) *constructive* : adverbium, ambarvalia, amburbium, conclave, ingluvies, interlunium, internecio, internundinum, intervallum, pomoerium, postliminium, proconsul, promunturium, pronomen, propraetor, subsellium, supellex, supercilium. (2) *adverbial* : abavus, abnepos, abneptis, administer, adminiculum, adnepos, agnomen, cognomen, coheres, commilito, compes, condiscipulus, conservus, consobrinus, contubernium, convallis ; deunx, dodrans ; ignominia, impluvium, incuria, intemperies, internuntius, interpres, interrex, interregnum ; nefas, negotium, nemo, persona, praenomen, praesaepe, proavus, progener, promulsis, pronepos, pronepotis, remora, subcenturio, subpromus, superficies.

B) Adjectives.

S. × *V.* chiefly poetic : from the following and other Verb-roots : cĭn- dĭc- fĕr- fĭc- frăg- flŭ- fŭg- gĕn- gĕr- lĕg- son- vaga- vom- : faticīnus, fatidĭcus, aurifer, munifĭcus, naufrăgus ; mellifluus, lucifŭgus, nubigĕnus, belliger, morigĕrus, florilĕgus, fluctisŏnus, nemorivăgus, flammivŏmus. Add arcitenens, velivolus, &c. ; armipotens, caelipotens, &c. See Examples of *P.* × *S.* in next page.

A. × *V.* : *N.* × *V.* : *P.* × *V.* : from the following and other Verb-roots : dĭc- fĭc- fĭd- flu- lŏqu- sci- son- vaga- vola- : veridĭcus, mirificus, multifidus, largifluus, vaniloquus, dulcisonus, solivagus, altisonus ; quadrifidus, septemfluus ; conscius, inscius, nescius, praescius, benefĭcus, malevŏlus, necopinus, innuba, &c. Horrisonus, terrificus, &c. take their determinative part from the rudiment of the Verbs horrere, terrere. Words like invidus, providus, profŭgus, &c., may be regarded as derivatives of the Verbs invideo, provideo, profugio, &c.

N. × *A.* : chiefly determined by semi-, a few by sesqui- and other numerals : semibarbarus, semihians, seminudus, sesquioctavus, trigeminus, &c.

3) *possessively* ; when the parts are

    A. × *S.* : *N.* × *S.* : magn-animus; centi-ceps.

    S. × *S.* : ali-pes ; igni-comus.

    P. × *S.* : when *S.* is not in the nature of a governed Case :

        con-cors, in-numerus, prae-ceps.

C) Verbs are compounded

    1) *constructively* ; when the parts are

    S. × *V.* : belli-gerare (= bellum gerere).

P. × *A.* :

com- implies *union* : compar, compos, consimilis, &c.

ex- intensifies : edurus, efferus, &c.

ob- implies '*coming in face* :' oblongus.

per- '*throughout, in a high degree* :' pervigil ; perdifficilis.

prae- (1) '*excess* :' praelongus, praecelsus; (2) '*priority* :' praecanus, *prematurely grey* ;' praeposterus, *last first, inverse* ; (3) '*extremity* :' praeustus, *burnt at the tip.*

pro- *forward* : procurvus, propatulus.

rĕ- rĕd- *back* : recurvus ; *again,* redivivus.

sub- diminishes : subobscurus, *rather dark,* subtristis, *somewhat sad.*

vē-=malĕ : vēsanus, *mad*=malesanus.

nĕ- is privative : nefandus, nefastus, *impious.*

in- (inseparable negative=Greek ἀν-) forms numerous Cp. Adjectives : impar, impotens, impius, ingratus, insanus, infidelis, inutilis, ignarus, ignavus, ignotus, ignobilis, illotus, irritus, &c. &c. &c.

A. × *S.* : *N.* × *S.* : *S.* × *S.* : unanim-is (us), '*having*' one *mind*, longi-manus, '*having*' *long hands* : tripes, '*having*' *three feet* : anguicomus, *snake-haired.* So aequaevus, longaevus, multiformis, misericors ; sollers ; biennis, bifrons, triceps, trilinguis, &c. &c. ; cornipes, sonipes, &c.

P. × *S.* (1) When *P.* is of adverbial nature :

anceps (ambi-ceps), *double-headed, doubtful.*

coaevus, *concurring in time* : cognominis, communis, concolor, confinis, consanguineus, consonus, consors, conterminus, &c. &c.

discolor, *divided (differing) in colour* ; discors, dissonus, &c.

imbellis, *unwarlike* ; imberbis, *beardless* ; immanis, implumis, importunus, inanimis (us), inerm-is (us), iners, infamis, informis, infrenis, illimis, illunis, inglorius, iniurius, insomnis, invius (but insignis from in *in, on*), &c. &c. &c.

obscenus, obscurus, obvius.

pervius.

praeceps, praesignis, praevius, &c.

proclivis, profundus, &c.

vecors.

(2) When *P.* has a prepositional nature : see p. 261. 1).

abnormis, amens, avius, &c.

acclivis, affinis, &c.

antelucanus, antemeridianus, antesignanus, &c.

circumforaneus.

cisalpinus, cisrhenanus, cispadanus, &c.

commodus.

declivis, decolor, deformis, degener, delirus, demens, devius, &c.

effrenus, effrons, egregius, elinguis, enervis, enodis, enormis, exanimis, excors, exheres, exlex, exsanguis, exsomnis, exsors, extorris, &c.

obnoxius, opportunus.

perduellis, perennis, perfidus, periurus, pernox, &c.

pomeridianus.

profanus, profestus, prosperus.

securus, sedulus, &c.

subdialis, subdolus, sublucanus, subsignanus, subsolanus, subterraneus, suburbanus, &c.

transalpinus, transmarinus, &c.

C) Verbs.

S. × *V.* : aedificare, significare ; litigare ; vociferari, morigerari.

A. × *V.* : aequi-parare (= aequum parare).

V. × *V.* : cale-facere (= calere facere), cale-fieri.

2) *adverbially* ; when the parts are

P. × *V.* : bene-dicere ; ne-quire ; ab-ducere, and all Verbs similarly compounded.

P. × *S.* or *P.* × *A.* : ef-feminare : e-rudire.[1]

Note. Words which have two Determinative parts are called Decomposita : im-per-turbatus. On Compound Words in Latin see M. *Lucr.* p. 312–313.

A. × *V.* : amplificare, gratificari, &c.

V. × *V.* : These are the Compp. of Verb-roots with facio, fio. See p. 217, and on the quantity of e see Prosody.

[1] The student may usefully test the force of Verbs compounded with Prepositions by comparing, with the help of a good Dictionary, the meanings and uses of the Compounds of the oldest and most obvious Simple Verbs : such as ago, cado, caedo, cano, capio, cedo, curro, dico, do (dhâ), duco, emo, eo, facio, fero, habeo, iacio, lĕgo, mitto, moveo, nosco, pleo, pono, porto, quaero, rego, rogo, sedeo, sto, sisto, sum, teneo, tendo, veho, venio, verto, video, voco.

Composition of Verbs with Prepositions.

When compounded with Verbs :

1. Ab, a, abs (*from, away*) always denotes '*separation*;' absum, *am away*; abeo, *go away*; aufero, *take away*; abstineo, *refrain from*, &c. Note abdīco (me magistratu), *resign office*; abrogo (legem, &c.), *repeal.* Abundo, *flow over, abound*; abutor, *use up, abuse*, contain the notion of *excess.*

2. Ad (*to, at, near*) generally denotes, (1) '*approach, presence at or near*;' adsum, *am present*; adeo, *go to*; advenio, *come to*; assideo, *sit by*; adsto, *stand by*, &c. : hence, (2) '*application to*:' adhibeo, *apply*; admoneo, *admonish*; afficio, *affect*; alloquor, *address*, &c. : (3) '*acquisition*,' as accipio, *receive*; adipiscor, *gain*; arrogo, *claim*, &c. : (4) '*addition*,' as addo, *add*; adnumero, *reckon with*; addisco, *learn besides*: (5) '*action to the full*:' admiror, *admire*; adedo, *eat up*; afficio, *affect*; agnosco, *recognise*; attondeo, *shear close*, &c. : (6) '*response, favour, sympathy*:' acclamo, *cheer*; adfleo, *weep with*; arrideo, *smile on*; annuo, *assent*: so affulgeo, *shine on*, &c. The Verb adimo, *take away* (quis te mihi casus ademit? Verg.), cannot be a true form. It is probably a vocal corruption of abĕmo, an ancient word cited by Festus, the sound of which would not be agreeable. Ar- was an old form of ad-, as arcesso, arbiter, arvorsum.

3. Cum, com-, con-, co- (*with, together*) implies, (1) '*union, coming, bringing, or acting together*:' coeo, *unite*; concurro, *run together*; confero, *bring together*; convenio, *meet*; convoco, *call together*, &c. For various purposes : (a) '*comparison*:' comparo, compono, confero, *compare*, &c. : (β) '*constraint*:' cohibeo, *restrain*; cogo, *compel*, &c. : (γ) '*friendly action*:' colloquor, *talk with*; concedo, *allow*; confido, *trust*; confiteor, *confess*; consolor, *console*; corrigo, *correct*: (δ) '*hostile action*:' confligo, *battle with*; colluctor, *struggle with*; so coarguo, convinco, *confute.* (2) In some words it implies '*combined thought, reflection*:' concipio, *conceive*; conicio, *guess*; computo, *reckon up.* (3) As implying a concurrence of parts or powers in action, this particle gives to many verbs the sense of *completeness* or *intensity*: cognosco, *learn*; conficio, *complete*; commoveo, *disturb*; compleo, *fill up*; corruo, *fall in*; consumo, *waste*; contendo, *strive*; converto, *turn round*: cohorresco, contremisco, *shudder all over*; convalesco, *get well*, &c. So consterno, *bestrew*; collino, *besmear.*

4. De (*down, down from, from*) implies, (1) '*action downward*:' decĭdo, *fall down*; deicio, *throw down*; depono, *lay down*: (2) '*absence, departure, removal, prevention*,' &c. : decedo, *depart*; detineo, *detain*; demo, *take away*; dehortor, *dissuade*; deterreo, *deter*; deprecor, *pray against*; desum, *am wanting*; deficio, *revolt, fail*, &c. : derogo, *abate* (a privilege by law ; see word in dictionary), &c. : (3) '*diminution, subtraction*:' depleo, *empty*; deperdo, *lose a part.* In the last word and others, as deerro, *stray*; decipio, *deceive*; deludo, *delude*; detero, *rub off*; detraho, *detract*, &c., the preposition carries a bad sense (deterioration). Debeo (dehibeo), *owe*, i.e. have a debt or minus quantity, to be subtracted : (4) '*negation or retractation*:' dedeceo, *misbeseem*; dedisco,

unlearn ; dedoceo, *unteach* ; despero, *despair.* (5) In numerous words it implies '*intensity* or *completeness*' (compare the phrase 'de haut en bas ') : deambulo, *walk up and down* ; deamo, *love exceedingly* ; defleo, *weep intensely* ; decerno, *decree* ; debello, *finish a war* ; defungor, *discharge* ; deleo, *blot out, destroy* ; deprendo, *catch* ; devenio, *arrive* ; devinco, *vanquish*, &c. (6) Such words as dedĭco, *dedicate* ; defero, *offer*, imply *humility* in the agent. Decurro means variously *run down, complete a course*, or *have recourse.*

5. Ex, e (*out of*) implies, (1) '*action out* or *from* :' exeo, *go out* ; eicio, *cast out* ; extendo, *stretch out* ; eximo, *take out, take away* : (2) '*manifest action* :' edico, *proclaim* ; exhibeo, *exhibit* ; exhorresco, *shudder visibly* ; exsisto, *stand forth, exist* : (3) '*achievement of action* :' edisco, *learn by heart* ; efficio, *effect* ; elaboro, *work out* ; enumero, *count up* ; evenio, *happen* ; evinco, *prove* ; existimo, *form opinion, think* : so effero, 1. *drive wild* ; effemino, *make womanish.* Note exaudio, *hear from far.*

6. In (*in, into, against, upon*) implies, (1) '*action in, being in* :' insum, *am in* ; inambulo, *walk in* ; incolo, *inhabit* ; inerro, *wander in* : (2) '*action into* :' ineo, ingredior, *enter* ; immitto, *send into*, &c. : (3) '*action onward* :' incedo, *move on* ; impello, *urge on*, &c. : (4) '*effective action*,' in many Transitive verbs : imminuo, *lessen, break* ; impetro, *obtain by prayer* ; impleo, *fill* ; incendo, *set on fire* ; inficio, *infect* ; instituo, informo, *instruct* ; instruo, *furnish* ; irrigo, *water*, &c. : (5) '*action upon, over, against*,' &c., in many Trajective Verbs : illido, *dash upon* ; impono, *place on* ; impertior, *impart* ; incumbo, *lean on* ; immineo, impendeo, *overhang* ; insurgo, *rise against*, &c. : (6) '*intensive action*,' especially in Inceptive Verbs : illucesco, *dawn* ; incalesco, *grow hot* ; ingravesco, *grow worse* ; intumesco, *swell up*, &c. Remark incipio, *begin* ; invenio, *find* (come upon) ; invideo, *envy* (look on with evil eye). An ancient form of in was endo, ĭndu (ἔνδον), which in old Latin appears in composition with a few words : endogredi or indugredi=ingredi ; endoperator or induperator=imperator. So ind-igeo ; ind-oles.

The negative particle in- appears in the compounds ignosco, *excuse, pardon*, and improbo, *disapprove.*

7. Inter (*between, among*) denotes, (1) '*action between* :' intercĭdo, *fall between* ; interpono, *place between* ; hence, (2) *interruption* : interpello, 1. *address abruptly* ; interrogo, *question* ; intervenio, *intervene* : (2) '*hindrance, stoppage* :' intercedo, *forbid* (by veto) ; intercludo, *shut off* ; interdico, *prohibit, exclude* : (3) '*concernment in* :' intersum, *am engaged in, am present at* ; interest, *it concerns.* Inter has a peculiar use in the words intermorior, intereo, interemo, interficio, *kill.* See Per. Also intellego, *perceive, understand.* Prof. Key (Philolog. Trans.) says that the notion of 'through' is often conveyed to Compounds by inter in Lucretius : interfodio, interfugio. See M. *Lucr.* iv. 716.

8. Ob (=ἐπί) seems to denote '*occupation of space in front* :' as, obeo, *go to encounter, perform, die*, &c. ; obicio, *cast in the way* ; occurro, *meet* ; offero, *offer, present.* This is sometimes hostile : as, obsideo, *besiege* ; obsto, *oppose* ; obsum, *harm* ; obruo, opprimo, *overwhelm* ; oppugno, *attack* ; obloquor, *speak against* : sometimes friendly : as, oboedio, obsĕquor, obtĕmpero, *obey.* '*Persistence*' is often implied by this particle : obstupesco, *stand amazed* ; obdormisco, *slumber* ; obsolesco, *become obsolete.* The use of obs is doubtful : obs-trudo in some MSS. of Plautus seems the only authority. Ostendo, *show*, may perhaps be a corruption of the old phrase ob os tendo, since obtendo, *stretch toward*, is an existing compound. Omitto, *leave off, omit, cease*, if for ob-mitto or om-mitto (which is phonetically possible), must be referred to the meaning of '*persistence*.' Operio, *cover*, is not (as a Latin verb) compounded with ob, but may contain its root.

Obs. Note the Adjj. obliquus, *athwart* ; obscurus, *dark* (having σκία, Prim. *sku*, in front).

9. Per has the general meaning, *through* ; percurro, *run through* : hence, *thoroughly* ; perdisco, *learn thoroughly.* Its use (see inter) is peculiar in pereo, *perish, am undone* (pessum eo) ; peremo, *kill* ; perdo, *ruin, destroy, lose*, for which in older Latin appears pessum do. These uses of per, inter, may perhaps grow out of some now forgotten custom or superstition.

10. Prae (*before*) expresses, (1) '*priority of place or rank* ;' as, praeeo, *go before* ; praeficio, *place in command* ; praesum, *am in command* ; praepono, *prefer* ; praeluceo, *outshine*, &c. : (2) '*priority of time* ;' as, praedĭco, *foretell* ; praemoneo, *forewarn* ; praevideo, *foresee* : (3) '*action in front* ;' as, praecingo, *gird in front* ; praebeo (for praehibeo), *hold in front, afford* ; praetendo, *hold out*, &c. : (4) '*passing along* :' praelabor, *glide by* ; praetexo, *skirt, border.*

11. Pro prod- (*forth, forward, before, for*) expresses, (1) '*motion or action forth, pub-licity :*' prodeo, *go forth* ; prodo, *give forth, surrender, betray* ; promo, *take forth* ; pro-fero, *bring forth* ; provoco, *call forth, challenge* ; proclamo, *proclaim*, &c. : (2) '*motion or action forward :*' procedo, *go forward* ; procumbo, *fall forward* ; promoveo, *promote* ; propello, *drive forward*, &c. : (3) '*action in front :*' prohibeo, *hold aloof, forbid* ; pro-pugno, *fight for* ; protego, *protect* ; protero, *trample down* (a) with the notion of advan-tage ; as, procuro, *care for* ; proficio, prosum, *profit* ; provenio, *come on, prosper*, &c. : (b) of prominence ; as, promineo, *jut out* ; propendeo, *hang forward* ; promereo, *deserve eminently* : (4) '*priority*' (rare) : proludo, *prelude* ; propino, *pledge a health* ; provideo, *look out, foresee*. The most noticeable verbs compounded with pro are, (a) promitto, lit. *send forth* ; which obtains the meanings *let grow* (*hair, beard*, &c.), *predict*, and hence its derived but most usual sense, *promise* : (b) prorogo, *put off* (to a forward time) by legal act ; *prorogue*.

12. Sub sus- (*under*) may imply, (1) '*being under :*' subsum, *am under, am at hand* ; subiaceo, *lie under* ; submergo, *dip under* ; subscribo, *write under* ; subsisto, *stand under* ; succumbo, *sink under* ; suffulcio, *prop* ; sustineo, *sustain* : (2) '*motion under :*' subdo, subicio, submitto, suppono, *put under* ; subeo, *go under, undergo* ; subigo, *bring under, subdue* ; suffundo, *pour under* : (3) '*motion from under :*' subduco, subtraho, subveho, *withdraw* ; submoveo, *remove* (from below) ; subverto, *overthrow* ; (*upward*) ; sublevo, *raise up* ; suscito, *rouse up* ; suspendo, *hang up* ; suspicio, *look up, look up to, suspect* ; suspiro, *sigh* : (4) '*motion in close sequence :*' subsequor, *follow close* ; succedo, *come after, succeed*, also means *go under, be successful*, &c. : (with a view to *help or sup-ply*) subvenio, succurro, *succour* ; sufficio, suppeto, suppleo, *supply* ; subrogo, *supply* (a legal successor). Sometimes sub implies '*secrecy :*' succenseo, *am angry* (in the heart) : surripio, *steal* : sometimes *slight action* ; subblandior, *fawn a little* ; subirascor, *am rather angry*.

13. Dis- di- (διά) (*apart, asunder*) implies '*division, severance, difference, distinction,*' &c. : diduco, *sever* ; disto, *stand apart, am distant* ; dido, *spread* ; diffindo, *cleave* ; dignosco, distinguo, *distinguish* ; differo, *sunder* or *differ* ; dimitto, *dismiss* , discedo, *depart* ; diribeo, dirimo, divido, *divide* ; disrumpo, *pull in pieces* ; discumbo, *recline apart* (of guests at table), &c. It is particularly used to express difference in argument, opinion, action : discepto, disputo, dissero, *argue, dispute, discuss* ; discrepo, dissentio, dissideo, *differ in sentiment, disagree* ; digladior, dimico, *contend in combat* : hence, diiudico, *judge between contending sides*. In some words dis- gives a negative sense : displiceo, *displease* ; diffiteor, *deny* ; diffido, *distrust* : in some it is intensive : disperdo, *ruin utterly* ; dispereo, *am utterly ruined* ; discrucio, *torture painfully*. The verb diligo, *love*, implies a choice between different persons.

14. The inseparable particle red- re- (*back, again*) conveys the two general meanings : I. '*reciprocated action :*' II. '*repeated action :*' but the shades of meaning are nume-rous, and will repay minute analysis with the aid of the dictionary.

I. If AB be a straight line, with motion from A to B, then red- or re- implies

1) '*recurrence from B to A :*' redeo, *return* ; recurro, *run back* ; reduco, *lead back* ; relabor, *slide back* ; remitto, *send back* ; redhibeo, repono, *replace* ; refero, reporto, *bring back* ; revoco, *call back* ; reddo, *give back, restore* ; redimo, *buy back, redeem, ransom* ; renuntio, *tell back, bring tidings* ; restituo, *restore*. Here rank compounds which ex-press reflected light, echoed or replying sound : respondeo, *answer* ; reluceo, *shine back* ; reboo, remugio, *rebellow* ; tidal reflux : refluo, redundo, *flow back*, &c. ; but in actions which by their nature imply recurrence, the particle loses emphasis : respiro, *breathe* : refulgeo, resplendeo, *shine, glitter*. Recaleo, *become warm* from being cold.

2) '*recurrence*' *from B towards A* : i.e. *backward action* : recumbo, *lean back, recline* ; resideo, *sit back, sit down* ; refringo, *break open* ; repello, *drive back* ; remaneo, *stay back, remain* ; remoror, retardo, *retard* ; relinquo, *leave behind* ; respicio, *look back* ; re-tineo, *hold back*, &c. In some verbs, re- (back)=*away* : relēgo, *send away* ; removeo, *move away, remove* : with implied care : recondo, *hide away, stow* : or force ; revello, *pluck away*. To this head belongs the group of words in which the particle (*against*) implies *resistance* : rebello, *war against, rebel* ; reclamo, *cry against* ; redarguo, refello, *refute* ; reluctor, *struggle against* ; (recuso), renuo, *refuse* ; repugno, resisto, *resist*.

II. '*Repeated action*' (*again, anew*) : recognosco, *examine anew* ; recalesco, *grow warm again* ; revalesco, reviresco : so, reparo, *repair* ; reficio (make again), *repair, renew, refresh* ; renovo, *renew* ; relevo, *raise again, relieve*. In refercio, *cram*, repleo, *fill full*, &c., the notion is that of repeating to excess. In recludo, retego, revelo, *uncover, open, disclose* ; refigo, *take down* ; resigno, *unseal*, re- has a force like that of de (*removal*). In revereor, *reverence* ; reticeo, *keep silence*, it implies *bashfulness* :

in redoleo, *smell of*, the idea is that of *giving back* to one who requires, as in renuntio. In some compounds re- gives various senses, as recipio : for which see dictionary.

15. Other Compounded Particles keep their proper force, and need but short notice : (*α*) ante (*before*): anteire, *to go before*: (*β*) circum (*around*): circumdo, *place round*: (*γ*) post (*after, behind*): posthabeo, postpono, *place behind*: (*δ*) praeter (*beside, beyond*): praeterlabor, *glide by* ; praetereo, *pass beyond, pass* ; praetermitto, *pass over, omit*: (*ε*) subter (*beneath*) : subterlabor, *glide under* : in subterfugio, *escape*, secrecy or slyness is implied (subterfuge): (*ζ*) super (*over, above*): superiacio, *throw over*: sometimes implies *excess* ; superfluo, *flow over, overflow*. Note supersum, *survive*, superstes, *surviving* (living over). Supersedeo (sit above) has the peculiar meaning, *disregard, dispense with* : see Ablative Case. (*η*) trans (*across, through*) is properly used of crossing a *river, mountain, road, region*, &c., hence tropically, of going or carrying over : transeo, *cross, pass beyond* : transfero, *carry across, transfer* ; transigo, *carry through, pierce, complete, transact*, &c. : (*θ*) se- sed- (*apart from*) : seduco, *draw aside* : seiungo, *separate* ; seligo, *select*, &c. : (*ι*) amb- am- an- (*around, about,* ἀμφί): ambio, *go round, canvass* ; ambigo, *doubt, question* ; anquiro, *question, search*. (*κ*) the adverbs bene, male, satis, intro, retro, in a few verbs : benedico, *bless* ; benefacio, *do kindness* ; maledico, *revile* ; malefacio, *do harm* ; satisdo, satisfacio, *satisfy* ; introeo, *go in* ; retrogredior, *retreat*.

Obs. 1. Many Verbs, of which the first element is a Preposition, are not Compounds in the same sense as those hitherto named, but belong to one or other of the three following classes :—

1) Derivatives of Compound Adjectives or Substantives : concinno 1. *arrange* (concinnus) ; concordo 1. *agree* (concors) ; discordo 1. *disagree* (discors) ; indignor 1. *am indignant* (indignus) ; infesto 1. *make dangerous* (infestus) ; effero 1. *drive wild* (efferus) ; obliquo 1. *slant* (obliquus) ; deliro 1. *am mad* (delirus) ; commodo 1. *lend* (commodus) ; incommodo 1. *inconvenience* (incommodus) ; praecipito 1. *fling headlong* (praeceps) ; pernocto 1. *pass the night* (pernox) ; insanio 4. *am mad* (insanus) ; consulo 3. *consult* (consul) ; concilio 1. *conciliate* (concilium).

2) Verbs compounded of Particle and a Noun which has no derived simple verb:—

recordor 1. *recollect* (re, cor) ; defaeco 1. *drain* (de, faex) ; infamo 1. *defame* (in, fama) ; so diffamo 1. ; effemino 1. *make womanish* (ex, femina) ; suffŏco 1. *choke* (sub, faux) ; digladior 1. *fight with sword* (di-, gladius) ; illaqueo 1. *ensnare* (in, laqueus) ; enervo 1. *weaken* (e, nervus) ; enucleo 1. *take out kernel* (e, nucleus) ; impedio 4. *hinder, entangle* (in, pes) ; expedio 4. *disentangle* (ex, pes) ; irretio 4. *ensnare* (in, rete) ; derivo 1. *draw off, derive* (de, rivus) ; erudio 4. *instruct* (e, rudis) ; exstirpo 1. *root out* (ex, stirps) ; exsurdo 1. *deafen* (ex, surdus) ; contemplor 1. *gaze at, observe* (cum, templum augural division of sky) ; praevaricor 1. *act dishonestly, deceive* (prae, varus) ; convaso 1. *pack up* (cum, vas) ; exubero 1. *abound* (ex, uber).

3) Compounds of lost or obsolete Verb-stems :—

ad-*ūl*-or 1. *flatter* (or- ?) ; amb-*ūl*-o 1. *walk* ; im-*bu*-o 3. *dye, steep* ; com-*bur*-o 3. *burn* ; in-*coh*-o 1. *begin* ; oc-*cūl*-o 1. *hide* ; in-*du*-o 3. *put on* ; ex-*u*-o (for ex-duo) 3. *put off* ; de-*fend*-o 3. ; of-*fend*-o 3. ; re-*frăg*-or 1. *oppose by vote* ; suf-*frăg*-or 1. *vote for* ; con-*gru*-o 3. *agree* ; in-*gru*-o 3. ; in-*vit*-o 1. *invite* ; ir-*rīt*-o 1. *provoke* ; pro-*mulg*-o 1. *publish* ; dis-*sip*-o 1. *scatter*. The verbs oc-*cup*-o 1. anti-*cip*-o 1. *anticipate*, re-*cip*-er-o, re-*cup*-er-o 1. *recover*, are forms modified from cap-, *take*. De-*stin*-o, *destine*, ob-*stin*-o, *keep firm*, are weakened from stan-, the root sta- strengthened with suffix **n**, like da-n-o from da-, and Gr. φθά-ν-ω from φθα.

Obs. 2. *a*) The primitive root of Growth is ar, al, which appears in Latin as **ar, al, or, ol** : sometimes, perhaps, as **er, el, ül**. It appears, (1) in a*l*o and its derived words, a*l*tus, co-a*l*esco, &c. : (2) in *or*ior and its forms: (3) in -*ŏl*eo, -*ŏl*esco and their compounds ado*l*esco, abo*l*esco, ino*l*esco, &c., proles (pro-*ol*es), subo*l*es, indo*l*es. Probably to this root may belong many names of common quick-growing, or tall, plants ; as ar-bor, ar-ista, (h)ar-undo, a*l*-ga, a*l*-nus, al-lium, (h)o*l*-us, o*l*-ea (o*l*-eum), o*l*-iva (o*l*-ivum), or-nus, er-vum, ἔρνος, *ll*-ex, u*l*-va, u*l*-mus : perhaps, also, ar-duus, ar-dea, A*l*-pis, ὄρ-ος, el-ephas, and other words.

It must be observed that the root of Smell, o*l*ēre, has no connection with that of Growth. In the former l represents d, as shewn in o*d*or (Gr. ὄδωδα), while in the latter l=r.

b) The root of Solidity appears in Latin chiefly as sol- (=Gr. ὁλ-), shewn in the words so*ll*us (ὅλος), sŏ*l*um, so*l*idus, so*ll*ers, so*ll*-i.citus, so*l*eo, with its compounds ob-so*l*esco, exo*l*esco, inso*l*esco, inso*l*ens. Obsolesco and exolesco have often been taken for compounds of olesco, the verb of growth ; but this is a mere error of grammarians.

CHAPTER VI.

THE USES OF WORDS.

SECTION I.

i. Figurate Construction.

(In this place it is convenient to describe certain variations of Construction.)

ii. Ellipsis and Zeugma: Pleonasm: Attraction: Synesis.

A) Ellipsis (ἔλλειψις) is the omission of one or more words which would be used if complete fullness of expression were necessary. This may be

1) When what is omitted appears from the context : ' Metuo tuam iram et patris' (*iram*), *I dread your anger and my father's.* 'Ego amo te et tu me' (*amas*), *I love you and you me.*

2) When usage or the exigence of meaning makes the omitted word evident: Falernum (i.e. vinum), *Falernian wine*; gelida (i.e. aqua), *cold water* : tum ego (i.e. inquam), *then said I.*

a) *Zeugma,* or the construction ἀπὸ κοινοῦ, is the connexion of one word with two words or with two clauses, to both of which it does not equally apply : so that for one of them, another word (to be gathered from the sense of the passage) must be mentally supplied. Zeugma is therefore a species of Ellipsis : 'Ex spoliis et torquem et cognomen induit,' C. 'Querimoniae conventusque habebantur,' C.

The agreement of a Verb or Adjective with one only of several Nouns forming one Subject, is also called Zeugma.[1]

---

[1] Ellipsis and Zeugma are brachylogical constructions ; that is, they abbreviate discourse. (In the following Examples words bracketed in italic type are explanatory merely.)

α) Where the words to be supplied are forms of another word in the sentence, the construction is Ellipsis of the first kind : 'Abi rus ergo hinc ; ibi ego te (*feram*), tu me feres,' Ter. *Haut.* iv. 2. 4. 'In Hyrcania plebs publicos alit canes, optimates domesticos' (*alunt*), C. *T. D.* i. 45. 'Paene ille timore (*corruit*), ego risu corrui,' C. *Qu. Fr.* ii. 10. 'Caper tibi salvus et haedi' (*salvi*), Verg. *B.* vii. 9. 'Hic illius arma (*fuere*), hic currus fuit,' Verg. *Ae.* i. 16. 'Hos tibi dant calamos, en accipe, Musae, Ascraeo quos ante seni' (*dedere*), Verg. *B.* vi. 69. 'Nisi facient quae illos aequum est' (*facere*), Ter. *Ad.* iii. 4. 8.

β) When the sense requires a different word, Ellipsis becomes Zeugma : 'Hoc tempus praecavere mihi me (*iubet*), non te ulcisci sinit,' Ter. *And.* iii. 5. 18. 'Fortuna qua illi florentissima (*usi videntur*), nos duriore conflictati videmur,' C. *Att.* x. 4. 'Alii naufragio (*periisse*), alii a servulis ipsius interfectum eum, scriptum reliquerunt,' Nep. *Hann.* viii. 'Quod arduum sibi (*sumpsit*), cetera legatis permisit,' Tac. *A.* ii. 20. 'Ne tenues pluviae (*corrumpant*) rapidive potentia solis Acrior aut Boreae penetrabile

B) Pleonasm (πλεονασμός) is the use of more words than seem necessary to the expression of a thought : 'Suo sibi gladio hunc iugulo,' *I slay this fellow with his own proper sword*, Ter. Ad. v. 8. So such phrases as plerique omnes; nemo unus; nihil quicquam; deinde postea; ubique gentium; praesensit prius.

C) Attraction occurs when a word, by the influence of another,

---

frigus adurat,' Verg. *G.* i. 93. 'Saepe velut qui, Currebat, fugiens hostem, persaepe velut qui Iunonis sacra ferret,' Hor. *S.* i. 3. 9 (i.e. saepe currebat velut qui fugiens hostem *curreret*, persaepe *tardus incedebat* velut *incederet is* qui Iunonis sacra ferret).

γ) An affirmative verb is understood from a negative: 'Ille quidem haud negat. Immo edepol negat profecto; neque se has aedis Philolachi vendidisse' (*dicit*), Plaut. *Most.* v. i. 3. 'Stoici negant bonum quicquam esse nisi honestum: virtutem autem nixam hoc honesto, nullam requirere voluptatem' (*dicunt*), C. *Fin.* i. 18. 'Nolo existimes me adiutorem huic venisse, sed auditorem et quidem aequum' (*volo existimes*), C. *N. D.* ∴ 7. Nostri Graece fere nesciunt, nec Graeci Latine (*sciunt*), C. *T. D.* v. 40. Qui fit, Maecenas, ut nemo quam sibi sortem Seu ratio dederit seu fors obiecerit illa Contentus vivat, laudet (=*sed ut quisque laudet*) diversa sequentis,' Hor. *S.* i. 1. 1. Compare Hor. *Epod.* v. 87.

δ) Justin has 'Provolutae deinde genibus Alexandri, non mortem, sed, dum Darii corpus sepeliant, dilationem mortis deprecantur,' vi. 9. 14 (i.e. non mortem deprecantur sed . . . . *precantur*). And 'Et caedem patris (*vindicavit*), et se ab insidiis vindicavit,' iii. 1. 9 (the same verb meaning *avenged* in the former clause, *freed* in the latter). But such licenses of a late age are not to be imitated.

Zeugma of the second kind requires a notice of the class of constructions called σύλληψις, when a Verb, Attribute, Apposite, Relative, &c. stands in relation to several Substantives or Pronouns which are often of different Numbers, Genders, Persons, &c.

The rules belong to the Syntax of Agreement (see this): but examples are : 'Pater mihi et mater mortui,' Ter. *Eun.* iii. 3. 'Cerere nati sunt Liber et Libera,' C. *N. D.* ii. 24. 'Attoniti . . . concipiunt Baucisque preces timidusque Philemon,' Ov. *Met.* viii. 681. 'Ptolemaeus et Cleopatra, reges Aegypti, L. xxxvii. 3. 'Sustulimus manus et ego et Balbus,' C. *Fam.* vii. 5. 'Errastis, Rulle, vehementer et tu et collegae tui,' C. *in Rull.* i. 'Ipse dux cum urbe et exercitu deleti,' Sall. 'Fregellis murus et porta de caelo tacta erant,' L. xxxii. 'Arbitrum habebimus Civilem et Veledam, apud quos pacta sancientur,' Tac. *H.* iv. 65. 'Favent pietati fideique di, per quae P. R. ad tantum fastigii venit,' L. xliv. 2.

In these examples the related words are all Plural; and Gender and Person are determined by consideration of all the Nouns. Zeugma occurs when the construction agrees with one of the Nouns only, whether in Number, Gender, Person, or all these: an Ellipsis being supposed of the other agreeing words. 'Filia (*capta*) atque unus e filiis captus est,' Caes. *B. G.* i. 26. 'Convicta est Messalina et Silius' (*convictus*), Tac. *A.* xii. 65. 'Utinam aut hic surdus (*factus*), aut haec muta facta sit,' Ter. *And.* iii. 4, 5. 'Et genus (*vilius*) et virtus, nisi cum re, vilior alga est,' Hor. *S.* ii. 5. 8. 'Populi (*liberati*) provinciaeque liberatae sunt,' C. *Phil.* v. 4. 'Et tu (*scis*) et omnes homines sciunt,' C. *Fam.* xiii. 8. 1. 'Et ego (*flagito*) et Cicero meus flagitabit,' C. *Att.* iv. 17. 3. In such examples agreement is with the nearer Noun; and thus it is a kind of Attraction.

Rarer instances occur of Zeugma, in which agreement is with the more distant word: 'Ego populusque Romanus populis priscorum Latinorum bellum indico facioque,' L. i. 32. 'Quibus ipse meique ante Larem proprium vescor,' Hor. *S.* ii. 6. 65.

B) Pleonasm, which expands discourse, belongs to the domain of rhetoric more than to that of grammar, and needs not to be dwelt on at length here. Periodic style, such as that of the Ciceronian speeches and treatises, is necessarily, to some extent, pleonastic: and the rounded fullness of Cicero's diction exposed him, even in his own times, to the charge of tumid Asiatic luxuriance. Two or three sentences will illustrate this tendency. 'Si fructibus et emolumentis et utilitatibus amicitias colemus, dubium est quin fundos et insulas amicis anteponamus?' *Fin.* ii. 26. 'Dicendi facultas non debet esse ieiuna atque nuda, sed aspersa atque distincta multarum rerum iucunda quadam varietate,' *Or.* i. 50. 'Quinctius orat atque obsecrat ut multis iniuriis iactatam atque agitatam aequitatem in hoc tandem loco consistere et confirmari patiamini,' *p. Quinc.* 2.

Examples of Attraction, Synesis, &c. will be found in various parts of the Syntax.

is diverted from the usual construction to a less usual one : 'Hic est quem quaero hominem,' *this is the man I seek* ; where the Subst. would usually be Nom., but, attracted by quem, becomes Accus. 'Thebae, quod Boeotiae caput est,' L. for 'Thebae, quae Boeotiae caput sunt;' the Complement caput (Neut. Sing.) attracting the Relative from its usual agreement in Gender and Number with the Antecedent (Thebae).

D) Synĕsis is when words are constructed in accordance with *meaning* (σύνεσις), not with form: 'Subeunt Tegeea iuventus auxilio tardi,' *the youth of Tegea come slow to the succour*, Stat. *Th.* vii. 605 : where iuventus (a Collective Noun Feminine and Singular) has the meaning of the Concrete iuvenes, *young men* (Masc. Plur.), with which meaning the Verb subeunt (Plur.) and the Adjective tardi (Masc. Plur.) agree in construction.

iii. Other Variations.

a) When a Verb or Adjective agrees with several Substantives (σύλληψις, see last Foot-note) : ' Pater, mater et filia capti sunt.'

b) When words are dislodged from the normal order (ὑπερ-βατόν) : 'Tu illas abi et traduce.'

An interposed clause is called παρένθεσις if not in construction with the rest : 'At tu—nam divum servat tutela poetas—Praemoneo, vati parce, puella, sacro,' Tibull. ii. 5. 113.

ç) When a Preposition follows its Case (ἀναστροφή) : Spemque metumque inter dubii, Verg.

d) When compound words are separated into their parts (τμῆσις) : 'Quae me cumque vocant terrae,' Verg. for quaecumque ; disque supatis for dissipatis ; ordia prima, Lucr. for primordia.

e) When one Part of Speech, Number, Case, Tense, &c., is used for another (ἐναλλαγή) : ' Vivere nostrum' for vita nostra ; 'Samnis' for Samnites, ' nos ' for ego : 'populus' for popule ; 'expectate' for expectatus ; ' mox navigo ' for navigabo, &c.

f) Interchange of Cases (ὑπαλλαγή) : ' Dare classibus Austros,' Verg. for 'dare classes Austris.' Or attribution of an Adjective to another than its natural Noun : 'Fontium gelidae perennitates,' C. for gelidorum : 'Tyrrhena regum progenies,' Hor. for Tyrrhenorum.

g) Expression of a complex notion by two Substantives, instead of Subst. and Adj. (ἐνδιαδυοῖν) : 'Pateris libamus et auro,' Verg. ii. *G.* 192, for pateris aureis.

h) That kind of Ellipsis which omits Annexive Conjunctions is called ἀσύνδετον : 'Abiit, excessit, evasit, erupit,' C. *Cat.* i. 1. Πολυσύνδετον is a kind of Pleonasm, which multiplies Conjunctions in poetry : 'Una Eurusque Notusque ruunt creberque procellis Africus,' Verg. *Ae.* i. 85.

i) *Archaism* is a form, phrase, or idiom borrowed from old writers (ἀρχαῖοι) : 'animaï; in cassum magnum.' Lucr.

k) *Graecism* (ἑλληνισμός) is a phrase or idiom borrowed from Greek : 'Amplexi habent,' Lucr., for amplexi sunt : 'Metuo fratrem ne intus sit,' Ter., for 'ne frater intus sit.'

The foregoing Variations (which grammarians call 'Figures') belong chiefly to Syntax.

iv. Metaphor and Metonymy.

(These are Figures of Rhetoric.)

I. *Metaphor* (μεταφορά, translatio) occurs when a term proper to one matter is transferred by analogy to another: volnus, *wound,* for damnum, *loss*; portus, *harbour,* for refugium, *refuge*; sentina reipublicae, *sink of the commonwealth,* for turpissimi cives, *vilest citizens*; ardeo, *I burn,* for amo, *I love,* &c.

A metaphor may be qualified by such expressions as quasi, tamquam, quidam, ut ita dicam, &c. : 'In una philosophia quasi tabernaculum vitae suae collocarunt,' *they have pitched as it were the tent of their life in philosophy alone,* C. d. Or. iii. 20. 'Caria et Phrygia asciverunt aptum suis auribus opimum quoddam et tamquam adipatae dictionis genus,' *the Carians and Phrygians chose a certain rich and as it were greasy style of diction suited to their peculiar taste,* C. Or. 8. 'Scopas, ut ita dicam, mihi videntur dissolvere,' *they seem to me to be untying, so to say, besoms,* C. Or. 71.

II. *Metonymy* (μετωνυμία) puts a related word for a proper one : (1) Cause for effect ; Mars for bellum ; Ceres for segetes ; 'Bacchus' for vinum ; 'Ianus' for Iani vicus or for Iani templum. (2) Material for work : 'argentum' for vasa argentea. (3) Abstract for concrete : 'civitas' for cives, 'cor Enni' for cordatus Ennius, *the sensible Ennius.* (4) Concrete for abstract : 'Cedant arma togae,' for 'cedat bellum paci.' (5) Country for inhabitants : 'Graecia' for Graeci : or the converse : 'In Persas ire,' for in Persidem, Nep. (6) The part is put for the whole (συνεκδοχή) : 'caput' for homo ; 'tectum' for domus. (7) Sometimes the whole for the part : 'Sal sextante erat,' for 'modius salis,' *salt was at two unciae the peck,* L.

SECTION II.

Uses of the Substantive.

(On certain classes of Singular and Plural Substantives see § **27**. iii.)

i. Singular Appellatives used collectively for Plural.

Such Appellatives are, (1) Material Objects. (2) Bodies civil or military. (3) People : occasional in Cato, Cic., Caes. : frequent in Liv., Tac., Curt. and poets.

Ex. rosa = rosae : pedes = pedites : Samnis = Samnites.

The Singular annexed to Plural is not earlier than Livy. He and Tacitus often use it : 'Hispani milites et funditor Baliaris,' L. xxvii. 2. 'Samnis Paelignusque et Marsi,' Tac. *H.* iii. 59.

ii. Plural words used with Singular collective sense in prose.

Ex. aquae, ardores, calores, frigora, frumenta, glacies, grandines, ignes, pecuniae, pluviae, praedae, pruinae, rores ; all in C.

In poetry this use of the Plural of Concretes is abundant : aconita, mella, colla, corda, currus, altaria, numina, litora, capitolia, tecta, &c.

It either heightens the image, or, still oftener, assists the metre.

iii. Plural of Appellatives expressing a 'genus' when individuals are implied.

Occasional in prose : 'Legati P. R.' (where Triarius alone is meant), C. *p. L. Man.* : frequent in poetry : 'Quas mulieres, quos tu parasitos loquere?' Plaut. *Men.* ii. 2 ; 'Barbaras regum est ulta libidines' (meaning Tereus), Hor. *C.* iv. 12.

iv. Plural of Proper Names used to express typical characters.

This is frequent in prose, occasional in poetry : 'Pauli, Catones, Galli, Scipiones, Phili,' C. *Lael.* 6. 'Decii Marii magnique Camilli,' Verg. *G.* ii. 169.

v. Abstract Substantives,[1] Verbal and Denominative, used in Plural.

This is frequent in prose, occasional in poetry.

1) When several kinds are implied : 'Tres constantiae,' C. *T. D.* iv. 6 ; 'Alia exitia,' C. *d. Fin.* v. 10 ; 'Sapiens nostras ambitiones levitatesque contemnit,' *the wise man despises our ambitious and shallow pursuits,* C. *T. D.* v. 36.

2) Several occurrences : 'Domesticae fortitudines,' C. *Off.* i. 22. So offices in L. and Tac. : 'Tribunatus et praeturae et consulatus,' Tac. *D.* 7.

    a) A material (aes, cera, &c.) may express in the Plural ornamental objects manufactured from it : 'Ephyreia aera,' *Corinthian bronzes,* Verg. *G.* ii. 463. 'Veteres cerae,' *old waxen busts,* Iuv. viii. 19. But aurum, argentum remain Singular always.

  ⋅ Draeger states that there are in Latin 3,814 abstract Substantives ; of which 2,889 are used in the Singular only, 925 in the Plural also. Of these latter 58 only are before Cicero, including 36 in Plautus, 6 in Terence : 383 are in Cicero ; a few only, 19, in Caesar, Sallust, Varro, and Auctor ad Herennium. The rest, 484, are distributed in Livy and subsequent prose writers, and in classical and later poetry. See his *Historische Syntax. der Lat. Spr.*, Part i. p. 9, where a full list of these Abstract Plurals is given.

3) When the abstract is related to Plural concretes : 'Conscientiae maleficiorum,' C. *Par.* 2.

4) When it is annexed to other Plurals : 'Tot artes, tantae scientiae, tot inventa,' C. *Cat. M.* 78.

vi. Abstract Substantives for Concrete in prose and poetry :

This may be in any of three ways :

1) Sing. Abstr. for Sing. Concr. } either or both.
   Plur. Abstr. for Plur. Concr. }

Ex. 'corruptela' = corruptor, Ter. *Ad.* v. 3. 7 ; 'desiderium' = res desiderata, Hor. *C.* i. 14. 18 ; 'servitia' = servi, C. *p. Flac.* 38 ; 'imperia' = imperatores, Caes. *B. C.* iii. 32 ; 'matrimonia' = uxores, L. x. 23. 'Mea festivitas,' *my delight,* App. ii. 10 ; so 'scelus' = *a wicked wretch,* 'scelera,' *scoundrels;* 'vigiliae' = vigiles ; 'excubiae' = excubitores.

2) Plur. Abstr. for Sing. Concr. : 'amores' = amatus or amata : 'Pompeius nostri amores,' C. *Att.* ii. 19. 'Acmen . . suos amores,' Catull. xlv. 1. So 'deliciae :' 'Amores et deliciae tuae Roscius,' C. *Div.* i. 36.

3) Sing. Abstr. for Plur. Concr. freq. in prose and poetry : 'amicitia' = amici, Tac. *A.* 271 ; 'barbaria' = barbari ; 'civitas' = cives ; 'coniuratio' = coniurati ; 'iuventus' = iuvenes ; 'nobilitas' = nobiles ; 'societas' = socii ; 'statio' or 'custodia' = custodes ; 'remigium' = remiges. So 'Canes amica vis pastoribus,' Hor. *Epod.* 6. 6. 'In hac tanta immanitate versari,' C. = inter tam immanis homines. 'Cum vestra aetate,' C. = cum vobis adulescentibus.

Obs. From the Plural use of Substantives we can hardly disconnect the 'Pluralis Modestiae,' which includes also Verbs and Pronouns, when a person speaks of himself in the Plural Number : 'Imperatores appellati sumus,' C. *Att.* v. 20. 'Poscimur, si quid vacui sub umbra lusimus,' Hor. *C.* i. 32. Sometimes Plur. and Sing. occur together : 'Ardeo incredibili cupiditate ut nomen nostrum scriptis illustretur tuis,' C. *Fam.* v. 12 ; 'Et flesti et nostros vidisti flentis ocellos,' Ov. *H.* v. 45.[1]

vii. Idioms of the Substantive chiefly Ciceronian :

1) Cicero describes state or action by a Verbal Abstract : 'Oratoris est languentis populi incitatio et effrenati moderatio,' *an orator's function is to rouse a languid, and restrain an infuriated, populace,* C. *d. Or.* ii. 9.

---

[1] The Plural of Majesty (we, our), used in the proclamations of modern princes and potentates, was unknown to classical Latin ; but it probably grew out of the use of the 'modest' Plural by Roman Emperors in such phrases as 'nostra mansuetudo,' 'nostra maiestas,' 'nostra excellentia,' &c.

2) A Denominative Abstract with Genitive is used for a Noun with Epithet. 'Vis flammae aquae multitudine opprimitur' (=flamma violenta plurima aqua opprimitur), C. *Cat. M.* 19. 'In consuetudine sermonis' (=in consueto sermone), *in ordinary conversation,* C. *Inv.* ii. 40.

3) A Noun takes a Genitive of another, to which it might be Apposite, if the other were constructed as Subject or Object. 'Est etiam deformitatis et corporis vitiorum satis bella materies ad iocandum,' *deformity also and bodily defects are a fine field for banter,* C. *d. Or.* ii. 59.

4) A Noun of quality or condition is used as Subject or Object with Genitive of the real Subject or Object, or with a Possessive Pronoun. 'Pupilli aetatem et solitudinem defendere praetor debuit,' *the praetor ought to have protected a young and orphan ward,* C. *Verr.* i. 58. 'Potest mihi denegare occupatio tua,' *your preoccupation* (=you being preoccupied) *may refuse me this,* C. *Fam.* v. 12. 8.

5) Cicero affects ornate periphrases and metaphors: 'Occasionis tarditas;' 'Etesiarum flatus;' 'naufragia fortunae;' 'summa luctus acerbitas:' 'mentis oculi;' 'philosophiae portus;' 'gloriae stimuli;' 'eius sceleri virtus M. Bruti obstitit.'

6) Stages of life and seasons of office are often expressed by the concrete words puer, adulescens, &c., consul, praetor, &c., rather than by the abstracts pueritia, consulatus, &c. 'Doctus a puero,' *learned from boyhood,* C. 'Ab parvulis,' *from their infancy,* Caes. 'Philosophiae multum adulescens temporis tribui,' *I gave much time to philosophy in my youth,* C. *Off.* ii. 4. 'Ante (post) me consulem,' *before (after) my consulship:* 'consule Planco,' *in the consulship of Plancus,* Hor. But the abstracts can be used.

7) Some Concrete Substantives, especially Verbals in -tor -trix, are used Adjectively. 'Ennius equi fortis et victoris senectuti comparat suam,' *Ennius compares his old age to that of a strong and victorious horse,* C. *Cat. M.* 5. 'Artifex stilus,' *an artistic style,* C. This idiom is especially poetic. 'Victrix causa deis placuit, sed victa Catoni,' *the conquering cause pleased the gods, but the conquered cause Cato,* Lucan. i. 128. 'Populum late regem,' *a far-ruling people,* Verg. *Aen.* v. 25.

8) Certain phrases assume the nature of single words: 'nomen Latinum' (=Latini), 'res Romanae' (=Roma). So 'res repetundae' (*extortion*), respublica, iusiurandum, &c.

9) In comparisons, by a peculiar brachylogy, names of Persons and Places stand for their works or properties: 'Percipietis voluptatem, si cum Graecorum Lycurgo et Dracone et Solone nostras leges conferre volueritis,' *you will find pleasure in comparing our laws with (those of) the Lycurgus and Draco and Solon of the Greeks,* C. *d. Or.* i. 44.

10) Verbal Substantives occasionally govern the same cases as their Verbs: Cicero has 'domum itio;' 'Narbone reditus;' 'obtemperatio legibus.' Constructions such as 'receptio virum meum,' 'curatio hanc rem,' are used by Plautus, but not subsequently.

viii. Ellipse of the Substantive:

Omitted Substantives are indicated

1) By Adjectives which are their Epithets :
   ager : in Tiburti, C.
   aqua : frigida, Quint. ; gelida, Hor. ; calida, Varr. ; decocta, Plin., Iuv.
   ars : dialectica, &c. C. musica.
   capilli : cani, C. and poets.
   caro: agnina, *lamb* ; anatina, *duck* ; aprugna, *wild-boar* ; bubula, *beef* : ferina, *venison* ; suilla, *pork* ; vitulina, *veal.*
   castra : aestiva ; hiberna ; stativa : C., Caes., L., Tac. &c.
   dies : natalis ; and in phrases postero, in posterum, &c.
   fabula : togata, *comedy* with Roman characters ; palliata, with Greek ; praetexta, trabeata, plays in which characters with these dresses appeared.
   familiaris : ' complexus inde Coriolanus suos dimittit,' L. ii. 40.
   febris : quartana, *quartan ague,* Iuv.
   feriae : Latinae, *the Latin holidays.*
   fodina : arenaria, argentaria, &c. C., L.
   fratres : gemini ; trigemini.
   funis : cereus, *a waxen torch.*
   hora : quarta, 10 *o'clock* ; octava, 2 *o'clock,* Iuv.
   lapis : molaris, *millstone,* Verg. ; ad quartum, *at the fourth milestone,* Tac. &c.
   liber: 'in T. Livii primo,' Quint. ; 'in tertio de Oratore,' do. ; 'ne in pontificiis quidem nostris,' C. *N. D.* i. 30.
   ludi : Circenses, Iuv.
   manus : dextra, laeva, sinistra.
   mare : Aegaeum ; Ionium ; altum ; profundum, &c.
   navis : triremis ; quinqueremis ; oneraria, C., L. ; Liburna, Hor., &c.
   nummus : aureus ; aereus ; denarius ; sestertius, &c.
   officina : coquina ; picaria ; figlina, &c. C., Plin.
   ordines : quattuordecim, the fourteen rows of the equites in the Roman theatre, Suet.
   ovis : bidens.
   partes : decumae, *tithes* : primae, secundae, &c., *the first, second,* &c. *parts* in a drama, C., Hor. &c.
   pecuniae : repetundarum, repetundis ; frequent : Cicero usually adds pecuniarum, pecuniis.
   porta : Coelimontana, Esquilina, Capena, &c., C., &c.
   praedium : Albanum, Antias, Tusculanum, &c., C.
   res : argentaria, pecuaria, topiaria, &c., C.
   sella : curulis, Tac.
   sol : occidens ; oriens.
   spolia : opima, Sen. Tr.
   telum : missile, L., Verg.
   tempus : brevi ; horno, Plaut.
   toga : praetexta, Hor. and later.
   tribus : Q. Verres Romilia, C. &c.
   usurae ; centesimae ; quincunces, besses, deunces, &c.
   vas : aënum ; fictile, Cat., Ov. &c.

ventus : Africus, Iapyx.
verba : multa, plura, &c.
versus, senarius.
via : Appia, Flaminia, Latina, &c.
vicibus : alternis, Lucr., Verg.
vinum : Caecubum, Falernum, Massicum, Sabinum, Surren-
tina (vina), &c. Hor. &c.

Also menstruum (*frumentum*), L.; nullas (*epistulas*), C.; molaris
(*dens*), Iuv.; Papia Poppaea (*lex*), Tac. Dialia, Liberalia, &c. (*festa*).

2) By Substantives which depend on those omitted :

aedes or *templum* : 'ad Apollinis;' 'ad Opis;' 'ad Iovis Statoris;' 'ad Vestae;' 'prope Cloacinae' (aedem), C., L. &c.
actor : 'Q. Arrius fuit M. Crassi quasi secundarum,' C. *Brut.*
69.
iter : 'castra aberant bidui,' C. *Att.* v. 16.
filius, filia : 'Faustus Sullae;' 'Caecilia Metelli;' 'Hannibal
Gisgonis.'
uxor : Terentia Ciceronis; Apicata Seiani, Tac.
homines : 'pergere ad Treveros et externae fidei,' Tac.
poculum : 'da noctis mediae,' &c. Hor. C. iii. 19.
servus : frequent in phrases : 'a manu' or 'ad manum,' *amanuensis* : 'ab epistulis,' *letter-writer* ; 'a potione,' *cup-bearer* ;
'a bibliotheca,' *librarian*, &c.

3) By Verbs, of which the omitted word is object or subject. See
§ 109, § 126.
Object omitted : mittere (*nuntium*); agere (*vitam*); obire (*mor·
tem*); merere (*stipendia*); movere (*castra*); ducere (*exercitum*)
appellere, conscendere (*navem, classem*), and others.
Besides Pronoun Subjects, the Nom. *homines* is constantly
omitted in the phrases aiunt, tradunt, narrant, &c.

**ix. Substantives are used with different kinds
of meaning (active or passive).**

alumn-us -a (usually qui alitur; sometimes qui alit) : clientela
(*clientship; clients; patronage*) : gloria (*glory; boasting, vanity*) :
hospes (*host; guest*) : fuga (*flight; exile*) : invidia (*envy; odium*) :
nuntius (*messenger; news*) : odium (*hatred* as feeling : *hated object*) : opinio (*opinion; credit*) : ruina (*ruin* suffered or inflicted) :
spes (*hope* as feeling ; as object) : tristitia (*sadness; gloom* inspiring
sadness) : tutela (*guardianship, guardian; that which is guarded,
ward*) : vector (qui vehit, *shipmaster*; qui vehitur, *passenger*), &c.

SECTION III.

Uses of the Adjective.

i. Adjectives used as Substantives. See § 15. *b*).

A) Masculine (and Feminine) Adjectives with personal meaning.

I. Singular :

a) in **arius, Ious, ānus, īnus,** &c., including Gentile words :
adversarius; consiliarius; librarius; ostiarius: sicarius; statuarius;

tabellarius ; vicarius, &c.; criticus, rusticus, vilicus, &c.; hortulanus ; paganus; publicanus; libertinus; vicinus, &c. ; Romanus, Sabinus, Atheniensis, &c. Also the terms for legionary soldiers : primanus, secundanus, &c.

b) Words of Kinship and Relation :

amicus, inimicus ; aequalis ; affinis ; agnatus, cognatus ; consanguineus; contubernalis; familiaris; gentilis; maritus; necessarius ; propinquus ; sodalis, socius.

c) Various ;

aemulus ; conscius ; consularis; luvenis ; insipiens ; stultus, &c. Cicero has, 'Meos partim inimicos partim invidos,' *p. Planc.* 'Nonnulli nostri iniqui,' do. 23. 'Omnibus iniquissimis meis,' *Verr.* v. 69.

d) Participles :

a) Present: adulescens ; amans ; sapiens.

β) Perfect Pass. : candidatus ; doctus ; praefectus ; nat-us (a) ; spons-us (a).

e) Generally, '*man*' may be omitted when any epithet implying it is used (Ellipsis) : 'Iacet corpus dormientis ut mortui,' *the body of a sleeper lies like that of a dead man,* C. *Div.* i. 30. 'Non de improbo, sed de callido improbo quaerimus,' *we are enquiring not about a knave, but about a cunning knave,* C. *Fin.* ii. 17. 'Neglegere quid de se quisque sentiat, non solum arrogantis est, sed omnino dissoluti,' *to be careless of what others think about him, indicates a man not arrogant only, but quite unprincipled,* C. *Off.* i. 28.

II. Plural :

Plural Adjectives and Participles still oftener express *men*; chiefly, but not exclusively, in the Nom. and Accus., because in these the Masc. is distinguished from the Neut. So

boni, divites, inferiores, infimi, iuniores, magni, maiores, minores, multi, mortales, nulli, optimi, omnes, pauci, plerique, posteri, proximi, summi, tenues, urbani ; nostri, sui, &c. &c.; adstantes, discentes, legentes, spectantes, &c. ; docti, indocti, imperiti, mortui, &c.

Participles are also used, especially in poetry, to describe, by some property, classes in natural history : balantes = oves ; natantes = pisces ; volantes = aves ; laniger = aries ; squamigeri = pisces.

Cicero has 'errantes' for 'planetae.'

B) Neuter Adjectives and Participles :

I. Singular :

a) It has been shewn in Ch. V. that a great number of Substantives in **arium, torium, sorium, tum, sum, āle, īle, āre**, &c., were originally Adjectival : as cibarium, deversorium, dictum, responsum, navale, ovile, talare, &c.

b) The Greek Article enables that language to convert any Neut. Adjective into an Abstract Noun (τὸ ἀγαθόν, τὸ καλόν). Latin authors, without this advantage, use a certain number of Neuter Adjectives Singular in this way : such are *a*) Moral Abstracts :

aequum, bonum, commodum, decorum, falsum, honestum, iustum, malum, nimium, pravum, rectum, ridiculum, utile, verum, &c.

β) Physical Abstracts :

album, aridum, calidum, canorum, umidum, igneum, inane, pingue, planum, serum, sudum, tranquillum, vacuum, &c.

γ) Ordinal Numerals :

primum, secundum, &c. extremum, medium, &c.

c) The most extensive Substantival use of Neuter Sing. Adjectives and Participles is with Prepositions ; forming phrases of an adverbial character.

Among the most usual phrases of this kind are :

ex adverso ; ex aequo ; ex ambiguo ; e contrario ; ex confesso ; ex imo ; ex obliquo ; ex occulto ; ex permisso ; ex propinquo ; ex transverso ; ex tuto ; ex vano; ex vero :—in abdito ; in alto ; in ambiguo ; in ancipiti ; in aperto ; in arduo ; in dubio ; in edito ; in incerto ; in integro ; in lubrico ; in medio ; in obscuro ; in plano ; in praecipiti ; in praesenti ; in propatulo ; in publico ; in sereno ; in secreto ; in sicco ; in solido ; in sublimi ; in tranquillo ; in turbido ; in tuto :—ab imo ad summum :—pro certo ; pro comperto ; pro indigno :—de alieno ; de cetero ; de communi ; de medio ; de publico ; de suo ; de vivo ;—in adversum ; in arduum ; in artum ; in commune ; in deterius ; in dubium ; in immensum ; in incertum ; in maius ; in medium ; in melius ; in obliquum ; in praeceps ; in plenum ; in sublime ; in tranquillum ; in transversum : and the temporal phrases, in aeternum ; in futurum ; in longum ; in posterum ; in perpetuum ; in praesens ; in serum :—ad certum, ad constitutum, ad immensum ; ad liquidum ; ad irritum, ad vanum ; ad vivum ; ad unum ; and the temporal phrases, ad extremum, ad (in) multum diei, ad ultimum.[1]

II. Plural :

Neuter Plural Adjectives are freely used in Latin as Abstract Nouns, signifying '*things*.'

bona, mala ; vera, falsa ; utilia, inutilia ; &c. &c.; multa, plurima, omnia, &c. ; ea, ista, haec, nostra, etc.

Some in *local* sense :

avia, devia, invia ; summa, infima, proxima, extrema, angusta ; aperta, secreta ; maritima, mediterranea, &c. &c. : often with a descriptive Genitive in history and poetry : secreta silvarum ; avia montium ; strata viarum ; deserta locorum, abdita vallium, &c.

---

[1] Draeger cites other instances :

Ex : abdito, alto, affluenti, antiquo, aperto, arido, communi, composito, conducto et locato, diverso, facili, patenti, praeparato, proximo, publico, solido, toto, &c.

In (Abl.) : aequo, angusto, arto, communi, conspicuo, excelso, expedito, extremo, facili, difficili, levi, occulto, pacato, privato, profano, promiscuo, summo, &c.

In (Accus.) : ambiguum, altum, angustum, cassum, contrarium, publicum, sublime, unum, &c.

ii. Adjectives used adverbially.

(1) 'Senatus frequens convenit,' *the senate met in force,* C.　So 'invitus (or libens) veni;' 'imprudens (or sciens) feci,' &c. Especially Adjectives of *time, order,* &c.: serus, citus, matutinus, nocturnus, vespertinus, prior, primus, princeps, proximus, ultimus, postremus, supremus, unus, multus, solus, totus, omnis, nullus, &c.

'Lupus gregibus nocturnus obambulat,' *the wolf prowls about the flocks at night,* Verg. G. iii. 538.　'Sulla multus aderat,' *Sulla shewed himself much,* Sall. *Iug.* 9.　'Philotimus nullus venit,' *Philotimus came not at all,* C. Fam. xi. 22.

(2) Virgil has 'tarda volventia plaustra' (for tarde), 'sublimem expulsum' (for sublime), 'inexpletus lacrimans' (for inexpletum); and similar examples abound in poetry.

iii. Partitive Attributes.

Primus, ultimus, summus, infimus, imus, intimus, extremus, postremus, novissimus, medius, reliquus, ceterus, are often used to designate one part of that to which they are attributed.

'Prima luce summus mons a Labieno tenebatur,' *at break of day the top of the mountain was occupied by Labienus,* Caes. *B. G.* i. 22.　'Maximum bellum Cn. Pompeius extrema hieme appararavit, ineunte vere suscepit, media aestate confecit,' *Gnaeus Pompeius prepared a mighty war at the close of winter, commenced it at the beginning of spring, completed it in the middle of summer,* C. *p. L. Man.* 12.　See M. *Lucr.* iii. 250.

iv. Proleptic Attributes.

An attribute is said to be proleptic when it indicates a quality not existing yet, but about to result from the action contained in the sentence: 'Ingentes tollent animos' (i.e. ut ingentes fiant), Virg. *G.* iii. 207.　This is an idiom of very frequent use in poetry.

v. Multiplication of Attributes.

1) Two or more Adjectives are not usually joinéd as Attributes to the same Substantive without an intervening Conjunction, unless one or more with the Substantive form one complex idea:

'Propter Ennam est spelunca 'quaedam ubi Syracusani festos dies anniversarios agunt,' *close to Enna is a certain cavern, where the people of Syracuse hold annual holidays,* C. *Verr.* iv. 52. 'Columna aurea solida sacrata est,' *a pillar of solid gold was dedicated,* L. xxiv. 3.　'Verri apud Mamertinos privata navis oneraria maxima publice est aedificata,' *a private yacht of very heavy tonnage was built for Verres in the Mamertine city at public cost,* C. *Verr.* iv. 52.　Here 'festos dies,' 'columna aurea,' 'navis oneraria maxima,' severally constitute one idea.　See M. *Lucr.* v. 13: 'Divina antiqua reperta;' and iv. 394, 'suo corpore claro.'

2) But any number of Adjectives may follow one Substantive, when each expresses a different kind of that Substantive:

'Auribus indicantur vocis genera permulta, candidum, fuscum, lene, asperum, grave, acutum, flexibile, lene,' C. *N. D.* ii. Or when intervening Conjunctions are supposed, not expressed:

'Animal hoc providum, sagax, multiplex, acutum, plenum rationis et consili, quem vocamus Hominem,' C. *Leg.* i. 7. 'Monstrum horrendum informe ingens,' Verg. *Aen.* iii. 658.

vi. Possessive Attributes.

The Latin language uses Denominative Epithets very largely, instead of Genitive Nouns, to express Origin, Possession, &c. : Anacreon Teïus, *Anacreon of Teos*; Hercules Xenophonteus, *Hercules in Xenophon*; erilis filius, *my master's son*; fraternus sanguis, *a brother's blood*; cursus maritimus, *a sea voyage*; bellum sociale, *a war with allies*; aliena vitia, *the faults of others*, &c.

vii. Idioms of the Superlative.

For those of the Comparative see Correlation (quam), and the Syntax of the Ablative.

1) The following example shews that the Superlative indicates any very high degree, though not the highest : 'Ego sum miserior quam tu quae es miserrima,' *I am more wretched than you, who are very wretched,* C. *Fam.* xiv. 3.

2) The force of the Superlative is increased by

    a) The Adverbs longe, multo, quam, vel : 'Ex Britannis omnibus longe humanissimi sunt, qui Cantium incolunt,' *of all the Britons, the most civilised by far are those who inhabit Kent,* Caes. *B. G.* v. 14. 'Alcibiades fuit omnium aetatis suae multo formosissimus,' *Alcibiades was much the handsomest man of his day,* Nep. *Alc.* I. 'Definitio quid sit id, de quo agitur, ostendit quam brevissime,' *definition shews as briefly as may be, what it is that is treated of,* C. *Or.* 33. Hence, quam primum (*as soon as possible*)`: 'Huic mandat, ut quam primum ad se revertatur,' *this man he directs to return to him as soon as possible,* Caes. *B. G.* iv. 21. 'In fidibus musicorum aures vel minima sentiunt,' *in luteplaying the ears of musicians perceive the very slightest errors,* C. *Off.* i. 41.

    b) The elliptical expressions, tam quam qui, tantum quantum qui, ut qui, qui qui, ut cum, cum: 'Tam sum mitis quam qui lenissimus,' *I am as mild as the very gentlest,* C. *p. Sull.* 31. 'Commendationi meae tantum tribue, quantum cui plurimum,' *assign to my recommendation the greatest weight you would to any,* C. *Fam.* xiii. 22. 'Grata ea res, ut quae maxime senatui unquam, fuit,' *that circumstance pleased the senate as much as anything had ever pleased them,* L. v. 25. 'Domus celebratur ita ut cum maxime,' *the house is thronged to its very utmost,* C. *Qu. F.* ii. 6.

    c) Quam, quantus, ut, with the verb possum: Aves quam possunt mollissime nidos substernunt, ut quam facillime ova serventur,' *birds line their nests as softly as they can, that the eggs may be preserved with the greatest ease,* C. *N. D.* ii. 52. 'Hannibal quantam maximam potest vastitatem ostendit,' *Hannibal exhibits the utmost desolation in his power,* L. xxii. 3. Ut potui brevissime dixi, *I spoke as briefly as I could.*

On unus as Superlative, and with Superlatives, see p. 153.

3) The Pronoun quisque (*each*), attached to the Superlative, imparts a universal notion: 'Epicureos doctissimus quisque contemnit,' *all the most learned men despise the Epicureans,* C. *T. D.* i. 31. Another Superlative is often added to increase the force: 'Maximae cuique fortunae minime credendum est,' *all the greatest fortunes are least to be trusted,* L. xxx. 30.

a) Ut quisque is used with one Superlative, ita following with another: 'Hoc maxime officii est, ut quisque maxime opis indigeat, ita ei potissimum opitulari,' *this is a special duty, according as men most need assistance, so by preference to assist them,* C. *Off.* i. 15. In other words, Indigentissimo cuique potissimum opitulandum est.

b) Quisque may likewise distribute the Comparative: 'Quo quisque est sollertior et ingeniosior, hoc docet iracundius et laboriosius,' *the greater a man's skill and genius, the more fervour and pains he throws into his teaching,* C. *p. Q. Rosc.* 11.

c) Quisque also distributes Ordinal numbers: Primus quisque, decimus quisque, &c.: 'Quinto quoque anno Sicilia tota censetur,' *a census of all Sicily is taken every fifth year,* C. *Verr.* ii. 56.

viii. Other Intensive Phrases.

1) Remark the attractions (imitated from Greek), mirum quantum, nimium quantum, immane quantum, &c. (*surprisingly, exceedingly,* &c.): 'Id mirum quantum profuit ad concordiam civitatis,' *this was marvellously conducive to the harmony of the citizens,* L. xi. 1. 'Vino et lucernis Medus acinaces immane quantum discrepat,' *between the lamp-lit carouse and the Median scimitar, vast is the difference,* Hor. *C.* i. 27. 5.

2) Praecipue, summe, valde, vementer, admodum, apprime, inprimis, sane, sanequam, perquam, egregie, oppido, enixe, perfecte, and similar Adverbs, give a Superlative force to a Positive Adjective or Adverb: 'Praecipue sanus,' *eminently healthy,* Hor. 'Iuvenis admodum,' *quite young,* Tac. (See p. 135, and QUAM.)

3) Some Positive Adjectives contain often an emphatic sense, like that given by the adverb nimis: 'At ne longum fiat videte,' *mind it be not too long* (i.e. tedious), C. *Leg.* ii. 10. 'Nihil arduum fatis,' *nothing is too hard for destiny,* Tac. *H.* ii. 82.

ix. Some Adjectives are used both in Passive and Active sense. Such are

ambiguus (*doubted; doubting*) ; angustus (*narrow ; narrowing*); anxius (*disturbed; disturbing*); caecus (*dark; blind*) ; credulus, incredulus ; docilis ; dubius ; flebilis ; formidolosus ; gnarus, ignarus ; gratus, ingratus ; gratiosus ; incautus ; infestus ; innocuus, innoxius ; inultus ; laboriosus ; memor ; nescius ; notus, ignotus ; odiosus ; operosus ; riguus, irriguus ; somniculosus ; surdus ; suspiciosus ; tristis, and others. See these in Dictionary.

SECTION IV.

Uses of Pronouns.

i. Personal and Possessive Pronouns.

64

Personal and Possessive Pronouns.

1) Pronouns and Verbs of the First Person Plural are often used by a single person speaking of himself. 'Noris nos: docti sumus,' *you should know me, I am a man of learning*, Hor. *S.* i. 9. See p. 272 *Obs.*

2) The Personal Pronouns are used with the Prepositions ad, apud, ab, to signify '*house*,' '*abode*:' 'Septimo Idus veni ad me in Sinuessanum,' *on the 7th of the Ides I came to my villa at Sinuessa*, C. *Att.* xvi. 10. 'Scaurum ruri apud se esse audio,' *I hear that Scaurus is at his country seat*, C. *de Or.* i. 49. 'Quisnam a nobis egreditur foras?' *who is coming out of our house?* Ter. *Haut.* iii. 2. 50.

3) Pronouns of 1st and 2nd Persons are sometimes hidden in an Apposite Noun ; 'Hannibal peto pacem,' *I, Hannibal, sue for peace*, L. xxx. 30. 'Omnes boni semper nobilitati favemus,' *all we conservatives ever regard noble birth with favour*, C. *p. Sest.* 9. 'Soli Tusculani vera arma invenistis,' *only you men of Tusculum have discovered genuine warfare*, L. vi. 26.

4) Latin uses Possessive Pronouns sparingly ; thus, for '*I see my father*,' the Latin is 'Patrem video,' omitting the Possessive unless required for perspicuity or emphasis : 'Quid vos uxor mea violarat?' *what wrong had my wife done you?* C. *p. Dom.* 25. Yet' the Possessive is sometimes introduced without obvious necessity :' Cum ita animum induxti tuum,' *as you have prevailed on yourself*, Ter. *An.* i. 2. 12. Pleonasm of other Pronouns occurs in poetry : 'Nec dulcis amores sperne puer, neque tu choreas,' *despise in boyhood neither sweet loves nor yet dances*, Hor. *C.* i. 9. 15. 'Sic oculos, sic ille manus, sic ora ferebat,' *thus he used to carry his eyes, his hands, his countenance*, V. *Ae.* iii. 490. For the pleonastic use of ille by Virgil in comparisons see *Ae.* x. 707, xi. 809, xii. 5, and notes there.

5) The Possessive Pronouns are used by poets in the sense *propitious* : 'Sed mihi tam facilis unde meosque deos?' *but whence can I obtain gods so easy and propitious?* Ov. *Her.* xii. 84. 'Ventis iturus non suis,' *about to sail with unpropitious winds*, Hor. *Epod.* ix. 30. 'Haud numine nostro,' V. *Ae.* ii. 396:

6) On the use of the Possessive Pronouns for the Personal, see Syntax of Genitive. Thus, 'Neque neglegentia tua neque odio id fecit tuo,' *this he did neither from disregard nor from hatred of you,* Ter. *Ph.* v. 9.

65
Demon-
strative
Pro-
nouns.

ii. Demonstrative Pronouns.

Of Demonstrative Pronouns, hic refers to what is near to the speaker's person, place, time, habits, &c. : ille to what is remote from these : iste to what is in near relation to those addressed.

Hic.　　1) 'Haec quae videtur esse accusatio mea,' *this which seems to be my prosecution,* C. *in Q. Caec.* 2. 'His meis litteris,' *by this letter of mine,* C. *Fam.* i. 3. 'Huic homini' (=mihi), Plaut. *Epid.* i. 2. 38. 'Chrysis vicina haec moritur,' *my neighbour Chrysis here died,* Ter. *An.* i. 1. 78. 'Hoc a te peto, ut subvenias huic meae sollicitudini et huic meae laudi studium dices,' *what I ask of you is to relieve my anxiety and study to support my honour in this matter,* C. *Fam.* ii. 6. 'His duobus mensibus,' *within the last two months,* C. *Fam.* vii. 1. 'Hic dies,' *to-day.* 'Licentia haec,' *this modern licence,* L. xxv. 40.

Ille.　　2) 'Si illos, Labiene, quos iam videre non possumus, neglegis, ne his quidem, quos vides, consuli putas oportere?' *if you disregard those, Labienus, whom we can see no longer, do you think no care should be taken even for these, whom you do see?* C. *p. Rab.* 11. 'Q. Catulus non antiquo illo more, sed hoc nostro, fuit eruditus,' *Quintus Catulus was learned not in that ancient manner, but in this later one of our own,* C. *Brut.* 35.

a) Ille may refer to what was erewhile, or what will be hereafter (hence its locative olim has both meanings): 'Illam veterem iudiciorum vim,' C. 'Sapiens non pendet ex futuris, sed exspectat illa, fruitur praesentibus,' *a wise man hangs not on future things, but looks for them, while he enjoys the present,* C. *Fin.* i. 19.

b) When special stress is laid on a proposition or fact, it is introduced by illud : 'Illud animorum corporumque dissimile, quod animi valentes morbo temptari non possunt, corpora possunt,' *there is this striking difference between minds and bodies, that healthy minds cannot be assailed by disease, bodies can,* C. *T. D.* iv. 14.

c) Ille is used to express fame or dignity : 'Medea illa,' *the celebrated Medea,* C. *p. L. Man.* 9. 'Veneramini illum Iovem, custodem huius urbis,' *adore that great Jupiter, guardian of this city,* C. *Cat.* ii. 12. So with an attribute : 'An censes omnium rerumpublicarum nostram veterem illam fuisse optimam?' *do you think that of all commonwealths that old one of ours was the best?* C. *Leg.* ii. 10. Or with other pronouns : 'Instat hic nunc ille annus egregius,' *there is coming on now this fine, famous year,* C. *Att.* i. 18. 'Ille ego liber, ille ferox, tacui,' *I, that free, that haughty one, was mute,* Ov. *Met.* i. 757.

d) Ille, *the other* (of two named) : 'Themistocles domino navis
qui sit aperit : at ille procul ab insula navem tenuit in
ancoris,' *Themistocles disclosed to the ship's captain who
he was : whereupon the other kept the vessel at anchor
some way from the island,* Nep. *Them.* 8.   Illi, *the other
side, the other party* : 'Illorum qui dissentiunt,' C. *p. L.
Man.* 23.

3) When hic and ille refer to two things, hic designates either Hic
with
ille.
what is last mentioned, or what is nearer to the speaker's mind :
ille, either what is first mentioned, or what is farther from the
speaker's mind : 'Idem et docenti et discenti propositum esse
debet, ut ille prodesse velit, hic proficere,' *the teacher and learner
ought to have the same object ; the former should desire to confer
advantage, the latter to obtain it,* Sen. *Ep.* 108.   'Scitum est illud
Catonis, melius de quibusdam acerbos inimicos mereri quam eos
amicos qui dulces videantur : illos saepe verum dicere, hos numquam,' *it is a shrewd saying of Cato, that keen-tongued enemies deserve better of some men, than those friends who seem sweet-spoken :
the former often tell the truth, the latter never,* C. *Lael.* 24.   'Melior est certa pax quam sperata victoria; haec in tua, illa in deorum
manu est,' *better is sure peace than hoped-for victory ; the one is in
your own power, the other in the power of the gods,* L. xxx. 30.

The two Pronouns are also used for distribution : hoc et illud,
this and that.   So ille aut ille, ille et ille, *this and that man,* C. *p.
Rosc. A.* 21.

4) Iste has the same relation to tu (vos) that hic has to ego Iste.
(nos).   'Quae est ista praetura?' *what sort of praetorship is
that of yours?* C. *Verr.* ii. 2. 18.   'De istis rebus exspecto tuas
litteras,' *I await a letter from you about affairs in your parts,* C.
Att. ii. 5.   'Adventu tuo ista subsellia vacuefacta sunt,' *as soon
as you arrived those benches* (next you) *were cleared,* C. *Cat.* i. 7.   In
Cicero's speeches iste often means 'the defendant,' or the person
attacked.

Contempt is not contained in the meaning of the Pronoun iste,
but it is implied sometimes, inasmuch as the speaker seems to repel
what he names from himself to some one else.   'Quid sibi isti
miseri volunt?' *what do those wretches want?* C.   'Errare malo
cum Platone quam cum istis vera sentire,' *I had rather be wrong
with Plato than hold true doctrine with that crew,* C. *T. D.* i. 17.

Is.

5) Is, the unemphatic Determinative Pronoun, is used

a) In reference to a Noun before mentioned : 'Veientes
regem creavere. Offendit ea res populorum Etruriae
animos, odio ipsius regis. Gravis iam is antea genti
fuerat,' *the people of Veii elected a king : that act dis-
pleased the population of Etruria, from their hatred of
the king himself : (for) he had already been oppressive to
the nation at a former time,* L. v. 1.   'Maximum orna-
mentum amicitiae tollit qui ex ea tollit verecundiam,' *he
takes away the chief grace of friendship, who takes from it
respectfulness,* C. *Lael.* 22.

Its oblique cases are often left to be understood: 'Eadem secreto ex aliis quaerit; reperit esse vera,' *he asks the same questions privately of others, and finds all true,* Caes. *B. G.* i. 18.

β) In correlation to a Relative, which it usually precedes, but often, for the sake of emphasis, follows: Is qui hoc fecit, *he who did this.* 'Magna sunt ea quae sunt optimis proxima,' *great are those things which are next to the best,* C. *Or.* 2. 'Bestiae, in quo loco natae sunt, ex eo se non commovent,' *beasts do not move from the place they were born in,* C. *Fin.* v. 15. It may be omitted: 'Qui e nuce nucleum esse vult, frangit nucem,' *he who wishes to eat the kernel out of the walnut, breaks the walnut,* Plaut. *Curc.* i. 1. 55. 'Semper in proelio maximum est periculum qui maxime timent,' *ever in battle their peril is most whose fear is greatest,* Sall. *Cat.* 58. 'Quidquid non licet, nefas putare debemus,' *whatever is unlawful we ought to think impious,* C. *Par.* 3.

γ) In the sense of '*one of a kind,*' '*such :*' in which sense it may relate to any person, and be followed by qui with Indic. or (more usually) Subjunctive, or by ut with Subj. : 'Atque haec omnia is feci, qui sodalis et familiarissimus Dolabellae eram,' *and I who did all this was one, who stood in the most intimate and familiar relations to Dolabella,* C. *Fam.* xii. 14. 'Neque enim tu is es qui quid sis nescias,' *for you are not the man to be ignorant of your own powers,* C. *Fam.* v. 12. 'Matris est ea stultitia, ut eam nemo hominem, ea vis, ut nemo feminam, ea crudelitas, ut nemo matrem appellare possit,' *such is that mother's folly that none can call her a human being ; such her violence that none can term her a woman ; such her cruelty that none can speak of her as a mother,* C. *p. Clu.* 70.

Obs. In such sentences as, '*The features of the mind are fairer than* those *of the body,*' where the Demonstrative (*those*) is used in English, the Latin idiom omits it : as 'Animi lineamenta pulchriora sunt quam corporis,' C. *Fin.* iii. 25. The use of an *emphatic* pronoun (hic or ille) is no real exception to this rule : 'Nullam virtus aliam mercedem laborum periculorumque desiderat, praeter hanc laudis et gloriae,' *virtue wants no other reward of its perils and toils, but this of praise and glory,* C. *p. Arch.* 11. So, '*Those dwelling at Rome*' is in Latin not, Ei Romae habitantes ; but either Romae habitantes, or Ei qui Romae habitant.

Idem. 6) The Definitive Pronoun idem (is-dem), '*the same,*' is often aptly rendered '*also :*' 'Quidquid honestum, idem est utile,' *whatever is morally right is also advantageous,* C. *Off.* ii. 3. 'Non omnes, qui Attice, eidem bene ; sed omnes, qui bene, eidem etiam Attice loquuntur,' *not all who speak in the Attic manner also speak well ; but all who speak well speak also in the Attic manner,* C. *Brut.* 84.

Sometimes it implies a contrast ('*but yet*') : 'Inventi multi sunt, qui vitam profundere pro patria parati essent, eidem gloriae iacturam ne minimam quidem facere vellent,' *many have been found who were prepared to yield up life for their country, yet would not choose to make the smallest sacrifice of glory*, C. *Off.* i. 24.

It is placed, like ipse, in apposition to other Pronouns: 'Tu idem dixisti,' *you also said*, C. *p. L. Man.* 17. So haec eadem, qui idem, &c.

Note 1. Et is, isque, atque is, et is quidem, et hic quidem, et idem, idemque, atque idem (*and that too*), nec is (*and that too not*), &c., are used to lay stress on some quality of a word before mentioned: 'Homo habet memoriam, et eam infinitam rerum innumerabilium,' *man has memory, and an infinite one too, of countless things*, C. *T. D.* i. 24. 'Apollonium cognovi optimis studiis deditum idque a puero,' *I have known Apollonius to be devoted to sound learning, and that from boyhood*, C. *Fam.* xiii. 16.

Note 2. The Adverb quidem is elegantly joined to Personal and Demonstrative Pronouns, especially to ille, when a concession is made, but immediately qualified by an adversative clause (sed); answering to the English '*certainly* . . . *but*:' 'Ignosco equidem (ego quidem) tibi, sed tu quoque velim mihi ignoscas,' *I pardon you certainly, but I would have you too pardon me*, C. *Q. Fr.* iii. 1, 3. 'Tuus dolor humanus is quidem, sed tamen magnopere moderandus,' *yours is a grief natural to man, I admit, but one which should be considerably modified*, C. *Att.* xii. 10. 'Ludo et ioco uti illo quidem licet, sed tum, cum seriis rebus satisfeceris,' *you may indulge in sport and amusement, I grant, but not till you have fulfilled serious engagements*, C. *Off.* i. 29. The adversative clause is omitted in C. *Off.* ii. 9: 'Quae sordidissima est illa quidem ratio,' &c., *a principle which is, I admit, of the meanest kind*. See § 64 (4).

Note 3. Redundance of Demonstrative Pronouns occurs: 'Parmenides, Xenophanes minus bonis quamquam versibus sed tamen illis versibus increpant eorum arrogantiam,' *Parmenides and Xenophanes reprove their arrogance in verses, which, though not very good, are verses nevertheless*, C. *Ac.* ii. 23. 'Ista animi tranquillitas ea ipsa est beata vita,' *that tranquillity of mind is itself happiness*, C. *Fin.* v. 8.

This peculiar redundance is especially remarkable in Relative clauses: 'Plato Titanum e genere statuit eos, qui, ut illi caelestibus, sic hi adversentur magistratibus,' *Plato assigns to the Titan race those men who oppose magistrates, as the Titans opposed the gods*, C. *Leg.* iii. 2. 'Est istius furor repellendus qui quae maiores voluerunt, ea iste labefactavit,' *we should put away from us his madness, who has shaken those institutions, which our ancestors thought proper to establish*, C. *p. Dom.* 42.

iii. The Reflexive Pronouns se, suus.

Personal and Possessive Pronouns of the First and Second Persons may be used reflexively: that is, they may be referred to a Subject of *their own* Person. But se and suus differ from the rest, inasmuch as they cannot be used unless there be a Noun of their own (the Third) Person, expressed or understood, to which they are referred. Although we can say, amat me, *he loves me*; amat te, *he loves thee*; we cannot say, amo se, amas se, but amo eum, *I love*

him; amas eum, *you love him*; not culpo suum factum, but culpo
eius factum, *I blame his deed.*

The general rules for the use of se, suus are these :—

1) First : they may be referred to a Subject Nominative of the
Third Person in their own Clause. 'Fur telo se defendit,' *the thief
defends himself with a weapon*, C. *p. Mil.* 3. 'Atticus incitabat
omnis studio suo,' *Atticus inspired all with his own zeal*, Nep.
Att. 1. 'Sentit animus se vi sua moveri,' *the soul feels that it is
moved by its own force*, C. *T. D.* i. 23. The Pronoun quisque is
a frequent Subject of se, suus : 'Ipse se quisque diligit, quod per
se sibi quisque carus est,' *everyone loves himself, because everyone by the law of his own nature is precious to himself*, C. *Lael.*
21.

2) Secondly : they may be referred to an Object (which usually
precedes) when this reference causes no ambiguity. 'Scipionem
impellit ostentatio sui,' *ostentation of self sways Scipio*, Caes. *B.
C.* i. 4. 'Caesarem sua natura mitiorem facit,' *Caesar's own character makes him milder*, C. *Fam.* vi. 13. 'Ei nunc alia ducendast
domum, sua cognata,' *he has now to marry another, his own kins-
woman*, Plaut. *Cist.* i. 1. 'Multa sunt civibus inter se communia,' *many things are common to fellow-citizens*, C. *Off.* i. 17.
'Scipio suas res Syracusanis restituit,' *Scipio restored to the
Syracusans their property*, L. xxix. 1. 'Apibus fructum restituo
suum,' *I restore to the bees their produce*, Phaed. iii. 13.

3) Thirdly, they may be referred to an Indefinite Object Case
(alicui, aliquem) understood : 'Habenda ratio non sua solum, sed
etiam aliorum,' *men must take account not of themselves alone, but
also of others.* Especially in conjunction with an Infinitive : 'De-
forme est de se ipsum praedicare,' *it is unseemly to vaunt of oneself*, C. *Off.* i. 38. 'Bellum est sua vitia nosse,' *it is a fine thing to
know one's own faults*, C. *Att.* ii. 17.[1]

---

[1] The principles stated above hold good when se, suus, occur in Participial, Gerundial
and other dependence. 'Multa mea in se collata, etiam sua in me proferebat officia,'
*he brought forward many services done by me to him, and also those done by himself to
me*, C. *p. Sull.* 6. 'Constituit igitur ut ludi, absente se, fierent suo nomine,' *he
therefore arranged that in his absence the games should be held in his name*, C. *Att.*
xv. 11. 'Tanto gratior populo fuit quanto doctior maioribus suis,' *he was more popular
in proportion as he was more learned than his ancestors*, Iust. xvii. 3. 'Si nulla
caritas erit quae faciat amicitiam ipsam sua sponte, vi sua, ex se et propter
se expetendam,' *if there is no love to make friendship desirable on the first offer, by its
own force, from itself, and for itself*, C. *Fin.* ii. 20. 'Itaque redimendi se captivis
copiam fecere,' *accordingly they gave the prisoners the opportunity of ransoming themselves*, L. xxii. 58. 'Mithridatem Tigranes excepit diffidentemque rebus suis confirmavit,' *Tigranes received and encouraged Mithridates, who was despairing of his
own resources*, C. *p. L. Man.* 9. From such bold constructions as those of the three
latter examples, in which the Reflexive is referred to the Object Case by virtue of an
intervening Verb Infinite (expetendam, redimendi, diffidentem), has arisen one yet
bolder, in which the Preposition cum is equivalent to a Relative Clause : 'Dicaear-
chum cum Aristoxeno, aequali et condiscipulo suo, omittamus,' *let us pass over
Dicaearchus, and Aristoxenus his contemporary and fellow-pupil*, C. *T. D.* i. 18, where
cum &c. =quocum coniungimus Aristoxenum . . suum. A similar idiom is extended to
places where the Preposition in (more rarely ad, ab, intra) follows such Verbs as remittere,
retinere, reverti, iubere, cogere, removere, &c. the formula of command being adopted by
the writer from the speaker's mouth. Thus, 'Caesar Fabium cum legione sua remittit
in hiberna,' *Caesar sends back Fabius and his legion to their winter encampment*, Caes.
B. G. v. 53, is equivalent to 'Caesar imperat, Fabius cum legione sua in hiberna rever-

a) The Cases of is (sometimes those of ipse) are used when se, suus, would be wrong : ' Chilius te rogat, et ego eius rogatu,' *Chilius asks you, and I at his request*, C. *Att.* i. 9. ' Aranti Quinctio nuntiatum est eum dictatorem esse factum,' *news came to Quinctius while ploughing, that he was appointed dictator*, C. *Cat. M.* 16.

b) The Reflexive when referred to the Pronoun quisque (either Subject or Object) generally stands immediately before it : ' Mors sua quemque manet,' *his death awaits every man*. 'Suus quoique mos,' *every one has his own fashion*, Ter. *Ph.* ii. 4. But sometimes after it : 'Quisque suos patimur Manis,' Verg. *Aen.* vi. 743. So, 'Ut quisque sibi maxime confidit,' C. *Lael.* 30.

c) The use of the Adjectival phrase suus quisque (though not noticed in Madvig's grammar) is explained and illustrated by him on C. *Fin.* v. 17 : 'Quia cuiusque partis naturae et in corpore et in animo sua quaeque vis sit,' *because every part of nature both in body and soul has its own particular power*. So 'suo quoque anno' on an Inscription. See M. *Lucr.* ii. 372.

d) The Plural Masculine sui is used for amici, familiares or milites so idiomatically, that it sometimes appears to transgress the laws of Pronominal reference : ' Is annus Crassi omnem spem atque omnia vitae consilia morte pervertit ; fuit hoc luctuosum suis,' *that year overthrew by death all the hope and all the life-plans of Crassus : it was an event full of sorrow to his friends*, C. *d. Or.* iii. 2. ' Iam perventum ad suos est ' (= iam pervenerant ad suos), L. xxxiii. 4.

On these Pronouns in Dependent Clauses see § 231—236.

iv. The Definitive Pronoun ipse.

1) This is of any person, and strengthens any Noun-term, especially a Personal or Demonstrative Pronoun, with which it is placed in attributive apposition : ' Ipse Pater dextra molitur fulmina,' *the Sire himself wields the lightnings with his right hand*,

---

tantur.' So : 'Carthaginienses Magonem cum classe sua copiisque in Italiam mittunt,' *the Carthaginians send Mago with his fleet and forces into Italy*, L. xxiii. 32. 'Corbulo, ut Armenios ad sua defendenda cogeret, exscindere . parat castella,' *Corbulo, in order to compel the Armenians to defend their possessions, prepares to destroy their forts*, Tac. *Ann.* xiii. 39, where Corbulo may be supposed to say, 'Armenios ad sua defendenda cogam.' In such instances, if the Subject of the sentence is of the Third Person, the word or words to which the Reflexive suus is referred will be found immediately before the Reflexive. If the Subject is not of the Third Person, or if reference to it would be absurd, this is unnecessary. 'In sua terra cogam pugnare eum,' *I will compel him to fight in his own land*, L. xxviii. 44. 'Suis flammis delete Fidenas,' *destroy Fidenae with its own flames*, L. iv. 33. 'Desinant insidiari domi suae consuli,' *they should cease to lay snares for the consul at his own house*, C. *Cat.* i. 13. In constructions, however, like some of those cited in this note, it is optional to use the Demonstr. instead of the Refl. ; and the following passages (cited by Madvig, *Gr.* § 490) shew that ancient writers often did so : 'Omitto Isocratem discipulosque eius Ephorum et Naucratem,' C. *Or.* 51. 'Pisonem nostrum merito eius amo plurimum,' C. *Fam.* xiv. 2. 'Deum agnoscis ex operibus eius,' C. *T. D.* i. 28.

Verg. *G.* i. 329. 'Tarde nosmet ipsos cognoscimus,' *we gain knowledge of ourselves slowly,* C. *Fin.* v. 15. 'Ego ipse cum eodem ipso non invitus erraverim,' *I myself would be wrong without reluctance in that very same man's company,* C. *T. D.* i. 17.

2) Ipse implies that the notion, which it thus accentuates, is opposed to some other, expressed or understood. Cicero writes, 'Nemo est qui ipse se oderit,' *there is no one who hates himself,* C. *Fin.* v. 10. If he had written Nemo est qui se ipsum oderit, the English would still be, *there is no one who hates himself.* Yet there is a difference between the two Latin sentences, for, in the former, ipse indicates the following contrast, 'utcumque alii eum oderint,' *however others may hate him*; in the latter the following: 'utcumque alios oderit,' *however he may hate others.* So, 'Non egeo medicina : me ipse consolor,' *I want no medicine, I comfort myself,* C. *p. Cael.* 3, where ipse with the subject implies, 'I and no other,' but 'me ipsum consolor' would mean 'I comfort myself but nobody else.'

1) The Pronoun, which ipse emphasises, may be understood : 'Quaeram ex ipsa,' *I will inquire of herself* (= ex ea ipsa), C. *p. Cael.* 14.

2) When ipse strengthens the Subject, and a Reflexive Pronoun is Object, that Pronoun usually stands before ipse : 'Artaxerxes se ipse reprehendit,' *Artaxerxes blamed himself,* Nep. *Dat.* 5. 'Artes se ipsae per se tuentur singulae,' *the several arts maintain themselves on their own grounds,* C. *de Or.* ii. 2. But after qui, quidam, &c., or for stronger emphasis, ipse may precede the Pronoun Object : 'Non sunt composita mea verba : ipsa se virtus satis ostendit,' *mine is no set speech : virtue of itself is conspicuous enough,* Sall. *Iug.* 85. 'Qui ipse sibi sapiens prodesse non quit, nequiquam sapit,' *the wise man who cannot benefit himself is wise in vain,* C. *Fam.* v. 6.

3) Ipse strengthens the Object usually, when something in the context is opposed to that Object. Thus, in the phrase *killed himself,* though ipse generally stands with the Subject ('Iulius Priscus se ipse interfecit,' Tac. *H.* iv. 11), yet it may sometimes distinguish the Object : 'Pompeianus miles fratrem suum, dein cognito facinore se ipsum interfecit,' *a soldier of Pompeius slew his brother, and then, discovering his crime, killed himself,* Tac. *H.* iii. 51. Cicero writes, 'Sunt qui dicant, foedus quoddam esse sapientum ne minus amicos quam se ipsos diligant,' *some say there is a kind of covenant among the wise to love their friends not less than themselves, Fin.* i. 20. Yet it is a peculiarity of his to connect ipse with the Subject, and so heighten its force, even when the opposition lies between the Pronoun and something else : 'Iste sic erat humilis atque demissus, ut non modo populo Romano, sed etiam sibi ipse condemnatus videretur,' *the man was so lowly and downcast, that not only to the Roman people but even to himself he seemed already condemned,* C. *Verr. Act.* i. 6. 'Non ita abundo ingenio, ut te consoler, cum ipse me non possim,' *I have not such excess of ability as to comfort you when I cannot comfort myself,* C. *Fam.* iv. 8.

4) Ipse is also used

    a) For ultro, *of one's own accord* : 'Ipsae lacte domum re-
ferent distenta capellae ubera,' *the she-goats of their own
accord will bring home their milk-swollen udders*, Verg.
B. iv. 21.

    b) To define time exactly : 'Cum Athenis decem ipsos dies
fuissem,' *when I had been at Athens exactly ten days*, C.
Fam. ii. 8. So, 'nunc ipsum,' *at this very moment*, C.
Att. xii. 16. 'Tunc ipsum,' *at that exact time*, C. *de Fin.*
ii. 20. On the other hand aliquis is used to state time
inexactly : 'Aliquos viginti dies,' *some twenty days*,
Plaut. *Men.* v. 5. 47.

    c) To express the chief person : 'Pythagorei respondere sole-
bant, Ipse dixit,' *the Pythagoreans used to reply, He
himself said so* (i.e. *Pythagoras*), C. *N. D.* i. 5. Hence
slaves used to call their master and mistress, ipse, ipsa :
and Catullus uses ipsa for era : 'Suamque norat Ipsam
tam bene quam catella matrem,' *and knew its mistress as
well as a kitten knows its mother*, iii. 6.

v. The Indefinite Pronouns.

1) The Indefinite Pronouns, quis, qui,[1] being Enclitic, cannot
begin a sentence. They usually follow some particle (si, nisi, ne,
an, num, ut, &c.) or a Relative. 'Si quis est sensus in morte,'
if there is any feeling in death, C. *Phil.* ix. 6. 'Si qui etiam
inferis sensus est,' *if even the shades below have any feeling*, C.
Fam. iv. 5. 'Oppida coeperunt munire et ponere leges, ne quis
fur esset, neu latro, neu quis adulter,' *they began to build towns
and establish laws, that none should be a thief or bandit or adulterer*,
Hor. *S.* i. 3. So numquis, ecquis, &c. The Particles are similarly combined, siqua, siquando, sicubi, necubi, ecquando, &c.

    a) Quis Indef. is often connected with a case of its own : 'Si
mala condiderit in quem quis carmina, ius est,' *if one
man has composed libellous verses on another, there is a
remedy at law*, Hor. *S.* ii. 1. 82. Or with Indef. Particle :
'si quando quis faceret,' &c., L.

---

[1] It has been stated (p. 140) that the Interrogative and Indefinite forms quis, quid, are
substantival, qui, quod, adjectival ; and the truth of this assertion is shown by the two
facts, that quis in old Latin is of both genders, and that quid and quod always retained
their distinct characters as Substantive and Adjective. But it is also true that quis
(quae) is often used adjectively, as quis campus, puer quis in Horace, sensus aliquis in
Cicero ; the reply to which is that other Substantives are also used adjectively, as rex,
regina, incola, indigena, raptor, &c.

Another difficulty is the distinction of the Feminine Singular and Neuter Plural forms
qua, quae, of quis (qui) Indefinite. Some suppose that qua belongs to quis, quae
to qui ; but this is mere conjecture without proof. Both forms are used adjectively,
and both (less often) substantively ; but adjectives may become substantives, and occasionally substantives take the place of adjectives. The question thus remains undecided.
Cicero writes : 'ecquae civitas ? ecqua religio ? si quae pars ; si qua natio ; si quae prava
sint ; ne qua discidia fiant ; aliqua significatio virtutis ;' but not 'aliquae,' which occurs in
Lucretius. Upon the whole it may be stated that the form qua (Indef. S. and Pl.) is
more usual than quae, but that quae is also classical.

b) Si quis, si qui, stand for the Relative with a shade of uncertainty : ' Errant si qui in bello omnis secundos rerum proventus expectant,' *they are wrong who in war expect all issues to be prosperous,* Caes. *B. G.* vii. 29.

c) Quis and qui indefinite are sometimes used without a Particle, but only when the context expresses uncertainty : ' Potest quis errare aliquando,' *a person may err now and then,* C. *Div.* i. 32. ' Etiam quis forsitan hostis haesura in nostro tela gerit latere,' *and already perhaps some foe carries darts that will fasten in my side,* Tib. i. 10. 13. Here forsitan favours the use of quis.

Nescio quis, nescio qui. 2) ' Nescio quis, nescio qui (I know not who or what =) *some or other,*' are used as Indefinite Pronouns : ' Fortasse non ieiunum hoc nescio quid quod ego gessi et contemnendum videbitur,' *perhaps this something which I have done will seem not barren and despicable,* C. *Fam.* xv. 17. Particles correspond in use, nescio quo, nescio quando, &c.

Aliquis, aliqui. 3) Aliquis, aliqui, *some,* are somewhat less indefinite than quis, qui, and imply a person or thing assumed to exist somewhere. They do not need a Particle : ' Semper aliqui anquirendi sunt quos diligamus,' *we must always seek some persons to love,* C. *Lael.* 27. ' Sensus morienti aliquis esse potest,' *one who is dying may have some sensation,* C. *Cat. M.* 20. But they can follow a Particle : ' Si est aliqui sensus in morte,' *if there is any kind of feeling in death,* C. *p. Ses.* 62. Aliquando, aliqua, alicubi, &c., correspond in use to aliquis.

a) Occasionally aliquis signifies ' a person of importance :' ' Sese aliquem credens,' *considering himself somebody* (of importance), Pers. i. 129.

b) Aliquis itself (with its particles) has always positive force : but may stand in a Negative sentence or clause : ' Cum scias . . . sceleri ac furori tuo non mentem aliquam aut timorem tuum, sed fortunam populi Romani obstitisse,' *knowing as you do that your wicked madness was not baulked by any right feeling or fear on your part, but by the good fortune of the Roman people,* C. *in Cat.* i. 6. Draeger (*Histor. Synt.* p. 23) exemplifies at great length the use of this Pronoun and its Particles.

Quispiam, quisquam, &c. 4) Quispiam is used with more emphasis than quis, and rather less than aliquis : ' Forsitan aliquis aliquando eiusmodi quidpiam fecerit,' *perchance somebody or other at some time or other may have done a thing of the kind,* C. *Verr.* ii. 32. Quispiam is used chiefly in positive sentences : quisquam chiefly in negative and dubitative sentences : nonnullus only in a positive, ullus only in a negative or dubitative construction. ' Dicat (dixerit) quispiam,' *some one may say,* C. ' Hereditas est pecunia, quae morte alicuius ad quempiam pervenit iure,' *an inheritance is money which by somebody's death has come to any one by right,* C. *Top.* 6. ' Zeuxis tabulas pinxit, quarum nonnulla pars usque ad

nostram memoriam mansit,' *Zeuxis painted pictures, some of which
have remained to our time,* C. *Inv.* ii. 1. 'Nihil attinet quicquam
sequi, quod assequi non queas,' *it avails not to pursue anything
which you cannot attain,* C. *Off.* i. 31. 'Heu, cadit in quemquam
tantum scelus?' *alas, occurs there to any one such great wickedness?*
Verg. *B.* ix. 17. 'Nihil est quod Deus efficere non possit, et quidem sine labore ullo,' *there is nothing which God cannot effect,
and indeed without any toil,* C. *N. D.* iii. 39. 'Indignor quicquam reprehendi non quia crasse compositum illepideve putetur,
sed quia nuper,' *I am indignant that any work should be censured,
not because it is supposed to be of coarse or tasteless, but of modern,
composition,* Hor. *Ep.* ii. 1. 76. See M. *Lucr.* i. 1077.

Uspiam corresponds in use to quispiam; usquam, umquam to
quisquam and ullus; nusquam, numquam, to non quisquam, non
nullus. Nemo = non quisquam; nullus = non ullus. Nemo quisquam
is used: also homo quisquam.

Rare instances occur of quispiam with negatives, of quisquam
in positive sense, and of qui, aliqui where ullus would be usual.

5) Quidam, *a certain one,* as opposed to aliquis, implies that the
subject is definitely known, though indefinitely described: thus we
should say, 'Quodam tempore natus sum: aliquo moriar,' *I was
born at a certain time; I shall die some time or other.* 'Accurrit
quidam notus mihi nomine tantum,' *a certain man runs up to me,
whom I only knew by name,* Hor. *S.* i. 9. 3. It is joined with epithets, like the English word '*certain*:' 'Erat spinosa quaedam et
exilis oratio,' *his was a certain prickly and lean style,* C. *Or.* i. 18.
It occasionally means '*some,*' as opposed to '*the whole*' or '*others*:'
'Nullis piscibus supra quaternas pinnae sunt, quibusdam
binae, aliquibus nullae,' *no fishes have more than four fins, some
two, a few none at all,* Pl. *N. H.* ix. 20. Hence it is used to qualify
an expression not meant to be taken strictly: 'In ideis Plato quiddam divinum esse dicebat,' *Plato used to say that in ideas there
is something divine,* C. *Ac.* i. 9.

Quidam also stands in contrast to quivis, quilibet, *any you will.*
'Ut saltatori motus non quivis sed certus quidam est datus,
sic vita agenda est certo genere quodam non quolibet,' *as to a
dancer is assigned not any optional movement, but a certain definite one, so must life be passed in a certain definite way, not in any
we please,* C. *Brut.* 50.

(margin: Quidam, quivis, &c.)

6) Quisque, quaeque, quicque, *each* of any number. Plautus
uses quisque = quisquis: 'Quemque offendero,' *whomsoever I find,'*
Capt. iv. 2. For its other uses, see pp. 280, 287. On quem quisque,
&c., see M. *Lucr.* i. 966.

(margin: Quis-que.)

7) The Universal Relatives, whether compounded with -cumque
or of the duplicated form (quisquis, &c.), have no special idioms
distinguishing them from other Relatives: 'Quoscumque de te
queri audivi, quacumque ratione potui placavi,' *I appeased in
whatever way I could all whom I heard complaining of you,* C. *Q.
Fr.* i. 2. 'Quidquid erit tibi erit,' *whatever there is shall be for
you,* C. *Fam.* ii. 10. 'Quantiquanti bene emitur quod necesse
est,' *what is necessary is well purchased at any price,* C. *Att.* xii.
24. On quicquid for quicque, *each thing,* see M. *Lucr.* i. 289.

(margin: Univer-sal Re-latives.)

vi. Pronominalia.

1) **Alter** is *one of two* : the forms in **-ter** (as -τερος in Greek) implying comparison of two. 'Agesilaus claudus fuit altero pede,' *Agesilaus was lame of one foot*, Nep. *Ag.* i. 'Epaminondas habuit collegas duos, quorum alter erat Pelopidas,' *Epaminondas had two colleagues, one of whom was Pelopidas*, Nep. *Ep.* 8. Thus it answers the question u-ter, *which of two ?* al-ter qui . . . *the one who*, alter qui . . . *the other who*. 'Consules inter se agitabant uti alter Samnites hostis, alter Etruscos deligeret, et uter ad utrum bellum dux idoneus magis esset,' *the consuls were discussing, how that one of the two should choose the Samnites for enemy, the other the Etruscans ; and which commander was more suitable for which war*, L. x. 14. So, 'quidquid negat alter et alter,' *whatever one denies, the other denies also*, Hor. *Epist.* i. 10. 4.

> *a)* Two cases of alter (as of alius) may stand in the same clause, distributing ambo, uterque, &c. 'Uterque horum medium quiddam volebat sequi : sed ita cadebat ut alter ex alterius laude partem, uterque autem suam totam haberet,' *both these men wished to attain a mean ; but it so fell out that one had a share of the other's credit, while each possessed his own entire*, C. *Brut.* 20. Uterque (*each of two*) ; alteruter (*one or the other of two*) : 'Non est tuae dignitatis atque fidei ut contra alterutrum, cum sis utrique coniunctissimus, arma feras,' *it squares not with your dignity and honour, to bear arms against one or the other, being nearly allied to both*, C. *Att.* ix. 10. Alter alterum amant, *they love one another*; also expressed, 'amant se invicem,' 'mutuo amant,' 'amant inter se.' Alteri . . . alteri, *one party . . . the other party*.

> *b)* Alter means '*a second*,' '*another*,' besides one named or implied : 'Solus aut cum altero,' *alone or with another*, C. *Att.* xi. 15. 'Me ipsum accuso, deinde te, quasi me alterum,' *I reproach myself, and then you, a sort of second self*, C. *Att.* iii. 15. 'Alter erit tum Tiphys,' *then will there be a second Tiphys*, Verg. *B.* iv. 34. 'Alter ab illo,' *next to him*, Verg. *B.* v. 49. Alterum tantum, *as much again*.

2) **Alius** repeated in successive clauses signifies *one . . . another*, &c., without limit of number. 'Aliud equo est e natura, aliud bovi, aliud homini,' *one thing is natural to a horse, another to an ox, another to a man*, C. *Fin.* v. 9. Contrast is similarly effected by the adverbs of alius ; aliter, alias, alibi, alio, &c. Alias contentius, alias remissius, *at one time more vigorously, at another more slackly*. Here too the repetition of alius in the same clause, or its juxtaposition with one of its adverbs, or two of these adverbs in the same clause, will denote a difference of the predicate for different subjects. 'Duo deinceps reges alius alia via civitatem auxerunt,' *two successive kings increased the civic body in different ways*, L. i. 21. 'Illi alias aliud isdem de rebus iudicant,' *those men judge one thing at one time, another at another, on the same questions*, C. *de Or.* ii. 30. 'Eadem aliter alibi nuncupantur,' *the same things are differently named in different places*, Pl. *N. H.* xxv. 4. Aliud ex alio, *one thing after another*.

SECTION V.

Uses of Prepositions.

i. Prepositions with an ACCUSATIVE Case.

I. Ad (*to, at,* &c.).

Usque ad is often used : usque ad Numantiam. Hor. has
'adusque supremum tempus,' *even to his last hour.* Also the Adv.
usque, omitting ad. 'Usque Puteolos,' *as far as Pozzuoli,* C. 'Tar-
sum usque,' C. 'Ab ovo usque ad mala,' *from the eggs to the
apples,* Hor., i.e. from the beginning to the end of dinner.

1) Local Use.

    a) Ad, *to,* takes a Case of Place or Person, after a Verb ex-
pressing or implying motion : as ire, adire, accedere, ducere, adducere a d urbem, &c. ; mittere, scribere a d aliquem, &c. For simple Dat.: 'Dulce rideat ad patrem,'
Catull. See M. *Lucr.* i. 750.

    b) Ad, *at,* takes a Case after a Verb not expressing motion :
esse a d urbem : ad pedes iacere : ad quartum lapidem ;
victoria a d Cannas ; Curio fuit a d me, *at my house* ; ad
iudices, *before the judges* ; ad vinum, *over wine* ; ad Opis,
at the temple of Ops, C.

2) Temporal Use.

    a) Limit of Time (*to*) : ad summam senectutem, *to extreme old
age* ; ad hosce dies, *to modern times* ; ad ultimum, *to the very
last* ; a mani usque ad vesperum, *from morning to evening* ; ad
multam noctem, *till late in the night.*

    b) Point of Time : ad lucem, *at daybreak* ; ad postremum, *at
last* ; ad summum, *in fine.* Time fixed beforehand : exspecto te ad
Kal. Febr., *I look for you by the* 1st *of February* ; dies praestituta
est quam ad solveres, *a day was appointed you for paying.*

    c) Time within which : ad tempus, *for a time,* or *at the right
time* ; ad breve tempus, *for a short time* ; ad decem annos, *ten
years hence.*

    3) Ad marks the limit of Number and Degree : ad octingentos ;
or adverbially, ad octingenti caesi, *about* 800 *were slain,* L. So,
ad unum omnes, *to a man* ; ad assem, *to the last farthing* ; ad
summam, *on the whole* ; ad summam impudentiam, *to the most
shameless height.*

    4) The derived uses are :

    a) Addition : ad haec vulnera ; ad hoc, *moreover.*

    b) Standard : ad fistulam canere, *to sing to the pipe* ; ad
verbum ediscere, *to learn word for word* ; ad eum modum,
of that kind ; ad unguem, *to a nicety* ; ad amussim, *accurately.*

    c) Comparison : nihil est ad Persium, *he is nothing to Persius.*

d) Respect: Insignis ad laudem, *honourably distinguished.* Ad speciem ; ad pondus. See M. *Lucr.* iii. 214.

e) Occasion : Ad famam obsidionis, *on report of the siege.* Ad ictum, *after the blow.* See M. *Lucr.* i. 185.

f) Reply : Ad illa respondeo, *to this I reply.*

g) Purpose : Ad eam rem, *for that purpose* : ad praedam, *for plunder* : especially with Gerund and Gerundive : ad vescendum, *for food*; ad agros colendos, *for agriculture.* So servus ad remum, *rower*, Liv., ad manum, *amanuensis* ; Lygdamus ad cyathos, *the cup-bearer Lygdamus*, Prop. ; ad limina custos, *a doorkeeper*, Verg. And with a Case of that *against* which precaution or remedy is used : ad morsus bestiarum, *for bites*, ad morbos, *against diseases.*

II. Adversus, adversum (advorsus, advorsum) express

1) Place (*over against, opposite*) : Adversus Pydnam, *opposite to Pydna.* Quis haec est quae me advorsum incedit ? *who is this woman coming face to face with me ?* Plaut. Ire advorsum alicui, *to go to meet some one* = obviam ire. Exadversus is found : exadversus Athenas, *opposite Athens.*

2) Relation (*towards, against*). Amor adversus parentes, *love towards parents.* Adversus solem ne loquitor, *you must not speak against the sun.*

III. Apud expresses near neighbourhood, generally to Persons, rarely to Place : Apud oppidum, *near the town:*

1) With Persons it is used in various senses : Apud Lycomedem, *in the house of Lycomedes*; apud me, *at my house.* Apud populum orationem habuit, *he spoke before the people*; apud iudices eosdem reus factus est, *he was arraigned before the same judges.* Apud priscos Romanos hic mos erat, *this was the custom among the old Romans.* Apud Ciceronem, *in the writings of Cicero* ; apud Homerum (but in Iliade Homeri, in Ciceronis Libro de Officiis).

2) In phrases : Apud animum cogito, *I am considering in my mind.* Haec apud me valent, *these things have weight with me.* Fac apud te sis, *keep your wits about you.*

IV. Ante (*before*) is applied to

1) Place : Hannibal ante portas est.

2) Time : Ante lucem, *before daybreak.* Ante urbem conditam, *before the foundation of the city.* Ante tris annos, *three years ago* (also tribus ante annis or tertio anno ante). Multo ante, *long before.* Paulo ante, *a short time before.* Ante domandum, *before taming*, Verg.

3) Order and Preference : Hunc ante me diligo, *I love him above myself.* Ante alios carissimus (or carior). Ante omnia placent silvae, *woods please above everything.*

V. Pone (pos-ne) (*behind*) : Pone castra pabulatum ibant, *they went behind the camp to forage.* Ante et pone, *before and behind.*

VI. Post (pos-te : see ante) describes

1) Place (*behind*) : Hostis post montem se occultabat, *the enemy was hiding behind the mountain.* Manus eius post tergum religatae sunt, *his hands were tied behind his back.*

2) Time (*after, since*) : Post cenam, *after supper.* Post urbem conditam, *after the foundation of the city.* Post Christum natum, *after the birth of Christ.* Post hominum memoriam, *since the memory of man.* Post paucos dies (or paucis post diebus), *a few days after.* Paulo post, *soon after.* Longo post tempore, *V.*

3) Of Order and Dignity (*after, behind*) : 'Neque erit Lydia post Chloen,' *nor shall Lydia be after Chloe,* Hor.

VII. Cis, citra (citera parte), (*on this side of, within*), is applied to

1) Place : Cis Alpis, cis Padum, citra Euphraten, citra mare.

2) Time (very rarely) : Cis paucos dies hostis aderit, *the enemy will be here within a few days.* Citra Kalendas Octobris, *before the 1st of October.*

Note.—Hence citra is used of measure in the sense of *without* (i.e. *without reaching*), *short of* : Citra controversiam, *without dispute.* Citra ebrietatem, *short of intoxication.*

VIII. Ultra, from the root il = ol = ul (ultera parte, *on yonder side, beyond*) describes

1) Place : Ultra Aethiopiam, *beyond Ethiopia.* Ultra Garamantas et Indos, *beyond the Garamantes and Indians.*

2) Measure : Ne sutor ultra crepidam (progrediatur), *the cobbler must not go beyond his last.* Ultra puerilis annos est, *he is past childhood.* Ultra feminam ferox, *fierce beyond the nature of woman.* So, ultra fas ; ultra fidem.

IX. Trans (*across, beyond*) is applied to seas, rivers, hills, &c. : Naves trans mare currunt, *ships glide across the sea.* Trans Euphraten, *beyond the Euphrates.* Trans Alpis. Trans caput, V.

X. 1. Circum (*round, about*) of Place : Terra circum axem vertitur, *the earth turns about its axis.* Circum haec loca commoror, *I am staying about these spots.* Turba circum regem, *a crowd around the king.*

2. Circa (not used before Livy), describes

1) Place (*round*) : Urbes circa Capuam occupavit, *he seized the cities around Capua.* Multos circa se habebat, *he kept many about him.* Circa vias discurritur, *there is a skurry about the streets.* Circa pectus, *round the bosom.*

2) Time and Number (*about*) : Circa Calendas Februarias, *about the 1st of February.* Circa quingentos capti sunt, *about five hundred were taken.*

3) Respect (*about, concerning*) in Post-Augustan Latinity : Varia circa haec opinio est, *there is variety of opinion on this subject.*

3. Circiter (*about*) denotes extension round, and is used of Time and Number : Circiter meridiem advenimus, *we came about noon*. Decem circiter milia passuum abest, *he is about ten miles away.*

XI. Contra (contera parte) denotes a tendency of two things to come together, and describes

1) Place (*over against*) : Carthago Italiam contra, *Carthage over against Italy*. Aspicedum contra me, *look me in the face.*

2) Relation (*against*) : Contra naturam, *against nature*. Contra legem, *against law*. Hoc contra ius fasque est, *this is against law and religion*. Quod contra fit a plerisque, *most people do just the contrary*. Non caru'st auro contra, *he's worth his weight in gold.*

XII. Erga (*towards*) is used of Relation : Tuam erga me benevolentiam agnosco, *I acknowledge your goodwill towards me*. Scio quomodo erga me affectus sis, *I know how you feel towards me*. Erga is once used of place by Plautus (=*facing*).

XIII. Extra (extera parte) describes

1) Place (*outside of, without*) : Extra urbem, *outside the city*. Extra teli iactum, *out of range of darts.*

2) Relation (*without, beyond, clear of*) : Extra culpam, periculum, iocum, ordinem, modum, causam, &c.

3) Exception (*except*) : Nemo extra eum, *nobody except him.*

XIV. Intra (intera parte) (*within*) describes

1) Place : Intra urbem factum est, *it happened within the city*. Intra montem Taurum, *within Mount Taurus* (for cis).

2) Time : Intra triginta dies, *within thirty days.*

3) Extent : Hortensii scripta intra famam sunt, *the writings of Hortensius are short of their reputation*. Intra modum, intra legem epulari, *to feast within measure, within law.*

The Adv. intus (*within*) is also used with Accus. Intus domum, Plaut. Intus cellam, L.

XV. Inter signifies extension inside, and is used of—

1) Place (*between*) : Inter urbem et fluvium, *between the city and river.*

2) Time (*between, during*) : Inter horam tertiam et quartam, *between nine and ten o'clock*. Inter prandendum (*or* inter cenam) curis vaco, *at dinner* (or *at supper*) *I am free from cares*. Inter tot annos, *during so many years*. Inter vias, *on the road.*

3) Relation (*between, among*) : Inter hominem et beluam multum interest, *there is much difference between a man and a brute*. Constat inter omnis, *all are agreed*. Inter arma silent leges, *amidst arms laws are silent*. Inter cetera et illud dixit, *among other things he said this too.*

And of mutual relation with se; as Inter se amant, *they love one another.* Inter haec = interea, *meanwhile.*

XVI. Infra (infera parte) (*beneath*) describes

1) Place : Infra lunam nihil est non mortale, *beneath the moon there is nothing not mortal.*
2) Time : Homerus non infra Lycurgum fuit, *Homer was not after Lycurgus.*
3) Number : Non infra novena, *not less than nine at a time.*
4) Measure : Uri magnitudine sunt paulo infra elephantos, *buffaloes are of a size rather under elephants.*
5) Worth : Infra dignitatem meam, *beneath my dignity.*

XVII. Supra (supera parte) (*above, over*) describes

1) Place : Caelum supra terram est, *heaven is above earth.* Saltu supra venabula fertur, *he bounds over the hunting spears.* Supra caput. Supra me erat Atticus, infra Verrius, *Atticus sat above me, Verrius below.*
2) Time : Supra hanc memoriam vixit, *he lived before these times.* Ut supra dixi, *as I said above.*
3) Number : Caesa sunt supra millia viginti, *more than twenty thousand were slain.* Supra belli Sabini metum, *over and above the dread of a Sabine war.*
4) Measure : Supra humanam formam altior, *taller than human form.* Supra modum, *above measure.*

XVIII. Iuxta (iugista parte, Corss.) describes

1) Place (*adjoining*) : Hortus meus iuxta viam est, *my garden adjoins the road.*
2) Order (*next to, as well as, akin to*) : Iuxta deos in tua manu positum est, *next to the gods it lies in your hands.* Inermes iuxta armatos trucidati sunt, *unarmed as well as armed men were slaughtered.* Celeritas iuxta formidinem est, *speed is akin to fear.* Iuxta seditionem ventum est, *things almost came to mutiny.* Solo caeloque iuxta gravi, *soil and climate being equally unhealthy.*

XIX. Ob describes

1) Place (*before*) : Ob oculos mihi mors versata est, *death was before my eyes.* Follem sibi obstringit ob gulam, *he ties a bladder on his throat.* Ob os trudere, *to thrust in one's face.*
2) Cause (*for, on account of, with a view to*) : Poenas ob stultitiam do, *I suffer punishment for my folly.* Pecuniam ob absolvendum accepit, *he received money to acquit.* Argentum ob asinos, *money to pay for the donkeys.* Ager oppositu'st pigneri ob decem minas, *the estate is mortgaged for ten minas.* Frustra an ob rem, *ineffectually, or to some purpose.* Ob industriam, *studiously.* Ob eam causam, *on that account.*

XX. Penes (*in the power of, resting with*) : Penes imperatorem est summum imperium, *supreme power rests with the commander-*

in-chief. Deum penes est custodia mundi, *the guardianship of the world rests with God.* Servi penes accusatorem sunt, *the slaves are in the prosecutor's power.* Culpa te est penes, *the fault lies with you.* Penes te es? *are you in your senses?*

XXI. **Praeter** means extension in front of, and has the uses

1) *Along, beside, before* : Praeter ripam, *along the bank.* Praeter oculos, *before their eyes.* Via una praeter hostis erat, *the only road was along the enemy's flank.*

2) *Besides, except* : Praeter se neminem amat, *he loves none besides himself.* Quod crimen dicis, praeter amasse, meum? *what crime do you call mine, except having loved?*

3) *Beyond* : Praeter modum, *beyond measure.* Praeter ceteros clarus, *renowned beyond others.*

4) *Contrary to* : Hoc praeter opinionem accidit, *this happened contrary to expectation.* So, praeter spem.

XXII. **Prope** (*near, nigh to*) : Prope viam aedificat, *he builds near the road.* Prope Kalendas Sextilis, *near the first of August.* Prope abesse ab aliquo, *to be near to some person* or *place.* Prope secessionem plebis res venit, *matters almost came to a secession of the commons.*

The Comparative propius, and Superlative proxime, also take an Accusative : Propius urbem, *nearer the city.* Proxime montem, *very near the mountain.*

XXIII. **Propter** (prope-ter) means 'extension near,' and describes—

1) Place (*near, alongside of*) : Volcanus tenuit insulas propter Siciliam, *Vulcan held the isles near Sicily.* Propter aquam ambulavimus, *we walked beside the water.* Propter te sedet, *he sits beside you.* Cubantes propter, *sleeping near.*

2) Cause or Object (*on account of*) : Sapiens non propter metum legibus paret, *the wise man obeys not the laws on account of fear.* Illa propter se expetenda sunt, *those things are desirable on their own account.*

XXIV. **Secundum,** from sequor, denotes *following,* and describes—

1) Place (*next behind*) : I secundum me, *go next to me.* Secundum aurem vulnus accepit, *he received a wound behind his ear.* (*Along*) : Secundum litus, *along the shore.*

2) Time (*after*) : Secundum Idus Ianuarias veniam, *I will come after the 13th of January.*

3) Rank (*next after*) : Secundum te nemo mihi amicior, *after you no man is more friendly to me.* Secundum vocem vultus valet, *countenance tells next after voice.*

4) Agreement (*according to, in favour of*) : Secundum naturam vive, *live according to nature.* Secundum Stoicos omnia vitia paria sunt, *according to the Stoics all faults are equal.* Pontifices secundum me decreverunt, *the priests decreed in my favour.*

XXV. **Per** (*through*) signifies Passage from one end to another, or in all directions, and describes—

1) Place : Per Macedoniam, *through Macedonia.* Sanguis per venas in omne corpus diffunditur, *blood is diffused through the veins into the whole body.*

2) Duration of Time (*throughout, during*) : Per tris annos, *for three years.* Per noctem cernuntur sidera, *the stars are seen all night.* Per somnum, *during sleep.*

3) Agency (*by, through*) : Per procuratorem non per se ipsum agit, *he acts by an agent, not personally.*

4) Manner or Means (*by*) : Eos per vim eiecit, *he turned them out by force.* Per simulationem amicitiae me perdidit, *he ruined me on pretence of friendship.* Per litteras certiorem te faciam, *I will acquaint you by letter.* So, per vices, *by turns,* per silentium, *in silence,* per iocum, *jocularly.*

5) Motive or Cause : Per avaritiam id fecit, *he did that through avarice.* Amicitia per se expetenda est, *friendship should be sought for its own sake.* Per me licet hoc agas, *you may do this with my free will.* Per leges non licet civem verberare, *the laws do not allow beating a citizen.* Per te stetit quominus ego discederem, *you were the cause of my not departing.*

6) Per is used in Prayers and Adjurations (*by*) : Per deos te oro, *I pray you by the gods.*

Note. Per is sometimes disjoined from the word with which it is compounded : as, Per mihi gratum est, *it is very agreeable to me.* Per ovilia turbans, V. Or from its case : Per ego te deos oro, *I pray you by the gods.*

XXVI. **Versus, versum** (anc. vorsus, vorsum) (*towards*), always follow their Case : Hannibal Romam versus contendit, *Hannibal marched towards Rome.* The best writers subjoin it to a case governed by ad or in : Ad meridiem versus ibimus, *we will go towards the south.* In Italiam versus se convertit, *he turned towards Italy.*

ii. Prepositions governing an ABL. Case.

I. **A, ab, abs,** express a 'proceeding from,' and describe—

1) Place :—(*a*) Motion from : Sidera ab ortu ad occasum commeant, *the stars move from east to west.* Ab nobis domo'st, *it comes from our house.*

b) Distance from : Mille passuum sex a Caesaris castris subsedit, *he halted six miles from Caesar's camp.* See Prope. A milibus passuum esse, *to be a mile off.* See M. *Lucr.* i. 554.

c) Position in regard to (*on, on the side of*) : A fronte, *in front.* A tergo, *in the rear.* A sinistro cornu, *on the left wing.* A Platone facio, *I am on the side of Plato.* Zeno et ab eo qui sunt, *Zeno and his disciples.* Hoc a me est, *this is in my favour.* A senatu stetit, *he took the senate's side.* See M. *Lucr.* i. 693, 935 ; v. 754, 1332 ; vi. 968.

Obs. Procul ab is used : Procul a patria, Verg. And procul without ab. Haud procul seditione, L.: Usque ab. Ab usque, V. Lucr. has ore foras, *out from the mouth*, iv. 554.

2) Time (*from*) : Ab antiquissimis temporibus hic mos invaluit, *this custom prevailed from the earliest times.* So, ab initio, a puero, a pueritia, ab incunabulis, a prima aetate, &c. A primo, *from the first* or *from the beginning.*

3) Rank (*after*) : Proximus a rege, *next after the king.* Alter ab illo. Alter ab undecimo, *the 12th.* Ab hoc sermone profectus est, *after this discourse he set out.* Ab exequiis. Ab igni, *after* (in consequence of) *fire.* M. *Lucr.* vi. 968.

4) Separation (*from*) : A poena liberi sumus, *we are free from punishment.* Defende te a periculo, *defend yourself from danger.* Non ab re fuerit ea narrare, *it will not be irrelevant to relate these things.* Abhorrere ab aliqua re, *to shrink from anything ; to dislike.*

5) Origin in general (*from*) : Pecuniam a me accepit, *he received the money from me.* Ab Egnatio solvet, *he will pay through Egnatius.* A te mihi salutem dixit, *he greeted me from you.* A superstitione animi vates adhibuit, *he called in seers from mental superstition.* M. *Lucr.* ii. 51.

6) Agent after Verbs Passive and Intransitive (*by*) : A cane non magno saepe tenetur aper, *a wild boar is often held by a small dog.* Oculi a sole dolent, *my eyes are pained by the sun.* Ab hoste vēnire, *to be sold by an enemy.*

7) Respect (*in, in point of, on the side of*) : Ab animo aeger fui, *I was sick in mind.* Firmus est ab equitatu, *he is strong in cavalry.* A doctrina instructus est, *he is well furnished in point of learning.* A patre nobilis erat, *he was noble on the father's side.*

To this use belong the phrases for the offices of slaves and freedmen at Rome, and the modern phrases for the posts in a royal household, &c. Thus, (servus) ab epistulis meant *a letter-carrier* or *estafette ;* (servus *or* libertus) a manu, *an amanuensis ;* a bibliotheca, *a librarian ;* a pedibus, *a footman ;* a potione, *a butler* or *cupbearer,* &c. So, Regi a secretis consiliis, *a privy counsellor of the king.* Reginae a sacris, *queen's chaplain.*

II. D e expresses

1) Place (*down from, from*) : De rostris descendit, *he came down from the rostra.* De manibus hostium effugit, *he escaped from the enemy's hands.* Susque deque, *up and down.*

2) Time (*ere the close of, at*) : De prima luce, *at daybreak.* De die, *in daytime.*[1] De nocte, *in the night.* De multa nocte, *in the dead of night.* De prandio, *after luncheon.* Diem de die exspecto, *I am waiting from day to day.*

---

[1] Cicero's *jeu de mots* (*Phil.* ii. 34), 'non solum de die sed in diem vivere,' links two common phrases, 'de die (potare),' *to carouse by daylight,* and 'in diem vivere,' *to live for the day,* so as to suggest that Antonius drank from before the evening of one day to the dawn of the next (de die in diem).

3) Origin : De summo loco, *of highest rank.* De scripto dixit, *he spoke from a written paper.* De facie eum novi, *I know him by sight.* Emi domum de Crasso, *I bought a house of Crassus.* Hoc audivi de patre, *this I heard from my father.* De marmore signum, *a bust of marble.* Fies de rhetore consul, *from a rhetorician you will become consul.*

4) Partition (*of*) : Una de multis, *one of many maidens.* Accusator de plebe, *a plebeian prosecutor.* De tuo illud addis, *you add of your own suggestion.* De meo, *at my expense.*

5) Respect (*concerning, of,* &c.) : Multa de eo scripta sunt, *much was written about him.* Legati de pace, *envoys to treat for peace.* De captivis commutandis, *concerning an exchange of prisoners.* De nihilo irasci, *to be angry about nothing.* Quid de me fiet? *what will become of me?* De Gallis triumphavit, *he triumphed over the Gauls.*

6) Cause (*for, from,* &c.) : Multis et gravibus de causis, *for many important reasons.* Hoc de communi sententia factum est, *this was done by common vote.* De via languebam, *I was ill from the journey.*

7) Manner (*according to, on*) in many phrases : De more, *according to custom.* De industria, *on purpose.* De improviso, *unexpectedly.* De novo, *anew.* De integro, *afresh,* &c. De gradu conari, *to combat on foot,* de genu, *on the knees.*

III. E, ex, describe—

1) Place (*out of, from, on,* &c.) : Ex urbe venio. Ex Italia discessit. Ex arbore pendet, *it hangs on a tree.* Ex equis pugnant, *they fight on horseback.* E longinquo, *from far.* Ex propinquo, *near.* Ex obliquo, *athwart.* E regione, *in a direct line with.* See M. *Lucr.* vi. 344.

2) Time (*from, since*) : Ex illo die numquam eum vidi, *since that day I never set eyes on him.* Ex Metello consule, *from the consulship of Metellus.* Ex itinere, *on arrival.*

3) Origin (*from, of*) : Ex eo audivi. Ex me quaesivit. Ex Pompeio sciam. Statua e marmore facta. Homo ex animo constat et corpore, *man consists of soul and body.*

4) Transition (*from, after*) : Ex oratore arator factus est. So, aliud ex alio, *one thing after another* : diem ex die, *from day to day.* Pallidum e viridi folium, *a palish green leaf.*

5) Partition (*of*) : Unus ex amicis meis, *one of my friends.*

6) Cause (*from, for, by,* &c.) : Ex quo manifestum est, *whence it is clear.* Ex lassitudine dormio, *I fall asleep from weariness.* E vino vacillat, *he staggers from the effects of wine.* Ex vulneribus mortuus est, *he died of his wounds.* Vir ex doctrina nobilis, *a man renowned for his learning.* Ex pedibus laborat, *he has gout in his feet.* Illud ex senatus consulto factum est, *that was done by vote of the senate.* Hoc mihi ex sententia evenit, *this happened to my heart's*

content. Ex animi sententia loqui, *to speak with sincerity.* So, ex ordine, ex composito, *by arrangement,* e re mea, *for my interest,* e republica, *for the good of the state,* with other phrases. See p. 277.

7) Manner, in many phrases : Ex occulto, *secretly,* ex improviso, ex insperato, *unexpectedly,* ex parte, *in part.* Heres ex asse, *heir to the whole property by will* ; heres ex deunce, heres ex semisse, &c.

IV. Cum (*with*) expresses

1) Company : Cum patre proficiscor, *I go with my father.* As a Sociative Particle : Romulus cum fratre Remo, *Romulus and his brother Remus.*

　　a) The Adv. simul is used with Abl. for simul cum. Simul his, *together with these,* Hor. Ore simul cervix, Ov.

2) Coincidence of Time : Pariter cum ortu solis, *exactly at sunrise.*

3) Community : Nihil mihi cum illo est, *I have nothing to do with him.* Bellum gessit cum Helvetiis, *he waged war with the Helvetii.* Tecum loquar, *I will speak with you.* Conferre, comparare cum, *to compare with.*

4) Coincident Circumstances : Homines cum gladiis adsunt, *men with swords are present.* Esse cum imperio, *to be in chief command.* Magno cum dolore loquor, *I speak with great pain.* Illud cum causa fecit, *he acted thus with reason.* Cum pernicie reipublicae, *to the ruin of the state.* Cum clamore. Cum silentio. Cum lacrimis. Madida cum veste, *in wet clothes,* 'as simple Abl.' See M. *Lucr.* i. 755.

Note the phrase : cum eo ut . . . *on condition that . . .* Liv.

V. Absque (*without*) is chiefly found in the Comic poets : Absque te esset, *were it not for you* ; sometimes in Cicero. Litterae absque argumento, *a letter devoid of matter.*

VI. Sine (*without*) : Vana est sine viribus ira, *anger without strength is fruitless.* Sine dubio, sine ulla dubitatione, *without any doubt.*

Lucr. uses seorsum (*apart from*) with Abl. : seorsum corpore.

VII. Palam (*in view of*) : Palam populo, *in the people's sight.*

VIII. Clam, clanculum (*without the knowledge of*) : Clam patre, *without his father's knowledge.* In Comedy with Accusative : Clam uxorem ; clanculum patrem.

IX. Coram (*in the presence of*) : Coram populo dixit, *he spoke before the people.* Coram loqui cum aliquo, *to speak with another face to face.*

X. Prae describes

1) Place (*before*) : I prae, sequar, *go forward, I will follow* ; but generally before a Pronoun, and after the Verbs ago,

fero, gero : as Pastores prae se agant gregem, *let shep-herds drive the flock before them.* Pugionem prae se fert, *he displays a dagger.* Also metaphorically : Speciem boni viri prae te fers, *you exhibit the appearance of a good man.*

2) Comparison (*compared with, before*) : Prae nobis beatus es, *you are happy compared with us.* Prae se neminem putat, *he thinks none his superior.* Utilitatis species prae honestate recte contemnitur, *the show of advantage is properly despised in comparison with moral rectitude.*

3) Cause (*owing to, for*) : Prae lacrimis scribere non possum, *I cannot write for tears.* Prae multitudine sagittarum solem non videbitis, *you will not see the sun for the number of arrows.* Prae laetitia lacrimae prosiliunt mihi, *tears start into my eyes for joy,* Plaut.

XI. Pro expresses

1) Place (*before*) : Pro foribus, *before the door.* Stabat pro litore classis, *the fleet was lying off the coast.* Pro rostris dicebat, *he was speaking from the rostra.* Pro contione laudatus est, *he was thanked in full assembly.*

2) Defence (*in behalf of, for*) : Hoc non modo non pro me, sed etiam contra me est, *this is not only not for me, but is even against me.* Pro Ligario dixit, *he spoke for Ligarius.* Pro patria mori, *to die for country.*

3) Substitution (*instead of, equivalent to,* &c.) : Mihi pro parente fuit, *he was as a father to me.* Vultus saepe pro omnibus verbis est, *countenance is often equivalent to any words.* Pro praetore fuit, *he was propraetor.*

4) Retribution (*for, in requital of*) : Pro istis factis te ulciscar, *I'll punish you for that conduct.*

5) Resemblance and Respect (*in the light of*) : Illam educavi pro mea, *I brought her up as my daughter.* Pro cive se gerit, *he comports himself as a citizen.* Pro certo hoc habui, *I held this as certain.* Pro comperto illud afferunt, *they inform me as an assured fact.*

6) Proportion (*according to*) : Pro tua temperantia vales, *your good health accords with your temperance.* Pro viribus contendam, *I will try my best.* Pro re nata me geram, *I will conduct myself as present circumstances dictate.* Pro re et tempore consilium capere, *to take counsel according to existing circumstances.* Pro multitudine hominum angustos habent finis, *their extent is small compared with their population.* Proelium atrocius quam pro numero pugnantium fuit, *the battle was more furious than might have been expected from the number of the combatants.*

XII. T e n u s (*as far as*), from root *tan, ten,* ' *stretch,*' follows its Case, and governs Abl. Sing. (rarely Plur.) and Plural Genitive : Capulo tenus abdidit ensem, *he buried his sword to the hilt.* Nutricum tenus, *as far as the breast.* Crurum tenus. Observe verbo tenus (*as far as words go*); quadam tenus (*a certain way, to some extent*); eatenus, hactenus, quatenus, understanding parte. The Abl. Pl. 'Pectoribus tenus' is found in Ovid : the Acc. S. 'Tanain tenus' in Valerius Flaccus.

72 **iii. Prepositions governing an ACCUSATIVE or ABLATIVE Case.**

I. :(*a*) In with ACCUSATIVE signifies motion *to*, and describes

1) Place (*into, to, upon, against*) : In carcerem coniectus est, *he was thrown into prison.* In aram confugit, *he fled for refuge to the altar.* In equum conscendit, *he got on horseback.* Ad urbem, vel potius in urbem, exercitum adduxit, *he led an army up to the city, or rather, into the city.*

By a Constructio praegnans (one Verb having the force of two) in with Accusative sometimes follows a Verb of Rest : Vitruvium in carcerem asservari iussit, *he ordered Vitruvius to be kept in prison.* Adesse in senatum iussit, *he bade him attend the senate.* Portus in praedonum potestatem fuere, *the harbours were in the power of pirates.*

2) Time (*for*) : In crastinum diem me invitavit, *he invited me for the morrow.* Comitia constituta sunt in Kalendas Ianuarias, *the elections were fixed for the* 1st *of January.* In perpetuum (*for ever*), in praesens (*for the present*), in posterum, *for the future,* &c.

3) Transition (*into*) : Mutatur in lapidem. In sollicitudinem versa fiducia est, *confidence turned to anxiety.*

4) Dimension (*to*) : In altitudinem pedum sedecim murum perducit, *he carries the wall to the height of sixteen feet.*

5) Distribution : Censores bini in singulas civitates descripti sunt, *two censors were appointed for each state.* Ad denarios quinquaginta in singulos modios, *at fifty denars the bushel.* Mutatur in dies et in horas, *he changes daily and hourly.* In aestatem, *every summer.* M. *Lucr.* vi. 712.

6) Relation (*towards, against,* &c.) : Liberalis in milites, *liberal towards the troops.* Merita in rempublicam, *services to the state.* Cicero in Verrem dixit, *Cicero spoke against Verres.* Viri in uxores potestatem habent, *husbands have power over their wives.* In te oculi omnium defiguntur, *all eyes are fixed on you.*

7) Manner (*in, after*) : In hunc modum locutus est, *he spoke after this fashion.* In verba imperatoris iuraverunt, *they swore allegiance to the general.* So, in universum, in commune, in vicem (*in turn*), in numerum, *in measured time.* M. *Lucr.* ii. 631.

8) Purpose (*for*) : Gladiatores in ludos locavit, *he engaged gladiators for the games.* Sontes in poenam dediti sunt, *the guilty were delivered for punishment.* Omnia in maius

celebravit, *he exaggerated everything.* Dabo tibi pecuniam in rem familiarem, *I will give you money for your household expenses.* Quae in rem tuam sunt, *what is for your interest.*

(*b*) In with an ABLATIVE signifies *rest in*, and describes

1) Place (*in*) : In Italia. In urbe. In sole. In ore omnium versaris, *you are in everybody's mouth.* In Miltiade erat summa humanitas, *in Miltiades there was the greatest courtesy.* In conspectu est exercitus. In manibus est Vergilius. So, in aprico est res, *the affair is all smooth.* In incerto. In difficili. In medio relictum est, *it has been left unsettled.* In luctu et squalore sum, *I am in sorrow and mourning.* In manu, *in hand.*

(*On*) : Agesilaus in ora consedit, *Agesilaus halted on the brink.* Nix est in summo monte, *snow is on the summit of the mountain.* Pons in flumine factus est, *a bridge was formed on the river.* In equo sedens, *on horseback.* Ponere curam, cogitationem, &c., in aliqua re, *to employ the mind on some object.*

(*Among*) : In magnis viris numeratur. Haec in bonis sunt habenda, *these must be counted among blessings.*

2) Time (*during, in*) : Ter in anno rus imus, *I go into the country thrice a year.* In praesenti nihil opus est, *there is no need at present.* In annonae caritate civitati subvenit, *when corn was dear he helped the city.* In tempore veni. Impraesentiarum, *under present circumstances,* is a corruption of 'in praesentia harum rerum,' chiefly used by elder and late authors, also by Nepos.

3) Circumstance (*amidst, in*) : In tanta perfidia veterum amicorum nihil supererat spei, *amidst such treachery of old friends no hope remained.* Etiam in summa bonorum civium copia timemus, *even amidst an abundance of good citizens I am alarmed.* In vino diserti sumus, *we are eloquent over wine.* In dicendo, in agendo. In honore, in pretio. Horridus in iaculis et pelle ursae. V.

(*In the case of*) : In hoc homine non accipio accusationem, *in this man's case I admit no charge.* Idem in bono servo dici solet, *the same is said of a good slave.*

4) Cause (*on the score of*) : In ea re gratias Deo agebamus, *for that we thanked God.* Pausanias in eo est reprehensus, *Pausanias was blamed on that score.*

II. (*a*) Sub with an ACCUSATIVE describes

1) Place (*under*) literally and metaphorically, when motion is implied : Armentum sub tecta referto, *take the herd back to shelter.* Sub ictum venire, *to come under fire.* Sub aciem primam succedere, *to come up with the van.* Sub iugum Romani missi sunt, *the Romans were made to pass under the yoke.* Sub oculos mihi venit, *he came under my view.* Sub iudicium cades, *you will be subject to trial.* Sub sensus subiecta, *within reach of the senses.*

x

2) Time (*immediately after* or *before, about, against*) : Sub eas litteras recitatae sunt tuae, *next after that letter yours was read.* Sub ortum lucis signa contulit, *at daybreak he engaged.* Cenam parat uxor sub adventum viri, *the wife prepares supper against her husband's arrival.* Sub lacrimosa Troiae funera, *just before Troy's sad destruction.*

(*b*) Sub with an ABLATIVE is applied to

1) Place (*under*), rest being implied : Talpae sub terra habitant, *moles dwell under the ground.* Iudaea sub procuratore erat, *Judea was under a procurator.* Sub hac condicione rediit, *under this condition he returned.* Sub oculis, *in view.*

2) Time (*about, at*) : Sub exitu anni, *about the end of the year.* Sub eodem tempore. See M. *Lucr.* iv. 545-785 ; vi. 413, 416.

III. (*a*) Super with an ACCUSATIVE expresses

1) Place (*over, above, beyond*) : Alii super vallum praecipitantur, *others fling themselves over the entrenchment.* Super navem turris exstructa est, *a tower was reared on the ship.* Super Sunium navigavit, *he sailed beyond Sunium.* Super ipsum, *above the host at table.*

2) Number (*besides*): Super bellum annona premit, *besides war, dearth causes distress.* Super haec. Super omnia, *over and above all else.* Super tris modios accepi, *I received above three bushels.* Alii super alios. Savia super savia, *kisses upon kisses.*

3) Comparison (*beyond*) : Res super vota fluunt, *matters proceed beyond our wishes.* Super, *principally*, V.

4) Time (*during*): Super cenam collocuti sumus, *during supper we conversed.*

Lucan uses desuper (*over*) with Accus. Desuper Alpis nubiferae collis, &c. i. 688.

(*b*) Super with an ABLATIVE expresses

1) Place (*over, upon*) : Ensis super cervice pendet, *a sword hangs over his neck.* Fronde super viridi requiescimus, *we rest on green foliage.*

2) Time (*during, at*) : Nocte super media, *at midnight.*

3) Subject Matter (*about*): Multa super Priamo rogitans, super Hectore multa, *asking much about Priam, much about Hector*, Verg.

IV. Subter (*under, below*), signifying extension under, generally governs an ACCUSATIVE, but sometimes in poetry an ABLATIVE : Amnes saepe subter terram vias occultas agunt, *rivers often pursue secret courses under ground.* Virtus omnia subter se habet, *virtue holds everything subject to itself.* Subter densa testudine, *under a compact pent-house.*

Note 1.—The following Prepositions are also used as Adverbs : ante, citra, circum, circa, circiter, contra, iuxta, infra, intra, pone, post, prae (rare), prope, subter, super, supra, ultra, coram, clam, palam.

Note 2.—Comminus ire, ' *to close with,*' is used by Propertius with Dat. and Accus. 'Haemonio comminus isse viro,' iii. 1. ' Agrestis comminus ire sues,' ii. 19. So Ov. *F.* v. 176.

Note 3.—Of the Prepositions the following are opposed in meaning :—

ante to post (pone)	infra to supra	sub to super
ad — ab	cis — (trans)	prope — procul
in — ex	citra — ultra	clam — palam

Note 4.—Prepositions may sometimes stand in good prose

1) Between Pronoun and Noun : qua in re; hanc ob causam; magno cum metu, &c.
2) After the Pronouns qui, hic, without Noun; quem contra dicit; quos inter, hunc adversus, &c. Not so found are, ab, cis, sub, pro, prae; seldom, ad, de, ex, in.
3) With one or more words interposed between Preposition and Case : 'in bella gerentibus;' 'in suum cuique tribuendo;' 'post autem Alexandri Magni mortem,' &c.

Poets often place Prepositions after their Cases, and sometimes aloof from them: 'Vitiis nemo sine nascitur,' Hor. *S.* i. 3, 68. See M. *Lucr.* i. 841 ; iii. 140.

(On Prepositions in composition, see § 52, § 59.)

SECTION VI.

Correlative Construction.

i. Pronominal Correlation.

The pronominal Root qui- quo- is the most influential word in Latin; for from it spring (1) Almost all Interrogative words ; (2) all Relative words; (3) most Subordinative Conjunctions.

A) 1) Every Interrogative word may question

Directly or Obliquely.

Direct.	Oblique.
quae est mulier?	rogo quae sit mulier
unde est mulier?	dic unde sit mulier
verumne est illud?	quaero verumne sit illud

Every Oblique Interrogative is Conjunctional, introducing a Subordinate Sentence.

2) Every Pronominal Interrogative has corresponding to it at least one Demonstrative Pronoun or Particle; and a Relative Pronoun or Particle.

Interr.	Dem.	Rel.	Interr.	Dem.	Rel.
quis ?	is	qui	quare ?	ideo	quod
ubi ?	ibi	ubi	quando ?	tum	quum (cum)

Every Relative Pronoun or Particle is Conjunctional, introducing a Subordinate sentence.

B) Hence the following Correlations : the first four of which are Adjectival, that is, they involve agreement with Substantives. The rest are Adverbial, but capable of being changed into Adjectival form : thus u b i = q u o in l o c o ? ubi . . . ibi = in eo loco . . . in quo.

1) Correlation of Person or Thing.

Direct Interrog.	Oblique Interrog.	Demonstr.	Rel.
a) quis qui } (est ?)	quis qui } (sit)	is, &c.	qui
who (is he ?)	*who (he is)*	*he*	*who*
b) quid (est ?)	quid (sit)	id, &c.	quod
what (is it ?)	*what (it is)*	*that*	*which*

(The forms ecquis, ecqui, ecquae, ecquid, ecquod are also used interrogatively.)

c) uter (est ?)	uter (sit)	is (alter)	qui
which of two (is he ?)	*which of two (he is)*	*that one*	*which*

2) Correlation of Quality.

qualis (est ?)	qualis (sit)	talis	qualis
of what kind (is he ?)	*of what kind (he is)*	*such*	*as*

3) Correlation of Quantity.

quantus (est ?)	quantus (sit)	tantus	quantus
how great (is he ?)	*how great (he is)*	*so great*	*as*

4) quot (sunt)	quot (sint)	tot	quot
how many (are they ?)	*how many they are)*	*so many*	*as*

(This includes quotiens? *how many times?* totiens . . . quotiens.)

5) Correlation of Place.

a) ubi (est ?)	ubi (sit)	ibi	ubi
where (is he ?)	*where (he is)*	*there*	*where*
b) unde (est?)	unde (sit)	inde	unde
whence (is he ?)	*whence (he is)*	*thence*	*whence*
c) quo (it ?)	quo (eat)	eo	quo
whither (goes he ?)	*whither (he goes)*	*thither*	*whither*
d) qua (it ?)	qua (eat)	ea	qua
by which way (goes he ?)	*by which way (he goes)*	*by that way*	*by which*

(These include quorsum, *whitherward,* &c., quousque? quoad? quatenus? *how far,* &c. ; compounded with quo, qua.)

6) Correlation of Manner.

ut (flet ?)	ut (fleat)	ita	ut
how (weeps he ?)	*how (he weeps)*	*so*	*as*
(Similarly quomodo ?		ita	quomodo
quemadmodum ?		ita	quemadmodum.)

7) Correlation of Degree.

Direct Interrog.	Oblique Interrog.	Demonstr.	Rel.
quam (celer est ?)	quam (c. sit)	tam	quam
how (swift is he ?)	*how s. (he is)*	*so*	*as*

(For tam . . . quam may be used aeque . . . atque (ac) and many other Demonstratives with atque (ac). In the Correlation of Inequality quam follows Comparatives and some other words which contain the idea of comparison.)

8) Correlation of Cause.

quare } (venit ?) cur }	quare } (veniat) cur }	ideo propterea }	quod quia }
why (comes he ?)	*why (he comes)*	*therefore*	*because*

9) Correlation of Time.

a) quando (it ?)	quando (eat)	tum	quum
when (goes he ?)	*when (he goes)*	*then*	*when*
b) quamdiu (ma-net ?)	quamdiu (ma-neat)	tamdiu	quam
how long (stays he ?)	*how long (he stays)*	*so long*	*as*

So quousque, quoad, quatenus, are answered demonstratively and relatively by several forms : as, eousque . . . dum (donec, quoad); usque . . . dum (donec, quoad); eatenus . . . dum (donec); tamdiu . . . quam, &c.

C) Examples of Direct Pronominal Interrogation.

1) 'Quis fuit horrendos primus qui protulit enses?' *who was it that first produced dreadful swords?* Tib. i. 10. 1. 'Qui cantus moderata orationis pronuntiatione dulcior inveniri potest? quod carmen artificiosa verborum conclusione aptius?' *what song can we find sweeter than a well-uttered speech? what poetry neater than a skilful period?* C. d. Or. ii. 8. 'Ecqui pudor est, ecqua religio, Verres? ecqui metus?' *have you any shame, Verres? any scruple? any fear?* C. Verr. iv. 8. 'Ubi aut qualis est tua mens?' *where or of what nature is your soul?* C. T. D. i. 27. 'Ut valet? ut meminit nostri?' *how is his health? how does he keep me in mind?* Hor. *Epist.* i. 3. (In exclamation :) 'Quam non est facilis virtus, quam vero difficilis eius diuturna simulatio !' *how far from easy is virtue, how difficult in truth the long-continued pretence of it !* C. *Att.* vii. 1. 'Quam timeo quorsum evadas !' *how I dread what you're coming to !* Ter. *An.* i. 1. 100. 'Gnaeus autem noster ut totus iacet !' *how totally prostrate is our friend Gnaeus !* C. *Att.* vii. 19. Quanti est sapere, *how valuable is wisdom !* Ter. Eun. iv. 7.

2) Several Interrogatives in one Sentence :

'Considera, Piso, quis quem fraudasse dicatur,' *consider, Piso, who is said to have defrauded whom,* C. p. Q. Rosc. 7. 'Uter utri insidias fecit ?' *which plotted against which ?* C. p. Mil. 9.

3) Quotus quisque literally is, '*each (unit) of what total number*' = '*one in how many,*' and might be answered : centensimus quisque, *one in a hundred* ; vicensimus quisque, *one in twenty* ; decimus quis-

que, *one in ten*, &c.   Hence it came to mean, *how small a proportion? how few?* 'Quotus enim quisque formosus est?' *how few men are handsome?* C. *N. D.* i. 28.

4) Quid is used in abrupt Interrogation with ellipse of a Verb : Quid? *well? how?* &c. quid multa? *why be prolix?* quid quaeris? *what would you have more?*   Quid tandem? *why pray?*   So, quid enim? quid ergo? quid tum?   quid quod . . .? *need I add that?*

5) Quin for qui non? 'Quin quod est ferendum fers?' *won't you bear what must be borne?* Ter. *Ph.* ii. 3. 82.   Quidni possim? *why can I not?* (=*to be sure I can*), C. *T. D.* v. 5.   Quippini? *why not? to be sure,* Plaut.   On quin with Indic., see M. *Lucr.* i. 588.

D) Correlation between Demonstrative and Relative :

1) 'Fere libenter homines id quod volunt credunt,' *men generally believe with readiness what they wish,* Caes. *B. G.* iii. 18. 'Quam quisque norit artem in hac se exerceat,' *let every one practise the profession he knows.*   'Non sunt tanti ulla merita quanta insolentia hominis quantumque fastidium,' *none of the man's deserts are on a par with the greatness of his insolence and pride,* C. *d. Or.* ii. 52.   'Ubi bene, ibi patria,' *country is where we are well off,* Inc.   'Ibit eo quo vis qui zonam perdidit,' *he who has lost his purse will go where you please,* Hor. *Epist.* ii. 2. 40.   'Quam audax est ad conandum tam est obscurus in agendo,' *he is as secret in action as he is bold in enterprise,* C. *Verr.* ii. 2.   'Ut magistratibus leges ita populo praesunt magistratus,' *as laws govern magistrates, so do magistrates the people,* C. *Leg.* iii. 1. 'Quid egeris tunc apparebit cum animam ages,' *what you have done will appear when you are at your last gasp,* Sen. *Ep.* 26.

2) Demonstrative with a Relative of different Correlation : 'In ea urbe es ubi (=in qua) nata et alta est ratio ac moderatio vitae,' *you are in that city wherein regulation and government of life were born and reared,* C. *Fam.* vi. 1.   'Ibi imperium erit unde victoria fuerit,' *empire will be on the side of victory,* L. i. 24.

3) Demonstrative understood : 'Donum redde unde accepisti, *render back the gift to the donor,* Ter. *Eun.* i. 2. 34.   This is the most frequent form.

4) The Correlation of cum and tum, originally of Time, is employed to distribute two notions, the one (with cum) general, the other (with tum) special, to which attention is thus invited. ' Multum cum in omnibus rebus tum in re militari potest fortuna,' *fortune can do much in all things, especially in war,* Caes. *B. G.* vi. 30.   'Exspecta hospitem cum minime edacem tum inimicum cenis sumptuosis,' *look for a guest who is not only a small eater, but also no friend to expensive dinners,* C. *Fam.* ix. 23.

74   ii. Correlations of Manner.

Ut (uti) is a Relative Particle (orig. = quod).   Its uses are :
 As Interrogative (*how?*).
 As a Subordinative Conjunction (*that,* &c.).
 As a Coordinative Conjunction of Comparison (*as*).

The Interrogative and Subordinative uses are elsewhere noticed.

1) As Coordinative, ut, as well as quomodo, quemadmodum
(*as*), is found in correlation usually with the Demonstratives ita,
sic, also with itidem, item, &c., eodem modo, ad eundem modum,
isto modo, &c.—pro eo: and compounded: sicut (sicuti); velut
(veluti). Or they may be used without a Demonstrative.

A) Correlation of ut, &c. with Demonstrative. (M. *Lucr.* ii. 901.)
'Ut optasti ita est,' *it is as you wished,* C. *Fam.* ii. 10. 'Ut
male posuimus initia, sic cetera sequentur,' *according to our bad
beginning, the rest will follow,* C. *Att.* x. 20. 'Ut vir doctissimus
fecit Plato item mihi credo esse faciendum,' *I think I should act
as the learned Plato did,* C. *p. Clu.* 24. 'Non ille ut plerique, sed
isto modo ut tu, distincte graviter ornate dicebat,' *he did not speak
as most do, but in that manner of yours, with clearness, power, and
elegance,* C. *N. D.* i. 21. 'Quemadmodum soles de ceteris rebus,
sic de amicitia disputa,' *argue concerning friendship, as you are
wont to do on other subjects,* C. *Lael.* 4. 'Necesse est, quo tu me
modo esse voles, ita esse, mater,' *I must be as you wish me,
mother,* Plaut. *Cist.* i. 1. 48. 'Ita ut fit,' *in the ordinary way.*

a) Ita . . . ut in asseverations: 'Ita me di ament ut ego
tam meapte causa laetor quam illius,' *so may the gods
love me as I rejoice on my own account as much as his,*
Ter. *Haut.* i. 3. 8. Also ita or sic without ut, parenthetically: 'Sollicitat, ita vivam, me tua valetudo,' *your
health, upon my life, makes me anxious,* C. *Fam.* xvi. 20.
See Hor. *C.* i. 3. 1.
b) Ut is used with concessive meaning in one clause, sic or ita
following with adversative force in another: 'Ut errare,
mi Plance, potuisti, sic decipi te non potuisse quis non
videt?' *err indeed you might, dear Plancus, but deceived
you could not have been,* C. *Fam.* x. 20.

B) Without Demonstrative:
'Praesertim ut nunc sunt mores,' *especially as fashions now are,*
Ter. *Ph.* i. 2. 5. Ut res dant sese, *in the present state of affairs.*
These Conjunctions are constantly used in parenthesis = id quod:
as, ut aiunt, *as they say*; ut opinor, *as I think*; ut videtur, *as you
please*; quemadmodum spero; quomodo mihi persuades, &c.
Also, ut nunc est, ut nunc quidem est (*under present circumstances*),
ut potest, ut potui, ut potero, (*as far as possible*).

2) Ut, sicut, in comparisons, usually express a more real likeness than quasi, tamquam: 'Sicut unus paterfamilias his de
rebus loquor,' *I speak on these subjects like any other head of a
family,* C. *d. Or.* i. 29. 'Inspicere tamquam in speculum in
vitas hominum,' *to look into men's lives, as into a mirror,* Ter. *Ad.*
iii. 3. 61.

3) Ut is used
a) To introduce a modifying expression, '*considered as being,*'
'*for,*' without a Verb: 'Clisthenes multum, ut temporibus illis, valuit dicendo,' *Clisthenes had great powers of
speaking for those times,* C. *Brut.* 7.
β) Also with a Causal force (*as being*): 'Apud me, ut
bonum iudicem, argumenta plus quam testes valent,'

*with me, as a discreet judge, circumstantial proofs have
more weight than witnesses,* C. d. Or. i. 38.

γ) Hence, with a Verb, to imply that some one fact is in
conformity with some other : 'Aiunt hominem, ut erat
furiosus, respondisse,' *they say the man, raging as he was,
replied,* C. p. Rosc. Am. 12. 'Horum auctoritate finitumi
adducti, ut sunt Gallorum subita et repentina consilia,
Trebium retinent,' *the neighbouring tribes, led on by these
men's influence, with the precipitation usual in the measures of the Gauls, detain Trebius,* Caes. B. G. iii. 8. This
sense may also be conveyed by the Relative qui (=quia
talis) or by the Preposition pro. Thus it is the same
thing to use any of these phrases :

Tu { ut es prudens / quā es prudentiā / quae tua est prudentia / pro tuā prudentiā } tacebas { *You / with your usual prudence / were silent* }

iii. Correlations of Likeness and Unlike-ness.

Atque, ac (not used before vowels), in the Correlation of Likeness follow the Adjectives and Pronouns, aequus, par, similis, talis,
idem, totidem; and the Adverbs, aeque, item, itidem, iuxta, pariter,
perinde, proinde, similiter, simul : in the Correlation of Unlikeness
they follow the Adjectives alius, contrarius, dissimilis, dispar, diversus ; and the Adverbs aliter, &c. contra, secus.

Ut is also found in the Correlation of Likeness after several of
the words cited : que after iuxta : et in both kinds : quam in the
Correlation of Unlikeness alone in the best age, but iuxta quam in
Livy, aeque, perinde quam in post-Augustan writers.

1) Correlation of Likeness :—'Modo ne in aequo hostes vestri
nostrique apud vos sint ac nos socii,' *provided our common enemies
be not on the same footing in your esteem as we your allies,* L. xxxix.
37. 'Animus te erga idem est ac fuit,' *the feeling towards you is
the same as it was,* Ter. Haut. ii. 1. 'Pari eum atque illos imperio
esse iussit,' *he ordered him to be equal in command with the others,*
Nep. Dat. 3. 'Aliquid ab illo simile atque a ceteris est factum,'
he did something like what others did, C. Phil. i. 4. 'Faxo eum
tali mactatum atque hic est infortunio,' *I will make him suffer
such a misfortune as this man has suffered,* Ter. Ph. v. 9. 'Pariter me nunc opera adiuvas ac re dudum opitulata es,' *you assist
me now with your zeal just as you helped me some time ago with
your money,* Ter. Ph. v. 3. 3. 'Hi quidem coluntur aeque atque
illi,' *these are worshipped equally with the former,* C. N. D. iii. 10.
'Simul atque natum animal est, gaudet voluptate,' *as soon as an
animal is born, it delights in pleasure,* C. Fin. ii. 10. 'Desiderium
absentium nihil perinde ac vicinitas acuit,' *nothing sharpens regret for the absent like neighbourhood,* Pl. Ep. vi. 1. 'Ostendant
milites se iuxta hieme atque aestate bella gerere posse,' *let the
troops shew they can wage war in winter as well as in summer,*

L. v. 6. ' Omnia in Themistocle fuerunt paria et Coriolano,' *all the facts in the case of Themistocles were like those in the case of Coriolanus*, C. *Br.* 11. ' Ad Luceriam iuxta obsidentis obsessosque inopia vexavit,' *scarcity distressed the besiegers at Luceria as much as the besieged*, L. ix. 13. ' Miltiades totidem navibus atque erat profectus Athenas rediit,' *Miltiades returned to Athens with as many ships as he had gone out with*, Nep. *Milt.* 7. So, ' Haud centensimam partem dixi atque possim exprimere,' *I have not said a hundredth part of what I could utter*, Plaut. *M. Gl.* iii. 1. Horace has plus ac, *more than*, Catullus non minus ac.

- *a*) Idem, iuxta, are used with Prep. cum and its Case : ' Eodem mecum patre genitus est,' *he has the same father as myself*, Tac. *A.* xv. 2. ' Quo in loco res nostrae sint iuxta mecum omnes intellegitis,' *the state of our affairs you all understand as well as I do*, Sall. *C.* 58.

  Horace uses idem with a Dative : ' Invitum qui servat idem facit occidenti,' *one who rescues a man against his will does the same as one who kills*, ad Pis. 467.

- *b*) Pro eo (*in proportion*) goes before ac, ut, quantum (*as*). ' Pro eo ac debui,' *as I was bound*, C. *Fam.* iv. 5. ' Pro eo ac mereor,' *according to my desert*, C. *in Cat.* iv. 2. ' Pro eo ut temporis difficultas tulit,' *as far as the existing difficulties allowed*, C. *Verr.* iii. 54. ' Pro eo quanti te facio,' *in proportion to my esteem for you*, C. *Fam.* iii. 31.

- *c*) Prout (*according as*). ' Prout ipse amabat litteras,' *in accordance with his own love of learning*, Nep. *Att.* 1.

- *d*) Praeut (*compared with*), praequam (*compared with*) are Comic : ' Praeut futurumst,' *compared with what is to be*, Plaut. *Bacch.* iv. 9. 5. ' Praequam quod molestumst,' *compared with the trouble*, Plaut. *Amph.* ii. 2. 3.

- *e*) Proquam is Lucretian, ii. 1137.

2) Correlation of Unlikeness :

' Illi sunt alio ingenio atque tu,' *they are of different temper from you*, C. *Leg.* ii. 7. ' Stoici multa falsa esse dicunt longeque aliter se habere ac sensibus videantur,' *the Stoics say many things are delusive and very different from what they seem to the senses*, C. *Ac.* ii. 31. ' Eadem sunt membra in utriusque disputatione, sed paulo secus a me atque ab illo distributa,' *there are the same members in the argument of each, but laid out by me somewhat differently from his method*, C. *d. Or.* iii. 30. ' Vides omnia fere contra ac dicta sint evenisse,' *you see that almost everything has turned out contrary to what was foretold*, C. *Div.* ii. 24. ' Brutus iuvenis erat longe alius ingenio quam cuius simulationem induerat,' *Brutus was a youth of very different character from that he had assumed*, L. i. 56. ' Multiplex quam pro numero damnum est,' *the loss is out of all proportion to the number*, L. vii. 8. ' Eruca diversae est quam lactuca naturae,' *colewort is of a different character from lettuce*, Pl. *N. H* xix. 8.

- *a*) Alius is used by Horace with Ablative : ' Neve putes alium sapiente bonoque beatum,' *and you will deem none other happy than the wise and good man*, *Epist.* i. 16. 20.

b) Contrast is also expressed by repeating alius, or any de-- rivative of alius : 'Aliud ratio est, aliud oratio,' *reason is one thing, speech another* = aliud est ratio atque (et) oratio. See p. 317.

76
Quam.

iv. Correlations of Degree with quam.

The uses of quam differ from those of quomodo and quem-- admodum.

As an Interrogative particle (*how*), it intensifies Adjectives, Ad- verbs, and a few Verbs of feeling. See pp. 279–80.

Correlative to tam expressed or understood (*as*), it compares the qualities of things in equal ratio. See p. 309.

Following Comparative words, quam (*than*) compares things in a ratio of inequality.

Following ante, prius, post, pridie, &c., quam forms Conjunctions represented by the English Conjunctions *before, after.* See SYNTAX (Compound Sentences of Time).

Quamdiu (correlative to tamdiu), *as long as*, is also used as a Conjunction of Time; but quam dudum, quam pridem, *how long ago*, are Interrogative only.

Com-
parison
of Equa-
lity.

A) Comparison of Equality with quam (*as*).

1) The idioms in which quam (*as, how*) is attracted to other Ad- verbs and to Adjectives are remarkable and of frequent use. Thus, it intensifies Positive words of quality (= *very*) ; where the full ex- pression might be tam quam potest. 'Ab eius summo, sicut palmae, rami quam late diffunduntur,' *the boughs spread very widely from its summit, like those of the palm-tree*, Caes. *B. G.* vi. 26. 'Cenam afferri quam opimam imperavit,' *he ordered a very splendid repast to be brought in*, Caes. *B. H.* 33. ' Sunt vestrum, iudices, quam multi, qui Pisonem cognoverunt,' *there are very many of you, gentlemen, who knew Piso*, C. *Verr.* iv. 25.

2) With a Verb quam = tam (tantum) quam : as in the Conjunc- tions quam-vis, quam-libet, *how you will, as much as you will*; 'quamvis multos,' *as many as you will*, C. *p. Rosc. A.* 16. So, 'Quam velit sit potens,' *be she as influential as she will*, C. *p. Cael.* 26. 'Quam volent in conviviis faceti sint,' *be they as witty as they please at dinner parties*, C. *p. Cael.* 28. Quam potest, *as much as possible.*

3) The Adjective or Adverb with quam is raised to the Superla- tive, in order to express the utmost intensity : ' Relinquebatur ut quam plurimos collis occuparet et quam latissimas regiones praesidiis teneret,' *it remained for him to occupy as many hills and hold by garrisons as large an extent of country as he could*, Caes. *B. C.* iii. 44. See p. 279.

4) Tam . . . quam with Superlative and Comparative words is an archaic construction. 'Magis quam id reputo tam magis uror,' *the more I think of it, the more I am annoyed*, Plaut. *Bac.* v. 1. 5. 'Quam pessime quisque fecit, tam maxime tutus est,' *the worse any man has acted, the safer he is*, Sall. *Iug.* 31.

5) Quam by a peculiar attraction (also frequent in Greek) follows a certain number of Positive Adverbs expressing intensity, espe-

cially mire, and, more rarely, admodum, nimis, oppido, per, sane, valde: Perquam doctus, *very learned*: 'Mire quam illius loci cogitatio delectat,' *I am wonderfully pleased with the very thought of the place*, C. *Att.* i. 11. 'Sane quam sum gavisus,' *I rejoiced exceedingly.* 'Suos valde quam paucos habet,' C. *Fam.* xi. 13.

B) The Comparison of Inequality with quam (*than*) is used after Comparative words unless an Ablative supplies its place.

Comparison of Inequality.

1) Plus, amplius, magis, minus, potius, non plus, non magis, non minus, &c., are used in this comparison, as tam in that of equality: 'Prodest plus imperator quam orator,' *a general is of more service than an orator*, C. *Br.* 73. Plus is used in quantitative comparison, magis in intensive, minus in both these; amplius in comparison of extension, potius in that of preference. Non amplius, haud amplius, are used; but amplius haud is quite inadmissible.

2) If two qualities of the same subject are to be compared, magis quam may connect the Adjectives. ' Celer tuus disertus magis est quam sapiens,' *your friend Celer is fluent rather than wise*, C. *Att.* xi. 10. Or, more elegantly, both are Comparative. 'Pauli Aemilii contio fuit verior quam gratior populo,' *the harangue of Paulus Aemilius was more truthful than popular*, L. xxii. 38. 'Romani bella quaedam fortius quam felicius gesserunt,' *the Romans waged some wars with more valour than success*, L. v. 43. Tacitus has 'vementius quam caute,' *Agr.* 4.

3) Often the Comparative implies some excess of the Positive quality: 'Senectus est natura loquacior,' *old age is naturally somewhat talkative* (or *rather too talkative*), C. *Cat. M.* 16. 'Themistocles liberius vivebat,' *Themistocles lived too freely*, Nep. *Them.* 1. So plures (i.e. uno) means *several*. ' In columba sentio pluris videri colores, nec esse plus uno,' *in the dove I notice a semblance of several colours, but not more than one actually*, C. *Ac.* ii. 25. In old Latinity, plures means *the departed, the dead.*

4) A Comparative and quam may be followed by Particles and Pronouns: 'Siculis plus frumenti imperabatur quam quantum exararant,' *the Sicilians were ordered to pay more corn than they had harvested*, C. *Verr.* iii. 23. See pro (PREPOSITIONS).

5) Quam may follow the verbs praestare, malle: 'Accipere quam facere praestat iniuriam,' C. *T. D.* v. 19.

6) In Plautus it follows a Positive: 'Tacita bona est mulier semper quam loquens,' *a woman is always better silent than speaking*, *Rud.* iv. 470.

7) An ellipse of quam is frequent after plus, amplius: plus annum, *more than a year*; amplius sex menses; amplius triennium, C. 'Plus quingentos colaphos infregit mihi,' *he inflicted on me more than five hundred blows*, Ter. *Ad.* ii. 1. 46.

Obs. In Correlation, a Nom. in the second member without verb expressed may answer to an Accus. in the first : Docui animam . . . minoribus esse principiis factam quam liquidus umor aquai aut nebula aut fumus, Lucr. iii. 426. See M. *Lucr.* iii. 456.

SECTION VII.

Coordination.

i. Coordination by Conjunctions.

Coordinate Sentences are introduced by the Coordinate Conjunctions enumerated § 57, or by the Relative and its Particles.

A) Annexive Conjunctions.

1) The First Class contains, (1) et, que, atque or (before consonants only) ac; (2) neque or nec, neve or neu.
Et associates things of equal importance.
Que appends a usual adjunct; being attached, as enclitic, to the word, or to the first word of the clause, which it annexes.[1]
Atque (ac) =ad-que, adds something important, as it were by afterthought.
Neque (nec), *nor, and not,* associates negative propositions; neve (neu) associates prohibitions.

2) The Second Class is Intensive, and associates emphatically. Such are etiam=et iam, *also, even,* for which et itself is often used; quoque, *also, even,* an emphatic que; item = eo modo, *likewise*; necnon, *also, moreover.* On etiam quoque, quoque etiam, &c., see M. *Lucr.* iii. 208.

3) The Annexive Conjunctions et, que, neque, neve, are frequently doubled in Distributive Correlation. The chief forms are: et . . . et, neque . . . neque, neve . . . neve: 'Et monere et moneri proprium est verae amicitiae,' *both advising and being advised is the property of true friendship,* C. *Lael.* 25. 'Illud neque taceri ullo modo neque dici pro dignitate potest,' *that matter can neither by any means be omitted from my speech, nor yet be spoken as it deserves,* C. *Verr.* ii. 1. 34. 'Carthaginiensibus condiciones pacis dictae, bellum neve in Africa neve extra Africam iniussu populi Romani facerent,' *the terms of peace dictated to the Carthaginians were that they should wage no war in or out of Africa, without authority from the Roman people,* L. xxx. 37.
Que . . . que, et . . . que, que . . . et, are poetic, but rare in prose. On et or que in protasis without conjunction in apodosis, see V. *Aen.* xi. 171.

4) Affirmative and Negative Propositions are associated by et . . . neque, neque . . . et, nec . . . que: 'Intellegitis Pompeio et animum praesto fuisse nec consilium defuisse,' *you perceive that Pompeius had both courage for the occasion, and no lack of counsel,* C. *Phil.* xiii. 6. 'Vitia erunt donec homines; sed neque haec continua, et meliorum interventu pensantur,' *vices will exist as long as men; but as, on the one hand, their operation is not perpetual, so also they find a counterpoise in the occasional action of better principles,* Tac. *H.* iv. 74. See M. *Lucr.* i. 280.

---

[1] -que sometimes stands after the second word, if the first is a Preposition or other small particle: in eoque; a meque; tam variisque, &c. And later still in poetry, to assist metre: multus ut in terras deplueretque lapis, Tib. ii. 5. 71.

5) Distributive association is likewise effected by the sequences, cum . . . tum; tum . . . tum; quā . . . quā; modo . . . modo; nunc . . . nunc; modo . . . nunc; simul . . . simul; partim . . . partim; pars . . . pars.

Also by alter . . . alter; alius . . . alius; and its particles, aliter . . . aliter; alias . . . alias; alibi . . . alibi; &c.

Examples :—'Agesilaus cum a ceteris scriptoribus, tum a Xenophonte collaudatus est,' *Agesilaus has been extolled both by other writers, and especially by Xenophon*, Nep. *Ag.* 1. 'Hae stellae tum occultantur tum rursus aperiuntur,' *these stars are at one time hidden, at another again displayed*, C. *N. D.* ii. 51. 'Socrates non tum hoc, tum illud, sed idem dicebat semper,' *Socrates did not say one thing at one time, another at another; but the same thing always*, C. *Lael.* 4. 'Scripsisti epistulam ad me plenam consili summaeque tum benevolentiae tum etiam prudentiae,' *you have written me a letter full of good advice, and of great kindness as well as prudence*, C. *Att.* ix. 5. 'Omnium Fabiorum, quā plebis, quā patrum, eximia virtus fuit,' *all the Fabii, both plebeians and senators, were men of eminent merit*, L. ii. 45. 'Animalia cibum partim oris hiatu et dentibus ipsis capessunt, partim unguium tenacitate arripiunt, partim aduncitate rostrorum; alia sugunt, alia carpunt, alia vorant, alia mandunt,' *some animals take their food by opening the mouth and applying the teeth, some seize it by their grasping claws, some by their crooked beaks, some suck, others peck, others swallow down, others chew*, C. *N. D.* ii. 47. 'Natura alterum alterius indigere voluit, quoniam quod alteri deest praesto plerumque est alteri,' *Nature would have one man stand in need of another, since what one lacks another generally has*, Colum. *Pr.* 6. 'Aliter cum tyranno, aliter cum amico vivitur,' *we live in one way with a tyrant, in another with a friend*, C. *Lael.* 10.

6) The Particles used to distribute thought in regular series (Ordinative) are, primum (*in the first place*), deinde (*in the next place*), variously followed by one or more of the words, tum, postea, mox, praeterea, porro, insuper: and often wound up with denique, *in short, finally*, or postremo (um), *in the last place*. *Ordinative Particles.*

'Primum latine Apollo nunquam locutus est; deinde ista sors inaudita Graecis est; praeterea Pyrrhi temporibus jam Apollo versus facere desierat; postremo Pyrrhus hanc amphiboliam versus intellegere potuisset nihilo magis in se quam in Romanos valere,' *in the first place Apollo never spoke in Latin; in the next the Greeks never heard of that oracle; moreover, in the times of Pyrrhus, Apollo had already ceased to make verses; in fine, Pyrrhus would have been able to perceive that the ambiguity in this verse told no more in his favour than in favour of the Romans*, C. *Div.* ii. 56.

Sometimes tum precedes deinde; and denique is followed by postremo. In Cic. *Fin.* v. 23 (where see Madvig), we find primum . . . tum . . . . deinde . . . post . . . tum . . . deinde, without denique or postremo. See also M. *Lucr.* iii. 529.

In these sequences primum is used; seldom primo, which means *originally, at first*, but sometimes *in the first place*, deinde following.

a) On Asyndeton and Polysyndeton see p. 269 *h*).

b) ANAPHORA is the construction which, instead of using An-nexive Conjunctions, repeats in each clause one or more words : ' Promisit, sed difficulter, sed subductis superciliis, sed malignis verbis,' *he promised, but hardly, with knitted brows, and in spiteful language*, Sen. *Ben.* i. 1. ' Si recte Cato iudicavit, non recte frumentarius ille, non recte aedium pestilentium venditor tacuit,' *if Cato judged rightly, then the corn-factor I cited was not rightly silent; nor yet the vendor of an unwholesome house*, C. *Off.* iii. 16.

78
Disjunctive Conjunctions.

B) Disjunctive or Alternative Conjunctions.

1) These are aut ; vel, -ve ; sive, seu.

Aut distinguishes notions, and opposes them to one another.

Vel (ancient Imperative of volo) and its enclitic -ve make optional distinction (*or, if you please*).

Sive (seu) sometimes means *or if*; but, as here cited, it implies a distinction of name rather than of fact.

' Audendum est aliquid universis, aut omnia singulis patienda,' *we must dare something as a body, or individually endure all things*, L. vi. 16. ' Sequimur vel antecedimus,' Curt. ' Ioco seriove,' *in jest or earnest*, L. 'Discessus sive potius fuga,' *departure or rather flight*, C.

2) Disjunctive Particles are doubled for the purpose of Distribu-tion : ' Aut nemo aut, si quisquam, Cato sapiens fuit,' *either no man or, if any, Cato was wise*, C. *Lael.* 2. 'Vel vi, vel clam, vel precario,' *either by force or by stealth, or by petition*, C. *p. Lig.* 3.

3) Vel may mean ' *even.*' 'Per me vel stertas licet,' *you may even snore if you will for me*, C. *Ac.* ii. 29. And ' *for instance.*' ' Amoris tui vestigia vel de Tigellio perspexi,' C. *Fam.* vii. 24.

Vel certe, *or at least* : vel etiam, *or perhaps.* See p. 279.

79
Adversative Conjunctions.

C) Adversative Conjunctions.

The Adversative Conjunctions are autem, sed ; verum, vero ; tamen ; at (ast), atqui ; ceterum.

1) Autem (akin to aut), the weakest of these, does not oppose strongly, but corrects slightly, adds, or continues, with the English *but, now,* or *and.* It is postpositive, following the first word or (after est, sunt) the second word in its clause : 'Magnes lapis est, qui ferrum ad se trahit : rationem autem, cur id fiat, afferre non pos-sumus,' *the magnet is a stone which attracts iron; but a reason for this effect we cannot assign*, C. *Div.* i. 86. ' Bonum est autem recta praecipere,' Lact.

a) Autem (followed by immo vero) is used with a word re-peated interrogatively, with a view to correction. 'Ferendus tibi in hoc meus error : ferendus autem? immo vero etiam adiuvandus,' *you must endure my mistake here: endure, do I say? you must even abet it*, C. *Att.* xii. 42.

2) Sed, a form of se- (*separate*), distinguishes with more or less of opposition. After a negative, it supplies an adverse or differing notion : ' Oti fructus est non contentio animi sed relaxatio,' *the advantage of leisure is not mental exertion, but relaxation*, C. *d.*

Or. ii. 5. Otherwise it is corrective : ' Contemno magnitudinem doloris. Sed si est tantus dolor quantus Philoctetae,' &c. *I despise greatness of pain. But suppose it as great as that of Philoctetes,* &c. C. *T. D.* ii. 19. Or it is used in passing on to new points or topics : ' Ego sane a Quinto nostro dissentio : sed ea quae restant audiamus,' *I quite differ from our friend Quintus. But let us hear what remains to be said,* C. *N. D.* ii. 1.

3) Verum (*but truly*) resembles sed in use, but is stronger : ' Non quid nobis utile, verum quid oratori necessarium sit, quaerimus,' *we are not inquiring what is profitable to us, but rather what is necessary for an orator,* C. *d. Or.* i. 60.

Sed and verum are praepositive, standing first in their clause.

4) Vero (*but in truth*) when used as a Conjunction is postpositive, and generally corrects by heightening the previous notion : ' Quidquid est quod bonum sit, id expetendum est ; quod autem expetendum, id certe approbandum ; quod vero approbaris, id gratum acceptumque habendum,' *whatever is good, is desirable ; what is desirable, is surely to be approved ; again what you approve must be deemed agreeable and acceptable,* C. *T. D.* v. 25.

5) Tamen (*yet, however, nevertheless*) detracts from the force of a concession, either expressed by etsi, quamvis, &c., or implied in the context. It stands in any part of the sentence where it may be most emphatic. See SYNTAX (Concessive Sentences).

Sed tamen, attamen, verumtamen, et tamen (*but yet*), are used.

6) At (anciently ast) is strongly adversative : and is used in objection, exclamation, interrogation, imprecation, &c.
' Non placet M. Antonio consulatus meus ; at placuit P. Servilio,' &c. *my consulship is not liked by Marcus Antonius, but it was liked by Publius Servilius,* &c. C. *Phil.* ii. 12. ' At te di deaeque perduint,' *may the gods and goddesses destroy thee!* Ter. *Hec.* i. 2. 59. ' Aeschines in Demosthenem invehitur : at quam rhetorice, quam copiose!' *Aeschines upbraids Demosthenes : aye, and how skilfully, how copiously,* C. *T. D.* iii. 26.

    a) At = at tamen : ' Si se ipsos illi nostri liberatores e conspectu nostro abstulerunt, at exemplum reliquerunt,' *if those champions of our freedom have removed themselves from our view, yet they have left us their example,* C. *Phil.* ii. 44.

    b) At enim, at vero, as well as at alone, are used, like ἀλλὰ νὴ Δία in Greek, to introduce an objection which must be answered. ' At enim ad Verrem pecunia ista non pervenit. Quae est ista defensio ?' &c. *but that money, it is urged, never reached Verres. What a lame defence is here ?* &c., C. *Verr.* ii. 10. ' At vero malum est liberos amittere. Malum, nisi hoc peius sit, haec sufferre et perpeti,' C. *Fam.* iv. 5. ' At ego, inquit, vobis rationem ostendam, qua tanta mala ista effugiatis,' Sall. *Cat.* 40.

    c) Atqui (*yes but, but indeed*) adds an objection which needs to be considered. ' O rem, inquis, difficilem atque inexplicabilem ! Atqui explicanda est,' *O what a difficult and inexplicable matter, you say ? Yes, but it must be explained,* C. *Att.* viii. 3. See M. *Lucr.* i. 755.

7) Ceterum (*but for the rest, but*) is used by historians. 'Qui Romanorum amicitiam colunt, multum laborem suscipiunt : ceterum ex omnibus maxime tuti sunt,' Sall. *Iug.* 14. So ceteroqui(n).

D) Causal Conjunctions.

1) Nam (*for, for instance, to be sure*) introduces a cause as explanatory ; enim (which follows the first or, after est, the second word of a clause) introduces a proof. Namque is a strengthened form of nam, etenim of enim : they are usually, in prose, the first words in their clause.

> *a*) Nam is used in urgent Interrogations, either appended to the Interrogative (quisnam, curnam, &c.), or, in old Latin chiefly, preceding it. 'Nam quid ego nunc dicam de patre?' *why what can I now say of my father?* Ter. *An.* i. 5, 17.

> *b*) Enim is linked with other Particles : etenim, *for*, neque enim, sed enim, at enim, verum enim, enimvero, verum enimvero. All these may begin a sentence. 'Enimvero, Dave, nihil loci'st segnitiae,' *why really, Davus, there is no room for laziness,* Ter. *An.* i. 3. 1.

> *c*) Enim may be emphatic (*yes*). 'Id enim est, inquies, ostentum,' C. *Div.* ii. 26. 'Tibi enim, tibi, maxima Iuno,' V. *Aen.* viii. 84.

E) Illative Conjunctions.

1) Igitur, ergo, *therefore*, itaque, proinde (proin). Igitur expresses a reasonable inference : ergo a necessary inference ; itaque (*and so*) an inference arising from the antecedence ; proinde (*so then*) an inference proportioned to the antecedence.

2) Ideo, idcirco, propterea (*on that account*), point to a ground of fact (quod). Hoc, *on this ground.* M. *Lucr.* iii. 531.

3) The Relative words quare, quamobrem, quapropter, quocirca, have a Conclusive sense : (*wherefore, on which account*).[1]

ii. Coordination by the Relative and its Particles.

1) The Relative itself may be equal to a Personal or Demonstrative Pronoun with a Particle (et, autem, enim, igitur, &c.). 'Res loquitur ipsa : quae (= et ea) semper valet plurimum,' *the fact itself speaks; and this always has most weight,* C. *p. Mil.* 20. 'Sunt igitur firmi et constantes eligendi : cuius (= eius autem) generis est magna penuria,' *firm and steady friends must be chosen: but of this class there is a great dearth,* C. *Lael.* 17. 'Multas ad res perutiles Xenophontis libri sunt, quos (= eos igitur) legite studiose,' *the works of Xenophon are useful for many purposes: read them then, I beg, with care,* C. *Cat. M.* 17.

Note. A Particle which appears with a Relative, belongs really to a Demonstrative understood (or expressed in another clause). 'Quod est bonum omne laudabile est ; quod autem laudabile

---

[1] The uses of Latin Adverbs and Conjunctions are a very extensive subject, which cannot be fully treated in a Grammar of moderate size. Hand's unfinished edition of *Tursel-linus de Particulis* extends only to the letter P, and fills four large octavo volumes.

est, omne est honestum; bonum igitur quod est, honestum est,' C. *Fin.* iii. 8, where autem and igitur belong to id understood.

2) The attraction of the Antecedent to the Relative Clause is a frequent idiom. Hence a peculiar use of the Relative arises. ' Moriar ni, quae tua gloria est, puto te malle a Caesare consuli quam inaurari,' *upon my life I think, such is your vanity, you would rather be consulted by Caesar than plated with gold,* C. *Fam.* vii. 13. 'Quanta potuit adhiberi festinatio,' L. xlv. 1.

3) When a Noun has an Attribute, especially a Superlative, and a Relative Clause further explaining it, the Attribute is often attracted to the Clause : 'Themistocles noctu de servis suis, quem habuit fidelissimum, ad Xerxem misit,' *Themistocles sent to Xerxes by night the most faithful slave he had,* Nep. *Them.* 4.

4) When the Relative Clause has another subordinate to it, the Relative may be constructed not with its own, but with its subordinate Clause : ' Aberat omnis dolor, qui si adesset (*for* quem si is adesset) non molliter ferret,' *all pain was absent, but had any been present, he would have borne it without weakness,* C. *Fin.* ii. 20.

5) A Relative may be connected with a Participial construction. ' Non sunt ea bona dicenda nec habenda, quibus abundantem licet esse miserrimum,' *those things ought not to be called or held good, amidst the overflow of which one may be utterly wretched,* C. *T. D.* v. 15.

With an Infinitive Clause. 'In eos, quos speramus nobis profuturos, non dubitamus beneficia conferre,' *we do not hesitate to confer benefits on those from whom we hope to derive advantage,* C. *Off.* i. 15.

With an Interrogation. 'Magnus orator fuit Demosthenes : quem quis umquam dicendo superavit?' *Demosthenes was a great orator : for who ever surpassed him in speaking ?* C.

6) The Relative not only connects Clauses with Principal Sentences, but it is used, especially by Cicero, in the beginning of Principal Sentences, to shew their *logical* connexion with something which has gone before. Such are the phrases quo facto, qua re cognita, quae cum ita sint, qua de causa, &c.

Also quod (*now, but, in fact,* &c.) stands before Conjunctions, si, nisi, etsi, quoniam, quia, quum, ubi, utinam, &c. : 'Fit protinus hac re audita ex castris Gallorum fuga : quod nisi crebris subsidiis ac totius diei labore milites fuissent defessi, omnes hostium copiae deleri potuissent,' *on this intelligence the Gauls forsook their camp : in fact, if our troops had not been worn out by frequent skirmishes and a whole day's fatigue, the entire forces of the enemy might have been destroyed,* Caes. *B. G.* vii. 88. See C. *Off.* i. 14, *Div.* ii. 62, *Fin.* i. 20; Liv. xxix. 34, xxxvi. 2.

7) Quod is also used (M. *Lucr.* ii. 248.)

   a) as quantum : ' Tu, quod poteris, nos consiliis iuvabis,' *you will help me with your advice as far as you can,* C. *Att.* x. 2. 'Epicurus se unus, quod sciam, sapientem profiteri est ausus,' *Epicurus is the only man, so far as I know, who ventured to profess wisdom,* C. *Fin.* ii. 3.

Y

b) opening a sentence in relation to something about to be stated (*as to*) : see M. *Lucr.* iv. 855 : 'Quod scribis te velle scire qui sit reipublicae status, summa dissensio est,' *as to the wish you express in your letter to know the condition of public affairs, all is discord,* C. *Fam.* i. 7.

c) as quare: 'Est quod te visam,' *there is something I must see you for,* Plaut. ' Credo ego vos mirari quid sit quod ego surrexerim,' *I imagine you are wondering for what reason I have stood up,* C.

d) occasionally for ex quo (*since*) : 'Dies tertius est quod audivi recitantem Augurinum,' *it is now three days since I heard Augurinus read,* Pl. *Ep.* iv. 27.

So cum : 'Multi anni sunt cum ille in aere meo est,' *it is many years that he is in my good books,* C. *Fam.* xv. 14.

And tantum quod for vix ubi, vixdum : 'Qui tantum quod ad hostis pervenerat, Datames signa inferri iubet,' *he had but just reached the enemy when Datames ordered the standards to advance,* Nep. *Dat.* 6. 'Tantum quod ex Arpinati veneram, cum mihi litterae a te redditae sunt,' *I had just arrived from my house at Arpinum, when a letter from you was delivered to me,* C. *Fam.* vii. 23.

Note 1. The transition by which the Relative quod (*which*) becomes the Conjunction of Fact quod (*that*) and the Causal Conjunction quod (*because*) is apparent from such examples. An analogous transition appears in the English *that*, and the Greek ὅτι.

Concedo quod postulas, *I grant* (the thing) *that you ask.*
Rectum est quod postulas, (the thing) *that you ask is right.*
Nefas est quod postulas, (the thing) *that you ask is a sin.*
Gaudeo quod venisti, *I am glad that you are come.*
Gratum est quod venisti, *it is a pleasure that you are come.*
Consolatio est quod venisti, *it is a comfort that you are come.*
Hoc consolatur quod venisti, *this comforts, that you are come.*
Fugit idcirco quod timet, *he flies because that he fears.*
Venit ideo quod pactus est, *he came because that he agreed.*
Felix est quod sapiens est, *he is happy in that he is wise.*

Note 2. On change of construction after Rel., see M. *Lucr.* i. 720, and Verg. *Aen.* vi. 284.

8) The place of the Relative can be taken by its Particles, ubi, unde, quo, qua, &c.

Ubi may stand for in quo, in qua, in quibus, of place, person, or thing : 'Porticus haec ipsa, ubi (= in qua) inambulamus,' *this very colonnade in which we are walking,* C. *d. Or.* ii. 5.

Unde stands for ex quo, qua, quibus, a quo, qua, quibus, &c., and is also referred to place, person, or thing : 'Fontes unde (ex quibus) hauriretis,' *sources from which you might draw,* C. *d. Or.* i. 46. 'Eloquentia, unde (= a qua) longe absum,' *eloquence, from which I am far removed,* C. *Brut.* 92.

Quo for ad quem, quam, quod, quos, quae, &c. 'Dignus Roma locus quo (= ad quem) deus omnis eat,' *Rome is a place worthy to be visited by every deity,* Ov. *F.* iv. 270.

Such Particles are connected with mood according to the same rules as the Relative Pronoun.

SECTION VIII.

Negative Words. 83
Nega-
tive
Words.

i. Ne and its Compounds.

1) From the Negative Root *na* come the Particles nĕ, nē.

Nĕ, the lighter form, is used as an enclitic Interrogative. Ne.
It enters into the composition of many words : nĕ-que (nec), ne-uter, ne-utiquam, non, nisi (for nĕ-si), nihil (for nĕ-hil), nemo (for nĕ-homo), nullus (ne-ullus), numquam (ne-umquam), nusquam (ne-usquam) : nĕ-queo, ne-scio, nolo (nĕ-volo), nĕ-fas and its derivatives : as nec, of nec-dum, nec-non, nec-opinus, neg-otium, neg-lego. On nec for non, see M. *Lucr.* ii. 23.

Nē, the strengthened form, is used in prohibitive and final construction, and in the phrases nē . . . quidem, nēdum, &c.

It enters into the composition of words : nē-ve (neu), nē-cubi, &c. ; nē-quaquam, nē-quiquam, nē-quam ; in old Latin more largely, as funera nē-funera in Catullus.

On ni, nei, as old forms of ne, see M. *Lucr.* ii. 734.

2) Non, haud (anc. haut), *not,* deny Predication or Attribution.
Non simply denies : haud somewhat more strongly.
Cicero rarely uses haud with a Verb, except in the phrase 'haud scio an' (often in MSS. hauscio an). But 'Haud equidem assentior,' *Leg.* iii. 11. See also *Cat. M.* xxiii. 82, *Div.* ii. 39.
The ordinary use of haud is with Adjectives and Adverbs. Thus in C. haud deterior, haud mediocris, haud sane, haud paulo, haud facile, haud fere quisquam, haud umquam. Comic poets use haud with Verbs, especially with possum : Virgil rarely with finite Verbs. Horace has 'haud mihi dero.'

3) Nihil (nil) may be used as a Particle (*in no wise*) : nihil opus est, nihil moror, nihil me fallis. Rarely with Adjectives and Participles : 'Nihil similis,' L. 'Senatus nihil sane intentus,' Sall. *Cat.* 17. 'Animos nil magnae laudis egentis,' Virg. *Ae.* v. 751.

4) So quicquam : 'Ne hoc quidem ipso quicquam opus fuit iudicio,' *even of this judgment there was no need,* C. d. *Inv.* ii. 27.

5) Nullus is used with the force of non. 'Sextus ab armis nullus discedit,' *Sextus does not lay down his arms,* C. *Att.* xv. 22.

6) The Substantive nemo (ne-homo) is used for nullus : as 'Nemo pictor,' *no painter,* C. 'Nemo fere adulescens,' *hardly any young man* ; even 'hominem neminem,' C. *Fam.* xiii. 55. 'Nemo unus,' *not one person,* L. iii. 12. So quisquam, though Substantival, is found with homo, civis, &c.
On the other hand, Gen. nullius, Abl. nullo, are used as Cases of nemo, rarely of nihil. 'Si iniuste neminem laesit, si nullius aures voluntatemve violavit, si nemini, ut levissime dicam, odio nec domi nec militiae fuit,' *if he has harmed no one unjustly, if he has done violence to no man, by word or act, if, to say the least, he has*

been disagreeable to none at home or abroad, &c., C. *p. Mur.* 40.
'Ut quisque sic munitus est ut nullo egeat,' *according as each man
is so provided as to want nobody's help,* C. *Lael.* 9.

a) Non ita, haud ita, are used as modified Negatives : non
ita pridem, haud ita pridem, (*not very long ago*).

Neutiquam (*not at all*) is chiefly found in Comedy : also in a
few places of Cicero and Livy. L. has neutique.

Nequiquam, (*to no purpose*). Nequaquam, haudquaquam, (*by
no means*).

b) Vix, *scarcely, hardly,* is a modified Negative.

c) Minus is used as nearly = non. 'Nonnumquam ea, quae
praedicta sunt, minus eveniunt,' *sometimes predictions fail
to turn out true,* C. *Div.* i. 14. Especially quominus (= ut
eo minus), and sin minus, *but if not.*

Minime (*least of all = not at all*) is a strong Negative.

d) The enclitic dum (*awhile, yet*) is compounded with all the
Negatives except nemo ; also with vix ; nondum, haud
dum, nullusdum, nihildum, vixdum.

ii. Succeeding Negatives.

1) A Negative precedes the word which it affects ; and if another
Negative follows within the same predication, the negation is an-
nulled, and the predication becomes Affirmative.

Hence arise new Pronominal forms ; some Indefinite :

nonnullus	nearly	=	aliqui
nonnemo	—	=	aliquis
nonnihil	—	=	aliquid
nonnumquam	—	=	aliquando

some Universal : as,

nullus non	nearly	=	omnis
nemo non	—	=	omnes or unusquisque
nihil non	—	=	omnia
numquam non	—	=	semper
nusquam non	—	=	ubique

So, neque . . . non is nearly = etiam (*also*).

2) Non followed by non forms a strong affirmative : thus, non
possum non = necesse est mihi. 'Non potui non dare litteras
ad Caesarem,' *I could not but write to Caesar,* C. *Att.* viii. 2.

So, nemo . . . non : nihil . . . non, &c. 'Tuum consilium nemo
potest non maxime laudare,' *nobody can help praising your design highly,* C. *Fam.* iv. 7.

Non modo, non tantum, *not only* ; modo non, tantum non, *only
not = all but* : 'Modo non montis auri pollicens,' *promising all
but mountains of gold,* Ter. *Ph.* i. 2. 18.

3) If a negative proposition branches into two clauses with
neque . . . neque, the proposition remains negative : 'Caesar
numquam neque fecit neque fecisset ea quae nunc ex falsis
eius commentariis proferuntur,' *Caesar never did nor would have
done the things which are produced from his spurious manuscripts,*
C. *Fam.* xiv. 13.

a) As the English '*and not*' is usually expressed by neque; and by 'et non' only when the negative belongs emphatically to the following word; so '*and none*,' '*and nothing*,' '*and nobody*,' '*and never*,' &c., are expressed by 'neque ullus,' 'neque quicquam,' 'nec quisquam,' 'nec umquam,' &c.; not by et nullus, et nihil, et nemo, et numquam, &c.: but if the negative is emphasised, the latter forms must be used: 'Domus temere et nullo consilio administratur,' *the household is conducted in a confused way, and without any plan*, C. d. Inv. i. 34.

b) Neque is used with vero, tamen, enim, rarely autem, to connect Adversative and Causal Sentences negatively.

iii. Ne ... quidem, nedum, non modo, &c.

1) Ne ... quidem = *not even*, takes the emphatic words between the particles. 'Ne ad Catonem quidem provocabo,' *I will not appeal even to Cato*, C. Att. iv. 1. Another negative may go before, with the predicative word: 'Non fugio ne hos quidem mores,' *I do not shun even these morals*, C. Verr. iii. 90.

Nec is rarely used for ne ... quidem. 'Esse aliquid manis et subterranea regna nec pueri credunt,' *that ghosts and subterranean realms have any existence not even boys believe*, Iuv. ii. 152.

2) Nedum indicates that a predication is out of the question. Hence with previous negative, it means '*much less*;' with affirmative (usually) '*not to say*.' 'Satrapa si siet amator, numquam sufferre eius sumptus queat, nedum tu possis,' *if a satrap were her lover, he could not support her expenses, much less can you*, Ter. *Haut*. iii. 1. 43. 'Nulla simulacra urbibus, nedum templis, sinunt,' *they allow no images to their cities, much less to their temples*, Tac. *H*. v. 5. 'Tu quoniam quartana cares et nedum morbum removisti sed etiam gravedinem, te vegetum nobis in Graecia siste,' *since you are free from quartan fever, and rid not to say of disease but even of languor, present yourself to us in Greece flourishing*, C. *Att*. x. 16.

Sometimes, but not in Cicero, nedum after an affirmative means '*much more not*.' 'Et consules bellicosos creatos, qui vel in pace bellum excitare possent, nedum in bello respirare civitatem forent passuri,' *warlike consuls had been elected, who could stir up war even in peace, much more in war would not suffer the state to take breath*, L. xlv. 29. See also Hor. *ad Pis*. 69.

3) When the principal sentence contains *not only*, an Adversative clause (*but*) succeeds. Hence non modo, non solum, are followed by sed, verum, sed etiam, verum etiam, &c.: 'Non solum verbis arte positis moventur omnes, verum etiam numeris ac vocibus,' *all men are affected not only by words skilfully arranged, but also by measures and sounds*, C. d. Or. iii. 50.

a) Also, non modo non, non solum non are followed by sed, sed etiam, &c., or by sed ne ... quidem, sed neque, &c.: 'Hoc non modo non pro me, sed contra me est potius,' *this is not only not for me, but even against me*, C. d. Or. iii. 20. 'Ego non modo tibi non irascor, sed ne reprehendo quidem factum tuum,' *I am not only not angry with you, but do not even blame your deed*, C. *p. Sull.* 18.

b) When both sentences have a common verb, non modo may be elliptically placed in the former, for non modo non : 'Talis vir non modo facere, sed ne cogitare quidem quicquam audebit, quod non honestum sit' (= sed etiam cogitare non audebit), *such a man will not venture, not merely to do, but even to conceive anything which is not morally right*, C. *Off.* iii. 19. 'Nihil eis Verres non modo de fructu, sed ne de bonis quidem suis reliqui fecit,' *Verres left them nothing, I do not say of their produce, but even of their property*, C. *Verr.* iii. 48.

c) The sentences are sometimes inverted, so that non modo = *much less* : 'Ne sues quidem id velint, non modo ipse,' *not even swine would desire that, much less himself,* C. *T. D.* i. 38.

d) Non tam, *not so much*, is followed by sed or sed magis. See M. *Lucr.* iii. 823.

SECTION IX.

Questions and Answers.

I. Questions (direct or oblique : see § 73).

Interrogation may be Single or Disjunctive.

·i. Single Interrogation without a Particle.

An Interrogation in English is indicated by the Verb at the beginning, ' *Will you go?*' But in Latin the sense or tone shews the distinction. 'Certe patrem tuum non occidisti?' *assuredly you did not kill your father?* Suet. *Aug.* 33, which suggests the reply, Certe non occidi. 'Infelix est Fabricius quod rus suum fodit?' *is Fabricius unhappy in having to dig his ground?* Sen. *Prov.* 3. Answer, Non est. Sometimes the question is remonstrative, and equivalent to a strong exhortation : 'Non pudet ad morem discincti vivere Nattae?' *are you not ashamed of living in the fashion of dissolute Natta?* Pers. iii. 31. Or attention is awakened : as 'Cernis odoratis ut luceat ignibus aether?' *seest thou with scented fires how shines the sky?* Ov. *F.* i. 75. 'Viden tu hunc?' Plaut. *Capt.* iii. 4. 25. Videtisne ut, &c.

ii. Single Interrogation with a Particle.

1) Num expects a negative answer ; nonne, an affirmative ; ne asks indifferently : 'Num formidulosus, obsecro, es, mi homo? —Egone formidulosus? nemo'st hominum, qui vivat, minus,' *are you in a fright, pray, my good fellow?—I in a fright? no man alive is less so*, Ter. *Eun.* iv. 6. 19. 'Nonne miseri sumus?'

a) Numne, numnam, are used: also ecquis, numquis: 'Deum ipsum **n u m n e** vidisti?' *have you seen God Himself?* (no), C. *N. D.* i. 31. 'N **umnam** ego perii?' *am I a lost man?* (I hope not), Ter. *Eun.* v. 4. 25. 'Ecquis me vivit hodie fortunatior?' *lives there any this day more lucky than I?* Ter. *Eun.* v. 8. 1. 'Numquis hic est? nemo est: numquis hinc me sequitur?' *is there any one here? nobody: is any one following me out?* Ter. *Eun.* iii. 5. 1.

2) An properly signifies '*or*,' and introduces the second and following members of double, triple, &c. questions. When it seems to introduce a single interrogation, it really refers to a previous question conceived in the mind ('*is this admitted or*,' &c.). Hence it confirms a statement by exhibiting the inadmissibility of the opposite notion: 'Oratorem irasci minime decet, simulare non dedecet. An tibi irasci tum videmur cum quid in causis acrius et vehementius dicimus?' *anger is unbecoming in an orator, the semblance of anger is not unbecoming.* (Do you allow this?) *or do you suppose we are really angry when we speak with more than usual vehemence?* C. *T. D.* iv. 25—meaning: 'we are not really angry when we so speak; the semblance therefore affords no argument against the maxim that anger is unbecoming in an orator.'

Sometimes an refers to aliudne understood: 'Quid dices? an Siciliam virtute tua liberatam?' *what will you say? that by your valour Sicily was freed?* C. *Verr.* v. 2. 5. (Will you say anything else, or, &c. = will you not probably say that, &c.) See § 87, Foot-note.

a) An has a peculiar use after Verbs expressing *uncertainty*, as nescio, haud scio, dubito. When in English we say, '*I know not whether he is coming*,' we imply a probability that '*he will not come*:' but in Latin, nescio an veniat usually means existimo eum venire. So, 'Nescio an modum excesserint,' *I am inclined to think they have overstepped the limit*, Iust. xiii. 2. Hence it is used almost adverbially: 'Sapientissimus et haud scio an omnium praestantissimus,' *the wisest and perhaps the most excellent of all*, C. *N. D.* ii. 4.

b) The doubled Conjunction may mark uncertainty: 'Hanc orationem in Origines suas rettulit paucis antequam mortuus est an diebus an mensibus,' *this speech he entered in his Origines a few days* (must we say) *or months before he died*, C. *Brut.* 23. This idiom is frequent in Tacitus.

c) If it were wished to express the meanings '*probably not*,' '*I am inclined to think not*,' &c., a Negative was introduced in the subordination: Nescio an non veniat, *I think he is not coming*. 'Quaere rationem cur ita videatur: quam ut maxime inveneris, quod haud scio an non possis, non tu ostenderis,' &c., *seek a ground for this opinion; but though you be ever so successful in finding one, which I rather think you cannot do, you will not have shewn*, &c., C. *Ac.* ii. 25. 'Contigit tibi, quod haud scio an nemini,' *there has happened to you what I rather think has befallen no one else*, C. *Qu. Fr.* i. 1. It is questioned whether the same sense is obtained by using, instead of Negatives, those Pronouns and Adverbs which are only found in negative or hypothetical sentences, quisquam, ullus, unquam, &c.; but, as the reading in all the places cited is doubtful, it is safer to use the Negatives for this purpose.

d) Writers of the Silver age sometimes give n e s c i o a n the negative force, '*I think not.*'

iii. D i s j u n c t i v e I n t e r r o g a t i o n has four varie- ties.

In First Member.						In Second Member.
1) utrum (utrumne)	.	.	.	.	.	an
2) ne	.	.	.	.	.	an
3) No Particle	.	.	.	.	.	an (anne)
4) No Particle	.	.	.	.	.	ne.[1]

1) 'U t r u m ea vestra an nostra culpa est?' *is that your fault or ours?* C. *Ac.* iv. 29. 'Quod nescire malum est agitamus, u t r u m n e divitiis homines a n sint virtute beati,' *we discuss, what it is an evil to be ignorant of, whether men are happy by riches or virtue,* Hor. *S.* ii. 6. 73.

2) 'Quod si dies notandus fuit, e u m n e potius notaret, quo natus, a n eum, quo sapiens factus est?' *now, if a day was to be marked, should he have marked that rather, on which he was born, or that on which he became wise?* C. 'Quaeritur virtus s u a m n e propter dignitatem an propter fructus aliquos expetatur,' *it is a question whether virtue be sought for its own worth or for some profits accruing,* C. *d. Or.* iii. 29.

3) 'Recto itinere duxisti exercitum ad hostis a n super omnes anfractus viarum?' *did you march your army straight to the enemy, or by every winding road?* L. xxxviii. 45. 'Refert oratorem qui audiant, senatus an populus a n judices, frequentes an pauci a n singuli,' *it is of moment who an orator's audience are, the senate or people or bench of judges; a crowd or a few persons or an individual,* C. *d. Or.* iii. 55.

4) 'Albus aterne fueris ignorans,' *not knowing whether you were white or black,* C. *Phil.* ii. 16. 'Tarquinius Superbus Prisci Tarquinii filius neposne fuerit, parum liquet,' *whether Tarquin the Proud was son or grandson of Tarquin the elder, is not certain,* L. i. 41. This form is only used in Oblique Interrogation.

a) An . . . an, ne . . . ne, are poetic, but rare in prose: 'Distat a n maturitas uvarum in torcularibus fiat a n in ramis,' *it makes a difference whether the grapes become ripe in the press-rooms or on the boughs,* Plin. *N. H.* xv. 1. 'Qui teneant . . . h o m i n e s n e f e r a e n e Quaerere consti-

---

[1] Madvig (*Opusc.* 230), with whom Hand concurs (*Turs.* iv. 321), denies that the form num . . . an can be classed with the other Disjunctive forms, in which one alternative must be affirmed. As n u m always points to a negative answer, a n, when annexed to it, becomes almost=annon. 'Num furis? an prudens ludis me obscura canendo?' *are you going mad? or do you purposely deceive me with dark oracles?* Hor. *S.* ii. 5. 59, implying that the latter is the fact.

tuit,' *he resolves to inquire who inhabit it . . . whether men or wild beasts*, Verg. Aen. i. 308.

b) If in the Second Member there is a Negation of the former, necne or annon is used, generally without, sometimes with, the Verb repeated : 'Fiat necne fiat id quaeritur,' *the question is whether it does happen or not*, C. Fam. i. 39. 'Di utrum sint necne sint quaeritur,' *it is in question whether gods exist or not*, C. N. D. iii. 7. 'Num tabulas habet annon?' *has he the accounts or not?* C. p. Qu. Necne is not used after num ; and only in Oblique Interrogation.

II. Answers.

i. Affirmative Answers in Latin are given in three ways.

1) By repeating the emphatic word of the question in the required person or case : 'Abiit Clitipho.—Solus? Solus,' *Clitipho is gone. Alone? Alone*, Ter. Haut. v. 1. 31. 'Virtutes narro.—Meas? Tuas.' *I talk of virtues. What, mine?—Yours*, Ter. Ad. iv. 1. 19. 'Tune negas? Nego hercle vero,' *do you deny it? Yes, upon my word, I do*, Plaut. Men. iv. 2. 67.

2) By some expression equivalent to a repetition of the emphatic word : 'Dic, Chaerea tuam vestem detraxit tibi? Factum,' *say, did Chaerea strip your coat off? He did*, Ter. Eun. iv. 4. 39. Or increasing the emphasis : 'Pater est? Ipsust,' *is it my father? Himself*, Ter. 'An voluptas in bonis habenda est? Atque in maximis quidem,' *is pleasure to be reckoned among goods? Ay, and among the greatest*, C.

3) By Affirmative Particles, either alone, or joined to the emphatic word. Such are, ita, sane, etiam, verum, utique, vero, certe, ita plane, ita enimvero, ita prorsus, omnino, admodum, recte, profecto. 'Numquid vis? Etiam,' *do you want anything? Yes*, Ter. 'Visne potiora tantum interrogem? Sane,' *would you have me ask only the principal matters? Exactly so*, C. 'Fuisti saepe, credo, cum Athenis esses, in scholis philosophorum? Vero, ac libenter quidem,' *you were often, I suppose, when you were at Athens, in the schools of the philosophers? Yes, and with pleasure*, C. T. D. ii. 11.

a) Nimirum, nempe, quippe, videlicet, scilicet (*obviously, to be sure, why*), express irony : 'Quem hunc appellas, Zeno? Beatum, inquit. Etiam beatissimum? Quippe, inquiet,' *what call you this man, Zeno? Happy, says he. Supremely happy, too? Why yes, he will say*, C. Fin. v. 28. 'Tibi ego possem irasci? Scilicet,' *could I have been angry with you? Very likely!* C. Qu. Fr. i. 3.

b) Certo always affirms positively (*for certain*) : certe sometimes affirms positively, sometimes restrictively (*at all events, at least*). Vero affirms positively (*of a truth*), or it may be used as an Adversative Particle. Vere means *verily, really, truly*.

ii. Negative Answers are also given in three ways.

1) By repeating the emphatic word with a Negative Particle: 'Estne frater intus? Non est,' *is my brother in? No,* Ter. *Ad.* iv. 2. 30.

2) By Negative Particles alone, such as non, non vero, non ita, minime, minime vero, nihil sane, nihil vero minus, nequaquam, ne id quidem, &c. 'Cognitorem adscribit Sthenio. Quem? Cognatum aliquem aut propinquum? Non. Thermitanum aliquem, honestum hominem ac nobilem? Ne id quidem. At Siculum, in quo aliquis splendor dignitasque esset? Minime,' *he assigns to Sthenius a defender. Whom? Was it some blood-relation or kinsman? No. Some inhabitant of Thermae, a man of honour and rank? Not even that. Well, but a Sicilian, possessing some eminence and dignity? Far from it,* C. *Verr.* ii. 43. 'Non opus est? Non hercle vero,' *is there no occasion? None, I assure you,* Ter. *Haut.* iii. 3. 50.

3) By immo (*nay rather* = the Greek μέν οὖν), when the answer is not simply Negative, but at the same time corrective of the opinion implied in the question: 'Ubi fuit Sulla, num Romae? Immo longe afuit,' *where was Sulla? was he at Rome? Nay, he was at a great distance from it,* C. *p. Sull.* 19. 'Visne adesse me una? Immo longe abi,' *would you like me to attend with you? No, keep at a distance,* Ter. 'Sicine hunc decipis? Immo enimvero hic me decipit,' *is it thus you deceive him? Nay, to tell the truth, he is deceiving me,* Ter. *Ph.* iii. 2. 43. Immo is also used when the answer admits the fact, but adds some heightening circumstance: as 'Hic tamen vivit. Vivit? Immo etiam in senatum venit,' *yet this man lives. Lives? Yea, even comes into the senate,* C. *Cat.* 1. 'Tenaxne est? Immo pertinax,' *is he tenacious? Yes, and pertinacious,* Plaut. *Capt.* ii. 2. 39.

    a) Recte, optime, are used not only affirmatively, but also as polite Negatives: 'Rogo numquid velit. Recte, inquit,' *I ask if he wants anything. All right, says he,* Ter. *Eun.* ii. 3. 4. So, benigne (*you're very kind*) is used as a polite mode of declining: as in French, *je vous remercie.* See Hor. *Epist.* ii. 7. 16.

SECTION X.

Uses of the Verb.[1]

(In Ch. III. Sections I.—III., Verbal uses have, to some extent, been explained along with the forms of the Verb. Throughout Syntax they again appear as affecting construction generally. The matter of the present Section is therefore limited to a few points.)

---

[1] Every finite Verb is a predicative word, having Number, Person, Mood and Tense. In regard of Number and Person, it is determined by its Subject: in regard of manner of action (Mood) and Time (Tense), it is determined by its relations to the speaker or narrator.

Thus when Dido in Virgil says, 'Veniet mihi fama,' *the report will come to me,*

i. The Indicative or Fact-Mood and its Tenses.

A. Mood.   See § 37.

The Indicative is the Fact-Mood, used to *declare* (state categorically) : scribo, *I write* ; scribam, *I will write*, &c.

Such declaration may be

1) Independent, in a principal sentence.

Scribo ad filium, *I write to my son* : non scripsi ad Lucium ; and (in the form of Interrogation), scribesne ad patrem ?

2) Subordinate, if the clause in which it stands is purely *objective* (independent of mental conception).

Thus the Indicative may be used in clauses of fact (quod), cause (quod, quia, &c.), condition (si, nisi), concession (etsi, quamquam, &c.), time (cum, quando, ubi, antequam, postquam, dum, donec, &c.) : and in clauses introduced by the Relative Pronoun or a Relative Particle ; whenever such clauses are free from those forms of thought which require (as hereafter shewn) the Subjunctive.

Examples : Gratum est quod vĕnis (venies, vēnisti, &c.). Gaudeo quod (cum, si, &c.) vĕnis, &c. Gaudebo si (cum) venies (vēneris). Non gaudebo nisi vĕnis (venies, vēneris). Gaudebam cum (quia) veniebas (vēneras). Mane dum redeo. Eo quamquam aeger sum. Ibo etsi tu noles (nolueris).

B. Tenses.

The relations of the Indicative Tenses Active (shewn § 38) may be thus re-stated.

Writing, as an action, is to me

I.   *a.* simply present : scribo, *I write.*
      b. —   past : scripsi, *I wrote.*
      c. —   future : scribam, *I shall write.*

II. 1. *a.* now present : scribo, *I am writing.*
      b. —   past : scripsi, *I have written.*
      c. —   future : scripturus sum, *I am about to write.*

   2. *a.* formerly present : scribebam, *I was writing.*
      b. —   past : scripseram, *I had written.*
      c. —   future : scripturus eram, *I was about to write.*

'veniet' is determined in Number (Sing.) and Person (3rd) by its Subject 'fama :' its Mood is Indicative and its Tense Future, because Dido *declares* what *will happen* to her. See § 37.

Had she said, 'Veniat mihi fama,' '*may the report come to me*,' 'veniat' would be related in the same respects to 'fama :' but its Mood (Conjunctive in Optative Sense) and Tense (C₁) would be determined by the fact that Dido states *a conceived wish* that something *may happen* to her in time coming.

If we suppose the expression to be, 'optabat Dido veniret sibi fama,' '*Dido wished the report* might *come to her*,' 'veniret' again follcws the Number and Person of 'fama ;' and is again Conjunctive in Optative Sense because a conceived wish is expressed ; but its Tense becomes C₃ because (instead of coming directly from the speaker's mouth as 'veniat' did) it depends on the narrator's statement, 'optabat,' which, being Past, requires (as hereinafter shewn) the Historic Consecution : and what is *stated* is, that Dido *in time past conceived a wish* that something *might happen* in time *then* future to her.

3. *a.* hereafter present : (scribam, *I shall be writing*).

   b. —   past : scripsero, *I shall have written.*

   c. —   future : scripturus ero, *I shall be about to write.*

Forms under I. are the Simple or Aorist (indefinite) Tenses.

Forms under II. are the Relative Tenses.

The Passive Tenses correspond similarly.

Note. 1. The form II. 1. *a.* (Present with Present relation) is seldom needed except when there is a clause with dum : 'Dum tu sectaris apros, ego retia servo,' *while you are chasing boars, I am watching nets*, Verg. *B.* iii. 74. 'Dum aes exigitur, dum mula ligatur, tota abit hora,' *while the fare is being taken, and the mule harnessed, a whole hour passes*, Hor. *S.* i. 5. 13.

The form 3. *a.* (Future with Present relation) is rarely needed.

A) The Present Tense expresses

1) Momentary Present action. 'Procumbit humi bos,' *the bull falls prostrate*, Verg. *Aen.* v. 481. 'Momento turbinis exit Marcus Dama,' *as soon as twirled he comes forth Marcus Dama*, Pers. v. 77.

2) Action or state occasionally, habitually, or permanently present. 'Domesticus otior,' *I lounge at home*, Hor. *S.* i. 6. 127. 'Honos alit artis,' *honour nurtures the arts*, C. *T. D.* i. 3. 'Deus est, qui sentit, qui regit et moderatur, et est aeternus,' *there is a god, who perceives, who rules and governs, and is eternal*, C. *Rep.* vi. 24.

3) The opinion or statement of an author, who is cited as if still living and speaking : 'Laudat Africanum Panaetius,' &c., C. 'Scribit Cato,' C. &c.

Peculiar uses of the Present are :

   a) The Anticipative Present, sometimes found as an emphatic substitute for the Future : 'Ni propere fit quod impero, vinciri vos iam iubeo,' *if what I command is not done with speed, I order you to be put in chains this moment*, L. xxxvi. 28. 'Abeo an maneo?' *shall I go or stay?* Ter. *Ph.* v. 1. 'Imusne sessum?' *shall we go and sit down?* C. *d. Or.* iii. 5.

   b) The Historic Present, used for the Past in animated and picturesque narrative, whether in history, oratory, or poetry : 'Dimisso senatu, decemviri prodeunt in contionem, abdicantque se magistratu, ingenti hominum laetitia,' *when the senate broke up, the decemvirs go forth to the assembled people, and resign office, to the great delight of the public*, L. iii. 54.

Note 2. Here may be noticed the idiom of the Historic Infinitive (Pres. Imperf.) used predicatively for a Finite Verb ; a construction analogous to the omission of the verb sum, inasmuch as it leaves out, like this, the expression of time, number, and person. Both *constructions* are found occurring together : 'Ceterum facies totius negotii varia incerta foeda atque miserabilis ; dispersi a suis pars cedere, alii insequi ; neque signa neque ordines observare; ubi quemque periculum ceperat, ibi resistere ac propulsare; arma, tela, equi, viri, hostes, cives permixti; nihil consilio neque imperio agi; fors omnia regere,' *now the aspect of the whole affair was confused, indecisive, shocking and pitiable; parties scattered from their comrades were some retiring, others advancing; observing neither standards nor ranks; where peril encountered each man, there was he resisting and repelling: arms, darts, steeds, men, foes, countrymen were intermingled, nothing was proceeding by counsel or command: chance directed all.* Sall. *Iug.* 51. This construction, in which the Infinitive may be considered Imperfect, is frequently used by poets as well as historians.

> c) The Historic Present is commonly used in a Temporal clause with dum, even when the Principal Sentence is Past or Future : 'Dum obsequor adolescentibus, me senem esse sum oblitus,' *in complying with young men, I have forgotten that I am old,* C. *d. Or.* ii. 4.

> d) The Present obtains a Past sense also when joined with iam, iam diu (dudum, pridem) : 'Annum iam audis Cratippum,' *you have now for a year been attending the lectures of Cratippus,* C. *Off.* i. 1. 'Iamdudum video,' *I have seen it this long time,* Hor. *Sat.* i. 9. 15. 'Iampridem cupio Alexandriam visere,' *I have been long desirous to visit Alexandria,* C. *Att.* ii. 5.

> e) Poets use the Historic Present with great license for the Perfect : 'Quantum mutatus ab illo Hectore, qui redit exuvias indutus Achillis,' *how changed from that Hector who returned clad in the spoils of Achilles,* Verg. *Aen.* ii. 275.

B) The Perfect Tense expresses

1) As Aorist, the simple statement of a past fact : 'Veni, vidi, vici,' *I came, I saw, I conquered,* Caes.

2) As Present with Past relation, the statement of a fact complete at the present moment. 'Dixi,' *I have spoken,* Cic. 'Venit summa dies,' *the last day is come,* Verg. *Aen.* ii. 324.

It is idiomatically used to express:

> a) The rapid completion of action (poetic) : 'Fugere ferae,' *beasts have fled,* Verg. *G.* i. 330.

> b) Cessation of existence (poetic): 'Fuimus Troes, fuit Ilium,' *we Trojans have been, Troy has been* (i.e. exists no longer), Verg. *Aen.* ii. 325.

> c) General habit: '(Rege) amisso rupere fidem constructaque mella diripuere,' *if the queen-bee is lost they break faith and pull down their honey stores,* Verg. *G.* iv. 213.
> Prose writers use this idiom in clauses with cum, si, &c. 'Cum fortuna reflavit affligimur,' *when fortune blows contrary, we are flung down,* C. *Off.* ii. 6.

> d) Anticipation, for the Future Perfect : 'Brutus si conservatus erit, vicimus,' *if Brutus shall have been saved, we have won the day,* C. *Fam.* xii. 6.

C) The Imperfect expresses

1) Action going on in time past along with other action (Past with Present relation) : 'Ibam forte Via Sacra . . . accurrit quidam,' &c., *I was walking by chance along the Sacred Road (when) a certain man ran up to me*, &c., Hor. *Sat.* i. 9. 1.

2) Action repeated or habitual in time past : 'Dicebat melius quam scripsit Hortensius,' *Hortensius used to speak better than he has written*, C. *Or.* 38. 'Noctes vigilabat ad ipsum mane, diem totum stertebat,' *he used to lie awake whole nights till daybreak, and snore all day long*, Hor. *S.* i. 3. 17.

3) Action in time past, intended or begun, but not completed : 'Aeneas . . . lenibat dictis animum,' *Aeneas was trying to soften her mind with his words*, Verg. *Aen.* vi. 468. 'Num dubitas id me imperante facere, quod iam tua sponte faciebas?' *do you hesitate to do at my command what you were already on the point of doing voluntarily?* C. *Cat.* i. 5. 'Huius deditionis ipse, qui dedebatur, suasor et auctor fuit,' *of this surrender the very man who was to be surrendered was the mover and adviser*, C. *Off.* iii. 30.

D) The Pluperfect expresses action past in a time itself past, and often stands in connection with other Tenses : 'Cum esset Demosthenes, multi oratores magni et clari fuerunt, et antea fuerant, nec postea defecerunt,' *in the time of Demosthenes there were many great and renowned orators, and there had been such before, nor did they fail afterwards*, C. *Or.* 2. 'Postquam lux certior erat, et Romani, qui caedibus superfuerant, in arcem confugerant, conticescebatque tumultus, tum Tarentinos convocari iubet,' *when the light became stronger, and the Romans, who had survived the massacre, had escaped into the citadel, and the uproar was getting quiet, he then orders the Tarentines to be convoked*, L. xxv. 10.

a) As Clauses expressing habit are in the Perfect with cum, si, ubi, simul ac, when the principal Verb is Present (see above *B c.*), so they are in the Pluperfect with the same Conjunctions, when the principal Verb is Imperfect. 'Gyges, cum palam eius anuli ad palmam converterat, a nullo videbatur, ipse autem omnia videbat; idem rursus videbatur cum in locum anulum inverterat,' *as often as Gyges turned the bezel of that ring towards his palm, he was visible to none, while he saw everything himself: moreover he came into sight again, as often as he turned the ring back to its place*, C. *Off.* iii. 9. 'Si hostis deterrere nequiverant, disiectos ab tergo circumveniebant,' *if they could not deter the enemy, they surrounded their divisions in the rear*, Sall. *Iug.* 50.

(The relations of the Past Indicative Tenses, also of the Historic Present and Infinitive, are well exemplified in C. *Verr.* iv. 27; Sall. *Iug.* 50-51.)

Tenses in letter-writing. *Note* 3. A Roman, writing a letter, arranged the Tenses with reference to the time when the letter would be received. Hence many facts, which to the writer were Present, are stated as Past in regard to the receiver. And other facts, which to the writer were Past, are stated in the Pluperfect, for the same reason. The English practice being different, a Roman letter must be translated not literally, but into our idiom : ' Pridie Idus haec scripsi ante lucem. Eo die apud Pomponium in eius nuptiis eram cenaturus,' *I have written this before daybreak on the day before the Ides. I am going to dine with Pomponius to-day at his wedding,* C. Q. F. ii. 3. ' Nihil habebam quod scriberem : neque enim novi quicquam audieram, et ad tuas omnis rescripseram pridie,' *I have nothing to write about : for I have heard no news, and I replied to all your letters yesterday,* C. *Att.* ix. 10. But matters which will remain present to the receiver, are stated in the Present : ' Ego hic cogito commorari, quoad me reficiam,' *I think of remaining here whilst I am recruiting my health,* C. *Fam.* vii. 26.

E) The Simple Future expresses what its name implies, simple action in the Future : ' Ut voles me esse, ita ero,' *I will be as you shall wish me to be,* Plaut. *Pseud.* i. 3

> *a*) It is often used as a polite Imperative : 'Quod superest, puerum Ciceronem curabis et amabis,' *for the rest, please to treat young Cicero with care and affection,* C. *Att.* iv. 7. See Hor. *Epist.* i. 18. 37–40.

F) The Future Perfect expresses action to be fulfilled in Future time : 'Qui Antonium oppresserit, is bellum confecerit,' *he, who shall have crushed Antonius, will have finished the war,* C. *Fam.* x. 20.

> *a*) It may be connected with the Simple Future, or used for the Simple Future, with a view to Emphasis : ' Ut sementem feceris, ita metes,' *as you shall have sown, so will you reap,* C. *d. Or.* ii. 65. 'Si quid acciderit novi, facies ut sciam,' *should anything new happen, please to let me know,* C. *Fam.* xiv. 8. 'Quid inventum sit, paulo post videro,' *what has been discovered, I shall very soon see,* C. *Ac.* ii. 24. 'A, si pergis, abiero,' *nay, if you go on, I shall be off,* Ter. *Ad.* i. 2. 47. 'Sitne malum dolor necne Stoici viderint,' *whether pain is an evil or not, the Stoics will have to see,* C. *T. D.* ii. 18.

G) In the Future Periphrastic Conjugation (-urus sum, eram, fui, fueram, ero, fuero, &c.) the Indicative Tenses are called Present, Perfect, &c., according to the forms of sum : and the general distinctions above stated apply to them, but not the idiomatic uses.

This Conjugation expresses

1) '*Being about to ;*' '*being on the point of :*' ' Apes evolaturae sunt,' *the bees are about to swarm,* Varr. *R. R.* iii. 16. 'Vos cum Mandonio arma consociaturi fuistis,' *you were on the point of allying your arms with Mandonius,* L. xxviii. 28.

2) '*Being likely to ;*' '*being sure to :*' ' Haec sine doctrina credituri fuerunt,' *this they were sure to believe without learning,* C. *T. D.* i. 21 (= '*they would have believed.*' See the use of this form, and of the Inf. -urum fuisse, in the Apodosis of Conditional Sentences).

3) '*Being destined to*' (*am to*, *are to*, &c.) : '*Si una interiturus* est animus cum corpore,' &c., *if the soul is to perish with the body*, &c., C. *Cat. M.* 22. '*Quidquid ex Agricola amavimus manet mansurumque est in animis hominum*,' *all that we have loved of Agricola abides and is destined to abide in the memory of men*, Tac. *Agr.* 46. '*Me ipsum ames oportet, si veri amici futuri sumus*,' *you must love me myself, if we are to be true friends*, C. *Fin.* ii. 26. See Conditional Sentences : and Consecution of Tenses.

(On the Gerundive Conjugation -ndus sum, -ndum est, &c., see Syntax of '*the Verb Infinite*.')

Note 4. Latin writers often use Verbs and phrases expressing *duty, necessity, propriety, possibility*, &c., in the Past Indicative Tenses instead of the Conjunctive, to indicate that it was proper or possible at that time to do something which however was not done.

1) Past Tenses of d e b e r e; d e c e r e; oportere; aequum (aequius, melius, par, utilius, &c.) esse; posse; malle; licere, &c. '*Omnibus eum contumeliis onerasti, quem patris loco colere debebas*,' *you have loaded with every insult one whom you ought to have revered as a father*, C. *Phil.* ii. 38. '*Ad mortem duci te iam pridem oportebat*,' *you ought long ago to have been dragged to death*, C. *in Cat.* i. 1. '*Ieci fundamenta reipublicae serius quam decuit*,' *I laid the foundations of the commonwealth at a later time than I should have done*, C. *Phil.* v. 11. '*Haec tecum coram malueram*,' *I would rather have discussed these things with you face to face*, C. *Fam.* vii. 3. '*Quanto melius fuerat promissum patris non esse servatum*,' *how much better had it been that the father's promise had not been kept*, C. *Off.* iii. 25. '*Hic tamen hanc mecum poteras requiescere noctem*,' *yet you might have rested here with me this night*, Verg. *B.* i. 80.

2) Periphrastic Past Tenses, Future and Gerundive : '*Romani Poenos depoposcerunt, qui Saguntum oppugnassent : deditos ultimis cruciatibus affecturi fuerunt*,' *the Romans demanded those Carthaginians who had besieged Saguntum; they would have executed them, if surrendered, with the uttermost tortures*, L. xxi. 44. '*Non Asiae nomen obiciendum Murenae fuit*,' *Murena should not have been reproached with the mention of Asia*, C. *p. Mur.* 5.

    a) Analogous idioms are the Indicatives p o s s u m, longum e s t, infinitum e s t, &c., where English idiom would write '*I could*,' '*it were tedious*,' &c. '*Possum persequi multa oblectamenta rerum rusticarum : sed ea ipsa quae dixi fuisse sentio longiora*,' *I could detail the many delights of farming operations; but even what I have said I feel to have been rather tedious*, C. *Cat. M.* 16. '*Longum est mulorum persequi utilitates et asinorum*,' *it were tedious to detail the advantages of mules and asses*, C. *N. D.* ii. 64. See M. *Lucr.* i. 400.

(On the Indicative in the Apodosis of Conditional Sumptio Ficti, see Syntax of Conditional Sentences.)

ii. The Imperative or Will-Mood. § 37.

1) The Imperative Present commands or entreats. 'Quae cum ita sint, Catilina, perge quo coepisti; egredere aliquando ex urbe; patent portae : proficiscere,' *such being the case, Catilina, proceed on your chosen path; quit the city at some time; the gates are open: go forth,* C. *in Cat.* i. 5. 'Pergite, adulescentes, atque in id studium, in quo estis, incumbite,' *go on, young men, and devote yourselves to that study, on which you are engaged,* C. *d. Or.* i. 8.

2) The Imperative forms in -to -tote may entreat or command : but they oftener command; being used in legal forms : 'Cum faciam vitula pro frugibus, ipse venito,' *when I shall be sacrificing a calf for the crops, you must come yourself,* Verg. *B.* iii. 77. 'Divis omnibus pontifices, singulis flamines sunto; virginesque Vestales in urbe custodiunto ignem foci publici sempiternum,' *all gods in common must have pontifices, each particular god a flamen; and the Vestal virgins in the city must guard for ever the fire of the public hearth,* C. *Leg.* ii. 20. 'Regio imperio duo sunto iique consules appellantor,' *there shall be two magistrates with royal power, and they shall be called consuls,* C. *Leg.* iii. 3. See Plaut. *Pseud.* iii. 2. 66, &c.

3) Ne with Imperative Present (ne crede, ne credite, Verg.) be-longs to poetry : but is rare in prose. L. has 'ne timete.' (See Conjunctive Mood.) With Imperative Future it is used in legal forms, 'Hominem mortuum in urbe ne sepelito neve urito,' *thou shalt not bury or burn a corpse in the city,* C. *Leg.* ii. 58.

4) A Periphrasis of the exhorting Imperative is made by fac, fac ut, cura ut, velim, with Subjunctive, and in poetry by memento with Subjunctive or Infinitive; and a Periphrasis of the forbidding Imperative by fac ne, cave, nolim, with Subjunctive; or by noli, and (poetically) parce, mitte, omitte, absiste, fuge, &c., with Infinitive.
'Magnum fac animum habeas,' *mind you have a lofty spirit,* C. *Qu. Fr.* i. 2. 5. 'Cura ut valeas,' *take care of your health,* C. 'Aequam memento rebus in arduis servare mentem,' *you must remember to keep an even mind in difficult circumstances,* Hor. *C.* ii. 3. 1. 'Cave facias,' *beware of doing it,* C. *Att.* xiii. 33. 'Hoc nolim me iocari putes,' *I would not have you think I say this in jest,* C. *Fam.* ix. 15. 'Nolite id velle, quod fieri non potest' *do not wish what cannot be,* C. *Phil.* vii. 9. 'Mitte sectari rosa quo locorum sera moretur,' *search not in what spot the rose lingers late,* Hor. *C.* i. 38. 3. 'Vos timere absistite,' *cease ye to fear,* Phaedr. iii. 2. 18. 'Fuge suspicari,' *do not suspect,* Hor.

5) Imperative forms are modified by the polite phrases sis, sultis, sodes, amabo, &c., *please, pray* (see p. 235). Sis is frequent in comedy (once in Cic.); sultis often in Plautus. Sodes, C. (once?); frequent in comic and other poets. Amabo, amabo te (= si me amas) in comedy often : and in Cic. So, Cave sis, vide sis, &c. 'Refer te sis ad veritatem,' C. 'Hoc agite sultis,' Plaut. 'Scin' quid te amabo ut facias?' *shall I tell you, please, what to do?* Plaut. 'Id agite, amabo,' C.

z

iii. The Conjunctive or Thought-Mood.

(On the Conjunctive as the mood of *mental conception* generally, and on its twofold use, (1) as *Pure* or independent Conjunctive ; (2) as *Subjunctive* or dependent, see § 37. 2.)

iv. The Thought-mood is properly termed **Conjunctive** by all German scholars, seeing that its use is to *join with* both the other Moods, and assist their power of expressing speech. It joins with the Indicative so as to state and question in a tone either contingent on a condition, or modified by mental reserve in the nature of a condition. It joins with the Imperative, so as to supply its deficient forms, and also to express the various shades of will-speech in modified tone. The Conjunctive Mood has four Tenses, called Present, Perfect, Imperfect, and Pluperfect, the powers and uses of which are best learnt from reading and practice. See p. 163. Though the Futures are wanting, all the Tenses are capable of referring to Future time, when required.

I. Pure Conjunctive of contingent or modified Statement (negation takes non, or haud).

A) When a condition is formally expressed, E am si moneas (monueris), *I will go, if you advise* : irem (issem) si moneres (monuisses), *I would have gone, if you had advised* : non eam nisi tu moneas (monueris), *I will not go unless you advise* ; non irem (issem) nisi tu moneres (monuisses), *I should not have been going (should not have gone) if you had not advised.* 'Tu, si hic sis, aliter sentias.' 'Improbe feceris nisi monueris,' Cic. 'Si luxuriae temperaret, avaritiam non timeres,' *had he curbed luxury, you would not have dreaded avarice in him,* Tac. ' Si redisset filius, pater ei veniam daret (dedisset),' *had the son come back, his father would have forgiven him.* 'Si non des, optet,' Hor. Si non dares (dedisses) optaret (optasset).

B) When a condition is informally expressed : see § 217, 3. E am (irem, issem) te monente, *if you advise (advised)*, or a te monitus, *if advised by you* : non eam (irem issem) te invito, *against your will*, or prohibitus a te, *if forbidden by you.* 'Optanti tibi divûm promittere nemo auderet,' *no god would have ventured to promise had you expressed the wish,* V. 'Non illi quisquam se impune tulisset obvius armato,' *no man would have encountered him, armed for battle, with impunity,* V. 'Sine Deo non esset mundus,' Cic. 'Ita laudem invenias et amicos pares,' Ter.

C) When a condition is implied, especially with Verb in 2nd Person. 'Migrantes cernas,' *you may see them on the move,* V. 'Marte videres fervere Leucaten,' *you might have seen Leucate boiling with war* (i.e. had you been present). 'Pelago credas innare revulsas Cycladas,' V. 'Nec quisquam . . . putet,' &c. V. *Aen.* viii. 704. 'Crederes victos,' L.

D) When modified to avoid positiveness or bluffness. 'Dubitem haud equidem,' V. Velim, nolim, vellem, nollem are frequently used on this ground. 'Nollem accidisset,' *I wish it had not happened,* C. *Fam.* iii. 30. 'Vellem adesse posset Panaetius,' *I wish Panaetius could have been present*, C. T. D. i. 33. Also with forsitan or fortasse : forsitan quaeratis; roges fortasse; 'forsitan et Priami fuerint quae fata requiras,' V. *Aen.* ii. 506. 'Vix verisimile fortasse videatur,' Cic. Especially C_2 is used to convey assertion or opinion moderately. Crediderim, *I am inclined to believe* : vix crediderim, *I can scarcely believe.* 'Non te transierim,' V. 'Ausim vel tenui vitem committere sulco,' V. *G.* ii. 289. And with forsitan.

This and the next use are sometimes called Potential.

II. *E*) Pure Conjunctive of the modified Question (Negation has non).

    a) A direct question of inquiry or of feeling implies more of mental dubitation when used in the Conjunctive. As in the Indicative, it may be of single or disjunctive form.

Quid hoc homine faciatis? *what are you to do with this man?* 'Quis Troiae nesciat urbem?' V. 'Quid dem, quid non dem,' Hor. 'Quid faciam? roger anne rogem?' Ov. 'Eloquar an sileam?' V. 'Tibi ego irascerer, mi frater? tibi ego possem irasci?' Cic. Quid facerem? quo fugerem? Iremusne annon? quare non iremus? issemne nisi voluissem?

III. Pure Conjunctive of modified Will-speech (Negation has ne).

    F) Concessive use : allowing, granting, &c.

        'Luant peccata,' *let them (they may) pay the penalty of their sins*, V. 'Vendat aedes vir bonus,' *suppose a good man has a house on sale.* Haec sint falsa sane, *granting this to be quite untrue.* 'Fuerit malus civis,' *suppose he was a bad citizen.* 'Ne sit summum malum dolor, malum certe est,' *allowing pain not to be the greatest evil, an evil it is at all events*, Cic. 'Verum anceps pugnae fuerat fortuna : fuisset; quem metui moritura?' *but the chance of war had been doubtful; suppose it were : whom could I fear with death in view?* V. *Aen.* iv.

    a) Ut is used in concession. 'Ut desint vires, tamen est laudanda voluntas,' *though strength be lacking, yet willingness is praiseworthy*, Ov. *Ep. P.* iii. 4.

    G) Optative and Precative Uses.

      1) The Optative use conveys a wish, and (when in direct construction without 'utinam') by C_1. (Negation has ne.)
        Sis felix, *may you be happy.* 'Valeant cives mei, sint florentes, sint beati,' Cic. ' Exoriare aliquis nostris ex ossibus ultor,' V. *Aen.* iv.
        It is frequently used in imprecation. 'Ne sim salvus si aliter loquor ac sentio,' *may I never be saved if I speak other than I think*, Cic. 'Moriar nisi vera loquor.' With ita (sic) . . . ut. 'Ita vivam ut te amo maxime.' And without ut. 'Ita culmo surgeret alto,' Hor. *S.* ii. 'Ita me di ament,' Cic.

a) Utinam, utinam ne (rarely non) are used with the Optative. With C_1 it expresses a possible wish : Utinam possim, *I wish I may be able* ; utinam ne adsit, *I wish he may not be present.* With C_3 an impracticable one : utinam possem, *I wish I could* (but I cannot); utinam ne adesset, *I wish he were not present* (but he is or was). With C_4 a bygone possibility : utinam potuissem, *I wish I had been able* (but I was not): utinam non adfuisset, *I wish he had not been present* (but he was).

b) Ut for utinam is sometimes found : Ut illum di deaeque perduint, *may the gods and goddesses destroy him,* Ter.

c) O si (rarely si alone) with Opt. is poetic. 'O mihi praeteritos referat si Iuppiter annos,' *O if Jove would bring back to me the past years,* V. *Aen.* viii. 560. See vi. 187. O utinam may be used.

2) The Precative use is chiefly in the Second Person, when a sacred being or a superior is addressed : 'Sis bonus o felixque tuis,' V. *Aen.* v. 65. 'Adsis o placidusque iuves et sidera caelo dextra feras,' V. *Aen.* iv. 578.

H) Hortative and Jussive Uses : exhorting, commanding, &c. Negative has ne.

The principal Hortative use is in the First Person Plural. The Jussive use in the Third Persons conveys a command more or less stringent. Thus 'naviget' (V. *Aen.* iv. 287) is a strong mandate : the instructions in the *Georgics* given in the Third Persons Conjunctive are precepts rightly called jussive. See *G.* iii. 300, 329.

1) 'Surgamus,' V. *E.* x. 'Eamus omnes,' Hor. *Ep.* 'Moriamur et in media arma ruamus,' V. *Aen.* ii. 'Aegritudinem depellamus,' Cic.

2) 'Ecferant quae secum huc attulerunt,' Ter. 'Vincat utilitas reipublicae.' 'Sit sermo lenis, insit in eo lepos,' Cic. 'Vilicus ne sit ambulator, sobrius sit semper, ad cenam ne quo eat, familiam exerceat, ne plus censeat sapere se quam dominum, parasitum ne quem habeat.' Cato. 'Donis impii ne placare audeant deos,' Cic. *Leg.* ii. 16.

The most remarkable examples are those which convey this use of the Will-speech Conjunctive into past time by C_3, C_4. 'Praediceres,' *you should have told me beforehand,* Plaut. 'Rem tuam curares,' *you should have been minding your own business,* Ter. 'Dictis, Albane *maneres,' you should have remained true to your word, O Alban,* V. 'Ne *poposcisses,' you ought not to have demanded,* Cic. This usage is not confined to the Second Person ; 'Animam ipse dedissem, atque haec pompa domum me, non Pallanta, referret,' V. *Aen.* xi. 162 ; see x. 854.

95
Second
Person
Con-
junctive.

a) Permissive and exhorting Use of Second Person Conjunctive. The Second Person of C_1 is often supposed to be Pure where it is really Subjunctive, depending on a Verb. Reddas, Hor. *C.* i. 3. 7; dones, i. 31. 18, depend on precor. Captes, Hor. *S.* ii. 5. 23, on dico. 'Sis . . .

sequare . . . cures,' C. *Fam.* x. 16, carry on the construction after 'hoc animo esse ut:' and the punctuation should shew this. 'Sis . . . scias,' L. xxvi. 50, depend on paciscor. 'Ne pigrere,' C. *Att.* xiv. 1, on quaeso.

b) Prohibitive use of Second Person Conjunctive.

Terence has 'Si certum est facere, facias; verum ne post culpam conferas in me,' *if you are bent on doing it, you may; but please not afterwards to throw the blame on me,* *Eun.* ii. 3. 97. In classical Latin this form (ne with Second Person of C_1) is not used as an independent prohibition, but ne with Second Person of C_2 is so used frequently. 'Quod dubitas ne feceris,' *what you doubt, do not perform,* Plin. *Ep.* i. 18. 'Illum iocum ne sis aspernatus,' *do not contemn that jest,* C. *Qu. F.* ii. 12. 'Tu ne quaesieris,' &c. Hor. *C.* i. 11. 1.

When Horace writes, 'Ne forte credas,' &c., he means *lest perchance you should believe,* C. iv. 9. 1. And so often.

On Periphrastic forms of exhortation and prohibition, see p. 337.

v. Examples of Pure Conjunctive:—

A) See Examples under § 213 β, γ, p. 408.

B) See § 217, 3, p. 473.

C) 'Pecuniae an famae minus parceret haud facile discerneres,' Sall. *Cat.* 25. 'Quo postquam venerunt, mirandum in modum, canes venaticos diceres, ita odorabantur omnia et pervestigabant,' C. *Verr.* iv. 13. 'Illum indignanti similem similemque minanti aspiceres,' V. *Aen.* viii. 650.

D) 'Tu velim sic existimes tibique persuadeas, omne perfugium bonorum in te esse positum, si, quod nolim, adversi quid evenerit,' C. *Fam.* xii. 6. 'Malim mihi Crassi unam pro Curio dictionem, quam castellanos triumphos duos,' C. *Br.* 73. 'Ego me Phidiam esse mallem quam vel optimum fabrum tignarium,' C. *Br.* 73. 'Vellem te ad Stoicos inclinavisses,' C. *Fin.* iii. 3. 'Hic quaerat quispiam, cuiusnam causa tanta molitio facta sit,' C. *N. D.* ii. 53. 'Primum ego me illorum, dederim quibus esse poetas, excerpam numero; neque enim concludere versum dixeris esse satis,' Hor. *S.* i. 4. 39. 'Forsitan quispiam dixerit; nonne sapiens, si fame ipse conficiatur, abstulerit cibum alteri?' C. *Off.* iii. 6.

E) 'Quid nunc te, asine, litteras doceam?' C. *Pis.* 30. 'Quid videatur ei magnum in rebus humanis, cui aeternitas omnis totiusque mundi nota sit magnitudo?' C. *T. D.* iv. 17. 'Quid enumerem artium multitudinem, sine quibus vita omnino nulla esse potuisset?' C. *Off.* ii. 4. 'Faveas tu hosti? bonorum spem virtutemque debilites? et te consularem aut senatorem aut denique civem putes?' C. *Phil.* vii. 20. 'Apud exercitum mihi fueris tot annos? forum non attigeris? a fueris tam diu? et, cum longo intervallo veneris, cum iis, qui in foro habitarunt, de dignitate contendas?' C. *Mur.* 9. 'Ego mihi putarem in patria non futurum locum?' C. *Mil.* 34. 'Putaresne unquam accidere posse ut mihi verba deessent?' C. *Fam.* ii. 11. 'Corinthiis bellum indicamus annon?' Cic.

F) 'At tamen dicat sine. Age dicat, sino,' Ter. *An.* v. 3. 24. 'Fuerint cupidi, fuerint irati, fuerint pertinaces: sceleris vero crimine, furoris, parricidi, liceat Cn. Pompeio mortuo, liceat multis aliis carere,' C. *Lig.* 6. 'Nemo is, inquies, umquam fuit. Ne fuerit,' Cic.

G. 1) 'Quod bonum faustum felixque sit populo Romano,' L. i. 28. 'Filiam despondi ego; di bene vertant!' Plaut. *Aul.* ii. 3. 'Tecum esse, ita mihi omnia quae opto contingant ut vehementer velim,' C. *Fam.* v. 21. 'Sollicitat, ita vivam, mi Tiro, me tua valetudo,' C. *Fam.* xvi. 20. 'Ne vivam, si tibi concedo, ut eius rei tu cupidior sis quam ego sum,' C. *Fam.* vii. 23. 'Ne istuc Iuppiter optimus maximus sirit,' L. xxviii. 28. 'Utinam tibi istam mentem dii immortales duint?' C. *Cat.* i. 9. 'Utinam, Quirites, virorum fortium atque innocentium copiam tantam haberetis, ut

v. The Subjunctive.

The Subjunctive is always a Mood of dependence, and, in most instances, of mental conception : but some of its functions in Latin are not of the latter description, especially its Consecutive use.

A Subjunctive Clause[1] sometimes has no link connecting it with the prior Verb : 'Sine te exorem,' *let me prevail on you.* 'Vellem adfuisses,' *I wish you had been present.* But usually it is introduced by a Conjunction or Relative.

I) A Finite Subordinate Clause, by classical usage, is always Subjunctive, when it contains

a) A dependent Consequence (*so that, such that*).
Such a clause may be introduced by ut, quin; or by the Relative qui consecutive. See Consecutive Clauses, and Ut-clause Enuntiative.

b) A dependent Purpose (*in order that, lest,* &c.).
Such a Clause may be introduced by ut, ne, quo, quominus; or by the Relative qui final : sometimes by a Particle of Time or Condition; antequam, dum, &c. See Final Clauses, and Petitio Obliqua.

c) A dependence on a Verb of Fear, introduced by ne, *lest,* or ut, *lest not.* See Petitio Obliqua.

d) A dependent Question, introduced by any Interrogative Pronoun or Particle. See Interrogatio Obliqua.

II) A Finite Subordinate Clause is Subjunctive, when it contains a mental conception

haec vobis deliberatio difficilis esset !' C. *L. Man.* 10. 'Illud utinam ne vere scriberem !' C. *Fam.* v. 17. 'Quod utinam ne Phormioni id suadere in mentem incidisset,' Ter. *Ph.* i. 3. 5. 'Utinam minus vitae cupidi fuissemus,' C. *Fam.* v. 17. 'Haec ad te die natali meo scripsi : quo utinam susceptus non essem, aut ne quid ex eadem matre postea natum esset !' C. *Att.* xi. 9.

2) 'Nihil ignoveris; nihil gratiae causa feceris; misericordia commotus ne sis,' C. *Mur.* 31. 'Ne fueris hic tu,' Hor. *Epist.* i. 6. 40. 'Cum te bene confirmaveris, ad nos venias,' C. *Fam.* xvi. 13. So teneas, L. xxii. 53. Afficias, xxvi. 50. Hor. *S.* ii. 3. 826 (*please to, pray*).

H. 1) 'Meminerimus, etiam adversus infimos iustitiam esse servandam,' C. *Off.* i. 13. 'Imitemur nostros Brutos, Camillos, Decios; amemus patriam, pareamus senatui, consulamus bonis, id esse optimum putemus, quod erit rectissimum,' C. *Sest.* 68.

2) 'Orator videat in primis, quibus de rebus loquatur; si seriis, severitatem adhibeat; si iocosis, leporem,' C. *Off.* i. 37. 'Sumatur nobis quidam praestans vir optimis artibus, isque animo parumper et cogitatione fingatur,' C. *T. D.* v. 24. 'Fortasse pater Cliniae aliquanto iniquior erat. Pateretur; nam quem ferret, si parentem non ferret suum ?' Ter. *Haut.* i. 2. 28. 'Forsitan non nemo vir fortis et acris animi magnique dixerit : Restitisses, repugnasses, mortem pugnans oppetisses,' C. *Sest.* 20. 'Ne quis tamquam parva fastidiat grammatices elementa,' Qu. i. 4. 'Neu desint epulis rosae,' Hor. *C.* i. 36. 15 'Tu ista ne asciveris neve fueris commenticiis rebus assensus,' C. *Ac.* ii. 40.

---

[1] The term Clause is used to signify 'any member of a Compound Sentence' which is not the 'Principal Sentence.' The 'Infinitive Clause' means what is often called 'Accusative and Infinitive.' See Enuntiatio Obliqua. Distinguished from this is 'a Finite Clause ;' that is, one of which the Verb is Finite.

a) Of Cause : introduced by c u m, *since*, by q u i causal (usually) ; by n o n q u o d, n o n q u i a, &c. See Causal Clauses.

b) Of Condition : after d u m, m o d o; or when s i, n i s i are related to a conceptive Apodosis : 's i p o s s i m v e l i m ;'
's i p o s s e m v e l l e m,' &c. See Conditional Sentences.

c) Of Concession : introduced by u t, l i c e t, and (usually) c u m,
q u a m v i s, *although*. Also when e t s i, e t i a m s i, t a m e t s i
are related to a conceptive Apodosis. 'E t s i p o s s e m,
nollem.' See Concessive Sentences.

d) Of Comparison : introduced by q u a s i, u t s i, &c., velut,
tamquam, &c. See Comparative Sentences.

III) A Finite Subordinate Clause is Subjunctive when it is really
dependent on

a) An Infinitive Clause (oratio obliqua).
'A u d i o t e a b e s s e q u o d a e g r o t e s.'

b) An assertion or opinion of some other than the writer or
speaker, implied but not formally expressed in the principal or prior Verb (*virtual* oratio obliqua).
'L a u d a t Africanum Panaetius q u o d f u e r i t abstinens,' Cic.
'A c c u s a t u s e s t Socrates q u o d c o r r u m p e r e t iuventutem,' Qu. See p. 345.
Obs. The Subjunctives *a* and *b* we call S u b o b l i q u e. They
may be introduced by any Conjunction, or by a Relative
Pronoun or Particle.

c) A Conjunctive Verb or prior Subjunctive (oratio obliqua).
'O m n i a d i x i s s e s q u a e in animo h a b e r e s.' 'Vellem omnia
d i x i s s e s q u a e in animo h a b e r e s.'

Note. The following are Idiomatic U s e s :—

a) A Subjunctive with c u m, *when* (rarely with other Temporal
Conjunctions) of a past action antecedent to another
past action (quasi-causal).
'In Cumano c u m e s s e m, venit ad me Hortensius,' *when I
was at my house in Cumae, Hortensius came to see me,* Cic.
'Decessit Agesilaus cum in portum venisset,' *Agesilaus
died after coming into harbour,* Nep. *Ag.*

β) A Subjunctive of repeated action (Iterative) with a Particle
or Relative. This construction is most frequent in past
time, historically, the principal verb being generally Imperfect : but it is very reasonably extended to time present
in philosophical statements by M. *Lucr.* iii. 736.

γ) A Subjunctive, generally of the Second Pers. Sing., in
dependence on a sentence containing a maxim (γνώμη).
See Madv. *Gr.* 370; M. *Lucr.* i. 327, ii. 36, 41.
'Bonus segnior fit ubi n e g l e g a s,' *a good person becomes
slacker, when you neglect him,* Sall. *Iug.* 31.

**vi. Classification of the Particles and Pro-
nouns which introduce Subordinate Clauses,
according to the Mood introduced.**

97

A) Pronouns and Particles which always, in classical Latin prose, introduce a Subjunctive.

a) Conjunctions:

1) Consecutive: ut; quin.
2) Final: ut; ne; quo; quominus.
3) Causal: cum, *since.*
4) Conditional: dum; modo, dummodo; *provided that.*
5) Concessive: licet, ut; cum, quamvis (usually).
6) Comparative: quasi; ut si; ac si; velut, tamquam, ceu, &c.

b) The Relative qui, or a Relative Particle, when used

1) Consecutively (= talis ut); 2) Finally (*in order that*);
3) Causally (= cum, *since*); 4) Concessively (*although*).

c) Interrogative Words, obliquely constructed: such are

1) Pronouns: quis; qui; uter; qualis; quantus; quot; quotus.
2) Particles: quam, quemadmodum, quomodo, ut, *how*; quare, cur, quamobrem, quapropter; quotiens; quando; ubi; unde; quo, quousque, quorsum; utrum, an, -ně, num.

d) Any Particle or Relative, when the Clause itself is in sense dependent on Oratio Obliqua, actual or virtual; or on a Conjunctive Mood.

See also the Iterative and Gnomic uses above, Note β. γ.

B) Pronouns and Particles which always (except in the circumstances above named) introduce an Indicative.

a) Conjunctions:

1) Causal: quod; quia; quoniam; quando; quandoquidem; siquidem.
2) Temporal: quando; ubi; ut (*when*, &c.); quotiens; simul ac; simul; postquam; dum, donec, quoad, *whilst.* Also cum, *when*: but see its idiom, Note, p. 343. *a.*
3) Concessive: quamquam; utut.

b) The Relative qui, and Relative Particles.

C) Particles which introduce an Indicative or a Subjunctive, according as the notion conveyed is one of fact or contingency.

1) Temporal: dum, donec, quoad, *until*; antequam, priusquam, which are used with Subjunctive when purpose is contained, or doubtfulness conveyed.

2) Conditional and Concessive: si, nisi; etsi, etiamsi, tametsi.

Obs. The reason of mood is independent of Conjunctions; but Conjunctions distinguish the relations of Clauses more clearly, as Prepositions distinguish the relations of Nouns.

98
Consecution
of
Tenses.

vii. Consecution of Tenses in Subjunctive Construction. See § 229.

The General Rule is that
Primary Tenses (S_1 S_2) follow Primary (Present; Future).
Historic — (S_3 S_4) — Historic (Past Tenses).

EXAMPLES ILLUSTRATING THE CONSECUTION OF TENSES.

I.

1) querĕris
  you complain

  querar-is (e)
  you may complain

  querēr-is (e)
  you will complain

  questus eris
  questus fueris }
  you will have complained

  questus sis
  questus fueris
  you may have complained

  questurus es (sis, &c.)
  *you are (may be, &c.) about
    to complain*

> quod te deseram
> *that I forsake you*
>
> quod te deseruerim
> *that I have forsaken you*
>
> quod te deserturus sim
> *that I am about to forsake you*
>
> quod tui memor non sim
> *that I am not mindful of you*
>
> quod tui memor non fuerim
> *that I have not been mindful of
>   you*
>
> quod tui memor non futurus sim
> *that I shall not be mindful of
>   you*
>
> quod tibi non succurram
> *that I do not succour you*
>
> quod tibi non succurrerim
> *that I have not succoured you*
>
> quod tibi non succursurus sim
> *that I am not about to succour
>   you*

2) querebar-is (e)
  you were complaining

  questus es
  you complained

  questus eras
  you had complained

  quererer-is (e)
  you would complain

  questus esses
  you would have complained

  questurus eras
  you were about to complain

> quod te desererem
> *that I was forsaking you*
>
> quod te deseruissem
> *that I had forsaken you*
>
> quod te deserturus forem
> *that I was about to forsake you*
>
> quod tui memor non essem
> *that I was not mindful of you*
>
> quod tui memor non fuissem
> *that I had not been mindful of
>   you*
>
> quod tui memor non futurus
>   essem
> *that I was not going to be mind-
>   ful of you*
>
> quod tibi non succurrerem
> *that I did not succour you*
>
> quod tibi non succurrissem
> *that I had not succoured you*
>
> quod tibi non succursurus fo-
>   rem
> *that I did not mean to succour
>   you*

II.

1) orant; orent orabunt; oraturi sunt oraverint; oranto	⎧ ne se deseram ⎨ ut sui memor sim ⎩ ut sibi succurram
2) orabant; orarent oraverunt; oraturi erant oraverant; oravissent	⎧ ne se desererem ⎨ ut sui memor essem ⎩ ut sibi succurrerem

Note. On the Verb Infinite see § 15 and § 40. Its further uses are most conveniently shewn in Syntax, Ch. I. II. III.

99
Ellipsis of Verb.

viii. Ellipsis of the Verb.

1) Est, sunt, esse, are often suppressed: sometimes other forms of the Verb of Being.

'Summum ius summa iniuria,' C. *Off.* i. 10 (s. *est*). 'Habenda ratio valetudinis, utendum modicis exercitationibus,' C. *Cat. M.* 11 (s. *est*). 'Omnia praeclara rara,' C. *Lael.* 21 (s. *sunt*). 'Iucundi acti labores,' C. *Fin.* ii. 32 (s. *sunt*). 'Aurum vestibus inlitum mirata,' Hor. *C.* iv. 9. 15 (for mirata est). 'Sed haec vetera (*sunt*): illud recens (*est*), Caesarem meo consilio interfectum' (*esse*), *but these are old stories: here is a new one, that Caesar was slain by my advice,* C. *Phil.* ii. 11. 'Ludi Romani biduum instaurati' (*sunt*), L. xxix. 38. ' Potest incidere comparatio, de duobus honestis utrum honestius' (*sit*), C. *Off.* i. 43.

    a) The Participle Perfect (Passive or Deponent) is often used in the Nom. Case with an Ellipsis of esse, being really a Prolative Infinitive dependent on fertur, dicitur, memoratur, narratur, &c. 'Sic miser instantis affatus dicitur undas,' Mart. *d. Spect.* 25. 5 (for affatus esse). 'Fertur Prometheus addere principi limo coactus particulam undique desectam,' Hor. *C.* i. 16. 13 (for coactus esse). 'Quidam memoratur Athenis . . . populi contemnere voces sic solitus,' Hor. *S.* i. 1. 64 (for solitus esse). 'Fabula qua Paridis propter narratur amorem Graecia barbariae lento collisa duello,' Hor. *Epist.* i. 2. 6 (for collisa esse). And often in prose: 'Q. Fabius Maximus sic eum proficiscentem allocutus fertur,' L. xxii. 38 (for allocutus esse). 'Capta eo proelio tria milia peditum et equites trecenti dicuntur,' L. xxii. 50. See Note at p. 428.

2) Inquit, inquam, &c. are omitted. 'At ille' . . . 'tum Brutus' . . . 'tum ego,' &c.

3) Forms of dicere, facere, fieri, &c. 'Scite Chrysippus' (*dicit*), C. 'Cave turpe quicquam' (*facias*), C. 'Ne quid crudeliter' (*fiat*), C. 'Cicero Attico salutem' (*dicit*), C. 'Crassus verbum nullum contra gratiam' (*dixit*), C. 'Expecto quid ad ista' (*dicturus sis*), C. 'Quas tu mihi intercessiones' (*narras*)? C. 'Finem ille' (*fecit*), C. 'Clamor inde concursusque' (*factus est*), L.

Forms of dicere are suppressed in the phrases, 'Quid multa?' 'Quid plura?' 'Ne multis,' &c. And forms of fieri in such phrases as 'Quid tum?' 'Quid postea?' &c.

Livy often uses the phrases, ' nihil aliud quam,' 'quid aliud quam,' in which forms of the verb fac ere may be supplied. ' Per biduum nihil aliud quam steterunt parati ad pugnandum,' *for two days they did nothing but stand in readiness for battle*, L. xxvi. 20. The phrase becomes adverbial = *merely, only.* ' N ihil aliud quam perfusis vano timore Romanis,' *the Romans being merely panicstruck*, L. ii. 63. ' Si nihil aliud,' *if nothing else comes of it.* ' Vincam silentium et, si nihil aliud (*faciam*), certe graviter interpellabo,' Curt. iv. 28.

4) Other Verbs are suppressed, which the mind can easily supply. ' Sed haec coram' (*tractabimus*), C. ' Litterarum aliquid interea' (*dabis*), C. ' A Chrysippo pedem nunquam' (*movet*), C. ' Sed ad ista alias' (*respondebo*), C. ' Sed non necesse est nunc omnia' (*commemorare*), C. ' Di meliora' (*dent*). ' A me C. Caesar pecuniam' (*postulat*)? C. ' Ad Tamum cogitabam' (*ire*), C. ' Unde mihi lapidem' (*petam*)? Hor. ' Nihil ad rem;' 'Quid ad me' (*attinet*)? With many more instances.

5) In the phrases, ' Quo mihi?' 'quo tibi?' ' usui' is to be supplied, quo being an old form of cui. ' Quo tibi, Pasiphae, pretiosas sumere vestis?' Ov. (= ' cui usui est tibi?'). But there is a further ellipse of habere or consequi: 'Quo mihi fortunam, si non conceditur uti?' Hor. (= cui usui est mihi habere fortunam?).

6) Proverbs, being generally known and understood, are often cited elliptically: 'Fortuna fortis' (*adiuvat*). 'Minima de malis' (*eligenda sunt*). 'Sus Minervam' (*docere vult*). 'Cuneus cuneum' (*trudit*). 'Manus manum' (*lavat*). 'Bis ad eundem' (*lapidem offendere*). 'Nec sibi nec alteri' (*prodest*). 'Cornici oculum' (*configere*). 'Bene tibi' (*dico*), &c. 'Bene Messallam' (*valere iubeo*), Tib.

PART II.

LATIN SYNTAX.

———

CHAPTER I.

THE DOCTRINE OF SENTENCES.

SPEECH in a connected series forms *DISCOURSE.*

As Words are the Parts of Speech, so the Parts of Discourse are *SENTENCES.*

100 Sentences.

1. Sentences are either AFFIRMATIVE or NEGATIVE.

Psittacus loquitur,	Psittacus non loquitur,
the parrot speaks.	*the parrot does not speak.*

2. Sentences are either SIMPLE or COMPOUND.

1) A SIMPLE SENTENCE is the expression of a single thought, and contains one Finite Verb :

Psittacus loquitur,	Psittacus non loquitur,
the parrot speaks.	*the parrot does not speak.*

2) A COMPOUND SENTENCE consists of two or more Simple Sentences forming one sentence. Of such Simple Sentences, one is the Principal Sentence, the others are Clauses.

    a) Psittacus hominem imitatur, itaque loquitur,
      the parrot imitates man, and so it speaks.
    b) Psittacus, quamvis hominem imitetur, non loquitur,
      the parrot does not speak, although it imitates man.

In (*a*) 'Psittacus hominem imitatur' is the Principal Sentence ; 'Itaque loquitur' a Coordinate Clause ; that is, connected but not constructively dependent. In (*b*) 'Psittacus non loquitur' is the Principal Sentence ; 'Quamvis hominem imitetur' a Subordinate Clause ; that is, constructively dependent.

3. Every SIMPLE SENTENCE is in one of three forms :

    I. *ENUNTIATIO* (statement) :
      Psittacus loquitur, *the parrot speaks.*

    II. *PETITIO* (will-speech) :
      Loquere, psittace, *speak, parrot.*
      Loquatur psittacus, *let the parrot speak.*

    III. *INTERROGATIO* (question) :
      Quid loquitur psittacus ? *what does the parrot speak ?*

4. Each of these forms, in the Principal construction of a Compound Sentence, is said to be R e c t a (direct). Oratio
Recta et
Obliqua.

If it is subordinated so as to become Subject or Object of the Principal Verb, it is called O b l i q u a (oblique or indirect).

I. *ENUNTIATIO OBLIQUA* (Indirect Statement) is mostly constructed as 'Accusative and Infinitive :'

> (Constat)
> (*it is a fact*)
> (Scimus)
> (*we know*) ⎫
> ⎬ psittacum loqui,
> ⎭ *that the parrot speaks.*

II. *PETITIO OBLIQUA* (Indirect Will-speech) is mostly constructed as 'Subjunctive with u t or n e :'

> (Poscitur)
> (*it is required*)
> (Rogamus)
> (*we ask*) ⎫
> ⎬ ut psittacus loquatur,
> ⎭ *that the parrot speak.*

III. *INTERROGATIO OBLIQUA* (Indirect Question) is constructed as 'Subjunctive after an Interrogative Pronoun or Particle :'

> (Incertum est)
> (*it is doubtful*)
> (Narra)
> (*declare*) ⎫
> ⎬ quid psittacus loquatur,
> ⎭ *what the parrot speaks.*

Obs. Clauses of these three kinds are called S u b s t a n t i v a l, because they stand, like Substantives, in the relation of Subject or Object, or in Apposition.

Note. As Discourse chiefly consists of Enunciations, Syntax chiefly considers Simple Sentences of this form. But its fundamental rules are equally applicable to the other two forms.

CHAPTER II.

THE SIMPLE SENTENCE.

i. The Simple Sentence has two essential members : 101
The
Simple
Sen-
tence.

1) The grammatical *SUBJECT*; that *of* which the action or state is predicated or declared ;

2) The grammatical[1] *PREDICATE*; that *by* which the action or state of the Subject is declared.

Subject.	Predicate.
Psittacus	loquitur,
the parrot	*speaks.*

---

[1] 'Grammatical' in contradistinction to 'logical.' A Predicate in formal logic is always a Nominal term Y : every X (some X, no X) *is* Y.

1) The SUBJECT must be—

(1) a Substantive, or that which takes the power of a Substantive ; as

(2) a Pronoun ⎫
(3) an Adjective ⎬ used Substantively.
(4) an Adverb ⎭

(5) a Verb-Noun Infinitive.

(6) a Vocable, or term cited as word or phrase merely.

(7) a Substantival Clause. See Ch. I. Obs.

2) As the Verb is the Part of Speech by which action or state is declared, the PREDICATE must be a Verb ; and, as action and state are predicated in Time, it must be a Finite Verb.

Examples :—

Subject.	Predicate.
(1) Deus	regnat,
God	*rules.*
(2) Nos	paremus,
we	*obey.*
(3) Omnia	florent,
all things	*bloom.*
(4) Satis temporis	datur,
enough time	*is given.*
(5) Navigare	delectat,
sailing	*gives delight.*
(6) 'Instant'	
they come	clamatur,
'Ad arma'	*is shouted.*
to arms	
(7) Quae sit natura lucis	ambigitur,
what is the nature of light	*is disputed.*

Such is the true Norm of Predication : that the Simple Sentence contains or implies a Subject and a Finite Verb.

This general truth is not overthrown by the following frequent exceptions :

I. Predication is made without a Subject expressed :

1) when Pronoun Subjects are implied in the Verb. See § 39.

2) in some of the constructions called Impersonal. See § 50.

II. Predication is made without a Verb expressed when the mind can be trusted to supply one. See § 99.

III. Predication is made by a Verb not Finite :

1) in the construction called the Historic Infinitive. See p. 332.

2) when a Participle stands for a Finite Verb, as often in poetry, and in Livy and Tacitus. See § 99, 1.

Examples of such Exceptions :

I. 1. Nec vēni, V. Venisti tandem, V.

2. Pudet pigetque facti. Quid agitur ? Statur, Ter.

II. Hic tibi certa domus, V. Quidam curiosior, Simonide, tu ex opibus nil sumis tuis ? Phaed.

III. 1. Tum sic affari et curas his demere dictis, V.

2. Fusi hostes, L. Extemplo turbati animi, V.

ii. Incomplete Predication.

Some Verbs do not make a complete predication. Of these the chief is the Verb of Being, sum, esse, which is completely predicative only when it denotes mere existence. Seges est ubi Troia fuit, *corn is where Troy was,* Ov.

Usually it is a COPULA, *coupling* the Subject with another term, called the COMPLEMENT, which qualifies the Subject: the Predicate being then Copula with Complement.

Subject.	Copula.	Predicate. Complement.
Seges	est	matura,
the corn	*is*	*ripe.*
Troia	fuit	urbs munitissima,
Troy	*was*	*a strongly fortified city.*

Verbs which so *couple* a Subject and Complement are called COPULATIVE VERBS.

Many other Verbs are (or may be) incompletely Predicative, if their predication is extended (or EXTENSIBLE) by an Infinitive (vii.). A few of these are also Copulative.

Verbs of incomplete Predication are, therefore—

1) Copulative, but not Extensible: (*a*) sum, forem, fio; and (sometimes) appareo, existo, evado, maneo, nascor; also (poetic) audio, *be called*; (*b*) many passive verbs of *being called* or *named*; appellor, vocor, nominor, nuncupor, usurpor, scribor, inscribor: *being chosen* or *declared*; creor, legor, eligor, sufficior, declaror, prodor, renuntior: *being known, deemed, counted, found*; cognoscor, iudicor, habeor, numeror, deprehendor, invenior, reperior.

2) Copulative and Extensible: videor (*seem*), dicor, memoror, censeor, credor, existimor, putor, perhibeor, arguor.

3) Extensible, but not Copulative: possum, nequeo, debeo; volo, malo, nolo, audeo; soleo, consuesco; coepi, incipio, meditor; desino; pergo; conor, laboro; with many more: a few passive verbs, as feror, narror, nuntior, trador. See vii. and § 180, where It is said that, if the Infinitive extending any Verb is Copulative, a nominal Complement following will agree with the Subject.

a. The Complement of a Copulative Verb may be—

(1) An Adjective agreeing with the Subject as its Attribute.
(2) A Substantive agreeing with the Subject as its Apposite.
(3) A Phrase: sometimes an Adverb.

Examples of Copula with Complement.

	Subject.	Predicate. Copul. Verb.	Complement.
(1)	Homo	est	mortalis
	man	*is*	*mortal*
	Puer	fiet	doctus
	the boy	*will become*	*learned*
	Vos	habemini	prudentes
	ye	*are held*	*prudent*

Examples of Copula with Complement (continued).

Subject.	Copul. Verb.	Complement.[1]
(2) Homines	sunt	animalia
men	*are*	*animals*
Mulier	evadit	victrix
the woman	*comes out*	*conqueress*
Isti	appellantur	philosophi
those men	*are called*	*philosophers*
(3) Bona	sunt	viri
the goods	*are*	*the husband's*
Facundia	censetur	magni
eloquence	*is counted*	*of great value*
Divitiae	numerantur	in bonis
riches	*are reckoned*	*among goods*
Navigare	est	voluptati
sailing	*is*	*a pleasure*
Conatus	fuerunt	frustra
endeavours	*were*	*in vain*

b. Examples of Nominative Complement after Infinitive.

Socrates parens philosophiae dici potest, C. *Fin.* ii. 1. Aelius Stoicus esse voluit, C. *Brut.* 56. Cato esse quam videri bonus malebat, Sall. *Cat.* 54. Xanthippe, Socratis uxor, morosa admodum fuisse fertur et iurgiosa, Gell. i. 17. Oracula evanuerunt postquam homines minus creduli esse coeperunt, C. *Div.* ii. 57. Brevis esse laboro; obscurus fio, H. *A.P.* 25. Animus hominis dives, non arca, appellari solet, C. *Par.* vi. 1. Tyndaridae fratres victoriae nuntii fuisse perhibentur, C. *Tusc.* i. 12. Piso minor haberi est coeptus postea, C. *Brut.* 69. Fisanus, et tamen vis formosa videri, H. *C.* iv. 13. L. Papirius Crassus primus Papisius est vocari desitus, C. *Fam.* ix. 21. Cum floret, existimari potest alba viola, Pl. iv. 11; vi. 22. Atilius prudens esse in iure civili putabatur, C. *Att.* vi. 1.[2]

Add to these the important examples of Participle Perf. (passive or deponent) used as Prolative Infinitive, esse being understood :. § 99a, and p. 428, Note.

---

[1] The term Complement must be understood to mean 'Predicative Complement,' that is, the word or phrase which *completes* predication, when the Verb is Copulative. French writers employ this term to denote the Cases which *complete* the construction of various Verbs: but, as these are sufficiently described by other names (Object; Recipient, &c.), it is better to reserve the word Complement for that which has no other appropriate name: as the term Predicate (in its logical sense) is applicable only in a few instances. Some German writers use the term 'Nominalprädikat.'

[2] In Oblique Oration, when the Verb becomes Infinitive, its Accusative Subject is called an Oblique Subject ; and if that Verb is Copulative, its Accus. Complement is called an Oblique Complement. Thus in 'Puto psittacum loqui ;' 'puto psittacum (esse) loquacem ;' psittacum is Oblique Subject, loquacem Oblique Complement. See § 108, p. 360.

(Note on § 103.) A *Phrase* means a few words (sometimes a single word idiomatically used) expressing a distinct notion, but not containing predication, formal or virtual. Thus in the sentences, Vir est magni ingeni: Caesar cum Balbo venit ; hoc nobis dedecori est ; we call 'magni ingeni,' 'cum Balbo,' and 'dedecori,' Phrases.

An *Enthesis* means a group of words not containing a formal predication, but convertible by a slight change of form into a Clause: 'ab exilio regressus ;' 'philosophus nobilis :' 'me absente.' See II. 2) p. 354.

A *Clause* has been explained to mean a coordinate or subordinate Simple Sentence.

iii. Relations in the Simple Sentence.

The Simple Sentence receives expansion from Words, Phrases, and Entheses used as Adjuncts, and standing in the various Relations which words in a Simple Sentence bear to one another. These Relations are:—

I. Predicative.   V. Circumstantive.

II. Qualitative.   VI. Proprietive.

III. Objective.   VII. Prolative.

IV. Receptive.   VIII. Annexive.[1]

I. The PREDICATIVE RELATION.

This subsists between the Finite Verb and the Subject. The Subject is (or is taken to be) a Nominative Case; and its Verb is so related as to agree with it in Number and Person.

a) A Subject Singular in form but Plural in sense is called a *Collective Subject,* and its Predication may agree with the sense and not with the form: 'Pars militum o c c i s i s u n t,' *part of the soldiers were slain.* See p. 269 *D*).

b) A Subject consisting of several Nouns in Annexive Relation is called a *Composite Subject,* and usually takes a Plural Predicate: 'Rex, regina, et regia classis p r o f e c t i s u n t,' *the king, queen and royal fleet set out.*

c) Impersonal Construction is a peculiar Predication, in which either an expressed Predicate implies an unexpressed Subject: pudet (= pudor pudet); curritur (= cursus curritur); or a Verb-form (Gerundive) becomes a Subject: parendum est. See § 50.

II. The QUALITATIVE RELATION.

(I.) Between an Attribute and the Noun to which it is in Attribution: 'magnae divitiae,' *great riches*; 'docti viri,' *learned men*; 'iste psittacus,' *that parrot.*

(2.) Between a Noun Apposite and the Noun to which it stands in Apposition: 'Cicero consul,' *Cicero the consul*; 'rex Croesus,' *king Croesus.*

The qualifying word will agree with its Noun as far as possible. See § 107. Verb-Nouns and Clauses are considered Neuter. See Examples on p. 360.[2]

---

[1] In the classifications of Language, each class does not exclude all the members of every other class. We find the same words ranked as Substantive and Adjective, as Noun and Verb, as Adverb and Preposition, &c. So the classification here given is not invalidated by the fact that some words, phrases, cases, &c., may be referred to more than one of these Relations: that the Complement, for instance, is both Predicative and Qualitative, the Genitive sometimes Qualitative, sometimes Objective, &c.

[2] Substantives receive as Adjuncts not only Attributes and Apposites, but many other qualifying expressions: Genitives Possessive, Qualitative, and Objective: Ablatives of Quality and Manner: frequently Prepositions with Cases: sometimes Adverbs.

Examples: Sullae exercitus; vir magni ingeni; senex promissa barba; philosophus nomine non re; obtemperatio legibus; domum reditio; mansio Formiis; interitus ferro, fame, frigore, pestilentia; excessus e vita; litterae a Caesare; liber de Officiis; colloquium cum Balbo; omnia ante bella; tua semper lenitas, &c.

This relation appears in four varieties :

1) Attribute or Apposite as Epithet : 'docti viri ;' 'rex Croesus.'

2) Attribute or Apposite as Enthesis : 'Cicero, ab exilio tandem regressus, in senatum venit,' *Cicero, having at length returned from exile, came into the senate* (regressus = ubi regressus erat). 'Socrates, philosophus in primis nobilis, veneno interiit,' *Socrates, an eminently renowned philosopher, died by poison* (philosophus = qui philosophus fuit).

3) Attribute or Apposite, agreeing with the Noun, but in close union with the Verb, in the manner of an adverb : 'Cicero primus in senatum venit,' *Cicero came first into the senate.* 'Caesar aedem Fortunae consul vovit,' *Caesar when consul vowed a temple to Fortune.*

4) Attribute or Apposite as Complement, already described and exemplified, p. 352.

III. The OBJECTIVE RELATION.

When the Predicate is a Transitive Verb, the predication is often without meaning until a word is added expressing that on which the Verb acts. This is called the Object, and its relation to the Verb and Subject is the Objective Relation.

Thus, 'Romulus interfecit,' *Romulus slew,* is deficient in sense until we add 'Remum,' *Remus.*

'Remum' is in the Accusative Case, as Object of the Verb interfecit, and in Objective Relation to that Verb and to its Subject Romulus. See Syntax of Accusative.

a) Anything which may be the Subject of a sentence may also be the Object : and when a Verb-noun, a Vocable, a Clause, or an Adverb, is used as Object, it is taken to be in the Accusative Case.

b) Verbs of *asking, teaching, concealing,* take two Objects, one of the Person, the other of the Thing : 'Doceo te litteras,' *I teach you letters.* See § 130.

c) Factive Verbs take a second Accusative in attribution or apposition as complement to the first : 'Socratem sapientissimum puto,' *I deem Socrates very wise.* 'Caesar Octavium scripsit heredem,' *Caesar left Octavius his heir.* See §§ 102, 131.

Such an Attribute or Apposite is called an Oblique Complement. See *Note,* p. 352.

IV. The RECEPTIVE RELATION.

The Dative is the Case of the Recipient, that is, of the person or thing interested in an action or state ; *for, to, upon,* or *against* which the action or state occurs : 'Non nobis sed reipublicae nati sumus,' *we are born not for ourselves, but for the commonwealth.* 'Do tibi librum,' *I give a book to you.* 'Pax grata civibus,' *a peace welcome to the citizens.* 'Poeni bellum inferunt Romanis,' *the Carthaginians wage war against the Romans.*

The Relation of such a Dative to the Verb or Adjective governing it, and to their Nouns, is the Receptive Relation.[1]

 a) The Dative of some Nouns is used as a Complement (Predicative Dative or Dative of the Purpose) :　See § 142.

  ' Hæc mihi voluptati sunt,' *these things are a pleasure to me.* ' Habet nos derisui,' *he holds us in derision.*

V. The CIRCUMSTANTIVE RELATION.

This limits the Verb and Adjective principally, also the Substantive and Adverb, by Adjuncts, which may be :

 (1) Adverbs;　(2) Noun-cases or Phrases;　(3) Entheses.

The chief Case of Circumstance is the Ablative; but also the Accusative, sometimes the Genitive, may express limiting circumstances.

Limiting Phrases are especially Prepositions with their Cases.

A frequent limiting Construction is the Ablative Absolute ; that is, a Noun with Participle (or with a second Noun) in the Ablative Case.

The Circumstances expressed in this relation are numerous : as,

Cause; Instrument; Agent; Price; Matter :—Respect; Measure; Manner; Condition; Quality; Time; Place Where :—Place Whence ; Separation ; Origin ; Comparison, &c.

Examples :

 1) ' O dea certe,' *O surely a goddess.* ' Vir longe optimus,' *a man by far the best.* ' Vixi hodie,' *I have lived to-day.*

 2) ' Gladiis certant,' *they contend with swords.* ' Vir procero corpore,' *a man of tall frame.* ' Fraude non vi periit,' *he died by fraud, not by force.* ' Centum annos vixit,' *he lived a hundred years.* ' Hic rus in urbe est,* *here is country in the city.* ' Remus a Romulo occisus est,' *Remus was killed by Romulus.* ' Vir natus ad gloriam,' *a man born for glory.*

 3) ' Occiso Gaio, Claudius imperavit,' *Gaius being slain, Claudius became emperor.* ' Sole cadente dormitant aves,' *when the sun sets, birds sleep.* ' Torquato consule natus est Horatius,' *Horace was born in the consulship of Torquatus.*　See §§ 161, 238, 239.

---

[1] Verbs or Adjectives which take a Dative for their appropriate case, as parcere, *to spare* ; placere, *to please* ; iucundus, *pleasant* ; odiosus, *hateful*, &c., are called TRAJECTIVE words.

If the Verb, as dare, *to give*, takes an Accusative also, it is a Trajective Verb Transitive.

Verbs may be classed according to the Cases they take :

Transitive Verbs	. . .	taking Accusative	. .	as Quid-Verbs.
Trajective Verbs	. . .	,,　　Dative	. . .	,, Cui-Verbs.
Trajective Verbs Transitive	,,	Acc. and Dative		,, Cui-Quid-Verbs.
Transitive Verbs taking Double		Accusative	. .	,, Quem-Quid-Verbs.
Factive Verbs	. . . .			,, Quid-Quale-Verbs.

The Accusative is often called the Case of the Nearer Object ; and the Dative the Case of the Remoter Object.

VI. The PROPRIETIVE RELATION.

When the Genitive Case of a Noun depends on another Noun which it has for *a possession, a part,* or, generally, as *a notion which it qualifies or determines.* See §§ 162–176.

Examples:

> 'Templum Minervae,' *the temple of Minerva.* 'Multi militum,' *many of the soldiers.* 'Vir magni ingeni,' *a man of great genius.* 'Cupido pecuniae,' *the desire of money.*

> *a)* The Proprietive Relation is, in some examples, a special instance of the Qualitative: thus, Vir magni ingeni = vir ingeniosissimus; in others it is a special instance of the Objective Relation; thus 'Cupido pecuniae' is nearly the same as 'cupere pecuniam.'

> *b)* Genitives of an Objective nature are joined to many Adjectives: 'Memor leti,' *mindful of death* ; and to some Verbs, 'Generis miseresce tui,' *pity thy offspring.*

VII. The PROLATIVE RELATION.

When Predication is *extended* (profertur) by an Infinitive adjoined to certain *extensible* Verbs and Participles or Adjectives.

Examples:

> 'Noli contendere,' *do not contend.* 'Ego videor videre res futuras,' *I seem to see future things.* 'Iussus confundere foedus,' *ordered to break the treaty.* 'Ludere pertinax,' *persisting to play.*

That such an Infinitive is not an Objective Verb-Noun appears from the fact that Infinitives of Copulative Verbs, so constructed, keep the Complement in the same Case with the Subject:

> 'Puer vult fieri doctus,' *the boy wishes to become learned.* 'Non omnes possumus esse philosophi,' *we cannot all be philosophers.* 'Homerus caecus fuisse creditur,' *Homer is believed to have been blind.*
> See § 180.

> *a)* Other uses of the Infinitive in the Simple Sentence fall under the Predicative or Objective Relation: Supines under the Circumstantive Relation; the Gerund is ranked according to its Case; Participles follow the rules of Adjectives.

> *b)* Cases of Nouns depend on the Infinite as well as on the Finite Verb.

VIII. The ANNEXIVE RELATION.

When a word is *annexed* to the construction of a similar word preceding, either by a Conjunction, or the Conjunction being omitted.

Examples:

> 'Pulvis et umbra sumus,' *we are dust and shade.* 'Non nobis nati sumus, sed patriae,' *we are not born for ourselves, but for our country.* 'Patriae nati sumus, non nobis,' *we are born for our country, not for ourselves.* 'Arma vi-

rumque cano,' *arms and the man I sing.* 'Pater et mater mortui sunt,' *my father and mother are dead.* 'Pater, mater, fratres periere,' *father, mother, brothers have perished.* 'Me amat ut fratrem suum,' *he loves me as his own brother.*

a) One Finite Verb annexed to another makes, strictly speaking, a new sentence: but is often conveniently ranked under this Relation:

'Odi profanum volgus et arceo,' *I hate and keep aloof the profane mob.* 'Abiit, excessit, evasit, erupit,' *he has departed, gone forth, escaped, burst out.*

iv. Interjections and Vocative.

104

1) To the forms constructed in a Simple Sentence under the eight Relations heretofore mentioned, must be added INTERJECTIONS and Interjectional utterances, especially the Case (of the person or thing addressed) called the VOCATIVE, which, with or without an Interjection, is attached to the Sentence, but not constructed with it; thus, with its adjuncts, forming an appendage, which may be called a Vocative Ecthesis. Thus Horace (*Carm.* i. 1. 1) begins with a Vocative Ecthesis of two lines:

Maecenas, atavis edite regibus,
O et praesidium et dulce decus meum,
Sunt quos curriculo pulverem Olympicum
Collegisse iuvat, &c.

2) Ecthesis appears also in the Accusative Case, with or without Interjection; in the Nominative Case, usually with Interjection; in the Dative, never without Interjection.

v. Notice of the Relative Pronoun.

105

The consideration of the RELATIVE belongs properly to the head of Compound Sentences; but it is introduced here so far as to establish its agreement in Gender, Number, and Person with its Antecedent, that is, with the Term in the Prior Sentence to which it stands related. To this extent the Relative Pronoun is Qualitative; but, as respects Case, it may (in its own clause) be Subject Nominative or fall under any of the following Relations: Objective, Receptive, Circumstantive, or Proprietive.

It corresponds to any Person. See §§ 108, 114, 204.

Note. The Relative Pronoun, qui, quae, quod, may be explained as standing between two Noun-terms, with the former of which it agrees in Gender, Number, and Person; with the latter in Case.

1) Sometimes both Noun-terms are expressed: 'Erant itinera duo, quibus itineribus exire possent,' *there were two roads by which they might go forth*, L.

2) Usually the latter is omitted: 'Animum rege, qui, nisi paret, imperat,' *rule the temper, which, unless it obeys, commands* (i. e. qui animus), Hor.

3) Sometimes the former is omitted in poetry: 'Sic tibi dent nymphae quae levet unda sitim,' *so may the nymphs give thee what water may assuage thirst* (i.e. undam quae unda), Ov.

4) Sometimes both: 'Sunt quibus in satira videor nimis acer,' *there are some to whom I seem too keen in satire* (i. e. homines quibus hominibus), Hor.

   b) The following scheme illustrates this principle.

     1) Vir *quem* virum vides rex est (full form).
     2) Vir *quem* .... vides rex est (usual form).
     3) ... *quem* virum vides rex est.
     4) ... *quem* .... vides rex est.

   c) Any Noun-term may be the Antecedent to a Relative.

vi. Rules for the Conversion of an Active into a Passive Sentence.

1) The Nominative of an Agent becomes Ablative (if expressed) with the Preposition a, ab :

    Act. Nos currimus,
    Pass. A nobis curritur, } *we run.*

Or the Person may be suppressed :

    Act. Sic imus ad astra, }
    Pass. Sic itur ad astra, } *thus we go to the stars.*

Obs. The Ablative of the Agent may also be used with the Quasi-Passive Verbs fio, vapulo, veneo :

    Haec a legionibus fiebant,
    these things were being done by the legions.

    Testis a reo vapulavit,
    the witness was beaten by the defendant.

    Nolim ab hoste vēnire,
    I would not be sold by an enemy.

2) The Nominative of an Instrument becomes Ablative without Preposition :

    Act. Flores caput ornant,
    Pass. Floribus caput ornatur, } *flowers adorn the head.*

3) The Object of a Transitive Verb becomes the Subject :

    Act. Deus mundum creavit,
    Pass. A Deo mundus creatus est, } *God made the world.*

4) If there are two Objects (Person and Thing) the Accusative of the Thing remains :

    Act. Rogas me sententiam,
    Pass. Rogor a te sententiam, } *you ask me my opinion.*

5) Factive construction becomes Copulative :

    A. Clodium plebs tribunum creavit, } *the plebeians elected*
    P. Clodius a plebe creatus est tribunus, } *Clodius tribune.*

6) Other Cases remain, and Intransitive Verbs become Impersonal.

Act. Pater librum filio dat,   } *the father gives a book to his*
Pass. A patre liber filio datur, } *son.*

Act. Medicinae indigemus,   }
Pass. Medicinae a nobis indigetur, } *we need medicine.*

Act. Mihi isti nocere non possunt, }
Pass. Mihi ab istis noceri non potest, } *they cannot hurt me.*

Note. On the Construction of Impersonal Verbs see § 50.

CHAPTER III.

CONSTRUCTIONS OF THE SIMPLE SENTENCE.

These fall into three Sections.   107

    I. Agreement.
    II. Case-construction.
    III. Verb-construction, so far as concerns the Simple Sentence.

SECTION I.

AGREEMENT.

AGREEMENT, in Syntax, is the assimilation of the   108
form of one word to that of another.   *Agreement.*

i. The Four Concords.

There are four Rules of Agreement, called CON-CORDS: namely,

Concord I.—A Finite Verb agrees with its Subject-Nominative in Number and Person.

Examples:
'Ego doceo; nos docemus.' 'Tu disces; vos discetis.'
'Magister hortetur; magistri hortentur.' 'Vivere est cogitare.' 'Omnia sunt recte.' 'Quod venisti gratum est.'

Concord II. — An Adjective agrees in Gender, Number, and Case with that to which it is in Attribution.

Concord III.—A Substantive agrees in Case with that to which it is in Apposition.

Obs.—Concords II. and III. are true for every various position of the Attribute or Apposite—whether they are Epithets, as in the examples marked (1) of the two lists which follow: Entheses, as in those marked (2); Adverbial, as in those marked (3); or Complements, as in those marked (4) and (5).

Examples.

II. (1) Vir bonus ille bonam hanc uxorem habet, *that good man has this good wife.*

(2) hirundo pullis suis orbata queritur, *the swallow bereft of its young complains.*

(3) quis vitā male actā felix moritur? *who, after a life ill-spent, dies happy?*

(4) cari sunt parentes; cara est patria, *dear are parents; dear is country.*

(5) pueri discendo fiunt docti, *boys by learning become learned,*

(6) haec est nobilis illa ad Trasimenum pugna, *this is that renowned battle at Lake Trasimenus.*

(7) quid sit futurum cras incertum est, *what will happen to-morrow is uncertain.*

(8) malim pueros esse quam videri bonos, *I would rather boys should be, than seem, good.*

(9) tacere aliquando utile putamus, *to be silent at times we deem expedient.*

(10) scire tuum nihil est, *your knowledge is nothing.*

Obs.—In (7) 'incertum' agrees with the Clause 'quid sit futurum cras.' In (8) 'bonos' (Oblique Complement) agrees with 'pueros,' which is Oblique Subject of each Infinitive. Hence it is seen that Copulative Verbs, Finite or Infinite, have the same case of *agreeing* words after as before them. Example (9) is of the same kind, for esse might be supplied to utile. See III. (6).

III. (1) Nos pueri patrem Lollium imitabimur, *we boys will imitate our father Lollius.*

(2) effodiuntur opes, irritamenta malorum, *riches are dug out, incentives of evil.*

(3) Cicero legem Maniliam praetor suasit, *Cicero recommended the Manilian law when praetor.*

(4) spes est expectatio boni, *hope is the expectation of good.*

(5) syllaba longa brevi subiecta vocatur iambus, *a long syllable following a short one is called iambus.*

(6) Athenas omnium doctrinarum inventrices esse credimus, *we believe Athens to be the inventress of all sciences.*

(7) cogita oratorem institui, rem arduam, *reflect that an orator is being formed, a difficult business.*

(8) Tungri sunt Galliae civitas, *the Tungri are a state of Gaul.*

Obs.—In (7) rem is in Apposition to the Clause 'oratorem institui.'

Concord IV.—The Relative Pronoun Qui, quae, quod, agrees with its Antecedent in Gender, Number, and Person ; but in Case it follows the construction of its own clause.   See § 105.

1. Tu, filia, quae nos amas, oboedies nobis, qui te amamus, *you, daughter, who love us, will obey us, who love you.*
2. Deum veneramur, qui nos creavit, *we worship God who created us.*
3. adsum quem quaeritis, *I am present whom ye seek.*
4. habeo quibuscum colloquar, *I have some to talk with.*
5. in tempore ad eam veni, quod rerum omnium est primum, *I came to her at the right moment, which is the most important thing of all.*
6. nos, id quod debent, virtutes delectant, *virtues delight us, as they ought.*

Obs.—In 3, the Antecedent is ego, in 4, aliquos, understood ; in 5, the Principal sentence is the Antecedent : in 6, id is in apposition to the sentence 'nos virtutes delectant.'   (Id quod = ut.)

ii. Ellipsis of the Subject.

1) Pronoun Subjects (ego, nos, tu, vos, is, ei) are omitted, unless required for emphasis : 'Si vales bene est, ego valeo,' *if you are well, I rejoice ; I am well,* C. *Fam.* xiii. 6. 'Odi profanum volgus et arceo,' *I hate and keep aloof the profane vulgar,* Hor. *C.* iii. 1. 1. 'Poscimur,' *we are required,* Hor. *C.* i. 32. 1.

2) When a Subject of the Third Person is omitted, it is generally known from the context.

On the omission of homines (Fr. *on,* Germ. *man*) before aiunt, ferunt, &c., see p. 275. 'Teque ferunt irae paenituisse tuae,' *and they say you have repented of your anger,* Ov. *A. A.* ii. 592. The adverb volgo sometimes accompanies this ellipsis : 'Volgo ex oppidis gratulabantur Pompeio,' *they came in crowds from the towns to congratulate Pompeius,* C. *T. D.* i. 35.

3) Impersonal Verbs have no Substantive or Pronoun expressed as Subject. But many have a Verb-noun Infinitive : 'Ire iuvat ; fugere dedecet,' &c. Many have a Clausular Subject : 'Oportet haec fieri :' 'interest ut te videam,' &c. The Subject of others is implied in the Verb itself : 'Pudet facti ; taedet vitae ; miseret hominis,' &c.: also in Pluit, tonat, grandinat, &c., and in Passive Impersonals, Itur, statur, vivitur, &c. See § 50.

On Ellipsis, see pp. 267, 274, 346.

iii. Attraction of the Verb.

1) A Copulative Verb sometimes agrees with the Complement. 'Amantium irae amoris integratio est,' *lovers' quarrels are the renewal of love,* Ter. *An.* iii. 3. 28. 'Quas geritis vestis sordida lana fuit,' *the clothes which ye wear were dirty wool,* Ov. *A. A.* iii. 222.

2) This Attraction may affect Gender. 'Non omnis error stultitia est dicenda,' *not every error must be called folly,* C. *Div.* ii. 43. 'Gens universa Veneti appellati,' *the entire race were called Veneti,* L. i. 1.

3) A Verb sometimes agrees with the Apposite rather than with the true Subject. 'Tungri Galliae civitas fontem habet insignem,' *Tongres, a city of Gaul, has a remarkable fountain,* Pl. *N. H.* xxxi. 2.

iv. Synesis in the first and second Concords. See p. 269.

1) Feminine or Neuter words implying males are found with Masculine agreement: 'Illa furia qui . . . &c. impunitatem est assecutus,' *the fury who* (namely Clodius) &c., *obtained impunity,* C. *Fam.* i. 9. 'Milia triginta capitum dicuntur capti,' *thirty thousand prisoners are said to have been taken,* L. xxvii. 16. 'Ubi illic est scelus, qui . . . ,' *where is that villain who . . . ?* Ter. *An.* iii. 5. Analogous to this is Livy's practice of mentioning the name of a town, and then continuing the construction as if he had mentioned the inhabitants: 'Saguntum civitas longe opulentissima ultra Iberum fuit. Oriundi a Zacyntho insula dicuntur mixtique,' &c., *the city of Saguntum was by far the wealthiest beyond the Ebro: they* (cives) *are said to have originated from the isle of Zante, and to have been mingled,* &c., L. xxi. 7.

2) Singular Collective Nouns, pars, multitudo, volgus, turba, vis, iuventus, nobilitas, plebs, &c., are used by Livy, Sallust, and the poets, with Plural Predicates, and agreement of Gender κατὰ σύνεσιν. 'Locros omnis multitudo abeunt,' *the whole number remove to Locri,* L. xxiv. 3. 'Pars perexigua, duce amisso, Romam inermes delati sunt,' *a very small portion, having lost their leader, were brought unarmed to Rome,* L. ii. 14. This construction is rare in Cæsar, not used by Cicero.

3) The Distributive words and phrases quisque, uterque, pars, alius . . . alium, alter . . . alterum, vir . . . virum, &c., are apparently used as Subjects to Plural Predicates, but may be explained as apposite to Plural Subjects understood: 'Uterque eorum exercitum e castris educunt,' *they both lead out an army from the camp,* Caes. *B. G.* iii. 30. 'At nostri, repentino metu perculsi, sibi quisque pro moribus consulunt; alii fugere, alii arma capere: magna pars volnerati aut occisi,' *but our men, seized with a sudden panic, provided for themselves according to their several habits; some fled, others took arms: a great portion were wounded or slain,* Sall. *Iug.* 57. 'Alius alii subsidium ferunt,' *they bring support one to another,* Caes. *B. G.* ii. 26. 'Vir virum legebant,' *each man picked another,* L. x. 38.

4) The Adverb partim is plurally constructed by Cicero, with Gender κατὰ σύνεσιν: 'Eorum partim in pompa partim in acie illustres esse voluerunt,' *some of them chose to be brilliant in procession, some on the battle-field,* C. *d. Or.* ii. 94. 'Partim e nobis

timidi sunt, partim a republica aversi,' *the one part of us are cowards, the other unfriendly to the state*, C. *Phil.* viii. 32.

5. Mille is generally Plural, sometimes Singular.   See § 34.

v. Composite Subject (σύλληψις).

Two or more Subjects united in one Predication are called a Composite Subject.   See p. 268.

A. 1) If the Subjects so united form an evidently Plural notion, the Predicate will be Plural: 'Pompeius, Lentulus, Scipio foede perierunt,' C. *Fam.* ix. 18. 'Castor et Pollux ex equis pugnare visi sunt,' C. *N. D.* ii. 2. 'Ius et iniuria natura diiudicantur,' *right and wrong are naturally distinguished*, C. *Leg.* i. 16. 'Aetas, metus, magister, prohibebant,' *age, timidity, and a tutor forbade*, Ter. *An.* i. 1. 27. Sometimes, when the Prep. cum unites the Subjects: 'Ipse dux cum aliquot principibus capiuntur,' *the commander himself with some leading men were captured*, L. xxi. 60. 'Ilia cum Lauso de Numitore sati,' Ov. *F.* iv. 55. But Cicero prefers the Singular in this last construction, 'Tu cum Sexto scire velim quid cogites,' *I should like to know what you and Sextus think, Att.* vii. 14.

2) If their union forms one complex Singular notion, the Verb may be Singular. 'Tempus necessitasque postulat,' C. *Off.* i. 23. 'Religio et fides anteponatur amicitiae,' C. *Off.* iii. 10. So 'Senatus populusque Romanus' forms one complex notion, and usually, but not always, takes a Singular Predicate.

3) If one of the Subjects is 1st Pers. Sing. (ego), the Predicate may be 1st Pers. Plur.
If one of the Subjects is 2nd Pers. Sing. (tu) and none 1st Pers., the Predicate may be 2nd Pers. Plur.
'Si tu et Tullia, lux nostra, valetis, ego et suavissimus Cicero valemus,' *If you and my darling Tullia are well, I and our sweet boy are in good health*, C. *Fam.* xiv. 5.

4) If the Subjects are sentient beings and of the same Gender, the Attributes follow that Gender ; if of different Genders, the Attributes are Plural Masculine.
'Non mihi venistis Semele Ledeve docendae,' *ye are not come a Semele or a Leda to be taught by me*, Ov. *A. A.* iii. 251. 'Pater mihi et mater mortui sunt,' *my father and mother are dead*, Ter. *Eun.* iii. 3. 11.

5) If they are non-sentient things and of the same Gender, that Gender may be kept by the Attributes, or these may be Neuter : if of different Genders, the Attributes are usually Neuter Plural.
'Grammatice quondam ac musice iunctae fuere,' *grammar and music were formerly combined*, Qu. i. 10. 17. 'Ira et avaritia imperio potentiora erant,' *anger and avarice were more powerful than authority*, L. xxxvi. 32. 'Fregellis murus et porta de caelo tacta erant,' *at Fregellae a wall and gate had been struck by lightning*, L. xxxii. 29. See M. *Lucr.* iii. 136.

6) If sentient beings and non-sentient things are combined, the former will sometimes regulate the Gender: 'Rex regiaque

classis una profecti,' *the king and the royal fleet set out together*, L. xxi. 50. But Neuter Attributes are more usual: ' Romani regem regnumque Macedoniae sua futura sciunt,' *the Romans know that the king and kingdom of Macedonia will be theirs*, L. xl. 10.

B. 1) Often, however, the Verb and Attributes are constructed with only one of the Subjects, and mentally supplied with the rest (zeugma). That one will be nearest to the Predication, and generally the most important. ' Nunc mihi nihil libri, nihil litterae, nihil doctrina prodest,' *now neither books nor literature nor learning avail me aught*, C. *Att.* x. 10. ' Homerus fuit et Hesiodus ante Romam conditam,' *Homer and Hesiod were before the foundation of Rome*, C. *T. D.* i. 1. ' Dicebat idem Cotta, Curio,' *Cotta said the same, and Curio*, C. *Off.* ii. 17. ' Cum quaesturam nos, consulatum Cotta, aedilitatem peteret Hortensius,' *when I stood for the quaestorship, Cotta for the consulship, Hortensius for the edileship*, C. *Brut.* 92. So, ' Et tu et omnes homines sciunt,' *you and all mankind know*, C. *Fam.* xiii. 8.

2) The agreement of Gender with a nearer word appears in this Example: ' Visae nocturno tempore faces ardorque caeli,' *meteors were seen in the night and a fiery sky*, C. *in Cat.* iii. 8.

3) Singular agreement with the more distant Noun is rare: 'Lucus quidem ille et haec Arpinatium quercus agnoscitur, saepe a me lectus in Mario,' *I recognise yonder grove, and this oak of the Arpinates, which I have often read of in the Marius*, C. *Leg.* i. 1.

4) ' Unus et alter' takes a Singular Verb: ' Unus et alter assuitur pannus' *one or two patches are stitched on*, Hor. *ad Pis.* 15.

5) When the Subjects are connected by aut, the Predicates sometimes appear as Singular, sometimes as Plural: ' Si Aeacus aut Minos diceret,' C. *Off.* i. 28. ' Si quid Socrates aut Aristippus ... fecerint locutive sint,' C. *Off.* i. 41. But with aut ... aut, the Singular alone is used. Et ... et, neque ... neque, usually lead to a Singular Predicate, but sometimes to a Plural.

In short, the construction of a Composite Subject exhibits every variety of usage.

6) Such instances as the following belong to Attraction: ' Ei cariora semper omnia quam decus et pudicitia fuit,' *everything was at all times dearer to him than decency and modesty*, Sall. *Cat.* 25.

vi. Idioms of Attribution and Apposition.

1) As Complement, the Adjective may be attributed to any Noun-term; as Epithet, chiefly to a Substantive: but sometimes to an Infinitive: ' Velle suum cuique est,' *every one has his own inclination.* ' Totum hoc displicet philosophari,' *all this philosophising they dislike*, Cic. *Fin.* i. 1. ' Me hoc ipsum nihil agere delectat,' *this ' far niente' itself is to me delightful*, C. *d. Or.* ii. 6.

2) Sometimes, in Copulative construction, an Adjectival Pronoun seems to take the place of Subject, and the Substantive, to which it refers, that of Complement. So placed, the Adjectival word usually agrees with the Substantive: 'H ae sunt fere de animis sententiae,' *these are pretty nearly the (current) opinions on the soul*, Cic. 'H ic murus aheneus esto, nil conscire sibi,' *let this be a wall of brass, to be conscious of nothing (wrong)*, Hor. *Epist.* i. 1. 61. But sometimes the Pronoun is substantively Neuter: 'Quod ego fui ad Trasimenum, ad Cannas, id tu hodie es,' *what I was at Trasimenus, at Cannae, you are now*, L. xxx. 30. 'Nunc scio quid sit amor,' *now know I what love is*, Verg. *B.* viii. 43.

3) The Adverbial and Proleptic uses of the Attribute and Apposite are important idioms, noticed p. 278.

 a) Attribute : 'Tum tu insiste audax muris,' *then do thou advance on the walls boldly*, L. iii. 26. 'Castris se pavidus tenebat,' *he kept himself within the camp timidly*, L. 'Vespertinus pete tectum,' *seek the roof at eventide*, Hor. *Epist.* i. 6. 20. 'Aeneas se matutinus agebat,' *Aeneas set himself in motion at morn*, Verg. *Aen.* viii. 465. 'Domesticus otior,' *I lounge at home*, Hor. *S.* i. 6. 127. 'Hostes rari se ostendere coeperunt,' *the enemy began to show themselves in small parties*, Caes. *B. G.* v. 17. 'Memini, tametsi nullus moneas,' *I remember, without any suggestion from you*, Ter. *Eun.* ii. 1. 10. 'Hannibal princeps in proelium ibat, ultimus conserto proelio excedebat,' *Hannibal used to be the first to go to battle, and after the engagement the last to quit the field*, L. xxi. 4. 'Omnem crede diem tibi diluxisse supremum,' *believe that every day that has dawned on you is your last*, Hor. *Epist.* i. 4. Thus, where the English generally uses a Relative Pronoun: *He was the first (last or only one) who came*, the Latin more concisely says Primus (ultimus, solus) venit.

 b) Adverbial Apposition limits the agency of the Subject in respect of *time, age, office, capacity*, &c.: 'Furius, noster familiaris, puer didicit quod discendum fuit,' *my intimate friend Furius learnt in boyhood what he had to learn*, C. d. *Or.* iii. 23. 'Cato senex scribere historiam instituit,' *Cato began to write history in old age*, Suet. *Ner.* 31. 'C. Iunius aedem Salutis, quam consul voverat, censor locaverat, dictator dedicavit,' *Gaius Junius dedicated in his dictatorship the temple of Salus, which he had vowed in his consulship, and given a contract for in his censorship*, L. x. 1. Under this head may be placed such phrases as, Ante me consulem (*before my consulship*), post me quaestorem (*after my quaestorship*). See p. 273.

4) If Neuter Adjectives are so constructed as to qualify Masculine or Feminine Nouns, they must be regarded as words which have acquired the nature of Substantives, and as standing in apposition : 'Turpe senex miles, turpe senilis amor,' *unseemly is an aged soldier, unseemly an old man's love*, Ov. *Am.* i. 9. 'Mors

omnium rerum extremum est, *death is the final close of all things,*
C. *Fam.* vi. 21. 'Turpitudo peius est quam dolor,' *dishonour is
worse than pain,* C. *T. D.* ii. 13. 'Patres et plebem, invalida et
inermia, ludificatur,' *he deludes the Senate and Commons, weak
and defenceless bodies,* Tac. *Ann.* i. 46.

5) The Apposite usually agrees in Number with its Noun, but
not necessarily: 'Tulliola, deliciolae nostrae, '*Tullia, my little
darling,* C. *Att.* i. 8. Substantiva Mobilia, having two forms, Masculine and Feminine, will agree, as far as possible, in Gender with
their Noun: Usus magister egregius,' *experience, an excellent
teacher,* Plin. *Epist.* i. 20. 'Vita rustica parcimoniae magistra
est,' *a country life is the teacher of thrift,* C. *p. S. Rosc.* 27. Such
words are also used as epithets, chiefly by poets: 'Regina pecunia,' *queen Money,* Hor. *Epist.* i. 6. 36. An Apposite may seem
to take a different case from its noun: 'Archias natus est Antiochiae, celebri quondam urbe,' *Archias was born at Antioch, a
once populous city,* C. *p. Arch.* 3.

6) Peculiar forms of Apposition :

a) Apposition to a Pronoun Subject understood :

'Hannibal peto pacem,' *I, Hannibal, sue for peace,* L. xxx.
30. 'Qualis artifex pereo!' *what an artist dies in me*
(lit. *I die*)! Suet. *Ner.* 49.

b) Apposition of the Part to the Whole :

'Galli Ruscinonem, aliquot populi, conveniunt,' *the Gauls,
a few tribes, meet at Ruscino,* L. xxi. 24. 'Duae filiae
harum, altera occisa, altera capta est,' *the two daughters
of these women, one was slain, the other captured,* Caes. *B.
G.* i. 53. 'Cetera multitudo sorte decimus quisque ad
supplicium lecti sunt,' *the remaining crowd were picked,
every tenth man, for execution,* L. ii. 59. 'Vos sibi quisque
consilium capitis,' *ye consult each for himself,* Sall. *C.* 52.

c) Apposition of the Proper Names of one Person :
P. Cornelius Scipio Africanus Aemilianus. See p. 193.

d) Apposition annexed by Conjunctions, such as ut, velut,
quasi, ceu, tamquam, quamvis :
'Aegyptii canem et felem ut deos colunt,' *the Egyptians
worship the dog and cat as deities,* C. *Leg.* i. 11. 'Herodotus
quasi sedatus amnis fluit,' *Herodotus flows as a calm
river,* C. *Or.* 12. 'Ficta omnia celeriter, tamquam flos-
culi, decidunt,' *all unreal things quickly droop like flowers,*
C. *Off.* ii. 12. 'Manlius filium suum, quamvis victorem,
occidit,' *Manlius slew his son, though conqueror,* Flor. i.

e) Apposition which requires a Noun answering a question to
be in the same case as the Noun which it answers :
'Quone malo mentem concussa? Timore deorum,' *by what
malady disturbed in mind?—By fear of the gods,* Hor. *S.*
ii. 3. 293. But here, too, the cases may seem to differ :
'Quanti emptum?—Parvo. Quanti ergo?—Octussibus,'
Hor. *S.* ii. 3. 155.

7) A single Adjective is seldom referred to more than one Noun except as Complement. When it is otherwise referred to more than one, and the Genders differ, it usually agrees with the nearest: 'Romanis cuncta maria terraeque patebant,' *all seas and lands were open to the Romans,* Sall. *C.* 10.

Sometimes it is Neuter Plural, like a Complement: 'Gallorum genti natura corpora animosque magna magis quam firma dedit,' *nature has given to the Gauls great rather than strong bodies and minds,* L. v. 44.

8) A Noun subdivided by more than one Singular Attribute is sometimes found Singular, sometimes Plural: 'Legio Martia quartaque rempublicam defendunt,' *the Martian legion and the fourth defend the commonwealth,* C. *Phil.* v. 17. 'In rabiem tractae prima ac vicesima legiones,' *the first and twentieth legions were drawn into the mad revolt,* Tac. *Ann.* i. 31.

A Noun in apposition to several others will be Plural in the same Case with them: 'Eupolis atque Cratinus Aristophanesque poetae,' *the poets Eupolis and Cratinus and Aristophanes,* Hor. *S.* i. 4. 1.

Sometimes the Nomen or Cognomen is in apposition to the Praenomina of two or more persons: 'M. et Q. Cicerones,' *the Ciceros, Marcus and Quintus*: 'C. et L. Memmii,' *the Memmii, Gaius and Lucius.*

vii. Synesis, Ellipsis and Attraction in Relative Construction.

1. *a)* The agreement of the Relative may follow meaning: 'Multitudo, qui convenerant...'

b) The agreement of a Relative with a Composite Subject is in principle the same as that of an Adjective. 'Pater et mater qui mortui sunt'... 'Fortuna, decus, honos, quae fortuita sunt. ...'

c) A Personal Pronoun as Antecedent may be implied in a Possessive: 'Omnes laudare fortunas meas, qui gnatum haberem tali ingenio praeditum,' *all were extolling my good fortune in having a son of such a character,* Ter. *An.* i. 1. 97.

2. *a)* Ellipsis of the Antecedent is frequent. See Concord iv. Ex. 3. 4. But that of the word or words which govern the Relative (when they are to be supplied from the antecedence) is less so: 'Nos imitamur quos cuique visum est (i.e. eos quos cuique visum est imitari),' *we imitate those, whom we severally think proper to imitate,* C. *Off.* i. 30. This idiom sometimes resembles Attraction: 'Si aliquid agis eorum quorum consuesti, gaudeo (i.e. eorum quorum aliquid agere consuesti),' *if you are pursuing any of your wonted occupations, I am glad,* C. *Fam.* v. 14.

b) When the Relative has been used in one Case, another Case of it is sometimes suppressed:

'Bocchus cum peditibus, quos filius eius adduxerat, neque in priore pugna adfuerant, postremam Romanorum aciem invadunt,' *Bocchus and the infantry, which his son had brought up, and which had not been present in the former battle, attack the rear of the Romans*, Sall. *I.* 101.

3. *a*) The Relative may agree with an Apposite, or not:

'Flumen Scaldis quod...' 'Flumen Rhodanus qui...'

b) The Relative may agree with the Complement of its own Clause, rather than with its Antecedent:

'Thebae, quod Boeotiae caput est,' L.

Madvig's rule is (*Gr.* § 319) that, if the Antec. is defined without the aid of the clause, the Rel. agrees with its Compl.; if not, with the Antec. But many exceptions occur.

c) The Antecedent is drawn into the same Clause and Case as the Relative: 'Quam artem novi, exerceo.' Or the Antecedent may remain in its own sentence, and be repeated in the Relative Clause: 'Dies instat, quo die . . .'

Sometimes the attracted Antecedent precedes the Relative: 'Urbem quam statuo vestra est,' V. *Aen.* i. 573.

Horace has a daring Attraction: 'Quis non malarum quas amor curas habet Haec inter obliviscitur?' *Epod.* ii.

d) An Attribute, especially unus, pauci and Superlatives, may be attracted to the Relative Case and Clause (§ 82. 3.):

'Tempestivis conviviis delector cum aequalibus, qui pauci admodum restant,' *I enjoy early dinners with contemporaries, very few of whom remain*, C. *Cat.* M. 14. 'Consiliis pare, quae nunc pulcherrima Nautes dat senior,' V. *Aen.* v.

e) Attraction of the Relative to the Case of the Antecedent is rare: 'Iudice quo nosti populo,' *in the judgment of that public with which you are acquainted*, Hor. *S.* i. 6. 15. This is sometimes complicated with Ellipsis of the Antecedent or of the governing word, or of both: 'Haec cadere possunt in quos nolis (i.e. in eos in quos nolis ea cadere),' C. *d. Or.* ii. 60.

viii. Qualis, quantus, quot.

Qualis (*such as*), quantus (*as great as*), follow the same rule as qui only when they are placed between two Cases (expressed or understood) of the *same* person or thing: 'Non sum qualis eram,' *I am not what I was*, Hor. *C.* iv. 1. 'Crocodilus parit ova quanta anseres,' *the crocodile lays eggs as big as geese lay*, Pl. *N. H.* xviii. 25. But if they are used to compare two *different* Nouns, they agree in Gender, Number, and Case with the latter; while their Demonstratives (talis, tantus) agree with the former: 'Talis est, qualem te esse video, *he is such as I see you are*, C. *p. Mur.* 14. 'Dixi tanta contentione quantum forum est,' *I spoke with exertion of voice as great as the forum is*, C. *Fam.* xii. 7. So tot . . . quot, which are undeclined.

Abnormal constructions are: 'Animae qualis neque candidiores terra tulit, neque quis me sit devinctior alter,' Hor. *S.* i. 5. 41. 'Nardo perunctum quale non perfectius meae laborarint manus,' Hor. *Epod.* v. 57.[1]

• Examples of the Rules of Agreement, for practice.

A. (Subject: Predicate: Complement: Attribution.) 'Mens peccat, non corpus,' L. i. 58. 'Nos consules desumus,' C. *Cat.* i. i. 'Nitimur in vetitum semper cupimusque negata,' Ov. *Am.* iii. 2. 'Natura tu illi pater es, consiliis ego,' Ter. *Ad.* i. 2. 'Haruspicum munus erat exta inspicere,' Val. M. i. i. 'Quid sit optimum neminem fugit,' Qu. xi. 2. 'Vivitur parvo bene,' Hor. *C.* ii. 16. 13. 'Iusta omnia decora sunt: iniusta contra, ut turpia, sic indecora,' C. *Off.* i. 94. 'Catilinae inerat satis eloquentiae, sapientiae parum,' Sall. *C.* 5. 'Vivere ipsum turpe est nobis,' C. *Att.* xiii. 28. 'Dulce satis umor,' Verg. *B.* iii. 13. 'Omnis ars imitatio est naturae,' Sen. *Ep.* 65. 'Terra altrix nostra diei noctisque effectrix eademque custos est,' C. *Univ.* 10. 'Servus, cum manu mittitur, fit libertinus,' Qu. vii. 3. 'De Amicitia eo libro dictum est, qui inscribitur Laelius,' C. *Off.* ii. 9. 'Athenis tenue caelum, ex quo acutiores etiam putantur Attici,' C. *Fat.* 4. 'Posteriores cogitationes, ut aiunt, sapientiores esse solent,' C. *Phil.* xii. 2. 'Omnia orta occidunt et aucta senescunt,' Sall. *Iug.* 1. 'Romam serae avaritia atque luxuria immigraverunt,' L. Praef. 'Scythae perpetuo intacti aut invicti mansere,' *Iust.* ii. 3. 'Marius, septimum consul, domi suae senex est mortuus,' C. *N. D.* iii. 32. Apud matrem recte est,' C. *Att.* i. 7. 'Sum Dyrrachii hoc tempore, et sum tuto,' C. *Fam.* xiv. 3. 'Nihil est tam angusti animi tamque parvi quam amare divitias,' C. *Off.* i. 20. 'Libertas et anima nostra in dubio est,' Sall. *C.* 52. 'Ne Pericles quidem dixit Attice, cui primae sine controversia deferebantur,' C. *Or.* 9.

B. (Synesis.) 'Pars in crucem acti, pars bestiis obiecti sunt,' Sall. *Iug.* 14. 'Volgus Macedonum Demetrium cum ingenti favore conspiciebant,' L. xxxix. 55. 'Samnitium caesi tria millia ducenti, capti quattuor milia ducenti,' L. x. 34. 'Optimus quisque iussis paruere,' Tac. *H.* iv. 25. 'Dux uterque pari culpa meritus adversa prosperis defuere,' Tac. *H.* iv. 34. 'Hic uterque me intuebatur, seseque ad audiendum significabant paratos,' C. *Fin.* ii. 1. (Cicero never has a Plural Verb with uterque: see Madvig ad l. c.)

C. (Composite Subject.) 'Dant veniam genitor coniunxque,' Ov. *F.* ii. 889. 'Spectantur in chartis tenuitas, candor, laevor,' Pl. *N. H* xiv. 12. 'Per interregem consules creati sunt Valerius et Horatius,' L. iii. 35. 'Ego ac tu simplicissime inter nos hodie loquimur,' Tac. *H.* i. 15. 'Haec neque ego neque tu fecimus,' Ter. *Ad.* i. 2. 23. 'Ex eo die ego et leo in eodem specu viximus,' Gell. v. 14. 'Quid est quod tu aut illa cum fortuna hoc nomine queri possitis,' C. *Fam.* iv. 5. 'Nec senatus gloriari nec princeps poterant,' Plin. *Ep.* 75. 'Effigiem nullam Vesta nec ignis habent,' Ov. *F.* vi. 298. 'Demosthenes cum ceteris populiscito in exsilium erant expulsi,' Nep. *Phoc.* 2. 'Dea Iuventus Terminusque deus id non sunt passi,' L. v. 54. 'Serpens, sitis, ardor, harenae, dulcia virtuti,' Lucan. ix. 402. 'Societas hominum et aequalitas et iustitia per se expetenda sunt,' C. *Leg.* i. 18. 'Omnibus in rebus temeritas ignoratioque vitiosa est,' C. *Fin.* iii. 21. 'Mens et animus et consilium et sententia civitatis posita est in legibus,' C. *p. Clu.* 53. 'Bene de republica mereri, laudari, coli, diligi, gloriosum est,' C. *Phil.* i. 14. 'Mihi magnae curae est ut tu ipse tuique omnes scire possint me tibi esse amicissimum,' L. xxix. 17. 'Tarquinius cum prole fugit,' Ov. *F.* ii. 851. 'Iane, face aeternos pacem pacisque ministros,' Ov. *F.* i. 287. 'O noctes cenaeque deum, quibus ipse meique ante lares proprios vescor,' Hor. *S.* ii. 6. 65.

D. (Apposition.) 'Alexander, victor tot regum atque populorum, irae succubuit,' Sen. *Ep.* 113. 'Quid dicam de thesauro omnium rerum memoria?'. C. *d. Or.* i. 5. 'Aquitania a Garumna flumine ad Pyrenaeos montis pertinet,' Caes. *B. G.* i. 1. 'Oppidum Genabum pons fluminis Ligeris continet,' Caes. *B. G.* vii. 11. 'Hostis hostem occidere volui,' L. ii. 12. 'Duo exercitus Aventinum insedistis,' L. ix. 34. 'Duo consules eius anni alter ferro alter morbo perierant,' L. xli. 18. 'Civilis omnium coniuges parvosque liberos consistere a tergo iubet, hortamenta victoriae vel pulsis pudorem,' Tac. *H.* iv. 61. 'Batavi machinas etiam, insolitum sibi, ausi,' Tac. *H.* iv. 23. 'Numquam ingenium ad res diversissimas,

SECTION II.

CASE-CONSTRUCTION.

A. *The Nominative Case.*

i. The NOMINATIVE is the Case of the Subject of a Finite Verb and of those words which agree in Case with the Subject. See Concords I. II. III.

ii. Thus the Nominative stands as Complement

1) Of Finite Copulative Verbs.
2) Of Copulative Verbs Infinite, prolatively used.

1) 'Galba medius inter Neronem et Othonem imperator exstitit,' *Galba was the emperor intervening between Nero and Otho,* Suet. *G.* 6. 'Subtilis veterum iudex et callidus audis,' *you are called a nice and shrewd critic of ancient authors,* Hor. *S.* ii. 7.

---

parendum atque imperandum, habilius fuit,' L. xxi. 4. 'Corioli oppidum captum est a Marcio,' L. ii. 23. 'Ludi Taurilia per biduum facti,' L. xxix. 22. 'Oculi tamquam speculatores altissimum locum obtinent,' C. *N. D.* ii. 140. 'Dies quo ceperat imperium Gaius Palilia vocatus est, velut argumentum rursus conditae urbis,' Suet, *Cal.* 16. 'Caelius historiam, ut homo neque doctus neque maxime aptus ad dicendum, ut potuit dolavit,' C. *d. Or.* ii. 54. 'Cottam cum Titurio legatos amisimus,' Flor. iii. 10. 'Duae urbes potentissimae Carthago atque Numantia ab eodem Scipione sunt deletae,' C. *p. L. Man.* 60. 'Soceri tibi Marsque Venusque contigerunt,' Ov. *M.* iii. 130. 'Duo fulmina Romani imperi subito in Hispania Cn. et P. Scipiones exstincti sunt,' C. *p. Balb.* 15. 'Acerrime deliciae meae Dicaearchus contra immortalitatem disseruit,' C. *T. D.* i. 77. 'Pompeius nostri amores ipse se afflixit,' C. *Att.* ii. 19. 'Cetera turba, nos, inquam, cenamus avis,' Hor. *S.* ii. 8. 26. 'Hoc dedimus nos tibi nomen eques (for equites),' Ov. *F.* ii. 128. 'Nec multo post diem obiit utroque liberorum superstite, Tiberio Drusoque Neronibus,' Suet. *Tib.* 4. 'Corinthi Achaiae urbe Vespasianus certos nuntios accepit de interitu Galbae,' Tac. *H.* ii. 1. 5. 'Quid meritu's? Crucem,' Ter. *An.* iii. 5. 15. 'Cuius es? Amphitruonis,' Plaut. *Amph.* v. 3. 222. 'Quanti emit? Vili,' Plaut. *Ep.* i. 1. 49.

E. (*Relative and Antecedent.*) a. 'Pax ita convenerat ut Etruscis Latinisque fluvius Albula, quam nunc Tiberim vocant, finis esset,' L. i. 8. 'Est locus in carcere, quod Tullianum appellatur, circiter duodecim pedes humi depressus,' Sall. *Cat.* 55. 'Veiens bellum exortum, quibus Sabini arma coniunxerant,' L. ii. 53. 'Habebam inimicum non C. Marium, sed duo importuna prodigia, quos egestas, quos aeris alieni magnitudo, quos levitas, quos improbitas tribuno plebis constrictos addixerat,' C. *p. Ses.* 16. 'Ad quadraginta milia militum, quod roboris in Samnio erat, convenerant,' L. x. 38. 'Illud, mi Tiro, te rogo, ne sumptui parcas ulla in re quod ad valetudinem opus sit,' C. *Fam.* xvi. 4. 'Iuniores, id maxime quod Kaesonis sodalium fuit, auxere iras in plebem,' L. iii. 14. 'Favent pietati fideique di, per quae populus Romanus ad tantum fastigi venit,' L. xliv. 2. 'Minime miror qui insanire occipiunt ex iniuria,' Ter. *Ad.* ii. 1. 43. 'En dextra fidesque quem secum patrios aiunt portare penatis,' Verg. *Aen.* iv. 598. 'Dividebat agros quibus volebat,' C. *Off.* i. 11. 'Lacedaemonii Agin regem, quod numquam antea apud eos acciderat, necaverunt,' C. *Off.* ii. 23. 'Raptim quibus quisque poterat elatis iam continens agmen migrantium impleverat vias,' L. i. 29. 'Pomptinus a te tractatus est praestanti ac singulari fide, cuius tui beneficii sum ego testis,' C. *Fam.* iii. 10. 'Accusator non ferendus est is, qui quod in altero vitium reprehendit in eo ipso deprehenditur,' C. *Verr.* iii. 2. 'Nullo modo animus audientis

101. 'Princeps in senatu tertium lectus est P. Scipio Afri-canus,' *Publius Scipio Africanus was for the third time chosen prince of the Senate*, L. xxxviii. 28. 'Amicitia virtutum adiu-trix a natura data est, non vitiorum comes,' C. *Lael.* 22.

2) 'Aristaeus inventor olei esse dicitur,' *Aristaeus is said to be the discoverer of oil*, C. *Verr.* iv. 57. 'Cato esse quam videri bonus malebat,' *Cato preferred being to seeming good*, Sall. C. 54. 'Socrates parens philosophiae iure dici potest,' *Socrates may justly be called the father of philosophy*, C. *Fin.* ii. 1. 'Ad auream arietis pellem profecti dicuntur Argonautae,' *the Argonauts are said to have gone after the golden fleece*, Varr. *R. R.* ii. 1 (esse being omitted).

iii. The Nominative may stand with the Inter-jections en, ecce, o, and others. 117

'En dextra fidesque!' *lo the right hand and the pledged faith!* Verg. *Aen.* iv. 597. 'Sed ecce nuntii, ecce litterae, Caesarem ad Corfinium,' *but lo couriers and letters stating that Caesar is at Corfinium*, C. *Att.* viii. 3. 'O vir fortis atque amicus!' *O the brave and friendly man!* Ter. *Ph.* ii. 2. 10.

B. *The Vocative Case.*

118
Vocative
Case.

i. The VOCATIVE is used without or with an Interjection: fili, Pompei, Iuppiter: O fili, O Pompei; pro Iuppiter.

ii. The Nominative takes the place of the Vocative: 119

1) When the Noun is Collective: 'I, pete virginea, populus, suffimen ab ara,' *go, people, seek incense from the virgin's altar*, Ov. *F.* iv. 731. 'O Pompilius sanguis,' Hor. *ad Pis.* 292.

2) When the word is an Attribute or Apposite enthetically or adverbially used: 'Tu quoque Cydon Dardania stratus dextra,' Verg. *Aen.* x. 320. 'Nudus iaciture sepulcro,' St. *Th.* vii. 777.

3) Yet poets sometimes keep the Vocative in such circum-stances: 'Sic venias hodierne,' *so mayst thou come to-day*, Tib. i. 7. 53. 'Rufe mihi frustra ac nequiquam credite amice,' *O*

---

aut incitari aut teneri potest, qui modus a me non tentatus sit,' C. *Or.* 38. 'Haec est quam Scipio laudat in libris et quam maxime probat temperationem reipublicae,' C. *Leg.* iii. 5. 'Poeta id sibi negoti credidit solum dari populo ut placerent quas fecisset fabulas,' Ter. *An. Pr.* 3. 'Tullia, qui illius in te amor fuit, hoc certe te facere non vult,' C. *Fam.* iv. 5. 'Cuius lenitatis est Galba, iam fortasse promisit,' Tac. *H.* i. 37. 'Qua es prudentia, nihil te fugiet,' C. *Fam.* xi. 13. (See p. 312.) 'Sarmatis neque conti neque gladii, quos praelongos utraque manu regunt, usui erant,' Tac. *H.* i. 79. 'Consul, qui unus supererat, moritur,' L. iii. 7.

b. 'Talis est quaecumque respublica qualis eius aut natura aut voluntas qui illam regit,' C. *Rep.* i. 31. 'Hoc bellum est, quale bellum nulla barbaria gessit,' C. *in Cat.* ii. 1. 'Videre mihi videor tantam dimicationem quanta numquam fuit,' C. *Att.* vii. 1.

Rufus vainly and to no purpose believed my friend, Catull. 75.
'Quibus Hector ab oris exspectate venis?' *from what shores,
Hector, comest thou expected?* Verg. Aen. ii. 282.　See Pers. iii. 28.
Ausonius has 'Iane, veni, novus anne, veni,' *Id.* viii. 1.

C. The Accusative Case.

i. The ACCUSATIVE is the Case of the Attained Nearer Object: also of the Contained Object.

Any Agent may become an Object: a striker may be struck, &c.
But not every Object can be an Agent in a proper sense.　Therefore it is that in Neuter Nouns (as bellum, regnum ; mel, far, &c.),
the Accusative is the primary, the Nominative only a secondary,
form.　Therefore also, when a Proposition (as, 'the parrot speaks')
quits the form of statement, and passes into an abstract notion
('the parrot's speaking'), while the Finite Verb becomes Infinitive
(loqui), the Nominative becomes Accusative (psittacum); that is,
the Subject of an Infinitive is an Accusative in Latin.　Such a
notion, 'psittacum loqui,' is essentially Objective, but, like the
Nominative of a Neuter word, it can, by a secondary use, become
the Subject of a Proposition ; 'psittacum loqui credibile est,' *the
parrot's speaking* (that the parrot speaks) *is credible.*

ii. Transitive Verbs of any class take an Accusative of the Attained Nearer Object.

　1. mater alit pullos,
　　　the mother nourishes the young ones.

　2. in primis venerare Deum,
　　　in the first place worship God.

　3. pudet me stultitiae,
　　　I am ashamed (lit. 'it shames me') *of my folly.*

The First Example, in Passive form, becomes
　　　　　　pulli a matre aluntur.

The Second (where the Verb is Deponent) and the Third (where
it is Impersonal) cannot assume the Passive form.

This is the standard Rule, because Transitive Verbs are so large
a class.　But to draw the line which divides Intransitive from
Transitive Verbs is not easy.　Intransitive Verbs are often used
with Transitive force: ardere, flere, pallere, sitire, &c.　Transitive Verbs may drop their Object and seem to be Intransitive:
amare, durare, obtinere, &c.

The following considerations may throw light on this subject.

---

[1] By the Attained Object is meant that which follows Transitive Verbs : by the Contained Object that which follows Intransitive Verbs.

iii. The Contained Object or Cognate Accusative.

₁) Every Verb has at least one Object, its own Activity, represented by its most abstract Verbal Noun in (ion-) **-io**: agere
actionem, stare stationem, ire itionem, narrare narrationem, &c.

This purest abstract form is not, however, used by Latin authors
in connection with Verbs.   But other Substantives, more concrete,
are so used with the Verbs to which they belong: the construction
being that called 'the Cognate Accusative,' or 'Accusative of the
Verbal Operation,' or 'Contained Accusative.'   Such instances
are :

Canere cantilenam, Ter. ; cenare cenam, Plaut.; furere furorem,
Verg.; gaudere gaudium, C.; iurare iusiurandum, C. ; insanire
insaniam, Sen.; ludere ludum, Hor.; nocere noxam, L.; ridere
risum, C.; servire servitutem, C.; somniare somnium, Plaut.;
vivere vitam, Plaut. ; moveri motus, Lucr.

When such expressions occur, the Substantive usually has an
epithet: Ludum insolentem ludere, Hor.

2) Instead of the purely Cognate Accusative, Intransitive Verbs
oftener take a Contained Accusative expressing some more limited
operation of the Verb:

Agere (*to pass*) aetatem ; agere (*to act*) partis ; cantare melos;
coronari Olympia (*to be crowned as an Olympian victor* = vincere
Olympia); currere stadium ; degere vitam, &c.; dormire noctem ;
errare litora ; ire viam, &c. ; iurare numen, &c. ; praelucere spem ;
ludere aleam ; ludere carmina ; militare bellum ; mentiri auspicia ;
natare aquas, &c. ; navigare aequor, &c.; prandere holus ; pugnare
proelia ; quadrare acervum ; respondere ius ; resonare Amaryllida
(alcyonen) ; saltare (moveri) Satyrum (Cyclopa) ; sonare vitium
(hominem), &c. ; triumphare hostem ; vagari terras ; vehi maria ;
vivere aetatem (Bacchanalia, Nestora), &c.; vigilare noctem ;
vincere causam (iudicium), &c.

Especially Verbs which express

a) Odour or flavour: olere crocos (pastillos, lampadem, anti-
quitatem, &c.), redolere flores ; spirare odorem ; exhalare
mephitim ; sapere mella (aprum, mare, plebeium, &c.).

b) Visible emanation: manare mella; depluere lacrimas;
spirare flammas ; stillare rorem ; sudare electra; erumpere liquores, &c.

Such constructions are chiefly poetic : but many of them occur
in prose.

3) Other Intransitive Verbs take a Contained Accusative only or
chiefly of Neuter Pronouns and Pronominal words:

Quod, quid, aliquid, quicquam, nescio quid, nihil, hoc, id,
idem, illud, istud, utrumque: quae, omnia, cuncta, eadem, multa,
pauca, &c.   See M. *Lucr.* vi. 404.

Among such Verbs are : cogere, dolere, dubitare, disserere,

gaudere, gloriari, laborare, laetari, obsequi, peccare, stomachari, succensere, &c.

And the expressions: animum advertere, auctor sum (*I advise*).

4) Out of this usage have grown a large number of Accusative phrases, which have an Adverbial use:

Cetera (alia, pleraque), multum, plus, plurimum, summum, aeternum, &c.; suam vicem; quod genus; id genus, omne genus; magnam partem; istuc (illud, id) aetatis; hoc noctis; id temporis, id auctoritatis, &c.

All these belong to prose style.

5) A Contained Accusative of the Neuter Adjective, Singular or Plural, is used by poets freely in an adverbial manner, especially with Verbs which express sensitive or sensible action:

Dulce ridere (loqui); immane spirare (sonare); suave resonare; perfidum ridere; turbidum laetari; lugubre rubere; immensum attolli (crescere); altum dormire; lene virere; suave olere; lucidum fulgere; falsum renidere; acerba tueri; sera comare; vana tumere; rauca gemere; crebra ferire; plura morari; insueta rudere; sollemnia insanire, with many more.

6) A form of the Contained Accusative, largely used by poets, sometimes by Livy and prose writers of the silver age, is 'the Accusative of Respect,' also called 'Accusativus Partis,' because it defines more nearly the *part affected* of the Object. Often an Ablative appears with it, sometimes a Dative.

This construction is taken by some Intransitive Verbs: tremere artus (ossa), torpere nervos, tumere colla, dolere caput (oculos), &c.

Oftener by Passive Verbs: suffundi ora rubore; expleri mentem; molliri ingenium; diduci animum; pingi alvum notis; 'Capita Phrygio velamur amictu,' V. *Aen.* iii.

Most frequently by Passive Participles and Adjectives:

Tectus caligine vultum; ornatus crinis apio; mutata mentem; labefactus animum; laniata genas, &c.; madidus unguento comam; os umerosque deo similis; crura thymo plenae; nudae bracchia et pedes.

Sometimes by Substantives:

Ora puer pulcherque habitum; cetera fossor.

iv. Medial Object.

123

Different from the Accusative of the Part, and having more the nature of an Attained Accusative, is that which poets often give to Passive Verbs and their Participles, used Reflexively, like the Greek Middle Verb. Thus cingi (=cingere se), indui (=induere se), exui (=exuere se), pasci (=pascere se), colligi (=colligere se), suspendi (=suspendere se), &c., take (as it were) a Second Object of the thing *girt on, put on, put off, fed on, gathered up, hung on,* &c. In prose this is rare, but sometimes found.

'Exuitur cornua,' *she puts off her horns,* Ov. *M.* ix. 52. 'Inutile ferrum cingitur,' *he girds himself with useless steel,* Verg. *Ae.* ii.

510. 'Pascuntur silvas,' *they graze on the forests,* Verg. *G.* iii. 314. 'Laevo suspensi loculos tabulamque lacerto,' *having their satchel and slate hung on their left arm,* Hor. *S.* i. 6. 74. So 'chlamydem circumdata,' *having a mantle thrown round her,* Verg. *Aen.* iv. 13. 7; 'saturata dolorem,' *having her resentment glutted,* Verg. *Aen.* v. 608.

v. The Accusative of Limiting Circumstances (Time, Space, Measure), § 103, V.

124

1) The Accusative of Duration of Time:

'Annum iam audis Cratippum,' *you have been a scholar of Cratippus for a year,* C. *Off.* i. 1. 'Pericles quadraginta annos praefuit Athenis,' *Pericles was prime minister of Athens forty years,* C. *d. Or.* iii. 34.

And after natus, expressing age:

'Dionysius quinque et viginti natus annos dominatum occupavit,' *Dionysius seized the government at the age of twenty-five years,* C. *T. D.* v. 20.

This last Accusative sometimes continues even when the Comparative (maior, minor) is introduced:

'Dionysius maior annos sexaginta decessit,' *Dionysius died when more than sixty years old,* Nep. *Eum.* 2.

2) The Accusative of Distance of Time past with abhinc:

'Pater abhinc duo et viginti annos est mortuus,' *the father died twenty-two years ago,* C. *Verr.* ii. 9.

3) The Accusative of Space traversed and of Distance:

'Milia tum pransi tria repimus,' *then after luncheon we crawl three miles,* Hor. *S.* i. 5. 25. 'Hadrumetum abest a Zama circiter milia passuum trecenta,' *Hadrumetum is about* 300 *miles from Zama,* Nep. *Hann.* 6.

4) The Accusative of Measure of Length, Breadth, Height, Depth, with the Adjectives longus, latus, altus: also of Weight with the word pondo:

Longum (latum, altum) ducentos pedes . . . quaterna cubita, &c., digitos sex, &c. So, libram pondo, *a pound weight.*

(The Ablative and Genitive are used in Constructions of Time, Space, and Measure: also Prepositions; per, ad, intra, supra, in, &c.)

vi. Accusative of Place Whither.

125

The Accusative of Place *whither* is chiefly used when the Place is a town or small island (sometimes, as by poets, more extensively); also when it is expressed by domum (*home*), rus (*into the country*).

'Legati Athenas missi sunt,' L. iii. 31. 'Caesar Narbonem profectus est,' Caes. *B. G.* iii. 7. 'Ibimus Afros,' Verg. *B.* i. 64. 'Veni consulis Antoni domum,' C. *Fam.* xi. 28. 'Ego rus ibo,' Ter. *Eun.* ii. 1. 10. So, domum itio, reditio, reditus. The phrases 'ire infitias,' *to deny,* 'ire exsequias,' *to attend a funeral,* are constructed on this model. The Prepositions ad, in, usque, are also much used in expressing Motion to a Place. See PREPOSITIONS.[1]

vii. Transitive Verbs used Intransitively.

The Subject of a Transitive Verb may be made its Object: Moveo me, moves te, movet se, &c.; and some Transitive Verbs may omit this Pronoun, and so become Intransitive. Such are,

Aequo, ago, abstineo, augeo, deflecto, duro, habeo, inclino, insinuo, lavo, minuo, moveo, muto, pasco, pono, praecipito, remitto, turbo, urgeo, verto, averto, vibro, volvo, and others. See M. *Lucr.* iii. 502 ; v. 931.

Ex. 'Abstineto irarum,' *abstain from angry feelings,* Hor. *C.* iii. 27. 69. 'A veritate deflectit,' *he swerves from truth,* C. *p. Caec.* 51. 'Bene habet,' *it is well,* Iuv. 'Nilus praecipitat ex altissimis montibus,' *the Nile dashes from very high mountains,* C. *S. Sc.* 13. 'Ubi nos laverimus lavato,' *when we have bathed, bathe,* Ter. *Eun.* iii. 5. 48. 'Minuente aestu,' *the heat moderating,* Caes. *B. G.* iii. 12. 'Res humanae semper in adversa mutant,' *human affairs always change to adversity,* Sall. *Iug.* 104. 'Remiserant dolores pedum,' *the pains of the feet had abated,* C. *Br.* 34. 'Iam verterat fortuna,' *fortune had now changed,* L. v. 49. 'Venti posuere,' *the winds have dropped,* Verg. *Ae.* vii. 27.

Conversely, many Passive forms are used reflexively:
Congregor, delector, effundor, exerceor, fallor, feror, lavor, moveor, mutor, oblector, pascor, versor, vertor, avertor, volvor, &c. See iv.

viii. Intransitive Verbs used Transitively.

The tendency of Intransitive Verbs to become Transitive is variously shewn.

1) Many Static Verbs take the cause or motive of the state as an Object, and so become Transitive. Such are

Doleo, lugeo, maereo, *grieve, grieve for*; tremo, *tremble, tremble at*; erubesco, *blush, blush for*; ardeo, *burn, burn for*; esurio, *hunger, hunger for*; sitio, *thirst, thirst for*; lateo, *lie hid, lie hid from*; maneo, *remain, await*; miror, *wonder, wonder at*; pereo, depereo, *die or waste away, die or waste for love of*; queror, *complain, complain of*; sileo, taceo, *am silent, am silent of*; audeo, *dare*; calleo, *am enured, am familiar with*; fastidio, *loathe*; horreo, horresco, *shudder*; paveo, pavesco, *quake*; palleo, pallesco, *turn pale,* &c.

Ex. 'Doleo casum tuum,' *I grieve for your misfortune,* C. 'Pontum palluit,' *she turned pale at the sea,* Hor. *C.* iii. 27, 26. 'Erubescit soloecismum,' *he blushes for his solecism,* Sen. *Ep.* 95. 'Nutum divitis horret,' *he shudders at the rich man's nod,* Hor. *Epist.* i. 18. 11.

---

[1] The Accusatives of Time, Space, Measure and Place, are in the nature of the Contained Accusative. Thus 'ire Romam' = 'ire iter Romae.'

2) Verbs of Intransitive action take as Object that which excites the action: latro, *bark, bark at*; sibilo, *hiss*; rideo, *laugh, laugh at*; fleo, *weep, weep for*; gemo, gemisco, *groan, groan for.*
'Populus me sibilat,' *the populace hiss me*, Hor. S. i. 1. 66.
'Flet necem fili,' *she weeps for her son's death*, Tac.

Note. Most in these classes have no personal Passive: ardeo, audeo, calleo, lateo, pereo, paveo, palleo, &c. A few are found Passive: 'Quo plus sunt potae plus sitiuntur aquae,' *water is thirsted for more, the more it has been drunk*, Ov. F. i. 216.

3) Various Verbs, usually Intransitive, take a Transitive force in certain senses:
Annuere, *grant*; adsuescere, consuescere, insuescere, *accustom*; desinere, *leave off*; censere, *enroll*; cunctari, *delay*; deproperare, festinare, maturare, properare, *speed*; iaculari, *shoot*; laborare, elaborare, *work out*; fugere, *escape from*; migrare, *transgress*; morari, *delay*; pergere, *continue;* plaudere, *pat*; putare, *reckon, prune*; sufficere, *supply*; ruere, proruere, *overthrow, rake up*; surgere, *rouse up*; vergere, *incline*, &c.

On the other hand, some Verbs, usually Transitive, have also a peculiar Intransitive use: such are,
Audire, *(hear) be called*; differre, *(sunder) disagree*; debere, *(owe) be bound (ought)*; superare, *(surpass) survive, remain.* Credere, *(entrust) believe*, takes Dat. or Acc. of *thing*, Dat. of *person*. Sortiri, *allot*, or *take by lot*, is Transitive in each sense.

4) Many Compounds of Intransitive Verbs, especially verbs of Motion, obtain a Transitive or Semitransitive force, chiefly when compounded with Prepositions governing an Accusative, ad, ante, circum, in, inter, ob, per, praeter, sub, trans:
Adire, aggredi, allabi, adsilire, anteire, antecedere, antecurrere, antegredi, antevenire, circumire, circumnavigare, circumvenire, inire, ingredi, illabi, innare, innatare, insilire, insultare, invadere, invehi, obire, obambulare, obequitare, perambulare, percurrere, permeare, praeterire, subire, transcurrere, transire, tranare, transgredi, transilire, transvolare, &c.

Some which do not contain motion:
Adiacere, accumbere, adstare, adsidere, alloqui, circumsonare, circumsedere, circumstare, impugnare, inclamare, incubare, insidere, instare, inundare, oppugnare, obsidere, occumbere, &c.

Many of these may take a Dative instead of an Accusative:
Allabi, illabi, innare, succedere, subrepere, incubare, instare, &c.

Some Verbs of motion, compounded with Prepositions which govern an Ablative, cum, e, prae, can be used as Transitive:
Coire, convenire, egredi, elabi, erumpere, evadere, excedere, exire, praecedere, praecurrere, praefluere, praegredi, praevenire:
And some not of motion:
Abnuere, aversari, edormire, expugnare, &c.
Most of these also vary their construction.

Note 1. We call those Verbs Semitransitive which, though they take an Attained Object, are not used Passively:
Adiacere, adsidere, and others in the preceding lists.

The test of an Active Transitive Verb is Personal use as Passive :
'Tamesis uno loco pedibus transiri potest,' *the Thames can be forded in one spot*, Caes. *B. G.* v. 18. 'Circumsedemur copiis omnibus,' *we are beset by all the forces*, C. *Att.* xv. 9. Therefore transeo and circumsedeo are used as Transitive Verbs.

So, 'Quidam oratores si arriderentur, esset id ipsum Atticorum,' *if certain orators were smiled on, this would be a true sample of Attic fashion*, C. *Opt. G. O.* 4.

Note 2. Intransitive Verbs which take a Contained Object are often used transitively in the third Persons Passive :
'Tota mihi dormitur hiemps,' *I sleep the whole winter*, Mart. xiii. 59. 'Noctes vigilantur amarae,' *there are bitter night-watches*, Ov. *H.* xii. 169. 'Tertia vivitur aetas,' *a third age of life is passing*, Ov. *M.* xii. 187. 'Multo pisce natantur aquae,' *the waters are swum by many a fish*, Ov. *A. A.* i. 48.

Rare instances of Trajective Verbs personally Passive are found : invideor in Horace ; imperor both in Horace and Cicero. But Impersonal Passive Construction is regular in such Verbs.

5) Sometimes the Preposition is repeated after Compound Verbs, or another introduced :
'Sestius ad urbem advolavit,' *Sestius flew to the city*, C. *p. Ses.* 4. 'Orator peragrat per animos hominum,' *an orator travels through the minds of men*, C. *d. Or.* i. 51. ' Pittacus accedere quemquam vetat in funus aliorum,' *Pittacus forbids anyone to approach the funeral of other people*, C. *Leg.* ii. 26.
This happens also with Prepositions governing the Ablative :
' Excedere ex urbe,' 'eripere ab aliquo pecuniam,' &c.

Hence some Compound Verbs, the Primitives of which are Transitive, have two Accusatives ; one of which is the Object of the Simple Verb, the other depends on the Preposition. The Prepositions admitting this construction are trans, ad, circum, praeter :
'Petreius iusiurandum adigit Afranium,' *Petreius makes Afranius* (take) *an oath*, Caes. *B. C.* i. 70. 'Postquam id animum advertit,' *when he turned his mind to this*, Caes. *B. G.* v. 18. 'Allobroges Pompeius sua praesidia circumduxit,' *Pompeius led the Allobroges round his posts*, Caes. *B. C.* iii. 61.

The Passive construction retains the Accusative governed by the Preposition : 'Scopulos praetervecta videtur oratio mea,' *my speech seems to have cleared the rocks*, C. *p. Coel.* 21.

128   **ix. Idiomatic Uses.**

1) The Abstract Verbal Noun itself appears in the Comic poets with an Accusative : 'Quid tibi hanc curatio est rem?' *what concern have you with this affair?* Plaut. *Amph.* i. 3. 21.

2) The Participial in -bundus is sometimes used with an Accusative : ' Populabundus agros,' *laying waste the lands*, Gell. xi. 15. Livy uses perosus, *hating*, with Accusative. Exosus and pertaesus are so used by writers of the silver age.

3) Comic poetry shews that it was an idiom of Roman conversation to begin a sentence with an unconstructed Accusative, antecedent to a Relative also in the Accusative:

'Naucratem quem convenire volui, in navi non erat,' *Naucrates whom I wished to meet was not on board*, Plaut. *Amph.* iv. 1. 1. 'Eunuchum quem dedisti nobis quas turbas dedit!' *that eunuch whom you gave us, what trouble he has given!* Ter. *Eun.* iv. 3. 11.

　　a) The Greek idiom was also used, by which the true Subject of a Relative Clause is made the Object of the principal sentence:

　　　'Scin' me in quibus sim gaudiis?' *do you know how overjoyed I am?* Plaut. *Bac.* iv. 6. 28. 'Servum meum Strobilum miror ubi sit,' *I wonder where is my slave Strobilus*, Plaut. *Aul.* iv. 7. 16.

Note. Many Verbs take a great variety of Objects, thus forming an extensive phraseology, which may be studied in good dictionaries with advantage. Such Verbs are: ago, capio, do, facio, fero, habeo, volo and their compounds.

x. The Exclamatory Accusative.

1) The Accusative may stand with one of the Interjections O, heu, eheu, pro, en, ecce, &c., or without an Interjection:

'O fallacem hominum spem fragilemque fortunam,' *O the deceitful hope of men and frail fortune*, C. d. *Or.* iii. 2. 7. 'En quattuor aras! Ecce duas tibi Daphni, duas altaria Phoebo,' *lo, four altars! behold two for thee, Daphnis, and two of higher elevation for Phoebus*, Verg. *B.* v. 65. 'Pro deorum atque hominum fidem,' C. *T. D.* v. 16. 'Heu stirpem invisam!' Verg. *Aen.* vii. 293. 'Me miserum!' C. *Fam.* xiv. 1. 'Operam tuam multam, qui et haec cures et mea expedias,' *how much trouble you take in both minding these affairs and expediting mine*, C. *Att.* xiii. 6.

2) This Accusative may take the form of an Interrogation:

'Huncine hominem? hancine impudentiam, iudices, hancine audaciam?' *what a man is this? what shamelessness, gentlemen, what audacity?* C. *Verr.* v. 25.

(On the Government of the Accusative by Prepositions, see § 70.)

xi. Accusative of two Objects.

1) Certain Verbs of teaching, asking, concealing, sometimes take two Accusatives, one Contained, of the Matter, the other Attained, of the Person.

'Quis musicam docuit Epaminondam?' *who taught Epaminondas music?* Nep. *Praef.* 'Numquam divitias deos rogavi,' *I never asked the gods for riches*, Mart. iv. 77. 1. 'Antigonus iter quod habebat omnis celat,' *Antigonus concealed from all the road he was taking*, Nep. *Eum.* 8.

Such Verbs are:

Doceo (and its compounds, edoceo, dedoceo), erudio (in poetry), rogo, interrogo, oro, exoro, posco, reposco, flagito, percontor, postulo, celo; and (in Horace) lacesso, veneror. Consulo with double Accusative is rare.

2) Moneo and its compounds, cogo, and some other Verbs, may have this construction when the Accusative of the Matter is a Neuter Pronoun or Pronominal:

'Illud me praeclare admones,' *you remind me of that fact excellently*, C. *Att.* ix. 9. 2. 'Multa extis admonemur,' *we are admonished of many things by entrails*, C. *N. D.* ii. 66. And this is the most common Accusative after Verbs of *asking*.

3) Verbs of *informing, warning, enquiring, concealing*, may take an Ablative of the Matter with de:

'De paratis incendiis senatum edocet,' *he informs the Senate of the intended conflagrations*, Sall. *C.* 48. 'Non est profecto de illo veneno celata mater,' *certainly his mother was not kept in ignorance of that poison*, C. *p. Clu.* 66.

4) Peto, contendo, take an Ablative of the Person with a, ab: which *may* also follow rogo, oro, exoro, posco, postulo, flagito:

'Hoc a te peto,' *this I ask of you*, C.

5) Quaero, scitor, sciscitor, percontor, exigo, take an Ablative of the Person with ab, ex: 'Zeuxis quaesivit ab iis quasnam virgines formosas haberent,' *Zeuxis enquired of them what beautiful maidens they had*, C. *d. Inv.* ii. 1.

6) The Contained Accusative of the Matter may remain in the Passive:

'In primis cultum agrorum docenda est vita,' *life must first be taught agriculture*, Pl. *N. H.* xv. 1. 'Livius est primus rogatus sententiam,' *Livius was first asked his opinion*, L. xxxvii. 14.

131　　**xii. Oblique Double Accusative with Verbs of making, thinking &c. (Factive).**

1) A simple Copulative Sentence, of which the Verb is sum, may become an Oblique Clause (Accusative with Infinitive), and (the Infinitive being omitted) the Clause may be made to depend on a principal sentence with one of these Verbs.

Examples:

Numa est rex; Numam esse regem; Numam regem:

'Populus Romanus Numam regem creavit,'
the Roman people elected Numa king.

Tu es doctus et prudens; te esse doctum et prudentem; te doctum et prudentem:

'Puto te doctum et prudentem,'
I count you learned and prudent.

Eumenes est sepeliendus; Eumenem esse sepeliendum; Eumenem sepeliendum:

'Antigonus Eumenem sepeliendum tradidit.'
Antigonus gave Eumenes to be buried.

Numam, te, Eumenem, are Oblique Subjects (becoming Objects).
Regem, doctum, prudentem, sepeliendum, are Oblique Complements. This use of the Gerundive is very frequent.

2) The Verbs which form this construction are:

    a) The Active forms of the Copulative Verbs enumerated
        on p. 351.
    b) Also many other Verbs:
        Adiungo, adscisco, arbitror, constituo, do, facio, impertior,
           monstro, peto, pono, praebeo, praesto (*exhibit, make*),
           reddo, sumo, tribuo, &c.

3) Instead of an Apposite or Attribute, the Complement in
any such form of Construction may sometimes be one of the Prepositions pro, in, with an Ablative Case, inter with Accusative, or
loco, numero, &c., with a Genitive.

Thus the English sentence, '*I hold Gaius my friend*,' may be
rendered in many ways:

          Gaium amicum habeo.
          Gaius a me amicus habetur.

                         (pro amico.
        Gaium habeo   {in amicis.
        Gaius a me habetur   {inter amicos.
                         (in amicorum numero.

Examples of Accusative.

ii. (*Attained Acc.*) 'Ea, quae leviter sensum voluptate movent, facillime fugi-
unt satietatem,' C. *d. Or.* iii. 25. 'Nulla ars imitari sollertiam naturae potest,'
C. *N. D.* i. 33. 'Solet Dionysium, cum aliquid furiose fecit, paenitere,' C. *Att.*
viii. 5.

iii. (*Contained Acc.*) 'Dentatus triumphavit triumphos novem, Gell. ii. 11.
'Magna voce iuravi verissimum pulcherrimumque iusiurandum, quod
populus idem magna voce me vere iurasse iuravit,' C. *Fam.* v. 2. 'Aquillius iuravit
morbum,' C. *Att.* i. 1. 'Quomodo tibi placebit Iovem lapidem iurare, cum scias,
Iovem iratum esse nemini posse?' C. *Fam.* vii. 12. 'Claudius aleam studiosissime
lusit,' Suet. *Claud.* 33. 'Curios simulant et Bacchanalia vivunt,' Iuv ii. 2. 'Qui
stadium currit, eniti et contendere debet ut vincat,' C. *Off.* iii. 10. 'Tigellius
noctes vigilabat ad ipsum mane,' Hor. *S.* i. 3. 17. 'Si Xerxes, cum tantis
classibus tantisque copiis mare ambulavisset, terram navigasset, mel se auferre
ex Hymetto voluisse diceret, certe sine causa videretur tanta conatus,' C. *Fin.* ii. 34.
'Nero sub exitu vitae palam voverat saltaturum se Vergilii Turnum,' Suet. *Ner.* 54.
'Inter alia prodigia carnem pluit,' L. iii. 10. 'Magis laudatur unguentum, quod
ceram, quam quod crocum olere videtur,' C. *d. Or.* iii. 25. 'Definitio genere ipso
doctrinam redolet,' C. *d. Or.* ii. 25. 'In Hispania multa in spartariis mella herbam
eam sapiunt,' Plin. *N. H.* xi. 8. 'Haud tibi voltus mortalis, nec vox hominem
sonat,' Verg. *Aen.* i. 308. 'Utrumque laetor, et sine dolore corporis te fuisse et
animo valuisse,' C. *Fam.* vii. 1. 'De Q. Fratre nihil ego te accusavi,' C. *Fam.* xiv. 1.
'Cetera assentior Crasso,' C. *d. Or.* i. 9. 'Q. Fabius Maximus moritur, exactae
aetatis; si quidem verum est, augurem dous et sexaginta annos fuisse, quod quidam
auctores sunt,' L. xxx. 26. 'Stupentis tribunos et suam iam vicem anxios libe-
ravit onere consensus populi Romani,' L. viii. 35. 'Suevi non multum frumento, sed
maximam partem lacte atque pecore vivunt,' Caes. *B. G.* iv. 1. 'Scis me orationes
aut aliquid id genus solitum scribere,' C. *Att.* xiii. 12. 'Si apud te plus auctoritas

D. The Dative Case.

i. The DATIVE is the Case of that which is interested in an action or state. It has three principal uses in Latin:

I. As Remoter Object, it completes the construction of many Verbs, Transitive and Intransitive ; of many Adjectives, sometimes of Adverbs, rarely of Substantives :

Dare librum (alicui); coronam capiti imponere ; placere, irasci (alicui); vicinus, carus, odiosus (alicui) : convenienter naturae : utiliter patriae : obtemperatio legibus.

---

mea valuisset, nihil sane esset quod nos paeniteret,' C. *ad Q. Fr.* i. 2.   Id nobis oneris, hominibus id aetatis, imponitur,' C. *d. Or.* i. 47.   'Romanorum nemo id auctoritatis aderat,' Tac. *Ann.* xii. 18.   'Cometae sanguinei lugubre rubent,' Verg. *Aen.* x. 273.   'Artabanus, ubi data fides a legatis reddendae dominationi venisse, adlevatur animum,' Tac. *Ann.* vi. 43.   'Arminius impetu equi pervasit oblitus faciem suo cruore ne nosceretur,' Tac. *Ann.* ii. 17.   'Hannibal, dum murum Sagunti incautius subit, adversum femur tragula graviter ictus cecidit,' L. xxi. 7.   'Non illa colo calathisve Minervae femineas adsueta manus,' Verg. *Aen.* vii. 805.

iv. (*Medial Obj.*) 'Dic quibus in terris inscripti nomina regum nascantur flores,' Verg. *B.* iii. 106. 'Septem et viginti virgines, longam indutae vestem, carmen in Iunonem reginam canentes ibant,' L. xxvii. 37. 'Domitianus sacellum Iovi conservatori aramque posuit casus suos in marmore expressam,' Tac. *H.* iii. 74.

v. (*Accus. of Time, Space, Measure.*) 'Multa saecula sic viguit Pythagoreorum nomen, ut nulli alii docti viderentur,' C. *T. D.* i. 16. 'Duodequadraginta annos tyrannus Syracusanorum fuit Dionysius, cum quinque et viginti annos natus dominatum occupavisset,' C. *T. D.* v. 20. 'Abhinc triennium commigravit huc viciniae,' Ter. *An.* i. 1. 43. 'A recta conscientia transversum unguem non oportet discedere,' C. *Att.* xiii. 20. 'Zama quinque dierum iter ab Karthagine abest,' L. xxx. 29. 'Milites aggerem, latum pedes trecentos, altum pedes octoginta exstruxerunt,' Caes. *B. G.* vii. 24.

vi. *Accus. of Place.*) 'Athenienses bello Persico sua omnia, quae moveri poterant, partim Salaminem, partim Troezenem asportarunt,' Nep. *Them.* 2. 'Hannibal in hiberna Capuam concessit,' L. xxiii. 18. 'Galli quondam longe ab suis sedibus Delphos usque ad oraculum orbis terrae spoliandum profecti sunt,' C. *p. Font.* 10. 'Pompeius Africam exploravit ; inde Sardiniam cum classe venit,' C. *p. L. Man.* 12. 'Aristoteles, Theophrastus, Zeno, innumerabiles alii philosophi numquam domum revertere,' C. *T. D.* v. 37. 'Scipio rus ex urbe, tanquam e vinculis, evolabat,' C. *d. Or.* ii. 6. 'Helvetii oppida sua omnia incendunt, ut, domum reditionis spe sublata, paratiores ad omnia pericula subeunda essent,' Caes. *B. G.* i. 5. 'Magni domum concursus ad Afranium fiebant,' Caes. *B. C.* i. 53. 'Hoc nemo eat infitias, Thebas, quamdiu Epaminondas praefuerit reipublicae, caput fuisse totius Graeciae,' Nep. *Ep.* 10. 'Exequias Chremeti, quibus est commodum, ire tempus est,' Ter. *Ph.* v. 8. 37.

vii. 'Terra dies duodequadraginta movit,' L. xxxv. 40. 'Aer movetur nobiscum,' C. *N. D.* ii. 33. 'Suevi lavantur in fluminibus,' Caes. *B. G.* iv. 1.

viii. 'Nemo tam ferus fuit quin Alcibiadis casum lacrimarit,' Nep. *Alc.* 6. 'Vel magistri equitum virgas ac securis dictatoris tremere atque horrere solent,' L. xxii. 27. 'Nec honores sitio, nec desidero gloriam,' C. *Q. Fr.* iii. 5. 'Commissa tacere qui nequit, hic niger est,' Hor. *S.* i. 4. 84. 'Ea quae disputavi disserere malui quam iudicare,' C. *N. D.* iii. 40. 'Risi nivem atram,' C. *Q. Fr.* ii. 13. 'Vigila illud, quod facile est, ne quid mihi temporis prorogetur,' C. *Fam.* ii. 10. 'Quis udo deproperare apio coronas curatve myrto?' Hor. *C.* ii. 7. 23. 'Quam expedita tua consilia, quam evigilata tuis cogitationibus!' C. *Att.* ix. 12. 'De natura deorum Cotta sic disputat, ut hominum non deleat religionem, credo, ne communia iura migrare videatur,' C. *Div.* i. 5. 'Matutine pater, seu Iane libentius audis,' Hor. *S.* ii. 6. 20. 'Me miseram! quid iam credas aut cui credas?' Ter. *Ad.* iii. 2. 'Insepulta membra different lupi,' Hor. *Epod.* v. 99. 'Haec cogitatione inter se differunt, re quidem

II. As Recipient or Acquisitive (Dativus Commodi et Incommodi) it is added to any Predication to express that *for* whom or *for* which something is, or is done:

Legere virgines Vestae : esse patrem urbi.

(The Datives I. II. oftener express persons than things.)

III. Idiomatically, the Latin Dative is used to express a Purpose in constructions which generally complete the construction of sum, do, habeo, fio, verto, venio, and other verbs.

Esse cordi, bono, usui, odio, honori, &c. ; vitio, culpae, crimini dare ; contemptui, derisui, habere ; auxilio, subsidio, venire, &c.

---

copulata sunt,' C. *T. D.* iv. 11. 'Aequa lege necessitas sortitur insignis et imos,' Hor. *C.* iii. 1. 15. 'Gens Claudia regnum in plebem sortita,' L. iii. 58. 'Hic tibi rostra Cato advolat,' C. *Att.* i. 14. 'Te nunc alloquor, Africane,' *Ad Herenn.* iv. 15. 'Appellitur navis Syracusas,' C. *Verr.* v. 25. 'Dictator triumphans urbem invehitur,' L. ii. 31. 'Creati consules Kalendis Sextilibus, ut tunc principium anni agebatur, consulatum ineunt,' L. iii. 6. 'Achaeos Aetoli, navibus per fretum, quod Naupactum et Patras interfluit, exercitu traiecto, depopulati erant,' L. xxvii. 29. 'Pythagoras multas regiones barbarorum pedibus obiit,' C. *Fin.* v. 29. 'Quaeritur, sitne honestum, gloriae causa mortem obire?' C. *d. Or.* iii. 29. 'Diligentissime semper illum diem et illud munus solitus es obire,' C. *Lael.* ii. 'Ad Antonium mittuntur qui nuntient ne Mutinam obsideat,' C. *Phil.* vi. 2. 'Euphrates Babyloniam mediam permeat,' Plin. *H. N.* v. 26. 'Non orat Roscius ut eam noctem pervigilet,' C. *p. S. Rosc.* 35. 'Populus solet nonnumquam dignos praeterire,' C. *p. Planc.* 3. 'Crassus Euphratem nulla belli causa transire voluit,' C. *Fin.* iii. 22. 'Hannibal cum reliquis copiis Pyrenaeum transgreditur,' L. xxi. 24. 'Haec Fetialis, quum finis suprascandit, haec portam ingrediens peragit,' L. i. 32. 'Germani intra annos quattuordecim tectum non subierant,' Caes. *B. G.* i. 36. 'Equites Pompeiani aciem Caesaris a latere aperto circumire coeperunt,' Caes. *B. G.* iii. 93. 'Angustias Themistocles quaerebat ne multitudine circumiretur,' Nep. *Them.* 3. 'Eumenes extremo tempore circumventus est,' Nep. *Eum.* 5. 'Themistocles adire ad magistratum noluit,' Nep. *Th.* 7. 'Ubii orabant ut Caesar exercitum modo Rhenum transportaret,' Caes. *B. G.* iv. 19. 'Transadigit costas et cratis pectoris ensem,' Verg. *Aen.* xii. 508. 'Hannibal nonaginta milia peditum duodecim milia equitum Iberum traduxit,' L. xxi. 23. 'Scipio colloquium haud abnuit,' L. xxx. 29. 'Verginius orabat ne se, ut parricidam liberum, aversarentur,' L. ii. 50. 'Utinam, Cn. Pompei, cum C. Caesare societatem aut numquam coisses, aut numquam diremisses!' C. *Phil.* ii. 10. 'Non eos solum convenire aveo, quos ipse cognovi, sed illos etiam, de quibus audivi et legi,' C. *Cat. M.* 23. 'Urbem unam mihi amicissimam declinavi,' C. *p. Planc.* 41. 'Struthiocameli altitudinem equitis insidentis equo excedunt,' Pl. *N. H.* x. 1. 'Edormi crapulam,' C. *Phil.* ii. 12. 'Historia non debet egredi veritatem,' Plin. *Ep.* vii. 33. 'Decius M. Livium pontificem praeire iussit verba, quibus se legionesque hostium pro exercitu populi Romani Quiritium devoveret,' L. x. 28.

x. 'En miserum hominem!' C. *Fin.* ii. 30. 'O hominem fortunatum,' C. *p. Quinc.* 25. 'Me caecum, qui haec ante non viderim,' C. *Att.* x. 10. 'Di vostram fidem!'

xi. (*Double Object.*) Eloquentia efficit ut ea quae scimus alios docere possimus,' C. *N. D.* ii. 57. Achaei quoque auxilia Philippum regem orabant,' L. xxviii. 5. 'Orationes me duas postulas,' C. *Att.* ii. 7. 'Pauca milites pro tempore hortatur,' Sall. *Iug.* 49. 'Rascilius de privatis me primum sententiam rogavit,' C. *Q. Fr.* ii. 1. 'Verres parentes pretium pro sepultura liberum poscebat,' C. *Verr.* i. 3. 'Ibo et consulam hanc rem amicos, quid faciundum censeant,' Plaut. *Men.* iv. 3. 26. 'Non te celavi sermonem Ampii,' C. *Fam.* ii. 16. 'Scito, me non esse rogatum sententiam,' C. *Att.* i. 13. 'Hoc nos celatos non oportuit,' Ter. *Hec.* iv. 4. 23. 'Non audimus ea quae a natura monemur,' C. *Lael.* 24.

xii. (*Factive Construction.*) 'Neminem pecunia divitem fecit,' Sen. *Ep.* 120. 'Interrex creatur M. Furius Camillus, qui P. Cornelium Scipionem interregem prodidit,' L. v. 31. 'Ciceronem universa civitas consulem declaravit,' C. *in Pis.* 1. 'Ubi illi tot di, si numeramus etiam caelum deum?' C. *N. D.* i. 13.

133 ii. (I) The Dative of the Remoter Object.

The Words which govern this Dative are Verbs or Adjectives containing the general notions of

1) Proximity and Remoteness.
2) Demonstration and Obscurity.
3) Gratification and Disfavour.
4) Rule and Subservience.

But many words, having these meanings, either take some other Case,[1] or, while they take a Dative, admit other constructions also. On this account it is desirable to name first those Verbs which take a Dative *only*, and then to add lists of Verbs with other varieties of Construction : and so in the Adjectives.

334 *A)* 1. Verbs with which a Remoter Object, if expressed at all, is always a Dative, are chiefly the following :

The Impersonal Verbs : accidit, conducit, contingit, convenit, expedit, libet, licet, liquet, placet, praestat, restat, usuvenit, vacat : (fas est, necesse est, opus est, usus est), &c.

Verbs of *affirming, relating, shewing, proving,* &c.—affirmo, confirmo, dico, exhibeo, indĭco, monstro, demonstro, narro, ostendo, patefacio, praecipio, probo, suadeo, persuadeo, dissuadeo, auctor sum, &c. (Trans.)

Appearing, being known, being near, &c.—appareo, innotesco, pateo, videor, obviam eo, praestŏ sum, &c. (Intrans.)

Giving, lending, paying, owing, entrusting, &c.—commodo, concedo, credo, divido, do, fero, and their compounds, mando, ministro, praebeo, praesto, pendo, redhibeo, relinquo, solvo, suppedito, trado, tribuo, debeo, committo, fido, confido, cedo, &c. (Trans.)

Promising, refusing, grudging—polliceor, promitto, recipio, spondeo, despondeo ;—nego, recuso, renuo, invideo, &c. (Trans.)

Congratulating, thanking ;—threatening : gratulor, grator, gratias (gratiam) ago, (refero, habeo) ;—minor, minitor, &c.

Dedicating, consecrating, sacrificing, vowing—dĭco, dedico, sacro, consecro, operor, immolo, sacrifico, voveo, devoveo, &c. (Trans.)

Assisting, favouring, benefiting, satisfying :—injuring, opposing : auxilior, benefacio, faveo, gratificor, medeor, opitulor, parco, patrocinor, prosum, satisdo, satisfacio,

---

'Montem Vesontione murus circumdatus arcem efficit,' Caes. *B. G.* i. 38. 'Socrates totius mundi se incolam et civem arbitrabatur,' C. *T. D.* v. 37. 'Nemo credit, nisi ei, quem fidelem putat,' C. *p. S. Rosc.* 39. 'Laelium Decimum cognovimus virum bonum et non illitteratum,' C. *d. Or.* ii. 6. 'Lentulus attribuit nos trucidandos Cethego, ceteros civis interficiendos Gabinio, urbem inflammandam Cassio, totam Italiam vastandam diripiendamque Catilinae,' C. *in Cat.* iv. 6.

[1] Thus delecto, iuvo, rego, though resembling in sense some of the Verbs hereafter recounted, are always Transitive, taking no Case but the Accusative.

studeo, subvenio, succurro :—adversor, incommodo, insidior, malefacio, noceo, obsto, obsum, officio, repugno, resisto, &c. (Intrans.)

Believing, flattering, assenting, pleasing :—distrusting, displeasing, upbraiding, reviling, being angry, &c.—credo, fido, confido, benedico, blandior, assentor, assentior, ignosco, indulgeo, placeo, morigeror, morem gero, convicior, diffido, obtrecto, displiceo, exprobro, irascor, maledico, stomachor, succensco, &c. (Chiefly Intrans.)

Ruling, commanding, obeying, serving—dominor, impero, regno :—ancillor, cedo, famulor, oboedio, pareo, servio, inservio, subservio, suffragor, supplico, &c. (Intrans.) Observe the expression, dicto audiens sum, *I obey.*

On nubo, vaco, see iii.

To these must be added numerous Verbs compounded with the particles :

Ad, ante, ab, con, de, e, in, inter, ob, post, prae, pro, re, sub, super, bene, male, satis :

Addo, addico, affulgeo, desum, indormio, impendeo, oppono, posthabeo, praefero, subiungo, satisfacio, &c.

Among such Compounds, however, some admit an Accusative where a Dative might stand : many repeat their Preposition with its Case, or admit another Preposition and Case, where a Dative might stand. Generally the Dative prevails in poetry, Prepositions in prose. But this is not true of all such Verbs : and as no Grammar can exhaust the combinations of Verbs and Cases, the student should observe these in reading, with the aid of a good Dictionary.

2. *a*) Verbs used with Dative or Accusative :

Adiaceo, adno, adstrepo, adsulto, adulor, aemulor, allatro, antecedo, anteeo, antevenio, assideo, ausculto, comitor, decet, deficio, inhio, innato, inno, insto, intervenio, lateo, medicor, moderor, obambulo, obequito, obstrepo, obtrecto, obumbro, occumbo, plaudo, praecedo, praecello, praecurro, praemineo, praesideo, praestolor, supersto, supervenio.

135

Observe mitto, nuntio, scribo, alicui or ad aliquem.

b) Verbs implying *agreement, communion, comparison,* &c., take either a Dative or, oftener in prose, the Preposition cum with its Case, or the phrase inter se. Such are

Coeo, cohaereo, communico, comparo, compono, concilio, confero, congrego ; also, apto, haereo, iungo, misceo, necto, socio, and their compounds with cum.

This applies also to Verbs of *contention,* certo, contendo, pugno, &c.

c) Verbs which imply *disagreement, disunion, difference, distance,* &c., take either a Dative or, often in prose, a Preposition with Case, usually ab, sometimes inter. Such are,

Absum, differo, discrepo, dissentio, dissideo, disto, &c.

d) Verbs which imply *taking away, defending, protecting from*, &c., take either a Dative of the Remoter Object or, oftener in prose, a Preposition with Ablative. Such are,

Abstraho, adimo, aufero, detraho, eripio, eximo; arceo, defendo, depello, propulso, &c.

e) Verbs which may take either a Dative of the Object with an Accusative of the Thing, or an Accusative Object with an Ablative of the Thing. Such are,

Adspergere, inspergere, circumdare, circumfundere, donare, munerare (i), exuere, induere, intercludere, impertire:

Dono tibi munus; dono te munere.

f) Interdico is best known in the phrase, 'interdicere alicui aqua et igni,' *to banish by the form of exclusion from fire and water*; but 'interdicere rem alicui' is a good Latin construction; also 'interdicere alicui de re.'

g) Verbs which may take Dative alone or Accusative of Thing with Dative of Person:

Condonare (*remit, forgive*); ignoscere (*excuse, pardon*); credere (*believe, lend*); gratulari (*congratulate*); imperare (*command*); indulgere (*grant, indulge*); minari, minitari (*threaten*); probare (*prove, make good*); suadere (*recommend*); persuadere (*persuade, convince*); invidere (*envy, grudge*). Also fidere, confidere (*trust*).

Persuadere alteri ut, &c., *to persuade one to*, &c.

Persuasit hoc mihi, *he convinced me of this.* Persuasum habeo; mihi persuasum est, *I am convinced*: hoc mihi persuasum est.

Invidere (*to grudge*) alteri re aliqua is a construction sometimes used.

Such Verbs cannot be so used in the Passive as to make that which was the Dative their Subject, though Horace has imperor; invideor: Lucr. officiuntur, ii. 156, where see Munro. Regularly, the Dative remains in the Passive: and, if there was an Accus., this becomes the Subject; if none, the Verb is Impersonal: 'Id mihi probatur:' 'Invidetur mihi.'

136   3. Examples of Verbs which vary construction with meaning:

Accedere (*to approach*) muris; muros, poet.; ad muros; in senatum. Accedere (*to join, concur with*) alicui. Accedere (*to be added*): aliquid accedit (accessit) alicui.

Aequare (*to level*) agrum. Aequare, aequiparare (*to make equal*) hunc illi; hanc rem illi. So adaequare, exaequare. Aequare, aequiparare (*to be equal to*) aliquem.

Cavere (*to take caution for*) securitati; agris; alicui. Cavere (*to beware of*) canem. Cavere a veneno.

Cedere (*to retire*) patria. Cedere (*to yield*) fortunae. Cedere (*to give up*) aliquid de iure suo alicui, &c.

Constare sibi (*to be consistent*). Constat (*it is an established fact*). Constare parvo, magno, &c., *to cost little, much*, &c.

Consulere: Si me consulis, ego tibi consulam, *if you consult me, I will consult for your interest.*

Convenire (*to suit*) alicui, in aliquem. Convenire (*to meet*) aliquem. Convenit mihi tecum, *you and I are agreed.* Inter se convenit ursis, *bears agree together.* Convenit, *it suits, it is agreed.*

Cupere (*to desire*) aliquid. Cupere (*to wish*) alicui (*in somebody's interest*).

Deficere (*to fail*) aliquem; alicui. Deficere ab aliquo, *to revolt from.*

Dare litteras alicui (*to give a letter for delivery*), rarely (*write to*). Dare litteras ad aliquem, *to post a letter to some one.*

Dolet mihi (*I grieve*): doleo rem.

Excusare, purgare (*to excuse, clear*) se alteri; se apud alterum. Excusare morbum, *to plead the excuse of illness.*

Imponere (*to lay on*) rem alteri; rem rei; aliquid in aliquid; aliquid in aliquo. Imponere alicui, *to cheat any one.*

Incumbere (*to lean on*) rei. Incumbere (*to devote oneself*) ad rem, in rem.

Interest inter (*there is a difference between*) hoc et illud. Interest omnium, nostra, &c., *it is the interest of all, of us,* &c. Interesse (*to be present at*) rei, in re.

Mactare (*to slaughter*) deo victimam, (*to sacrifice*) victimā. Mactare aliquem honoribus, *to grace with honours.* Mactare suppliciis, *to visit with punishment.*

Manere (*to remain*) alicui. Manere (*to await*) aliquem.

Metuere, timere, &c. (*to fear*) aliquem; aliquid; alicui (*for somebody*).

Moderari, temperare (*to curb*) rei. Moderari, temperare (*to govern*) rem. Temperare (*to refrain*) a re. Temperare (*to spare*) alteri.

Parcere (*to spare*) alteri. Parcere (*to forbear*) a re. Parcere (*to spare*) aliquid sibi, aliquid alteri.

Petere, precari (*to beg*) aliquid sibi; aliquid alteri. Petere (*to sue for*) consulatum, &c. Petere (*to entreat*) aliquid ab altero. Petere (*to seek*) locum.

Praeire (*to go before*) alicui. Praeire (*to recite*) verba alteri (*words for another to repeat*).

Praestare (*to excel*) alteri aliquā re. Praestare (*to assure, to warrant*) aliquid alicui. Praestare (*to prove, exhibit*) se talem.

Praevertere (*to prefer*) aliquid alicui rei. Praevertere (*to anticipate*) aliquid or aliquem. Praeverti (*to despatch first*) re͞.

Prospicere, providere (*to provide for the good of*) alicui. Prospicere, providere (*to foresee*) rem, de re.

Recipere (*to give assurance*) alicui. Recipere (*to receive*) aliquem.   Recipere (*to betake*) se aliquo.   Recipere (*to retake, recover*) res, urbem, &c.

Renuntiare (*to announce*) alicui aliquid (de aliqua re).   Re-nuntiare (*to proclaim*) aliquem consulem, &c.   Renuntiare (*to renounce*) alicui rei.

Solvere (*to pay*) alicui pecuniam, &c.   Solvere (*to release*) aliquem re.

Succedere (*to succeed*) alteri, alicui rei; in locum alicuius.   Succedere (*to come up to*) portas, muris, &c.

Sufficere (*to suffice*) alicui; alicui rei.   Sufficere (*to supply*) aliquem; aliquid.

Supersedere (*to sit upon*) rei; rem.   Supersedere (*to dispense with*) re; rarely rei.

Velle aliquem, *to want somebody*.   Bene velle alicui, *to wish well to somebody*.   Nolle alicui, *to wish ill to*.

137   *B*) The principal Adjectives used with a Dative Object are :

Cognatus, contiguus, conterminus, finitimus, praesens, pro-pinquus, propior, proximus, vicinus, &c., assuetus, con-suetus, &c., acclinis, aptus, accommodatus, commodus, congruens, consentaneus, conveniens, decorus, habilis, ho-nestus, idoneus, natus, necesse, necessarius, opportunus, promptus, proclivis, &c., aequalis, aemulus, idem, concors, consors, &c., concolor, &c. :—par, compar, similis, assi-milis, contrarius, diversus, insuetus, &c., incommodus, indecorus, inopportunus, turpis, &c., dispar, impar, inae-qualis, discors, dissimilis, dissonus, discolor, &c.

Apertus, certus, cognatus, compertus, conspicuus, evidens, liquidus, manifestus, notus, patens :—ambiguus, caecus, dubius, incertus, obscurus, &c.

Aequus, amicus, acceptus, benignus, benevolus, blandus, bonus, carus, clemens, dexter, dulcis, familiaris, fructuosus, gratus, iucundus, lenis, mitis, propitius, prosper, saluber, salutaris, secundus, suavis, utilis; expeditus, facilis, levis, obvius, pervius :—calamitosus, damnosus, exitialis, funestus, inutilis, malus, noxius, periculosus, pestifer; adversus, amarus, asper, crudelis, fatalis, hostilis, infensus, infestus, inimicus, iniquus, iratus, laevus, letalis, sinister, saevus; tristis, ingratus, invisus, molestus, odiosus, terribilis; in-credulus, infidus, infidelis; contumax, rebellis; arduus, difficilis, durus, gravis, invius, laboriosus, &c.

Imperiosus :— dicto-audiens, obnoxius, obsequiosus, sum-missus, supplex, &c.

138   *a*) Adjectives which take Dative or Genitive are :

Aequalis, affinis, alienus, communis, conscius, par, dispar, proprius, similis, dissimilis, superstes.

The following also may be treated as Substantives, and so take a Genitive :

Aemulus, amicus, inimicus, cognatus, necessarius, propinquus, socius, supplex, vicinus.

Alienus also takes an Ablative with or without ab.

Proprius is used by Cicero with Genitive only.

Propior, proximus are found with Accusative; also with ab and
its case.

β) Adjectives of *fitness*, aptus, commodus, idoneus, natus, proclivis, promptus, &c., may take ad (rem).

γ) Many Adjectives which express feeling or behaviour may
take in, erga (aliquem):

Acer, acerbus, crudelis, durus, iniquus, iniuriosus, saevus,
severus, &c.; benignus, comis, liberalis, mitis, pius, impius, gratus, ingratus, &c.

C) Adverbs derived from Adjectives are sometimes used with a　139
Dative:

Constanter sibi, convenienter naturae, utiliter patriae.

D) Verbal Substantives governing Dative rarely occur:　　　140
Obtemperatio legibus; remedia morbis, &c.

But such words as hostis, legatus, &c., being of an Adjectival
nature, are followed by a Dative; and others are so used when the
Dative is Acquisitive.

iii. (II) The Recipient or Acquisitive Dative.　141
(Dat. Commodi et Incommodi.)

'Pisistratus sibi non patriae Megarensis vicit,' *Pisistratus
conquered the Megarians for himself, not for his country*, Iust. ii. 8.
'Neque mihi ex cuiusquam amplitudine aut praesidia periculis
aut adiumenta honoribus quaero,' C. *p. L. Man.* 24. 'Filius
Blaesi militibus missionem petebat,' Tac. *Ann.* 1. 19. 'Cato . . .
urbi pater est urbique maritus,' Lucan. i.

1) Here may be ranked the Datives with vacare, *to be at
leisure* (alicui rei), nubere, *to wed*, properly '*to take the
veil for*' (viro), and those with Verbs of *care, caution,
fear*: consulere, studere, cupere, cavere, prospicere,
providere, metuere, timere, &c. (alicui), *to consult, look out,
fear* (for somebody or something).

2) Est, sunt, &c., with a Dative, express 'having:' Suus
cuique mos est,' *every one has his own custom*, Ter.
'Sex filii nobis, duae filiae sunt,' *we have six sons and
two daughters*, L. xlii. 34.

3) Facio, fio are used with a Dative:
'Quid facies huic?' C. 'Quid mihi futurum est?' C.

Also in the same sense, with de and Ablative:
Quid de me fiet? *what will become of me?* And with Abl.
alone: Quid me fiet? Quid te futurum'st? Ter.

4) The Dative of a Pronoun, loosely added, and expressing
general reference to a person, is called Dativus Ethicus:

'Quid mihi Celsus agit?' *how does my Celsus get on?* Hor. *Epist.* i. 3. 15. 'Quid ait nobis Sannio?' *what says our Sannio?*

5) Similar to this is the Dative with the Interjections hem, ecce: Hem Davum tibi, *see, here's Davus*: Ecce tibi Antonius, &c.

6) Hei, vae take a Dative:

'Hei misero mihi,' *alas for wretched me,* Ter. Vae victis, *woe to the conquered,* L.

7) A Recipient Dative, instead of an Ablative of the Agent, may be joined to Passive Participles, especially to Gerundives; also to Participials in -bilis:

'Formidatus Othoni,' *dreaded of Otho,* Iuv. 'Bella matribus detestata,' *wars abhorred by mothers,* Hor. 'Proelia coniugibus loquenda,' *battles for wives to talk of,* Hor. 'Non ulli affabilis,' Verg.

Poets extend this idiom to Personal Passive Verbs: 'Non intellegor ulli,' Ov. 'Carmina quae scribuntur aquae potoribus,' Hor. *Epist.* i. 19. 3.

In prose it is rare. 'Dissimillimis bestiis communiter cibus quaeritur,' C. *N. D.* ii. 48.

8) To such predications as 'Cui (huic) nomen est, quibus (his) nomen datur, damus,' &c., the Name itself is sometimes joined as an attracted Dative:

'Volitans, cui nomen asilo Romanum est,' *an insect whose Roman name is asilus,* Verg. *G.* iii. 147. 'In campis, quibus nomen erat Raudiis, decertavere,' *they fought in plains called the Raudian,* Vell. ii. 2.

(But a Nominative or Genitive of the Name is found: 'Ei morbo nomen est avaritia,' C. 'Nomen Mercuri est mihi,' Plaut. *Am. Prol.* 19.)

9) Analogous to this are the attractions: 'Hoc mihi volenti est,' Sall. 'Quibus bellum volentibus erat,' *who wished for war,* Tac.

10) When a Copulative Infinitive (esse, fieri, &c.) depends on a Verb with Dative Object, the Complement is generally Dative: 'Mihi non licet esse neglegenti,' C. *Att.* i. 17. 'Da mihi fallere, da iusto sanctoque videri,' Hor. *Epist.* i. 16. 61. But it may be Accusative: 'Primum ego me illorum, dederim quibus esse poetas excerpam numero,' Hor. *S.* iv. 39 (where Orelli reads poetis without authority or necessity).

Note. The Dative of Place Whither is poetic: 'It clamor caelo,' *a shout reaches the sky,* Verg. *Ae.* v. 451.

142 iv. (III) The Predicative Dative of Purpose.

This is usually found with a Second Dative of the Recipient:

Odio esse (cordi esse) alteri, *to be an object of hate* (liking) *to another*; vitio vertere alteri, *to impute as a fault to another.* So, commodo, dedecori, delectationi, emolumento, honori, voluptati, &c., esse alicui, crimini dare alteri; auxilio, subsidio venire alteri.

But a second Dative is not always used: Habere aliquem contemptui, derisui, ludibrio; habere rempublicam quaestui; ponere (opponere) aliquid pigneri, *to pawn, mortgage*; canere receptui, *to sound a retreat.*

(Akin to this construction is that of the Dative Gerund and Gerundive: solvendo esse, *to be solvent*; tresviri reipublicae constituendae, *three commissioners for settling the government.*)

In Personal Passive construction both Datives remain; Liber a patre filio dono datus est.[1]

Examples of the Dative Case.

I. (*Dative of Remoter Object.*) 'Zenoni placuit, bonum esse solum, quod honestum esset,' C. *T. D.* v. 11. 'Omnibus bonis expedit salvam esse rempublicam,' C. *Phil.* xiii. 8. 'Non vacat exiguis rebus adesse Iovi,' Ov. *Tr.* ii. 216. 'Cicero meus salutem tibi dicit,' C. *Att.* v. 9. 'Diem mihi dixerat, multam irrogarat,' C. *p. Mil.* 37. 'Qui sibi semitam non sapiunt, alteri monstrant viam,' Enn. 'Anguis Sullae apparuit immolanti,' C. *Div.* ii. 30. 'Tironem Dolabellae obviam misi,' C. *Att.* xii. 5. 'Dionysius nobis praesto fuit,' C. *Att.* iv. 12. 'Pompeio et Senatui pacis auctor fui,' C. *Att.* ix. 11. 'Quantum consuetudini famaeque dandum sit, id curent vivi,' C. *T. D.* i. 45. 'Is denique honos mihi videri solet, qui non propter spem futuri beneficii, sed propter magna merita claris viris defertur et datur,' C. *Fam.* x. 10. 'Iam non ago tibi gratias; cui enim re vix referre possum, huic verbis non patitur res satisfieri,' C. *ad Brut.* ii. 1. 'Attici neptem Caesar Tiberio Claudio Neroni privigno suo despondit,' Nep. *Att.* 19. 'Dissociatis animis civium, alii Sullanis, alii Cinnanis partibus favebant,' N. *Att.* 2. 'Omnino irasci amicis non temere soleo, ne si merentur quidem,' C. *Phil.* viii. 5. 'Tirones iureiurando accepto nihil iis nocituros hostis se Otacilio dediderunt,' Caes. *B. C.* iii. 28. 'Iudicis est innocentiae subvenire,' C. *p. Clu.* 1. 'Antiochus si parere voluisset consiliis Hannibalis, propius Tiberi quam Thermopylis de summa imperi dimicasset,' Nep. *Hann.* 8. 'Imperat aut servit collecta pecunia cuique,' Hor. *Epist.* i. 10. 47. 'Cur succumbis cedisque fortunae?' C. *T. D.* iii. 17. 'Non Caesari solum, sed etiam amicis eius omnibus pro Ligario exsule Cicero supplicavit,' C. *Fam.* vi. 14. 'Cui Gellius benedixit unquam bono?' C. *p. Sext.* 52. 'Tu verbis solves numquam quod mi re malefeceris,' Ter. *Ad.* ii. 1. 10. 'Pelopidas omnibus periculis adfuit,' Nep. *Pel.* 4. 'Erat nupta soror Attici Q. Tullio Ciceroni,' Nep. *Att.* 5. 'Venus nupsit Vulcano; Astarten Adonidi nupsisse proditum est,' C. *N. D.* iii. 23. 'Brutus collegae suo imperium abrogavit,' C. *Br.* 14. 'Sthenius est is, qui nobis assidet,' C. *Verr.* ii. 34. 'Leges omnium salutem singulorum saluti anteponunt,' C. *Fin.* iii. 19. 'Dionysius aureum Iovi Olympio detraxit amiculum, eique laneum pallium iniecit, cum id esse ad omne anni tempus diceret,' C. *N. D.* iii. 34. 'Est viri et ducis, non deesse fortunae praebenti se, et oblata casu flectere ad consilium,' L. xxviii. 44. 'Praetor interdixit de vi hominibus armatis,' C. *p. Caec.* 8. 'Hortensius veritus est ne Fufius tribunus plebis ei legi intercederet, quae ex senatus consulto ferebatur,' C. *Att.* i. 16. 'Ut Thucydidis concisis sententiis officit Theopompus elatione atque altitudine orationis suae, quod idem Lysiae Demosthenes, sic Catonis luminibus obstruxit posteriorum quasi exaggerata altius oratio,' C. *Br.* 17. 'Hannibal Alexandro Magno non postponendus est,' Iust. xxx. 4. 'Certis rebus certa signa praecurrunt,' C. *Div.* i. 52. 'Deus animum, ut dominum atque imperantem, oboedienti praefecit corpori,' C. *Univ.* 7. 'Nihil semper floret: aetas succedit aetati,' C. *Phil.* xi. 15. 'Numquam Atticus potenti adulatus est Antonio,' N. *Att.* 8. 'Non ita adulatus sum fortunam alterius, ut me meae paeniteret, C. *Div.* ii. 2. 'Lictores praetoribus anteeunt cum fascibus duobus,' C. *d. L. Agr.* ii. 34. 'Te semper anteit torva Necessitas,' Hor. *C.* i. 35. 17. 'Iis aemulamur, qui ea habent quae nos habere cupimus,' C. *T. D.* i. 19. 'Quod me Agamemnonem aemulari putas, falleris,' Nep. *Ep.* 5. 'Cui nullum probrum dicere poterat, eius obtrectare laudes voluit,' L. xlv. 37. 'Non id laboro, ut, si qui mihi obtrectent, a te refutentur,' C. *Fam.* ix. 11. 'Mihi ausculta; vide ne tibi desis,' C. *p. S. Rosc.* 36. 'Homines auscultant crimina,' Plaut. *Pseud.* i. 5. 12. 'In Formiano tibi praestolor,' C. *Att.* ii. 15. 'Curionis adventum L. Caesar filius ad Clupeam

---

[1] The saying 'Cui bono fuit?' *whose interest was it?* deserves special notice, because it is often erroneously cited in a different sense. See C. *p. Mil.* 12; *Phil.* ii. 14.

E. *The Ablative Case.*

i. The ABLATIVE is the Modal Case, or Case of Circumstances which modify the predication adverbially. Besides its proper Ablative functions (taken in Greek by the Genitive), it comprises those of the Primitive Instrumental (partly taken in Greek by the Dative) and most functions of the Locative Case.

Its uses may be conveniently taken in the following order:

I. Instrumental Ablative: comprising Cause; Instrument; Agent; Price; Matter.

II. Locative Ablative: comprising Respect;[1] Difference; Manner; Condition; Quality; Time When; Place Where and by Which.

III. Ablative Proper: comprising Place Whence; Separation; Origin; Thing Compared.

---

praestolabatur,' Caes. *B. C.* ii. 23. 'Aucta fama cladis ingens terror Patres invasit, dictatoremque dici placebat,' L. ix. 38. 'In Galliam Antonius invasit, in Asiam Dolabella,' C. *Phil.* xi. 2. 'Equidem ut veni ad urbem, mirus invaserat furor non solum improbis sed etiam his qui boni habentur ut pugnare cuperent,' C. *Fam.* xvi. 12. 'Est mihi magnae curae, ut ita erudiatur Lucullus, ut patri respondeat,' C. *Fin.* iii. 2. 'Respondebisne ad haec?' C. *Phil.* ii. 43. 'Si inest in oratione mixta modestiae gravitas, nihil admirabilius fieri potest,' C. *Off.* ii. 14. 'Inerant lunaria fronti cornua,' Ov. *M.* ix. 687. 'Caritati ipsius soli longo tempore assuescitur,' L. ii. 1. 'Assuetae sanguine et praeda aves,' Flor. i. 1. 'In omnia familiaria iura assuetus,' L. xxiv. 5. 'Natura vi rationis hominem conciliat homini,' C. *Off.* i. 4. 'Ratio et oratio conciliat inter se homines,' C. *Off.* i. 16. 'Ennius equi fortis et victoris senectuti comparat suam,' C. *Cat. M.* 5. 'Quaeso, pontifices, et hominem cum homine, et tempus cum tempore, et rem cum re comparate,' C. *p. Dom.* 50. 'Longe mea discrepat istis et vox et ratio,' Hor. *S.* i. 6. 92. 'Id a tuis litteris discrepabat,' C. *Att.* ii. 1. 'Duae leges inter se discrepant,' C. *d. Inv.* 2. 'Conexum sit principium consequenti orationi,' C. *d. Or.* ii. 80. 'Amicitia cum voluptate conectitur,' C. *Fin.* i. 20. 'Mamertini honorem debitum detraxerunt non homini, sed ordini,' C. *Verr.* iv. 11. 'Sacerdotem ab ipsis avis detraxisti,' C. *d. Har.* 13. 'Ille non cessat de nobis detrahere,' C. *Att.* xi. 11. 'Orationi adspergentur etiam sales, qui in dicendo nimium quantum valent,' C. *Or.* 26. 'Pythagoras ne Apollini quidem Delio hostiam immolare voluit, ne aram sanguine adspergeret,' C. *N. D.* 36. 'Dionysius fossam latam cubiculari lecto circumdedit,' C. *T. D.* v. 20. 'Deus animum circumdedit corpore,' C. *Univ.* 6. 'Equites Hannoni se circumfudere,' L. xxix. 34. 'Agesilaum amici, quod mel non habebant, cera circumfuderunt,' Nep. *Ag.* 3. 'Atticus Atheniensis universos frumento donavit,' Nep. *Att.* 2. 'Ciceroni populus Romanus aeternitatem immortalitatemque donavit,' C. *in Pis.* 3. 'In deversorio erant ea composita, quibus rex te munerare constituerat,' C. *p. Deiot.* 6. 'Di eam potestatem dabunt, ut beneficium benemerenti muneres,' Plaut. *Capt.* v. 1. 15. 'Doctrinis aetas puerilis impertiri debet,' Nep. *Att.* 1. 'Terentia impertit tibi multam salutem,' C. *Att.* ii. 12. 'Sto expectans si quid mihi imperent,' Ter. *Eun.* iii. 5. 46. 'Conon ad mare missus est, ut maritimis civitatibus navis longas imperaret,' Nep. *Ag.* 4. 'Matronis Medea persuasit ne sibi vitio verterent quod abesset a patria,' C. *Fam.* vii. 6. 'Hoc mihi non modo confirmavit, sed etiam persuasit,' C. *Att.* xvi. 5. 'Nihil facile persuadetur invitis,' Qu. iv. 3. 'Cato iis solis non invidebat, quibus nihil ad dignitatem posset accedere,' C. *Att.* vii. 3. 'Aliorum laudi atque gloriae maxime invideri solet,' C. *d. Or.* ii. 51. 'Africae solo oleum et

---

[1] Respect, Difference, Manner, Condition, Quality, Time, may be considered Locative, as logically limiting the position of that which they modify. In many examples it is not easy to say whether the Ablative should be referred to Cause, Instrument, Matter, or Manner.

ii. (I) Instrumental Ablative.

A) The Ablative of Cause answers the question *Owing to what ?*

1) It chiefly limits state; and is therefore joined to Verbs Intransitive or Passive, to their Participles, and to Adjectives.

vinum natura invidet,' Pl. *N. H.* xv. 2. 'Invidet igne rogi miseris,' Lucan. vii. 798.' 'Manus extrema non accessit operibus,' C. *Br.* 33. 'Nondum ad rempublicam accessi,' C. *p. S. Rosc.* 1. 'Dolor accessit bonis viris: virtus non est imminuta,' C. *Att.* i. 16. 'Rumore adventus nostri Cassio animus accessit,' C. *Att.* v. 20. 'Accedam in plerisque Ciceroni,' Qu. ix. 4. 2. 'Athenienses consuluerunt Apollinem Pythium, quas potissimum religiones tenerent,' C. *Leg.* ii. 16. 'Di consulunt rebus humanis,' C. *Div.* i. 51. 'Prudentia numquam deficit oratorem,' C. *Br.* 24. 'Cum iam amplius horis sex continenter pugnaretur, non solum vires, sed etiam tela nostris deficiebant,' Caes. *B. G.* iii. 5. 'Indulge valetudini tuae, cui quidem tu adhuc, dum mihi deservis, servisti non satis,' C. *Fam.* xvi. 18. 'Indulsit ornamenta consularia procuratoribus,' Suet. *Claud.* 24. 'Praestat honestas incolumitati,' C. *Inv.* ii. 58. 'Atheniensium civitas antiquitate, humanitate, doctrina praestabat omnis,' Nep. *Att.* 3. 'Ser. Sulpicius honorem debitum patri praestitit,' C. *Phil.* ix. 5. 'Trebatium obiurgavi, quod parum valetudini parceret,' C. *Fam.* xi. 27. 'Precantur ut et a caedibus et ab incendiis parceretur,' L. xxv. 25. 'Libros oratorios in manibus habeo, quos, ut spero, valde tibi probabo,' C. *Att.* iv. 14. 'Atticae meae velim me ita excuses, ut omnem culpam in te transferas,' C. *Att.* xv. 28. 'Quod te mihi de Sempronio purgas, accipio excusationem,' C. *Fam.* xii. 25. 'Antonius leges civitati per vim imposuit,' C. *Phil.* vii. 5. 'Metellum multi filii in rogum imposuerunt,' C. *T. D.* i. 35. 'Imposuistis in cervicibus nostris sempiternum dominum,' C. *N. D.* i. 20. 'Non recuso quin, si cuiquam Verres ulla in re umquam temperaverit, vos quoque ei temperetis,'C. *Verr.* ii. 6. 'Quis talia fando temperet a lacrimis?' Verg. *Ae.* ii. 8. 'Nobilitas Ser. Sulpicii hominibus litteratis et historicis erat notior, populo vero obscurior,' C. *p. Mur.* 7. 'Voluptatibus maximis fastidium finitimum est,' C. *d. Or.* iii. 15. 'Audivi te esse Caesari familiarem,' C. *Fam.* vii. 14. 'Omnis voluptas honestati est contraria,' C. *Off.* iii. 33. 'Fidelissimi ante omnia homini sunt canis atque equus,' Pl. *N. H.* viii. 40. 'Nec fertilis illa iuvencis, nec pecori opportuna seges nec commoda Baccho,' Verg. *G.* iv. 128. 'Romulus multitudini gratior fuit, quam Patribus; longe ante alios acceptissimus militum animis,' L. i. 15. 'Illa expugnatio fani antiquissimi Iunonis Samiae, quam luctuosa Samiis fuit, quam acerba toti Asiae !' C. *Verr.* i. 19. 'Ea virtus est praestantis viri, quae est fructuosa aliis, ipsi autem laboriosa, periculosa, aut certe gratuita,' C. *d. Or.* ii. 85. 'Sollertia pestifera multis admodum paucis salutaris est,' C. *N. D.* iii. 27. 'Falernum mihi semper idoneum visum est deversorio,' C. *Fam.* vi. 19. 'Verba innocenti reperire facile est; modum verborum misero tenere difficile,' Curt. vi. 10. 'Senatori necessarium est nosse rem publicam,' C. *Leg.* iii. 18. 'Epaminondas velut gratulabundus patriae exspiravit,' Iust. vi. 8. 'Syracusani nobis dicto audientes sunt,' C. *Verr.* v. 32. 'Apud Germanos probrosum est superstitem principi suo ex acie recessisse,' Tac. *G.* 14. 'Socrates nec patronum quaesivit ad iudicium capitis nec iudicibus supplex fuit,' C. *T. D.* i. 29. 'Ennio aequalis fuit Livius, qui primus fabulam dedit,' C. *Br.* 18. 'Aequalis temporum illorum,' C. *Div.* i. 20. 'Vetilius id dicit quod illi causae maxime est alienum,' C. *p. Caec.* 9. 'Ea scripsi ad te quae non aliena esse ducerem a dignitate,' C. *Fam.* iv. 7. 'Alienum dignitatis,' C. *Fin.* i. 4. 'Nihil est a me commissum, quod esset alienum nostra amicitia,' C. *Fam.* xi. 27. 'Omni aetati mors est communis,' C. *Cat. M.* 19. 'Haec ita iustitiae propria sunt ut sint virtutum reliquarum communia,' C. *Fin.* v. 23. 'Studium conservandi hominis commune mihi vobiscum esse debebit,' C. *p. Rab.* 1. 'Natus abdomini suo non laudi atque gloriae,' C. *in Pis.* 17. 'Ad laudem et ad decus nati sumus,' C. *Fin.* v. 22. 'Thracibus est ferrum et promptus libertati aut ad mortem animus,' Tac. *Ann.* iv. 46. 'T. Manlius perindulgens est in patrem, acerbe severus in filium,' C. *Off.* iii. 31. 'Iugurtha propior montem pedites collocat,' Sall. *Iug.* 49. 'Treviri proximi Rheno flumini sunt,' Caes. *B. G.* iii. 11. 'Ubii proximi Rhenum incolunt,' Caes. *B. G.* i. 54. 'Summum bonum a Stoicis dicitur, convenienter naturae vivere,' C. *Fin.*

Plecti neglegentia; mori senectute; pallescere culpa; impeditus morbo; pallidus ira; ardens amore; fessus inedia et fluctibus, &c.

It may limit Transitive Verbs, especially when it expresses feeling or motive:

Hac mente, hoc consilio, laetitia, odio, &c., facere, dicere aliquid, &c.

2) It includes the phrases: causā, gratiā, ergo, nomine, *for the sake of.* 'Quaestus causa,' *for the sake of gain*; but mea, tua, &c. causa. 'Turpitudinis effugiendae gratia,' *for the sake of avoiding disgrace.* 'Virtutis ergo (nomine),' *on the score of merit.*

---

iii. 7. 'Ex quibusdam stirpibus et herbis remedia morbis et vulneribus eligimus,' C. *N. D.* ii. 64.

II. (*Dativus Commodi et Incommodi.*) 'Non solum nobis divites esse volumus, sed liberis, propinquis, amicis, maximeque reipublicae,' C. *Off.* iii. 15. 'Si domus pulchra est, intellegimus eam dominis aedificatam esse, non muribus,' C. *in Caecil.* 3. 'Tibi aras, tibi occas, tibi seris, tibi eidem metis,' Plaut. *Merc.* i. 1. 71. 'Caesar reperiebat favere Dumnorigem et cupere Helvetiis propter affinitatem,' Caes. *B. G.* i. 18. 'Tibi favemus; tibi optamus eam rempublicam, in qua tuorum renovare memoriam atque augere possis,' C. *Br.* 97. 'Pro deum fidem, quid vobis vultis?' L. iii. 67. 'Atheniensis Clisthenes Iunoni Samiae, cum rebus timeret suis, filiarum dotes credidit,' C. *Leg.* ii. 16. 'Germani ab parvulis labori ac duritiae student,' Caes. *B. G.* vi. 21. 'Scabiem pecori et iumentis caveto,' Cato, *R. R.* 5. 'Bene mihi, bene vobis, bene omnibus nobis!' Plaut. *Pers.* v. 1. 20. 'Consulite vobis, prospicite patriae,' C. *in Cat.* iv. 2. 'Numa virgines Vestae legit, Salios item Marti Gradivo,' L. i. 20. 'Improbo et stulto et inerti nemini bene esse potest,' C. *Par.* 2. 'Tibi bene ex animo volo,' Ter. *Haut.* v. 2. 6. 'Multis de causis ego huic causae patronus exstiti,' C. *p. S. Rosc.* 2. 'Semper in civitate, quibus opes nullae sunt, bonis invident,' Sall. *Cat.* 37. 'An nescis longas regibus esse manus?' Ov. *Her.* xvii. 166. 'Filius meus si quid peccat, mihi peccat,' Ter. *Ad.* i. 2. 35. 'Quid mihi L. Pauli nepos quaerit, quo modo duo soles visi sint?' C. *Rep.* i. 19. 'Ecce tibi, qui rex populi Romani dominusque omnium gentium esse concupierit, idque perfecerit!' C. *Off.* iii. 21. 'Audita est Brenni, reguli Gallorum, intoleranda Romanis vox; Vae victis esse,' L. v. 48. 'Cui non sunt auditae Demosthenis vigiliae?' C. *T. D.* iv. 19. 'Mihi consilium captum iam diu est,' C. *Fam.* v. 19. 'Ut esse possem orator, magno studio mihi a pueritia est elaboratum,' C. *in Caecil.* 12. 'Legendus mihi saepius est Cato Maior,' C. *Att.* xiv. 21. 'Restat Chremes qui mihi exorandus est,' Ter. *An.* i. 1. 130. 'Hic tibi sit potius quam tu mirabilis illi,' Hor. *Epist.* i. 6. 23. 'Vix audior ulli,' Ov. *Ep. ex P.* iii. 9. 'Duo sunt Roscii, quorum alteri Capitoni cognomen est,' C. *p. S. Rosc.* 6. 'Attus Clausus, cui postea Appio Claudio fuit Romae nomen, ab Regillo magna clientium comitatus manu Romam transfugit,' L. ii. 16. 'Illis timidis et ignavis licet esse; vobis necesse est fortibus viris esse,' L. xxi. 44. 'Medios esse (nos) iam non licebit,' C. *Att.* x. 8.

III. (*Predicative Dative.*) 'Vitam rusticam tu probro et crimini putas esse?' C. *p. S. Rosc.* 17. 'Otho quidquid epistularum erat, ne cui periculo aut noxae apud victorem forent, concremavit,' Suet. *Oth.* 10. 'Spero homines intellecturos, quanto sit omnibus odio crudelitas, et quanto amori probitas et clementia,' C. *Fam.* xv. 19. 'Ampla domus dedecori domino saepe fit, si est in ea solitudo,' C. *Off.* i. 39. 'Vitio mihi dant quod mortem hominis necessarii graviter fero,' C. *Fam.* xi. 28. 'Pergite, ut facitis, adulescentes, atque in id studium, in quo estis, incumbite, ut et vobis honori, et amicis utilitati, et reipublicae emolumento esse possitis,' C. *d. Or.* i. 8. 'Flaminius consul ante signum Iovis Statoris sine causa repente concidit, nec eam rem habuit religioni,' C. *Div.* i. 35. 'Habere quaestui rempublicam turpe et nefarium est,' C. *Off.* ii. 22. 'Virtus sola neque datur dono neque accipitur,' Sall. *Iug.* 85.

3) Also the phrases ius su, iniussu, monitu, mandatu, permissu, rogatu, &c., ope, opera, beneficio, dolo, &c,

4) Cause may be expressed by the Prepositions ab, de, ex, per, prae.

Ab animi levitate; per aetatem; multis de causis; prae gaudio.

B) The Ablative of the Instrument answers the question 145 *By what means?*

1) It limits Verbs Active or Passive, and their Participles.
Pugnare gladiis; defendere se cornibus; lapide ictus; veneno exstingui, &c.

2) The Ablative of an Abstract Noun may be Instrumental:
'Forma et moribus conciliare aliquem.'

3) The Preposition **cum** with its Case is sometimes used as equivalent to a Participle with Instrumental Ablative:

'Homines cum gladiis'=homines gladiis armati.

C) The Ablative of the Personal Agent with the Preposi- 146 tion ab, *by*, answers the question *By whom?*

1) It is joined to Verbs Passive or Quasi-passive and their Participles:

'Mundus a Deo administratur;' ab hoste vēnire; ab improbis expulsus, &c.

2) The Preposition **per** is used to express both Instrument and Agent: Per dolum, per insidias capi; per bonos restitui, &c.

3) Abstract terms, though in general Instrumentally used in the Ablative, are sometimes treated as Agents:

'Piget dicere ut vobis animus ab ignavia atque socordia corruptus sit,' *it is sad to state how your mind has been corrupted by idleness and sloth*, Sall. *Iug.* 31; M. *Lucr.* i. 813.

D) The Ablative of Price answers the questions *For how* 147 *much? At what cost?*

1) It accompanies Verbs of *purchase, sale, barter, hiring, letting, bidding, costing*, &c., or any other with which Cost or Value can be connected. Such are

Emere and its compounds, mercari, opsonari, vendere, vēnire; conducere, locare, collocare; licere, liceri, licitari, &c., constare, stare, valere, esse, &c., aestimare, &c.

Also Adjectives implying *cost, dearness, cheapness*:
Venalis, vendibilis, parabilis, carus, vilis, &c.

Emere, &c., venalis esse, &c., pretio, grandi pecunia, centum nummis, viginti denariis, centum milibus, mille drachmis (minis, talentis), &c.

2) The following Ablatives of Cost are used with such words, the Noun pretio being understood:

Magno, parvo, minimo, paululo, plurimo, nimio, dimidio, duplo, vili, &c.

Tanto, quanto may be used; but Price is more usually expressed by their Genitives tanti, quanti, also by the Genitives pluris, minoris, maximi, which Adjectives are not used in the Ablative of Price without pretio.

a) Valuation is usually expressed by the Genitives magni, parvi, &c. (pretii), and others. See GENITIVE.

b) The Verbs mutare, commutare, permutare, vertere (*to exchange*), take either an Accusative of the thing parted with, and an Ablative of the thing taken: 'Mutare pacem bello,' *to exchange peace for war, i.e. to go to war*; or (especially in poetry) an Accusative of the thing taken, and an Ablative of the thing parted with: 'Permutare otio divitias,' *to take wealth in exchange for ease.*

148   *E*) The Ablative of Matter answers the questions *Wherewith?* (in a material sense ;) *Whereof?*

It accompanies a great number of Verbs and Adjectives:

1) Transitive Verbs of *sacrificing; adorning, enduing, arming; dignifying, afflicting, punishing; nourishing, supporting, delighting; fashioning, instructing, furnishing; binding,* &c.:

Facere, immolare, litare, libare, &c. victima, hostia, agno, &c. vino, lacte, &c. :—ornare, induere, armare, &c. veste, corona, ense, &c. :—afficere, mactare, &c. beneficio, honore, iniuria, poena, &c.: afficere admiratione; affici morbo, &c. :—alere, pascere, iuvare, delectare, oblectare, &c. opibus, sermonibus, &c.:—formare, informare, instituere, munire, &c. doctrina, bonis artibus, subsidiis, &c.:—obligare, devincire, obstringere, tenere, &c. iure-jurando, religione, &c.

2) Intransitive Verbs of *consisting, being made; being accustomed; depending; being strong, being distressed; flourishing, languishing; rejoicing, boasting, grieving; relying, distrusting;* &c.:

Constare, conflari, contineri, fieri; suescere, assuescere; pendere; pollere, valere, vigere, lascivire, laborare; florere, languescere; gaudere, laetari, exsultare, triumphare, gloriari; dolere, maerere; fidere, confidere, niti; (macte esto); diffidere, &c.

Constare also takes ex. 'Omnis ex re atque verbis constat oratio,' *all speech consists of matter and words,* C. d. *Or*. iii. 5.

3) Adjectives and Participles in meaning akin to some of these Verbs:

Compositus, conflatus, concretus, factus; praeditus (*endued*), beatus, felix, contentus, fretus (*relying*); laetus, superbus; fisus, diffisus, coniunctus, assuetus, assuefactus, insuetus, &c.

The last six also take a Dative.

4) **Dignus** (*worthy*), **indignus** (*unworthy*):
Sometimes also with Genitive.

They are applied either to person or to thing :
Vir dignus est laude : vox indigna est responsione.

Dignari, *to deem worthy*, or *to be deemed worthy* (honore, &c.), is always used passively by Cicero; by poets and later prose writers actively also.

5) **Opus est**, *there is need*, opus habere, *to have need* (consilio, prudentia, duce, &c.)
Generally used with Ablative, or with Genitive by poets.

Opus may also stand as Complement: ' Dux nobis et auctor opus est,' *we need a leader and adviser*, C. *Fam.* ii. 6.

Usus est, *there is occasion*, is sometimes found :
' Nunc viribus usus,' *now there is occasion for strength*, Verg. *Ae.* viii. 441.

Opus is used with Passive Participial words :
' Ita dictu opus est,' *so must we needs say*, Ter. *Haut.* v. 1. 68. ' Priusquam incipias, consulto opus est,' *ere you begin, there is need of consultation*, Sall. *Cat.* I. ' Opus fuit Hirtio convento,' *there was occasion for an interview with Hirtius*, C. *Att.* x. 14.

6) **Fungi**, *to perform, fulfil*, with compounds defungi, perfungi; **frui**, *to enjoy*, with perfrui; **uti**, *to use*, with abuti; **vesci**, *to feed on, eat*; **potiri**, *to acquire, gain possession of.*

The Ablative with these Verbs (which is properly instrumental) is construed like an Object. They were originally Reflexive, and are used with Accusative in E. L., hence they retain the Gerundive: ' Vita data est utenda.' ' Spes potiundorum castrorum,' Caes. See M. *Lucr.* iii. 956.

Utor is found in the sense of *possessing* :
' Valetudine utor non bona,' *I have poor health*, C. *Fam.* xiv. 5.
Being intimate with : ' Utebatur intime Q. Hortensio,' *he was intimate with Hortensius*, N. *Att.* v. 4.

Potior also takes a Genitive : sometimes an Accusative.

7) Transitive Verbs of *endowing, enriching, filling, increasing, loading, sating*, &c., *depriving, despoiling, emptying, stripping, releasing*, &c. :
Donare, munerare, dotare, ditare, locupletare, opulentare, complere, explere, implere, opplere, replere, augere, cumulare, onerare, farcire, confercire, refercire, satiare, exsatiare, saturare, exsaturare, &c., destituere, fraudare, privare, orbare, viduare, spoliare, despoliare, vacuare, nudare, levare, exonerare, laxare, liberare, solvere, exsolvere, expedire, exhaurire, emungere, exuere, &c. (re aliqua aliquem).

Intransitive Verbs of *abounding, overflowing*, &c., *wanting, being void being destitute*, &c.

Abundare, fluere, affluere, circumfluere, diffluere, exuberare, exundare, redundare, manare, stillare, pluere, scatere, &c., carere, egere, indigere, vacare (re aliqua).

Verbs of this class often take a Genitive in poetry; e g e r e, i n d i g e r e, prefer a Genitive in prose also.

Some are followed by the Preposition a b; levare, liberare, vacare (a re).

8) Adjectives of *abundance* and *want* :

Abundans, beatus, compos, dives, felix, ferax, fertilis, fecundus, fetus, frequens, gravis, gravidus, laetus, largus, locuples, nimius, onustus, opulentus, plenus, refertus, satur, tumidus, uber, &c., cassus, egenus, expers, immunis, inanis, inops, liber, mancus, nudus, orbus, pauper, purus, solutus, sterilis, truncus, vacuus, viduus, &c. (re aliqua).

Many of these may take a Genitive: compos, plenus, fecundus; expers, i n o p s, and some others; especially in poetry.

Some may take the Preposition a b: immunis, liber, purus, solutus, vacuus (a re); the case after such words being a true Ablative of Separation.

iii. (II) Locative Ablative.

149   *A*) The Ablative of Respect answers the question *In regard of what ?*

It is joined to any predication, especially to Substantives and Adjectives, denoting that particular in respect of which the predication is made:

'Nomine grammaticus, re barbarus,' *in name a grammarian, in fact a barbarian*; 'claudus altero pede,' *lame of one foot*; 'virtute et doctrina excellere;' 'contremere tota mente et omnibus artubus:' 'hae domo Carthaginienses sunt.' So, natu maior, *elder* (minor, maximus, minimus); grandis natu, *elderly*, &c.

150   *B*) The Ablative of Measure answers the question *By what measure ?*

1) It limits Measurement or Comparison:

'Sol multis partibus maior est quam terra,' *the sun is many times greater than the earth*, C. N. D. ii. 36.

2) It includes the Ablative of Space and Distance:

'Trium milium spatio (or tribus milibus passuum) distare,' &c., *to be three miles off*, &c.   Ab may be used with this Ablative of Distance:

'Naves ab milibus passuum octo vento tenebantur,' *the ships were kept by a wind eight miles off*, Caes. B. G. iv. 22.

3) The following Ablatives are used with Comparative and other words implying Comparison:

Hoc, eo, quo, tanto, quanto, aliquanto, multo, paulo, dimidio, nihilo, nimio, altero, &c. 'Eo gravior dolor quo culpa maior,' *the pain is heavier in proportion as the fault is greater.* Multo optimus; multo praestare; multo malle, &c., multo ante (post); paulo ante (post); tanto ante (post), &c. Multo aliter, secus, &c. See p. 279.

C) The Ablative of Manner answers the question *How?*

1) It is eminently adverbial, appearing in many phrases as a single word:

Ordine, ratione, via et ratione (*systematically*), dolo, fraude, vi, iure, iniuria, vitio (*faultily*), equo (*on horseback*), pedibus (*on foot*), &c. (Per might be used with some of these words in the same sense: per dolum, per vim.)

2) In some instances an unqualified Ablative may be used with or without cum:

Clamore, cum clamore; silentio, cum silentio.

But cum is generally used with an unqualified Ablative of Manner:

Cum dolore; cum gaudio; cum fide; cum cura.

3) Certain Ablatives, more, modo, ritu, take a Genitive if they have no epithet.

'More Sophoclis' or 'more Sophocleo,' *in the manner of Sophocles*; 'Herculis ritu,' *in the fashion of Hercules,* Hor.

4) With an Epithet the Ablative of Manner often stands without a Preposition, in some phrases always:

Hoc (eo) modo, nullo modo, nullo pacto, nullo ordine, nullo negotio, &c.

The Preposition seems to be used or omitted at discretion (on its frequency see M. *Lucr.* i. 755).

'Magno studio' or 'cum magno studio;' 'magno gaudio' or 'cum magno gaudio;' 'adesse omnibus copiis' or 'cum omnibus copiis,' &c.

D) The Ablative of Condition answers the question *On what terms?*

It is one form of the Ablativus Modi:

Pace tua, *by your leave,* bona tua venia, *with your indulgence,* meo iure, *by my own right,* mea sententia, *in my opinion,* &c.

E) The Ablative of Quality answers the question *Of what description?*

It always has an Epithet and defines a Substantive, to which it stands either as an Enthesis or as a Complement:

Murena, vir mediocri ingenio, &c. or 'Murena mediocri ingenio fuit.' See GENITIVE OF QUALITY.

154 *F*) The Ablative of Time answers the questions *When?* *Within what time?* Hieme, vere, aestate, primo vere, diluculo (*at dawn*), prima luce, hora quarta, tertia vigilia,[1] Kalendis Ianuariis, anno septimo, &c., centum annis, biennio, biduo, paucis diebus, &c.

1) Recurring solemnities may express *Time when* :

Ludis, *at the games*; gladiatoribus, *at the gladiators' show* ; comitiis, *at the comitia*; Liberalibus, *at the feast of Liber*, &c.

Rarer idioms are, Sereno, *in a calm* ; austro, *in a south wind*, &c.

Interdiu, noctu, mane (mani), luci, vesperi, heri, pridie, postridie, crastini die, are expressions of Time representing old Locatives.

2) The Preposition used to define *Time when*, is chiefly de (*beginning from, ere the close of, during*); de nocte, de multa nocte (*long before night ended*) ; de media nocte, de die, de mense Decembri.

In is used to express *time within which*: and often when the Ablative has another Numeral, Distributive or Quotientive, connected with it :

'Sol binas in singulis annis reversiones facit,' *the sun makes two turns annually*, C. *N. D.* ii. 40. 'Quidam oves in anno bis tondent,' *some shear sheep twice a year*, Varro. See also intra, sub.

3) The Pronouns hic, ille sometimes emphatically define the Ablative of *Time within which*.

His annis quadringentis, *within these last* 400 *years* ; hoc triennio, *within the next* (or *last*) *three years*; hoc biduo, *within the next* (or *last*) *two days*—the Tense determining whether hic refers to Future or Past Time.

4) Post is also used in answering the question *How soon?* paucis post diebus or paucos post dies, or post paucos dies, *within the next few days.*

5) *How long ago* is expressed by ante: paucis ante diebus, or paucos ante dies, or ante paucos dies. Also by abhinc with Accusative or Ablative of the Time : 'Abhinc triennium (or triennio) huc commigravit,' *she came here three years ago*, Ter. *An.* i. 1.

6) The occurrence of one of two facts before or after the other is variously expressed.

Thus the English, *I saw him three days before he died*, may be rendered by any of the following sentences :

Vidi eum tribus diebus (*or* triduo) antequam mortuus est.

Vidi eum tertio die antequam mortuus est.

Vidi eum ante tres dies (*or* ante triduum) quam mortuus est.

Vidi eum ante tertium diem quam mortuus est.

---

[1] The Romans divided the day (from 6 A.M. to 6 P.M.) into 12 hours, of whicn 7 A.M. was the first (prima hora). Noon was called meridies or sexta hora. The night (from 6 P.M. to 6 A.M.) they divided into four watches (vigiliae) of three hours each.

Pridie quam mortuus est, *the day before he died* (= ante diem quam).

Likewise, *he died six years after I saw him,* may be rendered by any of the following :

> Mortuus est sex annis (*or* sexennio) postquam eum videram.
>
> Mortuus est sexto anno postquam eum videram.
>
> Mortuus est sexto anno quam eum videram.
>
> Mortuus est post sex annos (*or* post sexennium) quam eum videram.
>
> Mortuus est post sextum annum quam eum videram.

Postridie quam eum vidi, *the day after I saw him* (= post diem quam).

Cum, quo, quibus, are used for postquam :

> 'Biduo quo (or cum) haec gesta sunt, *two days after these things were done,* Caes.

On multo, paulo, &c., with ante, post, see § 150.

7) The Accusative of Duration shews the space of time through which an action extends ; the Ablative, that within which it is contained.

G) The Ablative of Place Where generally takes 'in :'　　155

> 'In portu navigo,' *I am sailing in harbour,* Sen.

1) In is omitted in many instances : loco, multis locis, pluribus locis, &c. ; hoc libro, alio libro, &c. ; terra, mari ; tota Asia, *throughout Asia* ; dextra (parte), *on the right hand* ; laeva, sinistra, *on the left hand* ; media urbe, *in the middle of the city* ; medio aedium, *in the middle of the house* ; eodem statu (or in eodem statu).

Also with 'se tenere,' 'continere :' 'Pompeius se oppido tenet,' *Pompeius keeps in the town,* C. *Att.* ix. 11. 2.

2) Poets are more free in the omission : 'Silvisque agrisque viisque corpora foeda iacent,' *in forests and fields and roads lie revolting corpses,* Ov. *Met.* vii. 647. But this licence needs discrimination.

3) When a work is quoted, in is used : in Iliade Homeri ; in Andria Terentii ; in Gorgia Platonis.

But when the author only is cited, apud : apud Homerum ; apud Terentium ; apud Platonem.

4) If the Place is a town or small island, the question, *Where?* is answered by a Case in -ae, -i, Singular, -is Plural, when the Noun is of Decl. I. or II. : Romae, *at Rome,* Cypri, *at Cyprus,* Athenis, *at Athens,* Delphis, *at Delphi* ; but by a Case in -e or -i, Singular, -ibus, Plural, when the Noun is of Decl. III. : Babylone, *at Babylon,* Neapoli, *at Naples,* Gadibus, *at Cadiz.*

5) The Case of Place in -ae, -i is taken by the words militia, bellum, humus, domus, rus :

Militiae, belli, *at the wars,* humi, *on the ground,* domi, *at home,* ruri (or rure), *in the country.* Terrae, *on the earth,* is used by poets : 'Procubuit terrae,' Ov.

D D

6) That the Case in **-ae, -i** is not really a Genitive, was known even to the ancient grammarians, who call it an Adverb. But as it ends in **i** (Romai = Romae, militiai = militiae, domi, ruri, &c.), comparing the older forms of Place in Decl. III., Anxuri, Carthagini, Lacedaemoni, Tiburi, we cannot doubt the original existence of a Locative Case ending in **i** Sing. **s** Plur., in Latin as in Sanskrit.

Compare Die septimi, Plaut.; die crastini, Gell. (so die pristini, proximi); heri vesperi, C.

Some refer here the Case of the Part Affected: animi pendeo; maturus aevi, &c. Some that of Price.

7) A Gentile Adjective is sometimes found with the name of a town locatively constructed:

'Teani Apuli,' *at Teanum of Apulia,* C. 'Curibus Sabinis,' L. Other epithets are used in poetry: 'Doctas iam nunc eat, inquit, Athenas,' *let him forthwith go (says one) to learned Athens,* Ov. *Her.* ii. 83.

8) Apposition to à town without Attribute is generally with **in**: 'In urbe Antiochia.'

But when an Attribute is added, the name of the town usually precedes: 'Antiochiae, celebri quondam et copiosa urbe,' *at Antioch, a once populous and wealthy city,* C. *Arch.* 3. 'Neapoli in celeberrimo oppido,' *at Naples, a very populous town.* So, 'Syracusas in urbem florentissimam,' *to Syracuse, a very flourishing city,* C.

9) Domi, domum, admit the epithets **meus, tuus, suus, alienus,** also a Genitive of the Possessor:

'Nonne mavis sine periculo domi tuae esse quam cum periculo alienae?' *would you not rather be at your own house without peril than with peril at another's?* C. *Fam.* iv. 7. 'Clodius deprehensus est domi Caesaris,' *Clodius was caught at Caesar's house,* C. *Att.* i. 12. 'Alius alium domos suas invitant,' *they invite each other to their houses,* Sall. *Iug.* 66.

10) Prepositions are much used with names of towns:

In Epheso est; in Ephesum abii; 'has litteras a Brundisio dedi,' C. So ad, apud.

And with **humus, domus, rus**: 'Alcibiades educatus est in domo Periclis,' *Alcibiades was brought up in the house of Pericles,* Nep. *Alc.* 2.

Usque is joined to names of places with or without Prepositions: 'Ab Aethiopia est usque haec,' *she is as far as from Ethiopia,* Ter. 'Usque Ennam profecti sunt,' *they went as far as Enna,* C.

156 *H)* The Ablative of Direction of Motion has no Preposition: 'Ire Via Sacra,' *to walk on the Sacred Road,* Hor.; 'ingredi urbem porta Esquilina,' *to enter the city by the Esquiline gate.* L.

iv. (III) Ablative Proper.

A) The Ablative of Place Whence, if a town or small island, or domus, rus, humus, militia, is used without Preposition:

Redire Roma, Athenis, Epheso, Delphis, Tibure, Gadibus, militia, domo, rure, &c., *to return from Rome, Athens,* &c.

But Prepositions (ab, de, ex) may be employed.

1) The Ablative of Place Whence is used in dating letters:
'Litteras dederam Epheso pridie,' *I wrote yesterday from Ephesus,* C. 'Ego unas Capua litteras dedi,' *I have written once from Capua,* C.

2) Native place is sometimes expressed by this Ablative:
Cn. Magius Cremona, *Gnaeus Magius of Cremona,* Caes. *B. C.* i. 24; but more usually by an Adjective (Cremonensis); sometimes by ab: 'Turnus Herdonius ab Aricia,' L. i. 50. 'Pastor ab Amphryso,' V. *G.* iii. 2.

3) The name of the tribe is thus appended in inscriptions to that of a Roman citizen:
'Ser. Sulpicius Q. F. Lemonia Rufus,' *Servius Sulpicius Rufus, son of Quintus, of the Lemonian tribe.*

B) The Ablative of that From which Separation occurs depends on many Words either without or with a Preposition.

158

1) The usage of such Words must be carefully distinguished. Some either omit or take the Preposition in Prose:
Arcere, cedere, exsulare, movere, pellere, prohibere, solvere, summovere, removere: procul, alienus, &c.
Others prefer a Preposition (chiefly ab) in prose, but may omit it in poetry:
Alienare, discedere, disiungere, dispellere, distare, divellere, repellere, secernere, segregare, separare, &c. Horace writes 'alium sapiente bonoque,' *Epist.* i. 16. 20. On discrepo, differo, &c., see § 135.

2) Verbs compounded with ab, de, ex, can take an Abl. by means of the Preposition:
'Detrudit navis scopulo,' Verg.
But most of them, in prose, repeat their Preposition or add another:
Excedere ex urbe; a Roma abesse; ex equo desilire; a loco deicere.

3) Abstinere, *to abstain,* varies its construction thus:
Abstinere vino, &c., abstinere se vino, &c., abstinere a vino, &c.

4) Observe the legal phrases: Abdicare se magistratu, *to resign office,* movere senatu, tribu, &c., *to expel from the senate, the tribe,* &c. (an act of the Censor); 'interdicere aqua et igni,' *to banish by excluding from fire and water.*
Supersedere, *to dispense with,* generally takes an Ablative.

C) The Ablative of Origin is only a special instance of the Ablative of Separation.

159

1) It is joined to Verbs and Participles expressing or implying *descent, origination*, &c.   Such are

Nasci, oriri, gigni, with their compounds: and the Participles, editus, creatus, cretus, genitus, natus, prognatus, oriundus, ortus, satus (*born, sprung, descended*):

Nasci familia nobili; claris maioribus ortus; patre genitus illustri; sate sanguine divum, &c.

2) The usage of these words must be noted :

Most admit Prepositions (ab, de, ex), and some prefer this construction even in poetry :

'Prisco natus ab Inacho,' Hor. *C.* ii. 3. 21. 'Ilia cum Lauso de Numitore sati,' Ov. *F.* iv. 54. 'Edita de magno flumine nympha fui,' Ov. *Her.* v. 10.

160 *D*) The Ablative of the Thing Compared may be referred to the idea of Origin (or, as some think, to that of Respect).

1) It is attached to Comparative Adjectives or Adverbs in place of quam (*than*) with the Nominative or Accusative.

'Nihil est amabilius virtute,' *nothing is more amiable than virtue*, C. 'Lacrima nihil citius arescit,' *nothing dries sooner than a tear*, C. *Inv.* i. 55.

'Puto mortem dedecore leviorem,' *I think death easier than disgrace.*

2) In comparing the other Cases quam must be used :

'Nulli flebilior quam tibi, Vergili,' *to none more a cause of weeping than to thee, Vergilius*, Hor. *C.* i. 24. 10. 'Flagiti magis nos pudet quam erroris,' *we are more ashamed of the crime than of the blunder*, C. And often for perspicuity : 'Segnius homines bona quam mala sentiunt,' *men feel goods less keenly than evils*, L. xxx. 21. 'Brutum non minus amo quam tu, paene dixi quam te,' *I love Brutus not less than thou, I had almost said, than thee*, C. *Att.* v. 20. But poets do not always attend to this : 'Cur olivum sanguine viperino cautius vitat?' *Why does he shun oil more cautiously than viper's blood?* Hor. *C.* i. 8. 9. 'Ego possideo plus Pallante et Licinis,' Iuv. i. 108.

3) If the Comparative itself is in the Genitive or Dative, quam with a clause generally follows :

'Haec sunt verba Varronis doctioris quam fuit Claudius,' *these are the words of Varro, a more learned man than Claudius was*, Gell. x. 1.

4) The Ablatives aequo, iusto, dicto, solito, spe, opinione, necessario, follow Comparatives :

'Flagrantior aequo non debet dolor esse viri,' *a man's grief ought not to be more violent than is right*, Iuv. xiii. 11. 'Caesar opinione omnium celerius venturus est,' *Caesar will arrive sooner than is generally expected*, C. *Fam.* xiv. 23.

This Ablative elegantly falls out:

'Liberius vivebat (i.e. iusto),' *he lived too freely*, Nep. *Th.* 2. 'So, 'Res graviores' (i.e. solito), *matters of unusual importance.*

On quam after Comparatives, see § 76.

5) Inferior takes Ablative, and, in the Silver age, Dative:

Sapientia omnia inferiora virtute ducit,' *wisdom deems all things inferior to virtue*, C. *T. D.* iv. 26. 'Padus est nulli amnium claritate inferior,' *the Po is inferior to no river in clearness*, Pl. *N. H.* iii. 16.

6) The Prepositions ante, praeter, supra, prae, are used in Comparison:

'Pygmalion scelere ante alios immanior omnis,' *Pygmalion more monstrous in wickedness than* (lit. *before*) *all others*, Verg. *Aen.* i. 347. 'Crux praeter ceteras altior,' *a cross higher than* (lit. *beyond*) *the rest*, Suet. *Galb.* 9.

Obs. On several Ablatives with one Verb, see M. *Lucr.* i. 183. Madvig cites C. *Brut.* 91 : 'Menippus meo iudicio tota Asia illis temporibus disertissimus erat.'

v. Ablative Absolute.

1) The construction called Ablative Absolute (Ablativus Convenientiae) occurs when the Ablative of a Substantive or Pronoun takes for its adjunct another Ablative, which is either a Participle or an Adjective or a Substantive or (rarely) a Pronoun. Such an expression is equivalent to a Clause, often of Time:

Imperante Augusto, *when Augustus was emperor*; Caesare occiso, *when Caesar had been slain*; vivo patre, *while my father is* (*was*) *alive*; Camillo duce, *when Camillus is* (*was*) *commander*; Caninio consule, *in the consulship of Caninius*; hac iuventute, *when our young men are of this character.*

But the clause may express a condition, a concession, a cause, &c., according to the context. Thus te invito may mean, in various places, *if you are unwilling; though you are unwilling; since you are unwilling; without your consent.*

2) The Absolute Participle is often equivalent to the Gerund or Ablative of Manner:

'Tarquinius Turnum oblato falso crimine oppressit,' *Tarquinius crushed Turnus by imputing a false charge*, L. i. 51. 'Aruns Tarquinius et Tullia minor iunguntur nuptiis, magis non prohibente Servio quam approbante,' *Aruns Tarquinius and Tullia the younger marry rather without the opposition than with the approbation of Servius*, L. i. 56.

3) An Impersonal Participle is sometimes absolute:

Mihi, errato, nulla venia; recte facto, exigua laus proponitur,' *to me, if I blunder, no indulgence; if I succeed, small credit is offered*, C *d. L. Agr.* ii. 2. Errato = si erratum erit a me; recte facto = si recte factum erit a me.

Sometimes a Clause is absolute with a Participle:

'Excepto quod non simul esses, cetera laetus,' *cheerful in all respects, save that you are not with me*, Hor. *Epist.* i. 10. 50.

See § 237–240.

I. (*Instr. Abl.*) *A*) (*Causal.*) 'Lollius, aetate et morbo impeditus, ad testimonium dicendum venire non potuit,' C. *Verr.* iii. 25. 'Noli putare, pigritia me facere quod non mea manu scribam,' C. *Att.* xvi. 15. 'Consul dictatorem comitiorum causa T. Manlium Torquatum ex auctoritate senatus dixit,' L. vii. 26. 'Has familias honestatis amplitudinisque gratia nomino,' C. *p. S. Rosc.* 6. 'Demosthenes corona aurea donatus est virtutis ergo,' C. *O. G. Or.* 7. 'Senatus supplicationes consulum nomine decrevit,' L. iii. 63. 'Vestra magis hoc causa volebam quam mea,' C. *d. Or.* i. 35. 'Ad eum ipsius rogatu accersituque veneram,' C. *Lael.* 4.

B) *C*) (*Instr. Agent.*) 'Cornibus tauri, apri dentibus, morsu leones se tutantur,' C. *N. D.* ii. 50. 'Etesiarum flatu nimii temperantur calores,' C. *N. D.* ii. 53. 'Illud tibi affirmo, fore ut absens a multis, cum redieris ab omnibus collaudere,' C. *Fam.* i. 7. 'Nisi iam factum est aliquid per Flaccum, fiet a me,' C. *Fam.* iii. 11. 'Ingenium placida mollimur ab arte,' Ov. *A. A.* iii. 545.

D) (*Price.*) 'Plinius commentarios suos vendere poterat quadringentis milibus nummum,' Plin. *Ep.* iii. 5. 'Dareus mille talentis percussorem Alexandri emere voluit,' Curt. iv. 1. 'Aurea nunc vere sunt saecula; plurimus auro venit honos,' Prop. iii. 12. 'Mercatur tris libros nihilo minore pretio quam quod erat petitum pro omnibus,' Gell. i. 19. 'Seius in caritate annonae asse modium populo dedit,' C. *Off.* ii. 58. 'Vix drachmis opsonatum est decem,' Ter. *An.* ii. 6. 'Sextante sal et Romae et per totam Italiam erat,' L. xxix. 37. 'Cum esset frumentum sestertiis binis aut trinis, quibusvis locis provinciae duodenos sestertios exegisti,' C. *Verr.* ii. 3. 84. 'Aristidis, Thebani pictoris, unam tabulam centum talentis rex Attalus licitatus est,' Pl. *N. H.* vii. 37. 'Multo sanguine ac vulneribus ea Poenis victoria stetit,' L. xxiii. 30. 'Denis in diem assibus anima et corpus aestimantur,' Tac. *An.* i. 17. 'Notavit aliquos, quod pecunias levioribus usuris mutuatas graviori fenore collocassent,' Suet. *Aug.* 33. 'Triginta milibus Coelius habitat,' C. *p. Coel.* 7. 'Parvo fames constat, magno fastidium,' Sen. *Ep.* 17. 'Ei mandasti negotium, cui expediret, illud venire quam plurimo,' C. *Fam.* vii. 2. 'Ambulatiuncula dimidio pluris constabit,' C. *Att.* xiii. 29. 'Ego quaero, cur civis optimi bona tantulo venierint,' C. *p. S. R.* 45. 'Quanti emi potest? Minimo,' Plaut. 'Istuc verbum vile est viginti minis,' Plaut. *Most.* i. 3. 139. 'Clodii insula venalis est decem milibus,' C. *p. Coel.* 7. 'Quod non opus est asse carum est,' Sen. *Ep.* 94. 'Nefas duco victrice patria victam mutare,' L. v. 30. 'Tellus Chaoniam pingui glandem mutavit arista,' Verg. *G.* i. 18. 'Tauro mutatus membra rebello,' Ov. *M.* ix. 81. 'Fortuna praesens superbos vertere funeribus triumphos,' Hor. *Od.* i. 35. 4.

E) (*Matter.*) 'Germani Mercurium colunt, cui certis diebus humanis quoque hostiis litare fas habent,' Tac. *G.* 9. 'Romulum lacte, non vino libasse, indicio sunt sacra ab eo instituta,' Pl. *N. H.* xiv. 12. 'Hoc etiam maiore es malo mactandus, quod non solum facto tuo, sed etiam exemplo rempublicam vulnerasti,' C. *c. Vatin.* 15. 'Admiratione afficiuntur ii, qui anteire ceteros virtute putantur,' C. *Off.* ii. 10. 'Caesar Germanos, qui trans Rhenum incolunt, primus Romanorum maximis affecit cladibus,' Suet. *Caes.* 25. 'Summa difficultate rei frumentariae afficiebatur Caesaris exercitus, tenuitate Boiorum, indiligentia Aeduorum, incendiis aedificiorum,' Caes. *B. G.* vii. 17. 'Virgo inficitur teneras tota rubore genas,' Tibull. iii. 4. 31. 'Natura oculos tenuissimis membranis vestivit et saepsit,' C. *N. D.* ii. 57. 'Hippias gloriatus est pallium, quo amictus, soccos quibus indutus esset, se manu sua confecisse,' C. *d. Or.* iii. 32. 'Bonis artibus aetas puerilis ad humanitatem informari solet,' C. *p. Arch.* 3. 'Caesar Corfinium oppidum vallo castellisque circumvenire instituit,' Caes. *B. G.* i. 18. 'Indignum est in ea civitate, quae legibus tenetur, discedi a legibus,' C. *p. Clu.* 53. 'Quid de Tulliola mea fiet?' C. *Fam.* xiv. 4. 'Quid fecisti scipione?' Plaut. *Cas.* v. 4. 18. 'Quaero, si, qui velint vendere, non fuerint, quid pecunia fiet?' C. *d. L. Agr.* ii. 27. 'Delicto dolere, correctione gaudere oportet,' C. *Lael.* 24. 'Ut adulescentibus bona indole praeditis sapientes senes delectantur, sic adulescentes senum praeceptis gaudent, quibus ad virtutum studia ducuntur,' C. *Cat. M.* 8. 'Duobus vitiis, ava-

F. The Genitive Case.

i. The GENITIVE in Latin has for its main function to define or qualify a Noun on which it depends:

Pater pueri, *the father of the boy*; amor virtutis, *love of virtue*; pars militum, *part of the troops.*

ii. The uses of the Genitive may be considered as twofold:

A) SUBJECTIVE, when a predication is implied of which the Genitive word is Subject: hominum timor, *men's fear* (homines timent aliquid).

ritia et luxuria, Romana civitas laborabat,' L. xxxiv. 4. ' Nemo potest aut corporis firmitate aut fortunae stabilitate confidere,' C. *T. D.* v. 5. 14. ' Meis consiliis, monitis, studiis, auctionibus nituntur,' C. *Fam.* v. 8. 'Parvo est natura contenta,' C. *Fin.* ii. 28. 'Varus est homo summa religione et summa auctoritate praeditus,' C. *p. Clu.* 19. ' Non segetibus solum et pratis et vineis et arbustis res rusticae laetae sunt, sed etiam hortis et pomariis; tum pecudum pastu, apium examinibus, florum omnium varietate,' C. *Cat. M.* 15. ' Cimon Thasios, opulentia fretos, suo adventu fregit,' Nep. *Cim.* 2. ' I, decus Ausoniae, quo fas est ire superbas virtute et factis animas,' Sil. x. 573. 'Exclusus ab Antiochia Dolabella, nulla alia confisus urbe, Laodiceam se contulit,' C. *Fam.* xii. 15. ' Curionis patrio fuit instituto puro sermone assuefacta domus,' C. *Brut.* 59. 'Excellentium civium virtus imitatione, non invidia, digna est,' C. *Phil.* xiv. 6. ' Quam multi indigni luce sunt, et tamen dies oritur,' Sen. *Ben.* i. 1. ' Descendam magnorum haud umquam indignus avorum,' Verg. *Aen.* xii. 649. ' Haud equidem tali me dignor honore,' Verg. *Aen.* i. 535. ' Hi apud maiores nostros tali honore dignati sunt,' C. *Inv.* ii. 39. ' Nihil opus est simulatione et fallaciis,' C. *d. Or.* ii. 47. 'Auctoritate tua nobis opus est et consilio et etiam gratia,' C. *Fam.* ix. 25. 'Viginti iam usus est filio argenti minis,' Plaut. *Asin.* i. 1. ' An cuiquam est homini usus se ut cruciet,' Ter. *Haut.* i. 1. ' Ubi summus imperator non adest, citius quod non facto est usus fit quam quod facto est opus,' Plaut. *Am.* i. 3. ' Si quid, quod opus fuerit, Appio facies, ponito me in gratia,' C. *Fam.* viii. 6. 'Verres multa sibi opus esse aiebat, multa canibus suis, quos circa se haberet,' C. *Verr.* i. 48. ' Magna Helotarum multitudo agros Lacedaemoniorum colit, servorumque munere fungitur,' Nep. *Paus.* 3. ' Crassus, cum cognomine dives tum copiis, functus est aedilicio maximo munere,' C. *Off.* ii. 16. ' Hannibal Sosilo Lacedaemonio litterarum Graecarum usus est doctore,' N. xxiii. 13. 'Cum Phalerico portu neque magno neque bono Athenienses uterentur, Themistoclis consilio triplex Piraeei portus constitutus est,' Nep. *Them.* 6. ' Id est cuiusque proprium, quo quisque fruitur atque utitur,' C. *Fam.* vii. 30. ' Orgetorix Helvetiis persuasit, perfacile esse, cum virtute omnibus praestarent, totius Galliae imperio potiri,' Caes. *B. G.* i. 2. ' Numidae plerumque lacte et ferina carne vescebantur,' Sal. *Iug.* 89. ' Ad agrum fruendum etiam invitat senectus,' C. *Cat. M.* 16. ' Operam abutitur,' Ter. *An. Prol.* 5.

' Deus bonis omnibus explevit mundum,' C. *Univ.* 3. ' Crotoniatae quondam templum Iunonis egregiis picturis locupletare voluerunt,' C. *Inv.* ii. 1. ' Satia te sanguine quem sitiisti,' Iust. i. 8. ' Te autem quibus mendaciis homines levissimi onerarunt,' C. *Fam.* iii. 10. ' Abundarunt semper auro regna Asiae,' L. xxxv. 46. ' Metallis plumbi, ferri, aeris, argenti, auri tota ferme Hispania scatet,' Pl. *N. H.* iii. 3. ' Democritus dicitur oculis se privasse,' C. *Fin.* v. 29. ' Gravius est spoliari fortunis quam non augeri dignitate,' C. *p. Planc.* 22. ' Murus defensoribus nudatus est,' Caes. *B. G.* ii. 6. ' Non ante abscessum est quam castris exuerunt hostem,' L. xxix. 2. ' Omnium rerum natura cognita, levamur superstitione, liberamur mortis metu,' C. *Fin.* i. 19. ' Cotidie nos ipsa natura admonet, quam paucis, quam parvis rebus egeat, quam vilibus,' C. *T. D.* v. 35. ' Carere hoc significat, egere eo quod habere velis. Regno carebat Tarquinius, cum regno esset expulsus,' C. *T. D.* i. 36. ' Animi, quo maior est in eis praestantia, eo maiore indigent diligentia,' C. *T. D.* iv. 27. ' Virtus plurimae exercitationis indiget,'

B) OBJECTIVE; when a predication is implied of which the Genitive word is Object: timor hominum, *fear of men* (aliquis timet homines).

    a) One word may have both Genitives dependent on it:

      Hominum timor mortis, *men's fear of death*; Ciceronis defensio Gabinii, *Cicero's defence of Gabinius.*

    Among words capable of taking this double Genitive are:

      Amor, desiderium, iniuria, miseratio, obsequium, odium, studium, &c.

    b) One Genitive may depend on another:

      Africani sororis filius, *Africanus's sister's son.*

C. *Fin.* iii. 15. 'Gravitas morbi facit ut medicinae egeamus,' C. *Fam.* ix. 3. 'Plinius plenus annis, plenus honoribus obiit,' Plin. *Ep.* ii. 1. 'Habes epistulam plenam festinationis et pulveris,' C. *Att.* v. 14. 'Amor et melle et felle est fecundissimus,' Plaut. *Cist.* i. 1. 'Dives agris, dives positis in fenore nummis,' Hor. *in Pis.* 42. 'Sum dives pecoris, nivei sum lactis abundans,' Verg. *B.* ii. 20. 'Consules praeda ingenti compotem exercitum reducunt,' L. iii. 70. 'Numquam animus cogitatione et motu vacuus esse potest,' C. *Div.* ii. 128. 'Mamertini soli vacui, expertes, soluti ac liberi fuerunt ab omni sumptu, molestia, munere,' C. *Verr.* ii. 4. 10. 'Plerique patria, sed omnes fama atque fortunis expertes sumus,' Sall. *Cat.* 33. 'Caesari tradita urbs est nuda praesidio, referta copiis,' C. *Att.* vii. 13. 'Decius, Macti virtute, inquit, milites Romani, este,' L. vii. 36. 'Nunc cassum lumine lugent,' V. *Aen.* ii. 85.

II. (*Locative Abl.*) *A*) (*Respect.*) 'Agesilaus nomine non potestate fuit rex.' Nep. *Ag.* 1. 'Cn. Pompeius fuit forma excellens, innocentia eximius, sanctitate praecipuus, eloquentia medius,' Vell. ii. 29. 'Uri sunt magnitudine paulo infra elephantos, specie et colore et figura tauri,' Caes. *B. G.* vi. 28. 'Q. Maximum Cato adulescens colere coepit non admodum grandem natu, sed tamen iam aetate provectum,' C. *Cat. M.* 4. 'Persae mille numero navium classem ad Delum appulerunt,' C. *Verr.* i. 18. 'Cum illius temporis mihi venit in mentem, quo die mihi dicendum sit, non solum commoveor animo, sed etiam toto corpore perhorresco,' C. *in Caecil.* 13. 'Medius Polluce et Castore ponar,' Ov. *Am.* ii. 16. 13. 'Verres pretio, non aequitate iura describebat,' C. *Verr.* v. 11.

B) (*Measure.*) 'Messalla consul est egregius; ille alter uno vitio minus vitiosus,' C. *Att.* i. 14. 'Aesculapi templum quinque milibus passuum ab Epidauro distat,' L. xxv. 28. 'Belgae ad castra Caesaris omnibus copiis contenderunt, et ab milibus passuum minus duobus castra posuerunt,' Caes. *B. G.* ii. 7. 'Surculos demittito ita ut sex digitis de arbore exstent,' Columella, xxvi. 4. 'Numa Pompilius annis permultis ante fuit quam Pythagoras,' C. *d. Or.* ii. 37. 'Tribunus anno post fuit Crassus,' C. *Br.* 60. 'Tanto Pompeius superiores duces vicerat gloria quanto Caesar omnibus praestitit,' C. *p. Deiot.* 4. 'Meo iudicio multo stare malo quam omnium reliquorum,' C. *Att.* xii. 2. 'Hibernia dimidio minor est quam Britannia,' Caes. *B. G.* v. 13. 'Nimio plus quam velim nostrorum ingenia sunt mobilia,' L. ii. 37. 'Quinquiens tanto amplius Verres quam quantum in cellam sumere licitum erat civitatibus imperavit,' C. *Verr.* iii. 97. 'Alcibiades fuit omnium aetatis suae multo formosissimus,' Nep. *Alc.* 1.

C) (*Manner.*) 'Iniuria fit duobus modis, aut vi aut fraude,' C. *Off.* i. 13. 'Pace advenio, et pacem ad vos affero,' Plaut. *Am.* Prol. 32. 'Quod exemplo fit, id etiam iure fieri putant,' C. *Fam.* iv. 3. 'Arminius equo conlustrans cuncta, ut quosque advectus erat, reciperatam libertatem ostentabat,' Tac. *Ann.* ii. 45. 'Galli urbem cum clamore et impetu invadunt; patentis passim domos adeunt,' Fl. i. 13. 'Cur Pythagoras tantas regiones barbarorum pedibus obiit?' Cic. *Fin.* v. 29. 'Quantopere movemur, cum pie, cum amice, cum magno animo aliquid factum cognoscimus,' C. *Fin.* v. 22. 'Cultus deorum est optimus, ut eos semper pura integra incorrupta et mente et voce veneremur,' C. *N. D.* ii. 28. 'Parthi Euphratem transierunt cunctis fere copiis,' C. *Att.* v. 18. 'Scipio profectus in Siciliam est triginta navibus longis,' L. xxviii. 46. 'Mihi litterae redditae sunt, Pacorum cum permagno equitatu Parthico transisse Euphraten,' C. *Fam.* xv. 1. 'Magna

iii. *A*) SUBJECTIVE GENITIVE (Possessive ; Descriptive ; Partitive).

> I. Genitivus Auctoris et Possessoris.
> II. Genitivus Descriptionis.
> III. Genitivus Qualitatis.
> IV. Genitivus Rei Distributae et Demensae; with other
> Partitive Constructions.

Note 1. As Latin has an Ablative, its Genitive is more restricted
than the Greek ; but poets imitate the freedom of the Greek Gen.
In some instances the Abl. and Gen. concur (as in constructions
of Quality, Price, Matter); and Prepositional phrases are substituted

---

cum cura atque diligentia scripsit,' C. *Inv.* i. 39. ' Erit tum consul Hortensius
cum summo imperio et potestate,' C. *Verr.* i. 13. ' In summo apud Graecos
honore geometria fuit,' C. *T. D.* i. 2. ' Plancus in eam urbem rediit armis, e qua
excesserat legibus,' C. *Phil.* xiii. 12.

D) (*Condition.*) Optimo iure sunt ea praedia, quae optima condicione sunt,'
C. *d. L. Agr.* iii. 2. ' Auspicia nunc a Romanis auguribus ignorantur ; bona hoc
tua venia dixerim ; a Cilicibus tenentur,' C. *Div.* i. 15. ' Isocratis gloriam nemo,
meo quidem iudicio, est postea consecutus,' C. *Br.* 8. ' Meo iure te hoc beneficium
rogo ; nihil enim non tua causa feci,' C. *Att.* xiv. 13. ' Iam mater rure rediit ?
Responde mihi.—Sua quidem salute ac familiae maxuma,' Plaut. *Merc.* iv. 5. 9.

E) (*Quality.*) ' Fuit quidam summo ingenio vir, Zeno, cuius inventorum aemuli
Stoici nominantur,' C. *p. Mur.* 29. ' Iphicrates fuit et animo magno et corpore,
imperatoriaque forma,' Nep. *Iph.* 3. ' Erat apud Heium sacrarium, in quo signa
pulcherrima quattuor, summo artificio, summa nobilitate,' C. *Verr.* iv. 2.
' Magno timore sum ; sed bene speramus,' C. *Att.* v. 14.

F) (*Time.*) ' Nemo mortalium omnibus horis sapit,' Pl. *N. H.* vii. 40. ' Excur-
remus mense Septembri, ut Ianuario revertamur,' C. *Att.* i. 1. ' Hannibal, imperator factus, proximo triennio omnis gentes Hispaniae subegit,' Nep. *H.m.* 3.
' Abeunt hirundines hibernis mensibus,' Pl. *H. N.* 24. ' Septimo ferme anno
Caesar morabatur in Galliis, cum Iulia, uxor Pompeii Magni, decessit,' Vell. ii. 47.
' Erat consuetudo, ut quem ordinem interrogandi sententias consul Kalendis
Ianuariis instituisset, eum toto anno conservaret, Suet. *Caes.* 21. ' Claudius
neminem ultra mensem, quo obiit, consulem designavit,' Suet. *Claud.* 46. ' Brutus
consul collegam sibi comitiis centuriatis creavit P. Valerium,' L. ii. 2. ' Urbes
Africae post M. Atilium Regulum annis prope quinquaginta nullum Romanum
exercitum viderant,' L. xxix. 28. ' Nuntius hic decem horis nocturnis sex et quinquaginta milia passuum cisiis pervolavit,' C. *p. S. Rosc.* 7. ' Ecce autem repente, his
diebus paucis, eadem illa vetera consilia pecunia maiore repetuntur,' C. *Verr.* i. 6.
' Epistulam de nocte daturus eram, sicut dedi ; nam eam vesperi scripseram,' C.
Att. viii. 6. ' Lysander Atheniensis in Peloponnesios sexto et vicesimo anno
bellum gerentis confecit,' N. *Lys.* 1. ' Caesar compluris equitum turmas eo de media
nocte misit,' Caes. *B. G.* vii. 45. ' Fac ut naviges de mense Decembri (*before the
end of*),' C. *Qu. Fr.* ii. 1. ' De tertia vigilia castra movit,' Caes. *B. G.* i. 63.
' Artes in omni aetate cultae mirificos efferunt fructus,' C. *Cat. M.* 3. ' Nummos
tibi reponam in hoc triduo,' Plaut. *Pers.* i. 1. 33. ' Fere in diebus paucis quibus
haec acta sunt Chrysis vicina haec moritur,' Ter. *An.* 1. 1. ' Ego si semper haberem cui
darem litteras, vel ternas in hora darem,' C. *Fam.* xv. 16. ' Testamentum Augusti
ante annum et quattuor mensis quam decesserat factum est,' Suet. *Aug.* 101.
' Livius docuit anno ipso ante quam natus est Ennius,' C. *Brut.* 18. ' Aristides
decessit fere post annum quartum quam Themistocles Athenis erat expulsus,' N.
Ar. 3. ' Aristides sexto fere anno postquam erat expulsus, in patriam restitutus
est,' N. *Ar.* 1. ' Undecimo die postquam a te discesseram, hoc litterularum
exaravi,' C. *Att.* xii. 1. ' Dictator die octavo quam creatus erat, magistratu se
abdicavit,' L. iv. 47. ' Anno trecentesimo altero quam condita Roma erat,
iterum mutatur forma civitatis,' L. iii. 33. ' Andricus postridie ad me venit quam
exspectaram,' C. *Fam.* xvi. 14. ' Collegam triduo cum has dabam litteras exspecta-

for the Gen.: thus, una de multis, una e multis, una multarum, are equivalent.

Hence in French '*de*' is used as a Gen. and Abl. Preposition; in Italian, '*di*' is the Gen., '*da*' the Abl. Preposition.

Note 2. This Genitive is in the nature of an Attribute. Thus it is the same thing to say, 'Sullanus exercitus' or 'Sullae exercitus,' 'flamen Martialis' or 'flamen Martis.'

(Even for the Objective Gen. Adjectives are used: 'Timor externus' for 'timor exterorum.' And Possessive Pronouns: 'Tua fiducia,' *in reliance on you*, C. *Verr.* v. 58. 'Habenda ratio non sua solum, sed etiam aliorum,' *a man should take account not of himself alone but also of others*, C. *Off.* i. 39.)

'*Native of a place*' is usually expressed by an Adjective derived from the place: as, 'Dionysius Halicarnasseus,' for Dionysius Halicarnassi natus, *Dionysius of Halicarnassus*.

---

bam,' C. *Fam.* x. 23. 'Ipse, ut spero, octo diebus quibus has litteras dabam, cum Lepidi copiis me coniungam,' C. *Fam.* x. 18.

G) (*Place Where.*) 'Conon plurimum Cypri vixit, Iphicrates in Thracia, Timotheus Lesbi, Chares in Sigeo,' Nep. *Chab.* i. 3. 'Castra Gallorum opportunis locis erant posita,' Caes. *B. G.* vii. 69. 'Hi vagantur laeti atque erecti passim toto foro,' C. *p. Font.* 11. 'Ab Anco Marcio carcer ad terrorem increscentis audaciae media urbe imminens foro aedificatur,' L. i. 33. 'Ut Romae consules, sic Karthagine quotannis annui bini reges creabantur,' Nep. *Hann.* 7. 'Per eosdem dies quibus haec illi consultabant, consilium de iis Carthagini erat,' L. xxviii. 26. 'Dionysius, cum fanum Proserpinae Locris expilavisset, navigabat Syracusas,' C. *N. D.* iii. 34. 'Fuit Arganthonius quidam Gadibus qui octoginta regnavit annos,' C. *Cat. M.* 69. 'Scipio, L. Marcio Tarracone, M. Silano Karthagine Nova ad praesidium Hispaniae relictis, in Africam traiecit,' L. xxvjii. 17. 'Neapoli in celeberrimo oppido etiam senatores cum mitella saepe vidimus,' C. *p. Rab.* 10. 'A Romanis nihil belli domique nisi auspicato gerebatur,' L. i. 36. 'Manlius Titum filium ruri habitare iussit,' L. vii. 5. 'Manlius rure iuventam egit,' Pl. *N. H.* viii. 46. 'Nihil domi, nihil militiae per magistratus geritur sine augurum auctoritate,' C. *Leg.* ii. 12. 'Cadmus spargit humi iussos, mortalia semina, dentis, O. *Met.* iii. 105. 'Antonius intimus erat Clodio, cuius etiam domi quiddam molitus est,' C. *Phil.* ii. 19.

H) (*Place by Which.*) Demonstrabo iter; Aurelia via profectus est,' C. *Cat.* ii. 4. 'Cur non sancitis, ne vicinus patricio sit plebeius nec eodem itinere eat, ne idem convivium ineat, ne in foro eodem consistat?' L. iv. 4. 'Iam consul via Lavicana ad fanum Quietis erat,' L. iv. 41. 'Lupus Esquilina porta ingressus cum in forum decucurrisset, Tusco vico atque inde Germalo per portam Capenam prope intactus evasit,' L. xxxiii. 26. 'Legiones victrices Penninis Cottianisque Alpibus, pars monte Graio, traducuntur,' Tac. *H.* iv. 68.

III. (*Abl. Proper.*) A) (*Place Whence.*) 'Roma acceperam litteras, Milonem queri per litteras iniuriam meam,' C. *Att.* v. 8. 'Auximo Caesar progressus omnem agrum Picenum percurrit,' Caes. *B. G.* i. 15. 'Maiores nostri Capua magistratus, senatum, omnia denique insignia rei publicae sustulerunt, neque aliud quicquam nisi inane nomen Capuae reliquerunt,' C. *d. L. Agr.* i. 6. 'Dionysius Platonem Athenis accessivit,' N. *Di.* 3. 'Caesaris milites cogebantur Corcyra atque Acarnania pabulum supportare,' Caes. *B. C.* iii. 58. 'Princeps Academiae Philo cum Atheniensium optimatibus Mithridatico bello domo profugit, Romamque venit,' C. *Brut.* 89. 'Video rure redeuntem senem,' Ter. *Eun.* v. 5. 'Vix oculos attollit humo,' Ov. *Met.* iii. 448.

B) (*Separation.*) 'Censores omnis, quos senatu moverunt quibusque equos ademerunt, aerarios fecerunt et tribu moverunt,' L. xlii. 10. 'Hostis Antonius iudicatus Italia cesserat,' N. *Att.* 9. 'Apud Germanos quemcunque mortalium arcere tecto nefas habetur,' Tac. *G.* 21. 'Adolescentia a libidinibus arcenda est,' C. *Off.* i. 34. 'Avocat a rebus gerendis senectus,' C. *Cat. M.* 5. 'Di, talem terris avertite pestem,' Verg. *Aen.* iii. 620. 'Nisi is Antonium ab urbe avertisset, perissent omnia,' C. *ad. Br.* 3. 'Romano bello Fortuna Alexandrum abstinuit,' Liv. viii. 24. 'Tiberius et Augustus publico abstinuere, inferius

165
Gene-
tivus
Auctoris
et Pos-
sessoris.

I. 1) The Possessive Genitive expresses that which stands
in the relation of Author, Origin, or Proprietor to the Noun
on which it depends :

Oratio Ciceronis, leges civitatis, fortitudo militum, rex Ponti,
domus Periclis, &c. It may be rendered in English by
the Possessive Case in '*s*, or by the Preposition *of* :

Philippi filius, *Philip's son*, or *son of Philip*.

2) The Dativus Commodi is often substituted for it :

'In Palatio prima urbi fundamenta ieci,' *I laid the first
foundations of* (*for*) *my city on the Palatine hill*, L. i. 12.
'Natura tu illi pater es, consiliis ego,' *you are his sire by
nature, I by counsels*, Ter. *Ad.* i. 2. 46.

So advocatus, praefectus, legatus (properly Participles)
sometimes govern Gen., sometimes Dat. Likewise affinis,

---

maiestate sua rati,' Tac. *Ann.* iii. 3. 'Quale beneficium est, quod te abstinueris a
nefario scelere?' C. *Phil.* ii. 3. 'Alexander, cum interemisset Clitum, vix a se manus
abstinuit; tanta vis fuit poenitendi,' C. *T. D.* iv. 37. 'Abhorrent moribus
nostris,' Curt. vii. 8. 'Nostra aetas abhorret a castris, praesertim civilibus,' C.
Att. xiv. 19. 'Virtus numquam ulla vi labefactari potest, numquam demoveri loco,'
C. *Phil.* iv. 5. 'Miserum est exturbari fortunis omnibus,' C. *p. Quinct.* 31.
'Augur potest decernere ut magistratu se abdicent consules,' C. *Leg.* ii. 12.
'Hominis natura a reliquis animantibus differt,' C. *Off.* i. 27. 'Quindecim
milibus passuum Arabicus sinus distat ab Aegyptio mari,' Pl. *H. N.* ii. 68. 'Exculta
hominum vita distat a cultu et victu bestiarum,' C. *Off.* ii. 4. 'Temeritas a
sapientia dissidet plurimum,' C. *Off.* ii. 2. 'Alienum est magno viro, quod
alteri praeceperit, id ipsum facere non posse,' C. *ad. Br.* 9.

C) (*Origin.*) 'Nati sunt Carthagine, sed oriundi a Syracusis,' L. xxiv. 6. 'Ex
me is natus est,' Ter. *Haut.* v. 4. 'A parentibus, id quod necesse erat, parvus
sum creatus; a vobis natus sum consularis,' C. *post Red.* 2. 'E principio
oriuntur omnia: ipsum autem nulla ex re alia nasci potest,' C. *T. D.* i. 23.
'Qualis ille tibi videtur Tantalo prognatus Pelope natus?' C. *T. D.* iii. 12.
'Quidam parentibus nati sunt humilibus,' C. *Lael.* 19. 'Me equestri ortum
loco consulem videtis,' C. *Rep.* ii. 7.

D) (*Thing Compared.*) 'Deus maior est ac potentior cunctis,' Sen. *Ep.* 58.
'Lux sonitu velocior est,' Pl. *H. N.* ii. 54. 'Vilius argentum est auro, virtutibus aurum,' Hor. *Epist.* i. 1. 52. 'Quid est melius aut quid praestantius
bonitate et beneficentia?' C. *N. D.* 12. 'Demosthene nec gravior exstitit
quisquam nec callidior nec temperatior,' C. *d. Or.* 48. 'Recte auguraris de me,
nihil a me abesse longius crudelitate,' C. *Att.* ix. 16. 'Herodotum cur vera-
ciorem ducam Ennio?' C. *Div.* ii. 56. 'Neminem Lycurgo aut maiorem aut
utiliorem virum Lacedaemon genuit,' Val. Max. v. 13. 'Res aliquanto expecta-
tione omnium tranquillior fuit,' L. iv. 24. 'Voluptas cum maior est atque
longior, omne animi lumen exstinguit,' C. *Cat. M.* 12. 'Felix ante alias virgo,'
Verg. *Ae.* iii. 321. 'Prae nobis beatus videris,' Sulp. *ap.* C. *Fam.* iv. 4. 'Minor
quam pro tumultu caedes,' Tac. *H.* v. 15. 'Thais quam ego maiuscula est,' Ter.
Eun. iii. 3. 21.

E) (*Ablative Abs.*) 'Crastino die oriente sole redite in pugnam,' L. iii. 2. 'Solon
et Pisistratus Servio Tullio regnante viguerunt,' C. *Br.* 10. 'Caesare venturo,
Phosphore, redde diem,' Mart. viii. 21. 'Caesar inita hieme in Illyricum profectus
est,' Caes. *B. G.* iii. 7. 'Romani, Hannibale vivo, numquam se sine insidiis futuros
existimabant,' Nep. *Hann.* 12. 'Caninio consule scito neminem prandisse; nihil
tamen eo consule mali factum est,' C. *Fam.* vii. 30. 'Nil desperandum est Teucro
duce et auspice Teucro,' Hor. *C.* 1. 7. 27. 'Plebs Romana, Sicinio quodam
auctore, in Sacrum montem secessit,' L. ii. 32. 'Romana respublica, Cannensi
calamitate accepta, maiores animos habuit, quam umquam rebus secundis,' C.
Off. iii. 11. 'Germani pellibus utuntur, magna corporis parte nuda,' Caes. *B. G.*
vi. 21. 'Alia causa est eius, qui calamitate premitur, et eius, qui res meliores quaerit
nullis suis rebus adversis,' C. *Off.* ii. 18. 'Proxime, recenti adventu meo,
rem aliter institutam offendi ac mihi placuisset, si affuissem,' C. *Fam.* v. 17.

amicus, comes, consors, familiaris, hostis, inimicus, par, vicinus, &c., aequalis, communis, proprius, sacer, similis, dissimilis, &c.

3) This Genitive may depend on Neuter Adjectives and Pronouns used Substantively :

Amicorum omnia, C.; aliorum non me digna, C.; praeclarum hoc Thrasybuli quod, &c., N. Xerxi maxime
est illustre quod, &c., *the most famous feat of Xerxes is
that*, &c., N.

4) The Noun is in some instances omitted :

'Huius video Burriam,' *I see this man's (slave) Burria*, Ter.
An. iii. 2. See p. 275. 2).

Cicero has an ellipse of fundus, *estate* :

'Tu neque per Locustae neque per Varronis viam ducere
voluisti,' *you would not carry a road through either
Locusta's or Varro's property*, Qu. F. iii. 1.

5) Another Ellipse of the governing Noun before the Gen. is,
when that Noun occurs in a previous part of the sentence,
whether in the same or in a different case :

Meo iudicio stare malo, quam omnium reliquorum,' *I
would rather abide by my own judgment than by that of all
beside*, C. *Att.* xii. 21. 'Quis est qui possit conferre vitam
Trebonii cum Dolabellae?' *who can compare the life of
Trebonius with that of Dolabella?* C. *Phil.* xi. 4.

This takes place when two kinds of the same thing are
spoken of, or where the Noun is first used *specifically*, then
generally : but if first used *generally*, then *specifically*,
the Noun is repeated, or an *emphatic* Pronoun put for it :

'Nulla est celeritas quae possit cum animi celeritate contendere,' *there is no speed to vie with that of the mind*, C.
T. D. i. 9. 'Cum omnis arrogantia odiosa est, tum illa
ingeni atque eloquentiae multo molestissima,' *while
all assumption is odious, that* (suggested) *of genius and
eloquence is by far the most displeasing*, C. *in Caec.* 11.

6) The Pronouns meus, tuus, suus, noster, &c. must be
used Possessively instead of the Genitives, mei, &c.; but
with them may stand Pronominal or Participial Genitives
agreeing with the Gen. which the Possessives virtually
contain. Such are, ipsius, ipsorum, unius, solius, am-
borum, duorum, &c., besides Participles :

Respublica mea unius opera salva erat,' *the commonwealth was saved by my single exertion*, C. *in Pis.* 3.
'Aves fetus adultos suae ipsorum fiduciae permittunt,'
*birds entrust their grown young ones to their own self-
reliance*, Qu. ii. 6. 'Nostros vidisti flentis ocellos,' *you
saw the eyes of me weeping*, Ov. *Her.* v. 45.

7) The Possessive Genitive, being of Attributive nature, may
be used in Copulative or Factitive construction :

'Omnia, quae mulieris fuerunt, viri fiunt dotis nomine,'
all things that were the woman's become the husband's

under the title of dowry, C. *Top.* 4. 'Is Hercules dicebatur esse Myronis,' C. *Verr.* iv. 3. 'Iam me Pompeii totum esse scis,' *you know I am now Pompey's thorough partisan*, C. *Fam.* ii. 13. 'Popillius clavis portarum suae potestatis fecit,' *Popillius took possession of the keys of the gates*, L. xliii. 22.

8) Especially when the Subject of the Sentence is an Infin. and the Gen. may be supposed to depend on a suppressed notion, such as indicium, *token*, indoles, *nature*, munus, officium, *function, duty, part*, &c., proprium, *property* :

'Cuiusvis hominis est errare,' C. *Phil.* xii. 2. 'Honoris amplissimi esse puto miseros defendere,' *I deem it a function of highest office to defend the unfortunate*, C. *in Caec.* 21. 'Adulescentis est maiores natu vereri,' C. *Off.* i. 34. 'Tempori cedere semper sapientis est habitum,' C. *Fam.* iv. 9.

9) All these words are found before the Gen. :

'Id viri est officium,' C. *T. D.* ii. 21. 'Principum munus est resistere levitati multitudinis,' C. *p. Mil.* 8. 'Sapientis est proprium, nihil quod paenitere possit facere,' C. *T. D.* v. 28.

Pars itself is so used: as, 'Plura de extremis loqui pars ignaviae est,' *to dwell at length on the closing scene of life is a coward's part*, Tac. *H.* ii. 47.

10) For this Gen. are used Possessive Pronouns or other Adjectives indicating personal character :

'Nostrum est ferre modice populi voluntates,' C. *p. Planc.* 4. 'Et agere et pati fortia Romanum est,' L. ii. 12. 'Non est mentiri meum,' Ter. *Haut.* iii. 2. 38.

11) The Genitives moris, consuetudinis, arbitrii, iuris, tutelae, when Complements, may be explained by reference to proprium :

'Negavit moris esse Graecorum ut in convivio virorum accumberent mulieres,' *he said it was not a fashion of the Greeks for women to sit at table in a party of men*, C. *Verr.* i. 26. 'Est hoc Gallicae consuetudinis,' Caes. *B. G.* iv. 5. 'Victos tutelae nostrae duximus,' L. xxi. 41.

II. 1) The Descriptive Genitive expresses the specific class to which its governing Noun belongs, being often nearly equivalent to an Apposite, sometimes to an Epithet : *166 Genetivus Descriptionis.*

'Nomen regis; vox voluptatis; virtus continentiae; vitium ignorantiae; flos rosae; arbor fici; lauri nemus; montes auri; poena legis; oppidum Antiochiae; promunturium Miseni, &c. See Cic. *Off.* ii. 5. 'Ceteris causis enumeratis, eluvionis, pestilentiae,' &c.

a) This Gen. may be equivalent to a Preposition with Case :

Pyrrhi bellum = bellum cum Pyrrho or contra Pyrrhum; odium inimicitiarum = odium ob inimicitias, &c.

b) A Possessive and a Descriptive Gen. may depend on one and the same word :

'Exhaurietur ex urbe tuorum comitum magna et perniciosa sentina reipublicae,' *that great and mischievous sink of the commonwealth consisting of your companions shall be drained from the city,* C. p. S. Rosc. 5.

2) The Gen. with causā, gratiā, ergo, nomine, more, modo ritu, has been noticed.   Observe that with instar.

Instar (*image*) is a Substantive used to express *likeness, equivalence,* &c., either as Apposite, Complement, or after habere, obtinere, &c. :

'Instar montis equum,' Verg. *Ae.* ii. 15.   'Ille dies mihi immortalitatis instar fuit,' *that day was to me as good as immortality,* C. in Pis. 22.   'Unus is innumeri militis instar habet,' *he alone is worth countless troops,* Ov. Her. xvi. 368.   Ad instar is found in later Latin.

3) Here may be classed the Genitive of the Fact after Verbs, Participles and Adjectives expressing *accusation; conviction; condemnation* or *acquittal; criminality* or *innocence;* since it may be regarded as dependent on a suppressed Ablative such as crimine, nomine, causa, lege, iudicio; which often appear.

a) Such Verbs are :—

Accuso, ago, arguo, coarguo, appello, anquiro, arcesso, capto, cito, compello, defero, incuso, insimulo, interrogo, postulo, reum ago, reum facio, &c.

Alligo, adstringo, convinco, obligo, obstringo, prehendo, deprehendo, teneo, &c.

Damno, condemno, infamo, noto, &c.

Absolvo, libero, purgo ; also iudico, plecto, &c.

. . . (aliquem rei ; crimine rei ; nomine rei alicuius, &c.)

b) The Adjectives are :—

Affinis, reus, suspectus ; compertus, manifestus, noxius ; innocens, innoxius, insons.

c) The principal Genitives, expressing legal offences, which accompany such Verbs and Adjectives, are :

Ambitus (*bribery*), caedis, homicidi (*murder*), furti (*theft*), latrocinii (*robbery*), iniuriarum (*wrongs*), maiestatis, proditionis (*treason*), parricidii (*parricide*), repetundarum (*extortion*), sacrilegii (*sacrilege*), veneficii, veneni (*poisoning*), rei capitalis, rerum capitalium, &c.

The following forms have a Preposition : de vi (*violence, assault,* &c.), inter sicarios (*assassination*).

d) Such cases may be used with the legal terms above : reum esse, &c., furti, de vi, &c., furti nomine, crimine, &c.

e) Other phrases are : damnare capitis or capite, *to condemn capitally,* i.e. to death or disfranchisement : capitis minor, *a disfranchised person.*

Damnari voti, *to be condemned to pay what was vowed,* because the prayer has been granted.

Damnare quindecim millibus, *to condemn to a fine of* 15,000
sesterces; damnare octupli, *to condemn to a fine of eight
times the amount,* &c. Also with Dat., or with a d: damnare
morti; damnare ad bestias.

f) Anquirere capitis, capite, pecunia, &c., implies prosecution by the Tribunes, who specified the penalty beforehand.

g) Arguo, insimulo may be used in common parlance:
'Meque timoris argue tu, Drance,' *and do you, Drances,
undertake to convict me of cowardice,* Verg. *Ae.* xi. 383.

h) Damni infecti promittere, repromittere, stipulari, satisdare,
&c., are legal phrases: '*to give security against damage.*'

[II. *A.* 1) The Genitive of Quality is also Descriptive; but
it takes the place, not of an Apposite, but of a strengthened
Attribute.

168
Gene-
tivus
Quali-
tatis.

Vir excellentis ingeni = vir peringeniosus; Lucius est excellentis ingeni = Lucius est peringeniosus.

2) The Gen., then, like the Abl., of Quality, is a construction
by which one Substantive (in Latin always with Epithet)
is joined to another, for the purpose of describing it in
some particular:

Vir magni animi, corporis ingentis, spectatae virtutis, trium
litterarum (i.e. fur); adulescens bonae indolis, bonae spei,
summae audaciae; auctor sublestae fidei, *an author of
slight credit*; codex optimae notae, *a manuscript of the
best authority.*

3) This form of description may extend to Number, Measure,
Weight, Age, Time, Value, &c.:

Classis septuaginta navium; colossus triginta trium pedum;
lapis decem librarum pondo; puer quindecim annorum;
tempus viginti sex horarum; gemma maximi pretii.

4) In such examples the Noun which the Gen. qualifies is an
Appellative or Common Noun; and such it will be when
the Gen. of Quality is used as an Epithet merely; but if a
Finite Copulative Verb is joined (vir est, fuit, habetur,
habitus est, &c., magni animi, &c.), the Subject of such
sentence may be a Proper Name:

Lucius est (fuit, &c.) bonae indolis: Claudius erat somni
brevissimi; Sicilia est magnae fertilitatis, &c.

5) Rare instances occur, in which the Gen. of Quality accompanies a Proper Name enthetically:

'Tum T. Manlius Torquatus, priscae ac nimis durae
severitatis, ita locutus fertur,' *then Titus Manlius
Torquatus, a man of antique and over-rugged strictness, is
reported to have spoken thus,* L. xxii. 60.

6) A Possessive Gen. and a Gen. of Quality or Description may
depend on one Noun:

'Superiorum dierum Sabini cunctatio,' *Sabinus's delay of the preceding days,* Caes. *B. G.* iii. 10.

7) **Modi**, compounded with Pronouns, is a Gen. of Quality:

Huiusmodi, eiusmodi, istiusmodi, cuiusmodi, cuicuimodi, &c., *of this, that, which, whatever kind,* &c.

(It is hardly possible to discriminate nicely the uses of the Gen. and Abl. of Quality; the usage of writers differing, and some phrases being by custom assigned to the one, some to the other. Upon the whole it seems true that the Gen. oftener describes essential and permanent, the Abl. accessory and occasional circumstances. But many exceptions occur.)

169
Geneti-
vus Pre-
tii.

B. 1) The Genitive of Value and Price requires notice, because, though this is a particular instance of the Gen. of Quality, **pretii** is usually suppressed.

2) Price may be described after words which mean or imply *buying, selling, hiring, letting, costing,* &c., by the Genitives **tanti**, **quanti**, and their compounds, and by the Comparative Genitives **pluris**, **minoris** (rarely **maioris**); but other Positive and the Superlative Adjectives (**magno,** &c., **plurimo,** &c.) describe Price in the Abl.:

'**Quanti emptum? Parvo**,' Hor. *S.* ii. 3. 156. **Tanti est,** *it is worth while.* **Non tanti est,** *it is not worth the trouble.*

3) Valuation, after **ducere**, **habere**, **facere**, **pendĕre**, **putare**, **taxare**, **esse**, &c., is described by the Gen. of all the Adjectives above named: **aestimare** takes Gen. or Abl.

Parvi pendĕre aliquid; **magni** (**magno**) **aestimare.** See Madvig on C. *Fin.* iii. 3. 11.

4) Instead of **nullius pretii**, *of no value,* the Romans in common parlance (besides **nihili**) often, like ourselves, used such phrases with a Negative as, **assis** (**unius assis**), *a penny* (*a single penny*); **teruncii,** *a farthing*; **nauci, pili, flocci,** answering to the English phrases, *not a fig, not a rush,* &c. The phrase **huius** seems to imply a gesture, like snapping the fingers. **Non huius facio,** *I do not care* THAT *for it.*

5) To the Genitive of Value belong the phrases:

Lucri facere, *to make prize of*; **aequi boni facere,** *to take in good part*; **boni consulere,** *to make the best of.*

A Verre omnem illam pecuniam lucri factam videtis, *you see that all that money has been embezzled by Verres,* C. *Verr.* iii. 75. '**Animus meus totum istuc aequi boni facit,**' *my temper takes all that in good part,* C. *Att.* vii. 7. '**Hoc munus rogo, qualecumque est, boni consulas,**' *I beg you will make the best of this present, whatever its value,* Sen. *Ben.* i. 8.

170
Interest,
refert.

C. 1) The Constructions of the Impersonal Verbs, **interest**, *it imports, concerns,* **refert,** *it concerns,* are remarkable.

Interest may take a Genitive of the Person or Thing concerned: **interest omnium, interest reipublicae,** &c.

Refert does so less frequently; never in Cicero. '**Refert ipsorum,**' L. xxxiv. 27.

The ground of concernment is expressed, if at all, either by an Infinitive, or by an Infinitive Clause or its equivalent, or by an Oblique Interrogation:

'Interest omnium recte facere,' C. *Fin.* ii. 22. 'Salutis communis interest, duos consules in republica esse,' C. *p. Mur.* 2. 'Plurimum refert compositionis, quae quibus anteponas,' *it matters much to periodic construction, what words you place before what,* Qu. ix. 4.

2) But if what is concerned is in the First or Second Person, or to be expressed reflexively or relatively, then the Possessive forms meā, tuā, nostrā, vestrā, suā, cuiā, are used with these Verbs instead of a Genitive:

'Et meā et tuā maxime interest te valere,' C. *Fam.* xvi. 4. 'Quid nostrā id refert victum esse Antonium?' *what matters it to us that Antonius is conquered?* C. *ad Br.* 17.

3) These Verbs may be qualified by the Genitives of Value, magni, parvi, pluris, tanti, quanti:

'Utriusque nostrum magni interest ut te videam,' C. *Att.* xi. 22. 'Hoc non pluris refert quam si imbrem in cribrum geras,' *this matters no more than if you carry water to a sieve,* Plaut. *Pseud.* i. 1. 110.

Also by nihil, multum, tantum, quantum, quid, parum, &c., and by Adverbs: valde, magnopere, maxime, minime, vementer, &c. The Verbs may be used personally, as in the last example, with a Pronoun.

4) Interest and refert are constructed sometimes with ad, sometimes with a Dative: 'Magni ad honorem nostrum interest quam primum ad urbem me venire,' C. *Fam.* xvi. 1. 'Dic quid referat intra Naturae finis viventi iugera centum an mille aret,' Hor. *S.* i. 1. 14.

Refert is often without Case: as, 'Neque enim numero comprendere refert,' *nor indeed is it important to count them,* Verg. *G.* ii. 104.[1]

IV. *A.* 1) The Plural Genitive of the Thing Distributed is a divisible Whole, and depends on Partitive Words indicating that one or more Parts (or no Part) of such Whole are taken:

171
Genetivus Rei Distributae.

'Virtutum in alia alius mavult excellere,' *one prefers to excel in one virtue, another in 'another,* C. *Off.* i. 32. 'Neque stultorum quisquam beatus neque sapientium non beatus,' C. *Fin.* i. 18. 'Nunc iuvenum princeps deinde future senum,' Ov. 'Roma regionum Italiae media est,' L. v. 54.

2) The Partitive Words are:

a) Substantives which express Partition: pars, portio, nu-

---

[1] Interest is perhaps originally corrupted from in re est; and refert (not from refero) is from res and fert; with this Ablative re the Pronouns mea, &c., agree. Some suppose interest to be for inter rem est, refert for rem fert, and mea, &c., to be corruptions of meam, &c.

merus, multitudo, nemo, nihil, &c., and the Adverb partim.

β) Pronominals: alius, alter, uter and its compounds, ullus, nullus, plerique, multi, pauci, reliqui, ceteri, solus; qui, quis, and their compounds: tot, quot, and their derivatives.

γ) Numerals both Cardinal and Ordinal: also princeps, medius.

δ) Comparative and Superlative Adjectives; the former distributing two things: 'Maior Neronum;' or one class into two parts: 'Avium loquaciores,' *the noisier sort of birds*, Pl. *N. H.* Also Superlative Adverbs: 'Minime omnium.'

ε) Any Noun which can imply distribution: 'Sancte deorum;' 'lecti iuvenum;' 'piscium feminae.'

3) A Partitive Adjective, agreeing with that which is Part of a Whole, naturally follows the Gender of the Whole:

Beluarum nulla = beluarum nulla belua;

yet it is sometimes attracted to the Gender of the Subject.

'Indus est omnium fluminum maximus,' C. *N. D.* Or to that of the Person implied, by Synesis: 'Dulcissime rerum,' *my dearest friend*, Hor. *S.* i. 9. 4.

4) Partitives sometimes take the Gen. of a Collective Noun:

'Plato totius Graeciae doctissimus fuit,' C. *p. Rab.* 23 (Graeciae = Graecorum).

5) This Genitive is found in the place of a Complement:

'Fies nobilium tu quoque fontium,' Hor. *C.* iii. 13. 13.

Obs. 'Neque ille Sepositi ciceris nec longae invidit avenae,' Hor. *S.* ii. 6. 84, is a Graecism (πίνειν τοῦ οἴνου).

6) English idiom uses the Preposition *of* after Numeral words, when no *part* is taken, but the *whole* implied: as, '*there are two of us*:' but in Latin this would be, 'Nos duo sumus.' So, '*three hundred of them conspired*' is, 'Illi trecenti coniuraverunt;' '*kinsmen of whom I have few*,' 'Cognati quos paucos habeo.'

7) Distribution is also expressed by Prepositions:

'Nihil ex his, quae videmus, manet,' Sen. *Ep.* 58. 'Thales sapientissimus in septem fuit,' C. *Leg.* ii. 12. 'Inter Scythiae amnes amoenissimus Borysthenes,' Mela, 12. 'Ante omnis Turnus pulcherrimus,' Verg. *Ae.* vii. 65. 'Una de multis,' Hor. *C.* iii. 11. 33.

172
Geneti-
vus Rei
De-
mensae

B. 1) The Genitive of the Thing Measured depends on Quantitative Words, which imply that *so much* of a Whole is taken, not *so many*.

2) Such Quantitative Words are:

α) Substantives implying measurement of Quantity:

Amphora, *cask*; medimnus (um), *bushel;* modius, *peck* (frumenti, *of corn*); libra, *pound* (casei, *of cheese*), &c.; acervus, copia, numerus, pondus (auri), vis, &c.

β) Quantitative Neuter Adjectives and Pronouns:

Multum, plus, plurimum, amplius, minus, minimum, tantum, quantum, aliquantum, nimium, dimidium, nihil, aliud, id, &c., quod, quid, &c.

γ) Quantitative Adverbs:

Abunde, affatim, nimis, parum, partim, satis.

δ) The Adjectives and Adverbs are usually rendered in English as in agreement with the thing measured:

'Tantum vini,' *so much wine*; 'minus splendoris,' *less brilliance*; 'satis eloquentiae, sapientiae parum,' *eloquence enough, little wisdom*, Sall.; 'nimium pecuniae,' *too much money*; 'nihil mali,' *no evil.*

3) The Genitive may depend on a Demonstrative Pronoun understood from a following Relative.

'Medico mercedis quantum poscet promitti iubeto,' *you must order that as high a fee as he shall ask be promised to the physician*, C. *Fam.* xvi. 14. 'Vastatur agri quod inter urbem ac Fidenas est,' *all the land that is between the city and Fidenae is laid waste*, L. i. 14; M. *Lucr.* iv. 372.

4) Classes β and γ may also be constructed with the Genitive of a Neuter Adjective of the Second Declension; but an Adjective of the Third is commonly (but not always) put in the same case with the word of Quantity:

'Prima est historiae lex ut ne quid falsi dicere audeat, ne quid veri non audeat,' C. *d. Or.* ii. 62. 'Si quicquam in vobis, non dico civilis, sed humani esset,' L. v. 3. 'Nec viget quicquam simile aut secundum,' *and nothing exists like or in second rank*, Hor. *C.* i. 12. 18.

Note the Ciceronian phrase, 'Quod eius facere poteris,' *as far as you can* (but quoad for quod in some MSS.). 'Nihil reliqui facere,' *to leave nothing undone*; 'nihil pensi habere,' *to have no regard.*

5) The Genitive Pronouns nostrum, vestrum, are used with Partitive words; but, if an individual or human nature itself is quantitatively divided, mei, tui, sui, nostri, vestri may be used: 'Multa pars mei,' Hor. *C.* iii. 30. 6. 'Plus nostri superest rogo,' Sen. Tr.

6) The Genitives loci, locorum, gentium, terrarum, are used with Adverbs of Place, ubi, quo, unde, huc, eo, aliquo, usquam, nusquam, &c.:

'Ubi terrarum sumus,' *where on earth are we?* C. *p. Rab.* 37. 'An quisquam usquam gentium est aeque miser?' *is there anywhere in the world one so miserable?* Ter. *Hec.* iii. 1. 'Res eodem est loci ubi reliquisti,' *the affair is in the same position you left it in*, C. *Att.* i. 13.

Genitives not local are found with them, but not in Cicero:

'Eo deliciarum pervenimus ut nisi gemmas calcare noli-
mus,' *we have reached that pitch of luxury, that we will
not tread except on jewels,* Sen. *Ep.* 88. Tum (tunc) temporis occurs in Justin: interea loci (*meanwhile*) in the
Comic poets; minime gentium (*least in the world, by no
means*), postea loci, in Livy; inde loci, M. *Lucr.* v. 791.

'Pridie eius diei' (*the day before*), 'postridie eius diei' (*the
day after*), &c. Pridie, postridie also take Accus.

7) The Verb satago (*I am busy*) (sat and ago) takes a Gen. :

'Clinia rerum suarum satagit,' *Clinia has enough of his
own business,* Ter. *Haut.* iii. 1. 13. 'Nunc agitas sat
tute tuarum rerum,' *you have now affairs enough of your
own in hand,* Plaut. *Bac.* iv. 3. 23.

8) Neuter Adjectives of either Number, put abstractly for Substantives, sometimes govern a Genitive:

'Adulescens in lubrico aetatis est,' *a young man is at a
slippery time of life,* Plin. *Epist.* iii. 6. So medium diei,
serum diei. (On id temporis, id locorum, hoc aetatis,
&c., see ACCUSATIVE.)

Constructions like 'Incerta casuum,' 'occulta saltuum,'
'opaca locorum,' 'angusta viarum,' 'amara curarum,' are
not usual in Cicero; but they occur in Livy, abound in
Tacitus, and in poetry they are frequent. See p. 278.

**173
Geneti-
vus
Copiae
et Ino-
piae.**

C. 1) The Genitive of Abundance and Want is Partitive. See ABLATIVE, p. 397.

2) Verbs: egeo, indigeo prefer the Genitive in prose: compleo, expleo, impleo, take it occasionally: abundo, parti-
cipo, saturo, scateo: abstineo, careo, desino, desisto, levo,
libero, solvo, dissolvo, and others, chiefly in poetry.

'Indigere medicinae;' 'impleri veteris Bacchi:' 'abstinere
irarum;' 'desine querellarum,' &c.

Potior has a Genitive both in prose and poetry: apiscor,
adipiscor, in Tacitus; regno once in Horace.

3) Adjectives: fertilis, ferax, largus, plenus, refertus :—inanis, indigus, inops, ieiunus: often have Gen. in prose and
poetry; compos, particeps, exheres, expers, exsors,
almost always: potens, impos, impotens, no other Case:
benignus, dives, fecundus, locuples, prosper: pauper,
solutus, truncus, exsul, vacuus, &c., dignus, indignus,
are found in poetry with Genitive.

'Vita plena metus et insidiarum;' 'terra frugum fertilis;'
'compos mentis;' 'voti compos;' 'Musa potens lyrae;'
'rationis expers;' 'dives opum;' 'exsul patriae;' 'pauper
aquae Daunus,' &c.

D. Of a Partitive nature also are the Genitive of Respect
and that of the Part affected, which, in imitation of
Greek construction, is very freely used by poets and also
by prose writers of the silver age. Such phrases are:

'Consili certus;' 'militiae impiger, strenuus;' 'vetus sermonis;' all in Tac. :—'integer vitae,' Hor.; 'integer aevi,' Verg.; 'seri studiorum,' Hor. &c. Especially **animi**: 'Excruciari animi;' 'angi animi;' 'pendere animi,' C.: 'animi falli,' Lucr., Plaut. (desipere mentis, Plaut.): 'Animi anxius, aeger, audax, caecus, ferox, ingens, immodicus, infelix, laetus, promptus, turbidus, validus,' &c.

iv. *B*) OBJECTIVE GENITIVE.

This Genitive principally depends on Words which contain the Transitive force of Verbs from which they are derived. Such are :—

1) Substantives: **amor patriae**; cultus agrorum; scientia iuris; ignorantia recti; cura peculi; studium lucri; victor hostium.

Note 1. The Genitives nostrum, vestrum (in old Latin nostrorum, vestrorum) are used in Partitive Construction: mei, tui, &c., nostri, vestri, Quantitatively or Objectively.

But the phrases 'omnium nostrum,' 'omnium vestrum' are also used as Possessive Genitives: sometimes nostrum, vestrum alone. And mei, tui are sometimes found where the Possessive might have been expected: 'Fruitur fama sui,' Tac. *Ann.* ii. 13. Also the Possessives meus, tuus are sometimes used Objectively. See p. 410.

Note 2. An Objective Genitive (with Substantives derived from Transitive Verbs) must often be rendered in English by some other Preposition than *of*: 'Coelibis obsequium,' *attention* to *an unmarried man*, Hor. 'Praestantia animarum reliquarum,' *superiority* over *other souls*, Cic. 'Remedium irae,' *remedy* against *anger*, Cic. 'Misericordia pauperum,' *pity* for *the poor*. 'Quies laborum,' *rest* from *toils*.

2) Adjectives :

α) Verbal Adjectives in **ax**: capax, edax, ferax, fugax, pertinax, rapax, sagax, tenax, vorax, &c.

β) Present Participles used Adjectively: abundans, amans, appetens, contemnens, colens, cupiens, despiciens, diligens, efficiens, egens, experiens, fugiens, intellegens, metuens, neglegens, observans, patiens, impatiens, proferens, sciens, sitiens, timens, tolerans, benegerens, servantissimus, &c.

γ) Adjectives of *knowledge* and *ignorance*: assuetus, callidus, certus, certior, conscius, consultus, docilis, doctus, expertus, gnarus, memor, peritus, praescius, praesagus, providus, prudens, scitus, sollers; alienus, ambiguus, dubius, inscius, incertus, inexpertus, ignarus, immemor, imperitus, improvidus, imprudens, indoctus, insolens, insuetus, nescius, oblitus, rudis.

Here remark the phrase, 'Certiorem facere' (*to inform*): 'Pompeius me certiorem sui consili fecit,' *Pompeius informed me of his plan*. Cic. *Att.* ix. 2.

δ) *Care* and *carelessness*: aemulus, anxius, curiosus, certus, formidulosus, parcus, pavidus, sollicitus, timidus, trepidus, impavidus, incuriosus, incautus, intrepidus, interritus; profusus, prodigus, securus, socors.

ε) *Desire* and *dislike*: avarus, avidus, cupidus, studiosus fastidiosus.

ζ) Add superstes, supplex.

Obs. 1. Most of these are rendered with the sign *of*: except assuetus (*accustomed* to); insuetus, insolens (*unaccustomed* to); callidus, consultus, doctus, peritus, &c. (*skilled* in); indoctus, imperitus, &c. (*unskilled* in); scitus, prudens, expertus, &c. (*acquainted* with); imprudens, rudis, &c. (*unacquainted* with), and others.

Obs. 2. Many such Adjectives also take Prepositions: 'Callidus ad fraudem,' C. 'Prudens in iure,' C. 'Securus de bello Romano,' L. 'Certiorem fieri de re aliqua.' Some take other Cases: 'Peritus bello,' Vell. 'Dulcis docta modos,' Hor.

Obs. 3. A list of other Adjectives found with a Genitive is given in Stallbaum's *Ruddiman*, Pars II. p. 73. None are from Cicero but 'invidus laudis;' a few from Livy; many from Tacitus. Virgil has 'fessus rerum;' 'fidissima tui regina;' 'vanus veri,' &c. Lucr. has 'aversa viai,' i. 1081, see M.; Horace: 'lassus maris; divina avis imbrium; exsul patriae,' &c.; but most examples are from later poets, Statius, Silius, Claudian, &c. The student must distinguish prosaic from poetic usage, which admits Gen. freely.

175   3) A Genitive of the Matter, sometimes an Accusative, depends on Verbs of *remembering, forgetting, reminding*: memini (Gen. or Accus.), reminiscor (Gen. or Accus.), recordor (Accus., rarely Gen.), obliviscor (Gen. or Accus.); moneo, admoneo, commoneo, commonefacio (Accus. of person, Gen. of thing); mentionem facio (Gen.). (See memor, immemor, &c. above.)

'Vivorum memini, nec tamen Epicuri licet oblivisci,' *I remember the living, nor yet may I forget Epicurus*, C. *Fin.* v. 1. 'Res adversae admonent nos religionum,' *adversity reminds us of religious duties*, L. v. 51. 'Dulcis moriens reminiscitur Argos,' Verg. *Ae.* x. 782.

a) Verbs of Remembering sometimes take de: 'De Clodio ne meminisse quidem volo,' C. *Fam.* v. 3.

b) The phrase 'venit in mentem' is used impersonally, either with Genitive, or with Preposition: 'Venit mihi in mentem temporis illius, quo fuimus una,' C. *Fam.* vii. 3. 'Astute venit ei in mentem de speculo,' *he craftily remembered the mirror*, Plaut. *Most.* i. 3. Or personally: 'Non venit in mentem pugna apud Regillum lacum?' *do you not remember the battle at lake Regillus?* L. viii. 5.

4) A Genitive depends on the Verbs misereor 2. miseresco 3. (*feel pity*); but an Accusative in the best authors on miseror 1. commiseror 1. (*express pity, bewail*).

'Nil nostri miserere,' Verg. *B.* ii. 7. 'Arcadii miserescite regis,' Verg. *Ae.* viii. 573. 'Sortem miseratus iniquam,' Verg. *Ae.* vi. 332.

5) The Impersonal Verbs miseret (miserescit, miseretur), piget, pudet (veretur), paenitet, taedet, take an Accusative of the Nearer, with a Genitive of the Remoter, Object:

'Me tuarum miseritum est fortunarum,' *I pitied your fortunes*, Ter. *Haut.* iii. 1. 'Me civitatis morum piget taedetque,' *I am weary and sick of the manners of the state*, Sall. *Iug.* 4. 'Pudet me stultitiae,' *I am ashamed of my folly*, C. 'Me tui, mi pater, pudet,' *I am ashamed to face you, father*, Ter. *Ad.* iv. 5. 49. See C. *Att.* vii. 4 (veritus); *Fin.* ii. 13.

6) The Genitive of Cause in poetry is a Greek idiom: 176

'Iustitiaene prius mirer belline laborum?' Verg. *Ae.* xi. 126. 'Notus in fratres animi paterni,' Hor. *C.* ii. 2, 6. 'Felix, Bolane, cerebri,' Hor. *S.* i. 9. 11. 'Laudabat leti iuvenem,' Sil. iv. 160. 'O mihi nuntii beati,' Catull. ix. 5. 'Foederis heu taciti,' Prop. iv. 7. 13.

Examples of the Genitive Case.

A) (*Subjective.*) I. (*Possessive.*) 'Amore patriae nostrorum maiorum inventa nosse debemus, C. *d. Or.* i. 58. 'Sullae et Caesaris pecuniarum translatio a iustis dominis ad alienos non debet liberalis videri,' C. *Off.* i. 14. 'Nihil est quod multorum naufragia fortunae colligas,' C. *Verr.* v. 40. 'Consul es designatus, optima aetate, summa eloquentia, maxima orbitate reipublicae virorum talium,' C. *Fam.* x. 3. 'Egerius fratris filius erat regis,' L. i. 38. 'Polycleti signa plane perfecta sunt,' C. *Br.* 18. 'Singulorum facultates et copiae divitiae sunt civitatis,' C. *Off.* iii. 15. 'Pacis est comes otique socia, et iam bene constitutae civitatis quasi alumna quaedam, eloquentia,' C. *Br.* 12. 'Omnium est communis inimicus, qui fuit hostis suorum,' C. *Verr.* i. 15. 'In primis hominis est propria veri inquisitio,' C. *Off.* i. 11. 'Illa insula eorum deorum sacra putatur,' C. *Verr.* ii. 18. 'Phoebi Triviaeque sacerdos Deiphobe Glauci,' Verg. *Ae.* vi. 35. 'Dinomaches ego sum,' Pers. iv. 30. 'Paterae aureae ad Cereris positae,' L. x. 23. 'Quae in nostris rebus non satis honeste, in amicorum fiunt honestissime,' C. *Lael.* 16. 'Petulantia magis est adulescentium, quam senum; nec tamen omnium adulescentium, sed non proborum,' C. *Cat. M.* 11. 'Id maxime quemque decet, quod est cuiusque maxime suum,' C. *Off.* i. 31. 'Nolae senatus Romanorum, plebs Hannibalis erat,' L. xxiii. 39. 'Solon capite sanxit, si qui in seditione non alterius utrius partis fuisset,' C. *Att.* x. 1. 'Hannibal quod inter Alpis Apenninumque agri est suae dicionis fecit,' L. xxi. 53. 'Tardi ingeni est rivulos consectari, fontis rerum non videre,' C. *d. Or.* ii. 27. 'Qualis oratoris et quanti hominis in dicendo putas esse historiam scribere?' C. *d. Or.* ii. 12. 'Est proprium munus magistratus, intellegere, se gerere personam civitatis,' C. *Off.* i. 34. 'Quae est animo natura? propria, puto, et sua,' C. *T. D.* i. 29. 'Nulla mora est operae; vestrum dare, vincere nostrum est,' Ov. *F.* iv. 889. 'Tuum hominis simplicis pectus vidimus,' C. *Phil.* ii. 43. 'Noster duorum eventus ostendet utra gens bello sit melior, L. i. 7. 'Solius meum peccatum corrigi non potest,' C. *Att.* xi. 15. 'Dic mihi, Damoeta, cuium pecus, an Meliboei?' Verg. *B.* iii. 1.

II. (*Descriptive.*) 1) 'Stella Veneris Lucifer dicitur, cum antegreditur solem, cum subsequitur autem, Hesperus,' C. *N. D.* ii. 20. 'Non faciendo id, quod non decet, impudentiae nomen effugere debemus,' C. *d. Or.* i. 26. 'Duae sunt huius obscuritatis causae, una pudoris, altera sceleris,' C. *d. L. Agr.* ii. 24. 'Ea bona sunt generis, pecuniae, propinquorum, amicorum, opum, valetudinis, formae, ingeni,' C. *d. Or.* ii. 11.

2) 'Persuadent mathematici, terram ad universi caeli complexum quasi puncti instar obtinere,' C. *T. D.* i. 40. 'Quidam Romani habebant domos instar urbium,' Sen. *Ep.* 90.

SECTION III.

VERB-CONSTRUCTION.

(On Moods and Tenses see §§ 91-99.   On Verb Infinite, § 40.)

i. I) The Infinitive.

The Infinitive is at once a Verb and a Neuter Substantive.
As a Verb, it governs Cases.   As a Substantive it has Cases ; on
which see § 181 : and on its Tense-forms, § 40.

---

3) 'Labeo arguebatur male administratae provinciae aliorumque cri-
minum,' Tac. *Ann.* vi. 27.   'Cum capitis anquisivissent, duo milia aeris
damnato multam edixerunt,' L. ii. 52.   'Caesar Dolabellam repetundarum postu-
lavit,' Suet. *Caes.* 4.   'Defertur impietatis in Principem,' Tac. *Ann.* vi. 19.
'Legibus ambitus interrogati dederunt poenas,' Sall. *Cat.* 18.   'Alcibiades, postquam se capitis damnatum audivit, Lacedaemonem demigravit,' N. *Alc.* 4.
'Miltiades, capitis absolutus, pecunia multatus est,' N. *Milt.* 7.   'Recte con-
demnamus haruspices aut stultitiae aut vanitatis,' C. *Div.* i. 36.   'Coelius
iudex absolvit iniuriarum eum, qui Lucilium poetam nominatim laeserat,' Auct. *ad
Her.* ii. 19.   'Nomine sceleris coniurationisque damnati sunt multi,' C. *Verr.* v.
11.   'Miltiades crimine Pario est accusatus,' Nep. *Milt.*   'Silanus saevitiae
captarumque pecuniarum tenebatur reus,' Tac. *Ann.* iii. 27.   'De mani-
festis rerum capitalium more maiorum supplicium sumendum est,' Sall. *Cat.* 52.
Q. Sergius senator inter sicarios damnatus est,' C. *p. Clu.* 7.   'Furius damnatus
voti quum victor Romam revertisset, dictatura se abdicavit,' L. vii. 28.

III. (*Quality.*)   *a.* 'Tune trium litterarum homo me vituperas?' Plaut. *Aul.*
ii. 4. 46.   'Sp. Servilius, fervidi animi vir, periculum audacia discussit,' L. ii. 52.
'Themistocles persuasit populo ut classis centum navium aedificaretur,' N. *Th.* 2.
'Latini coronam auream in Capitolium tulere parvi ponderis,' L. iii. 57.   'Spes
unica imperi populi Romani L. Quinctius trans Tiberim quattuor iugerum colebat
agrum,' L. iii. 26.   'Caesar a fronte castrorum pedum quindecim fossam fieri
iussit,' Caes. *B. C.* i. 41.   'Hamilcar in Hispaniam secum duxit filium Hannibalem
annorum novem,' N. *Hann.* 8.   'C. Iulius Caesar annum ad solis cursum accommo-
davit ut trecentorum sexaginta quinque dierum esset,' Suet. *Caes.* 40.   'Servius Tullius iuvenis evasit vere indolis regiae,' L. i. 39.   'Magni iudicii,
summae etiam facultatis esse debet orator,' C. *Or.* 21.   'Nos in castra propera-
bamus, quae aberant bidui,' C. *Att.* v. 16.   'Agesilaus octoginta annorum in
Aegyptum profectus est,' N. *Ag.* 8.   'Admittenda est hominum cuiusquemodi
multitudo,' C. *Off.* i. 39.   'Eorum dierum consuetudo itineris nostri exercitus perspecta est,' Caes. *B. G.* ii. 17.

b. 'Ego a meis magni pendi postulo,' Ter. *Ad.* v. 4.   'Est hominis sapientis
maximi aestimare conscientiam mentis suae,' C. *p. Clu.* 58.   'Patrem tuum plurimi
feci, meque ille mirifice coluit,' C. *Att.* xvi. 19.   'Vendo meum frumentum non
pluris quam ceteri, fortasse etiam minoris, cum maior est copia,' C. *Off.* iii. 12.
'Nulla pestis humano generi pluris stetit quam ira,' Sen. *Ir.* i. 2.   'Mercatores non
tantidem vendunt quanti emerunt,' C. *Verr.* iii. 192.   'Noli spectare quanti
homo sit ; parvi enim pretii est qui iam nihili sit,' C. *Qu. Fr.* i. 2.   'Non quantum
quisque prosit, sed quanti quisque sit, pondera,' C. *Br.* 257.   'Quanti quisque
amicos facit, tanti fit ab amicis,' C. *Lael.* 16.   'Qui homo timidus erit in rebus
dubiis, nauci non erit,' Plaut. *Most.* v. 1. 1.   'Sapiens dolorem nihili facit,' C.
Fin. ii. 13.   'Ego, quae tu loquere, flocci non facio,' Plaut. *Rud.* iii. 5.   'Neque
fas neque fidem pensi habet,' Tac. *Ann.* xiii. 15.   'Te huius non faciam,' Ter.
Ad. ii. 1.   'Video quanta tempestas invidiae mihi immineat ; sed est mihi tanti,' C.
Cat. i. 9.   'Si vos non movet periculum ne serpat latius contagio eius mali, nos.

Livy (not C. or Caes.) uses a Past for a Present Infin. with such predications as satis est, melius est, satis habeo, contentus sum: also with possum, volo and some Impers. Verbs. 'Quiesse melius erit,' L. i. Poets take this license freely: 'Magnum si pectore possit excussisse deum,' Verg. *Ae.* vi. 78. 'Effugisse volunt longe longeque remosse,' Lucr. iii. 69. See M.

---

aequi bonique facimus,' L. xxxiv. 22. 'Haec, quaeso, consule missa boni,' Ov. *Ep. ex Pont.* iii. 8.

c. 'Caesar dicere solebat, non tam sua quam reipublicae interesse, uti salvus esset,' Suet. *Caes.* 86. 'Epistulis certiores facimus absentis, si quid est quod eos scire aut nostra aut ipsorum intersit,' C. *Fam.* ii. 4. 'Quid refert mea, cui serviam?' Phaedr. i. 35. 'Civitatum hoc multarum interfuit, antiquum vocum servare modum,' C. *Leg.* ii. 38. 'Semper Milo, quantum interesset Clodii, se perire, cogitabat,' C. *p. Mil.* 56. 'Quid, Chreme, tua, malum, id refert?—Magni, Demipho,' Ter. *Ph.* iv. 4. 'Quid id nostra?—Nihil (i.e. refert),' Ter. *Ph.* v. 7.

IV. (*Partitive.*) *a.* (*Thing Distributed.*) 'Nihil tam absurde dici potest quod non dicatur ab aliquo philosophorum,' C. *Div.* ii. 119. 'Incertum est, quam longa nostrum cuiusque vita futura sit,' C. *Verr.* i. 153. 'Equitum centum quinquaginta interfeci,' Curt. iii. 11. 'Erant Phocionis tempore duae factiones, quarum una populi causam agebat, altera optimatum,' N. *Phoc.* 19. 'Tarquinius Superbus septimus atque ultimus regum Romanorum fuit,' Eutr. i. 8. 'Rationem defectus solis apud Graecos investigavit primus omnium Thales Milesius,' Pl. *N. H.* ii. 12. 'Alexander seniores militum in patriam remisit,' Curt. x. 2. 'Quadrupedum talpis visus non est,' Pl. *N. H.* xi. 37. 'Canum degeneres caudam sub alvum reflectunt,' do. xi. 50. 'Lanarum nigrae nullum colorem bibunt,' do. viii. 48. 'Mardonius erat in primis omnium Persarum manu fortis,' N. *Ar.* 1. 'Sulpicius Gallus maxime omnium nobilium Graecis litteris studuit,' C. *Br.* 20. 'Trevirorum civitas longe plurimum totius Galliae equitatu valet,' Caes. *B. G.* ii. 3. 'Aliqui e nostris aliter existimant, quos quidem video esse multos sed imperitos,' C. *Fin.* i. 55. 'Quaeritur, quot sint species rerum publicarum, quas tris accepimus, quae populi, quae paucorum, quae unius potestate regerentur,' Qu. v. 10. 'De vera et perfecta amicitia loquor, qualis eorum, qui pauci nominantur, fuit,' C. *Lael.* 22. 'Numerate quot ipsi sitis,' L. vi. 18. 'Trecenti coniuravimus principes iuventutis Romanae,' L. ii. 12. 'Ex quinquaginta milibus Graecorum supersumus pauci,' Curt. v.

β. (*Thing Measured.*) 'Voluisti magnum agri modum censeri,' C. *p. Fl.* 32. 'In iugere Leontini agri medimnum fere tritici seritur,' C. *Verr.* iii. 47. 'Maximus vini numerus fuit, permagnum optimi pondus argenti,' C. *Phil.* ii. 27. 'Tantum quisque se in republica posse postulat, quantum habet virium,' C. *ad Brut.* i. 10. 'Rogo, ut de his rebus, quas tecum colloqui volo, annum mihi temporis des,' N. *Them.* 9. 'Romani castrorum oppugnatione, quia serum erat diei, abstinuere,' L. vii. 8. 'A te nihildum certi exquiro, sed quid videatur,' C. *Att.* vii. 12. 'Praemissus Caecina, ut occulta saltuum scrutaretur pontisque et aggeres humido paludum et fallacibus campis imponeret,' Tac. *Ann.* i. 61. 'Quid mulieris uxorem habes?' Ter. *Hec.* iv. 4. 'Velim, ut, quod eius fieri possit, praesentiae tuae desiderium meo labore minuatur,' C. *Fam.* v. 8. 'Ut adulescentem, in quo senile aliquid, sic senem, in quo est adulescentis aliquid, probamus,' C. *Cat. M.* 11. 'Ambulationem postmeridianam confecimus in Academia, maxime quod is locus ab omni turba id temporis vacuus esset,' C. *Fin.* v. 1. 'Dedi satis superque poenarum tibi,' Hor. *Epod.* 17. 'Armorum affatim erat Carthagine captorum,' L. xxvii. 17. 'Parentes abunde habemus, amicorum numquam satis,' Sall. *Iug.* 102. 'Multis in locis parum firmamenti et parum virium veritas habet,' C. *p. Clu.* 2. 'Ubi terrarum esses ne suspicabar quidem,' C. *Att.* v. 10. 'Qui virtutem adeptus erit, ubicumque erit gentium, a nobis diligetur,' C. *N. D.* i. 121. 'Rhodum aut aliquo terrarum migrandum est,' C. *Fam.* xi. 1. 'Mulier quaedam commigravit huc viciniae,' Ter. *An.* i. 1. 'Populus Romanus eo magnitudinis crevit, ut viribus suis conficeretur,' Flor. iii. 12. 'Postridie eius diei Ariovistus praeter castra Caesaris suas copias transduxit et milibus passuum duobus ultra eum castra fecit,' Caes. *B. G.* i. 48.

γ. (*Plenty and Want, &c.*) 'Celeriter adulescentem suae temeritatis implet,' L. i. 4. 'Me omnium laborum levas,' Plaut. *St.* i. 4. 'Helvetii totius Galliae se potiri

ii. The Infinitive Present and Past as Subject:

'Invidere non cadit in sapientem,' C. *T. D.* iii. 10. 'Inge-
nuas didicisse fideliter artes emollit mores,' Ov. *Ep. ex P.*
ii. 9.

Especially

1) Of an Impersonal Verb:
   'Libet semper discere,' C. *d. Or.* iii. 23

2) Of a Copulative Verb with Adj. or Adv. Complement:
   'Dulce et decorum est pro patria mori,' Hor. *C.* iii. 2. 13.

3) Of a Copul. Verb, when the Complement is a Subst. (either
Nom., or Possessive Gen., or Dat. of Purpose):
   'Tempus est maiora conari,' L. vi. 18. 'Tempori cedere
   semper sapientis est habitum,' C. *Div.* ii. 60. 'Laudi
   erit certasse.'

Obs. 1. If the Infin. is Copulative, and the principal Verb has an
Accus. Object, the Complement will be Accus.:
   'Dedecet hominem esse mendacem.'

If the Object is Dative, the Compl. may be Dat. or Accus.:
   'Licuit esse otioso Themistocli, licuit Epaminondae,' C. *T.
   D.* i. 15. 'Civi Romano licet esse Gaditanum,' C. *p. Balb.* 12.

Obs. 2. An Infin. is rarely found as Complement:
   'Docto homini et erudito vivere est cogitare,' C. *Fam.* vi. 1.

---

posse sperabant,' Caes. *B. G.* i. 3. 'Regio aeris ac plumbi uberrima,' Iust. xliv.
3. 'Plena errorum sunt omnia,' C. *T. D.* i. 5. 'Gallia adeo frugum homi-
numque fertilis fuit, ut abundans multitudo vix regi posse videretur,' L. v. 34.
'Roma externae opis indiga fuit,' Tac. *H.* ii. 48. 'Vis consili expers mole
ruit sua,' Hor. *C.* iii. 9. 'Certe omnes virtutis compotes beati sunt,' C. *T. D.* v.
39. 'Postquam Pompeius et consules ex Italia exierunt, non sum, mihi crede, mentis
compos,' C. *Att.* ix. 6. 'Eripite isti gladium, qui sui est impos animi,' Plaut.
Cas. iii. 5. 'Ira, ut insania, impotens sui est,' Sen. *Ir.* i. 1. 'Descendam magnorum
haud umquam indignus avorum,' Verg. *Ae.* xii. 649. 'Pacis eras mediusque
belli,' Hor. *C.* ii. 19. 28. 'Aevi maturus Acestes,' Verg. *Aen.* v. 73. 'Damnatus
longi Sisyphus Aeolides laboris,' Hor. *C.* ii. 14. 19. 'Fortunate animi,' St. *Th.* i.
638. 'Antipho me excruciat animi,' Ter. *Ph.* ii. 2. 10.

B) (*Objective.*) 'Iram bene Ennius initium dixit insaniae,' C. *T. D.* iv. 23. 'Me
tuae dignitatis non modo fautorem, sed etiam amplificatorem cognosces,' C.
Fam. x. 12. 'Epaminondas philosophiae praeceptorem habuit Lysim Tarenti-
num, Pythagoreum,' N. *Ep.* 2. 'Adhibenda est quaedam reverentia adversus
homines, et optimi cuiusque et reliquorum,' C. *Off.* i. 28. 'Patria est communis omnium nostrum parens,' C. *in Cat.* i. 7. 'Ais, Habe mei rationem: habe
tu nostrum (i.e. Romanorum : nostri would=mei),' C. *Att.* vii. 9. 'Habetis ducem
memorem vestri, oblitum sui,' C. *in Cat.* iv. 9. 'Nostri nosmet paenitet,'
Ter. *Ph.* i. 3. 'Nihil malo quam et me mei similem esse, et illos sui,' C. *Att.* ix. 16.
'Magna mei sub terras ibit imago,' Verg. *Ae.* iv. 654. 'Divi quorum est potestas
nostrorum hostiumque,' L. viii. 9. 'Cogor vestram omnium vicem unus consulere,' L. xxv. 38. 'Neque neglegentia tua neque odio id fecit tuo,' Ter. *Ph.*
v. 8. 'Galba omnium consensu visus est capax imperi, nisi imperasset,' Tac. *H.* i.
49. 'Natura tenacissimi sumus eorum quae rudibus annis percepimus,' Qu. i. 1.
'Tu me sitientem virtutis tuae deseruisti,' C. *p. Planc.* 5. 'Epaminondas adeo
fuit veritatis diligens ut ne ioco quidem mentiretur,' Nep. *Ep.* 3. 'Cum commode navigare poteris, ad nos amantissimos tui veni,' C. *Fam.* xvi. 7. 'Romani
semper appetentes gloriae praeter ceteras gentis atque avidi laudis fuerunt,'
C. *p. L. Man.* 3. 'Catilinae corpus erat patiens inediae, vigiliae, algoris,' Sall.
Cat. 9. 'Themistocles peritissimos belli navalis fecit Athenienses,' N. *Them.* 2.

iii. Infinitive as Object.

'Adimam cantare severis,' Hor. *Epist.* i. 19. 9.   'Mori nemo sapiens miserum duxit,' C. *Fam.* vi. 3.

Infin. with Attribute:

'Hoc ridere meum, tam nil, nulla tibi vendo Iliade,' Pers. i. 122.

With Preposition:

'Multum interest inter dare et accipere,' Sen. *Ben.* v. 2.

On the Historic Infinitive see p. 332 ; Infin. Clause, § 194.

iv. Prolative Infinitive.   (See § 102, § 103.)   180

(1) The 'Extensible' Verbs which take this Infinitive imply: *ability, learning, knowledge; duty; desire, dislike; daring, dread, hesitation; custom; endeavour, purpose, resolve; omission, neglect; beginning, continuing, ceasing; hastening, delaying; deserving.*

Also Passive Verbs of *seeming, being deemed, said, found,* &c.: with doceor, moneor, cogor, iubeor, vetor, prohibeor, impedior:

Possum (queo, debeo, volo, nolo, audeo, soleo, meditor, certo, coepi, desino, cogito, propero, moror, animum induco, videor, putor, dicor, reperior, doceor, iubeor, &c.) *currere, legere,* &c.

If the Infinitive depending on any such Verb is Copulative, the Complement will agree with the Subject:

Possum (debeo, volo, &c.; videor, putor, &c.; cogor, iubeor, vetor, &c.) *esse tranquillus, esse doctus, esse philosophus,* &c.

Obs. 1. Verbs of *Desire,* and oportet, take a Perf. Participle as Passive Infin.: 'Patriae consultum volo,' *I wish my country's good to be regarded.* 'Mansum oportuit,' *we ought to have remained.*   See § 203.

'In omnibus rebus est aliquid optimum, etiamsi latet, idque ab eo potest, qui eius rei gnarus est, iudicari,' C. *d. Or.* ii. 2. 'Orator ne physicorum quidem sit ignarus,' C. *Or.* 34. 'Evander vir erat venerabilis miraculo litterarum, rei novae inter rudis artium homines,' L. i. 7. 'Pecoris cupidissimi sunt barbari,' Caes. *B. G.* vi. 34. 'Urbanae militiae Proculus impiger fuit, bellorum insolens,' Tac. *H.* i. 87. 'Galli homines insueti laboris,' Caes. *B. G.* vii. 30. 'Utinam te, frater, non solum vitae sed etiam dignitatis meae superstitem reliquissem,' C. *Qu. F.* i. 3. 'Mihi quidem stultius nihil videtur, quam existimare eum studiosum tui, quem non noris,' C. *d. Pr. C.* 7. 'Caveant intemperantiam, meminerint verecundiae,' C. *Off.* i. 34. 'Plancii meriti in me recordor,' C. *p. Planc.* 28. 'Proprium est stultitiae, aliorum vitia cernere, suorum oblivisci,' C. *T. D.* iii. 73. 'Neque omnino huius rei meminit usquam poeta,' Qu. xi. 2. 'Admonitus sum huius aeris alieni,' C. *Top.* i. 5. 'Grammaticos officii sui commonemus,' Qu. i. 5. 'Venit mihi Platonis in mentem,' C. *Fin.* v. 1. 'Beneficia debet meminisse is, in quem collata sunt, non commemorare, qui contulit,' C. *Lael.* 20. 'Est operae pretium diligentiam maiorum recordari,' C. *d. L. Agr.* ii. 73. 'Obliviscor iniurias, depono memoriam doloris mei,' C. *p. Coel.* 50. 'Ea potius reminiscere, quae digna tua persona sunt,' C. *Fam.* iv. 5. 'Vive memor leti,' Pers. v. 153. 'Omnes immemorem beneficii oderunt,' C. *Off.* ii. 63. 'Qui misereri mei debent, non desinunt invidere,' C. *Att.* iv. 5. 'Tui me miseret, mei piget,' C. *Div.* i. 66. 'Numquam in re bona mali pudebit auctoris,' Sen. *Tranq.* 11. 'Numquam primi consili Deum paenitet,' Sen. *Ben.* 23. 'Me non solum piget stultitiae meae, sed etiam pudet,' C. *p. Dom.* 29. 'Prorsus vitae taedet; ita sunt omnia miseriarum plenissima,' C. *Att.* ii. 24. 'Postquam Alexander Clitum trucidaverat, pigere eum facti coepit,' Iust. xii. 6. 'Decemvirorum Romanos pertaesum est,' L. iii. 67.

Obs. 2. Habeo, do, idiomatically take Infin.: 'Tantum habeo polliceri,' C. *Fam.* i. 'Dare bibere,' L. Similarly, 'Dederat comam diffundere ventis, V. (for ad diffundendum).

Obs. 3. Coepit, incipit, desinit, debet, potest, solet, are impersonal with impers. Infinitives: 'Paenitere eum facti coepit,' 'Perveniri ad summa nisi ex principiis non potest,' Qu. x. 1.

'Coeptum est,' desitum est are so used with Pass. Infin.

(Coeptus sum, desitus sum are used personally with Pass. Infin.)[1]

Obs. 4. The construction of Infin. with Verbs of *motion* is found in poets: 'Ego huc missa sum ludere,' Plaut.

(2) The Infinitive extends also the construction of Adjectives in poetry, and in the prose of the Silver Age, especially in Tacitus. A few Adjectives are thus used by Cicero, Livy, &c., but the greatest number appear in poetry, especially in Horace:

'Audax omnia perpeti ;' 'impiger hostium vexare turmas.'

Other Adjectives so used are: aptus, blandus, bonus, callidus, catus, cautus, celer, doctus, durus, efficax, facilis, fortis, idoneus, impotens, largus, lenis, natus, neglegens, par, pernix, pertinax, potens, piger, praesens, prudens, segnis, sollers, timidus, &c.

181 Construction.

II) Cases of the Infinitive (Gerunds and Supines).

v. Gerundial Construction.

The base of the Latin Gerundial Construction (as of the partially corresponding Greek) is a Participial Adjective—the Gerundive in *dus*, which, as Pott says, is neither Active nor Passive exclusively: bibendus, *proper for drinking.* This serves three uses:

(1) By its Oblique Cases (called Gerunds) it completes (with the Supines) the Active Infinitive Verb-noun:

Sing. N. bibere, Acc. bibere (ad bibendum, bibitum), Gen. bibendi, Dat. bibendo, Abl. bibendo (in &c. bibendo), bibitu.

---

[1] Copulative Verbs Passive are oftener used personally with an Infinitive than with the Infin. Clause. Videtur errasse Cicero, not, videtur errasse Ciceronem. But nuntior, dicor, trador, credor can take the Clause. 'Nuntiatum est adesse Scipionem,' Caes. And Cic. once uses 'videtur mihi' with Clause: *T. D.* v. 5.

A Periphrastic or Combinate Infin. (-us esse, -urus esse, -ndus esse) frequently follows such Verbs; and esse as often as not is suppressed. 'Titus Manlius locutus fertur,' L. 'Affatus dicitur undas,' Mart. 'Creditur olim velificatus Athos,' Iuv. 'Secuturi vindicem libertatis videbantur,' L. 'Delectus habendus putatur.' This idiom has not been adequately noticed by grammarians and commentators: and hence words have been taken as Participles which are true Infinitives. Such in Horace are 'solitus,' *S.* i. 1. 66; 'collisa,' *Ep.* i. 2. 7, and perhaps 'adfatus,' *C.* i. 7. 24: especially 'coactus,' *C.* i. 16. 14, where the construction (undiscerned till lately) is, 'Prometheus fertur coactus ... et apposuisse ...,' *Prometheus is reported to have been compelled,* &c., *and to have attached,* &c. This explanation having been questioned by some on account of the coupling of Act. and Pass. Infin., the following instances (supplied by Mr. Munro) remove that objection. 'Aut tenui percussum verbere Circes *et* cum remigibus grunnisse Elpenora porcis,' Iuv. xv. 21. 'Bustis exisse feruntur *et* tacitae questi tempore noctis avi,' Ov. *F.* ii. 551. 'Emersisse iam e vadis *et* scopulos praetervecta videtur oratio mea, C. *p. Cael.* 21. 'Ne aut velificatus alicui dicaris, *aut* aliquid, quod referret scire, reticuisse,' Cael. *ap.* C. *Fam.* viii. 10. Also L. i. 11; Tac. *Ann.* i. 65: Sen. *Oed.* 768; Caes. *ap.* C. *Att.* x. 3; Cic. *Att.* ix. 11. So the omission of the finite est from Perfects Pass. and Dep., frequent as it is, has sometimes caused these to be mistaken for mere Participles: 'mirata,' Hor. *C.* iv. 9. 15; 'ausa,' Hor. *C.* i. 37. 25. See § 99.

(Its Adjectival origin appears in Gerundial Attraction.)

(2) Its Neuter Nom. with est becomes a Verb Impersonal, signifying *necessity, duty, meetness*: 'Nunc est bibendum.'

(3) As a Participle, it still signifies *necessity, duty, meetness,* but has the Adjectival Construction of Attribute or Complement:

Aqua bibenda: aqua est bibenda.

vi. The Gerunds.

(1) In the Gerunds, two things are to be considered:

A) The cases which depend on them as Verbs.

B) Their own dependence as Oblique Cases of Nouns.

A) A Gerund may govern the same Case as its Verb:

Spes satisfaciendi reipublicae.

A Transitive Gerund, in classic authors, does not generally take an Accus., except of Pronouns or Neuter Plural Adjectives: aliquid, multa, omnia, &c.   But it may do so when rhythm or perspicuity recommends:

'Salutem hominibus dando.'

The usual construction of a Transitive Gerund is that called Gerundial Attraction, by which the Gerund assumes the Gender and Number of its Object, and the Object assumes the Case of the Gerund:

For 'tuendi urbem' is written 'tuendae urbis.'
  „   'liberandi cives'   „   'liberandorum civium.'

B) Dependence of the four Gerunds:

a) The Accus. Gerund depends on Prepositions: ad, inter, ob; rarely ante, circa, post. Ad discendum; ad agros colendos ; inter ludendum ; ob rem iudicandam.

β) The Gen. Gerund depends, as Subjective, Descriptive, or Objective, on numerous Substantives: amor, ars, causa, (also causā, *for the sake*), &c.

As Objective, it depends on many Adjectives which govern a Genitive: capax, cupidus, ignarus, peritus, &c.

Ars canendi ; studium dicendi ; scientia civitatis regendae ; cupidus audiendi; conscius delendae tyrannidis; dux bene vivendi, &c.

γ) The Dat. Gerund as Dativus Commodi depends on

Verbs and Adjectives of *ability, attention,* and *adaptation*: praeesse, operam dare, sufficere, esse, &c.; aptus, utilis, &c.

Substantives : locus, materia, sedes, &c.

(Generally) on any predication implying purpose :

'Operam dedi pingendo;' 'Aqua utilis (inutilis) bibendo,' 'Studium aptum ingeniis acuendis,' &c.: solvendo non esse (*to be insolvent*).

The purpose of an office is stated in this form:

'Tiberius Gracchus triumvir dividendis agris creatus est,' *Tiberius Gracchus was elected one of three commissioners to divide the lands*, Flor.

δ) The Abl. Gerund is of *cause, instrument,* or *manner*; and with the Prepositions de, ex, in; rarely pro.

Mens alitur discendo, audiendis philosophis: in iubendo; a scribendo; de captivis commutandis, &c.

vii. Impersonal Gerundive Construction.

(2) This is not used transitively, but may be without Case:
'Bibendum est,' *we must drink,* Acc. bibendum esse:

or it may govern any Case but the Accusative:

'Serviendum est legibus:' 'utendum est aetate.'

In old Latin the Accus. was used:

'Aeternas quoniam poenas in morte timendum,' Lucr.

viii. Attributive Gerundive Construction.

(3) This is used by Transitive Verbs only:

'Aqua bibenda est,' *water should be drunk.*

Obs. The Gerundive may be an Epithet:

'Ridenda poemata,' *ridiculous poems,* Iuv. x.

but oftener takes a Dative Case (see p. 390):

'Proelia coniugibus loquenda,' *battles for wives to talk of,* Hor.

For this Dative an Ablative of the Agent with ab may be used if required for perspicuity.

ix. Notes on Gerund and Gerundive.

1) The Verbs fungor, fruor, utor, vescor, potior, may be used in Gerundive Construction, both attractional and attributive, because they were anciently Transitive:

'Officii fungendi causa.' 'Vita non fruenda sed utenda est.'

2) The Genitive Gerund is found with dependent Gen.:[1]

'Nobis fuit exemplorum eligendi potestas,' *we had the power of choosing examples,* C. d. Inv. ii. 2.

3) It appears in historians as causal:

'Regium imperium conservandae libertatis fuerat,' *the royal power had existed for the preservation of freedom,* Sall. Cat. 6.

A strange idiom is used by Tacitus: 'Vologesi vetus et penitus infixum erat arma Romana vitandi,' *Vologeses had an old and deeply rooted practice of shunning the Roman arms,* xv. 5.

4) The Attracted Abl. is found after a Comparative:

'Nullum officium referenda gratia magis necessarium est,' *no duty is more necessary than gratitude,* C. Off. i. 15.

---

[1] Madvig (on Cic. *Fin.* p. 112) says that this Gen. is always Plural. But this is disproved by Munro (on Lucr. v. 1225), and Wagner (on Ter. *Haut.,* Note 29).

5) The Gerundive is used as Oblique Complement with do, trado, conduco, loco, propono, curo, &c., to express purpose:

'Scriba quidam Cn. Flavius ediscendos fastos populo proposuit,' *one Flavius, a clerk, published the calendar for the people to learn by heart*, C. *p. Mur.* 11. 'Conon muros Athenarum reficiendos curat,' N. *Con.* 5. See § 131.

(So Pass.: 'Vita data est utenda,' *life was given to be used.*)

Poets use an Infin. for this Gerundive:

'Tristitiam et metus tradam protervis in mare Creticum portare ventis,' *sadness and terror I will deliver to the boisterous winds to carry into the Cretan Sea*, Hor. *C.* i. 26. 1.

x. The Two Supines.

These are Cases of Verb-nouns of the U-declension.

(1) The First or Accus. Supine (-**um**) implies Purpose after a Verb of actual or implied motion:

'Lusum it Maecenas, dormitum ego,' Hor. *S.* i. 5. 48.

a) It may take a Case:

'Hannibal defensum patriam revocatus est,' N. *Han.* 6.

b) Sometimes motion is rather implied than expressed:

'Coctum ego, non vapulatum conductus sum,' *I was hired to cook, not to be beaten*, Plaut. *Aul.* iii. 3. 3. 'Augustus filiam Iuliam primum Marcello, mox Agrippae nuptum dedit,' Suet. *Aug.* 63.

c) 'Ire' with this Supine means *to set about doing a thing*:

Perditum ire, raptum ire, ultum ire, &c.

Hence the use of the Impers. Infin. iri with the Supine to supply a Passive form for Infin. Fut.

'Audierat non datum iri filio uxorem suo,' Ter. *An.* i. 2. 6.

d) Other constructions oftener express the purpose of motion:

'Eunt consultum Apollinem.' For 'consultum' might be used, 'ut consulerent,' 'qui consulerent' 'ad consulendum,' 'consulendi causa:' less usually, 'consulturi.'

Livy uses this Supine most largely.

(2) The Second or Abl. Supine (-**u**) limits the undeclined Substantives fas, nefas, opus, and Adjectives which signify *good or evil, pleasantness or unpleasantness, fitness or unfitness,* &c.

'Nefas visu,' *horrible to behold.* 'Turpe dictu,' *shameful to say.*

a) After some words, ad with the Gerund is more elegant:

'Cibus facillimus ad concoquendum,' C. *Fin.* ii. 20.

b) In poetry the Infinitive may be used:

'Cereus in vitium flecti,' *waxlike in being moulded to vice*, Hor. *Pis.* 161.

c) The Supine in -u is rare after Verbs: 'Pudet dictu,' Tac.

d) Anciently it appears as an Ablative of Origin:

'Primus cubitu surgat vilicus, postremus cubitum eat,' *the bailiff should be the first to get up, the last to go to bed,* Cato.

---

188   Note on the Annexive Relation.

A Word is said to be in Annexive Relation to another, when it is so joined to it by a Conjunction (expressed or understood) as to take the same construction on the same grounds: 'Dis hominibusque visum est;' 'non mihi loquitur sed tibi;' 'Brutum non minus amo quam tu, paene dixi, quam te:' where tu, by being Nominative, shows that it is annexed to ego understood: te, by being Accusative, shows that it is annexed to Brutum.

Examples of Infinitive.

'Non attinet quicquam sequi quod assequi non queas,' C. *Off.* i. 31. 'Quo mihi fortunam, si non conceditur uti?' Hor. *Epist.* i. 5. 12. 'Flaccum numquam prospexisse vestrae saluti paenitebit,' C. *p. Fl.* 41. 'Bene sentire recteque facere satis est ad bene beateque vivendum,' C. *Fam.* vi. 1. 'Decet verecundum esse adulescentem,' Plaut. *As.* v. 1. 'Consulem fieri valde utile Mario videbatur,' C. *Off.* iii. 20. 'Iovis esse nepoti contigit haud uni,' Ov. *Met.* xi. 219. 'Mihi iurato dicere fas fuit,' C. *p. Mur.* 37. 'Vivere ipsum turpe est nobis,' C. *Att.* xiii. 28. 'Id primum videamus, beate vivere vestrum quale sit,' C. *Fin.* ii. 27. 'Neque mihi praestabilius quicquam videtur quam posse dicendo hominum voluntates impellere quo velit, unde autem velit deducere,' C. *d. Or.* i. 8. 'Honeste atque inhoneste vendere mos erat,' Sall. *Cat.* 30. 'Fas est et ab hoste doceri,' Ov. *M.* iv. 428.

'Aristo et Pyrrho inter optime valere et gravissime aegrotare nihil prorsus dicebant interesse,' C. *Fin.* ii. 13.

'Nondum fuga certa, nondum victoria erat; tegi magis Romanus, quam pugnare; Volscus inferre signa, urgere aciem, plus caedis hostium videre quam fugae,' L. iv. 37. See Sall. *B. Iug.* 50. 51. 75.

'Certos mihi finis terminosque constituam, extra quos egredi non possim, si maxime velim,' C. *p. Quinct.* 10. 'Perge reliqua; gestio enim scire omnia,' C. *Att.* iv. 11. 'Aelius Stoicus esse voluit, orator autem nec studuit umquam nec fuit,' C. *Br.* 56. 'Cato esse quam videri bonus malebat,' Sall. *Cat.* 54. 'Tu animum poteris inducere contra haec dicere?' C. *Div.* i. 13. 'Thraces, navibus committere se non ausi, domos dilapsi sunt,' L. xliv. 45. 'Miltiades Chersonesi manere decrevit,' Nep. *Milt.* 2. 'Desiderio Romuli populus Romanus regem flagitare non destitit,' C. *Rep.* ii. 12. 'Spartae pueri rapere discunt,' C. *Rep.* iv. 5. 'Vos sociis prospicere laboratis,' C. *Verr.* iii. 55. 'Sestii mortem ulcisceremini, si liberi esse cogitaretis,' C. *p. Sest.* 38. 'Datames Aegyptum proficisci parabat,' N. *Dat.* 4. 'Fortes et sapientes viri non tam praemia sequi solent recte factorum quam ipsa recte facta,' C. *p. Mil.* 35. 'Verus patriae diceris esse pater,' Mart. *Sp.* iii. 11. 'Amens mihi fuisse videor a principio,' C. *Att.* ix. 10. 'Barbara narratur venisse venefica tecum,' Ov. *H.* vi. 19. 'In Graecia primum humanitas, litterae, etiam fruges inventae esse creduntur,' Plin. *Ep.* viii. 24. 'Existimatur Caelius Catilinae nimium familiaris fuisse,' C. *p. Cael.* 4. 'Prometheus affixus Caucaso tradebatur,' C. *T. D.* v. 3. 'Commisisse cavet quae mox mutare laboret,' Hor. *in Pis.* 168. 'Romani pepercisse volunt,' L. xxxii. 21. 'Contenti sumus illud unum dixisse, quanti ille fuerit,' Vell. ii. 108. 'Si potuit meruisse necem, meruisse putetur,' Ov. *H.* xi. 109. 'Haec fere dicere habui de natura deorum,' C. *N. D.* iii. 39. 'Gallinis meridie bibere dato,' *Cat.* 89. 'Legati Celtiberorum nihil prius petierunt a praetore quam ut bibere sibi iuberet dari,' L. xl. 47. 'Lucere coepit,' C. *Div.* 1. 23. 'Non desiit paenitere me suscepti adversus Romanos belli,' L. xxiii. 13. 'Solet eum, cum aliquid furiose fecit, paenitere,' C. *Att.* viii. 5. 'Armis disceptari coeptum est de iure publico,' C. *Fam.* iv. 4. 'Iampridem contra eos desitum est disputari,' C. *Fin.* ii. 13. 'Comitia nostra haberi coepta sunt,' C. *Verr.* i. 9. 'Papirius Crassus primus Papisius est vocari desitus,' C. *Fam.* ix. 21.

'Glebae coepere moveri,' Ov. *M.* iii. 106. 'Is est maxime docilis qui attentissime est paratus audire,' C. *Inv.* i. 16. 'Reficit rates quassas, indocilis pauperiem pati,' Hor. *C.* i. 1. 'Maesta civitas fuit, vinci insueta,' L. iv. 31.

Examples of Gerunds and Gerundive.

I. (*Gerunds and Gerundial Attraction.*) 'Fuerunt apud Romanos qui assentando multitudini grassarentur,' L. xlv. 23. 'Diogenes dicebat, artem se tradere bene disserendi et vera ac falsa diiudicandi,' C. *d. Or.* ii. 38. 'Ita nati factique sumus, ut et agendi aliquid et diligendi aliquos, et libertatis, et referendae gratiae principia in nobis contineremus,' C. *Fin.* v. 15. 'Nulla causa iusta cuiquam esse potest contra patriam arma capiendi,' C. *Phil.* ii. 22. 'Legem doctissimi viri Graeco putant nomine a suum cuique tribuendo appellatam,' C. *Leg.* i. 16. 'Cernitur in delectu bonorum et malorum iustitia, et in suo cuique tribuendo,' C. *Fin.* v. 23. 'Non solum ad discendum propensi sumus, verum etiam ad docendum,' C. *Fin.* iii. 20. 'Oculus conturbatus non est probe affectus ad suum munus fungendum,' C. *T. D.* iii. 7. 'Mores puerorum se inter ludendum simplicius detegunt,' Qu. i. 3. 12. 'Flagitiosum est, eum, a quo pecuniam ob absolvendum acceperis, condemnare,' C. *Verr.* ii. 32. 'Homo magna habet instrumenta ad obtinendam adipiscendamque sapientiam,' C. *Leg.* i. 22. 'Eadem precor a dis immortalibus ob L. Murenae consulatum una cum salute obtinendum,' C. *p. Mur.* 1. 'Nihil Xenophonti tam regale videtur quam studium agri colendi,' C. *Cat. N.* 17. 'Veni consulis Antoni domum saepe salutandi causa,' C. *Fam.* xi. 28. 'Reliqua, ita mihi salus aliqua detur potestasque in patria moriendi, ut me lacrimae non sinunt scribere,' C. *Q. Fr.* i. 3. 'Iustitiae fruendae causa videntur olim bene morati reges constituti,' C. *Off.* ii. 12. 'Pythagoreorum more exercendae memoriae gratia quid quoque die dixerim, audierim, egerim, commemoro vesperi,' C. *Cat. M.* 11. 'Epaminondas, studiosus erat audiendi,' Nep. *Ep.* 3. 'Demosthenes Platonis studiosus audiendi fuit,' C. *d. Or.* i. 20. 'Homines bellandi cupidi magno dolore afficiebantur,' Caes. *B. G.* i. 2. 'Multi propter gloriae cupiditatem cupidi sunt bellorum gerendorum,' C. *Off.* i. 22. 'Multae res oratorem ab imperito dicendi ignaroque distinguunt,' C. *d. Or.* iii. 44. 'Mons pecori bonus alendo erat,' L. xxix. 31. 'Ver tamquam adulescentiam significat ostenditque fructus futuros: reliqua tempora demetendis fructibus et percipiendis accommodata sunt,' C. *Cat. M.* 19. 'Tu, Eruci, praeesse agro colendo flagitium putas?' C. *p. S. Rosc.* 18. 'Consul placandis dis dat operam,' L. xxii. 2. 'Galli Transalpini haud procul inde, ubi nunc Aquileia est, locum oppido condendo ceperunt,' L. xxxix. 22. 'Multarum civitatum principes ad me detulerunt, sumptus decerni legatis nimis magnos, cum solvendo civitates non essent,' C. *Fam.* iii. 8. 'Tributo plebes liberata est, ut divites conferrent, qui oneri ferendo essent,' L. ii. 9. 'Decemviros legibus scribendis intra hos decem annos et creavimus et e republica sustulimus,' L. iv. 4. 'Valerius consul comitia collegae subrogando habuit,' L. ii. 8. 'Hominis mens discendo alitur et cogitando,' C. *Off.* i. 30. 'Omnis loquendi elegantia augetur legendis oratoribus et poetis,' C. *d. Or.* iii. 10. 'Aristotelem non deterruit a scribendo Platonis amplitudo,' C. *d. Or.* 1. 'Multa de bene beateque vivendo a Platone disputata sunt,' C. *Fin.* i. 2. 'Ex providendo appellata est prudentia,' C. *Leg.* i. 23. 'Saepe plus in metuendo mali est, quam in illo ipso, quod timetur,' C. *Fam.* vi. 4. 'In voluptate spernenda virtus vel maxime cernitur,' C. *Leg.* i. 19. 'Reliquorum siderum quae causa collocandi fuerit, quaeque eorum sit collocatio, in alium sermonem differendum est,' C. *Tim.* 9. 'Agitur, utrum M. Antonio facultas detur opprimendae rei publicae, caedis faciendae bonorum, diripiendae urbis, agrorum suis condonandi,' C. *Phil.* v. 3. 'Aedui legatos ad Caesarem sui purgandi gratia mittunt,' Caes. *B. G.* vii. 43. 'Haec prodendi imperi Romani, tradendae Hannibali victoriae sunt,' L. xxvii. 9.

II. (*Impers. and Attrib. Gerundive.*) 'Hic vobis vincendum aut moriendum est, milites,' L. xxi. 43. 'Orandum est ut sit mens sana in corpore sano,' Iuv. x. 356. 'Non corpori soli subveniendum est, sed menti atque animo multo magis, C. *Cat. M.* 11. 'Suum cuique incommodum ferendum est potius, quam de alterius commodis detrahendum,' C. *Off.* iii. 6. 'Apud Pythagoram discipulis quinque annis tacendum erat,' Sen. *Ep.* 52. 'Tria videnda sunt oratori: quid dicat, et quo quicque loco, et quomodo,' C. *Or.* 14. 'Semper ita vivamus ut rationem reddendam nobis arbitremur,' C. *Verr.* ii. 11. 'Pietati summa tribuenda laus est,' C. *d. Or.* ii. 40. 'Quaeritur, praeponendane sit divitiis gloria,' C. *Top.* 22. 'Suo cuique iudicio est utendum,' C. *N. D.* iii. 1. 'Sentio moderandum mihi esse

CHAPTER IV.

THE COMPOUND SENTENCE.

SECTION I.

SUBORDINATION OF CLAUSES.

(See Chapter I. § 100.)

189
Subor-
dinate
Clauses.

Subordinate Clauses are of three kinds :

A) Substantival ; *B*) Adverbial ; *C*) Adjectival or Relative.

A) On Substantival Clauses see § 100, p. 349.

B) An Adverbial Clause qualifies the Principal Sentence like an Adverb, answering the questions *how, why, when,* &c.

Such Clauses are of seven kinds :

Consecutive (*so that*)	Conditional (*if, unless,* &c.)
Final (*in order that*)	Concessive (*although,* &c.)
Causal (*because, since,* &c.)	Comparative (*as if,* &c.)
Temporal (*when, whilst,* &c.)	

C) An Adjectival or Relative Clause is formed by the Relative qui or one of its Particles. When this contains some Adverbial sense (*so that, in order that, since, if, although*), it generally exhibits the Subjunctive Mood.

---

iam orationi meae,' C. *Verr.* iii. 43. 'Intellegite quibus credendum et a quibus cavendum sit,' L. xxxiv. 39. 'Aguntur bona multorum civium, quibus est a vobis et ipsorum et reipublicae causa consulendum,' C. *p. L. Man.* 2. 'Spectandus in certamine Martio,' Hor. *C.* iv. 14. 'Thrasybulus legem oblivionis non tantum ferendam curavit, sed etiam ut valeret effecit,' Nep. *Thras.* 3. 'Pueris sententias ediscendas damus,' Sen. *Ep.* 33. 'Redemptor columnam Iovis conduxerat faciendam,' C. *Div.* ii. 21.

Examples of Supines.

(*First Supine.*) 'Coriolanus in Volscos exsulatum abiit,' L. ii. 35. 'Legati ab Roma venerunt questum iniurias et ex foedere res repetitum,' L. iii. 25. 'Quid est, Crasse, inquit Iulius, imusne sessum? Etsi admonitum venimus te, non flagitatum,' C. *d. Or.* iii. 5. 'Cur te is perditum?' Ter. *An.* i. 1. 107. 'Ubi se flagitiis dedecoravere turpissimi viri, bonorum praemia ereptum eunt,' Sall. *Iug.* 85. 'In eam spem erecta civitas erat, in Africa eo anno debellatum iri,' L. xxix. 14. 'Dumnorix propinquas suas nuptum in alias civitates collocavit,' Caes. *B. G.* i. 18.

(*Second Supine.*) 'Narratio brevis erit, si non longius, quam quod scitu opus est, in narrando procedetur,' C. *Inv.* i. 20. 'Humanus animus cum alio nullo, nisi cum ipso deo, si hoc fas est dictu, comparari potest,' C. *T. D.* v. 13. 'Quid est tam iucundum cognitu atque auditu quam sapientibus sententiis gravibusque verbis ornata oratio?' C. *d. Or.* i. 8. 'Quod optimum factu videbitur, facies,' C. *Att.* vii. 22. 'Ad imitandum tam mihi propositum exemplar illud est quam tibi.' C. *p. Mur.* 31.

SECTION II.

SUBOBLIQUE CONSTRUCTION.

i. Oratio Obliqua.

190
Oratio
Obliqua.

1) Oratio Obliqua (in distinction from Oratio Recta, *direct oration*) is a term especially applied to Substantival Clauses, and, above all, to the Infinitive Clause and its substitutes.

2) A subordinate or dependent Clause may have another depending on it; and in a long Compound Sentence, or Period, there may thus be a *primary, secondary,* &c., dependence of clauses.

If the Verb (whether Infin. or Finite) of *a primary dependence* forms Oratio Obliqua, the Verb of *a following dependence* is 'Subordinate to Oratio Obliqua,' or (in one word) Suboblique.

ii. The first important Rule of dependent Construction is this:

I) A Suboblique Finite Verb is in the Subjunctive Mood.

This is seen by comparison of the two following passages:

Oratio Recta: 'Ars earum rerum est quae sciuntur; oratoris autem omnis actio opinionibus, non scientia, continetur: nam et apud eos dicimus, qui nesciunt, et ea dicimus, quae nescimus ipsi,' C. *d. Or.* ii. 7.

Oratio Obliqua: (Antonius apud Ciceronem docet:) Artem earum rerum esse, quae *sciantur*: oratoris autem omnem actionem opinione, non scientia, contineri; quia et apud eos *dicat*, qui *nesciant*, et ipse *dicat* quod *nesciat*.

Here 'artem esse,' 'actionem contineri,' form Oratio Obliqua, and the Finite Verbs in subsequent dependence (sciantur, dicat, nesciant, nesciat) are therefore Subjunctive.

iii. But, secondly, a *principal* Verb often contains more than is expressed by the mere form; not merely the writer's or speaker's declaration, but an implied *opinion* or *assertion* of some other; upon which the Verb of *the primary clause* may depend. Such a principal predication has been called by some writers 'Cogitatio Obliqua;' but a more convenient term is 'Virtual Oratio Obliqua:' from which it follows that the dependent Verb is Virtually Suboblique.

191
Virtual
Oratio
Obliqua.

Hence results the second Rule of dependent Construction: namely,

II) A Finite Verb virtually Suboblique is in the Subjunctive Mood.

Laudat Africanum Panaetius quod fuerit abstinens.

('Laudat' implies 'ait esse laudandum.')

Caesar Aeduos frumentum, quod polliciti essent, flagitabat.

(Flagitabat implies that *Caesar reminded* the Aedui of their promise. Hence the Mood of polliciti essent.)

F F 2

A mere change in the Mood of the dependent Verb may cause a change of reference to, or from, the writer or speaker:

'Themistocles noctu ambulabat in publico, quod somnum capere non posset.'

Here the mood of posset (and this alone) refers the clause to the mind of Themistocles, who *alleged* inability to sleep as the reason why he was in the habit of walking by night. Had poterat been written, the sentence would still be good Latin, but the cause would then rest on the assertion of the writer (Cicero).

iv. The principle of Rules II. and III. is, that *dependence on a conception must itself be conceptive* ; and, as the Conjunctive is the Mood of Conception, this leads to the third important rule:

192
Dependence on Conjunctive.

III) A Verb really dependent on a Conjunctive Verb is generally Subjunctive:

'Equidem illud molior, ut mihi Caesar concedat ut absim, cum aliquid in senatu contra Gnaeum agatur,' C. *Att.* ix. 6. 'Quaerimus qualis in bello praedonum praedo ipse fuerit Verres, qui in foro populi Romani pirata nefarius reperiatur?' C. *Verr.* i. 59. 'Erat in Hortensio memoria tanta ut, quae secum commentatus esset, ea sine scripto verbis eisdem redderet, quibus cogitavisset,' C. *Br.* 88.

Agatur is Subjunctive, being dependent on absim; reperiatur, on qualis fuerit; commentatus esset and cogitavisset, on redderet.

193
Exceptions.

v. Exceptions to the Law of Mood in Dependence.

1) A Clause which seems, by its position, to depend on Oratio Obliqua, may be independent; that is, it may contain a fact introduced by the author: in which case the Mood will be Indic.:

'Caesari nuntiatum est, Sulmonensis, quod oppidum a Corfinio septem milium intervallo abest, cupere ea facere, quae vellet, sed a Q. Lucretio senatore et Attio Paeligno prohiberi, qui id oppidum septem cohortium praesidio tenebant,' Caes. *B. C.* i. 18.

The Clauses quod ... abest and qui ... tenebant contain facts stated by the historian, and are not part of the message received by Caesar. But quae vellet is dependent.

2) A short Relative Clause, especially when it immediately follows a Demonstrative, is often constructed independently of Oratio Obliqua, being regarded as a mere epithet:

'Eloquendi vis efficit ut ea quae ignoramus discere, et ea quae scimus alios docere possimus,' C. *N. D.* ii. 59.

3) Dum (*whilst*) is sometimes constructed with Present Indic., even when subordinate to Oratio Obliqua:

'Quanto laudabilius periturum Pisonem, dum amplectitur rempublicam, dum auxilia libertati invocat!' Tac. *Ann.* xv. 59.

(Other reasons may occur, inducing an author to exempt a Clause from the general law and to keep the Indic. Mood.)

SECTION III.

SUBSTANTIVAL CLAUSES.

I) Indirect Statement (Enuntiatio Obliqua).

This has three forms : (1) first and principally the Infinitive Clause : (2) the Ut-clause : (3) the Quod-clause.

A. The Infinitive Clause, or Accusative with Infinitive.

1) This is introduced

As Object, by 'Verba Declarandi et Sentiendi,' Verbs which state or imply a *fact, feeling,* or *opinion.*

Such are: *a*) aio, dico, fateor, nego, scribo, &c., auctor sum; certiorem facio: *b*) audio, credo, disco, puto, scio, spero, &c., gaudeo, gratulor, &c.

As Subject, by the Passives of such Verbs; by Impersonal Verbs of those meanings: apparet, constat, interest, patet, placet, &c.; by est with many Adjectives, certum est, credibile (perspicuum, falsum, probabile, verum, verisimile, utile, &c.) est.

As Apposite, by Substantives and Pronouns : fama (mos, rumor, spes, fas, &c.) est ; illud certum est, illud nego, and the like.

2) The Tense of the Infinitive Verb will be such as sense and consecution require.

Dico (dicam, dixero)

eum venire, *that he* is *coming* ; eum venisse, *that he* has *come* ; eum venturum esse, *that he* will *come.*

Examples of Suboblique Construction.

I) 'Cato mirari se aiebat quod non rideret haruspex, haruspicem cum vidisset,' C. *Div.* ii. 24. 'Scito me, postquam in urbem venerim, redisse cum libris in gratiam,' C. *Fam.* ix. 1. 'Fateor me oratorem, si modo sim, ex Academiae spatiis exstitisse,' C. *Fin.* v. 5. 1. 'Sapientissimum esse dicunt eum, cui, quod opus sit, ipsi veniat in mentem ; propius accedere illum, qui alterius bene inventis obtemperet,' C. *p. Clu.* 31.

II) 'Quereris quod non, Cinna, bibamus idem,' Mart. xii. 28. 'Alium rogantes regem misere ad Iovem, inutilis quoniam esset qui fuerat datus,' Phaed. i. 2. 'Darius eius pontis, dum ipse abesset, custodes reliquit,' N. *Milt.* 3. 'In Hispania prorogatum veteribus imperatoribus est imperium cum exercitibus quos haberent,' L. xl. 18. 'Cum abessem, quotienscunque patria in mentem veniret, haec omnia occurrebant, colles campique et Tiberis et hoc caelum sub quo natus educatusque essem,' L. v. 54.

III) 'Dici non potest quin ii, qui nihil metuant, nihil angantur, nihil concupiscant, beati sint,' C. *T. D.* v. 17. 'Hirri necessarii fidem implorarunt Pompeii ; praestaret quod proficiscenti recepisset,' Caes. *B. C.* iii. 8. 'Miraretur qui cerneret,' L. xxxiv. 9. 'Isto bono utare dum adsit, cum absit ne requiras,' C. *Cat. M.* 10.

(*Exceptions.*) 'Themistocles Xerxem certiorem fecit id agi ut pons, quem in Hellesponto fecerat, dissolveretur,' N. *Th.* 9. 'Placet Stoicis eos anhelitus terrae, qui frigidi sunt, cum fluere coeperint, ventos esse,' C. *Div.* ii. 19. 'Dic, hospes, Spartae nos te hic vidisse iacentis, dum sanctis patriae legibus obsequimur,' ap. Cic. *T. D.* i. 42.

Copias mitti, *that forces* are *being sent*; copias missas esse, *that forces* have *been sent*; copias missum iri, *that forces* will *be sent.*

Dicebam (dixi, dixeram)

eum venire, *that he* was *coming*; eum venisse, *that he* had *come*; eum venturum (esse), *that he* would *come.*

Copias mitti, *that forces* were *being sent*; copias missas esse, *that forces* had *been sent*; copias missum iri (or missas fore), *that forces* would *be sent.*

For copias missum iri may also be used:

'Futurum (or fore) ut copiae mittantur (*will*) . . . mitterentur (*would*).'

If the Clause is to express that something *would have happened* or not, this is done by using,

For Active sense, the Future Participle with fuisse:

Dico (dixi) . . . eum venturum fuisse, *I say* (*said*) *that he would have come* (lit. *was about to come*).

For Passive sense, futurum fuisse ut with Passive Subjunctive:

Dico (dixi) futurum fuisse ut copiae mitterentur, *I say* (*said*) *that forces would have been sent* (lit. *it was about to happen that forces would be sent*).

3) Verbs, which by their meaning imply that the dependent action is Future, usually take a Future Infinitive Clause.

Such are Verbs of *promising, vowing, threatening, hoping*:

Polliceor, promitto, recipio, spondeo, voveo; minor, minitor; spero, despero, spes est:

Pollicentur, minantur se ita facturos.

Speramus, spes est eum venturum esse.

a) Such Verbs are also found with a Present Clause:

'Modo sum pollicitus ducere,' *I just now promised to marry her*, Ter. *An.* iii. 5. 7. 'Haec scripsi ut sperares te assequi id quod optasses,' C. *Fam.* ii. 10. See M. *Lucr.* i. 722.

And when spero implies *belief*:

'Spero nostram amicitiam non egere testibus,' C. *Fam.* ii. 2.

b) Posse after a Verb of *hoping* gives a Future character to the Clause:

'Vel me licet existimes desperare ista posse perdiscere,' *you may deem that even I have no hope that I can learn those things thoroughly*, C. *d. Or.* i. 36.

4) An Infinitive Clause, used Interrogatively without a principal Verb, expresses Indignation:

'Mene incepto desistere victam?' *what, I be vanquished, and abandon my design?* Verg. *Ae.* i. 37. 'O praeclarum imperatorem! tantumne vidisse in metu periculoque provinciae?' C. *Verr.* v. 5. 'Ita comparatam esse hominum naturam!' Ter. *H.* iii. 1.

Ut with a Subjunctive may be used for the same purpose:

'Te ut ulla res frangat?' *the idea that anything will humble you*, C. *Cat.* i. 1. 'Tibi ego ut credam, furcifer?' Ter. *An.* iii. 5.

5) In the Infin. Clause the following ellipses occur:

a) An Indefinite Subject understood in the Subjective Construction:

'Conveniet in dando munificum esse (aliquem),' C. *Off.* ii. 18.

b) A Reflexive Pronoun omitted:

'Ferre non posse clamabit,' C. *T. D.* ii. 17. 'Id nescire Mago dixit,' L. xxiii. 63.

Most frequently with the Fut. Infin.:

'L. Caecilius agrariae legi intercessorem fore professus est,' *Caecilius declared that he would interpose to forbid the agrarian law*, C. *p. Sull.* 13.

Esse is at the same time often omitted:

'Brutus populum iureiurando adegit, neminem Romae passuros regnare,' *Brutus made the people swear they would allow no one to be king at Rome*, L. ii. 1.

(Poets sometimes use the Greek idiom, by which the Nom. of the principal Verb becomes also the Subject of the Infin.

'Phaselus ille . . . ait fuisse navium celerrimus,' Catull. iv. 1. 'Sensit medios delapsus in hostis,' Verg. *Ae.* ii. 377. 'Vir bonus et sapiens dignis ait esse paratus,' Hor. *Epist.* i. 7. 23. 'Rettulit Aiax esse Iovis pronepos,' Ov. *M.* xiii. 141.

A far bolder instance is:

'Acceptum refero versibus, esse nocens,' Ov. *Tr.* ii. 10.

Compare Hor. *C.* i. 37. 31. iii. 16. 32.)

c) A Demonstr. Pronoun omitted if there is no ambiguity:

'Valerius dictatura se abdicavit. Apparuit causa plebi, suam vicem indignantem magistratu abisse,' *Valerius resigned the dictatorship: the motive was clear to the plebeians, that he quitted office from indignation on their account*, L. ii. 31.

d) A Verb omitted in a Correlative Clause, subordinate to Infinitive, its Noun being attracted to the Accusative:

'Te suspicor eisdem rebus, quibus me ipsum, interdum gravius commoveri,' *I suspect you are sometimes stirred too deeply by the same things which stir me*, C. *C. M.* 1.

Quibus me ipsum is for quibus ipse commoveor.

6) The ambiguous construction of two Accusatives, Subject and Object (as in the famous oracle, 'Aio te, Aeacida, Romanos vincere posse'), may be evaded by using the Passive Construction. Thus render, '*I believe that Marcus loves you*,' (not, 'Credo Marcum te amare,' but) 'Credo te a Marco amari.'

7) The English, '*it is said of Homer* that he was blind,' or '*they say of Homer* that he was blind,' or '*Homer, they tell us* (it is said), was blind,' is rendered by one of the constructions, 'tradunt (tra-

ditur) Homerum caecum fuisse,' or 'traditur Homerus caecus fuisse.' But the use of de is not inadmissible :

'De Tirone, video tibi curae esse,' C.

8) On the Personal Construction of Passive Copulative Verbs, see Note, p. 427.

9) 'Memini me videre' or 'memini videre,' *I remember seeing.* 'Memini me vidisse,' *I remember that I saw* (at a specific time). 'Memineram me vidisse,' *I remembered that I had seen.*

195
Ut-
Clause.

B. Ut-clause for Infinitive Clause.

Ut (*that*), with Subjunctive, for the Infin. Clause, is used as Subject, to express consecutiveness. It depends on

1) Impersonal Verbs : est, esto, abest, accedit, accidit, contingit, evenit, fit, interest, refert, relinquitur, restat, sequitur, superest, usu venit, &c. See M. *Lucr.* i. 442.

2) Est, with an Adj. or Adv. complement : aequum, consentaneum, consequens, extremum, iniquum, insitum, integrum, par, rarum, rectum, reliquum, tritum, usitatum, utile, verisimile, verum, &c. : prope, satis est, &c.

3) Est, with a Subst.: consuetudo, mos, vitium, and others. This Ut-clause is often in apposition to a Noun or Pronoun.

Examples : 'Est ut viro vir latius ordinet arbusta sulcis,' Hor. *C.* ii. 1. 'Ad Appii Claudii senectutem accedebat etiam ut caecus esset,' C. *Cat. M.* 6. 'Est hoc commune vitium . . . ut invidia gloriae comes sit,' C. *Verr.* ii. 65.

Obs. 1. Owing to the nature of this clause, it seldom contains a negative ; but if it does, the negatives are non, nihil, nullus, &c. 'Fuit hoc in Crasso, ut non tam existimari vellet non didicisse, quam . . . nostrorum hominum prudentiam Graecis anteferre,' C. *d. Or.* ii. 1. 'Soli hoc contingit sapienti ut nihil faciat invitus, nihil dolens, nihil coactus,' C. *Par.* v. 1. 'Est ut plerique philosophi nulla tradant praecepta dicendi, et habeant paratum tamen, quid de quaque re dicant,' C. *d. Or.* ii. 36.

Obs. 2. On the other hand, ut, implying *purpose* (as in Petitio Obliqua), takes ne, nequis, &c., in negation. See Examples, p. 446.

Certain predications may sometimes imply *consequence* only (introducing an Oblique Enunciation), sometimes *purpose* (introducing Oblique Petition). Such are facere, fieri, efficere, &c. ; expedit, interest, refert, placet, prodest, utile est, &c. ; condicio (consilium, ius, munus) est ; and others.

The following passage shews Obl. Petition and Obl. Enunciation dependent on the same word : 'Ex hoc efficitur non ut voluptas ne sit voluptas, sed ut voluptas non sit summum bonum,' *the result of this is not that pleasure will cease to be pleasure, but that pleasure is not the chief good,* C. *Fin.* ii. 8. The first result is *purposed* (ut ne sit), the second *consecutive* (ut non sit).

See the use of 'ita ne' in Consecutive Clauses.

Obs. 3. Ut Consecutive with predications of *affirming, thinking,* or *perceiving,* is confined to one or two expressions :

'Qui probari potest ut sibi animus mederi non possit?' *how can we be satisfied that the mind is unable to heal itself?* C. T. D. iii. 3.   Hence it rarely forms Objective Clauses.   See V. *Aen.* xi. 153.

Care must therefore be taken not to confound it with the Interrog. Particle ut (*how*), which often forms such clauses: 'Videmus ut luna solis lumen accipiat,' C. *d. Or.* iii. 5.   See § 202.

Obs. 4. Licet, oportet, necesse est, when they take the Subjunctive, usually omit ut: 'Licet pauca degustes,' *you may taste a few samples,* C. *Att.* xvi. 8. 'Me ipsum ames oportet,' C. *Fin.* ii. 28. 'Oratio, si res non subest, aut nulla sit necesse est aut omnium irrisione ludatur,' *a speech without matter must be either not delivered or laughed at by everybody,* C. *d. Or.* i. 12.

C. Quod-clause for Infin. Clause.

196
Quod-
clause.

Quod, *that*, with Indic. (but, if Suboblique, with Subjunctive) stands for the Infin. Clause, either to mark distinctly that a fact is expressed, or to shew that the Oratio Recta finds its *Cause* in a fact.

1) For the former purpose it appears

As Subject, with accedit, accidit, apparet, evenit, fit, interest, nocet, obest, occurrit, parum est, prodest, &c.; or with est and a Substantive: causa est, consolatio est, vitium est, &c.

As Object, with addo, adicio, animadverto, excuso, facio, mitto, nihil moror, non dico, omitto, praetereo, praetermitto, &c.

And in Apposition to Pronouns.

2) For the latter purpose it is joined to Verbs of Emotion, expressing *joy, sorrow, surprise, praise, blame, indignation,* &c.

As Subject, to dolet, iuvat, gratum (indignum, mirum, pergratum) est, &c.

As Object, to accuso, admiror, aegre (graviter, indigne, moleste) fero, angor, bene facio, delector, doleo, gaudeo, glorior, gratulor, ignosco, indignor, laetor, laudo, miror, obicio, queror, reprehendo, &c.

Examples: 'Accedit huc quod postridie ille venit,' C. *Fam.* viii. 2. 'Adde quod pubes tibi crescit omnis,' Hor. *C.* ii. 8. 'Magnum beneficium est naturae quod necesse est mori,' Sen. *Ep.* 103. 'Inter causas malorum nostrorum est, quod vivimus ad exempla,' C. *N. D.* ii. 53. 'Habet hoc optimum in se generosus animus, quod concitatur ad honesta,' *a noble mind has this chief merit, that its impulse is to virtue,* Sen. *Ep.* 39. 'Bene facis quod me adiuvas,' C. *Fin.* iii. 15. 'Gratum est quod patriae civem populoque dedisti,' Iuv. xiv. 70. 'Dolebam quod socium et consortem gloriosi laboris amiseram,' C. *Br.* 1. 'Quod spiratis, quod vocem mittitis, indignantur,' L. iv. 3. 'Caesar ad me scripsit gratissimum sibi esse quod quieverim,' C. *Fam.* viii. 11.

Obs. 1. After predications of Emotion in the 1st Pers., the Clause is often Indic., because the speaker states the ground of *his own* feeling. But after 2nd or 3rd Pers., often Subjunctive, when the writer or speaker ascribes the ground to the mind of another:

'Quereris quod non, Cinna, bibamus idem,' Mart. xii. 28. 'Nemo umquam est oratorem, quod Latine loqueretur, admiratus,' C. *d. Or.* iii. 14.

Obs. 2. Predications of Emotion are connected with the Infinitive Clause, or with quod, for which cum sometimes occurs:

$$\left.\begin{array}{l}\text{dolet mihi}\\ \text{angor animo}\end{array}\right\}\left\{\begin{array}{l}\text{te aegrotare}\\ \text{quod aegrotas}\\ \text{cum aegrotas}\end{array}\right\}\textit{I am sorry you are ill.}$$

$$\left.\begin{array}{l}\text{gaudeo}\\ \text{gratulor}\end{array}\right\}\left\{\begin{array}{l}\text{te convaluisse}\\ \text{quod convaluisti}\\ \text{cum convaluisti}\end{array}\right\}\textit{I am glad you are recovered.}$$

Obs. 3. On the use of quod in connecting sentences, see § 82.
'Quod scire vis qua quisque in te fide sit et voluntate, difficile dictu est de singulis,' C. *Fam.* i. 7.

Obs. 4. Quod, *that*, after a Verb of *thinking* or *declaring* (except in Apposition to a Pronoun) is **hardly classical**; but, in later Latin, it became a common barbarism.[1]

19,
Petitio
Obliqua.

II) Indirect Will-speech (Petitio Obliqua).

1) This Clause is the Oblique form of an Imperative Sentence.

It may be introduced by ut final, ut ne, ne (ne quis, &c.) with Subjunctive; depending (as Subject, Object, or Apposite) on predications expressing:

Concession, permission, demand, entreaty, exhortation; advice, persuasion, impulsion, compact (paciscor, rarely spondeo, debeo); *command, direction, will,* or any forms which may imply these (dico, mitto, monstro, nuntio, respondeo, scribo); also, *care, provision, endeavour; achieving, effecting, conducing,* &c. These include such phrases as condicio (ius, lex, munus, regula, &c.) est.[2]

2) Most of these predications can omit ut before the Subjunctive; but some always keep it:

Cogis (mones, scribis, auctor es, id agis, impetras, &c.) ut eam.
Oravi (suasi, hortatus sum, mandavi, &c.) ut adesses; adesses.

3) Such predications point to the *attainment* of an end. When they take ne, *prevention* is implied; and most can take ne, except iubeo, nolo, and a few more.

Rogas (imperas, operam das, efficis, &c.) ut ne (ne) quis eat.
Suasisti (pactus es, misisti, voluisti, &c.) ut ne (ne) abessem.

---

[1] A few words (accidit, evenit, interest, &c.) admit all three Enuntiative Clauses, while many are used with two of them. Care must be taken to note these uses, and to discriminate them where this is possible. But between some there seems little or no difference. We may write, 'Rectum est maiori parere minorem,' or 'Rectum est ut maiori minor pareat:' 'Gaudeo te salvum redisse,' or 'Gaudeo quod (cum) salvus redisti.'

[2] (*Verbs on which Petitio Obliqua depends*): concedo, do, patior, permitto, sino; oro, rogo, peto, postulo, contendo, precor, obsecro; hortor; cogo, impello, incito, induco, moneo, moveo, persuadeo, suadeo, auctor sum; censeo, decerno, edico, iubeo, impero, mando, praecipio; placet; caveo, curo, facio, id ago, nitor, enitor, operam do, prospicio, studeo, video, provideo; adipiscor, assequor, consequor, committo, efficio, perficio, impetro, evinco, pervinco; opto, volo, nolo, malo, &c. Blandior in L. and Lucr. ii. 173.

4) Another Class of Verbs points to the *prevention* of an end.

Of these c a v e o, when it means *beware*, takes or omits n e: 'Cave ne titubes' or 'cave titubes.'

Veto, *forbid*, takes ne, and very rarely omits it (in poetry).

P r o h i b e o, *forbid*, takes n e and q u o m i n u s; also deprecor, deterreo, dissuadeo, impedio, intercedo, interdico, invideo, obsto, officio, pugno, repugno, recuso, resisto, tempero, teneo, contineo, terreo, veto, and others of like import.   Some of these admit q u i n.

198
Quo-
minus.

5) Quominus.

Q u o m i n u s (= ut eo minus) with Subjunctive depends on predications implying *hindrance*.   Such predication is often negative or interrogative; but it may be positive.

To the Verbs above cited which take q u o m i n u s, may be added a b s t i n e o, a r c e o, cohibeo, defendo, moror, mora est, religio est, impedimentum est, &c.; fieri, stare per aliquem.

N u l l a religio est quominus a d s i m, *I have no scruple about coming.*

P e r te stetit quominus a d e s s e m, *you stood in the way of my coming.*

199
Quin.

6) Quin : see M. *Lucr.* i. 588.

The Consecutive Conjunction q u i n, *but that* (quî-ne = ut non, cur non), with Subjunctive depends on predications which *deny* (or go near to deny) a *preventing cause.*   Such predications are always either negative (non, haud, nihil, &c.), quasi-negative (vix, aegre, minimum, paulum), or interrogative (quid? num? &c.).

V e r b s and Phrases so constructed are numerous : *a*) (Non) dubito, dubium est, &c.   *β*)· (Non) contineor; retineor; resisto; tempero; possum; facere possum; fieri potest; abest; procul est, &c.: (nulla) causa (controversia) est, &c.   *γ*) N u m q u a m, with almost any Verb.

a) 'Non dubito . . . haud dubium est . . . nullus dubito . . . quis dubitet? q u i n f u e r i n t ante Homerum poetae,' *no doubt there were poets before Homer*, C.

β) A e g r e retentus sum . . . paulum afuit . . . temperare mihi vix potui q u i n f l e r e m, *I could hardly refrain from weeping.*

γ) N u m q u a m discedis aliquo q u i n te omnes d e s i d e r e n t, *you never go away but that all regret you.*

200
Fear.

7) Predications of *Fear.*·

M e t u o, timeo, vereor, pavidus sum, timor est, periculum est, &c., take n e with Subjunctive of that which it is feared will happen; u t, n e n o n, of that which it is feared will not happen.

Metuo (timeo, vereor, &c.) n e p e r e a s, *I fear you will perish.*

Metui ut (ne n o n) e f f u g e r e s, *I feared you would not escape.*

This ut is the Oblique Interrog. *how*, used idiomatically to avoid the harshness of a negative form.

201
Caution

8) Predications of *Caution*, c a v e o, v i d e o, c o g i t o, c o n s i d e r o, have some resemblance to those of Fear, so far as they introduce n e (which c a v e o can omit); but when ut follows them, they have the sense of c u r o, *take care, provide that.* See Examples.

9) Periphrastic phrases : non c o m m i t t e r e ut (*to act so that*), id agere, animum inducere, facere, efficere, fieri, fore, &c. ut (u t n e), n e. See M. *Lucr.* vi. 412–415.

III) Indirect Question (Interrogatio Obliqua).

1) If a Question, formed by an Interrogative Pronoun or Particle (quis es ?), becomes dependent upon another predication, its Verb becomes Subjunctive (quis sis). Such Interrogatives are : quis, qualis, quantus, quot, uter, quotus, unde, ubi, quando, quomodo, cur, quare, quamobrem, quam, num, ne, ut, an, utrum.

2) Predications on which such a Clause may depend are those of *inquiring, stating, hearing, knowing, perceiving, remembering, doubting, caring, considering, determining, concerning*, &c.

Quaero, dic, scio, &c., quid facias, feceris, facturus sis :
Quaesivi, &c., quid faceres, fecisses, facturus esses.

Examples of Substantival Clauses.

(Verbs which illustrate the rules of Oratio Obliqua are printed in Italics.)

I) Enuntiatio Obliqua.

(1) Infinitive Clause.

'Fac (*suppose*) animos non remanere post mortem; vides nos, si ita *sit*, privari spe beatioris vitae,' C. *T. D.* i. 33. 'Sic decet, te mea curare, tua me,' C. *Att.* xv. 2. 'Aequum est civis civibus parcere,' N. *Th.* 2. 'Meum gnatum rumor est amare,' Ter. *An.* i. 2.

'Solon furere se simulavit,' C. *Off.* i. 30. 'Metellum memini puer bonis esse viribus extremo tempore aetatis,' C. *Cat. M.* 9.

'Meministis, me ita initio distribuisse causam,' C. *p. S. Rosc.* 42. 'Thucydides non negat fuisse famam Themistoclem venenum sua sponte sumpsisse,' N. *Th.* 10. 'Hunc censes primis, ut dicitur, labris gustasse physiologiam, qui quicquam, quod ortum *sit*, *putet* aeternum esse posse? C. *N. D.* i. 8.

(See C. *Qu. F.* i. 8. 'Ac mihi quidem videtur . . . humanitatis.')

'Memineram, C. Marium, cum vim armorum *profugisset*, senile corpus paludibus occultasse,' C. *p. Sest.* 22.

'Plato tum demum beatum terrarum orbem futurum praedicavit, cum aut sapientes regnare aut reges sapere *coepissent*,' Val. Max. vii. 2. 'Exaudita vox est, futurum esse ut Roma caperetur,' C. *Div.* i. 45. 'Nisi nuntii de Caesaris victoria *essent* allati, existimabant plerique futurum fuisse ut oppidum amitteretur,' Caes. *B. C.* iii. 101.

'Lentulus consul senatui reique publicae se non defuturum pollicetur,' Caes. *B. C.* i. 1. 'Si quando parvis ludentes minamur praecipitaturos alicunde, extimescunt,' C. *Fin.* v. 11. 'Ad matrem virginis venit, iurans se illam ducturum domum.' Ter. *Ad.* iii. 4. 'Magna in spe sum nihil mihi temporis prorogatum iri,' C *Att.* vi. 2. 'Spes dabatur, pueros mergi posse,' L. i. 4. 'Iniecta mihi spes est velle mecum Sulpicium colloqui, C. *Att.* x. 7. 'Video te velle in caelum migrare, et spero fore ut contingat id nobis,' C. *T. D.* i. 82.

'Verminae responsum a legatis est : Si quid ad pacis leges addi, demi, mutarive *vellet*, rursus a senatu ei postulandum fore,' L. xxxi. ii. 'Semper ita vivamus ut rationem reddendam nobis arbitremur,' C. *Verr.* ii. 11.

'Me non cum bonis esse?' C. *Att.* ix. 6. 'Hasne tibi gratis, haec praemia digna rependi?' Stat. *Th.* viii. 50. 'Egone ut te interpellem?' C. *T. D.* ii. 18. 'Utne tegam spurco Damae latus?' Hor. *S.* ii. 5. 18.

'Confitere huc ea spe venisse,' C. *p. S. Rosc.* 22. 'Dissimulare etiam sperasti, perfide, tantum posse nefas?' Verg. *Aen.* iv. 305.

'Par est, primum ipsum esse virum bonum, tum alterum similem sui quaerere,' C. *Lael.* 22. 'Prima sequentem honestum est in secundis tertiisque consistere,' C. *Or.* 1.

'Tu fac, quod facis, ut me ames teque amari a me scias,' C. *Fam.* xiii. 47.

'De Antonio tibi scripsi, non esse eum a me conventum,' C. *Att.* xv. 1.

'Platonem ferunt idem sensisse quod Pythagoram,' C. *T. D.* i. 27.

'Pons in Ibero prope effectus nuntiabatur,' Caes. *B. C.* i. 62. 'Nuntiatur Afranio, magnos comitatus ad flumen constitisse,' Caes. *B. C.* i. 51.' 'Si Veios migrabimus, non reliquisse victores, sed amisisse victi patriam videbimur,' L. v. 53. 'Non mihi videtur ad beate vivendum satis posse virtutem,' C. *T. D.* v. 5.

3) An Oblique Interrogation must be carefully distinguished from an Adjectival (Relative) Clause.

The former depends on the principal Verb, and requires the Subjunctive: Intellego quae mihi narres, *I understand what things you are telling me*; where quae is from the Interrog. qui.

The latter is referred to a Demonstrative, expressed or understood, and does not require a Subjunctive: Intellego (ea) quae mihi narras, *I understand those things which you tell me*, where quae is from the Relative qui.

(Cp. *d. Or.* ii. 74. 299 ; *T. D.* v. 8, in which there is an irregular transition from the Personal construction to the Clause.)

(2) The Enuntiative Ut-clause.

'Quando fuit ut, quod *licet*, non liceret?' C. *p. Cael.* 20. 'Absit a nobis ut ex incommodo alieno nostram occasionem petamus,' L. iv. 58. 'Reliquum est ut certemus officiis inter nos,' C. *Fam.* vii. 21. 'Rarum est ut satis se quisque vereatur,' C. *p. Fl.* 27. 'Fit fere ut cogitationes sermonesque nostri pariant aliquid, in somno,' C. *Somn.* 1. 'Fieri potest ut recte quis sentiat et id, quod *sentit*, polite eloqui non possit,' C. *T. D.* i. 3. 'Valde optanti utrique nostrum cecidit ut in istum sermonem delaberemini,' C. *d. Or.* i. 21. 'Mos est hominum ut nolint eundem pluribus rebus excellere,' C. *Br.* 21. 'Quam habet aequitatem, ut agrum multis annis aut etiam saeculis ante possessum qui nullum habuit habeat, qui autem habuit amittat?' C. *Off.* ii. 22. 'Ut colloqui cum Orpheo, Musaeo, Homero, Hesiodo liceat, quanti tandem aestimatis?' C. *T. D.* i. 41.

(*Inf. Clause or* ut.) 'Si haec enuntiatio vera non est, sequitur ut falsa sit,' C. *Fat.* 12. 'Si, quod honestum est, id solum est bonum, sequitur vitam beatam virtute confici,' C. *T. D.* v. 8. 'Restat ut doceam, omnia, quae *sint* in hoc mundo, hominum causa facta esse,' C. *N. D.* ii. 61. 'Restat Bactra novis, restat Babylona tributis frenari,' Stat. *S.* i. 40. 'Omnibus bonis expedit, salvam esse rempublicam,' C. *Phil.* xiii. 8. 'Expedit omnibus ut singulae civitates sua iura et suas leges habeant,' L. xxxiv. 1. 'Puero opus est cibum ut habeat,' Plaut. *Truc.* v. 1. 'Nunc opus est te animo valere, ut corpore possis,' C. *Fam.* xvi. 14. 'Tris convenit res habere narrationem, ut brevis, ut dilucida, ut verisimilis sit,' *ad Her.* i. 9. 'Verisimile est, cum optimus quisque maxime posteritati *serviat*, esse aliquid, cuius is post mortem sensum *sit* habiturus,' C. *T. D.* i. 15. 'An verisimile est ut civis Romanus aut homo liber cum gladio in forum descenderit ante lucem?' C. *p. Sest.* 36. 'Potest illud esse falsum, ut circumligatus fuerit angui,' C. *Div.* ii. 31. 'Haud falsa sum nos odiosas haberi,' Ter. *Eun.* ii. 2.

(So credibile, aequum, rectum, verum est, and other adjective predications, can take either Clause.)

(3) The Enuntiative Quod-clause.

'Eumeni multum detraxit inter Macedones viventi quod alienae erat civitatis,' N. *Eun.* 1. 'Aristoteles laudandus est in eo quod omnia quae moventur aut natura moveri censuit aut vi aut voluntate,' C. *N. D.* ii. 16. 'Ex tota laude Reguli unum illud est admiratione dignum, quod captivos retinendos censuit,' C. *Off.* iii. 31. 'Quanta illa benignitas naturae, quod tam multa ad vescendum tam varia tamque iucunda gignit,' C. *N. D.* ii. 53. 'Mitto quod invidiam, quod omnis meas tempestates *subieris*,' C. (mitto=dicendum non puto).

(Quod, cum, *with Verbs of Emotion.*) 'Sane gaudeo quod te interpellavi,' C. *Leg.* iii. 1. 'Dolet mihi quod tu nunc stomacharis,' C. *ad Br.* 17. 'Gratulor tibi quod salvum te ad tuos recepisti,' C. *Fam.* xiii. 73. 'Laudo te cum isto animo es,' C. *p. Mil.* 36. 'Haec urbs laetari videtur quod tantam pestem *evomuerit*,' C. *Cat.* ii. 1. 'Memini gloriari solitum esse Q. Hortensium quod nunquam bello civili *interfuisset*,' C. *Fam.* ii. 16.

(*Inf. Clause with Verbs of Emotion.*) 'Gaudeo, id te mihi suadere, quod ego mea sponte *feceram*,' C. *Att.* xv. 27. 'Utrumque laetor, et sine dolore corporis te fuisse et animo valuisse,' C. *Fam.* vii 1. 'Lentulus se alterum fore, Sullam inter suos gloriatur,' Caes. *B. C.* i. 4. 'Gratulor Oechaliam titulis accedere nostris,' Ov. *Her.* ix. 1. 'Inferiores non dolere debent, se a suis superari,' C. *Lael.* 20.

4) Some examples, which at first sight seem to shew Indic. in Oblique Interr., really belong either to Interr. Recta:

'Quin tu uno verbo dic, quid est quod me velis?' *now tell me in one word, what do you want with me?* Ter. *An.* i. l. 18.

Or to Adjectival (Relative) construction:

'Nihil est admirabilius quam quomodo ille fili mortem tulit,' *nothing is more admirable than the manner in which he bore his son's death,* C. *Cat. M.* 4.

But the Comic poets use the Indic. in Oblique Interr. as an idiom of parlance; and some examples occur in later poets, but not in good Latin prose; for examples cited from Cicero are either corrupt readings or direct Interrogations.

(Cur *for* quod.) 'Primum illud reprehendo et accuso cur in re tam veteri tam usitata quicquam novi feceris,' C. *Verr.* iii. 7. 'Repeto me correptum ab avunculo cur ambularem: Poteras, inquit, has horas non perdere,' Plin. *Ep.* iii. 5. 'Miror cur philosophiae prope bellum indixeris,' C. *d. Or.* ii. 37.

(Ut *and* quod.) 'Accedit ut eo facilius animus evadat ex hoc aere, quod nihil est animo velocius,' C. *T. D.* i. 19. 'Accedit quod Caesar ingeniis excellentibus delectatur,' C. *Fam.* vi. 6. 'Accidit ut Athenienses Chersonesum colonos vellent mittere,' N. *Milt.* i. 'Accidit perincommode quod eum nusquam vidisti,' C. *Att.* i. 17. 'Evenit inquirant vitia ut tua rursus et illi,' Hor. *S.* i. 3. 28. 'Magna me spes tenet, bene mihi evenire quod *mittar* ad mortem,' C. *T. D.* i. 41. 'Invitus facio ut recorder ruinas reipublicae,' C. *in Vatin.* 8. 'Noli putare pigritia me facere quod non mea manu *scribam*,' C. *Att.* xvi. 15.

(Interest, refert take all three clauses, besides other constructions. See § 203.)

II) Petitio Obliqua.

'Petes a Crasso ut eam copiam in lucem proferat,' C. *d. Or.* i. 35. 'A te id, quod suesti, peto, me absentem diligas et defendas,' C. *Fam.* xv. 8. 'Non peto ut decernatur aliquid novi, sed ut ne quid novi decernatur,' C. *Fam.* ii. 7. 'Magnum documentum ne patriam rem perdere quis velit,' Hor. *S.* i. 4. 111. 'Exercitus Alexandrum lacrimis deprecatur, finem tandem belli faceret;' Iust. xii. 8. 'Alcibiades lacrimans supplex erat Socrati, ut sibi virtutem traderet turpitudinemque depelleret,' C. *T. D.* iii. 32. 'Id te rogo, ut valetudini tuae diligentissime servias,' C. *Qu. Fr.* i. 1. 'Cum magnum aliquod munus *susceperis*, hoc te rogo, ne demittas animum, neve te obrui tamquam fluctu, sic magnitudine negoti sinas,' C. *Qu. Fr.* i. 1. 'Decrevit quondam senatus, ut L. Opimius consul videret ne quid res publica detrimenti caperet,' C. *Cat.* i. 2. 'Gabinius egerat aliud nihil nisi ut urbes depopularetur,' C. *in Pis.* 17. 'Qui stadium currit, eniti et contendere debet ut vincat,' C. *Off.* iii. 10. 'Coeperunt ponere leges ne quis fur esset neu latro,' Hor. *S.* i. 3. 105. 'Vetus est lex illa iustae veraeque amicitiae, ut idem amici semper velint,' C. *p. Planc.* 1. 'Ariovistus respondit ius esse belli ut qui *vicissent* iis quos *vicissent*, quemadmodum *vellent*, imperarent. Factum est senatus-consultum, ut duo viros aedilis ex Patribus dictator populum rogaret,' L. vi. 42. 'Bene maiores nostri hoc comparaverunt, ut neminem regem, quem armis *cepissent*, vita privarent,' *ad Her.* iv. 16.

'Nuntia Patribus, urbem muniant, et Fabio, Aemilium et vixisse et adhuc mori,' L. xxii. 49. 'Dicam tuis ut librum tuum describant ad teque mittant,' C. *Fam.* xiii. 17. 'Dic ad cenam veniat,' Hor. 'Dicebam tibi ne matri consuleres male,' Plaut. *As.* v. 2. 'Rogo ergo scribas tuis, ut liberto villa, ut domus pateat,' Plin. *Ep.* v. 19. 'Caesar ad Lamiam scripsit, ut ad ludos omnia pararet,' C. *Att.* xiii. 45.

(Auctor sum, *I advise*, takes ut, ne; auctor sum, *I assure*, takes Infin. Clause.)

(Quominus.) 'Quid obstat quominus Deus sit beatus?' C. *N. D.* i. 34. 'Isocrati, quominus haberetur summus orator, non offecit quod infirmitate vocis ne in publico diceret impediebatur,' Plin. *Ep.* vi. 29. 'Nihil ne ego quidem moror quominus decemviratu abeam,' L. iii. 54. 'Praetor Samnitibus respondit: Nec quominus perpetua cum eis amicitia esset, per populum Romanum stetisse; nec contradici, quin amicitia de integro reconcilietur; quod

5) N e s c i o quis (qui), &c., followed by Indicative, is a special exception, being regarded as Pronominal = aliquis, aliqui. So mirum quantum, immane quantum, &c.

See § 86–97.

6) By Greek attraction the Subject of the Clause sometimes becomes Object of the Principal Verb: (See § 128, 3.)

'Sanguinem, bilem, pituitam, ossa videor posse dicere unde concreta sint,' *I think I can state what blood, bile, phlegm, and bones are formed from,* C. T. D. i. 24. 'Rem frumentariam ut satis commode supportari posset timere se dicebant,' *they said they were afraid the supply of corn could not be furnished easily,* Caes. B. G. i. 39.

---

ad Sidicinos *attineat,* nihil intercedi, quominus Samniti populo pacis bellique liberum arbitrium sit,' L. viii. 2. 'Qui domum meam, quominus ruat, fulcit, praestat mihi beneficium; ipsa enim domus sine sensu est,' Sen. *Ben.* v. 19. 'Saepe accidit in mari, ut naves teneantur quominus in portum pervenire possint,' Caes. B. G. iv. 22.

(Quominus, being a Final Particle, may also be represented by ne, with prohibeo, impedio, deterreo, deprecor, and many other Verbs.)

(Quin.) 'Non est dubium quin beneficium sit etiam invito prodesse,' Sen. *Ben.* v. 19. 'Numquam mihi dubium fuit quin a te diligerer,' C. *Att.* xvi. 19. 'Non dubito quin probaturus sim vobis defensionem meam,' C. p. *Mil.* 2. 'Quis dubitet quin in virtute divitiae positae sint?' C. *Par.* 6. 'Nolite dubitare quin (*do not hesitate to*) Pompeio uni credatis omnia,' C. p. L. M. 20. 'Temperare non potuit quin facti reminisceretur,' Suet. *Claud.* 4. 'Nihil abest quin sim miserrimus,' C. *Att.* ii. 15. 'Haud procul erat quin castra turbarentur,' L. v. 12. 'Vergilii et Livii scripta paulum afuit quin ex omnibus bibliothecis amoveret Caligula,' Suet. *Cal.* 34. 'Nihil praetermisi, quantum facere potui, quin Pompeium a Caesaris coniunctione avocarem,' C. *Phil.* ii. 2. 'Equidem numquam domum misi unam epistulam, quin esset ad te altera,' C. *Fam.* ii. 10.

(On 'non quin,' see Causal Clauses.)

(Dubito *also takes a Prol. Inf. or Inf. Clause, or Interr. Obl.*) 'Non dubitavi id a te per litteras petere,' C. *Fam.* ii. 6. 'Pompeius non dubitat, ea, quae de republica nunc *sentiat,* mihi valde probari,' C. *Att.* vii. 1. (See Interr. Obl.)

(*Fear.*) 'Metuo ne id consili ceperimus, quod non satis explicare *possimus,*' C. *Fam.* xiv. 12. 'Timor Romae grandis fuit, ne iterum Galli Romam redirent,' Eutr. v. 1. 'Pavor ceperat milites, ne mortiferum esset vulnus Scipionis,' L. xxiv. 42. 'Non vereor ne mea vitae modestia parum valitura sit contra falsos rumores,' C. *Fam.* xi. 28. 'Omnis labores te excipere video; timeo ut sustineas,' C. *Fam.* xiv. 2 'Hoc quia vos foedus non *iusseritis,* veretur Hiempsal ut satis firmum sit et ratum,' C. d. L. *Agr.* ii. 21. 'Veremur ne forte non aliorum utilitatibus, sed propriae laudi servisse videamur,' Plin. *Ep.* i. 8. 'Ne se penuria victus opprimeret metuebat,' Hor. *S.* i. 1. 98. 'Extimui ne vos ageret vesania discors,' Hor. *S.* ii. 3. 174.

(*Caution.*) 'Si vita in exsilio tibi commodior esse *videatur,* cogitandum tamen est ne tutior non sit,' C. *Fam.* iv. 9. 'Videamus ne beata vita ex sui similibus partibus effici debeat,' C. T. D. v. 15. 'Credere omnia vide ne non sit necesse,' C. *Div.* ii. 13. 'Ad rempublicam gerendam qui accedit, caveat ne id modo consideret, quam illa res honesta sit, sed etiam, ut (=ne non) habeat efficiendi facultatem,' C. *Off.* i. 21. (where considero is constructed like vereor.) 'Haec mea cura est, ne quid tu perdas neu sis iocus,' Hor. *S.* ii. 4. 36. (See Hor. *Epist.* i. 5. 21–28.)

(Caveo, *take care, is used with* ut: caveo, *beware, with* ne, *or suppressing* ne.) 'Caveamus ut ea, quae *pertinent* ad liberalem speciem et dignitatem, moderata sint,' C. *Off.* i. 39. 'Lege Cincia cavetur ne quis ob causam orandam pecuniam donumve accipiat,' Tac. *Ann.* xi. 5. 'Cave festines aut committas ut aut aeger aut hieme naviges,' C. *Fam.* xvi. 12.

(*Verbs which form periphrases.*) 'Non committam ut in scribendo neglegens fuisse videar,' C. *Fam.* v. 9. 'Numquam omnino periculi fuga committendum est ut imbelles timidique videamur,' C. *Off.* i. 24. 'Omne animal id agit ut se con-

**203
Verbs
vari-
ously
con-
struc-
ted.**

Note. Many of the Verbs included in II. III. of this Section admit a variety of dependent constructions.

The range of such variety is:

1. Ut.　2. Omission of ut.　3. Ne.　4. Infin. Clause.　4*a*. That form of Clause in which the Infin. is Perf. Pass., suppressing e s s e (nollem datum).　5. Object-case and Infin.; or Infin., suppressing Object-case (hortamur fari).　6. Prolative Infin., the Finite Verb being Active (vult ire).　7. Prolative. Infin., the Fin. Verb being Passive.　8. Oblique Interrogation.　9. Quominus.　9*a*. Quin.

---

servet,' C. *Fin.* v. 9. 'Potuit animum inducere ut se patrem esse obliviceretur,' C. *p. S. Rosc.* 15. 'Faciam (*will cause*) ex tragoedia comoedia ut sit,' Plaut. *Am. Prol.* 54. 'Invitus feci ut Flaminium e senatu eicerem (=invitus eieci),' C. *Cat. M.* 12. 'Omnes concedant oportet, numquam facturum (*allow himself*) virum bonum ut mendacium dicat,' *Qu.* xii. 15.　Fac (*suppose*), quaeso, qui ego *sim*, esse te,' C. *Fam.* vii. 23. 'Fac ut valeas,' C. 'Fac int ellegam, tu quid sentias,' C. *N. D.* 'Quid a me fieri potuit aut elegantius aut iustius, quam ut sumptus egentissimarum civitatum minuerem?' C. *Fam.* iii. 8. 'Faciendum mihi putavi ut litteris tuis breviter responderem,' do. 'M. Crassi consilio factum est ne fugitivi ad Messanam transire possent,' C. *Verr.* v. 2. 'Clamabant fore ut ipsi sese di ulciscerentur,' C. *Verr.* iv. 40. 'Quibus oculis animi intueri potuit vester Plato fabricam illam tanti operis, qua construi a deo atque aedificari mundum facit (*proves*)?' C. *N. D.* i. 8. 'Polyphemum Homerus cum immanem ferumque finxisset, cum ariete etiam colloquentem facit (*makes*), eiusque laudare fortunas, quod qua *vellet* ingredi *posset* et quae *vellet* attingere,' C. *T. D.* v. 39. 'Nati me coram cernere letum fecisti (*caused*),' Verg. *Ae.* ii. 538. 'Quae est Socratis oratio, qua facit (*makes*) eum Plato usum apud iudices iam morte multatum?' C. *T. D.* i. 40. 'Dolabella plus fecit (*made out*) Verrem accepisse, quam iste in suis tabulis habuit,' C. *Verr.* i. 39. 'Efficitur (*it results*) igitur fato fieri quaecumque *fiant*,' C. *Fat.* 10. 'Fides ut habeatur duabus rebus effici (*be achieved*) potest, si existimabimur adepti coniunctam cum iustitia prudentiam,' C. *Off.* ii. 9. 'Sol efficit (*causes*) ut omnia floreant et in suo quaeque genere pubescant,' C. *N. D.* ii. 15. 'Vos effici (*be brought about*) negatis sine divina posse sollertia ut innumerabilis natura mundos effectura sit, efficiat, effecerit,' C. *N. D.* i. 20. 'Potestis efficere ut male moriar; ne moriar, non potestis,' Plin. *Ep.* iii. 16.

III) Interrogatio Obliqua.

'Istud non est beneficium, sed fenus, circumspicere, non ubi optime ponas, sed ubi quaestuosissime habeas, unde facillime tollas,' Sen. *Ben.* iv. 3. 'Solon Pisistrato tyranno, quaerenti, qua tandem spe fretus sibi tam audaciter obsisteret, respondisse dicitur: Senectute,' C. *Cat. M.* 20. 'Sapiens videbit, ubi victurus sit, cum quibus, quomodo, quid acturus: cogitat semper, qualis vita, non quanta sit,' Sen. *Ep.* 70. 'Si vis gratus esse adversus Deum, recordare, quam multa sis consecutus; cum adspexeris, quot te antecedant, cogita, quot sequantur, cogita, quam multos antecesseris,' Sen. *Ep.* 15. 'Vides ut alta stet nive candidum Soracte,' Hor. *C.* i. 9. 1. 'Matri denarrat ut ingens belua cognatos eliserit,' Hor. *S.* ii. 3. 315 (see Hor. *Epist.* i. 8). 'A me consilium petis, quid tibi sim auctor, in Siciliane subsidas an ad reliquias Asiaticae negotiationis proficiscare?' C. *Fam.* vi. 8. 'Apud Germanos ea consuetudo erat ut matres familiae eorum sortibus et vaticinationibus declararent, utrum proelium committi ex usu esset necne,' Caes. *B. G.* i. 50. 'Non id quaeritur, sintne aliqui, qui deos esse *putent*: di utrum sint, necne sint, quaeritur,' C. *N. D.* iii. 7. 'Antigonus nondum statuerat, conservaret Eumenem necne,' N. *Eum.* 11. 'Di immortales, sit Latium deinde annon, in vestra manu posuerunt,' L. viii. 13. 'Metellus transfugas et alios opportunos,' Iugurtha ubi gentium, aut quid ageret, cum paucisne esset an exercitum haberet, exploratum misit,' Sall. *Iug.* 54. 'Quae parare et quaerere arduum fuit, nescio an tueri difficilius sit,' L. xxxvii. 54. 'Haud scio an quae dixit sint vera omnia,' Ter. *An.* iii. 2. 45. 'Si per se virtus sine fortuna ponderanda *sit*, dubito an Thrasybulum primum omnium ponam,' N. *Thr.* 1. (See Hor. *Epist.* i. 12. 16–20; i. 18. 96–103; *ad Pis.* 114–118. 307–315.)

(*Impersonal Verbs*: Interest, refert.) 'Illud mea magni interest, te ut videam,' C. *Att.* xi. 22. 'Illud permagni referre arbitror, ut ne scientem sentiat te id sibi dare,' Ter. *Haut.* iii. 1. 58. 'Epistulae inventae sunt, ut certiores faceremus absentis, si

Constructions within this range taken by certain Verbs.

  a) Impersonal Verbs:

  Interest and refert: 1. 2. 3. 4. 5. 8. Licet and necesse
  est: (1) 2. 4. 5. 6. Oportet: 2. 4. 4a. 5.

  b) Verbs of Desire:

  Volo: 1. 2. 3. 4. 4a. 5. 6. Malo: 1. 2. 4. 5. 6. Nolo: 1. 2.
  4. 4a. 6. Opto: 1. 2. 3. 4. 6. 7. Studeo: 1. 3. 4. 4a. 6.
  Cupio: 4. 4a. 6.

  c) Various:

  Iubeo: 1. 2. 4. 5. 7. Cogo: 1. 4. 5. 7. Patior: 1. 4. 6.
  Sino: 1. 2. 4. 5. 7. Concedo: 1. 2. 3. 4. 5. Permitto:
  1. 2. 4. 5. 8. Impero: 1. 2. 3. 4. 5. 7. 8. Mando: 1. 2.
  3. 4. Praecipio: 1. 2. 3. 5. 8. Veto: 3. 5. 7. 9. Prohibeo: 1. 3. 4. 5. 7. 9. 9a. Impedio: 3. 5. 9. Hortor
  and oro: 1. 2. 3. 5. Postulo: 1. 2. 3. 4. 5. 6. Suadeo
  and persuadeo: 1. 2. 3. 4. 5. Doceo: 1. 4. 5. 7. 8. Moneo: 1. 2. 3. 4. 5. 7. 8. Censeo: 1. 2. 3. 4. 5. Video: 1.
  3. 4. 7. 8. Curo: 1. 2. 3. 4. (espec. Gerundive) 5. 8.
  Statuo: 1. 3. 4. 6. 8. Dico: 1. 2. 3. 4. 7. 8.

---

quid esset, quod eos scire aut nostra aut ipsorum *interesset*,' C. *Fam.* ii. 4. 'Parvi
refert, vos publicanis amissis vectigalia postea victoria recuperare,' C. *p. L. Man.* 7.
'Theodori nihil interest humine an sublime putrescat,' C. *T. D.* i. 43. 'Aves
pascantur necne quid refert?' C. *Div.* ii. 35.

(Necesse est, oportet, licet.) 'Qui se metui volent, a quibus *metuentur*, eosdem
metuant ipsi necesse est,' C. *Off.* ii. 7. 'Animus oportet tuus te iudicet divitem,
non hominum sermo, neque possessiones tuae,' C. *Par.* vi. 1. 'Tollas licet,' Hor. *Ep.*
i. 16. 76. 'A Deo mundum necesse est regi,' C. *N. D.* ii. 30. 'Narrationem
oportet tris habere res, ut brevis, ut aperta, ut probabilis sit,' C. *Inv.* i. 20. 'Neque
nos lepore tuo, neque te, si quis est in me, meo frui licet propter molestissimas oc-
cupationes meas,' C. *Fam.* vii. 1. 'Non dubitabit, quid me sentire conveniat, cum,
quid mihi sentire necesse sit, *cogitarit*,' C. *d. Pr. C.* 1. 'Impetrabis a Caesare,
ut tibi abesse liceat et esse otioso,' C. *Att.* ix. 2. 'Is erat annus, quo per leges
ei consulem fieri liceret,' Caes. *B. C.* iii. 1. 'Adulescenti morem gestum oportuit,' Ter. *Ad.* ii. 2. 6.

(*Verbs of Desire.*) 'Maiores voluerunt, qui testimonium *diceret*, ut arbitrari se
diceret, etiam quod ipse *vidisset*; quaeque iurati iudices *cognovissent*, ea non ut esse
facta, sed ut videri pronuntiarent,' C. *Ac.* ii. 47. 'Nolo mentiare,' Ter. *Eun.* v.
2. 'Tu ad me de rebus omnibus scribas velim,' C. *Fam.* viii. 13. 'Vellem equidem
aut ipse Epicurus doctrinis fuisset instructior aut ne deterruisset alios a studiis,'
C. *Fin.* i. 7. 'Malo te sapiens hostis metuat quam stulti cives laudent,' L. xxii.
39. 'Caesar studebat maxime ut partem oppidi a reliqua parte urbis excluderet,'
Hirt. *B. A.* 1. 'Optandum est ut ii, qui *praesunt* reipublicae, legum similes sint,
quae ad puniendum non iracundia sed aequitate *ducuntur*,' C. *Off.* i. 25. 'Optavi
peteres caelestia sidera tarde,' Ov. *Trist.* ii. 57. 'Videmini intenta mala, quasi fulmen,
optare, se quisque ne attingant,' Sall. *Fr.*
  'Ego me Phidiam esse mallem quam vel optimum fabrum tignarium,' C. *Br.* 73.
'Cupio, me esse clementem; cupio, in tantis rei publicae periculis me non disso-
lutum videri,' C. *Cat.* i. 2. 'Quam multa passus est Ulixes in illo errore diuturno,
cum et mulieribus inserviret et in omni sermone omnibus affabilem et iucundum
esse se vellet,' C. *Off.* i. 31. 'Homo tenuis gratum se videri studet,' C. *Off.* ii. 20.
'Te mihi ipsum iamdudum optaram dari,' Ter. *H.* iv. 5.
  'Domestica cura te levatum volo,' C. *Qu. F.* iii. 9. 'Patres ordinem publicanorum
in tali tempore offensum nolebant,' L. xxv. 3. 'Nollem factum, *I'm sorry for it*,'
C. *Off.* i. 11. 'Duabus de causis a te potissimum petere constitui quod impetratum
maxime cupio,' Plin. *Ep.* ii. 13.
  'Volo is esse quem tu me esse voluisti,' C. *Fam.* i. 7. 'Nolo esse laudator ne

G G

videar adulator,' *ad Her.* iv. 21. 'Cato esse quam videri bonus malebat,' Sall. *Cat.* 54. 'Hunc videre optabamus diem,' Ter. *Hec.* iv. 4. 26. 'Scire studeo quid egeris, C. *Att.* xiii. 20. 'Cupio te consulem videre,' C. *Fam.* xv. 13.

(Iubeo.) 'L. Quinctius iussit ut, quae ex sua classe *venissent* naves, Euboeam peterent,' L. xxxii. 11. 'Velitis iubeatis Quirites, uti L. Valerius L. Titio iure legeque filius siet,' Gell. v. 19. 'Iube mihi denuo respondeat,' Ter. *Eun.* iv. 4. 24. 'Diogenes proici se iussit inhumatum,' C. *T. D.* i. 43. 'Iubeo gaudere te,' C. *Fam.* vii. 2. 'Iussi ei dari bibere,' Ter. *An.* iii. 2. 4. 'Transire in Epirum est iussus,' L. xxxv. 24.

(Cogo.) 'Quid Paris? ut salvus ŗegnet vivatque beatus cogi posse negat,' Hor. *Epist.* i. 2. 10. 'Nonne di ipsi cogent ab his virtutibus tanta vitia superari,' C. *in Cat.* ii. 11. 'Innumerabilia sunt ex quibus cogi (*be necessarily inferred*) possit nihil esse, quod sensum *habeat*, quin id intereat,' C. *N. D.* iii. 13. 'Num te emere coegit, qui ne hortatus quidem est,' C. *Off.* iii. 13. 'Neque cogi pugnare poterat rex,' L. xlv. 41.

(Patior.) 'Ne in turpi quidem reo patiendum est ut quicquam adversarii se minis proficere arbitrentur,' C. *p. Font.* 12. 'Consilium meum a te probari facile patior,' C. *Att.* xv. 2. 'Patior vel inconsultus haberi,' Hor. *Epist.* ii. v. 15.

(Sino.) 'Sivi animum ut expleret suum,' Ter. *An.* i. 2. 27. 'Sine te hoc exorem,' Ter. *An.* v. 3. 30. 'Germani vinum ad se importari non sinunt,' Caes. *B. G.* iv. 2. 'Sineres tu illum tecum facere haec?' Ter. *Ad.* iii. 3. 42. 'Accusare eum moderate a quo nefarie accusatur, non est situs,' C. *p. Sest.* 44.

(Concedo.) 'Concedo sit dives,' Catull. cxii. 5. 'Non concedam ut Attico nostro iucundiores tuae litterae fuerint quam mihi,' C. *Fam.* xiii. 18. 'Concede, nihil esse bonum, nisi quod honestum *sit*: concedendum est, in virtute sola positam esse beatam vitam,' C. *Fin.* v. 28. 'Concedunt plangere matri,' Stat. *Th.* v. 134. 'Quo mihi fortunam, si non conceditur uti,' Hor. *Epist.* ii. 5. 12.

(Permitto.) 'Quis Antonio permisit ut partis faceret?' C. *d. Or.* ii. 90. 'Permissum ipsi erat faceret quod e republica *duceret* esse,' L. xxxiii. 45. 'Ille meas errare boves, ut cernis, et ipsum ludere quae vellem calamo permisit agresti,' Verg. *B.* i. 9. 'Rex Cononi permisit quem vellet eligere,' N. *Con.* 4. 'Tibi permitto, responderene mihi malis, an universam orationem audire meam,' C. *N. D.* iii. 1.

(Impero.) 'Senatus imperavit decemviris ut libros Sibyllinos inspicerent,' L. vii. 27. 'Leto det imperat Argum,' Ov. *M.* i. 670. 'Mihi ne abscedam imperat,' Ter. *Eun.* iii. 5. 30. 'Pro serapionis libro tibi praesentem pecuniam solvi imperavi,' C. *Att.* ii. 4. 'Imperavi egomet mihi omnia assentari,' Ter. *Eun.* ii. 2. 21. 'Animo nunc iam otioso esse impero,' Ter. *An.* v. 2. 1. 'Haec ego procurare et idoneus imperor et non invitus,' Hor. *Epist.* i. 5. 21. 'In lautumias Syracusanas deduci imperantur,' C. *Verr.* v. 27. 'Imperabat coram quid opus facto esset,' Ter. *Ph.* i. 4.

(Praecipio.) 'Atheniensibus praecepit, ut Miltiadem sibi imperatorem sumerent; id si fecissent, incepta prospera futura,' Nep. *Milt.* 1. 'His praecipit omnis mortalis pecunia aggrediantur,' Sall. *Iug.* 30. 'Haec praecipienda videntur historiarum lectoribus, ne alienos mores ad suos referant, neve ea, quae ipsis leviora sunt, pari modo apud ceteros fuisse arbitrentur,' Nep. *Ep.* 1. 'Sunt qui praecipiant herbas satureia nocentis sumere,' Ov. *A. A.* ii. 415. 'Huic indici quid fieri vellent praeceperunt,' N. *Paus.* 4.

(Veto.) 'Pontus erat vetitus ne mergeret aequore terram,' Man. iv. 645. 'Vetabo qui Cereris sacrum *vulgarit* arcanae sub isdem sit trabibus,' Hor. *C.* iii. 2. 'Non ego, avarum cum veto te fieri, vappam iubeo aut nebulonem,' Hor. *Sat.* i. 1. 108. 'Desperatis etiam Hippocrates vetat adhibere medicinam,' C. *Att.* xvi. 15. 'Nolani muros portasque adire vetiti sunt,' L. xxxiii. 16. 'Sapientia nulla re quominus se exerceat vetari potest,' Sen. *Ep.* 9.

(Prohibeo.) 'Id potuisti prohibere ne fieret,' C. *in Caec.* 10. (One example of prohibere ut: 'Di prohibeant ut hoc . . . praesidium sectorum existimetur,' C. *p. S. Rosc.* 52.) 'Ignis fieri in castris prohibet,' Caes. *B. G.* v. 29. 'Peregrinos urbibus uti prohibent,' C. *Off.* iii. 11. 'Alii diurnum victum prohibiti quaerere,' Suet. *Ner.* 36. 'Hiemem credo adhuc prohibuisse quominus de te certum haberemus,' C. *Fam.* xii. 5. 'Neque me Iuppiter neque di omnes id prohibebunt quin sic faciam uti constitui,' Plaut. *An.* v. 3. 17.

(Impedio.) 'Isocrates infirmitate vocis ne in publico diceret impediebatur,' Plin.

Ep. v. 29. 'Cur iudices reipublicae munere impediantur quo setius suis rebus et commodis servire possint?' C. *Inv.* ii. 45. 'Aetas non impedit quominus litterarum studia usque ad ultimum tempus senectutis,' C. *Cat. M.* 17. (Impedire quin is rare and not good). 'Quid est quod me impediat ea quae mihi probabilia videantur sequi?' C. *Off.* ii. 2.

(Postulo.) 'Tribuni plebis postulant ut sacrosancti habeantur,' L. iii. 19. 'Postulo, Appi, etiam atque etiam consideres quo progrediare,' L. iii. 45. 'Legatos ad Bocchum mittit postulatum ne sine causa hostis populo Romano fieret,' Sall. *Iug.* 83. 'Postulant non ut ne cogantur statuere. Quid igitur? ut ipsis ne liceat,' C. *Verr.* ii. 60. 'Hic postulat se Romae absolvi,' C. *Verr.* iv. 60. 'Incerta haec si tu postules ratione certa facere, nihilo plus agas quam si des operam ut cum ratione insanias,' Ter. *Eun.* i. 1. 16. 'Postulat deus credi,' Curt. vi. 43. (Flagito has the same construction.)

(Suadeo. Persuadeo.) 'Caesar mihi ut sibi essem legatus non solum suasit, verum etiam rogavit,' C. *d. Pr. C.* 17. 'Dolabellae quod scripsi suadeo videas,' C. *Fam.* ii. 15. 'Pelopidas persuasit Thebanis, ut subsidio Thessaliae proficiscerentur, tyrannosque eius expellerent,' N. *Pel.* 5. 'Huic Albinus persuadet regnum Numidiae ab senatu petat,' Sall. *Iug.* 39. 'Duo tempora inciderunt quibus aliquid contra Caesarem Pompeio suaserim; unum ne quinquennii imperium Caesari prorogaret; alterum ne pateretur ferri ut absentis eius ratio haberetur: quorum si utrumvis persuasissem, in has miserias nunquam incidissemus,' C. *Phil.* ii. 19. 'Mihi ab adolescentia suasi nihil esse in vita magnopere expetendum nisi laudem atque honestatem,' C. *p. Arch.* 6. 'Mihi numquam persuaderi potuit animos, dum in corporibus *essent* mortalibus, vivere, cum *exissent* ex iis, emori,' C. *Cat. M.* 22. 'Nobis persuasum est, fore aliquando, ut omnis hic mundus ardore deflagret,' C. *Ac.* iv. 37. 'Saepes . . . somnum suadebit inire,' Verg. *B.* i. 56. 'Persuasum est facere cuius nunc me facti pudet,' Plaut. *Bacc.* iv. 9. 93. 'Dionysio persuasit Plato tyrannidis facere finem,' N. *Dion.* 3 (*rare*). See Verg. *Aen.* xii. 814.

(Doceo.) 'Philosophia nos cum ceteras res, tum quod est difficillimum, docuit, ut nosmet ipsos nosceremus,' C. *Leg.* i. 58. 'Orpheum poetam docet Aristoteles nunquam fuisse,' C. *N. D.* i. 28. 'Declamare doces,' Iuv. vii. 150. 'Graece loqui docendus sum,' C. *Fin.* ii. 3. 'Invideo magistro tuo, qui te tanta mercede nihil sapere docuit,' C. *Phil.* ii. 4. 'Ne litteras quidem ullas accepi, quae me docerent quid ageres,' C. *Fam.* iii. 6.

(Moneo.) 'Hanc habet vim praeceptum Apollinis, quo monet, ut se quisque noscat; non enim, credo, id praecipit, ut membra nostra, aut staturam figuramve noscamus,' C. *T. D.* i. 22. 'Caesar legatos monuit ad id tempus omnes res ab iis administrarentur,' Caes. *B. G.* iv. 28. 'Caesar cum a summo haruspice moneretur ne in Africam transmitteret, nihilominus transmisit,' C. *Div.* ii. 24. 'Caecos instare tumultus sol monet,' Verg. *G.* i. 464. 'Ratio ipsa monet amicitias comparare,' C. *Fin.* i. 20. 'Soror alma monet succedere Lauso Turnum,' Verg. *Aen.* x. 439. 'Moneo quid facto opus sit,' Ter. *Ad.* iii. 5. 65.

(Censeo, *judge, vote.*) 'Plerique censebant ut noctu iter facerent,' Caes. *B. G.* i. 57. 'Arcessas censeo omnis navalis terrestrisque copias,' L. xxxvi. 7. 'Stolida impudensque postulatio visa est, censere ne in Italiam transmittant Galli bellum,' L. xxi. 20. 'Aristoteles omnia aut natura moveri censet (*judges*) aut vi aut voluntate,' C. *N. D.* ii. 16. (The two next examples are idiomatic. 'Quid censes hunc ipsum Roscium, quo studio esse in rusticis rebus?' C. *p. S. Rosc.* 17. 'Quid censemus superiorem illum Dionysium, quo cruciatu timoris angi solitum?' C. *Off.* ii. 7.) 'Bona regis reddi censuerunt,' L. ii. 5. 'Regulus captivos in senatu reddendos non censuit,' C. *Off.* i. 13. 'Antenor censet belli praecidere causas,' Hor. *Epist.* i. 2. 9.

(Video.) 'Nos id videamus ut, quidquid *acciderit*, fortiter et sapienter feramus,' C. *Att.* xiv. 13. 'Vide ne,' &c.; see *Caution.* 'Volucris videmus fingere et construere nidos,' C. *d. Or.* ii. 6. 'Carneadem videre videor,' C. *Fin.* v. 2. 'Amens mihi fuisse videor a principio,' C. *Att.* ix. 10. 'Videamus primum deorumne providentia mundus regatur, deinde consulantne rebus humanis,' C. *N. D.* iii. 25.

(Curo, 1. 2. 3. 4. 5.) 'Cura ut valeas,' C. *Fam.* xiv. 5. 'Ante senectutem curavi ut bene viverem; in senectute ut bene moriar,' Sen. *Ep.* 61. 'Iam curabo sentiat quos attentarit,' *Phaed.* v. 2. 6. 'Cura ne quid mihi ad hoc negoti aut oneris accedat aut temporis,' C. *Fam.* iii. 8. 'Non verbum verbo curabis reddere,' Hor. *in Pis.* 133. 'Tu recte vivis, si curas esse quod audis,' Hor. *Epist.* i. 16. 17. 'Ex eo auro buculam curavit faciendam,' C. *Div.* i. 24. 'Nec hercle magno opere nunc curo quid Aetoli censeant,' L. xxxvi. 28.

SECTION IV.

ADVERBIAL AND ADJECTIVAL CLAUSES.

(These are properly considered in connexion, on account of the Adverbial character often taken by Adjectival Clauses.)

204
Relative
Clauses.

i. Relative or Adjectival Clauses.

1) A Relative Clause is called Adjectival, because it qualifies, like an Attribute, the Sentence on which it depends:

Deus est, qui regit mundum, qui creavit omnia, quem veneramur, = Deus est, mundum regens, creator omnium, veneratus a nobis.

2) A Clause may be introduced by a Relative Particle, equivalent to Pronoun with Preposition:

Roma est, ubi habito, quo proficiscor, unde venio, &c. = in qua habito, ad quam proficiscor, ex quâ venio, &c.

3) The Mood in a Relative Clause will be Indic., when no reason exists for another Mood. But the Subjunctive will be required, (1) if the Clause is actually or virtually Suboblique; (2) if it is Gnomic, or, sometimes, Iterative; (3) if the Clause contains a Consequence (*such that, so that*), a Purpose (*in order that*); often when it contains a conceived Cause (*since*), a Condition (*if*), or a Concession (*although*).

4) In the latter cases (3), as an Adjective may have Adverbial force (serus venit = sero venit), so an Adjectival Clause may become Adverbial: as when qui = ut ego, ut tu, ut is, &c.: quo = ut eo or eo quod: ubi = ut ibi, &c.

Hence, in considering Adverbial Clauses, it is proper, in each kind, to include those Relative (Adjectival) Clauses which contain Adverbial force, and always or usually require a Subjunctive.

205
Con-
secutive
Clauses.

ii. Consecutive Clauses.

Consecutive Clauses are so called because they express *consequence* or *result*.

A) An Adverbial Consecutive Clause is formed by the Conjunction ut, *that*, with Subjunctive; often following some Demonstrative word, but sometimes without Demonstr. (= *so that*).

1) Such Demonstratives are:

Adverbs: ita, tam, adeo, sic; tantum, tantopere, totiens; eo, huc, illuc.

Pronouns and Pronominals: is, hic, talis, tantus; tot, totidem; eiusmodi; huiusmodi.

Ut also follows the Adjectives dignus, indignus, idoneus, aptus.

Ut may follow a Comparative with quam (*than*): and sometimes ut falls out after quam, the Verb being still Subjunctive.

2) If Negation is required, the Negative words used are :
　　Non, nec, nihil, nemo, nullus, numquam, nusquam.

3) Ita miseri sunt ut fleant, fleverint (*have wept*), fleturi sint.
　Ita miseri erant ut flerent, fleturi essent.
　Ita miseri fuere ut fleverint (*they wept*).
　Quis tam durus est ut numquam fleat, fleverit, fleturus sit?
　Quis tam durus erat ut non fleret, fleturus esset?
　Quis tam durus fuit ut non fleverit?

[In Historic Consecution, if the *fact* is to be brought out, S_2 (fleverint) is used instead of S_3 (flerent). The following examples unite both constructions :—'Sicilia et classis Marcello evenit. Quae sors, velut iterum captis Syracusis, ita exanimavit Siculos, ut comploratio eorum flebilesque voces et extemplo oculos hominum converterent et postmodo sermones praebuerint,' L. xxvi. 29. 'Usque eo ut compluris dies milites frumento caruerint, et . . . extremam famem sustinerent,' Caes. *B. G.* vii. 17. S_2 will be *necessary*, when the consequence can only be referred to the time of the writer or speaker : 'Hortensius ardebat cupiditate dicendi sic ut in nullo unquam flagrantius studium viderim (*have seen*),' C. *Br.* 88.]

4) Idioms of Adverbial Consecution :

a) The phrase 'tantum abesse,' with an Enuntiative Ut-clause, may take also a Consecutive Clause, the meaning being *so far from . . . that*:

　'Tantum abest ut enervetur oratio compositione verborum ut aliter in ea nec impetus ullus nec vis esse possit,' *so far is a speech from being weakened by periodic arrangement, that otherwise there can be no movement or force in it*, C. *Or.* 68.

The Adverbial Clause after tantum abest is sometimes changed for a Principal Sentence:

　'Tantum afuit ut inflammares nostros animos, somnum isto loco vix tenebamus.'

b) The phrase 'in eo esse ut' means *to be on the point of* :
　'Iam in eo erat ut in muros evaderet miles,' L. ii. 17.

5) Ita ut is used with various shades of meaning : (*in such circumstances; on condition; with the understanding; with the feeling; with the exception*) *that*; &c. : 'Clodius Roma ita profectus est ut contionem turbulentam relinqueret,' C. *p. Mil.* 10. 'Huius ingenium ita laudo ut non pertimescam,' C. *in Caec.* 13. 'Caligula in adulescentia ita patiens laborum erat ut tamen nonnumquam subita defectione ingredi vix posset,' Suet. *Cal.* 48.

6) When ita or sic implies design, the Clause is rather Final than Consecutive, and, if Negative, takes ne : 'Hoc est ita utile ut ne plane illudamur,' *this is useful with a view to our being not altogether made a mock of*, C. *p. S. Rosc.* 10. Here ita is equivalent to idcirco.

7) Is . . . ut (*of the kind that*) is often used, though not so often as is . . . qui in the same sense: 'Non is sum ut mea me maxime delectent,' C. *ad. Brut.* 15.

B) An Adjectival Consecutive Clause with a Subjunctive occurs when qui or its Particle expresses (not the *individual* which, but) *the kind* which (= talis ut, ita ut, &c.).

Examples of Consecutive Clauses.

A) (*Adverbial.*) 'Galli dies natalis et mensium et annorum initia sic observant, ut noctem dies subsequatur (*succeeds to*),' Caes. *B. G.* vi. 18. 'Socratis responso sic iudices exarserunt ut capitis hominem innocentissimum condemnarent,' C. *d. Or.* i. 54. 'Talis est ordo actionum adhibendus ut in vita omnia sint (*may be*) apta inter se et convenientia,' C. *Off.* i. 40. 'Quis est tam demens ut sua voluntate maereat (*as to mourn*)?' C. *T. D.* iii. 29. 'Decori vis ea est ut ab honesto non queat (*cannot*) separari,' C. *Off.* i. 27. 'Non ita adulatus sum fortunam alterius ut me meae paeniteret (*as to regret*),' C. *Div.* ii. 2. 'Dolores, si qui incurrunt, numquam vim tantam habent, ut non plus habeat (*will not have*) sapiens, quod gaudeat, quam quod angatur,' C. *Fin.* i. 19. 'Hannibal petens Etruriam adeo gravi morbo adficitur oculorum, ut postea numquam dextro aeque bene usus sit,' Nep. *Hann.* 4. 'Iphicrates Atheniensis fuit talis dux, ut non solum aetatis suae cum primis compararetur sed ne de maioribus natu quidem quisquam anteponeretur. Multum vero in bello est versatus, saepe exercitibus praefuit, nusquam culpa sua male rem gessit; semper consilio vicit, tantumque eo valuit, ut multa in re militari partim nova attulerit, partim meliora fecerit,' Nep. *Iph.* 1. 'Quanta illa Scipionis fuit gravitas, quanta in oratione maiestas, ut (*so that*) facile ducem Romani populi diceres,' C. *Lael.* 25. 'Arboribus consita Italia est, ut tota pomarium videatur (*seems*),' Varro, 1. 'Cuius aures clausae veritati sunt, ut ab amico verum audire nequeat, huius salus desperanda est,' C. *Lael.* 24. 'In virtute multi sunt ascensus, ut is maxime gloria excellat (*excels*) qui virtute plurimum praestet,' C. *p. Planc.* 25. 'Data merces est erroris mei magna, ut me non solum pigeat stultitiae meae, sed etiam pudeat, qui non *intellexerim*, quibus, ut amicis, crederem,' C. *p. Dom.* 11. 'Maior sum quam ut mancipium sim (*too great to be*) mei corporis,' Sen. *Ep.* 65. 'Hoc videtur esse altius quam ut nos humi strati suspicere possimus (*too high for us to be able*),' C. *d. Or.* iii. 6. 'Galba parcior fuit quam conveniret principi,' Suet. *Galb.* 'Dignus es ut possis (*to be able*) totum servare clientem,' Mart. x. 34. 'Indigni ut a vobis redimeremur (*to be ransomed*) visi sumus,' L. xxii. 59. 'Tantum afuit ut Rhodiorum praesidio nostram firmaremus classem ut etiam a Rhodiis commeatu prohiberentur milites nostri,' C. *Fam.* xii. 15. 'Tantum abest ut nostra miremur ut usque eo difficiles ac morosi simus ut nobis non satisfaciat ipse Demosthenes,' C. *Or.* 29. 'Tantum abes a perfectione maximorum operum ut fundamenta nondum ieceris,' C. *p. Marc.* 8. 'Is, qui occultus et tectus dicitur, tantum abest ut se indicet, perficiet etiam ut dolere alterius improbe facto videatur,' C. *Fin.* ii. 17. 'Ita (*with this exception*) probanda est mansuetudo atque clementia ut adhibeatur reipublicae causa severitas,' C. *Off.* i. 25. 'Pythagoras et Plato mortem ita (*with this proviso*) laudant ut fugere vitam vetent,' C. *p. Scaur.* 2. 'Aristoteles ita non sola virtute finem bonorum contineri putat ut rebus tamen omnibus virtutem anteponat,' C. *Fin.* iv. 18. 'Ego tibi onus imponam, ita (*with the understanding*) tamen ut tibi nolim molestus esse,' C. *Fam.* xiii. 56. 'Ego a patre ita eram deductus ad Scaevolam ut a senis latere numquam discederem,' C. *Lael.* 1. 'Potest esse bellum, ut tumultus non sit (*without insurrection*), tumultus esse sine bello non potest,' C. *Phil.* viii. 1. 'Ita vobiscum amicitiam institui par est ne qua (*provided that no*) vetustior amicitia ac societas violetur,' L. vii. 31. 'Minucius sciebat ita se in provincia rem augere oportere ut ne quid de libertate deperderet,' C. *Verr.* ii. 30. 'Ea (*such*) invasit homines habendi cupido ut possideri magis quam possidere videantur,' Plin. *Ep.* ix. 30. 'Ea natura rerum est ut, qui sensum verae gloriae ceperit, nihil cum hac gloria comparandum putet,' C. *Phil.* v. 18. 'Non is (*the kind of man*) es, Catilina, ut te aut pudor a turpitudine aut metus a periculo aut ratio a furore revocarit,' C. *Cat.* i. 9.

B) (*Adjectival.*) 'Ea est Romana gens quae victa quiescere nesciat,' L. ix. 3. 'Non is sum qui, quidquid videtur, tale dicam esse quale *videatur*,' C. *Ac.* ii. 7. 'Innocentia est affectio talis animi quae noceat nemini,' C. *T. D.* iii. 8. 'Est aliquid quod non oporteat, etiamsi licet,' C. *p. Balb.* 3. 'Quotusquisque est

1) This may happen:

After the Demonstratives is, eiusmodi, huiusmodi, talis, tantus, tam, &c.:

'Habetis eum (eiusmodi, talem, tam bonum) consulem qui parere vestris decretis non dubitet,' *you have such a consul, as will not hesitate to obey your decrees*, C. *Cat.* iv. 11. 'Nihil tanti fuit quo venderemus fidem nostram et libertatem,' *nothing was so valuable that we should barter for it our honour and freedom*, C. *ad. Br.* 16. Wherever the Predication on which the Relative Clause depends might be explained by talis or tam: for instance, when it contains

a) Indefinite, Interrogative, Negative, and other Pronominal words: aliquis, quidam, &c., quis, quot, quotusquisque, &c., nemo, nihil, nullus ; unus, solus, primus, ultimus, &c. ; nonnulli, multi, pauci, &c.

b) Dignus, indignus, idoneus, aptus, &c.

c) A Comparative with quam.

d) A Verb, the Subject or Object of which (being the Antecedent) is not expressed, but left Indefinite. Such expressions are: est qui, sunt qui, reperitur qui, habeo, invenio, reperio qui, &c. : and many like phrases.

Even if the Antec. is expressed, the Rel. will take Subjunctive when it defines the *class* or *kind*.

---

qui voluptatem neget esse bonum?' C. *Div.* ii. 39. 'Nullum est animal praeter hominem, quod habeat notitiam aliquam Dei,' C. *Leg.* i. 8. 'Nihil est quod tam miseros faciat quam impietas et scelus,' C. *Fin.* iv. 24. 'Multae hodie sunt gentes quae tantum facie noverint caelum, quae nondum sciant cur luna deficiat,' Sen. *N. Qu.* vi. 25. 'Sapientia est una quae maestitiam pellat ex animis, quae nos exhorrescere metu non sinat,' C. *Fin.* i. 13. 'Sola est in qua merito culpetur Vespasianus pecuniae cupiditas,' Suet. *Vesp.* 16. 'Est quod differat inter iustitiam et verecundiam,' C. *Off.* i. 28. 'Sunt qui discessum animi a corpore putent esse mortem,' C. *T. D.* i. 9. 'Est quatenus amicitiae dari venia possit,' C. *Lael.* 17. 'Fuere qui crederent M. Licinium Crassum non ignarum Catilinae consili fuisse,' Sall. *Cat.* 17. 'Fuit cum mihi quoque initium requiescendi fore iustum arbitrarer,' C. *d. Or.* i. 1. 'Quid est cur virtus ipsa per se non efficiat beatos?' C. *T. D.* v. 6. 'Livianae fabulae non satis dignae sunt quae iterum legantur,' C. *Br.* 18. 'Mentem solam censebant idoneam cui crederetur,' C. *Ac.* i. 8. 'Campani maiora deliquerant quam quibus ignosci posset,' L. xxv. 12. 'Quid dulcius quam habere quicum omnia audeas sic loqui ut tecum?' C. *Lael.* 6. 'Non facile est invenire qui, quod sciat ipse, non tradat alteri,' C. *Fin.* iii. 20. 'Nihil difficilius quam reperire quod sit omni ex parte in suo genere perfectum,' C. *Lael.* 21. 'Nihil habeo quod incusem senectutem,' C. *Cat. M.* 5. 'Quid est quod tu cum fortuna queri possis?' C. *Fam.* iv. 5. 'Non est causa cur Epicurus fatum extimescat,' C. *Fat.* 9. 'Antonius quo se verteret non habebat,' C. *Phil.* ii. 25. 'Ne qui infans quidem est adsuescat sermoni qui dediscendus sit,' Qu. i. 1. 'Augusto prompta ac profluens, quae deceret principem, eloquentia fuit,' Tac. *Ann.* xiii. 3. 'Paci, quae nihil habitura sit insidiarum, semper est consulendum,' C. *Off.* i. 11. 'Quis est quin cernat quanta vis sit in sensibus?' C. *Ac.* ii. 7. 'Cleanthes negat ullum esse cibum tam gravem quin is die et nocte concoquatur,' C. *N. D.* ii. 9. 'Nemo tam ferus fuit quin Alcibiadis casum lacrimarit,' N. *Alc.* 6. 'Totas noctes dormimus, neque ulla est fere quà non somniemus,' C. *Div.* ii. 59. 'Nihil est tam sanctum quod non aliquando violet audacia,' C. *p. S. Rosc.* 70. 'Nulla tam detestabilis pestis est quae non homini ab homine nascatur,' C. *Off.* ii. 5. 'Non possunt una in civitate multi rem atque fortunas amittere, ut non pluris secum in eandem trahant cala-

Examples :

> Aliquis (quis? quotusquisque? nemo, unus, &c.) est qui sciat, *there is somebody (who is there? how many are there? there is nobody, there is one) who knows.*
>
> Dignus (indignus, idoneus) est qui imperet, *he is worthy (unworthy, fit) to rule.*
>
> ‘Maior fuit quam cui resisti posset,’ *he was too great to be resisted.*
>
> Sunt (reperiuntur, existunt, &c.) qui velint, *there are (are found, exist) those who will be willing.* Habui puerum quem mittere possem, *I had such a boy as I could send.* ‘Satis est causae cur timeamus.’

2) If a Relative Clause, depending on a Negative or Interrogative Predication, requires Negation itself, qui non (numquam, nusquam) may be used, or quin for qui non :

> Quis est (nemo est) quin (qui non) sues habeat? *who is there (there is nobody) that does not keep swine?*
>
> ‘Nihil est (quid est?) quin (quod non) male narrando possit depravari,’ *there is nothing (what is there?) that cannot be spoilt by telling it badly,’* Ter. Ph. iv. 4.
>
> ‘Nullum intermisi diem quin (= quo non) scriberem,’ *I let no day pass without writing,* C.

a) Quin rarely contains any Case of the Relative except Nom. or Abl. ; but a few exceptional instances are found :

> ‘Nego in Sicilia tota ullam picturam fuisse quin Verres conquisierit (=quam non),’ C. *Verr.* iv. 1.

b) Quin must be resolved into qui non whenever the Negative has a distinctive application to a part of the Clause, requiring special emphasis.

c) If another Relative Clause intervenes, quin = ut non, and a Demonstrative Pronoun follows :

> ‘Nihil est, quod sensum habeat, quin id intereat, *there is nothing that has feeling but it perishes,* C. *N. D.* iii. 13.

d) In some instances quin consecutive will be resolved into

---

mitatem,’ C. *p. L. Man.* 7. ‘Quod litteris exstet, Pherecydes Syrius primus dixit animos esse hominum sempiternos,’ C. *T. D.* i. 16. ‘Suae cuique utilitati, quod sine alterius iniuria fiat, serviendum est,’ C. *Off.* iii. 10. ‘Refertae sunt Catonis orationes amplius centum quinquaginta, quas quidem adhuc invenerim et legerim, et verbis et rebus illustribus,’ C. *Br.* 17.

(*Exceptions with Indic.*) ‘Tu es qui me tuis sententiis saepissime ornasti,’ C. *Fam.* xv. 4. ‘Sunt bestiae quaedam, in quibus inest aliquid simile virtutis, ut in leonibus, ut in canibus,’ C. *Fin.* v. 14. ‘Interdum volgus rectum videt: est ubi peccat,’ Hor. *Epist.* ii. 1. 63. ‘Gemmas . . . argentum . . . sunt qui non habeant, est qui non curat habere,’ Hor. *Epist.* ii. 2. 180 (where est qui implies the poet himself). ‘Sunt quibus e ramo frondea facta casa est,’ Ov. *F.* iii. 527. ‘Sunt nonnullae diciplinae, quae officium omne pervertunt,’ C. *Off.* i. 2. ‘Sunt multi, qui eripiunt aliis, quod aliis largiantur,’ C. *Off.* i. 14. ‘Duae sunt artes, quae possunt locare homines in amplissimo gradu dignitatis, una imperatoris, altera oratoris boni,’ C. *p. Mur.* 14.

ut non; if purpose is implied, ne takes its place; if
cause is implied, cur non, quare non, &c.:

'Quid fuit causae cur in Africam Caesarem non seque-
rere,' *what was the reason for your not following Caesar
into Africa?* C. *Phil.* ii. 29.

3) Qui with the Subjunctive is used parenthetically with a
sense of limitation: 'quod sciam,' *so far as I know* : in
which use the Relative is often modified by quidem:

'Antiquissimi fere sunt, quorum quidem scripta con-
stent, Pericles et Alcibiades,' *Pericles and Alcibiades are
about the most ancient orators of those at least whose
writings are known,* C. *Or.* 2. 'Omnium oratorum,
quos equidem cognoverim, acutissimum iudico Q.
Sertorium,' C. *Br.* 48.

Exceptions. The Demonstr. before a Relative may be so definite,
that the Relative, having no consecutive force, takes an Indicative.
Thus 'is est qui' may mean '*he is* the *person who*' (fecit, *did it*).
Even talis qui, eiusmodi qui are sometimes used with that definiteness which allows an Indic. : 'Mihi causa talis oblata est in qua
oratio deesse nemini potest,' *the case I speak for is of a sort in
which no man can be at a loss for words,* C. *p. L. Man.* I.

Sunt qui, sunt multi qui, sunt quidam qui, &c., are not always
indefinite : 'Sunt qui appellantur alces,' Caes. *B. G.* vi. 27.
'Sunt quidam qui molestas amicitias faciunt,' C. *Lael.* 20.
'Multa sunt quae dici possunt' (=ea quae dici possunt, sunt
multa). So est qui and sunt qui are constructed with Indic.
in poetry, in imitation of Greek idiom: 'Sunt quos curriculo pulverem Olympicum collegisse iuvat,' *some there are who delight
with the chariot to raise clouds of Olympian dust,* Hor. *C.* i. 1. 3.

iii. Final Clauses.[1]

A FINAL CLAUSE expresses an End or Purpose, and its Verb is
Subjunctive.

A) An Adverbial Final Clause is introduced by the Conjunction
ut (*in order that*), but if Negative by ne (*lest, that-not*), ut ne, ne
quis, necubi, nequando, &c.:

Venio ut videam ; veni ut viderem ; abito ne pereas, ut ne pereas, nequando pereas ; abiit ne periret, &c.

---

[1] Examples of Final Clauses (§§ 207-8).

A) (*Adverbial.*) 'Sessum it praetor: quid ut iudicetur?' C. *N. D.* iii. 30. 'Quid mereas
(*what would you take*) ut Epicureus esse desinas?' C. *N. D.* i. 24. 'Condiunt Aegyptii
mortuos ut quam maxime permaneant diuturna corpora,' C. *T. D.* i. 45. 'Platonem
ferunt, ut Pythagoreos cognosceret, in Italiam venisse,' C. *T. D.* i. 17. 'Inventa
sunt specula, ut homo se ipse nosceret,' Sen. *N. Qu.* i. 17. 'Dionysius, ne tonsori
collum committeret, tondere filias suas docuit,' C. *T. D.* v. 20. 'Hunc librum lege
convivis tuis, si me amas, hilaris et bene acceptis, ne in me stomachum erumpant,
cum sint tibi irati,' C. *Att.* xvi. 3. 'Caesar cum Pompeio Crassoque iniit societatem, ne
quid ageretur in republica, quod *displicuisset* ulli e tribus,' Suet. *Caes.* 19. 'Tu
quam plurimis de rebus ad me velim scribas, ut prorsus ne quid ignorem,' C. *Att.* iii.
10. 'Silanus signa quam maxime ad laevam iubebat ferri, necunde ab stationibus

1) Such Clauses may follow Demonstrative words or phrases: Eo, ideo, idcirco, propterea, ob eam rem, ob eam causam, eo consilio. Idcirco fugit, ut salvus sit. Ob eam rem fugerat, ne periret.

2) A Final Clause with ut or ne often stands parenthetically in such phrases as the following:
Ut ita dicam, *so to say*, ne dicam, *not to say*; ne longus sim, *not to be tedious*; ne te detineam, *not to detain you*, &c.

3) The construction of nedum with a Subjunctive is a peculiar instance of a Final Clause. See § 85.
(The idea of Purpose is often contained in certain Temporal Conjunctions, donec, dum, antequam, &c. See TEMPORAL CLAUSES.)

208   *B*) An Adjectival Final Clause is formed by a Relative or Relative Particle containing the notion of Purpose, and taking the Subjunctive:
'Clusini legatos Romam qui auxilium a senatu peterent misere,' L. v. 35. 'Ne illi sit cera, ubi facere possit litteras,' *let him have no wax to write upon*, Plaut. *As.* iv. 1. 22.

1) Quo is thus used, especially with a Comparative word:
'Medico puto aliquid dandum quo sit studiosior, *I think the physician should have something given to him that he may be more zealous*, C. *Fam.* xvi. 4.

209
Causal
Clauses.

iv. Causal Clauses.

A) ADVERBIAL CAUSAL CLAUSES are introduced by Conjunctions of three classes:

1) Quoniam, quando, quandoquidem, quandoque (*since*), siquidem, quatenus (*inasmuch as, seeing that*), of *admitted* Cause. The Verb is Indicative, if not Suboblique.

Punicis conspicerentur,' L. xxviii. 1. 'Haec eo scripsi ut potius relevares me,' C. *Att.* iii. 10. 'Eo perperam olim dixi ne vos forte imprudentes foris effutiretis,' Ter. *Ph.* v. 1. 18. 'Hanc ideo rationem subiecimus, ut hoc causae genus ipsum, de quo agimus, cognosceretur,' C. *Inv.* ii. 23. 'Suscipienda bella sunt ob eam causam ut sine iniuria in pace vivatur,' C. *Off.* i. 11. 'Legibus idcirco omnes servimus ut liberi esse possimus,' C. *p. Clu.* 53. 'Quid stultius est quam cetera parare, amicos non parare, optimam et pulcherrimam vitae, ut ita dicam, supellectilem?' C. *Lael.* 15. 'A te peto ut huic meae laudi vel, ut verius dicam, prope saluti, tuum studium dices,' C. *Fam.* ii. 6. 'Moleste ferebam tantum ingenium in tam levis, ne dicam ineptas, sententias incidisse,' C. *N. D.* i. 21. 'Ne te morer, audi quo rem deducam,' Hor. *S.* i. 1. 14. See Hor. *S.* i. 3. 137; *C.* iv. 9. 1. 'Vix in ipsis tectis et oppidis frigus hiemale infirma valetudine vitatur, nedum in mari et via sit facile abesse ab iniuria temporis,' C. *Fam.* xvi. 8.

B) (*Adjectival.*) 'Homini natura addidit rationem qua regerentur animi appetitus,' C. *N. D.* ii. 12. 'Hannibal tripartito Iberum copias traiecit, praemissis, qui Gallorum animos, qua traducendus exercitus *erat*, donis conciliarent, Alpium transitus specularentur,' L. xxi. 23. 'Subacto mihi ingenio opus est, ut agro non semel arato, sed novato et iterato, quo meliores fetus possit et grandiores edere,' C. *d. Or.* ii. 30. 'In funeribus Atheniensium sublata erat celebritas virorum ac mulierum, quo lamentatio minueretur,' C. *Leg.* ii. 26. (Horace has quo ne,' *S.* ii. 1. 37.)

2) Quod, quia (*because*), ascribe a Cause ; with Indic. normally.
But Causal Clauses are often Suboblique with quod, sometimes with quia :

'Mater irata est quia non redierim,' Plaut. *Cist.* i. 1. 105.

Quod, quia, may be strengthened by the same Demonstrative words or phrases as Final Conjunctions : eo, ideo,
propterea, &c.

3) Cum (*since*) expresses, usually, *conceived* Cause, with Subjunctive.

a) While quod and quia (=Greek ὅτι, διότι, and French
parceque) state a Cause *ascriptively*, cum (= Greek ἐπεί,
and French *puisque*) states it *conceptively*, hence taking
Subjunctive.

Hence too, when cum, after emotional expressions of *joy,
grief, surprise, praise, congratulation,* &c., assigns a fact
as cause, it takes an Indicative. See § 196.

(On cum in correlation with tum, see Temporal Clauses.)

b) The Subjunctive of a Verb *of thinking* is also used with
quod where the author doubtfully suggests the motive of
an action :

Helvetii, seu quod timore perterritos Romanos discedere
a se existimarent, sive eo quod re frumentaria inter-
cludi posse confiderent, nostros insequi ac lacessere
coeperunt,' Caes. *B. G.* i. 23.

c) And, by a very remarkable idiom, a Verb of *assertion* following quod is made Subjunctive, when the cause itself
(which is the really Suboblique notion) is contained in
the Infin. Clause dependent on that Verb.

Examples of Causal Clauses (§§ 209–10).

A) Adverbial.

(*Admitted Cause.*) 'Geramus, dis bene iuvantibus, quando ita videtur,
bellum,' L. xlii. 51. 'Dicite, quandoquidem in molli consedimus herba,' Verg.
B. iii. 55. 'Quandoque hice homines iniussu populi Romani Quiritium foedus
ictum iri spoponderunt, atque ob eam rem noxam nocuerunt, ob eam rem quo
populus Romanus scelere impio sit solutus, hosce homines vobis dedo,' L. ix. 10. 'Vos,
Quirites, quoniam iam nox est, in vestra tecta discedite,' C. *Cat.* iii. 12. 'Ea divi-
nationum ratio ne in barbaris quidem gentibus neglecta est, siquidem et in Gallia
Druidae sunt,' C. *Div.* i. 41. 'Audeat refrenare licentiam, clarus postgenitis, quatenus virtutem incolumem odimus,' &c. Hor. *C.* iii. 24. 28.

(*Alleged Cause.*) 'Codrus se in medios immisit hostis veste famulari, ne posset
agnosci, si esset ornatu regio ; quod oraculum erat datum, si rex interfectus esset,
victricis Athenas fore,' C. *T. D.* i. 48. 'Hae sordes susceptae sunt propter unum me,
quia meum casum luctumque doluerunt,' C. *p. Sest.* 69. 'Quia natura mutari non
potest, idcirco verae amicitiae sempiternae sunt,' C. *Lael.* 9. 'Feci e servo ut esses
libertus mihi propterea quod serviebas liberaliter,' Ter. *An.* i. 1. 10.

(*Suboblique.*) 'Comitiorum illi habendorum, quando minimus natu sit, munus consensu iniungunt,' L. iii. 35. 'Principes Trevirorum de suis privatis rebus petere coeperunt, quoniam civitati consulere non possent,' Caes. *B. G.* v. 3. 'Iugurthae
bellum illatum est, quod Adherbalem et Hiempsalem, Micipsae filios, interemisset,' Eutr. iv. 11. 'Nemo ipsam voluptatem, quia voluptas sit, aspernatur,' C.
Fin. i. 10. 'Nec quia sit honesta atque pulcherrima rerum eloquentia, petitur ipsa,
sed ad vilem usum et sordidum lucrum accingimur,' Qu. i. 12. 'Falso queritur de
natura genus humanum quod imbecilla atque aevi brevis forte potius quam virtute
regatur,' Sall. *Iug.* 1. 'Aristides nonne ob eam causam expulsus est patria, quod
praeter modum iustus esset?' C. *T. D.* v. 36. 'Plato escam malorum voluptatem
appellat, quod ea videlicet homines capiantur, ut hamo pisces,' C. *Cat. M.* 44.

'Ab Atheniensibus locum sepulturae intra urbem ut darent,
impetrare non potui, quod religione se impediri dicerent,'
C. *Fam.* iv. 12. 'Qui e Gallia veniunt, superbiam tuam
accusant, quod negent te percunctantibus respondere,'
C. *Fam.* vii. 16.

d) The ground of a writer's or speaker's present opinion will be
Indic., but that of his former opinion may take the Sub-
junctive, as if he were speaking of another person. See C.
T. D. ii. 3. cited by Madvig.

e) Non quod, non quia, non quo (less often non quoniam),
are used with the Subjunctive when the reason denied is
conceivable, but not real; sed generally following with the
true reason:

'Non idcirco librorum usum dimiseram, quod iis suc-
censerem; sed quod eorum me suppudebat,' *I had
not abandoned the intimacy of my books because I was
angry with them; but because I was a little ashamed of
my behaviour to them*, C. *Fam.* ix. 1. 'Numquam mihi
defuturam orationem, qua exercitum meum alloquerer,
credidi; non quo verba umquam potius quam res exer-
cuerim, sed quia assueram militaribus ingeniis,' *I never
supposed I should lack language to address my army; not
that I have ever practised words rather than deeds; but
because I had been accustomed to the tempers of soldiers*,
L. xxviii. 27.

f) If the cause denied is one which is *not conceivable*, non
quod, non quia take the Indicative:

'Ad urbem Scipioni majore resistitur vi; non quia plus

(*Conceived Cause.*) 'Cum sint in nobis consilium, ratio, prudentia, necesse est deos
haec ipsa habere maiora,' C. *N. D.* ii. 31. 'Cum in communibus suggestis consistere
non auderet Dionysius, contionari ex turri alta solebat,' C. *T. D.* v. 20. 'Cum Athenas
tamquam ad mercaturam bonarum artium sis profectus, inanem redire turpissimum
est,' C. *Off.* iii. 2.

(*Non quod, &c.*) 'Mihi apud vos de meis maioribus dicendi facultas non datur;
non quod non tales fuerint, qualis nos, illorum sanguine procreatos, videtis, sed
quod laude populari atque honoris vestri luce caruerunt,' C. *d. L. Agr.* ii. 1. 'Studium sapientiae mihi Latinis literis illustrandum putavi, non quia philosophia Graecis
litteris percipi non posset, sed meum semper iudicium fuit, omnia nostros accepta a
Graecis fecisse meliora,' C. *T. D.* i. 1. 'Saepe soleo audire Roscium, cum ita dicat, se
adhuc reperire discipulum, quem quidem probaret, potuisse neminem; non quo non
essent quidam probabiles, sed quia, si aliquid modo esset vitii, id ferre ipse non
posset, C. *d. Or.* i. 28. 'Crasso commendationem non sum pollicitus, non quin eam
valituram apud te arbitrarer, sed mihi egere commendatione non videbatur,' C.
Fam. xiii. 16. 'Ego me ducem in civili bello negavi esse, non quin rectum esset, sed
quia, quod multo rectius fuit, id mihi fraudem tulit,' C. *Att.* vii. 26.

B) Adjectival.

'Alexander cum in Sigeo ad Achillis tumulum adstitisset, O fortunate, inquit, adolescens, qui tuae virtutis Homerum praeconem inveneris,' C. *p. Arch.* 10. 'Cum
Dion non desisteret obsecrare Dionysium, ut Platonem Athenis arcesseret et eius consiliis
uteretur, ille, qui in aliqua re vellet patrem imitari, morem ei gessit,' N. *Di.* 3. 'O
magna vis veritatis, quae contra hominum calliditatem facile se per se ipsam defendat,'
C. *p. Cael.* 16. 'Numquam laudari satis digne philosophia poterit, cui qui pareat omne
tempus aetatis sine molestia possit degere,' C. *Cat. M.* 1. 'Habeo senectuti magnam
gratiam, quae mihi sermonis aviditatem auxit, potionis et cibi sustulit,' C. *Cat. M.*
13. 'Virtus est una altissimis defixa radicibus, quae numquam ulla vi labefactari
potest, numquam demoveri loco,' C. *Phil.* iv. 5. 'Callidus adulator non facile cognos-

animi victis est, sed melius muri quam vallum armatos arcent,' L. x. 41. See Hor. *S.* ii. 2. 89.

g) Non quin is used for non quo non or non quia non: 'Consilium tuum reprehendere non audeo, non quin ab eo dissentiam, sed,' &c., *I dare not blame your plan, not that I do not differ from it, but,* &c., C. *Fam.* iv. 7.

B) An ADJECTIVAL CAUSAL CLAUSE is formed by the Relative 210 qui, or one of its Particles.

Qui causal usually contains *conceived* Cause, with Subjunctive. Sometimes it contains quia, and takes Indic.

Quippe strengthens qui, cum, sometimes quod; the Mood being usually Subjunctive; but quippe qui is found with Indic. Ut qui, utpote qui, are rare, but found with each Mood: utpote cum with Subjunctive only.

v. Temporal Clauses. 211

Temporal Clauses

1) Temporal Conjunctions may be placed in four groups:

A) Ubi, *when,* ubi primum, simul ac, simul ut, simul, *as soon as*; ut, *when; from the time when*; ut primum, cum primum, &c., *since; as soon as*; quotiens, *as often as*; postquam, *after that, since.*

B) 1. Dum, donec, quoad, *whilst, as long as*; quamdiu, *as long as.*

2. Dum, donec, quoad, *until.*

C) Antequam, priusquam, *before that.*

D) Cum.

With most of these Conjunctions various Demonstrative Adverbs may be correlated, which are noticed in the Examples.

---

citur, quippe qui etiam adversando saepe assentetur,' C. *Lael.* 26. 'Animus fortuna non eget; quippe quae probitatem, industriam aliasque artis bonas neque dare neque eripere cuiquam potest,' Sall. *Iug.* 1. 'Sed de hoc tu videbis, quippe cum de me ipso ac de meis te considerare velim,' C. *Att.* vi. 13. 'Multa de mea sententia questus est Caesar, quippe quod etiam Crassum ante vidisset,' C. *Fam.* i. 9. 'Me incommoda valetudo, qua iam emerseram, utpote cum sine febri laborassem, tenebat Brundisii,' C. *Att.* v. 3. 'Nero inusitatae luxuriae fuit, ut qui retibus aureis piscaretur,' Eutr. vii. 9.

Examples of Temporal Clauses (§§ 211-12).

A) Ubi, &c., with Demonstratives, tum, tunc, tum demum, tum denique, ibi, iam, continuo, extemplo, ilico, ilicet, semel, statim, quamprimum, repente, &c.

(Ubi, *when,* ubi primum, *as soon as,* &c.) *a.* 'Miserum est opus fodere, ubi sitis fauces tenet,' Plaut. *Most.* ii. 1. 'Haec ubi aperuit ostium, continuo hic se coniecit intro,' Ter. *Haut.* ii. 2. 35. (Ubi nuntiata sunt, statim,' &c. C. *Verr.* v. 47. 'Ubi ... decessit, ilicet,' &c., Sall. *Iug.* 41.) 'Ubi Syracusanorum dolorem cognovi, tum eos hortatus sum,' &c., C. *Verr.* vi. 63. 'Ubi primum est licitum, ilico properavi abire de foro,' Plaut. *Men.* iv. 2. 34. 'Taleae ubi trimae sunt, tum denique maturae sunt,' Cato, *R. R.* 45. *β.* Divico ita cum Caesare agit: Si pacem populus Romanus cum Helvetiis faceret, in eam partem ituros atque ibi futuros Helvetios, ubi eos Caesar constituisset,' Caes. *B. G.* i. 13.γ. 'Id fetialis ubi dixisset, hastam in finis eorum mittebat,' L. i. 32. 'Ubi pretio non aequitate iura descripserat, Veneri iam et Libero reliquum tempus deberi arbitrabatur,' C. *Verr.* vii. 11.

2) Tense and Mood vary much in Temporal Clauses.

Variation of Tense is naturally due to the various combinations of Time in Clause and Sentence.

As to Mood, there is no Conjunction of Time which does not *normally* take the Indicative. But the Subjunctive often is required :

a) In Suboblique, Gnomic, and (in some styles) Iterative Construction.

b) When the notion of Time is complicated with that of Consequence, Purpose, Cause, or Concession. Thus, cum is constructed so as to express Consequence (Time of such a *kind* that), Cause (*since*), Concession (*although, whereas*); sometimes even Condition. Dum, donec, quoad (*until*), antequam, priusquam, &c. may imply Purpose.

The two latter sometimes take a Subjunctive which has no such internal reason ; and which may perhaps be explained by the Consec. use of quam. See § 205.

(The two last examples shew the difference of Iterative Pluperfect construction in Livy and Cicero : Subjunctive in the former, Indicative in the latter.)

(Quando, *when*=quo tempore.) 'Ubi satur sum, intestina nulla crepitant ; quando esurio, tum crepant,' Plaut. *Men.* v. 5. 27. 'Utinam tunc essem natus quando Romani dona accipere coepissent,' C. *Off.* ii. 27.

(Quotiens, *as often as.*) 'Heraclitus quotiens prodierat et tantum circa se male viventium, immo male pereuntium, viderat, flebat,' Sen. *Ir.* ii. 10. 'Quotiens patriam videret, totiens se beneficium meum videre dicebat,' C. *d. Or.* ii. 2.

(Ut, *when, as soon as*; ut primum, cum, cum primum.) 'Varro ut advenit, extemplo Hostilius legionem unam signa in urbem ferre iussit,' L. xxvii. 24. 'Ut Hostus cecidit, confestim Romana inclinatur acies,' L. i. 12. 'Cum primum sapere coepit, acerbissimos dolores percepit,' C. *Fam.* xiv. 1. 'Pompeius ut me primum vidit, complexus est,' C. *Fam.* x. 13. 'Ut vidi, ut perii,' Verg. *B.* viii. 41. 'Ut quisque me viderat narrabat,' &c. C. *Verr.* ii.

(Ut, *since, from the time when*=ex quo.) 'Ut tetigi Pontum, vexant insomnia,' Ov. *Tr.* iii. 8. 27. 'Ut sumus in Ponto, ter frigore constitit Ister,' Ov. *Tr.* v. 10. 1. See Hor. *C.* iv. 4. 42. 'Ut Athenas veneram, expectabam ibi iam quartum diem Pomptinum,' C. *Att.* v. 10.

(Simul, simul ac, simul ut, statim ut, *as soon as.*) 'Simul ac duraverit aetas membra animumque tuum, nabis sine cortice,' Hor. *S.* i. 4. 119. 'Ego statim habebo quod sentiam, simul ut videro Curionem,' C. *Att.* x. 4. 'Simul inflavit tibicen, carmen agnoscitur,' Caes. *B. G.* iv. 27. 'Statim ut ille praetor est factus . . . mira contentio est consecuta,' C. *Fam.* i. 9. 5. 'Simul ac annuisset, numeraturum se dicebat,' C. *p. Quinc.* 3.

(Postquam, posteaquam, *after that, since, when.*) 'Relegatus mihi videor posteaquam in Formiano sum,' C. *Att.* ii. 11. 'Postquam nec ab Romanis vobis ulla spes est, nec vestra iam arma vos defendunt, pacem affero necessariam,' L. xxi. 13. 'Quae postquam sunt audita et undique primores patrum consules increparent . . . tum T. Quinctius consules immerito increpari ait,' L. iv. 13. (In this place sunt audita simply marks time as stated by Livy, increparent adds the circumstance which caused Quinctius to feel and speak.) 'Hannibal anno tertio postquam domo profugerat, in Africam venit,' N. *Hann.* 8. 'Hoc scribis post diem quartum quam ab urbe discessimus,' C. *Att.* ix. 12. 'Scriptum a Posidonio est triginta annis vixisse Panaetium posteaquam illos libros edidisset,' C. *Off.* iii. 2. (In C. *Fam.* ii. 19, *p. L. Man.* 4, instead of posteaquam, postea cum is the right reading.)

B) 1. Dum, donec, quoad (*whilst, as long as*), often with Demonstratives, tamdiu, interea, interim, tantisper.

'Aegroto dum anima est, spes esse dicitur,' C. *Att.* ix. 10. 'Lacedaemoniorum gens fortis fuit, dum Lycurgi leges vigebant,' C. *T. D.* i. 42. 'Tiberius Gracchus tamdiu laudabitur, dum memoria rerum Romanarum manebit,' C. *Off.* ii. 12.

c) By Latin usage (cum historic), when, in narrative, an
   event is stated in the Perfect or Historic Present, a contemporary fact is expressed by cum with Imperfect Subjunctive; a preceding fact by cum with Pluperfect
   Subjunctive:

   Cum videret, ingemuit; cum vidisset, ingemuit.

d) The Iterative Subjunctive is used in Temporal, Relative,
   and Conditional Clauses, chiefly by historians. It occurs
   when an action *indefinitely repeated* in past time is expressed by the Clause, the Principal Verb being then
   generally in the Imperfect.

   'Cum cohortes ex acie procucurrissent, Numidae impetum nostrorum effugiebant,' Caes. *B. C.* ii. 41. 'Ignoti,
   faciem Agesilai cum intuerentur, contemnebant,'
   Nep. *Ag.* 8. 'Quemcumque lictor iussu consulis pre-
   hendisset, tribunus mitti iubebat,' L. iii. 11. 'Nec
   quisquam Pyrrhum, qua tulisset impetum, sustinere
   valuit,' Iust. xxv. 4. 'Ut quisque maxime laboraret
   locus, aut ipse occurrebat, aut aliquos mittebat,' L.
   xxxiv. 38.

And after si

   ' Ubi his ordinibus exercitus instructus esset, hastati omnium
   primi pugnam inibant. Si hastati profligare hostem non
   possent, pede presso eos retrocedentis in intervalla ordi-
   num principes recipiebant. Tum principum pugna erat.
   Si apud principes quoque haud satis prospere esset pug-
   natum, a prima acie ad triarios sensim referebantur,'
   L. viii. 8.

'Dum ad Antium haec geruntur, interim Aequi arcem Tusculanam capiunt,' L.
iii. 23. 'Dum is in aliis rebus erat occupatus, erant interea qui suis vulneribus
mederentur,' C. *p. S. Rosc.* 32. 'Ego te meum esse dici tantisper volo dum quod te
dignumst facies,' Ter. *Haut.* i. 1. 54. 'Sic se quisque hostem ferire, conspici, dum
tale facinus faceret, properabat,' Sall. *Cat.* 7. 'Donec eris felix, multos numerabis
amicos,' Ov. *Tr.* i. 8. 'Volgus trucidatum, donec ira et dies permansit,' Tac. *Ann.*
i. 68. 'Cato, quoad vixit, virtutum laude crevit,' Nep. *Att.* 2. 'Minucius praefectus
annonae, quoad res posceret, in incertum creatus,' L. iv. 13.

(Dum with Historic Present.) 'Dum haec in colloquio geruntur, Caesari nuntiatum est equites Ariovisti propius tumulum accedere,' Caes. *B. G.* i. 46. 'Quidam
tradunt, dum ad palum deligatur, quia parum inter strepitus audiri *possent* quae
vociferabatur, silentium fieri Flaccum iussisse,' L. xxvi. 16.

(*Suboblique.*) 'Dum in aestivis nos essemus, illum pueris locum esse bellissi-
mum duximus,' C. *Att.* v. 17. 'Nihil trepidabant elephanti, donec continenti velut
ponte agerentur,' L. xxi. 28.|

(*Purpose.*) 'Die insequenti quievere, dum praefectus iuventutem Apolloniatium
inspiceret,' L. xxiv. 40. 'Multa quoque et bello passus dum conderet urbem
inferretque deos Latio,' Verg. *Ae.* i. 5.

(Quamdiu.) 'Tamdiu requiesco quamdiu aut ad te scribo aut tuas litteras
lego,' C. *Att.* ix. 3. 'Deum atque hominum fidem implorabis, circumveniri Verrem,
quod accusator *nolit* tamdiu quamdiu *liceat* loqui,' C. *Verr.* ii. 1. 9.

2. Dum, donec, quoad, *until.* Demonstratives are eo usque, usque eo, tamdiu,
tantisper.

a. 'Retine Phormionem, dum huc ego servos evoco,' Ter. *Ph.* v. 7. 'Delibera hoc
dum ego redeo,' Ter. *An.* ii. 1. 'Ea mansit in condicione usque ad eum finem
dum iudices reiecti sunt,' C. *Verr.* i. 6. 'Caesar exanimis aliquamdiu iacuit, donec
lecticae impositum tres servuli domum rettulerunt,' Suet *Caes.* 82. 'Tarquinii tamdiu dimicaverunt donec Aruntem filium regis manu sua Brutus interfecit,' Flor. i.

e) The Indicative is so used, by Cicero generally, in the Pluperfect. But an Imperfect Subjunctive Clause in Iterative Sense is not unusual in Cicero: 'Zenonem, cum Athenis essem, audiebam frequenter,' *I used often to attend Zeno's lectures, when I was at Athens* (where he was more than once),' C. *N. D.* i. 2. This may happen even when tum precedes cum: 'Nos tum, cum maxime consilio nostro subvenire communi saluti oporteret, in senatum non vocabamur,' C. *Phil.* v. 1.

**212
Cum.**

3) Other uses of the Conjunction Cum:

a) Cum, *when*, is the most extensively used Temporal Conjunction, correlative to the Demonstrative tum, as dum to interea; and signifying a point of Time, as dum signifies extension of Time.

b) When the relation between the principal Sentence and the Clause is merely Temporal, cum takes an Indicative in the Present, Future (Simple or Exact), or Perfect Tense, according to the time required:

Cum venio, video; cum veniam (venero) videbo; cum veni, vidi (videbam, videram).

c) The time is more strongly defined by means of a Demonstrative (tum, eo tempore, nunc, iam, &c.).

'Vos tum paruistis cum paruit nemo,' C. *p. Lig.* 7.

d) Cum may take an Imperf. Indic., if an Imperf. is in the principal Sentence:

Cum veniebam, videbam:

Or, sometimes, if the point of time is to be strongly marked, the principal Verb may be Perfect:

---

10. 'Epaminondas ferrum usque eo in corpore retinuit quoad renuntiatum est vicisse Boeotios,' Nep. *Ep.* 9.

β. 'Expectandum putabant dum se res ipsa aperiret,' Nep. *Paus.* 3. 'Iratis subtrahendi sunt ii, in quos impetum conantur facere, dum se ipsi colligant,' C. *T. D.* iv. 18. 'Augustus rectorem solitus est apponere regibus aetate parvis ac mente lapsis, donec adolescerent aut resipiscerent,' Suet. *Aug.* 48. 'Thessalonicae esse statueram, quoad aliquid ad me scriberes,' C. *Att.* iii. 13. 'T. Quinctio consuli prorogatum in Macedonia imperium, donec successor ei venisset,' L. xxxii. 28.

C) (Antequam, priusquam.) α. 'Antequam de incommodis Siciliae dico, pauca mihi videntur esse de provinciae dignitate dicenda,' C. *Verr.* ii. 2. 'Priusquam de ceteris rebus respondeo, de amicitia pauca dicam,' C. *Phil.* ii. 3. 'Membris utimur priusquam didicimus cuius ea utilitatis causa habeamus,' C. *Fin.* iii. 66. 'Non ante finitum est proelium quam tribunus militum interfectus est,' L. xli. 2. 'Dociliora sunt ingenia priusquam obduruerunt,' Qu. ii. 11. 'Non defatigabor antequam illorum ancipites vias rationesque percepero,' C. *d. Or.* iii. 36.

β. 'Tempestas minatur antequam surgat,' Sen. *Ep.* 103. 'Tragoedi cotidie, antequam pronuntient, vocem cubantes sensim excitant,' C. *d. Or.* i. 59. 'Saepe magna indoles virtutis, priusquam reipublicae prodesse potuisset, exstincta fuit,' C. *Phil.* v. 17. 'Numidae, priusquam ex castris subveniretur, in proximos collis discedunt,' Sall. *Iug.* 54. 'Appius non ante continuando abstitit magistratu quam obruerent eum male parta, male gesta, male retenta imperia,' L. ix. 34. 'Providentia est, per quam aliquid videtur, antequam factum sit,' C. *Inv.* ii. 53. 'Nescire, quid anteaquam natus sis acciderit, id est semper esse puerum,' C. *d. Or.* 34. 'In omnibus negotiis, priusquam aggrediare, adhibenda est praeparatio diligens,' C. *Off.* i. 21. 'Priusquam incipias, consulto, et, ubi consulueris, mature facto opus est,' Sall. *Cat.* 1. (The three last Examples are Gnomic.)

'Nuper, cum te iam adventare arbitrabamur, repente abs te in mensem Quintilem reiecti sumus,' *lately, at the very moment we thought you were coming, we were thrown over by you suddenly to the month of July,* C. *Att.* i. 3. See Verg. *Aen.* xii. 736.

e) Cum may take Pluperf. Indic., when a Demonstrative marks the time :

'Tum cum in Asia res magnas permulti amiserant, scimus Romae fidem concidisse,' *at the very time when numerous persons had lost great properties in Asia we know that credit sank at Rome,* C. *p. L. Man.* 7.

f) Cum iterative (=quotiens) takes Plup. Indic. in Cicero, an Imperf. being in the principal Sentence, when repeated action is expressed : in which sense Livy has Subjunctive :

'Cum ad aliquod oppidum venerat, eadem lectica usque ad cubiculum deferebatur,' *as often as he came to any town, he was conveyed to his bed-chamber in the same sedan,* C. *Verr.* v. 11.

D. 1.) Examples of cum with Indicative. (§ 212.)

(Cum=quo tempore.) 'De te, Catilina, cum quiescunt, probant; cum patiuntur, decernunt; cum tacent, clamant,' C. *Cat.* i. 8. 'Lituo Romulus regiones direxit tum cum urbem condidit,' C. *Div.* i. 17. 'O praeclarum diem, cum in illud amicorum concilium coetumque proficiscar,' C. *Cat. M.* 23. 'Sed plura, cum ista cognoro,' C. *Att.* xv. 9. 'Regulus, tum cum vigilando necabatur, erat in meliore causa, quam si domi senex captivus, periurus consularis, remansisset,' C. *Off.* iii. 27. 'Cum Caesar in Galliam venit, alterius factionis principes erant Aedui, alterius Sequani,' Caes. *B. G.* vi. 12. 'Credo, tum cum Sicilia florebat opibus et copiis, magna artificia fuisse in ea insula,' C. *Verr.* iv. 21. 'Cum Collatino collegae Brutus imperium abrogabat, poterat videri facere injuste,' C. *Off.* iii. 10. 'Aliud est dolere, aliud laborare : cum varices secabantur C. Mario, dolebat, cum aestu magno ducebat agmen, laborabat,' C. *T. D.* ii. 15.

(Cum=quotiens, *with Plup. Indic.*) 'Cum palam eius anuli ad palmam converterat, a nullo videbatur,' C. *Off.* iii. 9. See *Ac.* ii. 47. Cum ver esse coeperat (cuius initium iste non a Favonio neque ab aliquo astro notabat, sed cum rosam viderat, tum incipere ver arbitrabatur), dabat se labori atque itineribus,' C. *Verr.* v. 10.

(Cum *put inversely.*) 'Piso ultimas Hadriani maris oras petivit, cum interim Dyrrachii milites domum, in qua eum esse arbitrabantur, obsidere coeperunt,' C. *in Pis.* 38. 'Evolarat iam e conspectu fere fugiens quadriremis, cum etiam tum ceterae naves uno in loco moliebantur,' C. *Verr.* v. 34. 'Hannibal iam scalis subibat muros Locrorum, cum repente patefacta porta Romani erumpunt,' L. xxix. 7. 'Commodum discesserat Hilarus cum venit tabellarius,' C. *Att.* xiii. 19. 'P. Sestius, fretus sanctitate tribunatus, venit in templum Castoris, obnuntiavit consuli : cum subito manus illa Clodiana, in caede civium saepe iam victrix, exclamat, incitatur, invadit,' C. *p. Sest.* 37. 'Iam dies consumptus erat, cum tamen barbari nihil remittere, atque, noctem pro se rati, acrius instare,' Sall. *Iug.* 98.

(Cum=ex quo tempore.) Permulti anni iam erant cum inter patricios magistratus tribunosque nulla certamina fuerant,' L. ix. 33. 'Nondum sex menses sunt cum huc commigravit,' Plaut. *Pers.* i. 3.

2) Examples of cum with Subjunctive. (§ 211.)

(*Iterative* cum *with Subjunctive.*) 'Saepe cum aliquem videret minus bene vestitum, suum amiculum dedit,' N. *Cim.* 4. 'Cum in ius duci debitorem vidissent, undique convolabant,' L. ii. 27. (Especially with cum diceret, cum dicat, following audio; an idiom which resembles the Consecutive use.) 'Ipsius Sulpicii nulla oratio est ; saepe ex eo audiebam, cum se scribere neque consuesse neque posse diceret,' Cic. *Br.* 56. 'Saepe soleo audire Roscium, cum ita dicat, se adhuc reperire discipulum, quem quidem probaret, potuisse neminem,' C. *d. Or.* i. 28.

g) The Inverse Construction with **cum** occurs in Narrative when the Clause seems to change places with the Principal Sentence, indicating that one action is interrupted, or quickly succeeded by another.

In this case, **cum** is often accompanied by such Adverbs as **repente, subito, interim, interea, iam,** &c., and the Verb is frequently Present Historic, now and then Historic Infinitive.

'Parata sententia consularis, **cum repente** ei affertur nuntius,' *the consul's opinion was just ready, when a sudden message reaches him,* C. *Phil.* xiii. 9. 'Id modo plebs agitabat, **cum interim** comitiorum mentio nulla fieri,' *that was what the commons were debating, while meantime no mention was being made of comitia,* L. iii. 37.

(Cum *Suboblique.*) 'Totiensne me litteras dedisse Romam, cum ad te nullas darem,' C. *Att.* v. 11. 'Quippe ius Laodiceae me dicere, cum Romae Aulus Plotius dicat,' C. *Att.* v. 15. 'Mihi non videbatur quisquam esse beatus posse, cum in malis esset,' C. *T. D.* v. 8.

(*Consecutive* cum=quali tempore.) 'Erit illud profecto tempus, cum tu unius post homines natos fortissimi viri magnitudinem animi desideres,' C. *p. Mil.* 26. 'Fuit quidem cum mihi quoque initium requiescendi fore iustum arbitrarer,' C. *Or.* i. 1. 'Ingressus est urbem cum dextra sinistra minaretur dominis, notaret domos,' C. *Phil.* xiii. 9. (But Indic. if cum =quo tempore.) 'Fuit quoddam tempus, cum in agris homines passim bestiarum more vagabantur et sibi victu fero vitam propagabant,' C. *Inv.* i. 2.

(Cum *causal.*) 'Quae cum ita sint, quid est quod de eius civitate dubitetis, praesertim cum aliis quoque in civitatibus fuerit adscriptus?' C. *p. Arch.* 5. (See Causal Clauses.)

(Cum *concessive.*) 'Atticus cum esset pecuniosus, nemo illo minus fuit emax, minus aedificator,' N. *Att.* 13. 'Cum multa sint in philosophia gravia et utilia, latissime patere videntur ea, quae de officiis tradita sunt,' C. *Off.* i. 2. 'His, cum facere non possent, tamen loqui licebat,' C. *p. Cael.* 17. (Specially frequent, when **tum** follows): 'Cole iustitiam quae, cum sit magna in parentibus et propinquis, tum in patria maxima est,' C. *d. Rep.* vi. 15. 'Cum plurimas et maximas commoditates amicitia contineat, tum illa nimirum praestat omnibus, quod debilitari animos non patitur,' Cic. *Lael.* 7. 'Haec urbs cum manu munitissima esset, tum loci natura terra ac mari claudebatur,' C. *Verr.* ii. 2.

(Cum *conditional is rare*): 'Haec neque cum ego dicerem, neque cum tu negares, magni momenti nostra esset oratio. Quo tempore igitur auris iudex erigeret animumque attenderet? Cum Dio ipse prodiret, cum reperiretur pecunias sumpsisse mutuas, cum tabulae virorum bonorum proferrentur,' C. *Verr.* i. 10.

(Cum *historic.*) 'Agesilaus, cum adversarios intra moenia compulisset, et ut Corinthum oppugnaret multi hortarentur, negavit id suae virtuti convenire,' N. *Ag.* 5. 'Socrates, cum paene in manu iam mortiferum illud teneret poculum, locutus ita est, ut non ad mortem trudi, verum in caelum videretur ascendere,' C. *T. D.* i. 29. 'Cimon Cyprum cum ducentis navibus imperator missus, cum eius maiorem partem insulae devicisset, in morbum implicitus, in oppido Citio est mortuus,' N. *Cim.* 5.

(Cum *historic* is found even after **tum**, where the Indicative might have been used.) 'Neque enim, si tibi tum, cum peteres consulatum, adfui, idcirco nunc, cum Murenam ipsum petis, adiutor eodem pacto esse debeo,' C. *p. Mur.* 3.

(In the following passage, the two Moods are used in succession; **haberent** being purely historic, **erant** appealing to later experience, shewn by **perspexeratis**): 'Unum hoc certe videor mihi verissime posse dicere: tum cum haberet haec res publica Luscinos, Calatinos, Acidinos, homines non solum honoribus populi rebusque gestis, verum etiam patientia paupertatis ornatos; et tum cum erant Catones, Phili, Laelii, quorum sapientiam temperantiamque in omnibus rebus perspexeratis, tamen huiuscemodi res commissa nemini est, ut idem iudicaret et venderet,' C. *d. L. Agr.* ii. 24.

h) Cum for ' ex quo tempore' takes the Indicative.

' Nondum centum et decem anni sunt cum de pecuniis repetundis a L. Pisone lata lex est,' *it is not yet·110 years since Lucius Piso brought in a law concerning extortion,* C. *Off.* ii. 21.

vi. Conditional Sentences.

1) The Conditional (Hypothetical) Conjunctions are : si, *if* (si non, *if not*); nisi, ni, *unless, if not.*

2) In the Compound CONDITIONAL SENTENCE, the Clause which contains the Condition is called Protăsis (quae praetenditur); the Principal Sentence is called Apodŏsis (quae redditur), the Conclusion.

These terms imply the logical assumption that the condition comes first, and that the conclusion is in the nature of a reply to the question, What then? But it is equally possible to regard the Protasis as an adverbial clause limiting a principal sentence : ' Maximas virtutes iacere omnes necesse est voluptate dominante,' C. = si voluptas dominetur.

I. Normal Forms of the Conditional Sentence.

Protasis.	Apodosis.
a. si das	negat
if you offer	*he refuses*
si dabis	negabit
if you shall offer	*he will refuse*

Normal Examples of Conditional Sentences.   (§ 213.)

a. (*Sumptio Dati.*) 'Si amitti beata vita potest, beata esse non potest,' C. *Fin.* ii. 27. 'Parvi sunt foris arma nisi est consilium domi,' C. *Off.* i. 22. 'Si noles sanus, curres hydropicus, et ni posces ante diem librum cum lumine, si non intendes animum studiis et rebus honestis, invidia vel amore vigil torquebere,' Hor. *Epist.* i. 2. 34. 'Si bellum omittimus, ɼace numquam fruemur,' C. *Phil.* v. 1. 6. 'Non si is, qui accepit, bene utitur, idcirco is qui dedit, amice dedit,' C. *N. D.* iii. 28. 'Si feceris id quod ostendis, magnam habebo gratiam; si non feceris, ignoscam,' C. *Fam.* v. 19. 'Nemo poterit esse omni laude cumulatus orator, nisi erit omnium artium scientiam consecutus,' C. *d. Or.* i. 6. 'Si in omnibus innocens fuero, quid mihi inimicitiae nocebunt?' C. *Verr.* iii. 69. 'Malevolentiae hominum in me, si poteris, occurres; si non potueris, hoc consolabere, quod me de statu meo nullis contumeliis deterrere possunt,' C. *Fam.* xi. 11. 'Telo si primam aciem praefregeris, reliquo ferro vim nocendi sustuleris,' Iust. vi. 8. 'Haud ergo, ut opinor, erravero, si a Zenone disputationis principium duxero,' C. *N. D.* ii. 21. 'Apud maiores magistratum non gerebat is qui ceperat, si patres auctores non erant facti,' C. *p. Planc.* 3. 'Cesseram, si alienam a me plebem fuisse vultis, quae non fuit, invidiae : si commoveri omnia videbantur, tempori ; si vis suberat, armis,' C. *p. Sest.* 30. 'Si licuit, patris pecuniam recte abstulit filius,' C. *p. Flacc.* 25. 'Si me amas, paulum hic ades,' Hor. *Sat.* i. 9. 38. 'Si vis amari, ama,' Sen. *Ep.* 9. Si quid novisti rectius istis, candidus imperti; si non, his utere mecum,' Hor. *Epist.* i. 6. 67. 'Si quid in te peccavi, ignosce,' C. *Att.* iii. 15. 'Causam investigato, si poteris,' C. *Div.* ii. 28.

'Mirer, inquit, si vana vestra ad plebem auctoritas est,' L. iii. 2. 'Etenim, si Lentulus putavit suum nomen fatale fore, cur ego non laeter?' C. *Cat.* iv. 1. 'Si sciens fallo, tum me, Iuppiter optime maxime, pessimo leto afficias,' L. xxii. 53. 'Si qui voluptatibus ducuntur, missos faciant honores, ne attingant rempublicam,' C. *p. Sest.* 66. 'Quod si meis incommodis laetabantur, urbis tamen periculo commoverentur' (*they should have been touched*—Hortative Past), C. *p. Sest.* 2.

β. si des (dederis)   neget (negaverit)
   if you were to offer *he would refuse*

γ. 1. si dares   negaret
   (lit.) *if you had been* *he would have been refusing*
   offering
   (often = *if you offered he would refuse*)

  2. si dedisses   negasset
    if you had offered *he would have refused*

  3. si dedisses   negaret
    if you had offered *he would have kept refusing*

β. (*Sumptio Dandi.*) 'Thucydidis orationes ego laudare soleo ; imitari neque possim, si velim, nec velim fortasse, si possim,' C. *Br.* 83. 'Si exsistat hodie ab inferis Lycurgus, gaudeat murorum Spartae ruinis, et nunc se patriam et Spartam antiquam agnoscere dicat,' L. xxxix. 37. 'Si gladium quis apud te sana mente deposuerit, repetat insaniens: reddere peccatum sit, officium non reddere,' C *Off.* iii. 25. 'Si scieris aspidem occulte latere uspiam, improbe feceris nisi monueris alterum ne assideat,' C. *Fin.* ii. 18. 'Nonne sapiens, si fame ipse conficiatur, abstulerit cibum alteri homini ad nullam rem utili? Minime vero,' C. *Off.* iii. 6. See Hor. *Epod.* ii. 39, &c. ; *Epist.* ii. 2. 1–17.

γ. (*Sumptio Ficti.*) 1. 'Si semper optima tenere possemus, haud sane consilio multum egeremus,' C. *Part.* 25. 'Si universi videre optimum et in eo consentire possent, nemo delectos principes quaereret,' C. *Resp.* i. 34. 'Si plane sic verterem Platonem aut Aristotelem, ut verterunt nostri poetae fabulas, male, credo, mererer de meis civibus, si ad eorum cognitionem divina illa ingenia transferrem,' C. *Fin.* i. 3.

2. 'Antiochus si tam in agendo bello parere voluisset consiliis Hannibalis, quam in suscipiendo instituerat, propius Tiberi quam Thermopylis de summa imperii dimicasset,' N. *Hann.* 8. 'Glebam commosset in agro decumano Siciliae nemo, si Metellus hanc epistulam non misisset,' C. *Verr.* iii. 18.

3. 'Nam si quam Rubrius iniuriam suo nomine ac non impulsu tuo et tua cupiditate fecisset, de tui comitis iniuria questum ad te potius quam te oppugnatum venirent,' C. *Verr.* i. 31. 'Esset Antonio certe statim serviendum, si Caesar ab eo regni insigne accipere voluisset,' C. *Phil.* iii. 5. 'Ulla si iuris tibi peierati poena, Barine, nocuisset unquam, dente si nigro fieres vel uno turpior ungui, crederem,' Hor. *C.* ii. 8. 1.

4. 'Consilium, ratio, sententia nisi essent in senibus, non summum consilium maiores nostri appellassent senatum,' C. *Cat. M.* 6. 'Mortuis tam religiosa iura maiores nostri tribuerunt, quod non fecissent profecto, si nihil ad eos pertinere arbitrarentur,' C. *Lael.* 4.

The following passages also strikingly illustrate the distinction between constructions β. and γ. 1.

(*a.*) 'Si vir bonus habeat hanc vim ut, si digitis concrepuerit, possit in locupletium testamenta irrepere, hac vi non utatur, ne si exploratum quidem habeat, id omnino neminem unquam suspicaturum. At dares hanc vim M. Crasso, ut digitorum percussione posset heres scriptus esse qui re vera non esset heres, in foro, mihi crede, saltaret,' C. *Off.* iii. 19. Here the first sentence (β) suggests a case which (though imaginary and really impossible) Cicero, by a fabulist's license, is entitled to represent as possible. The second falls into Construction γ. 1., because Crassus was dead at the time, and the condition, therefore, is a bygone possibility. Why then is not the Construction of the double Pluperfect Conj. used? Is it that the floating period of Crassus's public life is contemplated ; or that Cicero, taking Crassus as a mere type of unscrupulous greed, uses a form which includes an imaginary Future as well as an imagined Past? Compare Hor. *C.* iv. 8. 20 : 'Neque, si chartae sileant quod bene feceris, mercedem tuleris: quid foret Iliae Mavortisque puer, si taciturnitas obstaret meritis invida Romuli?'

(*b.*) 'Cur igitur Camillus doleret, si haec post trecentos et quinquaginta fere annos eventura putaret ; et ego doleam, si ad decem millia annorum gentem aliquam urbe nostra potituram putem?' C. *T. D.* i. 37. Here, as the first hypothesis respecting Camillus belongs to a floating past time, it rightly takes the form γ. 1, while the second, relating to the present and future of Cicero, takes β.

4. si civis esses   non negasset
  if you had been a citizen   he would not have refused

1) Class Alpha contains those Sentences with Indic. Protasis, in which it may be assumed that both Condition and Conclusion are real, because no suggestion is implied to the contrary.   Hence it is called Sumptio Dati, the Condition of Reality.

The Apodosis is usually either Indicative or Imperative; but it may be pure Conjunctive (C_1 or C_2) if it conveys a modest assertion, a wish, an exhortation, or prohibition.

The combinations of Tense in Class *a.* may be as large as the logic of language allows.

Examples :

si vis, do (dabo)	nisi vis, non do (dabo)
si voles, dabo (dedero)	nisi voles, non dabo (dedero)
si volueris, dedero (dabo)	nisi volueris, non dedero (dabo)
si volebas, dabam	nisi volebas, non dabam
si voluisti, dedi	nisi voluisti, non dedi
si dedisti, gaudeo	si non dedisti, doleo
si voluerat, dederat (dabat)	nisi voluerat, non dederat (dabat)

si vis (voles, volueris, voluisti), da (dato)
nisi (si non) vis (voles, &c.), ne dato (ne dederis)

mirer si non vincimus (vincemus, vicerimus)
si potes (poteris), velim adsis
ne vivam nisi te amo
si fas est (erit, fuerit), eamus.

2) In Classes *β.* and *γ.* the Condition and Conclusion are more or less unreal; but of this unreality there are two kinds: one which implies a possibility (more or less probable) of immediate or future realisation; the other, from which such possibility is excluded.

3) In Class *β.* Protasis and Apodosis may be C_1 or C_2, and the variation can make no difference in the English rendering.   This Class is called Sumptio Dandi, the condition of Possibility.

4) In Class *γ.* the Protasis often expresses a Condition which might possibly have occurred, but did not occur, in time past.   It is therefore purely imaginary; hence such a Sentence is called Sumptio Ficti.   The Mood of both Verbs is (normally) Conjunctive; the Tense of each may be Imperfect or Pluperfect, or one may be Imperfect, the other Pluperfect: the relations of time being what these Tenses express, as shewn in the examples.

5) It is, however, proper to observe that in the double Imperfect form of Sumptio Ficti (*γ.* I), the reference to past time is often faint, and the distinction between this form and Sumptio Dandi discernible only in the greater liveliness of the latter: which brings a Condition before the mind, as the Historic Present brings an Action, more vividly and picturesquely.   Hence Sumptio Dandi is a favourite construction of the terse and vivacious Horace.[1]

---

[1] Such a relation of these two constructions is well shewn in a passage of Cicero (*d. Or.* i. 48, 49) which treats of the definition of the Orator.   He begins by saying, 'Si forte quaereretur quae esset ars imperatoris, constituendum putarem,' &c. then: 'Sin autem quaereremus quis esset is qui ad rempublicam . . . studium

6) Thus the Construction of the double Imperfect (γ. 1.) exhibits a Condition as Present in Time Past; but such exhibition may take either of two shapes:

a) The Condition may belong only to the Past:

Si mehercule ex omni copia conventus Syracusani facere's potestatem aratori non modo reiciendi sed etiam sumendi recuperatores, tamen hoc novum genus iniuriae nemo ferre posset,' *if from your whole court at Syracuse you had allowed the farmer not merely to challenge but even to choose commissioners, yet could none have borne this novel kind of wrong*, C. *Verr.* iii. 13 (said of any time during the now past government of Verres).

b) The Condition may not only exist in Time Past, but continue, and be still valid, in Time Present.

'An possem vivere nisi in litteris viverem,' *could I have been living at all, if I lived not in literary studies?* C. *Fam.* ix. 26. Here Cic. refers not only to a portion of his life past, but also to his present circumstances and feelings.

214　　　II. Conjunctive Protasis with Indic. Apodosis.

1) An Indic. Past Tense is used in Apodosis to express an action begun, but hindered by another action which appears in a Conjunctive Protasis with nisi, ni, or si. Such an Apodosis generally stands before its Protasis.[1]

---

[1] Examples of Idiom 1. (§ 214.)

(*Imperf. in Apodosis.*) 'Labebar longius nisi me retinuissem,' C. *Leg.* i. 19. 'Auctoritas tanta plane me movebat, nisi tu opposuisses non minorem tuam,' C. *Ac.* ii. 20. 'Vincebat auxilio loci paucitas, ni iugo circummissus Veiens in verticem collis evasisset,' L. ii. 50. 'Iam fames quam pestilentia tristior erat, ni annonae foret subventum,' L. iv. 52. 'Atrox certamen aderat, ni Fabius consilio neutri parti acerbo rem expedisset,' L. iii. 1. 'Germanicus ferrum a latere diripuit elatumque deferebat in pectus, ni proximi pressam dextram vi attinuissent,' Tac. *Ann.* i. 35. Si in Cic. *Verr.* v. 49. 'Si per Metellum licitum esset, matres illorum sororesque veniebant.' (In the two following places an Indic. of being is understood in the Apodosis): 'Mitis legatio, ni praeferocis legatos habuisset,' L. v. 36. 'Suavis res, si non causas narraret earum et naturas dominus,' Hor. *S.* ii. 8. 92.

(*Perf. Apod.*, *usually with* paene *or* prope.) 'Pons Sublicius iter paene hostibus dedit, ni unus vir fuisset, Horatius Cocles,' L. ii. 10. 'Prope oneratum est sinistrum Romanis cornu, ni referentibus iam gradum consul pudore metum excussisset,' L. ii. 65. 'Paene imprudentia admissum facinus miserabile, ni utrimque praemissi equites rem exploravissent,' Sall. *B.* i. 53. 'Eadem nave paene Aethiopia tenus Aegyptum penetravit nisi exercitus sequi recusasset,' Suet. *Caes.* 52. Virgil has: 'Nec veni, nisi fata locum sedemque dedissent,' *Ae.* xi. 112.

(*Pluperfect Apodosis.*) 'Praeclare viceramus, nisi spoliatum, inermem, fugientem Lepidus recepisset Antonium,' C. *Fam.* xii. 10. 'Qui ante Latinos ne pro se quidem ipsis attingere arma passi sumus, nunc nisi Latini sua sponte arma sumpsissent, capti et deleti eramus, L. iii. 19. 'Me truncus illapsus cerebro sustulerat, nisi Faunus ictum dextra levasset,' Hor. *C.* iii. 17. 28. See iii. 6. 3. 'Perierat imperium, quod iam in extremo stabat, si Fabius tantum ausus esset quantum ira suadebat,' Sen. *Ir.* i. 11.

---

suum contulisset, definirem hoc modo,' &c. ; then, 'Sin autem quaereretur quisnam iurisconsultus vere nominaretur, eum dicerem,' &c., but next, 'Atque . . . si musicus, si grammaticus, si poeta quaeratur, possim similiter explicare,' &c. Here evidently the transition from Sumptio Ficti to Sumptio Dandi is not caused by any essential distinction in the nature of the hypotheses; though probably the use of examples to establish the first three led Cicero to choose the Imperf. form as most suitable for the purpose.

2) An Indic. Pres. Verb of *ability* or *duty* (possum, debeo), also est with longum, immensum, infinitum, or with Gerundive, may stand in Apodosis with Pres. Conjunctive Protasis.

3) The idiom by which Past Indic. Tenses of Verbs of *ability*, *duty*, *necessity*, *fitness*, &c. (including esse with Gerundive and other complements), can be used instead of Conjunctive forms, is noticed in p. 336. Such Verbs (except convenire, licere) retain the same idiom in the Apodosis of a Conditional Sentence with Conjunctive Protasis, so far as regards the Imperf. and Perf. Tenses (but the

---

(*Verb conditioned a dependent or suppressed Verb.*) 'Admonebat me res ut hoc quoque loco interitum eloquentiae deplorarem, ni vererer ne de me ipso aliquid viderer queri' (admonebat res ut deplorarem=re admonente deplorabam), C. *Off.* ii. 19. 'Obsistere ac retinere conati sunt ni strictis gladiis viri fortissimi inertes submovissent' (et retinuissent mentally supplied), L. xxii. 60. 'Volsci comparaverant auxilia quae mitterent Latinis, ni maturatum ab dictatore Romano esset '(supply 'et misissent '), L. ii. 22.

(*Analogous idiom.*) 'Numeros memini si verba tenerem ' (the mind supplies 'et canerem '), Verg. *B.* ix. 44.

Examples of Idiom 2 :—

'Hi te homines neque debent adiuvare si possint, neque possunt si velint,' C. *Verr.* iv. 9. 'Non potest iucunde vivi nisi cum virtute vivatur,' C. *Off.* 'Immensum est si velim singula referre,' Sen. *Ep.* 68. 'De quo iudicio si velim dicere omnia, multi appellandi laedendique sunt,' C. *Verr.* i. 60.

(Similarly) 'Si plus tibi promissa noceant quam illi prosint cui promiseris, non contra officium est (i.e. potest) maius anteponi minori,' C. *Off.* i. 10.

(Of like nature are the Gnomic constructions):

'Si valeant homines, ars tua, Phoebe, iacet (=iaceat necesse est),' Ov. *Tr.* iv. 3. 1. 'Ista discuntur facile, si et tantum sumas quantum opus sit, et habeas qui docere fideliter possit, et scias etiam ipse discere (discuntur=disci possunt),' C. *d. Or.* iii. 23. 'Si ridere concessum sit, vituperatur tamen cachinnatio,' C. *T. D.* iv. 31.

(*Pres. of Periphr. Fut. in Apod. with Conj. Protasis.*) 'Quid, si hostes ad urbem veniant, facturi estis? quid si plebs mox armata veniat?' L. iii. 52.

Examples of Idiom 3 :—

(*Imperfect.*) 'Omnibus eum contumeliis onerasti, quem patris loco, si ulla in te pietas esset, colere debebas ' (implies 'et nunc debes),' C. *Phil.* ii. 38. 'Si mihi pater succenseret, te maiorem fratrem pro minore deprecari oportebat. Ubi praesidium esse oportebat, ibi exitium est,' L. xl. 15. 'Poterat utrumque praeclare fieri, si esset fides, si gravitas in hominibus consularibus,' C. *Fam.* i. 17. 'Si verum respondere velles, haec erant dicenda,' C. *Fin.* iv. 23. 'Quantus imperator Aemilius fuerit, si ex alia re nulla aestimari posset, vel hoc satis erat,' L. xlv. 37. (With concessive meaning of si, *although*.) 'Quod si liceret, tamen non debebas,' C. *Fam.* vii. 27. 'Si Romae Pompeius privatus esset hoc tempore, tamen ad tantum bellum is erat deligendus atque mittendus,' C. *p. L. M.* 17. Nihil est necesse, et si quid esset, id necesse tamen non erat confiteri,' C. *Or.* 69.

(Cicero generally prefers the Conjunctive Apodosis when the Protasis is concessive.) 'Quae si maxime meminissem, tamen illius temporis similitudinem iam sequi deberem,' *Att.* ix. 13. (Especially when the Apodosis is posse.) 'Si tibi nemo responsurus esset, tamen ipsam causam demonstrare non posses,' *in Cael.* 13.

(*Perfect.*) 'Ne domi quidem, si sui iuris finibus matronas contineret pudor, quae leges hic rogarentur abrogarenturve curare decuit,' L. xxxiv. 2. 'Si ita esset, hac lege Iunium accusatum oportuit, qua accusatur Avitus,' C. *p. Clu.* 33. 'Ergo si viri illi arma habuissent, capi Roma me consule potuit?' L. iii. 67. 'An una fieri potuerunt, si una tribus non tulissent,' C. *p. Planc.* 22. 'Hanc urbem vos non hostium ducitis, ubi, si unum diem morati essetis, moriendum omnibus fuit,' L. ii. 38.

(With concessive force of si.) 'Debuisti, Vatini, etiam si falso venisses in suspicionem P. Sestii, tamen mihi ignoscere,' C. *in Vat.* 1.

Pluperf. in poetry only: ' Si di mihi parcere vellent, perdere debuerant,' Ov.). The Indic. lays stress on the duty, &c., as existing (Imperf.), or having existed (Perf.), independent of the Condition. Otherwise the Apodosis will be Conjunctive.

4) Especially, the Past Indic. Tenses of the Periphr. Fut. Conjugation are thus used in Apodosis.

215　　　III. Indicative Protasis with Conjunctive Apodosis.

1) Generally if the Protasis is Indicative and the Apodosis Conjunctive, this implies that if the former *is*, the latter *may be*.

Such are the instances, already given (p. 469), of modest assertions (dixerim, &c.), wishes (moriar, peream, ne vivam, &c.), exhortations, prohibitions, &c., in Apodosis with Indic. Protasis.

2) Some passages occur, in which, though the Verb in the Protasis is Indic., the true logical Protasis is a Conjunctive Verb implied in some adjunct, or to be otherwise mentally supplied.

' Si Caesaris causa in provinciam veniebatis, ad eum profecto exclusi provincia venissetis: venistis ad Pompeium,' *if you were coming into the province in Caesar's interest, no doubt when you were shut out of the province you would have come to him: you came to Pompey*, C. *p. Lig.* 8. Here veniebatis contains a fact: 'You were actually intending to come;' but the logical Protasis lies in the phrase, ' Caesaris causa,' 'had it been *in Caesar's interest* that you were intending to come.'

' Nisi Deiotarus revertisset, in eo conclavi ei cubandum fuisset, quod proxima nocte corruit. At id neque, si fatum fuerat, effugisset, nec, si non fuerat, in eum casum incidisset,' C. *Div.* ii. 8. Here the true Protases of the Conjunctive Verbs must be mentally supplied : ' had it been so destined, he would not have escaped, *even if he had turned back* : had it not been destined, he would not have met with that calamity, *even if he had not turned back.*'

Examples of Idiom 4.

(*Imperf. Indic. of Periphr. Fut. in Apod.*) ' Conclave illud, ubi mansurus erat, si ire perrexisset, proxima nocte corruit,' C. *Div.* i. 15. ' Illi ipsi aratores, qui remanserant, relicturi agros omnes erant, nisi ad eos Metellus Roma litteras misisset,' C. *Verr.* iii. 52. 'Quid? si ego morerer, mecum exspiratura respublica, mecum casurum imperium populi Romani erat?' L. xxviii. 28. ' Gravior ultor caedis, si superesset, rex futurus erat,' L. i. 40.

(*Perf. Indic. of Periphr. Fut. in Apod.*) ' Si P. Sestius occisus esset, fuistisne ad arma ituri? fuistisne vos ad patrium illum animum excitaturi? fuistisne aliquando rempublicam a funesto latrone repetituri?' C. *p. Sest.* 38. ' Quid futurum fuit, si illa plebs agitari coepta esset tribuniciis procellis?' L. ii. 1. ' Furius et Aemilius currum triumphalem me conscendere prohibent, quos ego, si tribuni me triumphare prohiberent, testis citaturus fui rerum a me gestarum,' L. xxxviii. 47.

(*Protasis virtually contained in a word or phrase.*) ' Quid tandem incensis futurum fuit?' (=si incensae essent), C. *Cat.* iv. 8. ' Haec sine doctrina credituri fuerunt,' C. *T. D.* i. 21. ' Quomodo trucidato te ipsi evasuri fuerunt?' L. xl. 14.

(*Duty,* &c. *strictly depending on Condition.*) ' Quod si bona Quinctii possideres, possidere omnia eo iure deberes' (i.e. nunc non debes), C. ' Omnino si id consilium placeret, necesse esset' (sed non placet), C. *Att.* xiii. 41. ' Nisi tu aliquid dixisses, nihil sane ex me quidem audire potuisses' (sed aliquid dixisti), C. *N. D.* i. 21. ' Sic faciendum fuisset si Gabinium accusassem' (sed non accusavi), C. *Qu. F.* iii. 4.

'Si domum tuam expugnaturus, capta domo dominum interfecturus eram, non temperassem vino in unum diem?' L. xl. 14. Here 'si expugnaturus (interfecturus) eram' may be regarded as equal to 'si voluissem expugnare (interficere),' because conditional force may exist in a Periphrastic Future.

IV. Abnormal Relation of Tenses.

216

Rare forms of Conditional Consecution occur in poetry:

'Carmina ni sint, ex humero Pelopis non nituisset ebur,' Tibull. i. 4. 63 (where a permanent condition affects a past fact).

'Et faceret si non aera repulsa sonent,' Tibull. i. 8. 22 (where faciat would be normal; but the poet wished to mark past time also as affected by the condition).

V. Protasis without si.

217

1) The Conjunctive Protasis often suppresses si.

'Rex velit honesta, nemo non eadem volet,' Sen. Tr. *Thy.* 214. 'Unum cognoris, omnis noris,' Ter. *Ph.* ii. 1. 35. 'Dedisses huic animo par corpus, fecisset quod optabat,' Plin. *Epist.* i. 12. 'Deciens centena dedisses huic parco, paucis contento, quinque diebus nil erat in loculis,' Hor. *Sat.* i. 3. 15.

2) A Categorical form takes the place of the Conditional.

'Ira exardescit, libido concitatur: in eandem arcem confugiendum est,' *anger flames out; lust is excited; to the same stronghold must we fly*, C. T. D. ii. 24. 'Negat quis; nego: ait; aio,' Ter. *Eun.* ii. 21.

3) Sine with Ablative, or an Ablative Absolute, or some phrase, may stand as Protasis instead of si with Verb:

'Sine Deo (Deo sublato) non esset mundus (= si Deum tolleres).' 'Neque agricultura, neque frugum fructuumque reliquorum perceptio et conservatio sine hominum opera ulla esse potuisset... nec lapides e terra exciderentur sine hominum labore et manu (i.e. nisi hominum opera, labor, manus accessissent),' C. *Off.* ii. 3. 'Animi magnitudo, remota communitate coniunctioneque humana, feritas sit quaedam et immanitas (i.e. si communitas remota sit),' C. *Off.* i. 44.

VI. Si in various senses.

218

1) The Protasis and Apodosis of a Condition may stand in the mutual relation of *premise* and *consequence*, or *cause* and *effect*. Hence si is found in correlation to ita, sic, tum, tum vero; ideo, idcirco.

'Hoc ita iustum est, si est voluntarium,' *this is just, on condition of its being voluntary*, C. *Off.* i. 9. 'A patribus acceptos deos ita placet coli si huic legi paruerint ipsi,' C. *Leg.* ii. 10. 'Haec si ages et senties, tum eris magnus consul et consularis; sin aliter, tum in istis amplissimis nominibus honorum non modo dignitas nulla erit, sed erit summa deformitas,' C. *Fam.* x. 6. 'Non, si Opimium defendisti, idcirco te isti bonum civem putabunt,' *they will not think you a good citizen because you defended Opimius*, C. d. Or. ii. 40.

2) Si is used in a peculiar Final Sense (=*to see* if ; *to try* if, &c.) :

'Ad Gonnum castra movet, si oppido potiri posset,' L. xlii. 67. 'Circumfunduntur hostes si quem aditum reperire possent (=ut possent, si possent),' *the enemy swarmed round to try if they could find any access*, Caes. *B. G.* vi. 37. ' Te adeunt fere omnes, si quid velis (=ut discant quid velis, si quid velis),' *nearly everybody calls on you to find out if you want anything*, C. *Fam.* iii. 9. 'Expectabam si quid ad me scriberes (=dum scriberes, si scriberes),' *I was waiting to see if you would write to me anything*, C.

Poets use a similar idiom with Indic. :

'Inspice si possum donata reponere laetus,' *examine me and see if I can cheerfully restore your gifts*, Hor. *Epist.* i. 7. 39. See Hor. *S.* ii. 5. 87.

3) Si is used in a Concessive Sense : si maxime, *though ever so much* ; si nihil aliud, *though nothing else* : which are often connected with the Demonstratives tamen, certe, &c.

'Vivorum memini : nec tamen Epicuri licet oblivisci, si cupiam,' C. *Fin.* v. 1. 'Caelestia si maxime cognita essent, nihil tamen ad bene vivendum conferrent,' C. *Ac.* i. 4. 'Si nihil aliud, gratorum certe nobis animorum gloriam dies haec dederit,' L. xxii. 29.

219 VII. Si in combination with various Pronouns and Particles.

1) Si is enclitically followed by many Particles and Indefinite Pronouns. Such combinations are :

Si quis, si qui, si quando, sicubi, &c. (also si quisquam, si aliquis, si unquam, &c.) ; si quidem, si modo, si tamen, si forte, si maxime, si vero, &c. ; sin (for si-ne), *but if*; sin autem, sin vero, &c.

2) Si quis = qui or quisquis : si quando = quandocumque, &c.

'Licet irridere si qui vult, plus apud me tamen vera ratio valebit quam vulgi opinio : neque ego umquam bona perdidisse dicam, si quis pecus aut supellectilem amiserit,' C. *Par.* 1. 'Si quod erat grande vas et maius opus inventum, laeti afferebant ; si minus eiusmodi quodpiam venari potuerant, illa quidem certe pro lepusculis, patellae, paterae, turibula,' C. *Verr.* iv. 21.

220 VIII. Idiomatic Uses.

1) A Clause with si (especially accompanied by an indefinite Pronoun or Particle) is used to imply that the Apodosis is as certain or remarkable as any similar case which could be cited :

'Si quid generis istiusmodi me delectat, pictura delectat,' *if anything of that kind charms me, painting does*, C. *Fam.* vii. 23. 'Si quando urbs nostra floruit, nunc maxime floret,' Plin. *Epist.* i. 10. 'Si tibi umquam sum visus in republica fortis, certe me in causa Clodiana admiratus esses,' C. *Att.* i. 16.

2) Hence si quidem sometimes becomes Causal = *inasmuch as* :

'Antiquissimum e doctis est genus poetarum, siquidem Homerus fuit et Hesiodus ante Romam conditam,' *of the learned classes, poets are the most ancient, seeing that Homer and Hesiod lived before Rome was founded*, C. *T. D.* i. 1.

But si quidem may also = si modo.

3) The Protasis with si is sometimes designed to correct the form of expression in the principal Sentence:

'Romae delectus habetur totaque Italia, si hic delectus appellandus est, cum ultro se offerunt omnes,' *a levy is going on at Rome and throughout Italy, if levy it can be called, when all present themselves unpressed,'* C. *Fam.* xi. 8.

4) Si modo, si tamen, si vero are used for a similar purpose; also si forte.

'Ea diligenter a me expressa acumen habent Antiochi, nitorem orationis nostrum, si modo is est aliquis in nobis,' C. *Att.* xiii. 19. 'Nunc incorrectum populi pervenit in ora, in populi quicquam si tamen ore meum est,' Ov. *Tr.* iii. 14.

5) Often si enforces an entreaty by suggesting a reason.

'Si me diligis, excita ex somno tuas litteras,' *if you have any regard for me, wake up your correspondence,* C. *Fam.* xvi. 14. 'Nihil amplius oro, Maia nate, nisi ut propria haec mihi munera faxis, si neque maiorem feci ratione mala rem, nec sum facturus vitio culpave minorem,' Hor. *Sat.* ii. 6. 4.

6) The phrase si quaeris, si quaeritis (*if you want to know*), also si quaerimus, apologises for a possibly superfluous statement:

Si dis placet (*save the mark! forsooth*) is an expression of slightly contemptuous surprise.

'Ea res, si quaeris, ei magno honori fuit,' C. *Off.* iii. 20. 'Et, si quaeritis, is, qui appellatur dicax, in hoc genere maxime excellit,' C. *d. Or.* ii. 62. 'Etiam Latini, si dis placet, hoc biennio dicendi magistri exstiterunt,' C. *d. Or.* iii. 24.

IX. Sive, Seu.

221

Sive, seu (*whether, or if, or*), are often used in Distributive construction, sive . . . sive, seu . . . seu, &c.   See CONJUNCTIONS.

'Si nocte sive luce, si servus sive liber faxit, probe factum esto,' L. xxii. 10. 'Veniet tempus mortis et quidem celeriter; et sive retractabis sive properabis,' C. *T. D.* i. 31. 'Mala et impia consuetudo est contra deos disputandi, sive ex animo id fit sive simulate,' C. *N. D.* ii. 67. 'Inviso semel principe seu bene seu male facta premunt,' Tac. *H.* i. 7. 'Illo loco libentissime soleo uti, sive quid mecum ipse cogito, sive quid aut scribo aut lego,' C. *Leg.* ii. 1. 'Utcumque haec, sive errore humano, seu casu, seu necessitate inciderunt, bonum animum habe,' L. xlv. 8. 'Iuxta periculoso ficta seu vera promeret, monuit Liviam,' Tac. *Ann.* i. 6.

X. Conditional Negation.

222

1) Nisi (*unless, except if*) denies a supposition: si non (*if not*) supposes a denial, the emphasis falling on the negative.

'Nemo fere saltat sobrius nisi forte insanit,' *hardly any sober person dances, unless perchance he is mad,* C. *p. Mur.* 6. 'Si non quaeret, nullus dixeris,' *if he shall not ask, you will say nothing,* Ter. *Hec.* i. 2. 4.

Si minus, sin minus, sin aliter, sin secus, are used for si non.

Nisi is strengthened by Adverbs: nisi tamen, nisi forte, nisi vero. &c.

2) One Conditional clause with si or si non following another without distinct reference to the former may express an alternative or contradictory hypothesis:

'Iudicia non metuis: si propter innocentiam, laudo; si propter vim, non intellegis ei, qui isto modo iudicia non timeat, quid timendum sit?' C. *Phil.* ii. 45. 'Si erunt in officio amici, pecunia non derit; si non erunt, tu efficere tua pecunia non poteris,' C. *Fam.* xiv. 1. 'Quid nos, quibus te vita si superstite iucunda, si contra gravis?' Hor. *Epod.* i. 5.

3) But sin, sin autem, sin aliter, are used in distinct reference to another Condition which has gone before, actually or virtually:

'Mercatura si tenuis est, sordida putanda est; sin magna et copiosa, non est admodum vituperanda,' C. *Off.* i. 42. 'Luxuria cum omni aetati turpis, tum senectuti foedissima est: sin autem libidinum intemperantia accesserit, duplex malum est,' C. *Off.* i. 34. 'Velim deinceps meliora sint; sin aliter fuerit, reipublicae vicem dolebo,' C. *ad Br.* 10.

4) Sin minus, si minus, sin secus, *if not,* may follow without repeating the Verb:

'Senatus consultum si erit factum, scribes ad me; sin minus, rem tamen conficiam,' C. *Att.* v. 4. 'Huic tu libro maxime velim ex animo, si minus, gratiae causa suffragere,' C. *Fam.* xii. 17.

Sin, sin autem, are sometimes used in the same way:

'Si Brutus conservatus erit, vicimus: sin, quod di omen avertant, omnis omnium cursus est ad vos,' C. *Fam.* xii. 6. 'Iniecta mihi spes quaedam est velle mecum Ser. Sulpicium colloqui. Si vir esse volet, praeclara συνοδία; sin autem, erimus nos qui solemus,' C. *Att.* x. 7.

5) Nisi is sometimes used in a sense resembling that of sed (*but*):

'Quid erat quod Capitonem primum scire voluerit? Nescio; nisi hoc video, Capitonem in his bonis esse socium,' *why was it that he wished Capito to be informed first? I can't say; but this I observe, that Capito is a partner in this property,* C. *p. S. Rosc.* 35.

In this sense nisi tamen, nisi quod are used.

6) Nisi is also used to set aside a possible objection:

'Adhuc certe, nisi ego insanio, stulte omnia et incaute,' *so far, certainly, if I am not out of my wits, all has been done foolishly and unwarily,* C. *Att.* vii. 10.

7) Nisi forte, nisi tamen, nisi vero, have an ironical use:

'Eruci criminatio tota, ut arbitror, dissoluta est, nisi forte expectatis ut illa diluam quae de peculatu obiecit,' C. *p. S. Rosc.* 29. 'Frangetis impetum vivi, cuius vix sustinetis furias insepulti; nisi vero sustinuistis eos qui cum facibus ad curiam cucurrerunt,' C. *p. Mil.* 33. 'Equidem nec cur Patro tantopere contendat video, nec cur tu repugnes: nisi tamen multo minus tibi concedi potest quam illi laborare sine causa,' C. *Fam.* xiii. 1.

8) On the other hand, nisi si stands for nisi when the exception is purely conditional; and often before quis, quando, &c.

'Miseros illudi nolunt, nisi si se forte iactant,' *they will not have the unfortunate ridiculed, unless, indeed, they vaunt themselves,* C. *d. Or.* ii. 58. 'Ambiguum admirationem magis quam risum movet, nisi si quando incidit in aliud genus ridiculi,' C. *d. Or.* ii. 62.

9) N i s i, as a mere annexive Conjunction, especially follows Negatives, Interrogatives, &c. :

'Nullum imperium est tutum, nisi benevolentia munitum,' Nep. *Di.* 5. 'Hoc sentio, nisi in bonis amicitiam esse non posse,' C. *Lael.* 5. 'Oleam Theophrastus negavit nisi intra xl. millia passuum a mari nasci,' Pl. *N. H.* xv. 1. 'Quicquamne putas me curare nisi ut ei ne desim,' C. *Att.* xii. 4. 'Erat historia nihil aliud nisi annalium confectio,' C. *d. Or.* ii. 12.

10) Hand (Tursellinus iv.) denies that n i is a contracted form of n i s i. He regards it as an ancient negative particle, which remains in use only in a conditional sense = si non.

'Neque eius pugnae memoria tradita foret, ni Marsi eo primum proelio cum Romanis bellassent,' *that battle would not have been recorded, had it not been the first in which the Marsi waged war with the Romans,* L. ix. 41. 'Ni virtus fidesque vestra spectata mihi foret, nequiquam opportuna res cecidisset,' *if I had not well tried your valour and fidelity, this opportunity would have occurred in vain,* Sall. *Cat.* xx. 'Respondere vadato debebat, quod ni fecisset, perdere litem,' *he was bound to appear in court to one who had taken bail from him, or, in default of appearing, to lose his cause,* Hor. *Sat.* i. 9. 37.

α) N i follows Optatives of Imprecation : 'Dispeream ni summosses omnis,' *upon my life you would have supplanted all,* Hor. *Sat.* i. 9.

β) N i is used in the formula of a wager : 'Lutatius, eques Romanus, sponsionem fecerat, ni vir bonus esset,' *Lutatius, a Roman knight, had laid a wager (on condition of losing) if he were not a good man,* C. *Verr.* iii. 59.

(This was the usual mode of settling disputes of personal honour at Rome. See Mommsen, *Rom. Hist.* B. iii. Ch. 12.)[1]

XI. The following table shews how to convert Conditional Sentences into Oratio Obliqua when the Apodosis becomes an Infin. Clause, and the Protasis is subordinate to it.

223

---

[1] Examples of nisi (ni), si non, &c. (§ 222.)

I. *a.* 'Actum de te est, nisi provides,' C. *Fam.* ix. 18. 'Opprimemini, nisi provideritis,' C. *ad Brut.* i. 2. 'Ni tua custodis, avidus iam haec auferet heres,' Hor. *S.* ii. 3. 151.

b. Te nusquam mittam, nisi das firmatam fidem,' Plaut. *M. Gl.* ii. 5. 'Doli non doli sunt, nisi astu colas, Plaut. *Capt.* ii. 1.

c. 'Nisi ego illum hominem perdo, perii,' Plaut. *Pers.* iv. 9. 'Moriar, nisi facete,' C. *Att.* xvi. 11. 'Mirum ni illa salva est,' Ter. *Haut.* iii. 5.

d. 'Cogere eum coepit, sponsionem facere cum lictore suo, ni furtis quaestum faceret,' C. *Verr.* v. 54. 'Da pignus, ni ea sit filia,' Plaut. *Epid.* v. 2. 'Da hercle pignus, ni omnia memini et scio,' Plaut. *Pers.* ii. 2.

e. 'Ausculta paucis, nisi molestum est, Demea,' Ter. *Ad.* v. 9. 'Impetrarim libenter, nisi molestum sit,' C. *T. D.* v. 29. 'Nisi molestum est, percontari hanc paucis hic vult,' Plaut. *Pers.* iv. 4.

Conditio Recta.	Conditio Obliqua.
Si peccas, doles.	Aio te, si pecces, dolere,
Si peccabis, dolebis. Si peccaveris, dolueris. Si pecces, doleas.	si { pecces, / peccaveris, / peccaturus sis, } doliturum (dolendum) esse.
Si peccares, doleres.	si peccares, doliturum (dolendum) esse
Si peccavisses, Si peccares, } doluisses.	si { peccavisses, / peccares, } doliturum (dolendum) fuisse.[1]

II. *a.* 'Et certe, nisi is Antonium ab urbe avertisset, perissent omnia,' C. *ad Br.* i. 3. 'Haec illius severitas acerba videretur, nisi multis condimentis humanitatis mitigaretur,' C. *p. Qu.* 1. 'Plures cecidissent, ni nox proelio intervenisset,' L. xxiii. 18.

b. 'Haec ego non ferrem, nisi me in philosophiae portum contulissem,' C. *Fam.* vii. 30. 'Nam ni vellent di, non fieret, scio,' Plaut. *Aul.* iv. 10. 'Agesilaus talem se imperatorem praebuit, ut omnibus apparuerit, nisi ille fuisset, Spartam futuram non fuisse,' Nep. *As.* 6.

c. 'Quod ni ita sit, quid veneramur, quid precamur deos?' C. *N. D.* i. 44. 'Quod ni ita se haberet, nec iustitiae ullus esset nec bonitati locus,' C. *Fin.* iii. 20.

III. 1. *a.* 'Si re publica non possis frui, stultum est nolle privata,' C. *Fam.* iv. 9. 'Vas factus est alter eius sistendi ut, si ille non revertisset, moriendum esset ipsi,' C. *Off.* iii. 10. 'Ego vero meum consilium, si praesertim tu non improbas, vehementer approbo,' C. *Qu. Fr.* iii. 4.

b. 'Si mundus universus non est deus, ne stellae quidem,' C. *N. D.* iii. 9. 'Quod si verisimile non est, ne illud quidem est, haec unde fluxerunt,' C. *N. D.* iii. 18.

'Si tot exempla virtutis non movent, nihil umquam movebit,' L. xxii. 60.

'Quae potest esse sanctitas, si di humana non curant?' C. *N. D.* i. 44.

'Si non tangendi copia est, eho, ne videndi quidem erit?' Ter. *Eun.* iv. 2.

c. 'Si illud non licet, saltim hoc licebit,' Ter. *Eun.* iv. 2. 'Si non urna, tamen iunget nos littera; si non ossibus ossa meis, at nomen nomine tangam,' Ov. *M.* xi. 706. 'Victi sumus igitur, aut, si vinci dignitas non potest, fracti certe et abiecti,' C. *Fam.* iv. 7.

'Dolorem iustissimum, si non potero frangere, occultabo,' C. *Phil.* xii. 8.

2. *a.* 'O miserum te, si intellegis, miseriorem, si non intellegis,' C. *Phil.* ii. 22. 'Bene si amico feceris, ne pigeat fecisse, at potius pudeat, si non feceris,' Plaut. *Trin.* ii. 2.

b. 'Si mihi veniam, quam peto, dederit, utar condicione; sin minus, impetrabo aliquid a me ipso,' C. *Att.* ix. 15.

'Sume, catelle; negat: si non des, optet,' Hor. *S.* ii. 3. 258.

c. 'Si affers, tum patent, si non est quod des, aedes non patent,' Plaut. *As.* i. 3.

d. 'Valerium iureconsultum valde tibi commendo, sed ita etiam si non est iureconsultus,' C. *Fam.* iii. 1.

3. *a.* 'Aes pro capite dent: si id facere non queunt, domum abeant,' Plaut. *Poen. Pr.*

b. 'Quid, si quis non sit avarus, continuon' sanus?' Hor. *S.* ii. 3. 159. 'Quid si non impetraro?' *C. Att.* ix. 2.

4. *a.* 'Hoc tamen nuntia, melius me morituram fuisse si non in funere meo nupsissem,' L. xxx. 15.

b. 'Interminatus est a minimo ad maximum, si quis non hodie munus misisset sibi, eum cras cruciatu maximo perbitere, Plaut. *Ps.* iii. 1.

c. 'Peream male si non optimum erat,' Hor. *S.* ii. 1. 6. 'Peream si non invitant omnia culpam,' Ov. *Her.* xvii. 183.

d. 'Iubet P. Quinctium sponsionem cum S. Naevio facere, si bona sua ex edicto praetoris dies xxx. possessa non essent,' C. *p. Qu.* 8.

e. 'Volo te verbis pauculis, si tibi molestum non est,' Plaut. *Ep.* iii. 4.

[1] Examples of Conditional Sentences in Oratio Obliqua. (§ 223.)

'Omnes intellegunt, si salvi esse velint, necessitati esse parendum,' C. *Off.* ii. 21. 'Equidem putabam virtutem hominibus, si modo tradi ratione possit, insti-

XII. Modo, dum, dummodo.

Modo (*only*) is used for si modo, *if only*; modo ut, *provided that*; with Negative, modo ne, *provided that . . . not.*

Tantum is similarly used in poetry.

Dum (*whilst*), dummodo (*whilst only*), may also signify, *provided that, provided that only*: and, if Negative, take ne.

All these Conjunctions require the Subjunctive.[1]

vii. Concessive Sentences.

These, like Conditional Sentences, have Protasis and Apodosis. They are called Concessive, because the Protasis *concedes* an objection: meaning *although, even if, however, granting that,* &c.

I. Concessive Conjunctions are of several classes.

(1) The strengthened forms of si (including si itself used concessively), etsi, etiamsi, tamen-etsi (usually written tametsi), *even if, although.*

The natural Demonstrative of these and of all Concessive forms is tamen, *nevertheless, yet*; certe, at, at certe, sed tamen, tamen, saltem, are also used

(2) The Universal Relative Adverbs, quamquam (*howsoever = although*), utut (*however*).

---

tuendo ac persuadendo tradi,' C. *d. Or.* i. 58. 'M. Claudius vociferatur: ita demum liberam civitatem fore, ita aequatas leges, si sua quisque iura ordo, suam maiestatem teneat,' L. iii. 63. 'Veneti legationem ad P. Crassum mittunt; si velit suos recipere, obsides sibi remittat,' Caes. *B. G.* iii. 7. 'Ariovistus respondit: si ipse populo Romano non praescriberet, quemadmodum suo iure uteretur, non oportere se a populo Romano in suo iure impediri,' Caes. *B. G.* i. 36. 'Additum decreto: si quis quid postea, quod ad notam ignominiamque Philippi pertineret, ferrent, id omne populum Atheniensium iussurum; si quis contra ignominiam prove honore eius dixisset fecissetve, qui occidisset eum iure caesurum,' L. xxx. 44. '(Hasdrubal Carthaginiensibus suadet) si ulla Hispaniae cura esset, successorem sibi cum valido exercitu mitterent,' L. xxiii. 27. 'Batavi praemisere qui Herennio Gallo mandata cohortium exponerent: si nemo obsisteret, innoxium iter fore; sin arma occurrant, ferro viam inventuros,' Tac. *H.* iv. 20. 'Ad ea Epicydes, si qua ad se mandata haberent, responsum eis ait daturum fuisse: . . . si bello lacessant, ipsa re intellecturos, nequaquam idem esse Syracusas ac Leontinos oppugnare,' L. xxiv. 33.

[1] Examples of modo, dum, &c., in Conditional Sense. (§ 224.)

'Manent ingenia senibus, modo permaneat studium et industria,' C. *Cat. M.* 7. 'Mediocritas in puniendo placet Peripateticis; et recte placet, modo ne laudarent iracundiam,' C. *Off.* i. 25. 'Modo ut haec nobis loca tenere liceat, bellissime mecum esse poteritis,' C. *Fam.* xiv. 2. 'Oderint, dum metuant,' Suet. *Calig.* 30. 'Sin autem ieiunitatem et siccitatem et inopiam, dummodo sit polita, dum urbana, dum elegans, in Attico genere ponit, hoc recte dumtaxat,' C. *Br.* 82. 'Mea nihil refert, dum potiar modo,' Ter. *An.* v. 1. 31. 'Ego si cui adhuc segnior esse videor, dum ne tibi videar, non laboro,' C. *Att.* viii. 11. 'Aliqui omnia recta et honesta neglegunt, dummodo potentiam consequantur,' C. *Off.* iii. 21. 'Sit summa in iure dicundo severitas, dummodo ea ne varietur gratia, sed conservetur aequabilis,' C. *Qu. Fr.* i. 1. 7.

(Dum non *used conditionally by Seneca.*) 'Omnia licet foris resonent, dum intus nihil tumultus sit, dum inter se non rixentur cupiditas et timor, dum avaritia luxuriaque non dissideant, nec altera alteram vexet; nam quid prodest totius regionis silentium, si affectus fremunt?' *Ep.* 56.

(Tantum *used by Virgil conditionally, like* modo.) 'Veniam quocumque vocaris, audiat haec tantum vel qui venit, ecce, Palaemon,' *B.* iii. 49. See do. 53, and *B.* ii. 28.

(3) The Verbal forms quamvis, quamlibet, quantumvis (*how you will = howsoever, although*), licet (*it may be that = although*), for which licebit is sometimes used.   See Hor. *Epod.* xv. 19.

(4) Ut in Concessive Sense (= concesso ut, *granting that*, i.e. *although*); with ne (= concesso ut ne, *granting that . . . not*). Also cum (*whereas*).

II. Mood in Concessive Clauses.

(1) Concessive Sentences which have etsi, etiamsi, tametsi, or si, in the Protasis, are subject to the same rules of Mood as Conditional Sentences, of which they are merely special instances.

(2) A Concessive Clause with quamquam, utut, will be Indicative ; but if Suboblique or Gnomic, Subjunctive.

By writers of the Silver Age, as Tacitus and Suetonius, quamquam is freely used with Subjunctive.

(3) A Concessive Clause with licet and Subjunctive is a special instance of Petitio Obliqua, in which ut is omitted.

Quamvis is used with Indicative once by Cicero ; sometimes by Nepos, Livy, and the poets : usually taking Subjunctive.

(4) Ut, ne, Concessively used, are also special instances of Petitio Obliqua, in which the Verb is suppressed.

Cum Concessive is found with both Moods.   On its use with Indic. see M. *Lucr.* i. 566

III. Idioms of Concessive Conjunctions.

1) Etsi, quamvis, rarely quamquam, are used adverbially to qualify words without affecting mood.   Licet, quamlibet are so used in poetry only.

'Si mihi obtemperatum esset, etsi non optimam, at aliquam rempublicam haberemus,' C. *Off.* i. 11.   'Haec mira quamquam fidem ex eo trahebant quod,' &c., Tac. *Ann.* vi. 30.   'Res bello gesserat, quamvis reipublicae calamitosas, attamen magnas,' C. *Phil.* ii. 45.   'Huic, licet ingratae, Tityrus ipse canam,' Prop. iii. 30. 74.   'Adiuvat infirmas quamlibet ira manus,' Ov.

2) Quamvis, quam vultis, quam volet, &c., are so used in the sense of quantumvis, *ever so* (*much*).

'Quasi vero mihi difficile sit quamvis multos (*ever so many*) nominatim proferre,' C. *p. Rosc.* 16.   'Exspectate facinus quam vultis improbum (*as dishonest as you please*), vincam tamen expectationem omnium,' C. *Verr.* v. 5.   'Quam volet iocetur,' *let him jest as he will*, C. *N. D.* ii. 17.

3) Quamvis licet, quantumvis licet with Subjunctive.

'Quamvis licet insectemur Stoicos ; metuo ne soli philosophi sint,' *we may rail at the Stoics as much as we please: I am afraid they are our only true philosophers*, C. *T. D.* iv. 24. 'Quamvis licet menti delubra et virtuti et fidei consecremus, tamen haec in nobis ipsis sita videmus,' *we may dedicate temples as much as we will to Intellect and Virtue and Faith; yet these are things we perceive to be resident in ourselves*, C. *N. D.* iii. 36. 'Non possis tu, quantumvis licet excellas, omnis tuos ad amplissimos honores perducere,' C. *Lael.* 20.

4) The Protasis with etsi or quamquam is sometimes added to modify or correct the Apodosis, and may be rendered '*and yet.*'

'Do, do poenas temeritatis meae: etsi quae fuit illa temeritas?' *I pay the penalty of my rashness: and yet what was that rashness?* C. *Att.* ix. 10. 'Puto mea non nihil interesse, quamquam id ipsum quid intersit non sane intellego,' *I think I have some interest in the matter; and yet I don't quite perceive what that interest is,* C. *Fam.* v. 21.

5) The Protasis of a Concessive Sentence may, without a Conjunction, be contained

a) In the Pure Conjunctive:

'Naturam expellas furca, tamen usque recurret,' Hor. *Epist.* i. 10. 24.

b) In the Indicative, especially with quidem:

'Matura res erat, consules tergiversabantur tamen,' L. ii. 45. 'Maxima est illa quidem consolatio, sed tamen necessaria,' C. *Fam.* vi. 2.

c) In an Adjectival or Participial Enthesis:

'Homo natura lenissimus stomachari tamen coepit,' C. *Ac.* ii. 4. 'A nigro album etiam nullo monente oculus distinguit,' Sen. *Ep.* 94.

(On the Concessive use of si see p. 474.)

Examples of Concessive Sentences. (§ 225.)

(*Etsi, etiamsi, tametsi.*) 'Viri boni faciunt quod rectum, quod honestum est, etsi nullum consecuturum emolumentum vident,' C. *Fin.* ii. 14. 'Cum tuis dare possem litteras, non praetermisi, etsi, quod scriberem, non habebam,' C. *Att.* xi. 19. 'Sunt qui, quod *sentiunt,* etsi optimum sit, tamen invidiae metu non audeant dicere,' C. *Off.* i. 25. 'Homo quod crebro videt non miratur, etiamsi cur fiat nescit,' C. *Div.* ii. 22. 'Cur nolint, etiamsi tacent, satis dicunt,' C. *in Caec.* 6. 'Rectum est in contentionibus, etiamsi nobis indigna audiamus, tamen gravitatem retinere, iracundiam repellere' (Gnomic), C. *Off.* i. 38. 'Equidem, etiamsi oppetenda mors esset, domi atque in patria mallem quam in externis atque alienis locis,' C. *Fam.* iv. 7. 'Mihi quidem, tametsi haudquaquam par gloria sequatur scriptorem et actorem rerum, tamen inprimis arduum videtur res gestas scribere' (Virt. Or. Obl. but some edd. have sequitur), Sall. *Cat.* 3.

(*Quamquam, utut.*) 'Quamquam sunt omnes virtutes aequales et pares; sed tamen est species alia magis alia formosa et illustris,' C. *d. Or.* iii. 14. 'Utut erga me meritus't, mihi cordi est tamen,' Plaut. *Cist.* i. 1. 111. 'Ut tu me carum esse dixisti senatui, sic ego te, quamquam sis omni civitate taeterrimus, tamen dico esse odio civitati,' C. *p. Vat.* 3. 'Vi quidem regere patriam, quamquam et possis et delicta corrigas, tamen est importunum,' Sall. *Iug.* 3.

(*Quamvis, licet.*) *a.* 'Quod turpe est, id, quamvis occultetur, tamen honestum fieri nullo modo potest,' C. *Off.* iii. 19. 'Licet ipsa vitium sit ambitio, frequenter tamen causa virtutum est,' Qu. i. 2. 22. 'Assentatio quamvis perniciosa sit, nocere tamen nemini potest, nisi ei qui eam recipit atque ea delectatur,' C. *Lael.* 26. 'Licet irrideat, si quis vult; plus apud me tamen ratio valebit, quam vulgi opinio,' C. *Par.* 1. 'Illa, quamvis ridicula essent, sicut erant, mihi tamen risum non moverunt,' C. *Fam.* vii. 32. 'Pompeius multa alia vidit, sed illud maxime, quamvis atrociter ipse tulisset, vos tamen fortiter iudicaturos,' C. *p. Mil.* 8. 'Licet tibi significarim, ut ad me venires, tamen intellego, te hic ne verbo quidem levare me posse,' C. *Att.* iii. 12.

b. 'Hoc ille natus, quamvis patrem suum numquam viderat, tamen et natura ipsa duce, quae plurimum valet, et assiduis domesticorum sermonibus in paternae vitae

I I

6) The Protasis is sometimes a Relative Clause, which may be Subjunctive or Indicative.

'Egomet, qui sero Graecas litteras attigissem, tamen, cum Athenas venissem, compluris ibi dies sum commoratus,' C. *d. Or.* i. 18. 'Oculorum, inquit Plato, est in nobis sensus acerrimus; quibus sapientiam non cernimus,' C. *Fin.* ii. 16.

227
Comparative Sentences.

viii. Comparative Sentences.

I. These, which, as special instances of conceived Condition, contain in the Protasis[1] the meaning *as if*, require the Verb of the Protasis to be Subjunctive.

They are introduced by the Comparative Conjunctions quam, ut, ac (see CORRELATION) going before (or supposing) si, and are usually preceded by one of the Demonstratives tam, ita, sic; vel; perinde, proinde, aeque, similiter, &c.: is, idem, itidem. Hence are obtained Conjunctional forms quasi (for quam si); quasi si (rare); tamquam si; tamquam (understanding si); velut si; velut (understanding si); also

perinde		ita	
proinde	ac si	perinde	quasi
aeque		proinde	
similiter		sic	ut si
is, idem, itidem		ita	

non aliter quam si, and similar forms: sometimes proinde ac, &c., without si; ac si, ut si, without Demonstrative.

similitudinem deductus est,' C. *p. Rab. Post.* 2. 'Miltiades inter suos potestate erat regia, quamvis carebat nomine,' N. *Milt.* 2. 'Quamvis cecidere trecenti, non omnis Fabios abstulit una dies,' Ov. *Ep. Pont.* i. 2.

(*Ut, ne, cum.*) 'Ut desint vires, tamen est laudanda voluntas,' Ov. *Ep. Pont.* iii. 4. 79. 'Ut rationem Plato nullam afferret, ipsa auctoritate me frangeret,' C. *T. D.* i. 21. 'Ne sit sane summum malum dolor: malum certe est,' C. *T. D.* ii. 5. 'Ne aequaveritis Hannibali Philippum, Pyrrho certe aequabitis,' L. xxi. 7. 'Cum omnibus virtutibus me affectum esse cupiam, tamen nihil est, quod malim, quam me et gratum esse et videri,' C. *p. Planc.* 33. 'Hoc ipso tempore, cum omnia gumnasia philosophi teneant, tamen eorum auditores discum audire quam philosophum malunt,' C. *d. Or.* ii. 5.

Examples of Comparative Sentences. (§ 227.)

'Stultissimum est, in luctu capillum sibi evellere, quasi calvitio maeror levetur,' C. *T. D.* iii. 26. 'Nisi forte idcirco numen esse non putant, quia non apparet, nec cernitur: proinde quasi (*just as if*) nostram ipsam mentem videre possimus,' C. *p. Mil.* 31. 'Quasi sua res aut honor agatur, ita diligenter Naevii cupiditati morem gerunt,' C. *p. Quinc.* 2. 'Educavit magna industria, quasi si esset ex se nata,' Plaut. *Cas. Prol.* 45. 'Sic Plancius quaestor est factus quam si esset summo loco natus,' C. *p. Planc.* 25. 'Sic cogitandum est, tamquam aliquis in pectus intimum inspicere possit,' Sen. *Ep.* 83. 'Antonius Plancum sic contemnit, tamquam si illi aqua et igni interdictum sit,' C. *Phil.* vi. 4. 'Tu, qui id quaeris, similiter facis ac si me roges, cur te duobus contuear oculis, quum idem uno assequi possim,' C. *N. D.* iii. 5. 'Quae perdifficilia sunt, perinde habenda saepe sunt ac si effici non possint,' C. *Part.* 24. 'Me iuvat, velut ipse in parte laboris ac periculi fuerim, ad finem belli Punici pervenisse,' L. xxxi. 1. 'Sequani absentis Ariovisti crudelitatem, velut si coram adesset, horrebant,' Caes. *B. G.* i. 32. 'Scipiades belli fulmen, Carthaginis

---

[1] The true Apodosis is a suppressed Conjunctive Verb. Thus, in the sentence Tam amo te quam si frater esses, the true Apodosis to si esses is amarem understood: *I love you as* (I should love you) *if you were my brother.*

II. Comparative Idioms.

1) Ceu is used for ceu si (*as if*) in poetry, and in the prose of the Silver Age. 'Natura dedit cornua convoluta arietum generi, ceu caestus daret,' Pl. *N. H.* xi. 37. Ceu si is used by Lucretius: 'Ceu lapidem si percutiat lapis,' vi. 160.

2) Quasi vero, quasi autem, like nisi vero, are used ironically (*as if forsooth*): 'Quasi vero id cupiditate defendendae nobilitatis fecerit,' C. *Fam.* iii. 7. 'Immo vero quasi tu dicas quasique ego autem id suspicer,' Plaut. *Pseud.* ii. 2. 40.

3) Quasi, tamquam, velut, ceu (like ut, sicut, si, nisi, etsi, quamvis, quamquam), may be used as mere annexive or adverbial Particles, not affecting Mood.

'Litteras Graecas avide arripui quasi diuturnam sitim explere cupiens,' C. *Cat. M.* 8. 'Servis respublica et quasi (*as it were*) civitas domus est,' Pl. *Ep.* viii. 16. 'Ex vita ita discedo tamquam (*as though*) ex hospitio, non tamquam ex domo,' C. *Cat. M.* 23.

Sometimes quasi is used for fere or circiter (*almost, about*): 'Quasi ad duo milia,' *about* 2,000, L. xxvii. 12.

SECTION V.

SUPPLEMENT TO COMPOUND CONSTRUCTION.

I. Consecution of Tenses.

229
Consecution of Tenses.

The Law that Primary Tenses are followed by Primary, Historic by Historic (see § 98), is illustrated by all the Examples in this Chapter, especially by those of Petitio and Interr. Obliqua, Consecutive and Final Clauses. On the use of the Tense S_2 (-erim), see § 204.

1) The two following passages shew that a Present Past admits either Consecution:

'Non ita generati a natura sumus ut ad ludum et iocum facti esse videamur,' C. *Off.* i. 29. 'Homines sunt hac lege generati, qui tuerentur illum globum . . . quae terra dicitur,' C. *Rep.* vi. 15.

It is, however, the prevailing idiom of Cicero, to construct the Present Past with Historic consecution:

'Adduxi hominem in quo satisfacere exteris nationibus possetis,' *I have brought a man before you, in dealing with whom you may do your duty to foreign nations,* Verr. i. 2. 'Quemadmodum officia ducerentur ab honestate satis explicatum arbitror,' *I consider that I have explained enough how duties are derived from moral principle,* Off. ii. 1.

---

horror, ossa dedit terrae, proinde ac famul infimus esset,' Lucr. iii. 1048. 'Eius negotium sic velim cures ut si esset res mea,' C. *Fam.* ii. 14. 'Egnati absentis rem ut tueare aeque a te peto ac si mea negotia essent,' C. *Fam.* xiii. 43. 'Qua de re quoniam nihil ad me scribis, perinde habebo ac si scripsisses nihil esse,' C. *Att.* iii. 13.

2) The Historic Present generally takes Historic Consecution: but sometimes Primary:

'Sulla suos h o r t a t u r uti fortem animum gererent,' Sall. *Iug.* 107. 'Pompeius, ne duobus c i r c u m c l u d e r e t u r exercitibus, ex eo loco d i s c e d i t,' Caes. *B. C.* iii. 30. 'Caesar c o h o r t a t u r milites ne labori s u c c u m b a n t,' Caes. *B. G.* vii. 86.

Transitions occur from the Historic to the Primary Consecution and conversely:

'M o n e b a n t etiam ne orientem morem pellendi reges inultum s i n e r e t : satis libertatem ipsam habere dulcedinis: nisi quanta vi civitates eam e x p e t a n t, tanta regna reges d e f e n d a n t, aequari summa infimis: nihil excelsum, nihil quod supra ceteros e m i n e a t in civitatibus fore,' *they warned him also not to leave unpunished the nascent custom of expelling kings: freedom* (they said) *was sweet enough in itself: if kings were not to defend their thrones as vigorously as states seek freedom, the highest were levelled with the lowest; there would be in communities nothing lofty, nothing to rise above the mass,* L. ii. 9. 'Novum in republica introductum exemplum q u e r i t u r, ut tribunicia intercessio armis n o t a r e t u r atque o p p r i m e r e t u r, quae superioribus annis armis e s s e t resti-tuta: Sullam, nudata omnibus rebus tribunicia potestate, tamen intercessionem liberam reliquisse: Pompeium, qui amissa resti-tuere v i d e a t u r, a d e m i s s e,' *he complains that a novel precedent has been introduced in the commonwealth, of censuring and putting down by arms the intercession of the tribunes, which in the pre-ceding years had been restored by arms: Sulla* (he said) *though he stripped the tribunician power of everything else, had yet left the veto free: while Pompeius, who seemed to be restoring what was lost, had taken it away,* Caes. *B. C.* i. 7.

3) When two Future actions are brought into connexion there are three possible varieties:

a) When both actions commence and continue together, both Verbs will be in the Simple Future: 'Profecto beati e r i m u s, cum corporibus relictis cupiditatum e r i m u s expertes,' C. *T. D.* The English idiom differs: 'We shall be happy, when we *are* free from desires.' So when we say, 'I will come if (when) I can,' the Latin construction is, Veniam si (cum) potero.

b) When one action will commence after the other is com-plete, one Verb will be in the Simple Future, the other in the Future Perf.: 'De Carthagine vereri non ante desi-n a m quam illam excisam esse c o g n o v e r o,' C. *Cat. M.* 6. Cum ego v e n i a m, tu d i s c e s s e r i s.

c) When both actions will be complete together, both Verbs are in the Future Perf.: 'Qui Antonium o p p r e s s e r i t, is hoc bellum taeterrimum c o n f e c e r i t, *whoever shall have crushed Antonius, will have concluded this most horrid war,* C. *Fam.* x. 19.

But if an action going on is the condition of a Future action, the Protasis may be Present:

'P e r f i c i e t u r bellum, si u r g e m u s obsessos,' *the war will be finished if we press the besieged,* L. v. 4.

4) As the Simple Future has no Subjunctive of its own, the Future Active form used in *immediate* consecution of Primary Tenses is -urus sim : that used in *immediate* consecution of Historic Tenses is -urus essem :

'Non debes dubitare quin aliqua republica sis futurus qui esse debes,' *you ought not to doubt that, while there is any republic, you will be what you ought to be,* C. *Fam.* vi. 1. 'Antea dubitabam venturaene essent legiones; nunc mihi non est dubium quin venturae non sint,' *I was in doubt before whether the legions would come; now I have no doubt they will not,* C. *Fam.* ii. 17.

But, in *secondary* subordination (futurity being expressed in the first), S_1 or (in Historic Consecution) S_3 will represent the Future Simple: S_2 or (in Historic Consecution) S_4 will represent the Future Perfect:

Examples:

(1) Qui hoc dicet errabit, subordinated, becomes :
Non dubito quin, qui hoc dicat, erraturus sit.
Credo eum, qui hoc dicat, erraturum esse.
Non dubitabam quin, qui hoc diceret, erraturus esset.
Credebam eum, qui hoc diceret, erraturum esse.

(2) Si ita fecero, me culpabis, becomes :
Non dubito quin, si ita fecerim, me culpaturus sis.
Non dubitabam quin, si ita fecissem, me culpaturus esses.

(3) Id faciemus, cum Lemnum veneris, becomes :
Respondent id se facturos, cum Lemnum venerit :
Respondebant id se facturos, cum Lemnum venisset.

5) If a Conditional Sentence in Sumptio Ficti, with Apodosis S_3, is subordinated by ut, ne, quin, &c., it may remain :

'Honestum tale est ut, vel si ignorarent id homines, vel si obmutuissent, sua tamen pulchritudine esset specieque laudabile,' *morality is such that, even if men were unacquainted with it or had been silent, it would still deserve praise for its own native loveliness,* C. *Fin.* ii. 15. 'Id ille si repudiasset, dubitatis quin ei vis esset illata?' *had he rejected it, have you any doubt that violence would have been offered to him?* C. *p. Sest.* 29.

6) When S_4, in the Apodosis of a Conditional Sentence, is subordinated so as to form a Consecutive Clause or Oblique Interrogation, the Perfect Subjunctive of the Conjugation in -urus takes its place :

'Hannibal, nisi fugae speciem timuisset, Galliam repetivisset,' becomes, 'Adeo inopia coactus est Hannibal, ut, nisi fugae speciem timuisset, Galliam repetiturus fuerit,' *Hannibal was so pressed by scarcity, that, if he had not dreaded the semblance of flight, he would have returned to Gaul,* L. xxii. 32. So, 'Dic agedum quidnam facturus fueris si eo tempore censor fuisses,' *just tell us what you would have done, had you been censor at that time,* L. ix. 33. 'Nec dubium erat quin, si tam pauci simul obire omnia possent, terga daturi hostes fuerint,' *there was no doubt that if so small a number could have done everything at once, the enemy would have taken flight,* L. iv. 38.

7) 'Might have' is expressed in a Consecutive Clause by potuerim: 'Captivi tantum timorem fecerunt, ut, si admotus extemplo exercitus foret, capi castra potuerint' (*the camp might have been taken*), L. xliii. 4.

'Ought or must have' is expressed by the Gerundive Perf. Subjunctive: 'Adeo aequa postulastis ut ultro vobis deferenda fuerint,' *you have made such fair demands that they ought to have been spontaneously offered you*, L. iii. 53. 'In eos versa peditum acies haud dubium fecit quin, nisi firmata extrema agminis fuissent, ingens in eo saltu accipienda clades fuerit' (*great loss must have been suffered*), L. xxi. 34.

These Constructions arise out of the idiom by which potuerunt is used for potuissent, and deferendum fuit for deferendum fuisset. See p. 336.

8) When an Infinitive (Present or Future), a Participle, Gerund, or Supine, intervenes, consecution is still dependent on the principal Verb:

Credo me intellegere . . {quid agas, egeris, acturus sis; quid agatur, actum sit, agendum sit.

Credebam me intellegere {quid ageres, egisses, acturus esses; quid ageretur, actum esset, agendum esset.

'Cato mirari se aiebat, quod non rideret haruspex, haruspicem cum vidisset,' C. *Div.* ii. 24. 'Cupido incessit animos iuvenum sciscitandi ad quem eorum regnum Romanum esset venturum,' L. i. 56.

But, if an Infinitive Perfect intervenes, the consecution is Primary or Historic according as the Infinitive is Present Past or Simple Past: 'Ita comparatam esse hominum naturam omnium, aliena ut melius videant et diiudicent quam sua,' *strange that the characters of men are so constituted that they see and decide the affairs of others better than their own*, Ter. *Haut.* iii. 1. 98. 'Liberatur Milo non eo consilio profectus esse, ut insidiaretur in via Clodio,' *Milo is acquitted of having gone with the design of lying in ambush on the high road for Clodius*, C. *p. Mil.* 18.

But to this Infinitive we must apply what was said above, 1):

'Satis videor docuisse, hominis natura quanto omnes anteiret animantis,' *I think I have sufficiently shewn how much the nature of man surpasses all animals*, C. *N. D.* ii. 51.

The same Rule applies to the Periphrastic Perfect Infin.:

'Quis est qui hoc non sentiat, quidvis prius futurum fuisse quam ut hi fratres diversas sententias fortunasque sequerentur?' *who can help feeling that anything would sooner have happened, than that these brothers should follow diverging sentiments and fortunes?* C.

9) As the Infinitive has no Conditional force of its own, it acquires this by means of the Future Participle.

'I knew that he would come if he could,' Sciebam eum venturum esse, si posset; 'I know that he would have come if he could,' Scio eum venturum fuisse si potuisset.

II. Narratio Obliqua.

When an author relates the speeches or writings of others not, as the speakers or writers delivered them, in the First Person, but in a series of Oblique constructions, dependent on his own statement that they so spoke or wrote, such use of Oblique Oration is called Narratio ·Obliqua.

Caesar almost always reports speeches obliquely, Sallust directly; Livy and Tacitus in both ways, often gliding from the indirect into the direct form. Enunciations are interspersed with Petitions and Interrogations ; and in general, when transition takes place from one form of Oratio Obliqua to another, a new Verb is not introduced, the original Verb (by Zeugma) supplying its meaning.

1) The Clauses are sometimes carried on in the Infin. Clause:

(1) After a Relative : ' Nam illorum urbem ut propugnaculum oppositam esse barbaris, apud quam (= nam apud eam) iam bis classis regias fecisse naufragium,' Nep. *Th.* 7.

(2) After various Conjunctions (quia, quamquam, cum, nisi forte, &c.): 'Ideo se moenibus inclusos tenere Campanos, quia si qui evasissent aliqua, velut feras bestias per agros vagari, et laniare et trucidare quodcumque obviam detur,' *they kept the Campanians shut up within their walls on this account, that, if any of them got out anywhere, they wandered over the country like wild beasts,*

Examples of Narratio Obliqua.   (§ 230.)

'Orat Tarquinius Veientis, ne se extorrem egentem ex tanto modo regno cum liberis adolescentibus ante oculos suos perire sinerent: alios peregre in regnum Romam accitos; se regem, augentem bello Romanum imperium, a proximis scelerata conjuratione pulsum: . . . patriam se regnumque suum repetere, et persequi ingratos civis velle: ferrent opem, adiuvarent; suas quoque veteris iniurias ultum irent, toties caesas legiones, agrum ademptum,' *Tarquinius entreats the people of Veii not to allow him with his grown-up children to die before their eyes, expelled in destitute condition from a royal station lately so eminent: (he says) that others had been invited to Rome from abroad to reign: that he, when king, and aggrandising the Roman empire in war, had been driven out by a wicked conspiracy of his nearest kin: that he wished to reclaim his country and kingdom, and to take vengeance on his ungrateful countrymen: (he entreats them) to lend their aid, to assist him: to set about avenging their own ancient wrongs, the frequent slaughter of their legions, the curtailment of their territory,* L. ii. 6.

'Docebat Caesar, quam veteres quamque iustae causae necessitudinis ipsis cum Aeduis intercederent; quae senatus consulta, quotiens, quamque honorifica in eos facta essent; ut omni tempore totius Galliae principatum Aedui tenuissent, prius etiam quam nostram amicitiam appetissent; populi Romani hanc esse consuetudinem, ut socios atque amicos non modo sui nihil deperdere, sed gratia, dignitate, honore auctiores velit esse: quod vero ad amicitiam populi Romani attulissent, id iis eripi quis pati posset?'· *Caesar shewed, what ancient and just grounds of friendship existed between themselves* (the Romans) *and the Aedui; what decrees of the senate had been made in their favour, how often, and in what honourable terms ; how the Aedui from time immemorial had held the first rank in Gaul, even before they had courted our friendship : (adding) that the custom of the Roman people was to resolve that its allies and friends should not only lose nothing of their own, but even be increased in influence, dignity, and honour: but (as to) what they had possessed at the time of contracting friendship with the Roman people, who could endure that this should be wrested from them?* Caes. *B. G.* i. 43.

and tore and slaughtered whatever came in their way, L. xxvi. 27.　　See ii. 13, xxxiii. 45.

2) Rhetorical questions belong to the primary clauses of Oratio Obliqua, and take the Infinitive:

'Plebs fremit: Quid se vivere, quid in parte civium censeri, si, quod duorum hominum virtute partum sit, id obtinere universi non possint?' *the plebeians murmured: Why were they living, why reckoned one portion of the citizens, if, what the valour of two persons had won, their entire body were unable to maintain?* L. vii. 18.

But Caesar generally throws such questions into the Conjunctive.

3) Questions, to which an answer is expected, are regularly put in the Conjunctive:

'Docet Caesar, latum ab decem tribunis, ut sui ratio absentis haberetur, ipso consule Pompeio; qui si improbasset, cur ferri passus esset? sin probasset, cur se uti populi beneficio prohibuisset?' *Caesar informed them, that the ten tribunes had brought in a bill, allowing him to rank as a candidate, though absent, in the very consulship of Pompeius; if Pompeius disapproved, why had he allowed the bill to be brought in? if he approved, why had he prevented him from taking advantage of the people's boon?* Caes. B. C. i. 32.

4) *a.* A Potential Sentence may become Oblique by means of the Verb possum; an Optative Sentence by means of volo.

Examples of the Conversion of Oratio Recta into Oratio Obliqua.

A. ENUNTIATIO		
1. Recta.	2. Obliqua post Praesens.	3. Obliqua post Praeteritum.
	Ait	Dixit
1. Eo.　2. Ibo.　3. Ivi.	se ire : iturum esse: isse.	se ire : iturum esse: isse.
4. Eo quia (cum, quo, si) iubes.	se (quia, &c.)ille iubeat, ire.	se(quia, &c.)ille iuberet, ire.
5. Ibo cum (quo, si) iusseris.	se (cum, &c.) ille iusserit, iturum.	se (cum, &c.) ille iussisset, iturum.
6. Ivi quo (cum, quia) iussisti.	se (quo, &c.) ille iusserit, isse.	se (quo, &c.) ille iussisset, isse.
7. Faciam quod voles.	se, quod ille velit, facturum.	se, quod ille vellet, facturum.
8. Feci quod voluisti.	se, quod ille voluerit, fecisse.	se,quod ille voluisset,fecisse.
9. Gratum est mihi quod quievisti.	gratum esse sibi quod ille quieverit.	gratum esse sibi quod ille quievisset.
10. Dum moraris, urbs capta est.	urbem, dum ille moratur, esse captam.	urbem, dum ille moratur, captam fuisse.
11. Non recuso quominus (quin) eas.	se, quominus (quin) ille eat, non recusare.	se, quominus (quin) ille iret, non recusare.
12. Edo ut vivam.	se, ut vivat, edere.	se, ut viveret, edere.
13. Expedit civitati ut redeam.	expedire civitati ut ipse redeat.	expedire civitati ut ipse rediret.
14. Quaeras quid agam.	quaerere illum posse quid ipse agat.	quaerere illum posse quid ipse ageret.
15. Moriar ni gaudeo.	velle se mori ni gaudeat.	velle se mori ni gauderet.
16. Si quid mihi, Caesar, a te opus esset, ipse ad te venirem(venissem): si quid tu me vis, ad me veni.	si quid ipsi a Caesare opus sit, sese ad eum venturum esse : si quid ille se velit, illum ad se venire oportere.	si quid ipsi a Caesare opus esset, sese ad eum venturum fuisse : si quid ille se vellet, illum ad se venire oportere.

231
Se,
suus.

b. An Imperative Sentence may become Petitio Obliqua; or it may be expressed by debeo, oportet, &c., or Gerundive Construction.

III. The Reflexive Pronouns in Clauses.

i. Se (Personal), suus (Possessive), are Reflexive Pronouns of the Third Person; implying reference to a Subject in that Person; which, in general, is the Subject of the Sentence. To supply their defect, and for distinction or emphasis, ipse is used.

Se, suus, are therefore Pronouns of Subjective Reference always; ipse, so far as it is used for them, or with them.

The Demonstratives is, ille, iste, hic, &c., are Pronouns of Objective Reference. See § 65.

The use of these Pronouns in Clauses is a difficult subject, respecting which certain general directions may be given.

A) First: Pronominal reference must be interpreted according to the logic of the passage.

This logical interpretation (the Reason of the thing) must be applied especially when in the same Clause, or in succeeding Clauses, Subjective reference is made by the Reflexive Pronouns to different Subjects.

Thus Caes. *B. G.* vii. 4, Veneti legationem ad P. Crassum mittunt: si velit suos recipere, obsides sibi remittat. Here 'the Reason of the thing' shews that suos must be

---

Examples of the Conversion of Oratio Recta into Oratio Obliqua.—*cont.*

B. PETITIO.		
1. Recta.	2. Obliqua post Praesens.	3. Obliqua post Praeteritum.
	Imperat (orat, hortatur)	Imperabat (orabat, hortabatur)
1. Abi quo vis.	abeat quo velit.	abiret quo vellet.
2. I quo condixi.	eat ille quo ipse condixerit.	iret ille quo ipse condixisset.
3. Utere vita dum potes.	vita, dum possit, utatur.	vita, dum posset, uteretur.
4. Ite, create consules ex plebe; transferte auspicia quo nefas est.	eant, creent consules ex plebe; transferant auspicia quo nefas sit.	irent, crearent consules ex plebe: transferrent auspicia quo nefas esset.

C. INTERROGATIO.		
1. Recta.	2. Obliqua post Praesens.	3. Obliqua post Praeteritum.
	Quaerit	Quaerebat
1. Quid tibi vis?	quid sibi velit ille? (velle illum?)	quid sibi vellet ille? velle illum?
2. Num bellum proderit?	num bellum profuturum sit (esse)?	num bellum profuturum esset (esse)?
3. Cur facitis quod vetitum est?	cur, quod vetitum sit, faciant?	cur, quod vetitum esset, facerent?
4. Cur fecistis quod vetitum est?	cur, quod vetitum sit, fecerint?	cur, quod vetitum esset, fecissent?
5. Quid deinde restat, si neque ex equis pepulimus hostem; neque pedites quicquam momenti facimus? Quam tertiam expectamus pugnam?	quid deinde restet, si neque ex equis pepulerint hostem, neque pedites quicquam momenti faciant? quam tertiam expectent pugnam?	quid deinde restaret, si neque ex equis pepulissent hostem, neque pedites quicquam momenti facerent? quam tertiam expectarent pugnam?

referred to Crassus (Subject of velit), sibi to Veneti (the Principal Subject).

B) Secondly: in some Clauses there is an intimate connexion between the use of the Reflexive Pronouns and that of the Subjunctive Mood; both being determined by the same law of Subjective relation.

Thus, if the following Clauses be compared:

(1) Marcus salvus rediit, quod ei peperceram:

(2) Marcus gratias mihi egit quod sibi pepercissem:

In (1), the Quod-clause is alleged by the speaker as the cause of an act on the part of Marcus *objectively* regarded (salvus rediit), for which reason the Demonstrative ei and Indicative peperceram are used:

In (2), the Quod-clause is cited as the cause *subjectively* felt and avowed by Marcus for an act of his own (gratias egit); therefore the Reflexive sibi and the Subjunctive pepercissem are used.

C) Thirdly: it often happens (principally in Adverbial and Adjectival Clauses, or in Participial Entheses, which stand for them) that a Subjective Pronoun is used when the writer wishes to refer the Clause to the mind of the Subject: though, if the Clause were only part of his own statement, he might have used an Objective Pronoun.

'Africanus, qui suo cognomine declarat, tertiam partem orbis terrarum se subegisse, tamen, si sua res ageretur, testimonium non diceret,' C. *p. S. Rosc.* 36. Here Cicero might have written eius for sua, if he had not wished to continue the Subjective construction, and to place the condition in the mind of Africanus (si mea . . . non dicerem).

232　ii. The use of Reflexive Pronouns in the various Clauses will now be noticed.

A) 1. In a Substantival Clause standing as Object, while the Principal Subject is in the 3rd Person, Pronominal reference to that Subject will be Subjective, unless the Clause has a Subject of its own, requiring Subjective reference to itself.

Marcus
- ait sibi et suis commodis serviendum esse (serviri).
- putat nos sibi et suis commodis obesse.
- queritur quod vos sibi et suis commodis obsistatis.
- vult ut se et sua commoda tueamur.
- orabat se et suos liberos defenderem.
- timet ne ipse et liberi sui neglegantur.
- non dubitat quin ipse et sua commoda spernantur.
- multa obstare putat quominus sibi suisque consulatur.
- videt quanta sibi suisque mala impendeant.

Such examples are frequent, and free from difficulty. As the Clauses have either no new Subject, or a new Subject

not of the Third Person, or a new Subject not admitting
Subjective Pronominal reference, there is nothing to disturb the reference of the Reflexive Pronouns to the Principal Subject Marcus.

2. But, when a Substantival Clause receives a new Subject
capable of Subjective Pronominal reference, many difficulties arise, the solution of which is generally derived from
'the Reason of the thing,' sometimes from the character of
the principal Verb, sometimes from that of the dependent
Verb.

a. The general Rule in such case is, that the Reflexive Pronouns are referred to the Subject, if capable, of the Clause
in which they stand; but if that Subject is not capable,
then to the Principal (or Prior) Subject.
The capability of the Clausular Subject is tested by seeing if
the Clause, converted into Oratio Recta, gives a good sense.
'Caesar reperit Dumnorigem his rebus suam rem familiarem auxisse,' *B. G.* i. 18. Here the converted Clause
would be: 'Dumnorix his rebus suam rem familiarem
auxit,' which gives a good sense, and so determines the
reference of suam to Dumnorigem; and this 'the Reason.
of the thing' demands.

Obs. Sometimes the reference to the Clausular Subject is
determined by quisque joined to the Reflexive: 'Natura
quidquid genuit in suo quodque genere perfectum esse
voluit,' C. *T. D.* v. 13.
Sometimes by other Indefinite Pronouns: 'Nec quemquam
nisi sua voce, utcumque quis posset, ac sine patrono
rationem vitae passus est reddere,' Suet. *Claud.* 16.

b. On the other hand, conversion of the Clause in such examples as the following shews that the Reflexive Pronouns cannot reasonably be referred to the Subject of the
Clause, but must go back to the Principal (or Prior)Subject.
'Datames audit Pisidas quasdam copias adversus se
parare,' Nep. *Dat.* 18. 'Ariovistus respondit, omnis
Galliae civitates contra se castra habuisse,' Caes. *B. G.*
i. 44. 'Caesar . . . docebat, illum (Ariovistum) . . .
beneficio ac liberalitate sua ac senatus ea praemia con-
secutum,' Cæs. *B. G.* i. 43. See i. 33.

B) If the Clause is an Oblique Petition, with a Subject of
its own allowing Subjective Pronominal reference, the
meaning of the Principal Verb will cause a difference. If
that Verb is one of *prayer, command,* or *endeavour,* the
Subjective reference in the Clause will be to the Principal
Subject; if it is one of *exhortation, advice,* or *persuasion,*
such reference will be to the Subject of the Clause.

Marcus   {orat (rogat, &c.) Aulum} (ut) sibi consulat (i.e.
         {Aulo imperat   }   Marco),
but
Marcus   {hortatur (admonet) Aulum} (ut) sibi consulat (i.e.
         {Aulo suadet (persuadet) }   Aulo).

This distinction lies in 'the Reason of the thing;' that is, in the assumption that we *pray* or *command* another for our own benefit, that we *exhort* or *advise* him for his own.

(1) Iste petit a rege et eum pluribus verbis rogat ut id ad se mittat,' C. *Verr.* iv. 28. 'Arverni Vercingetorigem obsecrant ut suis fortunis consulat, neu se ab hostibus diripi patiatur, praesertim cum videat omne ad se bellum translatum,' Caes. *B. G.* vii. 8.

(2) Caesar Nervios hortatur ne sui in perpetuum liberandi occasionem dimittant,' Caes. *B. G.* v. 38. 'Rex supplicem non prodidit, monuitque ut consuleret sibi,' Nep. *Th.* 8. 'Helvetii persuadent Rauracis ... uti, eodem usi consilio, oppidis suis vicisque relictis, una cum iis (Helvetiis) proficiscantur,' Caes. *B. G.* i. 5. (Persuadeo is found with Subjective reference in the Clause to the Principal Subject): 'Multa pollicendo persuadet Metellus (legatis) uti Iugurtham maxime vivum, sin id parum procedat, necatum sibi traderent,' Sall. *Iug.* 46.

Obs. A Case dependent on a Passive Verb or on sum is sometimes referred to as a Principal Subject, if it appears such when converted into Active form.

'A Caesare invitor (= Caesar me invitat) sibi ut sim legatus,' *Caesar invites me to be his lieutenant,* C. *Att.* ii. 18. 'Iam inde ab initio Faustulo spes fuerat (=' Faustulus speraverat) regiam stirpem apud se educari,' L. i. 5.

But if it cannot be so converted, the reference will be Objective:

'L. Quinctio Cincinnato in agro aranti nuntiatum est eum dictatorem esse factum,' C. *Cat. M.* 16.

In the following places it might seem that the reference ought to be Subjective:

'A Curione mihi nuntiatum est eum ad me venire,' C. *Att.* x. 4. 'Nuntiatum est nobis a M. Varrone venisse eum Roma pridie vesperi,' C. *Ac.* i. 1.

But the Prep. a means *from,* not *by :* a Curione (M. Varrone) missi nuntiarunt; the true Subjects, therefore, are the messengers.

234 C) Pronominal Reference in Adverbial and Adjectival Clauses :

1. If the Clause is Final, the Pronominal reference to the purposing Subject will usually be Subjective:

'Cuncti ad me saepe venerunt, ut suarum fortunarum omnium causam defensionemque susciperem,' C. *in Caec.* I. ' (Tiridates) mittebat oratores qui suo Parthorumque nomine expostularent, cur depelleretur,' Tac. *Ann.* xiii. 37.

Yet we find:

'Pompeius ... idoneum locum nactus ibi copias collocavit, suosque omnis in castris continuit, ignisque fieri prohibuit, quo occultior esset eius adventus,' Caes. *B. C.* iii. 30. 'Verres Milesios navem poposcit, quae eum praesidii causa Myndum prosequeretur,' C. *Verr.* i. 34.

2. In Ut-clauses of a Consecutive nature Pronominal reference to a Principal Subject will usually be Objective, because (result not purpose being implied) there is so far no subjectivity in the Clause.

'Ligarius in provincia pacatissima ita se gessit ut ei pacem esse expediret,' C. *p. Lig.* 2.   'Habet hoc virtus ut viros fortis species eius et pulchritudo etiam in hoste posita delectet,' C. *in Pis.* 32.

Yet if in a result a purpose is implied, the Subjective Pronoun may be used:

'(Agesilaus) locum delegit talem ut non multum obesse multitudo hostium suae paucitati posset,' N. *Ag.* 7.

In the following, the Reflexive is necessary for reference to the Subject of its Clause:

'Is enim sic se gerit ut sibi iam decemvir designatus esse videatur,' C. *d. L. Agr.* ii. 19.   'Caput est Heraclides ille Temnites, homo ineptus et loquax, sed, ut sibi videtur, ita doctus ut,' &c., C. *p. Flacc.* 18.

In the sentence, 'Tum mittit rex ad istum, Si sibi videatur, ut reddat,' C. *Verr.* iv. 29, the Reflexive seems strange, when we compare: 'Cum ei scriptam orationem orator Lysias attulisset, quam, si ei videretur, edisceret,' C. *d. Or.* i. 54.   'Reliquum a suis Tyndaridis peteret, si ei videretur,' C. *d. Or.* ii. 86.   But the direct message of the king, 'si tibi videtur, redde,' is rendered in oblique form.

Other special causes may make the reference in such Clauses Subjective: 'Ambiorix ad hunc modum locutus est: Sese, &c. . . . suaque esse eiusmodi imperia ut non minus haberet iuris in se multitudo quam ipse in multitudinem,' Caes. *B. G.* v. 27.   The use of se instead of eum is determined by sese preceding and by the antithesis se . . . ipse.

3. Suboblique Quod-clauses often require Subjective Pronominal reference to the Principal Subject:

'Scipionem Hannibal eo ipso quod adversus se dux potissimum lectus esset, praestantem virum credebat,' L. xxi. 39.   'Divitiacus ait, scire se illa esse vera, nec quemquam ex eo plus quam se doloris capere, propterea quod per se crevisset,' Caes. *B. G.* i. 20.

4. Pronominal reference in Conditional Clauses often follows the same rule: 'Domino navis qui sit (Themistocles) aperit, multa pollicens, si se conservasset,' Nep. *Th.* 8.   'Sed ausus est Furfanio dicere, si sibi pecuniam, quantam poposcerat, non dedisset, mortuum se in domum eius illaturum,' C. *p. Mil.* 27.

5. The Subjective reference to the Principal Subject is often kept in a Relative Clause, if 'the Reason of the thing' shews that the Reflexive cannot be referred to the Relative itself: 'Epaminondas ei, qui sibi ex lege praetor successerat, exercitum non tradidit,' C. *Inv.* i. 33.   'Dexio

hic non quae privatim sibi eripuisti, sed unicum abs te
filium flagitat,' C. *Verr.* v. 49. 'Epaminondas . . . eos
coegit superare Lacedaemonios, quos ante se imperatorem
nemo Boeotorum ausus fuit aspicere,' Nep. *Ep.* 8.
Yet in such places the Objective Pronoun would not have
been wrong ; and in the last cited example there seems
little justification for se instead of eum.
When Caesar writes : 'Ambiorix in Aduatucos, qui erant
eius regno finitimi, proficiscitur,' *B. G.* v. 38, he uses the
Objective Pronoun because the Clause is a statement of
his own, not referred to the mind of Ambiorix.

Obs. But, if the Relative Clause is Suboblique, it will often
happen that Subjective reference is made to the Relative itself or
its immediate Antecedent : 'Commemorant . . . errare eos, si quicquam ab his praesidii sperent, qui suis rebus diffidant,' Caes. *B.
G.* v. 41.

235　　iii. When Oratio Obliqua intervenes between the Principal Subject and Pronominal reference to it in a Clause, Latin authors,
having evidently much freedom of choice, often prefer the Objective reference, as less liable to confusion.

'Quod cum interrogatus esset Socrates, respondit, sese meruisse ut amplissimis honoribus et praemiis decoraretur, et ei
victus quotidianus in Prytaneo publice praeberetur,' C. *d. Or.* i.
54. 'Tarquinius e suis unum sciscitatum Romam ad patrem misit
quidnam se facere vellet, quandoquidem, ut omnia unus Gabiis
posset, ei di dedissent,' L. 54.

iv. When in the Clauses of a Compound Sentence Subjective
reference is made to more than one Subject, 'the Reason of the
thing' must determine to what Subjects the Pronouns are referred
severally.

'Scythae petebant ab Alexandro ut regis sui (i.e. Scytharum)
filiam matrimonio sibi (i.e. Alexandro) iungeret ; si dedignaretur
affinitatem, principes Macedonum cum primoribus suae gentis (i.e.
Scytharum) conubio coire pateretur,' Curt. viii. 1. 'Ariovistus respondit, Neminem secum (i.e. cum Ariovisto) sine sua (i.e. con-
tendentis) pernicie contendisse,' Caes. *B. G.* i. 36. 'Tarquinius
orabat Tarquiniensis ne se (i.e. Tarquinium) . . . ante oculos
236　suos (i.e. Tarquiniensium) perire sinerent,' L. ii. 6.
Ipse.
　　v. The Definitive Pronoun ipse, which may qualify Nouns or
Pronouns of any Person, assists in two ways the use of the Reflexive Pronouns in Clauses.

(1) By qualifying the Subject of a Clause in which a Reflexive
Pronoun occurs, so as to shew the reference of that Pronoun to the
Subject of the Clause rather than to the Principal Subject.

'Natura movet infantem ut se ipse diligat,' *nature prompts
an infant to love itself,* C. *Fin.* ii. 11. Without ipse the Pronoun
se might have been referred to natura. 'Clearchus ait . . . proinde
consulant sibi ipsi ; iubeant abire se,' Iust. xvi. 4 (sibi is referred
by ipsi to the Subject of consulant : se refers to the Principal
Subject Clearchus). 'Neque prius vim adhibendam putaverunt
(Ephori) quam se ipse (Pausanias) indicasset,' Nep. *Paus.* 4.

'Flaccus milites portis mūrisque sibimet ipsos tecta militariter coëgerat aedificare,' L. xxvii. 3.

(2) By standing for the Reflexive se, when antithetic to some other word; whether to a Substantive, to suus, or another Pronoun. In such use ipse refers to the Principal Subject, and the word to which it is antithetic is either the Subject of the Clause, or referred to the Subject of the Clause.

'Pertimuerunt ne ab ipsis desciscceret et cum suis in gratiam rediret,' Nep. *Alc.* 75. 'Caesar quaesivit, cur de sua (i.e. militum desperantium) virtute aut de ipsius (i.e. Caesaris) diligentia desperarent,' Caes. *B. G.* i. 40.

If no such antithesis exists, ipse refers to the next preceding Noun:

'Habemus a Caesare, sicut ipsius dignitas . . . postulabat, sententiam,' C. *Cat.* iv. 5.

Obs. The cases of ipse, when they appositively strengthen and define se, semet, &c., suus, suusmet, &c., assist Pronominal reference so far only as, by distinguishing Gender and Number, they often make the reference more clear and obvious.

'(Rex meminerat hos fratres) nuper praeter consuetudinem . . . admovisse semetipsos lateri suo . . . seque mirantem quod non vice sua tali fungerentur officio . . . ad armigeros recessisse . . . Iam temeritatem verborum, quae in semetipsum iacularentur, nihil aliud esse quam scelesti animi indicem ac testem,' Curt. vii. 2.

Note 1. Inter ipsos, in Cicero, is always preceded by a Case (Genitive or rarely Dative) dependent on some Noun which admits the notion of reciprocity: 'Id iam patebit, si hominum inter ipsos societatem coniunctionemque perspexeris,' C. *Leg.* i. 10. 'Latissime patens hominibus inter ipsos, omnibus inter omnis, societas haec est,' C. *Off.* i. 16.

In other writers inter ipsos appears without the preceding Case: 'Sed gloriae maximum certamen inter ipsos erat,' Sall. *Cat.* 7. 'Haec dum in India geruntur, Graeci milites, orta inter ipsos seditione, defecerant,' Curt. ix. 51.

Note 2. Inter se must be connected either with a Plural Adjective or with a Verb, or Participle, implying *likeness* or *unlikeness*, *agreement* or *disagreement*, &c., as, 'Omnes inter se dissimiles fuerunt,' C. *d. Or.* iii. 7.

IV. Participial Construction.

A PARTICIPLE is the Attribute of one that acts, or has acted, or will act; of one that is being acted on, or has been acted on, or will be acted on; to which must be added, of one that is meet for acting on. As Adjective, it agrees attributively with Nouns and Pronouns: as a Verb-form, it takes the same Case-constructions as its Verb.

A) 1. The want of a Perf. Participle Act. in Active Verbs is supplied in Latin either by the Finite Verb Active, with Relative or Particle, or by an Abl. Absolute Passive:

'Tarquinium regem qui non tulerim, Sicinium feram?' *having refused to endure Tarquin as king, shall I endure Sici-*

nius? L. ii. 34. 'Alexander, cum interemisset Clitum, vix a
se manus abstinuit,' *Alexander, having slain Clitus, hardly re-
frained from suicide,* C. *T. D.* iv. 37. 'Pompeius, captis Hiero-
solymis, victor ex illo fano nihil attigit,' *Pompeius, having taken
Jerusalem, in the very moment of victory, meddled with nothing
belonging to that temple,* C. *p. Flacc.* 28.

2. The want of a Pres. Participle Passive is supplied by the
Finite Passive Verb with Relative or Particle:

'Pueri, qui (cum, dum) docentur, discunt = Greek παῖδες
διδασκόμενοι μανθάνουσι, *children (by) being taught learn.*

Rarely the Perfect Participle Passive takes a Present Passive
sense: 'Sperata victoria' (= victoria quae speratur), L. xxx. 30.

3. A Fut. Participle Passive is not often used even in Greek.
In Latin the Finite Verb with Relative stands for it: 'Grata
superveniet quae non sperabitur hora,' Hor. *Epist.* i. 4. 14.

4. Some Participles are used as mere Adjectives. Such are,
neglegens, patiens, sapiens, doctus, horrendus, tremendus, vene-
randus, &c.

Many appear as Substantives: amans, adulescens, sponsus;
nupta, sponsa; coeptum, dictum, factum, praeceptum, &c.

Neuters such as the last named are sometimes modified by
Adverbs: 'Verum est fortis et sapientis viros non tam praemia
sequi solere recte factorum quam ipsa recte facta,' C. *p. Mil.* 35.

The Nouns, *man, men, things,* are frequently understood with
Participles: 'Grande locuturi nebulas Helicone legunto,' *they
that would utter a sublime strain must cull mists on Helicon,* Pers.
v. 7. 'Male parta male dilabuntur,' *ill gotten, ill go,* C. *Phil.* ii.
27. 'Beatos puto, quibus deorum munere datum est aut facere
scribenda, aut scribere loquenda,' Plin. *Ep.* vi. 16.

238　　*B)* A Participle may often be considered as an Enthesis or
Abbreviated Clause. Such use is of two kinds:

(1) Attributive, when the Subject of the Clause to be abbreviated is contained (in any Case, and expressed or understood) in the Principal Sentence, and the Participle agrees
with that word in Gender, Number, and Case:

'Alexander moriens (= cum moreretur) anulum suum
dederat Perdiccae,' *Alexander in his dying moments had
given his ring to Perdiccas,* Nep. *Eum.* 2. 'Spreta (= si
spreta est) in tempore gloria interdum cumulatior
redit,' *glory spurned at the right moment now and then
returns in ampler measure,* L. ii. 47. 'Animo nobis opus
est non abhorrente (= qui non abhorreat) a quietis
consiliis,' *we need a temper not averse from peaceful counsels,* L. xxx. 30. 'Servilius Ahala Sp. Maelium, regnum
appetentem (= quod appeteret) interemit,' *Servilius
Ahala slew Spurius Maelius, for aiming at royal power,*
C. *Cat. M.* 16.

(2) Absolute, when the Subject of the Clause to be abbreviated
is not contained in the principal Sentence, but is placed,
together with the Participle, in the Ablative Case. See
§ 161, and Examples, p. 411.

1) It appears therefore that the Ablative Absolute must not generally be used when a Noun-term for the Participle to agree with can be found in the Principal Sentence. For instance, we must not write: Nostra te legente, utere tuo iudicio ; but, ' Nostra legens utere tuo iudicio,' *when you read my works, use your own judgment,* C.

This rule is sometimes, but very rarely, violated, and then only for the sake of some peculiar emphasis.

'Vercingetorix, convocatis suis clientibus, facile incendit (eos),' Caes. *B. G.* vii. 4. 'Iugurtha fratre meo interfecto regnum eius sceleris sui praedam fecit,' Sall. *Iug.* 14.

2) The want of a Copulative Participle (*being*) enables the Abl. Abs. to consist of Substantive with Adjective : ' Caesare vivo,' *Caesar being alive,* or of two Substantives : ' Caesare duce,' *Caesar* being *commander* : ' Consule Planco.'

3) The Impersonal Passive construction (erratur, litatur, &c.) enables a Participle alone to be used Absolutely :

Errato (*a mistake having been made*), litato (*sacrifice having been duly performed*), &c.

4) A Clause may be Absolute with a Participle or Adjective. See § 161. 4.

C. The Participial Construction, Attributive and Absolute, is   **239** used to abbreviate

(1) Relative Clauses :

'Peloponnesus est peninsula, angustis Isthmi faucibus continenti adhaerens,' *the Peloponnesus is a peninsula, attached to the continent by the narrow pass of the Isthmus,* L. xxxii. 21. 'Sunt divitiae certae, in quacumque sortis humanae levitate permansurae,' *sure riches are those that will abide in whatsoever fickleness of human fortune,* Sen. *Ben.* vi. 3. 'Pisistratus Homeri libros, confusos antea, disposuit,' *Pisistratus arranged the books of Homer, which were heretofore confused,* C. *d. Or.* iii. 4. (Where adhaerens = quae adhaeret ; permansurae = quae permansurae sunt ; confusos = qui confusi erant.) 'Gaudentem ' (Hor. *C.* i. 1. 11) = ' hominem qui gaudet.'

(2) Adverbial Clauses :

1) Consecutive Clauses are represented by Participial construction (chiefly where this is accompanied by a Negative) :

Sapientis est, nihil contra mores, leges, instituta facientem, habere rationem rei familiaris,' *it is a wise man's duty to have regard to his private fortune, so that he do nothing contrary to morals, laws, and customs,* C. *Off.* ii. 15 (where nihil facientem = ita ut nihil faciat, *without doing anything*). 'Natura dedit usuram vitae, tamquam pecuniae, nulla praestituta die,' *nature has given the loan of life, as it were of money, without fixing any day for repayment,* C. *T. D.* i. 39.[1]

---

[1] Here observe the versions of the English idiom 'without,' followed by a Verb.

2) Final Clauses may be abbreviated by the Fut. Participle:
'Catilina ad exercitum proficiscitur, signa illaturus urbi,' *Catilina goes to the army, intending to march on the city,* Flor. iv. 1. 'Alexander Hephaestionem in regionem Bactrianam misit, commeatus in hiemem paraturum,' *Alexander sent Hephaestion into the Bactrian country to get provisions for the winter,* Curt. viii. 8. (Where illaturus = ut inferat ; paraturum = ut pararet.) See § 186.

3) Causal Clauses : 'Nihil affirmo dubitans plerumque et mihi ipse diffidens,' *I affirm nothing because I generally doubt and distrust myself,* C. *Div.* ii. 3 (dubitans = quia dubito, diffidens = quia diffido). 'Hephaestio longe omnium amicorum carissimus erat Alexandro, cum ipso pariter educatus,' *of all his friends Hephaestion was by far the dearest to Alexander, because he had been brought up with him,* Curt. iii. 12 (educatus = quia educatus erat). 'Flaminium Coelius religione neglecta cecidisse apud Trasimenum scribit,' *Coelius says, that Flaminius fell at Trasimenus, because he had neglected religion,* C. *N. D.* ii. 3 (i.e. quod religionem neglexisset).

4) Temporal Clauses : 'Herculem Germani, ituri in proelia, canunt,' *the Germans, when about to march to battle, chaunt Hercules,* Tac. *G.* 3 (i.e. cum ituri sunt). 'Tarquinius Ardeam oppugnans imperium perdidit,' *Tarquin lost his power, while besieging Ardea,* Eutr. i. 8 (oppugnans = dum oppugnat). 'Pleraeque scribuntur orationes habitae iam, non ut habeantur,' *most speeches are written after being delivered, not that they may be delivered,* C. *Br.* 91 (habitae = postquam habitae sunt). 'Iove tonante cum populo agi non est fas,' *when Jupiter thunders, it is against religion to transact affairs with the people,* C. *Phil.* v. 3 (i.e. cum Iuppiter tonat).

5) Conditional Clauses : 'Epistulae offendunt, non loco redditae,' *letters annoy, if not delivered in season,* C. *Fam.* xi. 16 (i.e. si non redduntur). 'Nihil, me sciente,

---

Marcus entered the city without being saluted by any one, may be variously rendered :
(1) Marcus nullo salutante urbem ingressus est.
(2) Marcus a nullo salutatus urbem ingressus est.
(3) Marcus insalutatus urbem ingressus est.
(4) Marcus sine cuiusquam salutatione urbem ingressus est.
(5) Marcus ita urbem ingressus est ut a nullo salutaretur.
(6) Marcus urbem est ingressus neque a quoquam salutatus est.

And, with a Negative, *Marcus never entered the city without being saluted*—

(7) Marcus numquam urbem ingressus est quin (*or* ut non) salutaretur.

This force of the Participle with a Negation may be illustrated by a few more examples : 'Epicurus, non erubescens, voluptates persequitur omnis nominatim,' *Epicurus without blushing details all pleasures by name,* C. *N. D.* i. 40. 'Constat Numam non petentem in regnum ultro accitum,' *it is well known that Numa, without being a candidate, was solicited to accept the royal office,* L. i. 35. 'In bello civili nihil accidit non praedicente me,' *in the civil war nothing has happened without my foretelling it,* C. *Fam.* vi. 6. 'Quis est qui nullis officii praeceptis tradendis philosophum se audeat dicere ?' *who will dare to call himself a philosopher without laying down any rules of duty ?* C. *Off.* i. 2.

frustra voles,' *you shall wish for nothing in vain, if I know it,* Sall. (i.e. dummodo ego sciam).

6) Concessive Clauses : 'Scripta tua iam diu exspectans, non audeo tamen flagitare,' *though I have long been looking for your writings, yet I dare not demand them,* C. *Ac.* i. I. (i.e. etsi exspecto).   'Perditis rebus omnibus, tamen ipsa se virtus sustentare potest,' *though all things be lost, yet virtue can support herself,* C. *Fam.* vi. I. (i.e. quamvis perditae sint).

Nisi, etsi, quamvis may annex a Participial Clause :

'Etsi aliquo accepto detrimento tamen summa exercitus salva locum quem petunt capi posse,' *though some loss would be sustained, yet the spot they aimed at might be occupied without the main army being destroyed,* Caes. *B. C.* i. 69.

7) In Comparative Participial Constructions the Particles are prefixed to the Participial Clause : 'Graecas litteras senex didici, quas quidem avide arripui, quasi diuturnam sitim explere cupiens,' *I learnt Greek in old age, and grasped it indeed with much zest, as if I wished to quench a protracted thirst,* C. *Cat. M.* 8.   'Antiochus securus de bello Romano erat, tamquam non transituris in Asiam Romanis,' *Antiochus was careless about the war with Rome, as imagining that the Romans would not come over to Asia,* L. xxxvi. 41.

D) Notes on Participial Construction.

1) The Participle Perfect Passive is used to express a past action continuing in its consequences, after such Verbs as habeo, teneo, possideo, &c. : 'Illud exploratum habeto, nihil fieri potuisse sine causa,' *consider it clear, that nothing could have been made without a cause,* C. *Div.* ii. 28. 'Hoc tibi persuasum habe,' *be persuaded of this,* C. 'Hoc cognitum comprehensumque habeo,' *this is thoroughly known and comprehended by me,* C.

2) It is used in older Latin with the Verbs do, reddo, curo, by way of Periphrasis : 'Stratas legiones Latinorum dabo,' *I will lay prostrate the legions of the Latins,* L. viii. 6. 'Hoc tibi effectum reddam,' *I'll get this done for you,* Ter. *An.* iv. 4. 'Inventum tibi curabo et mecum adductum Pamphilum,' *I'll look up Pamphilus for you and bring him with me,* Ter. *An.* iv. 4.

To the same idiom belong the phrases missum facere and fieri : 'Si qui voluptatibus ducuntur, missos faciant honores,' *if any are seduced by pleasures, they may bid farewell to honours,* C. *p. Sest.* 68. 'Legiones bello confecto missas fieri placet,' *I recommend that on the close of the war the legions be disbanded,* C. *Phil.* v. 19.

After volo, nolo, cupio, oportet, a Perf. Participle represents Infin. Pass., see p. 449. The constructions ' Properato opus est,' *hasty action is needed,* C.; ' Liberis consultum volumus,' *we would have the children's good regarded*, C.; 'Mansum oportuit,' Ter., arise from the Impers. use of. Passive Verbs.

3) The Participle Perfect is used attributively to supply the place of a Substantive expressing the action of the Verb:

'Prusiam regem suspectum Romanis et receptus Hannibal et bellum adversus Eumenem motum faciebat,' *both the reception of Hannibal and the commencement of war against Eumenes made King Prusias an object of suspicion to the Romans*, L. xxxix. 51. 'Labeo male administratae provinciae arguebatur,' *Labeo was charged with maladministration of the province*, Tac. *Ann.* vi. 29.

Hence Livy, Tacitus, and Lucan use the Neuter Participle Perf. Pass. to express the Substantival notion of the Passive Verb, which the Greeks expressed by the Article and Infinitive:

'Diu non perlitatum tenuerat dictatorem ne ante meridiem signum dare posset,' *the long-continued want of a well-omened sacrifice had withheld the dictator from being able to give the signal before noon*, L. vii. 8. So, tentatum, L. iv. 49. 'Summisque negatum stare diu,' Lucan, i. 70. 'Notum,' V. *Ae.* v. 6. 'Expectatum,' V. *G.* iii. 348.

4) The Gerundive Construction is more largely used in the place of Substantives expressing the transitive action of the Verb:

'Flagitiosum est ob rem iudicandam pecuniam accipere,' *it is scandalous to take money to give a verdict in court*, C. *Verr.* ii. 32. 'Temperantia constat ex praetermittendis voluptatibus corporis,' *temperance consists in abstinence from bodily pleasures*, C. *N. D.* iii. 15. 'Phocion cum Demade de urbe tradenda Antipatro consenserat,' *Phocion had agreed with Demades as to the surrender of the city to Antipater*, Nep. *Phoc.* 2.

In Livy's Preface we read 'ante conditam condendamve urbem,' which probably means 'before the actual or designed foundation of the city,' 'before the city was built or commenced.' See GERUNDIVE CONSTRUCTION.

5) Participles are sometimes equivalent to Gerundive Instrumental Construction:

'Aer effluens huc et illuc ventos efficit,' *the air, by flowing hither and thither, causes winds*, C. *N. D.* ii. 39. 'Crescit indulgens sibi dirus hydrops,' *the dreadful dropsy grows by self-indulgence*, Hor. *C.* ii. 2. 13. See § 161. 2.

6) A Participle and Verb are often best translated by two Verbs:

'Caesar scribit, se cum legionibus profectum celeriter adfore,' *Caesar wrote word that he had set out with his legions and would soon arrive*, Caes. *B. G.* v. 38. 'Iure interfectum Clitum Macedones decernunt, sepultura quoque prohibituri, ni rex humari iussisset,' *the Macedonians voted that Clitus was justly slain, and would even have denied him burial, had not the king ordered him to be interred*, Curt. viii. 2.

7) A Participle Present after such Verbs as audio, video, facio, pingo, &c., expresses the action or state of the Object heard, seen, &c.:

'Audivi eum dicentem, vidi eum ambulantem,' &c.

Analogous to this is the construction, 'Est apud Platonem Socrates . . . dicens,' &c., *we read in Plato of Socrates saying*, &c. C.

8) The Participle sometimes repeats the preceding Verb:

'Mars videt hanc visamque cupit,' *Mars sees, and seeing desires her*, Ov. *Fast.* iii. 21.

9) A Participial construction is often involved with an Oblique Interrogation or a Relative Clause:

'Cogitate quantis laboribus fundatum imperium, quanta virtute stabilitam libertatem una nox paene delerit,' C. *Cat.* iv. 9. Such a sentence cannot be rendered in English without paraphrase: *Consider how vast the toil that founded this empire, how great the valour that established this freedom, which a single night all but destroyed.*

CHAPTER V.

ARRANGEMENT OF WORDS AND STRUCTURE AND CONNEXION OF SENTENCES.

THE ORDER OF WORDS reflects the progress of a writer's ideas. This is true of modern languages, such as English and French, which, having lost their inflexions, are obliged in the arrangement of words to follow somewhat definite rules; but it is worthy of special attention in languages which, by inflecting the Nouns and Verbs, can abandon the syntactical order as often as emphasis or harmony requires. Latin is one of these languages, which are called Transpositive.

A. Since an unusual order indicates logical or rhetorical emphasis, it is necessary for adequate translation that the ordinary arrangement should be clearly understood.

We shall consider I. the beginning; II. the end; III. the middle of the Sentence.

I. 1. The Subject usually stands either first, or after the word definitive of time, place, or logical connexion:

Verres Siciliam vexavit. At ille in iudicium venit.

2. Everything logically connected with the Subject must be placed in close connexion with it:

*241
Arrangement of Words.*

The Aedui, since they were unable to protect themselves and their property, sent ambassadors to Caesar.

'Aedui legatos ad Caesarem mittunt, cum se suaque defendere non possent,' Caes.

Democritus was of course unable to distinguish between black and white, after he had lost his sight.

'Democritus, luminibus amissis, alba scilicet et atra discernere non poterat,' C.

Hence, if emphasis is to be thrown on the Subject, it must be placed in a striking position. Now the most striking position is that farthest removed from the ordinary one. Therefore it should be placed at the end of the Sentence: 'Scenicorum mos tantam habet verecundiam, ut in scenam sine subligaculo prodeat nemo,' C. 'Hannibal iam subibat muros, cum in eum erumpunt Romani,' L.

II. The end of the Sentence is occupied in general by the Verb, because this usually contains the main predication, and unites together the whole proposition. Such order is frequently observed throughout long paragraphs, as in L. ix. 40, 41.

This arrangement, however, should be abandoned:

1. If it is inharmonious in sound, as happens whenever several Verbs come together in a period: 'Constiterunt, nuntios in castra remissos, qui, quid sibi, quando praeter spem hostis occurrisset, faciendum esset consulerent quieti opperientes,' L. xxxiii. 6.

2. If it is necessary to give peculiar importance to the Verb, which, like other words, acquires emphasis from an unusual position: 'Offendit te, A. Corneli, vos, Patres conscripti, circumfusa turba lateri meo,' C.

3. Or to emphasise a word, which in the middle of the sentence would not have the requisite stress: 'Sicine vestrum militem ac praesidem sinitis vexari ab inimicis?' L.

4. To prevent the separation of closely connected words: 'Erant ei veteres inimicitiae cum duobus Rosciis Amerinis,' C.

5. To secure directness of expression in clauses introduced by enim or autem: 'Sed hoc vitium huic uni in bonum convertebat: habet enim flebile quiddam in quaestionibus,' C. 'Amicum aegrotantem visere volebat: habitat autem ille in parte urbis remotissima,' C.

6. To secure Antithesis by the figure Chiasmus: 'Aedes pestilentes sint, habeantur salubres,' C. 'Patriae salutem anteponet saluti patris,' C.

III. The middle of the sentence is usually occupied by the Adverb and other qualifying words; and by the Oblique Cases.

The Adverb, however, and the Oblique Cases, like other words, acquire emphasis from peculiarity of position: 'His Fabriciis semper usus est Oppianicus familiarissime,' C. 'Secuti estis alium ducem; sequemini nunc Camillum,' L.

242 *B.* Notes.

1) The Adjective or dependent Genitive usually follows its Substantive: 'Vir bonus. Moderatio animi.' But if it is emphatic

or imparts a specific meaning to an Adjective, or other word, it precedes it: M a g n u s Alexander, or M a g n u s ille Alexander. I u r i s prudens.

2) Usually Substantives having a Genitive belonging to them all, should not be separated, but all should follow or precede it: 'Huius autem orationis difficilius est e x i t u m q u a m p r i n c i p i u m invenire,' C. 'Honestum autem illud positum est in animi c u r a atque c o g i t a t i o n e,' C Similarly several Genitives depending on a single Noun either follow or precede it: 'Dedicatum est inter cellam I o v i s et M i n e r v a e,' L. 'Haec omnia h o n o r i s et a m-p l i t u d i n i s commodo compensantur,' C.

Yet closely connected words are frequently separated for the sake of emphasis: 'I u s t i t i a m cole et p i e t a t e m,' C. 'Quod et a e t a t i t u a e esset aptissimum et a u c t o r i t a t i m e a e,' C.

3) An Adjective qualifying a Substantive with dependent Geni-tive is placed first, the Genitive next: U n a l i t t e r a r u m signifi-catio. C o n s t a n s o m n i u m fama.
But an Attribute acquires emphasis by separation from its Noun: In m i s e r i a m nascimur s e m p i t e r n a m. 'Unum a Clu-entio profectae pecuniae v e s t i g i u m ostende,' C.

4) Contrasted words are rendered effective by juxtaposition :
'Ex bello tam t r i s t i l a e t a repente pax cariores Sabinas viris ac parentibus fecit,' L. 'M o r t a l i i m m o r t a l i t a t e m non arbitror contemnendam,' C.

5) Similarly, different cases of the same word, and words having a common derivation, are placed in juxtaposition :
'A l i u m a l i o nequiorem. Sint semper omnia h o m i n i h u-m a n a meditata. 'U t ad s e n e m s e n e x de senectute, sic hoc libro ad a m i c u m a m i c i s s i m u s de a m i c i t i a scripsi,' C. *Lael.*

6) Q u i s q u e should be placed in juxtaposition with s u u s and the cases of s u i : 'S u a c u i q u e v i r t u t i laus propria debetur.' 'Gallos Hannibal in civitates q u e m q u e s u a s dimisit,' L. xxi.

7) The directness of Latin expression requires that in Negative Sentences the Negative form should be stamped on the sentence at once :
'N e g a t Epicurus quemquam, qui honeste non vivat, iucunde posse vivere,' C. 'N i h i l est agricultura melius, n i h i l homine libero dignius,' C. 'V e t a t enim dominans ille in nobis Deus iniussu nos hinc suo demigrare,' C. 'N e m i n i quicquam negavit. N o n memini me umquam te vidisse.

Hence n o n is frequently separated by one or more words from m o d o, solum, tantum, minus, magis :
'I u s bonumque apud Scythas n o n legibus magis quam natura valebat,' C.

8) Similarly for the sake of emphasis a n t e and p r i u s are sepa-rated from q u a m, and the Demonstrative from its Relative :
'A n t e revertit quam expectaveram,' C. 'I l l u d quidem p o s t accidit quam discesseram,' C. 'H a n c esse perfectam philoso-phiam semper indicavi, q u a e de maximis quaestionibus, &c., C.

9) The Demonstrative Pronouns usually precede their Substan-tives :

'Eius disputationis sententias memoriae mandavi: quas hoc libro exposui meo arbitrio,' Cic.

Unless it is desirable to bring them into close connexion with the Relative:

'Numquam qui iratus accedet ad poenam mediocritatem illam tenebit, quae est inter nimium et parum,' C.

10) Prepositions are either placed immediately before their case, or at least are only separated from it by a Genitive belonging to the Case they govern:

'Sanguis a corde in totum corpus distribuitur,' C. 'Quid est tam inhumanum quam eloquentiam ad bonorum perniciem pervertere,' C.

11) Qualifying words, however, which form an essential part of the word governed by a preposition, may intervene between the preposition and its case:

Ob non redditos transfugas. De bene beateque vivendo. 'Ex illo caelesti Epicuri de regula et iudicio volumine,' C.

12) Disyllabic prepositions often follow their case, if it is a pronoun: is quem contra dico; sometimes also ad, de, per, post, follow their case. This, however, is usually to prevent the separation of the relative from its antecedent:

Illud, quo de agitur.

An Apposition to a Proper Name is commonly placed after the name, as conveying a subordinate idea:

'Q. Mucius augur multa narrare de C. Laelio, socero suo, solebat,' C. Agis rex; Cyprus insula; Hypanis fluvius; Orpheus poëta.

If, however, the Appellative is more important, and requires to be emphasised, it will precede the Proper Name:

'Obviam ei venerunt duo consules, C. Terentius Varro et L. Paullus Aemilius,' L.

C. The Connexion of Sentences.

243
Connexion of Sentences.

1) Latin writers not only paid great attention to the logical sequence of Clauses and Sentences, but made this logical connexion obvious by placing a particle as the first or second word in the sentence. Hence no sentence stands detached unless it is logically disconnected from what precedes. Sentences connected in thought form links of a chain, which only breaks off because the topic is altogether dismissed.

2) The Relative and its Particles are particularly useful for this connexion of sentences, and for avoiding monotonous repetition.

The Relative may be used for the Demonstrative with a Particle, and is therefore found with those Conjunctions which allow of connexion by means of a Particle. See COORDINATION.

Quod cum audissem; quod si fecissem; quod quamvis non ignorassem; for Et cum hoc, &c.

From this habit of connexion by Relatives, appears to have arisen the use of quod before many Conjunctions, as a merely Sociative Particle. It is most frequent before the conditional

Particles, si, nisi, and etsi, and is found also, though more rarely, before other Conjunctions: so quod cum, quod ubi, quod utinam; in all which the Conjunction alone would have been sufficient. Even before the Relative, we find quod thus used: 'Quod qui ab illo abducit exercitum, et respectum pulcherrimum et praesidium firmissimum adimit reipublicae,' C. See § 82.

3) Another peculiarity, which in Latin helps the connexion of Sentences, is the use of neque (nec). It stands for et with the Negation, in whatever form it occurs in the sentence, unless when it belongs exclusively to a single word in antithesis. This connexion is in Latin so common, that, for the sake of it, neque is joined to enim and vero, where in English we could not use *and*, and are, therefore, obliged to explain it by saying that neque = non.

D. The Period in Latin.

I. 1) A Period is a compound Proposition, consisting of at least two, generally of several Sentences, which are so connected, that grammatical construction is not complete before the last clause is added.

A Period (*ambitus* or *circuitus verborum*) is so called because the main proposition surrounds the interpolated clauses.

2) A Period is Simple, when it does not consist of more than two such Sentences, related to each other as Antecedent and Consequent (Protasis and Apodosis). It is Complex if it consists of several Sentences so related.

3) Thus the following sentences do not constitute Periods: Quemadmodum concordia res parvae crescunt, ita discordia vel maximae dilabuntur. Vitis natura caduca est, et claviculis quidquid est nacta complectitur. But they may readily be made to assume a simple Periodic form:

Constat, quemadmodum concordia res parvae crescant, ita discordia vel maximas dilabi. Vitis, quae natura caduca est, quidquid est nacta, complectitur.

The latter sentence, if we add to it, et nisi fulta sit, ad terram fertur, becomes a Complex Period, in which vitis complectitur is the principal sentence, quae natura caduca est, nisi fulta sit, ad terram fertur, quidquid est nacta, are the clauses.

It may be further enlarged as it stands in Cicero:

'Vitis, quae natura caduca est, et nisi fulta sit, ad terram fertur, eadem, ut se erigat, claviculis, quasi manibus, quidquid est nacta complectitur,' C. *Cat. M.* 15.

4) If the Subject of two Sentences united by a Conjunction is one and the same, the almost invariable practice in Latin is to form them into a Period:

'Antigonus, cum adversus Seleucum Lysimachumque dimicaret, in proelio occisus est,' Nep. *Eum.* 'Verres, simul ac tetigit provinciam, statim Messanam litteras dedit,' C. *Verr.* 1.

So also when the Object is the same for both Propositions:

'Quem ut barbari incendium effugisse viderunt, telis eminus emissis interfecerunt,' Nep. *Alc.*

5) The Clauses of a Period are modifications of the main proposition. By being grouped together in due order, they produce the effect of logical completeness, of sonorous and dignified expression, which accorded well with the gravity and majesty of the Roman character. The Periodic style is admirably fitted for the great oratorical efforts of an accomplished rhetorician like Cicero; and for history designed, as was Livy's, to celebrate the greatness and triumphs of the Roman people. Hence the style of the golden age of Latinity is essentially Periodic. It is, however, but ill adapted for an age in which a profusion of new ideas and fresh information demands the most rapid and facile expression. The modern style is on this account essentially unperiodic.

It will be easily understood that the Period is not suited for all subjects. It is out of place in the description of ordinary and trivial matter, in epistolary composition, in outbursts of passion, irony and denunciation.

245　　II 1) As the dignity of the Roman character delighted in the sonorous roll and fulness of the Period, so their practical sagacity and critical ear required that it should be well proportioned, rhythmical, unmonotonous, and above all, perspicuous and clear.

2) To secure the first of these requisites, a Period should consist of sentences of nearly equal length :

‘Et quisquam dubitabit | quin huic tantum bellum transmittendum sit | qui ad omnia nostrae memoriae bella capienda | divino quodam consilio natus esse videatur,’ C. ‘Stultitia etsi adepta est quod concupivit | numquam se tamen satis consecutam putat,’ C.

3) Roundness and regularity of sound is chiefly to be obtained by correspondence in the structure of sentences. Words, which are opposed to each other, should, as far as possible, be of the same kind, so that noun should answer to noun, verb to verb, &c. If possible, more than one important word should intervene between a parenthetic Clause and the end of a Sentence :

‘Magnitudo maleficii facit, ut, nisi manifestum parricidium proferatur, credibile non sit,’ C.

4) All good prose writing is rhythmical, that is, it flows on in such a manner as to satisfy and delight the ear. It is, however, especially necessary to attend to the cadence of a Sentence or Period, because the necessary pause at the close gives the ear time to criticise. The following is a table of cadences approved by Cicero and Quintilian :

Name	Meter	Meter	Example
Creticus cum Ditrocheo . .	– ∪ –	– ∪ – ∪	gloriam comparavit.
Trochaeus cum Molosso . .	– ∪	– – –	membra firmarunt.
Trochaeus cum Paeone Tertio	– ∪	∪ ∪ – ∪	esse videatur.
Creticus cum Cretico . . .	– ∪ –	– ∪ –	cogitans sentio.
Dochmius.	∪ – – ∪ –		. tui Scipio.
Tribrachys cum Spondeo .	∪ ∪ ∪	– –	. varietates.
Trochaeus vel Iambus cum Dispondeo . . }	∪ –	– – – – / – – – –	pluribus de causis. / virum condemnarunt.
Bacchius	∪ – –		videri.
Palimbacchius	– – ∪		novisse.

5) As the rhythm of prose is essentially distinct from that of

verse, all verse-endings should be avoided at the close of a sentence, particularly the hexameter termination of dactyl and spondee.

Such endings, therefore, as quo me vertam nescio; esse videtur; are carefully to be avoided. It should be observed, however, that the historians were less careful on this point than the orators and rhetoricians. Hexameter endings are frequently met with in Livy.

III. To prevent monotony in the periodic style, short detached sentences (*cola* or *commata*) are introduced. Such frequently occur in periodic style. To secure perspicuity and clearness of expression in constructing them, the following rules should be observed:

(1) That no Sentences be admitted into a Period but such as are logically connected together.

(2) That of these Sentences the leading thought form the main proposition.

(3) That the limitative and qualifying Sentence be placed in logical subordination. Hence in a narrative the accessory details should be arranged in the order of time.

(4) That every Period, indeed every Sentence, commence with the word in closest logical connexion with the preceding:

'Bellum propter nos suscepistis: susceptum quartum decimum annum pertinaciter geritis,' L. 'Quod si acciderit, facienda morum institutorumque mutatio est. Commutato autem genere vitae,' &c. C.

(5) Hence the Relative should be placed as near to the Antecedent as possible. To secure this, either the Relative Clause is introduced parenthetically after its Antecedent:

'Acilius autem, qui Graece scripsit historiam, pluris ait fuisse,' C.

Or the Antecedent is drawn into contact with the Relative by being placed at the end of the Principal Sentence:

'Dicebam habere eos actorem Q. Caecilium, qui praesertim quaestor in eadem provincia post me quaestorem fuerat,' C.

The same remark applies to hic, inde, unde, ibi, &c.:

'Hannibal tris exercitus maximos comparavit. Ex his unum in Africam misit (not unum ex his),' L.

Hence quamobrem and quare always begin a sentence.

IV. As, in the construction of a Simple Sentence, minor additions and circumstances are thrown into the middle, and the Verb closes the whole, so Clauses containing explanatory matter are thrown into the midde of the Period:

'Scipio, ut Hannibalem ex Italia deduceret, exercitum in Africam traiecit. Itaque, cum Romam venisset, statim imperatorem adiit,' L.

The usual arrangement of clauses in a Period is analogous to that of words in a Simple Sentence.

(1) The word or clause containing the Subject, with the words or clauses immediately connected with it. (2) The words or clauses explanatory of the time, place, motive, &c. (3) The word or clause expressing the remoter object. (4) The clause expressing the immediate object. (5) The principal Verb.

To this arrangement there are frequent exceptions, particularly in the position of the principal Verb, for, as was before stated, an agglomeration of finite Verbs at the end of a Period was especially distasteful to the Romans. Hence the principal Verb frequently precedes a Substantival, Final, or Consecutive Clause:

'Cum C. Licinius sacerdos prodisset, clara voce, ut omnis contio audire posset, dixit se scire illum conceptis verbis peierasse,' C.

'Commilitones appellans, orabat ne, quod scelus Ap. Claudii esset, sibi attribuerent,' L.

'Quam rem Tarquinius aliquanto quam videbatur aegrius ferens, confestim Turno necem machinabatur, ut eundem terrorem, quo civium animos domi oppresserat, Latinis inferret,' L.

V. Correlative construction is largely employed in forming Periods. If emphasis is sought, the Relative is placed before the Demonstrative:

'Quid? ii qui dixerunt totam de dis opinionem fictam esse ab hominibus reipublicae causa, ut, quos ratio non posset, eos ad officium religio duceret, nonne omnem religionem funditus sustulerunt?' C. 'Quod si, quam audax est ad conandum, tam esset obscurus in agendo, fortasse aliqua in re nos aliquando fefellisset,' C.

So qualis often precedes talis: quidquid id: and quo, hoc or eo. But this is not the universal practice.

248

VI. Grammatical Subject and Object in Periods.

1) The literature of the Romans is distinguished above all others by directness and lucidity of expression. This is mainly due to the practical sagacity which was their distinguishing characteristic; but partly also to the conditions under which their literary works were composed. There was then no eager public, demanding daily information and periodical criticism: consequently there was no popular literature. As reporters did not exist, we have no trustworthy remains of spontaneous eloquence. The orations that have come down to us are either masterpieces redacted by the orators themselves, or speeches attributed to eminent men by historians. Hence both in matter and form they are the products not of extemporaneous eloquence, but of literary labour.

Moreover, in the case of the ancients, the limited character of their scientific and other information, and the comparative want of fecundity and diversity of ideas, made artistic expression in every branch of art more easily attainable. The simplicity of conception and purity and unity of execution, which distinguish the great works of antiquity, are denied to a modern writer by the very profusion of thought and material which surrounds him.

2) To secure unity and directness of expression :

(1) The Subject remains in the same Case, as far as possible,
throughout a Period :

When they asked him *for his opinion, he replied.*
Rogatus sententiam respondit.

Hannibal allowed him to leave the camp ; but he soon
returned, *because* he said that *he had forgotten something.*

' Cum Hannibalis permissu exisset e castris, rediit paulo
post, quod se oblitum nescio quid diceret,' C.

(2) The introduction of several independent subjects in the
same Period is avoided. Hence sentences expressing the
time, condition, or means of accomplishing the main
action, are frequently thrown into the Ablative Absolute
or are introduced in a Subordinate Sentence, not coordi-
nated as they frequently are in English :

This was observed, and they altered their plan.
Id ubi vident, mutant consilium.

*The plan was universally approved, and the consul was
entrusted with the execution of it.*
Cunctis rem approbantibus, negotium consuli datur.

(3) If an Oblique Case of one sentence becomes the Subject
of the next, the change of Subject should be clearly indicated by a Pronoun :

' Huius filiam virginem auro corrumpit Tatius, ut armatos in arcem accipiat. Aquam forte ea tum sacris extra
moenia petitum ierat,' L. I.

' Principium defectionis ab Othone factum est. Is cum
magna popularium manu transfugit,' Tac.

(4) The Subject of discourse, in whatever case it may appear,
should receive prominence by being placed at the beginning of the Period. Four cases require illustration :

a) When the grammatical Subject of the principal sentence
and clauses is the same :

' Dionysius, cum gravior crudeliorque in dies civitati esset,
iterata coniuratione obsidetur,' Nep.

' Ea animi elatio, quae cernitur in periculis, si iustitia
vacat, in vitio est,' C.

b) When the Subject of the principal sentence is the Object
of the clauses :

' Galli, cum eos non caperent terrae, trecenta milia ad
novas sedes quaerendas miserunt,' L.

' Rex Prusias, cum Hannibali apud eum exsulanti de-
pugnari placeret, negabat se audere, quod exta prohiberent,' C.

c) When the Object of the principal sentence and of the
clause is the same :

' Praemia virtutis communi petitorum consensu tulit,
concessit autem Alcibiadi, quem magno opere dilexit.'

'Polyphemum Homerus cum immanem ferumque finxisset, cum ariete colloquentem facit,' C.

d) When the Object of the principal sentence is the Subject
of the clauses:

'Captis, cum paenitentiam profiterentur, ut parceretur
edixit,' L.

'Midae illi Phrygio, cum puer esset, dormienti formicae
in os tritici grana congesserunt,' C.

The forms *a*) and *c*) are most deserving of imitation, because they
possess greater directness and unity of expression. When, however, prominence is to be given to the motive or occasion of an act,
it may be necessary to employ the other forms.

249 VII. Historical narrative requires frequent change in statements
of time: to express which, historians have recourse to two resources
—the Participial construction, attributive and absolute, and the
Conjunctions, cum, ubi, postquam. By these Livy can unite,
without failure of perspicuity, in one Period, what in English must
be broken into three or more:

'Numitor, inter primum tumultum, hostis invasisse urbem
atque adortos regiam dictitans, cum pubem Albanam in arcem
praesidio armisque obtinendam avocasset, postquam iuvenes per-
petrata caede pergere ad se gratulantis vidit, extemplo advocato
consilio, scelera in se fratris, originem nepotum, ut geniti, ut
educati, ut cogniti essent, caedem deinceps tyranni, seque eius
auctorem ostendit,' L. i.

'His, sicut acta erant, nuntiatis, incensus Tarquinius non dolore
solum tantae ad irritum cadentis spei, sed etiam odio iraque, postquam dolo viam obsaeptam vidit, bellum aperte moliendum ratus,
circumire supplex Etruriae urbes,' L. ii.[1]

**250
Quali-
ties of
Style.**

E. Poetry and Prose alike require the virtues of Purity, Perspicuity, Simplicity, and Harmony.

1) Purity is violated by Barbarism or Solecism.
Barbarism is the use of a word not properly Latin, as, confiscare,
'*to confiscate*:' or (what is more to be guarded against as a more
easy error) the use of good Latin words in meanings they do not
bear: as, intentio, for 'an intention,' instead of consilium.

Solecism is a construction not allowed by Syntax: Parce me,
for parce mihi: Ita graviter aegrotavit ut paene mortuus est, for
mortuus sit.

2) Perspicuity of style requires that it be clear and intelligible,
free from confusion and ambiguity.

3) Simplicity of style requires it to be free from affectation, and
unencumbered by tawdry and tasteless ornament.

4) Harmony of style requires that harsh and unmusical sounds
be carefully avoided; that long and short words be well inter-
mixed, and that grave and important words close the sentences.[2]

---

[1] Compare with these a much less elegantly constructed Period in Caes. *B. C.* ii. 22:
'Massilienses . . . constituunt.'

[2] The style of Prose Composition admits a fourfold distinction: (1) The Didactic;
(2) the Epistolary; (3) the Oratorical; (4) the Narrative or Historic.

PART III.

LATIN PROSODY.

251
Prosody.

A. *PROSODIA*, of which the Latin *accentus* is a translation, denoted in classical Greek the accent of a word. In later times, when Accent became confounded with Quantity, the word was sometimes employed in its modern sense. In English and other languages Prosody now signifies that part of Grammar which deals with the quantity of syllables and the rules of metre.

I. Quantity and Rhythm.

252
Quantity and Rhythm.

1. In Latin, as in Greek, Verse depended on the Quantity of syllables, every syllable being either long or short; and the various metres resulted from the various relations of the long and short syllables to each other. We therefore first treat of the Quantity of syllables, so far as it can be reduced to rule; and then discuss the most important metres: the Heroic Hexameter first, as the leading and typical form of verse; next the Elegiac, and then the Lyric metres, mainly those of Horace and Catullus.

Of the first three styles, the model in Latin is Cicero, to whom, we may justly say, non viget quicquam simile aut secundum. (1) His Didactic writings are in the form of Treatise or of Dialogue. Of the Treatise, his work De Officiis is the best model; of his Dialogues, the Laelius or De Amicitia, and the Cato Maior or De Senectute, are best adapted to the young student, who may proceed afterwards to the Tusculan Disputations and the De Oratore (2) Cicero's Letters are either dignified or familiar. Of the dignified style, the letters to Lentulus and Lucceius, and the first Ad Quintum Fratrem may be taken as models; of the familiar, the First Book of Letters to Atticus. (3) Speeches are either Forensic or Public. Forensic speeches are for the Prosecution or for the Defence. Of the former, we have only Cicero's Verrine speeches, of which the Actio Prima may be taken as a sample. The latter are numerous; and of these the best samples for early study are Pro Archia Poeta, Pro Milone, and Pro Murena. Public speeches may be classed under the three heads of Exposition, Eulogy, or Invective. Hardly any of Cicero's Speeches belong entirely to the first class; but some of the Catilinarian and later Philippic Speeches approach it. Of Eulogy, Pro Lege Manilia is the best example. Of Invective, the First In Catilinam and the Second Philippic.

In History, the greatest Latin authors are Caesar, Livy, and Tacitus. Caesar's style is the clear, full, and unaffected narrative of an accomplished soldier. That of Livy is more ornate and picturesque, bespeaking a student of the Greek historians. The manner of Tacitus, though not without a Thucydidean tinge, is yet peculiar to himself—terse, vigorous, subjective, sternly moral, sometimes bitterly sarcastical; often rising to eloquence, here and there indulging in picturesque description, especially of gloomy and tumultuous scenes.

The student may further compare the following Periods in Livy and Cicero: Liv. i. 16, 'Romana pubes . . . obtinuit.' xxii. 3, 'Flaminius qui . . . proposuit.' xxiii. 25, 'Hac nuntiata clade . . . submitterent.' Cic. *p. S. Rosc.* 1, 'Credo . . . comparandus.' *p. Mil.* 4, 'Est enim . . . salutis.' *p. Caecin.* 1, 'Si quantum . . . audaciae.' *p. Mur.* 2, 'Quod si . . . subeundas,' *in Cat.* iii. 12, 'Sed quoniam . . . providere.' *in Cat.* i. 13, 'Ut saepe . . . ingravescet.' See also *Off.* i. 1. 1; *Fam.* iii. 8. 1.

He may also consult with advantage, 'Hints towards Latin Prose Composition' (Macmillan and Co.), by Alexander W. Potts, Esq., Head Master of the Fettes College, Edinburgh, who has afforded valuable assistance in the present chapter.

We learn from the ancient grammarians (Aristotle, Cicero, and Quintilian among them) that Rhythm, or a due admixture of long and short syllables, was of vital moment in prose as well as verse. As our ears and tongues can at the best discriminate imperfectly differences of Quantity, it is most important for us to acquire a mental ear and tongue, to be able to feel the beauty of Plato as well as Homer, of Cicero as well as Virgil. Cicero's technical writings will supply an excellent commentary on what is here meant.

2. Syllables are either Short or Long. A short syllable is technically denoted by this mark (˘), a long syllable by this (¯).

A short syllable was said to contain one Mora or *time*, a long syllable two Morae or *times*.

Syllables which at one period of the language were long, at another were short.

Certain classes of syllables, which might at the same period be either long or short, are called Doubtful.

In verse a long syllable is exactly equivalent to two short.

3. Long syllables have two main divisions, syllables long by nature, and syllables whose short vowel is lengthened by Position, that is to say by coming before a double consonant, or two or more consonants, whether in the same word or in two consecutive words. In the words fātō, māēstīs both syllables are long by nature: in fāctūs sūbsūnt the four syllables, whose vowels are short by nature, are all lengthened by position.[1]

4. H does not give position any more than the aspirate in Greek; and qu has only the power of a single letter.

5. In the older language final s, preceded by a short vowel, was slightly sounded, if at all; was often therefore not written, and

---

[1] Technically all long syllables and all short syllables are respectively equal, though the nature of the case and the testimony of the ancients prove that there is a great diversity in their real length. Fractus and factus have each their first syllable long, but the latter is only lengthened by position, the former is long by nature also; aquă and nequĕ have each the last syllable short, but the rules of elision, observed by the most careful poets, shew that ŏ was much lighter than ă. We are often ignorant of the natural quantity of Latin syllables lengthened by position. The η and ω, and sometimes the accent, gives us this knowledge in regard to Greek syllables, though we are sometimes at a loss even there in the case of α, ι, υ. The poet Accius introduced the practice of denoting naturally long vowels by doubling them. This was soon laughed out of fashion by Lucilius. We find some traces of this usage in inscriptions of that time: Maarcus, paastores and the like. Later such vowels were often marked by an apex (′); many traces of which we find in inscriptions of all ages; á, Mártis, dominéis, &c. Quintilian alludes to both these fashions. Attention to general laws of the language will enable us to determine the quantity of many vowels. Thus the vowel of the Supine and cognate parts of the Verb was long by nature (even if the vowel of the Present Indic. was short) when it was followed by a medial; the a of actus (for ag-tus) was long, of factus short by nature; the e of lectus (for leg-tus), Part. was long, of lectus, *bed*, short. Again, every vowel followed by ns or nf was long by nature, as in mens, sapiens, and other cases; while e was short in mentis, sapientis, &c. This is what Cicero means when he says in his *Orator*, 48: 'Inclitus dicimus brevi prima littera, insanus producta, inhumanus brevi, infelix longa: et, ne multis, quibus in verbis eae primae litterae sunt, quae in sapiente atque felice, producte dicitur *in*.' In many cases we know the length of the vowel by finding the Latin word written in Greek: Sestius (Σήστιος), Roscius ('Ρώσκιος) and many proper names; but Μάγνος, Γράκχος and the like show us that in such words the vowel was short by nature.

often with the older poets, including Lucretius and Cicero when young, did not give position: as, 'infantibŭs parvis,' 'torvŭs draco.'

6. An important exception to the rule of position is this:

A vowel short by nature, coming before a mute followed by a liquid in the same word, may either remain short, or be lengthened by position: tenĕbrae or tenēbrae, rĕtro or rētro, trĭplex or trīplex. In the same verse Virgil has pătris, pātrem; Lucretius pătribus, pātres; Horace nīgris, nīgroque; Ovid volŭcri, volūcris.

7. Before **gm, gn,** a vowel cannot remain short: tēgmen, āgnus. In genuine Latin words not compounded, the other mutes do not precede **m, n.** Thus the older writers, such as Plautus, wrote drăcŭma, mĭna, cŭcĭnus, lŭcĭnus, Alcŭmēna, Tĕcŭmessa, and the like, for the corresponding Greek words. The learned poets, copying the Greeks, did not object to cўcnus, Tĕcmessa, Prŏcne, &c. It is worth noting, too, that Plautus, Terence, &c., following no doubt the usage of common life, seem never to have lengthened a short vowel before a mute and liquid; while the Augustan and later poets preferred to lengthen one, when the mute was a medial, **b** or **g**; writing lābra, nīgro rather than lăbra, nĭgro. With this we might compare on the one hand the repugnance of Aristophanes to lengthen a short vowel before a mute and liquid, unless he is parodying a serious poet, and on the other the great frequency with which this is done by the tragedians; while Homer nearly always lengthens the vowel in such cases, unless constrained by the metre.

8. The older poets, among them Lucretius, do not hesitate to leave a vowel short before a word beginning with **sc, sp, sq, st, x, z, gn.** The more careful poets avoid such positions, not choosing either to lengthen the vowel or to leave it short. Virgil has only one instance of such a lengthening—'date telā, scandite ;' and once only leaves the vowel short—' Ponitĕ : spes ;' in each case the license seems to be used for effect. Horace has no instance of either license in his Odes or Epistles ; but several in his Satires. As in the case of mutes and liquids, this would seem to point to a studied contrast between the usage of common life and the more stately pronunciation of the higher poetry. In a few Greek words, such as Scamander, Zacynthus, zmaragdus, some of the poets follow the Greeks in a rare exceptional license. Catullus in his two pure Iambic poems three times lengthens a short **a** before a mute and liquid of the following word : as, 'impotentiā freta :' ' Propontidā trucemque . . . ; ultimā Britannia.' The peculiar metre seems to have influenced him in this.

II. Quantity of Inner Syllables.

253.

The Quantity of Final Syllables may be reduced to rules ; but that of Syllables in the body of words is so indefinite, that we must confine ourselves to pointing out a few general principles, with the leading exceptions to these.

1. Where two vowels are contracted into one, the syllable is long: cōgo, cōperio, tibīcen, bōbus, iūnior, bīgae, mōmentum.

In semi, ante, and a few other particles, the vowel does not coalesce, but is altogether elided, when followed by a vowel in a compound word. The syllable is therefore not lengthened: semi-hŏmo, ant(e)ĕo, antĕa, &c., whether the vowel be omitted or not in writing. Forms like 'grave olens,' 'suave olens,' 'magno opere,' 'summo opere,' are better written as two words.

2. All diphthongs are long: Grāīus, āūra, harpȳīa.

Except prae in composition before a vowel, as in prăĕustus, prăĕeunte. Ovid once wrote 'Măĕotis;' but in exile.

Statius once uses prăēiret; and in Catullus the **prae** of 'prae-optarit' coalesces into one syllable with the **op.**

3. A vowel before another vowel in the same word, but a different syllable, is short: trăho, mĕae, vĭa, ĭo, bŏant, tŭus.

Exceptions:

(1) Gāĭus, dīus, Rhĕā (Silvia), but Rhĕā ('Ρέα), ōheu; āer is Greek usage: and there are hundreds of other Greek words, adopted by the poets, chiefly proper names, which keep a vowel long before another: Ĭo, cycnēus, &c. Dĭana, ŏhē are doubtful: also some Greek words: as, daedalĕus and daedalēus, chorēa and chorĕa.[1] Academīa, long in Greek and the best Latin, is shortened by some later poets.

(2) The ĭ of fīo is long, except when followed by **er**, as fĭeri, fĭeret; though Plautus and Terence sometimes have fĭĕri, &c.

(3) The **a** of the old Genitive of the 1st Declension is long: terrāi, aulāi, purpureāi.

(4) The **e** of the Gen. and Dat. of the 5th Declension is long in dīēi, fīdēi (Plautus, Ennius, Lucr.), but fīdĕi in Manilius and later writers; rēi (Lucr.), rĕi (Hor.). Lucretius and others sometimes make rei a monosyllable. In Terence, spei seems always monosyllabic, but spĕi in Seneca. In Latin poetry no other Gen. or Dat. in -**ei** seems to be found, neither speciei, materiei, nor any such. Lucretius has ēi, Catullus ĕi, for the Dat. of the Pronoun is.

(5) The ĭ of Genitives in **ius** is doubtful: illĭus or illīus, and so with istĭus, ipsĭus, ullĭus, nullĭus, solĭus (solīus, Ter.). But always alīus, which is contracted. In later writers alterĭus; but alterīus sometimes in Plautus. Utrĭus, utrĭusque.

By comparing Cicero (*d. Or.* iii. 183) with Quintilian (i. 5. 18), we learn the interesting fact that in the time of the former the prose pronunciation was illĭus, unĭus, &c.; in the time of the latter illīus, unīus, as he with all the later grammarians held the shortening to be a poetic license.

---

[1] In Latin i seems often to have been doubled in pronunciation and to have served for a vowel and consonant at once: thus in Cicero's time Pompeius and such words were often written with **ii**; and so Troi-ia-nus, ei-ius, cui-ius; and hence perhaps the quantity of the two last words. In compounds of iacio it was usual to write i only once, as in ē-ĭcit, āb-ĭcit, though the i was equivalent to ji. We can thus account for the quantity of rē-ĭcio, where the ĭ formed a diphthong with the **e** of **re**, and also a separate syllable. On the other hand ei-cit, rei-cit, are sometimes disyllabic, and āb-ĭcit, ăd-ĭcit are found with their first syllable short. In the older writers, too, eius, cuius are often monosyllabic, and sometimes have the quantity cūĭŭs, ēĭŭs.

4. Derivatives are said to follow as a rule the quantity of the words from which they are derived. But this rule has many exceptions, some systematic, some which seem to be accidental.

(1) Disyllabic Perfects and their compounds, with the tenses formed from them, have the first syllable long: vīdi, invīdi, vīderam; but vĭdeo, vĭderem, &c.; lēgi, lēgissem; but lĕgo, lĕgam.

Except bĭbi, dĕdi, (fĭdi) diffĭdi, (scĭdi) discĭdi, &c., stĕti, (stĭti) constĭti, &c., tŭli, attŭli, &c.

But these exceptions are perhaps only apparent, as the Perfects seem either to be actually reduplicated, as dedi, steti, or to have once been so, as tuli, &c. (tetuli, Lucr., &c.).

(2) Some apparent derivatives are illusory: rex rēgis, rēgina, do not come from rĕgo. Cŏma (κόμη) has no connection with cōmo.

(3) Disyllabic Supines, with the parts of the Verb formed from them, are also long: vīsum, vīsurus, &c. Except dătum, ĭtum, lĭtum, quĭtum, rătum, (rŭtum) dirŭtum, &c., stătum from sisto; but stātum from sto; cĭtum from cieo; but cītus from cio.

(4) Other apparent or real discrepancies might perhaps be explained, if we had the required knowledge: lux, lūcis, lūceo, but lŭcerna; mōles, mŏlestus; sōpio, sŏpor; hūmanus, hŏmo; iūro, peiĕro.

(5) We find not a few variations of quantity in the same word: Lucret. has 'lĭquidis' and 'līquida' in the same verse; he has 'līquor aquai,' all others lĭquor (subst.), but līquor (verb); he has 'flŭvidus' and 'flūvidus,' 'glōmere,' but 'glŏmero,' &c. with other instances. Silius derives Săbini from Săbus; Māmurra (Catull.), Māmurra (Hor., Mart.). Lūceres (Prop.), Lŭceribus (Ov.). Lemŭres and Lemūria (Ov.). Mamūri (Prop.), Mamŭrium (Ov.). Cātillus (Verg.), Cătĭlus (Hor.), Cătillus (Stat.). Vertrăgus (Mart.), vertrāga (Gratius). Cōturnices (Plaut., Lucr.), cŏturnices (Ov., Iuven.). Vatĭcanus (Hor.), Vatĭcanus later. Pălatia, Pălatinus, usually, but pālatia (Iuv.). Often conūbia; often also conŭbia, conŭbio, conŭbiis, &c. It is an error to regard the latter forms as trisyllabic. See Munro *on Lucr.* iii. 776.

(6) Sometimes the consonant is or is not doubled: văcillo, but vāccillo (Lucr., Cic.). Compare făr, farris, fărina; mamma, mămilla; offa, ŏfella; tintĭno, tintĭnnabulum, Porsenna, Porsĕna; and perhaps currus, cŭrulis, quattuor, quăter; littera, lĭtura.

(7) The penult of the 3rd Pers. Plur. Indic. Perf. is long: amavērunt, legērunt. But the poets not unfrequently shorten it; and dedĕrunt (Lucr. Hor.), fuĕrunt (Lucr. Prop.), tulĕrunt (Verg.), vertĕrunt (Hor.), locavĕrunt (Plaut.) prove that this was not done from metrical necessity merely.

(8) The penult of the 1st and 2nd Pers. Plur. of the Fut. Perf. Indic. and the Perf. Subj. is doubtful: viderĭmus (Lucr.), egerĭmus (Verg.), fecerĭmus (Catull.); viderĭtis, dixerĭtis but dederītis

(Ov.). The poets appear to have been determined solely by the requirements of their metre.

As ı and u are both vowels and consonants, from necessity of the verse the vowel sometimes passes into its corresponding consonant: ār-iĕ-tĕ for ărĭĕtĕ, āb-iĕ-tĕ for ăbĭĕtĕ, tēn-uĭ-ă for tĕnŭĭă. Sometimes without such necessity we have āb-iē-gnus, tēnvis for tĕnŭis, and the like. Trisyllabic in Horace is once princīp-ium, once consīl-ium, in Virgil flūv-iōrum; Lucr. has flūtant. Sometimes the ı is suppressed between two long syllables: vindēm-ıātor, stēl-io, taen-iıs. Lucretius once makes ŏr-iūn-dī a trisyllable with short o. The third syllable of fortuītus, gratuītus seems doubtful: Statius certainly has grātŭĭtus. Promontōrium is an error: the real form is promuntŭrĭum. On the other hand v sometimes becomes ŭ: sŏlŭo, dissŏlŭo, vŏlŭo, &c.: Hor. has sĭlŭae and mīlŭus. But rēlĭcuus is the genuine form (Lucr., Plaut., &c.): rēlĭquŭs does not appear before the Silver Age. The Augustan poets abstain from using it, perhaps from a dislike to lengthening the first syllable.

(9) Vēmens, vēmenter are the only genuine forms: vĕhĕmens, &c. never appear in good writers.

(10) Many Crases occur in the poets, like aurêı, ferrêı, even omn-iă as disyllabic, precant-iă as trisyllabic.

(11) In words like deinde, dein, deesse, deest, deerrarunt, the first e is altogether elided, as in antehac, anteactus, &c.; so numquam, nusquam, nullus for neumquam, &c. In neutiquam, neu becomes diphthongal.

(12) Eodem, eaedem, eosdem, are disyllabic or trisyllabic; but disyllabic only where the second vowel is long by nature: eundem, eandem, are always trisyllabic. Idem (plur.) and isdem are disyllabic in the best writers; ĕīsdem seems to occur first in Juvenal: ei (nom.) or ii, eis or iis are avoided by the poets.

(13) A few words like suesco, suetus, deorsum, seorsus are either disyllabic or trisyllabic: suo is twice monosyllabic in Lucr., who has sis for suis after Ennius.

Note. The quantity is doubtful in many Proper Names, adopted from the Greek, in which short vowels are often lengthened for metrical reasons, as Prĭamides.

254 ### III. Quantity of Final Syllables.

(I) 1. Monosyllables ending in a vowel are long: except the enclitics quĕ, vĕ, nĕ, and quă (Nom. and Accus.), which is also an enclitic (sīquă, nēquă).

2. It is perhaps most convenient to say that monosyllables ending in a consonant are also long.

Exceptions:

(1) Such as end in b, d, l, t, are short, two only, sāl and sōl, being long (aut and haud, as diphthongs, are of course long).

(2) Făc, nĕc, ăn, ĭn, fĕr, pĕr, tĕr, vĭr, cŏr, bĭs, cĭs, ĭs (Pron.), quĭs (Nom.).

(3) Also ĕs (sum): ēs is found in Plautus, &c.: but es (edo) is circumflexed and long.

(4) Hĭc (Pron.) is doubtful: hoc (Nom. and Acc.) is doubtful in the old scenic, long in the later, poets.

(5) Ac in good writers never comes before a vowel, and its quantity is uncertain. Very late writers seem to use it both long and short.

(II) 2. In words of more than one syllable:

a. **A** final is long—

(1) In the Abl. Sing. of 1st. Decl.: as, mensā.

(2) In the Imperative of 1st Conj.: amā, monstrā; but pută is used parenthetically.

(3) In the Numerals trigintā, &c.

(4) In Prepositions and Adverbs: circā, contrā, ergā, frustrā, intrā, suprā, intereā, posteā, praetereā, postillā; which are really Ablatives, and therefore regularly long, as may be proved by forms like posthāc, antehāc, praeterhāc; and by the forms extrād, suprād, arvorsum eād (adversum ea), in old inscriptions. But ită, quiă are short: eia or heia is perhaps doubtful, certainly short.

β. **A** final is short in all Noun-Cases but the Ablative: except

(1) In Greek words ending in *ă*, the **a** is sometimes retained in Latin, but there is a strong tendency to shorten it: philomelă; elegīā Ov.); elegīă (Mart. Stat.); Electrā (Cic. Ov.), Electră (Sen.). Phaedrā and Phaedră (Ov.); Phaedră (Sen.). For Greek Nominative in *ăς*, we find Tiresiā (Lucil.), Tiresiă, Peliă (Sen.). But when **a** represents η, it is short: as, nymphă; so, Nom. Atridă (Prop.).

(2) In Vocatives of Greek names in **as**, *ā* is long: Aeneā, Pallā; but doubtful in Vocatives from Nom. in **es**: Atridă (Hor.), Anchisā (Verg.), Cecropidă (Ov.).

E final is short: except

(1) Abl. Sing. of 5th Decl.: diē (hodiē, &c.), rē (quārē); so famē, which in this case at least belongs to this Decl.

(2) 2nd Pers. Sing. Imper. of 2nd Conj.: as, gaudē, monē. But căvĕ (Hor. Ov.); though these have also căvē; vidĕ (Phaedr. Pers.).[1]

(3) Adverbs from Adjectives of the 2nd Decl.: valdē, aegrē, doctē; and in fermē, ferē, ohē. But benĕ, malĕ, infernĕ (Lucr.), supernŏ (Lucr. Hor.), are short. Temerĕ follows the general rule, as is proved negatively by

---

[1] The Latins had a strong tendency to shorten the final in familiar iambic words: compare pută above, and other examples, ending in i and o; and this is especially true and important in the old scenic prosody. In 'valē vale inquit' (Verg.), 'mane inquii' (Catull.), 'fave Ilithyia' (Ov.), the e is long and only shortened by a vowel following.

e being always elided in Hexameter poets; positively by its frequently occurring with ŏ in Seneca.

(4) When it represents η : nymphē, Hebē, Antigonē, tempē, &c.

ɪ final is long : except

(1) ɪ is doubtful in mihĭ, tibĭ, sibĭ, ibĭ, ubĭ; short in nisĭ, quasĭ, necubĭ, sicubĭ.

Obs. The ɪ of utī (= ut) is always long ; sicuti dactyl is a fiction; ibīdem always in Hexameter poets; the second ɪ is doubtful in the scenic poets; utĭque, utĭnam are short. So ubĭnam, ubĭvis; but ubīque.

(2) The ɪ of Vocatives which represent ι is short : Daphnĭ, Adonĭ; also Thybrĭ.

(3) The ɪ of Datives, representing ι, is short in Minoidĭ, Tethyĭ (Catull.), Iasonĭ, Palladĭ (Stat.). But Thetidī, Paridī, &c., have ɪ long ; and these are the more numerous.

o final is long : except [1]

(1) The archaic endŏ is short : also citŏ (adv.), modŏ (adv.), duŏ, egŏ, cĕdŏ, owing to the tendency to shorten the final of familiar Iambic words. Yet modō as well as modŏ is in Lucr.; egō occasionally in Plautus.

(2) Homŏ is doubtful, generally short.

(3) Scio and nescio, which have o doubtful in the scenic writers, for metrical reasons have it short in Hexameter poets, &c.

ʊ final is long : except in the archaic indŭ (= in), and nenŭ (= ne oenum = ne unum = non).

ʏ, a purely Greek letter, is short in the few words adopted from Greek : as, molȳ, Tiphȳ.

ᴄ final lengthens the Vowel : except donĕc.

---

[1] The final o continued always inflexibly long in Datives and Ablatives of the 2nd Decl., and when it represented a final ω (Cliō); but in Verbs and Nominatives of the 3rd Decl. it became doubtful; though still in most cases generally long. Seneca, indeed, Juvenal, and others, venture to shorten the Gerund in do (vincendŏ, vigilandŏ, &c.), and Juvenal even postremŏ, though these appear at least analogous to the Dat. and Abl. in o ; so indeed is quomodŏ (Hor.).

As might be inferred from the laws of Latin pronunciation, this shortening first took place in Cretic and Iambic words. Virgil, an anxious metrist, only ventures to shorten Polliŏ (three times), nuntiŏ and audeŏ. In all these instances the o is elided ; but, as he never elides the final of a Cretic, preferring hiatus, as, insŭlă Ionio, he evidently did not regard the o as long. It is probable, however, that the elision was a compromise, and that the vowel was to him neither precisely long nor short, something, in fact, like a final m, which he occasionally elides in Cretic words, audiam ĕt, omnium ĕgenos. Horace, in his Odes as careful a metrist as Virgil, shortens only Polliŏ, but in his Satires and Epistles he has, besides this word, eŏ, rogŏ, vetŏ, dixerŏ, obsecrŏ, mentiŏ, quomodŏ. But before them Catullus has volŏ, dabŏ, and putŏ, when, like pută, it is a quasi adverb. Tibullus desinŏ, Propertius caeditŏ, and even findŏ. Ovid always shortens Sulmŏ, Nasŏ ; and we find in him examples of amŏ, canŏ, negŏ, petŏ, regŏ, leŏ, conferŏ, desinŏ, oderŏ, Curiŏ, Galliŏ, Scipiŏ, estŏ, credŏ, tollŏ, rependŏ, nemŏ, ergŏ. In most poets of the Silver Age this ŏ is frequent enough : we find quandŏ, porrŏ, serŏ, ambŏ, octŏ, &c. In all ages quandŏquidem.

D final shortens the Vowel.

L final shortens the Vowel.

> In nihĭl it is doubtful; generally short, but occasionally long in Ov. Lucr. Some only use contracted nīl; Virgil seems only twice to use the disyllable, each time before a consonant: *B.* ii. 6.; *Ae.* ii. 287. But there are some 18 instances in which it might be said that he wrote nĭhĭl, not nīl.

[**M** final is treated of under the head of Elision.]

N final shortens the Vowel.

> The only Exceptions are Greek words.
>
> Those in **ēn** are long, as they represent ην: hymēn, &c. Those in **on** are long, which represent ων; short, which represent ον: Tritōn, Troilŏn. Those in **an, in, yn**, are long or short, as they are long or short in Greek: Electrān, but Iphigenĭăn; chelўn, but Tethýn.

R final shortens the Vowel: except

(1) Celtibĕr is doubtful.

(2) Compounds of p a r are long, as dispār, impār.

(3) When **-er** represents ηρ it is long, as āēr. But **or**, even when representing ωρ, follows the general rule: Hectŏr, rhētŏr.

As final is long: except

> The Nom. Sing. and Accus. Plur. of Nouns taken from the Greek, which have -ăς: Pallăs (-ădis), lampădăs, &c.

Es final is long: except

(1) penĕs.

(2) Nouns of Decl. 3 which increase short, as milĕs milĭt-, obsĕs obsĭd-, segĕs segĕt-. But pēs and compounds, Cerēs, abiēs, ariēs, pariēs, remain long.

(3) Compounds of ĕs, as potĕs, adĕs.

(4) Words representing Greek ες; as cacŏēthĕs (Neut.), Arcadĕs (Nom. Plur.).

Is final is short: except

(1) Dat. and Abl. Plur. in **-īs**: terrīs, dominīs, vobīs.

(2) Accus. Plur. of 3rd Decl. in **-īs** (=ēs): omnīs, gentīs.

(3) 2nd Pers. Sing. Pres. Subj. in **-īs**: adsīs, velīs.

(4) Compounds of vīs, as mavīs, quamvīs.

(5) Nominatives which increase long: as, Samnīs (-ītis); and from Greek ῑς: as, Salamīs (-īnis)

(*a*) The **-is** of the Fut. Perf. and Perf. Subj. is doubtful: as, dixerĭs (Hor.), dederīs (Ov.). Compare the quantity of the 1st and 2nd Persons Plur. in these tenses.

(*b*) S a n g u i s has **īs** always in Lucretius; though usually short in and after the Augustan age, it is long more than once in Ovid, Lucan, Silius ; and once in Verg. Tibull. Seneca, Valérius Flaccus, and in the 'Aetna.' Virgil has only pulvīs.

Os final is long : except

(1) Exŏs (Lucr.), compŏs, impŏs.

(2) Greek words which end in ος, as Chiŏs, Phasidŏs.

Us final is short : except

(1) Nominatives in **us** with **ū** in Gen.; virtūs (-ūtis), tellūs (-ūris), (palŭs in Horace's *Ars P.* must be corrupt).

(2) Gen. Sing. and Nom. and Acc. Plur. of the 4th Decl. gradūs.

(3) When **-ūs** represents Greek -ους: Panthūs, Mantūs (Verg.).

Ys final is short, occurring only in a few Greek proper names, as Tiphўs. Except Tethўs (Verg. Ov.), and chrysophrўs.

T final shortens the Vowel.

Except contracted Perfects, disturbāt (Lucr.), petīt, obīt. The final of the uncontracted petiit, iit and its compounds, as rediit, is often long ; some say always, and do not admit exīit and the like.

255   IV. Quantity of Words in Composition.

Generally words in composition retain the quantity they had in their simple form.[1] Thus :—

(1) Prŏ is long in composition.

But there are many exceptions : prŏcella, prŏfanus, prŏficiscor, prŏfecto, prŏfugus, prŏfundus, prŏfiteor, prŏfari, prŏtervus (also prōtervus in Plaut.), prŏnepos, prŏneptis, prŏfundo (but profundo, Catull.) ; prŏpello twice in Lucr., elsewhere prōpello ; prŏcuro, prŏpino, prŏpago (Verb and Subst.) are doubtful ; Prōserpina, but Prŏserpina once in Horace, once in his imitator Seneca. In Greek words προ remains short, as Prŏpontis. Yet prōlogus in Plautus and Terence.

(2) Nē- is long ; nēquaquam ; but short in nĕque, nĕqueo, nĕfas, nĕfandus, nĕfarius, &c.

(3) Rŏ in composition is short, unless lengthened by position merely, as rēscribo. The four Perfects, rēccidi, rēpperi, rēppuli, rēttuli, have always rē, as they are really reduplications, and should have the consonant doubled. As the old quantity was rē, rēd, generally, rēddūco or rēduco always appear in Lucr. Plaut.

---

[1] In many cases, however, compound words have undergone such organic changes as remove them from the domain of prosody ; they belong to the general grammar and history of the language. We might ask again why we have ŏmitto, not ŏbmitto, as in ŏbmoveo, ŏbmurmuro ; hŏdie, not hŏddie (hoc-die) : Īdem (neut.), not īddem, as īdem (is-dem). But as such quantities are invariable in all periods of the language, we must take them for granted, assuming that the tendency of the language was to shorten such syllables in familiar words. This tendency, unchecked in old times, was artificially resisted by more educated ages.

Ter. Compare rĕddo. Rēccĭdo is in Ov. Prop. Iuv. (Virgil does not use the word). Isolated cases occur of rēllatus, rēllictus. The Hexameter poets always have rēligio, rēlicuus, rēliquiae·from metrical necessity; but also rĕligio, rĕlicuus, rĕliquiae in Plaut. Ter. Phaedrus, &c.; and in later poets always rĕliquus.

(4) In that peculiar compound Verb, formed with facio and words like căle- rāre- (where by the, way the word had a double accent, as cále-fécit, ráre-fécit), the quantity of the e is very variable. Lucretius has many of them with these quantities: rārēfieri, rārēfacere, expergēfactus, confervēfacit, putrē-factus, vacēfit, patēfecit once, patēfiet once, but oftener patĕf., liquēfit, but liquĕfactus, calĕfecit, cinĕfactus, labĕfacto, tepĕfactus, timĕfactus, conlabĕfactus, conla-bĕfiunt. It will be seen that the e is always long where a long syllable precedes; but generally short where a short syllable goes before; and this tendency to shorten the e is even greater in later poets. We see from the form calfacio how short the e was in this word, the most usual of the class. Ritschl says that in Plautus the e is long where the preceding syllable is long; short, where it is short. We have thus another instance of the tendency to shorten the finals of iambic words in common use, the e in all these words having been originally long. This tendency has a powerful influence, as will appear, on the old scenic poetry. Vidēlicet, long in Hexameter poetry, shortens the e in Plautus and Terence.

V. Elision.

(1) Elision, sometimes termed by Grammarians Synaloepha, sometimes Ecthlipsis, is an important modifying principle of Quantity. Shortly stated it is this. In a Latin verse, when one word ends in a vowel or diphthong or **m**, and the following word begins with a vowel or **h**, such final vowel or diphthong or **m** with its vowel is elided, that is to say, does not count in the verse.[1]

---

[1] This general principle, however, is subject to many limitations. Much depends on the age of the writer, much on the style of verse. Plautus, or Ennius himself in his dramas, will freely employ elisions which the latter, to judge from the fragments, would never admit in his Annals, written in heroic verse. Virgil has many elisions which Ovid never admits: nay, Horace in his later Odes abstains from elisions found in the earlier books, in his Epistles from elisions which often appear in the Satires. We have room here only for a few remarks. There is not evidence to show in what precise way the elision took place; how far the former vowel was modified or destroyed; whether some short vowels, as ŏ in indeclinable words, benĕ, quĕ, atquĕ, &c., disappeared altogether; whether a long vowel formed a kind of diphthong with a following long vowel; whether a long vowel, elided before a short, was first shortened, and then formed a kind of synaeresis with the other; how it fared with syllables ending in **m**, and the like. As elision, especially of long vowels, continued to become rarer and rarer with careful writers, in the higher kinds of verse, it is probable from this, as well as from other facts, that the artificial cultivation of the language produced a more distinct sounding of final syllables. In a single verse of Plautus or Terence five or six elisions, even of long or middle syllables in **m**, are usual enough. The quantity of syllables in **m** is somewhere between that of a long and a short syllable.

That, as some suppose, the former vowel or diphthong was lost altogether in pronunciation, and the accent thrown a syllable back, seems impossible: for then many verses of the best poets would cease to be verses at all: such as Virgil's 'Sublimem expulsam eruerent,' 'Insontem infando indicio.' The latter would then be equivalent to 'Insons infans indicio,' which has no rhythm.

(2) Elision is very rare when a vowel or diphthong immediately precedes the elided syllable, though we find in Virgil, 'Alpheae ab origine;' in Horace's Satires, 'fio et mersor.'

(3) Monosyllables, long or ending in **m**, should not be elided before a short vowel, except a few, such as me, te, se, tu, si, cum, tum, iam, sum but not sim, qui sing. not plur. Here, and in what precedes and follows, we are not speaking of the old scenic poets.

(4) Iambic words (⏑–) are never elided before a short vowel: seldom (never by some poets, such as Ovid in his Elegiacs) even before a long vowel. Lucretius so elides only once, 'equi atque hominis.' Virgil, however, makes use of this license, but yet under limitations.

(5) Careful poets, as Virgil, abstain from eliding the ultima of a Cretic (– ⏑ –), because this can be only before a short syllable. The style of verse, however, makes a difference. Horace does this in his Satires, as 'tantŭli ĕget,' not elsewhere; Catullus in his Lyrics and Elegiacs, not in his Heroics. So elision of words in **m**, like omnium, is rare, yet occurs in the best writers: as, 'omnium egenos' (Verg.), 'fluminum amores' (Ov.), 'principum amicitias' (Hor.).

(6) There are many distinctions in the elision even of short vowels. Thus ŏ or ĭ elide more freely than ă or ŏ before a short vowel. Many poets will hardly thus elide ă except in the first foot of a verse or before another ă: Flūmĭna ămem is a much easier elision than Flūmĭna ĕrant. The ĕ of indeclinable words, such as quĕ, vĕ, atquĕ, nequĕ, benĕ, malĕ, temerĕ, is the easiest of all elisions. A poet like Ovid will only admit the elision even of a short vowel in the last half of the Pentameter with very great limitation, and such elisions as a rule occur only in the first foot of this half; elisions like 'insula habet,' 'resistere equos,' are quite exceptional. In the final syllable of the verse Elision is unknown.

(7) An apparent, not a real, exception to what is said must be noted. We often see est at the end or in other parts of a verse, where Elision would be inadmissible: 'dolori est,' 'laborum est,' 'meo est,' 'sua est,' and the like. Here est is enclitic, and we ought to write, or at least pronounce, dolorist, laborumst, meost, suast. Also es sometimes is an enclitic in the same way.

Virgil, moved perhaps by his love of the older poets, frequently elides long vowels, but generally in the first half of the verse or in the middle of the fourth foot; not at the very beginning of the line: 'Si ad vitulam spectes,' in one of his earliest Eclogues, being a singular exception.

But between Virgil and Ovid a great change was going on: the latter has hardly one elision of a long vowel for ten of Virgil's: his elisions too of syllables in **m** are much rarer. The most careful poets, such as Martial, follow Ovid; though Virgil's authority had weight with some of the later Epic poets. As an illustration of what is said, it is to be noted that Horace, in the Fourth book of his Odes, only once elides a long syllable: 'Quod spiro et placeo;' and even here the **o** may have become doubtful, though spondaic words did not so soon begin to shorten the final. Horace, however, freely elides here syllables in **m**.

A. Exceptions to the law of Elision, forming Hiatus.　See
§ **12.** xxxi. p. 52.

(*a*) The monosyllabic interjections ā, ō, heu, for manifest reasons are not elided by the dactylic poets.　Ovid once has
the Greek Interjection **ai ai** unelided; once, too, he
writes: 'Et bis ĭō Arethusa vocavit ĭō Arethusa,' for a
peculiar effect, and Catullus leaves ĭō unelided in his
Epithalamium.　Others do not allow a vowel to follow ĭō.

(*b*) Sometimes a long vowel is left unelided and long in the
arsis of a foot.　Virgil employs this license more than
others, clearly in imitation of the Greeks ; but there is not
more than one instance to several hundred verses. 'Stant
et iuniperī et castaneā̆e hirsutae' gives two in one verse.
Often it occurs in Greek words ; sometimes for poetical
effect: 'Ter sunt conatī imponere Pēlĭŏ Ossam;' 'Si
pereō, hominum manibus.'　Once and once only he leaves
a syllable thus long, in the thesis of the foot: 'Glaucō et
Panopeae ĕt Inoo Melicertae:' a manifest Greek rhythm,
as in Homer a vowel is very often thus left long in the
thesis of the first foot.

Ovid keeps an unelided vowel more rarely than Virgil, and
in deference to him.　Many poets abstain from it altogether: Horace has it very rarely: 'capitī ĭnhŭmato.'
'Daedaleō ōcior' is not genuine ; for the **ō** would then
remain long in thesis.

This license is very rare in middle syllables in **m**, and most
of the examples admit of easy correction, as in Propertius,
'O me felicēm, o nox mihi candida' (read nox o).

(*c*) In thesis, too, a long vowel is sometimes shortened before
a short vowel, but generally in the case of Iambic or
Cretic words, which would hardly admit of elision, many
of them being Greek or Proper Names.　It is sometimes
united with the other kind of hiatus in the same line ; see
some of the examples given above ; and Virgil's 'Hy̆lā
Hy̆lă omne sonaret.'　Virgil has 'vălē vălĕ inquit,' 'In-
sŭlăe Ĭonio,' &c.; Lucretius, 'Remigī oblitae,' 'etesiā̆e
esse ;' Ennius has, 'Scipiŏ invicte ;' Cicero, 'etesiā̆e in
vada,' who in his 'Orator' speaks of it as a license very
rare in Latin, common in Greek.

Such license is scarcely allowable in polysyllables in **m**,
though Ennius has 'Dum quidĕm unus homo,' 'militŭm
octo,' and Lucilius 'sordidŭm omne.'　Instances given to
Lucretius have no foundation.

Virgil's two examples of such a hiatus with a short syllable,
'Addam cerea prună hŏnos erit,' and 'patuit dĕă Ĭlle
ubi,' may perhaps be defended by the pause, but are
almost unparalleled ; for the 'mălĕ ōminatis' assigned
by some to Horace, and the 'mălĕ, o miselle passer'
given by others to Catullus, are impossible.

(*d*) Long monosyllables and those in **m** are sometimes shortened in thesis before a short vowel: Virgil has 'quĭ

ămant,' 'tŏ ămice,' 'ŏ Ălexi ;' Horace 'mŏ ămas,' 'nŭm
ădest.' Lucretius has eleven instances of this license;
which is frequent in the comic poets, but there only in
arsis.

(*e*) A license, resembling that of hiatus, is the lengthening of a
short syllable ending in a consonant before a vowel.
Virgil has many examples, in imitation of Homer and
Ennius, the license often taking place in or before a
Greek word : 'Pectoribūs ĭnhians,' 'Altius ingreditūr et,'
'fultūs hўăcintho.' Lucretius has only two examples,
'fulgēt āuro,' 'scirēt ănĭmoque ;' Catullus three, all
coming before the Greek word hymenaeus.

(*f*) Virgil, if his text is right, thus lengthens a short syllable
ending in a vowel : 'graviā sectoque elephanto ;' but
'animā ātque istius inscia culpae,' where there would be
hiatus also, is condemned by all sound critics, as well as
'supervacuā āut' in Juvenal.

(*g*) Virgil, however, has one singular license : sixteen times he
lengthens que in arsis, though que is one of the shortest
syllables in the language and eminently susceptible of
elision; and he has induced hardly any one else to follow
his example. But, in fifteen of the sixteen cases, que is
in the arsis of the second foot, as 'Terraequē tractusque ;'
once in the arsis of the fifth, 'Noemonaquē Prўtănimque,'
with Greek words. Clearly it is a mere imitation of
Homer's lengthening of τε in the second and fifth foot.
In fourteen of the cases, too, the next word begins with a
double consonant.[1]

B. Having discussed the laws of Quantity generally,
we proceed to apply them to the chief kinds of Verse
employed by the Latin poets, which are all borrowed
from the Greeks.

The poets, however, with whom we need concern ourselves, have
with great tact confined themselves to a few of the simpler kinds of
verse, discarding the more complicated feet, rhythms, and verses, as
unsuitable to their language. Those, however, which they have
selected, they have adapted with great skill to all its peculiarities.

I. Verse and Metre.

1. A Verse (versus, *line*) is composed of a certain number of
Feet.

A Foot (pes) contains a certain number of morae, three at
least.

---

[1] In all the above instances a purely short syllable is artificially lengthened. Virgil
employs this license, so far as we know, much more than his predecessors. It is not,
therefore, a reminiscence of the time when such syllables were long: once on a time
perhaps every final in the language was long. It is manifestly an imitation of Greek
rhythm. When a syllable in Latin is really doubtful, it is used indifferently long or short
in all places of the verse : comp. Virgil's 'Ante ŏră pătris pātrem qui obtruncat ad aras ;'
Martial's 'Captŏ tŭam, pudet heu, sed captŏ, Pontice, cenam.' Here lengthening as
well as shortening takes place in thesis.

Each simple Foot has two parts, one of which is said to have the ictus upon it, and is called arsis (marked $\acute{\smile}$); the other part is called thesis. The relation of these parts to one another determines the nature of the Foot, and thereby of the Verse.

2. There are, properly speaking, only four distinct Feet with which we need concern ourselves. Two of these have the arsis and thesis equal, each consisting of two morae. Two have them unequal, the arsis containing two, the thesis one mora.

The first two are,

    1. Dactylus . . . . . . $-\smile\smile$ . . .   lītŏră.
    2. Anapaestus . . . . $\smile\smile-$ . . .   pătŭlāē.

The last two are,

    3. Trochaeus (or Choreus) $-\smile$ . . .   ārmă.
    4. Iambus . . . . . . $\smile-$ . . .   cănō.

These are the genuine Feet ; but for the Dactyl often appears in every kind of Dactylic verse.

Also
    5. Spondeus . . . . . . $--$ . . .   fātō.

    6. Tribrachys . . . . $\smile\smile\smile$ . . .   tĕmĕrĕ

can take the place of either the Iambus or the Trochee.

Therefore the Spondee and the Tribrach are representative Feet.[1]

In most kinds of Trochaic and Iambic verse, a Spondee may be used for the Trochee or Iambus in certain parts of the verse; and sometimes it may be represented by an Anapaest or a Dactyl.

In Dactylic and Trochaic verse the arsis is on the first part of each foot: lítora, árma. In Anapaestic and Iambic on the last: patulaé, canó.

The arsis therefore falls on a long syllable; in regular Dactylic verse invariably. When, however, a Dactyl is used for an Anapaest, the arsis falls on the first short syllable, litóra: when a Tribrach or Anapaest takes the place of a Trochee, the arsis is on the first syllable, témere, pátulae; when a Tribrach or Dactyl is used for an Iambus, the arsis is on the second syllable, temére.[2]

II. Verses.

1. The Dactylic Hexameter occupies as large a space in Latin poetry as all other Verses together, and is of more *relative* importance than the Homeric Hexameter is in Greek.

---

[1] In Anapaestic verses both the Spondee and the Dactyl may stand for the Anapaest.
[2] A full list of (so-called) Feet is subjoined for reference.

(a) Of two Syllables—

$\smile\smile$ Pyrrhichius: pătĕr	$-\smile$ Trochaeus: vīdĭt
$\smile-$ Iambus: ămānt	$--$ Spondeus: lātōs

(b) Of three Syllables.

$\smile\smile\smile$ Tribrachys: rĕgĕrĕ	$\smile--$ Amphibrachys: lătīnŭs
$\smile\smile-$ Anapaestus: ănĭmōs	$\smile--$ Bacchius: rĕgēbānt
$-\smile\smile$ Dactylus: cōrpŏră	$--\smile$ Palimbacchius: rēxīssĕ
$-\smile-$ Creticus: dīxĕrānt	$---$ Molossus: dīcēbās

This famous Verse, as well as the Elegiac couplet, was first adapted from the Greek by Ennius, who died B.C. 169 ; was gradually improved, until it attained an admirable perfection in the hands of Virgil, Ovid, and others ; and continued for many centuries to be the favourite form, until the total extinction of the old classical world. It may be defined as a Dactylic Hexameter Catalectic (catalecticus in disyllabum), the last Dactyl losing its final syllable, It consisted therefore of five Dactyls and a Trochee.

But as the final syllable of a Verse (except when connected closely by Synaphea [1] with the following Verse, as in the Anapaestic system and the Glyconic of Catullus) was indifferently long or short, the final Trochee might always be a Spondee. And indeed, while in Greek the last syllable is indifferent, in all the most careful Latin writers it is much oftener long than short. For Ennius, followed by the rest, seems to have thought the last Foot a real Spondee, and, from mistaking Homer, to have even introduced occasional Hypermetrical Verses. In this he has been followed by Virgil and most Latins, though to Homer this licence is unknown. In him we feel that the last Foot is a Trochee or curtailed Dactyl ; while the best Latin Verse lets us see that in the writer's mind the last Foot was rather a genuine Spondee.

Of the five Dactyls which remain, the fifth must, as a rule, always remain a Dactyl, probably to keep in view the Dactylic nature of the Verse. The first four may be indifferently Dactyls or Spondees ; and, contrary to the rule in Greek, in Latin the Spondees are somewhat the more numerous, owing perhaps to the character of the language.

Sometimes not only the older poets, but, for poetical effect, Virgil and, in imitation of him, Ovid and others have a Spondee in the fifth foot ; but then (to give weight to the exceptional rhythm) the two last feet are generally contained in a single word, and the fourth foot is in most cases a Dactyl. Sometimes a purely Greek rhythm, the words being often Greek, is introduced ; in which cases a Spondee now and then appears in the fourth foot. These three instances from Virgil will illustrate what is meant :

'Cara deum suboles, magnum Iovis incrementum.'
'Lamentis gemituque et femineo ululatu.'
'Nereidum matri et Neptuno Aegaeo.'

(c) Of four Syllables (compound)—

˘ ˘ ˘ ˘ Proceleusmaticus : hŏmĭnĭbŭs	— ˘ — ˘ Ditrocheus : cōndĭdīssĕ
— ˘ ˘ ˘ Paeon Primus : cōndĭdĭmŭs	— ˘ ˘ — Choriambus : ōppŏsĭtīs
˘ — ˘ ˘ Paeon Secundus : ămābĭmŭs	˘ — — ˘ Antispastus : rĕgēbāmŭr
˘ ˘ — ˘ Paeon Tertius : nĕmŏrālĭs	˘ — — — Epitritus Primus : ămāvīstī
˘ ˘ ˘ — Paeon Quartus : rĕgĭmĭnī	— ˘ — — Epitritus Secundus : aūdĭēbās
˘ ˘ — — Ionicus a Minore : mĕtŭēntēs	— — ˘ — Epitritus Tertius : aūdīvĕrānt
— — ˘ ˘ Ionicus a Majore : tērrēbĭmŭs	— — — ˘ Epitritus Quartus : rēxīssēmŭs
˘ — ˘ — Diiambus : prŏtērvĭtās	— — — — Dispondeus : sūspēxērūnt

The Pyrrhich is not properly a Foot. The Trochee is also called Choreus, the Cretic Amphimacer : this has a second arsis. The Ionic a Minore is used by Horace and Catullus. The Proseleusmatic is occasionally put for its equivalent Spondee or Anapaest by the old scenic poets, and even by Seneca.

[1] Synaphea (συνάπτειν) is said to exist in any system of Verses, when the last syllable of each verse is influenced by the first syllable of the following verse, as it would be if the two words stood in one and the same verse.

The two following :

> 'Cum patribus populoque, penatibus et magnis dïs.'
> 'Cum sociis gnatoque, penatibus et magnis dis,'

are reminiscences of Ennius.

These Versus σπονδειάζοντες are proportionally more frequent in Catullus from imitation of the Alexandrine poets.

In the fragments of Ennius we find one or two verses without a single Dactyl. The only instance in later writers seems to be one in Catullus :

> 'Si te lenirem nobis neu conarere.'

But to make a verse it is not enough to place side by side six feet of the kind mentioned ; as in these verses of Ennius : **260 Caesura.**

> 'Poste recumbite vestraque pectora pellite tonsis.'
> 'Sparsis hastis longis campus splendet et horret.'

Both verses are rude attempts to make the sound point the sense ; but we might apply to them the 'horret et alget,' which Lucilius jocularly proposed for the end of the second.

For the beauty and harmony of a verse CAESURA is necessary.

(1) CAESURA is the technical term for the law that in some part or parts of the verse the end of a word must coincide with the middle of a foot.[1]

---

[1] Explanation may here be given of various technical terms.

A. Hemimeris (ἡμίμερις) means ½.

Hence one foot and a half (3⁄2) is called Trihemimeris :

two feet	,,	(4⁄2)	,,	Penthemimeris ;
three	,,	(6⁄2)	,,	Hephthemimeris ;
four	,,	(8⁄2)	,,	Ennehemimeris.

Hence :

(a) Caesura after 1½ feet is called Trihemimeral ;
(b)   ,,   ,, 2½ ,,   ,,   Penthemimeral ;
(c)   ,,   ,, 3½ ,,   ,,   Hephthemimeral :
(d)   ,,   ,, 4½ ,,   ,,   Ennehemimeral ;

Examples :

	a		b	c	d	
1. Fúdit equúm	magnó	tellús	percússa	tridénti.—Verg.
2. Aut ámite	lévi	rára	téndit	rétia.—Hor.

In 1 (a Dactylic Hexameter) the caesuras a, b, c, being after an arsis, are *strong* ; but d, being after a thesis, is *weak*.

In 2 (an Iambic Trimeter) all the caesuras are after thesis, and therefore *weak*.

In contradistinction to Caesura (which is the coincidence of the close of a word with the *middle* of a foot) the coincidence of the close of a word with the *close* of a foot may be called 'Dialysis :'

> Lumina | labentem caelo quae | ducitis | annum.

B. Metre (μέτρον, *measure*) is used in two senses.

I. Metre, in the first place, means the verse or system of verses used by a poet in any composition (Heroic, Elegiac, Alcaic, Sapphic Metre).

(a) A Metre which contains only one kind of verse is called Monocolum ;

,,	,,	two kinds	,,	,,	Dicolum ;
,,	,,	three	,,	,,	Tricolum.

(from μόνος, *single* ; κῶλον, *member*).

(b) When two kinds of verse alternate, they form Distichum (from δίς, *twice* ; στίξ, *row*), a Distich or couplet.

(2) The best and most common caesura in the Dactylic Hexameter is the penthemimeral or semiquinarian, where the coincidence takes place after two feet and a half, or five half-feet:

> Tityre tu patulae | recubans sub tegmine fagi.

The caesura in question has place after p a t u l a e, though the verse has also two subordinate cæsuras, after t u and r e c u b a n s.

When recurrence takes place after four verses, these form Tetrastichum, a Tetrastich (stanza).

(c) Thus the Dactylic Hexameter (Heroic), Iambic Trimeter, Trochaic Tetrameter, and others, are found as Metra Monocola.
The Elegiac Metre and many others are Dicola Disticha.
The Sapphic and some others are Dicola Tetrasticha.
The Alcaic is Tricolum Tetrastichum.

II. Metre, in the second place, is used to express a given portion of a Verse in some Rhythms: as the Dactylic, the Trochaic, the Iambic, and the Anapaestic.

(a) In a Dactylic Verse, one foot constitutes a Metre.
In Trochaic, Iambic, and Anapaestic Rhythms two feet (διποδία) constitute a Metre.

(b) A Verse comprised in a single Metre is called Monometer; in two, Dimeter; in three, Trimeter; in four, Tetrameter; in five, Pentameter; in six, Hexameter.

(c) Wanting one syllable to complete its metres a Verse is called Catalectic (καταληκτικός); in syllabam, if the incomplete foot retains one syllable; in disyllabum, if it retains two.
Wanting two syllables, Brachycatalectic (βραχυκατάληκτος):
Having a syllable above its metres, Hypercatalectic (ὑπερκατάληκτος):
Having its metres complete, Acatalectic (ἀκατάληκτος).

(d) A Verse may also be called according to the number of feet: Binarius (2), as the Adonian; Ternarius (3), as the Pherecratean; Quaternarius (4), as the Trochaic or Iambic Dimeter: Senarius (6), as the Dactylic Hexameter or the Iambic Trimeter; Septenarius (7), as the Trochaic Tetrameter Catalecticus; Octonarius (8), as the Trochaic Tetrameter Acat. of the scenic poets.

(2) Or a Verse may be called according to the number of its syllables, as Phalaecius Hendecasyllabus (11). So the Alcaic Strophe consists of two Alcaic Hendecasyllabi (11), one Alcaic Enneasyllabus (9), and one Alcaic Decasyllabus (10).

C. (a) A syllable at the beginning of a Verse before the just Rhythm is called Anacrusis (ἀνάκρουσις, back-stroke): as (according to one mode of scansion),

> O | magna Carthago probrosis.

(b) Two syllables so preceding the just Rhythm are called a Base, which may be trochaic:

> Lūte | umve papaver;

or spondaic:

> Dūrăm | difficilis mane.

(c) A double Base is trochee+spondee, as in the Sapphic Verse:

> Illĕ mĭ pār | esse deo videtur.

This may have Anacrusis before it, as in the Alcaic Hendecasyllable:

> Mŏrs | ĕt fŭgacĕm | persequitur virum.

D. (a) A Verse is called Asynartete (ἀσυνάρτητος) which is really composed of two different verses welded, as it were, together:

> Tu vina Torquato move ‖ consule pressa meo.

(b) A Verse which has one syllable more than its regular constitution, elided before a vowel at the beginning of the next verse, is Hypermetrical (Hypermeter):

> Sors exitura et nos in aetern | um
> Exitium impositura cumbae.

This caesura, however, is so powerful that it is alone sufficient for a perfectly harmonious verse :

> Illius immensae | ruperunt horrea messes.

Or the verse may equally have two or three caesuras, as in the one quoted, and

> Silvestrem | tenui | Musam | meditaris avena.

Caesura after the first half-foot seems to have no force ; and 'Quid faciat laetas segetes' seems equivalent to 'Conficiat laetas segetes.'

However, there is a weak trochaic caesura, after the trochee or second syllable of the dactyl ; so that a verse may in a way have five caesuras :

> Una | salus | victis | nullam | sperare | salutem.

But in all these instances the penthemimeral is the one important caesura. As a quite exceptional rhythm, we might find 'viam | vi,' for instance, instead of 'salutem,' which would give one more caesura. This verse of Lucretius :

> Augescunt | aliae | gentes | aliae | minuuntur,

in which are four strong caesuras, is faulty. See (11), p. 530.

(3) But, to avoid monotony, the best poets seek variety of rhythm by other caesuras. Next in power to the penthemimeral is the hephthemimeral or semiseptenarian caesura, coming, that is, after three and a half feet, or seven half-feet. But, to give a proper verse, this caesura must be combined with one or more others. In this verse,

> Quid faciat | laetas | segetes | quo sidere terram,

it may be said the principal pause is at the hephthemimeris. But the verse has its character really determined by the penthemimeral caesura.

(4) When the latter is absent, the next best form is obtained by uniting with the hephthemimeral caesura the trihemimeral, in the middle of the second foot, and also the weak caesura which falls between the two short syllables of a dactyl in the third foot :

> Formosam | resonare | doces | Amaryllida silvas.

(5) Less perfect, though coming perhaps next to the above, is that form which has only the trihemimeral and hephthemimeral :

> Despiciens | mare velivolum | terrasque iacentes.

(6) It is less common to find the caesura at the third trochee together with only the trihemimeral ; though sometimes a pleasing effect is thus produced ; as in this verse :

> Praecipitat | suadentque | cadentia sidera somnos ;

yet in Greek this is perhaps the normal type of the Hexameter.

(7) The caesura at the third trochee by itself is still rarer and is usually intended for poetical effect :

> Aequora concussitque | micantia sidera mundus.
> Falleret indeprensus | et inremeabilis error.

M M

(8) This caesura, preceded by one at the second trochee, produces an unpleasant rhythm :

O crudelis | Alexi | nihil mea carmina curas ;

unless it is designed for effect :

Una Eurusque | Notusque|ruunt creberque procellis

and even Horace's familiar style will not reconcile us to

Dignum mente | domoque | legentis | honesta | Neronis.

But the alternation of the trochaic with the stronger caesuras is often pleasing :

Quantus | Athos | aut quantus | Eryx | aut ipse | coruscis :
Marsa | manus | Paeligna | cohors | Vestina | virum | vis.

(9) Sometimes, but rarely, the preposition beginning a compound word serves for a quasicaesura ; as in this verse of Horace,

Vestrum praetor, is intestabilis et sacer esto.

Virgil, or Lucretius, would mask the harshness by elision :

Conplerunt, | magno indignantur murmure clausi :

and thus in Virgil's

Magnanimi | Iovis ingratum ascendere cubile,

the main caesura is hephthemimeral not penthemimeral ; while in both verses the rhythm is helped by the trihemimeris.

(10) The effect of Elision generally on the caesuras and rhythm of a verse, as was said above, is not easy to determine. It seems clear that the elided syllable did not disappear altogether, and that the rhythm of such a verse as this for example :

Monstrum | horrendum | informe | ingens | cui lumen | ademptum :

was not identical with

Hic | vertex | nobis | semper | sublimis | at illum.

The elisions, which in this case were designed for effect, must have had some intermediate influence.

(11) The close of the verse should have a free open movement, in contrast, as it were, to the involution caused by the caesuras in the middle of the verse. Good Latin verse indeed exhibits only two main types of rhythm here : 1. where the fifth dactyl is wholly contained in one word and ends with that word : 'sidere terram,' 'adiungere vites ;' 2. where caesura takes place between the two short syllables ; 'cultus | habendo,' 'primus | ab oris.'

The verse, as a rule, is faulty, when caesura takes place in the middle of the dactyl ; as 'aliae | minuuntur' in the verse quoted above from Lucretius ; unless the dactyl contains two entire words, as 'ac tua nautae' in Virgil. Lucretius and the older writers often violate this law ; Virgil very seldom, and then with his usual skill for the sake of effect :

Ne saturare fimo pingui pudeat | sola neve.
Quam pius Aeneas et quam magni | Phryges et quam.

As this rhythm is much more frequent in Greek, Virgil and Ovid are fond of using it with Greek words, like h y m e n a e u s, h y a c i n-t h u s.

(12) The last foot should be contained in one 'word; though occasionally it may consist of two monosyllables, as in the line just quoted. Here again artists like Virgil use exceptional cadences like 'procumbit humi bos,' 'praeruptus aquae mons,' 'atque hominum rex,' to produce exceptional effects.

(13) Lucretius often comprises the two last feet in one word, like principiorum, materiai; Virgil and Ovid very rarely, and then always for a special purpose, as 'perfractaque quadrupedantum;' or with Greek words in imitation of the Greeks. Elisions in this part of the verse should be of the easiest kinds: ĕ or ĭ: ergo age in the fifth foot has its special excuse. Virgil has two or three endings like 'mentem animumque,' 'hoc animo hauri,' which strike by their rarity and are perhaps in compliment to Lucretius. Elisions within the sixth foot are still rarer: Virgil elides ĕ in 'huc turbidus atque huc,' 'hinc comminus atque hinc:' Horace in his *satires* ventures to say, 'iugera centum an.' As shewn above, est at the end of a verse makes no elision.

(14) Hypermetrical verses were introduced by Ennius, probably, as was said above, from his misapprehending Homer. A supernumerary syllable at the end of one verse is supposed to be elided by a vowel at the beginning of the next, sometimes even when a full stop intervenes. Lucretius has only one instance, 'concurrere deber|e:' Catullus only one or two. Virgil has more of them: que is generally the superfluous syllable, and a long syllable precedes. But if his MSS. are to be trusted, he has these two endings: 'vivaque sulpur|a,' 'arbutus horrid|a.'

(15) The part also of the verse which precedes the caesura must be properly connected with the rest. If there is no trihemimeral caesura, the end of the second foot should not coincide with the end of a word. Exceptions to this rule are exceedingly rare in Virgil; still rarer in Ovid. In the former we find, 'Scilicet omnibus est labor impendendus.' 'Armentarius Afer.' 'Sed tu desine velle.' 'Spargens umida mella.' 'Per conubia nostra:' the second foot being always a dactyl. Lucretius has very many instance s, and sometimes a spondee in the second foot, if a monosyllable follow: 'Sive voluptas est.' Such a commencement as 'Et quaecumque coloribu' sint,' is also very exceptional. Once he makes sound echo sense by a most exceptional but felicitous rhythm: 'Et membratim vitalem deperdere sensum.' Horace, aiming at a conversational style, has a few negligent rhythms.

2. The ELEGIAC DISTICH[1] (Dactylic Hexameter with so-called Pentameter) comes next in importance. Borrowed by Ennius from the Greeks, it passed to Catullus, Gallus, Tibullus and Propertius, and attained its final polish in the hands of Ovid: he and the two last mentioned being always looked upon as its greatest masters.

261
The
Elegiac
Distich.

---

[1] Rhythm of the Elegiac Distich :

(1) Dactylic Hexameter.

(2) $- \cup \cup \,|\, - \cup \cup \,|\, -\|\, - \cup \cup \,|\, - \cup \cup \,|\, -$

(1) The Elegiac Hexameter is subject to the same laws as the Heroic. But Ovid indulges in very few licences, fewer even than in his own Heroic, though there he is stricter than Virgil. He seldom deviates from one or other of the two best types of caesura; and abstains from harsh elisions. Catullus' Elegiacs, on the other hand, are much harsher in their elisions than his Heroics are.

(2) The second verse of the couplet, called the Pentameter from a strange fancy of the ancient grammarians, has been brought by Ovid and others under much stricter rules than the Greek verse from which it is derived. It consists of two Dactylic Penthemimers, which must be kept quite distinct, and the sentence, or at least a distinct clause, must close with the couplet.[1]

The first Penthemimer corresponds precisely with that of a Hexameter, ending with a distinct, penthemimeral caesura, never followed by an elision; for a verse like Propertius's 'Quaerere: non impune illa rogata venit,' never occurs in Ovid.

The second of the two Penthemimers gives the Latin Elegiac its peculiar character. Like the Greek, the two full feet must be dactyls; but the Latin, unlike the Greek verse, ought to end with an Iambic word.[2] This restricts the rhythm to very few types, which do not differ essentially in their general effect. The rest of the penthemimer must either be contained in one word, like delituisset; excutiatque; or in two: ut videare; arte regendus; praebuit ille (excutiat sit would be inadmissible); or in three: tu mihi sola; quo sit amanda; quisquis es, adde; ille vel alter; or in four: as, mens sit et apta.

Ovid's Elisions in this part of the verse are the easiest and slightest, as of ĕ or ĭ; if ă, only before another **a**. They have place too only in the middle of the first dactyl, or else between its two short syllables. Elision between the two dactyls is very rare, except in the case of quĕ. In the second dactyl it is very exceptional, as 'insula habet,' 'resistere equos.' At the end it is utterly inadmissible, except before the enclitic est (es) spoken of above. Ovid in this part of the verse never elides any long or even doubtful syllable. With him, therefore, Ennius's 'me aequiparare queat,' or Propertius' 'si altera talis erit,' would not be possible. Catullus, however, has very harsh elisions in this half of the verse, especially in his short vituperative Elegiacs: 'me pretio atque malo;' even 'ploxemi habet veteris.'

As the Romans definitively accepted the strict Ovidian type for the Elegiac, we are bound to do the same. It commends itself, however, by its own intrinsic merits, its marvellous ease and

---

[1] Very rarely the Subject is in one distich, and the Verb in the next: as,

> Languor et immodici nullo sub vindice somni
> Aleaque et multo tempora quassa mero
> Eripiunt omnis animo sine vulnere nervos, Ov.

[2] In Versus Elegiacus a final trisyllable is rare and ungraceful: a final word of four or five syllables is less ungraceful, but rare in Ovid: as,

> Maxima de nihilo nascitur historia, Prop.
> Lis est cum forma magna pudicitiae, Ov.

The final disyllable should be a Verb, Substantive, or Pronoun; rarely an Adverb; more rarely still an Adjective or Participle, and only when a strong emphasis falls on it:

> Hoc faciet positae te mihi, terra, levem, Ov.

buoyancy. Propertius in his earlier poems has a very distinct style of his own : in his later, influenced doubtless by the example of his younger friend, he approaches much nearer to the Ovidian movement.

3. Lyric Metres.

(1) The Lyric poetry of the Romans is far less in amount than their Heroic and Elegiac. It is of much less importance also than that of the Greeks. The same is true of their Iambic and Trochaic poetry, if we omit the old scenic verse. The peculiar excellence, however, of the two chief representatives of these styles, Catullus and Horace, gives to them an important rank in Latin literature.

Catullus and Horace saw that Latin was unfitted for the rich and complicated variety of choral rhythm, so brilliantly worked out by the Greeks, and confined themselves to the simpler and more manageable melodies of Alcaeus and Sappho, and, in the case of Catullus, of the Alexandrine school. They subjected even these to stricter laws, in conformity with the genius of their language, as had been done by Virgil, Ovid, and others in the metres cultivated by them. They also both made use of Iambic measures, but in different ways.

Horace and Catullus are the only important models in these styles, with two exceptions. Each had a follower ; Catullus a very brilliant one in Martial, who has largely employed in his Epigrams the Phalaecian Hendecasyllable and the Iambic Scazon, increasing the strictness of their laws on principles of metre akin to those of Ovid. Seneca in his numerous choruses copies the lyrical measures of Horace, especially Asclepiads and Sapphics, but with little skill and often in a very hybrid fashion.

(2) Though it is so much used by the old scenic writers, and was always the favourite measure in popular chants, and seems so well adapted to the genius of the language, and is so common in Greek, the Trochaic Tetrameter Catalectic is hardly found in the extant learned poets. Seneca has very few of them: the ' Pervigilium Veneris,' though brightly burnished, is of the copper age. Anapaests, too, found little favour, if we except Seneca, Plautus, the old Tragic fragments and those of Lucilius.

(3) Both Horace and Catullus must have tried many metres, before they finally decided which were best adapted to their genius and purpose; but such they seem to have found at last. The Odes of Horace are 104 in number: of these, ninety-seven are Alcaic, Sapphic, or Asclepiad; of which last he employs five different systems.

But his Epodes preceded his Odes in time; and here the Iambic is the prevailing type. Only one, however, the 17th and last, is in continuous Trimeter Iambics. Horace has here imitated strictly the Greek Trimeter. The caesuras are very precise: generally the penthemimeral, now and then the hephthemimeral. Of resolved feet he admits the dactyl in the first, and the tribrach in any of the next three places. It is remarkable, too, that he observes the law of the Greek tragic pause in the fifth, with one exception only in the eighty-one verses, in which the rhythm is designed for a peculiar effect; in which, too, elision disguises the violation :

Alítibus atque cánibus homicídam Hectorem.

He must have felt, however, that the regular Greek trimeter was not effective, alone and unrelieved; and has not repeated the experiment.

(4) Catullus, too, with his nice tact, must have felt the same. He has but one poem (52), of four lines, in ordinary trimeters, two of the four being pure Iambics. Like Horace, he would nòt have liked to recall the old scenic verse with its spondees, effective in its way, but to them inartistic. He has therefore obviated the monotony by two opposite methods.

Two of his best poems, the 4th and 29th, are in pure Iambics, to which his taste and skill give lightness, force, and variety.

In contrast to this, eight of his poems are in the Scazon, or limping Trimeter (Choliambus) of Hipponax:

$$\bar{\smile}\, \acute{\smile}\, \smile\, \_\, \bar{\smile}\, \acute{\smile}\, \smile\, \_\, \smile\, \acute{}\, \_\, \_$$

Misér Catulle | désinas inéptire,
Et quód vides perísse | perditúm ducas.

The peculiar movement produced by the inversion of rhythm at the end is very effective. The caesura is indifferently penthemimeral or hephthemimeral, but always one or other. He has a dactyl once in the first, once in the third place; but no other resolved feet. Martial after him uses the Scazon often and with equal success.

(5) To avoid the monotony of the continuous ordinary Trimeter, Horace has composed the first ten Epodes in Iambic couplets, this Trimeter alternating with a Dimeter, resolved feet being very rare. In the remaining six Epodes he has sought still further variety by coupling in five of them the regular Heroic with some other metre —in two (14, 15) with the Iambic Dimeter just spoken of; in one (16) with a pure Iambic Trimeter; in one (12) with a Dactylic Tetrameter Catalecticus in disyllabum, in which metre he has also composed two of his Odes (i. 7 and 28). In the fifth (13) he has joined the Heroic with an Asynartete verse, the Iambelegus, composed of a Dimeter Iambic followed by a Dactylic Penthemimer. In the remaining Epode (11) he has united a Trimeter Iambic with the reverse Asynartete, a Dactylic Penthemimer followed by an Iambic Dimeter.

264   Besides the above, he has single examples of five other metres in his Odes: namely i. 4; i. 8; ii. 18; iii. 12; iv. 7. The first contains a peculiar Verse (Dactylic Tetrameter going before three Trochees) alternating with an Iamb. Trim. Cat.: the second, a verse consisting of Dactyl and two Trochees alternating with Iamb. Trim. Cat.; the third, Trochaic Hephthemimer alternating with Iamb. Trim. Cat.; the fourth, a pure Ionic a Minore system; the fifth, Dactylic Hexameter alternating with Dactylic Penthemimer.

Most of the foregoing systems have technical names from their supposed inventors or chief cultivators. See Table of Metres.

(6) But all these seem to have·been but experiments, and he confined himself chiefly to three Lyric types of metre, one which was mainly Dactylic, one which joined this with the Trochaic movement, and a third which united the Dactylic, Iambic, and Trochaic rhythms.

(7) Of the first, or ASCLEPIAD, Horace employed five systems, each consisting of one or several kinds of the following verses.

1. The Glyconic:

Síc te díva poténs Cypri.

2. The Pherecratean:

Gráto Pýrrha sub ántro.

3. The Lesser Asclepiad:

Maécenás atavís | édite régibus.

4. The Greater Asclepiad:

Tú ne quaésierís | scíre nefás | quém mihi, quém tibi.

In all these four varieties, out of which he has composed 34 of his 104 Odes, Horace tenaciously keeps a Spondee for the base, with perhaps one exception, ' Ignīs Iliacas domos ;' whereas with the Greeks and with Catullus the Trochee is the typical base of the Glyconic verse. But in his one poem, written in the greater Asclepiad, Catullus also has a Spondaic base.

Horace too in both 3 and 4 is most tenacious of the penthemimeral caesura, as we have marked in our scheme ; not so Catullus and other Greeks. In the two apparent exceptions :

Dum flagrantia de|-torquet ad oscula :
Arcanique fides | prodiga per|-lucidior vitro :

the preposition gives a quasicaesura. He has but one real exception :

Non incendia Car|thaginis impiae,

occasioned perhaps by the proper name.

Out of these four kinds of verse he has composed five different Asclepiad systems :

1. The Lesser Asclepiad alone, as i. 1.

2. The Greater Asclepiad alone, as i. 11.

3. A stanza composed of three Lesser Asclepiad verses, followed by one Glyconic, as i. 6.

4. A couplet of alternate Glyconics and Lesser Asclepiads, as i. 3.

5. A stanza of which the first two lines are Lesser Asclepiads, the third a Pherecratean, in which the last syllable is always long; the fourth Glyconic ; as i. 5.

In two of these five systems the metre shews they are in stanzas of four verses. In the other three kinds, as in the Odes generally of Horace, the Odes are multiples of four, except in one Ode, written in the Lesser Asclepiad, iv. 8. But such divisions in the case of the uniform metres, and of those which run in couplets, is of no practical importance, as there is no necessary pause at the end of each fourth, any more than of the other verses.

Catullus has employed the Glyconic with great happiness in his long 'Epithalamium,' and in one other poem, the 34th. The stanza in the former consists of four Glyconics, followed by a Pherecratean:

$$\acute{\smile}\; \bar{\smile}\; \acute{\smile}\; \smile\; \smile\; \acute{\smile}\; \smile\; \_ \quad \text{(four times)}$$
$$\acute{\smile}\; \bar{\smile}\; \acute{\smile}\; \smile\; \smile\; \acute{\smile}\; \smile \quad \text{(once)}$$

in the latter, of three Glyconics followed by the Pherecratean. But his rhythm is nearer the Greek than is Horace's, as he prefers a Trochee for the base; and in one stanza the four lines are connected by synaphea, the last syllable of the Glyconic being always long, while that of the Pherecratean is doubtful; in the other stanza the first three and last two lines are similarly connected. The light Trochaic base, and the point given by the final long syllable together produce a beautiful and powerful metre, hypermetrical syllables sometimes suffering elision at the end of a line.

Horace's earlier Asclepiads seem to suffer from the number of weak short syllables at the end of verses; and to a feeling of this we refer the occurrence of such lines as these in the 4th book:

> Cur facunda parum decor|o (hypermetrical)
> Sed cur heu, Ligurine, cur;
> Lentum sollicitas ille virentis et
> Audivere Lyce di mea vota di

and even the Alcaic:

> Ne forte credas interitura quae.

266
Sapphic
Verses. (8) The SAPPHIC stanza, consisting of three Sapphic Hendecasyllables, followed by a Dactyl. Dim. Catal. in disyllabum (Versus Adonius):

$$\acute{\smile}\; \smile\; \smile\; \acute{\smile}\; \bar{\smile}$$
Rísit Apóllo.

In his first three books Horace rarely departs from the following rhythm in the Sapphic Hendecasyllable:

$$\acute{\smile}\; \smile\; \_\; \_\; \acute{\smile}\; |\; \smile\; \smile\; \acute{\smile}\; \smile\; \_\; \bar{\smile}$$
Iám satis terrís | nivis átque dirae,

differing in this exceedingly from Sappho. The monotony is increased by his always having a Spondee in the second foot. He seems himself at least to have felt the faultiness of his monotonous caesura, and in his fourth book and 'Carmen Saeculare' often substitutes the caesura at the third Trochee: as,

> Liberum munivit | iter daturus.

But the stiffness is thus increased and the monotony not much diminished.

He sometimes, like Sappho and Catullus, has hypermetrical verses; sometimes too, like them, he has no break between the third and fourth verse: as,

> Labitur ripa Iove non probante u-
> xorius amnis.

Catullus has two Sapphic Odes, one a very early poem, a translation of Sappho; the second written with reference to this, and, as it were, a defiant retractation of it. He is less regular in his rhythm than Horace, and three times has a Trochee in the second foot.

But he seems to have felt the futility of competing with Sappho, and has with brilliant success made a variation of the Sapphic his own, by adopting in forty out of fifty-nine of his Lyric and Iambic poems the Phalaecian Hendecasyllable, which differs from the Sapphic in this, that the Dactyl forms the second instead of the third foot. This difference, however, has enabled him to wield it with marvellous grace and at the same time freedom, as it has no regular caesura, which is apt in a short verse to cause monotony :

Quoi dono lepidum novum libellum
Arĭda modo pumice expolitum?
Mĕas esse aliquid putare nugas.

Martial has adopted it with equal success; but the first foot with him is always a Spondee ; and we learn from the elder Pliny that a Spondee in his time was alone admitted. In his 55th poem Catullus has tried the experiment of occasionally substituting a Spondee for the Dactyl, but the result is not happy.

(9) Horace's most successful stanza is that in which he has adapted to Latin forms the famous system called after Alcaeus. It consists of (I. 2) two Hendecasyllabic verses of this form, **267 Alcaic Stanza.**

Qui rore puro Castaliae lavit.

(3) an Enneasyllabic verse of this form,

Dumeta natalemque silvam.

completed by (4) an Alcaic Decasyllable :

Delius et Patareus Apollo.

This varied metre, combining Dactylic, Iambic, and Trochaic forms, has gained by the restrictions to which the poet has subjected it. In the three first verses of the stanza he has admitted an Iambus rarely in the first foot, and not at all in his 4th Book. The fifth syllable too of verses I, 2, which Alcaeus uses as doubtful, is always long, with one single exception :

Si non perirĕt immiserabilis.

In those verses the Penthemimeral Caesura is strictly observed, with only these two exceptions :

Mentemque lymphatam Mareotico.
Spectandus in certamine Martio ;

though more than once he has the quasicaesura after the Preposition of a compound word ; as,

Hostile aratrum ex|-ercitus insolens.

Verse 3. too gains stateliness and weight by rejecting the most usual Iambic movements ; thus,

Hunc Lesbio sacrare plectro

is the only instance of the second Iambus being contained in a word thus ending in an Iambus; and only in the earlier books does it ever end with a word of four syllables, like barbarorum. Its most normal rhythms are:

> Breunosque velocis et arcis.
> Commisit immanisque Raetos.
> Quantis fatigaret ruinis;

and next to these:

> Vexare turmas et frementem.

In the verse 'Non decoloravere caedes,' there is probably a pause after the preposition de.

This verse is sometimes hypermetrical: as, 'Cum pace delabentis Etruscum | In mare.'

In Verse 4 these seem the best rhythms:

> Vindelici didicere nuper.
> Alpibus impositas tremendis.
> Auspiciis pepulit secundis;

or modifications of these:

> Stravit humum sine clade victor.

268
Galliam-
bus.
The Galliambus of Catullus is worth considering from the celebrity of his sixty-third poem. Varro and others used this metre in poems now lost. Its nature, often misunderstood, is simple enough. We may take as its type an Ionic a minore Tetram. Cat. with an unvarying caesura at the end of the second foot:

$$\smile\smile\acute{-}\,\_\,\smile\smile\acute{-}\,\_\,|\,\smile\smile\acute{-}\,\_\,\smile\smile\acute{\underline{\smile}}$$

No whole verse of Catullus is of this primary form.

Of the first part an example is

> Et earum omnia adirem:

of the second,

'stadio et gymnasiis;' but Catullus probably wrote guminasiis.

As a rule, in each part what is called Anaclasis occurs, that is to say, the last long syllable of the first foot changes place with the first short syllable of the second foot; and the same occurs between the third and fourth feet: we then get this form:

$$\smile\smile\acute{-}\,\smile\acute{-}\,\smile\acute{-}\,\_\,|\,\smile\smile\acute{-}\,\smile\acute{-}\,\smile\acute{\underline{\smile}}$$

> Aliena quae petentes | velut exules loca.

This is the most common form for the first part; but usually in the second part a further change takes place: the second long syllable is resolved into two short ones; and we then get the regular type of the verse:

> Super alta vectus Attis | celeri ratĕ mǎria.

Occasional variations of this type occur.

> Tībīcĕn ŭbĭ canit Phryx | cūrvo gravĕ calamo,

gives in one verse three of these variations:

> Ibi marĭă vasta visens | lacrĭmantibus oculis,

gives the fourth.

TABLE OF CLASSICAL LATIN VERSES AND METRES.

269

I. SINGLE VERSES.

A. DACTYLIC RHYTHMS.

(1) Trimeter Catalecticus in Syllabam (Penthemimer) called Archilochius Minor:

$$-\,\smile\,\smile\,|\,-\,\smile\,\smile\,|\,-$$

Arbori|busque co|mae, Hor.

(2) Tetrameter Catalecticus in Disyllabum, called Alcmanius:

$$-\,\smile\,\smile\,|\,-\,\smile\,\smile\,|\,-\,\smile\,\smile\,|\,-\,\smile$$

Mobili|bus po|maria | rivis, Hor.

In the case of a Proper Name Horace has a Spondee in third foot:

Menso|rem cohi|bent, Ar|chyta.

(3) On the Hexameter and the Elegiac Pentameter. see §§ 259–261.

B. TROCHAIC RHYTHMS.

(1) Dimeter Catalecticus:

$$-\,\smile\,|\,'-\,\smile\,|\,-\,\smile\,|\,-$$

Non tra|bes Hy|metti|ae, Hor.

(2) The Tetrameter Catalectic or Septenarius was used by the Greek Tragic and Comic Poets; also by Plautus and Terence. The Latin Poem (of uncertain age and author) called Pervigilium Veneris, is a Monocolum in this metre; of which the following is the scheme:

Cras a|met qui | nunquam a|mavit ‖ quique a|mavit | cras a|met. Dialysis after the 4th foot is essential.

In Comedy the license of feet is vastly wider (see Note, p. 474); but a Trochee or its equivalent, a Tribrach, must precede the final syllable. Plautus also uses the Tetrameter Acatalectic or Octonarius with similar license, but always with final Trochee.

C. IAMBIC RHYTHMS.

(1) Dimeter Acatalectus:

Forti | seque|mur pec|tore, Hor.
Canidi|a tra|ctavit | dapes, Hor.

(2) Alcaicus Enneasyllabus : Iamb. Dim. Hyperc.,

$$\breve{u} - | \smile - | - - | \smile - \breve{u}$$

Periu|ra pu|gn|acis | Achivos, Hor.

Caesura after the 3rd syllable is required.　See § 267.

(3) (Trimeter Acatalectus, or Senarius, which sometimes consists of six Iambic feet (Hexapodia Iambica) :

Suis | et i|psa Ro|ma vi|ribus | ruit, Hor.
Gemel|le Cas|tor et | gemel|le Cas|toris, Catull.

But usually Spondees are admitted into the first, third, and fifth places ; a Tribrach may stand in any place but the last for an Iambus ; a Dactyl in the first place, and an Anapaest in the first (rarely in the fifth) for a Spondee :

Pater|na ru|ra bo|bus ex|ercet | suis, Hor.
Aliti|bus at|que cani|bus homi|cidam Hec|torem, Hor.
Pavidum|que lepo|rem et ad|venam | laqueo | gruem, Hor.

A penthemimeral or hephthemimeral caesura is necessary to the harmony of the Verse.　This Verse may form a Metrum Mono-colum, as Hor. *Epod.* 17.

Note. The Comic Poets, Plautus and Terence, admit Spondees, Dactyls, and Anapaests, in every place but the last, sometimes even Proceleusmatics ; with numerous other licenses.

The Iambic Trimeters of the fabulist Phaedrus resemble these, but take fewer feet of three syllables and fewer licenses.

(4) Scazon, or Choliambus ; which is an Iambic Trimeter with a Spondee in the sixth, and an Iambus in the fifth, place ; as,

Miser | Catul|le de|sinas | ine|ptire, Catull.

Used as a Metrum Monocolum, but not by Horace.　The cae-suras as in (3).

(5) Trimeter Catalecticus :

$$\underset{\smile}{\breve{\smile}} - | \smile - | \underset{\smile}{\breve{\smile}} - | \smile - | \smile \smile | \breve{u}$$

Mea | reni|det in | domo | lacu|nar, Hor.
Iunctae|que nym|phis Gra|tiae | decen|tes, Hor.

The penthemimeral caesura is essential.

(6) Versus Hipponacteus (Dimeter + Hephthemimer).

Depren|sa na|vis in | mari ‖ vesa|nien|te ven|to, Catull.

Dialysis after the Dimeter.　This verse forms a Metrum Mono-colum, not used by Horace.

D. IONIC RHYTHMS.

(1) Ionicus a minore Dimeter Acatalectus :

$$\smile \smile - - | \smile \smile - -$$

Patruae ver|bera linguae, Hor.

(2) Ionicus a minore Tetrameter Acatalectus :

$$\smile \smile - - | \smile \smile - - | \smile \smile - - | \smile \smile - -$$

Miserarum est | neque amori | dare ludum, | neque dulci, Hor.

(3) Versus Galliambus.　See § 266.

E. Mixed Rhythms.

1. **Logaoedic.** Logaoedic Rhythms are those in which Dactyls are followed by Trochees.[1] A Base often begins them, and sometimes a Choriambus is inserted.

(1) Adonius : Dactyl. Dim. Cat. in Disyll.

$$ - \smile \smile \mid - \smile $$

Risit A|pollo, Hor.

(2) Aristophaneus (Dactylus simplex dupliciter Trochaicus) :

$$ - \smile \smile \mid - \smile \mid - \smile $$

Lydia | dic per | omnis, Hor.

Dialysis after the Dactyl.

(3) Pherecrateus ; an Adonius with Base, which, in Horace, is Spondaic, in Catullus, chiefly Trochaic :

Base
$$ \genfrac{}{}{0pt}{}{- -}{- \smile} \mid - \smile \smile \mid - \smile $$

Vix du|rare ca|rinae, Hor.
Lute|umve pa|paver, Catull.

(4) Glyconeus ; the Base of which, in Horace, is Spondaic, in Catullus, usually Trochaic :

Base
$$ \genfrac{}{}{0pt}{}{- -}{- \smile} \mid - \smile \smile \mid - \smile - $$

Mater | saeva Cu|pidinum, Hor.
Tardat | ingenu|us pudor, Catull.

(5) Asclepiadeus Minor, the Base being Spondaic.

Base
$$ - - \mid - \smile \smile - \mid - \smile \smile \mid - \smile - $$

Maece|nas atavis‖edite | regibus, Hor.

Elision at Penthemimer is rare : as,

Audi|tam modere|re arbori¦bus fidem, Hor.

It is used as Metrum Monocolum (Asclepiadeum Primum).

(6) Asclepiadeus Maior, the Base being Spondaic :

Base
$$ - - \mid - \smile \smile - \| - \smile \smile - \| - \smile \smile \mid - \smile - $$

Nullam|Vare sacra | vite prius | severis | arborem, Hor.

Caesuras after 6th and 10th syllables. This is Metrum Monocolum.

(7) Alcaicus Decasyllabus :

$$ - \smile \smile \mid - \smile \quad \mid - \smile \mid - \smile $$

Nec vete|res agi|tantur | orni, Hor.

(8) Phalaecius Hendecasyllabus ; Metrum Monocolum, not used by Horace.

---

[1] As the last syllable of a verse is doubtful, a final Trochee can pass into a Spondee. In the Pherecrateans of Horace it always does so ; and in his verses generally a final long syllable is preferred.

Base
$$- - \mid - \smile \smile \mid - \smile \mid - \smile \mid - \breve{\upsilon}$$

Soles | occide|re et re|dire | possunt, Catull.

Sometimes an Iambus appears as Base, seldom a Trochee:
Mĭnister vetuli puer Falerni, Catull.
Arĭda modo pumice expolitum, Catull.

A Spondee is sometimes put for the Dactyl, but very inharmoniously.

(9) Archilochius Maior: Dactylic Tetrameter with Dactyl in fourth place, where is Dialysis, and three Trochees:

$$- \smile \smile \mid - \smile \smile \mid - \smile \smile \mid - \smile \smile \parallel - \smile \mid - \smile \mid - \breve{\upsilon}$$

Solvitur | acris hi|emps gra|ta vice ‖ veris|et Fa|voni, Hor.

(10) Sapphicus Minor, consisting of a Dactyl and two Trochees preceded by Trochee + Spondee (called by some a double Base):

$$- \smile - - \mid - \smile \smile \mid - \smile \mid - \breve{\upsilon}$$

Nota quae se|des fue|rat co|lumbis, Hor.

Sappho, the inventor of this verse, as also Catullus, often began with a double Trochee: but Horace always lengthens the fourth syllable.
The strong caesura after the fifth syllable is usual; occasionally the weak caesura is found after the sixth (short) syllable:

Non semel dicemus ‖ io triumphe, Hor.

One or other is essential to the harmony of the verse.

(11) Sapphicus Maior; which only differs from the last in having a Choriambus between the Spondee and Dactyl:

$$- \smile - - \mid - \smile \smile - \mid - \smile \smile \mid - \smile \mid -$$

Saepe trans fi|nem iaculo | nobilis | expe|dito, Hor.

(12) Versus Alcaicus Hendecasyllabus, in which an Iambic Penthemimer ($\breve{\upsilon} - \smile - -$) is followed by Dactyl and $- \smile \breve{\upsilon}$:

$$\breve{\upsilon} - \smile - - \mid - \smile \smile \mid - \smile -$$

Mors et fugacem ‖ persequi|tur virum, Hor.
Vides ut alta ‖ stet nive | candidum, Hor.

The first syllable is seldom short. The penthemimeral caesura is observed. Elision sometimes occurs there:

Regum timendo ‖ rum in proprios greges, Hor.

(13) Versus Priapeius of Catullus: Metrum Monocolum.

$$- \smile \mid - \smile \smile \mid - \smile - \parallel - \smile \mid - \smile \smile \mid - \breve{\upsilon}$$

O co|lonia|quae cupis‖ponte|ludere|longo,
Quendam | munici|pem meum ‖ de tu|o volo | ponte, Catull.

2. **Asynartete.**

(1) Iambelegus Archilochius : Iamb. Dim. Dactyl. Penthem.

$$\overset{\smile}{=} \mid \smile - \mid \overset{\smile}{=} \mid \smile - \| - \smile \smile \mid - \smile \smile \mid \overline{\smile}$$

Tu vi|na Tor|quato | move ‖ consule | pressa me|o, Hor.

(2) Elegiambus Archilochius, Dactyl. Penthem. Iamb. Dim.

$$- \smile \smile \mid - \smile \smile \mid - \| \overset{\smile}{=} \mid \smile - \mid \overset{\smile}{=} \mid \smile \overline{\smile}$$

Iussus ab|ire do|mum ‖ fere|bar in|certo | pede, Hor.

There is a Dialysis at the end of the Penthemimer.

Note a. The Anapaestic Rhythm is the converse of the Dactylic. It admits however Spondees and Dactyls ; in which the arsis falls on the second syllable. The most usual verse is the Dimeter, having a break after the second foot :

O va|ne pudor ‖ falsum|que decus.
Decies|nivibus‖canuit|Ide, Sen. Tr.

The Greek dramatic poets used this verse in systems ending with a Dimeter Catalectic, called Versus Paroemiacus ; but Seneca has not in this imitated them ; nor does he admit a Dactyl at the close of a line. A Monometer is sometimes introduced (in Greek always before the Paroemiacus), called a Base. In Anapaestic metre the last syllable of the Dimeter is not indifferent, and makes position with the succeeding verse (Synaphea).

Note b. The Saturnian Verse was an old Roman measure, not used in the best ages. The following is cited as its purest type :

Dabunt | malum | Metel|li ‖ Naevi|o po|etae.

But great license was taken in its form.

II. STROPHIC METRES.

a. DICOLA DISTICHA or DISTROPHA.

On the Elegiac Distich, see § 261.

(1) Metrum Hipponacteum.

Troch. Dim. Cat. + Iamb. Trim. Cat

Non ebur neque aureum
Mea renidet in domo lacunar, Hor. ii. 18.

(2) Metrum Iambicum Senarium Quaternarium.

Iamb. Trim. Acat. + Iamb. Dim. Acat.

Beatus ille qui procul negotiis
Ut prisca gens mortalium, Hor. *Epod.* 2.

(3) Metrum Archilochium Primum.

Dact. Hex. Cat. in Disyll. + Archilochius Minor.

Diffugere nives ; redeunt iam gramina campis,
Arboribusque comae, Hor. *Od.* iv. 7.

(4) Metrum Archilochium Secundum.

Dact. Hex. Cat. in Disyll. + Iambelegus Archilochius.

> Horrida tempestas caelum contraxit, et imbres
> Nivesque deducunt Iovem ; nunc mare nunc siluae,
>> Hor. *Epod.* 13.

(5) Metrum Archilochium Tertium.

Iamb. Trim. Acat. + Elegiambus Archilochius.

> Petti, nihil me, sicut antea, iuvat
> Scribere versiculos amore percussum gravi,
>> Hor. *Epod.* 11.

(6) Metrum Archilochium Quartum.

Archilochius Maior + Iamb. Trim. Cat.

> Solvitur acris hiemps grata vice veris et Favoni,
> Trahuntque siccas machinae carinas, Hor. *Od.* i. 4.

(7) Metrum Pythiambicum Primum.

Dact. Hex. Cat. in Disyll. + Iamb. Dim. Acat.

> Mollis inertia cur tantam diffuderit imis
> Oblivionem sensibus, Hor. *Epod.* 14.

(8) Metrum Pythiambicum Secundum.

Dact. Hex. Cat. in Disyll. + Hexapodia Iambica.

> Altera iam teritur bellis civilibus aetas,
> Suis et ipsa Roma viribus ruit, Hor. *Epod.* 16.

(9) Metrum Alcmanium.

Dact. Hex. Cat. in Disyll. + Dact. Tetram. Alcmanius.

> Laudabunt alii claram Rhodon aut Mitylenen
> Aut Ephesum bimarisve Corinthi,
>> Hor. *Od.* i. 7 ; *Epod.* 7.

(10) Metrum Asclepiadeum Secundum.

Versus Glyconeus + Versus Asclepiadeus Minor.

> Sic te diva potens Cypri,
> Sic fratres Helenae lucida sidera, Hor. *Od.* i. 3.

Horace has twelve Odes in this measure.

(11) Metrum Sapphicum Maius.

Versus Aristophaneus + Sapphicus Maior.

> Lydia, dic per omnes
> Te deos oro Sybarin cur properes amando, Hor. *Od.* i. 8.

b. Dicola Tetrasticha or Tetrastropha.

(1) Strophe Sapphica Minor.

Terni Sapphici Minores + Adonius.

> Integer vitae scelerisque purus
> Non eget Mauris iaculis neque arcu
> Nec venenatis gravida sagittis,
> Fusce, pharetra, Hor. *Od.* i. 22.

Horace has twenty-six Sapphic Odes.

The Adonian Verse is so intimately connected with the third Sapphic line that Hiatus at the close of the latter is unusual, and words are sometimes divided between the two verses: as,

Thracio bacchante magis sub inter-
lunia vento, Hor.

An Hypermeter is sometimes found among the Sapphic lines: as

Dissidens plebi numero beator|um
Eximit virtus, Hor.

(2) Metrum Asclepiadeum Tertium.

Terni Asclepiadei Minores + Glyconeus.

Iam veris comites, quae mare temperant,
Impellunt animae lintea Thraciae:
Iam nec prata rigent, nec fluvii strepunt
Hiberna nive turgidi, Hor. *Od.* iv. 12.

Horace has nine Odes in this measure.

(3) Strophe Glyconea Catulliana.

Terni Glyconei Catulliani + Pherecrateus Catullianus.

Sis quocumque placet tibi
Sancta nomine, Romulique
Antiquam, ut solita es, bona
Sospites ope gentem, Catull. 34.

Synaphea is kept in this Metre.

Catullus in Poem 61 uses this Metre as Pentastichon.

Namque Iulia Manlio,
Qualis Idalium colens
V̆enit ad Phrygium Venus
Iudicem, bona cum bona
Nubit alite virgo.

Here Synaphea is observed between lines 1, 2, 3, and between 4, 5.

c. TRICOLA TETRASTICHA.

(1) Metrum Asclepiadeum Quartum.

Bini Asclepiadei Minores + Pherecrateus + Glyconeus.

Prima nocte domum claude: neque in vias
Sub cantu querulae despice tibiae:
Et te saepe vocanti
Duram difficilis mane, Hor. *Od.* iii. 7 29.

Horace has seven Odes in this Metre.

Although the Pherecratean ends, in theory, with a Trochee, yet in the usage of Horace a final long syllable is adopted.

(2) Strophe Alcaica.

Bini Alcaici Hendecasyllabi + Alcaicus Enneasyllabus + Alca-icus Decasyllabus.

N N

Qui rore puro Castaliae lavit
Crinis solutos, qui Lyciae tenet
Dumeta natalemque silvam
Delius et Patareus Apollo, Hor. *Od.* iii. 4. 6**1.**

Horace has thirty-seven Odes in this Metre.

NOTE.

The metres of the Comic poets, Plautus and Terence, are too large a sub-ject to be treated in this grammar. We will merely observe that many final syllables (**ar, or, at, et, ĭt**), short in later poets, are lengthened by Plautus and Terence ; Iambic words, on the other hand (such as h a b e n t, b o n i s), are often scanned as Pyrrhichs; the law of position is often vio-lated ; and long initial syllables slurred into short quantity, when they follow monosyllables or elided Pyrrhichs. Add to these licenses the most extensive synizesis and the free use of Spondee, Dactyl, Anapaest, even Proceleusmatic for Iambus or Trochee (always excepting the final foot), and it will be seen at once in how wide a field of rhythm the old scenic poets ranged. See p. 56.

APPENDIX.

————+————

A. LATIN ORTHOGRAPHY.

ORTHOGRAPHY is defined by Suetonius (*Oct.* 88), as 'the form and method of writing taught by grammarians,' and by Quintilian (i. 7), more shortly, as 'the science of writing correctly.' We may blend the two definitions, and say that Orthography is 'the science of writing in correct form the words of any language.'

The Greeks settled their orthography with reference to four considerations : (1) analogy ; (2) etymology ; (3) dialect ; (4) history. The Latins left dialect out of question, but had regard to the other three points. Yet, owing to the fluctuating character of their language, and its many changes during the seven centuries between the first Punic war and the fall of the Roman empire, the settlement of a solid Latin orthography is a work of difficulty. The labours of Ritschl, Lachmann, and others have indeed during the last few years thrown much light on this subject. Ritschl justly selects the age of Quintilian's great work (about the close of the first century, A.D.) as the standard of Latin orthography ; but, unfortunately; it is only by an inductive process, often uncertain, that the forms of words can, generally speaking, be referred to this age. Inscriptions, of course, have the greatest value ; but they are often inconsistent even when contemporaneous. The earliest MSS. are several centuries later than the Christian era ; and they also disagree. The opinions of old grammarians are not less various. Hence it often happens that the classical form of a word can be determined only by a balance of conflicting evidence ; and different minds will strike the balance differently. A few probable results, compendiously stated, must suffice here. The student may compare Munro's *Introd. to Lucretius*, and Ribbeck's *Proleg. to Virgil.*

Here forms assumed to be most classical are named first : others of nearly equal authority are added with ' or:' those of minor authority are within brackets ; those which seem inadmissible follow ' not,' and are in italic type.

1) **a, e** : defatigo or defetīgo ; depeciscor (depaciscor).

2) **e, ae, oe** : caecus, not *coecus* ; caelum, *heaven*, not *coelum* ; also caelum &c. *graving-tool* ; caementum (cementum) ; caerimonia, not *ceremonia* ; caespes, not *cespes* ; Camena, not *Camoena* ; cena &c., not *coena* &c. ; ceteri, not *caeteri* ; faenum (fenum?), not *foenum* ; fecundus, not *foecundus* ; femina, not *foemina* ; fetus &c., not *foetus* ; fenus (foenus) ; foedus, *treaty* ; glaeba ; heres, not *haeres* ; lēvis, not *laevis* ; maerere and maestus, not *moerere* and *moestus* ; oboedire (obedire) ; obscenus, not *obscaenus obscoenus* ; Paelignus,

not *Pelignus* ; paelex, not *pellex* ; paenitet, not *poenitet,* but poena ; paenula, not *penula* ; pomaerium (pomerium) ; prelum, not *praelum* ; proelium, not *praelium* ; raeda, not *reda rheda* ; saeculum, not *seculum* ; saepes &c., not *sepes* &c. ; scaena (scena).

3) **e, i**: benevolus (benivolus) ; deminuere &c., not *diminuere* &c. ; di (dei), dis (deis) ; genetrix, not *genitrix* ; heri (here) ; intellego (intelligo) ; neglego (negligo) ; protinus or protenus, but quatenus ; valetudo (valitudo) ; Vergilius, not *Virgilius.*

As respects -īs (eis) or -es, Accus. Plur. of I-nouns, admitting that in the republican age -īs was the more usual, as it is certainly truer in formation, yet we believe that, before the age of Quintilian, -ēs was in general use ; and this, with its superior convenience, has led to its frequent retention. On -ĕ or -ī in Abl. of I-nouns, see § 24. 5.

4) **i, u**: The middle tone between ĭ and ŭ (see § 11. p. 8 ; § 12. p. 33), led to the existence of a large number of double forms : aestimare (aestumare) ; Brundĭsium (Brundŭsium) ; inclutus (inclitus) ; lŭbet &c. or lĭbet &c. ; recŭperare (recĭperare) ; Dat. Pl. of Decl. 4 : grad-ĭbus &c. (gradŭbus &c. § 25) ; maxĭmus (maxŭmus), and all Superlatives ; vicensĭmus (vicensumus), and other Ordinals in -ĭmus (-ŭmus) ; so maritĭmus (maritŭmus) ; monimentum or monŭmentum ; tegĭmen or tegŭmen ; and other similar derivatives. But the ŭ-form in many of these was archaic in the Augustan and following age, which wrote carnĭfex rather than carnŭfex ; lacrĭma rather than lacrŭma ; clĭpeus rather than clŭpeus ; optĭmus rather than optŭmus, except perhaps in old formulas ; mancipium, not *mancupium* ; victima, not *victuma.*

5) **e, u**: -endus (-undus) in Gerundive forms : -undus was the ancient form, but superseded by -endus in the Imperial age.

6) **o, u**: adulescens (Noun), adolescens (Part.) ; epistula or epistola ; suboles (soboles). The earlier Latins, even to the Augustan age, wrote **o** rather than **u** when **u** preceded : but **u** was received under the emperors : hence vult (volt) ; avus (avos) ; equus (equos), &c. But Ribbeck in Virgil almost always avoids **uu, vu**. See 12.

7) **e, o**: vertere (vortere) ; versus (vorsus) ; vertex (vortex). The forms in **o** are comparatively archaic. But fenoris or feneris, feneror ; iecinoris or iecineris ; pignoris or pigneris, pigneror.

8) **i, y**: **y** is not properly a Latin letter, but introduced in Cicero's age to represent Greek *v*. Therefore, such forms as *clypeus, hyems, inclytus, ocyus, satyra, stylus, sylva, Sylla,* are now justly exploded, the true forms being clipeus (clupeus), hiemps, inclutus (inclitus), ocius, satira, stilus, silva, Sulla. But, where Greek *v* is represented by **y**, this letter holds its proper place : lyra, Nympha, Syrus, Syria, Tyrus, &c.

9) **guo** or **go**: lingĕre (linguere) ; ningit (ninguit) ; stinguere and compounds, not *stingere* ; tingĕre (tinguere) ; ungĕre (unguere), but unguentum, unguen ; urgēre (urguēre).

10) **g** or **c**: vicensimus (vigensimus), trĭgensimus or tricensimus, but quadragensimus, &c. ; so ducenti, trecenti, sescenti, but quadringenti or quadrigenti ; quingenti, &c. ; viceni, triceni, but quadrageni, &c. ; duceni, treceni, sexceni or sesceni, but quadringeni, quingeni, &c. See NUMERALIA, § 33. Cycnus or cygnus ; Cnosus or Gnosus.

11) **gn** or **n**: nasci not *gnasci* ; natus (gnatus), but agnatus, cognatus, &c. ; noscere not *gnoscere* ; but agnoscere, cognoscere, &c.

12) **c** or **q** (qu): cotidie or cottidie, not *quotidie*; coquus (anc. cocus, coqus); equus (anc. ecus, equs, equos); pecunia (anc. pequnia); locutus (anc. loqutus); secutus (anc. sequtus); loquuntur, sequuntur (anc. locuntur, secuntur); cui (anc. quoi, quoei); cur (anc. qur, quor); quum or cum, conj. (anc. qum, quom); cum, prep. (anc. qum, quom). The form cum is good for preposition and conjunction; quom was used for both to the Augustan age: after which the dislike of **uu** seems to have gone out of fashion; and the form quum is often used for the conjunction. But qu was uttered as **c**. Ribbeck in Virgil commonly edits ecus, ecum (or -quos, -quom) locuntur, secuntur, &c., instead of the forms with qu.

13) **b** for **v**: ferbui or fervi; to avoid **vu**.

14) **h** initial present or absent: Hadria, not *Adria*; alucinari (halucinari); Hammon (Ammon); harena (arena); harundo or arundo; haruspex or aruspex; hariolus, not *ariolus*; have (ave); hedera, not *edera*; erus, era, or herus, hera; heres (eres); herciscĕre, not *erciscere*; holus (olus); Hiber (Iber); Hister (Ister); umēre, umor, &c., rather than *humēre, humor*, &c.; umerus, not *humerus*.

15) **h** interior: aëneus, &c. (aheneus, &c.); cohors or cors; incohare (inchoare); nihil or nil; prendo (prehendo); vemens, not *vehemens*.

16) euphonic **p**: compsi, comptum, &c. (comsi, comtum, &c.), and others; hiemps (hiems).

17) **ci** or **ti** before a vowel. Authority favours dicio, condicio, solacium, patricius, tribunicius, &c., not *ditio*, &c.; and contio, fetialis, indutiae, nuntius, nuntiare, &c., setius; not *concio*, &c. Also convitium rather than convicium; suspitio (Subst.), rather than suspicio; but the forms of these with **ci** were also used. See Corssen, I. 56.

18) **b** or **p**: caelebs (caeleps): urbs (urps), &c., obsonium, obsonari (opsonium, opsonari); obtulit (optulit); subter (supter). But **bs** was sounded as **ps**, **bt** as **pt**.

19) **d** or **t** final. In Quintilian's time the endings in **d**, haud, sed, apud, &c., had become general in preference to the archaic **t**, haut (hau), set, aput, &c. But **d** final was sounded as **t**.

20) **-icĕre** or **-iicere**. The compounds of iacĕre have been elsewhere noticed. To the Augustan age the single **i** seems to have prevailed: adicere, deicere, conicere, reicere, &c. But in imperial times **ii** was at least admissible: adiicere, coiicere or coniicere, &c., the former **i** being a consonant. And in adicere, &c. **i** did double duty as consonant and vowel = ad-yi-cere, &c.

21) **ct** or **t**: artus not *arctus*; autumnus, not *auctumnus*; but auctor.

22) **n** kept or omitted: conectere, conexus, coniti, conivēre, conixus, conūbium, not *connectere*, &c. (M. *Lucr.* i. 633): coniunx (coiunx coiux): **n** before **s** was liable to elimination: thus Numeral Adverbs in **-ens** passed into **-es**; the earlier form being, however, generally preserved: quotiens (quoties); totiens (toties); miliens (milies), &c. So vicensimus (vicesimus). Such omissions of **n** abound in Inscr. as cosol for consol, cesor for censor. See Corssen, I. 249, &c.

23) Consonants singled or doubled: on this point documents are especially discrepant. We find Britannia or Brittannia; cottidie or cotidie; Iuppiter (Iupiter); littera (litera); loquella or loquela; querella or querela: but medēla, suadēla, &c., also cautēla, tutēla, reliquiae (relliquiae), but relicuus (later reliquus); religio (relligio): causa (caussa): paulum (paullum). But nummus (nūmus); bracchium, not *brachium*; Messalla, not *Messala*; sollemnis, not *solennis*;

sollers, &c., not *solers*, &c. ; sollicitus, not *solicitus*, &c. ˜Yet anulus[rather than annulus ; culeus rather than culleus, &c. ; litus, not *littus* ; ilico rather than illico ; vilicus rather than villicus ; stilicidium. Pliny wrote mille but milia ; Augustus, however, writes millia, milliens ; and Corssen, I. 226, prefers the **ll.** Reppuli, repperi, rettuli, seem better than repuli, &c., which are, however, used.

24) Assimilation : quidquid (quicquid) ; quicquam (quidquam), quicque (quidque) ; quamquam (quanquam) ; tamquam (tanquam) ; umquam, numquam (unquam, nunquam) ; -cumque (cunque) ; quendam not *quemdam* ; eundem not *eumdem* ; tantundem not *tantumdem* ; quorundam not *quorumdam* ; eorundem not *eorumdem*. When **m** remains before the guttural or dental, it is sounded as **n** : quamquam = quanquam when uttered.

25) Assimilation of Compounded Prepositions. This is received or rejected in MSS. and Inscr. with such apparently free option in most instances, that no safe rules on the point can be laid down. Thus we read in imperial times adlectus and allectus, collapsus and conlapsus, collegium and conlegium, illustris and inlustris, impendium and inpendium, irritus and inritus, even imperium and inperium, &c. On the whole assimilation prevails. See Brambach, *Neugestaltung der Latein. Orthographie*, p. 300, &c.

26) Not less uncertainty exists in regard to words beginning with **s**, when compounded with ex (ecs : c. ἐκ, ἐξ). We find exspectare and expectare, exspirare and expirare ; exsequi, exsequiae, and exequi, exequiae ; exsecrari, &c., and execrari, &c. ; exserere and exerere ; exsilire and exilire ; exsultare and exultare ; especially exsul, exsulare, exsilium with exul, exulare, exilium. In some words, it is perhaps better to retain the **s** ; but exul, &c., have ample authority ; and excidium (from exscindo) is better established than exscidium.

27) Accessory Note :

' We have now (writes Mr. Munro) an accurate transcription of the large fragments of the Ancyra monument, containing no doubt an exact copy of the "Res gestae" of Augustus, which, as Tacitus (*Ann.* i. 11) tells us, he had written out with his own hand, a short time probably before his death. The spelling is interesting, as Suetonius says that Augustus was a purist on such points.

' He always admits **uu** : rivus, vivus, as well as annuus ; but he writes Phrates, praerant.

' In Gen. Plur. we find denarium, sestertium, deum, nummum ; triumvirum, but xv virorum. In Gen. Sing. always **i**, not **ii** ; proeli, Iuli, Pompei, congiari. In Dat. Abl. Plur. of Decl. 1 and 2, both **is** and **iis** : dis, colonis, provincis, &c. ; but also consiliis, &c. ; both municipis and municipiis. Dalmateis, emeriteis, quadrigeis : but oftener **is** in Dat. and Abl. Plur. Sometimes **is**, but oftener **es** in Accus. Plur. of 3rd Decl. : once pluris in Nom. Plur.

' Honos, incohare, Messalla, plebis Gen. Sing., but plebei Dat., sescenti, valetudo.

' Always **i**, not **u**, in the fluctuating instances : legitimus, septimus, frequentissimus, reciperare, manibiae, &c. Compare what Suetonius (ch. 87) says of his writing sĭmus for sumus. Perhaps it was this love of consistency which makes him always spell millia, milliens ; though he writes militum, militare. He has absens, not apsens ; adque, apud, sed, aliquod, with **d** not **t** ; cumque, but nunquam. Always quotiens, not quoties ; milliens, vicensimus, &c. Caussa, claussum ; also clausum, inclusum.

' Generally he writes **x**, not **xs**, as exilium : compare Quintilian (i. 7, 4), who speaks of it as an affectation to write exspecto for expecto. But Augustus has exstinguere and sexsiens.

' He writes immortalis, but inmissus ; collaticius ; once collegium, five times conlega or conlegium ; accipere, oppressus, but adsignare ; imperator, impendere ; but inpensa in the heading written not by Augustus, but probably by Tiberius.'

These interesting extracts shew that spelling had a large license even in the Augustan age.

B. LATIN PRONUNCIATION.

In the year 1872, the Latin Professors of Oxford and Cambridge (then Messrs. Palmer and Munro) issued the following Syllabus, in compliance with request.

'If it were thought advisable to adopt any existing pronunciation, we should be inclined for many reasons to recommend the Italian with perhaps a few modifications. But not to speak of other difficulties, the tyranny of accent over quantity is at least as marked in the Italian as in the English reading of Latin ; and we hold with the most experienced teachers that to distinguish between long and short syllables is an essential part of a reform in pronunciation. At the same time Italian appears to us to offer many valuable aids which should not be neglected ; as English in its tones and vocalisation seems so different from old Latin, that often it is not easy to find in it even single sounds to give as adequate representations of an old Latin sound. The Italian of literature has been fixed for six centuries, and manifestly approximates to the Latin of the 7th or 8th century.

'There can be little doubt that during the best ages the writing, as seen in inscriptions, was meant to represent exactly the sounding of words, and that a difference of spelling implied so far a difference of pronouncing.

'We propose then that the letters of Latin should be sounded as follows :

' I. *Vowels and Diphthongs :—*

' $\bar{a}$, as the accentuated Italian *a* : i.e. as the middle *a* of *amata*, or as the *a* of *father*.

' $\breve{a}$, as the unaccentuated Italian *a* : i.e. as the first and last *a* of *amata*. It is not easy to represent this sound in English : we know nothing better than the first *a* in *away, apart, aha*.

' $\bar{e}$, as the Italian closed *e* : *arena* ; nearly as *ai* in English *pain* :

' *ae*, as the Italian open *e* : *secolo* ; nearly as the first *e* in English *there*, or French *père*.

' $\breve{e}$, the same sound shortened : nearly as in English *men*, or our sounding of μέν. A wide induction, extending from classical times to the present, would support what is said of *e, ae* : thus Italians represent Latin *ae* always by their open *e*, and as a rule $\bar{e}$ by closed *e*, $\breve{e}$ by open *e*.

' $\bar{i}$, as accentuated Italian *i* : i.e. as the first *i* of *timidi*, or the *i* of *machine* : $\breve{i}$, as unaccentuated Italian *i* : i.e. as the two last *i*'s of *timidi*, or the *i* of *pity*. The way in which Latin $\breve{i}$ is represented in Greek on the one hand, and in Italian on the other, and its history in Latin itself, would tend to shew that its actual sound approximated to that of *e*, and was something between the *i* of *pity* and the *e* of *petty*.

' *ō*, as Italian closed *o* : nearly as in German *ohne*, English *more*.

' *ŏ*, as Italian open *o* shortened : nearly as in German *gold* ; less nearly as in English *corn*. The English and English-Latin *o* is very peculiar, in most cases hardly an *o* at all : compare our *honos, domos* ; and our *non, bos, pons* on the one hand with *nos, hos, donum* on the other.

' Perhaps, comparing Italian, we should pronounce *ō*, when it precedes *r*, or when it represents *au*, as the Italian open *o* : *gloria, victoria, plostrum, Clodius.*

' *ū*, as accentuated Italian *u* : as the first *u* of *tumulo*, the second of *tumulto*, or as *u* in *rule, lure*.

' *ŭ*, as unaccentuated Italian *u* : as the second *u* of *tumulo*, the first of *tumulto*, the *u* of *fruition*.

' *au*, as Italian *au* : nearly as *ow* in English *power*.

' In genuine Latin words the other diphthongs are very rare, except in archaisms where *ei, oe, oi, ou* are common enough.

' *eu*, as Italian *eu*, or Latin *ĕ* quickly followed by Latin *ŭ*. Of Latin words we find perhaps only *heu, ceu, seu* ; and we do not feel competent to propose a different sound for it in the many Greek words adopted into Latin.

' *oe* is also very rare in Latin words : for them, as well as for Greek words, we should prefer a sound like the German *ö* : as an alternative we propose the open Italian *e* for *oe*, as before for *ae*.

' *ei* too as a diphthong is very rare : we would give it the Latin *ĕ* sound quickly followed by a Latin *ĭ* sound.

' But in a large class of words containing *ae, ei, oi*, or *ui*, the *i* is a semi-consonant, and should be sounded like English *y* : pronounce *Graius, maior, Troia, eius, Pompeius, Seianus, cuius*, as *Grā-yus, mā-yor, Trō-ya, ē-yus, Pompē-yus, Sē-yanus, cū-yus : eicit, reicit*, as *ē-yicit, rē-yicit*. The *o* or *e* of *proin, prout, dein, deinde*, when not forming a distinct syllable, does not form a diphthong, but is elided, and must be treated as a final vowel is treated, when it is elided before an initial vowel : so in *neŭtiquam e* is elided.

' II. *In a fuller Discussion more might be said of the Consonants : a few Remarks must suffice for the present.*

' *c*, always as *k* : in *Cicero, facies*, as well as *Cacus*.

' *g*, always as *g* in *get* : in *gero, gingiva, gyrus* as well as *gaudeo*.

' *s*, at the beginning and end of words, and at the beginning of syllables, and before consonants, is always sharp (as the *s* of *sin*) in Italian and should be so in Latin : *sol, stella, de-sero, ni-si, nos, sonus*.

' *s*, between two vowels, has in Italian a soft *z* sound, as in our *rose* : we would thus sound in Latin *rosa, musa, miser*. But words of this kind in Latin are but few : much more numerous are those where *s* might also be written *ss*, a lost consonant having been assimilated and the vowel always lengthened : *causa, casus, visus, odiosus, divisio* (see Quintilian 1, 7, 20). Italian is here very suggestive ; and in all these words *s* should be sharp.

' *t* is always a pure dental, in *ratio* as in *ratis*, in *notio* as in *notus*, in *vitium* as in *vita*.

' *bs, bt* should be sounded (and generally written) as *ps, pt : lapsus, aps, apsens, optulit, supter*.

' *j*, or consonant *i*, as *y* in *yard*.

'As to consonant *u*, or *v*, we believe that its sound was as near as possible to that of the vowel *u* : i. e. like the *ou* of the French *oui*, not differing much therefore from English *w*. But as there is great diversity of opinion on this point, we propose to leave it an open question, whether it shall be pronounced in this way, or as the English and Italian *v*.

'*y*, *z*, *ch*, *ph*, *th* were brought into the language to represent Greek sounds : *z*, *ph*, *th* we propose should be sounded as at present: *ch* should never be pronounced as in our *charter* : it would be better to give it a *k* sound succeeded by an *h* sound ; but it must follow the fortunes of Greek χ. *y*, or Greek *υ*, had some middle sound between Latin *u* and *i*, perhaps resembling either French *u* or German *ü* ; but *ȳ* and *ў* came probably much nearer to *ī* and *ĭ* than to *ū* and *ŭ*.

' In our Latin pronunciation quantity is systematically neglected: attention to it seems essential in any reformed method : *ā* and *ă* should be distinguished in *matris* and *patris*, as in *mater* and *pater*. The ancients observed the natural length of vowels, when the syllable was also long by position : as in *Marcus*, *pastor* : Cicero tells us that every vowel when followed by *ns* or *nf* became long by nature : as in *infimus*, *insanus*: *gn* seems to have had the same power over the preceding vowel. Often too an extruded consonant leaves a naturally short vowel long : *e* from *ex: es*, *est* from *edo* : *Sestius* (Σήστιος), but Sextius (Σέξτιος). On the other hand the long vowel of many final syllables in time became short ; and we can scarcely suppose that, while the naturally long vowel in *amat*, *docet* was shortened, it always remained long in *amant*, *docent* : it seems certain also, whatever the reason may be, that the *e* was short in *docentis*, etc., as much as in *legentis*, *audientis*.

' Following the tradition of the Italians, we fortunately keep the accent in most cases on the right syllable, though the loss of quantity has changed its nature. In a summary like this we cannot dwell on the exceptions.

' In respect of elision we may see, by comparing Plautus and Terence with Ovid, how much the elaborate cultivation of the language had tended to a more distinct sounding of final syllables. We must not altogether pass over the elided vowel or the elided syllable which ends in *m*, except perhaps in the case of *ĕ* in common words, *que*, *neque*, and the like. How far too final *m* was mute, or nasal, it is not easy to determine. *Est* 'is' seems often in pronunciation (and in writing) to have lost its *e* and become an enclitic *st* after a vowel or *m* : thus *tuo est*, *meum est* can end an Ovidian pentameter, *labori est* an Hexameter : we must therefore pronounce *tuost*, &c.'

To the foregoing suggestions of these eminent scholars the present Editor assents generally. Only, (1) He cannot conceive that **oe** ought to be sounded in the same manner as **ae**, even alternatively ; (2) It is not to his mind an open question, whether Latin **v** had the sound of English **v**. His principal reasons for believing that Latin **v** had always the sound, or nearly the sound, of English **w** are given in a foot-note on pp. 66–7.

C. AFFINITIES IN THE ARYAN FAMILY.

I. As a stimulus to the interesting study of Comparative Philology, examples are here given of the affinity between words in Latin, Greek, and Indic (Sanskrit).

1) Nouns.

L.	Gr.	I.	L.	Gr.	I.
aes	—	ayas (*iron*)	mater	μητήρ	mâtar
aevum	αἰϜών	âyus (*life*)	medius	μέσσος	madhyas
ager	ἀγρός	ajras	nasus	ῥίς	nas, nâs
anguis	ἔχις	ahis	navis	ναῦς	naus
animus	ἄνεμος	anilas	novus	νέϜος	navas
anser	χήν	hansas	nox (noct-)	νύκτ-	naktam
aurora	αὐ(σ)ώς	ushâs	nubes	νέϜος	nabhas
bos	βοῦς	gaus	oci-or	ὠκύς	âśus
can-is	κύων	śvan	oc-ulus	ὀπ-	akshi
cor(d-)	καρδία	hrid, hard	opus	—	apas
cuculus	κόκκυξ	kokilas	os (oss-)	ὀστε-ον	asthi
dens	ὀδόντ-	dant	ovis	ὄϜις	avis
deus }	θεός }	div- devas }	pater	πατήρ	pitar
divus }	Ζεύς }	dyaus }	pes (pĕd-)	πόδ-	pâd
dexter	δεξιτερός	dakshiṇas	primus	πρόμος	prathamas
domus	δόμος	damas	sal	ἅλ-ς	saras
ego	ἐγώ	aham	somnus	ὕπνος	svapnas
equus	ἵππος	aśvas	stella }	ἀ-στήρ }	star
fores	θύρα	dvâr	a-strum }	ἄστρον }	
frater	φράτηρ	bhrâtar	soror	—	svasar
fumus	θυμός	dhûmas	sua-vis	ἡδύς	svâdus
genu	γόνυ	jânu	suus	ἑός	svas
gravis	βαρύς	gurus	taurus	ταῦρος	sthûras (*strong*)
hiem-s	χειμών	himam	umerus	ὦμος	aṇsas
ignis	—	agnis	ulna	ὠλένη	aratni
imber	ὄμβρος	abhram	ursus	ἄρκτος	ṛikshas, arkshas
iecur	ἧπαρ	yakṛit, yakart	ver	ἔαρ	vasantas
laus	κλέϜος	śravas	Vesta	ἑστία	vasta, vâstu
levir	δαήρ	devar	vestis	ἐσθής	(vasti)
lupus	λύκος	vṛikas, varkas	vidua	—	vidhava
lux (luc-)	λυκ-	ruć	virus	ἰός	vishas
mag-n-us	μέγας	mahâ			

2) Verbs.

L.	Gr.	I.	L.	Gr.	I.
aest-uo	αἰθ-	indh	flagro }	φλέγω	bhrâj
ait	ἠ-	âha	fulgeo }		
ago	ἄγω	aj	frigo	φρύγω	bhrajj
apiscor	—	âp	fu-	φύω	bhû
aro	ἀρόω	(âr)	fugio	φεύγω	bhuj (*bow*)
bibo	πο-	pâ (pibâmi)	gigno	γεν-	jan
cano	(καν-)	kvaṇ	iungo	ζεύγ-νυμι	yuj
cio	κι-	śi	linquo	λείπω	rić
cluo	κλύω	śru	loquor	λακ-	lap
coquo	πέπτω	pać	lubet	—	lubh
credo	—	(śrad-dadhâmi)	luo	λύω	lû
creo	κραίνω	kṛi, kar	men- }	μεν- }	
dico }	δεικ-	diś	moneo, &c. }	μον- }	man
-dico }				μαν- }	
do	δί-δω-μι	dâ (da-dâ-mi)	metior	μετρέω	mâ
(-dere)	τί-θη-μι	dhâ (da-dhâ-mi)	minuo	μινύθω	mî, mî-nâmi
domo	δαμάω	dam	misceo	μίσγω	miśr
ĕdo	ἔδ-ω	ad	morior	(μορ-)	mṛi, mar
i (eo)	ἰ (εἶμι)	i (emi)	mulgeo	ἀμέλγω	mṛij, marj
fallo	σφάλλω	sphal	mungo	μύσσω	muć
fari	φά-ναι	bhâsh	(g)nosco	γι-γνώσκω	jnâ
fero	φέρω	bhṛi, bhar	pac-iscor	παγ-	paś

2) Verbs—*continued*.

L.	Gr.	I.		L.	Gr.	I.
·pleo	πίμ-πλημι	pṛi, par		tego	στέγω	sthag
·quie-sco	κεῖ-μαι	śi		ten-do	τεν- ταν	tan
scindo	σχίζω	ćhid		terreo	τρέω	tras
·sedeo	ἐδ-	sad		tollo	ταλ- τλα-	tul
sequor	ἕπομαι	sać		uro, ussi	—	ush
serpo	ἕρπω	sṛip, sarp		veho	Ϝὸχέω	vah
·spec-	σκεπ-	spaś		verto	—	vṛit, vart
sterno	στρώννυμι	stṛi, star		vestio	Ϝέω	vas
sto	στα-	sthâ (stâ)		video	Ϝιδ-	(vid, *know*)
·suo		siv		volvo	Ϝελύω	(val ?)
·(e)s-um (esse)	ἐσ-μι	as-mi		vomo	Ϝεμέω	vam

3) Particles.

L.	Gr.	I.		L.	Gr.	I.
ab	ἀπό	apa		ob	ἐπί	abhi
ante	ἀντί	anti		per	περί	parí
at, et	ἔτι	at-i		pro	πρό	pra
bis	δίς	dvis		quando	κότε	kadâ
heri	χθές	hyas		semi-	ἡμι-	sâmi
in	ἐν	ni (ani ?)		simul	ἅμα	sam-
in-	ἀ- ἀν-	a- an-		sub	ὑπό	upa
·intus	ἐντός	antar		super	ὑπέρ	upari
·ne	μή	ma, na				

4) Numerals.　See § 34, vi.

In the Sanskrit words palatal k' is expressed by c' (sounded as ch in 'child'); the softly aspirated sibilant (often representing Latin c, Greek κ) by s'. The vowel ṛi may be rendered by ar (vṛit = vart).

II. Grimm's Law teaches that the Mute Consonants of Latin, Greek, and (generally) Indic, when they pass into Low Dutch and High Dutch languages respectively, undergo certain definite changes ; namely :—

When L., Gr., I. have	sonant	surd	aspirate
Low Dutch has	surd	aspirate	sonant
High Dutch has	aspirate	sonant	surd

1. Among Low Dutch languages are Gothic, Friesic, Dutch, English ; High Dutch are Old, Middle, and present German.

2. The Surds are c, q, k, t, p ; the Sonants, g, d, b, v ; the Aspirates, ch, th, z, ss, ph, f, pf.

Examples.

	L.	ego	Goth.	ik	Germ.	**ich**
1.	L.	cord-	Eng.	heart	Germ.	**herz**
	L.	ob	Eng.	up	Germ.	**auf**
2.	L.	tacere	Goth.	**thahan**	M. G.	**dagen**
	L.	tu	Eng.	**thou**	Germ.	**du**
	L.	pater	Eng.	**father**	Germ.	**vater**
3.	Gr.	λείχειν	Goth.	laigon	Germ.	**leoken**
	Gr.	θυγάτηρ	Goth.	**dauhtar**	Germ.	**tochter**
	Gr.	κεφαλή	Goth.	**haubith**	Germ.	**haupt**

(This law is subject to exceptions.)

D. THE ANCIENT DIALECTS OF ITALY.

On the ancient races and dialects of Italy, see T. Mommsen's *History of Rome,* bk. i. ch. 2. 3. 9. 13. 14. Mommsen comes to the following conclusion : ' that from the common cradle of peoples and languages there issued a stock which embraced in common the ancestors of the Greeks and the Italians ; that from this, at a subsequent period, the Italian branched off, and these again into the western and eastern stocks, while at a still later date the eastern became subdivided into Umbrians and Oscans.' As to the Etruscans, who called themselves Ras or Ras-ennae, he says they were not, according to the story, Lydian emigrants from Asia ; they perhaps had their earlier abode in the Raetian Alps, thence migrating into Italy and driving out the Umbrians from the land afterwards called Etruria. Their name (Rasennae) seems to have passed into Tursennae, Turseni, Tyrrheni, which the Umbrians changed into Tursci, the Romans into Tusci and Etrusci. Their language (he adds) differs as widely from all the Graeco-Italian dialects as did the languages of the Kelts or of the Sclavonians. Yet he thinks they may have belonged to the Aryan family. They received a modification, or rather several modifications, of the Semitic alphabet, from which their neighbours, the Umbrians and Sabellians, obtained their oldest letters.

Our knowledge of the early dialects of Italy is chiefly gained from extant inscriptions, some of which are sepulchral, some dedicatory, while others contain laws, decrees, or religious formularies. Besides Latin and Etruscan, the dialects of which the most specimens survive are the Umbrian and the Oscan, the former in eastern and north midland Italy ; the latter chiefly in its south midland districts. Between these the Sabellian forms a link : while Faliscan (a relic of Umbrian in Etruria) and Volscian, south of the Roman plain, and cognate to Oscan, appear in a few remaining fragments.

A) The Umbrian Dialect.

The most important remains are the Eugubine Tables, seven in number, discovered in the 15th century near Gubbio (Iguvium). They are a code of religious ceremonies, engraved partly in letters of an alphabet borrowed from Etruria, partly in Roman letters. The ancient letters contain an older, the Roman a later Umbrian dialect. Old Umbrian is without the letters o, g, d, q, x. Of these o is represented by u ; d by a peculiar form of r (here marked **r**), which in New Umbrian becomes rs. Old Umbrian has k, but not hard c ; it has a soft c (here marked **c**), which in New Umbrian we mark as s. Final z = ts.

(New Umbrian forms stand between brackets. Latin equivalents follow =.)

a) Umbrian Vowels.

Diphthongs faded into long vowels in New Umbrian: as, (quêstur) = quaestor. Ai = aj ; ei is medial between ī and ē ; au between ū and ō, usually becoming o : (toru) = taurus. Sometimes i takes the place of u : (si-m) = suem ; (mani) = manu. Compounds seldom weaken a into i : thus, (proca̖nurent) = proca̖nuerint. Vowels are dropt by Syncope and Apocope : thus, pihaz = piatus ; katel = catulus. Iu (io) becomes i ; tertis = tertius : so in old Latin alis = alius, alid = aliud.

b) Umbrian Consonants.

P represents Latin qu : pis = quis :—r (rs) = d : arveitu = advehito, **rere** = dedit :—nd is changed into nn or n, (pihanêr) for (pihandêr) = piandi ; panupei for pandupei = quandoque. B stands for v : benest = veniet : for p : kabru for kapru = caprum. R for s is frequent : eru (erom) for esum = esse ; -arum for -asum ; (totar) for tutas ; but asa = ara ; fust = fuerit, &c. M and s final are weaker than in Latin, and generally fall off : kapru or kabru = caprum ; puplu (poplo) = populus : also t falls off : facia = faciat ; **rere** for dedet = dedit.

Thus we see in this early language that Italian tendency to reject consonant terminations, which, checked for many centuries by the intervention of classical Latin, set in again with the decay of Rome, and culminated in the modern Italian.

The chief final consonants in Umbrian are r, t, s, m (all weak and perhaps hardly sounded when written) ; rarely n, z ; f in Accus. Plur. ; k in a few pronouns, p (= Latin que) in a few particles.

c) Umbrian Nouns.

1) First or A-Declension.
Sing. N. a, u (o). Acc. am. G. as (ar). D. e. Abl. a. Loc. amem, emem (eme, e).
Plur. N. as (ar). Acc. af. G. arum. D. Abl, es. Loc. afem, afe.
Examples : tuta (tota) or tutu (toto), *a state, people* ; asa = ara ; (cesna) = cena ; (peica) = pica, &c.

2) Second or O-Declension (regular form).
Sing. N. us (os). Voc. e. Acc. um (om). G. es (er). D. e. Abl. u (o). Loc. umem (omem).
Plur. N. us (ur, or). Acc. uf (of). G. um (om). D. Abl. es (er, ir, eir). Loc. ufem (ofem).
Examples : puplus (poplos) ; kaprus (kapros), &c.
Syncopated forms occur : ins (is) : Ikuvins (Ikovis) for Ikuvinus ; az (os) : pihaz (pihos) for piatus, &c. ; and apocopated forms : katel = catulus ; (ager), &c. Neuters in um (om) differ only as in Latin ; having Pl. N. Acc. in a, u, o.

3) Third or Consonant and I-Declension.
Sing. N. masc. fem. s or none. Acc. m. G. es (er). D. e. Abl. e, i (ei). Loc. emem.
Plur. N. masc. fem. es (er). Acc. f. G. um (om). D. Abl. es, is (eis). Loc efem.
Examples : Cons. Noun, kvêstur (quêstur) ; I-Noun, ukar (okar), Nom. S. (okris), *a mountain.*
Neuters, which are rare, have a in Accus. Pl.

U-Nouns are few: manu = manus; vutu = vultus: D. S. manu; Abl. S. mani, for manu.

d) Umbrian Verbs.

Verb of Being: erum (erom) = esse. Besides this form are extant only est = est; (sent) = sunt; (sir) = sis; (si) = sit; (sins) = sint.

From root fu- are extant: fuia = fiat; fuiest = fiet; fust = fuerit; furent = fuerint; futu = fito; (fututo) = fitote.

Umbrian has the Consonant, A, and E-Conjugations. Huschke attempts a paradigm of the Tenses, which Donaldson cites (*Varron.* p. 104). A few well-established forms must suffice here.

Pres. Ind. -u = -o: sestu = sisto; (suboca-u) = subvoco; stahu = sto. Pass. emantur.

Pres. Conj. façia = faciat, tera (dersa, dirsa) = det or rather di-det, the Verb being a reduplicated form of da; (dirsans, dirsas) = dent, (porta-i-a) = portet; (etaians, etaias) = itent; habia = habeat; arhabas = adhibeant. Pass. mugatu = mugiatur.

S. Fut. benes = venies; ferest = feret; (eest) = ibit; habiest = habebit; staheren = stabunt.

Perf. Indic. -fi = -vi; pihafi = piavi.

Fut. Perf. -ust = -uerit; -urent = -uerint; (benust) = venerit; terust, (dirsust) = dederit; (iust) = ierit; fakust = fecerit; (andersesust) = interstiterit; dersikust = dixerit; (portust) = portaverit; (habust) = habuerit;— ambrefurent = ambiverint; (procanurent) = procinuerint; pihaz fust = piatus fuerit; cersnatur furent = cenati fuerint.

Imperative: -tu = -to; -tuta -tutu (-tuto) = -tote; aitu = aieto; tertu (dirstu, ditu) = dato; teitu (deitu) = dicito; feitu, fetu = facito; am-prehtu = ambito; enetu = inito; upetu = obito; kuveitu = convehito; (etuto) = eunto; aitutu = aiunto; habetu = habeto; habetutu (habituto) = habento.

Partic. Perf. Pass. -tu -to = -tus: declined as noun: (screhto) = scriptum; (comohota) = commota.

Gerundive: probably -nus = -ndus: pihanêr = piandi.

Infin. Pres. Act. -um = ěre; ferum = ferre; façiu, for façiu-m, = facere. There are also traces of Supines -um -u.

e) Umbrian Numerals.

1) Cardinal: *one*, unu = unus: *two*, du = duo; from which Nom. m. dur, Acc. m. duf, f. tuf, n. tuva; Abl. tuves:—*three*, Acc. m. f. tref, tre (trif treif), n. trija, Abl. tris. We find the word (petor-pursus) = quadrupedibus: therefore petor = quattuor (whenc petor-ritum, *a four-wheeled carriage*, Hor.). We find semenies (seh-menier, sehemenier) = semestribus; therefore se (sehe) = sex: also (desendut) = duodecim; therefore deçen (desen) = decem. Others are not extant: but, under 1000, a general correspondence with Latin numerals may be inferred.

2) Ordinal: prumu (promo) = primus: tertiu (tertio) = tertius: tuplu = duplus. Others are not extant.

f) Umbrian Pronouns.

1) Personal. First (mehe) = mihi. Second: Acc. S. tiu (tio, tiom) = te: (tefe) = tibi. Reflex. (seso) = sibi.

2) Possessive. Abl. S. tuer (tover) = tuo: tuā = tuā; vestrā = vestrā.

3) Demonstrative. Various cases occur of the following:

Ere, erek (erec) = is; (esto) = iste; (eso) = hic; (ero) = ille. Probably also (ho) = hic; this occurs only in the affix -hunt (-hont) attached to some forms of erek and ero, like -ce in Latin.

4) Relative and Interrogative.

Rel. (poe) f. pu=qui, quae; svepu=siqua. Another Rel. is pure (porse). Of these only a few forms are extant. Pis=quis? pisi =quis indef. ; pisipumpe=quicumque.

g) Umbrian Particles.

1) Adverbs: (rehte)=recte; superne; (nesimei)=proxime. Eruk, erak=illic; esuf=istic; ife=ibi; if-ont=ibidem. Enuk, enu (eno), enumek, erek (erse)=tunc, tum; panupei=quandoque; este, isek, itek=ita; neip=non, nec.

2) Prepositions: Separable, ar (ars)=ad; (ehe, eh)=ex; hutra (hondra)=infra; kum (com) ku (co)=cum, con- co-; pus (post) =post; pustin (posti)=post-in; pre=prae; (sei)=se; super; (subra)=supra; tra (tref, trahef, traha)=trans: per=περί, pro, is appended to its case: tutaper Ikuvina=pro civitate Eugubina. Inseparable: an=in (negative); amb- ampr- (ambr-)=ambi: ah (aha), perhaps=ab; anter (ander)=inter; en=in; up, us (os) re; sub for up-s, =ob, os; pru (pro)=pro; pur=por- in porrigo, &c.

3) Conjunctions: Coordinative: et; several others also, ene, enu, &c. =et; neife=neque; ute (ate)=aut; heris—heris=vel—vel; (surur, sururont)=dein, deinde (?).

Subordinative: ape (apei)=ubi; (arnipo)=donicum, donec (?); prepa=priusquam; pus-pane=postquam; pune=quum; pufe =ubi; pere (perse, pirse)=quippe; (pirsi)=quando; puze (puse, pusei)=quasi; sve=si; (nosve)=nisi; svepis=siquis; svepu (svepo)=siqua.

Note. The following Latin Verb-roots occur in Umbrian: (ag-); aj-= ai-ere; ben-=venire; der (ders-) or ded- reduplicated from da-; dik-, deik- =dicere; i-, e-=ire; em-=emere; es-=esse; fak-=facere; fer-=ferre; fing-=fingere; frek-=fricare; fu-; gna-=g-nasci; (gno-)=g-noscere; habe-=habēre; hera=velle; kan-=canere; cave-=cavēre; krema-= cremare; kura-=curare; ci-=cire; (loka-)=locare; mal-=molere; (move-)=movere; muge-=mugire; ning-=ningere; ug- (og-)=augere; ul- (ol-); ur- (or-)=oriri; par=parĕre; penn=pendēre; pese; ple-= plere; (porta-)=portare; ques-=quaerere; seka-=secare; sere-=servare; skreh-=scribere, (sona-)=sonare; stahe-=stare; sum-=sumere; take-= tacere; tene-=tenere; tenn-=tendere; terg-=tergere; trem-=tremere; turse-=torrere; vei- veh-=vehere; vel-=velle; vert-=vertere; vire-= videre; (v-oka)=vocare. Perhaps also the root tu- (to-) represents Indian dhâ, Gr. θε-, Lat. -de-re.

B) The Oscan Dialect.

Of the Oscan inscriptions some are in the old Umbro-Oscan characters borrowed from Etruria, others in the Roman, a few in Greek letters. The chief fragment is the Tabula Bantina found in 1793, containing Roman laws for the Apulian town of Bantia.

The old Oscan is without o, q, x: its other letters generally agree in power, though not in shape, with the corresponding Latin. It had however two forms of i, and two of u. The second form of i, which inclined to e or ei, is here noted as ı, and the second form of u, which inclined to o, as ᴜ. In the Tabula Bantina they are not distinguished from i, o.

(New Oscan forms stand between brackets.)

a) Oscan Vowels.

The Oscan diphthongs agree generally with the Latin : aí = ae, anciently ai ; eí = ei ; uí = oe, anciently oi.

Weakening of vowels is less frequent than in Latin : thus (fefacust) = fecerit : Syncope and Apocope often occur, especially in Decl. 2 : tuvtiks = tuticus ; Bantins = Bantinus ; Pumpaiians = Pompeianus ; cevs = civis ; hurs = hortus ; Mutil = Mutilus, &c. Also Heírennis = Herennius ; Puntiís = Pontius, &c. Oscan often inserts a vowel between a liquid and another ·consonant : ter-*e*-mniss = terminos ; ar-*a*-getud = argento ; also i before i or ·a : tiurri = turrim ; Viínikiís = Vinicius.

b) Oscan Consonants.

Here we find much resemblance to Umbrian. Thus p = q : pam = quam, Πόμπτιες = Quintius ; ben- = ven- : kumbened = convenit ; nn = nd : ·upsannam = operandam ; ht = ct, saahtum = san(c)tum ; ehtrad = extra ; ft = pt ; (scriftas) = scriptæ ; multas (moltas) = multæ. T remains after ns : (censtur) = censor ; ti before a vowel = s : (Bansae) = Bantiae. S remains between vowels : asa = ara ; but in Gen. Pl. (-azum) = -arum : here and in -azet for uerit z = soft s ; but in hurz = hortus z = ts ; in (zicolom) = dieculum z = ds. V may come between u and a consonant : tuvtiks = tuticus. Final m, s, t, do not fall off as in Umbrian. We find the ending d in Abl. S., as in old Latin ; toutad ; suvad = suā ; (dolud) = dolo ; also in some 3rd Persons of Verbs, as deded = dedit ; in the Imperative : likítud = liceto ; ·estud = esto ; and in Adverbs : amprufid = improbe ; ehtrad = extra.

c) Oscan Declensions.

1) First or A-Declension.

Sing. N. masc. as, a, fem. u (o). Acc. am. G. masc. ai, fem. as. D. aí. Abl. ad. Loc. aí (ae).
Plur. N. as ? Ac. as. G. (azum). D. Abl. aís.

Examples : tuvta (touta) tuvtu (touto), *a state or people* ; viu = via.

2) Second or O-Declension.

Sing. N. us (os, us). Acc. um (om). G. eís. D. uí. Abl. ud (ud). Loc. eí.
Plur. N. us. Acc. uss. G. um. Abl. uís (ois).

Example : status ; (dolus).

As in Umbrian, the Nom. S. often takes other forms : ins for inus ; ans for anus ; ís for ius, &c.
The variation of Neuters resembles that in Latin.

3) Third or Consonant and I-Nouns.

Sing. N. s or none. Acc. ím. D. eí. Abl. id.
Plur. N. ss or none. Acc. D. Abl. íss.
The Neuters have no distinctive peculiarities.

Note. 'Meddís (meddix, medix) tuvtíkus' (tuticus) is the Oscan name for the chief magistrate, or mayor, of a town. See Liv. xxiii. 35, xxiv. 19, xxvi. 6.

d) Oscan Verbs :

Verb of Being : root es ; sum ; ísí = est ; (set) = sit ; estud = esto : root fu : (fuid) = fiat : fusíd (fust) = fiet ; fufans = fuerunt.

The Conjugations are Consonant and A only : Pres. Ind. Act. (anget) = agit ; amfret = ambit ; (dat) ; faamat = habitat ; eítuns = eunt. Pass. (vincter) = vincitur ; sakarater = sacratur.

Pres. Conj. Act. (angit) = agat ; (hipid) = habeat, (pruhipid) = prohibeat;
stait = stet ; (dat) = det : Plur. 3rd P. -ins.

Pass. sakahiter = sacretur.

S. Fut. Ind. Act. (didest) = didet, (deivast) = iurabit.

Perf. Ind. Act. prufatted = probavit ; (deicans) = dixerunt.

Fut. Perf. Act. (dicust) = dixerit ; (hipust) = habuerit; (fefacust) =
fecerit.

Imperat. Act. likitud (licitud) = liceto ; factud = facito.

Infin. Pres. (deicum) = dicere ; (moltaum) = multare ; (censamur) =
censeri.

Part. Perf. P. (censto) = censo ; pusst = positus ; (deivatud) = iurato.
Gerundive : upsannam = operandam.

e) Oscan Pronouns.

1) Possessive : suveis = sui ; suvad = suā ; (sivom, siom) = suum, n.
2) Demonstrative : izik (izic), iuk, idik (idic) = is, ea, id : in (ionc)
   = eum ; isidum = idem : ekik (exeic) = illud, with other case-forms of
   the same pronoun, of which Nom. S. is not extant, but supposed by
   Mommsen to be ekus, eksus, by Aufrecht eiso (eizo), Umbr. eso = hic.
3) Relative and Interrogative.
   S. Pus (pos) pai (pae) pud (pod) = qui quae quod : (phim) pam pud
   (pod) = quem quam quod : puv = quo. Pl. pus = qui ; (pous) =
   quibus. Pis, pid = quis quid? (pieis) = cuius? ; (pitpit) = quidquid ;
   -pid = -que ; puturus-pid = utrique, pl.

f) Oscan Particles :

1) Adverbs : (amprufid) = improbe ; ip = ibi ; (mais) = magis ; (min) =
   minus ; pruf = probe ; fortis = forte.
2) Prepositions : Separable : az = ante ; anter = inter ; ehtrad = extra ;
   kum (com) = cum, com ; (contrud) = contra ; up (op) = ob, apud ;
   (perum) = per ; pust (post) = post. Inseparable : (an- am- a-) =
   in- ; (-en) = in ; pru- = pro.
3) Conjunctions : Coord. ; avt (aut) = at ; (auti) = aut; ekkum = item ;
   inim (inim), in (in), &c. = et ; (-ni) = ne ; nep (ne, nei, neip) =
   non, ne. Subord. pun (pon) = quom, cum ; (pam, pan) = quam ;
   (pruter-pam pruter-pan) = priusquam ; puf = ubi ; pukkapid (pocapit)
   = quandoque ; sva (sve) = si.

Note. The chief Latin Verb-roots found in Oscan are : ag- ; c-ben- =
venire ; kumben- = convenire ; censa- = censere ; da- ; deic- dic- = dicere ;
(deiva-) = iurare ; e- i- = ire ; em- ; es- ; fac- ; fu- ; habe- haf- (hip-) =
habere (pruhip- = prohibere) ; liga- = legare ; (molta-) = multare ; pat- =
pandere ; prufa- = probare ; pus-(pos-) = ponere ; rega- = regere ; sac- =
sancire ; sakara- = sacrare ; sta- ; vinc- = vincere.

[The fullest account of the Umbrian dialect will be found in Aufrecht
and Kirchhoff's *Umbrische Denkmäler* : of the Oscan, Sabellian, &c. in
T. Mommsen's *Die Unteritalischen Dialekte.* The student should also consult Schleicher's *Vergleichende Grammatik*, Corssen's *Aussprache*, &c., and
various papers in Kühn's *Zeitschrift* by Corssen and other scholars.
Donaldson's *Varronianus* gives much valuable information : but some of its
theories must be cautiously viewed. See Peile's *Introduction to Greek and
Latin Etymology.*]

C) Specimens of Ancient Latin, taken from Corpus Inscriptionum
Latinarum (Ritschl and Mommsen).

I. Epitaph of L. Cornelius Scipio Consul B.C. 259.

Honc oino ploirume cosentiont R[omai]
duonoro optimo fuise uiro uiroro

Luciom Scipione : filios Barbati
consol censor aidilis hic fuet a[pud uos :]
hec cepit Corsica Aleriaque urbe [pucnandod :]
dedit Tempestatebus aide mereto[d uotam.] 32.

[In Classical Latin : Hunc unum plurimi consentiunt Romae bonorum optimum fuisse virum virorum Lucium Scipionem : filius Barbati consul censor aedilis hic fuit apud vos : hic cepit Corsicam Aleriamque urbem pugnando, dedit Tempestatibus aedem merito votam.]

II. Epitaph of another L. Cornelius Scipio.

L. Cornelio Gn. F. Gn. N. Scipio.
Magna sapientia multasque uirtutes
aetate quom parua posidet hoc saxsum.
quoiei uita defecit, non honos, honore,
is hic situs quei nunquam uictus est uirtutei.
annos gnatus uiginti is Diteist mandatus :
ne quairatis honore quei minus sit mandatus. 34.

[In Classical Latin : L. Cornelius Gnaei filius, Gnaei nepos, Scipio : magnam sapientiam multasque virtutes aetate cum parva possidet hoc saxum : cui vita defecit non honos honorem (?) is hic situs est qui nunquam victus est virtute : annos natus viginti is Diti est mandatus, ne quaeratis honorem (eius) qui non sit mandatus.]

III. The Columna Rostrata in honour of C. Duilius, Consul B.C. 260, which seems to be an antiquarian restoration of the Empire, is restored and explained by the learned editors, I. 195. But every line and sentence is mutilated. No consonants are doubled ; c stands for g, as lecioneis ; exem*et* for exemit ; we find max*i*mosque macistratos, but [max]*u*mas copias ; castreis, socieis ; numei ; naveis, claseis, but also navales, clases ; exfociont = effugiunt.

Extract : Ma[celam . .] pucnandod cepet enque eodem mac[istratod prospere r]em navebos marId consol prImos c[eset c]lasesque navales prImos ornavet, cumque eis navebos claseis Poenicas om[nes . . ·max] umasque copias Cartaciniensis praesente[d maxumod d]ictatored o[lor]om in altod marId puc[nandod vicet].

[In Classical Latin : Macelam urbem pugnando cepit, inque eodem magistratu prospere rem navibus mari consul primus gessit, classesque navales primus ornavit, cumque eis navibus classes Punicas omnes . . maximasque copias Carthaginienses praesente maximo dictatore illorum in alto mari pugnando vicit.] I = ī.

In the second 'navebos' the stonecutter had engraved u first, then o over it.

IV. Extract from the Senatusconsultum de Bacchanalibus, B.C. 186.

Haice utei in conventionid exdeicatis ne minus trinum noundinum ; senatuosque sententiam utei scientes esetis . . . eorum sententia ita fuit : sei ques esent, quei arvorsum ead fecisent quam suprad scriptum est, eeis rem caputalem faciendam censuere . . . atque utei hoce in tabolam ahenam inceideretis, ita senatus aiquom censuit ; uteique eam figier ioubeatis, ubei facilumed gnoscier potisit ; atque utei ea Bacanalia, sei qua sunt, exstrad quam sei quid ibei sacri est, ita utei suprad scriptum est, in diebus X. quibus vobeis tabelae datai erunt faciatis utei dismota sient in agro Teurano, I. 196.

[In Classical Latin : Haec ut in contione edicatis ne minus trinum nundinum ; senatusque sententiam ut scientes essetis . . . eorum sententia ita fuit : si qui essent qui adversum ea fecissent quam (i.e. aliter quam) supra scriptum est, eis rem capitalem faciendam censuere . . . atque ut hoc in tabulam ahenam incideretis, ita senatus aequum censuit ; utque eam figi iubeatis, ubi facillime nosci possit ; atque ut ea Bacchanalia, si qua sunt, extra quam si quid ibi sacri est, ita ut supra scriptum est, in diebus X. quibus vobis tabulae datae erunt, faciatis ut dimota sint in agro Teurano.]

V. Extract from the Lex Iulia Municipalis, enacted by C. Iulius Caesar, B.C. 49.

Queiquomque inmunicipieis coloneis praefectureis conciliabuleis c. R. IIvir. IIIIvir. erunt aliove quo nomine mag. potestatemve sufragio eorum, quei quoiusque municipi coloniae praefecturae fori conciliabuli erunt, habebunt, neiquis eorum quem in eo municipio colonia praefectura foro conciliabulo in senatum decuriones conscriptosve legito neve sublegito neve coptato neve recitandos curato nisi indemortuei damnateive locum eiusne quei confessus erit se senatorem decurionem conscreiptumve ibei h. l. esse non licere, I. 206.

[Here c. R. = civium Romanorum ; mag. = magistratum ; IIvir. = duumviri ; IIIIvir. = quattuorviri ; h. l. = hac lege. Observe ei for ī in Abl. and Nom. Pl. ; neiquis for nequis ; su*f*ragio ; conscr*ei*ptum ; and the Prep. 'in' proclitically joined to its case: inmunicipieis, indemortuei locum.]

E. POETIC FORMS AND IDIOMS.

Although the general Rules of Grammar are applicable to poetry as well as to prose, yet poetry has many words, phrases, constructions, and collocations peculiar to itself. A few of these will here be mentioned.

I. ETYMOLOGY AND USE OF WORDS.

1) The archaic Gen. of 1st Decl. in *ai* is used by the Epic poets, Lucretius and Virgil, as, aulai, aquai.

2) Virgil and Horace always contract the Gen. of 2nd Decl. in *ii* : otî, tugurî, ingenî, imperî. The elegiac poets retain *ii* generally.

3) The contraction of the Gen. *arum*, *orum* into *ûm* is confined to Masculine Substantives: agricolûm, sociûm ; and of Adjectives to a few polysyllables only : magnanimûm heroum.

4) Many Genitives in *ium* are contracted into *um* : ăpûm, cohortûm. This may be done in Present Participles : amantûm. Words of the form ‿◡‿, as nūbĭum, seldom lose i ; but mensûm, sedûm are found.

5) The Dat. in *ui*, and the Gen. and Dat. in *ei*, may be contracted into *u, e* : victu for victui, fide for fidei.

6) The Imperf. of the 4th Conj. in *ibam*, and the Fut. in *ibo*, are archaisms occasionally used by Virgil : vestibat for vestiebat, This is not done in lyric verse, rarely in elegiac. The Infin. Pass. in *ier* is an archaism used occasionally in epic poetry ; not allowable in elegiac, rare in lyric. Other archaic forms are found.

7) Such forms as amaram amasse, fleram flesse, noram nosse, audieram audisse are of usual occurrence.

8) Tmesis is frequent, as Q u a e me c u m q u e vocant terrae, Verg. ; in q u e li g a t u s, Verg. Cum tu argento p o s t omnia p o n a s, Hor.

9) (*a*) Substantive is used for Adjective or Participle : Victor equus ; fabulae manes ; populus late rex.

(*b*) Participle or Adjective for Substantive : volitans, *an insect* ; volantes, *birds* ; natantes, *fishes* ; praeceps, *a precipice* ; planum, *a level surface*; inane, *the* (*void*) *air.* So, Opaca domorum, strata viarum, &c.

(*c*) Neuter Adjective for Adverb; Lugubre rubens; perfidum ridens; transversa tuentes, &c.

10) The Plural Number for the Singular: as, Tua numina posco; sibila colla tumens. And the Singular for the Plural: as, Thyna merce beatum; late loca milite complet.

11) Transitive Verbs are used intransitively: Venti posuere, Verg. Intransitives used transitively: Horret iratum mare, Hor. Even Passives sometimes assume a Transitive force: Fontis avertitur, Verg.

12) The use of the Simple for the Compound Verb is a poetic idiom: Pone moras for depone; tendere for contendere; tenere for retinere, &c.

13) In regard to tenses, the Historic Present for the Preterite is often used; also the Preterite Aorist for the Present to express habit or frequency; the Perf. Infin. for the Pres. Infin.

14) Many words are purely poetic, not being used in prose. They are too numerous to be here specified, but should be noted in reading.

II. SYNTAX.

1. Agreement. A Neuter Complement with Masc. and Fem. Substantives: Turpe senex miles; and Synesis, are frequent in poetry.

2. Government.

   1) The Accusative of Respect after Adjectives and Verbs is very frequent: Cetera laetus; sibila colla tumens.
   2) The Dative after Compound Verbs is favoured by the poets. Verbs of *contending, repelling, differing, uniting,* have a Dative in poetry; but in prose, for the most part, a Preposition with its Case: Mihi contendere noli; solstitium pecori defendite; scurrae distabit amicus; verba sociare chordis, &c.
   A Dative after a Verb of Motion is peculiar to poetry, but rare: It clamor caelo. A Dative after a Finite Passive Verb is poetic: Neque cernitur ulli.
   3) A large number of Adjectives govern a Genitive in poetry only: Inane lymphae, nimius pugnae, gravis morum, integer aevi, &c.
   4) The Infinitive Mood after Adjectives is frequent in poetry, and rare in good prose: Callidus condere, catus iaculari, audax omnia perpeti, &c. After some Substantives: Causa perire, tempus abire, &c. After Verbs of motion: Populare penatis venimus: of entreaty; Hoc petit esse suum: of feeling; Furit reperire, dedignata teneri: of hastening; Trepidat claudere, &c. Est is used for licet with Infin.: Aenean cernere erat: Nec sit mihi credere tantum. The use of the Participle after Verbs of Sense for the Accusative and Infinitive is a poetic Graecism: Sensit medios delapsus in hostis. The Infinitive Active is used poetically where a prose writer would use the Participle in *dus*; Dat ferre talentum; quem sumis celebrare, &c.
   5) Many instances of Ellipsis and Pleonasm are found in Poetry, too numerous to be here cited.

Note.—Historians, as Sallust, Livy, above all Tacitus, often heighten their style by the intermixture of poetic imagery and expression, especially when a narrative is picturesque, or a speech impassioned.

III. COLLOCATION.

The Collocation of words in poetry is much more free than that of prose, but will be better learnt by reading and practice than by any attempt to reduce the subject to rules.

F. SUPPLEMENT TO FIGURATE CONSTRUCTION. § 61.

1. *Anacoluthon* is the passing from one construction to another before the former is completed: 'Si, ut Graeci dicunt, omnes aut Graios esse aut barbaros, vereor ne Romulus barbarorum rex fuerit,' C. 'Quae qui in utramque partem excelso animo magnoque despiciunt, cumque aliqua his ampla et honesta res obiecta est, totos ad se convertit et rapit; tum quis non admiretur splendorem pulchritudinemque virtutis?' C. Anacoluthon is often due to Attraction.

2. *Hysteron-Proteron* is when, of two things, that which naturally comes first is mentioned last: 'Moriamur et in media arma ruamus,' Verg. *Ae.* ii. 353.

The following Figures belong to Rhetoric :—

3. *Synecdoche* puts the part for the whole: 'Caput for homo; tectum for domus,' &c. Sometimes the whole stands for a part: 'Sal sextante est' (Liv.), for modius salis.

4. *Allegoria* is a chain of metaphors: 'Claudite iam rivos, pueri, sat prata biberunt,' Verg. *B.* iii. 111. Meaning, 'Cease to sing, O shepherds; sufficient recreation has been taken.'

5. *Hyperbole* magnifies beyond credibility: 'Sudor fluit undique rivis,' Verg. *Ae.* v. 200.

6. *Litotes* states less than is actually meant: Non laudo, for culpo.

7. *Ironia* says one thing and means another, but so as to let the real meaning be understood: 'Egregiam vero laudem et spolia ampla refertis tuque puerque tuus,' Verg. *Ae.* iv. 93.

8. *Climax* rises by gradations, like the steps of a ladder: 'Quod libet iis, licet; quod licet, possunt; quod possunt, audent,' C.

9. *Polyptoton* brings together cases of the same Noun: 'Iam clipeus clipeis, umbone repellitur umbo; ense minax ensis, pede pes et cuspide cuspis,' Stat.

10. *Paronomasia* is a play upon the sound of words: 'Tibi parata erunt verba, huic verbera,' Ter.

11. *Antithesis* contrasts opposites: 'Urbis amatorem Fuscum salvere iubemus ruris amatores,' Hor.

12. *Chiasmus* places a double Antithesis in introverted order: 'Ratio nostra consentit, repugnat oratio,' C. *Fin.* iii. 3. 'Non video quomodo sedare possint mala praesentia praeteritae voluptates,' C. *T. D.* v. 26. 'Alba ligustra cadunt, vaccinia nigra leguntur,' Verg. *B.* ii. 18.

13. *Oxymoron* unites seeming contraries: 'Temporis angusti mansit concordia discors,' Lucan i. 98.

14. *Periphrasis* describes a simple fact by various attending circumstances. Thus, instead of 'now night is approaching,' Virgil says, 'Et iam summa procul villarum culmina fumant, maioresque cadunt altis de montibus umbrae,' *B.* i. 83. See the beautiful periphrases of old age and death in Ecclesiastes, ch. xii.

15. *Simile* or *Parabole* illustrates a statement by an apt comparison: 'Per urbis Hannibal Italas ceu flamma per taedas vel Eurus per Siculas equitavit undas,' Hor. *C.* iv. 4. 42.

16. *Apostrophe* is an appeal to some person or thing: 'Quid non mortalia pectora cogis auri sacra fames?' Verg. *Ae.* iii. 56.

17. *Prosopopoeia* represents inanimate things as living and acting: 'Te Spes et albo rara Fides colit velata panno,' Hor. *C.* i. 35. 21. 'Belli ferratos rupit Discordia postis,' *Enn.*

18. *Aposiopesis* suppresses the conclusion of a thought: 'Quos ego— sed motos praestat componere fluctus,' Verg. *Ae.* i. 135.

Most of these Figures (to which might be added others) are used in Prose as well as in Poetry.

G. MONEY, WEIGHT, AND MEASURE.

I.

'As' was the Roman unit of weight and measure. See its duodecimal division, § 34. viii.

II. Money.

1. Cattle were the earliest Italian medium of exchange. The word 'pecunia' (from 'pecus') preserved the memory of this fact, as Engl. *chattel* and *fee*, from Germ. *vieh*, point to the same custom in the Teuton branch. Cattle fines are noticed in ancient laws as commuted for sums of money; a sheep being rated at 10 'asses librales,' an ox at 100.

2. The metals used for agricultural implements, iron and (in Italy) copper, were the next medium of exchange. These were at first weighed out roughly (the 'libra' or pound being the unit of this 'aes rude'), then cut in bars of various shapes and sizes, corresponding to the weights, and bearing generally some mark, as an ox, a swine, &c. This was called 'aes signatum.' Its origin is referred to the reign of Servius, that is, to a time before authentic history. 'Aestimare,' *to value*, is derived from 'aes;' and the act of weighing copper continued in later times to be the legal form of 'mancipatio' in sales, repayments, and in one matrimonial solemnity (per aes et libram). The bit of unwrought copper with which the purchaser struck the scale was called 'raudus' or 'rodusculum.'

3. About the year B.C. 451, U.C. 303, copper money was first coined, with impressions obverse and reverse, by the Decemviri. Their coinage comprised the 'as libralis,' and some of its fractional parts, 'semis,' 'triens,' 'quadrans,' 'uncia,' and 'semuncia.' It had an alloy of about 7 per cent. of tin, not reducing its intrinsic value; but, later, another alloy of about 23 per cent. of lead, by which the value was reduced, lead being in proportion to copper as 1 : 2. Varro says: 'Libram pondo as valebat': and in theory, this copper 'as' was libral, equivalent to a pound of 12 ounces: but in practice existing specimens shew variation from 8 or 9 to 14 ounces, giving an average of about 10. Hence this coinage, on a scale nominally duodecimal, was really decimal.

4. It continued in use nearly 200 years: but shortly before the first Punic War, about B.C. 269, U.C. 485, a mint was established in the temple of Juno Moneta, and three commissioners were appointed (triumviri monetales auro argento aere flando feriundo), who began to coin silver money; the coins being the denarius (nominally 10 asses), the quinarius or half-denar (nominally 5 asses), and the sestertius or quarter-denar (nominally 2½ asses). About the same time, a revolution was made in the copper money itself. The libral as (nominally of 12, but actually 10 ounces on the average) was reduced from the libral to the triental standard, that is, to the weight of 4 ounces. Nevertheless, the old libral standard was occasionally used or referred to, under the title of 'aes grave.' As the

denarius represented 10 asses of the triental standard, =40 unciae, its quarter part, the sestertius, was equal to 10 unciae, which was the average value of the libral as. Thus it came to pass that, in the new monetary system, the silver sesterce represented the old copper 'as,' so that any numerical sum 'aeris gravis' (as in Livy) may be counted at the same number of sesterces, under the triental standard.

5. Between the first and second Punic Wars, the value of silver in proportion to copper fell considerably. In consequence, the triental 'as' sank first to the sextantar, and then, B.C. 217, U.C. 537, by the Flaminian law, to the uncial standard. At the same time the denarius was raised, by way of compensation, to the value of 16 (uncial) asses, making the sestertius equal to 4. The weight of this denarius was $\frac{1}{84}$ of a pound; that of the older one, $\frac{1}{72}$, and the smaller silver coins in proportion. Among these was a coin called 'victoriatus,' from the figure of Victory stamped on it. The original value of this was $\frac{3}{4}$ of the denarius; but by the Clodian law, B.C. 104, U.C. 650, it was reduced to the same value as the 'quinarius,' or $\frac{1}{2}$ of the 'denarius.'

6. Although the sesterce, when =4 uncial or semuncial asses, ceased to possess the ancient value of the libral as, it still continued to represent the popular calculation of 'aes grave.' During the first Civil Wars, B.C. 86, U.C. 668, the Marian Consul Valerius Flaccus carried an iniquitous law (afterwards repealed by Sulla), enabling debtors to clear themselves by paying one coined 'as' ($\frac{1}{4}$ of the sesterce) in place of one ancient 'as,' or the sesterce itself. In other words, debtors might discharge themselves from all liability by paying 25 per cent. of their debts, or, as we commonly say, five shillings in the pound.

7. After the second Punic War silver became so abundant that it thenceforward constituted the chief Roman currency, and copper money was, as among ourselves, small change only. This led to a further reduction of the copper 'as,' which, by the Papirian Law, B.C. 89, U.C. 665, fell to a semuncial standard, indicating a rise in the value of copper as compared with silver. From this date copper coinage ceased for half a century, being resumed during the second Civil Wars. Besides the copper coins heretofore mentioned, the following were also in use from time to time: the 'dupondius,' in value 2 'asses'; 'tressis,' 3 'asses'; 'decussis' 10, &c. 'Centussis' was not a coin, but a sum; and when Persius says, 'Centum Graecos curto centusse licetur,' he means that the rude centurion would not give an 'as' apiece for 100 Greek philosophers.

8. Gold coinage in the republican times was occasional but not frequent, chiefly for the purpose of military donations. The 'aureus' of Sulla was $\frac{1}{30}$ of a lb. of gold; that of Pompey $\frac{1}{36}$; that of C. Julius Caesar $\frac{1}{40}$; that of Augustus $\frac{1}{42}$. This last and most important coin was made equal to 25 denarii or 100 sesterces. Mommsen values it at 1*l.* 1*s.* 5*d.*, Hultsch at 1*l.* 1*s.* 9*d.* Thus it corresponds nearly to the English guinea. This rate makes the Augustan denarius about 10·4*d.* and the sesterce 2·6*d.*, though before the gold coinage they were severally about 8·4*d.* and 2·1*d.* Some writers have been led into error by confounding the intrinsic value, or weight, of these two coins with their current or relative value. Finding the oldest republican denarius to have contained $\frac{1}{72}$ of a pound of silver, the later republican and Augustan $\frac{1}{84}$, the Neronian $\frac{1}{96}$, they have fallen into the mistake of assuming a corresponding depreciation of the *current* value of the coins. As between the older and later republican coinage, silver being the standard of both, such calculation would be just; but, when the Augustan gold standard came in, the current values of the silver (and gold) denar and of the brass sesterce (its fourth part) then coined were determined by their several relations to the

'aureus' as $\frac{1}{25}$ and $\frac{1}{100}$. At that time (see Mommsen, p. 766, &c.) gold was not quite ten times as valuable as silver, while now it exceeds silver in the proportion of more than 15 : 1. As the relative values changed, derangement of the coinage would result ; but the calculations here given hold good for at least two centuries after Augustus (allowing for the simultaneous reduction of the intrinsic value of the coins by Nero). For the further details of this intricate subject the student must consult T. Mommsen's 'Geschichte des Römischen Münzwesens,' of which a convenient abridgment is found in Hultsch's 'Griechische und Römische Metrologie,' though with calculations of value sometimes not agreeing with those of Mommsen. We now set down a few practical rules, enabling the student to appreciate, at least approximately, the coins and sums cited by classical authors, especially by Livy, Cicero, and Tacitus.

9. The 'sestertius' ('semis-tertius' because 2½ asses originally, though afterwards = 4) is often called 'nummus' (a term borrowed from the Sicilian coinage, νόμος), sometimes 'sestertius nummus.' It forms the basis of all pecuniary calculation after the following manner :—

(*a*) Sums under 1,000 sesterces are named in sesterces ('sestertii' or 'nummi'): 'decem sestertios (nummos)' = 10 *sesterces* ; 'quinos sestertios (nummos)' = 5 *sesterces each*, &c.

(*b*) In sums above 1,000 sesterces, the thousands may be described as consisting of sesterces: 'duo milia sestertiorum (sestertiûm, nummûm) ;' 2,000 *sesterces* ; 'sexagena milia nummum (sestertium),' 60,000 *sesterces each*.

Or a (supposable) noun sestertium, only found in the Plural 'sestertia,' may be used, where each of the 'sestertia' counted means a *sum* (not a coin) of about 1,000 sesterces. 'Sexcenta sestertia' = 600,000 *sesterces* ; 'duodena sestertia' = 12,000 *sesterces each*, &c.

Or, again, both 'milia' and 'sestertia' can be used : 'dena milia sestertia' = 10,000 sesterces. And, in poetry, 'milia' is used with ellipse of 'sestertium :' 'mullum sex milibus emit,' *he bought a mullet for* 6,000 *sesterces*, Juv. Horace has 'bis dena sestertia nummum,' = 20,000 *sesterces*.

On the mode of writing compound numerals see § 34, vii. Thus 'sestertia tria milia et quadringenti octoginta nummi' = 3,480 *sesterces* ; 'xxxi milium quingentorum lx nummorum' = 31,560 sesterces.

(*c*) The last mentioned mode of calculation extends to all sums under a million. For a million, and all higher amounts, must be used the Numeral Adverbs ; see § 34. vii. *e.* But the words centum (centena) milia are frequently understood, not expressed, in pecuniary calculations, with these Adverbs. Thus may be written deciens sestertium (sestertii, sestertio) or deciens (understanding sestertium), to express 1,000,000 sesterces. In Cicero we also find 'deciens centena milia,' and in Horace 'deciens centena' to express this sum. The normal sum 'centena milia' is rated by Hultsch at 875*l.* for the republican age, and 1,087*l.* 13*s.* 4*d.* for the Augustan. As this is probably a high estimate, we may take these sums approximately at 870*l.* and 1,080*l.* When an amount is described with more than one Adverb, the numbers they contain must be added together if the larger Numeral stands first, but multiplied when the smaller is first ; care being taken not to reckon the 'centena milia,' which is understood, more than once. Thus 'miliens quingentiens' = 150,000,000 *sesterces*, but 'quaterdeciens miliens' = 1,400,000,000 *sesterces*.

(d) For the Gen. 'sestertiûm' may be written its symbol HS, for IIS, $2\frac{1}{2}$ (or, as some say, for LLS), the cross line indicating. the Pl. 'asses,' as the Pl. 'librae' is indicated by our ℔, £.

(e) If the sums are described by cypher, it is sometimes difficult to distinguish whether sesterces, or sestertia, or centena milia sestertium are meant, unless the rule mentioned (§ 34, vii. 2) be observed. Thus, when Livia Augusta bequeathed to Galba 'sestertium quingentiens,' Tiberius reduced the amount to 'sestertia quingenta, quia notata non perscripta erat summa.' That is, he chose to read HS$\overline{D}$ for HS|$\overline{D}$|.

Examples :—

'HS deciens et octingenta milia' = 1,800,000 *sesterces.*

Viciens ducenta triginta quinque milia quadringentos decem et septem nummos' = 2,235,417 *sesterces.*

(Hultsch cites a place in which mille is used for deciens.)

10) The following rules, of a roughly practical nature, will enable the student to calculate approximately the sums which occur in classical authors :—

1) For sums in 'aes grave' (often in Livy) count the amount 'aeris gravis' as the same amount of sesterces, and count the sesterce = 2·4*d.* Thus 'milia aeris gravis' = 1,000 sesterces = 2,400*d.* = 10*l.*

2) For sums under the silver currency from B.C. 217—B.C. 30, U.C. 537—U.C. 624, cited by Cicero and other writers, count the sesterce = 2·1*d.*

If 'sestertia' (i.e. 'milia sestertium') are to be regarded as an exact total of 1,000 sesterces, this would give them the current value of 8*l.* 15*s.*, and this is a convenient figure, though Hultsch rates it somewhat higher, 8*l.* 15*s.* 6*d.*

This calculation, as already stated, gives to 'centena milia (sestertium)' an approximate value of 870*l.*, which will be the multiple understood with the Adverbs in -iens. Thus 'deciens' = 8,700*l.*, 'centiens' = 87,000*l.*, 'miliens' = 870,000*l.*, &c., approximately.

3) Under the gold standard from B.C. 30 to A.D. 200, count the sesterce, as above stated, 2·6*d.*, 'sestertia' at 10*l.* 16*s.*, 'centena milia' at 1,080*l.* approximately. Thus 'deciens' = 10,800*l.*, 'centiens' = 108,000*l.*, 'miliens,' = 1,080,000*l.*, approximately.

III. INTEREST.

The As and its fractional parts were used to calculate interest. Thus (interest being paid monthly at the rate of so much per 100 Asses) :—

Unciae usurae = $\frac{1}{12}$ per cent. per month =			1 per cent. per annum
Sextantes	= $\frac{1}{6}$,,	,,	= 2 ,,	,,
Quadrantes	= $\frac{1}{4}$,,	,,	= 3 ,,	,,
&c.		&c.		&c.
Asses usurae = 1 per cent. per month = 12 per cent. per annum.				

Asses usurae were also called centesimae ; and binae centesimae = 2 per cent. per month = 24 per cent. ; so quaternae centesimae = 48 per cent. per annum. Horace says : 'Quinas hic capiti mercedes exsecat' (i.e. quinas centesimas), *this man slices off* 60 *per cent. from the capital* ; because in lending money he deducts from it interest at the rate of 5 per cent. per month = 60 per cent. per annum.

Unciarium fenus, the yearly interest legalised by the Twelve Tables, was probably 1 uncia per As (=$8\frac{1}{3}$ per cent.) for the old year of 10 months.

Note. The silver sesterce of republican times had also the following fractional parts : 'libella = $\frac{1}{10}$ sest. (quinque libellae = $\frac{1}{2}$) ; sembella ($\frac{1}{2}$ libella) = $\frac{1}{20}$ sest. ; teruncius ($\frac{1}{2}$ sembella) = $\frac{1}{40}$ sest. Cicero (*Att.* vii. 2) uses these terms to express fractional parts of an inheritance ($\frac{1}{10}$, $\frac{1}{20}$, $\frac{1}{40}$ severally). See Mommsen, p. 199.

IV. WEIGHT.

The Unit or As of weight was the 'libra' or Roman pound (the supposed weight which a man could support on his hand horizontally extended). It was duodecimally divided (see § 34, viii.), the 'uncia,' *ounce*, being its 12th part, and the scriptulum or scripulum, *scruple*, its 288th part. Its exact relation to English weight is a debated question. See Smith's *Dict. Ant.* under *Libra* and *Pondera*, where it is calculated at about 5050 grains. Hultsch (with Böckh and Mommsen) rates it at 327·453 grammes (French) = 5044 grains English nearly. *Metrol.* § 21.

V. MEASURE OF LENGTH.

(*a*) The Unit or As of length was 'pes,' *the foot* : the human body furnishing the first or technical measurement. 'Digitus' was *a finger-breadth* : 'palmus,' *a hand-breadth*, = 4 digits : 'pes,' *a foot*, = 4 palms = 16 digits.

(*b*) In the second, or duodecimal division, of the foot (§ 34, viii.), 'uncia,' the 12th part, was *an inch*. Hence 3 unciae = 4 digits = 1 palmus.

We find 2 feet sometimes called 'dupondius ;' $2\frac{1}{2}$ feet 'sestertius' (also 'gradus') ; $1\frac{1}{2}$ 'sesquipes.'

(*c*) Coming to larger measures,

'Palmipes' = pes + palmus = $1\frac{1}{4}$ foot = 20 digits.

'Cubitus,' *cubit* (measured from the elbow to the tip of the middle finger), = $1\frac{1}{2}$ foot = 6 palms = 24 digits.

'Ulna, *ell*, is often a synonym of 'cubitus,' $1\frac{1}{2}$ foot : but it sometimes means the full span of the human arms, reckoned = 6 feet.

(*d*) Land was measured out by the 'pertica' or 'decempeda,' a measuring rod of 10 feet. An 'actus' of length = 12 decempedas.

(*e*) For the measurement of roads the unit was 'passus,' *a pace or double step* = twice $2\frac{1}{2}$ feet or 2 'gradus' = 5 feet.

'Mille passus' (or 'milia passuum' or 'milia'), 1,000 *paces*, expressed the Roman *mile* (miliarium) = 5,000 *feet*.

'Stadium,' *a furlong* (borrowed from Greece), was $\frac{1}{8}$ of a mile = 625 feet.

The Roman mile was about $\frac{1}{5}$ of the geographical mile, and less than an English mile by about $\frac{1}{13}$.

(*f*) The relation of the Roman 'pes' to modern feet is a difficult problem. See Hultsch, *Metr.* § 15. Smith's *Dict. Ant.* states it as less than the English foot by $\frac{3}{16}$ of an inch.

According to Hyginus, a standard foot (pes monetalis) was kept in the temple of Juno Moneta.

VI. MEASURE OF SURFACE.

The As of superficial measure was the 'iugerum' or Roman acre : which Smith's *Dict. Ant.* states at about $\frac{5}{8}$ of an English acre. Hultsch's statement is the same. It contained 2 square 'actus' = 28,800 square feet. It

was duodecimally divided, like the 'libra' and 'pes.' Of the fractions of
the 'iugerum' the most important is the 'scripulum' (scruple) or 'decempeda quadrata' = 100 square feet. Of these the 'clima' contained 36, and
the 'actus' 144. Surfaces exceeding the iugerum were: heredium =
2 iugera : centuria = 100 heredia ; saltus = 4 centuriae.

All these surfaces were squares, except the 'iugerum' itself, which was
the sum of two equal squares. The sides of these squares were related to
each other as follows, the decempeda here counting as 1 :

dec.	clima	actus	hered.	cent.	salt.
1	6	12	24	240	480

The following Table (given by Hultsch) shews the relations fully :

saltus	1					
centuria	4	1				
heredium	400	100	1			
iugerum	800	200	2	1		
actus	1600	400	4	2	1	
clima	6400	1600	16	8	4	1
scripulum	230400	57600	576	288	144	36

VII. MEASURES OF CAPACITY.

i. Liquid Measure.

(a) The Romans took for their standard a vessel of a cubic foot in content, called 'quadrantal,' afterwards (from the Greek ἀμφορεύς)
'amphora.' Its parts (which are chiefly Greek) are thus exhibited
by Hultsch, *Metr.* § 17. 3 :

amphora	1						
urna	2	1					
congius	8	4	1				
sextarius	48	24	6	1			
hemina	96	48	12	2	1		
quartarius	192	96	24	4	2	1	
acetabulum	384	192	48	8	4	2	1
cyathus	576	288	72	12	6	3	1½

(b) The 'sextarius' (less than a pint) was an As duodecimally divided,
like the 'libra,' 'pes,' and 'iugerum,' the 'cyathus' being its
'uncia' (not quite half an ordinary wineglass). Hence are to be
understood the following passages, cited by Hultsch :

'Interponis aquam subinde, Rufe,
Et, si cogeris a sodale, raram
Diluti bibis unciam Falerni.'
Mart. i. 106.

'Quotiens largissime se invitaret, senos sextantes non excessit.'
Suet. *Aug.* 77.

(Seni sextantes, i.e. 12 cyathi, fall short of a full pint of wine.)
'Poto ego sextantes, tu potas, Cinna, deunces,
Et quereris quod non, Cinna, bibamus idem.'
Mart. xi. 36.

Martial also speaks of one who was 'septunce multo perditus.' In the
following epigram he alludes to the custom of drinking to the health
of a person as many 'cyathi' as there were letters in his name.

Quincunces et sex cyathos bessemque bibamus,
Gaius ut fiat Iulius et Proculus.—Mart. x. 36.

(*c*) The 'semuncia' was called 'ligula,' *a spoon* carrying ½ 'cyathus;' the 'sicilicus' was 'cochleare', carrying ¼ 'cyathus.'

(*d*) 'Culeus' ('culleus') was a wine-vat, holding 20 amphoras. The 'amphora' itself was an earthen vessel with two handles, whence its name.

(*e*) 'Cadus' is sometimes used in the same sense as 'amphora;' but usually it means a cask of no definite size.

ii. Dry Measure.

The 'modius' approached 2 gallons (¼ bushel) English. Its divisions were—

modius	1					
semodius	2	1				
sextarius	16	8	1			
hemina	32	16	2	1		
quartarius	64	32	4	2	1	
acetabulum	128	64	8	4	2	1
cyathus	192	96	12	6	3	1½

Again the 'sextarius' is duodecimally divisible, its 'uncia' being 'cyathus,' its 'semuncia' being 'ligula.'

Larger measures are 'trimodius' (3 'modii') and 'decemmodius' (10 'modii').

The 'sextarius' is sometimes called 'librarius.'

H. COMPUTATION OF TIME.

A. The Julian Calendar agrees with the English, except in the manner of naming the days of the month. Every Roman month had three chief days : Kalendae or Calendae (Calends), Nonae (Nones), Idus (Ides). The Calends were always the 1st day of the month ; the Nones were on the 5th : the Ides on the 13th ; except in March, May, July, and October, in which months the Nones were on the 7th, the Ides on the 15th.

> March, May, July, October, these, we say,
> Make Nones the seventh, Ides the fifteenth day.

These three days, the Calends, Nones, and Ides, were taken as points, from which the other days were reckoned backwards. That is, the Romans did not say, such and such a day *after*, &c., but such and such a day *before* the Calends, or Nones, or Ides.

Calendae from calare, *to call*; Nonae, *ninth* before Ides; Idus from iduere (=div-idĕre), *to divide*. See Hor. *C.* iv. 11. 14.

B. If January be taken as a sample, the first day was Kalendae Ianuariae. The 2nd must be reckoned backwards from the Nones, which in January fell on the 5th, Nonae Ianuariae. But in this reckoning the day of the Nones itself must be included. Therefore our 4th of January was the 2nd day before the Nones, called pridie (ante) Nonas Ianuarias. The 3rd of January was 'tertio (ante) Nonas Ianuarias;' the 2nd, 'quarto (ante) Nonas Ianuarias;' or, abbreviated, 'III. Non. Ian.,' 'IV. Non. Ian.' To obtain the Roman name for the 6th of January, the reckoning must be made backwards from the Ides, which fell on the 13th, 'Idus Ianuariae.' Thus the 12th was 'pridie Id. Ian. ;' the 11th, 'III. Id. Ian ;' the 10th, 'IV. Id. Ian.,' &c. ; the 6th was therefore 'VIII. Id. Ian.' To obtain the name for the 14th of January, the reckoning is back from the Calends of the next month, Kalendae Februariae. Thus, January 31st was 'pridie Kal. Feb. ;' January 30th, 'III. Kal. Feb.,' &c. &c. ; January 14th was, therefore, 'XIX. Kal. Feb.'

C. From these observations it appears that the Roman name for any given English day may be found by the following rules :—

1) If the given day is between the Calends and Nones of the Roman month, subtract its English number from the English number of the day on which the Nones fall, increased by one ; the remainder will give that number before the Nones by which the day is called in Latin.

2) Similarly, if the given day is between the Nones and Ides of the Roman month, subtract its English number from the English number of the day on which the Ides fall, increased by one ; the remainder will give that number before the Ides by which the day is called in Latin.

Thus, to find the Roman name for the 4th of June, the Nones of June falling on the 5th, subtract 4 from 5 + 1, or 6 ; the remainder is 2 (pridie) ; therefore the 4th of June is 'pridie Non. Iun.' Again ; to find the Roman name for the 10th of May, the Ides of May falling on the 15th, subtract 10 from 15 + 1, or 16 ; the remainder being 6, the 10th of May is called 'VI. Id. Mai.'

3) But if the given day is between the Ides of the given month and the Calends of the next, then subtract its English number from the total number of days in the given month, increased by two ; the remainder will give that number before the Calends of the next month by which the day is called in Latin.

Thus, to find the Roman name for the 18th of August ; subtract 18 from 31 + 2, or 33, the remainder is 15, and August 18th is called 'XV. Kal. Sept.' For April 21st, subtract 21 from 30 + 2, or 32, there remains 11 ; and April 21st is called XI. Kal. Mai. For February 25th, subtract 25 from 28 + 2, or 30, there remains 5 ; and February 25th is called 'V. Kal. Mart.'

D. As regards Construction, the forms Kalendis, Nonis, Idibus, are used as Ablatives of time ; and when tertio, quarto, &c., Kalendas, &c. are used, the words d i e a n t e are understood. But Cicero does not employ these latter phrases: he writes (for instance) 'ante diem tertium Kalendas Ianuarias,' or, in abbreviated form, 'a.d. III. Kal. Ian.,' to express December 30th, and so in every case.

Here the Preposition a n t e has, by a corruption of custom, quitted its proper place before K a l e n d a s, to stand before d i e m, which it does not govern. So merely idiomatic is this mode of expression, that it is used in dependence on Prepositions: 'Consul Latinas in ante diem tertium Idus Sextilis edixit,' *the Consul proclaimed the Latin holidays for the 11th of August*, L. xli. 16. 'De Quinto fratre nuntii nobis tristes venerant ex ante diem iii. Non Iun. usque ad pridie Kal. Sept.,' *I have sad news of my brother Quintus from the 3rd of June down to the 31st of August,* C. *Att.* v. 17.

E. The names of the months are all Adjectives agreeing with m e n s i s understood: Ianuarius, Februarius, Martius, Aprilis, Maius, Iunius, Iulius (so called from Julius Caesar, but before his time Quintilis), Augustus (so called from Augustus Caesar, but before his time Sextilis), September, October, November, December. With the words Kalendae, Nonae, Idus, they are used attributively, very seldom as Possessive Genitives: 'Natus est Augustus IX. K a l e n d a s O c t o b r e s,' *Augustus was born on the 23rd of September*, Suet. *Aug.* 5. 'Memoriā tenent, me a.d. XIII. K a l e n d a s I a n u a r i a s principem revocandae libertatis fuisse,' *they remember that on the 20th of December I took the lead in restoring freedom,*

Days of English Month	MARTIUS, MAIUS, IULIUS, OCTOBER, 31 Days	IANUARIUS, AUGUSTUS, DECEMBER, 31 Days	APRILIS, JUNIUS, SEPTEMBER, NOVEMBER, 30 Days	FEBRUARIUS, 28 Days—in every fourth year 29
1	KALENDIS	KALENDIS	KALENDIS	KALENDIS
2	a.d. VI.	a.d. IV.	a.d. IV.	a.d. IV.
3	a.d. V.	a.d. III.	a.d. III.	a.d. III.
4	a.d. IV.	Pridie	Pridie	Pridie
5	a.d. III.	NONIS	NONIS	NONIS
6	Pridie	a.d. VIII.	a.d. VIII.	a.d. VIII.
7	NONIS	a.d. VII.	a.d. VII.	a.d. VII.
8	a.d. VIII.	a.d. VI.	a.d. VI.	a.d. VI.
9	a.d. VII.	a.d. V.	a.d. V.	a.d. V.
10	a.d. VI.	a.d. IV.	a.d. IV.	a.d. IV.
11	a.d. V.	a.d. III.	a.d. III.	a.d. III.
12	a.d. IV.	Pridie	Pridie	Pridie
13	a.d. III.	IDIBUS	IDIBUS	IDIBUS
14	Pridie	a.d. XIX.	a.d. XVIII.	a.d. XVI.
15	IDIBUS	a.d. XVIII.	a.d. XVII.	a.d. XV.
16	a.d. XVII.	a.d. XVII.	a.d. XVI.	a.d. XIV.
17	a.d. XVI.	a.d. XVI.	a.d. XV.	a.d. XIII.
18	a.d. XV.	a.d. XV.	a.d. XIV.	a.d. XII.
19	a.d. XIV.	a.d. XIV.	a.d. XIII.	a.d. XI.
20	a.d. XIII.	a.d. XIII.	a.d. XII.	a.d. X.
21	a.d. XII.	a.d. XII.	a.d. XI.	a.d. IX.
22	a.d. XI.	a.d. XI.	a.d. X.	a.d. VIII.
23	a.d. X.	a.d. X.	a.d. IX.	a.d. VII.
24	a.d. IX.	a.d. IX.	a.d. VIII.	a.d. VI.
25	a.d. VIII.	a.d. VIII.	a.d. VII.	a.d. V.
26	a.d. VII.	a.d. VII.	a.d. VI.	a.d. IV.
27	a.d. VI.	a.d. VI.	a.d. V.	a.d. III.
28	a.d. V.	a.d. V.	a.d. IV.	Pridie
29	a.d. IV.	a.d. IV.	a.d. III.	
30	a.d. III.	a.d. III.	Pridie	
31	Pridie	Pridie		

Column MARTIUS, MAIUS, IULIUS, OCTOBER — Nonas and Idus grouped to Oct. Iul. Mai. Mart.; Kalendas grouped to Apr. Iun. Aug. Nov.

Column IANUARIUS, AUGUSTUS, DECEMBER — Nonas and Idus grouped to Dec. Aug. Ian.; Kalendas grouped to Feb. Sep. Ian.

Column APRILIS, JUNIUS, SEPTEMBER, NOVEMBER — Nonas and Idus grouped to Apr. Iun. Sept. Nov.; Kalendas grouped to Mai. Iul. Oct. Dec.

Column FEBRUARIUS — Nonas and Idus grouped to Feb.; Kalendas grouped to Mart.

C. *Phil.* xiv. 7. 'Capuam venire iussi sumus a d N o n a s F e b r u a r i a s,' *we were ordered to come to Capua by the 5th of February,* C. *Att.* v. 17. 'VII. I d u s M a i a s aestatis initium,' *the 9th of May is the commencement of summer,* Colum. xi. 2.

Feast-days are sometimes used to express the dates of letters : 'L i b e r a l i- b u s litteras accepi tuas,' *I received your letter on the day of the Feast of Liber,* C. *Att.* ix. 5.

In Leap-year, the twenty-fourth of February (a.d. VI. Kal. Mart.) was reckoned twice over ; hence this day came to be called DIES BISSEXTUS, and Leap-year itself was called ANNUS BISSEXTUS.

K. SIGLARIUM ROMANUM, OR ABBREVIATIONS USED IN LATIN.

1. PRÆNOMINA.

A. Aulus.	K. Kaeso.	P. Publius.	SP. Spurius.
C. Gaius.[1]	L. Lucius.	Q. Quintus.	T. Titus.
CN. Gnaeus.[1]	M. Marcus.	SER. Servius.	TI. Tiberius.
D. Decimus.	M'. Manius.	SEX. Sextus.	

Women's names were expressed by inverting the character : as, Ɔ, Gaia.

2. TITLES.

Cos. Consul.   Coss. Consules or Consulibus.
DES. Designatus.
D. Divus.
IMP. Imperator.
III. V. R. C. Triumvir Reipublicae Constituendae.
P. C. Patres Conscripti.

P. M. Pontifex Maximus.
PRC. Proconsul.
S. P. Q. R. Senatus Populusque Romanus.
TR. PL. Tribunus Plebis.
X. V. Decemvir.
XV. V. S. F. Quindecimviri Sacris Faciundis.

3. IN VOTING ON TRIALS AND ELECTIONS.

A. Absolvo.   C. Condemno.
N. L. Non liquet.

A. P. Antiquam (legem) probo.
V. R. Uti rogas.

4. ON TOMBS.

F. C. Faciundum curavit.
H. C. E. Hic conditus est.
H. S. E. Hic situs est.

OB. Obiit.
P. C. Poni curavit.
V. Vixit.

5. MISCELLANEOUS.

A. U. C. Anno Urbis Conditae.
D. D. Dono dedit.
DD. Dederunt.
D. D. D. Dat, dicat, dedicat.
D. M. Dis Manibus.
F. Filius.
F. F. F. Felix, faustum, fortuna-tum.

O. M. Optumus Maxumus.
S. C. Senatusconsultum.
S. D. Salutem dicit.
S. P. D. Salutem plurimam dicit.
S. V. B. E. E. Q. V. Si vales, bene est, ego quoque valeo.
TR. POT. Tribunicia Potestate.

---

[1] These names are written in MSS. Gaius, Gnaeus, but abbreviated C., Cn.

6. MODERN.

A. C. Anno Christi.
A. D. Anno Domini.
A. M. Anno Mundi.
a. C. n. ante Christum natum.
Cf. Confer or Conferatur.
Coll. Collato or Collatis.
Cod. Codex. Codd. Codices.
Del. Dele or Deleatur.
Ed. Editio. Edd. Editiones.
e.g. Exempli gratia.
Etc. or &c. Et cetera.
h. e. hoc est.
I. C. Iesus Christus.
Ictus. Iurisconsultus.
ibid. ibidem.
i. e. id est.
i. q. idem quod.
L. or Lib. Liber.
L. B. Lectori benevolo.
l. c. loco citato.
p. C. n. post Christum natum.

C. P. P. C. Collatis pecuniis poni curaverunt
Cet. Cetera.
l. l. loco laudato.
leg. lege or legatur.
MS. Manuscriptus (Liber).
MSS. Manuscripti (Libri).
N. B. Nota bene.
N. T. Novum Testamentum.
Obs. Observa or observetur.
PS. Postscriptum.
q. v. quod vide.
sc. scilicet.
s. v. sub voce.
vid. vide or videatur.
v. l. vide locum.
viz. videlicet.
V. Cel. Vir Celeberrimus.
V. Cl. Vir Clarissimus.
V. T. Vetus Testamentum.

7. ACADEMICAL.

A. B. Artium Baccalaureus.
A. M. Artium Magister.
D. Doctor.
LL.D. Legum Doctor.
M. D. Medicinae Doctor.

Mus. D. Musicae Doctor.
S. T. P. Sanctae Theologiae Professor (which = D. D. Doctor of Divinity).

---

[1] 'It was always supposed that the Universities gave two kinds of Degrees or Certificates of proficiency—in Arts and in the Faculties. The inferior or preparatory Degree in each department was that of "Bachelor" (baccalaureus), a barbarous title derived from the French Bas Chevalier, which primarily denoted a Knight Bachelor, one who sat at the same table with the Bannerets, but, being of inferior rank, was "mis arrière,"·or "plus bas assis:" hence it came to denote the unfinished apprentice, the unmarried man, and the semigraduate. The complete degree in Arts was that of Magister, *Master*—in the Faculties, Doctor, *Teacher*; two titles equivalent to one another and to the common designation of Professor, or claimant of complete knowledge. The Arts were seven in number (Grammatica, *Grammar*; * Dialectica, *Logic*; Rhetorica, *Rhetoric*—which were called Trivium; Musica, *Music*; Arithmetica, *Arithmetic*: Geometria, *Geometry*; Astrologia, *Astrology*—which four were called Quadrivium); and are summed up in the technical lines:—

> GRAM- loquitur; DIA- vera docet; RHET- verba colorat;
> MUS- canit; AR- numerat; GE- ponderat; AS- colit astra.

Music from an Art has passed into a Faculty, and has special Degrees. The older Faculties are Divinity, Law, Medicine: the first of which was supposed to include all Arts.'—Donaldson, *Lat. Gr.* p. 470.

---

* When Public Schools were first established to prepare boys for the studies of the University, the subject mainly taught in them was the first and fundamental Art—that of language—Grammatica. Hence such a school was called Schola Grammaticalis, *a Grammar School*; and, when founded by Royal Charter, it was declared to be Libera Schola Grammaticalis, *a Free Grammar School*, i.e. *free* from all superiority but that of the Crown.

SUPPLEMENTARY NOTES.

I. (§ 6, p. 5.) 'Primitive Sound or Root.'

It seems necessary to explain more distinctly the sense in which the word 'Primitive' is here used.

When a root appears with some variety of form in several kindred languages (as Latin, Greek, and Sanskrit), it is natural to ask which of the forms is earlier than the rest, and whether such earlier form is to be regarded as 'primitive,' or a still earlier one is to be assumed as once existing, though disused. To determine these points certainly or with high probability, the various forms must be carefully compared, and tested by well-ascertained principles and facts of language. Among such principles and facts are the following:

(1) Guttural Letters sounded from the throat with the lips apart are primitive, as compared with all others.

Thus the vowel a, having its proper sound, either from the back of the throat, as in Indian ăk (= English ŭk), or from the front, as in English ăk (for the sounds in English 'ale,' 'all,' are diphthongal), is *the* great primitive vowel, into which no other passes by strengthening, though itself may be weakened into others. Such weakening is either by closure of the lips, as in the series ă, ŏ, ŭ, or by employment of the palate and tongue, as in the series ă, ĕ, ĭ. Hence it follows that

If an a-sound compete with another vowel-sound, the a-sound belongs to the primitive form.

Example. The Sanskrit stem signifying 'father' is pitar, the Latin pătĕr, the Greek (πᾰτήρ) πᾰτέρ-. We are hence able to infer that the primitive stem is pătăr, of which Sanskrit (in pĭtăr) has weakened the first syllable, Latin and Greek the second.

(2) A long vowel is the sum of two short vowels.

Hence it appears that a root with long vowel is the development of another with short vowel, which is therefore the earlier of the two.

Example. The 'foot' of man or any other animal is expressed in Latin and Greek by the root pĕd- πŏδ-, but in Sanskrit the word is pâd, nom. pâd-as m. This shews, what we might have been pretty sure of, that the vowel of the root is a; but here we find long â; so we are led to expect an earlier root with short ă, from which â is developed. And this we find in the Sanskrit verb-root păd, 'to go,' which has derivatives with ă, pădă, pădă-m, 'a pace,' 'a step.' The Latin and Greek Nominatives pēs, πούς, have the same quantity as pâd, and so in Compounds Sk. dvipâd, Lat. bipēs, Gr. δίπους, &c. But the verb-form păd does not exist in Latin and Greek (unless bitere and πατεῖν can be referred to it).

(3) Guttural Consonants, by (1), antecede the rest. Others are not changed into them, though they are represented by others.

Hence if a guttural form compete with another, the guttural may be regarded as primitive.

P P

Examples. In Sanskrit, c′ (soft ch) and s′ often represent k, c ; s′v may represent kv, qu ; sometimes Lat. p, π, τ, represent a guttural ; Sk. j represents g. See pp. 59–61.

(4) Of the Consonant trills r, l, so often interchanged (p. 64), r must be considered the earlier.

(5) Sanskrit words beginning with h have lost an initial which preceded it.

(6) The vocalized r-trill is expressed in Sanskrit by the vowel ṛi (ṛî), but this in Latin and Greek is usually represented by ar, er, or. Even in Sk. ar is the earlier form, and Professor Cowell has pointed out to me (since this Grammar was reprinted) that the great Sanskrit Dictionary, now being published at St. Petersburgh by the Russian Government, rejects ṛi from verb-roots, and receives ar as the true form, though the ṛi-form is that which Indian scholars use. Terminal diphthongs are also rejected. The words of the editors are : ‘ Wir haben aus den Verbal-würzeln die Vocale ṛi, ṛî und li vollständig verbannt ; desgleichen die Diphthonge vom Auslaut derselben ; ṛi im Auslaut von Nominalthemen haben wir durch ar ersetzt.’

Hence they write bhar not bhṛi, kart not kṛit, pitar not pitṛi, da not ‘de’ or ‘do.’

The following instances may suffice to illustrate the principles stated ; the suggested primitive form being placed in the fourth column :

Lat.	Gr.	Sk.	Pr.
coqu-	πεπ-	pac′	pak (kak ?)
quinque	πέντε	panc′an	pankan (kankan?)
li(n)qu-	λιπ-	ric′	rik
equ-us	ἵππος	as′vas	akva-s
gno-	γνο-	jnâ	gna
vert		vṛit, vart	vart
cord-	καρδ-ία	hṛid, hard	khard ?
serp-	ἑρπ-	sṛip, sarp	sarp
lup-us	λύκ-ος	vṛika-s, varka-s	varka-s
urs-us	ἄρκτ-ος	ṛiksha-s, arksha-s	arksa-s
levi-s	ἐ-λαχύ-s	laghu-s, raghu-s	raghu-s
(for leg-vis)			

Raghu-s is a derivative of the verb-root ranh, or ran-gh, to move fleetly.

Exemplifying these principles further from other roots and words cited in p. 554, we are led to infer that the following, among others, are the primitive forms : ăg drive ; ăp acquire ; kru hear ; kăr make ; dhă, place ; dă give ; dĭk shew ; bhăr bring ; bhŭ be ; găn produce ; măn think ; mă measure ; măr fade, die ; săd sit ; săk follow ; stăr strew ; stă stand ; stăg cover ; tăn stretch ; văs clothe ; ghans goose ; kvăn dog ; dvăr· door ; ăvĭs sheep, &c. Many of these forms will be seen to differ in some respect or other from the Sanskrit, while others agree, as man, sad, tan, vas, avis, &c. The only two which agree exactly with Greek or Latin are ag, ap. Thus it is shewn how primitive forms are deduced with probability from a comparison of kindred languages.

An instructive example may be added : the derivative word Sk. s′ravas, Gr. κλέος, L. laus. The root is (Prim. kru) Sk. s′ru, Gr. κλυ-, L. clu- hear. The derived forms may be compared letter by letter :

$$\text{Sk. s' } r \ a \ v \ a \ s = \text{s'ravas.}$$
$$\text{Gr. } \kappa \ \lambda \ \epsilon \ (\digamma) \ o \ s = \kappa\lambda\epsilon(\digamma)os.$$
$$\text{L. } \text{—} \ l \ a \ v \ \text{—} \ s = \text{laus.}$$

Here it is seen that ·

(a) in Sanskrit : the primitive k passes (as often) into s′ ; r remains ; ăv from u is a constant formation ; ăs is a Noun-ending.

(b) in Greek : k remains in κ ; the rough liquid r passes into the soft λ av is weakened into ϵF, and the F (= v) is lost in later Greek ; *os* n. is the weakened ending for ăs n.

(*c*) in Latin : k falls off (p. 44) ; r passes into l, av is vocalized into au ; and as the ending ŭs is hereby precluded, a suffix d is brought in, and the nom. lau-d-s (= laus) is formed, which, by Latin analogy, becomes Fem.

A similar word is hravas (clearly for dhravas from root dhvṛi, or dhurv, 'to bend' or 'make crooked') = Latin fraus ; fr corresponding to dhr, the rest as in s'ravas and laus.

The following is a list of Sanskrit roots corresponding to most of those cited on pages 14–17 :

English.	Sanskrit.	English.	Sanskrit.
to *yoke*	yuj	*know*	jnâ
hear	s'ru	*hide*	kûl
float	plu	*slip*	lamb
cleanse	pû	*measure*	mâ
stink	pûy	*fasten*	pas'
bray, sound	ru	*rule*	râj
shine	ruc'	*bathe*	snâ
cover	sku	*stand*	sthâ
sew	siv	*strew*	stṛi, star
be strong	tu	*seize*	hṛi, har
shew	dis'	*make, create*	kṛi, kar
shine	div	*sit*	sad
go	i	*cover*	sthag
that	i	*cover*	vṛi, var, **val**
lie down	s'î	*move*	val
adhere	lî	*sound*	svan
spy	spas'	*sleep*	svap
three	tri	*the sun*	svar
love, desire	lubh	*speak*	vac'
drive	aj	*fill*	pṛi, par, pur
shine	bhâ, bhâs	*fade, die*	mṛi, mar
beget	jan	*be*	bhû

The roots duc- *lead,* nu- *nod,* fid- *trust,* ac- *sharpen,* sa- *sow,* mar- *glitter,* are not represented in Sanskrit.

We find push, *nurture,* and putra *a son* in Sanskrit, with which L. puer and its cognates are probably connected.

Sanskrit has the Adjective rudh-ira *red,* but not the verb rudh *to be red;* yet to such a root we must refer the words ruber, rufus, ἐ-ρυθ-ρός, &c.

The Latin verbs luo, lavo *to wash,* and f-luo *to flow,* are probably related to Sk. plu *to float.*

To break is in Sk. bhanj : if this is the root of Gr. Ϝραγ, L. frang-, it has developed r in those languages.

L. sero, *connect,* may be from the Causal of Sk. sṛi sar, *to proceed.*

That Sk. sarva, *all,* is of the same family as the Latin words of solidity, salus, solum, sollus, sōlus, sollers, &c., appears certain : and they are referred by some to the root sṛi, sar.

Sk. svar, *the sun,* may indicate a verb-root svar or sur, *to shine* : but such root is not extant.

II. 'Relations in the Simple Sentence, §§ 103–105, pp. 352-8.'

In the belief that the meaning of these sections will be most clearly shewn by the analysis of a passage according to the principles laid down in them, the first Ode of Horace (*C.* i. 1.) is chosen for that purpose.

Horace, presenting three Books of Carmina to his illustrious friend

Maecenas in the year B.C. 19, U.C. 735, places this Ode first by way of dedication. The outline of what he says is this :

'O Maecenas, my beloved protector, *various are the delights of men.* Some *who, like the Greeks, love excitement, display and barren honour,* are glad to win the great Olympian chariot-race.[1] *Romans* having large landed property are overjoyed, one, if the popular vote exalts him to the three offices of state ; another, if he is enabled to acquire unrivalled wealth. The yeoman farmer would not be tempted by the riches of Attalus to forsake the tillage of his hereditary fields. The merchant captain, amidst the perils of shipwreck, may regret his native village ; but let him return there, and restless greed soon drives him back to sea. *The Epicurean* quaffs his wine, and takes life easily from day to day. The soldier is all for camps and battles ; the huntsman for the hardships of the chase. As for me [2]—*at Rome* I enjoy, as a learned man, the society of the great ; *elsewhere,* the haunted forest and the favour of the Muses. But if, *after reading what I now send,* you rank me among lyric poets, I shall reach the very zenith of delight.'

> Maecenas atavis edite regibus,
> o et praesidium et dulce decus meum,
> sunt quos curriculo pulverem Olympicum
> collegisse iuvat, metaque fervidis
> evitata rotis palmaque nobilis.[1]   5
> terrarum dominos evehit ad deos
> hunc, si mobilium turba Quiritium
> certat tergeminis tollere honoribus,
> illum, si proprio condidit horreo
> quidquid de Libycis verritur areis.   10
> gaudentem patrios findere sarculo
> agros Attalicis condicionibus
> numquam dimoveas, ut trabe Cypria
> Myrtoum pavidus nauta secet mare.
> luctantem Icariis fluctibus Africum   15
> mercator metuens otium et oppidi
> laudat rura sui : mox reficit rates
> quassas, indocilis pauperiem pati.
> est qui nec veteris pocula Massici
> nec partem solido demere de die   20
> spernit, nunc viridi membra sub arbuto
> stratus, nunc ad aquae lene caput sacrae.
> multos castra iuvant et lituo tubae
> permixtus sonitus bellaque matribus
> detestata.   manet sub Iove frigido   25
> venator tenerae coniugis immemor,
> seu visa est catulis cerva fidelibus,
> seu rupit teretes Marsus aper plagas.
> me [2] doctarum hederae praemia frontium
> dis miscent superis, me gelidum nemus   30
> nympharumque leves cum satyris chori
> secernunt populo, si neque tibias
> Euterpe cohibet nec Polyhymnia
> Lesboum refugit tendere barbiton.
> quodsi me lyricis vatibus inseris,   35
> sublimi feriam sidera vertice.

The following Syntactic Analysis is thus arranged :—

In the Predicative Relation (I) both related words, Nominative and Verb, are placed together. In II–VII, one word is stated ; and that to which it is related by agreement or government is added within brackets, sometimes by its initial only, but so as not to be mistaken. With Annexed words (VIII) the Conjunction, if any, is given, the related words following. Words to be mentally supplied are in italic type. Numerals by § or page refer to the Rules, as given in the Syntax or Uses of Words.

I. Predicative Relation. (§ 108. Concord I. § 115.)

3. Sunt *homines* (§ 114. 2, § 206. note). 4. collegisse iuvat (§ 177–8). 6. *illud* evehit si, &c. (when si nearly = quod, the Protasis forms a Substantival Clause which may be, as here, the Subject of the Apodosis).[1] 7–8. turba certat. 9. *ille* condidit. 10. quidquid verritur. 13. *tu* dimoveas. 14. *ille* secet. 16–17. mercator laudat. 17. *ille* reficit. 19. est *homo*. 19–21. qui spernit. 23. castra iuvant. 25. venator manet. 27. cerva visa-est. 28. aper rupit. 29. hederae miscent. 30–2. nemus chorique secernunt (§ 112). 33. Euterpe cohibet. 33–4. Polyhymnia refugit. 35. *tu* inseris. 36. *ego* feriam (p. 350, § 109).

II. Qualitative.

(1) Attribution (§ 108. Concord II.).

α. As Epithet (p. 354).

2. Meum dulce (d.). 3. Olympicum (p.). 4. fervidis (r.). 5. nobilis (p.). 7. hunc (*dominum*, see note). 7. mobilium (Q.). 8. tergeminis (h.). 9. proprio (h.). 10. Libycis (a.). 11. patrios (agr.). 12. Attalicis (c.). 13. Cypria (t.). 14. pavidus (n.). Myrtoum (m.). 15. Icariis (f.). 17. sui (o.). 18. quassas (r.). 19. veteris Massici (*vini*). 20. solido (die). 21. viridi (a.). 22. lene (c.). sacrae (a.). 23. multos (*homines*). 25. frigido (I.). 26. tenerae (c.). 27. fidelibus (c.). 28. Marsus (a.). teretes (p.). 29. doctarum (f.). 30. superis (dis). gelidum (n.). 31. leves (c.). 34. Lesboum (b.). 35. lyricis (v.). 36. sublimi (v.).

β. As Enthesis (p. 354. See also § 237–9).

1. Edite (M. = qui editus es). 5. evitata (m. = quae evitata est). 11. gaudentem (*virum* = qui gaudeat). 15. luctantem (A. = dum luctatur or qui luctetur). 16. metuens (merc. = cum metuit). 18. indocilis (merc. = quia indocilis est). 22. stratus (qui = cum straverit, *having stretched*). 24. permixtus (s.). 25. detestata (b.). 26. immemor (v.).

(2) Apposition (§ 108. Concord III.).

α. As Epithet (p. 354).

1. Regibus (atavis, which is the principal noun here : *royal ancestors*).

β. As Enthesis (p. 354).

2. Praesidium (M. = qui es praesidium . . . meum). 15. nauta (*ille* = *factus* nauta). 29. praemia (h. = quae sunt praemia).

III. Objective. Nearer Object. (§ 120–1. See § 237.)

3. Quos (iuvat). 3. pulverem (coll.). 6. dominos (evehit, see note). 7. hunc (evehit, see note). 8. *eum* (tollere). 9–10. *frumentum* (condidit). 11. *virum* (dimov.). 12. agros (f.). 14. mare (s.). 15. Africum (met.). 16. otium (laud.). 17. rates (r.). pauperiem (pati). 19. pocula (sp.). 20. partem (dem.). 21. membra (stratus, § 122. 6). 23. *homines* (iuv.). 28. plagas (r.). 29. me (misc.). 30. me (sec.). 32. tibias (c.). 33. barbiton (t.). 35. me (i.). 36. sidera (f.).

IV. Receptive (§ 132–3, &c. See § 237).

15. Fluctibus (l. § 135. b. c.). 23. lituo (p. § 135. b.). 24. matribus (d. § 141. 7). 27. catulis (v. § 134. 1). 30. dis (misc. § 135. b.). 35. vatibus (i. p. 385).

V. **Circumstantive.** (§ 143, &c. Ablative : Adverbs : Prepositions.)

1. Atavis (ed. § 159). 3. curriculo (coll. § 145). 5. rotis (evit. § 145, or § 151). 6. ad deos (eveh. § 70. 1.). 8. honoribus (tollere, § 151). 9. horreo (c. § 155. 2.). 10. de areis (§ 71, p. 300). 11. sarculo (f. § 145). 12. condicionibus (dim. § 145). 13. numquam (d.). 14. trabe (s. § 145). 17. mox (r.). 20. de die (§ 71, p. 300). 21-2. nunc—nunc (str. p. 317). sub arbuto (str. § 71, p. 306). ad caput (str. § 70. 1.). 25. Sub Iove (m. § 71, p. 306). 31. cum satyris (ch. § 71. IV.). 32. populo (sec. § 158). 36. vertice (f. § 145).

VI. **Proprietive** (§ 162, &c.).

6. Terrarum (dom. § 174). 7. Quiritium (t. § 166). 16. oppidi (r. § 165). 19. *vini* (pocula, § 166). 22. aquae (c. § 165). 23. tubae (s. § 165). 26. coniugis (i. § 174, 2. γ.). 29. frontium (p. § 165). 31. nympharum (ch. § 166).

VII. **Prolative** (§ 180).

8. Tollere (c.). 11. findere (g.). 18. pati (indocilis). 34. tendere (r.).

VIII. **Annexive** (§ 188).

2. Et decus (praesidium). 4-5. metaque palmaque (collegisse). 9. illum (hunc). 17. et rura (otium). 20. nec demere (pocula). 23-4. et sonitus bellaque (castra). 31. chorique (nemus).

(A) **Vocative** (§ 118) Interjections (§ 104) and Conjunctions.

1. Maecenas (§ 104, § 118). 2. O (§ 104. 118) et (§ 77. 3). 7-9. si—si (see note). 13. ut ('*so that he, &c.*' § 205 : or, if to dimoveas be given the sense of persuading, 'ut secet' may be referred to § 197). 20-1. nec—nec (§ 77. 3). 27-8. seu—seu (§ 221). 32-3. si neque—nec (§ 77. 3.)

(B) **Relative Construction** (§ 108.   Concord IV. § 105).

3. Quos (agrees with antecedent *homines*, § 108. case is governed by iuvat, § 121). 10. quidquid (*omne frumentum* is suppressed antec. On Case, see I.) 19. qui (agrees with antecedent *homo* : is nom. subject of spernit). 35. quod si, *but if* (=*as to which, if*, &c. See § 82. 6).

[*Notes.* [1] l. 5. A full stop is placed after 'nobilis,' and no stop after 'deos' in l. 6, with Macleane and Munro. Horace would tolerate nowhere, much less in the opening lines of his First Ode, such a construction as 'hunc—illum' dependent on 'iuvat' or 'evehit' supplied from a previous and specially distinct sentence. 'Nobilis' forms a beautiful ending to the sentence 'sunt quos,' &c.; and 'evehit,' having for its subjects the two clauses 'si mobilium,' &c., 'si proprio,' &c., is an exquisite, though not frequent construction. As to 'terrarum dominos,' opinions will probably be divided between making it an apposition to 'deos' and taking it as object of 'evehit,' in the sense of 'Roman landlords.' The latter explanation, supported by Lucan's 'terrarum dominos,' *Phars.* viii. 208, which Orelli cites, is here preferred.

[2] l. 29, &c. The reading 'te,' which some suggest for the first 'me,' is tempting, because Maecenas was learned : see *C.* iii. 8. 4. But perhaps Horace in these lines speaks of his own two modes of life, both delightful : one, which, as a scholar favoured by the great (di superi, *i.e.* Augustus, perhaps including Maecenas : see *C.* iii. 3, 11.—5, 2. iv. 5, 33), he enjoyed at Rome ; the other, in his Sabine villa near Tibur. See iv. 3, the most exquisite of all his poems, where he expresses similar feelings in another form, and exults in having gained that which in the present ode he declares to be the summit of his hopes—to be called 'Romanae fidicen lyrae.']

INDEX I.

SUBJECTS.

[Reference is made sometimes to Sections, §: sometimes to Pages. An asterisk marks a term introduced in modern works on Latin Grammar. Italics with asterisk mark a term introduced in this Grammar or its companion works.]

A

A, the standard guttural Vowel, § 12. Its sound; strength, 10, 11; forms diphthongs with i, u, 12; weakenings, 20–32. See CONTENTS.

*A-Nouns, Decl. I., § 22. See § 20–21.

*A-Verbs, Conj. I., § 43–47. § 53.

Abbreviations (Siglarium Romanum). Appendix *K.*, 575.

Ablativus Casus (auferre, *to take away*), the Ablative Case, so called from one of its uses (separation), § 19. Its form in the Declensions, § 20. Governed by Prepositions, § 71–72. In *Circumstantive Relation*, § 103. V. Syntactic uses, § 143–161. See CONTENTS.

Ablativus Absolutus (absolvere, *to release*), the Ablative Absolute, so called because it stands released, as it were, from government. Also called *Ablativus Convenientiae*, § 161. § 238–240.

Ablative Supine, § 40. § 187.

Abstract Names, 71, 125, 272.

Abundance in Nouns, § 27.

Acatalectus (ἀ, *not*, καταλήγειν, *to stop short*), Versus, 528.

Accentus (accinere, *to intone*), Accent, Acute or Circumflex, 7.

Accentuation, § 10. 511.

Accusativus Casus (accusare, *to accuse*), the Accusative Case, so called because the accused is the *Object* of prosecution. Gr. αἰτιατικὴ πτῶσις, § 19. Its form in the Declensions, § 20. Governed by Prepositions, § 70. § 72. *Objective Relation*, § 103. III. Syntactic uses, § 119–131. See CONTENTS.

Active Voice (agere, *to do*), § 36.

Active Sentence, how changed to Passive Form, § 106.

Adaptation or Partial Assimilation of Consonants, 42.

Adjectivum, Adjective (quod adicitur

APO

Substantivo). Gr. ἐπίθετον (*epithet*), § 15. Declension of Adjectives in Decl. II. and I., 93; in Decl. III., 115–119. Irregularities, § 28. Comparison, § 29. Derivation, § 59. Uses, § 63. In *Qualitative Relation*, § 103. II. See Agreement; also CONTENTS.

*Adjectival Clause, § 189. Adjectival (Relative) Clauses, § 204–210.

Adonius Versus, 541.

Adverbium, Adverb (quia ad Verbum est), § 15. Comparison of Adverbs, § 30. Correlation of, § 54. Table of, 228–230. Derivation of, 255–258. Strengthen Superlative and other Adjectives, 279.

*Adverbial Attribute and Apposite, 278, 365.

*Adverbial Clause, § 189. (*B.*) Adverbial Clauses, § 204–227. See CONTENTS.

Adversative Conjunctions, § 57. 318.

Affirmative Answers, § 88.

Agreement, § 108–114. See CONTENTS.

Alcaic Verse, § 267. § 269.

Alphabet, the letters of any language, so called from Alpha, Beta, the first two Greek letters. Latin Alphabet, § 7. § 12.

Anacoluthon, a Figure of Syntax, 565.

Anapaestus, Anapaest, ◡ ◡ ´, a metrical Foot, 525.

Anapaestic Rhythm, 543.

Anaphora, 318.

Animals, names of, their gender, 76, 77.

Annexive Relation in the Sentence, § 103, VIII. 432. Conjunctions, 316.

Answers, Affirmative and Negative, § 88–89.

Antecedent, 357, 361. Agreement of Relative with, § 108. 361, 367, 368.

*Apodŏsis (ἀποδιδόναι, *to render back*). If a Predication is so limited by a

Clause, that the Clause can be stated first, the Predication afterwards, such Predication is called Apodosis, while the Clause is called Protăsis (προτείνειν, *to stretch before*). These terms are chiefly used in regard to Compound Conditional and Concessive Sentences (*if, although*) ; *if, although—I stand* (Protasis), *I see* (Apodosis). But there would be no impropriety in applying them when the Clause is Temporal or Causal, '*when—because—I stand, I see*,' or when it is Relative, as '*whoever stands—he will see.*' Any such clause is conditionally limitative, and is a Protasis ; because a condition precedes in logical order that of which it is the condition. But in grammar the terms Apodosis and Protasis are applied to the principal sentence and condition severally, in whatever order placed.

Appellativa (appellare, *to call by name*), Common Names, 71.

*_Apposite_ (apponere, *to place by*), a Substantive attributed to another Substantive, 71, 353.

Apposition, 71, 353, 359, 360, 364–367.

Arsis (αἰρειν, *to lift*), that Syllable in a Foot on which 'ictus' falls, § 258.

Articles (ἄρθρα), none in Latin, 73.

*Aryan Affinities, Append. *C.*, 554.

*Aryan Family of Speech, § 2.

As, Compounds of, 149 ; parts of, 157. Appendix *G.*, 556, &c.

Asclepiad Metres, § 265. ; 544, &c.

*Assimilation of Vowels, 32–35 ; of Consonants, 41–43.

Asynartetus (ἀ, *not*, συναρτᾶν, *to link*), Versus, 528, 543.

Atonic or Baryton Syllables, § 10.

*Attraction (attrahere, *to draw to*), a very important usage in Syntax, § 61. § 110. § 114.

Attributum (attribuere, *to assign*), Attribute, 71. In Qualitative Relation, 353, 354. Concord, § 108.

Attribution, Idioms of, § 113.

B, a medial labial mute **Consonant**, Relations of, 63. Euphonically inserted, 44 (note).

Base in metre, 528 (note).

*_Being_, Verb of (sum, esse), § 42.[1]

C, a tenuis guttural mute **Consonant**, modified from Γ. Sounded as K., 9, 60 (note). Relations of, 59–64.

Caesura (caedere, *to cut*), § 260. and note.

Calendar (Roman), Appendix *H.*, 572.

Cardinalia (cardo, *hinge*), Cardinal Numerals, § 33. Uses of, § 34.

Case, § 19.

Cases, Formation of, § 20. See Declensions.

Case-construction, § 115–176. See CONTENTS.

Catalecticus (καταλήγειν, *to stop short*), Versus, 528.

Causal Conjunctions : Coordinative and Subordinative, § 57.

Causal Coordination, 320.

*Causal Clauses, Adverbial and Adjectival, § 209–210.

*Character (χαρακτήρ, *impressed mark*) of a Stem or Root, 70.

*_Circumstantive Relation_, § 103. V.

*_Clause_, 352.

*_Clipt Stem_, 30, 170.

*Coalition, 53.

Collective Nouns or Nouns of multitude, 71. Their construction, 362.

*_Combinate Tense-forms_, § 38.

Common Gender, § 18.

Common Names (Appellativa), 71

Comparatives and Superlatives, their formation, 42 (note).

Comparative Constructions, 314, 315, 404, 405.

Comparative Conjunctions, Coordinative and Subordinative, § 57.

*Comparative Sentences, § 227–228.

Comparison, § 29–30.

*Compensation, 18.

*Complement (complere, *to complete*), the (Predicative), that which completes the construction of a Sen-

---

[1] The term '*Substantive Verb*,' as used to denote ' sum, esse,' has every disadvantage which a term can have. (1) It is a false translation of its Greek original, ῥῆμα ὑπαρκτικόν (verbum existens). (2) It tends to confuse learners, who ought to consider a *Substantive* one part of speech and a *Verb* another. (3) If any form could claim the term Substantive Verb, it would be the Infinitive, which partakes of each character (Verb-noun). These evils are aggravated by the modern practice of saying Súbstantive Verb, not Substántive, which was the universal pronunciation of the Adjective formerly, in accordance with Johnson's authority (a substántive proposition). There is no more reason to obliterate his wise distinction by applying the general rule of pronunciation to this word in both its senses, than to accent the first syllable in *adjacent, subjective*, and hundreds more.

COM

tence, when the Verb is copulative, § 102. *Oblique Complement*, 351, 360, § 131. See Predicate.

Composite Subject, 268, 353, § 112.

Composition of Words, § 60.

Composition of Verbs, § 52, § 60.

*Compound Sentence, § 100, § 198–228. See CONTENTS.

Concessive Conjunctions, § 57.

*Concessive use of Conjunctive Mood, 339.

*Concessive Sentences, § 225–226.

Concords, Four, § 108.

Concrete Names, 71.

Conditional Conjunctions, § 57.

Conditional Sentences, § 213–224. See CONTENTS.

Conjugation (coniugare, *to yoke together*), the Flexion of Verbs, 72. Periphrastic, § 47.

Conjugations, the four, § 43. Their Paradigms, § 44–50.

Conjugating, method of, § 43.

Coniunctio (coniungere, *to unite*), Conjunction, Gr. σύνδεσμος, 73. § 57. Coordination by, 77–81. See CORRELATION and COMPOUND SENTENCES.

*Coniunctivus Modus, Conjunctive Mood, § 37. Pure Conjunctive, Examples of, 174. § 93–95.

*Consecutio Temporum, Consecution of Tenses, § 98. § 229.

*Consecutive Conjunctions, § 57.

*Consecutive Clauses, § 205, 206.

Consonants, § 7. Scheme of, 8. Affections of, 41–58. Relations in Latin, Greek, and Sanskrit, § 12. xxxv. See CONTENTS.

*Consonant Nouns, § 20. § 24.

*Consonant Verbs, § 43–47. § 53.

Contraction, 52, 56.

*Coordination by Conjunctions, § 77–81. By Relative, § 82.

*Copulative Verbs (copulare, *to couple*). List of, § 101.

*Correlation, § 73–76.

*Correlative Pronouns and Particles, § 31.

D, a medial dental mute Consonant, 63. Sounded as t when final. T written for final d, 63. Interchanged with l, 65.

Dactylic Hexameter, § 259–260.

Dativus Casus, Dative (Receptive) Case, § 19, 20. In Receptive Relation, § 103. IV. Constructions, § 132–142. See CONTENTS.

Declension (declinare, *to slope down*), § 19.

Declensions of Substantives, the Five,

ENG

§ 20. Their Case-endings, § 21. First Decl., § 22. Second Decl., § 23. Third Decl., § 24. Fourth Decl., § 25. Fifth Decl., § 26. Declensions of Adjectives, 93, 94, 115–119. Irregularities of Declension, § 27–28.

Defective Nouns, § 27. Defective Adjectives, § 28. Defective Verbs, § 49.

Deminutiva, Diminutives, 247.

*Dental Consonants, 8, 63.

Deponent Verbs, § 36. Their Conjugation, § 45. Paradigm, § 171. Deponents of First Conj., 207–208. Of Second Conj., 214. Of Fourth Conj., 215. Of Third Conj., 225.

Derivation, § 59. Of Nouns, 235–253. Of Verbs, 254. Of Particles, 255–259.

Desiderative Verbs (desiderare, *to desire*), 206.

Dialects of Italy. Append. *D.*, 556.

Diphthongs (δίς, φθόγγος, *sound*), 6, 12, 13.

Disjunctive Conjunctions, § 57.

Disjunctive Coordination, 318.

*Dissimilation of Vowels, 34. Of Consonants, 43.

Distributive Numerals, § 33.

Double Object Verbs, their construction, 354, 379.

*Dubitative Sense of Conjunctive, 339.

Duration of Time in Accus., 375; Abl., 401.

E, medial Vowel between a and i. Its sound and strength, 11, 19. Forms diphthongs with i, u, 12. Various affections of, 24–28, 38.

*E-Nouns, Fifth Declension, § 20. 21. § 26.

*E-Verbs, Conj. II., § 43–47. § 53.

*Ecthesis (ἐκτιθέναι, *to place out*), a word or words standing out of the predication with which they are in context; as, a Vocative Case, or an Interjection, with their adjuncts, § 104.

Elegiac Distich, § 261.

*Elision (elidere, *to strike out*), the removal of a final Syllable before a word beginning with a Vowel, 52, § 256.

Ellipsis (ἐλλείπειν, *to omit*), omission of one or more words in construction, § 61. 274, 346, 367.

*Enclitic words (ἐγκλίνειν, *to lean on*), those which throw back accent on the word which they follow, 7, 259.

Ending, § 14.

English Language, 2.

ENT

Enthesis (ἐντιθέναι, *to place in*), 352.

Enuntiatio (enuntiare, *to declare or state*), *a statement*, § 100.

Enuntiatio Obliqua, the First Class of Substantival Clauses, § 100, 189, 194–203. See CONTENTS.

Epicoene words, 77.

Epithet (ἐπίθετον, *placed on to*), an Adjective in simple Attribution ; as, vir b o n u s, § 15. See Attribute.

Etymology (ἔτυμος λόγος, *true account*), § 1. § 6.

*Euphonic Insertion of Consonants, 44.

*Euphony, 19.

Exclusion of Consonants followed by Contraction of Vowels, 56–58.

Extensible Verbs, § 102. § 103, VII., § 180.

F, an aspirate spirant Consonant ; its sound uncertain, 9. Corresponds to bh, dh, gh ; φ, θ, χ, 61, 62. Passes into h, 62.

*Factive Verbs, 351. Their construction with Accusative (Oblique Clause), 380–381.

Families of Language, § 2.

Figures of Syntax and Rhetoric, § 61. Appendix *F.*, 565.

*Final Conjunctions (finis, *end, purpose*), § 57.

*Final Clauses, Adverbial and Adjectival, § 207–208.

*Finite Verb, § 35.

*Flexion (flexio, *a bending*), § 14–15.

Foot, § 258. List of Feet, 525 (note).

Fractions, how expressed, 157.

Frequentative Verbs, 205.

Futurum Tempus, Future Tense, Simple and Perfect, § 38. Their uses, § 90. 229. Consecution, 484, 485. See Periphrastic Conjugation, § 47.

G, a medial guttural mute Consonant, § 12. 9. Its Relations and utterance, 61.

Galliambus of Catullus, 538.

Gender (genus), § 18.

Generic Names, 74.

Genetivus Casus, the Genitive (Proprietive) Case, Gr. γενική πτῶσις, § 19. Formation of, in Sing. and Plur., § 20. Genitive in Proprietive Relation, § 103. VI. Syntax of Genitive, § 162–176. See CONTENTS.

Gentile or Clan Names ; also from People, Cities, &c., 252.

Gerundia, Gerunds, § 40. Construction, § 181–184.

INF

Gerundive Forms, 23 (note).

Glyconic Metre, 536.

Gnomic Use of Subjunctive, 343.

Grammar, divisions of, § 1.

Greek ; its influence on Latin, 2. Affinities, Append. *C.*, 554.

Greek Nouns in First Decl., § 22. In Second Decl., 92. In Third Decl., 112–115.

*Guna, 12.

*Guttural Consonants, 8, 61.

H, an aspirate guttural Consonant, 9. Relations of, 61–62.

Hexameter (Dactylic), § 259–260.

*Hiatus, 52–53, § 257.

*Historic Infinitive, 332–333.

*Historic Present, 332.

*Historic Tenses, 164, § 98.

Homonymous Verb-forms (ὁμώνυμα, *having same name*), § 227.

*Hortative and Jussive uses of Conjunctive Mood, § 95.

I (j), Vowel and Consonant, 9, 10. Its sound and strength as i-vocalis ; weakest Vowel, 11. Forms diphthongs when strengthened by a, e, o, 12. Selection of i, 29, &c. Weakens a and e, § 12.

I as a vincular or link-vowel, 11, 30–32. I and u, 31.

*I-Consonans (j), 9, 10–68. Sound, Append. *B.*

*I-Nouns in Third Decl., § 24.

*I-Verbs, Conj. IV., § 43–47. 214–216.

Iambic Rhythms, § 263. 539–540.

Illative Conjunctions, § 57. Coordination by, 320.

Imperative Mood (imperare, *to command*), § 37. Its Tenses, 163. How used, § 92.

Imperfect Tense, § 38. Imperfect Indic., its uses, § 90. Subjunctive, § 229.

Impersonalia Verba, Impersonal Verbs, so called because they cannot take a Personal Pronoun as Subject, § 50. § 109.

Impersonal use of Passive Verbs, § 50. 359. Of Gerundive Construction, § 50. § 181.

Inceptive or Inchoative Verbs, 196, § 53.

Indicative Mood (indicare, *to shew*) in Verbs, for categorical or absolute statement, § 37. Uses of, § 90.

*Infinite Verb, § 35. § 40. § 177–188. See p. 169.

Infinitivum, the Infinitive, § 35. § 40. Its constructions, § 177–188.

INF

*Infinitive Clause (Accusative with Infinitive), § **194**.

Interest, Calculation of, Append. *G.*, 569–570.

Interjection (intericere, *to throw between*), Interjection, § **58**, 357.

Interrogations, § **86–87**.

*Interrogatio Obliqua, the Third Class of Substantival Clauses, 100, § **202**.

Interrogative Particles, § **86–87**.

Intransitive Verbs, 159, § **122–127**.

-io-Verbs of Third Conj., § **46**.

Irregular Nouns, § **27–28**.

Italian Dialects, Append. *D.*, 556.

Iterative Construction with Subjunctive, 343, 463 ; with Indic., 464.

K, a guttural tenuis mute Consonant, gradually disused in Latin, 9.

Kalendae or Calendae, the Calends of the Roman month. Append. *H.*, 572–574.

L, a dental liquid Consonant = lisped r. Its Relations, 64, 65.

*Labial Consonants, 8.

Language, Families of, 1. Languages derived from Latin, 2.

Latin, § **2**. Literature, § **5**.

Letters, § **7–12**.

*Letter-change, § **12**.

Letter-writing, Tenses in, § **90**.

*Locative Case, § **20**, § **155**. See Declensions.

Logaoedic Rhythms, 541.

Loss of Initial and Final Letters, 44–47. Of Inner Consonants by concurrence with other Cons., 47–50. Of Inner Vowels before Consonants, 50–52. Of Inner Vowels with Consonants, 54.

Lyric Metres, § **262**.

M, a labial nasal Consonant. Euphonically inserted, 44. Its Relations, 64.

Metaphor (μεταφέρειν, *to transfer*), a Figure of Rhetoric, 270.

Metonymy (μετὰ, ὄνομα), a Figure of Rhetoric, 270.

Metre, § **258**.

*Mobilia Substantiva, Substantives which have Feminine as well as Masculine Form, 74.

Money, Computation of, Appendix *G.*, 566.

Month, Roman, Appendix *H.*, 572.

Moods, § **37**. § **90–97**.

*Morphology (μορφή, *form*, λόγος, *account*), Wordlore, § **8**. § **13**.

Multiplicative Numerals, 148.

*Mutation of Letters, § **12**.

PAR

N, a nasal Consonant, usually dental, but before Gutturals becoming guttural or palatal ; its Relations, 64.

Names (Roman), 252. How abbreviated, Appendix *K.*, 575.

*Narratio Obliqua, § **230**.

*Nasalization, insertion of n, 19.

Negative Particles and Pronouns, § **83–85**.

Negative Answers, 330.

Neuter Adjectives, their Substantival use, § **63**. 365.

Nomen, Noun, § **15**. Gr. ὄνομα.

Nominative Case, ὀνομαστικὴ πτῶσις, § **19**. Formation of, in Sing. and Plur., § **20**. Uses of, § **115–117**. See Predicative Relation.

Number, § **17**. § **39**. § **62**.

Numeralia, Words of Number, § **33–34**.

Numeral Series, Declension, Table, § **33–34**.

O, medial Vowel between a and u. Its sound and strength, 11. Forms. Diphthongs with i, 12. Weakening into u, 21.

*O-Nouns, Second Declension, § **20**. § **23**.

*O-Verbs (fragments of), 221.

*Obiectum (obicere, *to cast in the way*), Object (correlated to Subiectum, *subject*), that on which a Subject acts. It may be Nearer Object (Accus. Case), or Remoter (usually Dative, sometimes Accus.) See Accusative, Dative, and Objective Relation.

*Objective Relation, § **103**, III.

*Objective Genitive, § **163**. § **174**.

*Obliqua Oratio, § **190–193**.

*Oblique Subject or Complement (the Subject or Complement of an Oblique Infinitive Clause), 352 (note), § **131**.

Optative use of Conjunctive, § **95**.

Order of Words in a Sentence, § **241–243**.

Ordinalia, Ordinal Numerals, § **33**.

Ordinative Particles, 317.

Orthography, Append. *A.*, 547.

*Oscan Dialect, Append. *D.*

P, a labial tenuis mute Consonant, § **12**. Euphonically inserted, 59, 63.

*Parasitic u (v) joined to q, 10, 58.

Part affected, Accusative of, 374

Participles (partem capere), 165

Participial Construction, § **237–240**. See CONTENTS.

PAR

Particulae, Particles or Small Parts of Speech, a name given to the four undeclined Parts, including some which are inseparable, or only used in Compounds : ambi-, dis-, in-, re-, se-, § 24. § 54–58. 255–259

Partitive (partiri, *to divide*), words which take a Genitive of the Thing Distributed, § 171. See Genitive in CONTENTS.

Parts of Speech or Words, § 14. § 16.

Passiva Vox (pati, *to suffer*), Passive Voice in Verbs, § 36.

Patronymic (πατήρ, *father*, ὄνομα, *name*), a name expressing descent from a father or ancestor, 75.

Perfect Tense (perficere, *to complete*), § 38. Disyllabic Perfect, 18. Its double use in Latin, 164. Its uses in the Indic. M., 162. In pure Conjunctive M., § 90. § 95. In Subjunctive, § 204. § 229.

Perfect-Stem and Character, § 41. Its Formation, § 51. § 53.

Period (περίοδος, *circuit*) and Periodic Style in Discourse, § 244–249.

*Periphrastic Conjugation, a term used to express the forms of predication obtained by connecting the Participles with the Verb sum : especially the Future Active Participle in -urus and the Gerundive in -ndus, § 47. The term would be equally applicable to the Combinate Passive Tenses with sum and Perf. Part., but is not usually given to these. See p. 164, § 47.

Person, § 39.

*Petitio (petere, *to seek*), that Form of a Simple Sentence in which the Imperative Mood is used, § 100.

*Petitio Obliqua, *Indirect Will-speech*, the second of the three kinds of Substantival Clauses, 349, § 197.

Phalaecian or Hendecasyllable Verse, 537.

Pherecrateus Versus, 535.

Phonetic Decay, 11.

*Phonology (φωνή, *sound*, λόγος, *account*), Soundlore, § 7–12.

Phrase (φράσις, from φράζειν, *to speak intelligibly*), 352 (note).

Place, Adverbs of, § 55. Constructions of, § 155–157. See CONTENTS.

Plautus and Terence, 3. Their Prosody, 56, 546.

Pleonasm (πλεονάζειν, *to exceed*), a Figure of Syntax, § 61.

Pluperfect Tense (plus quam perfectum, *more than complete*), § 38. Its use in the Indic. M., § 90. Conjunctive and Subjunctive, § 229.

PRO

Plural Number (plures, *more*), § 17. Peculiar uses of, § 62.

Plural only ; words generally without Singular, 125.

Plural, variation of meaning in, 128.

Poetic Forms and Idioms, Append. *E.*, 563.

Position, a Term used in Prosody to express that a vowel is long, short, or doubtful in quantity by coming before certain letters, 512.

Potential Use of Conjunctive, 338.

Praeteritiva Verba, Verbs not conjugated with Present-Stem, § 49.

*Predicate (praedicare, *to declare*), that member of a Sentence by which something is declared of the Subject. Writers on Logic resolve every proposition into Subject, Copula, and Predicate. But in Grammar this would only mislead, for it is not in such form that authors write. Neither sum, nor any other Copulative Verb, exactly corresponds to the logical Copula ; and the word, which such Verb links to the Subject, is often not identical with a logical Predicate. For these reasons (while Madvig and most other Grammarians are followed in allowing the term Predicate in Grammar to a Finite Verb) the term Complement is used to express the word or phrase linked by a Copulative Verb to the Subject, and so *completing* a Simple Sentence, § 101–102.

*Predicative Relation, § 103, I.

Prefix, 70.

Preposition (praeponere, *to place before*), Gr. πρόθεσις, 72. Table of Prepositions, § 56. Prepositions in composition with Nouns, § 60. With Verbs, § 52–60. Use of Prepositions with Cases, § 70–72.

Present Tense, § 38. Its uses in Indic. M., § 90. In Conjunctive M., § 94. In Consecution, § 229.

Present Stem and Character, § 41. Affections of Present Stem, § 51. See CONTENTS.

*Primary Tenses, § 38. § 95.

*Primitive Roots, § 5. Supplementary Notes, 577.

*Proclitica (προκλίνειν, *to lean forward*), Particles which merge their accent in the following word, 7.

Prohibition, forms of, § 92. § 95.

*Prolative Relation (proferre, *to extend*), that in which Predication is extended by an Infinitive added to Verbs, Participles, or Adjectives, 356.

*Prolative Infinitive, § 180.

PRO

Pronoun (Gr. ἀντωνυμία), § **15**. Pronouns, § **32**. Use of, § **64–69**. See CONTENTS.

Pronominalia, 137, 142, 292, 368. § **73**.

Pronunciation of Vowels and Diphthongs, § **12**. Of Latin generally, Append. *B*.

Proper Names ; Names peculiar to Persons or Places, 71.

Proportional Numerals (duplus, &c.), 148.

Proprietive Relation*, that of the Genitive to the Noun on which it depends, 356. § **103.

Prosodia (προσᾴδειν, *to sing in accord*), Prosody, 1, § **251–269**.

*Protasis. See Apodosis.

Punctuation, § **11**.

*Pure or Independent Conjunctive Mood, § **37**. Uses of, § **93–95**.

Q, a guttural tenuis mute Consonant, only used with parasitic u (v), 9, 10. Its Relations, 59–61. Sounded as c before u, Append. *A*.

Qualitative Relation*, that in which Attributes orApposites stand to their Nouns, § **103, II.

Quality, Ablative of, § **153**. Genitive of, § **168**.

Quantitative Words, taking Genetivus Rei Demensae, § **172**.

Quantity of Syllables, § **8**. § **252–255**.

**Quasi-Passive Verbs*, 160.

Questions. See Interrogatio.

R, a dental liquid Consonant, § **12**. Its relations, 64–66. Substituted for s, 65.

Receptive Relation*, that in which a Dative Case stands to a Trajective or other Verb or Noun on which it depends, § **103, IV.

*Recta Oratio (distinguished from Obliqua O.), Direct Discourse in a Principal Sentence, § **100**, § **190**.

Reduplication (reduplicare, *to redouble*), a peculiar mutation, by which the form and sense of words is varied in Greek, Latin, and other languages, 40. Reduplication in Present-Stem, § **51**. In Perfects, § **51**. Loss of, 118.

Reflexive Pronouns (reflectere *to bend back*), se with its Possessive suus ; so called because they 'bend back' their reference to a preceding Subject of the Third Person, § **32**. Their use, § **66**. In Clauses, § **231–235**.

*Relations of construction existing

SUB

between words in Simple Sentences, § **103**.

Relative Pronoun (referre, *to refer*) qui quae quod, so called because referred to an Antecedent nounterm, § **32**. The root of most Subordinative Conjunctions and of numerous Adverbs, § **59**. Coordination by Relative, § **82**. Agreement of Relative with Antecedent, § **108**, Concord IV. Notes on, § **114**.

*Relative (Adjectival) Clauses, § **204**. Consecutive, § **206**. Final, § **208**. Causal, § **210**.

Rhythm (ῥυθμὸς), modulated flow or measure in verse or prose, 512. Prose rhythm, 506. Rhythms in Verse, § **269**.

*Root, § **14**. § **59**. Supplementary Notes, 577.

S, a dental sibilant Consonant. Relations, § **12**. Passes into r, 66.

*Sanskrit, 1, § **6**. Append. *E*. Suppl. Notes, 577.

Sapphic Stanza in Horace and Catullus, § **266**.

Sapphic Metres, 542–544.

Selection, 20–32.

*Semiconsonants, 9–10.

**Semideponent Verbs*, 160.

Semitic Family of Language, § **2**.

Sententia (sentire, *to express thought*), a Sentence, § **100**.

Sentences. The Parts of Discourse ; their kinds, § **100**. Order of Words in a Sentence, § **241**.

Shortening of Vowels, 55, &c.

Simple Sentence ; three forms of, § **100**. Its parts, **101–103**. Constructions of, § **107–188**. See CONTENTS.

Singular Number, § **17**. § **27**. § **62**.

Singular only, words without plural, 125.

*Soundlore (Phonology), § **7–12**. See CONTENTS.

*Stem, § **14**. The three Stems in Verbs, § **41**. § **51**. § **53**.

*Strengthening, § **12**. 12–19.

Strophe or Stanza (στρέφειν, *to turn*), Strophic Metres, 528 (Note), 543–546.

*Subiectum, *Subject*, that member of a Sentence of which action or state is predicated, § **102**.

Subiunctivus Modus (subiungere, *to subjoin*), the Subjunctive Mood, a name given to the Conjunctive Mood when subordinated to another Verb, § 37. 175. § 96–98. In Suboblique Construction, § 190–193. In Compound Sentences, § 194–228. Seé CONTENTS.

Suboblique Construction, the Construction of Verbs in Subordination to Oratio Obliqua, real or virtual, § 190–193.

*Substantival Clauses, why so called : their varieties, § 100. Construction, § 194–203. See CONTENTS.

Substantive (substare, *to stand beneath*), the first of the inflected Parts of Speech, § 15. Declensions of, § 17–26. Irregularity in, § 27. Uses of, § 62.

*Suffix, § 14. List of Noun-suffixes, § 58. Suffixes of Particles, § 59.

Superlativus gradus (superferre, *to carry above*), the highest Degree of Comparison in Adjectives and Adverbs, § 29, 30. Idioms of, 279.

Supine, an unmeaning term, applied to the two Cases of the Verb Infinite which end in um and u, 165. Their construction, § 185–186.

Supine-Stem, § 41. Its formation, § 51.

Syllaba (συλλαμβάνειν, *to take together*), a Syllable, § 7.

Syllabation, 9.

Synaphea, 520 (note).

*Synesis (συνιέναι, *to understand*; σύνεσις, *meaning*), a Figure of Syntax, by which meaning rather than form determines the construction, § 61. § 111. § 114.

Syntax (συντάσσειν, to *construct*), a Division of Grammar, § 1. § 100–250.

T, a dental tenuis mute Consonant, 8, 63.

Tenses, § 38. § 90–98. Consecution of, § 98. § 229.

Temporal Clauses (Adverbial), § 211–212. See CONTENTS.

Temporal Conjunctions, § 57. § 211.

Thesis in Verse, § 253.

Time of Syllables (Mora), § 8, § 512.

Time, Constructions of, § 124. § 154. Computation of, Appendix *H.*, 572.

Tmesis, 35, 299, 563.

Towns, Names of; their Gender, § 18. Their constructions, § 125. § 155–157.

*Trajective (traicere, *to throw over*). Verbs and Adjectives which by their meaning suggest a Remoter Object, 355, 384.

Transitive Verbs, 159, § 121–126.

Transposition of Consonants, 44.

U-V, Vowel and (Spirant) Consonant, its uses in each character, 10.

U as weakening of a, o, 11, 21.

*U-Nouns (Fourth Decl.), § 26.

*U-Verbs (in Third Conj.), § 43. § 53. 224.

*Umbrian Dialect, Appendix *D.*

Universal Relatives, 141, 146, 291. § 73.

V, a soft Labial Spirant, 8, 10, 67. Sound of, 66 (note). Appendix *B.*

Variant meaning of Plural Substantives, 128.

Verb, Gr. ῥῆμα, § 15. § 35–53. § 59. 254. § 60. § 90–98.

Verse, § 258, &c.

*Vinculation, 11, 30.

Vocales, Vowels, § 7–12. Scheme of, 8.

Vocative Case (vocare, *to call*), §19. § 20. Vocative Ecthesis, § 104. § 118, 119.

Voice (also called Genus), that form by which Verbs are marked as doing or suffering, § 36.

*Vowel-change, § 12. See CONTENTS.

Vowel-weakening in Compounds, 35–39. See CONTENTS.

*Vṛiddhi, 12.

*Weakening, § 12. § 19, &c. See CONTENTS.

Words, § 14–19.

*Wordlore (Morphology), § 13–99.

X, double Consonant=cs ; not in the older Latin Alphabet, 9, 68.

Y represents Gr. υ, introduced with z (=ζ) in Cicero's age, 9. Its sound, Appendix *B.*

Z, introduced with y, only used in latinised Greek words, 9.

Zeugma, § 61.

INDEX II.

LATIN WORDS.

a, ab, abs, 202, 231, 263, 299–300
abicio, conicio, eicio, &c., 10, 549
abiete, ariete, pariete, 10, 27
absque, 302
ac, atque, 233, 312, 313, 316
accestis, 55
accipiter, 77
acer, 16
ac si, 482
acetabulum, 571–572
acipens-is, -er, 29
actus, 570–571
acus, acuo, 16
ad; 232, 263, 293
adamantinus, 29
adeps, 65
adfatim, ad-amussim, 26, 105, 256
*adimo (for abimo?), 263
adiuris, 57
admodum, 135, 256, 329
*adolere, abolere, &c., 210
adorea, 102
adulescens, adolescens, 548
adultus, 160
advers-us, -um, 232, 294
aeque ac, 312
aequi boni facere, 416
aerugo, 36
aes, 56, 566
aes grave, 566–569
Aesculapius, 29
aestimare (aestumare), 548, 566
aetas, 54
Agaue, Agave, 130
age, apage, agesis, &c., 191
agmen, agmin-, 25
ago, 16, 61
aheneus, aëneus, 50, 549
ai, 12

aidilis, 12
aio, 13, 48, 190
ain tu ? 190
ala, 48
Alcumena, 29
ales, 27
alias . . . alias, 292
aliquis, aliqui, 289, 290
alis, 144
aliter, 292, 314, 421
alius, 142, 292, 314, 362
alter, 42, 142, 144, 154, 292, 362
alteruter, 141, 260, 292
alucinari, 549
alumnus, 23
amabo, 235, 337
amb-, 203, 266
ambissint, 55
ambo, 151
amentum, ames, 50
amphora, 571–572
amphorum, &c., 87
amplus, 50
ampulla (amphorula), 23
an, annon, 326–329
ancora, 21
anguis, anguilla, 50
animans, 76
anser, 61
ante, 232, 251, 255, 294
ante diem, 573
antecedo, anticipo, 31
antequam, priusquam, 464
anulus, 550
apio, 189 (note)
apis, 109
apprime, in primis, prae-cipue, &c., 280
Aprilis, 51
apsens, optuli, &c., 42
apud, 232, 294
aquilā, 33 (note)
aranea, 47, 64
arbiter, 65

arbos, arbustum, 24
arceo, arx, 4
arcesso, 65
armentum, 28
artus (part.), 549
arx, 46, 64
as, 157, 566–570
asses usurae, 569
at, atqui, 259, 319
Athenis, 87
attinet, pertinet, 192
au, 12, 13
auceps, 27, 52, 57
audeo, 52, 57
audieram, &c., 58
Aurelii, 63
auris, 66
Aurora, 66
ausim, 55
aut, 259
aut, vel, ve, 318
autem, 259, 314
autumnus, 549
avariti-a, -es, 33
avos, &c., 34
avus, avia, 74

balanus, &c., 29 (note)
balneum, 52
-bam -bo, &c., 51, 63
barbarus, 40
bardus, 65
belli, humi, &c., 83, 91
belli gerundi, 23
bellicus, 30
bellum, 46, 63
bene, bonus, 20, 34
benigne, 330
benignus, 51
-bero -beri, &c., 51, 63
bibo, 40
biceps, 54
bicessis, 54
bidens, biennium, bifa-riam, &c., 149

biduum, triduum, &c., 15, 52, 149
bigae, quadrigae, 56
bilanx, 149
bimus, &c., 149
binarius, &c., 148
bini, 153, 155
bis, 44, 63, 153
bissextus, 575
bobus, bubus, 57
bonus, 44, 63
bos, 63, 67
brevis, 48
bruma, 57
Brundisium (Brundusium), 548
bubo, 77
bulbus, 23

cadus, 572
caecus, 547
caelebs, 27
caelum, 45, 547
caementum, 49, 547
caerimonia, 547
caeruleus, 43
caespes, 547
calamitosus, 54
calcar, 45
calfacere, 51, 263
caligo, 16
camena, 50, 547
candidus, 30
canis, 59
canis, iuvenis, vates, 109
capella, 51
*capio, 189 (note)
capsis, 187
carnifex, 548
caro, 65
Carthagini, 83
casa, 45
cauda, 45
caupo, copa, 74
causa (caussa), 14, 55, 56
causā, 394, 414
cautum, fautum, &c., 10, 57
cave with Subj., cave sis, vide sis, 337
caveo, 14, 443
cāvi, fāvi, fōvi, &c., 18
cavus, 45
cedo, cette, 52, 191
cella, 16
cello, fallo, pello, 67
celo, clam, &c., 16
celsus, 28
cena, 50, 547
cenatus, 160
censeo, 451
centum, 59, 152, 154

centuria, 571
centussis, 36
Cerealis, 66
Ceres, 17, 25
cerno, crimen, cribrum, &c., 17, 65
certe, certo, 329
ceteri, 547
ceu, neu, seu, 13, 45
Charisin, 43
Chalybōn, 113
cicindela, 40
ciconia, 40
cincinnus, 40
cinis, 25, 29
circuit, 53
circum, circa, circiter, 266, 295–296
circumago, 53
cis, citra, 133, 151, 294
cithara, 25
citimus, 42, 151
civis, 15, 76
clam, clanculum, 16, 256
clandestinus, 43, 251
claustrum, 43
clepsit, 55
cliens, clienta, 53, 74
clima, 571
clipeus, 548
cludo, 13
cluo, 14, 44, 64
coalituᶜ, 160
cochleare, 572
codex, &c., 13, 27
coëmo, 53
coepi, coeptus sum, 189
cogo, 450
cohors, cors, 56, 549
color, colos, &c., 66
columna, 41
colurnus, 44
comedo, 53
comes, 27
comminiscor, 190
con, com, 203, 251, 263
concedo, 450
condicio, 549
conectere, conubium, &c., 549
congius, 571
coniunx, coiunx, 76
consuetudo, 54
consul, 22, 36
consulo, consilium, 34
contamino, 48
contio, 57, 549
contra, 251, 296
contumelia, contumax, 39
convitium (convicium), 34 (note), 549
copia, 35
copis, 53

coquo, 59, 578
cor, 46
coram, 256, 302
cordi esse, odio esse, &c., alteri, 390
corpulentus, 50
cotidie, cottidie, 155, 255, 549
creare, crescere, &c., 17
credo, 216
Cres, Cressa, 75
cretus, 160, 404
crudus, crudelis, crustum, &c., 141
cubitus, 570
cuculus, 40
cucumis, 29
cui bono fuit ? 391
cuicuimodi, 144
culest, 53
culeus, 572
cum (prep.), 233, 263, 302
cum, or quum (conj.) : for quod, 442 ; causal, *since*, 449 ; temporal, *when*, 463–467 ; concessive, *although*, 480, 482
cum, quum (quom), 549.
cum-tum, tum-tum, &c., 317
cuncti, 56
cupio, 449
cupressus, 28, 50
cur, quare, &c., 36, 53
cura, 14
cura ut, 337
curculio, 40
curia, 57
curo, 451
custos, cutis, &c., 14
cyathus, 571–572
cygnus, 43

-dam -dem -do -dum, &c., 259
damnas, 131
Dareus, Darius, 10
de, 251, 263, 277, 300
de, deterior, deterrimus, 133, 251
deabus, filiabus, &c., 84, 87
debeo, 56, 263, 427
decem, 59, 152–153
decempeda, 570
decennis, 53
decenter, 257
decet, dedecet, 192
decies, decies centena, &c., 156, 568–569
decuria, 57

decurro, 264
decussis, 36
deesse, &c., 53
defetigo (defatigo), 36, 547
deflagratus, 160
deiero, 25, 39
dein, deinde, &c., 13, 46
deminuere, 548
demum, 259
denarius, 567-8
deni, 47
denique, 259
denuo, 257
depeciscor (depaciscor), 547
deram, dero, &c., 53
deses, 28
deus, divus, &c., 15, 33
dextans, 56
dexter, dexterior, dextimus, 42, 133
di (dei), dis (deis), 548
Diana, 15
dic, duc, fac, fer, &c., 45
dĭcare, dĭcere, 115
dĭcio, dĭcis, 15, 549
die crastini, 120, 400
dies, diu, &c., 15
digitus, 570
dignus, 15
diluvies, 36
diribeo, dirimo, 66
dis- dir-, 203, 265
dis (dives), 57
disco, 48 (note)
diu, *by day* ; diu, *long*, 257
diurnus, 66
divisse, 55
dixti, 54
do (Sk. dâ), -do (Sk. dhâ), 206
doceo, 451
doctrina, 50
dodrans, 57
Dolabella, 51
doleo quod, 441
domi, 83, 120
domine, 26
domus, 120
donec (donicum), 259, 461-463
dracuma, 29
dubito an, 327
duellum, 45
dulcedo, 30
dulcis, 65
dum, 259 ; dum, donec, quoad, *whilst*, 461-463 ; *until*, 461-464
dum, dummodo, *provided that*, 479

dumtaxat, 259
dumus, 50
dupondius, 570
dux, duco, edūco, &c.,15

e, ex, 133, 251, 264, 301
ebur, ebor-, 21
ecce, en, 235, 259
eccum, ellum, &c., 140
ecquis, 141
edepol, epol, pol, 235
ĕdo, 189
ēdus, &c., 12
ego, 61
eheu, heu, 235
ei, 12, 13
eice, reice, 10
elephus, elephantus, 77
-endus, -undus, 548
enim, etenim, 259, 320
eo (v.), 189
eo (adv.), 229, 308
eo, quo, tanto, quanto, &c., with compar., 399
epigrammatōn, 113
epistula, epistola, 548
Epona, 59 (note)
equester, 28
equidem, 259
equus, 59
erepsemus, 54
erga, 296
ergo, 320
erus, era (herus, hera), 17, 62
ēs, 52
ēsse, 51
et is, &c., 285
et, que, 259, 316
et, neque, 316
etiam, quoque, 316
Etrusci, Tusci, 65
etsi, etiamsi, 479-482
eu, 12, 13
examen, 48
examussim, 106
excubiae, 79
exin, 46
existimo, 39
exosus, 160
exspecto, expecto, exsul, exul, &c., 550
exta, 52
exterior extremus, 42, 133
extinxem, 54
extra, 296

faba, 63
fac with Infin. Clause, 444

fac (ut, ne), 337, 444
facies, 16
facio, 16
facio, efficio, 448
facit are, 35
facul, 46
faenum, 547
faginus, 29
Falisci, Falerii, 65
fallo, 45
famul, 46
far, 42, 46
fari, 14, 191
fas, 16
fateor, 16
fax, 16
faxo, faxim, faxitur, 55
febris, 50
fecundus, 23, 547
fel, 46, 63
femina, 29, 547
fendo, 60
fenus, fener- fenor-, feneror, 25, 547, 548
ferbui, fervi, 549
feriae, 65
fero, 62, 184-5, 217
ferre, 51
fers, 52
fetialis, 549
fetus, 547
fĭdes, fĭdo, &c., 15
figlinus, 51
finis, 49
fio, 185-6
firmus, 62
flagro, 62
flamen, 48
flamma, 41
fluo, fluvius, &c., 15
foedus (s.), 15, 547
fomentum, 57
foras, 256
fore, 21
fore ut, futurum ut, with Subjunctive, 444
foris, 62
formosus, 50
fors, forte, 259
forsitan, fortasse, 259
fossa, 41
frango, 16
fra(n)go, iu(n)go, &c., 19
frater, 62
frigo, 62
frigus frigor-, 25
frivolus, 22
*frugi, 131, 133
frustra, 39
fugio, 62
fui, 58 (note), 62
fulcrum, 28 (note)
fulgeo, 62

fulmen, 47
fumus, 62
fundo, 63
funebris, 50
fungor, fruor, utor, vescor, with Abl., 397
funus, funer-, 25
furfur, 40
Furius, 65

Gaius, 9, 13
gallus, gallina, 75
gaudeo, 52, 57
gaudeo, gratulor quod, 441
genitor, genetrix, 30, 547
gen-va, 10
Georgicōn, 92
gero, 65
gigno, genus, &c.,16, 40, 61
glacialis, 53
Gnaeus, 9
gnarus, &c., 16
gnasci, 44
gnatus, &c., 16
gnavus, &c., 16
gnosco, &c., 16, 44
gradior, 180
gradus, 570
grando, 64
gratiā, 394, 414
gravor, 159

habeo, with part. perf., 499
Hadria, 62, 549
Hammon (Ammon), 549
harena (arena), 62, 65, 549
hariolus, 549
harundo (arundo), 62, 549
haruspex (aruspex), 62, 549
haud, haut, hau, 323, 549
haudquaquam, 324
haud scio an, 323
haurio, 65
hauscio, 46
have (ave), 191, 549
hebetudo, 54
hedera, 549
hei, vae, hem, 235, 390
hemina, 571-572
herciscere, 549
Hercules, 29
heredium, 569
heres, 17, 62, 158, 547
heri (here), 61, 257, 400, 548

hesternus, 65
Hiber (Iber), 549
hibernus, 44 (note)
hic, 139, 144, 282
hic, ille, 283
hiemps, 61, 548, 549
hilaris, hilarus, 31
hilla, 50
hirundo, 17, 64
hirudo, 17
Hister (Ister), 549
hodiernus, 66
holus (olus), 62, 549
homicida, 54
homo, 19, 69, 76
homullus, 23
honestus, 28
hornus, 57
horsum, 57
hortor, 442
huiusque, huiusce, 59
humi, humo, 83

iacio, 10
Ianus, 45
ibi, illic, 228, 308
id aetatis, id temporis, &c., 374
idcirco, ideo, propterea, 320, 458, 459
idem, 50, 284, 313
idūs, 572
iecur, ieciner- iecinor-, 59, 548
igitur, 320
ignis, 20
ignosco, 50
ilicet, 259
ilico (illico), 39
Ilithyia, 12
ille, 26, 139, 144, 258,283
illinc, 258
imberbus, imberbis, 31
immo, 257, 259, 330
impedio, 450
impero, 264, 450
impetrassere, 55
impubis, 115
imus, 56
in-, 262
in- (Pr.), 202, 251, 264, 304-305
in eo esse ut, &c., 453
inciens, 53 (note)
incitas, 130
inclutus (inclitus), 548
incohare, 549
induor, exuor, with Accus., 374, 549
industrius, 53 (note)
indutiae, 53
infimus, 42, 151

infitias īre, exsequias īre, 376
infra, 133, 297
inger, 45
in promptu, in procinctu, 130
inquam, 188
inquilinus, 34, 59
inquinare, 39, 59
instar, 130, 414
instigo, 17
intellego, 203, 264, 548
inter, 42, 265, 296-297
inter ipsos ; inter se, 495
interea loci, &c., 420
intercludo, &c., 264
interdius, interdiu, 257, 400
*intereo, interemo, interficio, 264
interest, refert, 193, 416-417, 449
interior, intimus, 42, 151
intra, 133, 151, 296
intus, 29, 136
invideo, 264, 384
iocus, 15
ipse, 288-289, 494-495
iracundus, 30
ire, iri, with supine, 186
is, 139, 283-285
is, eiusmodi, talis, &c., ut (qui), &c., 452, 455, &c.
iste, 140, 283
ita, itaque, 258, 320
ita ut, 452
item, itidem, 258, 312,313
iterum, tertium, &c., 149
itur, 188
iubeo, 450
iucundus, 14
iudex, 50
iug-, iungere, iŭgum, iūgis, &c., 14
iugerum, 157, 570-571
iumentum, 14, 48, 57
iunior, 133
Iuppiter, 15, 45, 57
iuratus, 160
iurgor, 52
iuvat, 15, 193
iuvenis, 76
iuxta, 52, 297, 313

Kaeso, 9
Kalendae, 9, 527
Kalumnia, 9
Kartago, 9

lăbare, lābi, 16
Labienus, 34
lac, 44, 46

lăcer, 64
lacrima, 65, 548
lama, 471
lamentum, 44
lamna, 52
lana, 47
lanius, 47
lanx, 45
lapicidina, 54
Lares, 65
latrocinium, 54
latus, 45
laus, 14, 44, 578
lavo, 14
Lemuria, 43
leo, lea, leaena, 64, 75
levir, 65
lĕvis, 48, 64, 578
lēvis, 64, 547
libella, 570
libera schola, 576
libet, lubet, 9, 15, 192, 548
libīdo, 30
libra, 566, &c.
librarius, 572
licet, 66, 192, 441, 449
ligula, 572
lilium, 64
limax, 15
limus, 15
linere, 15
lingo, 61
lingua, 65
linquo, 59, 64
liquere, liquet, liquor, 17, 192
lis, 45
littera, lĭtura, līnea, 15, 549
litus, 550
locuples, 54
locus, 45
loquella (loquela), 549
luci, 83
lucifer, 31
lucinus, 29
lupus, 45
luscinia, 14, 44, 64
lux, lūceo, lūna, lŭcerna, Lucina, 14, 64
lynx, 77

machina, 29
macte, macti, 131, 235
maerere, maestus, 547
mage, magis, 26, 42, 136
magister, 25
maiestas, 28
maior, 13, 48
Maius, 13, 48
māla, 48
maleficus, malificus, 31
Mamers, 40

manceps, 50
mancipium, 79, 548
mane, mani, 257, 400
malo, 57, 186-187, 449
manibiae, 54
mansuetudo, 54
manus, 16
margo, margin-, 29
maritimus (maritumus), 548
marmor, 40
Maspiter, 35
matertera, 53
maximus, 42
meā, tuā, &c., 417
mecastor, mehercule, medius fidius, 235
medicus, 30
meditor, 65
medius, 63
mel, 46
melior, melius, 21
memini, 189, 422
mensa, 16
mensis, 16
meridies, 65
mētior, 16, 216
mĕto, 16, 220
mi, 56
militiae, Romae, &c., 83, 87
mille, millia (milia), 41, 152, 159
millia passuum, 570
mina, 29
Minerva, 29, 66
minime, 324, 330
minister, 28
minor, minimus, 42
minus (=non), 324
mirum quantum, &c., 280
misceo, 48 (note)
misereor, miseror, miseret, 192, 422-423
misti, 54
modestus, 28
modium, medimnum, &c., 91
modius, 572
modo, 324
modo . . . modo, 317
modo non, 324
modus, &c., 16
mōles, mŏlestus, 48
momentum, 57
moneo, 451
monimentum, monumentum, 548
monstro, monstrum, 44
morior, 180
mos, &c., 16
mostellaria, 50

mostis, 57
mox, 259
mulsum, 24
multimodis, 50
murmur, 21, 40

nae (nē), nae tu, nae ille, &c., 235
nam, namque, 258, 320
nare, nătare, &c., 16
naris, nasus, &c., 16, 65
narrare, 44, 54
nascor, natio, &c., 16, 44, 548
nasturtium, 52
nauci, 416
nausea, 33
nauta, 52, 57
navis, 67
-nĕ, 326
nē, 323
nē prohibitive, 337-342
nē in Pet. Obl., 442-443, 446-451
nē in Fin. Cl., 457-458
ne . . . quidem, 325
nec, neque, 316, 325
nec (=ne . . . quidem), 325
necdum, 323
necesse, 26
necesse est, 441, 449
necne, 329
necnon, 316, 323
necubi, 323
nedum, 323, 325
nefas, nefarius, 65
negassim, 55
neglego, 43, 548
negotium, 43
nemo, 56, 323
nemo unus, 268, 323
nemo non, &c., 324
nempe, 255
nepos, neptis, 52, 74
*nequam, 131, 323
nequaquam, 324, 330
nequeo, 188
nequiquam, 324
nescio quis, 290
neuter, 323
neutiquam, 323, 324
neve, 316, 323
nihil, nil, 34, 56, 323, 549
nihil dum, nullus dum, &c., 324
nihil non, 324
nihil quicquam, 268
nimirum, 259
nimius, 34
ningo, ninguo, nix, 43, 548
nisi, 323, 475-477

noli, 337
nolo, 54, 57, 186–187, 449
nomenclator, 52
nomen Latinum, 273
non, 256, 323, 330
non modo, non solum, 325
non modo non, 325
non quia, non quod, 460
nonae, 572
nonne, 323
nonnemo, 324
nonnihil, nonnullus, &c., 324
non possum non, 324
nonus, 152
nos, 141
nosco, nŏta, nōmen, 16, 548
nostri, nostrum, 141
novem, 20
nubes, 26, 63
nucleus, 52
nudius, 259
nullus, 142, 323
num, numne, 326, 328
numen, numin-, 29
Numerius, 65
nummus, 568
numquis, 141, 143
nunc, 57
nuncupo, 54
nundinae, 57
nunquam, &c., 52, 323, 324
nuntio, 57
nuo, numen, nutus, &c., 15
nuper, 57
nurus, 66

O, 235
O, heu, pro, en, ecce, &c., 379
ob, 203, 264, 297
obĭt, 58
*obliquus, obscenus, 39, 264, 547
*(obs), 203 (note), 264
oboedire, 39, 547
*obscurus, 14, 39
*obsolesco, exolesco, insolesco, 203, 266
obsoletus, 160
obviam, 256
occulo, 16
occupo, 22, 266
ocior, ocissimus, 16, 134
octavus, 152
odi, 189
oi, oe, 12, 13
olere, 65
olla, 50
omen, 50
omitto, 264
omnino, 257

onustus, 28
operae, 79
operio, 264
oportet, 192, 446, 449
optime, 331
optimus, 42
opto, 449
opus, usus, 197
orior, 180
oro, 449
ōs, 46
*ostendo, 203, 264
ou, 12, 13
ovare, 191
ovis, 20, 21

păciscor, pax, &c., 16
paelex, 547
Paelignus, 547
paenitet, 192, 548
paenula, 548
pala, 48
palam, 256, 302
palma, 50
palmipes, 570
palmus, 570
palumbes, 59
palus, 48
papaver, 40
Papirii, 65
par, pariter, 312
Parilia, 43
parricida, 41
pars, portio, 20
pars, plebs, &c., 362
partim, 105, 256
parum, 136, 256
parvulus, 22
paterfamilias, &c., 86
patior, 450
patricius, 549
patrocinium, 54
pauper, 54
pavo, 59, 77
pecu, 120
peiero, 25, 39
peior, 35
penes, 297
penitus, 136
penna, 41
peperi, 25
per, 299
-per, 259
per-, 262, 299
*perdo, peremo, pereo, 54 (note), 160, 264
perendie, 257
pergo, 54
perinde ac, 312
perinde quam, 312
per mihi gratum est, per mihi placet, 35
permitto, 450

perosus, 160
perperam, 256
perquam, 135
Perses, Perseus, 114
persona, 17
pertaesus, 160
pes, 157, 570
pes monetalis, 570
pessimus, 42
pessulus, 22
pessum, 130
pestis, 50
picus, 15
pietas, 34
piget, 192
pila, 48
pignoris, pigneris, pigneror, 548
Pinarii, 65
pinguis, 61
pinus, 47
pistrinum, 50
placitus, 160
plaustrum, 43
plebs, 17, 63
plenus, 47
plerique, 131, 142
plerique omnes, 268
pluo, pluvia, &c., 14
plus, plurimus, 42, 136
poëmatorum, poematis, 113
poena, 547
pomeridianus, 46
pomoerium, 46, 548
Pompeius, 13, 59
Pomponius, &c., 59
pondo, 130, 575
pone, 50, 294
pono, 50, 220
Pontius, &c., 59
popina, 59
populare, 41
pŏpulus (popolus), 17, 21, 40
pōpulus, 40
porro, 65
posco, 206
possum, 54, 184
post, 133, 151, 294
postea, posthac, 256
posterior, postremus, postumus, 42, 133
postquam, posteaquam, 462
postridie, 257, 400
postulo, 451
potes, 54
potestas, 28
potior (v.), 186
potior, potius, 134, 136
potis, pote, 20, 27, 31, 134, 184

potus, 160
prae, 133, 151, 264, 302-3
praebeo, 56
praeceps, 27
praecipio, 450
praecipue, 280
praeco, 54
praeda, 56
praefiscine, 230
Praeneste, 28, 79
praes, 57
praestigiae, 128
praesto (adv.) 52
praeter, 251, 298
praetor, praetura, 24
praeterea, 256
praeut, 313
pransus, 160
prece, procus, 20
precor, 448
prehendo, prendo, 56, 549
prelum, 548
pridie, 400, 573
primanus, 148
primarius, 148
primo, primum, 149
primum, deinde, &c., 317
prior, primus, 42, 133
princeps, 43
pristis, 44
priusquam, 464
pro, prod-, 251, 265, 303
pro (interj.), 235
pro eo ac, 313
procul, 299
prodeo, prodesse, 203
proelium, 548
prohibeo, 443, 450
prohibessit, 55
proin, proinde, 13, 53, 482
proles, 53
promo, 53
prope, propior, proximus, 42, 133, 298
propediem, 259
propter, 298
propterea. 458, 459
prosa, 50, 57
protenus (protinus), 548
prout, 313
prudens, 57
pūbes, 14
pubis, puber, 29
publicus, 40, 43
pŭdet, 14, 192
puer, 14
puerpera, 25
puertia, 52
pulmo, 65
pulvis, 25, 29
pūnio, pūrus, 14
pūpa, 14

purgo, 52
pŭsillus, 14
pūsio, 14
pŭter, pŭteo, pūs, 14
pŭto, pŭtus, 14

quadrupes, 76
quaero, quaeso, quaesivi, 65
quaeso, 191
qualis, 142, 145
qualis. quantus, &c., 308, 368, 388
qualus, 48, 50
quam, *how*, 309
quam, *as*, 314
quam, *than*, 315, 404
quamdiu, 461, 463
quamdudum, quampridem, 314
quamquam, utut, 479, 481-482
quamvis, quamlibet, quantumvis, quamvis licet, 480, 482
quando, 309, 458
quandoque, 458
quandoquidem, 458
quantillus, 51
quantus, 42, 142, 145, 308
quantuscumque, quantusquantus, 291
quare, cur, 36, 309
quare, quamobrem, &c., 320
quartarius, 571-572
quasi, 50, 482-483
quatenus, 458, 548
quattuor, 59
que, 59, 316
quemadmodum, quomodo, 308
queo, nequeo, 188
querimonia, 30, 69
querquetum, quercetum, 59
qui = ut ego, ut tu, &c. &c., 452; (consec.), 454-457
quia (coord.), 320, 459
quicumque, 291
quidam, 291
quidem, 285
quies, 15
quin, 45, in subst. sent., 443, in adj. sent., 455, &c.
quina-vicenaria (lex), 148
quindecim, 54
quinetiam, 447
quinque, 26, 59
quippe, 329

quippe qui, 441
Quirites, 59
quis, 59
quis, qui, 140-141, 289-290, 308
quisnam, uternam, 141
quispiam, 290-291
quisquam, 290-291
quisque, 280, 291, 362
quisquiliae, 130
quisquis, 291
quivis, quilibet, 291
quo, *in order that*, 458
quo, eo, &c., 308, 399
quoad, 461, 463
quocirca, 49
quŏd, *that*, 322, 441
quod, quia, *because*, 459
quoimodi, 144
quom, 59
quominus, 443, 447
quoniam, 458
quoque, 316
quorsum, 230
quot, 308, 368
quotannis, 155
quotiens (quoties), 33, 461, 549
quotus, 42
quotusquisque, 309-310
quousque, 230, 308
quum (*see* cum, conj.)

radix, 45, 67
raeda, 548
ramentum, 49
rana, 47
raucus, 14
raudus, 14
re red-, 204, 265
rēcidi reccidi, &c., 54
recipio, 37, 266
reciprocus, 251
recte, 329
recuperare (recip-), 548
recuso, 39
redivivus, 15
rēfert, 193, 416-417, 449
rego, regio, 16
relligio, &c., 41 (note), 549
remus, 50
repente, subito, &c., 466
repetundarum, 130
repperi, 25, 550
res repetundae, res Romana, res publica, 273
retro, 251
rex, 16
rima, 48
rogo, 448
rosa, 45

rostrum, 43
ruber, rūbigo,rufus,14,62
rŭdis, 14
rŭdo, rūmor, 14
rumpo, 64
rumusculus, 24
rursus, rursum, &c., 51
rus, rure, ruri, 375, 401, 403

saeculum, 548
saepe, 136, 256
saepes, 548
sal, 64
salix, 66
saltus, 571
saltem, saltim, 26, 256
salus, salve, salvus, 17, 191
Samnium, 43
sane, 329
sanequam, 314-315
sanguis, 50, 99
sanguisuga, 50
satis, abunde, &c., 419
satin? 45
scaena (scena), 548
scala, 50
scilicet, 259
scopulus, 22
scripulum, 158, 571
scutum, 14
se- sed-, 204, 251, 266
se, 136
se, suus, 285-287, 489-494
seco, 17
secundum, 298
secundus, 154
secus (s.), 130
secus (adv.), 136, 256
sed, 319
sedecim, 48
sēdi, vīdi, vēni, 18
seges, 27
segmentum, 43
selibra, 54
sella, 41
sembella, 570
semel, 152
semestris, 50
semi, 66
semis, 53
semodius, 572
semper, 259
sempiternus, 50
semuncia, 158
senex, senior, 69, 133
seni, 48
septem, 26
sequester, 31
sequor, 59
serenus, 17

ero, series, &c., 17, 66
sero,sēmen,&c., 16,40,65
serpo, 66
serum, 66
serus, 17
servasso, 55
sescenti, 154
sescuncia, 158
sescuplus, &c., 148
sesqui, 54, 148
sesquialtera ratio, 158
sesquipes, 570
sestertius, sestertium, 48, 566-570
Sestius, 48
setius, 136, 549
sex, 66
sextarius, 571, 572
sextula, 158
si, 66, 467-475
sica, 17
sicilicus, 158
sicubi,si quando, &c.,474
si dis placet, 475
silua, 10
silva, 64, 66
similis, similiter ac, 312
si maxime, 474
si minus, 474
si modo, si tamen, si vero, 475
simplex, 152
simul, 66, 152
simul, simul ac, 312, 462
singuli, 152, 153
sine, 302
*sinister (next the sinus), 28, 133
sinistimus, 42
si quis, &c., 474
sino, 450
si non, nisi, 475-477
si quaeris, si quaerimus, 475
siquidem, 474
siris, 57
Sirius, 17
sis, sultis, 57, 187, 337
sisto, 40
sive, seu, 318, 475
soboles, suboles, 34, 548
socer, 21, 24, 174
socors, 34
sodes, 235, 337
sol, 17, 21
solacium, 519
*soleo, 214, 266
sollers, 266, 550
sollemnis, 550
sollicitus, 266, 550
sollus, &c., 66, 266
solor, 17
solvendo esse, 391

solus, 142
somnulentus, 23 (note)
somnus, sopor, 17, 43
sonus, &c., 17, 21
sorbeo, 65
soror, 21
spero, spes, 65
spolium, 59
sponsor, 76
sponte, 130
spurius, 65
stadium, 570
stare, statio, &c., 17
statim, 258
statim ubi, &c., 462
statuo, 448
stella, 50
stercus, 59 (note)
sterno, &c., 17
sterquilinium, 59
stĭlus, 17, 548
stipendium, 54
sto, 206
strigilis, 64
studeo, studium, 59 (note), 449
suadeo, persuadeo, 451
suavis, 49, 66
sub, sus-, 202, 251, 265, 305-306
subtemen, 48
subter, 251, 306
successor, 76
sudor, 66
suffōco, 39
sultis, 187
sum (esse), 58 (note), 167-168
sumen, 48
suo, sūtor, subula,&c.,14
supellex, 105
super, 66, 251, 306
supersedeo, 265
supra, 133, 251, 297
superior, supremus, summus, 42, 133, 251
surgo, 54
surpui, 54
surrexe, 55
sus (s.), 66
susurrus, 21, 40
suspitio (suspicio), 34 (note), 549
suus, 66, 489-494

tabuleis publiceis, 12
taedet, 14, 192
talentum, 28
talis, 455
talpa, 59, 77
tam, adeo, sic, 452
tamen, 319, 479-481

tametsi, tamenetsi, 480
tamquam (tanquam), 43, 482
tantum, 452
tantum abesse ut, 453
tantus, 145
taurus, 45, 64
tego, 17, 45, 61
tegula, 17, 45
Teïus, 13
tela, 48
temo, 47
temperi, tempori, temperius, 25, 136
templum, 51
ten-via, 10
tenus, 304
teruncius, 570
tibicen tibicina, 53, 75
timeo, metuo, vereor (ne, ut), 443, 447
titulus 40
tollo, 217
-tor -trix (subst.), 75
tormentum, 47
torqueo, 65
torus, 45, 129
tot, 145, 308
totus, 15
trans, 203, 251, 266, 295
traxe, 55
tres, ter, &c., 15, 65, 151, 154
tribunicius, 549
triginta, 54
trinundinum, 54
Troia, 13
Troïus, 13
Tros, Troas, 75
trucido, 54
tum-cum, 456
tuber, 15
tugurium, 34
tumeo, &c., 15
turbassitur, 55
turris, 42
turtur, 40
Tydides, 13

uber, 63
ubi, *when*, 461
ubi, unde, &c., 285, 308 = Relative, 452
udus, 57
ui, 12
Ulixes, 65
udus, 41, 51, 142
ulna, 64, 570
ulterior, ultimus, 42, 133
ultra, ultro, 251, 295
ululo, 40

umere, umor, 62, 549
umerus, 549, 621
uncia, 151, 566–572
unciarium fenus, 570
unde, 308
undecim, 54
ungere, unguere, &c., 548
unguis, 61
unus, 150, 152, 153, 157
unus et alter, 364
uni, trini, &c., 155
urbes, urbis, urbeis, 13
urbs, urps, 549
urna, 571
upilio, 57
upupa, 22
uro, 65, 224
ursus, 48
usura, *interest*, 569
-us -a, &c. (subst.), 75
ut (*that*) in Subst. Cl., 440–441; in Petitio Obl., 442–451; in Consec. Cl., 452–454; in Final Cl., 457–458
ut, *how*, 309, 441
ut, *as*, 312–313
ut si, 482–483
ut, *when, since*, 461–462
ut, *granting that*, 339, 480–482
utare, utaris, 19
utcumque, utut, 479
uter, 230, 259, 308
uterque, 141, 362
utervis, uterlibet, 141
utinam, ut, 339
ut non, 440–441, 452–455
ut ne, 442–451, 453, 457–458
ut qui, utpote qui, 461
ut quisque, 280
utrimque, 230
utrum, 328
uxor, 74

valde, 125
vale, 191
Valerii, 65
valetudo (valitudo), 548
vallum, 17
vanus, 47
vapor, 44
vapulo, 160
-ve, 318
vē-, 262
vehemens, vemens, 56, 549

veho, 61
vel, 318
velle, 51
vello, 28
velo, 17
velox, 17
velut si, velut, veluti, 482
vendo, venumdo, 54, 160
veneficium, 54
veneo, 160
venere, venerunt, 19
venio, 18
ver, 66, 67
vere, vero, 329
verecundus, 30
vereor, 17, 443, 447
vermis, 64
verna, 66
versus, versum, vorsum, 299, 548
verto (vorto), 548
verum, vero, &c., 319
verus, 17
vespera, 67
vesperi, vespere, 83, 91, 102, 157, 400
Vesta, 67
vestis, 67
vestri, vestrum, 421
veternus, 66
veto, 450
vetus, 118
Veturii, 65
via, 33
vicem, 256
vicesimus, 50
victima, 548
videlicet, 259
viden?, 45
video, 447, 451
vidua, 63
viginti, 45, 541, 61, 152
vilicus, 550
villum, 50
viola, 67
violentus, 22
vir, 69
virus, 66
vis (s.), 65, 67
vis (v.), 52
vivere vitam, &c., 373
vivo, 45, 222
vix, vixdum, 324
voco, vox, 17, 21, 59, 67
volgus, vulgus, 22
volnus, vulnus, 20, 21
volo, nolo, malo, 64, 186–7, 449
volucris, 109
volvo, 67
vomer, vomis, 25
vomo, 67

Printed in the United Kingdom
by Lightning Source UK Ltd.
136542UK00001B/148/P